BASIC CRIMINAL PROCEDURE
CASES, COMMENTS AND QUESTIONS

Thirteenth Edition

. . . ■

By
Yale Kamisar
Clarence Darrow Distinguished University Professor Emeritus of Law,
University of Michigan
Distinguished Professor Emeritus of Law, University of San Diego

Wayne R. LaFave
David C. Baum Professor Emeritus of Law
and Center for Advanced Study Professor Emeritus,
University of Illinois

Jerold H. Israel
Ed Rood Eminent Scholar Emeritus,
University of Florida, Fredric G. Levin College of Law
Alene and Allan F. Smith Professor Emeritus,
University of Michigan

Nancy J. King
Lee S. & Charles A. Speir Professor of Law
Vanderbilt University Law School

Orin S. Kerr
Professor of Law
The George Washington University Law School

Eve Brensike Primus
Professor of Law
University of Michigan

AMERICAN CASEBOOK SERIES®

WEST®
A Thomson Reuters business

Mat #40901756

American Casebook Series is a trademark registered in the U.S. Patent and Trademark Office.

COPYRIGHT © 1965, 1966, 1969, 1974, 1994 WEST PUBLISHING CO.
COPYRIGHT © 1980, 1986, 1990 YALE KAMISAR, WAYNE LaFAVE, JEROLD H. ISRAEL
© West, a Thomson business, 1999, 2002, 2005, 2008
© 2012 Thomson Reuters
    610 Opperman Drive
    St. Paul, MN 55123
    1–800–313–9378
Printed in the United States of America

ISBN: 978–0–314–91166–7

PREFACE TO THE THIRTEENTH EDITION

Aside from two introductory chapters on the right to, and the role of, counsel, this volume—based on our much larger *Modern Criminal Procedure* (13th ed. 2012)—deals almost exclusively with "police practices" and other investigative alternatives (see Ch.11, dealing with grand jury investigations). The success of the previous editions of *"Basic"* confirms our belief that when allocated 30 (or even 45) class hours for criminal procedure (or a third or half of the crowded first-year criminal law course for procedural problems), many teachers will find it more useful and meaningful to explore in depth a few fundamental and closely related areas (e.g., search and seizure, right to counsel, confessions and lineups) than to make a whirlwind tour through the investigatory process, joinder and severance, speedy trial, "trial by newspaper" (and TV), criminal discovery, sentencing appeals, post-conviction review and all of the other topics treated in the 29 chapters of our larger book, we have kept the first twelve chapters intact and omitted all others.

Some instructors will welcome Ch. 11 (grand jury investigations) for providing an opportunity to compare and contrast police work with other investigative alternatives. However, we suspect other instructors, pressed for time, will pass quickly through Ch. 11 or even skip it entirely. But particular attention should be paid to the last section of of this chapter: Fifth Amendment history and values. This section is designed to facilitate exploration of the general policies underlying the privilege against compelled self-incrimination. There is much to be said for taking up this material with the confessions chapter.

A final point about the organization of these materials. Although we have a separate chapter on the scope of the exclusionary rules (Ch. 12), which includes a section on the "fruit of the poisonous tree," we believe the *Miranda* "poisoned fruit" cases, *Patane* and *Seibert*, shed so much light on the significance of *Dickerson*, the case that reaffirmed *Miranda*'s constitutional status (or perhaps one should say shed so much light on the lack of significance of *Dickerson*) that we decided to place *Patane* and *Seibert* in the confessions chapter, a few pages after *Dickerson*.

This volume includes significant developments up to January 31, 2012. This has permitted inclusion of such major rulings from the Supreme Court's 2011–12 Term as *United States v. Jones*, and *Perry v. New Hampshire*. Important developments thereafter will appear in annual supplements, which will also contain relevant federal court rules and statutory materials. The first annual supplement to this book, which will be published about two months after this volume appears, will contain all notable cases handed down by the Supreme Court during the 2011–12 Term. It will also include various extracts from the new criminal procedure literature.

Case citations in the text and the footnotes of judicial opinions and in the writings of commentators have been omitted without so specifying. Numbered footnotes are from the original materials; lettered footnotes are ours.1 Omissions from the text of the original are indicated by asterisks and brackets.

If there are cross-references to cases beyond pages 930 (the end of *Basic Criminal Procedure*), the citations to these cases can be found in the Table of Cases. We have continued the tradition of an exceptionally detailed index, in part because students have found that detail useful in reviewing for exams.

One or more of the authors has been fortunate enough to participate actively in four major criminal procedure projects: The American Bar Association's *Standards for Criminal Justice*; The American Law Institute's *Model Code of Pre–Arraignment Procedure*; The National Conference of Commissioners on Uniform State Laws' *Uniform Rules of Criminal Procedure*; and the ongoing revision of the *Federal Rules of Criminal Procedure*. We are indebted to the members of the various committees with whom we have worked for providing us with many leads and insights. We are also indebted to the many users of this book who have offered helpful suggestions on content as to this edition and previous editions. That list, like the list of our student research assistants over the years, has now grown far too long to mention each person individually.

We are especially appreciative of the outstanding secretarial assistance provided on the thirteenth edition, too often under great stress, by Karen Kays, Dorothy Kryskowski, Mary Lebert and Selah Woody. We are also indebted to Aurora Maoz for her valuable research assistance.

YALE KAMISAR

WAYNE R. LaFAVE

JEROLD H. ISRAEL

NANCY J. KING

ORIN S. KERR

EVE BRENSIKE PRIMUS

P.S. An additional note from Yale Kamisar, Wayne LaFave, Jerold Israel, Nancy King and Orin Kerr. We are delighted that Eve Brensike Primus has agreed to join us in this venture. We greatly appreciate the important contributions she has made to the new edition.

May 2012

ACKNOWLEDGEMENTS

Excerpts from the following books and articles appear with the kind permission of the copyright holders.

Arenella, Peter, Foreword: O.J. Lessons, 69 S.Cal. 1233 (1996). Copyright © 1996 by the University of Southern California. Reprinted by permission.

Beale, Sara Sun, Reconsidering Supervisory Power in Criminal Cases: Constitutional and Statutory Limits on the Authority of the Federal Courts, 84 Colum.L.Rev. 1433 (1984). Copyright © 1984 by the Columbia Law Review Association. Reprinted by permission.

Berman, Mitchell, Constitutional Decision Rules, 90 Va. L.Rev. 1 (2004). Copyright © 2004 by the University of Virginia Law Review. Reprinted by permission.

Bloom, Robert M., Inevitable Discovery: An Exception beyond the Fruits, 20 Am.J.Crim.law 79 (1992). Copyright © 1992 by the American Journal of Criminal Law. Reprinted by permission.

Bradley, Craig M., On Custody, Trial Magazine, Feb. 2005, p. 58. Copyright © 2005 by Trial. Reprinted by permission.

————, Should American Courts Heed the 'English Warnings'?, Trial Magazine, Dec. 2007, p. 62. Copyright © 2007 by Trial. Reprinted by permission.

Caplan, Gerald M., Questioning *Miranda*, 38 Vand.L.Rev. 1417 (1985). Copyright © 1985 by the Vanderbilt Law Review. Reprinted by permission.

Cassell, Paul G., The Paths Not Taken: The Supreme Court's Failures in *Dickerson*, 99 Mich.L.Rev. 898 (2001). Copyright © 2001 by the Michigan Law Review Association. Reprinted by permission.

Cloud, Morgan; Shepherd, George B.; Barkoff, Alison Nodwin; and Shur, Justin V., Words Without Meaning: The Constitution, Confessions, and Mentally Retarded Suspects, 69 U.Chi.L.Rev. 495 (2002). Copyright © 2002 by the University of Chicago Law Review. Reprinted by permission.

Colb, Sherry F., Why the Supreme Court Should Overrule the *Massiah* Doctrine and Permit *Miranda* Alone to Govern Interrogations, Findlaw's Writ at <http://writ.news.findlaw.com/colb/20010509.html> (May 9, 2001). Copyright © 2001 by Findlaw's Writ. Reprinted by permission.

Davies, Sharon, Profiling Terror, 1 Ohio St. J. Crim. L. 45 (2003). Copyright © by the Ohio State Journal of Criminal Law. Reprinted with permission.

————, The Reality of False Confessions—Lessons of the Central Park Jogger Case, 30 NYU Review of Law & Social Change 209 (2006). Copyright © 2006 by the NYU Review of Law & Social Change. Reprinted by permission.

Dershowitz, Alan M., Torture Without Visibility and Accountability Is Worse than with It, 6 U.Pa.J.Const.L. 326 (2003). Copyright © 2003 by the University of Pennsylvania Journal of Constitutional Law. Reprinted by permission.

————, The Torture Warrant: A Response to Professor Strauss, 48 N.Y. Law Sch.Rev. 275 (2004). Copyright © 2004 by the New York Law School Review. Reprinted by permission.

Dressler, Joshua, and Michaels, Alan C., Understanding Criminal Procedure (5th ed. 2010). Copyright © 2010 by Matthew Bender & Co. Inc. Reprinted by permission.

Dripps, Donald A., Constitutional Theory for Criminal Procedure: *Miranda, Dickerson*, and the Continuing Quest for Broad–But–Shallow, 43 Wm. & Mary L. Rev. 1 (2001). Copyright © 2001 by the William and Mary Law Review. Reprinted by permission.

Drizin, Steven and Leo, Richard A., The Problem of False Confessions in the Post–DNA World, 82 North Carolina Law Review 891 (2004). Copyright © by the North Carolina Law Review. Reprinted by permission.

Friedman, Barry, The Wages of Stealth Overruling (with Particular Attention to Miranda v. Arizona), 99 Geo.L.J. 1 (2001). Copyright © by Professor Barry Friedman. Reprinted by permission.

Garrett, Brandon L., Convicting the Innocent: When Criminal Prosecutions Go Wrong (2011). Harvard University Press. Copyright © 2011 by the President and Fellows of Harvard College. Reprinted by permission.

Israel, Jerold H., LaFave, Wayne R., King, Nancy J., & Kerr, Orin S., Criminal Procedure Treatise (3d ed. 2007). Copyright © 2007 by Thomson/West. Reprinted by permission.

Kainen, James, The Impeachment Exception to the Exclusionary Rules: Policies, Principles, and Politics, 44 Stan.L.Rev. 1301 (1992). Copyright © 1992 by the Board of Trustees of the Leland Stanford Junior University. Reprinted by permission of the Stanford Law Review and Fred B. Rothman & Co.

Kamisar, Yale, Another Look at Patane and Seibert, the 2004 *Miranda* "Poisoned Fruit" Cases, 2 Ohio St. J. Crim. L. 97 (2004). Copyright © 2004 by the Ohio State Journal of Criminal Law. Reprinted with permission.

————, The Warren Court and Criminal Justice, in the Warren Court: A Retrospective 116, 140–43 (B. Schwartz ed. 1996). Copyright © 1996 by the Oxford University Press. Reprinted with permission.

————, On the Fortieth Anniversary of the *Miranda* Case, 5 Ohio St. J. Crim. L. 163 (2007). Copyright © 2007 by the Ohio State Journal of Criminal Law. Reprinted by permission.

Kerr, Orin S., King, Nancy J., LaFave, Wayne R., & Israel, Jerold H., Criminal Procedure Treatise (3d ed. 2007). Copyright © 2007 by Thomson/West. Reprinted by permission.

King, Nancy J., LaFave, Wayne R., Israel, Jerold H., & Kerr, Orin S., Criminal Procedure Treatise (3d ed. 2007). Copyright © 2007 by Thomson/West. Reprinted by permission.

Klarman, Michael J., The Racial Origins of Modern Criminal Procedure, 99 Mich.L. Rev. 48 (2000). Copyright © 2000 by the Michigan Law Review Association. Reprinted by permission.

Kreimer, Seth F., Too Close to the Rack and the Screw: Constitutional Constraints on Torture in the War on Terror, 6 U.Pa.J.Const.L. 278 (2003). Copyright © 2003 by the University of Pennsylvania Journal of Constitutional Law. Reprinted by permission.

LaFave, Wayne R., Israel, Jerold H., King, Nancy J., & Kerr, Orin S., Criminal Procedure Treatise (3d ed. 2007). Copyright © 2007 by Thomson/West. Reprinted by permission.

LaFave, Wayne, Search and Seizure: A Treatise on the Fourth Amendment (4th ed. 2004). Copyright © 2004 by Thomson/West. Reprinted by permission.

Leo, Richard A., Police Interrogation and American Justice (2008). Copyright © 2008 by Richard A. Leo. Reprinted by permission.

_____, and Drizin, Steven, The Problem of False Confessions in the Post–DNA World, 82 North Carolina Law Review 891 (2004). Copyright © by the North Carolina Law Review. Reprinted by permission.

Loewy, Arnold, Police–Obtained Evidence and the Constitution: Distinguishing Unconstitutionally Obtained Evidence from Unconstitutionally Used Evidence, 87 Mich.L.Rev. 907 (1989). Copyright © 1989 by the Michigan Law Review. Reprinted by permission.

Maclin, Tracey, "Black and Blue Encounters"—Some Preliminary Thoughts about Fourth Amendment Seizures: Should Race Matter?, 26 Val. U.L.Rev. 243 (1991). Copyright © by the Valparaiso Law Review. Reprinted by permission.

Marcus, Paul, It's Not Just About Miranda: Determining the Voluntariness of Confessions in Criminal Cases, 40 Valparaiso Law Review 601 (2006). Copyright © by the Valparaiso Law Review. Reprinted by permission.

Michaels, Alan C., and Dressler, Joshua, Understanding Criminal Procedure (5th ed. 2010). Copyright © 2010 by Matthew Bender & Co. Inc. Reprinted by permission.

Mosteller, Robert P., The Duke Lacrosse Case, Innocence, and False Identifications: A Fundamental Failure to "Do Justice," 76 Ford.L.Rev. 1337 (2007). Copyright © 2007 by the Fordham Law Review. Reprinted by permission.

Orfield, Myron, Deterrence, Perjury and the Heater Factor: An Exclusionary Rule in the Chicago Criminal Courts, 63 U.Colo.L.Rev. 75 (1992). Copyright © 1992 by the University of Colorado Law Review. Reprinted by permission.

Parry, John T., and White, Welsh S., Interrogating Suspected Terrorists: Should Torture Be An Option?, 63 U.Pitt.L.Rev. 743 (2002). Copyright © 2002 by the University of Pittsburgh Law Review. Reprinted by permission.

Primus, Eve Brensike, Structural Reform in Criminal Defense: Relocating Ineffective Assistance of Counsel Claims, 92 Cornell L. Rev. 679 (2007). Copyright © 2007 by the Cornell Law Review. Reprinted by permission.

Rosenthal, Lawrence, Against Orthodoxy: Miranda Is Not Prophylactic and the Constitution Is Not Perfect, 10 Chapman L. Rev. 579 (2007). Copyright © 2007 by the Chapman Law Review. Reprinted by permission.

Schulhofer, Stephen J., Reconsidering *Miranda*, 54 U.Ch.L.Rev. 435 (1987). Copyright © 1987 by the University of Chicago Law Review. Reprinted by permission.

Seidman, Louis Michael, *Brown* and *Miranda*, 80 Calif.L.Rev. 673 (1992). Copyright © 1992 by the California Law Review, Inc. Reprinted by permission.

Slobogin, Christopher, Toward Taping, 1 Ohio St.J.Crim.L. 309 (2003). Copyright © 2003 by the Ohio State Journal of Criminal Law. Reprinted by permission.

Slobogin, Christopher & Whitebread, Charles, Criminal Procedure (5th ed. 2008). Copyright © 2000 by The Foundation Press, Inc. Reprinted by permission.

Smith, Stephen F., Activism as Restraint: Lessons from Criminal Procedure, 80 Texas L.Rev. 1056 (2002). Copyright © 2002 by the Texas Law Review. Reprinted by permission.

Strauss, Marcy, Torture, 48 N.Y. Law Sch.Rev. 203 (2004). Copyright © 2004 by the New York Law School Review. Reprinted by permission.

Stuntz, William J., The Uneasy Relationship Between Criminal Procedure and Criminal Justice, 107 Yale L.J. (1997). Copyright © 1997 by the Yale Law Journal Co., Inc. Reprinted by permission of the Yale Law Journal Company and William S. Hein Company from *The Yale Law Journal*, Vol. 107, pages 1–76.

———, Waiving Rights in Criminal Procedure, 75 Va.L.Rev. 761 (1989). Copyright © 1989 by the Virginia Law Review. Reprinted by permission.

———, Warrants, and Fourth Amendment Remedies, 77 Va.L.Rev. 881 (1991). Copyright © 1991 by the Virginia Law Review. Reprinted by permission.

———, *Miranda*'s Mistake, 99 Mich.L.Rev. 975 (2001). Copyright © 2001 by the Michigan Law Review Association. Reprinted by permission.

Thomas, George C. III, Stories about *Miranda*, 102 Mich. L. Rev. 1959 (2004) Copyright © 2004 by the Michigan Law Review. Reprinted by permission

Weisselberg, Charles D., Mourning *Miranda*, 96 Calif.L.Rev. 1521 (2008). Copyright © 2008 by the California Law Review, Inc. Reprinted by permission.

White, Welsh S., and Parry, John T., Interrogating Suspected Terrorists: Should Torture Be An Option?, 63 U.Pitt.L.Rev. 743 (2002). Copyright © 2002 by the University of Pittsburgh Law Review. Reprinted by permission.

Whitebread, Charles, and Slobogin, Christopher, Criminal Procedure (5th ed. 2008). Copyright © 2008 by The Foundation Press, Inc. Reprinted by permission.

Summary of Contents

                                                                                          Page
Preface to the Thirteenth Edition -- iii
Acknowledgements-- v
Table of Cases -- xxxv
Table of Authorities --- liii

PART ONE. INTRODUCTION

Chapter
 1. On Studying the Legal Regulation of the Criminal Justice Process ----   2
 2. Sources of Criminal Procedure Law--- 25
 3. Some General Reflections on Criminal Procedure and Its
          Administration -- 49
 4. The Right to Counsel--- 74
 5. The Performance of Counsel-- 131

PART TWO. POLICE PRACTICES

 6. Arrest, Search and Seizure --- 222
 7. Undercover Investigations --- 470
 8. Network Surveillance --- 501
 9. Police Interrogation and Confessions --- 543
10. Lineups, Showups and Other Pre-Trial Identification Procedures ----- 760
11. Grand Jury Investigations-- 791
12. The Scope of the Exclusionary Rules--- 879

Index-- [1]

TABLE OF CONTENTS

PREFACE TO THE THIRTEENTH EDITION -- iii

ACKNOWLEDGEMENTS--- v

TABLE OF CASES --- xxxv

TABLE OF AUTHORITIES -- liii

PART ONE

INTRODUCTION

CHAPTER 1. ON STUDYING THE LEGAL REGULATION OF THE CRIMINAL JUSTICE PROCESS-------------------------- 2

1. *THE CHAPTER'S OBJECTIVES* --- 2
2. *THE STEPS IN THE PROCESS* -- 3
    Step 1 (pre-arrest investigation) through Step 18 (collateral remedies) 6
3. *DIVERSITY IN LEGAL REGULATION* -- 19
    Fifty-two lawmaking jurisdictions-- 19
    Unifying role of federal constitution regulation---------------------------- 19
    Natural divergence --- 21
    Describing common patterns--- 21
    Models--- 22
    Procedural subsets --- 22
4. *DIVERSITY IN ADMINISTRATION* --- 23
    Significance of discretion--- 23
    Discretion and diversity --- 23

CHAPTER 2. SOURCES OF CRIMINAL PROCEDURE LAW------ 25

1. *THE "FUNDAMENTAL FAIRNESS," "TOTAL INCORPORATION" AND "SELECTIVE INCORPORATION" THEORIES*--------------- 25
    McDonald v. City of Chicago-- 25
    Duncan v. Louisiana-- 26
2. *THE PROBLEM OF BODILY EXTRACTIONS: ANOTHER LOOK AT THE "DUE PROCESS" AND "SELECTIVE INCORPORATION" APPROACHES*-- 27
    Rochin v. California --- 28
    Breithaupt v. Abram -- 29
    Schmerber v. California --- 30
    County of Sacramento v. Lewis --- 31
    Jerold Israel—Free-Standing Due Process and Criminal Procedure --- 32
3. *IS THERE A DUE PROCESS RIGHT TO TECHNOLOGY THAT MIGHT ESTABLISH ONE'S INNOCENCE?*--------------------------- 32
    District Attorney's Office v. Osborne --- 33
4. *THE FEDERAL COURTS' "SUPERVISORY POWER" OVER THE ADMINISTRATION OF FEDERAL CRIMINAL JUSTICE* -------- 34
    McNabb v. United States -- 34

4.   THE FEDERAL COURTS' "SUPERVISORY POWER" OVER THE
     ADMINISTRATION OF FEDERAL CRIMINAL JUSTICE—
     Continued
          Sara Sun Beale—Reconsidering Supervisory Power in Criminal
              Cases-- 34
              United States v. Payner -- 35
              United States v. Hasting --- 36
5.   TRENDS AND COUNTERTRENDS: THE "NEW FEDERALISM IN
     CRIMINAL PROCEDURE" AND NEW LIMITATIONS ON
     STATE RIGHTS PROTECTIONS -- 38
          Michigan v. Long -- 38
          Charles Whitebread & Christopher Slobogin—Criminal
              Procedure -- 39
6.   DUE PROCESS, INDIVIDUAL RIGHTS AND THE WAR ON
     TERRORISM: WHAT PROCESS IS CONSTITUTIONALLY
     DUE A CITIZEN WHO DISPUTES HIS ENEMY-COMBATANT
     DESIGNATION? -- 40
          Hamdi v. Rumsfeld -- 40
          Rasul v. Bush --- 41
          Hamdan v. Rumsfeld--- 41
          Boumediene v. Bush --- 43

**CHAPTER 3.   SOME GENERAL REFLECTIONS ON CRIMINAL
              PROCEDURE AND ITS ADMINISTRATION** --------- 49
     Michael J. Klarman—The Racial Origins of Modern Criminal Procedure 49
     Yale Kamisar—The Warren Court and Criminal Justice ---------------- 51
     Donald A. Dripps—Constitutional Theory for Criminal Procedure---- 53
     Peter Arenella—Foreword: O. J. Lessons ------------------------------- 53
     William J. Stuntz—The Uneasy Relationship Between Criminal
          Procedure and Criminal Justice-------------------------------------- 54
     Justice David H. Souter—Dissenting in Kansas v. Marsh --------------- 57
     Justice Antonin Scalia—Concurring in Kansas v. Marsh --------------- 59
     Brandon L. Garrett—Convicting the Innocent ----------------------------- 59
     Tracey Maclin—"Black and Blue Encounters"—Some Preliminary
          Thoughts about Fourth Amendment Seizures: Should Race Matter? 64
     Sharon L. Davies—Profiling Terror ------------------------------------- 66
     A Note on the Justice Department's Policy Guidance Regarding Racial
          Profiling -- 67
     According to a Vera Institute Study, Post-9/11 Law Enforcement
          Policies Have Caused Deep Fears and Distrust Among
          Arab-Americans -- 68

CHAPTER 4.   THE RIGHT TO COUNSEL-------------------------------- **74**
1.   THE RIGHT TO APPOINTED COUNSEL AND RELATED PROB-
     LEMS-- 70
     A.   The Right to Appointed Counsel in Criminal Proceedings--------- 70
              James Tomkovicz—The Right to the Assistance of Counsel 70
              Betts v. Brady--- 71
                   The Aftermath of *Betts v. Brady* -------------------------- 73
              Gideon v. Wainwright--- 73
                   Argersinger v. Hamlin------------------------------------ 80

1. *THE RIGHT TO APPOINTED COUNSEL AND RELATED PROB-LEMS*—Continued

    Scott v. Illinois ---- 81

    Bruce R. Jacob—Memories of and Reflections about Gideon v. Wainwright ---- 82

    Donald A. Dripps—About Guilt or Innocence ---- 83

    Nichols v. United States ---- 83

    Alabama v. Shelton ---- 84

  B. The "Beginnings" of the Right to Counsel: "Criminal Prosecutions" and "Critical Stages" ---- 85

    Rothgery v. Gillespie County ---- 85

    United States v. Gouveia ---- 86

    Estelle v. Smith ---- 92

2. *THE RIGHT TO APPOINTED COUNSEL IN PROCEEDINGS OTHER THAN CRIMINAL PROSECUTIONS: THE CONTINUED VITALITY OF THE BETTS v. BRADY APPROACH* ---- 93

  A. Probation and Parole Revocation Hearings; Juvenile Court Proceedings; Parental Status Termination Proceedings; Contempt Hearings ---- 93

    Gagnon v. Scarpelli ---- 93

    In re Gault ---- 95

    Lassiter v. Dep't of Social Services ---- 96

    Lawrence J. Siskind—Civil Gideon: An Idea Whose Time Has Not Come ---- 97

3. *THE GRIFFIN-DOUGLAS "EQUALITY" PRINCIPLE* ---- 99

    Griffin v. Illinois ---- 99

  A. Application (or extension) of *Griffin* ---- 99

    Mayer v. Chicago ---- 100

  B. The Impact of the "Equality" Principle on Those Who Cannot Afford Counsel or Other Forms of Assistance ---- 100

    Douglas v. California ---- 100

    Ross v. Moffitt ---- 102

    On the Meaning of *Ross* ---- 105

    Yale Kamisar—Poverty, Equality, and Criminal Procedure ---- 105

    Halbert v. Michigan ---- 105

4. *WAIVER OF THE RIGHT TO COUNSEL: THE RIGHT TO PROCEED PRO SE* ---- 107

    Faretta v. California ---- 107

    Erica J. Hashimoto—Defending the Right of Self-Representation: An Empirical Look at the Pro Se Felony Defendant ---- 110

    Martinez v. Court of Appeal of California ---- 111

    McKaskle v. Wiggins ---- 111

    Anne Bowen Poulin—The Role of Standby Counsel ---- 113

    Warning Requirements and the Waiver of the Right to Counsel ---- 114

    Iowa v. Tovar ---- 115

    Godinez v. Moran ---- 117

4. *WAIVER OF THE RIGHT TO COUNSEL: THE RIGHT TO*
    PROCEED PRO SE—Continued
            Limits of the Right to Self-Representation--------------------- 118
            Indiana v. Edwards --- 118
            Christopher Slobogin—Mental Illness and Self-
            Representation -- 120
5. *THE RIGHT TO "COUNSEL OF CHOICE"*--------------------------------- 121
            United States v. Gonzalez-Lopez ----------------------------- 121
            Morris v. Slappy --- 128
            Caplin & Drysdale Chartered v. United States --------------- 129

CHAPTER 5.   THE PERFORMANCE OF COUNSEL ------------------ 131
1. *THE INEFFECTIVE ASSISTANCE OF COUNSEL (IAC) CLAIM:*
    BASIC FEATURES-- 131
            Cuyler v. Sullivan --- 131
            United States v. Cronic-- 134
2. *THE* STRICKLAND *STANDARDS* --------------------------------------- 136
            Strickland v. Washington ------------------------------------ 137
            Notes and Questions on *Strickland* --------------------------- 147
            Bobby v. Van Hook --- 151
            Padilla v. Kentucky -- 151
            Kimmelman v. Morrison -- 152
            Lockhart v. Fretwell -- 153
3. STRICKLAND *APPLIED*--- 154
            Harrington v. Richter-- 155
            Section 2254(d)(1) deference ----------------------------------- 163
            Establishing "counsel's actual thinking ---------------------- 164
            Supreme Court rulings--- 164
            Counsel's "actual thought" and "objective reason-
            ableness" -- 165
            The isolated error--- 165
            Section 2254(d)(1) deference ----------------------------------- 163
            The limits of tactical decision making ------------------------ 166
            Mitigating Evidence and Capital Sentencing -------------------- 166
            Wiggins v. Smith --- 167
            Rompilla v. Beard --- 168
            Cullen v. Pinholster --- 172
4. *THE* CRONIC *EXCEPTIONS AND OTHER POSSIBLE PER*
    SE VIOLATIONS--- 173
            United States v. Cronic------------------------------------- 173
            Bell v. Cone -- 174
            Challenges to the Defense Delivery System Deficiencies --- 176
            Hurrell-Harring v. State of New York----------------------- 177
            Strickland and systemic challenges ---------------------------- 182
            Duncan v. State-- 182
            Compensation for appointed attorneys-------------------------- 183
            Lawyer withdrawal --- 183
            The Right to the Assistance of Experts------------------------ 183
            Ake v. Oklahoma --- 183

4. *THE* CRONIC *EXCEPTIONS AND OTHER POSSIBLE PER*
     SE VIOLATIONS—Continued
       The Sixth Amendment vs. Fourteenth Amendment
          due process -- 185
       Other basic tools --- 185
       Local law alternatives -- 186
       Reversible error --- 186
5. *CONFLICTS OF INTEREST* --- 186
   A.   Potential Conflicts and the Duty to Inquire -------------------- 186
       Range of conflicts-- 186
       Conflicts and professional responsibility standards ---------------- 187
       Prohibiting representation in potential conflict situations-------- 188
       Non-constitutional requirement of judicial inquiry ---------------- 188
       Constitutional duty of inquiry-------------------------------------- 188
          Holloway v. Arkansas -- 188
          Cuyler v. Sullivan -- 189
   B.   Postconviction Review-- 191
   Mickens v. Taylor --- 191
       Burger v. Kemp --- 201
   C.   Disqualification of Counsel -- 202
   Wheat v. United States --- 202
       William J. Stuntz—Waiving Rights in Criminal Procedure ------ 207
       Bruce A. Green—"Through a Glass Darkly": How the Court Sees
          Motions to Disqualify Criminal Defense Lawyers -------------- 207
       "Manufactured conflicts" -- 208
       Disqualifications in other conflict settings -------------------------- 208
       Waivers -- 208
6. *CLIENT CONTROL*--- 209
       Self-representation vs. attorney control----------------------------- 209
       Identifying "strategic" and "personal" decisions -------------------- 210
       The Nixon ruling --- 211
          Florida v. Nixon --- 211
       Nixon and personal decisions--------------------------------------- 212
       Nixon and consultation-- 213
       Ineffective assistance and acceptance of defendant's directions- 213
       Gonzalez v. United States -- 214
       Justice Scalia's concurring opinion in *Gonzalez* --------------------- 215
       Failing to consult and per se prejudice ------------------------------ 216
          Roe v. Flores-Ortega -- 216
       Lawyer/client disagreements and the replacement of counsel---- 217
       Appointed Counsel and the Frivolous Appeals ---------------------- 218
          Anders v. California --- 218

PART TWO

POLICE PRACTICES

CHAPTER 6.   ARREST, SEARCH AND SEIZURE ---------------------- 222
1. *THE EXCLUSIONARY RULE*--- 222
   Wolf v. Colorado --- 222
   Mapp v. Ohio--- 224
   United States v. Leon-- 229

1.   *THE EXCLUSIONARY RULE*—Continued

Arnold H. Loewy—Distinguishing Unconstitutionally Obtained Evidence from Unconstitutionally Used Evidence --------------- 238

Myron W. Orfield—Deterrence, Perjury and the Heater Factor: An Exclusionary Rule in the Chicago Criminal Courts --------- 238

Massachusetts v. Sheppard-- 239

Groh v. Ramirez -- 240

John Kaplan—The Limits of the Exclusionary Rule --------------- 241

Burger, C.J., dissenting in Bivens -- 242

Illinois v. Krull--- 243

Davis v. United States -- 244

United States v. Caceres --- 246

Notes on the "Dimensions" of the Exclusionary Rule-------------------- 247

United States v. Calandra --- 247

Pennsylvania Board of Probation and Parole v. Scott -------------- 247

One 1958 Plymouth Sedan v. Pennsylvania ------------------------- 248

United States v. Janis-- 248

I.N.S. v. Lopez-Mendoza -- 249

Burdeau v. McDowell -- 249

United States v. Jacobsen --- 249

Arizona v. Evans-- 250

United States v. Verdugo-Urquidez ----------------------------------- 251

Hudson v. Michigan --- 252

Herring v. United States-- 258

Wayne R. LaFave—The Smell of *Herring*-------------------------------- 263

2.   *PROTECTED AREAS AND INTERESTS*------------------------------- 264

Katz v. United States -- 264

Fourth Amendment interests --- 267

Garbage -- 267

California v. Greenwood --- 267

"Curtilage" vs. "open fields"--- 269

Oliver v. United States --- 269

Florida v. Riley-- 270

Other premises--- 272

Hudson v. Palmer--- 272

Vehicles--- 273

Effects--- 273

Bond v. United States --- 273

Enhancing the senses -- 274

Thermal imaging -- 274

Kyllo v. United States --- 274

The canine nose--- 274

United States v. Place -- 277

Illinois v. Caballes --- 277

Photographic magnification--- 278

Dow Chemical Co. v. United States-------------------------------------- 278

United States v. Jones -- 279

ALPR cameras -- 285

Data aggregation and mining--- 285

Gouled v. United States -- 286

2. *PROTECTED AREAS AND INTERESTS*—Continued
    Andresen v. Maryland ---- 286
        Zurcher v. Stanford Daily ---- 288
        O'Connor v. Johnson ---- 291
        A.L.I.—Model Code of Pre-Arraignment Code ---- 291
        Tattered Cover v. City of Thornton ---- 291
        The PATRIOT Act ---- 292
        United States v. Rayburn House Office Building ---- 292
3. *"PROBABLE CAUSE"* ---- 292
    Spinelli v. United States ---- 292
    Illinois v. Gates ---- 295
        Massachusetts v. Upton ---- 304
        United States v. Grubbs ---- 306
        Franks v. Delaware ---- 307
    Notes on the Informer's Privilege ---- 308
        McCray v. Illinois ---- 308
    Maryland v. Pringle ---- 310
    Notes on Other Sources of Probable Cause ---- 314
4. *SEARCH WARRANTS* ---- 316
    A. Issuance of the Warrant ---- 316
        Coolidge v. New Hampshire ---- 316
        Shadwick v. City of Tampa ---- 316
        Maryland v. Garrison ---- 317
        United States v. Bradley ---- 319
        Groh v. Ramirez ---- 320
    B. Execution of the Warrant ---- 321
        Gooding v. United States ---- 321
        Richards v. Wisconsin ---- 322
        United States v. Banks ---- 323
        Ybarra v. Illinois ---- 324
        Los Angeles County v. Rettele ---- 325
        Michigan v. Summers ---- 325
        Muehler v. Mena ---- 327
        Horton v. California ---- 325
        Wilson v. Layne ---- 328
    C. Special Problems: Computer Searches ---- 329
    D. The "Preference" for Warrants ---- 332
5. *WARRANTLESS ARRESTS AND SEARCHES OF THE PERSON* - 332
    United States v. Watson ---- 332
        Atwater v. City of Lago Vista ---- 337
        Tennessee v. Garner ---- 339
        Scott v. Harris ---- 340
        Gerstein v. Pugh ---- 340
        County of Riverside v. McLaughlin ---- 342
    United States v. Robinson ---- 343
    Notes and Questions on Unnecessary, Pretextual, and Arbitrary
        Arrests ---- 348
        Gustafson v. Florida ---- 348

5. *WARRANTLESS ARRESTS AND SEARCHES OF THE*
      PERSON—Continued
       Atwater v. City of Lago Vista ------------------------------------ 348
       Whren v. United States--- 353
       United States v. Botero-Ospina ---------------------------------- 356
    Notes and Questions on Other Searches of the Person ----------------- 359
       United States v. Edwards-- 359
       Schmerber v. California --- 360
       Winston v. Lee --- 360
6. *WARRANTLESS ENTRIES AND SEARCHES OF PREMISES* ----- 362
   Chimel v. California--- 363
       Maryland v. Buie --- 366
       Washington v. Chrisman--- 367
       Arizona v. Hicks -- 368
   Kentucky v. King -- 368
       Vale v. Louisiana --- 372
       Segura v. United States --- 373
       Illinois v. McArthur--- 374
       Mincey v. Arizona -- 375
       Brigham City v. Stuart -- 375
   Payton v. New York --- 376
       Welsh v. Wisconsin-- 381
       Steagald v. United States --------------------------------------- 382
7. *WARRANTLESS SEIZURES AND SEARCHES OF VEHICLES*
      AND CONTAINERS-- 383
   California v. Carney--- 383
   California v. Acevedo-- 388
       Wyoming v. Houghton --- 393
       Illinois v. Andreas --- 397
   Arizone v. Gant -- 398
       Colorado v. Bertine --- 407
       Florida v. Wells -- 408
8. *STOP AND FRISK* --- 408
   Terry v. Ohio--- 408
   The Significance of the Stop-and-Frisk Cases ----------------------------- 415
   A.   Police Action Short of a Seizure----------------------------------- 415
       United States v. Drayton-- 415
       California v. Hodari D.--- 416
       Brendlin v. California --- 417
   B.   Grounds for Temporary Seizure for Investigation------------------- 419
       United States v. Cortez-- 419
       United States v. Hensley--- 420
       United State v. Sokolow --- 421
       Illinois v. Wardlow --- 421
       Tracey L. Meares & Bernard E. Harcourt—Transparent
         Adjudication and Social Science Research in Constitutional
         Criminal Procedure --- 422
       Florida v. J. L. --- 422
   C.   Permissible Extent and Scope of Temporary Seizure--------------- 425
       Florida v. Royer -- 425

8. *STOP AND FRISK*—Continued
       United States v. Sharpe ---- 426
       Hiibel v. Sixth Judicial District Court ---- 427
       Illinois v. Caballes ---- 428
       United States v. Everett ---- 429
       Ohio v. Robinette ---- 431
   D. Temporary Seizure of Effects ---- 432
       United States v. Place ---- 433
   E. Protective Search ---- 434
       Arizona v. Johnson ---- 434
       David A. Harris—Frisking Every Suspect: The Withering of Terry 435
       Minnesota v. Dickerson ---- 436
       Michigan v. Long ---- 436
   F. Other Brief Detention for Investigation ---- 437
       Davis v. Mississippi ---- 437
       Dunaway v. New York ---- 438
9. *ADMINISTRATIVE INSPECTIONS AND REGULATORY SEARCHES: MORE ON BALANCING THE NEED AGAINST THE INVASION OF PRIVACY* ---- 439
       Camara v. Municipal Court ---- 439
       Michigan Dep't of State Police v. Sitz ---- 442
       New Jersey v. T.L.O. ---- 442
       National Treasury Employees Union v. Von Raab ---- 443
       Skinner v. Railroad Labor Executives' Ass'n ---- 443
       Board of Education v. Earls ---- 444
   Samson v. California ---- 444
       United States v. Kincade ---- 452
       Illinois v. Lidster ---- 453
10. *CONSENT SEARCHES* ---- 454
   A. The Nature of "Consent ---- 454
       Schneckloth v. Bustamonte ---- 454
       Notes on the Relevant Factors in Determining the Validity of a Consent ---- 459
          Bumper v. North Carolina ---- 459
          Florida v. Jimeno ---- 460
   B. Third Party Consent ---- 462
       Illinois v. Rodriguez ---- 462
          United States v. Andrus ---- 465
       Notes on Who May Consent ---- 466
          Frazier v. Cupp ---- 467
       Notes on Limits on Third-Party Consent ---- 467
       Georgia v. Randolph ---- 467

CHAPTER 7.   UNDERCOVER INVESTIGATIONS ---- 470
1. *SECRET AGENTS AND THE FOURTH AMENDMENT* ---- 470
   Hoffa v. United States ---- 470
       United States v. White ---- 474
       Undercover agents and recording devices ---- 475
       Undercover Agents and the Supervisory Power ---- 477
       Government infiltration of groups engaged in First Amendment activities ---- 477

1.   *SECRET AGENTS AND THE FOURTH AMENDMENT*—Continued
       The Attorney General's Guidelines on the Use of Confidential
              Informants --- 478
       Undercover Agents and the Scope of Consent ------------------------ 478
2.   *THE ENTRAPMENT DEFENSE*-- 479
       A.   Introduction -- 479
              Sorrells v. United States -- 479
       B.   Inducement -- 480
              Sherman v. United States ------------------------------------ 480
              The meaning of "inducement" ------------------------------------ 485
              United States v. Gendron-- 485
              Subjective versus objective approaches ------------------------- 486
              United States v. Russell --- 487
              A common myth about entrapment -------------------------------- 489
       C.   Predisposition-- 489
              Jacobson v. United States ----------------------------------- 490
              How much predisposition is enough? -------------------------------- 496
              What does predisposition measure? ------------------------------- 496
              The timing of predisposition evidence --------------------------- 497
              Private, vicarious and derivative entrapment ------------------ 498
              "To Catch a Predator" and internet entrapment------------------ 499

CHAPTER 8.   NETWORK SURVEILLANCE --------------------------------- 501
1.   *THE FOURTH AMENDMENT*-- 501
       A.   Rights in Content Information ------------------------------------- 501
              United States v. Warshak ------------------------------------ 501
              Postal mail privacy--- 505
              Ex parte Jackson --- 505
              The history of telephone privacy ------------------------------------ 505
              Olmstead v. United States--- 505
              Berger v. New York-- 507
              Katz v. United States -- 507
              Cordless telephone privacy--- 507
              Private search doctrine-- 509
              Materials posted on the World Wide Web-------------------------- 509
       B.   Rights in Non-content Information ------------------------------- 510
              Smith v. Maryland-- 510
              Mail covers and postal mail privacy --------------------------------- 515
              Internet addresses -- 515
              United States v. Forrester ------------------------------------ 515
              Protection for stored account records--------------------------- 516
2.   *STATUTORY PRIVACY LAWS* --- 518
       A.   Introduction -- 518
       B.   The Wiretap Act ("Title III")--------------------------------------- 520
              United States v. Turk --- 520
              Interception of communications ------------------------------------ 522
              Contents and non-content information------------------------------ 522
              Bugging and oral communications------------------------------------ 523
              Obtaining wiretap orders -- 524
              Covert entry-- 525
              Use and disclosure of intercepted information ------------------ 525
              Bartnicki v. Vopper --- 525

2. *STATUTORY PRIVACY LAWS*—Continued
       Remedies for violations of the Wiretap Act -------------------------- 526
       Exceptions to the Wiretap Act -------------------------------------- 526
       Deal v. Spears --- 526
       The consent exception --- 526
       The extension telephone exception --------------------------------- 530
       Packet sniffers and "Carnivore" ----------------------------------- 531
  C. The Pen Register Statute -- 532
  D. The Stored Communications Act --------------------------------------- 534
       Entities regulated by the Act -------------------------------------- 535
       The rules for compelling opened e-mail ----------------------------- 536
       Why does the Act have lower protections for remote computing
         services and for storage for more than 180 days? ----------------- 537
       Why does the Act limit voluntary disclosure only for services
         available to the public? --- 538
       Note on National Security Monitoring and the Foreign Intelli-
         gence Surveillance Act --- 539

CHAPTER 9. POLICE INTERROGATION AND CONFESSIONS - 543
1. *HISTORICAL BACKGROUND* --- 543
  A. The Third Degree (and Torture) ------------------------------------- 543
       Richard Leo—Police Interrogation and American Justice --------- 543
  B. Police Professionalism and the Rise of the Police Interrogation
       Manual -- 545
       Fred E. Inbau—Police Interrogation -------------------------------- 546
       Fred Inbau & John Reid—Criminal Interrogation and Confes-
         sions -- 546
  C. The Interests Protected by the Due Process "Voluntariness"
       or "Totality of Circumstances" Test for Admitting
       Confessions --- 547
  D. The Shortcomings of the "Voluntariness" Test ---------------------- 551
       Louis Michael Seidman—*Brown* and *Miranda* ---------------------- 553
       Culombe v. Connecticut -- 553
  E. The *McNabb*—*Mallory* Rule: Supervisory Authority Over Federal
       Criminal Justice vs. Fourteenth Amendment Due Process ---- 554
  F. The Right to Counsel and the Analogy to the Accusatorial,
       Adversary Trial -- 556
       Crooker v. California --- 556
       Cicenia v. La Gay --- 556
       Spano v. New York --- 556
  G. *Massiah* and *Escobedo*: The Court Closes in on the "Confession
       Problem" -- 557
       Massiah v. United States -- 557
       Escobedo v. Illinois -- 559
       On the Meaning of *Escobedo* -------------------------------------- 563
  H. A Late Arrival on the Scene: The Privilege Against Self-
       Incrimination -- 564
       Malloy v. Hogan -- 565
2. *THE MIRANDA "REVOLUTION"* --- 566
    Oral Arguments in *Miranda* and Companion Cases ------------------ 566
    Miranda v. Arizona --- 571

2. *THE MIRANDA "REVOLUTION"*—Continued

Justice Kennedy's Question about *Miranda*'s Constitutional Status - 588

Can (Did) Congress "Repeal" *Miranda*? (and why treatment of this
issue should be postponed) -- 589

Forty-six Years with *Miranda*: An Overview ----------------------------- 589

    Michigan v. Tucker --- 590

    New York v. Quarles -- 593

    Oregon v. Elstad -- 593

    Dickerson v. United States --------------------------------------- 594

    Berghuis v. Thompkins --- 595

    Barry Friedman—The Wages of Stealth Overruling (with
particular attention to Miranda v. Arizona)---------------------- 595

Applying and Explaining *Miranda* -------------------------------------- 596

  1. "Intelligent" waivers vs. "wise" ones ------------------------------ 596

    State v. McKnight --- 596

  2. Do the Miranda warnings actually induce some suspects to
talk? --- 596

    Steven Duke—Does *Miranda* Protect the Innocent or the
Guilty? -- 596

  3. Adequacy of warnings -- 597

    Duckworth v. Eagan--- 597

  4. Need for admonitions in addition to the four *Miranda* warnings 599

    Colorado v. Spring -- 599

  5. "Custody" vs. "focus"--- 601

    Beckwith v. United States -- 601

  6. What constitutes "custody" or "custodial interrogation"? -------- 602

    J.D.B. v. North Carolina ------------------------------------ 603

  7. What constitutes "interrogation" within the meaning of
Miranda?-- 608

    Rhode Island v. Innis-- 600

    Arizona v. Mauro -- 613

  8. The "jail plant" situation; "surreptitious interrogation" ---------- 615

    Illinois v. Perkins --- 615

  9. **Pennsylvania v. Muniz**: What constitutes "testimonial" evidence?
What questions fall within the "routine booking question"
exception to *Miranda*? --- 617

  10. When does a response to an officer's question present a reasonable danger of incrimination? ----------------------------------- 619

    Hiibel v. Sixth Judicial Court ----------------------------------- 619

  11. Questioning prompted by concern for "public safety"------------ 621

    New York v. Quarles --- 621

  12. Is the Quarles "public safety" exception insufficient when it
comes to dealing with suspected terrorists?---------------------- 625

  13. When should interrogators be allowed to use "torture" in
order to obtain information from suspected terrorists? -------- 625

    Marcy Strauss—Torture -- 625

    Alan Dershowitz—The Torture Warrant: A Response to
Professor Strauss --- 626

    Seth Kreimer—Too Close to the Rack and Screw ------------------ 627

    Alan Dershowitz—Torture Without Visibility and Account-
ability Is Worse Than With It ----------------------------------- 627

2.   *THE MIRANDA "REVOLUTION"*—Continued

      John T. Parry & Welsh White—Interrogating Suspected Ter-
        rorists: Should Torture Be an Option? ------------------------------ 628

14. Meeting the "heavy burden" of demonstrating waiver: should
      tape recordings of the warnings and police questioning be
      required? -- 628

      Richard Leo—Police Interrogation and American Justice--------- 628

15. Implied waiver -- 631

      North Carolina v. Butler -- 631

16. Why do so many suspects waive their rights? ------------------------ 632

      George C. Thomas—Stories about *Miranda* ------------------------- 632

      David Simon—Homicide: A Year on the Killing Streets ----------- 632

      Yale Kamisar—On the Fortieth Anniversary of the Miranda
        Case -- 632

17. "Qualified" or "Conditional" Waiver ------------------------------------ 633

      Connecticut v. Barrett -- 633

18. What Constitutes an Invocation of *Miranda* Rights? ---------------- 634

      Fare v. Michael C. -- 634

19. The Scope of "second-level" *Miranda* Safeguards -------------------- 635

      Michigan v. Mosley --- 635

      Edwards v. Arizona --- 636

      Arizona v. Roberson -- 636

20. When do the Edwards protections come to an end? What
      constitutes a "break in custody"? ----------------------------------- 637

      Maryland v. Shatzer --- 637

21. What constitutes "initiating" further communication with the
      police? --- 642

      Oregon v. Bradshaw --- 642

22. How direct, assertive and unambiguous must a suspect be in
      order to invoke the right to counsel? --------------------------------- 645

      Janet Ainsworth—In a Different Register: The Pragmatics
        of Powerlessness in Police Interrogation --------------------------- 645

      Davis v. United States --- 646

23. Another look at implied waiver: the distinction between the
      right to remain silent and the right not to be interrogated ---- 648

      Oral arguments in Berghuis v. Thompkins -------------------------- 649

      Berghuis v. Thompkins -- 651

24. The *Miranda–Edwards* rule and the Sixth Amendment
      right to counsel compared and contrasted --------------------------- 659

      Montejo v. Louisiana -- 659

25. "Anticipatorily" invoking the *Miranda–Edwards–Roberson* right
      to counsel --- 663

26. Does the failure to inform a suspect that a lawyer is trying to see
      him vitiate the waiver of Miranda rights? ------------------------- 665

      Moran v. Burbine --- 665

27. Use of a pretrial psychiatric examination at a capital sentencing
      proceeding -- 670

      Estelle v. Smith --- 670

28. *Miranda* and mentally retarded suspects: the Cloud–Shepherd–
      Barkoff–Shur study --- 671

2.   *THE MIRANDA "REVOLUTION"*—Continued

    29.   Juveniles --- 672

    30.   Comparing and contrasting *Miranda* with (a) the prohibition against the use of involuntary statements and (b) the Fourth Amendment exclusionary rule ----------------------------------- 672

          Withrow v. Williams --- 673

    31.   The failure of the police to notify the consular post of a detainee's home country that he has been arrested ---------------------- 674

          Sanchez-Llamas v. Oregon --------------------------------------- 674

    32.   Other *Miranda* problems --------------------------------------- 675

    Can (Did) Congress "Repeal" *Miranda*? ---------------------------- 676

    Title II of the 1968 Crime Control Act (§ 3501) ------------------------ 676

    Dickerson v. United States --------------------------------------- 657

        1. Reconciling the prophylactic-rule cases with *Miranda* --------- 677

          Donald A. Dripps—Constitutional Theory for Criminal Procedure -- 685

        2. Foolish confessions -- 685

        3. Why did Chief Justice Rehnquist come to the rescue of *Miranda*? --- 685

        4. Does Dickerson leave *Miranda* incoherent? ---------------------- 686

          Paul G. Cassell—The Paths Not Taken ------------------------ 686

        5. Is constitutional law filled with "prophylactic rules"? On the other hand, as Justice Scalia defines "prophylactic rules," is *Miranda* such a rule? ------------------------------------- 687

          Mitchell N. Berman—Constitutional Decision Rules ------- 687

        6. "The advantages of reactivism" ------------------------------- 687

          Stephen F. Smith—Activism as Restraint: Lessons from Criminal Procedure ------------------------------------ 687

        7. Does *Dickerson* represent an opportunity missed? -------------- 688

          William J. Stuntz—*Miranda*'s Mistake ------------------------ 688

        8. Is Congress still free to replace *Miranda* warnings with other procedures? -- 689

          Yale Kamisar—*Miranda* Thirty-Five Years Later ------------ 689

        9. Unrepentant dissenters -- 690

          Dripps, supra --- 690

3.   *MIRANDA, THE PRIVILEGE AGAINST COMPELLED SELF-INCRIMINATION AND FOURTEENTH AMENDMENT DUE PROCESS: WHEN DOES A VIOLATION OF THESE SAFEGUARDS OCCUR?* -- 690

    Chavez v. Martinez --- 690

        Alan Dershowitz—Is There a Right to Remain Silent ---------------- 696

        Thomas Y. Davies—The Recharacterization of the Right Against Self-Incrimination as a "Trial Right" in Chavez v. Martinez -- 696

4.   *THE PATANE AND SEIBERT CASES: IS PHYSICAL EVIDENCE OR A "SECOND CONFESSION" DERIVED FROM A FAILURE TO COMPLY WITH THE MIRANDA RULES ADMISSIBLE? THE COURT'S ANSWERS SHED LIGHT ON DICKERSON* --- 697

    Oregon v. Elstad -- 697

    Oral Arguments in the *Patane* case --------------------------------- 698

4. *THE PATANE AND SEIBERT CASES: IS PHYSICAL EVIDENCE OR A "SECOND CONFESSION" DERIVED FROM A FAILURE TO COMPLY WITH THE MIRANDA RULES ADMISSIBLE? THE COURT'S ANSWERS SHED LIGHT ON DICKERSON—* Continued

United States v. Patane -- 699

    Yale Kamisar—Another Look at *Patane* and *Seibert*, the 2004 *Miranda* "Poisoned Fruit" Cases ------------------------------------ 701

Missouri v. Seibert -- 702

    Notes and Questions on *Seibert* ------------------------------------ 708

5. *SOME FINAL QUESTIONS ABOUT MIRANDA* --------------------------- 709

  A. Was the *Miranda* Ruling a Straightforward Interpretation of the Fifth Amendment? --- 709

    Justice Byron White—Recent Developments in Criminal Law --- 709

  B. Are the *Miranda* Warnings Overplayed? Does *Miranda* Contain Three Different Holdings? --- 710

    Stephen Schulhofer—Reconsidering *Miranda* ----------------------- 710

  C. The "Stealth Overruling" of *Miranda* --------------------------------- 712

    Barry Friedman—The Wages of Stealth Overruling (with Particular Attention to Miranda v. Arizona) ----------------------- 712

  D. Should We Recognize that *Miranda* has Turned out to be A Failure and Start Over? -- 713

    Charles Weisselberg—Mourning *Miranda* --------------------------- 713

  E. What If *Miranda* were Abolished? ------------------------------------- 715

    Yale Kamisar—On the Fortieth Anniversary of the *Miranda* Case --- 715

6. *THE "DUE PROCESS"–"VOLUNTARINESS" TEST REVISITED* -- 717

    The Significance of the "Voluntariness" Test in the Post-*Miranda* era --- 717

    Stephen J. Schulhoffer—Confessions and the Court --------------- 717

    Paul Marcus—It's Not Just About *Miranda* ------------------------- 718

  A. *Miller v. Fenton*: What Kinds of Trickery or Deception If Any, May the Police Employ After a Suspect Has Waived His Rights? 718

    Welsh S. White—Police Trickery in Inducing Confessions -------- 719

    Miller v. Fenton --- 719

    Phillip Johnson—A Statutory Replacement for the *Miranda* Doctrine --- 724

    United States v. LeBrun --- 724

    Fabrication of Scientific Evidence-------------------------------------- 726

    Arizona v. Fulminante --- 727

  B. *Colorado v. Connelly*: Did the Court Decline to Expand the "Voluntariness" Test or Did It Revise the Test Significantly? 728

    Colorado v. Connelly --- 728

    What if the Ku Klux Klan had kidnapped and tortured a murder suspect? --- 731

    Laurence Benner—Requiem for *Miranda*: The Rehnquist Court's Voluntariness Doctrine in Historical Perspective ---------------- 731

6.   *THE "DUE PROCESS"–"VOLUNTARINESS" TEST REVISITED—*
      Continued
            Suppose Connelly had phoned a Denver police officer from Boston
                and—with the "voice of God" ringing in his ears—confessed? 732
            Does *Connelly* mark the decline and fall of the "reliability"
                element? -- 733
            The Central Park Jogger Case—and False Confessions
                Generally -- 734
            Sharon Davies—The Reality of False Confessions—Lessons of
                the Central Jogger Case -- 735
            Steven Drizin & Richard Leo—The Problem of False Confessions
                in The Post-DNA World --------------------------------------- 736
            Richard Leo—Police Interrogation and American Justice -------- 736
            Lawrence Rosenthal—Against Orthodoxy: *Miranda* is not
                Prophylactic and the Constitution Is Not Perfect -------------- 738
7.   *MASSIAH REVISITED; MASSIAH AND MIRANDA COMPARED*
      AND CONTRASTED-- 738
      A.   The Revivification of *Massiah* ---------------------------------- 738
           Brewer v. Williams (Williams I) ------------------------------ 739
           United States v. Fellers--- 746
           Patterson v. Illinois--- 746
           Maine v. Moulton--- 749
      B.   "Passive" vs. "Active" Secret Agents --------------------------- 750
           United States v. Henry --- 750
           Kuhlmann v. Wilson--- 751
           H. Richard Uviller—Evidence From the Mind of the Criminal
                Suspect-- 752
           James Tomkovicz—An Adversary System Defense of the Right
                to Counsel Against Informants----------------------------------- 753
           Once the Sixth Amendment Right to Counsel Arises, Does it
                Attach to All Other Offenses Closely Related to the Particular
                Offense Charged? --- 754
      Texas v. Cobb-- 754
           Should *Massiah* Be Overruled? --------------------------------- 758
           Sherry Colb—Why the Supreme Court Should Overrule the
                Massiah Doctrine and Permit *Miranda* Alone to Govern
                Interrogations --- 758

CHAPTER 10.   LINEUPS, SHOWUPS AND OTHER PRE-TRIAL
                IDENTIFICATION PROCEDURES -------------------- 760
Commentary on how many mistaken eyewitness identifications lead to
      wrongful convictions --- 760
1.   *WADE AND GILBERT: CONSTITUTIONAL CONCERN ABOUT*
      THE DANGERS INVOLVED IN EYEWITNESS IDENTIFICA-
      TIONS-- 761
           United States v. Wade--- 761
           On the Meaning of the Lineup Decisions ------------------------ 764
           Model Pre-Arraignment Code ------------------------------------ 765
           A.J. Davis—The Role of the Defense Lawyer at a Lineup -------- 767

2.   *THE COURT RETREATS: KIRBY AND ASH* ------------------------ 769
     Kirby v. Illinois --- 769
     United States v. Ash --- 770
3.   *DUE PROCESS LIMITATIONS* -------------------------------- 773
        Stovall v. Denno -- 773
     Manson v. Braithwaite -- 774
        Notes on the Stovall-Brathwaite Due Process Test ------------------ 779
        Gary L. Wells & Deah S. Quinlivan—Suggestive Eyewitness
           Identification Procedures and the Supreme Court's Relia-
           bility Test in Light of Eyewitness Science: 30 Years Later ---- 780
     Perry v. New Hampshire --------------------------------------- 780
4.   *SOCIAL SCIENCE RESEARCH ON IDENTIFICATION PRO-
     CEDURES AND THE NEED FOR REFORM* ------------------------- 786
        Estimator variables --- 786
        System variables -- 787
        Changes in identification procedures -------------------------- 787
        Expert testimony -- 789
        Jury instructions --- 789
        Preventing resort to the ultimate punishment------------------- 790

CHAPTER 11.   GRAND JURY INVESTIGATIONS -------------------- 791
1.   *THE ROLE OF THE INVESTIGATIVE GRAND JURY* ---------------- 791
     A. The Investigative Authority of the Grand Jury -------------------- 791
         Dual Functions --- 791
         Historical developments -------------------------------------- 792
         Current status --- 794
     B. Investigative Advantages ------------------------------------- 794
         1. Subpoena ad testificandum --------------------------------- 795
         2. Psychological pressure ------------------------------------ 795
         3. Immunity grants --- 796
         4. Subpoena duces tecum -------------------------------------- 797
         5. Secrecy --- 798
         6. Maintaining public confidence ----------------------------- 800
     C. Alternative Routes to Investigation by Subpoena ------------------ 800
         1. Alternative criminal investigative authority -------------- 800
         2. Civil administrative subpoenas --------------------------- 801
         3. Legal similarities and differences ----------------------- 802
     D. Judicial Regulation: Some Differing Perspectives ---------------- 802
         Wayne LaFave, Jerold Israel, Nancy King & Orin Kerr—Criminal
            Procedure Treatise -- 802
         Blair v. United States -- 804
         In re Grand Jury Proceedings (Schofield I) ------------------- 804
         United States v. Williams ------------------------------------ 805
2.   *FOURTH AMENDMENT CHALLENGES TO THE INVESTIGATION* 806
     A. The Initial Approach --------------------------------------- 806
         Boyd v. United States ------------------------------------ 806
            The significance of *Boyd* -------------------------------- 810
     B. The Overbreadth Doctrine ----------------------------------- 811
         1. Hale v. Henkel -- 811
         2. Explaining the overbreadth doctrine----------------------- 812
         3. Applying the overbreadth doctrine ------------------------ 814

2. *FOURTH AMENDMENT CHALLENGES TO THE INVESTIGATION—*
  Continued
    4. Third-party objections -- 815
  C. Compelling Testimony (and Identification Exemplars) ------------ 816
    United States v. Dionisio -- 816
      Notes on the meaning and scope of Dionisio ------------------ 821
      United States v. Calandra -------------------------------------- 822
3. *OTHER OBJECTIONS TO THE INVESTIGATION* ------------------ 823
  United States v. R. Enterprises, Inc. -------------------------------- 823
    Notes on reasonableness requirements---------------------------- 827
    In re Grand Jury Proceedings ------------------------------------ 827
    "Chilling effect": First Amendment objections ---------------------- 830
    "Chilling effect": Attorney subpoenas ------------------------------ 832
    Oppressive burdens-- 833
    Notes on Misuse Objections -------------------------------------- 833
    Notes on Third Party Subpoenas -------------------------------- 835
      1. Third party subpoenas ------------------------------------ 835
      2. Target standing -- 835
      3. Target notification -------------------------------------- 836
      4. Legislative grants of standing and notification ---------- 837
4. *GRAND JURY TESTIMONY AND THE PRIVILEGE AGAINST*
  SELF-INCRIMINATION --- 838
  A. Grand Jury Testimony -- 838
    1. Application of the privilege------------------------------------ 838
      Counselman v. Hitchcock-------------------------------------- 838
    2. The nature of "incriminating testimony" ------------------------ 839
      Hoffman v. United States -------------------------------------- 839
    3. Incrimination under the laws of another sovereign ------------ 840
      Murphy v. Waterfront Comm. ---------------------------------- 840
      United States v. Balsys-- 840
    4. Waiver -- 841
      Rogers v.United States -- 841
    5. Exercise of the privilege by the target ---------------------------- 842
    6. Self-incrimination warnings ------------------------------------ 843
      United States v. Mandujano ------------------------------------ 843
    7. Target warnings-- 845
      United States v. Washington ------------------------------------ 845
    8. Constitutional right to counsel ---------------------------------- 846
      United States v. Mandujano ------------------------------------ 846
    9. Federal practice-- 847
    10. State practices-- 847
    11. The location of counsel -- 848
  B. Immunity Grants -- 848
    Constitutionality -- 848
    Scope of the immunity-- 849
      Murphy v. Waterfront Comm. ---------------------------------- 849
      Kastigar v. United States-------------------------------------- 850
    Subsequent prosecution -- 851
    Prosecutorial discretion -- 852

5.   *SELF-INCRIMINATION AND THE COMPELLED PRODUCTION*
     OF DOCUMENTS--- 852
    A.   The Dismantling of *Boyd* ------------------------------------- 852
       Self-incrimination and Boyd ------------------------------- 852
       The entity exception-- 853
          Hale v. Henkel -- 853
          United States v. White ---------------------------------- 854
       Required records exception ------------------------------- 855
       Testimonial limitation ------------------------------------- 855
          Schmerber v. California ---------------------------------- 855
          Doe v. United States (Doe II)---------------------------- 855
       "Personal compulsion" limitation -------------------------- 856
       Act-of-production analysis --------------------------------- 856
    B.   The Act-of-Production Doctrine ------------------------------- 856
       Fisher v. United States ----------------------------------- 856
       The demise of Boyd --------------------------------------- 863
          United States v. Doe (Doe I)----------------------------- 863
       The foregone conclusion doctrine ------------------------- 864
          Robert Mosteller—Simplifying Subpoena Law: Taking the
          Fifth Amendment Seriously------------------------------- 865
       Potential incrimination------------------------------------- 865
       Act of production immunity-------------------------------- 866
          Braswell v. United States ------------------------------- 866
       The non-documentary act-of-production-------------------- 869
       United States v. Hubbell---------------------------------- 870
       Establishing a foregone conclusion ----------------------- 876
          In re Grand Jury Subpoena, April 18 -------------------- 876
          United States v. Ponds ---------------------------------- 877
       Act-of-production immunity -------------------------------- 878
       Compelled-to-give evidence--------------------------------- 878

CHAPTER 12.   THE SCOPE OF THE EXCLUSIONARY RULES-- 879
1.   *"STANDING" TO OBJECT TO THE ADMISSION OF EVIDENCE*   879
    A.   Historical Background and Overview------------------------- 879
          Alderman v. United States ------------------------------- 880
       Daniel Meltzer—Deterring Constitutional Violations by Law
       Enforcement Officials ------------------------------------- 880
       Joshua Dressler & Alan Michaels—Understanding Criminal
       Procedure --- 880
          United States v. Payner---------------------------------- 881
          "Automatic" standing ------------------------------------ 882
          United States v. Salvucci -------------------------------- 882
          Residential premises ------------------------------------- 883
          Business premises --------------------------------------- 883
    B.   The Current Approach ------------------------------------- 884
       Can a Passenger in a Car other than His Own Challenge
       the Legality of a Search of that Car? ----------------------- 884
       Rakas v. Illinois--- 884
       Rawlings v. Kentucky------------------------------------ 884

1.   *"STANDING" TO OBJECT TO THE ADMISSION OF EVIDENCE*—
     Continued
                    Wayne LaFave—Search and Seizure-------------------------- 886
                    Can a Passenger in a Car Other than Her Own Challenge
                       the Legality of a Police Stop of that Car? -------------------- 887
                    Brendlin v. California -------------------------------------- 887
                    Under What Circumstances Can a Guest or Visitor in
                       another Person's Home Challenge the Legality of a
                       Search of that Home? -------------------------------------- 889
                    Minnesota v. Carter -------------------------------------- 889
2.   *THE "FRUIT OF THE POISONOUS TREE"*------------------------- 893
     A.   Historical Background and Overview------------------------------- 893
                    Wong Sun v. United States --------------------------------- 894
                    Brown v. Illinois --- 895
                    Dunaway v. New York-------------------------------------- 897
                    United States v. Crews ------------------------------------- 898
                    New York v. Harris-- 899
                    Segura v. United States ------------------------------------ 900
                    Murray v. United States ----------------------------------- 901
                    Craig M. Bradley—The Bell Tolls for the Search Warrant
                       Requirement --- 902
                    United States v. Ceccolini ---------------------------------- 903
     B.   The "Inevitable Discovery" Doctrine: The Sequel to *Brewer* v.
             Williams--- 903
          Nix v. Williams (Williams II) ----------------------------------- 903
                    1. Must the independent line of investigation be underway? 905
                    2. Primary evidence vs. secondary evidence ------------------ 906
                    Robert M. Bloom—Inevitable Discovery: An Exception
                       beyond the Fruits-- 906
                    3. The significance of Murray v. United States -------------- 906
                    4. The relatively easy case --------------------------------- 906
                    5. Inevitable discovery and the warrant requirement ------ 906
                    6. More on the "inevitable discovery" exception and the
                       "attenuation" doctrine----------------------------------- 907
                    Hudson v. Michigan --------------------------------------- 907
     C.   Is a Confession Obtained in Violation of the *Miranda* Rules a
             "Poisonous Tree"? --- 909
                    United States v. Patane------------------------------------- 909
                    Missouri v. Seibert--- 909
     D.   Is a "Second Confession" Following a Failure to Comply with
             the *Massiah* Doctrine Admissible?-------------------------------- 909
                    United States v. Fellers ------------------------------------ 910
3.   *USE OF ILLEGALLY OBTAINED EVIDENCE FOR IMPEACHMENT
        PURPOSES* --- 910
     A.   The Expansion of a Once-Narrow Exception------------------------- 910
                    Walder v. United States ------------------------------------ 910
                    Harris v. New York--- 911
                    Oregon v. Hass--- 912
                    United States v. Havens ------------------------------------ 912
                    James v. Illinois --------------------------------------- 913

3. *USE OF ILLEGALLY OBTAINED EVIDENCE FOR IMPEACHMENT
     PURPOSES*—Continued
                    The "Pinocchio defense witness" ---------------------------------- 915
                    James Spira—A Halt to the Expansion of the Impeachment
                        Exception -- 916
                    James Kainen—The Impeachment Exception to the
                        Exclusionary Rules-- 916
        B.   What Kinds of Constitutional or Other Violations Are
                Encompassed Within the Impeachment Exception?-------------- 916
                    Kansas v. Ventris -- 917
        C.   Use of Defendant's Prior Silence for Impeachment Purposes ---- 918
                    Doyle v. Ohio -- 919
                The "English Warnings" -- 919
                    Craig Bradley—Should American Courts Heed the "English
                        Warnings"? -- 919
                    Jenkins v. Anderson-- 919
                    Fletcher v. Weir --- 920
        D.   Use of Post-*Miranda* Warnings Silence or Assertion of Rights to
                Rebut Insanity Defense of Insanity---------------------------------- 921
                Wainwright v. Greenfield --- 921
        E.   How Much Leeway Do the "Impeachment" Cases and "Fruit of
                the Poisonous Tree" Cases Give A "Bad Man of the Law"?---- 921
                Albert W. Alschuler—Failed Pragmatism: Reflections on the
                    Burger Court --- 921
                Charles Weisselberg—Saving *Miranda* -------------------------------- 922
4. *ALLOCATION OF THE BURDENS OF PROOF*------------------------- 922
   People v. Berrios-- 922
                How common is police "falsification"? -------------------------------- 924
                Lego v. Twomey-- 927
                Colorado v. Connelly -- 928
                Jackson v. Denno--- 929
                Watkins v. Sowders -- 930

Index--- [1]

TABLE OF CASES

The principal cases are in bold type. Cases cited or discussed in the text are roman type. References are to pages. For Commonwealth v. _____, People v. _____, State v. _____, United States v. _____, see the name of the other party. For Ex parte _____, In re _____, Matter of _____, see the name of the party. For Commonwealth ex rel _____, People ex rel. _____, State ex rel. _____, United States ex rel. _____, see the name of the first party. Where a case is discussed in another case, reference is made only to the first page at which it is cited. No reference is made to discussion of a principal case in the Notes and Questions that follow that case.

Acosta v. State, 233 S.W.3d 349 (Tex.Crim. App.2007), 202

Adams, People v., 53 N.Y.2d 241, 440 N.Y.S.2d 902, 423 N.E.2d 379 (N.Y.1981), 790

Adams v. United States ex rel. McCann, 317 U.S. 269, 63 S.Ct. 236, 87 L.Ed. 268 (1942), 109

Adams v. Williams, 407 U.S. 143, 92 S.Ct. 1921, 32 L.Ed.2d 612 (1972), 424, 435

Administrative Subpoena, In re, 253 F.3d 256 (6th Cir.2001), 801

Agnello v. United States, 269 U.S. 20, 46 S.Ct. 4, 70 L.Ed. 145 (1925), 363, 910, 911, 913

Aguilar v. Texas, 378 U.S. 108, 84 S.Ct. 1509, 12 L.Ed.2d 723 (1964), 292, 298, 305, 307

Agurs, United States v., 427 U.S. 97, 96 S.Ct. 2392, 49 L.Ed.2d 342 (1976), 143

Ake v. Oklahoma, 470 U.S. 68, 105 S.Ct. 1087, 84 L.Ed.2d 53 (1985), **183,** 186, 1322

Alabama v. Shelton, 535 U.S. 654, 122 S.Ct. 1764, 152 L.Ed.2d 888 (2002), **84**

Alabama v. White, 496 U.S. 325, 110 S.Ct. 2412, 110 L.Ed.2d 301 (1990), 422, 423, 424

Albitez v. Beto, 465 F.2d 954 (5th Cir.1972), 316

Alderman v. United States, 394 U.S. 165, 89 S.Ct. 961, 22 L.Ed.2d 176 (1969), 230, 279, 282, 879, **880,** 883

Almeida–Sanchez v. United States, 413 U.S. 266, 93 S.Ct. 2535, 37 L.Ed.2d 596 (1973), 441

Alston v. Redman, 34 F.3d 1237 (3rd Cir.1994), 665

Alvarez–Machain, United States v., 504 U.S. 655, 112 S.Ct. 2188, 119 L.Ed.2d 441 (1992), 246

Alvarez–Sanchez, United States v., 511 U.S. 350, 114 S.Ct. 1599, 128 L.Ed.2d 319 (1994), 677

Amey v. Long, 1808 WL 1848 (KB 1808), 876

Amos v. United States, 255 U.S. 313, 41 S.Ct. 266, 65 L.Ed. 654 (1921), 459

Anders v. California, 386 U.S. 738, 87 S.Ct. 1396, 18 L.Ed.2d 493 (1967), 106, 133, 210, **218,** 219, 220

Andersen Consulting LLP v. UOP, 991 F.Supp. 1041 (N.D.Ill.1998), 538

Anderson v. Charles, 447 U.S. 404, 100 S.Ct. 2180, 65 L.Ed.2d 222 (1980), 919

Anderson v. Creighton, 483 U.S. 635, 107 S.Ct. 3034, 97 L.Ed.2d 523 (1987), 242

Andresen v. Maryland, 427 U.S. 463, 96 S.Ct. 2737, 49 L.Ed.2d 627 (1976), **286,** 811, 814, 856, 864

Andrus, United States v., 483 F.3d 711 (10th Cir.2007), 465

Angivoni, Commonwealth v., 383 Mass. 30, 417 N.E.2d 422 (Mass.1981), 460

Ankeny, United States v., 490 F.3d 744 (9th Cir.2007), 257

Apodaca v. Oregon, 406 U.S. 404, 92 S.Ct. 1628, 32 L.Ed.2d 184 (1972), 27

Application for Pen Register and Trap/Trace Device with Cell Site Location Authority, In re, 396 F.Supp.2d 747 (S.D.Tex.2005), 533

Application of (see name of party)

Argersinger v. Hamlin, 407 U.S. 25, 92 S.Ct. 2006, 32 L.Ed.2d 530 (1972), **80,** 81, 82, 84, 94, 100

Arizona v. Evans, 514 U.S. 1, 115 S.Ct. 1185, 131 L.Ed.2d 34 (1995), **250,** 251, 256, 258, 264

Arizona v. Fulminante, 499 U.S. 279, 111 S.Ct. 1246, 113 L.Ed.2d 302 (1991), 123, **727,** 734

Arizona v. Gant, 556 U.S. 332, 129 S.Ct. 1710, 173 L.Ed.2d 485 (2009), 245, 366, **398**

Arizona v. Hicks, 480 U.S. 321, 107 S.Ct. 1149, 94 L.Ed.2d 347 (1987), 275, 328, 330, **368,** 437, 439

Arizona v. Johnson, 555 U.S. 323, 129 S.Ct. 781, 172 L.Ed.2d 694 (2009), 429, 432, **434**

Arizona v. Mauro, 481 U.S. 520, 107 S.Ct. 1931, 95 L.Ed.2d 458 (1987), **613,** 614, 615

Arizona v. Roberson, 486 U.S. 675, 108 S.Ct. 2093, 100 L.Ed.2d 704 (1988), 593, **636,** 638, 647, 663, 664, 679

Arkansas v. Sanders, 442 U.S. 753, 99 S.Ct. 2586, 61 L.Ed.2d 235 (1979), 389, 391, 396, 397

Arkansas v. Sullivan, 532 U.S. 769, 121 S.Ct. 1876, 149 L.Ed.2d 994 (2001), 358

Armstrong, United States v., 517 U.S. 456, 116 S.Ct. 1480, 134 L.Ed.2d 687 (1996), 357

Arnold, United States v., 533 F.3d 1003 (9th Cir.2008), 441

Arvizu, United States v., 534 U.S. 266, 122 S.Ct. 744, 151 L.Ed.2d 740 (2002), 419

Ash, United States v., 413 U.S. 300, 93 S.Ct. 2568, 37 L.Ed.2d 619 (1973), **770,** 772, 773

Ashcraft v. Tennessee, 322 U.S. 143, 64 S.Ct. 921, 88 L.Ed. 1192 (1944), 52, 548, 549, 550, 551

Ashcroft v. al–Kidd, ___ U.S. ___, 131 S.Ct. 2074, 179 L.Ed.2d 1149 (2011), 353, 358, 451

Atwater v. City of Lago Vista, 532 U.S. 318, 121 S.Ct. 1536, 149 L.Ed.2d 549 (2001), **337, 348,** 351, 352

Awadallah, United States v., 349 F.3d 42 (2nd Cir.2003), 352

Bacon v. United States, 449 F.2d 933 (9th Cir.1971), 352

Baldasar v. Illinois, 446 U.S. 222, 100 S.Ct. 1585, 64 L.Ed.2d 169 (1980), 83

Baldwin v. New York, 399 U.S. 117, 90 S.Ct. 1914, 26 L.Ed.2d 446 (1970), 27

Balsys, United States v., 524 U.S. 666, 118 S.Ct. 2218, 141 L.Ed.2d 575 (1998), 840, 841

Baltimore City Dept. of Social Services v. Bouknight, 493 U.S. 549, 110 S.Ct. 900, 107 L.Ed.2d 992 (1990), 620, 869

Bank of Nova Scotia v. United States, 487 U.S. 250, 108 S.Ct. 2369, 101 L.Ed.2d 228 (1988), 38

Banks, United States v., 514 F.3d 769 (8th Cir.2008), 315

Banks, United States v., 540 U.S. 31, 124 S.Ct. 521, 157 L.Ed.2d 343 (2003), **323**

Barker, United States v., 988 F.2d 77 (9th Cir.1993), 773

Bartelt, People v., 241 Ill.2d 217, 349 Ill.Dec. 949, 948 N.E.2d 52 (Ill.2011), 273

Bartnicki v. Vopper, 532 U.S. 514, 121 S.Ct. 1753, 149 L.Ed.2d 787 (2001), **525**

Beckwith v. United States, 425 U.S. 341, 96 S.Ct. 1612, 48 L.Ed.2d 1 (1976), **601**

Beets v. Scott, 65 F.3d 1258 (5th Cir.1995), 194

Bell v. Burson, 402 U.S. 535, 91 S.Ct. 1586, 29 L.Ed.2d 90 (1971), 342

Bell v. Cone, 535 U.S. 685, 122 S.Ct. 1843, 152 L.Ed.2d 914 (2002), 174, 175

Bell v. Wolfish, 441 U.S. 520, 99 S.Ct. 1861, 60 L.Ed.2d 447 (1979), 272

Bellis v. United States, 417 U.S. 85, 94 S.Ct. 2179, 40 L.Ed.2d 678 (1974), 852, 854, 855, 859

Benbo, State v., 174 Mont. 252, 570 P.2d 894 (Mont.1977), 555

Benchimol, United States v., 471 U.S. 453, 105 S.Ct. 2103, 85 L.Ed.2d 462 (1985), 1295

Bennett, United States v., 409 F.2d 888 (2nd Cir.1969), 858

Berger v. New York, 388 U.S. 41, 87 S.Ct. 1873, 18 L.Ed.2d 1040 (1967), 322, 507, 518

Berghuis v. Thompkins, ___ U.S. ___, 130 S.Ct. 2250, 176 L.Ed.2d 1098 (2010), 595, 648, **651**

Bergmann, State v., 633 N.W.2d 328 (Iowa 2001), 278

Berkemer v. McCarty, 468 U.S. 420, 104 S.Ct. 3138, 82 L.Ed.2d 317 (1984), 427, 428, 602

Berrios, People v., 28 N.Y.2d 361, 321 N.Y.S.2d 884, 270 N.E.2d 709 (N.Y.1971), **922**

Betts v. Brady, 316 U.S. 455, 62 S.Ct. 1252, 86 L.Ed. 1595 (1942), 26, **71,** 74, 75, 76, 81, 94, 95, 96, 100, 556, 576

Bin Laden, United States v., 126 F.Supp.2d 264 (S.D.N.Y.2000), 540

Binney v. State, 384 S.C. 539, 683 S.E.2d 478 (S.C.2009), 136

Bishop, State v., 289 Minn. 188, 183 N.W.2d 536 (Minn.1971), 927

Bittaker v. Woodford, 331 F.3d 715 (9th Cir. 2003), 136

Bivens v. Six Unknown Named Agents of Federal Bureau of Narcotics, 403 U.S. 388, 91 S.Ct. 1999, 29 L.Ed.2d 619 (1971), 240, 242, 254, 358

Blackburn v. Alabama, 361 U.S. 199, 80 S.Ct. 274, 4 L.Ed.2d 242 (1960), 549, 551, 729, 730

Blackburn, State v., 266 Or. 28, 511 P.2d 381 (Or.1973), 317

Blair v. United States, 250 U.S. 273, 39 S.Ct. 468, 63 L.Ed. 979 (1919), 802, **804,** 817

Blake, United States v., 888 F.2d 795 (11th Cir.1989), 461

Blakeney, United States v., 942 F.2d 1001 (6th Cir.1991), 318

Block, People v., 103 Cal.Rptr. 281, 499 P.2d 961 (Cal.1971), 367

Blockburger v. United States, 284 U.S. 299, 52 S.Ct. 180, 76 L.Ed. 306 (1932), 755

Bloyd, People v., 416 Mich. 538, 331 N.W.2d 447 (Mich.1982), 426

Board of Education of Independent School District No. 92 of Pottawatomie County v. Earls, 536 U.S. 822, 122 S.Ct. 2559, 153 L.Ed.2d 735 (2002), 444

Bobby v. Van Hook, ___ U.S. ___, 130 S.Ct. 13, 175 L.Ed.2d 255 (2009), **151,** 160

Bolte, State v., 115 N.J. 579, 560 A.2d 644 (N.J.1989), 382

Bond v. United States, 529 U.S. 334, 120 S.Ct. 1462, 146 L.Ed.2d 365 (2000), **273**

Borden Co., Petition of, 75 F.Supp. 857 (N.D.Ill.1948), 815

Botero–Ospina, United States v., 71 F.3d 783 (10th Cir.1995), 356, 420

Boukater, United States v., 409 F.2d 537 (5th Cir.1969), 459

Boumediene v. Bush, 553 U.S. 723, 128 S.Ct. 2229, 171 L.Ed.2d 41 (2008), **43,** 48

Boyd v. United States, 116 U.S. 616, 6 S.Ct. 524, 29 L.Ed. 746 (1886), 248, 286, 287, 710, **806,** 810, 811, 818, 852, 853, 855, 856, 859, 863, 864, 866, 876, 878

Boyette, United States v., 299 F.2d 92 (4th Cir.1962), 288

Boykin v. Alabama, 395 U.S. 238, 89 S.Ct. 1709, 23 L.Ed.2d 274 (1969), 211

Bradley, United States v., 644 F.3d 1213 (11th Cir.2011), **319**

Brady v. Maryland, 373 U.S. 83, 83 S.Ct. 1194, 10 L.Ed.2d 215 (1963), 160

Bram v. United States, 168 U.S. 532, 18 S.Ct. 183, 42 L.Ed. 568 (1897), 548, 565, 575, 678, 721, 724, 725

Brand, United States v., 467 F.3d 179 (2nd Cir.2006), 499

Branzburg v. Hayes, 408 U.S. 665, 92 S.Ct. 2646, 33 L.Ed.2d 626 (1972), 817, 830, 831, 832

Braswell v. United States, 487 U.S. 99, 108 S.Ct. 2284, 101 L.Ed.2d 98 (1988), **866,** 869, 870

Breithaupt v. Abram, 352 U.S. 432, 77 S.Ct. 408, 1 L.Ed.2d 448 (1957), 30, 31

Brendlin v. California, 551 U.S. 249, 127 S.Ct. 2400, 168 L.Ed.2d 132 (2007), **417,** 432, 434, **887**

Brewer v. Williams, 430 U.S. 387, 97 S.Ct. 1232, 51 L.Ed.2d 424 (1977), 86, 91, 558, 609, 613, 738, **739,** 757, 769, 903, 918

Briggs v. American Air Filter Co., Inc., 630 F.2d 414 (5th Cir.1980), 526

Brigham City, Utah v. Stuart, 547 U.S. 398, 126 S.Ct. 1943, 164 L.Ed.2d 650 (2006), 375

Brinegar v. United States, 338 U.S. 160, 69 S.Ct. 1302, 93 L.Ed. 1879 (1949), 296, 464

Britt v. North Carolina, 404 U.S. 226, 92 S.Ct. 431, 30 L.Ed.2d 400 (1971), 100, 105

Brochu, State v., 237 A.2d 418 (Me.1967), 462

Brookhart v. Janis, 384 U.S. 1, 86 S.Ct. 1245, 16 L.Ed.2d 314 (1966), 210, 212, 215

Brooks v. Gaenzle, 614 F.3d 1213 (10th Cir. 2010), 417

Brooks v. Tennessee, 406 U.S. 605, 92 S.Ct. 1891, 32 L.Ed.2d 358 (1972), 176

Brooks v. United States, 159 A.2d 876 (D.C.Mun.App.1960), 314

Brooks, United States v., 427 F.3d 1246 (10th Cir.2005), 331

Brower v. County of Inyo, 489 U.S. 593, 109 S.Ct. 1378, 103 L.Ed.2d 628 (1989), 887

Brown v. City of Oneonta, New York, 221 F.3d 329 (2nd Cir.2000), 68

Brown v. Illinois, 422 U.S. 590, 95 S.Ct. 2254, 45 L.Ed.2d 416 (1975), 231, 592, 893, **895,** 897, 898, 900

Brown v. Mississippi, 297 U.S. 278, 56 S.Ct. 461, 80 L.Ed. 682 (1936), 49, 50, 548, 549, 553, 565, 678, 729, 731

Brown, United States v., 64 F.3d 1083 (7th Cir.1995), 907

Brown v. United States, 365 F.2d 976, 125 U.S.App.D.C. 43 (D.C.Cir.1966), 314

Brown v. Walker, 161 U.S. 591, 16 S.Ct. 644, 40 L.Ed. 819 (1896), 848, 849

Bryant, State v., 287 Minn. 205, 177 N.W.2d 800 (Minn.1970), 272

Bumper v. North Carolina, 391 U.S. 543, 88 S.Ct. 1788, 20 L.Ed.2d 797 (1968), 459, 461, 926

Burdeau v. McDowell, 256 U.S. 465, 41 S.Ct. 574, 65 L.Ed. 1048 (1921), 249, 250

Burdine v. Johnson, 262 F.3d 336 (5th Cir. 2001), 175

Burdo, People v., 56 Mich.App. 48, 223 N.W.2d 358 (Mich.App.1974), 338

Burger v. Kemp, 483 U.S. 776, 107 S.Ct. 3114, 97 L.Ed.2d 638 (1987), 164, 168, 187, **201**

Burgess, United States v., 576 F.3d 1078 (10th Cir.2009), 393

Burkley, United States v., 591 F.2d 903, 192 U.S.App.D.C. 294 (D.C.Cir.1978), 496

Burnett, State v., 42 N.J. 377, 201 A.2d 39 (N.J.1964), 309

Burns v. Ohio, 360 U.S. 252, 79 S.Ct. 1164, 3 L.Ed.2d 1209 (1959), 99, 102

Burns v. Reed, 500 U.S. 478, 111 S.Ct. 1934, 114 L.Ed.2d 547 (1991), 242

Burrows v. Superior Court, 118 Cal.Rptr. 166, 529 P.2d 590 (Cal.1974), 518

Bursey v. United States, 466 F.2d 1059 (9th Cir.1972), 831, 832

Bustamonte v. Schneckloth, 448 F.2d 699 (9th Cir.1971), 459

Bute v. Illinois, 333 U.S. 640, 68 S.Ct. 763, 92 L.Ed. 986 (1948), 73

Byers, United States v., 740 F.2d 1104, 239 U.S.App.D.C. 1 (D.C.Cir.1984), 92, 620

Caceres, United States v., 440 U.S. 741, 99 S.Ct. 1465, 59 L.Ed.2d 733 (1979), 246

Cady v. Dombrowski, 413 U.S. 433, 93 S.Ct. 2523, 37 L.Ed.2d 706 (1973), 384

Cahan, People v., 44 Cal.2d 434, 282 P.2d 905 (Cal.1955), 52

Calandra, United States v., 414 U.S. 338, 94 S.Ct. 613, 38 L.Ed.2d 561 (1974), 230, 247, 248, 256, 259, 805, **822,** 825, 894

Caldwell v. Mississippi, 472 U.S. 320, 105 S.Ct. 2633, 86 L.Ed.2d 231 (1985), 185

California v. Acevedo, 500 U.S. 565, 111 S.Ct. 1982, 114 L.Ed.2d 619 (1991), **388**

California v. Beheler, 463 U.S. 1121, 103 S.Ct. 3517, 77 L.Ed.2d 1275 (1983), 592, 602

California v. Byers, 402 U.S. 424, 91 S.Ct. 1535, 29 L.Ed.2d 9 (1971), 620, 621

California v. Carney, 471 U.S. 386, 105 S.Ct. 2066, 85 L.Ed.2d 406 (1985), 332, **383,** 387

California v. Ciraolo, 476 U.S. 207, 106 S.Ct. 1809, 90 L.Ed.2d 210 (1986), 268, 274, 279, 285

California v. Greenwood, 486 U.S. 35, 108 S.Ct. 1625, 100 L.Ed.2d 30 (1988), 222, **267,** 269, 331

California v. Hodari D., 499 U.S. 621, 111 S.Ct. 1547, 113 L.Ed.2d 690 (1991), **416,** 418

California v. Prysock, 453 U.S. 355, 101 S.Ct. 2806, 69 L.Ed.2d 696 (1981), 597

California v. Stewart, 384 U.S. 436, 86 S.Ct. 1602, 16 L.Ed.2d 694 (1966), 571

California Bankers Ass'n v. Shultz, 416 U.S. 21, 94 S.Ct. 1494, 39 L.Ed.2d 812 (1974), 518

Camara v. Municipal Court of City and County of San Francisco, 387 U.S. 523, 87 S.Ct. 1727, 18 L.Ed.2d 930 (1967), 322, 411, 439, 440, 441, 442

Caplin & Drysdale, Chartered v. United States, 491 U.S. 617, 109 S.Ct. 2646, 105 L.Ed.2d 528 (1989), **129,** 130

Cardwell v. Lewis, 417 U.S. 583, 94 S.Ct. 2464, 41 L.Ed.2d 325 (1974), 273, 384, 386

Carey v. Nevada Gaming Control Bd., 279 F.3d 873 (9th Cir.2002), 427

Carey, United States v., 172 F.3d 1268 (10th Cir.1999), 331

Carmichael, United States v., 489 F.2d 983 (7th Cir.1973), 308

Carnley v. Cochran, 369 U.S. 506, 82 S.Ct. 884, 8 L.Ed.2d 70 (1962), 560, 579

Carrillo, United States v., 16 F.3d 1046 (9th Cir.1994), 624

Carroll, State v., 322 Wis.2d 299, 778 N.W.2d 1 (Wis.2010), 348

Carroll v. United States, 267 U.S. 132, 45 S.Ct. 280, 69 L.Ed. 543 (1925), 363, 383, 387, 388, 389

Carruthers, State v., 35 S.W.3d 516 (Tenn. 2000), 121

Cassidy v. Chertoff, 471 F.3d 67 (2nd Cir. 2006), 442

Cayward, State v., 552 So.2d 971 (Fla.App. 2 Dist.1989), 726

Ceccolini, United States v., 435 U.S. 268, 98 S.Ct. 1054, 55 L.Ed.2d 268 (1978), 231, **903**

Certain Chinese Family Benevolent and District Associations, Application of, 19 F.R.D. 97 (N.D.Cal.1956), 815

Chadwick, United States v., 433 U.S. 1, 97 S.Ct. 2476, 53 L.Ed.2d 538 (1977), 386, 389, 391, 396, 397

Chalmers (John) v. HM Advocate, 1954 WL 15494 (HCJ 1954), 580

Chamberlain, People v., 229 P.3d 1054 (Colo. 2010), 406

Chambers v. Maroney, 399 U.S. 42, 90 S.Ct. 1975, 26 L.Ed.2d 419 (1970), 384, 388

Chandler v. Fretag, 348 U.S. 3, 75 S.Ct. 1, 99 L.Ed. 4 (1954), 73, 76

Chandler v. Miller, 520 U.S. 305, 117 S.Ct. 1295, 137 L.Ed.2d 513 (1997), 443

Chapman v. California, 386 U.S. 18, 87 S.Ct. 824, 17 L.Ed.2d 705 (1967), 764, 928

Chapman v. United States, 365 U.S. 610, 81 S.Ct. 776, 5 L.Ed.2d 828 (1961), 466

Chase, Commonwealth v., 599 Pa. 80, 960 A.2d 108 (Pa.2008), 420

Chavez v. Martinez, 538 U.S. 760, 123 S.Ct. 1994, 155 L.Ed.2d 984 (2003), 229, 624, 659, 674, **690,** 699, 838

Chimel v. California, 395 U.S. 752, 89 S.Ct. 2034, 23 L.Ed.2d 685 (1969), 347, 362, **363,** 377, 398, 407, 926

Chmiel, Commonwealth v., 558 Pa. 478, 738 A.2d 406 (Pa.1999), 136

"Christian burial speech" case (see Brewer v. Williams)

Cicenia v. La Gay, 357 U.S. 504, 78 S.Ct. 1297, 2 L.Ed.2d 1523 (1958), **556**

City of (see name of city)

Clyburn, United States v., 24 F.3d 613 (4th Cir.1994), 307

Coleman v. Alabama, 399 U.S. 1, 90 S.Ct. 1999, 26 L.Ed.2d 387 (1970), 91

Coleman v. Thompson, 501 U.S. 722, 111 S.Ct. 2546, 115 L.Ed.2d 640 (1991), 133

Collins v. Beto, 348 F.2d 823 (5th Cir.1965), 895

Collins v. Brierly, 492 F.2d 735 (3rd Cir.1974), 596

Colorado v. Bannister, 449 U.S. 1, 101 S.Ct. 42, 66 L.Ed.2d 1 (1980), 384

Colorado v. Bertine, 479 U.S. 367, 107 S.Ct. 738, 93 L.Ed.2d 739 (1987), 332, 354, 358, 359, **407,** 408, 439

Colorado v. Connelly, 479 U.S. 157, 107 S.Ct. 515, 93 L.Ed.2d 473 (1986), 460, 543, 547, 548, 551, 652, **728,** 729, 731, 732, 733, **928,** 929

Colorado v. Spring, 479 U.S. 564, 107 S.Ct. 851, 93 L.Ed.2d 954 (1987), **599,** 601

Colorado Supreme Court, United States v., 189 F.3d 1281 (10th Cir.1999), 832

Colyer, United States v., 878 F.2d 469, 278 U.S.App.D.C. 367 (D.C.Cir.1989), 278

Combs, People v., 19 A.D.2d 639, 241 N.Y.S.2d 104 (N.Y.A.D. 2 Dept.1963), 181

Commonwealth v. _____ (see opposing party)

Commonwealth ex rel. v. _____ (see opposing party and relator)

Comprehensive Drug Testing, Inc., United States v., 621 F.3d 1162 (9th Cir.2010), 331, 835

Comprehensive Drug Testing, Inc., United States v., 579 F.3d 989 (9th Cir.2009), 331

Comprehensive Drug Testing, Inc., United States v., 513 F.3d 1085 (9th Cir.2008), 331

Conklin v. Schofield, 366 F.3d 1191 (11th Cir. 2004), 186

Connally v. Georgia, 429 U.S. 245, 97 S.Ct. 546, 50 L.Ed.2d 444 (1977), 316

Connecticut v. Barrett, 479 U.S. 523, 107 S.Ct. 828, 93 L.Ed.2d 920 (1987), 633

Cook, United States v., 657 F.2d 730 (5th Cir. 1981), 318

Coolidge v. New Hampshire, 403 U.S. 443, 91 S.Ct. 2022, 29 L.Ed.2d 564 (1971), 316, 327, 367, 386, 457, 469

Copenhefer, Commonwealth v., 526 Pa. 555, 587 A.2d 1353 (Pa.1991), 331

Corley v. United States, 556 U.S. 303, 129 S.Ct. 1558, 173 L.Ed.2d 443 (2009), 555

Cortez, United States v., 449 U.S. 411, 101 S.Ct. 690, 66 L.Ed.2d 621 (1981), 296, **419**

Couch v. United States, 409 U.S. 322, 93 S.Ct. 611, 34 L.Ed.2d 548 (1973), 287, 537, 856, 857

Coughlin, United States v., 338 F.Supp. 1328 (E.D.Mich.1972), 359

Counselman v. Hitchcock, 142 U.S. 547, 12 S.Ct. 195, 35 L.Ed. 1110 (1892), 710, 838, 839, 844, 849, 850

County of (see name of county)

Crane v. Kentucky, 476 U.S. 683, 106 S.Ct. 2142, 90 L.Ed.2d 636 (1986), 929

Creighton, United States v., 639 F.3d 1281 (10th Cir.2011), 380

Crews, United States v., 445 U.S. 463, 100 S.Ct. 1244, 63 L.Ed.2d 537 (1980), 247, 898, 899

Cromedy, State v., 158 N.J. 112, 727 A.2d 457 (N.J.1999), 789

Cronic, United States v., 466 U.S. 648, 104 S.Ct. 2039, 80 L.Ed.2d 657 (1984), 133, **134,** 142, 149, 152, **173,** 174, 175, 176, 180, 196, 216

Crooker v. California, 357 U.S. 433, 78 S.Ct. 1287, 2 L.Ed.2d 1448 (1958), **556,** 557

Crovedi, People v., 65 Cal.2d 199, 53 Cal.Rptr. 284, 417 P.2d 868 (Cal.1966), 132

Cullen v. Pinholster, ___ U.S. ___, 131 S.Ct. 1388, 179 L.Ed.2d 557 (2011), 150, 164, 165, 167, **172**

Culombe v. Connecticut, 367 U.S. 568, 81 S.Ct. 1860, 6 L.Ed.2d 1037 (1961), **553,** 554, 565

Cupp v. Murphy, 412 U.S. 291, 93 S.Ct. 2000, 36 L.Ed.2d 900 (1973), 360, 362

Cuyler v. Sullivan, 446 U.S. 335, 100 S.Ct. 1708, 64 L.Ed.2d 333 (1980), **131,** 142, 173, **189,** 190, 191, 200, 201

Dalia v. United States, 441 U.S. 238, 99 S.Ct. 1682, 60 L.Ed.2d 177 (1979), 306, 331, 525

Darden, People v., 34 N.Y.2d 177, 356 N.Y.S.2d 582, 313 N.E.2d 49 (N.Y.1974), 310

Davenport, Commonwealth v., 471 Pa. 278, 370 A.2d 301 (Pa.1977), 555

Davila, People v., 27 Misc.3d 921, 901 N.Y.S.2d 787 (N.Y.Sup.2010), 285

Davis v. Mississippi, 394 U.S. 721, 89 S.Ct. 1394, 22 L.Ed.2d 676 (1969), **437,** 438, 767, 817, 820

Davis, State v., 872 So.2d 250 (Fla.2004), 166

Davis v. United States, 512 U.S. 452, 114 S.Ct. 2350, 129 L.Ed.2d 362 (1994), **646,** 651

Davis, United States v., 346 F.Supp. 435 (S.D.Ill.1972), 317

Davis, United States v., 458 F.2d 819, 147 U.S.App.D.C. 400 (D.C.Cir.1972), 315

Davis v. United States, ___ U.S. ___, 131 S.Ct. 2419, 180 L.Ed.2d 285 (2011), **244,** 263

Deal v. Spears, 980 F.2d 1153 (8th Cir.1992), **526,** 529

Dean, People v., 39 Cal.App.3d 875, 114 Cal. Rptr. 555 (Cal.App. 4 Dist.1974), 624

Decoster, United States v., 624 F.2d 196, 199 U.S.App.D.C. 359 (D.C.Cir.1976), 136, 137, 139

Defore, People v., 242 N.Y. 13, 150 N.E. 585 (N.Y.1926), 226

Deitchman, People v., 695 P.2d 1146 (Colo. 1985), 240

Delaware v. Prouse, 440 U.S. 648, 99 S.Ct. 1391, 59 L.Ed.2d 660 (1979), 441

Delgado, State v., 188 N.J. 48, 902 A.2d 888 (N.J.2006), 788

Dennis, United States v., 183 F.2d 201 (2nd Cir.1950), 473

Department of Justice v. Reporter's Committee for Freedom of the Press, 489 U.S. 749 (1989), 285

Derichsweiler v. State, 348 S.W.3d 906 (Tex. Crim.App.2011), 419

DeSantis, United States v., 870 F.2d 536 (9th Cir.1989), 637

Devenpeck v. Alford, 543 U.S. 146, 125 S.Ct. 588, 160 L.Ed.2d 537 (2004), 337

Dickerson, United States v., 166 F.3d 667 (4th Cir.1999), 677, 686, 687, 688, 690

Dickerson v. United States, 530 U.S. 428, 120 S.Ct. 2326, 147 L.Ed.2d 405 (2000), 53, 588, 589, 594, 652, **677,** 684, 685, 696, 698, 699, 702, 705, 714, 754

DiModica, United States v., 468 F.3d 495 (7th Cir.2006), 461

Dionisio, United States v., 410 U.S. 1, 93 S.Ct. 764, 35 L.Ed.2d 67 (1973), 438, 768, 799, 802, 805, **816,** 821, 822, 823, 825, 832, 836, 842

Diozzi, United States v., 807 F.2d 10 (1st Cir. 1986), 208

Di Re, United States v., 332 U.S. 581, 68 S.Ct. 222, 92 L.Ed. 210 (1948), 311, 333, 394, 396

District Attorney's Office for Third Judicial Dist. v. Osborne, 557 U.S. 52, 129 S.Ct. 2308, 174 L.Ed.2d 38 (2009), 33, 63

District of Columbia v. Heller, 554 U.S. 570, 128 S.Ct. 2783, 171 L.Ed.2d 637 (2008), 25

Dixon, People v., 392 Mich. 691, 222 N.W.2d 749 (Mich.1974), 338

Dixon, United States v., 509 U.S. 688, 113 S.Ct. 2849, 125 L.Ed.2d 556 (1993), 755

Doe v. United States, 487 U.S. 201, 108 S.Ct. 2341, 101 L.Ed.2d 184 (1988), 855, 863, 874

Doe, United States v., 465 U.S. 605, 104 S.Ct. 1237, 79 L.Ed.2d 552 (1984), **863,** 864, 866, 869, 874

Doe, United States v., 455 F.2d 1270 (1st Cir. 1972), 834, 855

Dominguez–Martinez, State v., 321 Or. 206, 895 P.2d 306 (Or.1995), 356

Donovan, People v., 13 N.Y.2d 148, 243 N.Y.S.2d 841, 193 N.E.2d 628 (N.Y.1963), 575

Dorman v. United States, 435 F.2d 385, 140 U.S.App.D.C. 313 (D.C.Cir.1970), 377, 380, 381

DoubleClick Inc. Privacy Litigation, In re, 154 F.Supp.2d 497 (S.D.N.Y.2001), 537

Douglas v. California, 372 U.S. 353, 83 S.Ct. 814, 9 L.Ed.2d 811 (1963), **100,** 101, 102, 105, 106, 132, 133, 219, 560, 578

Dow Chemical Co. v. United States, 476 U.S. 227, 106 S.Ct. 1819, 90 L.Ed.2d 226 (1986), 278, **285**

Dowling v. United States, 493 U.S. 342, 110 S.Ct. 668, 107 L.Ed.2d 708 (1990), 32

Doyle v. Ohio, 426 U.S. 610, 96 S.Ct. 2240, 49 L.Ed.2d 91 (1976), 679, 919, 920, 921

Draper v. United States, 358 U.S. 307, 79 S.Ct. 329, 3 L.Ed.2d 327 (1959), 294, 299

Drayton, United States v., 536 U.S. 194, 122 S.Ct. 2105, 153 L.Ed.2d 242 (2002), **415,** 462

Dreier v. United States, 221 U.S. 394, 31 S.Ct. 550, 55 L.Ed. 784 (1911), 853

Dubose, State v., 285 Wis.2d 143, 699 N.W.2d 582 (Wis.2005), 790

Duckworth v. Eagan, 492 U.S. 195, 109 S.Ct. 2875, 106 L.Ed.2d 166 (1989), **597,** 598, 642

Dunaway v. New York, 442 U.S. 200, 99 S.Ct. 2248, 60 L.Ed.2d 824 (1979), 425, **438,** 592, 897

Duncan v. Louisiana, 391 U.S. 145, 88 S.Ct. 1444, 20 L.Ed.2d 491 (1968), 26

Duncan v. State, 284 Mich.App. 246, 774 N.W.2d 89 (Mich.App.2009), **182**

Dunlap, Commonwealth v., 596 Pa. 147, 941 A.2d 671 (Pa.2007), 315

Dunn, United States v., 480 U.S. 294, 107 S.Ct. 1134, 94 L.Ed.2d 326 (1987), 270

Duran, United States v., 957 F.2d 499 (7th Cir.1992), 466

Dusky v. United States, 362 U.S. 402, 80 S.Ct. 788, 4 L.Ed.2d 824 (1960), 117, 118, 119

Dyke v. Taylor Implement Mfg. Co., 391 U.S. 216, 88 S.Ct. 1472, 20 L.Ed.2d 538 (1968), 408

Edwards v. Arizona, 451 U.S. 477, 101 S.Ct. 1880, 68 L.Ed.2d 378 (1981), 593, 598, 608, 635, **636,** 637, 638, 642, 643, 644, 645, 646, 647, 648, 660, 662, 663, 664, 745, 748, 755

Edwards v. Lamarque, 475 F.3d 1121 (9th Cir. 2007), 120, 164

Edwards, United States v., 415 U.S. 800, 94 S.Ct. 1234, 39 L.Ed.2d 771 (1974), 359, 361

Elkins v. United States, 364 U.S. 206, 80 S.Ct. 1437, 4 L.Ed.2d 1669 (1960), 227, 248, 358

Elrod, United States v., 441 F.2d 353 (5th Cir.1971), 459, 460

Entick v. Carrington and Three Other King's Messengers, 19 How. St. Tr. 1029 (C.P. 1765), 406

Erving L., United States v., 147 F.3d 1240 (10th Cir.1998), 729

Escobedo v. Illinois, 378 U.S. 478, 84 S.Ct. 1758, 12 L.Ed.2d 977 (1964), 550, 554, **559,** 560, 561, 562, 564, 566, 569, 570, 571, 575, 580, 582, 583, 601, 667, 678, 716, 718, 738, 739, 769, 846

Estelle v. Smith, 451 U.S. 454, 101 S.Ct. 1866, 68 L.Ed.2d 359 (1981), 92, **670,** 671

Everett, United States v., 601 F.3d 484 (6th Cir.2010), **429,** 430

Evers, State v., 175 N.J. 355, 815 A.2d 432 (N.J.2003), 329

Evitts v. Lucey, 469 U.S. 387, 105 S.Ct. 830, 83 L.Ed.2d 821 (1985), 132

Ewing v. California, 538 U.S. 11, 123 S.Ct. 1179, 155 L.Ed.2d 108 (2003), 447

Ex parte (see name of party)

Falon, United States v., 959 F.2d 1143 (1st Cir.1992), 319

Fare v. Michael C., 442 U.S. 707, 99 S.Ct. 2560, 61 L.Ed.2d 197 (1979), **634**

Faretta v. California, 422 U.S. 806, 95 S.Ct. 2525, 45 L.Ed.2d 562 (1975), **107,** 111, 114, 115, 116, 118, 120, 209, 210, 747, 748

Fellers, United States v., 397 F.3d 1090 (8th Cir.2005), **746,** 769, 910

Fellers v. United States, 540 U.S. 519, 124 S.Ct. 1019, 157 L.Ed.2d 1016 (2004), 745, 746, 910

Ferguson v. City of Charleston, 532 U.S. 67, 121 S.Ct. 1281, 149 L.Ed.2d 205 (2001), 449

Ferguson v. Georgia, 365 U.S. 570, 81 S.Ct. 756, 5 L.Ed.2d 783 (1961), 73, 76, 176, 452, 453

Fernandez, United States v., 18 F.3d 874 (10th Cir.1994), 431

Fields, United States v., 113 F.3d 313 (2nd Cir.1997), 383

Finch, State v., 137 Wash.2d 792, 975 P.2d 967 (Wash.1999), 624

Fingerprinting of M. B., In re, 125 N.J.Super. 115, 309 A.2d 3 (N.J.Super.A.D.1973), 438

Finley, United States v., 477 F.3d 250 (5th Cir.2007), 347

Fisher v. United States, 425 U.S. 391, 96 S.Ct. 1569, 48 L.Ed.2d 39 (1976), 287, 288, 802, 853, **856,** 874, 876, 877, 878

Fletcher v. Weir, 455 U.S. 603, 102 S.Ct. 1309, 71 L.Ed.2d 490 (1982), 590, 919, 920

Flippo v. West Virginia, 528 U.S. 11, 120 S.Ct. 7, 145 L.Ed.2d 16 (1999), 375

Flores–Montano, United States v., 541 U.S. 149, 124 S.Ct. 1582, 158 L.Ed.2d 311 (2004), 441

Florida v. Bostick, 501 U.S. 429, 111 S.Ct. 2382, 115 L.Ed.2d 389 (1991), 417, 460, 887, 888

Florida v. Jimeno, 500 U.S. 248, 111 S.Ct. 1801, 114 L.Ed.2d 297 (1991), 459, 461

Florida v. J.L., 529 U.S. 266, 120 S.Ct. 1375, 146 L.Ed.2d 254 (2000), **422,** 424, 435

Florida v. Meyers, 466 U.S. 380, 104 S.Ct. 1852, 80 L.Ed.2d 381 (1984), 384

Florida v. Nixon, 543 U.S. 175, 125 S.Ct. 551, 160 L.Ed.2d 565 (2004), 210, 211, 212, 213, 214

Florida v. Powell, ___ U.S. ___, 130 S.Ct. 1195, 175 L.Ed.2d 1009 (2010), 598

Florida v. Riley, 488 U.S. 445, 109 S.Ct. 693, 102 L.Ed.2d 835 (1989), **270,** 273

Florida v. Royer, 460 U.S. 491, 103 S.Ct. 1319, 75 L.Ed.2d 229 (1983), 64, **425,** 425, 427

Florida v. Wells, 495 U.S. 1, 110 S.Ct. 1632, 109 L.Ed.2d 1 (1990), 354, 358, 408

Florida v. White, 526 U.S. 559, 119 S.Ct. 1555, 143 L.Ed.2d 748 (1999), 387, 388

Flowers v. Fiore, 359 F.3d 24 (1st Cir.2004), 425

Flynn, State v., 92 Wis.2d 427, 285 N.W.2d 710 (Wis.1979), 437

Forrester, United States v., 512 F.3d 500 (9th Cir.2008), **515**

Fort, State v., 660 N.W.2d 415 (Minn.2003), 428

Franks v. Delaware, 438 U.S. 154, 98 S.Ct. 2674, 57 L.Ed.2d 667 (1978), 231, 260, **307,** 308, 358

Fraser v. Nationwide Mut. Ins. Co., 135 F.Supp.2d 623 (E.D.Pa.2001), 537

Frazier v. Cupp, 394 U.S. 731, 89 S.Ct. 1420, 22 L.Ed.2d 684 (1969), 457, 467, 718, 719, 721

Frazier, United States v., 476 F.2d 891, 155 U.S.App.D.C. 135 (D.C.Cir.1973), 633

Fregoso, United States v., 60 F.3d 1314 (8th Cir.1995), 517

French v. Jones, 282 F.3d 893 (6th Cir.2002), 175

Frisbie v. Collins, 342 U.S. 519, 72 S.Ct. 509, 96 L.Ed. 541 (1952), 246

Fry, People v., 271 Cal.App.2d 350, 76 Cal. Rptr. 718 (Cal.App. 4 Dist.1969), 467

Fuller v. Oregon, 417 U.S. 40, 94 S.Ct. 2116, 40 L.Ed.2d 642 (1974), 79

Fulton, United States v., 5 F.3d 605 (2nd Cir. 1993), 202, 209

Futch, Commonwealth v., 447 Pa. 389, 290 A.2d 417 (Pa.1972), 555

Gagnon v. Scarpelli, 411 U.S. 778, 93 S.Ct. 1756, 36 L.Ed.2d 656 (1973), **93,** 95, 96, 98

Gall, People v., 30 P.3d 145 (Colo.2001), 330

Garcia, State v., 147 N.M. 134, 217 P.3d 1032 (N.M.2009), 417

Gardner v. Broderick, 392 U.S. 273, 88 S.Ct. 1913, 20 L.Ed.2d 1082 (1968), 674

Garrity v. New Jersey, 385 U.S. 493, 87 S.Ct. 616, 17 L.Ed.2d 562 (1967), 710

Gault, Application of, 387 U.S. 1, 87 S.Ct. 1428, 18 L.Ed.2d 527 (1967), 95, 96

Geders v. United States, 425 U.S. 80, 96 S.Ct. 1330, 47 L.Ed.2d 592 (1976), 176

Gelbard v. United States, 408 U.S. 41, 92 S.Ct. 2357, 33 L.Ed.2d 179 (1972), 823

Gendron, United States v., 18 F.3d 955 (1st Cir.1994), **485,** 496

Gentile v. United States, 419 U.S. 979, 95 S.Ct. 241, 42 L.Ed.2d 191 (1974), 460

Georgia v. Randolph, 547 U.S. 103, 126 S.Ct. 1515, 164 L.Ed.2d 208 (2006), **467,** 468, 469

Gerber, United States v., 994 F.2d 1556 (11th Cir.1993), 321

Gerstein v. Pugh, 420 U.S. 103, 95 S.Ct. 854, 43 L.Ed.2d 54 (1975), 13, 89, 91, 246, **340,** 342, 343, 639

Gervato, United States v., 474 F.2d 40 (3rd Cir.1973), 322

Giacalone v. Lucas, 445 F.2d 1238 (6th Cir. 1971), 366

Gideon v. Wainwright, 372 U.S. 335, 83 S.Ct. 792, 9 L.Ed.2d 799 (1963), 26, 52, 57, **73,** 80, 81, 82, 83, 93, 94, 95, 96, 100, 101, 123, 131, 177, 560, 562, 578, 584, 710

Gilbert v. California, 388 U.S. 263, 87 S.Ct. 1951, 18 L.Ed.2d 1178 (1967), 456, 761, 762, 763, 764, 766, 767, 768, 769, 773, 777

Gillard v. Schmidt, 579 F.2d 825 (3rd Cir. 1978), 466

Gilmore v. Gonzales, 435 F.3d 1125 (9th Cir. 2006), 442

Gines–Perez, United States v., 214 F.Supp.2d 205 (D.Puerto Rico 2002), 509

Glasser v. United States, 315 U.S. 60, 62 S.Ct. 457, 86 L.Ed. 680 (1942), 131, 186, 187, 188, 193, 204

Glazner v. Glazner, 347 F.3d 1212 (11th Cir. 2003), 531

Glover, Commonwealth v., 266 Pa.Super. 531, 405 A.2d 945 (Pa.Super.1979), 466

Glover v. United States, 531 U.S. 198, 121 S.Ct. 696, 148 L.Ed.2d 604 (2001), 154

G. M. Leasing Corp. v. United States, 429 U.S. 338, 97 S.Ct. 619, 50 L.Ed.2d 530 (1977), 388

Go–Bart Importing Co. v. United States, 282 U.S. 344, 51 S.Ct. 153, 75 L.Ed. 374 (1931), 318, 363

Godinez v. Moran, 509 U.S. 389, 113 S.Ct. 2680, 125 L.Ed.2d 321 (1993), **117,** 118, **119,** 119, 120

Goldman v. United States, 316 U.S. 129, 62 S.Ct. 993, 86 L.Ed. 1322 (1942), 265, 523

Gonzalez, State v., 290 Kan. 747, 234 P.3d 1 (Kan.2010), 833

Gonzalez v. United States, 553 U.S. 242, 128 S.Ct. 1765, 170 L.Ed.2d 616 (2008), **214,** 215, 245

Gonzalez–Lopez, United States v., 548 U.S. 140, 126 S.Ct. 2557, 165 L.Ed.2d 409 (2006), 73, **121,** 127, 128, 149, 203, 244

Gonzalez–Valle, State v., 385 So.2d 681 (Fla. App. 3 Dist.1980), 467

Gooding v. United States, 416 U.S. 430, 94 S.Ct. 1780, 40 L.Ed.2d 250 (1974), 321

Goodwin, Commonwealth v., 458 Mass. 11, 933 N.E.2d 925 (Mass.2010), 454

Gordon v. United States, 518 F.3d 1291 (11th Cir.2008), 166

Goss v. Lopez, 419 U.S. 565, 95 S.Ct. 729, 42 L.Ed.2d 725 (1975), 342

Gouled v. United States, 255 U.S. 298, 41 S.Ct. 261, 65 L.Ed. 647 (1921), 286, 471, **478**

Gourde, United States v., 440 F.3d 1065 (9th Cir.2006), 331

Gouveia, United States v., 467 U.S. 180, 104 S.Ct. 2292, 81 L.Ed.2d 146 (1984), 86, 87

Government of Virgin Islands v. Weatherwax, 77 F.3d 1425 (3rd Cir.1996), 213

Graham v. Connor, 490 U.S. 386, 109 S.Ct. 1865, 104 L.Ed.2d 443 (1989), 31, 32, 339

Grand Jury, In re, 111 F.3d 1066 (3rd Cir. 1997), 836

Grand Jury, In re, 619 F.2d 1022 (3rd Cir. 1980), 836

Grand Jury 87–3 Subpoena Duces Tecum, In re, 955 F.2d 229 (4th Cir.1992), 831

Grand Jury Investigation of Possible Violation of 18 U.S.C. § 1461 et seq., In re, 706 F.Supp.2d 11 (D.D.C.2009), 831

Grand Jury Matters, In re, 751 F.2d 13 (1st Cir.1984), 832

Grand Jury Proceedings, In re, 814 F.2d 61 (1st Cir.1987), 835, 837

Grand Jury Proceedings, In re, 486 F.2d 85 (3rd Cir.1973), **804**

Grand Jury Proceedings, In re, 616 F.3d 1186 (10th Cir.2010), 827

Grand Jury Proceedings: Subpoenas Duces Tecum, In re, 827 F.2d 301 (8th Cir.1987), 517, 833

Grand Jury Proceedings (T.S.), In re, 816 F.Supp. 1196 (W.D.Ky.1993), 822

Grand Jury Subpoena, In re, 646 F.2d 963 (5th Cir.1981), 856

Grand Jury Subpoena, Dated April 18, 2003, In re, 383 F.3d 905 (9th Cir.2004), 876

Grand Jury Subpoena Duces Tecum Dated Nov. 15, 1993, In re, 846 F.Supp. 11 (S.D.N.Y.1994), 815

Grand Jury Subpoena Duces Tecum Served Upon Underhill, In re, 781 F.2d 64 (6th Cir.1986), 855

Grand Jury Subpoena Issued June 18, 2009, In re, 593 F.3d 155 (2nd Cir.2010), 869

Grand Jury Subpoenas, April, 1978, at Baltimore, In re, 581 F.2d 1103 (4th Cir.1978), 834

Gray, United States v., 78 F.Supp.2d 524 (E.D.Va.1999), 331

Grayson, Ex parte, 479 So.2d 76 (Ala.1985), 183

Greenslit, State v., 151 Vt. 225, 559 A.2d 672 (Vt.1989), 362

Gregoire, United States v., 638 F.3d 962 (8th Cir.2011), 330

Griffin v. California, 380 U.S. 609, 85 S.Ct. 1229, 14 L.Ed.2d 106 (1965), 36, 37, 689, 711

Griffin v. Illinois, 351 U.S. 12, 76 S.Ct. 585, 100 L.Ed. 891 (1956), 69, **99,** 100, 101, 102, 105, 560, 571

Griffin v. Wisconsin, 483 U.S. 868, 107 S.Ct. 3164, 97 L.Ed.2d 709 (1987), 445, 452, 453

Griggs, People v., 152 Ill.2d 1, 178 Ill.Dec. 1, 604 N.E.2d 257 (Ill.1992), 670

Grizzle, People v., 140 P.3d 224 (Colo.App. 2006), 500

Groban, Petition of, 352 U.S. 330, 77 S.Ct. 510, 1 L.Ed.2d 376 (1957), 803, 846

Groh v. Ramirez, 540 U.S. 551, 124 S.Ct. 1284, 157 L.Ed.2d 1068 (2004), 240, **320,** 329

Grosso v. United States, 390 U.S. 62, 88 S.Ct. 709, 19 L.Ed.2d 906 (1968), 855

Grubbs, United States v., 547 U.S. 90, 126 S.Ct. 1494, 164 L.Ed.2d 195 (2006), **306,** 329, 331

Grummel, United States v., 542 F.2d 789 (9th Cir.1976), 373

Guevara v. Superior Court, 7 Cal.App.3d 531, 86 Cal.Rptr. 657 (Cal.App. 2 Dist.1970), 367

Gustafson v. Florida, 414 U.S. 260, 94 S.Ct. 488, 38 L.Ed.2d 456 (1973), 348

Guy, United States ex rel. v. McCauley, 385 F.Supp. 193 (E.D.Wis.1974), 360

Gwynn, Commonwealth v., 555 Pa. 86, 723 A.2d 143 (Pa.1998), 425

Halbert v. Michigan, 545 U.S. 605, 125 S.Ct. 2582, 162 L.Ed.2d 552 (2005), **105**

Hale v. Henkel, 201 U.S. 43, 26 S.Ct. 370, 50 L.Ed. 652 (1906), 287, 811, **812,** 813, 814, 815, 816, 818, 853, 854, 859

Hamdan v. Rumsfeld, 548 U.S. 557, 126 S.Ct. 2749, 165 L.Ed.2d 723 (2006), **41,** 48

Hamdi v. Rumsfeld, 542 U.S. 507, 124 S.Ct. 2633, 159 L.Ed.2d 578 (2004), **40,** 46, 48

Hamilton v. Alabama, 368 U.S. 52, 82 S.Ct. 157, 7 L.Ed.2d 114 (1961), 73, 174

Hamilton, Commonwealth v., 445 Pa. 292, 285 A.2d 172 (Pa.1971), 609

Hamilton, People v., 359 Mich. 410, 102 N.W.2d 738 (Mich.1960), 555

Hammond v. Hall, 586 F.3d 1289 (11th Cir. 2009), 165

Hampton v. United States, 425 U.S. 484, 96 S.Ct. 1646, 48 L.Ed.2d 113 (1976), 35

Hargus, United States v., 128 F.3d 1358 (10th Cir.1997), 330

Harrington v. Richter, ___ U.S. ___, 131 S.Ct. 770, 178 L.Ed.2d 624 (2011), 150, **155**

Harris v. Commonwealth, 266 Va. 28, 581 S.E.2d 206 (Va.2003), 428

Harris v. New York, 401 U.S. 222, 91 S.Ct. 643, 28 L.Ed.2d 1 (1971), 590, 591, 679, **911,** 921

Harris, People v., 124 Cal.Rptr. 536, 540 P.2d 632 (Cal.1975), 426

Harris v. South Carolina, 338 U.S. 68, 69 S.Ct. 1354, 93 L.Ed. 1815 (1949), 549

Harris, United States v., 403 U.S. 573, 91 S.Ct. 2075, 29 L.Ed.2d 723 (1971), 301

Harris v. United States, 331 U.S. 145, 67 S.Ct. 1098, 91 L.Ed. 1399 (1947), 363, 404

Hartwell, United States v., 436 F.3d 174 (3rd Cir.2006), 442

Hasting, United States v., 461 U.S. 499, 103 S.Ct. 1974, 76 L.Ed.2d 96 (1983), 35, **36**

Havens, United States v., 446 U.S. 620, 100 S.Ct. 1912, 64 L.Ed.2d 559 (1980), **912**

Hayes v. Florida, 470 U.S. 811, 105 S.Ct. 1643, 84 L.Ed.2d 705 (1985), 430, 437, 438, 767

Haynes v. Washington, 373 U.S. 503, 83 S.Ct. 1336, 10 L.Ed.2d 513 (1963), 550, 565

Hedgepeth ex rel. Hedgepeth v. Washington Metropolitan Area Transit Authority, 386 F.3d 1148, 363 U.S.App.D.C. 260 (D.C.Cir. 2004), 352

Henderson, People v., 33 Ill.2d 225, 210 N.E.2d 483 (Ill.1965), 459

Henderson, State v., 208 N.J. 208 (N.J.2011), 779, 785, 786, 789, 790

Henderson v. United States, 390 F.2d 805 (9th Cir.1967), 440

Hendrix, State v., 782 S.W.2d 833 (Tenn.1989), 375

Henry v. Ryan, 775 F.Supp. 247 (N.D.Ill.1991), 822

Henry, United States v., 447 U.S. 264, 100 S.Ct. 2183, 65 L.Ed.2d 115 (1980), 745, **750,** 751, 752

Hensley, United States v., 469 U.S. 221, 105 S.Ct. 675, 83 L.Ed.2d 604 (1985), **420,** 425

Herman S., In re, 79 Misc.2d 519, 359 N.Y.S.2d 645 (N.Y.Fam.Ct.1974), 419

Herrera v. Collins, 506 U.S. 390, 113 S.Ct. 853, 122 L.Ed.2d 203 (1993), 60

Herrera, United States v., 444 F.3d 1238 (10th Cir.2006), 452

Herring v. New York, 422 U.S. 853, 95 S.Ct. 2550, 45 L.Ed.2d 593 (1975), 176

Herring v. United States, 555 U.S. 135, 129 S.Ct. 695, 172 L.Ed.2d 496 (2009), 251, **258**

Hester v. United States, 265 U.S. 57, 44 S.Ct. 445, 68 L.Ed. 898 (1924), 269

Higgins v. United States, 209 F.2d 819, 93 U.S.App.D.C. 340 (D.C.Cir.1954), 460

Hiibel v. Sixth Judicial Dist. Court of Nevada, Humboldt County, 542 U.S. 177, 124 S.Ct. 2451, 159 L.Ed.2d 292 (2004), 427, 428, 430, 437, **619,** 620, 621, 839

Hill v. California, 401 U.S. 797, 91 S.Ct. 1106, 28 L.Ed.2d 484 (1971), 457, 464

Hill v. Lockhart, 474 U.S. 52, 106 S.Ct. 366, 88 L.Ed.2d 203 (1985), 147

Hill, United States v., 252 F.3d 919 (7th Cir. 2001), 115

Hobson, People v., 39 N.Y.2d 479, 384 N.Y.S.2d 419, 348 N.E.2d 894 (N.Y.1976), 559

Hoffa v. United States, 385 U.S. 293, 87 S.Ct. 408, 17 L.Ed.2d 374 (1966), **470,** 507, 513, 529, 601, 615, 753

Hoffman v. United States, 341 U.S. 479, 71 S.Ct. 814, 95 L.Ed. 1118 (1951), 289, 619, 620, 621, **839,** 839, 866

Hollingsworth, United States v., 27 F.3d 1196 (7th Cir.1994), 496, 497

Holloway v. Arkansas, 435 U.S. 475, 98 S.Ct. 1173, 55 L.Ed.2d 426 (1978), **188,** 189, 190, 192, 204

Horowitz, In re, 482 F.2d 72 (2nd Cir.1973), 812

Horton v. California, 496 U.S. 128, 110 S.Ct. 2301, 110 L.Ed.2d 112 (1990), **327,** 328

Horton, People v., 65 Ill.2d 413, 3 Ill.Dec. 436, 358 N.E.2d 1121 (Ill.1976), 369

Hubbell, United States v., 530 U.S. 27, 120 S.Ct. 2037, 147 L.Ed.2d 24 (2000), 620, 699, **870**

Hudson v. Michigan, 547 U.S. 586, 126 S.Ct. 2159, 165 L.Ed.2d 56 (2006), **252,** 899, 906, **907**

Hudson v. Palmer, 468 U.S. 517, 104 S.Ct. 3194, 82 L.Ed.2d 393 (1984), 257, 258, 272, 445

Hudspeth, United States v., 459 F.3d 922 (8th Cir.2006), 330

Hufnagel, People v., 745 P.2d 242 (Colo.1987), 366

Huie, United States v., 593 F.2d 14 (5th Cir. 1979), 515

Hunt, State v., 275 Kan. 811, 69 P.3d 571 (Kan.2003), 790

Hurrell–Harring v. State, 15 N.Y.3d 8, 904 N.Y.S.2d 296, 930 N.E.2d 217 (N.Y.2010), 92, **177**

Hyde, Commonwealth v., 434 Mass. 594, 750 N.E.2d 963 (Mass.2001), 530

Ianniello, People v., 21 N.Y.2d 418, 288 N.Y.S.2d 462, 235 N.E.2d 439 (N.Y.1968), 847

Illinois v. Allen, 397 U.S. 337, 90 S.Ct. 1057, 25 L.Ed.2d 353 (1970), 773

Illinois v. Andreas, 463 U.S. 765, 103 S.Ct. 3319, 77 L.Ed.2d 1003 (1983), 397

Illinois v. Caballes, 543 U.S. 405, 125 S.Ct. 834, 160 L.Ed.2d 842 (2005), 273, 277, 327, **428,** 429, 430, 431

Illinois v. Gates, 462 U.S. 213, 103 S.Ct. 2317, 76 L.Ed.2d 527 (1983), 39, 229, 237, **295,** 305, 313

Illinois v. Krull, 480 U.S. 340, 107 S.Ct. 1160, 94 L.Ed.2d 364 (1987), **243,** 245, 250, 259

Illinois v. Lafayette, 462 U.S. 640, 103 S.Ct. 2605, 77 L.Ed.2d 65 (1983), 347, 359, 407

Illinois v. Lidster, 540 U.S. 419, 124 S.Ct. 885, 157 L.Ed.2d 843 (2004), 453

Illinois v. McArthur, 531 U.S. 326, 121 S.Ct. 946, 148 L.Ed.2d 838 (2001), 374, 381, 425, 427, 430

Illinois v. Perkins, 496 U.S. 292, 110 S.Ct. 2394, 110 L.Ed.2d 243 (1990), **615,** 616, 617, 728, 745

Illinois v. Rodriguez, 497 U.S. 177, 110 S.Ct. 2793, 111 L.Ed.2d 148 (1990), 459, **462,** 468

Illinois v. Wardlow, 528 U.S. 119, 120 S.Ct. 673, 145 L.Ed.2d 570 (2000), **421,** 422

Indiana v. Edwards, 554 U.S. 164, 128 S.Ct. 2379, 171 L.Ed.2d 345 (2008), 111, **118**

Indianapolis, City of v. Edmond, 531 U.S. 32, 121 S.Ct. 447, 148 L.Ed.2d 333 (2000), 358, 449, 453

In re (see name of party)

I.N.S. v. Lopez–Mendoza, 468 U.S. 1032, 104 S.Ct. 3479, 82 L.Ed.2d 778 (1984), 239, 248, 249, 252, 256

Iowa v. Tovar, 541 U.S. 77, 124 S.Ct. 1379, 158 L.Ed.2d 209 (2004), **115,** 116, 117

Irvine v. People of California, 347 U.S. 128, 74 S.Ct. 381, 98 L.Ed. 561 (1954), 29

Jackson, Ex parte, 96 U.S. 727, 6 Otto 727, 24 L.Ed. 877 (1877), 269, 503, **505,** 506

Jackson v. Denno, 378 U.S. 368, 84 S.Ct. 1774, 12 L.Ed.2d 908 (1964), 929, 930

Jacobsen, United States v., 466 U.S. 109, 104 S.Ct. 1652, 80 L.Ed.2d 85 (1984), 249, 278

Jacobson v. United States, 503 U.S. 540, 112 S.Ct. 1535, 118 L.Ed.2d 174 (1992), **490**

James v. Illinois, 493 U.S. 307, 110 S.Ct. 648, 107 L.Ed.2d 676 (1990), **913,** 916

James v. Strange, 407 U.S. 128, 92 S.Ct. 2027, 32 L.Ed.2d 600 (1972), 79

Janis, United States v., 428 U.S. 433, 96 S.Ct. 3021, 49 L.Ed.2d 1046 (1976), 230, 248, 249, 256

Jarrett, United States v., 338 F.3d 339 (4th Cir.2003), 509

J.D.B. v. North Carolina, ___ U.S. ___, 131 S.Ct. 2394, 180 L.Ed.2d 310 (2011), 418, **603**

Jeffers, United States v., 342 U.S. 48, 72 S.Ct. 93, 96 L.Ed. 59 (1951), 471

Jenkins v. Anderson, 447 U.S. 231, 100 S.Ct. 2124, 65 L.Ed.2d 86 (1980), 590, 919

Jennings, United States v., 985 F.2d 562 (6th Cir.1993), 357

Jetblue Airways Corp. Privacy Litigation, In re, 379 F.Supp.2d 299 (E.D.N.Y.2005), 535

Jimenez v. Wood County, Tex., 621 F.3d 372 (5th Cir.2010), 361

J.M., In re, 619 A.2d 497 (D.C.1992), 418

Johns, United States v., 469 U.S. 478, 105 S.Ct. 881, 83 L.Ed.2d 890 (1985), 330, 384, 390

Johnson, Commonwealth v., 420 Mass. 458, 650 N.E.2d 1257 (Mass.1995), 790

Johnson v. Eisentrager, 339 U.S. 763, 70 S.Ct. 936, 94 L.Ed. 1255 (1950), 44

Johnson v. Quander, 440 F.3d 489, 370 U.S.App.D.C. 167 (D.C.Cir.2006), 453

Johnson v. State, 282 Md. 314, 384 A.2d 709 (Md.1978), 555

Johnson v. Zerbst, 304 U.S. 458, 58 S.Ct. 1019, 82 L.Ed. 1461 (1938), 70, 71, 75, 76, 108, 114, 115, 116, 156, 456, 579, 584, 647, 742

Jones v. Barnes, 463 U.S. 745, 103 S.Ct. 3308, 77 L.Ed.2d 987 (1983), 210, 211, 213

Jones, United States v., 58 F.3d 688, 313 U.S.App.D.C. 128 (D.C.Cir.1995), 321

Jones v. United States, 362 U.S. 257, 80 S.Ct. 725, 4 L.Ed.2d 697 (1960), 284, 882, 883, 884, 892

Jones, United States v., __ U.S. __, 132 S.Ct. 945, 181 L.Ed.2d 911 (2012), **279,** 388

Julius, United States v., 610 F.3d 60 (2nd Cir.2010), 263

Kaluna, State v., 55 Haw. 361, 520 P.2d 51 (Hawai'i 1974), 359

Kaminski, United States v., 703 F.2d 1004 (7th Cir.1983), 497

Kansas v. Marsh, 548 U.S. 163, 126 S.Ct. 2516, 165 L.Ed.2d 429 (2006), 49, **57, 59,** 63, 910

Kansas v. Ventris, 556 U.S. 586, 129 S.Ct. 1841, 173 L.Ed.2d 801 (2009), **917**

Karo, United States v., 468 U.S. 705, 104 S.Ct. 3296, 82 L.Ed.2d 530 (1984), 275, 278, 285, 307, 892

Kastigar v. United States, 406 U.S. 441, 92 S.Ct. 1653, 32 L.Ed.2d 212 (1972), 701, 848, **850,** 851, 858, 868, 872

Katz v. United States, 389 U.S. 347, 88 S.Ct. 507, 19 L.Ed.2d 576 (1967), **264,** 268, 269, 271, 274, 276, 279, 417, 474, 475, 503, 507, 511, 514, 515, 516, 518, 818, 858, 887, 889

Kee v. City of Rowlett, Tex., 247 F.3d 206 (5th Cir.2001), 523

Kelley, Matter of, 433 A.2d 704 (D.C.1981), 822

Kentucky v. King, __ U.S. __, 131 S.Ct. 1849, 179 L.Ed.2d 865 (2011), **368**

Ker v. Illinois, 119 U.S. 436, 7 S.Ct. 225, 30 L.Ed. 421 (1886), 246

Kimmelman v. Morrison, 477 U.S. 365, 106 S.Ct. 2574, 91 L.Ed.2d 305 (1986), **152**

Kincade, United States v., 379 F.3d 813 (9th Cir.2004), 452

King, United States v., 509 F.3d 1338 (11th Cir.2007), 508, 509

Kirby v. Illinois, 406 U.S. 682, 92 S.Ct. 1877, 32 L.Ed.2d 411 (1972), 86, 667, 741, **769,** 770, 846

Knights, United States v., 534 U.S. 112, 122 S.Ct. 587, 151 L.Ed.2d 497 (2001), 444, 452, 460

Knotts, United States v., 460 U.S. 276, 103 S.Ct. 1081, 75 L.Ed.2d 55 (1983), 280, 285

Knowles v. Iowa, 525 U.S. 113, 119 S.Ct. 484, 142 L.Ed.2d 492 (1998), 361, 362

Knowles v. Mirzayance, 556 U.S. 111, 129 S.Ct. 1411, 173 L.Ed.2d 251 (2009), 158

Knox, United States v., 112 F.3d 802 (5th Cir.1997), 497

Konop v. Hawaiian Airlines, Inc., 302 F.3d 868 (9th Cir.2002), 522

Krause v. Commonwealth, 206 S.W.3d 922 (Ky. 2006), 461

Krom, People v., 61 N.Y.2d 187, 473 N.Y.S.2d 139, 461 N.E.2d 276 (N.Y.1984), 624

Kuhl v. United States, 370 F.2d 20 (9th Cir. 1966), 164

Kuhlmann v. Wilson, 477 U.S. 436, 106 S.Ct. 2616, 91 L.Ed.2d 364 (1986), **751**

Kyllo v. United States, 533 U.S. 27, 121 S.Ct. 2038, 150 L.Ed.2d 94 (2001), **274,** 278, 907

LaGrone, United States v., 43 F.3d 332 (7th Cir.1994), 461

Lalor, United States v., 996 F.2d 1578 (4th Cir.1993), 306

Lance W., In re, 210 Cal.Rptr. 631, 694 P.2d 744 (Cal.1985), 879

Lankford v. Gelston, 364 F.2d 197 (4th Cir. 1966), 382

Lassiter v. Department of Social Services of Durham County, N. C., 452 U.S. 18, 101 S.Ct. 2153, 68 L.Ed.2d 640 (1981), 96

Lavallee v. Justices In Hampden Superior Court, 442 Mass. 228, 812 N.E.2d 895 (Mass.2004), 183

Leavell v. Commonwealth, 737 S.W.2d 695 (Ky. 1987), 313

LeBrun, United States v., 363 F.3d 715 (8th Cir.2004), **725**

Ledbetter, State v., 275 Conn. 534, 881 A.2d 290 (Conn.2005), 789

Lee, United States v., 73 F.3d 1034 (10th Cir. 1996), 356

Lefkowitz v. Cunningham, 431 U.S. 801, 97 S.Ct. 2132, 53 L.Ed.2d 1 (1977), 674

Lefkowitz, United States v., 285 U.S. 452, 52 S.Ct. 420, 76 L.Ed. 877 (1932), 363

Lego v. Twomey, 404 U.S. 477, 92 S.Ct. 619, 30 L.Ed.2d 618 (1972), 729, 926, **927,** 928, 929, 930

Leis v. Flynt, 439 U.S. 438, 99 S.Ct. 698, 58 L.Ed.2d 717 (1979), 127

Lender, United States v., 985 F.2d 151 (4th Cir.1993), 417

Leon v. State, 410 So.2d 201 (Fla.App. 3 Dist. 1982), 625, 750

Leon, United States v., 468 U.S. 897, 104 S.Ct. 3405, 82 L.Ed.2d 677 (1984), 39, **229,** 243, 244, 250, 252, 258, 307, 316, 321, 661

Lewis v. United States, 385 U.S. 206, 87 S.Ct. 424, 17 L.Ed.2d 312 (1966), 461

Leyra v. Denno, 347 U.S. 556, 74 S.Ct. 716, 98 L.Ed. 948 (1954), 550

Linkletter v. Walker, 381 U.S. 618, 85 S.Ct. 1731, 14 L.Ed.2d 601 (1965), 879

Lockhart v. Fretwell, 506 U.S. 364, 113 S.Ct. 838, 122 L.Ed.2d 180 (1993), 153

Lo–Ji Sales, Inc. v. New York, 442 U.S. 319, 99 S.Ct. 2319, 60 L.Ed.2d 920 (1979), 233, 316

Long v. District Court of Iowa, In and For Lee County, Fort Madison, Iowa, 385 U.S. 192, 87 S.Ct. 362, 17 L.Ed.2d 290 (1966), 99, 105

Longoria, United States v., 177 F.3d 1179 (10th Cir.1999), 476

Lopez v. United States, 373 U.S. 427, 83 S.Ct. 1381, 10 L.Ed.2d 462 (1963), 472, 489

Los Angeles, City of v. Lyons, 461 U.S. 95, 103 S.Ct. 1660, 75 L.Ed.2d 675 (1983), 65

Los Angeles County, California v. Rettele, 550 U.S. 609, 127 S.Ct. 1989, 167 L.Ed.2d 974 (2007), 325

Losavio v. Kikel, 187 Colo. 148, 529 P.2d 306 (Colo.1974), 800

Loucks, United States v., 806 F.2d 208 (10th Cir.1986), 388

Lugo, United States v., 978 F.2d 631 (10th Cir.1992), 407

Luisi, United States v., 482 F.3d 43 (1st Cir. 2007), 498

Lynch, State v., 796 P.2d 1150 (Okla.1990), 183

Lynumn v. Illinois, 372 U.S. 528, 83 S.Ct. 917, 9 L.Ed.2d 922 (1963), 550

MacWade v. Kelly, 460 F.3d 260 (2nd Cir. 2006), 442

Mahnke, Commonwealth v., 368 Mass. 662, 335 N.E.2d 660 (Mass.1975), 717, 731

Maine v. Moulton, 474 U.S. 159, 106 S.Ct. 477, 88 L.Ed.2d 481 (1985), **749,** 751, 758

Maldonado v. State, 528 S.W.2d 234 (Tex.Crim. App.1975), 388

Malinski v. New York, 324 U.S. 401, 65 S.Ct. 781, 89 L.Ed. 1029 (1945), 550

Malley v. Briggs, 475 U.S. 335, 106 S.Ct. 1092, 89 L.Ed.2d 271 (1986), 239, 242

Mallory v. United States, 354 U.S. 449, 77 S.Ct. 1356, 1 L.Ed.2d 1479 (1957), 52, **555,** 556, 575, 676, 677

Malloy v. Hogan, 378 U.S. 1, 84 S.Ct. 1489, 12 L.Ed.2d 653 (1964), 26, 30, 31, 564, **565,** 566, 575, 678, 701, 710, 841

Mancusi v. DeForte, 392 U.S. 364, 88 S.Ct. 2120, 20 L.Ed.2d 1154 (1968), 883, 884

Mandujano, United States v., 425 U.S. 564, 96 S.Ct. 1768, 48 L.Ed.2d 212 (1976), 601, 842, **843,** 845, **846,** 847

Maness v. Meyers, 419 U.S. 449, 95 S.Ct. 584, 42 L.Ed.2d 574 (1975), 289

Mankani, United States v., 738 F.2d 538 (2nd Cir.1984), 274

Manson v. Brathwaite, 432 U.S. 98, 97 S.Ct. 2243, 53 L.Ed.2d 140 (1977), **774,** 779, 780, 781, 784, 785, 786, 790, 930

Mapp v. Ohio, 367 U.S. 643, 81 S.Ct. 1684, 6 L.Ed.2d 1081 (1961), 27, 29, 30, 31, 52, 56, 76, **224,** 235, 248, 252, 258, 584, 673, 688, 879, 923

Mara, United States v., 410 U.S. 19, 93 S.Ct. 774, 35 L.Ed.2d 99 (1973), 438, 819, 822

Marbury v. Madison, 5 U.S. 137, 2 L.Ed. 60 (1803), 680

Marin–Buitrago, United States v., 734 F.2d 889 (2nd Cir.1984), 307, 321

Marquez, United States v., 410 F.3d 612 (9th Cir.2005), 442

Marron v. United States, 275 U.S. 192, 48 S.Ct. 74, 72 L.Ed. 231 (1927), 363, 811

Marshall v. Barlow's, Inc., 436 U.S. 307, 98 S.Ct. 1816, 56 L.Ed.2d 305 (1978), 440

Martin, Commonwealth v., 358 Mass. 282, 264 N.E.2d 366 (Mass.1970), 467

Martin, People v., 45 Cal.2d 755, 290 P.2d 855 (Cal.1955), 879

Martinez v. Court of Appeal of California, Fourth Appellate Dist., 528 U.S. 152, 120 S.Ct. 684, 145 L.Ed.2d 597 (2000), 110, **111,** 129

Martinez–Fuerte, United States v., 428 U.S. 543, 96 S.Ct. 3074, 49 L.Ed.2d 1116 (1976), 441, 448

Maryland v. Buie, 494 U.S. 325, 110 S.Ct. 1093, 108 L.Ed.2d 276 (1990), 257, **366,** 401

Maryland v. Dyson, 527 U.S. 465, 119 S.Ct. 2013, 144 L.Ed.2d 442 (1999), 387

Maryland v. Garrison, 480 U.S. 79, 107 S.Ct. 1013, 94 L.Ed.2d 72 (1987), 317, 464

Maryland v. Pringle, 540 U.S. 366, 124 S.Ct. 795, 157 L.Ed.2d 769 (2003), **310**

Maryland v. Shatzer, ___ U.S. ___, 130 S.Ct. 1213, 175 L.Ed.2d 1045 (2010), **637**

Maryland v. Wilson, 519 U.S. 408, 117 S.Ct. 882, 137 L.Ed.2d 41 (1997), 361

Massachusetts v. Sheppard, 468 U.S. 981, 104 S.Ct. 3424, 82 L.Ed.2d 737 (1984), 239, 240, 241, 250, 259, 321

Massachusetts v. Upton, 466 U.S. 727, 104 S.Ct. 2085, 80 L.Ed.2d 721 (1984), **304**

Massenburg, United States v., 654 F.3d 480 (4th Cir.2011), 315

Massiah v. United States, 377 U.S. 201, 84 S.Ct. 1199, 12 L.Ed.2d 246 (1964), 37, 38, 461, 554, **557,** 558, 559, 561, 562, 563, 564, 609, 616, 671, 738, 739, 742, 744, 745, 746, 747, 749, 750, 751, 753, 758, 769, 910, 917, 918

Master, United States v., 614 F.3d 236 (6th Cir.2010), 263, 316

Matlock, United States v., 415 U.S. 164, 94 S.Ct. 988, 39 L.Ed.2d 242 (1974), 463, 467

Matter of (see name of party)

Mayer v. City of Chicago, 404 U.S. 189, 92 S.Ct. 410, 30 L.Ed.2d 372 (1971), **100,** 105

Mayer, United States v., 503 F.3d 740 (9th Cir.2007), 477

McCane, United States v., 573 F.3d 1037 (10th Cir.2009), 245

McCauley, United States ex rel. Guy v., 385 F.Supp. 193 (E.D.Wis.1974), 360

McCoy v. Court of Appeals of Wisconsin, Dist. 1, 486 U.S. 429, 108 S.Ct. 1895, 100 L.Ed.2d 440 (1988), 220

McCray v. Illinois, 386 U.S. 300, 87 S.Ct. 1056, 18 L.Ed.2d 62 (1967), 301, **308,** 310

McDermott, Commonwealth v., 448 Mass. 750, 864 N.E.2d 471 (Mass.2007), 331

McDonald v. City of Chicago, Ill., ___ U.S. ___, 130 S.Ct. 3020, 177 L.Ed.2d 894 (2010), **25**

McFarland v. Scott, 512 U.S. 1256, 114 S.Ct. 2785, 129 L.Ed.2d 896 (1994), 82, 83, 84, 167

McKane v. Durston, 153 U.S. 684, 14 S.Ct. 913, 38 L.Ed. 867 (1894), 103

McKaskle v. Wiggins, 465 U.S. 168, 104 S.Ct. 944, 79 L.Ed.2d 122 (1984), **111,** 113, 118, 123, 170, 172

McKnight, State v., 52 N.J. 35, 243 A.2d 240 (N.J.1968), **596**

McMann v. Richardson, 397 U.S. 759, 90 S.Ct. 1441, 25 L.Ed.2d 763 (1970), 139

McNabb v. United States, 318 U.S. 332, 63 S.Ct. 608, 87 L.Ed. 819 (1943), **34,** 38, 51, 52, 483, **554,** 555, 556, 565, 575, 676, 677

McNeil v. Wisconsin, 501 U.S. 171, 111 S.Ct. 2204, 115 L.Ed.2d 158 (1991), **663,** 664, 754

McNulty, United States v., 47 F.3d 100 (4th Cir.1995), 508

Medina v. California, 505 U.S. 437, 112 S.Ct. 2572, 120 L.Ed.2d 353 (1992), 32, 33

Medrano v. State, 914 P.2d 804 (Wyo.1996), 425

Melgar, United States v., 139 F.3d 1005 (4th Cir.1998), 664

Melvin, In re, 546 F.2d 1 (1st Cir.1976), 822

Mempa v. Rhay, 389 U.S. 128, 88 S.Ct. 254, 19 L.Ed.2d 336 (1967), 93

Mendenhall, United States v., 446 U.S. 544, 100 S.Ct. 1870, 64 L.Ed.2d 497 (1980), 888

Mesa, United States v., 62 F.3d 159 (6th Cir. 1995), 356

Mesa, United States v., 638 F.2d 582 (3rd Cir.1980), 554, 602, 624

Michigan v. Clifford, 464 U.S. 287, 104 S.Ct. 641, 78 L.Ed.2d 477 (1984), 440

Michigan v. DeFillippo, 443 U.S. 31, 99 S.Ct. 2627, 61 L.Ed.2d 343 (1979), 243

Michigan v. Fisher, ___ U.S. ___, 130 S.Ct. 546, 175 L.Ed.2d 410 (2009), 376

Michigan v. Jackson, 475 U.S. 625, 106 S.Ct. 1404, 89 L.Ed.2d 631 (1986), 86, 659, 660, 663, 756

Michigan v. Long, 463 U.S. 1032, 103 S.Ct. 3469, 77 L.Ed.2d 1201 (1983), **38,** 361, 366, **436**

Michigan v. Mosley, 423 U.S. 96, 96 S.Ct. 321, 46 L.Ed.2d 313 (1975), 39, 592, 593, 608, **635,** 636, 656, 745

Michigan v. Payne, 412 U.S. 47, 93 S.Ct. 1966, 36 L.Ed.2d 736 (1973), 683

Michigan v. Summers, 452 U.S. 692, 101 S.Ct. 2587, 69 L.Ed.2d 340 (1981), **325,** 328

Michigan v. Thomas, 458 U.S. 259, 102 S.Ct. 3079, 73 L.Ed.2d 750 (1982), 384

Michigan v. Tucker, 417 U.S. 433, 94 S.Ct. 2357, 41 L.Ed.2d 182 (1974), 256, 576, 590, 591, 594, 597, 679, 921

Michigan Dept. of State Police v. Sitz, 496 U.S. 444, 110 S.Ct. 2481, 110 L.Ed.2d 412 (1990), 442

Mickens v. Taylor, 535 U.S. 162, 122 S.Ct. 1237, 152 L.Ed.2d 291 (2002), 122, 189, 190, **191**

Middendorf v. Henry, 425 U.S. 25, 96 S.Ct. 1281, 47 L.Ed.2d 556 (1976), 96, 98

Miller v. Fenton, 796 F.2d 598 (3rd Cir. 1986), **719,** 725

Miller v. Fenton, 474 U.S. 104, 106 S.Ct. 445, 88 L.Ed.2d 405 (1985), 551

Miller v. Idaho State Patrol, 150 Idaho 856, 252 P.3d 1274 (Idaho 2011), 360

Miller, State v., 429 N.W.2d 26 (S.D.1988), 321

Miller, United States v., 425 U.S. 435, 96 S.Ct. 1619, 48 L.Ed.2d 71 (1976), 285, 504, 513, **517,** 518, 815, 835

Mills, People v., 178 N.Y. 274, 70 N.E. 786 (N.Y.1904), 479

Mincey v. Arizona, 437 U.S. 385, 98 S.Ct. 2408, 57 L.Ed.2d 290 (1978), 375, 552, 693, 733, 917

Minnesota v. Carter, 525 U.S. 83, 119 S.Ct. 469, 142 L.Ed.2d 373 (1998), 276, **889**

Minnesota v. Dickerson, 508 U.S. 366, 113 S.Ct. 2130, 124 L.Ed.2d 334 (1993), 436

Minnesota v. Murphy, 465 U.S. 420, 104 S.Ct. 1136, 79 L.Ed.2d 409 (1984), 603

Minnesota v. Olson, 495 U.S. 91, 110 S.Ct. 1684, 109 L.Ed.2d 85 (1990), 883, 886, 889, 890

Minnick v. Mississippi, 498 U.S. 146, 111 S.Ct. 486, 112 L.Ed.2d 489 (1990), 593, 637, 640

Miranda v. Arizona, 384 U.S. 436, 86 S.Ct. 1602, 16 L.Ed.2d 694 (1966), **571,** *passim*

Miranda, State v., 104 Ariz. 174, 450 P.2d 364 (Ariz.1969), 581

Missouri v. Seibert, 542 U.S. 600, 124 S.Ct. 2601, 159 L.Ed.2d 643 (2004), 594, 675, 701, **702,** 712, 713, 746, 769, 909

Mitchell v. United States, 321 U.S. 756, 64 S.Ct. 485, 88 L.Ed. 1056 (1944), 51

Mitchell v. W. T. Grant Co., 416 U.S. 600, 94 S.Ct. 1895, 40 L.Ed.2d 406 (1974), 342

Mobley, United States v., 40 F.3d 688 (4th Cir.1994), 637

Mohabir, United States v., 624 F.2d 1140 (2nd Cir.1980), 37, 38, 747

Monell v. Department of Social Services of City of New York, 436 U.S. 658, 98 S.Ct. 2018, 56 L.Ed.2d 611 (1978), 242, 254

Monia, United States v., 317 U.S. 424, 63 S.Ct. 409, 87 L.Ed. 376 (1943), 844

Monroe v. Pape, 365 U.S. 167, 81 S.Ct. 473, 5 L.Ed.2d 492 (1961), 254

Montejo v. Louisiana, 556 U.S. 778, 129 S.Ct. 2079, 173 L.Ed.2d 955 (2009), **659**

Montoya de Hernandez, United States v., 473 U.S. 531, 105 S.Ct. 3304, 87 L.Ed.2d 381 (1985), 441

Moore v. Dempsey, 261 U.S. 86, 43 S.Ct. 265, 67 L.Ed. 543 (1923), 49, 50

Moore v. Illinois, 434 U.S. 220, 98 S.Ct. 458, 54 L.Ed.2d 424 (1977), 88

Moran v. Burbine, 475 U.S. 412, 106 S.Ct. 1135, 89 L.Ed.2d 410 (1986), 39, 600, **665,** 747, 748

Morris v. Slappy, 461 U.S. 1, 103 S.Ct. 1610, 75 L.Ed.2d 610 (1983), 128

Morris, State v., 668 P.2d 857 (Alaska App. 1983), 307

Morrissey v. Brewer, 408 U.S. 471, 92 S.Ct. 2593, 33 L.Ed.2d 484 (1972), 93, 94, 445

Morton Salt Co., United States v., 338 U.S. 632, 70 S.Ct. 357, 94 L.Ed. 401, 46 F.T.C. 1436 (1950), 824

Mosley, Michigan vs., (see Michigan v. Mosley)

Muehler v. Mena, 544 U.S. 93, 125 S.Ct. 1465, 161 L.Ed.2d 299 (2005), 327

Munkus v. Furlong, 170 F.3d 980 (10th Cir. 1999), 114

Munson, State v., 594 N.W.2d 128 (Minn. 1999), 425

Murphy v. Waterfront Com'n of New York Harbor, 378 U.S. 52, 84 S.Ct. 1594, 12 L.Ed.2d 678 (1964), 575, 673, 840, 841, 849, 850, 856, 858, 866

Murray v. Carrier, 477 U.S. 478, 106 S.Ct. 2639, 91 L.Ed.2d 397 (1986), 162

Murray v. Giarratano, 492 U.S. 1, 109 S.Ct. 2765, 106 L.Ed.2d 1 (1989), 98

Murray v. United States, 487 U.S. 533, 108 S.Ct. 2529, 101 L.Ed.2d 472 (1988), **901,** 902, 906, 909

Nardone v. United States, 308 U.S. 338, 60 S.Ct. 266, 84 L.Ed. 307 (1939), 893, 894, 908, 927

Nathanson v. United States, 290 U.S. 41, 54 S.Ct. 11, 78 L.Ed. 159 (1933), 293, 298

National Treasury Employees Union v. Von Raab, 489 U.S. 656, 109 S.Ct. 1384, 103 L.Ed.2d 685 (1989), 443

Nawrocki, People v., 6 Mich.App. 46, 150 N.W.2d 516 (Mich.App.1967), 462

Neder v. United States, 527 U.S. 1, 119 S.Ct. 1827, 144 L.Ed.2d 35 (1999), 126

Neely, State v., 261 Mont. 369, 862 P.2d 1109 (Mont.1993), 321

Neil v. Biggers, 409 U.S. 188, 93 S.Ct. 375, 34 L.Ed.2d 401 (1972), 775, 780, 784, 790

Nepstead, United States v., 424 F.2d 269 (9th Cir.1970), 321

Newell, United States v., 315 F.3d 510 (5th Cir.2002), 209

New Jersey v. Portash, 440 U.S. 450, 99 S.Ct. 1292, 59 L.Ed.2d 501 (1979), 916

New Jersey v. T.L.O., 469 U.S. 325, 105 S.Ct. 733, 83 L.Ed.2d 720 (1985), 251, 442, 443

New York v. Belton, 453 U.S. 454, 101 S.Ct. 2860, 69 L.Ed.2d 768 (1981), 244, 245, 350, 391, 398, 405, 406, 407

New York v. Burger, 482 U.S. 691, 107 S.Ct. 2636, 96 L.Ed.2d 601 (1987), 354, 358, 440

New York v. Class, 475 U.S. 106, 106 S.Ct. 960, 89 L.Ed.2d 81 (1986), 273

New York v. Harris, 495 U.S. 14, 110 S.Ct. 1640, 109 L.Ed.2d 13 (1990), **899,** 908, 911, 912, 913, 916, 917

New York v. P.J. Video, Inc., 475 U.S. 868, 106 S.Ct. 1610, 89 L.Ed.2d 871 (1986), 290

New York v. Quarles, 467 U.S. 649, 104 S.Ct. 2626, 81 L.Ed.2d 550 (1984), 593, 594, 602, **621,** 624, 625, 679, 682, 686, 700, 893

New York Tel. Co., United States v., 434 U.S. 159, 98 S.Ct. 364, 54 L.Ed.2d 376 (1977), 512

Nicholas v. Goord, 430 F.3d 652 (2nd Cir. 2005), 453

Nichols v. United States, 511 U.S. 738, 114 S.Ct. 1921, 128 L.Ed.2d 745 (1994), **83**

Nix v. Whiteside, 475 U.S. 157, 106 S.Ct. 988, 89 L.Ed.2d 123 (1986), 153, 154

Nix v. Williams, 467 U.S. 431, 104 S.Ct. 2501, 81 L.Ed.2d 377 (1984), 623, 743, 746, 769, 895, 901, **903,** 905, 906, 907, 908, 909, 910, 927

Nixon, United States v., 418 U.S. 683, 94 S.Ct. 3090, 41 L.Ed.2d 1039 (1974), 824

Norris v. Alabama, 294 U.S. 587, 55 S.Ct. 579, 79 L.Ed. 1074 (1935), 49, 50

Norris v. Premier Integrity Solutions, Inc., 641 F.3d 695 (6th Cir.2011), 444

North, United States v., 910 F.2d 843, 285 U.S.App.D.C. 343 (D.C.Cir.1990), 851

North Carolina v. Butler, 441 U.S. 369, 99 S.Ct. 1755, 60 L.Ed.2d 286 (1979), **631,** 633, 649, 650, 652

North Carolina v. Pearce, 395 U.S. 711, 89 S.Ct. 2072, 23 L.Ed.2d 656 (1969), 683

North Georgia Finishing, Inc. v. Di–Chem, Inc., 419 U.S. 601, 95 S.Ct. 719, 42 L.Ed.2d 751 (1975), 342

O'Connell v. United States, 40 F.2d 201 (2nd Cir.1930), 842

O'Connor v. Johnson, 287 N.W.2d 400 (Minn. 1979), 291

O'Connor v. Ortega, 480 U.S. 709, 107 S.Ct. 1492, 94 L.Ed.2d 714 (1987), 890

O'Hagen, State v., 189 N.J. 140, 914 A.2d 267 (N.J.2007), 453

Ohio v. Reiner, 532 U.S. 17, 121 S.Ct. 1252, 149 L.Ed.2d 158 (2001), 840

Ohio v. Robinette, 519 U.S. 33, 117 S.Ct. 417, 136 L.Ed.2d 347 (1996), **431,** 431, 432, 456

Oklahoma Press Pub. Co. v. Walling, 327 U.S. 186, 66 S.Ct. 494, 90 L.Ed. 614 (1946), 812

Oliver v. United States, 466 U.S. 170, 104 S.Ct. 1735, 80 L.Ed.2d 214 (1984), **269,** 270

Oliver, United States v., 683 F.2d 224 (7th Cir.1982), 352

Olmstead v. United States, 277 U.S. 438, 48 S.Ct. 564, 72 L.Ed. 944 (1928), 227, 235, 265, **505,** 507, 810

Oman v. State, 737 N.E.2d 1131 (Ind.2000), 813

O'Neal, United States v., 17 F.3d 239 (8th Cir.1994), 239

One 1958 Plymouth Sedan v. Commonwealth of Pa., 380 U.S. 693, 85 S.Ct. 1246, 14 L.Ed.2d 170 (1965), 248

Oregon v. Bradshaw, 462 U.S. 1039, 103 S.Ct. 2830, 77 L.Ed.2d 405 (1983), **642,** 643, 645

Oregon v. Elstad, 470 U.S. 298, 105 S.Ct. 1285, 84 L.Ed.2d 222 (1985), 594, 677, 679, **697,** 698, 700, 703, 709, 746, 769, 910, 921

Oregon v. Hass, 420 U.S. 714, 95 S.Ct. 1215, 43 L.Ed.2d 570 (1975), 590, 682, 912, 913, 916, 917, 921

Oregon v. Mathiason, 429 U.S. 492, 97 S.Ct. 711, 50 L.Ed.2d 714 (1977), 592, 602, 718

Orozco v. Texas, 394 U.S. 324, 89 S.Ct. 1095, 22 L.Ed.2d 311 (1969), 589, 602, 681

Ortiz, United States v., 422 U.S. 891, 95 S.Ct. 2585, 45 L.Ed.2d 623 (1975), 441

Padilla v. Kentucky, ___ U.S. ___, 130 S.Ct. 1473, 176 L.Ed.2d 284 (2010), 150, **151,** 159

Padilla, United States v., 508 U.S. 77, 113 S.Ct. 1936, 123 L.Ed.2d 635 (1993), 880

Palko v. Connecticut, 302 U.S. 319, 58 S.Ct. 149, 82 L.Ed. 288 (1937), 71, 76

Parsley v. Superior Court, 109 Cal.Rptr. 563, 513 P.2d 611 (Cal.1973), 323

Paszek, State v., 50 Wis.2d 619, 184 N.W.2d 836 (Wis.1971), 314

Patane, United States v., 542 U.S. 630, 124 S.Ct. 2620, 159 L.Ed.2d 667 (2004), 594, 595, 623, 675, 684, 698, **699,** 706, 712, 713, 746, 909

Patterson v. Illinois, 487 U.S. 285, 108 S.Ct. 2389, 101 L.Ed.2d 261 (1988), 38, 116, **746,** 748

Paulino v. State, 399 Md. 341, 924 A.2d 308 (Md.2007), 347

Payne v. Arkansas, 356 U.S. 560, 78 S.Ct. 844, 2 L.Ed.2d 975 (1958), 727

Payner, United States v., 447 U.S. 727, 100 S.Ct. 2439, 65 L.Ed.2d 468 (1980), **35,** 38, 881, **882**

Payton v. New York, 445 U.S. 573, 100 S.Ct. 1371, 63 L.Ed.2d 639 (1980), 365, **376, 899,** 900

Peart, State v., 621 So.2d 780 (La.1993), 176

Pennsylvania v. Finley, 481 U.S. 551, 107 S.Ct. 1990, 95 L.Ed.2d 539 (1987), 98, 133

Pennsylvania v. Mimms, 434 U.S. 106, 98 S.Ct. 330, 54 L.Ed.2d 331 (1977), 361

Pennsylvania v. Muniz, 496 U.S. 582, 110 S.Ct. 2638, 110 L.Ed.2d 528 (1990), **617,** 619, 620

Pennsylvania v. Ritchie, 480 U.S. 39, 107 S.Ct. 989, 94 L.Ed.2d 40 (1987), 32

Pennsylvania Bd. of Probation and Parole v. Scott, 524 U.S. 357, 118 S.Ct. 2014, 141 L.Ed.2d 344 (1998), 247, 252, 258, 259, 446

People v. _____ (see opposing party)

People ex rel. v. _____ (see opposing party and relator)

Perry v. New Hampshire, ___ U.S. ___, 132 S.Ct. 716, 181 L.Ed.2d 694 (2012), **780,** 786

Perry, People v., 47 Ill.2d 402, 266 N.E.2d 330 (Ill.1971), 365

Pervaz, United States v., 118 F.3d 1 (1st Cir. 1997), 531

Peterson, State v., 314 Wis.2d 192, 757 N.W.2d 834 (Wis.App.2008), 129

Petition of (see name of party)

Pickens v. State, 96 Wis.2d 549, 292 N.W.2d 601 (Wis.1980), 120

Place, United States v., 462 U.S. 696, 103 S.Ct. 2637, 77 L.Ed.2d 110 (1983), 267, 277, 278, **433**

Ponds, United States v., 454 F.3d 313, 372 U.S.App.D.C. 117 (D.C.Cir.2006), 876, 877, 878

Powell v. Alabama, 287 U.S. 45, 53 S.Ct. 55, 77 L.Ed. 158 (1932), 49, 50, 70, 71, 74, 75, 76, 123, 131, 149, 174, 847, 918

Powell v. Barrett, 541 F.3d 1298 (11th Cir. 2008), 361

Powell v. Nevada, 511 U.S. 79, 114 S.Ct. 1280, 128 L.Ed.2d 1 (1994), 343

Powell v. Texas, 492 U.S. 680, 109 S.Ct. 3146, 106 L.Ed.2d 551 (1989), 671

Prall, People v., 314 Ill. 518, 145 N.E. 610 (Ill.1924), 318

Price v. Turner, 260 F.3d 1144 (9th Cir.2001), 508

Procter & Gamble Co., United States v., 356 U.S. 677, 78 S.Ct. 983, 2 L.Ed.2d 1077 (1958), 798, 799

Quirin, Ex parte, 317 U.S. 1, 63 S.Ct. 1, 87 L.Ed. 3 (1942), 42

Rabinowitz, United States v., 339 U.S. 56, 70 S.Ct. 430, 94 L.Ed. 653 (1950), 363, 404, 406, 407

Raettig v. State, 406 So.2d 1273 (Fla.App. 1 Dist.1981), 274

Raffel v. United States, 271 U.S. 494, 46 S.Ct. 566, 70 L.Ed. 1054 (1926), 919

Rakas v. Illinois, 439 U.S. 128, 99 S.Ct. 421, 58 L.Ed.2d 387 (1978), 230, 879, 880, 882, 883, **884,** 885, 886, 887, 889

Ramirez, State v., 817 P.2d 774 (Utah 1991), 790

Ramirez, United States v., 523 U.S. 65, 118 S.Ct. 992, 140 L.Ed.2d 191 (1998), 322

Ramos–Oseguera, United States v., 120 F.3d 1028 (9th Cir.1997), 407

Ramsey, United States v., 431 U.S. 606, 97 S.Ct. 1972, 52 L.Ed.2d 617 (1977), 440

Rasul v. Bush, 542 U.S. 466, 124 S.Ct. 2686, 159 L.Ed.2d 548 (2004), **41,** 43

Rathbun v. United States, 355 U.S. 107, 78 S.Ct. 161, 2 L.Ed.2d 134 (1957), 530, 531

Rawlings v. Kentucky, 448 U.S. 98, 100 S.Ct. 2556, 65 L.Ed.2d 633 (1980), 362, 883, **885,** 886, 887, 897

Rayburn House Office Building, Room 2113, Washington, D.C. 20515, United States v., 497 F.3d 654, 378 U.S.App.D.C. 139 (D.C.Cir.2007), 292

Reck v. Pate, 367 U.S. 433, 81 S.Ct. 1541, 6 L.Ed.2d 948 (1961), 551

Rehberg v. Paulk, 598 F.3d 1268 (11th Cir. 2010), 504, 505

R. Enterprises, Inc., United States v., 498 U.S. 292, 111 S.Ct. 722, 112 L.Ed.2d 795 (1991), 801, 815, 822, **823**

Reynolds, People v., 55 Cal.App.3d 357, 127 Cal.Rptr. 561 (Cal.App. 2 Dist.1976), 467

Rhode Island v. Innis, 446 U.S. 291, 100 S.Ct. 1682, 64 L.Ed.2d 297 (1980), **608,** 624, 645, 745

Riccardi, United States v., 405 F.3d 852 (10th Cir.2005), 329, 330

Richards v. Wisconsin, 520 U.S. 385, 117 S.Ct. 1416, 137 L.Ed.2d 615 (1997), 253, **322,** 323, 383

Richardson, State v., 204 Conn. 654, 529 A.2d 1236 (Conn.1987), 310

Ricketts v. Adamson, 483 U.S. 1, 107 S.Ct. 2680, 97 L.Ed.2d 1 (1987), 31

Riley, United States v., 554 F.2d 1282 (4th Cir.1977), 505

Rinaldi v. Yeager, 384 U.S. 305, 86 S.Ct. 1497, 16 L.Ed.2d 577 (1966), 79

Riverside, County of v. McLaughlin, 500 U.S. 44, 111 S.Ct. 1661, 114 L.Ed.2d 49 (1991), **342,** 343, 350, 639

Robbins v. California, 453 U.S. 420, 101 S.Ct. 2841, 69 L.Ed.2d 744 (1981), 402

Roberson, United States v., 6 F.3d 1088 (5th Cir.1993), 356

Roberts v. LaVallee, 389 U.S. 40, 88 S.Ct. 194, 19 L.Ed.2d 41 (1967), 99, 105

Roberts, United States v., 333 F.Supp. 786 (E.D.Tenn.1971), 335

Robinson, People v., 104 Cal.Rptr.3d 727, 224 P.3d 55 (Cal.2010), 263

Robinson, United States v., 414 U.S. 218, 94 S.Ct. 467, 38 L.Ed.2d 427 (1973), 39, **343,** 349, 354, 359, 367

Rochin v. California, 342 U.S. 165, 72 S.Ct. 205, 96 L.Ed. 183 (1952), **28,** 30, 31, 241, 472, 487, 549

Rodney, United States v., 956 F.2d 295, 294 U.S.App.D.C. 9 (D.C.Cir.1992), 461

Roe v. Flores–Ortega, 528 U.S. 470, 120 S.Ct. 1029, 145 L.Ed.2d 985 (2000), **216**

Rogers v. Richmond, 365 U.S. 534, 81 S.Ct. 735, 5 L.Ed.2d 760 (1961), 549, 550

Rogers v. United States, 340 U.S. 367, 71 S.Ct. 438, 95 L.Ed. 344 (1951), 579, 841, 842

Rogers v. Zant, 13 F.3d 384 (11th Cir.1994), 150

Romero, State v., 191 N.J. 59, 922 A.2d 693 (N.J.2007), 789

Rompilla v. Beard, 545 U.S. 374, 125 S.Ct. 2456, 162 L.Ed.2d 360 (2005), 151, 166, **168,** 172

Rooker v. Commonwealth, 508 S.W.2d 570 (Ky. 1974), 316

Ropp, United States v., 347 F.Supp.2d 831 (C.D.Cal.2004), 524

Rosales, People v., 68 Cal.2d 299, 66 Cal.Rptr. 1, 437 P.2d 489 (Cal.1968), 383

Rosenbaum v. Washoe County, 654 F.3d 1001 (9th Cir.2011), 337

Ross v. Moffitt, 417 U.S. 600, 94 S.Ct. 2437, 41 L.Ed.2d 341 (1974), **102,** 106, 132, 133, 184

Ross, United States v., 456 U.S. 798, 102 S.Ct. 2157, 72 L.Ed.2d 572 (1982), 384, 388, 393, 394, 401

Rothgery v. Gillespie County, Tex., 554 U.S. 191, 128 S.Ct. 2578, 171 L.Ed.2d 366 (2008), **85,** 178, 769

Rubin, United States v., 474 F.2d 262 (3rd Cir.1973), 374

Rumsfeld v. Padilla, 542 U.S. 426, 124 S.Ct. 2711, 159 L.Ed.2d 513 (2004), 41

Rupnick, State v., 280 Kan. 720, 125 P.3d 541 (Kan.2005), 330

Ruscoe, State v., 212 Conn. 223, 563 A.2d 267 (Conn.1989), 328

Russell, United States v., 411 U.S. 423, 93 S.Ct. 1637, 36 L.Ed.2d 366 (1973), 35, **487**

Russell v. United States, 408 F.2d 1280, 133 U.S.App.D.C. 77 (D.C.Cir.1969), 769, 770

R.V., In re, 89 Cal.Rptr.3d 702 (Cal.App. 1 Dist.2009), 454

Rytman, United States v., 475 F.2d 192 (5th Cir.1973), 318

Sacramento, County of v. Lewis, 523 U.S. 833, 118 S.Ct. 1708, 140 L.Ed.2d 1043 (1998), **31,** 32, 339, 416, 888

Safford Unified School Dist. No. 1 v. Redding, 557 U.S. 364, 129 S.Ct. 2633, 174 L.Ed.2d 354 (2009), 442

Salsman, State v., 112 N.H. 138, 290 A.2d 618 (N.H.1972), 318

Salvucci, United States v., 448 U.S. 83, 100 S.Ct. 2547, 65 L.Ed.2d 619 (1980), 882

Samson v. California, 547 U.S. 843, 126 S.Ct. 2193, 165 L.Ed.2d 250 (2006), 439, **444,** 460

Sanchez–Llamas v. Oregon, 548 U.S. 331, 126 S.Ct. 2669, 165 L.Ed.2d 557 (2006), 674

Sanders, People v., 2 Cal.Rptr.3d 630, 73 P.3d 496 (Cal.2003), 448

Santana, United States v., 427 U.S. 38, 96 S.Ct. 2406, 49 L.Ed.2d 300 (1976), 380

Sawyer, United States v., 799 F.2d 1494 (11th Cir.1986), 319

Scales, State v., 518 N.W.2d 587 (Minn.1994), 630

Scharfman, United States v., 448 F.2d 1352 (2nd Cir.1971), 318

Schipani, United States v., 315 F.Supp. 253 (E.D.N.Y.1970), 247

Schmerber v. California, 384 U.S. 757, 86 S.Ct. 1826, 16 L.Ed.2d 908 (1966), 30, 31, **360,** 440, 617, 618, 767, 817, 855, 856, 859, 878

Schmidt v. State, 659 S.W.2d 420 (Tex.Crim. App.1983), 306

Schneckloth v. Bustamonte, 412 U.S. 218, 93 S.Ct. 2041, 36 L.Ed.2d 854 (1973), 431, 446, **454,** 460, 529, 550, 602

Schneyder v. Smith, 653 F.3d 313 (3rd Cir. 2011), 353

Schriro v. Landrigan, 550 U.S. 465, 127 S.Ct. 1933, 167 L.Ed.2d 836 (2007), 213

Schwartz v. Texas, 344 U.S. 199, 73 S.Ct. 232, 97 L.Ed. 231 (1952), 518

Schwarz, United States v., 283 F.3d 76 (2nd Cir.2002), 209

Scott v. Harris, 550 U.S. 372, 127 S.Ct. 1769, 167 L.Ed.2d 686 (2007), **340,** 343

Scott v. Illinois, 440 U.S. 367, 99 S.Ct. 1158, 59 L.Ed.2d 383 (1979), **81,** 100, 101, 133

Scott, United States v., 975 F.2d 927 (1st Cir. 1992), 269, 331

Scott v. United States, 436 U.S. 128, 98 S.Ct. 1717, 56 L.Ed.2d 168 (1978), 354

Sealed Case, In re, 310 F.3d 717 (Foreign Int. Surv.Ct.Rev.2002), 540

S.E.C. v. Jerry T. O'Brien, Inc., 467 U.S. 735, 104 S.Ct. 2720, 81 L.Ed.2d 615 (1984), 836

See v. City of Seattle, 387 U.S. 541, 87 S.Ct. 1737, 18 L.Ed.2d 943 (1967), 272

Segura v. United States, 468 U.S. 796, 104 S.Ct. 3380, 82 L.Ed.2d 599 (1984), 373, **900,** 901, 902, 908

Sells Engineering, Inc., United States v., 463 U.S. 418, 103 S.Ct. 3133, 77 L.Ed.2d 743 (1983), 836

Shadwick v. City of Tampa, 407 U.S. 345, 92 S.Ct. 2119, 32 L.Ed.2d 783 (1972), 316

Shapiro v. United States, 335 U.S. 1, 68 S.Ct. 1375, 92 L.Ed. 1787 (1948), 855

Sharpe, United States v., 470 U.S. 675, 105 S.Ct. 1568, 84 L.Ed.2d 605 (1985), **426,** 427

Sherman v. United States, 356 U.S. 369, 78 S.Ct. 819, 2 L.Ed.2d 848 (1958), **480,** 493, 498

Sibron v. New York, 392 U.S. 40, 88 S.Ct. 1889, 20 L.Ed.2d 917 (1968), 419, 434, 435

Silverman v. United States, 365 U.S. 505, 81 S.Ct. 679, 5 L.Ed.2d 734 (1961), 265, 471

Silverthorne Lumber Co. v. United States, 251 U.S. 385, 40 S.Ct. 182, 64 L.Ed. 319 (1920), 893, 894, 895

Simmons v. United States, 390 U.S. 377, 88 S.Ct. 967, 19 L.Ed.2d 1247 (1968), 774, 882

Simpson, State v., 95 Wash.2d 170, 622 P.2d 1199 (Wash.1980), 408

Skaggs, State v., 903 So.2d 180 (Ala.Crim.App. 2004), 245

Skinner v. Railway Labor Executives' Ass'n, 489 U.S. 602, 109 S.Ct. 1402, 103 L.Ed.2d 639 (1989), 443, 449

Slough, United States v., 641 F.3d 544, 395 U.S.App.D.C. 178 (D.C.Cir.2011), 852

Smith v. Bennett, 365 U.S. 708, 81 S.Ct. 895, 6 L.Ed.2d 39 (1961), 99, 102

Smith v. Maryland, 442 U.S. 735, 99 S.Ct. 2577, 61 L.Ed.2d 220 (1979), 268, **510,** 519, 532, 533

Smith v. Murray, 477 U.S. 527, 106 S.Ct. 2661, 91 L.Ed.2d 434 (1986), 147

Smith v. Robbins, 528 U.S. 259, 120 S.Ct. 746, 145 L.Ed.2d 756 (2000), 219

Smith, State v., 124 Ohio St.3d 163, 920 N.E.2d 949 (Ohio 2009), 347

Sokolow, United States v., 490 U.S. 1, 109 S.Ct. 1581, 104 L.Ed.2d 1 (1989), 421

Soldal v. Cook County, Ill., 506 U.S. 56, 113 S.Ct. 538, 121 L.Ed.2d 450 (1992), 267, 280, 283

Sorrells v. United States, 287 U.S. 435, 53 S.Ct. 210, 77 L.Ed. 413 (1932), **479,** 481, 488, 493

South Dakota v. Neville, 459 U.S. 553, 103 S.Ct. 916, 74 L.Ed.2d 748 (1983), 610, 919

South Dakota v. Opperman, 428 U.S. 364, 96 S.Ct. 3092, 49 L.Ed.2d 1000 (1976), 384, 407

Spano v. New York, 360 U.S. 315, 79 S.Ct. 1202, 3 L.Ed.2d 1265 (1959), 549, 551, **556,** 557, 558, 564

Spevack v. Klein, 385 U.S. 511, 87 S.Ct. 625, 17 L.Ed.2d 574 (1967), 710

Spinelli v. United States, 393 U.S. 410, 89 S.Ct. 584, 21 L.Ed.2d 637 (1969), **292,** 296, 305

Springer, United States v., 460 F.2d 1344 (7th Cir.1972), 559

Stanley v. Georgia, 394 U.S. 557, 89 S.Ct. 1243, 22 L.Ed.2d 542 (1969), 328

Stansbury v. California, 511 U.S. 318, 114 S.Ct. 1526, 128 L.Ed.2d 293 (1994), 602

State v. _____ (see opposing party)

State ex rel. v. _____ (see opposing party and relator)

Steagald v. United States, 451 U.S. 204, 101 S.Ct. 1642, 68 L.Ed.2d 38 (1981), 318, 382

Steed, United States v., 465 F.2d 1310 (9th Cir.1972), 316

Steele v. United States, 267 U.S. 498, 45 S.Ct. 414, 69 L.Ed. 757 (1925), 317

Steeves, United States v., 525 F.2d 33 (8th Cir.1975), 306

Steiger, United States v., 318 F.3d 1039 (11th Cir.2003), 509

Stephan v. State, 711 P.2d 1156 (Alaska 1985), 630

"Stomach-pumping" case (see Rochin v. California)

Stone v. Powell, 428 U.S. 465, 96 S.Ct. 3037, 49 L.Ed.2d 1067 (1976), 152, 153, 230, 256, 259, 673

Stoner v. California, 376 U.S. 483, 84 S.Ct. 889, 11 L.Ed.2d 856 (1964), 464, 466

Stovall v. Denno, 388 U.S. 293, 87 S.Ct. 1967, 18 L.Ed.2d 1199 (1967), 761, 762, **773,** 774, 775, 780, 781, 783, 790

Street v. Surdyka, 492 F.2d 368 (4th Cir.1974), 339

Strickland v. Washington, 466 U.S. 668, 104 S.Ct. 2052, 80 L.Ed.2d 674 (1984), 122, 126, 133, 134, 136, **137,** 151, 152, 153, 154, 155, 158, 163, 164, 165, 166, 167, 168, 169, 170, 171, 172, 173, 174, 175, 176, 177, 182, 192, 202, 211, 212, 213, 216, 217

Sullivan, State v., 340 Ark. 315, 16 S.W.3d 551 (Ark.2000), 358

Taglia, United States v., 922 F.2d 413 (7th Cir.1991), 135

Tague v. Louisiana, 444 U.S. 469, 100 S.Ct. 652, 62 L.Ed.2d 622 (1980), 631

Tamalini v. Stewart, 249 F.3d 895 (9th Cir. 2001), 129

Tattered Cover, Inc. v. City of Thornton, 44 P.3d 1044 (Colo.2002), 291

Taylor v. Alabama, 457 U.S. 687, 102 S.Ct. 2664, 73 L.Ed.2d 314 (1982), 592, 897

Taylor v. Illinois, 484 U.S. 400, 108 S.Ct. 646, 98 L.Ed.2d 798 (1988), 211

Taylor, United States v., 933 F.2d 307 (5th Cir.1991), 113

Telfaire, United States v., 469 F.2d 552, 152 U.S.App.D.C. 146 (D.C.Cir.1972), 789

Tennessee v. Garner, 471 U.S. 1, 105 S.Ct. 1694, 85 L.Ed.2d 1 (1985), **339,** 355

Terry v. Ohio, 392 U.S. 1, 88 S.Ct. 1868, 20 L.Ed.2d 889 (1968), 277, 325, 326, 332, 344, 357, 361, 366, **408,** 416, 417, 419, 420, 421, 423, 424, 425, 426, 427, 428, 430, 431, 432, 433, 434, 435, 436, 437, 438, 439, 441, 461, 535, 620

Texas v. Brown, 460 U.S. 730, 103 S.Ct. 1535, 75 L.Ed.2d 502 (1983), 367, 397, 398

Texas v. Cobb, 532 U.S. 162, 121 S.Ct. 1335, 149 L.Ed.2d 321 (2001), 663, 740, **754**

The New York Times Co. v. Gonzales, 459 F.3d 160 (2nd Cir.2006), 836

Theodor v. Superior Court, 104 Cal.Rptr. 226, 501 P.2d 234 (Cal.1972), 308

Theofel v. Farey–Jones, 359 F.3d 1066 (9th Cir.2004), 537

Thibodeau, State v., 317 A.2d 172 (Me.1974), 466

Thickstun, United States v., 110 F.3d 1394 (9th Cir.1997), 496, 498

Thomas, State v., 187 W.Va. 686, 421 S.E.2d 227 (W.Va.1992), 313

Thomas, United States v., 757 F.2d 1359 (2nd Cir.1985), 278

Thompkins case (see Berghuis v. Thompkins)

Thompson v. Louisiana, 469 U.S. 17, 105 S.Ct. 409, 83 L.Ed.2d 246 (1984), 375

Thompson v. Whitman, 85 U.S. 457, 21 L.Ed. 897 (1873), 416

Thornton v. United States, 541 U.S. 615, 124 S.Ct. 2127, 158 L.Ed.2d 905 (2004), 399, 406

Tidwell v. Superior Court, 17 Cal.App.3d 780, 95 Cal.Rptr. 213 (Cal.App. 1 Dist.1971), 461

Tom, United States v., 330 F.3d 83 (1st Cir. 2003), 489

Town of (see name of town)

Townsend v. Sain, 372 U.S. 293, 83 S.Ct. 745, 9 L.Ed.2d 770 (1963), 548, 729, 730, 732

Trapnell v. United States, 725 F.2d 149 (2nd Cir.1983), 144

Trudeau, People v., 385 Mich. 276, 187 N.W.2d 890 (Mich.1971), 359

Truong Dinh Hung, United States v., 629 F.2d 908 (4th Cir.1980), 539

Trupiano v. United States, 334 U.S. 699, 68 S.Ct. 1229, 92 L.Ed. 1663 (1948), 363

Tucker case (see Michigan v. Tucker)

Turk, United States v., 526 F.2d 654 (5th Cir.1976), **520**

Turner v. Commonwealth of Pa., 338 U.S. 62, 69 S.Ct. 1352, 93 L.Ed. 1810 (1949), 549

Turner v. Rogers, ___ U.S. ___, 131 S.Ct. 2507, 180 L.Ed.2d 452 (2011), **97**

Tyler v. Berodt, 877 F.2d 705 (8th Cir.1989), 508

Tyrell J., In re, 32 Cal.Rptr.2d 33, 876 P.2d 519 (Cal.1994), 452

Underwood v. State, 252 P.3d 221 (Okla.Crim. App.2011), 453

Ungar v. Sarafite, 376 U.S. 575, 84 S.Ct. 841, 11 L.Ed.2d 921 (1964), 127

United States v. _____ (see opposing party)

United States Dept. of Justice v. Reporters Committee For Freedom of Press, 489 U.S. 749, 109 S.Ct. 1468, 103 L.Ed.2d 774 (1989), 285

United States ex rel. v. _____ (see opposing party and relator)

United States for an Order Authorizing use of A Pen Register and Trap On (XXX) Internet Service Account/User Name, (xxxxxxxx@xxx.com), In re Application of, 396 F.Supp.2d 45 (D.Mass.2005), 523

Upham, United States v., 168 F.3d 532 (1st Cir.1999), 331

Upton, Commonwealth v., 394 Mass. 363, 476 N.E.2d 548 (Mass.1985), 305

U.S. Dist. Court for Eastern Dist. of Mich., Southern Division, United States v., 407 U.S. 297, 92 S.Ct. 2125, 32 L.Ed.2d 752 (1972), 539

Vale v. Louisiana, 399 U.S. 30, 90 S.Ct. 1969, 26 L.Ed.2d 409 (1970), 365, **372,** 373, 374

Valencia, United States v., 645 F.2d 1158 (2nd Cir.1980), 498

Valenzuela–Bernal, United States v., 458 U.S. 858, 102 S.Ct. 3440, 73 L.Ed.2d 1193 (1982), 143

Van Leeuwen, United States v., 397 U.S. 249, 90 S.Ct. 1029, 25 L.Ed.2d 282 (1970), 432

Ventresca, United States v., 380 U.S. 102, 85 S.Ct. 741, 13 L.Ed.2d 684 (1965), 332

Verdugo v. United States, 402 F.2d 599 (9th Cir.1968), 247

Verdugo–Urquidez, United States v., 494 U.S. 259, 110 S.Ct. 1056, 108 L.Ed.2d 222 (1990), 41, 251, 252, 539

Vest, United States v., 813 F.2d 477 (1st Cir. 1987), 526

Vignera v. New York, 384 U.S. 436, 86 S.Ct. 1602, 16 L.Ed.2d 694 (1966), 571, 582, 584

Villamonte–Marquez, United States v., 462 U.S. 579, 103 S.Ct. 2573, 77 L.Ed.2d 22 (1983), 354

Villegas, United States v., 899 F.2d 1324 (2nd Cir.1990), 322

Virginia v. Harris, ___ U.S. ___, 130 S.Ct. 10, 175 L.Ed.2d 322 (2009), 424

Virginia v. Moore, 553 U.S. 164, 128 S.Ct. 1598, 170 L.Ed.2d 559 (2008), 316, 351, 362

Vollhardt, State v., 157 Conn. 25, 244 A.2d 601 (Conn.1968), 555

Von Lusch v. C & P Tel. Co., 457 F.Supp. 814 (D.Md.1978), 512

Von Moltke v. Gillies, 332 U.S. 708, 68 S.Ct. 316, 92 L.Ed. 309 (1948), 117, 197

Wade, United States v., 388 U.S. 218, 87 S.Ct. 1926, 18 L.Ed.2d 1149 (1967), 91, 456, 630, **761,** 763, 764, 765, 766, 767, 768, 769, 770, 771, 772, 773, 776, 780, 781, 782, 784, 785, 926, 927, 928

Wainwright v. City of New Orleans, Louisiana, 392 U.S. 598, 88 S.Ct. 2243, 20 L.Ed.2d 1322 (1968), 336

Wainwright v. Greenfield, 474 U.S. 284, 106 S.Ct. 634, 88 L.Ed.2d 623 (1986), 921

Wainwright v. Sykes, 433 U.S. 72, 97 S.Ct. 2497, 53 L.Ed.2d 594 (1977), 922

Wainwright v. Torna, 455 U.S. 586, 102 S.Ct. 1300, 71 L.Ed.2d 475 (1982), 132, 133

Walberg v. Israel, 766 F.2d 1071 (7th Cir. 1985), 202

Walder v. United States, 347 U.S. 62, 74 S.Ct. 354, 98 L.Ed. 503 (1954), 230, 256, 910, 911, 912, 913, 915

Walters, In re, 126 Cal.Rptr. 239, 543 P.2d 607 (Cal.1975), 342

Ward, State v., 62 Haw. 509, 617 P.2d 568 (Hawai'i 1980), 274

Ward v. Texas, 316 U.S. 547, 62 S.Ct. 1139, 86 L.Ed. 1663 (1942), 550

Warden v. Hayden, 387 U.S. 294 (1967), 286, 287

Warden, Md. Penitentiary v. Hayden, 387 U.S. 294, 87 S.Ct. 1642, 18 L.Ed.2d 782 (1967), 286, 290, 380, 811, 859

Warshak, United States v., 631 F.3d 266 (6th Cir.2010), **501,** 504, 505, 536

Warshak v. United States, 490 F.3d 455 (6th Cir.2007), 815

Washington v. Chrisman, 455 U.S. 1, 102 S.Ct. 812, 70 L.Ed.2d 778 (1982), **367**

Washington v. Glucksberg, 521 U.S. 702, 117 S.Ct. 2258, 138 L.Ed.2d 772 (1997), 32

Washington, United States v., 431 U.S. 181, 97 S.Ct. 1814, 52 L.Ed.2d 238 (1977), 845

Watkins v. Sowders, 449 U.S. 341, 101 S.Ct. 654, 66 L.Ed.2d 549 (1981), **930**

Watson, United States v., 423 U.S. 411, 96 S.Ct. 820, 46 L.Ed.2d 598 (1976), 332, **332,** 377, 380, 460

Watts v. Indiana, 338 U.S. 49, 69 S.Ct. 1347, 93 L.Ed. 1801 (1949), 52, 549, 583

Webster v. State, 59 Del. 54, 213 A.2d 298 (Del.Supr.1965), 555

Weeks v. United States, 232 U.S. 383, 34 S.Ct. 341, 58 L.Ed. 652 (1914), 222, 223, 225, 235, 248, 255, 259, 344, 363, 471

Weese, State v., 424 A.2d 705 (Me.1981), 190

Weikert, United States v., 504 F.3d 1 (1st Cir.2007), 451

Welsh v. Wisconsin, 466 U.S. 740, 104 S.Ct. 2091, 80 L.Ed.2d 732 (1984), 339, 350, 355, **381,** 382

Werking, United States v., 915 F.2d 1404 (10th Cir.1990), 431

West Covina, City of v. Perkins, 525 U.S. 234, 119 S.Ct. 678, 142 L.Ed.2d 636 (1999), 329

Westover v. United States, 384 U.S. 436, 86 S.Ct. 1602, 16 L.Ed.2d 694 (1966), 571, 582, 584

Wheat v. United States, 486 U.S. 153, 108 S.Ct. 1692, 100 L.Ed.2d 140 (1988), 121, 122, 188, **202**

White, United States v., 401 U.S. 745, 91 S.Ct. 1122, 28 L.Ed.2d 453 (1971), 39, 266, **474, 475,** 478, 529

White, United States v., 322 U.S. 694, 64 S.Ct. 1248, 88 L.Ed. 1542 (1944), 852, **854,** 867

Whiteley v. Warden, Wyo. State Penitentiary, 401 U.S. 560, 91 S.Ct. 1031, 28 L.Ed.2d 306 (1971), 307, 315, 420

Whren v. United States, 517 U.S. 806, 116 S.Ct. 1769, 135 L.Ed.2d 89 (1996), 55, 337, 350, 351, **353,** 356, 357, 358, 369, 376, 429, 432, 451

Wiggins v. Smith, 539 U.S. 510, 123 S.Ct. 2527, 156 L.Ed.2d 471 (2003), 150, 151, 161, 164, 166, **167,** 169, 213

Williams v. Florida, 399 U.S. 78, 90 S.Ct. 1893, 26 L.Ed.2d 446 (1970), 27

Williams, People v., 63 Mich.App. 398, 234 N.W.2d 541 (Mich.App.1975), 437

Williams, State v., 248 Or. 85, 432 P.2d 679 (Or.1967), 461

Williams v. Taylor, 529 U.S. 362, 120 S.Ct. 1495, 146 L.Ed.2d 389 (2000), 154

Williams, United States v., 504 U.S. 36, 112 S.Ct. 1735, 118 L.Ed.2d 352 (1992), 38, **805**

Wilson v. Arkansas, 514 U.S. 927, 115 S.Ct. 1914, 131 L.Ed.2d 976 (1995), 322, 323, 328, 355, 908

Wilson v. Layne, 526 U.S. 603, 119 S.Ct. 1692, 143 L.Ed.2d 818 (1999), 328

Wilson, United States v., 953 F.2d 116 (4th Cir.1991), 418

Wilson v. United States, 221 U.S. 361, 31 S.Ct. 538, 55 L.Ed. 771 (1911), 853, 855, 860, 867

Wimberly v. Superior Court, 128 Cal.Rptr. 641, 547 P.2d 417 (Cal.1976), 388

Winship, In re, 397 U.S. 358, 90 S.Ct. 1068, 25 L.Ed.2d 368 (1970), 927

Winston v. Lee, 470 U.S. 753, 105 S.Ct. 1611, 84 L.Ed.2d 662 (1985), 355, 360

Wise v. Murphy, 275 A.2d 205 (D.C.1971), 438

Withrow v. Williams, 507 U.S. 680, 113 S.Ct. 1745, 123 L.Ed.2d 407 (1993), **673,** 674, 677, 692, 700

Wolf v. People of the State of Colo., 338 U.S. 25, 69 S.Ct. 1359, 93 L.Ed. 1782 (1949), 26, 29, **222,** 225, 256, 457

Wong Sun v. United States, 371 U.S. 471, 83 S.Ct. 407, 9 L.Ed.2d 441 (1963), 231, 305, 460, 703, 764, **894,** 895, 896

Wood v. Allen, ___ U.S. ___, 130 S.Ct. 841, 175 L.Ed.2d 738 (2010), 165, 190, 192, 193

Wood v. Georgia, 450 U.S. 261, 101 S.Ct. 1097, 67 L.Ed.2d 220 (1981), 190

Wood, United States v., 981 F.2d 536, 299 U.S.App.D.C. 47 (D.C.Cir.1992), 417

Woolverton v. Multi–County Grand Jury Oklahoma County, 859 P.2d 1112 (Okla.Crim. App.1993), 822

Wyatt, United States v., 179 F.3d 532 (7th Cir.1999), 664

Wyoming v. Houghton, 526 U.S. 295, 119 S.Ct. 1297, 143 L.Ed.2d 408 (1999), 312, 313, 338, **393,** 407, 893

Wyrick v. Fields, 459 U.S. 42, 103 S.Ct. 394, 74 L.Ed.2d 214 (1982), 643

Yarborough v. Alvarado, 541 U.S. 652, 124 S.Ct. 2140, 158 L.Ed.2d 938 (2004), 603

Yarborough v. Gentry, 540 U.S. 1, 124 S.Ct. 1, 157 L.Ed.2d 1 (2003), 161, 165

Ybarra v. Illinois, 444 U.S. 85, 100 S.Ct. 338, 62 L.Ed.2d 238 (1979), 311, **324,** 394, 395, 437, 439

Young, People v., 21 Mich.App. 684, 176 N.W.2d 420 (Mich.App.1970), 927

Zehrung v. State, 569 P.2d 189 (Alaska 1977), 359

Zicarelli v. New Jersey State Commission of Investigation, 406 U.S. 472, 92 S.Ct. 1670, 32 L.Ed.2d 234 (1972), 850

Zurcher v. Stanford Daily, 436 U.S. 547, 98 S.Ct. 1970, 56 L.Ed.2d 525 (1978), **288,** 291

TABLE OF AUTHORITIES

Bold type indicates major extracts

A.B.A., Gideon's Broken Promise: America's Continuing Quest for Equal Justice (2004), 78, 91

ABA Canons of Professional Ethics, Canon 9, p. 559

A.B.A., Model Rules of Professional Conduct Rule 1.7, p. 187

A.B.A. Model Rules of Professional Conduct, Rule 3.1, p. 218

A.B.A., Model Rules of Professional Conduct Rule 3.8, p. 832

A.B.A. Standard 5-7.2, p. 79

A.B.A. Standard 18-7.5, p. 95

A.B.A., Standards for Criminal Justice, § 4–4.1, p. 169

A.B.A., Standards for Criminal Justice, § 5–1.4, p. 185

A.B.A. Standards Relating to the Defense Function (1971), 136

ABA Standing Committee on Ethics and Professional Responsibility, Formal Opinion 10–456, p. 136

American Bar Association, Standing Committee on Legal Aid and Indigent Defendants, Gideon's Broken Promise (Exec. Summary) (2004), 78

Administrative Office of the United States Courts, 2006 Wiretap Report, 525

Ainsworth, Janet E., In a Different Register: The Pragmatics of Powerlessness in Police Interrogation, 103 Yale L.J. 259 (1993), 645

A.L.I., Model Code of Pre–Arraignment Procedure (1975), 288, 291, 394, 556, 765, 750

A.L.I., Model Code of Pre–Arraignment Procedure (Tent.Draft No. 1, 1966), 586

A.L.I., Model Penal Code (1985), 480

Allen, Francis A., Griffin v. Illinois: Antecedents and Aftermath, 25 U.Chi.L.Rev. 151 (1957), 99

Allen, Francis A., The Judicial Quest for Penal Justice: The Warren Court and the Criminal Cases, 1975 U.Ill.L.F. 518, p. 590

Allen, Francis A., The Supreme Court, Federalism, and State Systems of Criminal Justice, 8 DePaul L.Rev. 213 (1959), 73, 548

Allen Report, The, Attorney General's Committee on Poverty and the Administration of Federal Criminal Justice, Report (1963), 578

Allen, Ronald J., et al., Clarifying Entrapment, 89 J.Crim.L. & Criminology 407 (1999), 486

Allen, Ronald J., Tribute to Fred Inbau, 89 J.Crim.L. & Criminology 1271 (1999), 717

Alschuler, Albert W., A Peculiar Privilege in Historical Perspective: The Right to Remain Silent, 94 Mich.L.Rev. 2625 (1996), 564, 689

Alschuler, Albert W., Constraint and Confessions, 74 Denv.U.L.Rev. 957 (1997), 551, 715, 733

Alschuler, Albert W., Failed Pragmatism: Reflections on the Burger Court, 100 Harv. L.Rev. 1436 (1987), 688, 921

Alschuler, Albert W., The Exclusionary Rule and Causation: Hudson v. Michigan and Its Ancestors, 93 Iowa L.Rev. 1741 (2008), 906

Amar, Akhil Reed, Slate article: The Battle of Hudson Heights, June 19, 2006, p. 908

Amar, Akhil Reed & Lettow, Renée B., Fifth Amendment First Principles: The Self–Incrimination Clause, 93 Mich.L.Rev. 857 (1995), 689

Amsterdam, Anthony G., Perspectives on the Fourth Amendment, 58 Minn.L.Rev. 349 (1974), 266, 514, 881

Amsterdam, Anthony G., The Supreme Court and the Rights of Suspects in Criminal Cases, 45 N.Y.U.L.Rev. 785 (1970), 543

Amsterdam, Anthony G., Trial Manual for the Defense of Criminal Cases (5th ed. 1989), 926

Anderson, James M. & Heaton, Paul, How Much Difference Does the Lawyer Make? The Effect of Defense Counsel on Murder Case Outcomes, RAND Working Paper (Dec. 2011), 78

Arenella, Peter, Foreword: O.J. Lessons, 69 S.Cal.L.Rev. 1233 (1996), 53

Arenella, Peter, Schmerber and the Privilege Against Self–Incrimination: A Reappraisal, 20 Am.Crim.L.Rev. 31 (1982), 610

Ashdown, Gerald D., The Fourth Amendment and the "Legitimate Expectation of Privacy," 34 Vand.L.Rev. 1289 (1981), 892

Associated Press Report, Death Moratorium Backed, April 10, 2001, p. 167

Attorney General's Committee on Poverty and the Administration of Federal Criminal Justice, Report (1963) (Allen Report), 578

Avery, Michael, Rudovsky, David & Blum, Karen, Police Misconduct: Law and Litigation v. (3d ed.2005), 254

Bacigal, Ronald J., Dodging a Bullet, But Opening Old Wounds in Fourth Amendment Jurisprudence, 16 Seton Hall L.Rev. 597 (1986), 360

Bagley D., & Mendelsohn, H., Minorities and the Police 107 (1969), 65

Baker, Liva, Miranda: Crime, Law & Politics (1983), 581

Barnes, Harry Elmer, Battling the Crime Wave (1931), 52

Barrett, Edward, Criminal Justice: The Problem of Mass Production, in The American Assembly, Columbia University, The Courts, the Public, and the Law Explosion (H.W. Jones ed. 1965), 336

Barrett, Edward L., Police Practices and the Law—From Arrest to Release or Charge, 50 Calif.L.Rev. 11 (1962), 586

Bazelon, David, The Defective Assistance of Counsel, 42. U.Cin.L.Rev. 1 (1973), 149

Beale, Sara Sun, Reconsidering Supervisory Power in Criminal Cases: Constitutional and Statutory Limits on the Authority of the Federal Courts, 84 Colum.L.Rev. 1433 (1984), 34, 554

Beale, Sara Sun & Bryson, William E., Grand Jury Law and Practice (1st ed. 1986), 825, 845, 847, 850

Beale, Sara Sun, et al., Grand Jury Law and Practice (2d Ed. 1997), 791

Bedau and Radelet, Miscarriages of Justice in Potentially Capital Cases, 40 Stan.L.Rev. 21 (1987), 59

Benner, Laurence A., Requiem for Miranda: The Rehnquist Court's Voluntariness Doctrine in Historical Perspective, 67 Wash. U.L.Q. 59 (1989), 543, 565, **731**, 732

Berger, Mark, Compromise and Continuity: Miranda Waivers, Confession Admissibility, and the Retention of Interrogation Protections, 49 U.Pitt.L.Rev. 1007 (1988), 929

Berger, Mark, Taking the Fifth (1980), 543

Berman, Mitchell N., Constitutional Decision Rules, 90 Va.L.Rev. 1 (2004), 687

Bibas, Transparency and Participation in Criminal Procedure, 81 N.Y.U.L.Rev. 911 (2006), 59

Black's Law Dictionary 1227 (6th ed. 1990), 538

Blauner, B., Black Lives, White Lives 110 (1989), 65

Bloom, Robert M., Inevitable Discovery: An Exception beyond the Fruits, 20 Am. J.Crim.L. 79, 87 (1992), 906

Bloom, Robert M. & Fentin, David H., "A More Majestic Conception": The Importance of Judicial Integrity in Preserving the Exclusionary Rule, 13 U.Pa.J.Const.L. 47 (2010), 254

Bradley, Craig M., Behind the Dickerson Decision, Trial (2000), 685

Bradley, Craig M., Havens, Jenkins, and Salvucci, and the Defendant's "Right" to Testify, 18 Am.Crim.L.Rev. 419 (1981), 920

Bradley, Craig M., Murray v. United States: The Bell Tolls for the Search Warrant Requirement, 64 Ind.L.J. 907 (1989), 902

Bradley, Craig M., Seas, Bogs and Police Interrogation, Trial, p. 71 (2001), 757

Bradley, Craig, Red Herring or the Death of the Exclusionary Rule?, 45 Trial 52 (April 2009), 263

Bradley, Craig M., Should American Courts Heed the 'English Warnings'?, Trial, Dec. 2007, p. 919

Bradley, Craig M., The Fourth Amendment's Iron Triangle: Standing, Consent and Searchability, Trial, p. 75 (1999), 893

Bradley, Craig M., The "Good Faith" Exception Cases: Reasonable Exercises in Futility, 60 Ind.L.J. 287 (1985), 239

Braga, Anthony, et al., Moving the Work of Criminal Investigations Toward Crime Control (2011), 7, 8

Brennan, William J., State Constitutions and the Protection of Individual Rights, 90 Harv.L.Rev. 489 (1977), 38

Brenner, Susan W. & Shaw, Lori E., Federal Grand Jury: A Guide to Law & Practice (2d ed. 2006), 791

Breyer, Stephen, Democracy Work (2010), 48

Bristow, Police Officer Shootings—A Tactical Evaluation, 54 J.Crim.L.C. & P.S. 93 (1963), 344, 435

Bryson, William E. & Beale, Sara Sun, Grand Jury Law and Practice (1st ed. 1986), 791, 825

Cameron, James D. & Lustiger, Richard, The Exclusionary Rule: A Cost–Benefit Analysis, 101 F.R.D. 109 (1984), 241

Caplan, Gerald M., Questioning Miranda, 38 Vand.L.Rev. 1417 (1985), 543, 552, **561**, 563, 716

Cassell, Paul G., Miranda's Social Costs: An Empirical Reassessment, 90 Nw.U.L.Rev. 387 (1996), 629

Cassell, Paul G., The Paths Not Taken: The Supreme Court's Failure in Dickerson, 99 Mich.L.Rev. 898 (2001), 686

Cassell, Paul G., The Statute that Time Forgot: 18 U.S.C. § 3501 and the Overhauling of Miranda, 58 Iowa L.Rev. 175 (1999), 714

Chin, Gabriel J. & Wells, Scott C., "The Blue Wall of Silence" As Evidence of Bias and Motive to Lie: A New Approach to Police Perjury, 59 U.Pitt.L.Rev. 233 (1998), 924

Choper, Jesse H., et al., The Supreme Court: Trends and Developments, 1979–80 (1981), 613, 645, 752

Claerhout, The Pen Register, 20 Drake L. Rev. 108 (1970), 512

Cloud, Morgan, Judges, "Testilying," and the Constitution, 69 S.Cal.L.Rev. 1341 (1996), 924

Cloud, Morgan, Torture and Truth, 74 Texas L.Rev. 1211 (1996), 731

Cloud, Morgan, et al., Words Without Meaning: The Constitution, Confessions, and Mentally Retarded Suspects, 69 U.Chi.L.Rev. 495 (2002), 671, 714

Clymer, Steven D., Are Police Free to Disregard Miranda?, 112 Yale L.J. 447 (2002), 624

Cohen, Fred, Miranda and Police Deception in Interrogation, 26 Crim.L.Bull. 534 (1990), 616

Cohen, Fred, Sentencing, Probation, and the Rehabilitative Ideal, 47 Texas L.Rev. 1 (1968), 95

Cohen, Thomas H., Who's Better at Defending Criminals? Does Type of Defense Attorney Matter in Terms of Producing Favorable Case Outcomes (2011), 78

Cohen, Thomas H. & Reeves, Brian A., Felony Defendants in Large Urban Counties, 2002, p. 925

Colb, Sherry F., Profiling With Apologies, 1 Ohio St.J.Crim.L. (2004), 67

Colb, Sherry F., Why the Supreme Court Should Overrule the Massiah Doctrine and Permit Miranda Alone to Govern Interrogations (2001), 758

Colb, Sherry, Kansas v. Ventris: The Supreme Court Misconstrues the Right to Counsel, (June 10, 2009), 910, 918

Colbert, Douglas L. Colbert, Prosecution Without Representation, 59 Buff. L. Rev. 333 (2011), 91

Cole, David, No Equal Justice (1999), 148

Commentary to the Model Pre–Arraignment Code, 765

Commentary to § 160.5 of the Model Pre–Arraignment Code, 780

Congressional Research Service, USA PATRIOT Act Improvement and Reauthorization Act of 2005: A Legal Analysis, 292

Cruz, R. Ted, In Memoriam: William H. Rehnquist, 119 Harv.L.Rev. 10 (2005), 685

Cutler, Brian L. & Penrod, Steven D., Mistaken Identification: The Eyewitness, Psychology, and the Law (1995), 789

Dallas Police Dep't, Dallas Police Department General Order § 304.01 (2009), 789

Darmer, M.K.B., Lessons from the Lindh Case: Public Safety and the Fifth Amendment, 68 Brooklyn L.Rev. 241 (2002), 637

Dateline NBC, "To Catch A Predator", 499

Davies, Sharon L., Profiling Terror, 1 Ohio St.J.Crim.L. 45 (2003), 66

Davies, Sharon L., The Reality of False Confessions—Lessons of the Central Park Jogger Case, 30 NYU Rev. of Law & Social Change 209, 215 (2006), 735

Davies, Sharon L. & Scanlon, Anna B., Katz in the Age of Hudson v. Michigan: Some Thoughts on "Suppression as a Last Resort," 41 U.C. Davis L.Rev. 1035 (2008), 909

Davies, Thomas Y., A Hard Look at What We Know (and Still Need to Learn) About the "Costs" of the Exclusionary Rule: The NIJ Study and Other Studies of "Lost" Arrests, 1983 A.B.F.Res.J. 611, p. 229

Davies, Thomas Y., Farther and Farther from the Original Fifth Amendment: The Recharacterization of the Right Against Self-Incrimination as a "Trial Right" in Chavez v. Martinez, 70 Tenn. L.Rev. 987 (2003), 696

Davies, Thomas Y., The Fictional Character of Law-and-Order Originalism: A Case Study of the Distortions and Evasions of Framing–Era Arrest Doctrine in Atwater v. Lago Vista, 37 Wake Forest L.Rev. 239 (2002), 338

Davis, A.J., The Role of the Defense Lawyer at a Lineup in Light of the Wade, Gilbert and Stovall Decisions, 4 Crim. L.Bull. 273 (1968), 767

Dean, John W., The Rehnquist Choice (2001), 590

Dershowitz, Alan M., Is There a Right to Remain Silent? (2008), 696

Dershowitz, Alan M., The Torture Warrant: A Response to Professor Strauss, 48 N.Y. Law Sch.L.Rev. 275 (2004), 625

Dershowitz, Alan M., Torture Without Visibility and Accountability Is Worse Than with It, 6 U.Pa.J.Const.L. 326 (2003), 627

Dershowitz, Alan M., Why Terrorism Works (2002), 625

Dershowitz, Alan M. & Ely, John Hart, Harris v. New York: Some Anxious Observations on the Candor and Logic of the Emerging Nixon Majority, 80 Yale L.J. 1198 (1971), 911, 912

Developments in the Law—Race and the Criminal Process, 101 Harv.L.Rev. 1472 (1988), 64

Devenport, Jennifer L. & Cutler, Brian L., Impact of Defense–Only and Opposing Eyewitness Experts on Juror Judgments, 28 Law & Hum. Behav. 569 (2004), 789

Denver Police Dep't, Operations Manual § 104.44 (2006), 789

Dillickrath, Thomas, Expert Testimony on Eyewitness Identification: Admissibility and Alternatives, 55 U. Miami L.Rev. 1059 (2001), 789

Dix, George, Federal Constitutional Confession Law: The 1986 and 1987 Supreme Court Terms, 67 Tex.L.Rev. 231 (1988), 733

Doernberg, Donald, "The Right of the People": Reconciling Collective and Individual Interests under the Fourth Amendment, 58 N.Y.U.L.Rev. 259 (1983), 880

Dorf, Michael C. & Friedman, Barry, Shared Constitutional Interpretation, 2001 Sup.Ct. Rev. 61, p. 685

Dressler, Joshua & Michaels, Alan, Understanding Criminal Procedure (5th ed. 2010), 880, 885, 909

Dressler, Joshua & Michaels, Alan, 2007 Supplement to Dressler & Michaels, Understanding Criminal Procedure, 909

Dripps, Donald A., About Guilt or Innocence (2003), 83

Dripps, Donald A., At the Borders of the Fourth Amendment: Why A Real Due Process Test Should Replace the Outrageous

Government Conduct Defense, 1993 U.Ill. L.Rev. 261, p. 28

Dripps, Donald A., Constitutional Theory for Criminal Procedure: Dickerson, Miranda, and the Continuing Quest for Broad–But–Shallow, 43 Wm. & Mary L.Rev. 1 (2001), 53, 685

Dripps, Donald A., Police, Plus Perjury, Equals Polygraphy, 86 J.Crim.L. & C. 693 (1996), 924

Dripps, Donald A., The Case for the Contingent Exclusionary Rule, 38 Am.Crim.L.Rev. 1 (2001), 243

Dripps, Donald A., The "New" Exclusionary Rule Debate: From "Still Preoccupied with 1985" to "Virtual Deterrence," 37 Fordham Urb.L.J. 743 (2010), 242

Drizin, Steven A. & Colgan, Beth A., Let the Cameras Roll: Mandatory Videotaping of Interrogations is the Solution to Illinois' Problem of False Confessions, 32 Loyola U. Chi. L.J. 337 (2001), 629, 630

Drizin, Steven A. & Leo, Richard A., The Problem of False Confessions in the Post–DNA World, 82 N.C.L.Rev. 891 (2004), 672, 736, 737

Duke, Steven B., Does Miranda Protect the Innocent or the Guilty?, 10 Chapman L.Rev. 551 (2007), 596, 733

Duke, Steven B., The Right to Appointed Counsel: Argersinger and Beyond, 12 Am. Crim.L.Rev. 601 (1975), 81

Durose Matthew R., et al., Contacts between Police and the Public, 2005 (U.S. Dep't of Justice, 2007), 356

Elliot, Andrea, After 9/11, Arab–Americans Fear Police Acts, Study Finds, N.Y. Times, June 12, 2006, p. 68

Elsen, Sheldon & Enker, Arnold, Counsel for the Suspect: Massiah v. United States and Escobedo v. Illinois, 49 Minn.L.Rev. 47 (1964), 564

Elsen, Sheldon & Rosett, Arthur L., Protections for the Suspect under Miranda v. Arizona, 67 Colum.L.Rev. 645 (1967), 599, 718

Ely, John Hart & Dershowitz, Alan, Harris v. New York: Some Anxious Observations on the Candor and Logic of the Emerging Nixon Majority, 80 Yale L.J. 1198 (1971), 911

Enker, Arnold & Elsen, Sheldon, Counsel for the Suspect: Massiah v. United States and Escobedo v. Illinois, 49 Minn.L.Rev. 47 (1964), 564

Federal Rules of Evidence, Rule 901, pp. 865, 866

Flynn, John J., Panel Discussion on the Exclusionary Rule, 61 F.R.D. 259 (1972), 571

Frankel, Marvin, From Private Rights to Public Justice, 51 N.Y.U.L.Rev. 516 (1976), 689

Fried, Charles, Order and Law: Arguing the Reagan Revolution—A Firsthand Account (1991), 714

Friedman, Barry, The Wages of Stealth Overruling (with Particular Attention to Miranda v. Arizona), 99 Geo.L.J. 1 (2010), 595, 712

Friendly, Henry J., The Bill of Rights as a Code of Criminal Procedure, 53 Calif.L.Rev. 929 (1965), 28, 259

Friendly, Henry J., The Fifth Amendment Tomorrow: The Case for Constitutional Change, 37 U.Cin.L.Rev. 671 (1968), 689

Fulda, Joseph S., Data Mining and Privacy, 11 Alb.L.J.Sci. & Tech. 105 (2000), 286

Garcia, Alfredo, Is Miranda Dead, Was It Overruled, or Is It Irrelevant?, 10 St. Thomas L.Rev. 461 (1988), 714

Garrett, Brandon L., Convicting the Innocent: Where Criminal Prosecutions Go Wrong (2011), 61, 629, 760

Gaynes, Elizabeth A., The Urban Criminal Justice System: Where Young + Black + Male = Probable Cause, 20 Ford.Urb.L.J. 621 (1993), 64

Geller, William A., Videotaping Interrogation and Confessions, in The Miranda Debate: Law, Justice and Policing 303 (Richard A. Leo & George C. Thomas III eds. 1998), 629

Gershman, Bennett, The New Prosecutors, 53 U.Pitt.L.Rev. 393 (1992), 38

Gershowitz, Adam M., The Phone Meets the Fourth Amendment, 56 UCLA L.Rev. 27 (2008), 347

Glater, Jonathan, New Profile Policy: Is Less Really Less?, N.Y. Times, June 2, 2003, p. 68

Godsey, Mark A., Reformulating the Miranda Warnings in Light of Contemporary Law & Understandings, 90 Minn.L.Rev. 781 (2006), 599, 632

Godsey, Mark A., Rethinking the Involuntary Confession Rule: Toward a Workable Test for Identifying Compelled Self–Incrimination, 93 Calif.L.Rev. 465 (2005), 710

Gohara, Miriam S., A Lie for a Lie: False Confessions and the Case for Reconsidering the Legality of Deceptive Interrogation Techniques, 33 Ford.Urb.L.J. 791 (2006), 726

Goldfoot, Josh, The Physical Computer and the Fourth Amendment, 16 Berkeley J.Crim.L. 112 (2011), 330

Graham, Fred, The Self–Inflicted Wound (1970), 51

Graham, Kenneth W., What Is "Custodial Interrogation"?, 14 U.C.L.A.Rev. 59 (1966), 601

Grano, Joseph D., Confessions, Truth, and the Law (1993), 543, 565, 716

Grano, Joseph D., Kirby, Biggers, and Ash: Do Any Constitutional Safeguards Remain Against the Danger of Convicting the Innocent?, 72 Mich.L.Rev. 717 (1974), 767, 768

Green, Bruce A., "Through a Glass, Darkly": How the Court Sees Motions to Disqualify Criminal Defense Lawyers, 89 Colum.L.Rev. 1201 (1989), 207

Gross, Samuel R., et al., Exonerations in the United States 1989 Through 2003 (2004), 58, 60, 761

Gross, Samuel, Response to Justice Scalia, 105 Michigan Law Review First Impression (2006), 61

Gross, Samuel R., "Souter Passant, Scalia Rampant: Combat in the Marsh," 105 Michigan Law Review First Impression 67 (2006), 63

Gross, Samuel R. & Livingston, Debra, Racial Profiling Under Attack, 102 Colum.L.Rev. 1413 (2002), 67

Guiora, Amos N., Relearning Lessons of History: Miranda and Counterterrorism, 71 Louisiana L.Rev. 1 (2011), 625

Hancock, Catherine, Due Process before Miranda, 70 Tul.L.Rev. 2195 (1996), 543, **548, 552**

Harcourt, Bernard E. & Meares, Tracey L., Transparent Adjudication and Social Science Research in Constitutional Criminal Procedure, 90 J.Crim.L. & Criminology 733 (2000), 422

Harris, David A., Driving While Black and All Other Traffic Offenses: The Supreme Court and Pretextual Traffic Stops, 87 J.Crim.L. & C. 554 (1997), 357

Harris, David A., Factors for Reasonable Suspicion: When Black and Poor Means Stopped and Frisked, 69 Ind.L.J. 659 (1994), 64

Harris, David A., Frisking Every Suspect: The Withering of Terry, 28 U.C. Davis L.Rev. 1 (1994), 435

Harris, David A., Good Cops (2005), 66

Harris, David A., Racial Profiling Revisited: "Just Common Sense" in the Fight Against Terrorism?, Criminal Justice, Summer 2002, p. 66

Hashimoto, Erica J., Defending The Right of Self–Representation: An Empirical Look at the Pro Se Felony Defendant, 85 N.C.L.Rev. 423 (2007), 110

Henderson, Stephen E., Learning From All Fifty States: How To Apply The Fourth Amendment And Its State Analogs To Protect Third Party Information From Unreasonable Search, 55 Cath. U. L. Rev. 373 (2006), 517

Henning, Peter, Finding What Was Lost: Sorting Out the Custodian's Privilege Against Self–Incrimination From the Compelled Production of Records, 77 Neb. L.Rev. 34 (1998), 869

Henning, Peter, The Conundrum of Corporate Criminal Liability: Seeking A Consistent Approach to the Constitutional Rights of Corporations in Criminal Prosecutions, 63 Tenn.L. Rev. 793 (1996), 853

Herman, Lawrence, The Supreme Court and Restrictions on Police Interrogation, 25 Ohio St.L.J. 449 (1964), 559, 565

Herman, Lawrence, The Supreme Court, the Attorney General, and the Good Old Days of Police Interrogation, 48 Ohio St.L.J. 733 (1987), 547

Herman, Lawrence & Thompson, Charles A., Scott v. Illinois and the Right to Counsel: A Decision in Search of a Doctrine?, 17 Am. Crim.L.Rev. 71 (1979), 82

Hiemstra, V.G., Abolition of the Right Not to be Questioned, 80 South African L.J. 187 (1963), 564

Higgins, Michael, Looking the Part, 48 A.B.A.J. 48 (Nov. 1997), 357

Hogan, James E. & Snee, Joseph M., The McNabb–Mallory Rule: Its Rise, Rationale and Rescue, 47 Geo.L.J. 1 (1958), 51, 555

Holder, Eric, U.S. Att'y Gen., Remarks at the Brennan Legacy Awards Dinner, Brennan Center for Justice (Nov. 17, 2009), 69

Holmes, O.W., The Path of the Law, 10 Harv. L.Rev. 457 (1897), 921

Hopkins, Ernest, Our Lawless Police 193–95 (1931), 564

Inbau, Fred E., A Forum on the Interrogation of the Accused, 49 Corn.L.Q. 382 (1964), 557

Inbau, Fred E., Police Interrogation—A Practical Necessity, 52 J.Crim.L.C. & P.S. 16 (1961), 546

Inbau, Fred E. & Reid, John, Criminal Interrogation and Confessions 216 (3d ed. 1986), 546, 572

Inbau, Fred E. & Reid, John, Lie Detection and Criminal Interrogation 185 (3d ed. 1953), 546

International Association of Chiefs of Police, Training Key #600: Eyewitness Identifications (2006), 760, 789

Israel, Jerold H., Criminal Procedure, the Burger Court, and the Legacy of the Warren Court, 75 Mich.L.Rev. 1320 (1977), 602, 715

Israel, Jerold H., Free-Standing Due Process and Criminal Procedure: The Supreme Court's Search for Interpretive Guidelines, 45 St. Louis U.L.J. 303 (2001), 32

Israel, Jerold H., Gideon v. Wainwright: The "Art" of Overruling, 1963 Sup.Ct. Rev. 211, p. 76

Israel, Jerold H., King, Nancy J., Kerr, Orin S. & LaFave, Wayne R., Criminal Procedure Treatise (3d ed. 2007), (passim)

Jacob, Bruce R., Memories of and Reflections About Gideon v. Wainwright, 33 Stetson L.Rev. 181 (2003), 72, **82,** 96

Joh, Elizabeth E., The Paradox of Private Policing, 95 J. Crim.L. & Criminology 49 (2004), 249

Johnson, Phillip E., A Statutory Replacement for the Miranda Doctrine, 24 Am.Crim. L.Rev. 303 (1987), 725

Johnson, Phillip E., The Return of the "Christian Burial Speech" Case, 32 Emory L.J. 349 (1983), 905

Johnson, Sheri Lynn, Race and the Decision to Detain a Suspect, 93 Yale L.J. 214 (1983), 64

Johnson, Sheri Lynn, Unconscious Racism and the Criminal Law, 73 Cornell L.Rev. 1016 (1988), 64

Jonakait, Randolph N., Reliable Identification; Could the Supreme Court Tell in Manson v. Brathwaite?, 52 U.Colo.L.Rev. 511 (1981), 788

Kadish, Sanford H., Methodology and Criteria in Due Process Adjudication—A Survey and Criticism, 66 Yale L.J. 319 (1957), 28

Kainen, James, The Impeachment Exception to the Exclusionary Rules: Policies, Principles and Politics, 44 Stan. L.Rev. 1301 (1992), 913, **916**

Kamisar, Yale, Brewer v. Williams, Massiah and Miranda: What is "Interrogation"? When Does it Matter?, 67 Geo.L.J. 1 (1978), 609, 615

Kamisar, Yale, "Comparative Reprehensibility" and the Fourth Amendment Exclusionary Rule, 86 Mich.L.Rev. 1 (1987), 241

Kamisar, Yale, Does (Did) (Should) the Exclusionary Rule Rest on a "Principled Basis" Rather than an "Empirical Proposition"?, 16 Creighton L.Rev. 565 (1983), 882

Kamisar, Yale, Duckworth v. Eagan: A Little-Noticed Miranda Case that May Cause Much Mischief, 25 Crim.L.Bull. 550 (1989), 598

Kamisar, Yale, Equal Justice in the Gatehouses and Mansions of American Criminal Procedure (1965), 578

Kamisar, Yale, Foreword: Brewer v. Williams—A Hard Look at a Discomfiting Record, 66 Geo.L.J. 209 (1977), 741

Kamisar, Yale, Gideon v. Wainwright A Quarter–Century Later, 10 Pace L.Rev. 343 (1990), 97

Kamisar, Yale, How Much Does It Really Matter Whether Courts Work Within the "Clearly Marked" Provisions of the Bill of Rights or With the "Generalities" of the Fourteenth Amendment?, 18 J.Contemp. Legal Issues 513 (2009), 288

Kamisar, Yale, In Defense of the Search and Seizure Exclusionary Rule, 26 Harv. J.L. & Pub. Pol'y 119 (2003), 255

Kamisar, Yale, Kauper's Judicial Examination of the Accused Forty Years Later—Some Comments on a Remarkable Article, 73 Mich.L.Rev. 15 (1974), 689

Kamisar, Yale, Miranda Thirty–Five Years Later: A Close Look at the Majority and Dissenting Opinions in Dickerson, 33 Ariz.St.L.J. 387 (2001), 686, **689**

Kamisar, Yale, On the Fortieth Anniversary of the Miranda Case, 5 Ohio St. J. Crim. L. 163 (2007), 632, **715**

Kamisar, Yale, On the "Fruits" of Miranda Violations, Coerced Confessions, and Compelled Testimony, 93 Mich.L.Rev. 929 (1995), 689

Kamisar, Yale, Police Interrogation and Confessions, 548, 552, **553**, 558, **562**, 614, 668, 669, **739**, 744

Kamisar, Yale, Postscript: Another Look at Patane and Seibert, the 2004 Miranda "Poisoned Fruit" Cases, 2 Ohio St.J.Crim.Law 97 (2004), 701

Kamisar, Yale, Poverty, Equality, and Criminal Procedure, in National College of District Attorneys, Constitutional Law Deskbook 1–97 to 1–100 (1977), 105

Kamisar, Yale, Remarks of, in Choper, Kamisar & Tribe, The Supreme Court: Trends and Developments 1982–83 (1984), 645

Kamisar, Yale, Remembering the "Old World" of Criminal Procedure: A Reply to Professor Grano, 23 U.Mich.J.L.Ref. 537 (1990), 670

Kamisar, Yale, The "Police Practice" Phases of the Criminal Process and the Three Phases of the Burger Court, in The Burger Years (Herman Schwartz ed. 1987), 670

Kamisar, Yale, The Right to Counsel and the Fourteenth Amendment: A Dialogue on "the Most Pervasive Right" of an Accused, 30 U.Chi.L.Rev. 1 (1962), 73, 95

Kamisar, Yale, The Warren Court and Criminal Justice, in The Warren Court: A Retrospective (B. Schwartz ed. 1996), 51

Kamisar, Yale, The Warren Court (Was It Really So Defense–Minded?), the Burger Court (Is It Really So Prosecution–Oriented?) and Police Investigatory Practices, in The Burger Court: The Counter–Revolution That Wasn't 62 (V. Blasi ed. 1983), 636

Kamisar, Yale, What is an "Involuntary" Confession?, 17 Rutgers L.Rev. 728 (1963), 543, **548**

Kamisar, Yale, et al., Gideon at 40: Facing the Crisis, Fulfilling the Promise, 41 Am.Crim. L.Rev. 131 (2004), 76

Kaplan, John, The Limits of the Exclusionary Rule, 26 Stan.L.Rev. 1027 (1974), 241

Katz, Daniel M., Institutional Rules, Strategic Behavior, and the Legacy of Chief Justice Rehnquist: Setting the Record Straight in Dickerson v. United States, 22 J.Law & Politics 303 (2006), 685

Kauper, Paul, Judicial Examination of the Accused—A Remedy for the Third Degree, 30 Mich.L.Rev. 1224 (1932), 689

Kaye, D.H. & Smith, Michael E., DNA Identification Databases: Legality, Legitimacy, and the Case for Population—Wide Coverage, 2003 Wis.L.Rev. 413, p. 453

Keeney, John & Walsh, Paul, The American Bar Association's Grand Jury Principles: A Critique From A Federal Criminal Justice Perspective, 14 Idaho L.Rev. 545 (1978), 796

Kennedy, Randall L., The State, Criminal Law, and Racial Discrimination: A Comment, 107 Harv.L.Rev. 1255 (1994), 64

Kerr, Orin S., A User's Guide to the Stored Communications Act—And a Legislator's Guide to Amending It, 72 Geo.Wash.L.Rev. 1208 (2004), 537

Kerr, Orin, Ex Ante Regulation of Computer Search and Seizure, 96 Va.L.Rev. 1241 (2010), 331

Kerr, Orin S., Searches and Seizures in a Digital World, 119 Harv.L.Rev. 531 (2005), 331

Kerr, Orin S., Fourth Amendment Seizures of Computer Data, 119 Yale L.J. 700 (2010), 330

Kerr, Orin S., The Fourth Amendment in Cyberspace: Can Encryption Create A Reasonable Expectation of Privacy?, 33 Conn. L. Rev. 503 (2001), 508

Kerr, Orin S., Good Faith, New Law, and the Scope of the Exclusionary Rule, 99 Geo.L.J. 1077 (2011), 245

Kerr, Orin S., LaFave, Wayne R., Israel, Jerold H., King, Nancy J., Criminal Procedure Treatise (3d ed. 2007), (*passim*)

Kidd, W.R., Police Interrogation 47 (1940), 545

King, Nancy J., LaFave, Wayne R., Israel, Jerold H. & Kerr, Orin S., Criminal Procedure Treatise (3d ed. 2007), (*passim*)

Klarman, Michael J., The Racial Origins of Modern Criminal Procedure, 99 Mich.L.Rev. 48 (2000), 49, 731

Klein, Susan R., Identifying and (Re)Formulating Prophylactic Rules, Safe Harbors, and Incidental Rights in Constitutional Criminal Procedure, 99 Mich.L.Rev. 1030 (2001), 685, 687

Koosed, Margery Malkin, The Proposed Innocence Protection Act Won't—Unless It Also Curbs Mistaken Eyewitness Identifications, 63 Ohio St.L.J. 263 (2002), 790

Krauss, Stanton D., The Life and Times of Boyd v. United States (1886–1976), 76 Mich.L.Rev. 184 (1977), 810

Kreimer, Seth F., Too Close to the Rack and the Screw: Constitutional Constraints on Torture in the War on Terror, 6 U.Pa.J.Const.L. 278 (2003), 627

Kris, David S. & Wilson, J. Douglas, National Security Investigations and Prosecutions (2007), 539

Kuckes, Niki, The Useful Dangerous Fiction of Grand Jury Independence, 41 Amer.Crim. L.Rev. 1 (2004), 802

Kuhns, Richard B., The Concept of Personal Aggrievement in Fourth Amendment Standing Cases, 65 Iowa L.Rev. 493 (1980), 880

LaFave, Wayne R., Arrest: The Decision to Take a Suspect into Custody (1965), 586

LaFave, Wayne R., Search and Seizure § 4.13(e) (4th ed. 2004), 813

LaFave, Wayne R., Search and Seizure: A Treatise on the Fourth Amendment (4th ed.2004), 222, 261, 400, 451

LaFave, Wayne R., The "Routine Traffic Stop" From Start to Finish: Too Much "Routine," Not Enough Fourth Amendment, 102 Mich. L.Rev. 1843 (2004), 428

LaFave, Wayne R., The Smell of Herring: A Critique of the Supreme Court's Latest Assault on the Exclusionary Rule, 99 J.Crim.L. & Criminology 757 (2009), 263, 264

LaFave, Wayne R., Israel, Jerold H., King, Nancy J. & Kerr, Orin S., Criminal Procedure Treatise (3d ed. 2007), (*passim*)

Langston, Lynn, & Farole, Jr., Donald J., Public Defender Offices, 2007–Statistical Tables, Bureau of Justice Statistics (June 2010), 77

Lanier & Acker, Capital Punishment, the Moratorium Movement, and Empirical Questions, 10 Psychology, Public Policy & Law 577, 593 (2004), 58

Lefcourt, Gerald, The Blank Lineup: An Aid to the Defense, 14 Crim.L.Bull. 428 (1978), 788

Leib, Michael S., E-mail and the Wiretap Laws: Why Congress Should Add Electronic Communication To Title III's Statutory Exclusionary Rule and Expressly Reject A "Good Faith" Exception, 34 Harv. J. on Legis. 393 (1997), 526

Leiken, Lawrence S., Police Interrogation in Colorado: The Implementation of Miranda, 47 Denver L.J. 1 (1970), 633

Leo, Richard A., Police Interrogation and American Justice (2008), 58, 543, 544, 545, 547, 628, 630, 631, 672, 725, **736,** 737

Leo, Richard A., Questioning the Relevance of Miranda in the Twenty–First Century, 99 Mich.L.Rev. 975 (2001), 685

Leo, Richard A., The Impact of Miranda Revisited, 86 J. Criminal Law and Criminology 621 (1996), 716

Leo, Richard A. & Drizin, Steven A., The Problem of False Confessions in the Post–DNA World, 82 N.C.L.Rev. 891 (2004), 672, 734, 736

Leo, Richard A. & White, Welsh S., Adapting to Miranda: Modern Interrogators' Strategies for Dealing with the Obstacles Posed by Miranda, 84 Minn.L.Rec. 397 (1999), 632, 633

Lettow, Renée B. & Amar, Akhil Reed, Fifth Amendment First Principles: The Self–Incrimination Clause, 93 Mich.L.Rev. 857 (1995), 689

Lewis, Anthony, Gideon's Trumpet, 223–38 (1964), 76

Lichtlau, Eric, Two Groups Charge Abuse of Witness Law, N.Y. Times, June 27, 2005, p. A10 (Nat'l ed.), 352

Linde, Hans, First Things First: Rediscovering the States' Bill of Rights, 9 U.Balt.L.Rev. 379 (1980), 38

Liptak, Adam, Longtime Death Case Lawyer Appeals Ouster, N.Y. Times (Mar. 24, 2003), 129

Liptak, Adam, New Scrutiny for Law on Detaining Witnesses, N.Y. Times, Mar. 22, 2006, p. A18 (Nat'l ed.), 352

Loewy, Arnold H., Police-Obtained Evidence and the Constitution: Distinguishing Unconstitutionally Obtained Evidence from Unconstitutionally Used Evidence, 87 Mich.L.Rev. 907 (1989), 238

Maclin, Tracey, "Black and Blue Encounters"—Some Preliminary Thoughts About Fourth Amendment Seizures:

Should Race Matter?, 26 Valparaiso U.L.Rev. 243 (1991), 64, 418

Maclin, Tracey, New York v. Class: A Little–Noticed Case With Disturbing Implications, 78 J.Crim.L. & C. 1 (1987), 273

Maguire, John MacArthur, Evidence of Guilt (1959), 551, 764, 894

Marcus, Paul, It's Not Just About Miranda: Determining the Voluntariness of Confessions in Criminal Cases, 40 Val.U.L.Rev. 601 (2006), 718, 725

Marcus, Paul, Presenting Back From the [Almost] Dead, the Entrapment Defense, 47 Fla.L.Rev. 205 (1995), 497

Marquis, Joshua, The Innocent and the Shammed, N.Y. Times, Jan. 26, 2006, p. A23, p. 61

Marquis, Joshua, The Myth of Innocence, 95 J.Crim.L. & C. 501 (2006), 61

Mayers, Lewis, Shall We Amend the Fifth Amendment? (1959), 566

McCormick, Charles T., Evidence 226 (1954), 547

McCormick, Charles T., The Scope of Privilege in the Law of Evidence, 16 Texas L.Rev. 447 (1938), 547

McGowan, Carl, Constitutional Interpretation and Criminal Identification, 12 Wm. & Mary L.Rev. 235 (1970), 768

McPhie, David, Almost Private: Pen Registers, Packet Sniffers, and Privacy at the Margin, 2005 Stan. Tech. L. Rev. 1, p. 531

Meares, Tracey L. & Harcourt, Bernard E., Transparent Adjudication and Social Science Research in Constitutional Criminal Procedure, 90 J.Crim.L. & Criminology 733 (2000), 422

Meltzer, Daniel J., Deterring Constitutional Violations by Law Enforcement Officials: Plaintiffs and Defendants as Private Attorneys General, 88 Colum.L.Rev. 247 (1988), 880

Michaels, Alan & Dressler, Joshua, Understanding Criminal Procedure (5th ed. 2010), 880, 885, 909

Model Code of Pre-Arraignment Procedure (see A.L.I.)

Model Penal Code (see A.L.I.)

Model Rules of Professional Responsibility, Rule 3.8, p. 832

Monaghan, Henry P., Foreword: Constitutional Common Law, 89 Harv.L.Rev. 1 (1975), 686

Morgan, Edmund M., The Privilege Against Self–Incrimination, 34 Minn.L.Rev. 1 (1949), 585

Mosteller, Robert, Cowboy Prosecutors and Subpoenas for Incriminating Evidence: The Consequences and Corrections of Excess, 58 Wash. & Lee L.Rev. 487 (2001), 876

Mosteller, Robert, Simplifying Subpoena Law: Taking the Fifth Amendment Seriously, 73 Va.L.Rev. 1 (1987), 865

Mosteller, Robert P., The Duke Lacrosse Case, Innocence, and False Identifications: A Fundamental Failure to "Do Justice", 76 Ford L.Rev. 1337 (2007), 786

Murphy, James, An Evaluation of the Arguments Against the Use of Expert Testimony on Eyewitness Identification, 8 U.Bridgeport L.Rev. 21 (1987), 789

Nagareda, Richard A., Compulsion "To Be a Witness" and the Resurrection of Boyd, 74 N.Y.U.L.Rev. 1575 (1999), 852, 875

Nixon, Richard, Toward Freedom from Fear (1968), 590

Nowak, John E., Due Process Methodology in the Postincorporation World, 70 J.Crim.L. & C. 397 (1979), 28

Office of the Attorney Gen., Wis. Dep't of Justice, Model Policy and Procedure for Eyewitness Identification (2005), 788

Office of the Inspector General, A Review of the Federal Bureau of Investigation's Use of National Security Letters (2007), 541

Office of the Inspector General, A Review of the Federal Bureau of Investigation's Use of Section 215 Orders for Business Records 17 (2007), 541

Ofshe, Richard J. & Leo, Richard A., The Decision to Confess Falsely: Rational Choice and Irrational Action, 74 Denv.U.L.Rev. 979 (1997), 715

O'Hara, Charles, Fundamentals of Criminal Investigation, (1959), p. 572

Orfield, Myron W., Deterrence, Perjury, and the Heater Factor: An Exclusionary Rule in the Chicago Criminal Courts, 63 U.Colo.L.Rev. 75 (1992), 238

Park, Roger, The Entrapment Controversy, 60 Minn.L.Rev. 163 (1976), 486

Parry, John T. & White, Welsh S., Interrogating Suspected Terrorists: Should Torture Be An Option?, 63 U.Pitt.L.Rev. 743 (2002), 628

Patriot Act, as amended in 2006, 18 U.S.C.A. § 3103a, App. B, 322

Paulsen, Monrad, The Fourteenth Amendment and the Third Degree, 6 Stan.L.Rev. 411 (1954), 551

Peart, Nicholas K., Why Is the N.Y.P.D. After Me?, N.Y. Times, Dec. 18, 2011 (Opinion of the Week), p. 6, p. 66

Pitler, Robert, "The Fruit of the Poisonous Tree" Revisited and Shepardized, 56 Calif.L.Rev. 579 (1968), 894, 895

Pizzi, William, The Privilege Against Self–Incrimination in a Rescue Situation, 76 J.Crim.L. & C. (1985), 624, 625

Police Chiefs' Ass'n of Santa Clara County, Line-up Protocol for Law Enforcement (2002), 789

Posner, Richard A., Excessive Sanctions for Governmental Misconduct in Criminal Cases, 57 Wash.L.Rev. 635 (1982), 242

Posner, Richard A. & Yoon, Albert H., What Judges Think of the Quality of Representation, 63 Stan.L.Rev. 317 (2011), 148

Poulin, Anne Bowen, The Role of Standby Counsel in Criminal Cases: In the Twilight Zone of The Criminal Justice System, 76 N.Y.U.L.Rev. 676 (2000), 113

Priar & Martin, Searching and Disarming Criminals, 45 J.Crim.L.C. & P.S. 481, p. 410

Primus, Eve Brensike, Disentangling Administrative Searches, 111 Colum.L.Rev. 254 (2011), 439

Primus, Eve Brensike, Structural Reform in Criminal Defense: Relocating Ineffective Assistance of Counsel Claims, 92 Cornell L.Rev. 679 (2007), 135, 136

Pulaski, Charles, Jr., Neil v. Biggers: The Supreme Court Dismantles the Wade Trilogy's Due Process Protection, 26 Stan.L.Rev. 1097 (1974), 775

Reid, John & Inbau, Fred E., Criminal Interrogation and Confessions (1962), 546, 572

Report of the National Right to Counsel Committee, Justice Denied: America's Continuing Neglect of Our Constitutional Right to Counsel (April 2009), 91

Rhodes, Deborah L., Simpson Sound Bites: What Is and Isn't News About Domestic Violence, in Postmortem: The O.J. Simpson Case 83 (Jeffrey Abramson ed. 1996), 54

Rosen, Richard A., Reflections on Innocence, 2006 Wis.L.Rev. 237, p. 786

Rosenberg, Irene & Rosenberg, Yale, In the Beginning: The Talmudic Rule Against Self–Incrimination, 63 N.Y.U.L.Rev. 955 (1988), 574

Rosenthal, Lawrence, Against Orthodoxy: Miranda Is Not Prophylactic and the Constitution Is Not Perfect, 10 Chapman L.Rev. 579 (2007), 738

Rosett, Arthur L. & Elsen, Sheldon, Protections for the Suspect under Miranda v. Arizona, 67 Colum.L.Rev. 645 (1967), 597, 718

Rothblatt & Rothblatt, Police Interrogation: The Right to Counsel and to Prompt Arraignment, 27 Brooklyn L.Rev. 24 (1960), 555

Saltzburg, Stephen A., Foreword: The Flow and Ebb of Constitutional Criminal Procedure in the Warren and Burger Courts, 69 Geo.L.J. 1512 (1980), 920

Saltzburg, Stephen A., Miranda v. Arizona Revisited: Constitutional Law or Judicial Fiat, 26 Washburn L.J. 1 (1986), 565

Saltzburg, Stephen A., Standards of Proof and Preliminary Questions of Fact, 27 Stan. L.Rev. 271 (1975), 928

Saulny, Susan, Why Confess to What You Didn't Do?, N.Y.Times, Dec. 8, 2002, at 5, p. 737

Schaefer, Walter V., Federalism and State Criminal Procedure, 70 Harv.L.Rev. 1 (1956), 69, 552

Schaefer, Walter V., The Suspect and Society (1967), 554, 686

Schulhofer, Stephen J., Confessions and the Court, 79 Mich.L.Rev. 865 (1981), 550, 551, 554, 717

Schulhofer, Stephen J., Miranda, Dickerson and the Puzzling Persistence of Fifth Amendment Exceptionalism, 99 Mich. L.Rev. 941 (2001), 690, 710

Schulhofer, Stephen J., Miranda's Practical Effect: Substantial Benefits and Vanishingly Small Social Costs, 90 Nw. U.L.Rev. 500 (1996), 629, 714

Schulhofer, Stephen J., Reconsidering Miranda, 54 U.Chi.L.Rev. 435 (1987), 710, 716

Seamon, Richard H., Kyllo v. United States and the Partial Ascendance of Justice Scalia's Fourth Amendment, 79 Wash.U.L.Q. 1013 (2001), 276

Seidman, Louis Michael, Brown and Miranda, 80 Calif.L.Rev. 673 (1992), 553, 686

Shaw, Lori E. & Brenner, Susan W., Federal Grand Jury: A Guide to Law & Practice (2d ed. 2006), 791

Simon, David, Homicide: A Year on the Killing Streets (1991), 632

Sklansky, David A., The Fourth Amendment and Common Law, 100 Colum.L.Rev. 1739 (2000), 338

Skolnick, Jerome H., Justice Without Trial (1966), 315, 374

Slobogin, Christopher, Mental Illness and Self–Representation: Faretta, Godinez, and Edwards, 7 Ohio St. J. Crim. L. 391 (2009), 120

Slobogin, Christopher, Privacy at Risk (2007), 816

Slobogin, Christopher, Subpoenas and Privacy, 54 DePaul L.Rev. 805 (2005), 814, 815

Slobogin, Christopher, Testilying: Police Perjury and What to Do About It, 67 U.Colo. L.Rev. 1037 (1996), 925

Slobogin, Christopher, Toward Taping, 1 Ohio St.J.Crim.L. 309 (2003), 630

Slobogin, Christopher & Whitebread, Charles H., Criminal Procedure (5th ed. 2008), 39, 767, 884

Smith, Abbe, The Difference in Criminal Defense and the Difference It Makes, 11 Wash. U.J.L. & Pol'y. 83 (2003), 149

Smith, Maxwell C., Quiet Eyes: The Need for Defense Counsel's Presence at Court–Ordered Psychiatric Evaluations, 16 Cap. Def. J. 421 (2004), 92

Smith, Michael E. & Kaye, D.H., DNA Identification Databases: Legality, Legitimacy, and the Case for Population—Wide Coverage, 2003 Wis.L.Rev. 413, p. 453

Smith, Stephen F., Activism as Restraint: Lessons from Criminal Procedure, 80 Texas L.Rev. 1056 (2002), 687

Snee, Joseph M. & Hogan, James E., The McNabb–Mallory Rule: Its Rise, Rationale and Rescue, 47 Geo.L.J. 1 (1958), 51, 555

Spira, James, James v. Illinois: A Halt to the Expansion of the Impeachment Exception, 15 So.Ill.U.L.J. 27 (1990), 916

Starkman, David, The Use of Eyewitness Identification Evidence in Criminal Trials, 21 Crim. L.Q. 361 (1979), 789

Stein, Edward, The Admissibility of Expert Testimony About Cognitive Science Research on Eyewitness Identification, 2 Law, Probability & Risk 295 (2003), 789

Stephens, Otis, The Supreme Court and Confessions of Guilt (1973), 543

Stone, Geoffrey R., The Miranda Doctrine in the Burger Court, 1977 Sup.Ct.Rev. 99, pp. 552, **554,** 590, 591, 636, 911, 912

Strauss, David A., Miranda, The Constitution and Congress, 99 Mich.L.Rev. 958 (2001), 687, 690

Strauss, David A., The Ubiquity of Prophylactic Rules, 55 U.Chi.L.Rev. 190 (1988), 687

Strauss, Marcy, Reconstructing Consent, 92 J.Crim.L. & Crimin. 211 (2002), 462

Strauss, Marcy, Torture, 48 N.Y. Law Sch. L.Rev. 203 (2004), 625

Strauss, Marcy, Understanding Davis v. United States, 40 Loyola of L.A.L.Rev. 1011 (2007), 648

Stuntz, William J., Local Policing After the Terror, 111 Yale L.J. 2137 (2002), 67

Stuntz, William J., Miranda's Mistake, 99 Mich.L.Rev. 975 (2001), 629, 633, 686, **688**

Stuntz, William J., O.J. Simpson, Bill Clinton, and the Transubstantive Fourth Amendment, 114 Harv.L.Rev. 842 (2001), 814

Stuntz, William J., Privacy's Problem and the Law of Criminal Procedure, 93 Mich.L.Rev. 1016 (1995), 810, **814**

Stuntz, William J., The Substantive Origins of Criminal Procedure, 105 Yale L.J. 393 (1995), 810

Stuntz, William J., The Uneasy Relationship Between Criminal Procedure and Criminal Justice, 107 Yale L.J. 1 (1997), 54

Stuntz, William J., Waiving Rights in Criminal Procedure, 75 Va.L.Rev. 761 (1989), 207

Stuntz, William J., Warrants and Fourth Amendment Remedies, 77 Va.L.Rev. 881 (1991), 332

Sutherland, Arthur, Crime and Confession, 79 Harv.L.Rev. 21 (1965), 53

Symposium, In re Gault: A 40 Year Retrospective on Children's Rights, 44 Crim.L.Bull. 302 (2008), 95

Taipale, K. A., Data Mining and Domestic Security: Connecting the Dots to Make Sense of Data, 5 Colum.Sci. & Tech.L.Rev. 2 (2003), 285

Taylor, Stuart, Jr., Politically Incorrect Profiling: A Matter of Life or Death, National Journal, p. 3406 (2001), 67

Thomas, George C., III, Regulating Police Deception During Interrogation, 39 Tex.Tech. L.Rev. 1293 (2007), 672, 724

Thomas, George C., III, Separated at Birth but Siblings Nonetheless: Miranda and the Due Process Cases, 99 Mich. L. Rev. 1081 (2001), 632

Thomas, George C., III, Stories about Miranda, 102 Mich.L.Rev. 1959 (2004), 632

Thomas, George C., III, Terrorism, Race and a New Approach to Consent Searches, 73 Miss.L.J. 525 (2003), 462

Thomas, III, George C. & Leo, Richard A., Confessions of Guilt (2012), 548, 658

Thompson, Sandra Guerra, Evading Miranda: How Seibert and Patane Failed to "Save" Miranda, 40 Val.U.L.Rev. 645 (2006), 595

Tomkovicz, James, An Adversary System Defense of the Right to Counsel Against Informants: Truth, Fair Play, and the Massiah Doctrine, 22 U.C.Davis L.Rev. 1 (1988), 753

Tomkovicz, James J., Hudson v. Michigan and the Future of Fourth Amendment Exclusion, 93 Iowa L.Rev. 1819 (2008), 909

Tomkovicz, James, Standards for Invocation and Waiver of Counsel in Confession Contexts, 71 Iowa L.Rev. 975 (1986), 596, 644

Tomkovicz, James, The Right to the Assistance of Counsel 1 (2002), 70

Tribe, Laurence H., American Constitutional Law (2d ed. 1988), 105

Uniform Rule of Criminal Procedure 212(b), 633

Uniform Rule of Criminal Procedure 243, p. 633

Uniform Rule of Criminal Procedure, Commentary 321(b), 83

United States Attorneys' Manual, 823, 842, 843, 847, 846, 852

United States Dep't of Justice, Eyewitness Evidence: A Guide For Law Enforcement (1999), 789

United States Department of Justice, Policy Guidelines Regarding Racial Profiling (2003), 67

United States Department of Justice, Searching and Seizing Computers and Obtaining Electronic Evidence in Criminal Investigations (July 2002), 537

United States Department of Justice, The Attorney General's Guidelines Regarding the Use of Confidential Informants, 478

Utter, Robert, State Constitutional Law, the United States Supreme Court, and Democratic Accountability, 64 Wash.L.Rev. 19 (1989), 39

Uviller, H. Richard, Evidence from the Mind of the Criminal Suspect, 87 Colum.L.Rev. 1137 (1987), 752

Uviller, H. Richard, Fisher Goes On The Quintessential Fishing Expedition and Hubbell is Off the Hook, 91 J.Crim.L. & Criminology 311 (2001), 877

Uviller, H. Richard, The Role of the Defense Lawyer at a Lineup in Light of the Wade, Gilbert and Stovall Decisions, 4 Crim. L.Bull. 273 (1968), 767

Walker, Samuel, Taming the System: The Control of Discretion in Criminal Justice 1905-1990, p. 51 (1993), 255

Wall, Patrick E., Eye-Witness Identification in Criminal Cases (1965), 772

Wasserstrom, Silas J. & Mertens, William J., The Exclusionary Rule on the Scaffold: But Was it a Fair Trial?, 22 Am.Crim.L.Rev. 85 (1984), 905

Wechsler, Herbert, A Caveat on Crime Control, 27 J.Crim.L. & Criminology (1937), 52

Weisberg, Bernard, Police Interrogation of Arrested Persons: A Skeptical View, 52 J.Crim.L. & P.S. 21 (1961), 560, 628

Weisselberg, Charles D., Mourning Miranda, 96 Calif.L.Rev. 1519 (2008), 595, 658, 713

Weisselberg, Charles D., Saving Miranda, 84 Cornell L.Rev. 109 (1998), 576, 674, 922

Wells, Gary L., et al., Eyewitness Identification Procedures: Recommendations for Lineups and Photospreads, 22 L. & Hum. Behavior 603 (1998), 787

Wells, Gary L. & Quinlivan, Deah S., Suggestive Eyewitness Identification Procedures and the Supreme Court's Reliability Test in Light of Eyewitness Science: 30 Years Later, 33 Law & Hum. Behav. 19 (2009), 780, 785, 790

Wells, Gary L. & Seelau, Eric P., Eyewitness Identification: Psychological Research and Legal Policy on Lineups, 1 Psychology, Pub. Pol'y. & L. 765 (1995), 760, 787

White, Byron R., Recent Developments in Criminal Law, Address before the Conference of Chief Justices (Aug. 3, 1967) in Council of State Governments, Proceedings of the 19th Annual Meeting of the Conference of Chief Justices (1967), 709

White, Welsh S., Defending Miranda: A Reply to Professor Caplan, 39 Vand.L.Rev. 1 (1986), 552

White, Welsh S., Interrogation without Questions, 78 Mich.L.Rev. 1209 (1980), 613

White, Welsh S., Miranda's Failure to Restrain Pernicious Interrogation Practices, 99 Mich. L.Rev. 1211 (2001), 686

White, Welsh S., Miranda's Waning Protections (2001), 736

White, Welsh S., Police Trickery in Inducing Confessions, 127 U.Pa.L.Rev. 581–90 (1979), 719

White, Welsh S., What is an Involuntary Confession Now?, 50 Rutgers L.Rev. 2001 (1998), 717

White, Welsh & Parry, John T., Interrogating Suspected Terrorists: Should Torture Be An Option?, 63 U.Pitt.L.Rev. 743 (2002), 628

Whitebread, Charles H. & Slobogin, Christopher, Criminal Procedure (5th ed. 2008), 39, 767, 884

Wickersham Commission Report (1931), 545

Wigmore, Evidence §§ 817–26 (Chadbourn rev. 1970), 543, 551

Wigmore, John Henry, Evidence (3d ed. 1940), 30, 547

Wigmore, John Henry, Evidence (McNaughton rev. 1961), 566

Wilkes, Donald E., Jr., More on the New Federalism in Criminal Procedure, 63 Ky.L.J. 873 (1975), 38

Wilkes, Donald E., Jr., The New Federalism in Criminal Procedure in 1984: Death of the Phoenix?, in Developments in State Constitutional Law 166 (B. McGraw ed. 1985), 39, 555

Wilkes, Donald E., Jr., The New Federalism in Criminal Procedure: State Court Evasion of the Burger Court, 62 Ky.L.J. 421 (1974), 38

Wu, Frank H., Profiling in the Wake of September 11: The Precedent of the Japanese American Internment, Criminal Justice, Summer 2002, p. 66

Younger, Irving, The Perjury Routine, The Nation (1967), 310

Basic Criminal Procedure

Cases, Comments and Questions

Thirteenth Edition

PART 1

INTRODUCTION

■ ■ ■

CHAPTER 1

ON STUDYING THE LEGAL REGULATION OF THE CRIMINAL JUSTICE PROCESS

■ ■ ■

SECTION 1. THE CHAPTER'S OBJECTIVES

This chapter provides the introduction for three different books—*Modern Criminal Procedure*, *Basic Criminal Procedure* (containing chapters 1–12 of *Modern*), and *Advanced Criminal Procedure* (containing chapters 1–5 and 13–29 of *Modern*). All three books are designed for use in courses on the legal regulation of the "criminal justice process"—that is, the process through which the substantive criminal law is enforced. That process starts with the investigation of possible criminality and the apprehension of the suspected criminal, the primary subjects considered in *Basic Criminal Procedure* and in the first half of *Modern Criminal Procedure*. The process then progresses through the charging decision, a variety of pre-adjudication proceedings, the adjudication of the charge, the imposition of sentence upon a defendant found guilty, and any subsequent challenges to the conviction and sentence. These subjects are considered in *Advanced Criminal Procedure* and in the second half of *Modern Criminal Procedure*.

Single courses on the criminal justice process typically concentrate on only a portion of the process. Thus, a course may cover the investigative stages (as in a "police practices" course) or concentrate on the post-investigative stages of the process (as in the course commonly described as "the adversary process" or the "bail to jail" course), or it may treat selective parts of both the investigative and post-investigative stages of the process (as in the courses that concentrate on the various constitutional provisions regulating the process). Yet, a general understanding of the totality of the process often is needed to place in context the law regulating any particular portion of the process. For that legal regulation is likely to be framed in light of the interplay of the procedures applied at one stage with procedures applied at various other stages of the process. Section two of this chapter seeks to provide that "big picture" understanding through an overview of the various steps that carry the process from its initiation to its completion.

The section two overview takes account, at several points, of the differences among states in the types of procedures they apply to a particular stage in the process. That, however, is only one aspect of the divergence in the legal regulation of the criminal justice process from one jurisdiction to another. Variations also are found in the regulations of identical procedures by different states (and sometimes even in a single state's regulation of a particular procedure as applied to different types of offenses). Section three of this chapter provides a brief introduction to the division of lawmaking authority that produces this diversity in legal regulation, and explains how that diversity is treated in our descriptions of the patterns of legal regulation in later chapters.

2

Even greater diversity is found in the administration of the criminal justice process. Legal regulations typically are accompanied by broad grants of discretion, often producing striking variations in the administration of the process from one local agency to another in the same state, although each agency is operating within the same legal structure. Section four of this chapter provides a brief summary of the factors that contribute to this diversity in the administration of the process.

Each of the sections that follow in this chapter hopefully will assist you in placing in context the materials presented in the remaining chapters. At times, those materials will explicitly direct your attention to one of the three features of the criminal justice process discussed in this chapter—i.e., (1) the relationship of any particular procedure to the overall structure of the process, (2) the potential for diversity in legal regulation from one jurisdiction to another, and (3) the potential for substantial administrative diversity, even within a single jurisdiction. These three features should be kept in mind, however, even when not explicitly cited, as they will bear upon the likely administrative impact of the particular legal standards under discussion.

In common with the chapters that follow, the topics considered in Chapter One are treated in far more detail in the seven volume treatise, *Criminal Procedure* (3d ed.2007), by Wayne LaFave, Jerold Israel, Nancy King, and Orin Kerr. That treatise is available in Westlaw, under the database CRIMPROC (and the treatise is hereafter cited, in this chapter and in later chapters, simply as CRIMPROC). Students interested in further documentation supporting the general descriptions of the law presented in our commentary, in citations to additional literature, or in a more comprehensive review of the relevant caselaw or statutes, should look to the CRIMPROC sections dealing with the topic under consideration. Those sections can readily be identified by using the topic as your search term in the "prelim & caption" field of the CRIMPROC database.

SECTION 2.   THE STEPS IN THE PROCESS

This section presents an overview of the procedural steps that carry the process from start to finish in an individual case. The basic objectives of the overview are to position each step within a "typical" progression of the process, to introduce the relevant terminology, and to briefly describe what occurs at each step. The chapters that follow discuss the legal standards that apply to many but not all these procedural steps. The focus there is on the procedures that commonly are the subject of litigation. This overview, in contrast, encompasses procedures that are rarely, if ever, seen as presenting legal difficulties, but nonetheless are important elements in the overall structure of the process.

There is no "standard" set of procedures that are potentially applicable to all cases in all jurisdictions. What the overview describes is the "typical" procedural steps in the progression of a "typical felony case" in a "typical" jurisdiction. That objective incorporates several important limitations, which should be kept in mind.

Initially, the overview concentrates on the procedural steps adopted in a substantial majority of our fifty-two lawmaking jurisdictions (i.e., the fifty states, the District of Columbia, and the federal system, see Note 1, p. 19). Where the jurisdictions are fairly evenly divided, that division will be noted, but where only a small group of states depart from the majority position, that minority position will not be noted. In addition, the overview describes the majority position by reference only to the basic components of a procedure; it ignores variations in other aspects of the procedure. Thus, it lumps together all states requiring grand jury issuance of a charging instrument, ignoring state variations in such matters as the composition of the grand jury and the evidentiary standard applied by the grand jury in deciding to charge.

As discussed in Note 6, p. 22, jurisdictions often draw substantial distinctions in the procedures applied to "minor" and "major" offenses, with the critical line of distinction commonly drawn between misdemeanors and felonies.[a] Our overview is limited to the processes applied to non-capital felony cases. It thus encompasses almost all basic procedures for serious crimes (special procedures for capital offenses are omitted, but capital offense prosecutions are relatively few in number). It does not, however, consider the sometimes quite different procedures applicable in misdemeanor cases, which far outnumber felonies.[b]

As discussed in Section 4, the exercise of discretion determines in large part which procedures are applied in a particular case. A procedure may be authorized under the law of a particular jurisdiction, but not required, making its use dependent upon the discretionary choice of an enforcement official (police or prosecutor), a judicial official (magistrate or trial judge), or a defendant. Our overview, in large part, looks only to whether a procedure is authorized. Where available statistics indicate that a widely authorized procedure is rarely utilized in practice in a substantial group of states, however, the overview will take note of that pattern of discretionary choice.

In describing the administrative functions of the police, prosecutors, magistrates, and trial courts, the overview concentrates on the basic authority common to the particular group, ignoring the institutional differences that bear upon the exercise of that authority. Thus, where the overview speaks of "police officers," it encompasses a wide array of personnel, in a variety of government agencies, who are assigned to the task of enforcing part or all of the criminal law and given the authority that distinguishes "sworn officers" from "civilian" personnel (basically, the authority to make arrests and to carry weapons).[c] It focuses on the general role of such officers, ignoring, for example, the distinctions that may exist in the

---

a. All but a handful of jurisdictions utilize one of two seemingly distinct standards to distinguish between felonies and misdemeanors. The federal system and roughly half of the states classify as felonies all crimes punishable by a term of incarceration of more than one year; crimes not punishable by incarceration, or punishable by incarceration for a maximum term of one year or less, are misdemeanors. Most of the remaining states look to the location of the possible sentence of incarceration. If the offense is punishable by incarceration in a penitentiary, it is a felony; offenses punishable by incarceration only in a jail are misdemeanors. States using this distinction, however, commonly also provide for possible incarceration in a penitentiary only if the offense of conviction carries a maximum term of incarceration exceeding one year. Thus, both standards, in practice, will classify as felonies all offenses punishable by a term of imprisonment of more than one year.

b. In a 2007 survey, local prosecutors nationally reported closing 2.9 million prosecutions charging felonies. No similar national counting exists for prosecutions charging only misdemeanors, in large part because of lapses in tracking prosecutions for ordinance violations, that duplicate state misdemeanor offenses and carry similar penalties. See CRIMPROC § 1.8(d) (noting that some states treat such ordinance violation proceedings as "quasi-criminal"). Many states, however, do provide complete data on both felony and misdemeanor prosecutions (including ordinance violations), and theses states "typically have a ratio of at least 4 to 1 of misdemeanors to felonies" CRIMPROC § 1.2(f). That ratio can be quite higher if the state does not follow the dominant position of treating as civil infractions (rather than misdemeanors) the violation of all but a small group of traffic offenses. The ratio is also significantly impacted by the state's treatment as a misdemeanor or felony different grades of the top two offenses (measured by number of arrests)—"driving under the influence" and drug possession.

c. In the state criminal justice systems, agencies employing "police officers," using this traditional definition, include: municipal police departments; county sheriffs' offices; state police departments (e.g., the state highway patrol); special-unit enforcement agencies (e.g., campus police departments, conservation departments); and regulatory agencies enforcing a limited class of criminal prohibitions (e.g., crimes relating to businesses selling liquor). The 50 states combined have over 18,000 agencies employing police officers, with even a small state likely to have close to 100 different police agencies. See CRIMPROC § 1.4(c), (d).

jurisdictional reach and specific responsibilities of such different types of officers as the detective in a city police department and the park ranger. Similarly, the overview speaks generally of "prosecutors," a term encompassing government attorneys of several different types of agencies to which a state may grant the authority to initiate and present criminal prosecutions.[d] The overview's references to "magistrates" likewise encompasses judges of a variety of different courts, the common denominator being their assignment to the initial portions of the processing of felony cases and their lack of trial jurisdiction in felony cases.[e] The overview's references to "trial courts" encompasses judges of a less varied group of courts (typically the jurisdiction's basic court of general jurisdiction) having trial authority over felony charges.[f]

Finally, our overview will not take account of variations in chronology. It will assume the chronology that occurs in the majority of felony cases, although many

---

The federal criminal justice system has over 50 agencies employing police officers. However, a half dozen agencies, located either in the Department of Justice (DOJ) or Homeland Security (HS), account for the vast majority of federal prosecutions. Those agencies are: the Federal Bureau of Investigation (DOJ); Customs and Border Protection (HS) (by far the largest federal police agency); the Drug Enforcement Agency (DOJ); the Bureau of Alcohol, Tobacco, Firearms, and Explosives (DOJ); the Secret Service (HS); Immigration and Customs Enforcement (HS); and the United States Marshalls Service (DOJ).

d. In all but a few states, the dominant prosecuting agency is the office of an elected county or multi-county official (titles include "county prosecutor," "district attorney," and "state's attorney"). There are roughly 2,300 such local prosecuting agencies in these states. Most often, their prosecuting authority is not exclusive. The Attorney General will have an independent authority to initiate prosecution. Even where the Attorney General's authority is quite broad, however, tradition and staffing limitations will restrict its use to a limited group of offenses (often crimes having a statewide impact). Also, in many states, prosecutions for ordinance violations that are essentially misdemeanors (see fn. b., p. 4) may be brought by city attorneys as well as local prosecutors. In the few states that do not utilize local prosecutors, a state agency has authority over all criminal prosecutions, but that agency typically will operate through local offices. See CRIMPPROC § 1.4(e).

In the federal system, all criminal prosecutions are brought by attorneys who are part of the Department of Justice. The vast majority of prosecutions are brought by the United States Attorney assigned to an individual federal judicial district. The United States Attorneys are subordinate to the Attorney General, although traditionally given considerable independence. Federal prosecutions for certain limited groups of offenses (e.g., antitrust or civil rights) are brought by specialized divisions within the Department of Justice. See CRIMPROC § 1.4(e).

e. These judges are commonly described as "magistrates" because they perform functions that were assigned to magistrates in the English common law system. In most state systems, magistrates are judges of courts of limited jurisdiction (in particular, their trial jurisdiction in criminal cases is limited to some or all misdemeanors). Magistrate courts have a variety of different titles, including "municipal courts," "county courts," "justice of the peace courts," or "district courts." Many states have more than one type of magistrate court, with different courts of limited jurisdiction operating in different parts of the states (e.g., a municipal court in urban areas and a "j.p. court" in rural areas). In some of these states, judges in certain courts of limited jurisdiction need not be lawyers.

In other states, magistrates are judges of a consolidated trial court that combines the authority of courts of limited jurisdiction and courts of general jurisdiction. Here, a separate division of that single court is assigned to trial jurisdiction over minor crimes and to the processing of the preliminary stages of felony cases.

In the federal system, United States magistrate judges are a part of the federal district court. They often are given considerably broader authority over the preliminary processing of felony cases than state magistrates. Thus, federal magistrate judges may be authorized to hold hearings and make rulings (subject to review by the district court trial judge) as to various issues described in the overview as considered by the state trial court after the felony prosecution reaches that court (see e.g., step 13 infra). See generally CRIMPROC § 1.4(g).

f. In the state systems, these courts are commonly described as "superior courts," "circuit courts," or "district courts" (where that title is not used for courts of limited jurisdiction). Variations exist, in particular, as to whether their criminal trial jurisdiction includes some types of misdemeanors as well as felonies, and as to the character of their appellate jurisdiction with respect to rulings of the magistrate courts. In the federal system, the 94 United States District Courts are the felony trial courts. See CRIMPROC § 1.4(h).

felony cases do not follow that chronology. Similarly, the overview discusses each step as occupying a specific place in the progression of a case, but that is not true of all procedures. While some steps have a definite starting and ending point, others are continuing and overlap other steps in the process. For example, the decision on pretrial release, though it comes initially at the first appearance, is subject to possible reconsideration at several points as the case progresses.

Step 1: Pre–Arrest Investigation. Investigation, by the police or prosecutor, is the initial administrative stop in the processing of what eventually will become a felony prosecution. Investigation is an ongoing process that continues after the second step noted below (the arrest), and sometimes beyond the filing of charges (see steps 6 and 11) as well. Because the arrest facilitates certain investigative techniques that are not earlier employed, we distinguish in this overview between pre-arrest and post-arrest investigations (see step 4). However, many of the investigative procedures described as part of pre-arrest investigation (e.g., inter-viewing witnesses) will also be included in post-arrest investigations.

The vast majority of pre-arrest investigations are undertaken entirely by the police. Various characteristics distinguish different police investigative procedures. One of the most significant, though not formally recognized in the law governing investigations, is the distinction between "reactive" and "proactive" investiga-tions. A reactive investigation is aimed at solving a past crime, while a proactive investigation is aimed at placing the police in a position to respond to an unknown but anticipated ongoing or future crime. The discussion that follows treats separately the investigative procedures most commonly associated with reactive and proactive aspects of investigation. It also considers separately the special investigative tools within the exclusive authority of prosecutors.

Reactive Investigations. General purpose police agencies (e.g., local police departments), who employ over 85% of the police officers in this country, tradi-tionally have devoted the vast majority of their investigative efforts to reactive investigations. This is an "incident driven" or "complaint-responsive" style of policing, flowing from various aspects of local policing, including the neighborhood patrol and the 911 emergency telephone link. The police receive a citizen report of a crime (typically from the victim or an eyewitness), or they discover physical evidence indicating that a crime has been committed, and they then proceed to initiate an investigation responsive to that "known crime."[g] Depending upon the type of information that initially identifies the crime, the pre-arrest investigative activity will have one or more of the following objectives: (1) determining that the crime actually was committed; (2) determining who committed the crime; (3) collecting evidence sufficient to support the arrest of the offender (and if readily available, additional evidence that will be sufficient to support a trial conviction); and (4) locating the offender so that he may be arrested. A wide variety of investigative activities may be utilized to achieve these objectives. Those activities include: (1) the interviewing of victims; (2) the interviewing of other witnesses present when the officer arrives at the crime scene; (3) canvassing the neighbor-hood for (and interviewing) still other persons with relevant information; (4) the interviewing of suspects, which may require a physical stopping of the suspect on the street and a frisking of the suspect (i.e., pat-down of the outer clothing) for

---

g. National and state crime statistics include in the "known crime" category (sometimes described as "reported crimes") those crimes reported by the public (whether or not they result in an arrest) and those crimes witnessed by the police which result in an arrest. Where an arrest is made for a crime, that crime is further identified as "cleared" (although crimes also can be listed as cleared where the police conclude that the crime has been "solved," but an arrest is not practicable, e.g., the offender is dead or already in prison for another offense). The clearance designation is based strictly on the police department's own evaluation, so a crime may be listed as cleared even though the prosecutor decided not to charge the arrestee, or a charge was brought but subsequently was dismissed or resulted in an acquittal.

possible weapons; (5) examining the crime scene and collecting physical evidence (including possible forensic evidence) found there (and where the offenses involved physical contact with the victim, also collecting possible forensic evidence from the person of the victim); (6) checking departmental records and computer files; (7) seeking information from informants; (8) searching for physical evidence of the crime (e.g., stolen property or weapons) in places accessible to the suspect (e.g., his home or automobile) and seizing any evidence found there; (9) surveillance of a suspect (including electronic surveillance) aimed at obtaining leads to evidence or accomplices; and (10) using undercover operatives to gain information from the suspect.

While the variation among investigations is far too great to characterize any single combination of investigative procedures as "typical," it is clear that prearrest investigations rarely take on the characteristics of popular depictions of the crime solving process. In general, investigations do not involve the use of scientific methods of investigation,[h] violent confrontations with crafty criminals, or reliance upon informants. Indeed, many of the commonly depicted prearrest investigative procedures are used infrequently. Perhaps the most extreme example is the use of court-ordered electronic surveillance through wiretaps and "bugs," a common feature of television dramas, but actually utilized in less than 3,500 of the millions of felony investigations conducted annually throughout the United States.

So too, while pre-arrest investigations obviously include those procedures cited above that are subject to significant legal regulation (e.g., searches), the central role of such procedures in the legal materials discussed in later chapters does not warrant the assumption that they similarly are central to pre-arrest felony investigations generally. Initially, in one quite common scenario, police hardly engage in any reactive pre-arrest investigation; the officer is present when the crime is committed, and responding to what he has seen, or has been told by an apparent victim, makes an immediate on-scene arrest. Where significant investigative steps are needed to identify the offender, a variety of factors will influence the choice of investigative procedures. Different types of crimes leave different potential leads, such as eyewitnesses, forensic evidence, distinctive

---

h. While television's infatuation with CSI units clearly exaggerates the significance of forensic evidence in the totality of police investigations, over the past few decades, forensic evidence has played an increasingly important role in the investigation of certain types of crimes. Over that period, major advances in technology, and the development of three readily accessible national databases (CODIS for DNA, AFIS for fingerprints, NIDIN for ballistics), has made it substantially easier to both collect forensic evidence and obtain from it "probative evidence" (i.e. admissible evidence that helps in establishing the identity of the offender). As a result, studies of police departments in mid-sized and large cities conclude that forensic evidence typically is collected in a very high percentage of homicide investigations (e.g., 85–95%) and in a majority of sexual assault investigations (e.g., 50–65%) and produces probative evidence in over half of those cases. On the other hand, as for other offenses that involve confrontations with the victim, the percentages for collection are much lower (varying from 8–25% for robbery investigations and 5–30% for aggravated assault investigations). Although burglary is an exception (with forensic evidence collected in 15–30% of all investigations), forensic evidence is rarely collected in investigating offenses that do not involve such confrontations (e.g., the typical property offense). See CRIM-PROC § 1.10(b).

Very often, forensic evidence is used to identify a completely unknown offender, rather than to confirm the identity of a suspected offender. Other evidence collected by the police tends to serve the latter function. See Anthony Braga, et.al., Moving the Work of Criminal Investigations Toward Crime Control (2011) (available at www.ncjrs.gov) (describing the findings of three "seminal research studies," conducted in the 1970's and 1980's on the investigation of high volume serious crimes—burglary, larceny, assault, and robbery): "Contrary to fictional portrayals, detectives do not work from facts to identification of suspects; they work from identification of suspects back to facts that are necessary to prosecute and convict them. The primary job of detectives is not to find unknown suspects, but to collect evidence required for a successful prosecution of known suspects."

methods of operation, and hidden fruits of the crime or other contraband. The presence or absence of these potential "traces" of the crime will exclude certain techniques as clearly inapplicable and suggest that, among those that might be helpful, some are far more likely to succeed than others. The eventual police choice among potentially useful procedures may be influenced by other factors as well, including; (1) the division of investigative responsibility between patrol officers and assigned investigators (with patrol officers generally looking to a more limited range of investigative options); (2) policies of the department (e.g., a department "solvability formula" may exclude certain techniques based on cost considerations outweighing usefulness or the less serious nature of the offense); (3) the special expertise of units assigned to particular types of investigations; and (4) legal requirements (choosing a technique that presents no legal difficulties over techniques that may not be available without a further grounding or that may be legally questionable). The end result is that, for a great many crimes, the first pre-arrest investigative step will be one that is not subject to significant legal regulation (e.g., interviewing the victim and eyewitnesses), and for some offenses, all relevant pre-arrest investigative steps are likely to fall in that category.

Proactive Investigations. Although general purpose police agencies traditionally have concentrated their investigative efforts on solving known crimes, those agencies also have regularly used, in a limited fashion, proactive investigations. Indeed, in recent years, many local police departments in large communities have sharply increased their utilization of proactive investigative procedures. Also, many special-function police agencies (such as the federal Drug Enforcement Administration) traditionally have devoted a quite substantial portion of their resources to proactive investigations.

Proactive investigations are aimed at uncovering criminal activity that is not specifically known to the police. The investigation may be aimed at placing the police in a position where they can observe ongoing criminal activity that otherwise would both be hidden from public view and not reported (as typically is the case with offenses that prohibit the possession of contraband or proscribe transactions between willing participants). It may be aimed at inducing persons who have committed crimes of a certain type, including many unknown to the police, to reveal themselves (as in a "fencing sting"). Proactive investigations also often are aimed at anticipating future criminality and placing police in a position to intercept when the crime is attempted. This approach is facilitated by computer programs which use data-mining to identify high crime areas that are particularity troublesome ("hot spots") and the characteristics of both repeat victims and high-rate offenders.[i]

A variety of different procedures may be used in a proactive investigation, with the choice of procedure largely tied to the specific objective of the investigation. Deception is a common element of many proactive procedures. In traditional undercover operations, the police assume a false identity and present themselves as willing to participate in criminal activities (as where undercover agents "set up" fencing operations or narcotics transactions). So too, deception is the key to a "decoy tactic" of providing what appears to be an easy target for victimization (e.g., a drunk with an exposed wallet or a business of the type that is readily subject to extortion). Deception commonly also is critical to the effective use of informants. Where police utilize as informants persons whose activities expose them to a criminal milieu, they are counting on the criminals associating with

---

i. See Braga et al., fn. h. supra (research suggests "that crime tends to cluster among a few problem places, offender, and victims," with one study estimating "that 10 percent of the victims in the U.S. are involved in 40 percent of victimizations, 10 percent of offenders are involved in more than 50 percent of serious crimes, and 10 percent of places are the sites of about 60 percent of calls for service").

those persons being deceived by a belief that those persons will not take what they have learned to the police (usually because the persons are themselves engaged in criminal activity, gain their livelihood in part from criminals, or have social ties to the criminals). Surveillance through stakeouts, covert patrols, and electronic monitoring also rests on deception by hiding the surveillance.

Other proactive techniques rely on intrusive confrontations designed to place police in a position where they can observe what otherwise would be hidden or to elicit nervous or unthinking incriminatory responses that will provide a legal grounding for taking further investigative action (e.g., an arrest or stop). Thus, police following an aggressive motorized patrol strategy will fully utilize traffic laws to maximize stops of motorists, thereby gaining greater opportunity to peer into car windows, to ask questions, and to request consent to a search of the vehicle. Similarly, under a practice of heavy field interrogation, police will frequently approach pedestrians and initiate questions to determine who they are and what they are doing. Such intrusive confrontations are most often used on a selective basis, with police concentrating their efforts on those characteristics of the social environment that suggest to them possible criminality (e.g., high-crime neighborhood, suspicious class of persons, unusual behavior). In general, such proactive investigative procedures are more resource intensive, more intrusive, arguably more likely to foster community opposition, and clearly pose more legal problems than typical reactive investigative procedures.

Prosecutorial Investigations. Not all prearrest investigations are conducted by police. For certain types of crimes, the best investigatory tool is the subpoena—a court order directing a person to appear in a particular proceeding for the purpose of testifying and presenting specified physical evidence (e.g., documents) within his possession. The subpoena authority typically is available for the general investigation of crime only through the grand jury, although many jurisdictions also grant a limited subpoena authority to enforcement agencies charged with regulating particular types of potentially criminal activities. The grand jury, although it tends to be known more for its screening function in reviewing the prosecution's decision to charge (see step 10), also has authority to conduct investigations into the possible commission of crimes within the judicial district in which it sits. In carrying out this function, the grand jurors, being a group of laypersons with no special expertise in investigation, quite naturally rely heavily on the direction provided by their legal advisor, who is the prosecutor. Thus, grand jury investigations become, for all practical purposes, investigations by the prosecutor.

Grand jury investigations tend to be used where (1) witnesses will not cooperate with the police (they can be compelled by subpoena to testify before the grand jury and given immunity to replace their self-incrimination privilege should they refuse to testify on that ground); (2) the critical evidence of the crime is likely to be a "paper trail" buried in voluminous records of business dealings (as the subpoena can be used to require production of such records where the police lack the necessary probable cause predicate for obtaining those documents through a search); or (3) the area of investigation is especially sensitive, reflecting a strong need to keep the ongoing investigation from the public gaze (an objective facilitated by grand jury secrecy requirements) or to ensure public confidence in the integrity of the investigation (an objective facilitated by the participation of the lay grand jurors). Criminal investigations presenting such special needs tend to deal with crimes of public corruption (e.g., bribery), misuse of economic power (e.g., price-fixing), or widespread distribution of illegal services or goods (e.g., organized crime operations).

Step 2: Arrest. Once a police officer has obtained sufficient information to justify arresting a suspect (i.e., probable cause to believe the person has committed a crime), the arrest ordinarily becomes the next step in the criminal justice process. The term "arrest" is defined differently for different purposes. We refer here only to the act of taking a person into custody for the purpose of charging him with a crime (the standard commonly used in the reporting of arrest statistics). This involves the detention of the suspect (by force if necessary) for the purpose of first transporting him to a police facility and then requesting that charges be filed against him. As an alternative to such a "full custody" arrest, many jurisdictions authorize the officer in certain situations to briefly detain the suspect and then release him upon issuance of an official document (commonly titled a "citation," "summons" or "appearance ticket") which directs the suspect to appear in court on a set date to respond to the charge specified in the document. In most communities, this release-on-citation alternative is only infrequently used (if at all) for felonies (in contrast to misdemeanors, where its use is fairly common).

Where there is no immediate need to arrest a suspect, an officer may seek to obtain an arrest warrant (a court order authorizing the arrest) prior to taking the person into custody. Arrest warrants in most jurisdictions are issued by magistrates. To obtain a warrant, the police must establish, to the satisfaction of the magistrate, that there exists probable cause to believe that the prospective arrestee committed the crime for which he will be arrested. The showing of probable cause may be made by affidavits or live testimony of either the investigating officer or a witness (usually the victim). The vast majority of arrests for felonies are made without first seeking a warrant (and are therefore described as "warrantless arrests").

While the arrest is part of the charging process, it contributes to the investigation. Initially, it provides an opportunity for the investigative practices that depend on the suspect's custody (see step 4 below). It also can provide significant evidence through what is described as the "search incident to the arrest." Contemporaneously with the arrest, the arresting officer usually will search the arrestee's person and remove any weapons, contraband, or evidence relating to a crime (although some police agencies encourage use of only a frisk for weapons, rather than a full search, in certain arrest situations). Under appropriate circumstances, this searching authority may be extended beyond the person of the arrestee to include a contemporaneous search of: containers being carried by the arrestee (e.g. a purse of package); the passenger compartment of a vehicle and containers therein, in the case of a roadside arrest of the driver or passenger; and that portion of a room that is within the reaching distance of the arrestee where the arrest is made within a structure (e.g. a residence or office).

Step 3: Booking. After the arrestee has been secured and the contemporaneous search incident to the arrest completed, the arrestee will be transported, by the arresting officer or other officers called to the scene, to a police station or similar "holding" facility. It is at this facility that the arrestee will be taken through a process known as "booking". Initially, the arrestee's name, the time of his arrival and the offense for which he was arrested are noted in the police "blotter" or "log". This is strictly a clerical procedure, and does not control whether the arrestee will be charged or what charge may be brought. If it is determined that the arrestee is a juvenile, however, the arrestee will be transferred at this point to a juvenile facility and thereafter processed through the juvenile process (absent a subsequent decision to treat the juvenile as an adult), where that option is available under state law. The record left by the booking process typically includes more than the notation of the arrest. Felony arrestees ordinarily will be photographed and fingerprinted (and in some jurisdictions, an appropriate sample for DNA testing will also be taken).

Once the booking process is complete, the arrestee ordinarily will be allowed one telephone call. After that, the arrestee will be placed in a "lockup" (usually some kind of cell) pending his subsequent presentation at a first appearance (step 8). Before entering the lockup, the arrestee will be subjected to another search, often more thorough than that conducted incident to the arrest, with his personal belongings removed and inventoried. In some jurisdictions, persons arrested on lower-level felonies can gain release from the lockup by meeting the prerequisites of a "stationhouse bail program" (i.e., making a cash deposit, in an amount specified by a judicially approved "bail schedule," and agreeing to certain conduct-restrictions, including appearance in court on a specified date).

Step 4: Post–Arrest Investigation. One critical source made available by the arrest itself is the person of the arrestee. That source allows police, for example, to obtain eyewitness identification by placing the arrestee in a lineup, having a witness view the arrestee individually (in a showup), or taking the arrestee's picture and showing it to witnesses (usually with photographs of other persons in a "photographic lineup"). Similarly, the police may obtain from the arrestee identification exemplars, such as handwriting or hair samples, that can be compared with evidence found at the scene of the crime. As the arrestee is now in police custody, police questioning of the arrestee also is greatly facilitated (although custodial interrogation does require that the arrestee be advised of certain rights, including the right not to respond, and that he agree to forego those rights). Other post arrest investigative procedures will be similar to the procedures employed in pre-arrest investigations (e.g., witness interviews), but they will build upon information collected in the course of the arrest and the custodial investigative procedures.

Step 5: The Decision to Charge. For the vast majority of felony cases, the initial decision to charge a suspect with a crime is made when a police officer makes a warrantless arrest of the suspect. That decision may be reversed on internal review within the police department, typically by a "booking officer." Police departments vary in their willingness to utilize this authority. Some will decide against charging (and immediately release the arrestee) only where the arrest clearly is in error; some will more fully evaluate the available evidence; and some will decide against charging even where the evidence is sufficient if the reviewing officer concludes that the offense can more appropriately be handled by a "stationhouse adjustment" (e.g., reconciliation with a family-member victim, or the arrestee's willingness to become an informant). Even where the police agency is willing to exercise such broad review authority, only a very small percentage of felony arrests will be rejected within the police department (although a somewhat larger percentage of felony arrestees are likely to have their booking charge reduced to a misdemeanor).

The ultimate authority over charging rests with the prosecutor, rather than the police. The prosecutor is engaged in an ongoing evaluation of the charge throughout the criminal justice process, but a prosecutor's decision not to go forward on a charge requires a different processing action depending upon whether that decision is made: (1) prior to the filing of complaint (step 6); (2) after the complaint is filed, and prior to the filing of an indictment or information (step 11); or (3) after the filing of the indictment or information. A decision not to proceed at the first stage simply results in the complaint not being filed (leading to the common description of that decision as a "no-paper decision"), and the release of the arrestee from police custody without any involvement of the judiciary. A decision not to proceed at the second stage commonly occurs in connection with the prosecutor's review of the case against the defendant prior to presenting it to a magistrate at a preliminary hearing (step 9) or to a grand jury (step 10). This decision commonly is formalized in a prosecution motion before the magistrate to withdraw the complaint (although, where grand jury review is being used, the prosecutor can ask the grand jury to vote against indicting, which similarly terminates the prosecution). A decision not to proceed further at the third stage (i.e., following the filing of an indictment or information) requires a prosecutor's *nolle prosequi* motion, which must be approved by the trial court.

Prosecutorial review of the police charging decision prior to the filing of the complaint must occur in a short time span, as the arrested defendant must be brought before the magistrate within 24 or 48 hours (see step 8), and the complaint must have been filed at that point. Not surprisingly, there is considerable variation among prosecutors' offices as to the scope of their review at this stage, with some largely leaving the decision to file the complaint to the police, and delaying their initial review of the charge in most felony cases until the second stage noted above.

Where a prosecutor decides against proceeding in the prosecutor's initial screening of the police department's charging decision (whether before or after the filing of the complaint), that conclusion most often will have been based upon anticipated difficulties of proof (e.g., the evidence is insufficient to convict, the victim is reluctant to testify, or key evidence was obtained illegally and therefore will not be admissible). However, the prosecutor also may decide against prosecution, even though the evidence clearly is sufficient, because there exists an adequate alternative to prosecution (e.g., the arrestee is willing to participate in a diversion program,[j] or the arrestee is on probation and can be proceeded against more expeditiously by revoking his probation), or special circumstances render prosecution not "in the interest of justice". A decision not to proceed made on reexamination of an earlier decision to prosecute (the typical situation where the prosecutor decides to drop charges at the third stage) is most likely to be the product of a change in circumstances that has either eliminated the need for prosecution (e.g., the defendant has been convicted on other charges) or substantially reduced the likelihood of success (e.g., a critical witness is no longer available).

Complete statistics on prosecutor screening are available only for a relatively small group of states. These statistics show considerable variation among prosecutors' offices as to the frequency of their decisions not to prosecute at any one stage of the process. At the same time, however, the statistics present a fairly consistent picture of the significance of the totality of the non-prosecution decisions made by prosecutors through the totality of the process. In all of the states providing statistics on the disposition of felony arrests, prosecutorial non-prosecution decisions account for the second highest percentage of dispositions, trailing only guilty pleas (albeit, trailing by a wide margin. e.g., 25% non-prosecutions to 65% guilty pleas). So too, in the many more states with statistics tracing only the dispositions of informations and indictments (thereby excluding the typically much larger body of earlier non-prosecution decisions), dismissals based on the prosecution's motion still constitute the second most common disposition, although now trailing guilty pleas by a much larger margin.

---

j. A diversion program offers the arrestee the opportunity to avoid conviction if he or she is willing to perform prescribed "rehabilitative steps" (e.g., making restitution to the victim, undertaking a treatment program). The diversion agreement operates, in effect, to place the arrestee on a probationary status without conviction. In many jurisdictions, this is achieved by the prosecutor promising not to file charges if the arrestee complies with the prescribed conditions. In others, charges initially are filed with the court, then held in abeyance for the period during which the arrestee is to meet the prescribed conditions, and dismissed with prejudice once the arrestee meets those conditions. If the arrestee fails to meet the prescribed conditions, the prosecution against the arrestee proceeds (with the charges then filed, if that had not been done previously).

Where the prosecutor in the initial screening process decides in favor of criminal prosecution, other decisions also must be made. Initially, the prosecutor must determine whether the proposed charge is set at the correct level, or whether there is a need to reduce or raise the offense-level recommended by the police. In many instances, the prosecutor must also consider the potential for charging multiple separate offenses (as where the arrested person allegedly committed several separate crimes in a single criminal transaction or engaged in more than one criminal transaction). Here the prosecutor must determine whether the charging instrument should allege all offenses or simply some of the offenses (e.g., only the most serious, or only those easiest to prove). Where the prosecutor chooses to proceed on more than one charge, the law may give to the prosecutor another choice—whether to bring the charges in a single prosecution or in multiple, separate prosecutions. A similar choice must be made where several people have been arrested for participating in the same crime, as each can be proceeded against separately or the group can be prosecuted jointly through a single charging instrument naming multiple defendants.

Step 6: Filing the Complaint. Assuming that the police decide to charge and that decision is not overturned in a pre-filing prosecutorial review, the next step is the filing of charges with the magistrate court, which must be done prior to the arrestee's scheduled first appearance (see step 8). The initial charging instrument commonly is called a "complaint". For most offenses, the complaint will be a fairly brief document. Its basic function is to set forth concisely the allegation that the accused, at a particular time and place, committed specified acts constituting a violation of a particular criminal statute. The complaint will be signed by a "complainant," a person who swears under oath that he or she believes the factual allegations of the complaint to be true. The complainant usually will be either the victim or the investigating officer. When an officer-complainant did not observe the offense being committed, but relies on information received from the victim or other witnesses, the officer ordinarily will note that the allegations in the complaint are based on "information and belief." With the filing of the complaint, the arrestee officially becomes a "defendant" in a criminal prosecution.

Step 7: Magistrate Review of the Arrest. Following the filing of the complaint and prior to or at the start of the first appearance (see step 8), the magistrate must undertake what is often described as the *"Gerstein* review." As prescribed by the Supreme Court's decision in *Gerstein v. Pugh,*[k] if the accused was arrested without a warrant and remains in custody (or is subject to restraints on his liberty as a condition of stationhouse bail), the magistrate must determine that there exists probable cause for the offense charged in the complaint. This ordinarily is an *ex parte* determination, similar to that made in the issuance of an arrest warrant and based on the same sources of information (see step 2). If the magistrate finds that probable cause has not been established, she will direct the prosecution to promptly produce more information or release the arrested person. Such instances are exceedingly rare, however. Since a judicial probable cause determination already has been made where an arrest warrant was issued, a *Gerstein* review is not required in such cases (or in cases in which the arrestee was indicted by a grand jury prior to his arrest).

Step 8: The First Appearance. An arrestee who is held in custody, or who otherwise remains subject to custodial restraints (as where released on stationhouse bail), must be presented before the magistrate court within a time period typically specified as either 24 or 48 hours. Since the arrestee is now a defendant (the complaint having been filed), and this is his initial appearance in that capacity, this proceeding before the magistrate is described in many jurisdictions

---

k.   Discussed at p. 340 of *Modern* and *Basic,* and Note 1, p. 1011 of *Modern* and *Advanced.*

as the "first appearance," (although other jurisdictions use "initial presentment," "preliminary arraignment," or "arraignment on the complaint"). Where the accused person was not arrested by the police, but issued a citation (see step 2), the 24 or 48 hour timing requirement does not apply and the first appearance may be scheduled a week or more after the issuance of the citation.

The first appearance in a felony case commonly is a quite brief proceeding. Initially, the magistrate will inform the defendant of the charge in the complaint, of various rights possessed by the defendant, and of the nature of further proceedings. The range of rights and proceedings mentioned will vary from one jurisdiction to another. Commonly, the magistrate will inform the defendant of his right to remain silent, and warn him that anything he says to the court or the police may be used against him at trial. The defendant always will be informed of at least the very next proceeding in the process, which usually will be a preliminary hearing. The magistrate also will set a date for the preliminary hearing unless the defendant at that point waives his right to that hearing.

Where the felony defendant is not represented by counsel at the first appearance, the magistrate's responsibilities include making certain that the defendant is aware of his right to be represented by counsel, including the right to counsel funded by the state if the defendant is indigent. In some jurisdictions the indigency determination is made at the first appearance, and the magistrate initiates the appointment of state-funded counsel on a finding of indigency. In others, the indigency determination will be made prior to the first appearance, by a court administrator or public defender, and the counsel assigned to the indigent defendant will be present at the first appearance.

One of the most important first-appearance functions of the magistrate is to fix the terms under which the defendant can obtain his release from custody pending the disposition of the charges against him. This process is still described at "setting bail," although release today often is conditioned on non-financial requirements (e.g., a promise to appear and a restriction on travel) rather than traditional "bail" (i.e., the posting of a security, such as cash or a bond). As discussed in chapter 13, setting bail requires consideration of information relating to both the alleged offense and the defendant. This information may be collected prior to the first appearance (typically by a pretrial services agency) or at the first appearance itself. Where the magistrate imposes a financial condition (e.g., requires a bailbond), and the defendant is not prepared to meet that condition, the defendant will be held in custody in a jail and will remain there until the financial condition is met or there is a final disposition of the charges. Many jurisdictions have a "preventive detention" exception to the setting of bail for certain types of felonies. Here, upon a necessary finding of danger or likely flight, the magistrate does not set release terms, but instead orders that the defendant continue to be held in custody pending final disposition of the charges.

Step 9: Preliminary Hearing. Following the first appearance, the next scheduled step in a felony case generally is the preliminary hearing (sometimes called a preliminary "examination"). All but a handful of our fifty-two jurisdictions grant the felony defendant a right to a preliminary hearing, to be held within a specified period (typically, within a week or two if the defendant does not gain pretrial release and within a few weeks if released). However, the actual use of the preliminary hearing varies considerably from one jurisdiction to another (and sometimes from one judicial district to another in the same jurisdiction). In most jurisdictions, the prosecution, if it so chooses, can preclude a preliminary hearing by obtaining a grand jury indictment prior to the scheduled date of the hearing. Also, in some jurisdictions, defendants who intend to plead guilty commonly waive the hearing and move directly to the trial court. The end result is that among the many jurisdictions recognizing preliminary hearings, the hearings are held in almost all felony prosecutions in some, in a substantial majority in others, in a significant minority in still others, and almost never in several.

Where the preliminary hearing is held, it will provide, like grand jury review, a screening of the decision to charge by a neutral body. In the preliminary hearing, that neutral body is the magistrate, who must determine whether, on the evidence presented, there is sufficient evidence to send the case forward. Ordinarily, the magistrate will already have determined that probable cause exists as part of the *ex parte* screening of the complaint (see step 7). The preliminary hearing, however, provides screening in an adversary proceeding in which both sides are represented by counsel. Typically, the prosecution will present its key witnesses and the defense will limit its response to the cross-examination of those witnesses (although the defense has the right to present its own witnesses and may occasionally do so).

If the magistrate concludes that the evidence presented is sufficient for the prosecution to move forward (usually that it establishes probable cause), she will "bind the case over" to the next stage in the proceedings. In an indictment jurisdiction (see step 10), the case is bound over to the grand jury, and in a jurisdiction that permits the direct filing of an information (see step 11), the case is bound over directly to the general trial court. If the magistrate finds that the evidence supports only a lesser charge (e.g., a misdemeanor), the charge will be reduced. If the magistrate finds that the evidence is insufficient to support any charge, the prosecution will be terminated.

Step 10: Grand Jury Review. Although almost all fifty-two jurisdictions still have provisions authorizing grand jury screening of felony charges, such screening is mandatory only in those jurisdictions requiring felony prosecutions to be instituted by an indictment, a charging instrument issued by the grand jury. In a majority of the states, the prosecution is now allowed to proceed either by grand jury indictment or by information at its option. Because prosecutors in these states commonly choose to prosecute by information, the states providing this option commonly are referred to as "information" states. Eighteen states, the federal system, and the District of Columbia currently require grand jury indictments for all felony prosecutions. These jurisdictions commonly are described as "indictment" jurisdictions. Four additional states are "limited indictment" jurisdictions, requiring prosecution by indictment only for their most severely punished offenses (capital, life imprisonment, or both).

The grand jury is selected randomly from the same pool of prospective jurors (the "venire") as the trial jury. Unlike the trial jury, however, it sits not for a single case, but for a term that may range from one to several months. As in the case of the magistrate at the preliminary hearing, the primary function of the grand jury is to determine whether there is sufficient evidence to justify a trial on the charge sought by the prosecution. The grand jury, however, participates in a screening process quite different from the preliminary hearing. It meets in a closed session and hears only the evidence presented by the prosecution. The defendant has no right to offer his own evidence or to be present during grand jury proceedings.

If a majority of the grand jurors conclude that the prosecution's evidence is sufficient, the grand jury will issue the indictment requested by the prosecutor. The indictment will set forth a brief description of the offense charged, and the grand jury's approval of that charge will be indicated by its designation of the indictment as a "true bill." If the grand jury majority refuses to approve the proposed indictment, the charges against the defendant will be dismissed.

Step 11: The Filing of the Indictment or Information. If an indictment is issued, it will be filed with the general trial court and will replace the complaint as the accusatory instrument in the case. Where a grand jury indictment either is not required under the law of the jurisdiction, or has been waived, an information will be filed with the trial court. Like the indictment, the information is a charging instrument which replaces the complaint, but it is issued by the prosecutor rather than the grand jury.

Step 12: Arraignment on the Information or Indictment. After the indictment or information has been filed, the defendant is arraigned—i.e., he is brought before the trial court, informed of the charges against him, and asked to enter a plea of guilty, not guilty, or, as is permitted under some circumstances, *nolo contendere* (a plea in which the defendant accepts a judgment of conviction, but does not admit guilt). In the end, most of those felony defendants whose cases reach the trial court will plead guilty. At the arraignment, however, they are likely to enter a plea of not guilty. Where there has not been a preliminary hearing, defense counsel probably will not be fully apprized of the strength of the prosecution's case at this point in the proceedings. Also, in the vast majority of jurisdictions, guilty pleas in felony cases are the product of plea negotiations with the prosecution, and in many places, that process does not start until after the arraignment. When the defendant enters a plea of not guilty at the arraignment, the judge will set a trial date, but the expectation generally is that the trial will not be held.

Step 13: Pretrial Motions. In most jurisdictions, a broad range of objections must be raised by a pretrial motion. Those motions commonly present challenges to the institution of the prosecution (e.g., claims regarding the grand jury indictment process), attacks upon the sufficiency of the charging instrument, challenges to the scope, location, and timing of the prosecution (claiming improper joinder of charges or parties, improper venue, or violation of speedy trial require-ments), requests for discovery when there is a dispute over what is discoverable,[1] and requests for the suppression of evidence allegedly obtained through a consti-tutional violation. While some pretrial motions are made only by defendants who intend to go to trial, other motions (e.g., for discovery) may benefit as well defendants who expect in the end to plead guilty. Nevertheless, pretrial motions are likely to be made in only a small portion of the felony cases that reach the trial court. Their use tends to vary with the nature of the case. In narcotics cases, for example, motions to suppress are quite common. In the typical forgery case, on the other hand, pretrial motions of any type are quite rare.

Step 14: Guilty Plea Negotiation and Acceptance. Guilty pleas in felony cases most often are the product of a plea agreement under which the prosecution offers certain concessions in return for the defendant's plea. The offering of concessions lies in the discretion of the prosecutor, and as discussed in chapter 22, there is considerable variation among prosecutors' offices as to what types of concessions will be offered to defendants charged with particular offenses. There also is considerable variation as to the negotiation process itself (e.g., whether the prosecutor will actually "bargain," or simply present a "take-it-or leave-it offer"). Where a plea is entered as result of an agreement with the prosecutor, that agreement must be set forth on the record before the trial court. The trial judge will review the agreement to ensure that its terms are within the law, but cannot second-guess its soundness as a matter of criminal justice policy.

---

1. Discovery is a process whereby the prosecution discloses to the defense some or all of the evidence it intends to use at trial and certain other evidence within its possession or control that may be useful to the defense. Jurisdictions vary considerable as to the range of discovery that the prosecution must provide. They generally require the defense to reciprocate by providing somewhat narrower discovery to the prosecution. This may lead to pretrial prosecution motions challenging the defense's failure to provide discovery.

The trial judge's primary responsibility in accepting a guilty plea is to ensure that the defendant understands both the legal consequences of entering a guilty plea and the terms of the plea agreement. If that understanding is present, and there exists a factual basis for the plea (typically provided by the defendant admitting in court the acts constituting the offense), the plea will be accepted and a date set for sentencing.

Step 15: The Trial. Assuming that there has not been a dismissal and the defendant has not entered a guilty plea (or a *nolo contendere* plea), the next step in the criminal process is the trial. In most respects, the criminal trial resembles the civil trial. There are, however, several distinguishing features that are either unique to criminal trials or of special importance in such trials. These include: (1) the presumption of defendant's innocence; (2) the requirement of proof beyond a reasonable doubt; (3) the right of the defendant not to take the stand; (4) the exclusion of evidence obtained by the state in an illegal manner; and (5) the more frequent use (by the prosecution) of incriminating statements previously made by the defendant (often to police).

As noted previously, the vast majority of felony charges will be disposed of either by a guilty plea or a dismissal, with guilty pleas dominating. Nationally, trials account for only a small percentage of all dispositions in cases originally charged as felonies (e.g., 3% in 2007). That low percentage, however, is still likely to produce over 75,000 felony trials annually.

In felony cases, the defendant is entitled to a trial by jury, but in many jurisdictions, for certain types of offenses, defendants commonly will waive the jury, in favor of bench trial. Where the trial is to a jury, the verdict, whether for acquittal or conviction, in all but a few states, must be unanimous. Where the jury cannot reach agreement, it is commonly described as a "hung jury". Such a jury is discharged without reaching a verdict, and the case may be retried.

The median time frame from the arrest of the defendant to the start of the felony trial can exceed a year in judicial districts with slow moving dockets, but for most judicial districts, it is likely to fall within the range of 5–8 months. The median will be influenced, in particular, by the mix of jury and bench trials, as the time frame tends to be considerably longer for jury trials. While most jurisdictions have speedy trial requirements that impose time limits of 6 months or less, there are various excludable time periods (for factors such as witness unavailability and the processing of motions) which commonly extend the time limit by at least a few months.

In state courts, most jury trials will be completed within 2–3 days. A key variable in setting the length of the trial is the case type, as certain types of offenses (most notably capital homicides) produce trials substantially longer than the typical felony. Thus, the special character of the federal docket (in particular, the complex conspiracy and white collar offenses) explains in large part why trials lasting a week or more are so common in the federal courts. In general, trials to the bench are considerably shorter, and in state courts, unlikely to last more than a day.

Whether a criminal case is tried to the bench or the jury, the odds favor conviction over acquittal. A fairly typical ratio for felony charges will be 3 convictions for every acquittal. That ratio may vary significantly, however, with the nature of the offense. Thus, the rate of conviction at trial tends to be substantially lower for an offense such as rape than an offense such as drug trafficking.

Step 16: Sentencing. Following conviction, the next step in the process is the determination of the sentence. In all but a handful of jurisdictions (which allow for jury sentencing, even apart from capital punishment), the sentence determination is the function of the court. Basically three different types of sentences may be used: financial sanctions (e.g., fines, restitution orders); some form of release into the community (e.g., probation, unsupervised release, house arrest); and incarceration in a jail (for lesser sentences) or prison (for longer sentences). The process applied in determining the sentence is shaped in considerable part by the sentencing options made available to the court by the legislature. For a particular offense, the court may have no choice. The legislature may have prescribed that conviction automatically carries with it a certain sentence and there is nothing left for the court to do except impose that sentence. Most frequently, however, legislative narrowing of options on a particular offense does not go beyond eliminating the community release option (by requiring incarceration) and setting maximums (and sometimes mandatory minimums) for incarceration and fines. However, states vary considerably in shaping the court's authority to choose within available options, particularly as to the length of incarceration. Their approaches include: allowing the sentencing judge considerable discretion within a broad range set by the legislature; narrowing the range subject to discretion by requiring the court to make specified additions to the minimum sentence where certain aggravating factors are present; and channeling discretion through the use of sentencing guidelines that look to specified offender and offense characteristics.

The process utilized in felony sentencing varies to some extent according to whether judicial discretion is broad or is channeled or limited by guideline or legislative reference to specific sentencing circumstances. In all jurisdictions, the process is designed to obtain for the court information beyond that which will have come to its attention in the course of trial or in the acceptance of a guilty plea. That information is provided primarily through a presentence report prepared by the probation department, although the prosecution and defense commonly will be allowed to present additional information and to challenge the information contained in the presentence report. The presentation of this information is not subject to the rules governing the presentation of information at trial. The rules of evidence do not apply, and neither the prosecution nor the defense has a right to call witnesses or to cross-examine the sources of adverse information presented in the presentence report or in any additional documentation presented by the opposing side. However, where the sentencing authority of the judge is restricted or channeled by reference to specific factors, a judge commonly is required to make a preponderance-of-the-evidence finding as to those factors. Here, if relevant facts are in dispute, the court commonly will find it necessary to hold an evidentiary hearing and to utilize trial-type procedures to resolve that dispute.

Step 17: Appeals.[m] For criminal convictions imposed by the general trial court, the initial appeal is to the intermediate appellate court. If the state has no intermediate appellate court, then the initial and final appeal within the state system is to the state's court of last resort. All states allow the convicted defendant to appeal his conviction, and many allow an appeal as to sentence as well. The vast majority of appeals in felony cases are taken by convicted defendants who were sentenced to imprisonment. Imprisoned defendants convicted on a guilty plea are a part of this group, but their portion of the appeals is likely to be small where appeals may only challenge the conviction (the potential grounds for challenging a guilty plea conviction being considerably narrower than the poten-

---

m. The focus here is on defense appeals from a conviction. The prosecution may appeal from certain types of dismissals, but may not appeal from an acquittal. Since the percentage of dismissals over the objection of the prosecution is low, and prosecutors do not regularly appeal such rulings (even when they could do so), prosecution appeals are infrequent as compared to defense appeals.

tial grounds for challenging a trial conviction). Reversals of conviction on appeal vary with the jurisdiction, but a reversal rate in the 5–10% range is fairly typical (with the rate somewhat higher when reversals in part—not overturning the entire conviction—are added).

Step 18: Collateral Remedies. After the appellate process is exhausted, imprisoned defendants may be able to use postconviction procedures to challenge their conviction, although the grounds for challenge tend to be limited (e.g., to constitutional violations). Since these procedures are separate from the basic criminal justice process (indeed, some are viewed as civil in nature), they are described as a group as "collateral remedies." Perhaps the most prominent of these collateral remedies is the federal writ of habeas corpus (discussed in chapter 29), which Congress has expanded to allow state prisoners to raise federal constitutional challenges to their state convictions in federal courts.

SECTION 3.   DIVERSITY IN LEGAL REGULATION

1. *Fifty-two lawmaking jurisdictions.* Under the United States' version of federalism, each of the fifty state governments retains the authority to enact its own criminal code. Each state also retains the power to provide for the enforcement of that criminal code through agencies and procedures that it creates. That authority has been used in each state to establish what is basically a single, general criminal justice process applicable throughout the state (although that process may vary with the level of the offense, as discussed in Note 7 infra). Congress has added to these fifty state criminal justice processes its two distinct federal criminal justice processes. First, it has created a separate criminal justice process for the District of Columbia, used to enforce a separate criminal code that applies only in the District. Second, it has created a criminal justice process for the enforcement of the general federal criminal code, which applies throughout the country. This process utilizes the national law enforcement agencies and relies on prosecutions brought in the federal district courts.

In many fields in which both state and federal governments exercise regulatory authority, the enforcement of federal law by federal officials so clearly dominates the field that law school courses focus almost exclusively on the federal enforcement system. A similar focus would be most inappropriate in the field of criminal procedure. While the federal criminal justice system may be the most prominent of the nation's fifty-two criminal justice systems, the traditional statistical measures of criminal justice systems rank it simply as one of the larger, but hardly the largest, of our fifty-two systems. Moreover, when the federal system is compared to the state systems as a group, the combined state systems clearly dominate, as they account for the vast bulk of the nation's criminal justice workload (e.g., roughly 97% of all felony prosecutions and over 99% of all misdemeanor prosecutions). Thus, to understand the criminal justice process in its everyday operation, one must take account of the laws regulating the fifty state criminal justice processes, as well as the two federal processes.

2. *The unifying role of federal constitutional regulation.* Taking account of fifty-two different criminal justice systems would be a less daunting task if the fifty-two jurisdictions were subject to a single source of law that mandated an exclusive, comprehensive regulation of the process in all fifty-two jurisdictions. But there is no such law. The regulation provided by the federal constitution (as interpreted by the Supreme Court) does, however, provide a common foundation that shapes major portions of the process in all fifty-two jurisdictions.

The Bill of Rights of the Federal Constitution includes a large number of guarantees dealing specifically with the criminal justice process—all the guarantees of the Fourth, Sixth, and Eighth Amendments, and with the inclusion of the Fifth Amendment's due process clause (which clearly applies to criminal proceedings, although extending also to certain non-criminal proceedings), all but one of the guarantees (the just compensation guarantee) of the Fifth Amendment. As discussed in chapter 2, these provisions bear upon the state criminal justice processes as well as the federal. Applying a "selective incorporation" reading of the Fourteenth Amendment's due process clause (which explicitly governs state governmental activities), the Court has concluded that almost all of these criminal-process Bill of Rights guarantees are fully applicable to the state criminal justice processes. The Supreme Court also has held that the due process clauses of the Fifth and Fourteenth Amendment have an independent content, extending beyond the guarantees specifically directed at the criminal process, and imposing further constitutional limitations upon the state and federal criminal justice processes.

In light of their scope and their applicability to all fifty-two jurisdictions, the applicable federal constitutional guarantees constitute the traditional starting point for describing the law regulating the criminal justice processes of the United States. All fifty-two jurisdictions must, at a minimum, meet the requirements of these guarantees (as interpreted by the Supreme Court). Constitutional regulation, however, is neither comprehensive nor exclusive. Initially, constitutional regulation does not govern all aspects of the criminal justice process. As to many steps in the process, constitutional regulation is limited to only a few aspects of the applicable procedures. Secondly, even where the constitutional regulation is comprehensive, the states remain free to go beyond the constitutionally mandated minimum and impose more rigorous safeguards.

The significance of federal constitutional regulation varies with the different stages of the criminal justice process. Three models provide a rough picture of that variation. First, as to some procedures (e.g., the preliminary hearing), the Constitution says very little. Here, legal regulation comes primarily from the laws of the individual jurisdiction. Second, as to other procedures, such as searches, the constitutional regulation is so comprehensive as to rival the Internal Revenue Code in its detail and complexity. Here, constitutional standards tend to dominate. Some jurisdictions may add more rigorous standards, and many may add their own requirements as to minor aspects of administration, but the constitutional standards provide the critical legal standards for the vast majority of the fifty-two jurisdictions in regulating the particular procedure. Third, for still other elements of the process, the federal constitution provides a substantial set of regulations, but those regulations are not comprehensive in their scope and are not dominant in shaping state law. Here, a fairly large group of states will impose under their own laws standards more rigorous than the constitutional prerequisites, and almost all states will seek in their state law to regulate other aspects of the particular element that are not treated by the constitutional standard.

Our discussion of a particular step in the process will always start by considering applicable federal constitutional requirements (if any). When our coverage concentrates entirely on the constitutional standards, as set forth by the Supreme Court, it can be assumed that the second model prevails, i.e., the number of jurisdictions that add substantial requirements of their own is fairly small, and for the vast majority of the fifty-two jurisdictions, the federal constitutional standards provide the basic legal regulation. Where the constitution provides very little direction, or many jurisdictions establish standards more rigorous than the constitutional standard, our discussion will go beyond the constitutional standards and consider the general patterns of regulation under the laws of the fifty-two jurisdictions (as discussed in Note 4 infra).[a]

3. *Natural divergence.* With each jurisdiction regulating through its own laws, some degree of diversity is almost inevitable. The English common law provided a common starting point for the criminal justice systems of the original states and the federal system, and continues to provide an element of commonality even to this day. However, as the common law concepts have been adjusted to accommodate new developments in the administrative structure of the process (such as the creation of police departments), and as the process has been reshaped to accommodate new concerns, various factors have led the different jurisdictions to take diverse approaches on common issues. Four factors, in particular, point toward different states adopting somewhat different legal regulations: (1) criminal procedure is not one of those areas of lawmaking in which a need for reciprocity or the interaction of transactions forces the states to seek uniformity; a lack of uniformity in the criminal justice processes of adjoining states is not likely to be a deterrent to the free flow of goods, services, or persons between the states or to restrain economic development within the state; (2) the criminal justice process must be shaped in light of the state's administrative environment, including the demography of the population, the resources available to the process, and the structure of the institutions responsible for the administration of the process (particularly police, prosecutor, and judiciary); states vary considerably as to that administrative environment, particularly in the division between states that are largely urban and largely rural; (3) criminal process issues tend to be issues of high visibility and, often, high emotional content, leading to lawmaking decisions (at least legislative lawmaking decisions[b]) that are influenced more by symbolic politics (which tend to vary with the ideological assumptions of the local constituency) than the views of those with presumed technical expertise; and (4) the integrated components of the criminal justice process means that a divergence between states in their laws governing one part of the process most likely will necessitate further differences at other stages of the process.

4. *Describing common patterns.* The laws of the fifty-two jurisdictions are most likely to vary where (1) federal constitutional regulation is not comprehensive and detailed, and (2) the particular procedure was either unknown at common law or its common law form has been substantially modified as a result of institutional and process changes not anticipated by the common law. Even here, however, if the focus is on the basic structure of the regulation, and not upon administrative refinements, the legal regulations applicable in the vast majority of the fifty-two jurisdictions usually can be characterized as following one or the

---

a. While federal statutes regulating criminal procedure generally apply only to the federal system, Congress in a few instances has utilized its regulatory authority (e.g., its authority over interstate commerce) to prescribe criminal process standards that govern in both the federal and state systems. The prime example is the federal law governing wiretapping and other forms of electronic surveillance. Where such a statute is applicable, our discussion (as in chapter 8) focuses on that federal statute rather than the laws of the states.

Federal treaties (particularly multinational conventions) also present the potential for regulating state criminal procedure. However, current treaties that deal with the subject of criminal justice have been construed as not having that effect, either because they are not self-executing, do not create judicially enforceable private remedies, or are subject to a reservation that limits the treaty's scope to rights otherwise protected by the federal constitution. See CRIMPROC § 1.7(c).

b. Legislative lawmaking plays a critical role in the field of criminal procedure as every state has an extensive group of statutes regulating the criminal justice process (commonly described as a "code of criminal procedure"). Judicial lawmaking through common law rulings, once the most common form of criminal process lawmaking, today plays a very limited role. Judicial lawmaking more commonly occurs in the adoption of court rules, with roughly two-thirds of the states having a comprehensive set of court rules of criminal procedure (i.e., rules equivalent in scope, or sometimes even broader than, the Federal Rules of Criminal Procedure, discussed infra). See CRIMPROC § 1.7(e),(f),(h). Of course, courts also may be viewed as engaged in judicial lawmaking in their interpretation of constitutions (federal and state), statutes, and court rules.

other of two or three alternative approaches. We will not attempt in this single volume to go beyond describing these basic patterns that differentiate one major grouping from another. It should be kept in mind, however, that there will almost always be a few jurisdictions that take an entirely different approach. So too, jurisdictions described as following the same general approach commonly will present some variation in their implementation of that approach; a description of that approach as applied in a particular jurisdiction cannot be carried over in its entirety to all other jurisdictions adopting the same basic approach.

5.   *Models.* Very often a basic pattern followed by a substantial grouping of jurisdiction is the product of states emulating reforms adopted in a particular jurisdiction. The federal law of criminal procedure is undoubtedly the most important model in this regard. Notwithstanding significant distinctions in the role and administrative institutions of the federal criminal justice system, as to almost every one of the basic elements of that system, a substantial group of states, ranging from a significant minority to an overwhelming majority, have copied in large part the standards of the relevant federal statutes (see Appendix B of the Supplement) or the Federal Rules of Criminal Procedure (see Appendix C of the Supplement). Thus, the discussion in later chapters of the nonconstitutional federal law of criminal procedure is presented not only because of its significant role in regulating the federal criminal justice system, but because it usually reflects also the governing state law in a substantial group of states.

The American Bar Association's *Standards for Criminal Justice* provide another important model. Now in their third edition, the *A.B.A. Standards* have been cited thousands of times by appellate courts and have been followed by numerous states in formulating their court rules and statutes. Unlike the Federal Rules, however, the *A.B.A. Standards* have been incorporated into state law on a piecemeal basis, with the state reforms typically looking either to an individual standard or a grouping of standards dealing with a particular aspect of the process (e.g., pretrial discovery). Accordingly, the Standards are not included in Appendix B, but are cited (and quoted) in the text discussion of those topics on which they have been especially influential.

6.   *Procedural subsets.* Even within a single jurisdiction the law governing the criminal justice process will not be the same for each and every case. All fifty-two jurisdictions utilize at least a few lines of division that produce procedural subsets (i.e., different classes of cases governed by different procedural standards). The most common is the line drawn between felonies and misdemeanors (see fn.a, p. 4). All jurisdictions distinguish between felonies and misdemeanors as to some procedures. Indeed, some states add an additional subset for certain procedures by drawing a distinction between lower level misdemeanors (e.g., punishable by 90 days in jail or less) and higher level misdemeanors (which then may or may not be treated in the same manner as felonies). We will always take note of differences in the federal constitutional standards applicable to misdemeanors and felonies (or certain types of misdemeanors and more serious charges). As to distinctions drawn by state law, however, only the most significant differences in the treatment of misdemeanors will be cited. Our focus primarily is on describing the law applicable to felony prosecutions.

A similar approach will be taken as to state laws creating another procedural subset based on penalty—the distinction drawn, as to various procedures, between felonies subject to capital punishment (limited to certain types of murder) and all other felonies. Our focus will be on the processing of the non-capital case, although here again, distinctions drawn in constitutional regulation between capital and non-capital prosecutions will always be noted.

SECTION 4. DIVERSITY IN ADMINISTRATION

1. ***Significance of discretion.*** Commentators commonly speak of the immense gap existing between the law of criminal procedure "on the books" and the law of criminal procedure "in action." Part of that gap is attributable to administrative deviance—that is, the failure of public administrators (particularly police, but also prosecutors, magistrates, and trial court judges) to adhere to the law in administering the process. The larger part of the gap, however, is a product of a narrow view of the "governing law," a view which fails to take account of discretion. As commonly defined, discretion flows from the authorization, explicit or implicit, of the law. Discretion exists where the law fails to prescribe standards and thereby either explicitly or implicitly leaves the administrator to his or her own standards. When commentators, in describing "the law," refer only to the various procedures recognized in constitutional provisions, statutes, court rules, and legal decisions, disregarding the discretionary options that are given to administrators as to the use of those procedures, they tend to characterize every failure to utilize a procedure as a departure from the "law on the books." What they are describing, however, is only a departure from the expectation that the law will mandate procedures, rather than simply authorize procedures to be used at the discretion of different participants in the process. The law of criminal procedure frequently departs from that expectation.

Discretion is a common component of almost all aspects of the criminal justice process. The law grants enforcement officials (police and prosecutor) the authority to institute certain procedures under specified conditions, but typically also grants those officials the discretion not to exercise that authority even when these conditions exist. The law authorizes, for example, the search of the arrested person incident to his arrest, but the police officer has discretion not to exercise that authority if he so chooses. On occasion, the law even grants to the enforcement official the discretion to control the procedural rights made available to a suspect or defendant (as where the prosecutor may determine whether the charges against the defendant are screened by a magistrate at a preliminary hearing or by a grand jury, see § 2, step 9).

The defendant's rights are also subject to the defendant's authority to relinquish those rights. Thus, there is no true gap between the "law" and the "practice" when most prosecutions are resolved without a trial. The law gives the defendant not only a right to a trial, but a right also to waive the trial and plead guilty. Also, the law does not prohibit the government from offering incentives to encourage such waivers.

2. ***Discretion and diversity.*** When there exists a legal normlessness or a legal norm so broad as to allow reference to personal values,[a] diversity in the

---

a. Discretionary decisions are not necessarily decisions totally unregulated by the law, but decisions to which the law grants the actor sufficient leeway to look to personal value judgments. The leeway granted to the administrator tends to be broadest where the decision is not to exercise governmental power adversely to the individual (sometimes described as "ameliorative discretion"). Yet, even here, there usually are some legal limits. A prosecutor has great latitude, for example, in deciding not to prosecute, but that decision cannot be based on a bribe.

Where the official is authorized to choose between different procedures in the exercise of power adverse to the individual (e.g., the police officer's decision, after deciding to charge a misdemeanant, as to whether to issue a summons, which will result in immediate release, or proceed through the arrest process by taking the person into custody), the governing law tends to offer somewhat less latitude. Here the law typically will specify some general prerequisites for taking action, but then give the administrator a choice, based upon an open-ended standard, between the different alternatives. Open-ended standards, such as that requiring that an action be consistent with "the

exercise of authority is inevitable, as it can hardly be expected that all actors performing the same function will look to the same values in exercising their discretion. Numerous studies suggest, however, that to considerable extent, the values of the individual administrator are shaped and confined by a combination of institutional influences, producing what is commonly described as the "dominant administrative culture," and it is this culture that more often than not guides the exercise of discretion. In the state systems, that culture tends to vary from one local community to another since the primary administrative units (police agencies, prosecutors' offices, and magistrate and trial courts) are either a part of local government or organized as local units of a statewide agency. A variety of factors will shape the local administrative culture, including: (1) the structure, management, and basic approach to task (the "organizational ethos") of police departments and prosecutors' offices (and, to a lesser extent, of multi-judge courts and public defender offices); (2) the interactions of administrators (particularly the recurring interactions of prosecutor, public defender, and judge where assigned to the same courtroom); (3) the character and values of the local community, particularly as they bear upon agencies headed by (or responsive to) elected officials; and (4) the extent to which the local administration of the criminal justice process is subject to "caseload pressures" (i.e., quantitative demands that exceed the resources of the local administrative units).

With the administrative culture varying from one community to another (and where more than one agency performs the same role, varying as well within the community, depending on which agency is involved), it is not surprising that the criminal justice process, as applied, will differ in many respects even where the same legal standards govern. For example, in five different communities in a single state, the standard police response to otherwise similarly situated first offenders caught shoplifting, may be quite different: (1) in one community, the shoplifter may be sent on his way with a "warning"; (2) in another the shoplifter will be proceeded against, but released on a summons; (3) in another, the shoplifter will be taken into custody and transported to the police station, but without being frisked or searched; (4) in another, the shoplifter will be frisked when taken into custody; and (5) in another, the shoplifter taken into custody will be subjected to a complete search. Moreover, the differences in approach are not likely to be limited to this initial police reaction. Where the shoplifter is proceeded against, further variations are likely to be found as to such matters as the availability of diversion, the use of plea bargains, the defense waiver of jury trial in cases that go to trial, and the exercise of sentencing discretion. In addition, while certain approaches on these issues may be "standard" for the particular community, the potential always exists for individual participants to exercise their discretion in a manner that deviates from that "standard."

Where the exercise of discretion plays a major rule in the application of a particular step in the criminal justice process, our commentary usually will offer illustrations of some alternative modes of exercising that discretion. Those illustrations come from studies which focus on the exercise of discretion in particular localities. Ordinarily, it can be assumed that something close to the same administrative environment can be found in many other communities and the same style of discretionary decisionmaking probably prevails there as well. But it also must be kept in mind that the illustrations hardly cover the full range of possibilities, and that there are many communities in which a quite different administrative environment and quite different use of discretion will be found.

---

interests of justice," commonly are seen as allowing for basically "discretionary" decisionmaking, though subject to limited judicial review (typically, under an "abuse of discretion" standard).

CHAPTER 2

SOURCES OF CRIMINAL PROCEDURE LAW

■ ■ ■

The law of criminal procedure has a number of sources. (For a brief discussion of sources not covered in this chapter, see pp. 19–22 supra.) Foremost is the Constitution of the United States, and specifically various provisions of the Bill of Rights (such as the Fourth, Fifth, and Sixth Amendments) as well as the Due Process Clause of the Fourteenth Amendment. In federal cases the federal court's supervisory power over the administration of the federal criminal justice system provides an occasional source of authority. In state cases, state constitutional provisions that (as interpreted by the state courts) furnish an individual more protection then does the U.S. Constitution (as interpreted by the U.S. Supreme Court) can also be important. Finally, the cases involving Guantanamo Bay detainees (see pp. 40 to 48) raise the question whether—and to what extent—the inherent powers of the President in matters of military operations and foreign affairs enable him to dispense with normal or traditional procedure safeguards.

SECTION 1. THE "FUNDAMENTAL FAIRNESS," "TOTAL INCORPORATION" AND "SELECTIVE INCORPORATION" THEORIES

In McDonald v. City of Chicago, the Court Looks Back on Its "Incorporation" of Bill of Rights Guarantees

In *District of Columbia v. Heller*, 554 U.S. 570 (2008), the Court held that the Second Amendment protects the right to keep and bear arms for the purpose of self-defense. Thus, the Court struck down a District of Columbia law that banned the possession of handguns in the home. After *Heller* was decided, petitioners filed a federal suit against the City of Chicago, maintaining that the City's handgun ban violated the Second and Fourteenth Amendments. In McDONALD v. CITY OF CHICAGO, 130 S.Ct. 3020 (2010), a 5–4 majority agreed.

Justice Alito announced the judgment of the Court and delivered the opinion of the Court with respect to Parts I, II–A, II–B, II–D, III–A, and III–B, in which the Chief Justice, Justices Scalia, Kennedy and Thomas joined, and an opinion with respect to Parts II–C, IV, and V, in which the Chief Justice and Justices Scalia and Kennedy joined.

Justice Thomas agreed that the Second Amendment is "fully applicable to the States," "fundamental" to the American "scheme of ordered liberty" and "deeply rooted in the Nation's history and tradition." However, he could not agree that the Second Amendment is enforceable against the States through a clause that speaks only to "process." Instead, he viewed the right to keep and bear arms as a

25

privilege of American citizenship applicable to the States through the Fourteenth Amendment's Privileges or Immunities Clause.

In Part II–D of his opinion, speaking for a majority of the Court at this point, Justice Alito looked back on various cases dealing with the relationship between the Bill of Rights and Fourteenth Amendment Due Process:

"[During an earlier era], even when a right set out in the Bill of Rights was held to fall within the conception of due process, the protection or remedies afforded against state infringement sometimes differed from the protection or remedies provided against abridgement by the Federal Government. To give an example, in *Betts v. Brady* [p. 71 infra] the Court held that, although the Sixth Amendment required the appointment of counsel in all federal criminal cases in which the defendant was unable to retain an attorney, the Due Process Clause required appointment of counsel in state criminal proceedings only where 'want of counsel in [the] particular [case] resulted in a conviction lacking [in] fundamental fairness.' Similarly, in *Wolf v. Colorado* [p. 222 infra], the Court held that the 'core of the Fourth Amendment' was implicit in the concept of ordered liberty and thus 'enforceable against the States through the Due Process Clause,' but that the exclusionary rule, which applied in federal cases, did not apply to the States.

"An alternative theory regarding the relationship between the Bill of Rights and § 1 of the Fourteenth Amendment was championed by Justice Black. This theory held that § 1 of the Fourteenth Amendment totally incorporated all of the provisions of the Bill of Rights. [As] Justice Black noted, the chief congressional proponents of the Fourteenth Amendment espoused the view that the Amendment made the Bill of Rights applicable to the States * * *. Nonetheless, the Court never has embraced Justice Black's 'total incorporation' theory.

"While Justice Black's theory was never adopted, the Court eventually moved in that direction by initiating what has been called a process of 'selective incorporation,' i.e., the Court began to hold that the Due Process Clause fully incorporates particular rights contained in the first eight Amendments. See, e.g., *Gideon v. Wainwright* (1963) [p. 73]; *Malloy v. Hogan* (1964) [p. 565]; *Duncan v. Louisiana* (1968) [set forth at p. 1348].

"The decisions during this time abandoned three of the previously noted characteristics of the earlier period. The Court made it clear that the governing standard is not whether *any* 'civilized system [can] be imagined that would not accord the particular protection.' *Duncan*. Instead, the Court inquired whether a particular Bill of Rights guarantee is fundamental to *our* scheme of ordered liberty and system of justice. * * *

"The Court also shed any reluctance to hold that rights guaranteed by the Bill of Rights met the requirements for protection under the Due Process Clause. The Court eventually incorporated almost all of the provisions of the Bill of Rights. Only a handful of the Bill of Rights protections remain unincorporated.[13]

"Finally, the Court abandoned the 'notion that the Fourteenth Amendment applies to the States only a watered-down, subjective version of the individual guarantees of the Bill of Rights', stating that it would be 'incongruous' to apply

---

13. In addition to the right to keep and bear arms (and the Sixth Amendment right to a unanimous jury verdict, see n.14, infra), the only rights not fully incorporated are (1) the Third Amendment's protection against quartering of soldiers; (2) the Fifth Amendment's grand jury indictment requirement; (3) the Seventh Amendment right to a jury trial in civil cases; and (4) the Eighth Amendment's prohibition on excessive fines. * * *

We never have decided whether the Third Amendment or the Eighth Amendment's prohibition of excessive fines applies to the States through the Due Process Clause. * * * Our governing decisions regarding the Grand Jury Clause of the Fifth Amendment and the Seventh Amendment's civil jury requirement long predate the era of selective incorporation.

different standards 'depending on whether the claim was asserted in a state or federal court.' *Malloy*.[a] Instead, the court decisively held that incorporated Bill of Rights protections 'are all to be enforced against the States under the Fourteenth Amendment according to the same standards that protect those personal rights against federal encroachment.' Id. See also *Mapp v. Ohio* [p. 224].[14]

"Employing this approach, the Court overruled earlier decisions in which it had held that particular Bill of Rights guarantees or remedies did not apply to the States. See, e.g., *Mapp*; *Gideon*; and *Malloy*."

SECTION 2.   THE PROBLEM OF BODILY EXTRACTIONS: ANOTHER LOOK AT THE "DUE PROCESS" AND "SELECTIVE INCORPORATION" APPROACHES

As noted in the previous section [fn. a], dissenting in *Baldwin* and concurring in *Williams,* Justice Harlan maintained that "the difference between a 'due process' approach [and] 'selective incorporation' is not an abstract one whereby different formulae achieve the same results." But he made this observation in the context of the applicability to the states of the Sixth Amendment right to trial by

---

a.   In *Malloy,* the Court applied the Fifth Amendment's privilege against self-incrimination to the states to the same extent it applied to the federal government. Justice Brennan observed for a majority of the Court that recently various provisions of the Bill of Rights had been applied to the states according to the same standards protecting these rights against federal encroachment. He mentioned "the guarantees of the First Amendment, the prohibition of unreasonable searches and seizures of the Fourth Amendment [*Mapp v. Ohio*, p. 224], and the right to counsel guaranteed by the Sixth Amendment, *Gideon v. Wainwright* [p. 73]."

Justice Harlan repeatedly voiced his opposition to this approach. "The consequence," he protested, dissenting in *Malloy*, "is inevitably disregard of all relevant differences which may exist between state and federal criminal law and its enforcement. The ultimate result is compelled uniformity, which is inconsistent with the purpose of our federal system and which is achieved either by encroachment on the State's sovereign powers or by dilution in federal law enforcement of the specific protections found in the Bill of Rights."

Matters were brought to a head by the "right to jury trial" cases: *Baldwin v. New York*, 399 U.S. 117 (1970) (no offense can be considered "petty," thus dispensing with the Fourteenth and Sixth Amendment rights to jury trial, where more than six months incarceration is authorized); *Williams v. Florida*, 399 U.S. 78 (1970) (the fact that a jury at common law was made up of precisely 12 is an "historical accident," one unnecessary to carry out the purposes of the jury system, and therefore a 6–person jury in criminal cases does not violate the Sixth Amendment as applied to the state via the Fourteenth).

Dissenting in *Baldwin* and concurring in *Williams,* Justice Harlan protested: "[Rather] than bind the States by the hitherto undeviating and unquestioned federal practice of 12–member juries, the Court holds, based on a poll of state practice, that a six-man jury satisfies the guarantee of a trial by jury in a federal criminal system and consequently carries over to the States. This is a constitutional *renvoi*. With all respect, I consider that before today it would have been unthinkable to suggest that the Sixth Amendment's right to a trial by jury is satisfied by a jury of six, or less, as is left open by the Court's opinion in *Williams*, or by less than a unanimous verdict, a question also reserved in today's decision."

14.   There is one exception to this general rule. The Court has held that although the Sixth Amendment right to trial by jury requires a unanimous jury verdict in federal criminal trials, it does not require a unanimous jury verdict in state criminal trials. See *Apodaca v. Oregon* (1972) [discussed in Chapter 23]. [But] that ruling was the result of an unusual division among the Justices, not an endorsement of the two-track approach to incorporation. In *Apodaca*, eight Justices agreed that the Sixth Amendment applies identically to both the Federal Government and the States. Nonetheless, among those eight, four Justices took the view that the Sixth Amendment does not require unanimous jury verdicts in federal and state criminal trials. Justice Powell's concurrence in the judgment broke the tie, and he concluded that the Sixth Amendment requires juror unanimity in federal, but not state, cases. *Apodaca,* therefore, does not undermine the well-established rule that incorporated Bill of Rights protections apply identically to the States and Federal Government. * * *

jury, which had, or was thought to have, a relatively rigid meaning. Most language in the Bill of Rights, however, is rather vague and general, at least when specific problems arise under a particular phrase. In such cases, does dwelling on the literal language simply *shift the focus of broad judicial inquiry* from "due process" to, e.g., "freedom of speech," "establishment of religion," "unreasonable searches and seizures," "excessive bail," "cruel and unusual punishments," and "the assistance of counsel"? See Donald A. Dripps, *At the Borders of the Fourth Amendment: Why A Real Due Process Test Should Replace the Outrageous Government Conduct Defense*, 1993 U.Ill.L.Rev. 261 (defending, "as both more faithful to conventional sources of constitutional law and more consonant with the political values of a free society, a revitalized due process test"); John E. Nowak, *Due Process Methodology in the Postincorporation World*, 70 J. Crim. L. & C. 397, 400–01 (1979) (arguing that decisions based on specific guarantees tend to rely on definitional analysis and fail to explore the interest at stake). Consider too, Note 1, p. 31. See also Henry J. Friendly, *The Bill of Rights as a Code of Criminal Procedure*, 53 Calif.L.Rev. 929, 937 (1965); Sanford H. Kadish, *Methodology and Criteria in Due Process Adjudication—A Survey and Criticism*, 66 Yale L.J. 319, (1957); Yale Kamisar, *How Much Does It Really Matter Whether Courts Work Within the "Clearly Marked" Provisions of the Bill of Rights or With the "Generalities" of the Fourteenth Amendment?*, 18 J.Contemp. Legal Issues 513 (2009).

In considering whether the right to counsel "begins" at the time of arrest, preliminary hearing, arraignment, or not until the trial itself, or includes probation and parole revocation hearings or applies to juvenile delinquency proceedings, deportation hearings or civil commitments, or, where the defendant is indigent, includes the right to *assigned* counsel or an assigned psychiatrist at state expense, how helpful is the Sixth Amendment language entitling an accused to "the assistance of counsel for his defense"? Is the specificity or direction of this language significantly greater than the "due process" clause?

To turn to another cluster of problems—which form the basis for this section—in considering whether, and under what conditions, the police may direct the "pumping" of a person's stomach to uncover incriminating evidence, or the taking of a blood sample from him, without his consent, do the "specific guarantees" in the Bill of Rights against "unreasonable searches and seizures" and against compelling a person to be "a witness against himself" free the Court from the demands of appraising and judging involved in answering these questions by interpreting the "due process" clause?

ROCHIN v. CALIFORNIA, 342 U.S. 165 (1952), arose as follows: Having "some information" that Rochin was selling narcotics, three deputy sheriffs "forced open the door of [his] room and found him sitting partly dressed on the side of the bed, upon which his wife was lying. On a 'night stand' beside the bed the deputies spied two capsules. When asked 'Whose stuff is this?' Rochin seized the capsules and put them in his mouth. A struggle ensued in the course of which the three officers 'jumped upon him' and [unsuccessfully] attempted to extract the capsules. [Rochin] was handcuffed and taken to a hospital. At the direction of one of the officers, a doctor forced an emetic solution through a tube into Rochin's stomach against his will. This 'stomach pumping' produced vomiting. In the vomited matter were found two capsules which proved to contain morphine. [Rochin was convicted of possessing morphine] and sentenced to sixty days' imprisonment. The chief evidence against him was the two capsules."

The Court, per Frankfurter, J., concluded that the police conduct violated fourteenth amendment due process: "This is conduct that shocks the conscience. Illegally breaking into the privacy of the petitioner, the struggle to open his mouth and remove what was there, the forcible extraction of his stomach's contents—this course of proceeding by agents of government to obtain evidence is bound to offend even hardened sensibilities. They are methods too close to the rack and the screw to permit of constitutional differentiation.

"It has long since ceased to be true that due process of law is heedless of the means by which otherwise relevant and credible evidence is obtained. [The confession] decisions [are] only instances of the general requirement that States in their prosecutions respect certain decencies of civilized conduct. Due process of law, as a historic and generative principle, precludes defining, and thereby confining, these standards of conduct more precisely than to say that convictions cannot be brought about by methods that offend 'a sense of justice.' It would be a stultification of the responsibility which the course of constitutional history has cast upon this Court to hold that in order to convict a man the police cannot extract by force what is in his mind but can extract what is in his stomach.

"[E]ven though statements contained in them may be independently established as true, [c]oerced confessions offend the community's sense of fair play and decency. So here, to sanction the brutal conduct which naturally enough was condemned by the court whose judgment is before us, would be to afford brutality the cloak of law. Nothing would be more calculated to discredit law and thereby to brutalize the temper of a society."

Concurring Justice Black reasoned that the Fifth Amendment's protection against compelled self-incrimination applied to the states and that "a person is compelled to be a witness against himself not only when he is compelled to testify, but also when as here, incriminating evidence is forcibly taken from him by a contrivance of modern science." He maintained that "faithful adherence to the specific guarantees in the Bill of Rights insures a more permanent protection of individual liberty than that which can be afforded by the nebulous [Fourteenth Amendment due process] standards stated by the majority."

In a separate concurring opinion, Justice Douglas also criticized the majority's approach. He contended that the privilege against self-incrimination applied to the states as well as the federal government and because of the privilege "words taken from [an accused's] lips, capsules taken from his stomach, blood taken from his veins are all inadmissible provided they are taken from him without his consent. [This] is an unequivocal, definite and workable rule of evidence for state and federal courts. But we cannot in fairness free the state courts from the [restraints of the Fifth Amendment privilege against self-incrimination] and yet excoriate them for flouting the 'decencies of civilized conduct' when they admit the evidence. This is to make the rule turn not on the Constitution but on the idiosyncracies of the judges who sit here."

Irvine v. California, 347 U.S. 128 (1954), limited *Rochin* to situations involving coercion, violence or brutality to the person.[a] BREITHAUPT v. ABRAM, 352

---

a. In *Irvine* the police made repeated illegal entries into petitioner's home, first to install a secret microphone and then to move it to the bedroom, in order to listen to the conversations of the occupants—for over a month.

Jackson, J., who announced the judgment of the Court and wrote the principal opinion, recognized that "few police measures have come to our attention that more flagrantly, deliberately, and persistently violated the fundamental principle declared by the Fourth Amendment as a restriction on the Federal Government," but adhered to the holding in *Wolf v. Colorado* (1949), p. 222, that the exclusionary rule in federal search and seizure cases is not binding on the states. (*Wolf* was overruled in *Mapp v. Ohio* (1961), p. 224.) Nor did Justice Jackson deem *Rochin* applicable: "However obnoxious are the facts in the case before us, they do not involve coercion, violence or brutality to the person [as did *Rochin*], but rather a trespass to property, plus eavesdropping."

Because of the "aggravating" and "repulsive" police misconduct in *Irvine,* Frankfurter, J., joined by Burton, J., dissented, maintaining that *Rochin* was controlling, not *Wolf.* (He had written the majority opinions in both cases.) Black, J., joined by Douglas, J., dissented separately, arguing that petitioner had been convicted on the basis of evidence "extorted" from him in

U.S. 432 (1957), illustrated that under the *Rochin* test state police had considerable leeway even when the body of the accused was "invaded." In *Breithaupt,* the police took a blood sample from an unconscious person who had been involved in a fatal automobile collision. A majority, per Clark, J., affirmed a manslaughter conviction based on the blood sample (which showed intoxication), stressing that the sample was "taken under the protective eye of a physician" and that "the blood test procedure has become routine in our everyday life." "[T]he interests of society in the scientific determination of intoxication, one of the great causes of the mortal hazards of the road," outweighed "so slight an intrusion" of a person's body.

Dissenting Chief Justice Warren, joined by Black and Douglas, JJ., deemed *Rochin* controlling and argued that police efforts to curb the narcotics traffic, involved in *Rochin,* "is surely a state interest of at least as great magnitude as the interest in highway law enforcement. * * * Only personal reaction to the stomach pump and the blood test can distinguish the [two cases]."

Justice Douglas, joined by Black, J., also wrote a separate dissent, maintaining that "if the decencies of a civilized state are the test, it is repulsive to me for the police to insert needles into an unconscious person in order to get the evidence necessary to convict him, whether they find the person unconscious, give him a pill which puts him to sleep, or use force to subdue him."

Nine years later, even though in the meantime the Court had held in *Mapp* that the federal exclusionary rule in search and seizure cases was binding on the states and in *Malloy v. Hogan,* supra, that the Fifth Amendment's protection against compelled self-incrimination was likewise applicable to the states, the Court still upheld the taking by a physician, at police direction, of a blood sample from an injured person, over his objection. SCHMERBER v. CALIFORNIA, 384 U.S. 757 (1966).[b] In affirming the conviction for operating a vehicle while under the influence of intoxicating liquor, a 5–4 majority, per Brennan, J., ruled: (1) that the extraction of blood from petitioner under the aforementioned circumstances "did not offend 'that "sense of justice" ' of which we spoke in *Rochin,*" thus reaffirming *Breithaupt;* (2) that the privilege against self-incrimination, now binding on the states, "protects an accused only from being compelled to testify against himself, or otherwise provide the State with evidence of a testimonial or communicative nature and that the withdrawal of blood and use of the analysis in question did not involve compulsion to these ends";[c] and (3) that the protection against unreasonable search and seizure, now binding on the states, was satisfied because (a) "there was plainly probable cause" to arrest and charge petitioner and to suggest "the required relevance and likely success of a test of petitioner's blood for alcohol"; (b) the officer "might reasonably have believed that he was confront-

violation of the Fifth Amendment's privilege against compelled self-incrimination, which he considered applicable to the states. Douglas, J., dissenting separately, protested against the use in state prosecutions of evidence seized in violation of the Fourth Amendment.

Speaking for himself and Chief Justice Warren, Justice Jackson suggested that copies of the Court's opinion and the record in the case be sent to the U.S. Attorney General for possible federal prosecution. The FBI did conduct an investigation which revealed that the officers who placed the microphone in Irvine's home were acting under orders of the Chief of Police and with the full knowledge of the local prosecutor. Thus, concluded the Department of Justice, "it would be both useless and inadvisable to present [the] matter to the Federal grand jury." See Comment, 7 Stan.L.Rev. 76, 94, fn. 75 (1954).

b. For other aspects of *Schmerber,* see p. 360.

c. In fn. 7 to its opinion, the Court compared "Wigmore's view, 'that the privilege is limited to testimonial disclosure. It was directed at the employment of legal process *to extract from the person's own lips* an admission of guilt, which would thus take the place of other evidence.' 8 Wigmore, *Evidence* § 2263 (McNaughton rev. 1961)." "Our holding today," noted the Court, "is not to be understood as adopting the Wigmore formulation." But see Note 5, p. 767.

ed with an emergency, in which the delay necessary to obtain a warrant, under the circumstances, threatened 'the destruction of evidence' "; and (c) "the test chosen to measure petitioner's blood-alcohol level was a reasonable one * * * performed in a reasonable manner."

Dissenting Justice Black, joined by Justice Douglas, expressed amazement at the majority's "conclusion that compelling a person to give his blood to help the State to convict him is not equivalent to compelling him to be a witness against himself." "It is a strange hierarchy of values that allows the State to extract a human being's blood to convict him of a crime because of the blood's content but proscribes compelled production of his lifeless papers."[d]

NOTES AND QUESTIONS

1. In light of *Rochin*, *Breithaupt* and *Schmerber*, when courts decide consti- tutional questions by "looking to" the Bill of Rights, to what extent do they proceed, as Justice Black expressed it in *Adamson*, "within clearly marked constitutional boundaries"? To what extent does resort to these "particular standards" enable courts to avoid substituting their "own concepts of decency and fundamental justice" for the language of the Constitution?

2. Did *Mapp* and *Malloy*, decided in the interim between *Breithaupt* and *Schmerber*, affect any Justice's vote? Did the applicability of the "particular standards" of the Fourth and Fifth Amendments inhibit Justices Black, Douglas or Brennan from employing their own concepts of "decency" and "justice" in *Schmerber?* After *Schmerber*, how much force is there in Justice Black's view, concurring in *Rochin*, that "faithful adherence to the specific guarantees in the Bill of Rights assures a more permanent protection of individual liberty than that which can be afforded by the nebulous standards stated by the majority"?

3. Applying the "shocks-the-conscience" test first articulated in the *Rochin* case, COUNTY OF SACRAMENTO v. LEWIS, 523 U.S. 833 (1998), held, per SOUTER, J., that a police officer did not violate substantive due process by causing death through "reckless indifference" to, or "reckless disregard" for, a person's life in a high-speed automobile chase of a speeding motorcyclist. (The chase resulted in the death of the motorcyclist's passenger when the police car skidded into the passenger after the cycle had tipped over). In such circumstances, concluded the Court, "only a purpose to cause harm unrelated to the legitimate object of arrest will satisfy the element of arbitrary conduct shocking to the conscience, necessary for a due process violation [and for police liability under 42 U.S.C. § 1983]." Regardless of whether the officer's behavior "offended the reasonableness held up by tort law on the balance struck in law enforcement's own codes of practice, it does not shock the conscience."

The Court recalled that it had held in *Graham v. Connor*, 490 U.S. 386 (1989), that "where a particular amendment provides an explicit textual source of constitutional protection against a particular sort of government behavior, that Amendment, not the more generalized notion of substantive due process, must be the guide for analyzing [claims of substantive due process violations]." But the "more-specific-provision" rule of *Graham* did not bar respondents' lawsuit be- cause neither the high-speed chase of the motorcycle nor the accidental killing of the motorcycle passenger constituted a Fourth Amendment "seizure."[a]

---

d. Warren, C.J., and Douglas, J., dissented in separate opinions, each adhering to his dissenting views in *Breithaupt*. In a third dissenting opinion, Fortas, J., maintained that "petitioner's privilege against self-incrimination applies" and, moreover, "under the Due Process Clause, the State, in its role as prosecutor, has no right to extract blood from an accused or anyone else, over his protest."

a. Concurring in the judgment, Scalia, J., joined by Thomas, J., would not have decided the case by applying the "shocks-the-conscience" test but "on the ground that respondents offer no

4. Continued application of "free-standing" due process. As indicated in *County of Sacramento*, the Court in the "post-incorporation era" has continued to apply the independent content of due process that exists apart from the selectively incorporated guarantees (also described as "free-standing" due process). The applicable standard for cases presenting issues of procedural due process (in contrast to substantive due process) has been whether the state practice "offends some principle of justice so rooted in the traditions and conscience of our people to be ranked as fundamental." *Medina v. California*, 505 U.S. 437 (1992). Jerold Israel, *Free-Standing Due Process and Criminal Procedure: The Supreme Court's Search for Interpretive Guidelines*, 45 St. Louis U.L.J. 303 (2001), reviews the Court's application of that standard in the post-incorporation decades. The article concludes that while the Court has set forth various guidelines for determining the independent content of due process, it has not been consistent in applying those guidelines. The Court has noted that "beyond the specific guarantees enumerated in the Bill of Rights, the Due Process Clause has limited operation" and will be "construed very narrowly." *Dowling v. United States*, 493 U.S. 342 (1990). This position rests on the ground that, since the "Bill of Rights speaks in explicit terms to many aspects of criminal procedure," the expansion of constitutional regulation under the "open-ended rubric of the Due Process Clause * * * invite[s] undue interference with both considered legislative judgments and the careful balance that the constitution strikes between liberty and order." *Medina v. California*, supra. Notwithstanding such statements, free-standing due process has emerged as: (1) the dominant source of constitutional regulation of the pre-trial and post-trial stages of the process (most notable as to guilty pleas and sentencing); (2) a major source of constitutional regulation of the trial; (3) a lesser, but still significant source of regulation of police practices (see e.g., ch. 10, § 3). So too, while the Court has repeatedly stressed that the historical acceptance of a practice is a strong indicator that the practice does not offend fundamental fairness, it has on various occasions relied on deductive reasoning (often tied to the character of a "fair hearing") to hold unconstitutional practices that were entirely consistent with the common law (typically without discussing historical acceptance). Most often, the Court has described free-standing due process as looking to the circumstances of the particular case and resting, at least in part, on fact-sensitive determinations (particularly as to a likelihood of prejudicial impact), but in several areas, the Court has relied on free-standing due process to formulate per se prohibitions and automatically presume prejudice. The Court at times has advance a procedural due process counterpart of *Graham v. Connor*, but at other times has turned to free-standing due process without first considering the possible application of a specific guarantee (indeed, even announcing a preference for relying on free-standing due process in *Pennsylvania v. Ritchie*, p. 1260).

SECTION 3.   IS THERE A DUE PROCESS RIGHT TO TECHNOLOGY THAT MIGHT ESTABLISH ONE'S INNOCENCE?

Looking to the *Medina* standard, DISTRICT ATTORNEY'S OFFICE v. OSBORNE, 129 S.Ct. 2308 (2009), rejected the claim of a convicted defendant that state law violated due process in the prerequisites it imposed for granting him

---

textual or historical support for their alleged due process right." The concurring Justices maintained that in *Washington v. Glucksberg*, 521 U.S. 702 (1997) (upholding a criminal prohibition against physician-assisted suicide), "the Court specifically rejected the method of substantive-due-process analysis employed by Justice Souter in that case, which is the very same method employed by Justice Souter in his opinion for the Court today."

Justice Kennedy, joined by O'Connor, J., joined the opinion of the Court, but also wrote separately. They "share[d] Justice Scalia's concerns about using the phrase 'shocks the conscience' in a manner suggesting that it is a self-defining test." The phrase, they observed, "has the unfortunate connotation of a standard laden with subjective assessments. In that respect, it must be viewed with considerable skepticism."

access to biological evidence for the purpose of applying DNA testing more sophisticated than what was available at the time of his conviction. The Court (per Roberts, C.J.) noted:

"Osborne's * * * approach would take the development [in] this area out of the hands of legislatures and state courts shaping policy in a focused manner and turn it over to federal courts applying the broad parameters of the Due Process Clause. There is no reason to constitutionalize the issue in this way. * * * Forty-six States have already enacted statutes dealing specifically with access to DNA evidence. [The] Federal Government has also passed the Innocence Protection Act of 2004, which allows federal prisoners to move for court-ordered DNA testing under certain specified conditions. That Act also grants money to States that enact comparable statutes.

"[These] laws recognize the value of DNA evidence but also the need for certain conditions on access to the State's evidence. A requirement of demonstrating materiality is common, but is not the only one. The federal statute, for example, requires a sworn statement that the applicant is innocent. States also impose a range of diligence requirements. Several require the requested testing to have been technologically impossible at trial. Others deny testing to those who declined testing for tactical reasons. * * * Alaska is one of a handful of States yet to enact legislation specifically addressing the issue of evidence requested for DNA testing. But that does not mean that such evidence is unavailable for those seeking to prove their innocence. Instead, Alaska courts are addressing how to apply existing laws for discovery and postconviction relief to this novel technology. * * *

"A criminal defendant proved guilty after a fair trial does not have the same liberty interests as a free man. At trial, the defendant is presumed innocent and may demand that the government prove its case beyond reasonable doubt. But [o]nce a defendant has been afforded a fair trial and convicted of the offence for which he was charged, the presumption of innocence disappears. * * * The State accordingly has more flexibility in deciding what procedures are needed in the context of postconviction relief. * * * The question is whether consideration of Osborne's claim within the framework of the State's procedures for postconviction relief "offends some principle of justice so rooted in the traditions and conscience of our people as to be ranked as fundamental," or "transgresses any recognized principle of fundamental fairness in operation." *Medina v. California.*

"[We] see nothing inadequate about the procedures Alaska has provided to vindicate its state right to postconviction relief in general, and nothing inadequate about how those procedures apply to those who seek access to DNA evidence. Alaska provides a substantive right to be released on a sufficiently compelling showing of new evidence that establishes innocence. It exempts such claims from otherwise applicable time limits. The State provides for discovery in postconviction proceedings, and has—through judicial decision—specified that this discovery procedure is available to those seeking access to DNA evidence. These procedures are not without limits. The evidence must indeed be newly available to qualify under Alaska's statute, must have been diligently pursued, and must also be sufficiently material. These procedures are similar to those provided for DNA evidence by federal law and the law of other States. * * * * "

"His attempt to sidestep state process through a new federal lawsuit puts Osborne in a very award position. If he simply seeks the DNA through the State's discovery procedures, he might well get it. If he does not, it may be for a perfectly adequate reason, just as the federal statute and all state statutes impose conditions and limits on access to DNA evidence. It is difficult to criticize the State's procedures when Osborne has not invoked them. [These] procedures are adequate on their face, and without trying them. Osborne can hardly complain that they do not work in practice."[a]

SECTION 4. THE FEDERAL COURTS' "SUPERVISORY POWER" OVER THE ADMINISTRATION OF FEDERAL CRIMINAL JUSTICE

As the Court, per FRANKFURTER, J., observed in McNABB v. UNITED STATES (1943) (more extensively discussed at p. 554), "while the power of this Court to undo convictions in *state* courts is limited to the enforcement of those 'fundamental principles of liberty and justice' secured by [fourteenth amendment due process]" (emphasis added), the standards of *federal* criminal justice "are not satisfied merely by observance of those minimal historic safeguards." Rather, "[i]n the exercise of its supervisory authority over the administration of criminal justice in the federal courts, [this Court has] formulated rules of evidence to be applied in federal criminal prosecutions." Thus, in *McNabb*, the Court held incriminating statements obtained during prolonged and hence unlawful detention (i.e., while the suspect was held in violation of federal statutory requirements that he be promptly taken before a committing magistrate) inadmissible in federal courts "[q]uite apart from the Constitution."

For a long, hard look at *McNabb* itself and the federal "supervisory power" generally, see Sara Sun Beale, *Reconsidering Supervisory Power in Criminal Cases: Constitutional and Statutory Limits on the Authority of the Federal Courts,* 84 Colum.L.Rev. 1433 (1984). Professor Beale maintains, inter alia, that "the supervisory power has blurred the constitutional and statutory limitations on the authority of the federal courts [and] fostered the erroneous view that the federal courts exercise general supervision over federal prosecutors and investigators"; and that "there is no statutory or constitutional source of authority broad enough to encompass all of the supervisory power decisions." Id. at 1434–35.

"In cases not involving questions of judicial procedure or a statutory violation," concludes Beale, id. at 1521–22, the federal courts lack the authority "to exclude evidence or to dismiss a prosecution unless the government's conduct violated the Constitution. This analysis requires the federal courts to decide some constitutional issues they are now able to avoid—or at least defer—by grounding their rulings on supervisory power. [Requiring the federal courts to ground

---

a. Responding to the four dissenters, Justice Alito, in a concurring opinion added: "Justice Stevens [dissent] argues that the State should welcome respondent's offer to perform modern DNA testing (at his own expense) on the State's DNA evidence; the test will either confirm respondent's guilt (in which case the State has lost nothing) or exonerate him (in which case the State has no valid interest in detaining him). Alas, it is far from that simple. First, DNA testing—even when performed with modern STR technology and even when performed in perfect accordance with protocols—often fails to provide 'absolute proof' of anything. * * * Second, the State has important interests in maintaining the integrity of its evidence, and the risks associated with evidence contamination increase every time someone attempts to extract new DNA from a sample. * * * Third, even if every test was guaranteed to provide a conclusive answer, and even if no one ever contaminated a DNA sample, that still would not justify disregarding the other costs associated with the DNA-access regime proposed by respondent. * * * Even without our creation and imposition of a mandatory-DNA-access regime, state crime labs are already responsible for maintaining and controlling hundreds of thousands of new DNA samples every year. * * * The resources required to process and analyze these hundreds of thousands of samples have created severe backlogs in state crime labs across the country."

decisions on a constitutional basis] would be likely to result in eliminating some restrictions on federal investigators and prosecutors that have been grounded solely on supervisory power. This is as it should be.

"But this approach need not straitjacket the courts. Where there has been a legislative grant of authority, such as the rules enabling legislation, the power of the courts is extensive. Amendments to the Federal Rules of Criminal Procedure may properly regulate some matters that have been the subject of highly question-able supervisory power rulings. * * * But the concept of separation of powers dictates that federal prosecutors and investigators, like their state counterparts, should perform their duties subject only to the requirements imposed by the federal Constitution and statutes, not subject to the federal judiciary's preference for particular policies and practices."

In *United States v. Russell* (1973) (discussed at p. 487), in the course of rejecting respondent's argument that he had been "entrapped" because there had been an intolerable degree of government involvement in the criminal enterprise, the Court, per Rehnquist, J., observed:

"[Several lower federal court decisions] have undoubtedly gone beyond this Court's [precedents] in order to bar prosecutions because of what they [consid-ered] 'overzealous law enforcement.' But the [entrapment defense] was not intended to give the federal judiciary a 'chancellor's foot' veto over law enforce-ment practices of which it does not disapprove. The execution of the federal laws under our Constitution is confined primarily to the Executive Branch of the Government, subject to applicable constitutional and statutory limitations and to judicially fashioned rules to enforce those limitations."

When a three-justice plurality (Rehnquist, J., joined by the Chief Justice and White, J.,) quoted the "chancellor's foot" passage with approval in another entrapment *Hampton v. United States* (1976), 425 U.S. 484 (1976), concurring Justice Powell, joined by Blackmun, J., observed:

"The plurality's use of the 'chancellor's foot' passage from *Russell* may suggest that it also would foreclose reliance on our supervisory power to bar conviction of [a defendant predisposed to commit the crime] because of outrageous police conduct. * * * I do not understand *Russell* to have gone so far. There we indicated only that we should be extremely reluctant to invoke the supervisory power in cases of this kind because that power does not give the 'federal judiciary a 'chancellor's foot' veto over law enforcement practices of which it [does] not approve.' * * * I therefore am unwilling to join the plurality in concluding that, no matter what the circumstances, neither due process principles nor our supervi-sory power could support a bar to conviction in any case where the Government is able to prove predisposition [to commit the crime]."[a]

Whatever the implications of the "chancellor's foot" passage, both in *Payner,* infra, and in *Hasting,* infra, the Court left no doubt that it took a dim view of the federal courts' exercise of their "supervisory power."

UNITED STATES v. PAYNER, 447 U.S. 727 (1980), arose as follows: An IRS investigation into the financial activities of American citizens in the Bahamas focused on a certain Bahamian bank. When an official of that bank visited the United States, IRS agents stole his briefcase for a time, removed hundreds of documents from the briefcase and photographed them. As a result of this "brief-case caper," defendant Payner was convicted of federal income tax violations.

---

a. Dissenting Justice Brennan, joined by Stewart and Marshall, JJ., agreed with Justices Powell and Blackmun that *"Russell* does not foreclose imposition of a bar to conviction—based upon our supervisory power or due process principles—where the conduct of law enforcement authorities is sufficiently offensive, even though the individuals entitled to invoke such a defense might be 'predisposed.' "

Because Payner lacked "standing" to challenge the "briefcase caper" under the Court's Fourth Amendment precedents (see Ch. 11, § 1), the federal district court invoked its supervisory power to exclude the tainted evidence. The district court found, and these findings were undisturbed by the higher courts, that "the Government counsels its agents that the Fourth Amendment standing limitation permits them to purposefully conduct an unconstitutional search and seizure of one individual in order to obtain evidence against third parties who are the real targets of the government intrusion" and that IRS agents "transacted the 'briefcase caper' with a purposeful, bad faith hostility toward the Fourth Amendment rights of [the bank official] in order to obtain evidence against persons like Payner." But a 6–3 majority, per Powell, J., held that the supervisory power "does not authorize a federal court" to exclude evidence that did not violate the defendant's Fourth Amendment rights:

"[T]he interest in deterring illegal searches does not justify the exclusion of tainted evidence at the instance of a party who was not the victim of the challenged practices. The values assigned to the competing interests do not change because a court has elected to analyze the question under the supervisory power instead of the Fourth Amendment. In either case, the need to deter the underlying conduct and the detrimental impact of excluding the evidence remain precisely the same. [The] district court's reasoning, which the [Sixth Circuit] affirmed, amounts to a substitution of individual judgment for the controlling decisions of this Court. Were we to accept this use of the supervisory power, we would confer on the judiciary discretionary power to disregard the considered limitations of the law it is charged with enforcing."

Dissenting Justice Marshall, joined by Brennan and Blackmun, JJ., maintained that the Court's holding "effectively turns the standing rules created by this Court for assertions of Fourth Amendment violations into a sword to be used by the Government to permit it deliberately to invade one person's Fourth Amendment rights in order to obtain evidence against another person. Unlike the Court, I do not believe that the federal courts are unable to protect the integrity of the judicial system from such gross government misconduct." Continued the dissent:

"The Court's decision to engraft the standing limitations of the Fourth Amendment onto the exercise of supervisory powers is puzzling not only because it runs contrary to the major purpose behind the exercise of the supervisory powers—to protect the integrity of the court—but also because it appears to render the supervisory powers superfluous. In order to establish that suppression of evidence under the supervisory powers would be proper, the Court would also require Payner to establish a violation of his Fourth or Fifth Amendment rights, in which case suppression would flow directly from the Constitution. This approach is totally unfaithful to our prior supervisory power cases, which, contrary to the Court's suggestion, are not constitutional cases in disguise."

UNITED STATES v. HASTING, 461 U.S. 499 (1983), arose as follows: Five defendants were convicted of kidnapping and transporting women across state lines for immoral purposes. Concluding that the prosecutor had violated *Griffin v. California* (p. 1450, fn. a) by, in effect, commenting on the failure of any defendant to take the stand in his own defense, the U.S. Court of Appeals for the Seventh Circuit reversed. The Seventh Circuit was motivated at least in part by what it perceived to be continuing violations of *Griffin* by the prosecutors within its jurisdiction. Although impermissible comment on a defendant's failure to take the stand is subject to a "harmless error" doctrine (see p. 1558), the Seventh Circuit declined to apply that doctrine, stating that its application "would impermissibly compromise the clear constitutional violation of the defendants' Fifth Amendment rights." The Court, per Burger, C.J., reversed:

"[W]e proceed on the assumption that, without so stating, the court was exercising its supervisory powers to discipline the prosecutors of its jurisdiction. * * * We hold that the [harmless error doctrine] may not be avoided by an assertion of supervisory power, simply to justify a reversal of these criminal convictions.

"[I]n the exercise of supervisory powers, federal courts may, within limits, formulate procedural rules not specifically required by the Constitution or the Congress. The purposes underlying use of the supervisory powers are threefold: to implement a remedy for violation of recognized rights; to preserve judicial integrity by ensuring that a conviction rests on appropriate considerations validly before the jury; and finally, as a remedy designed to deter illegal conduct.

"[These goals] are not, however, significant in the context of this case if, as the Court of Appeals plainly implied, the errors alleged are harmless. Supervisory power to reverse a conviction is not needed as a remedy when the error to which it is addressed is harmless since by definition, the conviction would have been obtained notwithstanding the asserted error. Further, in this context, the integrity of the process carries less weight, for it is the essence of the harmless error doctrine that a judgment may stand only when there is no 'reasonable possibility that the [practice] complained of might have contributed to the conviction.' Finally, deterrence is an inappropriate basis for reversal where, as here, the prosecutor's remark is at most an attenuated violation of *Griffin* and where means more narrowly tailored to deter objectionable prosecutorial conduct are available."[5]

Justice Brennan, joined by Marshall, J., concurred in part and dissented in part, observing:

"[Various cases] indicate that the policy considerations supporting the harmless error rule and those supporting the existence of an appellate court's supervisory powers are not in irreconcilable conflict. Both the harmless error rule and the exercise of supervisory powers advance the important judicial and public interest in the orderly and efficient administration of justice. [If] Government prosecutors have engaged in a pattern and practice of intentionally violating defendants' constitutional rights, a court of appeals certainly might be justified in reversing a conviction, even if the error at issue is harmless, in an effort to deter future violations. If effective as a deterrent, the reversal could avert further damage to judicial integrity. * * * Convictions are important, but they should not be protected at any cost."

NOTES AND QUESTIONS

1. Under the *Massiah* doctrine (p. 557), an indicted defendant has a Sixth Amendment right to counsel as well as his *Miranda* safeguards. Stressing that the "strict standard" governing waiver of counsel at trial should apply to an alleged waiver of the *Massiah* right to counsel as well, in *United States v. Mohabir*, 624 F.2d 1140 (2d Cir.1980), the court invoked its federal supervisory power to hold that a "valid waiver of the Sixth Amendment right to have counsel present during post-indictment interrogation must be preceded by a federal judicial officer's

---

5. Here, for example, the court could have dealt with the offending argument by directing the District Court to order the prosecutor to show cause why he should not be disciplined, or by asking the Department of Justice to initiate a disciplinary proceeding against him. The Government informs us that in the last three years, the Department of Justice's Office of Professional Responsibility has investigated 28 complaints of unethical conduct and that one assistant United States attorney resigned in the face of an investigation that he made improper arguments to a grand jury. The Court also could have publicly chastised the prosecutor by identifying him in its opinion.

explanation of the content and significance of this right." However, in *Patterson v. Illinois* (1988) (p. 746), the Supreme Court specifically rejected *Mohabir*'s holding that warnings in addition to the *Miranda* warnings are required to effectuate a waiver of the *Massiah* right (see fn. 8 in *Patterson*), without mentioning that *Mohabir* was an exercise of the Second Circuit's federal supervisory power.

2. The *Hasting* Court noted that, within limits, federal courts may exercise their "supervisory power [to] formulate procedural rules not specifically required by the Constitution or the Congress." After *Payner* and *Hasting, what* procedural rules? Consider Note 4, p. 805 and *United States v. Williams*, p. 1063 (exercise of federal supervisory power over grand juries). After *Payner* and *Hasting,* may the federal courts still *exclude evidence* or reverse a conviction based in part on inadmissible evidence if such exclusion or reversal is not required by the Constitution or the Congress? Cf. *Bank of Nova Scotia v. United States*, 487 U.S. 250 (1988) (Note 2, at p. 1076).

3. Why has the effort to impose "extraconstitutional" standards on federal law enforcement officials, best illustrated by *McNabb* and its progeny, fared so badly in recent decades? Consider Bennett Gershman, *The New Prosecutors*, 53 U.Pitt.L.Rev. 393, 432 (1992): "First, [the supervisory power] required judges to impose on government officials their own notions of 'good policy.' The judiciary has resisted this invitation. Second, supervisory power increasingly has been viewed as an unwarranted judicial intrusion into the exclusive domain of a coordinate branch of the government. Finally, once supervisory power became subservient to the harmless error rule, it became largely irrelevant."

SECTION 5.   TRENDS AND COUNTERTRENDS: THE "NEW FEDERALISM IN CRIMINAL PROCEDURE" AND NEW LIMITATIONS ON STATE RIGHTS PROTECTIONS[a]

When the Warren Court's "criminal procedure revolution" came to a halt, a number of state courts "greeted the Burger Court's retreat from activism not with submission, but with a stubborn independence that displays a determination to keep alive the Warren Court's philosophical commitment to protection of the criminal suspect." Donald E. Wilkes, *More on the New Federalism in Criminal Procedure,* 63 Ky.L.J. 873 (1975). The most influential article on the subject of state constitutional rights is Justice William Brennan's *State Constitutions and the Protection of Individual Rights,* 90 Harv.L.Rev. 489 (1977), one of the most frequently cited law review articles of modern times. See, too, Justice Brennan's updated views in *The Bill of Rights and the States: The Revival of State Constitutions as Guardians of Individual Rights,* 61 N.Y.U.L.Rev. 535 (1986). See also Hans Linde, *First Things First: Rediscovering the States' Bill of Rights,* 9 U.Balt.L.Rev. 379 (1980).

A state supreme court bent on providing the accused with greater protection than that said to be required by the federal constitution must be careful to make it clear that it is resting its ruling on an independent state ground. As the Court, per O'Connor, observed in MICHIGAN v. LONG, 463 U.S. 1032 (1983), "when the adequacy and independence of any possible state law ground is not clear from the face of the opinion, we will accept as the most reasonable explanation that the state court decided the case the way it did because it believed that federal law

---

a. The phrase "new federalism in criminal procedure" was coined by Professor Donald E. Wilkes, Jr., in his 1974 article, *The New Federalism in Criminal Procedure: State Court Evasion of the Burger Court*, 62 Ky.L.J. 421.

required it to do so." Thus, in order to insulate its decision from U.S. Supreme Court review, the state court, to quote *Long* again, must indicate "clearly and expressly" that its ruling is based on "separate, adequate and independent" state grounds.

Justice Brennan and Marshall, who often found themselves in a dissenting role in the 1970's, frequently pointed to—and approved and encouraged—the practice of some state courts (a distinct minority) to interpret state procedural rights more expansively than does the current U.S. Supreme Court. See especially Justice Brennan's dissenting opinion in *Michigan v. Mosley* (p. 635). Justice Brennan also forcefully stated his views on this matter in his 1977 law review article, supra, emphasizing that "the decisions of the [U.S. Supreme] Court are not, and should not be, dispositive of questions regarding rights guaranteed by counterpart provisions of state law. [A]lthough in the past it might have been safe for counsel to raise only federal constitutional issues in state courts, plainly it would be most unwise these days not also to raise the state constitutional questions."

Justice Brennan's advice has not gone unheeded. A dozen years after Brennan wrote his first article on state constitutional rights, Washington Supreme Court Justice Robert Utter, *State Constitutional Law, the United States Supreme Court, and Democratic Accountability,* 64 Wash.L.Rev. 19, 27 (1989), reported that "more than 450 published state court opinions [had interpreted] state constitutions as going beyond federal constitutional guarantees."

Consider CHARLES H. WHITEBREAD & CHRISTOPHER SLOBOGIN, Criminal Procedure § 34.02(c) (5th ed. 2008):

"State court reaction against the Supreme Court has been particularly energetic with respect to search and seizure, perhaps because the post–1970 Supreme Court has been especially antagonistic to the Fourth Amendment. Indeed, the first Supreme Court criminal procedure decision to encounter significant state court resistance involved a search and seizure issue. In *United States v. Robinson* [set forth at p. 343], the Supreme Court held that a full search is permissible after a lawful custodial arrest, regardless of the crime giving rise to the arrest. Within four years of *Robinson,* four different state courts had held, based on state constitutional language, that the nature of the offense is relevant to whether a full search is justified. Similarly, the courts of at least four states refused to follow *United States v. White* [set forth at p. 474], on state law grounds. [At] least three states' courts, again relying on their constitutions, have declined to adopt the Supreme Court's totality of the circumstances approach to the probable cause inquiry established in *Illinois v. Gates* [set forth at p. 295].ᵃ

" * * * A factor that could severely curtail the New Federalism, however, is the hostile reaction of state citizens to their courts' activism. Chief Justice Burger, for one, sought to encourage this reaction while he was on the Court. [He pointed out] that 'when state courts interpret state law to require more than the Federal Constitution requires, the citizens of the state must be aware that they have the power to amend state law to ensure rational law enforcement.' [In] at least two states [California and Florida] the electorate has exercised this power."ᵇ

---

a. In addition, a number of states have declined to adopt the Supreme Court's position in *United States v. Leon* (set forth at p. 229) (adopting a "good faith exception to the fourth amendment exclusionary rule and *Moran v. Burbine*) (set forth at p. 665) (police need not inform a custodial suspect that a lawyer retained by friends or relatives is trying to reach him).

b. See also Donald E. Wilkes, *The New Federalism in 1984: Death of the Phoenix?,* in DEVELOPMENTS IN STATE CONSTITUTIONAL LAW 166, 169 (B. McGraw ed. 1985).

SECTION 6. DUE PROCESS, INDIVIDUAL RIGHTS AND THE WAR ON TERRORISM: WHAT PROCESS IS CONSTITUTIONALLY DUE A CITIZEN WHO DISPUTES HIS ENEMY–COMBATANT DESIGNATION?

Consider HAMDI v. RUMSFELD, 542 U.S. 507 (2004), which arose as follows: Petitioner Yasar Hamdi is an American citizen who by 2001 resided in Afghanistan. In the immediate aftermath of the al Qaeda terrorist attacks of September 11, 2001, Congress passed a resolution authorizing the President to "use all necessary and appropriate force" against "nations, organizations or persons" that he determines "planned, authorized, committed or aided" in the September 11 attacks. Authorization for Use of Military Force (AUMF). A short time later, the President ordered the Armed Forces to subdue al Qaeda and oust the ruling Taliban regime. At a time when American forces were engaged in active combat, Hamdi was seized late in 2001 by a military group opposed to the Taliban government, and, according to a declaration by a Defense Department official, turned over to the U.S. military as a Taliban fighter been captured on the battlefield. He was initially taken to the American naval base at Guantanamo Bay, Cuba, but when it was learned that he was an American citizen, he was transferred to a naval brig in the United States. In detaining Hamdi, the government took the position that he was an "enemy combatant," who had fought against the United States and its allies, and that his enemy combatant status justifies the U.S. in holding him indefinitely without bringing any formal charges against him.

Hamdi's father filed a habeas petition, alleging, inter alia, that the Government was holding his son in violation of the fifth and fourteenth amendments. He also claimed that his son's detention was prohibited by the Non–Detention Act, 18 U.S.C. § 4001(a), which forbids any imprisonment or detention of an American citizen "except pursuant to an Act of Congress." According to Hamdi's father, less than two months before the September 11 attacks his son went to Afghanistan to do "relief work" and could not have received any military training. The Government responded with a declaration from a Defense Department official (the Mobbs declaration) asserting in conclusory terms that Hamdi was affiliated with a Taliban army unit during a time when the Taliban was fighting U.S. allies. The Government maintained that Hamdi's habeas corpus petition should be dimissed on the basis of the Dobbs declaration.

There was no opinion of the Court. The principal opinion was written by Justice O'Connor, joined by Chief Justice Rehnquist and Justices Kennedy and Breyer. Although she concluded that the initial detention of Hamdi was authorized by the AUMF, and that the Non–Detention Act was satisfied because Hamdi's detention was "pursuant to an Act of Congress"—the AUMF—Justice O'Connor rejected the government's argument that Hamdi could be held indefinitely, without formal charges or proceedings. Justice Souter, joined by Ginsburg, J., disagreed with the O'Connor plurality that if Hamdi's designation as an enemy combatant were correct, his detention, at least for some period of time, was authorized by the AUMF. According to Souter, not only was the detention of a citizen like Hamdi unauthorized by the AUMF, but it was forbidden by the Non–Detention Act. Therefore, maintained Justice Souter, Hamdi was entitled to immediate release. However, in order to "give practical effect" to the conclusions of eight Justices rejecting the government's position, he "join[ed] with the plurality in ordering remand on terms closest to those I would impose."

According to dissenting Justice Scalia, joined by Stevens, J., absent suspension of the writ of habeas corpus by Congress, an American citizen accused of waging war against his country could not be imprisoned indefinitely; he had to be prosecuted for treason or some other crime. The AUMF did not suspend the writ and, noted Justice Scalia, nobody claims that it did. Absent suspension of the writ by Congress, the Executive's assertion of military exigency is not sufficient to permit detention without charge. Dissenting Justice Thomas was the only member of the Court who believed Hamdi's habeas challenge should fail. He maintained that the Executive Branch had acted "with explicit congressional approval" and that Hamdi's detention "falls squarely within the Federal Government's war powers."

––––––

Two other war-on-terrorism cases decided the same day as *Hamdi* settled important questions involving the jurisdiction of the federal courts to review the detentions of suspected terrorists, but they did not resolve any substantive constitutional issues. RASUL v. BUSH, 542 U.S. 466 (2004), per Stevens, J., rejecting the government's reliance on a World War II precedent., ruled that U.S. courts have jurisdiction under the same habeas corpus statute involved in *Hamdi* to consider challenges to the legality of the detentions of foreign nationals captured abroad and imprisoned at a U.S. naval base at Guantanamo Bay, Cuba. Significantly, however, the Court left open the question of what substantive rights the detainees might assert. Cf. *United States v. Verdugo–Urquidez*, 494 U.S. 259 (1990) (fourth amendment does not apply to property detained by a nonresident alien and located in another century) (also discussed at p. 251 infra). Neither did *Rasul* make it wholly clear whether its opinion would apply to prisoners detained by the U.S. in foreign locations other than Guantanamo, on which the U.S. has a permanent lease. Justice Scalia, joined by Rehnquist, C.J., and Thomas, J., dissented, maintaining that the federal courts lacked statutory jurisdiction to review the Guantanamo detentions at all.

Rumsfeld v. Padilla, 542 U.S. 426 (2004), ruled only that an American citizen seized in the U.S. and held as an enemy combatant had brought his legal challenge in the wrong federal district court. If thus left open the question whether the "enemy combatant" designation would be applied to an American citizen who, unlike Hamdi, was apprehended in the U.S. and not on a foreign battlefield.

––––––

HAMDAN v. RUMSFELD, 548 U.S. 557 (2006), arose as follows: In November, 2001, while the United States was engaged in active combat with the Taliban, the President issued an order (the November 13 Order), which gave the Secretary of Defense the authority to appoint military commissions. Shortly after American forces invaded Afghanistan, militia forces captured Hamdan, a Yemini national, and turned him over to the Americans. Hamden was then transported to Guantanamo. In July of 2003, the President announced his determination that Hamdan was subject to the November 13 Order and thus triable by military commission. A year later, he was charged with having "conspired and agreed" with al Quaeda to commit offenses "triable by military commission," including "attacking civilians" and "terrorism."

Hamdan conceded that a court-martial constituted in accordance with the Uniform Code of Criminal Justice (UCMJ) would have authority to try him, but maintained that the military commission convened by the President did not. A federal district court granted habeas relief, but the U.S. Court of Appeals for the

District of Columbia Circuit (in an opinion joined by future Chief Justice Roberts)* reversed.

A 5–3 majority, per Stevens, J., held that, because its structure and procedures violated both the UCMJ and the Geneva Conventions, the military commission lacked power to proceed. Four Justices (the majority minus Justice Kennedy) also concluded that the conspiracy offense with which Hamdan had been charged "is not an 'offense that by [the] law of war may be tried by military commissions.' "[a]

In December, 2005, a month after the Supreme Court had granted certiorari to decide whether the military commission convened to try Hamdan had the authority to do so, Congress enacted the Detainee Treatment Act of 2005 (DTA), which provides that no court shall have jurisdiction to consider a habeas corpus application filed by a Guantanamo Bay detainee. However, the DTA did not shut out the courts completely, vesting in the U.S. Court of Appeals for the D.C. Circuit the "exclusive jurisdiction" to determine the validity of any final decision rendered pursuant to a military order implementing the November 13 Order. Review is of right for any alien sentenced to death or 10 years or more in prison, but is otherwise at the Court of Appeals' discretion. Review is limited to whether the final decision of the military commission was "consistent with the standards and procedures specified in the [aforementioned] military order" and "with the Constitution and laws of the United States."

On the basis of the DTA, the Government moved to dismiss the writ of certiorari, maintaining that the Act repealed federal jurisdiction, inter alia, over habeas actions "then pending in any federal court—including this Court." The Court concluded, however, that "ordinary principles of statutory construction suffice to rebut the Government's theory—at least insofar as this case, which was pending at the time the DTA was enacted is concerned."[b]

The Court then concluded that the military commission at issue was not authorized by any congressional Act: "Together, the UCMJ, the AUMF, and the DTA at most acknowledge a general Presidential authority to convene military commissions in circumstances where justified under the 'Constitution and laws,' including the law of war. Absent a more specific congressional authorization, the task of this Court is, as it was in *Quirin*, to decide whether Hamdan's military commission is so justified."

The Court then concluded that the UCMJ barred Hamdan's commission from proceeding: "The UCMJ conditions the President's use of military commissions on compliance with the rest of the UCMJ itself and with the 'rules and precepts of the law of nations, including the four Geneva conventions signed in 1949.' [But] the procedures that the Government has decreed will govern Hamdan's trial by commission violate these laws.[c] [At] a minimum, [a] military commission "can be 'regularly constituted' by the standards of our military justice system only if some practical need explains deviation from court-martial practice [and] no such need has been demonstrated here."

---

* The Chief Justice took no part in the consideration or decision of the Supreme Court case.

a. In dissent, Justice Thomas, joined by Justice Scalia, and in part by Justice Alito, concluded that Hamdan had been charged with a "violatio[n] of the law of war cognizable before a military commission."

b. Justice Scalia, joined by Justices Thomas and Alito, reached a contrary conclusion in his dissent.

c. Justice Thomas, joined in dissent by Justices Scalia and Alito, disagreed with the majority's conclusion that UCMJ Article 21 requires compliance with the Geneva Convention, and also concluded that the Convention does not create judicially enforceable rights of individuals. Justice Thomas and Scalia also concluded that, in any event, common Article 3 does not apply to the conflict with Al Qaeda.

Then, speaking at this point for four Justices (the majority minus Justice Kennedy), Justice Stevens concluded that because the rules governing Hamdan's commission dispense with the principles of international law (as set forth in Protocol 1 to the Geneva Convention) that "an accused must, absent disruptive conduct or consent, be present for his trial and must be privy to the evidence against him," they violate Common Article 3's standard—a "regularly constituted court *affording all the judicial guarantees which are recognized as indispensable by civilized peoples* (emphasis added)."

The Court, per Stevens, J., then concluded: "It bears emphasizing that Hamdan does not challenge, and we do not today address, the Government's power to detain him for the duration of active hostilities in order to prevent [great] harm. But in undertaking to try Hamdan and subject him to criminal punishment, the Executive is bound to comply with the Rule of Law that prevails in this jurisdiction."

BOUMEDIENE v. BUSH

553 U.S. 723, 128 S.Ct. 2229, 171 L.Ed.2d 41 (2008).

JUSTICE KENNEDY delivered the opinion of the Court.

[In prosecuting the War on Terrorism, the United States has apprehended a number of foreign nationals that it has subsequently designated as "enemy combatants" and detained at the United States Naval Station at Guantanamo Bay, Cuba (GTMO)]. In *Rasul v. Bush* [p. 41], the Court held that the then existing statutory scheme vested the United States district court in Washington, D.C., with statutory habeas corpus jurisdiction to review the lawfulness of the Guantanamo detainees' incarceration as enemy combatants. In response to *Rasul* and a subsequent decision, Congress enacted the Military Commissions Act of 2006 (MCA), which purported to strip all United States courts of habeas corpus jurisdiction over the Guantanamo detainees. As a substitute for habeas corpus— the traditional mechanism by which courts have ruled on the lawfulness of executive detentions of persons not convicted of crimes by civilian courts— Congress provided a limited form of review by the D.C. Circuit. Under the Detainee Treatment Act of 2005 (DTA), the D.C. Circuit could exercise review only after so-called Combatant Status Review Tribunals (CSRT's) had found detention to be warranted on the ground that the detainees were enemy combatants, with review limited to whether the CSRTs had acted in accordance with applicable law and procedures.

[Petitioners argue that the MCA's withdrawal of habeas corpus jurisdiction violated the Suspension Clause, Art. I, § 9, cl. 2, which provides that "The Privilege of the Writ of Habeas Corpus shall not be suspended, unless when in Cases of Rebellion or Invasion, the public Safety may require it," and thereby implicitly guarantees that the writ must be available unless Congress validly suspends it. In response, the Government did not argue that Congress had invoked its Art. I, § 9, cl. 2 power to suspend the writ on grounds of "Rebellion or Invasion," but contended instead that the Suspension Clause did not guarantee the availability of the writ to noncitizens held outside the United States and thus conferred no right on the petitioners. Even if the Clause did apply, the Government further argued, the withdrawal of habeas jurisdiction did not violate it, because the DTA provided enough judicial review to qualify as a constitutionally adequate substitute for habeas corpus.]

[P]rotection for the privilege of habeas corpus was one of the few safeguards of liberty specified in a Constitution that, at the outset, had no Bill of Rights. In the system conceived by the Framers the writ had a centrality that must inform proper interpretation of the Suspension Clause.

[The Court rejected the argument that the Suspension Clause affords petitioners no rights because the United States does not claim sovereignty over the place of detention.] The necessary implication of the argument is that by surrendering formal sovereignty over any unincorporated territory to a third party, while at the same time entering into a lease that grants total control over the territory back to the United States it would be possible for the political branches to govern without legal constraint.

Our basic charter cannot be contracted away like this. The Constitution grants Congress and the President the power to acquire, dispose of and govern territory, not the power to decide when and where its terms apply. * * * Abstaining from questions involving formal sovereignty and territorial governance is one thing. To hold the political branches have the power to switch the Constitution on or off at will is quite another. [If] the privilege of habeas corpus is to be denied to the detainees now before us, Congress must act in accordance with the requirements of the Suspension Clause. * * *

[The government relies heavily on *Johnson v. Eisentrager,* 339 U.S. 763 (1950), where habeas relief was sought by enemy aliens who had been convicted of violating the laws of war. They were incarcerated in Landsberg prison in Germany during the Allied Powers postwar occupation.] True, the court in *Eisentrager* denied access to the writ, [but] because the United States lacked both *de jure* sovereignty and plenary control over Landsberg Prison, it is far from clear that the *Eisentrager* Court used the term sovereignty only in the narrow technical sense and not to connote the degree of control the military asserted over the facility.

[It] is true that before today the Court has never held that non-citizens detained by our Government in territory over which another country maintains *de jure* sovereignty have any rights under our Constitution. But the cases before us lack any historical parallel. They involve individuals detained by executive order for the duration of a conflict that, if measured from September 11, 2001, to the present, is already among the longest wars in American history. The detainees, moreover, are held in a territory that, while technically not part of the United States, is under the complete and total control of our Government. Under these circumstances, the lack of precedent on point is no barrier to our holding. * * *

We do not endeavor to offer a comprehensive summary of the requisites for an adequate substitute for habeas corpus. We do consider it uncontroversial, however, that the privilege of habeas corpus entitles the prisoner to a meaningful opportunity to demonstrate that he is being held pursuant to 'the erroneous application or interpretation' of relevant law. And the habeas court must have the power to order the conditional release of an individual unlawfully detained— though release need not be the exclusive remedy and is not the appropriate one in every case in which the writ is granted.

[To] determine the necessary scope of habeas corpus review, * * * we must access the CSRT process, the mechanism through which petitioners' designation as enemy combatants became final. [The] most relevant [deficiency in the CSRTs] are the constraints upon the detainee's ability to rebut the factual basis for the Government's assertion that he is an enemy combatant. [The] detainee has limited means to find or present evidence to challenge the Government's case against him. He does not have the assistance of counsel and may not be aware of the most critical allegations that the Government relied upon to order his detention. The detainee can confront witnesses that testify during the CSRT proceedings. But given that there are in effect no limits on the admission of hearsay evidence [the] detainee's opportunity to question witnesses is likely to be more theoretical than real.

[Although] we make no judgment as to whether the CSRTs, as currently constituted, satisfy due process standards, we agree with petitioners that, even when all the parties involved in this process act with diligence and in good faith, there is considerable risk of error in the tribunal's findings of fact. [And] given that the consequence of error may be detention of persons for the duration of hostilities that may last a generation or more, this is a risk too significant to ignore.

[Accordingly,] for the writ of habeas corpus, or its substitute, to function as an effective and proper remedy in this context, the court that conducts the habeas proceeding must have the means to correct errors that occurred during the CSRT proceedings. This includes some authority to assess the sufficiency of the Government's evidence against the detainee. It also must have the authority to admit and consider relevant exculpatory evidence that was not introduced during the earlier proceeding.

[The] cases before us * * * do not involve detainees who have been held for a short period of time while awaiting their CSRT determinations. Were that the case, or were it probable that the Court of Appeals could complete a prompt review of their applications, the case for requiring temporary abstention or exhaustion of alternative remedies would be much stronger. [In] some of these cases [,however,] six years have elapsed without the judicial oversight that habeas corpus or an adequate substitution demands. And there has been no showing that the Executive faces such onerous burdens that it cannot respond to habeas corpus actions. To require these detainees to complete Detainee Treatment Act (DTA) review before proceeding with their habeas corpus actions would be to require additional months, if not years, of delay. The first DTA review applications were filed over a year ago, but no decisions on the merits have been issued. While some delay in fashioning new procedures is unavoidable, the costs of delay can no longer be borne by those who are held in custody. The detainees in these cases are entitled to a prompt habeas corpus hearing.

Our decision today holds only that the petitioners before us are entitled to seek the writ; that the DTA review procedures are an inadequate substitute for habeas corpus; and that the petitioners in these cases need not exhaust the review procedures in the Court of Appeals before proceeding with their habeas actions in the District Court. The only law we identify as unconstitutional is MCA § 7. [Accordingly,] both the DTA and the CSRT process remain intact. [The] CSRT process is the mechanism Congress and the President set up to deal with these issues. Except in cases of undue delay, federal courts should refrain from entertaining an enemy combatant's habeas corpus petition at least until after the Department, acting via the CSRT, has had a chance to review his status.

[The] laws and Constitution are designed to survive, and remain in force, in extraordinary times. Liberty and security can be reconciled; and in our system they are reconciled within the framework of the law. The Framers decided that habeas corpus, a right of first importance, must be a part of that framework, a part of that law. * * *

JUSTICE SOUTER, with whom JUSTICES GINSBURG and BREYER join, concurring.

[It] is in fact the very lapse of four years from the time *Rasul v. Bush* put everyone on notice that habeas process was available to GTMO prisoners, and the lapse of six years since some of these prisoners were captured and incarcerated, that stand at odds with the repeated suggestions of the dissenters that these cases should be seen as a judicial victory in a contest for power between the Court and the political branches. [After] six years of sustained executive detentions in

GTMO, subject to habeas jurisdiction but without any actual habeas scrutiny, today's decision is no judicial victory, but an act of perseverance in trying to make habeas review, and the obligation of the courts to provide it, mean something of value both to prisoners and to the Nation.

CHIEF JUSTICE ROBERTS, joined by SCALIA, THOMAS, AND ALITO, J.J., dissenting.

[The] majority is adamant that the GTMO detainees are entitled to the protections of habeas corpus—its opinion begins by deciding that question. [I] agree with Justice Scalia's analysis of our precedents and the pertinent history of the writ, and accordingly join his dissent. The important point for me, however, is that the Court should have resolved these cases on other grounds. Habeas is most fundamentally a procedural right, a mechanism for contesting the legality of executive detention. The critical threshold question in these cases, prior to any inquiry about the writ's scope, is whether the system the political branches designed protects whatever rights the detainees may possess. If so, there is no need for any additional process, whether called "habeas" or something else.

[The] majority's overreaching is particularly egregious given the weakness of its objections to the DTA. Simply put, the Court's opinion fails on its own terms. The majority strikes down the statute because it is not an "adequate substitute" for habeas review, but fails to show what rights the detainees have that cannot be vindicated by the DTA system.

Because the central purpose of habeas corpus is to test the legality of executive detention, the writ requires most fundamentally an Article III court able to hear the petitioner's claims and, when necessary, order release. [Beyond] that, the process a given prisoner is entitled to receive depends on the circumstances and the rights of the prisoner. [After] much hemming and hawing, the majority appears to concede that the DTA provides an Article III court competent to order release. The only issue in dispute is the process the GTMO prisoners are entitled to use to test the legality of their detention. *Hamdi* concluded that American citizens detained as enemy combatants are entitled to only limited process, and that much of that process could be supplied by a military tribunal, with review to follow in an Article III court. That is precisely the system we have here. It is adequate to vindicate whatever due process rights petitioners may have. * * *

Today's Court opines that the Suspension Clause guarantees prisoners such as the detainees "a meaningful opportunity to demonstrate that [they are] being held pursuant to the erroneous application or interpretation of relevant law." Further, the Court hold that to be an adequate substitute, any tribunal reviewing the detainee' cases 'must have the power to order the conditional release of an individual unlawfully detained.' The DTA system—CSRT review of the Executive's determination followed by D.C. Circuit review for sufficiency of the evidence and the constitutionality of the CSRT process—meets these criteria.

[For] all its eloquence about the detainees' right to the writ, the Court makes no effort to elaborate how exactly the remedy it prescribes will differ from the procedural protections detainees enjoy under the DTA. The Court objects to the detainees' limited access to witnesses and classified material, but proposes no alternatives of its own. Indeed, it simply ignores the many difficult questions its holding presents. What, for example, will become of the CSRT process? The majority says federal courts should *generally* refrain from entertaining detainee challenges until after the petitioner's CSRT proceeding has finished. [But] to what deference, if any, is that CSRT determination entitled?

There are other problems. Take witness availability. What makes the majority think witnesses will become magically available when the review procedure is labeled "habeas"? Will the location of most of these witnesses change?—will they suddenly become easily susceptible to service of process? * * * Speaking of witnesses, will detainees be able to call active-duty military officers as witnesses? If not, why not?

The majority has no answers for these difficulties. What it does say leaves open the distinct possibility that its "habeas" remedy will, when all is said and done, end up looking a great deal like the DTA review it rejects. * * *

So who has won? Not the detainees. The Court's analysis leaves them with only the prospect of further litigation to determine the content of their new habeas right, followed by further litigation to resolve their particular cases, followed by further litigation before the D. C. Circuit—where they could have started had they invoked the DTA procedure. Not Congress, whose attempt to 'determine—through democratic means—how best' to balance the security of the American people with the detainees liberty interests has been unceremoniously brushed aside. Not the Great Writ, whose majesty is hardly enhanced by its extension to a jurisdictionally quirky outpost, with no tangible benefit to anyone. Not the rule of law, unless by that is meant the rule of lawyers, who will now arguably have a greater role than military and intelligence officials in shaping policy for alien enemy combatants. And certainly not the American people, who today lose a bit more control over the conduct of this Nation's foreign policy to unelected, politically unaccountable judges.

JUSTICE SCALIA, with whom THE CHIEF JUSTICE, JUSTICE THOMAS, and JUSTICE ALITO join, dissenting.

[The] writ of habeas corpus does not, and never has, run in favor of aliens abroad; the Suspension Clause thus has no application, and the Court's intervention in this military matter is entirely *ultra vires*.

[The terrorist threat is grave, and the Court's opinion] will make the war harder on us. It will almost certainly cause more Americans to be killed. [At least 30 of the prisoners previously released from GTMO Bay have returned to the battlefield, and some have committed atrocities. And these] were detainees whom *the military* had concluded were not enemy combatants. Their return to the kill illustrates the incredible difficulty of assessing who is and who is not an enemy combatant in a foreign theater of operations where the environment does not lend itself to rigorous evidence collection. Astoundingly, the Court today raises the bar, requiring military officials to appear before civilian courts and defend their decisions under procedural and evidentiary rules that go beyond what Congress has specified.

[But] even when the military has evidence that it can bring forward, it is often foolhardy to release that evidence to the attorneys representing our enemies. [During] the 1995 prosecution of Omar Abdel Rahman, federal prosecutors gave the names of 200 unindicted co-conspirators to the "Blind Sheik's" defense lawyers; that information was in the hands of Osama Bin Laden within two weeks. In another case, trial testimony revealed to the enemy that the United States had been monitoring their cellular network, whereupon they promptly stopped using it, enabling more of them to evade capture and continue their atrocities.

[What] competence does the Court have to second-guess the judgment of Congress and the President on [the questions in issue with respect to the necessity and wisdom of the scheme that Congress created]? None whatever.

[The] Court admits that it cannot determine whether the writ historically extended to aliens held abroad, and it concedes (necessarily) that GTMO lies outside the sovereign territory of the United States. Together, these two concessions establish that it is (in the Court's view) perfectly ambiguous whether the common-law writ would have provided a remedy for these petitioners. If that is so, the Court has no basis to strike down the Military Commissions Act, and must leave undisturbed the considered judgment of the coequal branches.

[The Court relies on *Johnson v. Eisentrager*, 339 U.S. 763 (1950), from which it purports to derive a "functional" test for the extraterritorial reach of the writ, but its claim of support is falsified by the plain language of Justice Jackson's Court opinion]: "We are cited [to] no instance where a court, in this or any other country where the writ is known, has issued it on behalf of an alien enemy who, at no relevant time and in no stage of his captivity, has been within its territorial jurisdiction. Nothing in the text of the Constitution extends such a right, nor does anything in our statutes." [*Eisentrager*] mentioned practical concerns [only] to support *its holding* that the Constitution does not empower courts to issue writs of habeas corpus to aliens abroad *in any circumstances*.

[Putting] aside the conclusive precedent of *Eisentrager*, it is clear that the original understanding of the Suspension Clause was that habeas corpus was not available to aliens abroad. [The] Court finds it significant that there is no recorded case *denying* jurisdiction to such prisoners. [But] a case standing for the remarkable proposition that the writ could issue to a foreign land would surely have been reported, whereas a case denying such a writ for lack of jurisdiction would likely not. At a minimum, the absence of a reported case either way leaves unrefuted the voluminous commentary stating that habeas was confined to the dominions of the Crown.

Today [the Court] breaks a chain of precedent as old as the common law that prohibits judicial inquiry into detentions of aliens abroad absent a statutory authorization. And, most tragically, it sets our military commanders the impossible task of proving to a civilian court, under whatever standards the Court devises in the future, that evidence supports the confinement of each and every prisoner.

The Nation will live to regret what the Court has done today. * * *

Justice Breyer's Reflections on Supreme Court Cases Growing out of the "War on Terror"

In his recent book, *Making Our Democracy Work* (2010), Justice Stephen Breyer discusses four Supreme Court cases that grew out of the "War on Terror": *Rasul v. Bush* (2004), *Hamdi v. Rumsfeld* (2004), *Hamdan v. Rumsfeld* (2006), and *Boumediene v. Bush* (2008). He then suggests that the way in which the Court decided these cases may have contributed to their "widespread public acceptance" (id. at 212): "The Court sought to respect the roles of other government branches. It sought to recognize the practical security needs that underlie enemy combatant detention. * * * It decided the ultimate constitutional issue presented in *Boumediene* only after the Court had engaged in a dialogue with the other government branches through other case decisions over a period of several years."

For material on the retroactive effect of a holding of unconstitutionality and related matters, see Ch. 29, § 5, *infra*.

CHAPTER 3

SOME GENERAL REFLECTIONS ON CRIMINAL PROCEDURE AND ITS ADMINISTRATION

■ ■ ■

In the early 20th Century, civil rights abuses of African–Americans—brought to light in criminal prosecutions against them in the South—led the U.S. Supreme Court to assume a more active role in the regulation of the criminal justice system. This involvement in the rights of the accused reached its peak during the Warren Court era, especially in the 1960s. After the 1960s, the High Court's involvement in constitutional-criminal procedure reduced significantly. It is fair to say that neither Congress nor President Nixon (whose successful 1968 campaign included harsh criticism of *Miranda* and other famous Warren Court decisions) nor the four justices Nixon appointed to the Supreme Court (Burger, Blackmun, Rehnquist and Powell) were enamored of the Warren Court's "revolution" in American civil procedure. As both the Warren Court and post-Warren Court eras demonstrate, the law of criminal procedure has had to take into account the leading political issues of the day—from how to deal with racial injustice to how to deal with terrorism.

Finally, the dissenting and concurring opinions in the recent case of *Kansas v. Marsh*, pp. 57–61 infra, raise some old questions: How many "actually innocent" persons are convicted of capital offenses (or serious crimes generally)? Have we done everything possible to reduce the number of wrongful convictions to an insignificant minimum? How many convictions of the innocent are tolerable in a criminal justice system?

MICHAEL J. KLARMAN—THE RACIAL ORIGINS OF MODERN CRIMINAL PROCEDURE
99 Mich.L.Rev. 48, 52, 82–83, 93–94 (2000).

[*Moore v. Dempsey*, 261 U.S. 86 (1923), overturning a conviction obtained through a mob-dominated trial; the related cases of *Powell v. Alabama*, 287 U.S. 45 (1932) (holding that, under the circumstances of this capital case, due process required the appointed of counsel) and *Norris v. Alabama*, 294 U.S. 587 (1935) (reversing a conviction under the Equal Protection Clause where blacks had been intentionally excluded from the jury); and *Brown v. Mississippi*, 297 U.S. 278 (1936), marking the first time the Supreme Court overturned a state conviction based on coerced confessions] arose out of three quite similar episodes. Southern black defendants were charged with serious crimes against whites—either rape or murder. All three sets of defendants nearly were lynched before their cases could be brought to trial. * * * Lynchings were avoided only through the presence of state militiamen armed with machine guns surrounding the courthouse. There was a serious doubt—not just with the aid of historical hindsight, but at the time of the trial—as to whether any of the defendants were in fact guilty of the crime charged. * * * Trials took place quickly after the alleged crimes in order to avoid a lynching. [The] trials were completed within a matter of hours [and] the jurors, from which blacks were intentionally excluded * * *, deliberated for only a matter of minutes before imposing death sentences. * * *

It is impossible to measure the amount of physical coercion employed by southern sheriffs to extract confessions from black suspects, and thus one cannot say for sure what effect *Brown v. Mississippi* had on this practice. Supreme Court cases from the 1940s, however, make it clear that beating blacks into confessing remained a common practice in the South after *Brown*. For a variety of reasons, *Brown* had, at most, a limited impact on southern police practices. First, it must be recalled that the deputy sheriff who had administered the beatings in *Brown* made no effort to hide his behavior. The likeliest effect of the Supreme Court's decision, then, was to reduce the candor of state law enforcement officials. * * * Tortured confessions, if detected, might eventually be reversed by the Supreme Court or even by a state appellate court, but the vast majority of criminal cases never made it that far in the system. Thus, most convictions based on coerced confessions were unlikely to be overturned. Moreover, the narrow construction provided to federal civil rights statutes at this time made it very difficult to prosecute law enforcement officials who used physical violence against black suspects. Even in those unusual cases where a federal violation could be established, convincing all-white southern jurors to indict and convict law enforcement officials who had mistreated black defendants proved virtually impossible. * * *

[The rulings in *Moore, Powell, Norris* and *Brown*] support the claim made by several recent commentators that the Supreme Court's constitutional interventions tend to be less countermajoritarian than is commonly supposed. [The four rulings] almost certainly were consonant with dominant national opinion at the time. Even within the South, significant support existed for the results in these cases. [These] rulings only bound the southern states to abstract norms of behavior that they generally had embraced on their own. In the North, meanwhile, although blacks suffered oppressive discrimination in housing, employment, and public accommodations, the criminal justice system approached somewhat nearer to the ideal of colorblindness. Thus, it is erroneous to conceive of these landmark criminal procedure cases as instances of judicial protection of minority rights from majoritarian oppression. Rather, they better exemplify the paradigm of judicial imposition of a national consensus on resistant state outliers (with the qualification that even the southern states generally accepted these norms in the abstract).

Relatedly, these criminal procedure decisions raise the interesting possibility that during the interwar period the Supreme Court reflected national opinion on racial issues better than did Congress. These rulings imposed constitutional constraints on southern lynch law at almost precisely the same time that the national legislature was debating the imposition of statutory constraints on lynching. The House of Representatives approved anti-lynching bills three times, in 1922, 1937, and 1940. But these measures never survived in the Senate, mainly because that institution's antimajoritarian filibuster rules enabled intensely committed southern Senators (with the aid of some largely indifferent westerners) to block passage. Similarly, the House approved anti-poll tax bills five times in the 1940s, but they never passed the Senate, while the Supreme Court that same decade struck a momentous blow for black suffrage by invalidating the white primary.

YALE KAMISAR—THE WARREN COURT
AND CRIMINAL JUSTICE

Reprinted in The Warren Court: A Retrospective 116, 140–43 (B. Schwartz ed. 1996).

Did the Warren Court's Reform Effort Come at a Bad Time?
Could It Have Come at a Better Time?

In his lively book, *The Self–Inflicted Wound* (1970) (an account of the Warren Court's revolution in criminal procedure), former *New York Times* Supreme Court reporter Fred Graham observes: "History has played cruel jokes before, but few can compare with the coincidence in timing between the rise in crime, violence and racial tensions [and] the Supreme Court's campaign to strengthen the rights of criminal suspects against the state. [The] Court's reform effort could have come at almost any time in the recent past * * * [at a time] when it could have taken root before crime became the problem that it has become."

When was that? According to the media, the claims of law enforcement officials, and the statements of politicians, we have *always* been experiencing a "crime crisis"—*at no time* in our recent, or not-so-recent, past has there *been a time* when "society" *could afford* a strengthening or expansion of the rights of the accused.

In 1943, the Court held in *McNabb v. United States* [p. 554], in the exercise of its supervisory authority over the administration of federal criminal justice, that voluntary confessions should be excluded from evidence if they were obtained while the suspect was being held in violation of federal requirements that arrestees be promptly taken before a committing magistrate. The *McNabb* Court tried to do for the federal courts what, a quarter-century later, *Miranda* was designed to do for state, as well as federal, courts: bypass the frustrating "swearing contests" over the nature of the secret interrogation and reduce, if not eliminate, both police temptations and opportunity to coerce incriminating statements. The *McNabb* doctrine sought to do so by focusing on a relatively objective factor—the length of time a suspect was held by the police before being brought to a judicial officer to be advised of his rights.

Although it placed lesser restrictions on federal police than *Miranda* was to place on all police a quarter-century later, the *McNabb* rule was severely criticized by many law enforcement authorities and many members of Congress for barring the use of voluntary confessions. For example, in his testimony before a House subcommittee, the then head of the District of Columbia Police Department called *McNabb* "one of the greatest handicaps that has ever confronted law enforcement officers."

Police officials and politicians were not the only ones unhappy with the *McNabb* decision. Most of the judges of the lower federal courts "were unsympathetic, if not openly hostile, toward a rule which suppressed evidence not only relevant but also cogent and often crucial in order to effectuate what seemed to them to be an exaggerated concern for individual rights."[206]

A year after the *McNabb* decision, at a time when a bill to repudiate it was gathering much support, the Court took another look at the doctrine in the *Mitchell* case.[207] With one eye on Congress, and stung by strong criticism from the bench and bar, as well as from police and prosecutors, the Court backed off; it wrote an opinion that could be read as limiting *McNabb* to its particular facts.

---

206. Hogan & Snee, *The McNabb–Mallory Rule: Its Rise, Rationale and Rescue*, 47 Geo.L.J. 1, 5 (1958).

207. Mitchell v. United States, 321 U.S. 756 (1944).

[Although the Supreme Court reaffirmed the *McNabb* rule fourteen years later in *Mallory v. United States* (p. 555)], the storm of controversy over the rule never subsided. * * * More bills were introduced to repeal, or at least soften, the doctrine, and in 1968 a law was finally enacted that badly crippled it. [See p. 676.] (Because the *McNabb-Mallory* doctrine was a rule of evidence formulated in the exercise of the Court's supervisory authority over the administration of federal criminal justice, it was subject to repeal or revision by the Congress.)

The experience with the *McNabb-Mallory* rule is strong evidence that the 1940s and 1950s were hardly auspicious times for the Court to do what it was to do in *Miranda*—deem custodial interrogation by state police, as well as federal, "inherently coercive." Indeed, when, in the 1944 case of *Ashcraft v. Tennessee* [p. 548], a majority of the Court called *thirty-six hours of continuous relay interrogation* "inherently coercive," it evoked a powerful dissent by three Justices who severely criticized the majority for departing from the traditional "voluntariness" test.

In another coerced confession case, one decided in 1949 (*Watts v. Indiana*), concurring Justice Robert Jackson warned that our Bill of Rights, as interpreted by the Court up to that time, imposed "the maximum restrictions upon the power of organized society over the individual that are compatible with the maintenance of organized society itself"—good reason for not indulging in any further expansion of them.[a]

Were the 1950s a good time to impose the search-and-seizure exclusionary rule on the states? When the California Supreme Court adopted the exclusionary rule on its own initiative in 1955,[217] the cries of protest were almost deafening. Prominent law enforcement officials called the exclusionary rule "the 'Magna Carta' for the criminals" and "catastrophic as far as efficient law enforcement is concerned" and warned that it had "broken the very backbone of narcotics enforcement."

What of the 1930s? In 1935 [New York] Governor Herbert Lehman opened a conference on crime by warning: "There is no question that in recent years there has come a substantial increase in organized crime. The professional criminal has become bolder. * * * We must take steps to increase the certainty of punishment following crime. * * * We must have fewer legal technical loopholes in trials and appeals."

The New York gathering on crime was not a unique event in those troubled times. The U.S. attorney general also called a conference on crime, and similar conferences were held in various states.[220] The public was so alarmed by the apparent increase in crime that a U.S. Senate investigating committee, chaired by Royal Copeland of New York, scoured the country for information and advice that could lead to a national legislative solution. At these 1933 congressional hearings, witnesses attacked virtually every procedural safeguard found in the Bill of Rights.

Going back still further, in 1931 the famous criminologist Harry Elmer Barnes voiced fear that the repeal of prohibition would trigger "an avalanche of crime"—as thousands of crooks, chased out of the booze business, would return to their old rackets.[223] He warned that "the only effective check we can think of

---

a. Consider that this observation was made—and many agreed—more than a decade *before* such cases as *Gideon v. Wainwright* (p. 73), *Mapp v. Ohio* (p. 224) and *Miranda* (p. 571) were decided.

217. People v. Cahan, 282 P.2d 905 (Cal.1955).

220. See Wechsler, *A Caveat on Crime Control*, 27 J.Crim.L. & Criminology 629 (1937).

223. Barnes, *Battling the Crime Wave* 87–88 (1931).

[would] be to turn our cities over for the time being to the United States Army and Marines." Transferring the Marines from Central America to the streets of Chicago, added Barnes, "might not only promote the checking of the crime menace but also solve at one and the same time our diplomatic relations with Central America."

"Every generation supposes that its own problems are new, unknown to its forefathers."[226] To most of those who lived during that period, the 1930s (as usual) was *not* a time for strengthening the rights of the accused. Rather it seemed to be a period when (as usual) criminal procedure safeguards had already been stretched to the breaking point.

DONALD A. DRIPPS—CONSTITUTIONAL THEORY FOR CRIMINAL PROCEDURE: *DICKERSON, MIRANDA,* AND THE CONTINUING QUEST FOR BROAD-BUT-SHALLOW
43 Wm. & Mary L.Rev. 1, 45–46 (2001).

American legislatures consistently have failed to address defects in the criminal process, even when they rise to crisis-level proportions. For example, when the *Miranda* Court invited Congress and the states to experiment with alternatives to traditional backroom police interrogation, Congress responded by adopting Title II,[a] which stubbornly insisted on the traditional practice. To this day only two American jurisdictions, Alaska and Minnesota, require taping interrogations. In both instances the state courts, rather than the state legislature, were the sources of reform.

Legislatures across the United States have found billions of dollars for prisons, but the support for indigent defense is shamefully inadequate. No legislature has adopted reforms of police identification procedures, even though we have known since the 1930s that mistaken identification is the leading cause of false convictions. Legislatures have not filled the voids created by contemporary pro-government criminal procedure rulings. They have not, for instance, adopted statutory regulations of undercover operations, even though the Court has left such operations unregulated by the Fourth Amendment. They have not adopted statutory requirements for judicial warrants, or the preservation of exculpatory evidence, or plugged holes in the exclusionary rule, let alone delivered the effective tort remedy exclusionary rule critics have advocated for decades.

The record is not an accident, but the product of rational political incentives. Almost everyone has an interest in controlling crime. Only young men, disproportionately black, are at significant risk of erroneous prosecution for garden-variety felonies. Abuses of police search and seizure or interrogation powers rarely fall upon middle-aged, middle-class citizens. When powerful interest groups are subject to the exercise of police powers that pale in comparison to what is visited on young black men luckless enough to reside in a "high crime area," things are different. [But] so long as the vast bulk of police and prosecutorial power targets the relatively powerless (and when will that ever be otherwise?), criminal procedure rules that limit public power will come from the courts or they will come from nowhere.

PETER ARENELLA—FOREWORD: O. J. LESSONS
69 S.Cal.L.Rev. 1233, 1234–35 (1996).

Lawyers control adversarial trials. They decide what evidence to present and how to massage it into a story of guilt, innocence, or reasonable doubt. In such a

---

226. Sutherland, *Crime and Confession,* 79 Harv.L.Rev. 21, 32–33 (1965).

a. The relevant provision of Title II (which purported to "overrule" *Miranda* and reinstate the old due process-voluntariness test) is set forth at p. 676. The provision was struck down in *Dickerson v. United States* (2000), set forth at p. 677.

lawyer-dominated system, the trial's outcome may hinge on which side has the superior resources to pay for the best investigators, experts, and counsel. Money can have a greater impact on the verdict than the "facts" because it dictates how those "facts" are transformed into legally admissible and persuasive evidence.

This resource factor usually favors the state because most criminal defendants are poor. The prosecutor can use law enforcement agencies, state and private forensic laboratories, and experts on the public payroll to develop, shape, and present her evidence. Crime victims and witnesses usually cooperate with the prosecution. If they do not, the prosecutor can command their appearance before a grand jury and compel their testimony.

In contrast, a skilled and experienced public defender is lucky if she gets an investigator to spend a few hours investigating the "facts." Crime victims and civilian witnesses frequently refuse to answer the investigator's questions. If the public defender needs expert assistance, she must petition the court for funds to pay for the expert's time. The one or two state-funded experts she may obtain won't be [the caliber of O. J. Simpson's experts] and they will rarely spend hundreds of hours looking for flaws in the state's case.

This resource imbalance is particularly egregious in death penalty prosecutions. Given the horrific nature of these crimes, the defendant's life often depends on the defense's ability and capacity to make the client's humanity apparent to the jury deciding his fate at the sentencing phase of the trial.[4] Far too often, underpaid defense lawyers in capital cases spend less time and effort on death penalty cases than the Simpson defense team expended prepping for his preliminary hearing.

The "trial of the century" illustrated this resource imbalance problem in reverse. One of [O. J. Simpson's defense lawyer's] wisest decisions was to hire some of this country's leading medical, forensic, and legal experts before Simpson was even arrested. With the aid of [these experts], the defense's forensic attorney team * * * transformed incriminating hair, blood, DNA, and fiber data into evidence of police and criminalist incompetence and corruption. While defense counsel for the indigent can read the Simpson trial transcripts and learn new ways to attack forensic evidence, they lack the resources to buy the experts whose prestige and skills made the "garbage in-garbage out" strategy so effective.[a]

WILLIAM J. STUNTZ—THE UNEASY RELATIONSHIP BETWEEN CRIMINAL PROCEDURE AND CRIMINAL JUSTICE
107 Yale L.J. 1, 3–12, 72–76 (1997).

[The] criminal justice system is dominated by a trio of forces: crime rates, the definition of crime (which of course partly determines crime rates), and funding

---

4. This is no easy task. Explaining how one's client became a killer will not work unless the defendant's life story includes factors that trigger the jury's compassion. Constructing such a story requires extensive investigation into the offender's past, documentation of whatever factors "victimized" the offender at an early age, evidence of how the "system" failed to address these factors, and expert testimony explaining why these factors diminished the offender's capacity to control his anti-social impulses. Accounts of the offender's early victimizations may well fall on deaf ears unless the defense can also make some showing of why the offender is not beyond redemption.

a. See also Deborah L. Rhodes, *Simpson Sound Bites: What Is and Isn't News About Domestic Violence*, in Postmortem: The O. J. Simpson Case 83, 84 (Jeffrey Abramson ed. 1996). After observing that a single public defender often handles hundreds of cases per year and usually lacks adequate time or resources for investigation and expert testimony, Professor Rhode continues: "By contrast, in the Simpson case, [the] complete defense bill, including legal fees, may have reached $10 million. That figure exceeds what some states spend on appointed counsel for thousands of indigent defendants."

decisions—how much money to spend on police, prosecutors, defense attorneys, judges, and prisons. These forces determine the ratio of crimes to prosecutors and the ratio of prosecutions to public defenders, and those ratios in turn go far toward determining what the system does and how the system does it. But the law that defines what the criminal process looks like, the law that defines defendants' rights, is made by judges and Justices who have little information about crime rates and funding decisions, and whose incentives to take account of those factors may be perverse. High crime rates make it easy for prosecutors to substitute cases without strong procedural claims for cases with such claims. Underfunding of criminal defense counsel limits the number of procedural claims that can be pressed. Both phenomena make criminal procedure doctrines seem inexpensive to the appellate judges who define those doctrines. Unsurprisingly, given that regulating the criminal justice system has seemed cheap, the courts have done a lot of regulating—more, one suspects, than they would have done in a world where defendants could afford to litigate more often and more aggressively, or where prosecutors could not so easily substitute some cases for others. Criminal procedure is thus distorted by forces its authors probably do not understand.

The distortion runs both ways. As courts have raised the cost of criminal investigation and prosecution, legislatures have sought out devices to reduce those costs. Severe limits on defense funding are the most obvious example, but not the only one. Expanded criminal liability makes it easier for the government to induce guilty pleas, as do high mandatory sentences that serve as useful threats against recalcitrant defendants. And guilty pleas avoid most of the potentially costly requirements that criminal procedure imposes. These strategies would no doubt be politically attractive anyway, but the law of criminal procedure makes them more so. Predictably, underfunding, overcriminalization, and oversentencing have increased as criminal procedure has expanded.

Nor are the law's perverse effects limited to courts and legislatures. Constitutional criminal procedure raises the cost of prosecuting wealthier defendants by giving those defendants more issues to litigate. The result, at the margin, is to steer prosecutors away from such defendants and toward poorer ones. By giving defendants other, cheaper claims to raise, constitutional criminal procedure also raises the cost to defense counsel of investigating and litigating factual claims, claims that bear directly on their clients' innocence or guilt. The result is to steer defense counsel, again at the margin, away from those sorts of claims and toward constitutional issues. More Fourth, Fifth, and Sixth Amendment claims probably mean fewer self-defense claims and mens rea arguments. This turns the standard conservative criticism of the law of criminal procedure on its head. Ever since the 1960s, the right has argued that criminal procedure frees too many of the guilty. The better criticism may be that it helps to imprison too many of the innocent.

* * * In a world where trivial crimes stay on the books, or one where routine traffic offenses count as crimes, the requirement of probable cause to arrest may mean almost nothing. Officers can arrest for a minor offense—everyone violates the traffic rules—in order to search or question a suspect on a major one.[6] This allows arrests and searches of suspected drug dealers without any ex ante support for the suspicion, the very thing the probable cause standard is supposed to forbid. In a world where sodomy laws remain valid long after their enforcement has ceased, prosecutors can induce guilty pleas in some problematic sexual assault

---

6. See *Whren v. United States* (1996) [p. 353] (holding that police can detain motorists where there is a probable cause to believe that they have violated traffic laws, regardless of whether the stop is pretextual).

cases—the need to prove nonconsent disappears, and with it (again, in some cases) the ability to mount a plausible defense. This amounts to convicting defendants of sexual assault without proving the crime, by pointing to another crime that serves as the excuse for punishment, but not the reason.

[Legislatures] fund the system. Legislatures decide how many police officers, prosecutors, and judges to have, and how much to pay them. They also decide how generously to fund criminal defense counsel in those cases (the majority) in which the court appoints counsel. * * *

Over the course of the past couple of decades, legislatures have exercised this funding power to expand substantially the resources devoted to law enforcement, though the budget increases appear less substantial in light of parallel increases in crime. * * * [N]otwithstanding nominal budget increases, spending on indigent defendants in constant dollars per case appears to have declined significantly between the late 1970s and the early 1990s. The predictable result is public defenders' offices with very large ratios of cases to lawyers.

[There] are a great many constitutional rules, most of which are highly contestable. The rules are produced by a court system that acts quite independently of legislative preference, at least in this area. (*Mapp v. Ohio* and *Miranda v. Arizona* were hardly examples of majoritarian lawmaking.) Perhaps more so than anywhere else in constitutional law, in criminal procedure the broad exercise of judicial power tends to be justified precisely by legislators' unwillingness to protect constitutional interests. Yet these judge-made rules are enforced through the efforts of criminal defense counsel who, in most cases, are paid by the state—the same state whose preferences the rules purport to trump. By buying less criminal defense, the state can buy less enforcement of constitutional criminal procedure. It can, to some degree, trump the trump. Of course, if it does so it necessarily also buys less of whatever else criminal defense counsel do. * * *

* * * Constitutional law has focused relentlessly on the sorts of issues that are susceptible to legal analysis—how to select juries, when to require warrants, which mistrials permit retrial and which ones mean the defendant must go free. These are classic lawyers' issues; they give rise to classic lawyers' arguments. But courts' decisions on those issues are embedded in a system shaped by more open-ended—and more flagrantly political—judgments: How bad should something be before we call it a crime? How much money should we spend on criminal defense? Perhaps courts would do a sufficiently poor job of making these open-ended political judgments that we are better off leaving them to other actors. That is the system's current premise, and the premise is entirely plausible. But if that premise is right, those other actors—chiefly legislators and prosecutors—are able to defeat courts' work on courts' own turf: All those judge-made procedural rules are likely not to work the way they are supposed to. In the criminal justice system's three-legged stool—procedure, substance, and money—procedure is the least stable leg, the one that most depends on the others for support.

So criminal procedure may be no more than an instance of courts properly recognizing the need to intervene in a system that imposes terrible costs on large numbers of people, and then doing what comes naturally, regulating the kinds of things courts are used to regulating. That includes avoiding a kind of decision-making that, for courts, seems unnatural. All of which might be fine if the judicially regulated sphere could be isolated from the rest of the system. Sadly, it cannot. * * *

[The law of criminal procedure prevents some serious wrongs and produces other benefits, some of which are quite familiar.] Yet there are substantial tradeoffs, and the tradeoffs are not so familiar. The criminal process is much harder to control than courts suppose; it is driven by forces the courts do not, and perhaps cannot, direct. When courts do act, their actions are shaped by those forces in ways the courts themselves may not understand, ways that are at best ambiguous and at worst bad. Some part of what the Fourth, Fifth, and Sixth Amendments protect has probably come at the cost of a criminal justice system that is less focused on the merits and hence more likely to convict innocents, a system that disproportionately targets the poor, and a system that convicts for "crimes" that cover vastly more than anyone would wish to punish. The merits of this bargain are at least open to question. * * *

[For] the past thirty-five years, the legal system's discussion of criminal defendants' rights has suffered from an air of unreality, a sense that all goals can be satisfied and all values honored—that we can, for example, have the jury selection process we want at no cost to anything else we might want. * * *

That should change. It is time to acknowledge the tradeoffs, to take seriously the nature of the system the law of criminal procedure regulates and the ways in which that system can evade or undermine the regulation. In a regime like ours, countermajoritarian restraints on the criminal process can succeed only at a cost, the cost is probably substantial, and it is disproportionately imposed on those who least deserve to bear it. Leaving more of the process to majoritarian institutions might be better, not least for some of the defendants the process is designed to protect.

That need not mean leaving defendants to the mercies of state legislatures and local prosecutors. If constitutional law's response to criminal justice has failed, it has failed not just from too much intervention but from too little as well. Making *Gideon* a formal right only, without any ancillary funding requirements, has produced a criminal process that is, for poor defendants, a scandal. Courts' reluctance to police legislatures' criminalization and sentencing decisions—coupled with the way those legislative decisions can be used in a system that gives prosecutors blanket authority to choose whom to go after and for what—has produced its own scandals. Defendants' interests might best be protected by less procedure, coupled with a much more activist judicial posture toward funding, the definition of crime, and sentencing—all areas where judges have been loath to take dramatic stands.

This judicial reticence seems to have been motivated by a desire not to trench on the prerogatives of the politicians, a desire to stick to the more law-like and presumably less contentious ground of process. That the 1960s produced a revolution in criminal *procedure* may testify to the underrated conservatism of Warren Court constitutional thought, to that radical Court's willingness to confine its intervention to conventional categories. If so, in this area these conservative instincts may have been misplaced—as, perhaps, was the Court's reformist (procedural) zeal. The system might be better off today had Warren and his colleagues worried less about criminal procedure, and more about criminal justice.[a]

JUSTICE DAVID H. SOUTER—DISSENTING
IN KANSAS v. MARSH[b]
548 U.S. 163, 126 S.Ct. 2516, 2541, 165 L.Ed.2d 429, 460 (2006).

[The question presented was whether a Kansas statute requiring a jury to impose the death penalty if it found beyond a reasonable doubt that one or more aggravating circumstances (as defined by statute) existed and was "not out-

---

a. For more recent commentary by Professor Stuntz on these issues, see William J. Stuntz, *The Collapse of American Criminal Justice* (2011).

b. Stevens, Ginsburg and Breyer, JJ., joined Justice Souter's dissenting opinion.

weighed by any mitigating circumstances [found] to exist" satisfied the Eighth Amendment. The state supreme court had construed the provision to require imposition of the death penalty "in the event of equipoise," i.e., if the jury determined that the balance of any aggravating and mitigating circumstances "weighed equal." Given this construction, the state court struck down the law on the ground that the Eighth Amendment requires that "a tie" go to the defendant "when life or death is at issue." A 5–4 majority of the Supreme Court, per Thomas, J., disagreed.]

[Justice Souter, joined by Stevens, Ginsburg, and Breyer, JJ., dissented. Extracts from Souter's dissenting opinion appear immediately below. Justice Scalia, who joined the opinion of the Court, also wrote separately in response to Justice Souter's concerns about the risks inherent in capital punishment. Extracts from Scalia's concurring opinion appear immediately after Souter's dissent.]

* * * Today a new body of fact must be accounted for in deciding what, in practical terms, the Eighth Amendment guarantees should tolerate, for the period starting in 1989 has seen repeated exonerations of convicts under death sentences, in numbers never imagined before the development of DNA tests.

[A] few numbers from a growing literature will give a sense of reality that must be addressed. When the Governor of Illinois imposed a moratorium on executions in 2000, 13 prisoners under death sentences had been released since 1977 after a number of them were shown to be innocent. During the same period, 12 condemned convicts had been executed. Subsequently the Governor determined that 4 more death row inmates were innocent. Illinois had thus wrongly convicted and condemned even more capital defendants than it had executed, but it may well not have been otherwise unique; one recent study reports that between 1989 and 2003, 74 American prisoners condemned to death were exonerated, Gross, et al., *Exonerations in the United States 1989 Through 2003*, 95 J.Crim.L & C. 523, 531 (2006) (hereinafter Gross), many of them cleared by DNA evidence.[3] Another report states that "more than 110" death row prisoners have been released since 1973 upon findings that they were innocent of the crimes charged, and "[h]undreds of additional wrongful convictions in potentially capital cases have been documented over the past century." Lanier & Acker, *Capital Punishment, the Moratorium Movement, and Empirical Questions*, 10 Psychology, Public Policy & Law 577, 593 (2004). Most of these wrongful convictions and sentences resulted from eyewitness misidentification, false confession, and (most frequently) perjury, Gross, and the total shows that among all prosecutions homicide cases suffer an unusually high incidence of false conviction, probably owing to the combined difficulty of investigating without help from the victim, intense pressure to get convictions in homicide cases, and the corresponding incentive for the guilty to frame the innocent.[a]

We are thus in a period of new empirical argument about how "death is different": not only would these false verdicts defy correction after the fatal moment, the Illinois experience shows them to be remarkable in number, and they are probably disproportionately high in capital cases. While it is far too soon for

---

3. The authors state the criteria for their study: "As we use the term, 'exoneration' is an official act declaring a defendant not guilty of a crime for which he or she had previously been convicted. [The] authors exclude from their list of exonerations" any case in which a dismissal or an acquittal appears to have been based on a decision that while the defendant was not guilty of the charges in the original conviction, he did play a role in the crime and may be guilty of some lesser crime that is based on the same conduct. For our purposes, a defendant who is acquitted of murder on retrial, but convicted of involuntary manslaughter, has not been exonerated. We have also excluded any case in which a dismissal was entered in the absence of strong evidence of factual innocence * * *.

a. See also the extract from Professor Leo's book at p. 737 infra.

any generalization about the soundness of capital sentencing across the country, the cautionary lesson of recent experience addresses the tie-breaking potential of the Kansas statute: the same risks of falsity that infect proof of guilt raises questions about sentences, when the circumstances of the crime are aggravating factors and bear on predictions of future dangerousness.

In the face of evidence of the hazards of capital prosecution, maintaining a sentencing system mandating death when the sentencer finds the evidence pro and con to be in equipoise is obtuse by any moral or social measure. And unless application of the Eighth Amendment no longer calls for reasoned moral judgment in substance as well as form, the Kansas law is unconstitutional.

JUSTICE ANTONIN SCALIA—CONCURRING IN KANSAS v. MARSH
548 U.S. 163, 126 S.Ct. 2516, 2529, 165 L.Ed.2d 429, 447 (2006).

* * * There exists in some parts of the world sanctimonious criticism of America's death penalty, as somehow unworthy of a civilized society. (I say sanctimonious, because most of the countries to which these finger-waggers belong had the death penalty themselves until recently—and indeed, many of them would still have it if the democratic will prevailed.[3]) It is a certainty that the opinion of a near-majority of the United States Supreme Court to the effect that our system condemns many innocent defendants to death will be trumpeted abroad as vindication of these criticisms. For that reason, I take the trouble to point out that the dissenting opinion has nothing substantial to support it.

It should be noted at the outset that the dissent does not discuss a single case—not one—in which it is clear that a person was executed for a crime he did not commit. If such an event had occurred in recent years, we would not have to hunt for it; the innocent's name would be shouted from the rooftops by the abolition lobby. The dissent makes much of the new-found capacity of DNA testing to establish innocence. But in every case of an executed defendant of which I am aware, that technology has *confirmed* guilt. * * *

Instead of identifying and discussing any particular case or cases of mistaken execution, the dissent simply cites a handful of studies that bemoan the alleged prevalence of wrongful death sentences. One study (by Lanier and Acker) is quoted by the dissent as claiming that 'more than 110' death row prisoners have been released since 1973 upon findings that they were innocent of the crimes charged, and 'hundreds of additional wrongful convictions in potentially capital cases have been documented over the past century.' " [For] the second point, [Lanier and Acker] cite only a 1987 article by Bedau and Radelet. See *Miscarriages of Justice in Potentially Capital Cases*, 40 Stan.L.Rev. 21. [This] 1987 article has been highly influential in the abolitionist world. Hundreds of academic articles, including those relied on by today's dissent, have cited it. [The] article therefore warrants some further observations.

[The 1987 article's] conclusions are unverified. And if the support for its most significant conclusion—the execution of 23 innocents in the twentieth century—is any indication of its accuracy, neither it, nor any study so careless as to rely upon it, is worthy of credence. The only execution of an innocent man it alleges to have occurred after the restoration of the death penalty in 1976—the Florida execution

---

3. It is commonly recognized that "[m]any European countries [abolished] the death penalty in spite of public opinion rather than because of it." Bibas, *Transparency and Participation in Criminal Procedure*, 81 N.Y.U.L.Rev. 911, 931–932 (2006). Abolishing the death penalty has been made a condition of joining the Council of Europe, which is in turn a condition of obtaining the economic benefits of joining the European Union. * * *

of James Adam in 1984—is the easiest case to verify. [Justice Scalia then discusses the impressive evidence of Adams' guilt, evidence which the article failed to mention.]

[As for other cases of execution of alleged innocents,] the authors of the 1987 study later acknowledged, "We agree with our critics that we have not 'proved' these executed defendants to be innocent; we never claimed that we had." [One] would have hoped that this disclaimer of the study's most striking conclusion, if not the study's dubious methodology, would have prevented it from being cited as authority in the pages of the United States Reports. But alas, it is too late for that. Although today's dissent relies on the study only indirectly, the two dissenters who were on the Court in January 1993 have already embraced it. "One impressive study," they noted (referring to the 1987 study), "has concluded that 23 innocent people have been executed in the United States in this century, including one as recently as 1984." *Herrera v. Collins*, 506 U.S. 390 (1993) (Blackmun, J., joined by Stevens and Souter, JJ., dissenting).

Remarkably avoiding any claim of erroneous executions, the dissent focuses on the large numbers of *non*-executed "exonerees" paraded by various professors. It speaks as though exoneration came about through the operation of some outside force to correct the mistakes of our legal system, rather than *as a consequence of the functioning of our legal system*. Reversal of an erroneous conviction on appeal or on habeas, or the pardoning of an innocent condemnee through executive clemency, demonstrates not the failure of the system but its success. Those devices are part and parcel of the multiple assurances that are applied before a death sentence is carried out.

Of course even in identifying exonerees, the dissent is willing to accept anybody's say-so. It engages in no critical review, but merely parrots articles or reports that support its attack on the American criminal justice system. [The] dissent claims that [the Illinois] Report identifies 13 inmates released from death row after they were determined to be innocent. To take one of these cases, discussed by the dissent as an example of a judgment "as close to innocence as any judgments courts normally render," the defendant was twice convicted of murder. [The state supreme court overturned his conviction] because it found that the evidence was insufficient to establish guilt beyond a reasonable doubt. The court explained:

> "[A] not guilty verdict expresses no view as to a defendant's innocence. Rather, [a reversal of conviction] indicates simply that the prosecution has failed to meet its burden of proof."

This case alone suffices to refute the dissent's claim that the Illinois Report distinguishes between "exoneration of a convict because of actual innocence, and reversal of a judgment because of legal error affecting conviction or sentence but not inconsistent with guilt in fact." The broader point, however, is that it is utterly impossible to regard "exoneration"—however casually defined—as a failure of the capital justice system, rather than as a vindication of its effectiveness in releasing not only defendants who are innocent, but those whose guilt has not been established beyond a reasonable doubt.

Another of the dissent's leading authorities on exoneration of the innocent is Gross, et al., *Exonerations in the United States 1989 Through 2003*, 95 Crim.L. & C. 523 (2006). [Among] the article's list of 74 "exonerees" is a school principal who earned three death sentences for slaying one of his teachers and her two young children. [His] retrial for triple murder was barred on double jeopardy grounds because of prosecutorial misconduct during the first trial. [But he] had the gall to sue, under 42 U.S.C. § 1983, for false imprisonment. The Court of Appeals for the Third Circuit affirmed the jury verdict for the defendants, observing along the way that "our confidence in Smith's convictions is not diminished in the least. We remain firmly convinced of the integrity of those guilty verdicts."

[The] Gross article hardly stands alone; mischaracterization of reversible error as actual innocence is endemic in abolitionist rhetoric, and other prominent catalogues of "innocence" in the death-penalty context suffer from the same defect. * * *

Of course, even with its distorted concept of what constitutes "exoneration," the claims of the Gross article are fairly modest: Between 1989 and 2003, the authors identify 340 "exonerations" *nationwide*—not just for capital cases, mind you, nor even just for murder convictions, but for various felonies. Gross 520. Joshua Marquis, a district attorney in Oregon, recently responded to this article as follows:

> "[L]et's give the professor the benefit of the doubt: let's assume that he understated the number of innocents by roughly a factor of 10, that instead of 340 there were 4,000 people in prison who weren't involved in the crime in any way. During that same 15 years, there were more than 15 million felony convictions across the country. That would make the error rate .027 percent— or, to put it another way, a success rate of 99.973 percent." *The Innocent and the Shammed*, N.Y. Times, Jan. 26, 2006, p. A23.[a]

[Since] 1976 there have been approximately a half million murders in the United States. In that time, 7,000 murderers have been sentenced to death; about 950 of them have been executed; and about 3,700 inmates are currently on death row. See Marquis, *The Myth of Innocence*, 95 J.Crim.L. & C. 501, 518 (2006). As a consequence of the sensitivity of the criminal justice system to the due-process rights of defendants sentenced to death, almost two-thirds of all death sentences are overturned. "Virtually none" of these reversals, however, are attributable to a defendant's "actual innocence." Most are based on legal errors that have little or nothing to do with guilt. The studies cited by the dissent demonstrate nothing more. * * *

Like other human institutions, courts and juries are not perfect. One cannot have a system of criminal punishment without accepting the possibility that someone will be punished mistakenly. That is a truism, not a revelation. But with regard to the punishment of death in the current American system, that possibility has been reduced to an insignificant minimum. * * *

BRANDON L. GARRETT—CONVICTING THE INNOCENT
Pp. 5–12; 262–64 (2011).

Since DNA testing became available in the late 1980s, more than 250 innocent people have been exonerated by postconviction DNA testing.

Who were these innocent people? The first 250 DNA exonerees were convicted chiefly of rape, in 68% of the cases (171), with 9% convicted of murder (22), 21% of both murder and rape (52) and 2% convicted of other crimes like robbery (5). Seventeen were sentenced to death. Eighty were sentenced to life in prison. They served an average of thirteen years in prison. These people were typically in their twenties when they were convicted. Twenty-four were juveniles. All but four were male. At least eighteen were mentally disabled. Far more DNA exonerees were minorities (70%) than is typical among the already racially skewed populations of rape and murder convictions. Of the 250 exonerees, 155 were black, 20 Latino, 74 white and 1 Asian.

---

a. *Cf.* the extract from Professor Rosenthal's article at p. 738 infra. But see Professor Samuel Gross's response to Justice Scalia, 105 *Michigan Law Review First Impression*, 67 (2006).

DNA testing did more–it also identified the guilty. In 45% of the 250 postconviction DNA exonerations (112 cases), the test results identified the culprit. This most often occurred through a "cold hit" or a match in growing law enforcement DNA data banks. The damage caused by these wrongful convictions extends far beyond the suffering of the innocent. Dozens of criminals continued to commit rapes and murders for years until DNA testing identified them.

Before the invention of DNA testing, the problem of convicting the innocent remained largely out of sight. Many doubted that a wrongful conviction could ever occur. Justice Sandra Day O'Connor touted how "our society has a high degree of confidence in its criminal trials, in no small part because the Constitution offers unparalleled protections against convicting the innocent." Judge Learned Hand famously called "the ghost of the innocent man convicted" an "unreal dream." Prosecutors have from time to time claimed infallibility, announcing, "Innocent men are never convicted."

[When] I analyzed the trial records, I found that the exonerees' cases were not idiosyncratic. The same problems occurred again and again. * * * [Almost all of the] exonerees who falsely confessed had contaminated confessions statements [i.e., had disclosed specific details about the crime known only to the real killer or rapist, details that must have been improperly disclosed to them, most likely by the police].

* * * [C]elebrated constitutional rights, such as the requirement that jurors find guilty beyond a reasonable doubt and that indigent defendants receive lawyers, provide crucial bulwarks against miscarriages of justice. But those rights and a welter of others the Court has recognized, like the *Miranda* warnings, the exclusionary rule, and the right to confront witnesses, are procedural rules that the State must follow to prevent a conviction from being overturned. Few rules, however, regulate accuracy rather than procedures. Such matters are typically committed to the discretion of the trial judge. * * *

Why did victims and other eyewitnesses testify that they were certain that they saw innocent people commit crimes?

* * * I expected eyewitnesses to have been confident by the time of the trial. I never expected to find that in most of these cases, eyewitnesses admitted at trial that earlier they were not so certain and that police had used unreliable and suggestive procedures. * * * Once again, criminal procedure offered little guidance; the Supreme Court decades ago adopted a very flexible "reliability" standard that allows police to use highly suggestive procedures. * * *

Why did informants testify against innocent people? * * * Informants played an unsavory supporting role in 21% of these trials. Most were jailhouse informants, and they did not just lie, as I expected. Instead, they did something more pernicious–they claimed to have overheard telling details about the crime. * * *

Why didn't appeals or habeas corpus review set innocent people free? * * * One might expect that judges would look for serious mistakes like the ones in these exonerees' cases. However, judges only reluctantly review the evidence after a conviction. After all, most constitutional rights relate to procedure and not accuracy. Most exonerees did not try to challenge flawed trial evidence, and when they did they almost always failed. Judges typically refused to grant a new trial, and some were so sure that these people were guilty that they called the evidence of guilt "overwhelming."

Why did it take so long for innocent people to be exonerated? * * * Most of the exonerees fought for years to obtain access to DNA testing and exoneration. The word *exoneration* refers to an official decision to reverse a conviction based on new evidence of innocence. An exoneration occurs if the judge, after hearing the new evidence of innocence, vacates the conviction and there is no retrial, or there is an acquittal at a new trial, or if a governor grants a pardon. The 250 exonerees spent an average of thirteen years in prison. It took longer, an average of fifteen years, for them to be exonerated. Judges and prosecutors sometimes opposed requests for DNA testing. Judges sometimes initially refused to exonerate these people even after DNA tests provided powerful proof of their innocence. * * *

* * * These 250 exonerees are just the tip of the iceberg. The submerged bulk of that iceberg lurks ominously out of view. The most crucial question about these exonerations cannot be answered. We do not know and we cannot know how many other innocent people languish in our prisons. They remain invisible. One of the most haunting features of these exonerations is that so many were discovered by chance. Most convicts who seek postconviction DNA testing cannot get it. Some jurisdictions still deny convicts access to DNA testing that could prove innocence. In our fragmented criminal justice system, exonerations hinge on cooperation of local police, prosecutors, and judges. * * *

Some hardened souls will remain untroubled by DNA exonerations. For example, Justice Scalia has suggested that known wrongful convictions are an inconsequential percentage, an error rate of ".027 percent—or, to put it another way, a success rate of 99.973 percent," if one divides exonerations by the fifteen million felony convictions during the same time period.[82] But should we really be so reassured by the numbers?

If you eat at a fine restaurant and complain of a large bug in your soup, you are not reassured if the waiter tells you, "Don't worry, it will not happen again too often. There have only been a few hundred reported cases of bugs in soup in the United States. While human error is inevitable, with millions of bowls of soup served every year, we have an unparalleled sanitary soup rate." The waiter adds, before turning away with a flourish, "Because we found the bug in your soup, the system worked."

You had better ask to talk to the manager. The restaurant did not find that bug—you did. The system did not work. What system was there? * * *

DNA testing is done chiefly in rape cases, and rape convictions that result in prison sentences make up less than 2% of felony convictions. However, the right comparison group for DNA exonerees is even smaller. Exonerees were almost all convicted of rapes involving a stranger-perpetrator, in which there was a real question about who committed the crime. They received long sentences; on average they served thirteen years before DNA exonerated them. There is no good data on rape convictions in the 1980s. We do know that only a quarter of rape prosecutions involve stranger-perpetrators, and rape convicts overwhelmingly pleaded guilty and received much shorter prison sentences than these exonerees did. So the right control group for the exonerees would be stranger-rape cases from the 1980s in which the defendant took his case to trial. The number of these cases is much, much lower than the fifteen million total felonies cited by Justice Scalia, most likely in the low tens of thousands, making the number of exonerations quite troubling.[a]

---

82. *Kansas v. Marsh*, 548 U.S. 163, 194–195 (2006) (Scalia, J., concurring). Much of the thrust of his opinion, however, concerns a separate topic, the degree of error in our system of capital punishment, which he argued has been "reduced to an insignificant minimum," or at least that the public is comfortable with the risks of error that exist. * * * This book does not squarely address such debates, as I do not examine any set of capital convictions. However, * * * seventeen DNA exonerees had been sentenced to death, some multiple times, before their exoneration. For a discussion of the debate between Souter and Scalia, see Samuel R. Gross, "Souter Passant, Scalia Rampant: Combat in the Marsh," 105 *Michigan Law Review First Impression* 67 (2006).

a. Is there a due process right to technology that might establish one's innocence? See *District Attorney's Office v. Osborne*, p. 33 supra.

TRACEY MACLIN—"BLACK AND BLUE ENCOUNTERS"—SOME PRELIMINARY THOUGHTS ABOUT FOURTH AMENDMENT SEIZURES: SHOULD RACE MATTER?[a]

26 Valparaiso U.L.Rev. 243, 250, 252–61, 265–70 (1991).

* * * I submit that the dynamics surrounding an encounter between a police officer and a black male are quite different from those that surround an encounter between an officer and the so-called average, reasonable person. My tentative proposal is that the Court should disregard the notion that there is an average, hypothetical, reasonable person out there by which to judge the constitutionality of police encounters. When assessing the coercive nature of an encounter, the Court should consider the race of the person confronted by the police, and how that person's race might have influenced his attitude toward the encounter.

* * * [The] Supreme Court has said over and over that *all citizens*—not just rich, white men from the suburbs—are free to ignore a police officer who accosts them. In *Florida v. Royer* [p. 425], Justice White explained that: "The person approached ... need not answer any question put to him; indeed, he may decline to listen to the questions at all and may go on his way. He may not be detained even momentarily without reasonable, objective grounds for doing so; and his refusal to listen or answer does not, without more, furnish those grounds."[43]

This is what the law is supposed to be; black men, however, know that a different "law" exists on the street. Black men know they are liable to be stopped at anytime, and that when they question the authority of the police, the response from the cops is often swift and violent. This applies to black men of all economic strata, regardless of their level of education, and whatever their job status or place in the community.

* * * Black males learn at an early age that confrontations with the police should be avoided; black teenagers are advised never to challenge a police officer, even when the officer is wrong. Even if a police officer has arguable grounds for stopping a black male, such an encounter often engenders distinct feelings for the black man. Those feelings are fear of possible violence or humiliation.

To be sure, when whites are stopped by the police, they too feel uneasy and often experience fear. [But] I wonder whether the average white person worries that an otherwise routine police encounter may lead to a violent confrontation. When they are stopped by the police, do whites contemplate the possibility that they will be physically abused for questioning why an officer has stopped them? White teenagers who walk the streets or hang-out in the local mall, do they worry about being strip-searched by the police? Does the average white person ever see himself experiencing what Rodney King or Don Jackson went through during their encounters with the police?

---

a.   See also RANDALL L. KENNEDY, RACE, CRIME AND THE LAW 158–60 (1997). Elizabeth A. Gaynes, *The Urban Criminal Justice System: Where Young + Black + Male = Probable Cause*, 20 Ford.Urb.L.J. 621 (1993); David A. Harris, *Factors for Reasonable Suspicion: When Black and Poor Means Stopped and Frisked*, 69 Ind.L.J. 659 (1994); David A. Harris, *Driving While Black and All Other Traffic Offenses: The Supreme Court and Pretextual Traffic Stops*, 87 J.Crim.L. & C. 554 (1997); Sheri Lynn Johnson, *Race and the Decision to Detain a Suspect*, 93 Yale L.J. 214 (1983); Sheri Lynn Johnson, *Unconscious Racism and the Criminal Law*, 73 Cornell L.Rev. 1016 (1988); Randall Kennedy, *The State, Criminal Law, and Racial Discrimination: A Comment*, 107 Harv.L.Rev. 1255 (1994); *Developments in the Law—Race and the Criminal Process*, 101 Harv. L.Rev. 1472 (1988).

43.   Florida v. Royer [p. 425], (1983) (plurality opinion) * * *.

Police officers have shown [that] they will not hesitate to "teach a lesson" to any black male who, even in the slightest way challenges his authority. For example, in Los Angeles, even before [the Rodney King beating], blacks knew not to argue with the police unless they wanted to risk death in a police choke-hold that seemed to be applied more frequently in the case of black males than other citizens.[56]

In addition to fear, distrust is another component that swirls around encounters between black males and the police. Over the years, black males have learned that police officers have little regard for their Fourth Amendment rights. Two years ago in Boston, for instance, a city learned what can happen when a police department is encouraged to ignore the constitutional rights of a targeted class of individuals—black males. In the aftermath of a tragic shooting of a white couple and the declaration of a "war" against teenage gangs and their associates, black males were subjected to what one state judge called "martial law"[57] tactics by a police department that offered no apologies for its disregard of constitutional liberties.[58] * * *

* * * [B]eing black constitutes a "double-brand" in the mind of the police. Black men are associated with "crimes against the person, with bodily harm to police officers, and with a general lack of support for the police."[67] Also, because of their race, black males "are bound to appear discordant to policemen in most of the environment of a middle-class white society. For this reason, black males doubly draw the attention of police officers."[68] In essence, the police officer "identif[ies] the black man with danger."[69]

From the perspective of the black man, however, these police attitudes only reinforce the view that " '[t]he police system is a dictatorship toward the black people.' "[70] * * * Black men are considered suspicious and targeted for questioning not because of any objective or empirical evidence that they are involved in criminality, but because of police bias and societal indifference to the plight of black males who are on the receiving-end of aggressive police tactics. In effect, black men are accorded "sub-citizen" status for Fourth Amendment purposes.

* * * Currently, the Court assesses the coercive nature of a police encounter by considering the *totality of the circumstances* surrounding the confrontation. All I want the Court to do is to consider the role race might play, along with the other factors it considers, when judging the constitutionality of the encounter. * * *[a]

---

56. See City of Los Angeles v. Lyons, 461 U.S. 95, 116 n. 3 (1983) (Marshall, J., dissenting) ("'[S]ince 1975 no less than sixteen persons have died following use of a chokehold by an LAPD police officer. Twelve have been Negro males. [Thus] in a city where Negro males constitute nine per cent of the population, they have accounted for seventy-five per cent of the deaths resulting from the use of chokehold."). * * *

57. Commonwealth v. Phillips and Woody, No. 080275-6, Memorandum and Order, at 3 (Suffolk Sup.Ct. Sept. 17, 1989) (Judge Cortland Mathers found that a police order that all known gang members and their associates would be searched on sight was "a proclamation of martial law in Roxbury for a narrow class of people, young blacks, suspected of membership in a gang or perceived by the police to be in the company of someone thought to be a member."). * * *

58. Boston Police Deputy Superintendent William Celester had been quoted as saying: " 'People are going to say we're violating their [gang members'] constitutional rights, but we're not too concerned about that.... If we have to violate their rights, if that's what it takes, then that's what we're going to do." * * *

67. D. Bagley & H. Mendelsohn, *Minorities and the Police* 107 (1969).

68. Id.

69. J. Skolnick, *Justice Without Trial* 49 (1966).

70. B. Blauner, *Black Lives, White Lives* 110 (1989).

a. Twenty years after Professor Maclin wrote his article on "Black and Blue Encounters," a black college student who had been stopped and frisked by New York City police officers at least five times maintained that young black men continue (to use Maclin's words) to be "accorded

SHARON L. DAVIES—PROFILING TERROR

1 Ohio St.J.Crim.L. 45, 46–48, 51–53, 85, 99–100 (2003).

Following the attack on the World Trade Center on September 11, 2001, the nation's debate over racial profiling turned an abrupt corner. [The] public's view of racial profiling lurched from dramatically against the practice to decidedly in its favor. * * *

Even as it became apparent that ethnicity figured most heavily into the government's post–9/11 investigation than it first cared to admit, one popular reaction was: so what? After all, nineteen of the 9/11 suicide hijackers were nationals of Middle Eastern states. Didn't simple common sense mandate that government investigators of the events factor the shared ethnicity of additional suspects into their decisions of whom to question, detain, arrest or search? Post 9/11 polls showed that many believed the answer was yes. * * *

This Article rejects the suggestion that Arab or Middle Eastern heritage provides an appropriate basis of suspicion of individuals in the aftermath of the September 11 attacks. In a nation that claims upwards of 3.5 million persons of Arab ancestry, the ethnic characteristic of Arab descent, standing alone, possesses no useful predictive power for separating the September 11 terrorists' accomplices and other terrorist wannabees from innocent Americans.[a] It is a variable that is incapable of sufficiently narrowing what I call the "circle of suspicion" to warrant the kind of reliance pro-profiling arguments would place upon it. * * *

[Even] were we to assume that Middle Eastern origin had some value for distinguishing terrorists from non-terrorists, that ethnic fact would have no value for distinguishing between law-abiding and non-law-abiding persons of Middle Eastern descent. Put slightly differently, even if it had some minimal value for excluding certain people from the "circle of suspicion" (a point that this Article

---

'sub-citizen' status for Fourth Amendment purposes." See Nicholas K. Peart, *Why Is the N.Y.P.D. After Me?*, N.Y. Times, Dec. 18, 2011 (Sunday Review, p. 6).

    a. See also Frank H. Wu, *Profiling in the Wake of September 11: The Precedent of the Japanese American Internment*, Criminal Justice, Summer 2002, pp. 52, 58: "Most Arab Americans are not Muslim; most Muslims in the United States are South Asian or African American; and the post-September 11 backlash of violence has revealed our collective carelessness in assaulting Indian Sikhs—neither Arab nor Muslim but persons who look like they might be Arab or Muslim because of skin color, accents, and dress. * * *

    "[It] may well be that respective probabilities that a random older, white, Protestant American woman and the probability that a younger, Arab Muslim immigrant male are wrongdoers are not the same. But even were there a thousand sleeper agents of Arab descent or Muslim faith, ready to rise up in arms against democracy, they would constitute far less than a fraction of one-tenth of 1 percent of the Arab and Muslim populations of the United States. It is worth disputing whether the disparity in the chances are great enough to offset the tremendous cost to not just Arab Americans and Muslims but all of us is we relinquish our principle of individualism and presumption of innocence."

    Consider, too, David A. Harris, *Racial Profiling Revisited: "Just Common Sense" in the Fight Against Terrorism?*, Criminal Justice, Summer 2002, pp. 36, 40–41: "[If] we are to avoid attacks in the future by al-Qaeda operatives based on our own soil, we need to do much better in the intelligence arena than we did before September 11. And that, of course, means we will have to get information from those likely to know the Arab, Muslim, and Middle Eastern men we might suspect. This information is going to have to come not from the population at large, but from the Middle Eastern communities themselves; there is simply no avoiding this. It stands to reason, then, that what we need most right now are good, solid relations with the Arab and Muslim communities in the United States. Profiling that focuses on Arab and Muslim heritage will effectively communicate to these very same communities that we regard all their members not as our partners in law enforcement and terror prevention, but just the opposite: as potential terrorists. * * * [It] is not hard to imagine the result: alienation and anger toward the authorities at a time when we can least afford it." See also DAVID A. HARRIS, GOOD COPS 1–12 (2005).

contests), it would have no value for moving individual Middle Easterners inside that circle * * *.

A public convinced of its vulnerability might well be willing to endure greater police intrusions in exchange for greater security, even in the absence of hard evidence that the privacy-impairing measures it contemplates will actually deliver that security. But surely public acceptance cannot by itself supply the justification for a law enforcement policy that subscribes to racially-biased policing. The public "consented" to the forced relocation of over 100,000 persons of Japanese ancestry during World War II, but no thoughtful scholar today would defend the government's internment decisions on the basis of that consensus.

[Some have concluded that the Department of Justice's campaign to interview thousands of Middle Eastern men after 9/11] was *not* profiling "to the extent that the agents [were] pursuing case-specific information about the September 11 attacks, albeit in a dragnet fashion." This suggests that whenever an investigative effort derives in some (even remote) sense from an actual crime in which specific information about the racial or ethnic identity of the perpetrator (or perpetrators) is available, it will not technically be profiling, even if the police "dragnet" entire communities of persons with the same racial or ethnic characteristic in an effort to nab those responsible.[207]

Yet this argument surely excuses too much. [This] type of over-reliance on racial and ethnic information is extremely unlikely in a diverse society to yield those responsible for crimes. Even where such racial information is logically relevant to a criminal investigation, its value is largely limited to excluding groups of individuals from the circle of suspicion rather than moving any particular individual possessing that racial or ethnic characteristic inside that circle. Once we lose sight of this point, the door to using racial and ethnic information is opened far too wide: the police officer who has arrested a Latino male for involvement in a drug conspiracy can use this as a reason to stop other Latinos anywhere and everywhere.[b]

A NOTE ON THE JUSTICE DEPARTMENT'S POLICY GUIDANCE REGARDING RACIAL PROFILING

The Justice Department's June 2003 *Policy Guidance Regarding Racial Profiling* condemns racial profiling because it "sends the dehumanizing message to our citizens that they are judged by the color of their skin and harms the criminal justice system by eviscerating the trust that is necessary if law enforcement is to effectively protect our communities." The Justice Department guidelines point out that "even in the national security context, reliance upon generalized stereotypes is restricted by the Constitution." "Of course," adds a Justice Department release, "federal law enforcement officers may continue to rely upon

---

207. It is sheer fiction that the bulk of the ethnic focus of the government's post–9/11 investigation has been designed to bring to justice the perpetrators of the horrendous events of that single day. The plain focus of the government's ongoing law enforcement efforts is to investigate and prevent *future*, not past, terrorist conduct, and the question for legal thinkers is how far can it go in doing that, and down what sorts of paths?

b. Reasonable people can differ about "national-origin" or "ethnic" or "racial" profiling in the wake of the September 11 attacks—and a goodly number have. For other thoughtful views on this subject, see e.g., Sherry Colb, *Profiling With Apologies*, 1 Ohio St.J.Crim.L. (2004); Samuel R. Gross & Debra Livingston, *Racial Profiling Under Attack*, 102 Colum.L.Rev. 1413 (2002); William Stuntz, *Local Policing After the Terror*, 111 Yale L.J. 2137 (2002); Stuart Taylor Jr., *Politically Incorrect Profiling: A Matter of Life or Death*, National Journal, March 3, 2001, p. 3406.

specific descriptions of the physical appearance of criminal suspects, if a specific description exists in that particular case." One of the guidelines points out that when, as they often do, "federal officers have specific information [to] 'be on the lookout' for specific individuals identified at least in part by race or ethnicity, [the] officer is not acting based on a generalized assumption about persons of different races; rather, the officer is helping locate specific individuals previously identified as involved in crime."

Consider Jonathan Glater, *New Profile Policy: Is Less Really Less?*, N.Y. Times, June 2, 2003, § 4, p. 2: "The policy is the Bush administration's effort to deal with a controversial subject, racial profiling, in a way that earns points with members of minorities but that does not restrict the government's options in the battle against terrorism. But relying as it does on the difference between suspect descriptions (which it approves) and race-based profiles (which it doesn't), the policy restrictions on profiling may have little impact." After quoting a law professor, who comments that "the distinction falls apart very easily" because "most areas of law enforcement do not fall neatly into either [category]," the *Times* article continues: "The use of a suspect's description can have the same effect as racial profiling, either because the description is too broad or because the police use it to stop too many people."[a]

ACCORDING TO A VERA INSTITUTE STUDY, POST-9/11 LAW ENFORCEMENT POLICIES HAVE CAUSED DEEP FEARS AND DISTRUST AMONG ARAB-AMERICANS

The concerns of Sharon Davies, David Harris, Frank Wu and other commentators about the harm being done to the relationship between Arab–Americans and law-enforcement by post–9/11 enforcement tactics appear to be confirmed by a national study released in June, 2006.

According to the two-year study conducted by the Vera Institute of Justice, in the aftermath of September 11, Arab–Americans have a greater fear of racial profiling and immigration enforcement than of falling victim to hate crimes. Moreover, post–9/11 measures threaten destroy decades of work by police departments to build trust in Arab–American communities. See Andrea Elliot, *After 9/11, Arab–Americans Fear Police Acts, Study Finds*, N.Y. Times, June 12, 2006, p. A15. About 100 Arab–Americans and more than 100 law enforcement personnel (both police officers and FBI agents) took part in the study, which was conducted from 2003–05. (Approximately two-thirds of Arab–Americans are Christians.) The study was paid for by the National Institute of Justice, a research agency of the Justice Department.

New York Times reporter Elliot summed up the study's findings as follows: "Arab–Americans reported an increasing sense of victimization, suspicion of government and law enforcement, and concerns about protecting their civil liberties." Post 9/11 law enforcement tactics "have sown the deepest fear among Arab–Americans, including unease about the USA Patriot Act, voluntary interviews of thousands of Arab–Americans by federal agents, and an initiative known as Special Registration, in which more than 80,000 immigrant men were fingerprinted, photographed and questioned by authorities."

---

a. See *Brown v. City of Oneonta*, 221 F.3d 329 (2d Cir. 2000).

CHAPTER 4

THE RIGHT TO COUNSEL

■ ■ ■

"Of all the rights that an accused person has, the right to be represented by counsel is by far the most pervasive, for it affects his ability to assert any other rights he may have. [Procedural rules] are designed for those who know [them], and they can become a source of entrapment for those who do not. Substantive criminal law also presents difficulties to the uninitiated."

—Justice Walter V. Schaefer of the Supreme Court of Illinois, *Federalism and State Criminal Procedure*, 70 Harv.L.Rev. 1, 8 (1956).

"Ours is an adversarial system of justice—it requires lawyers on both sides who effectively represent their client's interests, whether it's the government or the accused. When defense counsel are handicapped by lack of training, time, and resources—or when they're just not there when they should be—we rightfully begin to doubt the process and we start to question the results. We start to wonder: Is justice being done? Is justice being served?"

—Eric Holder, U.S. Att'y Gen., Remarks at the Brennan Legacy Awards Dinner, Brennan Center for Justice (Nov. 17, 2009)

———

The right to counsel is relatively simple for the defendant who has the money to pay for an attorney. But what about the many defendants—indeed, the majority of defendants—who do not? Justice Black once said that "[t]here can be no equal justice where the kind of trial a man gets depends on the amount of money he has." *Griffin v. Illinois*, 351 U.S. 12 (1956). But how far does this principle carry?

Does it apply to misdemeanor cases as well as felony cases? Does it apply to appeals as well as trials? Should we provide indigent defendants with counsel all the way up to, and including, the U.S. Supreme Court? Should a probationer or parolee at a revocation hearing be provided with counsel? What about an indigent parent facing the loss of custody of her child in a parental status termination proceeding? For those individuals who are provided counsel, when are they entitled to counsels' assistance? Are they entitled to counsel of their own choosing? And what if they do not want to be represented by counsel? Under what circumstances can a defendant waive the right to counsel?

These questions and others are addressed in this chapter.

SECTION 1. THE RIGHT TO APPOINTED COUNSEL AND RELATED PROBLEMS

A. THE RIGHT TO APPOINTED COUNSEL IN CRIMINAL PROCEEDINGS

INTRODUCTION

A look at early English law reveals that the right to counsel had "surprisingly modest beginnings." James Tomkovicz, *The Right to the Assistance of Counsel* 1 (2002). Originally only those accused of minor offenses could be represented by counsel. (Evidently the monarch believed that permitting representation by defense counsel generally would prevent the successful prosecution of serious cases.) However, against a background of a decade of false treason charges against the Whigs, the Treason Act of 1695 provided that those prosecuted for high treason should be allowed to defend themselves by "counsel learned in the law." Thus, at the time of the adoption of the U.S. Constitution, England recognized a right to *retain* counsel to argue matters of fact only for those accused of misdemeanors or high treason.[a]

From the earliest times, the general practice in serious criminal cases in the American colonies was self-representation, not representation by counsel. But by the time the nation was about to ratify the Constitution, most states had granted criminal defendants the right to be represented by a lawyer. No state, however, guaranteed the right to *appointed* counsel. As Professor Tomkovicz has observed, "[i]t seems highly probable that the Sixth Amendment was designed to grant a legal representative of one's own choosing [thereby rejecting the restricted British approach], but no right to have counsel provided by the government."

One hundred and fifty-one years after the ratification of the Sixth Amendment and some sixty years after the adoption of the Fourteenth, the Supreme Court handed down its first significant opinion concerning the right to counsel— *Powell v. Alabama*, 287 U.S. 45 (1932). Although the *Powell* opinion contains sweeping, much-quoted language (such as "the right to be heard would be in many cases of little avail if it did not comprehend the right to be heard by counsel") the Court dwelt on the special circumstances—"above all that [the defendants] stood in peril of their lives." In a case *such as this* the Court told us, "the failure of the trial court to give [the defendants] reasonable time and opportunity to secure counsel was a clear denial of due process." *And in a case with these facts*, "the right to have counsel appointed [is] *a logical corollary of the constitutional right to be heard by counsel*." (Emphasis added.)

Powell, of course, was a state case. Six years later, in *Johnson v. Zerbst*, 304 U.S. 458 (1938), the Court held, without discussing the likely intent of the Sixth Amendment, that the Amendment guaranteed indigent *federal* defendants (at least all felony defendants) a right to *appointed* counsel. But it would take another twenty-five years before the Court would conclude that the Constitution guaranteed *state* defendants the same unqualified right.

---

a. At some point in the development of the right to counsel in England, retained counsel could appear on behalf of a felony defendant to argue, but only to argue, matters of law. "When it came to presenting evidence and arguing as to the strength of the evidence, the felony defendant was on his own." CRIMPROC § 1.5(b). However, the distinction between matters of fact and matters of law was hazy and by the middle of the nineteenth century "questions of law" seem to have been extended to include both direct examination and cross-examination. See id.

BETTS v. BRADY

316 U.S. 455, 62 S.Ct. 1252, 86 L.Ed. 1595 (1942).

JUSTICE ROBERTS delivered the opinion of the Court.

Petitioner, an indigent, was indicted for robbery. His request for counsel was denied because local practice permitted appointment only in rape and murder prosecutions. Petitioner then pled not guilty and elected to be tried without a jury. At the trial he chose not to take the stand. He was convicted and sentenced to eight years imprisonment.

[The] due process clause of the Fourteenth Amendment does not incorporate, as such, the specific guarantees found in the Sixth Amendment although a denial by a state of rights or privileges specifically embodied in that and others of the first eight amendments may, in certain circumstances, [deprive] a litigant of due process of law in violation of the Fourteenth. [Due process] formulates a concept less rigid and more fluid than those envisaged in other specific and particular provisions of the Bill of Rights. Its application is less a matter of rule. Asserted denial is to be tested by an appraisal of the totality of facts in a given case.

[Petitioner] says the rule to be deduced from our former decisions is that, in every case, whatever the circumstances, one charged with crime, who is unable to obtain counsel, must be furnished counsel by the state. Expressions in the opinions of this court lend color to the argument, but, as the petitioner admits, none of our decisions squarely adjudicates the question now presented.

In *Powell v. Alabama,* 287 U.S. 45 [1932], ignorant and friendless negro youths, strangers in the community, without friends or means to obtain counsel, were hurried to trial for a capital offense without effective appointment of counsel on whom the burden of preparation and trial would rest, and without adequate opportunity to consult even the counsel casually appointed to represent them. [This] court held the resulting convictions were without due process of law. It said that, in the light of all the facts, the failure of the trial court to afford the defendants reasonable time and opportunity to secure counsel was a clear denial of due process. The court stated further that "under the circumstances [the] necessity of counsel was so vital and imperative that the failure of the trial court to make an effective appointment of counsel was likewise a denial of due process," but added: "whether this would be so in other criminal prosecutions, or under other circumstances, we need not determine. All that it is necessary now to decide, as we do decide, is that in a capital case, where the defendant is unable to employ counsel, and is incapable adequately of making his own defense because of ignorance, feeblemindedness, illiteracy, or the like, it is the duty of the court, whether requested or not, to assign counsel for him as a necessary requisite of due process of law."

[We] have construed the [Sixth Amendment] to require appointment of counsel in all [federal] cases where a defendant is unable to procure the services of an attorney, and where the right has not been intentionally and competently waived. [*Johnson v. Zerbst,* 304 U.S. 458 (1938)].[b] Though [the] amendment lays

---

b. In holding that the Sixth Amendment required appointment of counsel, the Court, per Black, J., had reasoned: "The Sixth Amendment stands as a constant admonition that if the constitutional safeguards it provides be lost, justice will not 'still be done.' Cf. *Palko.* It embodies a realistic recognition of the obvious truth that the average defendant does not have the professional legal skill to protect himself when brought before a tribunal with power to take his life or liberty, wherein the prosecution is presented by experienced and learned counsel. [The] Sixth Amendment withholds from federal courts, in all criminal proceedings, the power and authority to deprive an accused of his life or liberty unless he has or waives the assistance of counsel."

down no rule for the conduct of the states, the question recurs whether the constraint laid by the amendment upon the national courts expresses a rule so fundamental and essential to a fair trial, and so, to due process of law, that it is made obligatory upon the states by the Fourteenth Amendment. Relevant data on the subject are afforded by constitutional and statutory provisions subsisting in the colonies and the states prior to the inclusion of the Bill of Rights in the national Constitution, and in the constitutional, legislative, and judicial history of the states to the present date.

[I]n the great majority of the states, it has been the considered judgment of the people, their representatives and their courts that appointment of counsel is not a fundamental right, essential to a fair trial. On the contrary, the matter has generally been deemed one of legislative policy.

[In] this case there was no question of the commission of a robbery. The State's case consisted of evidence identifying the petitioner as the perpetrator. The defense was an alibi. Petitioner called and examined witnesses to prove that he was at another place at the time of the commission of the offense. The simple issue was the veracity of the testimony for the State and that for the defendant. As Judge Bond [the author of the state court opinion below] says, the accused was not helpless, but was a man forty-three years old, of ordinary intelligence and ability to take care of his own interests on the trial of that narrow issue. He had once before been in a criminal court, pleaded guilty to larceny and served a sentence and was not wholly unfamiliar with criminal procedure. It is quite clear that in Maryland, if the situation had been otherwise and it had appeared that the petitioner was, for any reason, at a serious disadvantage by reason of the lack of counsel, a refusal to appoint would have resulted in the reversal of a judgment of conviction.

[To] deduce from the due process clause a rule binding upon the states in this matter would be to impose upon them, as Judge Bond points out, a requirement without distinction between criminal charges of different magnitude or in respect of courts of varying jurisdiction. As he says: "Charges of small crimes tried before justices of the peace and capital charges tried in the higher courts would equally require the appointment of counsel. Presumably it would be argued that trials in the Traffic Court would require it."

[While] want of counsel in a particular case may result in a conviction lacking [in] such fundamental fairness, we cannot say that the [Fourteenth Amendment] embodies an inexorable command that no trial for any offense, or in any court, can be fairly conducted and justice accorded a defendant who is not represented by counsel.

The judgment is affirmed.

JUSTICE BLACK, dissenting, with whom JUSTICE DOUGLAS and JUSTICE MURPHY concur.

[The] petitioner [was] a farm hand, out of a job and on relief. [The] court below found that [he] had "at least an ordinary amount of intelligence." It is clear from his examination of witnesses that he was a man of little education.

If this case had come to us from a federal court, it is clear we should have to reverse it, because the Sixth Amendment makes the right to counsel in criminal cases inviolable by the federal government. I believe that the Fourteenth Amendment made the sixth applicable to the states. But this view [has] never been accepted by a majority of this Court and is not accepted today. [I] believe, however, that under the prevailing view of due process, as reflected in the opinion just announced, a view which gives this Court such vast supervisory powers that I am not prepared to accept it without grave doubts, the judgment below should be reversed.

[The] right to counsel in a criminal proceeding is "fundamental." *Powell v. Alabama.* [A] practice cannot be reconciled with "common and fundamental ideas of fairness and right" which subjects innocent men to increased dangers of conviction merely because of their poverty. Whether a man is innocent cannot be determined from a trial in which as here, denial of counsel has made it impossible to conclude, with any satisfactory degree of certainty, that the defendant's case was adequately presented.

THE AFTERMATH OF BETTS v. BRADY— NOTES AND QUESTIONS

1. ***Was Betts "prejudiced"?*** When the Court reviewed Betts' case, he had appellate counsel, but his lawyer was confident—too confident—that the Court would apply the full measure of the Sixth Amendment right to counsel to the states. Thus he did not make any analysis of the trial and present any specific examples of how Betts might have been prejudiced by the absence of counsel. For the view that a number of such examples could have been shown and that competent trial counsel could have raised many more issues than "the simple issue [of] the veracity of the testimony for the State and that for the defendant," see Kamisar, *The Right to Counsel and the Fourteenth Amendment,* 30 U.Chi. L.Rev. 1, 42–56 (1962).

2. ***The "flat" requirement of counsel in capital cases.*** In *Bute v. Illinois,* 333 U.S. 640 (1948), and subsequent noncapital cases, the Court suggested that there was a "flat" requirement of counsel in capital cases. In *Hamilton v. Alabama,* 368 U.S. 52 (1961), holding that arraignment is so critical a stage in Alabama procedure that denial of counsel at that stage in a capital case violates due process, a unanimous Court declared, per Douglas, J., that "when one pleads to a capital charge without benefit of counsel, we do not stop to determine whether prejudice resulted. [T]he degree of prejudice can never be known." For an explanation and criticism of the Court's distinction between capital and noncapital cases, see Francis A. Allen, *The Supreme Court, Federalism, and State Systems of Criminal Justice,* 8 DePaul L.Rev. 213, 230–31 (1959).

3. ***The absolute right to retained counsel.*** During the *Betts* reign, the Court made it clear that denying a defendant the assistance of *his own lawyer* on *any* issue in the trial of *any* case, constituted a per se violation of "fundamental fairness." Thus, in *Chandler v. Fretag,* 348 U.S. 3 (1954), the Court stamped the right of petitioner "to be heard through his own counsel" as "unqualified." And *Ferguson v. Georgia,* 365 U.S. 570 (1961), held, in effect, that a state may not deny a criminal defendant the right to have his own counsel guide him on direct examination. More recently, the Supreme Court emphasized in *United States v. Gonzalez–Lopez,* 548 U.S. 140 (2006), that "the Sixth Amendment right to counsel of choice . . . commands, not that a trial be fair, but that a particular guarantee of fairness be provided—to wit, that the accused be defended by the counsel he believes to be best." For a discussion of the limits on the right to retained counsel of one's choosing, see infra Section 5.

GIDEON v. WAINWRIGHT
372 U.S. 335, 83 S.Ct. 792, 9 L.Ed.2d 799 (1963).

JUSTICE BLACK delivered the opinion of the Court.

Petitioner was charged in a Florida state court with having broken and entered a poolroom with intent to commit a misdemeanor. This offense is a felony under Florida law. Appearing in court without funds and without a lawyer, petitioner asked the court to appoint counsel for him, whereupon the following colloquy took place:

"The Court: Mr. Gideon, I am sorry, but I cannot appoint Counsel to represent you in this case. Under the laws of the State of Florida, the only time the Court can appoint Counsel to represent a Defendant is when that person is charged with a capital offense. * * *

"The Defendant: The United States Supreme Court says I am entitled to be represented by Counsel."

Put to trial before a jury, Gideon conducted his defense about as well as could be expected from a layman. He made an opening statement to the jury, cross-examined the State's witnesses, presented witnesses in his own defense, declined to testify himself, and made a short argument "emphasizing his innocence to the charge contained in the Information filed in this case." The jury returned a verdict of guilty, and petitioner was sentenced to serve five years in the state prison. [Since] 1942, when *Betts v. Brady* was decided by a divided Court, the problem of a defendant's federal constitutional right to counsel in a state court has been a continuing source of controversy and litigation in both state and federal courts. To give this problem another review here, we granted certiorari [and] appointed counsel to represent [petitioner].

We accept *Betts*'s assumption, based as it was on our prior cases, that a provision of the Bill of Rights which is "fundamental and essential to a fair trial" is made obligatory upon the States by the Fourteenth Amendment. We think the Court in *Betts* was wrong, however, in concluding that the Sixth Amendment's guarantee of counsel is not one of these fundamental rights. Ten years before *Betts,* this Court, after full consideration of all the historical data examined in *Betts,* had unequivocally declared that "the right to the aid of counsel is of this fundamental character." *Powell*. While the Court at the close of its *Powell* opinion did by its language, as this Court frequently does, limit its holding to the particular facts and circumstances of that case, its conclusions about the fundamental nature of the right to counsel are unmistakable.

[The] fact is that in deciding as it did—that "appointment of counsel is not a fundamental right, essential to a fair trial"—the [*Betts* Court] made an abrupt break with its own well-considered precedents. In returning to these old precedents, sounder we believe than the new, we but restore constitutional principles established to achieve a fair system of justice. Not only these precedents but also reason and reflection require us to recognize that in our adversary system of criminal justice, any person haled into court, who is too poor to hire a lawyer, cannot be assured a fair trial unless counsel is provided for him. This seems to us to be an obvious truth. Governments, both state and federal, quite properly spend vast sums of money to establish machinery to try defendants accused of crime. Lawyers to prosecute are everywhere deemed essential to protect the public's interest in an orderly society. Similarly, there are few defendants charged with crime, few indeed, who fail to hire the best lawyers they can get to prepare and present their defenses. That government hires lawyers to prosecute and defendants who have the money hire lawyers to defend are the strongest indications of the widespread belief that lawyers in criminal courts are necessities, not luxuries. The right of one charged with crime to counsel may not be deemed fundamental and essential to fair trials in some countries, but it is in ours. From the very beginning, our state and national constitutions and laws have laid great emphasis on procedural and substantive safeguards designed to assure fair trials before impartial tribunals in which every defendant stands equal before the law. This noble ideal cannot be realized if the poor man charged with crime has to face his accusers without a lawyer to assist him.

[The] Court in *Betts* departed from the sound wisdom upon which the Court's holding in *Powell* rested. Florida, supported by two other States, has asked that *Betts v. Brady* be left intact. Twenty-two States, as friends of the Court, argue that *Betts* was "an anachronism when handed down" and that it should now be overruled. We agree.

JUSTICE CLARK, concurring in the result.

[T]he Constitution makes no distinction between capital and noncapital cases. The Fourteenth Amendment requires due process of law for the deprival of "liberty" just as for deprival of "life," and there cannot constitutionally be a difference in the quality of the process based merely upon a supposed difference in the sanction involved. How can the Fourteenth Amendment tolerate a procedure which it condemns in capital cases on the ground that deprival of liberty may be less onerous than deprival of life—a value judgment not universally accepted—or that only the latter deprival is irrevocable?

JUSTICE HARLAN, concurring.

I agree that *Betts* should be overruled, but consider it entitled to a more respectful burial than has been accorded, at least on the part of those of us who were not on the Court when that case was decided. I cannot subscribe to the view that *Betts* represented "an abrupt break with its own well-considered precedents." [In *Powell*] this Court declared that under the particular facts there presented— "the ignorance and illiteracy of the defendants, their youth, the circumstances of public hostility [and] above all that they stood in deadly peril of their lives"—the state court had a duty to assign counsel for the trial as a necessary requisite of due process of law. It is evident that these limiting facts were not added to the opinion as an afterthought; they were repeatedly emphasized [and] were clearly regarded as important to the result.

Thus when this Court, a decade later, decided *Betts,* it did no more than to admit of the possible existence of special circumstances in noncapital as well as capital trials, while at the same time to insist that such circumstances be shown in order to establish a denial of due process. The right to appointed counsel had been recognized as being considerably broader in federal prosecutions, see *Johnson v. Zerbst,* but to have imposed these requirements on the States would indeed have been "an abrupt break" with the almost immediate past. The declaration that the right to appointed counsel in state prosecutions, as established in *Powell,* was not limited to capital cases was in truth not a departure from, but an extension of, existing precedent.

The principles declared in *Powell* and in *Betts,* however, had a troubled journey throughout the years that have followed first the one case and then the other.

[In] noncapital cases, the "special circumstances" rule has continued to exist in form while its substance has been substantially and steadily eroded. In the first decade after *Betts,* there were cases in which the Court found special circumstances to be lacking, but usually by a sharply divided vote. However, no such decision has been cited to us, and I have found none, [after] 1950. At the same time, there have been not a few cases in which special circumstances were found in little or nothing more than the "complexity" of the legal questions presented, although those questions were often of only routine difficulty. The Court has come to recognize, in other words, that the mere existence of a serious criminal charge constituted in itself special circumstances requiring the services of counsel at trial. In truth the *Betts* rule is no longer a reality.

This evolution, however, appears not to have been fully recognized by many state courts, in this instance charged with the front-line responsibility for the enforcement of constitutional rights. To continue a rule which is honored by this Court only with lip service is not a healthy thing and in the long run will do disservice to the federal system.

The special circumstances rule has been formally abandoned in capital cases, and the time has now come when it should be similarly abandoned in noncapital cases, at least as to offenses which, as the one involved here, carry the possibility of a substantial prison sentence. (Whether the rule should extend to *all* criminal cases need not now be decided.)[c]

NOTES AND QUESTIONS

1. *The significance of Powell v. Alabama and Johnson v. Zerbst.* Did the Court in *Betts* make, as Justice Black asserts in *Gideon,* "an abrupt break with its own well-considered precedents"? Did *Powell* furnish a steppingstone to either a *Betts* or a *Gideon,* depending on how far and fast the Supreme Court was willing to use the opinion's potential for expansion? Did the *Palko* doctrine constitute a clear warning that the Court would not impose the same requirements for appointed counsel upon the states as it had upon the federal government in *Johnson v. Zerbst?* See Israel, *Gideon v. Wainwright: The "Art" of Overruling,* 1963 Supreme Court Rev. 211, 234–38, 240–41.

2. *Alternative techniques of overruling available in Gideon.* Among the traditional arts of overruling are the arguments that (a) the old precedent has not withstood the "lessons of experience" and (b) that its rejection is required by later "inconsistent precedents." See e.g., *Mapp v. Ohio,* p. 224. Were these arguments available in *Gideon?* As to (b) reconsider, for example, the *Chandler* and *Ferguson* cases, establishing the unqualified right to the assistance of counsel *one can hire;* and the post-*Betts* development of the "automatic right" to appointed counsel in capital cases and its implicit admission of the unsoundness of the "fair trial" rule. As to (a), consider how, in the two decades since *Betts,* the assumption that a lawyerless defendant would usually be able to defend himself had fared in light of the constant expansion of the "special circumstances" concept; and how the assumption that a "special circumstances" test was more consistent with the "obligations of federalism" than an "absolute rule" had stood up in the face of the proliferation of federal habeas corpus cases produced by the *Betts* rule and the resulting friction between state and federal courts. See generally Israel, supra at 242–69.

3. *Why did the Gideon opinion take the route it did?* If the foregoing techniques of overruling were available in *Gideon,* why did Justice Black fail to utilize them? Would it have been most desirable to emphasize that the overruling of *Betts* was not attributable to recent changes in personnel, but that it constituted the product of a long line of Justices who, over two decades, participated in various decisions undermining *Betts?* See Israel, supra at 225, 269. Is the failure to employ the usual overruling "arts" in *Gideon* attributable to Justice Black's personal interest in vindicating his own dissenting opinion in *Betts?* Or his

---

c. Bruce Jacob, now Dean Emeritus and Professor at the Stetson University College of Law, was almost fresh out of law school when he argued the *Gideon* case for the State of Florida. Abe Fortas, later a Supreme Court Justice, argued the case for Gideon. After the Supreme Court reversed his case, Gideon was retried, this time with appointed counsel, and acquitted. See Anthony Lewis, *Gideon's Trumpet* 223–38 (1964). For an interesting look back on the *Gideon* case and what has happened to the *Gideon* principle, see Bruce R. Jacob, *Memories of and Reflections About Gideon v. Wainwright,* 33 Stetson L.Rev. 181 (2003). For another look back at *Gideon,* see Yale Kamisar, Abe Krash, Anthony Lewis & Ellen Podgor, *Gideon at 40: Facing the Crisis, Fulfilling the Promise,* 41 Am.Crim.L.Rev. 131 (2004).

reluctance to admit even the *original validity* of a decision that exemplifies the evils (to him) of the "fundamental rights" interpretation of the fourteenth amendment? See id. at 270–72.

4. *Federal delivery systems after Gideon.* In 1964, Congress enacted the Criminal Justice Act, 18 U.S.C.A. § 3006A, requiring federal district courts to adopt a local plan for furnishing counsel to indigent defendants. The Act mandated that the plans include the appointment of "private attorneys," but also allowed almost all districts to add an alternative delivery system of a Federal Public Defender Organization (a governmental entity established within the judicial branch) or a Community Defender Organization (a private non-profit organization, established by the local legal aid society or local bar association). All but a handful of the 94 federal judicial districts have used this alternative (with a substantial majority opting for a public defender organization). The Criminal Justice Act precludes, however, utilizing the public or community defender organization as the exclusive or almost-exclusive provider of government-funded representation, as it requires that "private attorneys shall be appointed in a substantial portion of the cases." Those private attorneys (commonly described as "panel attorneys," because they are selected from a court-approved panel of "qualified attorneys") typically are used in a "substantial minority" of the indigent-defense cases. They usually are assigned to the individual case by the clerk of the court or the defender organization, rather than by a judge. See CRIMPROC § 1.4(f).

5. *State delivery systems after Gideon.* State structures used to provide government-funded counsel tend to vary in several respects from the structure of the Criminal Justice Act. Initially, the choice of delivery system commonly is made by the governmental unit providing the funding, rather than the local court. That governmental entity traditionally has been the county, but over the past few decades, many states have shifted to primary or exclusive state funding.[d] The three most common delivery systems are: (1) individually appointed private attorneys, (2) public defender offices, and (3) contract-attorney organizations (typically a private law firm or a non-profit entity, sponsored by the local bar association or legal aid society, which contracts to provide representation for a large group of cases).

Public defender agencies have long been favored in metropolitan areas, and a fairly recent survey of the 100 most populous counties found that 90 percent had public defender programs. Where states provide the funding, they commonly establish a statewide program, with regional offices (and, in some instances, a separate appellate agency). Other public defender offices are local agencies. The staff of larger offices commonly includes investigators and social workers as well as lawyers and paralegals. Systems using defender offices typically assign to those offices almost all indigent-defense cases, with the primary exceptions being (1) cases in which a potential conflict of interest precludes defender representation [see Note 3, p. 188], and (2) "overflow cases" (where additional cases would exceed an agency-imposed caseload limit). Representation in these non-defender cases typically is provided through individual appointments, although some jurisdictions use a contract attorney program for such cases.

A substantial number of mid-size counties and most smaller counties do not have public defender offices. Here, indigent defense needs traditionally have been filled through individual appointments. In some judicial districts, appointment is made by the court, with the judge either exercising discretion in choosing counsel or relying upon a "neutral rotation system." In other districts, the court is

---

d. As of 2007, 22 states had state-based public defender programs, while the remaining states and the District of Columbia administered public defender offices at the county level. See Lynn Langston & Donald J. Farole, Jr., *Public Defender Offices, 2007–Statistical Tables*, Bureau of Justice Statistics (June 2010).

removed from the appointment process, with a rotation system administered by an independent official. In recent years, a growing number of mid-sized and small counties have moved to the contract system, with the contract firm agreeing to cover almost the entire indigent-defense docket, or a specific number of cases, for a flat fee or an hourly fee with caps (the typical fee system for individually appointed counsel).

Although commentators have expressed diverse viewpoints as to whether one appointment system or another is more likely to provide better representation, see CRIMPROC § 1.4(f), recent studies suggest that defendants represented by assigned counsel are more likely to be convicted and are more likely to receive longer sentences than those represented by public defenders. See, e.g., Thomas H. Cohen, *Who's Better at Defending Criminals? Does Type of Defense Attorney Matter in Terms of Producing Favorable Case Outcomes* 45 (2011), *available at* http://ssrn.com/abstract=1876474; James M. Anderson & Paul Heaton, *How Much Difference Does the Lawyer Make? The Effect of Defense Counsel on Murder Case Outcomes*, RAND Working Paper 870 (Dec. 2011). Anderson & Heaton supra offers some possible reasons for this observed difference: "We find that, in general, appointed counsel have comparatively few resources, face more difficult incentives, and are more isolated than public defenders. The extremely low pay reduces the pool of attorneys willing to take the appointments and makes doing preparation uneconomical."

6. *To what extent has the dream of Gideon been realized?* Consider the conclusion reached by the American Bar Association's Standing Committee on Legal Aid and Indigent Defendants after a series of public hearings involving testimony from 32 expert witnesses familiar with the delivery of indigent defense services throughout the states: "Forty years after *Gideon v. Wainwright*, indigent defense remains in a state of crisis, resulting in a system that lacks fundamental fairness and places poor persons at constant risk of wrongful conviction. [T]housands of persons are processed through America's courts every year either with no lawyer at all or with a lawyer who does not have the time, resources, or in some cases the inclination to provide effective representation. All too often, defendants plead guilty, even if they are innocent, without really understanding their legal rights or what is occurring. Sometimes the proceedings reflect little or no recognition that the accused is mentally ill or does not adequately understand English. The fundamental right to a lawyer that Americans assume appl[ies] to everyone accused of criminal conduct effectively does not exist in practice for countless people across the United States." *Gideon's Broken Promise: America's Continuing Quest for Equal Justice*, Exec. Summary at iv–v (2004).

Commentators agree that "the adequacy of the time and resources at defense counsel's disposal" is a critical factor related to the quality of defense representation, see CRIMPROC§ 1.4(f), and that state defense delivery systems are inadequately funded and overwhelmed with unmanageable caseloads. See Challenges to the Defense Delivery System Deficiencies, infra p. 176. In recent years, a growing number of states have created state oversight commissions to prescribe standards for all types of delivery systems within the state. While these commissions vary in their authority, some have mandated qualifications for appointed counsel, caseload limits for defender offices, and attorney training requirements for all government-funded defense counsel. In jurisdictions with capital sentences, states commonly impose, by court rule or commission directive, special standards for death penalty representation (e.g., appointment of two attorneys, with specified experience requirements).

7. *Indigency standards*. The Supreme Court did not explain in *Gideon* when a defendant is "indigent" and therefore entitled to appointed counsel. Most jurisdictions have legislation, court rules, or administrative regulations that set forth (often in considerable detail) the standards to be used in determining whether a defendant is financially eligible to receive government-funded counsel. See CRIMPROC § 11.2(g). Many states rely heavily on presumptive eligibility criteria (e.g., income below 125% of the current federal HHS poverty guideline), while others simply direct attention to a series of relevant factors (e.g., possible complexity of the case, family responsibilities, liquidity of assets). While the final say remains with the court, many jurisdictions assign the initial (and typically uncontested) determination to a public defender office, court clerk, or social service agency. Notwithstanding the variations in procedures and standards, the end results from state to state are fairly consistent for demographically similar communities. Thus, a study of defense representation in felony prosecutions in the 75 largest counties found a roughly standard rate of government-funded counsel, in the neighborhood of 82% (as contrasted to 66% for federal felony defendants in the same counties). See CRIMPROC § 1.4(f).

**8. *When Must Indigent Defendants Reimburse the Government?* ** *Rinaldi v. Yeager,* 384 U.S. 305 (1966), invalidated a New Jersey statute which required only those indigent defendants who were sentenced to prison to reimburse the state for the cost of a transcript on appeal, finding an "invidious discrimination" between those convicted defendants and others sentenced only to pay fines or subject only to a suspended sentence or to probation. *James v. Strange,* 407 U.S. 128 (1972), held that a Kansas recoupment statute (which applied whether or not the indigent defendant was convicted) violated equal protection because the indigent defendant could not avail himself of restrictions on wage garnishments and other protective exemptions afforded to other civil judgment debtors.

Fuller v. Oregon, 417 U.S. 40 (1974), however, upheld an Oregon recoupment statute which, under certain circumstances, authorized repayment to the state of the costs of a free legal defense as a condition of probation. A 7–2 majority, per Stewart, J., stressed that "the recoupment statute is quite clearly directed only at those convicted defendants who are indigent at the time of the criminal proceedings against them but who subsequently gain the ability to pay the expenses of legal representation. Defendants with no likelihood of having the means to repay are not put under even a conditional obligation to do so, and those upon whom a conditional obligation is imposed are not subjected to collection procedures until their indigency has ended and no 'manifest hardship' [to defendant or his immediate family] will result."

Dissenting Justice Marshall, joined by Brennan, J., protested that "the important fact which the majority ignores" is that because the repayment of the indigent defendant's debt to the state can be made a condition of his probation, as it was in this case, "[p]etitioner's failure to pay his debt can result in his being sent to prison. In this respect the indigent defendant in Oregon, like [his counterpart in *James*], is treated quite differently from other civil judgment debtors."

Notwithstanding the *Fuller* case, A.B.A. *Standards* § 5–7.2 (commentary) "recommends that defendants be ordered to [make reimbursement] for their defense only in instances where they have made fraudulent representations for purposes of being found eligible for counsel. [The] offer of free legal assistance is rendered hollow if defendants are required to make payments for counsel for several years following conviction. Reimbursement requirements also may serve to discourage defendants from exercising their right to counsel * * *."

EXTENDING *GIDEON* TO MISDEMEANOR CASES

In ARGERSINGER v. HAMLIN, 407 U.S. 25 (1972), the Court, per Douglas, J., struck down a Florida rule (following the line marked out in the jury trial cases) requiring that counsel be appointed only "for nonpetty offenses punishable by more than six months imprisonment," and held that "absent a knowing and intelligent waiver, no person may be *imprisoned* for any offense, whether classified as petty, misdemeanor, or felony unless he was represented by counsel" (emphasis added):

"While there is historical support for limiting the [right] to trial by jury [to] 'serious criminal cases,' there is no such support for a similar limitation on the right to assistance of counsel. [Thus,] we reject [the] premise that since prosecutions for crimes punishable by imprisonment for less than six months may be tried without a jury, they may always be tried without a lawyer. [The] requirement of counsel may well be necessary for a fair trial even in a petty offense prosecution. We are by no means convinced that legal and constitutional questions involved in a case that actually leads to imprisonment even for a brief period are any less complex than when a person can be sent off for six months or more. * * *

"We must conclude, therefore, that the problems associated with misdemeanor and petty offenses often require the presence of counsel to insure the accused a fair trial. [In his concurring opinion,] Mr. Justice Powell suggests that these problems are raised even in situations where there is no prospect of imprisonment. We need not consider the requirements of the Sixth Amendment as regards the right to counsel where loss of liberty is not involved, however, for here, petitioner was in fact sentenced to jail * * *.

"Under the rule we announce today, every judge will know when the trial of a misdemeanor starts that no imprisonment may be imposed, even though local law permits it, unless the accused is represented by counsel. He will have a measure of the seriousness and gravity of the offense and therefore know when to name a lawyer to represent the accused before the trial starts."

Analyzing the problem in terms of general due process rather than the sixth amendment right to counsel, concurring Justice Powell, joined by Rehnquist, J., concluded that "there is a middle course, between the extremes of Florida's six month rule and the Court's rule, which comports with the requirements of the Fourteenth Amendment"—"fundamental fairness" requires that a defendant have the assistance of counsel in petty cases when, but only when, "necessary to assure a fair trial":

"[The] rule adopted today [is] limited to petty offense cases in which the sentence is some imprisonment. The thrust of the Court's position indicates, however, that when the decision must be made, the rule will be extended to all petty offense cases except perhaps the most minor traffic violations. If the Court rejects on constitutional grounds, as it has today, the exercise of any judicial discretion as to need for counsel if a jail sentence is imposed, one must assume a similar rejection of discretion in other petty offense cases. * * *

"I would hold that the right to counsel in petty offense cases is not absolute but is one to be determined by the trial courts exercising a judicial discretion on a case-by-case basis. * * * [T]hree general factors should be weighed. First, the court should consider the complexity of the offense charged. Second, the court should consider the probable sentence that will follow if a conviction is obtained. The more serious the likely consequences, the greater is the probability that a lawyer should be appointed. Third, the court should consider the individual factors peculiar to each case. These, of course, would be the most difficult to anticipate. One relevant factor would be the competency of the individual defendant to present his own case. The attitude of the community toward a particular defendant or particular incident would be another consideration. * * *

"Such a rule is similar in certain respects to the special circumstances rule applied to felony cases in *Betts,* which this Court overruled in *Gideon.* One of the reasons for seeking a more definitive standard in felony cases was the failure of many state courts to live up to their responsibilities in determining on a case-by-case basis whether counsel should be appointed. But this Court should not assume that the past insensitivity of some state courts to the rights of defendants will continue. Certainly if the Court follows the course of reading rigid rules into the Constitution, so that the state courts will be unable to exercise judicial discretion within the limits of fundamental fairness, there is little reason to think that insensitivity will abate."

————

Petitioner, an indigent, was charged with shoplifting merchandise valued at less than $150, punishable by as much as a $500 fine, or one year in jail, or both. He was not provided counsel. After a bench trial he was convicted of the offense and fined $50. The Supreme Court of Illinois declined to "extend *Argersinger*" to a case where one is charged with an offense for which imprisonment upon conviction is authorized but not actually imposed. A 5–4 majority of the Supreme Court, per Rehnquist, J., agreed, SCOTT v. ILLINOIS, 440 U.S. 367 (1979):

"[W]e believe that the central premise of *Argersinger*—that actual imprisonment is a penalty different in kind from fines or the mere threat of imprisonment—is eminently sound and warrants adoption of actual imprisonment as the line defining the constitutional right to appointment of counsel. * * * We therefore hold that the Sixth and Fourteenth Amendments [require] only that no indigent criminal defendant be sentenced to a term of imprisonment unless the State has afforded him the right to assistance of appointed counsel in his defense."

Concurring Justice Powell noted that "the drawing of a line based on whether there is imprisonment (even for overnight) can have the practical effect of precluding provision of counsel in other types of cases in which conviction can have more serious consequences." He also thought that an "actual imprisonment" rule "tends to impair the proper functioning of the criminal justice system in that trial judges, in advance of hearing any evidence and before knowing anything about the case except the charge, all too often will be compelled to forego the legislatively granted option to impose a sentence of imprisonment upon conviction." Nevertheless, Justice Powell joined the opinion of the Court because "[i]t is important that this Court provide clear guidance to the hundreds of courts across the country that confront this problem daily." He hoped, however, "that in due time a majority will recognize that a more flexible rule is consistent with due process and will better serve the cause of justice."

Justice Brennan, joined by Marshall and Stevens, JJ., dissented:

"[*Argersinger*] established a 'two dimensional' test for the right to counsel: the right attaches to any 'non-petty' offense punishable by more than six months in jail and in addition to any offense where actual incarceration is likely regardless of the maximum authorized penalty. See Steven B. Duke, *The Right to Appointed Counsel: Argersinger and Beyond,* 12 Am.Crim.L.Rev. 601 (1975).

"The offense of 'theft' with which Scott was charged is certainly not a 'petty' one. It is punishable by a sentence of up to one year in jail. Unlike many traffic or other 'regulatory' offenses, it carries the moral stigma associated with common-law crimes traditionally recognized as indicative of moral depravity. The State indicated at oral argument that the services of a professional prosecutor were considered essential to the prosecution of this offense. Likewise, nonindigent defendants charged with this offense would be well advised to hire the 'best lawyers they can get.' Scott's right to the assistance of appointed counsel is thus plainly mandated by the logic of the Court's prior cases, including *Argersinger* itself.

"Perhaps the strongest refutation of respondent's alarmist prophecies that an authorized imprisonment standard would wreak havoc on the States is that the standard has not produced that result in the substantial number of States that already provide counsel in all cases where imprisonment is authorized—States that include a large majority of the country's population and a great diversity of urban and rural environments. * * * It may well be that adoption by this Court of an authorized imprisonment standard would lead state and local governments to re-examine their criminal statutes. A state legislature or local government might determine that it no longer desired to authorize incarceration for certain minor offenses in light of the expense of meeting the requirements of the Constitution. In my view this re-examination is long overdue. In any event, the Court's actual imprisonment standard must inevitably lead the courts to make this re-examina-tion, which plainly should more properly be a legislative responsibility."

In a separate dissent, Justice Blackmun maintained that the right to counsel "extends at least as far as the right to jury trial" and thus that "an indigent defendant in a state criminal case must be afforded appointed counsel whenever the defendant is prosecuted for a nonpetty criminal offense, that is, one punisha-ble by more than six months' imprisonment, *or* whenever the defendant is actually subjected to a term of imprisonment."

NOTES AND QUESTIONS

1. *Justice Powell's view.* Were Justice Powell's reasons for switching from his position in *Argersinger* to the "actual confinement" approach in *Scott*—to "provide clear guidance" to lower courts and to reach a result consistent with *Argersinger*—persuasive? Did Justice Powell explain why the "actual confine-ment" test provides clearer guidance than the alternative to it? Did he explain why he declined to join Justice Blackmun's dissenting opinion? Of all the opinions in *Scott*, does the Blackmun opinion diverge least from the views Powell expressed in *Argersinger?* See Lawrence Herman & Charles A. Thompson, *Scott v. Illinois and the Right to Counsel: A Decision in Search of a Doctrine?* 17 Am.Crim.L.Rev. 71, 94 (1979).

2. *How important are misdemeanor cases when no imprisonment is actually imposed?* Consider Bruce R. Jacob, *Memories of and Reflections about Gideon v. Wainwright*, 33 Stetson L.Rev. 180, 284 (2003) (writing forty years after he had argued the losing side in *Gideon*): "The stigma of any criminal conviction, including a misdemeanor conviction that results in a fine, is significant. Any misdemeanor conviction in a person's past, except for a minor traffic offense, makes it difficult for that person to gain entry into medical school or law school, to obtain certain jobs, or to enter the military service. Imposing a fine is a taking of property under [Fourteenth Amendment Due Process]. [Now] that the right to counsel has been incorporated into the Fourteenth Amendment, an indigent defendant in a misdemeanor case, facing a possible fine as punishment, should be entitled to the appointment of counsel."

3. Are unrepresented defendants likely to waive their right to a jury trial, hoping that a judge who sits as factfinder will be able to provide assistance? If so,

how in a *non-jury* case, can a judge *properly* make an intelligent pre-trial determination as to whether the sentence is likely to include incarceration, at least where he will hear the case? Isn't a considerable amount of potentially prejudicial information likely to be injected into the factfinding process? If an indigent defendant charged with an offense usually punished only by a fine is appointed counsel, would a *different* judge hearing the case assume that a colleague had found that the defendant had a "bad record" or had committed the minor offense in an egregious manner? See Commentary to Unif.R.Crim.P. 321(b); Note, 1979 U.Ill.L.F. 739, 752.

4. May the problems raised in Note 3 never be reached because of judicial reluctance to conduct pretrial inquiries about the likely sentence? Consider Note, 93 Harv.L.Rev. 82, 87 (1979): "It seems far more likely that, due to the sheer volume of misdemeanor cases, judges simply will not appoint counsel, thereby relinquishing their discretion to impose the penalty of imprisonment." If so, would this constitute improper judicial interference with the legislature's judgment concerning the appropriate range of penalties? See id.

5.   *State practices.* A number of states need not apply the *Scott* standard, because they provide counsel to any indigent defendant charged with an offense that carries a potential jail sentence. However, at least half the states use the *Scott* "actual imprisonment" standard when determining whether to appoint counsel for at least some category of misdemeanors. For a breakdown of how different states approach this issue, see CRIMPROC § 11.2(a).

6.   *Gideon revisited—and criticized.* Although he recognizes that "probably no decision in the field of constitutional criminal procedure enjoys anything like the unqualified and unanimous approval" that *Gideon* has received, Professor Dripps criticizes the case for focusing on the language of the Sixth Amendment rather than taking a more general due process approach. Donald A. Dripps, *About Guilt or Innocence* 117 (2003):

"[*Gideon*] took a Procrustean approach to the Sixth Amendment. Where the amendment says the defendant may appear through counsel, *Gideon* stretches the amendment to cover subsidizing counsel for the poor. Where the amendment says ['in *all* criminal prosecutions'], *Gideon* reduces the amendment to covering [felony cases and only those misdemeanor cases leading to incarceration]. Would the Court now or ever uphold a federal statute that forbade a misdemeanor defendant from appearing through privately-retained counsel? If not, how can 'all' mean 'all' when the issue is prohibiting appearance through counsel, but mean 'some' when the issue is providing indigent defense? * * * [By] relying on the Sixth Amendment (albeit in a distorted fashion) the Warren Court deflected attention from instrumental reliability in favor of a formalistic focus on the textually-referenced 'assistance of counsel.' The incorporation approach necessarily failed to describe Gideon's constitutional right with appropriate generality. There is nothing *intrinsically* valuable about lawyers; that is why subsequent cases have developed the idea, if not the reality, that defense counsel's assistance must be *effective.* * * * Gideon's right was not to a lawyer, but to a trial that ran no more than some practically irreducible risk of falsely convicting him."

7.   *Can an uncounseled misdemeanor conviction still be used to enhance a prison sentence when, after being given counsel, a defendant is convicted of a second crime?* Overruling an earlier decision (*Baldasar v. Illinois*, 446 U.S. 222 (1980)), the Court, per Rehnquist, C.J., held in NICHOLS v. UNITED STATES, 511 U.S. 738 (1994), that a "logical consequence" of *Scott* is that "an uncounseled conviction valid under *Scott* [because no prison term was imposed] may be relied upon to enhance the sentence for a subsequent offense, even though that sentence entails imprisonment. Enhancement statutes, whether in the nature of criminal history provisions such as those contained in the Sentencing Guidelines, or recidivist statutes that are commonplace in state criminal laws, do not change the penalty imposed for the earlier conviction." (Seven years earlier, when not represented by counsel, Nichols had pled *nolo contendere* to a state misdemeanor (DUI) and paid a $250 fine. This misdemeanor conviction was used to enhance his sentence when he was subsequently convicted of a federal drug offense.)

The Chief Justice pointed out: "[Nichols] could have been sentenced more severely based simply on evidence of the underlying conduct that gave rise to the previous DUI offense. And the state need prove such conduct only by a preponderance of the evidence. Surely, then, it must be constitutionally permissible to consider a prior uncounseled conviction based on the same conduct where that conduct must be proved beyond a reasonable doubt."

Blackmun, J., joined by Stevens and Ginsburg, JJ., dissented: "It is more logical, and more consistent with the reasoning in *Scott*, to hold that a conviction that is invalid for imposing a sentence for the offense remains invalid for increasing the term of imprisonment imposed for a subsequent conviction. [That] the sentence in *Scott* was imposed in the first instance and the sentence here was the result of an enhancement statute is a distinction without a constitutional difference. * * *"

8. *If an indigent defendant is not provided counsel, can he be given a suspended sentence or placed on probation?* Consider ALABAMA v. SHELTON, 535 U.S. 654 (2002), which arose as follows: After being convicted of a misdemeanor, third-degree assault, Shelton, an indigent defendant who had not been afforded counsel, was sentenced to a jail term of 30 days, which the trial court immediately suspended. Shelton was then placed on two years unsupervised probation. The Supreme Court of Alabama took the position that a suspended sentence constitutes a "term of imprisonment" within the meaning of *Argersinger* and *Scott* even though incarceration is not immediate or inevitable. Accordingly, the court affirmed Shelton's conviction and the monetary portion of his punishment, but invalidated "that aspect of his sentence imposing 30 days of suspended jail time." By reversing Shelton's suspended sentence, the court also vacated the two-year term of probation. A 5–4 majority, per GINSBURG, J., affirmed:

"A suspended sentence is a prison term imposed for the offense of conviction. Once the prison term is triggered, the defendant is incarcerated not for the probation violation, but for the underlying offense. The uncounseled conviction at that point 'result[s] in imprisonment'; it 'ends up in the actual deprivation of a person's liberty.' This is precisely what the Sixth Amendment as interpreted in *Argersinger* and *Scott* does not allow.

"[On the basis of figures suggesting that conditional sentences are commonly imposed but rarely activated,] *amicus* argues that a rule requiring appointed counsel in every case involving a suspended sentence would unduly hamper the States' attempts to impose effective probationary punishment. A more 'workable solution,' he contends, would permit imposition of a suspended sentence on an uncounseled defendant and require appointment of counsel, if at all, only at the probation revocation stage, when incarceration is imminent.

"[Amicus] does not describe the contours of the hearing, that, he suggests, might precede revocation of a term of probation imposed on an uncounseled defendant. [In] Alabama, however, the character of the probation revocation hearing currently afforded is not in doubt. The proceeding is an 'informal' one at which the defendant has no right to counsel, and the court no obligation to observe customary rules of evidence. More significant, the sole issue at the hearing—apart from determinations about the necessity of confinement—is whether the defendant breached the terms of probation. [The] validity or reliability of the underlying conviction is beyond attack. * * *

"We think it plain that a hearing so timed and structured cannot compensate for the absence of trial counsel, for it does not even address the key Sixth Amendment inquiry: whether the adjudication of guilt corresponding to the prison sentence is sufficiently reliable to permit incarceration. Deprived of counsel when tried, convicted, and sentenced, and unable to challenge the original judgment at a subsequent probation revocation hearing, a defendant in Shelton's circumstances faces incarceration on a conviction that has never been subjected to 'the crucible of meaningful adversarial testing.' "

Justice SCALIA, joined by the Chief Justice and Justices Kennedy and Thomas, dissented:

"[What procedures the Alabama courts will adopt if Shelton someday violates the terms of probation and the state decides to deprive him of his liberty] is not the [question] before us, and the Court has no business offering an advisory opinion on its answer. We are asked to decide whether 'imposition of a suspended or conditional sentence in a misdemeanor case invoke[s] a defendant's Sixth Amendment right to counsel.' Since *imposition* of a suspended sentence does not deprive a defendant of his personal liberty, the answer to *that* question is plainly no. In the future, *if and when* the State of Alabama seeks to imprison respondent on the previously suspended sentence, we can ask whether the procedural safeguards attending the imposition of that sentence comply with the Constitution. But that question is *not* before us now.

"[Surely] the procedures attending reimposition of a suspended sentence would be adequate if they required, upon the defendant's request, complete retrial of the misdemeanor violation with assistance of counsel. By what right does the Court deprive the State of that option? It may well be a sensible option, since most defendants will be induced to comply with the terms of their probation by the mere threat of a retrial that could send them to jail, and since the expense of those rare, counseled retrials may be much less than the expense of providing counsel initially in all misdemeanor cases that bear a possible sentence of imprisonment. And it may well be that, in some cases, even procedures short of complete retrial will suffice."

B. THE "BEGINNINGS" OF THE RIGHT TO COUNSEL: "CRIMINAL PROSECUTIONS" AND "CRITICAL STAGES"

ROTHGERY v. GILLESPIE COUNTY
554 U.S. 191, 128 S.Ct. 2578, 171 L.Ed.2d 366 (2008).

JUSTICE SOUTER delivered the opinion of the Court.

[Relying on erroneous information that petitioner Rothgery had a previous felony conviction, Texas police arrested him and brought him before a magistrate judge for what is sometimes called an "article 15.17 hearing." At this hearing the Fourth Amendment probable-cause determination is made, bail is set and the defendant is apprised of the accusation against him. In Rothgery's case the magistrate judge concluded that probable cause existed and bail was set at $5,000. Rothgery was committed to jail, from which he was released after posting a security bond. Rothgery had no money for a lawyer and made several unheeded requests for appointed counsel.

[Approximately six months later, Rothgery was indicted by a Texas grand jury for unlawful possession of a firearm by a felon, resulting in his rearrest the next day. When bail was increased to $15,000, Rothgery could not post it. As a result, he was placed in jail and remained there for three weeks.

[Shortly thereafter, Rothgery was finally assigned a lawyer. The lawyer's work led to the dismissal of the indictment. Rothgery then brought this 42 U.S.C. § 1983 action, claiming that if the county had provided him a lawyer within a reasonable time after the hearing, he would not have been indicted, rearrested, or jailed. He maintained that the county's unwritten policy of denying appointed counsel to indigent defendants out on bail until an indictment is entered violated his Sixth Amendment right to counsel. The Court of Appeals concluded, however, that the Sixth Amendment right to counsel did not attach at the Article 15.17 hearing because "the relevant prosecutors were not aware or involved in Rothgery's arrest or appearance" and there was "no indication" that the police alone "had any power to commit the state to prosecute."]

The Sixth Amendment right of the "accused" to assistance of counsel in "all criminal prosecutions" is limited by its terms: "it does not attach until a prosecution is commenced." We have, for purposes of the right to counsel, pegged commencement to "the initiation of adversary judicial criminal proceedings— whether by way of formal charge, preliminary hearing, indictment, information, or arraignment," *United States v. Gouveia*, 467 U.S. 180 (1984). [The] rule is [a] recognition of the point at which "the government has committed itself to prosecute" [and] the accused "finds himself faced with the prosecutorial forces of organized society, and immersed in the intricacies of substantive and procedural criminal law." *Kirby v. Illinois*, 406 U.S. 682 [1972]. The issue is whether Texas's article 15.17 hearing marks that point, with the consequent state obligation to appoint counsel within a reasonable time once a request for assistance is made.

[We] have twice held that the right to counsel attaches at the initial appearance before a judicial officer, see *Michigan v. Jackson*, 475 U.S. 625 [1986]; *Brewer v. Williams*, 430 U.S. 387 [1977]. This first time before a court, also known as a "preliminary arraignment" or "arraignment on the complaint," is generally the hearing at which "the magistrate informs the defendant of the charge in the complaint and of various rights in further proceedings," and "determine[s] the conditions for pretrial release." Texas's article 15.17 hearing is an initial appearance. * * * *Brewer* and *Jackson* control. * * *

[The *Jackson* case] flatly rejected the distinction between initial arraignment and arraignment on the indictment. [Our] conclusion was driven by the same considerations the Court has endorsed in *Brewer*: by the time a defendant is brought before a judicial officer, is informed of a formally lodged accusation, and has restrictions imposed on his liberty in aid of the prosecution, the State's relationship with the defendant has become solidly adversarial. And that is just as true when the proceeding comes before the indictment (in the case of the initial arraignment on a formal complaint) as when it comes after it (at an arraignment on an indictment).

[The] overwhelming consensus practice conforms to the rule that the first formal proceedings is the point of attachment. We are advised without contradiction that not only the Federal Government, including the District of Columbia, but 43 States take the first step toward appointing counsel "before, at, or just after initial appearance." [To] the extent [that 7 States] have been denying appointed counsel on the heels of the first appearance, they are a distinct minority. * * * Neither *Brewer* nor *Jackson* said a word about the prosecutor's involvement as a relevant fact, much less a controlling one. [An] attachment rule that turned on determining the moment of a prosecutor's first involvement would be "wholly unworkable and impossible to administer." [And] it would have the practical effect of resting attachment on such absurd distinctions as the day of the month an arrest is made [or] "the sophistication or lack thereof, of a jurisdiction's computer intake system."

[What] counts as a commitment to prosecute is an issue of federal law unaffected by allocations of power among state officials under a State's law, [and] under the federal standard, an accusation filed with a judicial officer is sufficiently formal, and the government's commitment to prosecute it sufficiently concrete, when the accusation prompts arraignment and restrictions on the accused's liberty to facilitate the prosecution.

The County [argues] that in considering the significance of the initial appearance, we must ignore prejudice to a defendant's pretrial liberty, reasoning that it is the concern, not of the right to counsel, but of the speedy-trial right and the Fourth Amendment. * * * We think the County's reliance on *United States v. Gouveia* is misplaced, and its argument mistaken. The defendants in *Gouveia* were prison inmates, suspected of murder, who had been placed in an administrative detention unit and denied counsel up until an indictment was filed. [They] argued that their administrative detention should be treated as an accusation for purposes of the right to counsel because the government was actively investigating the crimes. * * * We [saw] no basis for "depart[ing] from our traditional interpretation of the Sixth Amendment right to counsel in order to provide additional protections for [the inmates]." *Gouveia*'s holding that the Sixth Amendment right to counsel had not attached has no application here. [Since] we are not asked to extend the right to counsel to a point earlier than formal judicial proceedings (as in *Gouveia*), but to defer it to those proceedings in which a prosecutor is involved, *Gouveia* does not speak to the question before us. * * *

[According] to the County, our cases (*Brewer* and *Jackson* aside) actually establish a "general rule that the right to counsel attaches at the point that [what the County calls] formal charges are filed," with exceptions allowed only in the case of "a very limited set of specific preindictment situations." The County suggests that the latter category should be limited to those appearances at which the aid of counsel is urgent and "the dangers to the accused of proceeding without counsel" are great. Texas's article 15.17 hearing should not count as one of those situations, the County says, because it is not of critical significance, since it "allows no presentation of witness testimony and provides no opportunity to expose weaknesses in the government's evidence, create a basis for later impeachment, or even engage in basic discovery."

We think the County is wrong. * * * Attachment occurs when the government has used the judicial machinery to signal a commitment to prosecute as spelled out in *Brewer* and *Jackson*. Once attachment occurs, the accused at least is entitled to the presence of appointed counsel during any "critical stage" of the postattachment proceedings; what makes a stage critical is what shows the need for counsel's presence. Thus, counsel must be appointed within a reasonable time after attachment to allow for adequate representation at any critical stage before trial, as well as trial itself.

[The County] makes an analytical mistake in its assumption that attachment necessarily requires the occurrence or imminence of a critical stage. On the contrary, it is irrelevant to attachment that the presence of counsel at an article 15.17 hearing, say, may not be critical, just as it is irrelevant that counsel's presence may not be critical when a prosecutor walks over to the trial court to file an information. * * *

Our holding is narrow. We do not decide whether the 6–month delay in appointment of counsel resulted in prejudice to Rothgery's Sixth Amendment rights, and have no occasion to consider what standards should apply in deciding this. We merely affirm what we have held before and what an overwhelming

majority of American jurisdictions understand in practice: a criminal defendant's initial appearance before a judicial officer, where he learns the charge against him and his liberty is subject to restriction, marks the start of adversary judicial proceedings that trigger attachment of the Sixth Amendment right to counsel.
* * *

CHIEF JUSTICE ROBERTS, with whom JUSTICE SCALIA joins, concurring.

Justice Thomas's analysis of the present issue is compelling, but I believe the result here is controlled by *Brewer v. Williams* and *Michigan v. Jackson*. A sufficient case has not been made for revisiting those precedents, and accordingly I join the Court's opinion.

I also join Justice Alito's concurrence, which correctly distinguishes between the time the right to counsel attaches and the circumstances under which counsel must be provided.

JUSTICE ALITO, with whom THE CHIEF JUSTICE and JUSTICE SCALIA join, concurring.

I join the Court's opinion because I do not understand it to hold that a defendant is entitled to the assistance of appointed counsel as soon as his Sixth Amendment right attaches. As I interpret our precedents, the term "attachment" signifies nothing more than the beginning of the defendant's prosecution. It does not mark the beginning of a substantive entitlement to the assistance of counsel.

[The] Sixth Amendment provides [that] "[i]n all criminal prosecutions, the accused shall enjoy the right [to] have the Assistance of Counsel for his defence." The Amendment thus defines the scope of the right to counsel in three ways: It provides *who* may assert the right ("the accused"); *when* the right may be asserted ("[i]n all criminal prosecutions"); and *what* the right guarantees ("the right [to] have the Assistance of Counsel for his defence").

It is in the context of interpreting the Amendment's answer to the second of these questions—when the right may be asserted—that we have spoken of the right "attaching." In *Kirby v. Illinois*, a plurality of the Court explained that "a person's Sixth and Fourteenth Amendment right to counsel attaches only at or after the time that adversary judicial proceedings have been initiated against him." A majority of the Court elaborated on that explanation in *Moore v. Illinois*, 434 U.S. 220 (1977) [(holding that the defendant's Sixth Amendment right to counsel had attached at a preliminary hearing)].

[When] we wrote in *Kirby* and *Moore* that the Sixth Amendment right had "attached," we evidently meant nothing more than that a "criminal prosecutio[n]" had begun. Our cases have generally used the term in that narrow fashion.

[As] the Court, notes, however, we have previously held that "arraignments" that were functionally indistinguishable from the Texas magistration marked the point at which the Sixth Amendment right to counsel "attached." It does not follow, however, and I do not understand the Court to hold, that the county had an obligation to appoint an attorney to represent petitioner within some specified period after his magistration. To so hold, the Court would need to do more than conclude that petitioner's criminal prosecution had begun. It would also need to conclude that the assistance of counsel in the wake of a Texas magistration is part of the substantive guarantee of the Sixth Amendment. That question lies beyond our reach, petitioner having never sought our review of it. [To] recall the framework laid out earlier, we have been asked to address only the *when* question, not the *what* question. Whereas the temporal scope of the right is defined by the words "[i]n all criminal prosecutions," the right's substantive guarantee flows from a different textual font: the words "Assistance of Counsel for his defence."
* * *

We have thus rejected the argument that the Sixth Amendment entitles the criminal defendant to the assistance of appointed counsel at a probable cause hearing. See *Gerstein v. Pugh* (1975) [p. 340]. [At] the same time, we have recognized that certain pretrial events may so prejudice the outcome of the defendant's prosecution that, as a practical matter, the defendant must be represented at those events in order to enjoy genuinely effective assistance at trial [referring to the lineup cases at pp. 761 & 770]. [We] have also held that the assistance of counsel is guaranteed at a pretrial lineup, since "the confrontation compelled by the State between the accused and the victim or witnesses to a crime to elicit identification evidence is peculiarly riddled with innumerable dangers and variable factors which might seriously, even crucially, derogate from a fair trial." Other "critical stages" of the prosecution include pretrial interrogation, a pretrial psychiatric exam, and certain kinds of arraignments.

* * * I interpret the Sixth Amendment to require the appointment of counsel only after the defendant's prosecution has begun, and then only as necessary to guarantee the defendant effective assistance at trial. * * * Texas counties need only appoint counsel as far in advance of trial, and as far in advance of any pretrial "critical stage," as necessary to guarantee effective assistance at trial.

[The] Court expresses no opinion on whether Gillespie County satisfied that obligation in this case. Petitioner has asked us to decide only the limited question whether his magistration marked the beginning of his "criminal prosecutio[n]" within the meaning of the Sixth Amendment. Because I agree with the Court's resolution of that limited question, I join its opinion in full.

JUSTICE THOMAS, dissenting.

* * * Because the Court's holding is not supported by the original meaning of the Sixth Amendment or any reasonable interpretation of our precedents, I respectfully dissent.

[After examining the historical background of the term, Justice Thomas concludes that history furnishes] strong evidence that the term "criminal prosecutio[n]" in the Sixth Amendment refers to the commencement of a criminal suit by filing formal charges in a court with jurisdiction to try and punish the defendant. And on this understanding of the Sixth Amendment, it is clear that petitioner's initial appearance before the magistrate did not commence a "criminal prosecutio[n]." No formal charges had been filed. The only document submitted to the magistrate was the arresting officer's affidavit of probable cause. [As] the Court notes, our cases have "pegged commencement" of a criminal prosecution to "the initiation of adversary judicial criminal proceedings—whether by way of formal charge, preliminary hearing, indictment, information, or arraignment," *Kirby v. Illinois* (plurality opinion). The Court has repeated this formulation in virtually every right-to-counsel case decided since *Kirby*. * * *

[Rothgery's] initial appearance was not what *Kirby* described as an "arraignment." An arraignment, in its traditional and usual sense, is a postindictment proceeding at which the defendant enters a plea. Although the word "arraignment" is sometimes used to describe an initial appearance before a magistrate, that is not what *Kirby* meant when it said that the right to counsel attaches at an "arraignment." Rather, it meant the traditional, postindictment arraignment where the defendant enters a plea. * * *

[It] is clear that when *Kirby* was decided in 1972 there was no precedent in this Court for the conclusion that a criminal prosecution begins, and the right to counsel therefore attaches, at an initial appearance before a magistrate. The Court concludes, however, that two subsequent decisions—*Brewer v. Williams* and *Michigan v. Jackson*—stand for that proposition. Those decisions, which relied almost exclusively on *Kirby*, cannot bear the weight the Court puts on them. * * *

Even assuming, [that] the arraignment in *Brewer* was functionally identical to the initial appearance here, *Brewer* offered no reasoning for its conclusion that the right to counsel attached at such a proceeding. [There] is no indication that *Brewer* considered the difference between an arraignment on a warrant and an arraignment at which the defendant pleads to the indictment.

[The] only rule that can be derived from the face of the opinion in *Jackson* is that if a proceeding is called an "arraignment," the right to counsel attaches. That rule would not govern this case because petitioner's initial appearance was not called an "arraignment" (the parties refer to it as a "magistration"). And that would, in any case, be a silly rule. The Sixth Amendment consequences of a proceeding should turn on the substance of what happens there, not on what the State chooses to call it. But the Court in *Jackson* did not focus on the substantive distinction between an initial arraignment and an arraignment on the indictment. Instead, the Court simply cited *Kirby* and left it at that. In these circumstances, I would recognize *Jackson* for what it is—a cursory treatment of an issue that was not the primary focus of the Court's opinion.

[Neither] petitioner nor the Court identifies any way in which petitioner's ability to receive a fair trial was undermined by the absence of counsel during the period between his initial appearance and his indictment. Nothing during that period exposed petitioner to the risk that he would be convicted as the result of ignorance of his rights. Instead, the gravamen of petitioner's complaint is that if counsel had been appointed earlier, he would have been able to stave off indictment by convincing the prosecutor that petitioner was not guilty of the crime alleged. But the Sixth Amendment protects against the risk of erroneous *conviction*, not the risk of unwarranted *prosecution*. See *Gouveia* (rejecting the notion that the "purpose of the right to counsel is to provide a defendant with a preindictment private investigator").

[We] have never suggested that the accused's right to the assistance of counsel "for his defence" entails a right to use counsel as a sword to contest pretrial detention. To the contrary, we have flatly rejected that notion, reasoning that a defendant's liberty interests are protected by other constitutional guarantees.

[In] sum, neither the original meaning of the Sixth Amendment right to counsel nor our precedents interpreting the scope of that right supports the Court's holding that the right attaches at an initial appearance before a magistrate. * * *

NOTES AND QUESTIONS

1. Triggering the right to counsel versus requiring the presence of counsel. A defendant is not entitled to the assistance of counsel under the Sixth Amendment unless two conditions exist. First, there must be a "criminal prosecution" as defined by *Rothgery*—meaning that adversarial judicial criminal proceedings must have been commenced through a first formal hearing, a formal charge, a preliminary hearing, an indictment, an information, or an arraignment (whichever comes first). At that point, a defendant's Sixth Amendment right to counsel *attaches*, but that does not mean that the defendant is necessarily entitled to a lawyer's assistance at that very moment. Rather, counsel must be appointed "within a reasonable time after attachment" and the defendant is only entitled to the assistance of that counsel at "critical stages" in the criminal proceeding.

2. What is a reasonable time? The *Rothgery* Court notes that "counsel must be appointed within a reasonable time after attachment to allow for adequate representation at any critical stage before trial, as well as trial itself," but what is a reasonable time? Rothgery had to wait six months before he got his lawyer. Is that reasonable? What about the 50–year-old woman who was charged with shoplifting in Mississippi who spent 11 months in jail waiting for a lawyer to be appointed? Or the woman charged with stealing $200 from a slot machine who spent 8 months in jail waiting for a lawyer? See Report of the National Right to Counsel Committee, *Justice Denied: America's Continuing Neglect of Our Constitutional Right to Counsel* 86–87 (April 2009) (describing these and other cases). According to recent reports, in some states defendants routinely remain in pretrial detention for weeks or even months before counsel is appointed. See *Gideon's Broken Promise* at 23; see also Douglas L. Colbert, *Prosecution Without Representation*, 59 Buff. L. Rev. 333, 410 & 428–53 (2011) (documenting state delays).

The *Rothgery* Court did not address what, if any, remedy these defendants would have if they were able to demonstrate an unreasonable delay in the provision of counsel. The Court did suggest in dicta, however, that the defendant would have to show prejudice to his Sixth Amendment rights. How would one show prejudice? Would the defendant have to point to specific evidence that was lost due to the delay? Should a defendant's later guilty plea be vacated if there was unreasonable delay in appointing counsel? Consider Colbert at 387–88: "A lawyer's ... early investigation, and evaluation of the State's case allow a detainee to believe in an assigned counsel's dedication to the case and to consider a trial option. In contrast, the longer the delay before counsel appears ..., the greater the client's reasonable anxiety about the assigned lawyer's competence and commitment to defend. Many defendants, particularly those in custody, ultimately lose the will to fight and opt to plead guilty because they lack confidence in the late arriving, appointed lawyer."

    3. *What makes a stage critical?* A criminal defendant's trial is obviously the most critical stage of a criminal prosecution, but the Supreme Court has also held that pretrial corporeal identifications (*United States v. Wade*, p. 761), police questioning (*Brewer v. Williams*, p. 739), and certain kinds of arraignments and preliminary hearings (*Coleman v. Alabama*, p. 1017; *White v. Maryland*, 373 U.S. 59 (1963)) are critical stages that require the presence of counsel. At times, the Court has used broad language to describe what constitutes a critical stage. For example, in *Wade*, Justice Brennan, writing for the Court, explained that the Sixth Amendment ensures that the accused "need not stand alone against the State at any stage of the prosecution, formal or informal, in court or out, where counsel's absence might derogate from the accused's right to a fair trial." *United States v. Wade*, 388 U.S. at 226–27. At the same time, however, the Court has held that probable cause hearings (*Gerstein v. Pugh*, p. 340) and pretrial photographic identification procedures (*United States v. Ash*, p. 770) are not critical stages requiring the presence of counsel. In refusing to recognize photographic identifications as "critical stages," the Supreme Court, per Justice Blackmun, observed that the right to counsel has always been limited to "trial-like confrontations" between prosecuting authorities and the accused where the lawyer acts as "a spokesman for, or advisor to the accused." Concurring Justice Stewart emphasized that "a photographic identification is quite different from a corporeal lineup, for there are substantially fewer possibilities of impermissible suggestion when photographs are used, and those unfair influences can be readily constructed at trial."

    Do you think that the Texas magistration hearing is a "critical stage" at which Rothgery should be entitled to the presence of a lawyer? The majority in *Rothgery* suggests (and Justice Alito's concurrence explicitly claims) that it is not. Why not?

    4. *Bail hearings as critical stages.* Only ten states guarantee counsel to defendants at the initial bail review hearing. Another ten states deny counsel at bail review hearings while the practices in the remaining thirty states vary by county. The Supreme Court has yet to decide whether a bail review hearing is a "critical stage" in a criminal prosecution. What do you think? For a strong argument that it should be deemed critical, see Colbert supra, discussed further in Note 7, p. 941.

5. *Pre-trial psychiatric examinations as critical stages.* In *Estelle v. Smith*, 451 U.S. 454 (1981), the Supreme Court held that the Sixth Amendment guarantees defendants the opportunity to consult with counsel before deciding whether to submit to a pretrial psychiatric examination. The Court avoided the question whether the defendant would have a Sixth Amendment right to have counsel *present* during the psychiatric examination and, in dicta, suggested that it might be disruptive. See id. at 471 n.14. The lower courts are divided regarding whether a pretrial psychiatric examination is a "critical stage" that entitles defendants to the presence of counsel. Consider the statements of then-judge Scalia in *United States v. Byers*, 740 F.2d 1104, 1118–19 (D.C. Cir. 1984):

"[For an encounter to be considered a 'critical stage,'] the defendant must be confronted *either* with the need to make a decision requiring distinctively legal advice—which may occur even in a context in which the prosecutor or his agents are not present—*or* with the need to defend himself against the direct onslaught of the prosecutor—which may require some skills that are not distinctively legal, such as the quality mentioned in *Wade,* of being 'schooled in the detection of suggestive influences.'

"[It] is obvious that neither condition exists here. [At] the psychiatric interview itself, [the defendant] was not confronted by the procedural system; he had no decisions in the nature of legal strategy or tactics to make. [The] only conceivable role for counsel at the examination would have been to observe."

But see Judge Bazelon's response in dissent:

"A court-ordered clinical interview is clearly a 'confrontation' in the sense that the accused is present and is the object of the inquiry. [The] psychiatrists and other behavioral experts who conduct court-ordered clinical interviews are clearly professional adversaries. They are experts employed by the government. They meet with the accused after he has been charged with a crime and while he is in criminal custody. Their reports are transmitted to the government and may be used by it to help prove the defendant's guilt. They routinely testify on behalf of the government.

"A typical psychiatric or other clinical interview is a complex event, in which the accused exhibits a host of subtle but important behaviors. [The] expert cannot be a completely objective and reliable informant even with respect to the bare 'facts' of the interview. The same intellectual presuppositions and personal and institutional biases that affect his or her evaluation of the data also affect his or her conscious or unconscious decisions regarding what sort of behavior to notice, remember, and record. And what is left out in that process may—in the minds of other equally competent behavioral scientists—cast serious doubt on the validity of the interviewer's conclusions."

Who is right? For a more recent discussion of the split in the lower courts and the policy arguments involved, see Maxwell C. Smith, *Quiet Eyes: The Need for Defense Counsel's Presence at Court–Ordered Psychiatric Evaluations*, 16 Cap. Def. J. 421 (2004).

6. *The period between arraignment and trial as a critical stage.* Consider *Hurrell-Harring v. State of New York*, 904 N.Y.S.2d 296, 930 N.E.2d 217, 224 (N.Y. 2010) (also discussed infra p. 177): "Also 'critical' for Sixth Amendment purposes is the period between arraignment and trial when a case must be factually developed and researched, decisions respecting grand jury testimony made, plea negotiations conducted, and pretrial motions filed. Indeed, it is clear that 'to deprive a person of counsel during the period prior to trial may be more damaging than denial of counsel during the trial itself.' [This] complaint contains numerous plain allegations that in specific cases counsel simply was not provided at critical stages of the proceedings. [These] allegations state a claim [for] basic denial of the right to counsel under *Gideon*."

SECTION 2.   THE RIGHT TO APPOINTED COUNSEL IN PROCEEDINGS OTHER THAN CRIMINAL PROSECUTIONS: THE CONTINUED VITALITY OF THE *BETTS v. BRADY* APPROACH

A.   PROBATION AND PAROLE REVOCATION HEARINGS: JUVENILE COURT PROCEEDINGS; PARENTAL STATUS TERMINATION PROCEEDINGS; CONTEMPT HEARINGS

GAGNON v. SCARPELLI, 411 U.S. 778 (1973), arose as follows: After pleading guilty to armed robbery, Scarpelli was sentenced to 15 years imprisonment. However, his sentence was suspended and he was placed on probation. A month later, he and a "known criminal" were apprehended while burglarizing a house. Probation was revoked without a hearing on the stated grounds that (a) Scarpelli had associated with known criminals in violation of probation conditions and (b) while associating with a known criminal he had been involved in a burglary. The Court held, per POWELL, J., that an indigent probationer or parolee has no unqualified due process right to be represented by counsel at revocation hearings:[e]

"In *Mempa v. Rhay*, 389 U.S. 128, 88 S.Ct. 254, 19 L.Ed.2d 336 (1967), the Court held a probationer is entitled to be represented by appointed counsel at a combined revocation and sentencing hearing.[f] Reasoning that counsel is required 'at every stage of a criminal proceeding where substantial rights of a criminal accused may be affected,' and that sentencing is one such stage, the Court concluded that counsel must be provided an indigent at sentencing even when it is accomplished as part of a subsequent, probation revocation proceeding. But this line of reasoning does not require a hearing or counsel at the time of probation revocation in a case such as the present one, where the probationer was sentenced at the time of that trial.

"[The] introduction of counsel into a revocation proceeding will alter significantly the nature of the proceeding. If counsel is provided for the probationer or parolee, the State in turn will normally provide its own counsel; lawyers, by training and disposition, are advocates and bound by professional duty to present all available evidence and arguments in support of their clients' positions and to contest with vigor all adverse evidence and views. The role of the hearing body itself, aptly described in *Morrissey* as being 'predictive and discretionary' as well as fact-finding, may become more akin to that of a judge at a trial, and less

---

e. Since Scarpelli did not attempt to *retain* counsel, the Court reserved judgment on "whether a probationer or parolee has a right to be represented at a revocation hearing by retained counsel in situations other than those where the State would be obliged to furnish counsel for an indigent."

f. Initially, the petitioners' sentencing was deferred subject to probation. The prosecutor subsequently moved to have their probation revoked on the ground that they had committed other crimes. At the hearings, petitioners' probation was revoked and they were sentenced to a term of imprisonment on their original convictions.

attuned to the rehabilitative needs of the individual probationer or parolee. In the greater self-consciousness of its quasi-judicial role, the hearing body may be less tolerant of marginal deviant behavior and feel more pressure to reincarcerate rather than continue nonpunitive rehabilitation. Certainly, the decision-making process will be prolonged, and the financial cost to the State—for appointed counsel, counsel for the State, a longer record, and the possibility of judicial review—will not be insubstantial.

"In some cases, these modifications in the nature of the revocation hearing must be endured and the costs borne because [the] probationer's or parolee's version of a disputed issue can fairly be represented only by a trained advocate. But due process is not so rigid as to require that the significant interests in informality, flexibility, and economy must always be sacrificed.

"In so concluding, we are of course aware that the case-by-case approach to the right to counsel in felony prosecutions adopted in *Betts* [was] later rejected in favor of a *per se* rule. [But we do not] draw from *Gideon* and *Argersinger* the conclusion that a case-by-case approach to furnishing counsel is necessarily inadequate to protect constitutional rights asserted in varying types of proceedings: there are critical differences between criminal trials and probation or parole revocation hearings, and both society and the probationer or parolee have stakes in preserving these differences.

"In a criminal trial, the State is represented by a prosecutor; formal rules of evidence are in force; a defendant enjoys a number of procedural rights which may be lost if not timely raised; and, in a jury trial, a defendant must make a presentation understandable to untrained jurors. In short, a criminal trial under our system is an adversary proceeding with its own unique characteristics. In a revocation hearing, on the other hand, the State is represented not by a prosecutor but by a parole officer with the orientation described above; formal procedures and rules of evidence are not employed; and the members of the hearing body are familiar with the problems and practice of probation or parole. The need for counsel at revocation hearings derives not from the invariable attributes of those hearings but rather from the peculiarities of particular cases. * * *

"We [find] no justification for a new inflexible constitutional rule with respect to the requirement of counsel. We think, rather, that the decision as to the need for counsel must be made on a case-by-case basis in the exercise of a sound discretion by the state authority charged with responsibility for administering the probation and parole system. * * * Presumptively, it may be said that counsel should be provided in cases where, after being informed of his right to request counsel, the probationer or parolee makes such a request, based on a timely and colorable claim (i) that he has not committed the alleged violation of the conditions upon which he is at liberty; or (ii) [that] there are substantial reasons which justified or mitigated the violation and make revocation inappropriate and that the reasons are complex or otherwise difficult to develop or present. In passing on a request for the appointment of counsel, the responsible agency also should consider, especially in doubtful cases, whether the probationer appears to be capable of speaking effectively for himself. * * *

"We return to the facts of the present case. Because respondent was not afforded either a preliminary hearing or a final hearing, the revocation of his probation did not meet the standards of due process prescribed in *Morrissey*.[g] [Accordingly,] respondent was entitled to a writ of habeas corpus. [Because of

---

g. *Morrissey v. Brewer*, 408 U.S. 471 (1972), held that even though the revocation of parole is not a part of the criminal prosecution, the loss of liberty involved is a serious deprivation requiring that the parolee be accorded due process. That means a preliminary and a final revocation hearing under the conditions specified in *Morrissey*.

respondent's assertions regarding his confession to the crime] we conclude that the failure [to] provide [him] with the assistance of counsel should be reexamined in light of this opinion."

NOTES AND QUESTIONS

1. **Are probationers better off without lawyers?** The Court seemed to suggest so in *Gagnon* when it noted that judges might be "less tolerant" and "feel more pressure to reincarcerate" defendants if counsel were introduced in probation revocation hearings. This is not the first time that it has been suggested that defendants would be better off without lawyers. The Assistant Attorney General of Alabama made exactly that argument when he argued against a categorical right to counsel in *Gideon*. See Oral Arg. Tr. ("[A]n indigent appearing without aid of counsel really [stands] a better chance of getting a lighter sentence or even an outright acquittal than one who does have an attorney. . . . [G]enerally speaking indigents charged with crime are not as unfortunately situated as the critics of *Betts* versus *Brady* would have us believe."). Do you think that is true? If so, what does it say about the role of lawyers and the behavior of judges in our criminal justice system?

2. **Betts, Gideon and Gagnon compared.** How likely is it that a probationer or parolee will be able to convince a court, *without* the benefit of counsel, on the basis of a record made *without* the assistance of counsel, that there are "substantial reasons which justified or mitigated the violation" or that "the reasons are complex or otherwise difficult to develop or present"? How many probationers or parolees will know *what* to point to or look for and *why?* How intelligent a decision can be made as to whether "the probationer appears to be capable of speaking effectively for himself" without knowing what justifications or mitigations a competent lawyer might have raised or developed? Can *Gagnon* escape the criticism of *Betts?* Consider *ABA Standards* § 18–7.5 (commentary); Kamisar, *The Right to Counsel and the Fourteenth Amendment: A Dialogue on "the Most Pervasive Right" of an Accused,* 30 U.Chi.L.Rev. 1, 53, 65 (1962).

3. **Juvenile court proceedings.** The *Gagnon* Court talked about "the rehabilitative needs of the individual probationer or parolee" and viewed the probation or parole officer's function "not so much to compel conformance to a strict code of behavior as to supervise a course of rehabilitation." But compare *In re Gault*, 387 U.S. 1 (1967), holding that, in respect to juvenile delinquency proceedings that may result in loss of the juvenile's freedom, fourteenth amendment due process requires that "the child and his parent [be] notified of the child's right to be represented by [retained counsel] or, if they are unable to afford counsel that counsel will be appointed to represent the child." The Court stressed the need for counsel to assure a fair hearing in a proceeding "comparable in seriousness to a felony prosecution." It rejected the state's suggestion that the probation officers, parents, and judge might be relied on to "represent the child," finding "no material difference in this respect between adult and juvenile proceedings of the sort involved here."

Gault was hailed as demonstrating the Court's reluctance to be "hemmed in by such artificial labels as 'criminal,' 'civil', or 'quasi-administrative,' " and for taking the position that "a desire to help—the rehabilitation ideal—no longer will serve as the incantation before which procedural safeguards must succumb." Fred Cohen, *Sentencing, Probation, and the Rehabilitative Ideal,* 47 Texas L.Rev. 1, 2 (1968). For a close look at the legacy of *Gault*, see *Symposium, In re Gault: A 40 Year Retrospective on Children's Rights*, 44 CRIM.L.BULL. 302 (2008).

4. Summary courts-martial. In *Middendorf v. Henry*, 425 U.S. 25 (1976), a 7–2 majority held there is no right to appointed counsel at summary courts-martial, even though the officer conducting these proceedings can impose a maximum punishment of 30 days confinement at hard labor. In rejecting even the view that counsel must be provided in "special circumstances," the Court, per Rehnquist, J., observed:

"[E]ven were the Sixth Amendment to be held applicable to court-martial proceedings, the summary court-martial provided for in these cases was not a 'criminal prosecution' within the meaning of that Amendment. [T]he fact that the outcome of a proceeding may result in loss of liberty does not by itself, even in civilian life, mean that the Sixth Amendment's guarantee of counsel is applicable. In *Gagnon,* the respondent faced the prospect of being sent to prison as a result of the revocation of his probation, but we held that the revocation proceeding was nonetheless not a 'criminal proceeding.' [In *Gault*] the juvenile faced possible initial confinement as a result of the proceeding in question, but the Court nevertheless based its conclusion that counsel was required on [Fourteenth Amendment due process], rather than on any determination that the hearing was a 'criminal prosecution' within the meaning of the Sixth Amendment."

5. Parental status termination proceedings. Over the dissenters' protest that "the unique importance of a parent's interest in the care and custody of his or her child cannot constitutionally be extinguished through formal judicial proceedings without the benefit of counsel" and the dissenters' charge that the Court was "reviv[ing] an ad hoc approach thoroughly discredited nearly 20 years ago in *Gideon,*" in *Lassiter v. Department of Social Services*, 452 U.S. 18 (1981), a 5–4 majority, per Stewart, J., rejected the view that due process requires the appointment of counsel in every parental status termination proceeding involving indigent parents. Thus, the Court left the appointment of counsel in such proceedings to be determined by the state courts on a case-by-case basis.

"The pre-eminent generalization that emerges from the Court's precedents on an indigent's right to appointed counsel," observed the Court, "is that such a right has been recognized to exist only where the litigant may lose his physical liberty if he loses the litigation. * * * Significantly, as a litigant's interest in personal liberty diminishes, so does his right to appointed counsel. [Thus, *Gagnon*] declined to hold that indigent probationers have, *per se*, a right to counsel at revocation hearings, and instead left the decision whether counsel should be appointed to be made on a case-by-case basis."

The Court then examined the termination hearing and found it to be fundamentally fair. "In light of the unpursued avenues of defense, and of the experiences petitioner underwent at this hearing," the dissenters found the Court's conclusion "virtually incredible." Consider Bruce R. Jacob, *Memories of and Reflections about Gideon v. Wainwright*, 33 Stetson L.Rev. 180, 287 (2003): "[Whether counsel is to be appointed in cases involving the termination of parental rights] is to be made on a case-by-case basis, in the same way decisions such as this were made under the *Betts* rule. The rule of *Betts* was considered unworkable by the Court. That was one of the main reasons for the decision in *Gideon*. [If] *Betts* was not workable in 1963, why is it workable now?"

6. Where to draw the line. Was the *Lassiter* Court's greatest concern where to draw the line? If the state must provide indigents counsel in parental termination proceedings, why not in a child custody fight growing out of a divorce action when one parent is indigent? Why not in an eviction proceeding, when an indigent is about to lose his place of residence? Is there a stronger case for providing counsel in parental termination proceedings than in these other proceedings? Why (not)? See Kamisar, *Gideon v. Wainwright A Quarter–Century Later,* 10 Pace L.Rev. 343, 357–59 (1990).

7. *Should Gideon apply to civil cases?* In 2006, the American Bar Association adopted a resolution urging federal and state governments to create a right to counsel in civil cases where "basic human needs are at stake." Although a number of states have taken steps to provide limited civil representation, in 2009 California became the first state to enact sweeping legislation recognizing a civil right to counsel and establishing funding for a pilot project designed to provide poor individuals with lawyers in an array of civil cases including child custody, housing, and domestic abuse cases as well as cases involving claims of neglect of the elderly and disabled. While many celebrate California's law, others are deeply skeptical of it. Consider Lawrence J. Siskind, *Civil Gideon: An Idea Whose Time Should Not Come,* American Thinker (August 6, 2011):

"Considering the sorry state of Criminal Gideon, one would expect proponents of a government entitlement program for poor civil litigants to have chosen a different title from 'Civil Gideon.' It's a badly tarnished brand.

"Providing criminal counsel at public expense has ensured that deserving cases are lost in the sea of undeserving ones. The same will happen in the civil sphere if Civil Gideon proponents have their way, and the screening function now provided by legal aid societies is removed.

"Apart from a lack of screening, a government entitlement program is also a bad idea because of plain economics. Economists may not agree on much, but they do agree on one basic idea. If you price a good or service below the market rate, people will want more of it. If civil litigation is free, there will be more of it. And that's not necessarily good for the litigants themselves, or for society as a whole. [Making] counsel available for free, to any party below a certain income level, ensures that many ordinary disputes, once settled by discussions, will become clogs in an increasingly overloaded justice system.

"Finally, Civil Gideon is a bad idea today because the states cannot afford it. [In] 2007, the California State Bar's 2007 Commission on Access to Justice Report found a $394–million gap in unfunded civil legal services. Ironically, that figure is about the same size as the recent budget cut. If California cannot afford its current legal budget, where is it going to find the money for a new legal entitlement program?"

Do you agree? Given the states' financial inability to adequately fund counsel in criminal cases, why should we think that they can adequately fund access in civil cases? Which is more important or is there another way (other than the civil versus criminal divide) to decide which individuals should be entitled to publicly-funded assistance of counsel?

8. *Civil contempt hearings.* When a State enforces its child support orders by threatening with incarceration for civil contempt those who are (1) subject to such an order, (2) able to comply with it, but (3) fail to do so, is the State required to provide counsel at a civil contempt hearing for an *indigent* person potentially faced with such incarceration? The Court addressed this issue in TURNER v. ROGERS, 131 S.Ct. 2507 (2011), a case where the noncustodial parent (Turner) was found in civil contempt of court for failing to make child support payments and sentenced to (and served) 12 months in prison. Neither Turner nor the child's mother were represented by counsel at his brief civil contempt hearing. The judge who sentenced Turner to prison failed to make any finding as to his ability to pay or to indicate on the contempt order form whether he was able to make child support payments.

A 5–4 majority, per Justice Breyer, concluded that "where as here the custodial parent [the one entitled to receive the support] is unrepresented by counsel, the State need not provide counsel to the noncustodial parent." However, the Court "attach[ed] an important caveat, namely, that the State must nevertheless have in place alternative procedures that assure a fundamentally fair determination of the incarceration-related question, whether the supporting parent is able to comply with the support order."

In the Court's view, "a categorical right to counsel in proceedings of [this kind] would carry with it disadvantages (in the form of unfairness and delay) that, in terms of ultimate fairness, would deprive it of significant superiority over the alternatives that we have mentioned. We consequently hold that the Due Process Clause does not *automatically* require the provision of counsel at civil contempt proceedings to an indigent individual who is subject to a child support order, even if that individual faces incarceration (for up to a year)." This is especially so "where the opposing parent or other custodian (to whom support funds are owed) is not represented by counsel and the State provides alternative procedural safeguards equivalent to those we have mentioned (adequate notice of the importance of ability to pay, fair opportunity to present, and to dispute, relevant information and court findings)."

However, "[the] record indicates that Turner received neither counsel nor the benefit of alternative procedures like those we have described. [The] court nonetheless found Turner in contempt and ordered him incarcerated. Under these circumstances Turner's incarceration violated the Due Process Clause."

Dissenting Justice Thomas (joined by Roberts, C.J., and Scalia and Alito, JJ.) protested that although the Court recognizes that appointed counsel was not required in this case, "it nevertheless vacates the judgment of the [state supreme court] on a different ground, which the parties have never raised. Solely at the invitation of the United States as amicus curiae, the majority decides that Turner's contempt proceedings violated due process because it did not include 'alternative procedural safeguards.' " He noted that "[e]ven when the defendant's liberty is at stake, the Court has not concluded that fundamental fairness requires that counsel also be appointed if the proceeding is not criminal," citing *Gagnon v. Scarpelli* and *Middendorf v. Henry*.

The balancing test utilized by the majority, maintained Justice Thomas, "weighs an individual's interest against that of the Government itself," but fails to "account for the interests of the child and custodial parent, who is usually the child's mother. But their interests are the very reason for the child support obligation and the civil contempt proceedings that enforce it."

Thomas observed that "[the] interests of children and mothers who depend on child support are notoriously difficult to protect. [That] some fathers subject to a child support agreement report little or no income 'does not mean they do not have the ability to pay any child support.' [Rather,] many 'deadbeat dads' opt to work in the underground economy to 'shield their earnings from child support enforcement efforts.' [The] States that use civil contempt with the threat of detention find it a 'highly effective' tool for collecting child support when nothing else works."

B. COLLATERAL ATTACK PROCEEDINGS

As is discussed more extensively elsewhere in this book (see Ch. 29, § 1), an indigent prisoner has no federal constitutional right to assigned counsel in postconviction proceedings. See *Pennsylvania v. Finley*, 481 U.S. 551 (1987). A 5–4 majority held in *Murray v. Giarratano*, 492 U.S. 1 (1989) that this rule applies no differently in capital cases than in noncapital cases.

SECTION 3. THE *GRIFFIN-DOUGLAS* "EQUALITY" PRINCIPLE

GRIFFIN v. ILLINOIS: "THERE CAN BE NO EQUAL JUSTICE WHERE THE KIND OF TRIAL A MAN GETS DEPENDS ON THE AMOUNT OF MONEY HE HAS"

Prior to GRIFFIN v. ILLINOIS, 351 U.S. 12 (1956), full direct appellate review could only be had in Illinois by furnishing the appellate court with a bill of exceptions or report of the trial proceedings, certified by the trial judge. Preparation of these documents was sometimes impossible without a stenographic transcript of the trial proceedings, but such a transcript was furnished free only to indigent defendants sentenced to death. *Griffin* upheld by a 5–4 vote the contention that the due process and equal protection clauses of the fourteenth amendment require that *all* indigent defendants be furnished a transcript, at least where allegations that manifest errors occurred at the trial are not denied. See generally Francis A. Allen, *Griffin v. Illinois: Antecedents and Aftermath,* 25 U.Chi.L.Rev. 151, 152 (1957).

There was no opinion of the Court in *Griffin*. Justice Black announced the Court's judgment in a four-justice opinion; Justice Frankfurter concurred specially. In the course of his opinion, Justice Black observed:

"In criminal trials a State can no more discriminate on account of poverty than on account of religion, race, or color. Plainly the ability to pay costs in advance bears no rational relationship to a defendant's guilt or innocence and could not be used as an excuse to deprive a defendant of a fair trial. [It] is true that a State is not required by the federal constitution to provide appellate courts or a right to appellate review at all. [But] that is not to say that a State that does grant appellate review can do so in a way that discriminates against some convicted defendants on account of their poverty. * * *

"All of the States now provide some method of appeal from criminal convictions, recognizing the importance of appellate review to a correct adjudication of guilt or innocence. Statistics show that a substantial proportion of criminal convictions are reversed by state appellate courts. Thus to deny adequate review to the poor means that many of them may lose their life, liberty or property because of unjust convictions which appellate courts would set aside. Many States have recognized this and provided aid for convicted defendants who have a right to appeal and need a transcript but are unable to pay for it. A few have not. Such a denial is a misfit in a country dedicated to affording equal justice to all and special privileges to none in the administration of its criminal law. There can be no equal justice where the kind of trial a man gets depends on the amount of money he has. Destitute defendants must be afforded as adequate appellate review as defendants who have money enough to buy transcripts."

A. APPLICATION (OR EXTENSION) OF *GRIFFIN*

In the decade and a half following *Griffin,* its underlying principle was broadly applied. See *Burns v. Ohio,* 360 U.S. 252 (1959) (state cannot require indigent defendant to pay filing fee before permitting him to appeal); *Smith v. Bennett,* 365 U.S. 708 (1961) (extending ban on filing fees to state post-conviction proceedings); *Long v. District Court of Iowa,* 385 U.S. 192 (1966) (indigent must be furnished a free transcript of a state habeas corpus hearing for use on appeal from a denial of habeas corpus, although availability of transcript not a sine qua non to access to the appellate court); *Roberts v. LaVallee,* 389 U.S. 40 (1967) (indigent defendant entitled to free transcript of preliminary hearing for use at trial, even though both defendant and his counsel attended preliminary hearing and no indication of use to which preliminary hearing transcript could be put—points stressed by dissenting Justice Harlan); *Britt v. North Carolina,* 404 U.S. 226 (1971) (recognition that under ordinary circumstances indigent would be entitled to free transcript of previous trial ending with a hung jury because such a transcript would be "valuable to the defendant" as a discovery device and "as a tool at the [second] trial itself for the impeachment of prosecution witnesses").

In MAYER v. CHICAGO, 404 U.S. 189 (1971), a unanimous Court, per Brennan, J., carried the *Griffin* principle further than it ever has the *Gideon* principle by holding that an indigent appellant "cannot be denied a 'record of sufficient completeness' to permit proper consideration of his claims" because he was convicted of ordinance violations punishable by fine only. "The size of the defendant's pocketbook bears no more relationship to his guilt or innocence in a non-felony than in a felony case." Nor was the Court impressed with the argument that appellant's interest in a transcript in a case where he is not subject to imprisonment is outweighed by the State's fiscal and other interests in not burdening the appellate process:

"*Griffin* does not represent a balance between the needs of the accused and the interests of society; its principle is a flat prohibition against pricing indigent defendants out of as effective an appeal as would be available to others able to pay their own way. The invidiousness of the discrimination that exists when criminal procedures are made available only to those who can pay is not erased by any differences in the sentences that may be imposed. The State's fiscal interest is, therefore, irrelevant.

"We add that even approaching the problem in the terms the city suggests hardly yields the answer the city tenders. The practical effects of conviction of even petty offenses of the kind involved here are not to be minimized. A fine may bear as heavily on an indigent accused as forced confinement.[h] The collateral consequences of conviction may be even more serious, as when (as was apparently a possibility in this case) the impecunious medical student finds himself barred from the practice of medicine because of a conviction he is unable to appeal for lack of funds."[i]

B. THE IMPACT OF THE "EQUALITY" PRINCIPLE ON THOSE WHO CANNOT AFFORD COUNSEL OR OTHER FORMS OF ASSISTANCE

Prior to *Gideon,* the *Griffin* case posed a challenge to *Betts:* How could the *Betts* line of cases be reconciled with the language, if not the holding, of *Griffin?* Since there was an unqualified right to have one's own paid counsel of his choosing at state trial, capital or not, did *Griffin* not imply that an indigent also has this unqualified right? By requiring *special circumstances* to exist before the indigent was entitled to appointed counsel in non-capital state cases, was the indigent not denied equal protection of the law? When the Supreme Court finally overruled the *Betts* case, somewhat surprisingly, it did not rely on *Griffin* at all, but *Douglas v. California,* infra, decided the same day, is another story.

DOUGLAS v. CALIFORNIA, 372 U.S. 353 (1963), arose as follows: Indigent defendants requested, and were denied, the assistance of counsel on appeal. In

---

h. But cf. *Argersinger v. Hamlin,* p. 80; *Scott v. Illinois,* p. 81.

i. Chief Justice Burger joined the Court's opinion, but in a separate opinion emphasized that "there are alternatives in the majority of cases to a full verbatim transcript of an entire trial."

accordance with a California rule of criminal procedure, the California District Court of Appeals stated that it had "gone through" the record and had come to the conclusion that "no good whatever could be served by appointment of counsel." Under the California procedure, appellate courts had to appoint counsel only if in their opinion it would be helpful to the defendant or the court. A 6–3 majority, per Justice Douglas, viewed the denial of counsel on appeal to an indigent under these circumstances "a discrimination at least as invidious as that condemned in [*Griffin*]:"

"[Whether the issue is a transcript on appeal or the assistance of counsel on appeal] the evil is the same: discrimination against the indigent. For there can be no equal justice where the kind of an appeal a man enjoys 'depends on the amount of money he has.' * * *

"When an indigent is forced to run this gantlet of a preliminary showing of merit, the right to appeal does not comport with fair procedure. [T]he discrimination is not between 'possibly good and obviously bad cases,' but between cases where the rich man can require the court to listen to argument of counsel before deciding on the merits, but a poor man cannot. There is lacking that equality demanded by the Fourteenth Amendment where the rich man, who appeals as of right, enjoys the benefit of counsel's examination into the record, research of the law, and marshalling of arguments on his behalf, while the indigent, already burdened by a preliminary determination that his case is without merit, is forced to shift for himself. The indigent, where the record is unclear or the errors are hidden, has only the right to a meaningless ritual, while the rich man has a meaningful appeal."[j]

Justice Harlan, whom Stewart, J., joined, dissented,[k] maintaining that "the Equal Protection Clause is not apposite, and its application to cases like the present one can lead only to mischievous results." He thought the case "should be judged solely under the Due Process Clause" and that the California procedure did not violate that provision. In rejecting the equal protection argument, Harlan observed:

"Laws such as these do not deny equal protection to the less fortunate for one essential reason: the Equal Protection Clause does not impose on the States 'an affirmative duty to lift the handicaps flowing from differences in economic circumstances.' To so construe it would be to read into the Constitution a philosophy of leveling that would be foreign to many of our basic concepts of the proper relations between government and society. The State may have a moral obligation to eliminate the evils of poverty, but it is not required by the Equal Protection Clause to give to some whatever others can afford.

"[I]t should be noted that if the present problem may be viewed as one of equal protection, so may the question of the right to appointed counsel at trial, and the Court's analysis of that right in *Gideon* [is] wholly unnecessary. The short way to dispose of *Gideon*, in other words, would be simply to say that the State deprives the indigent of equal protection whenever it fails to furnish him with legal services, and perhaps with other services as well, equivalent to those that the affluent defendant can obtain."[l]

---

j. The Court pointed out it was dealing "only with the first appeal, granted as a matter of right," not deciding whether a state had to provide counsel for an indigent seeking discretionary review.

k. Justice Clark wrote a separate dissenting opinion.

l. One may ask, too, why the Court failed even to discuss the applicability of the *Griffin-Douglas* "equality" principle to the issue raised in *Scott v. Illinois* p. 81. Since it is plain that one charged with an offense *punishable* by incarceration may *retain* counsel for his defense, does not the "equality" principle suggest that the "actual imprisonment" standard, even if it defensibly

ROSS v. MOFFITT

417 U.S. 600, 94 S.Ct. 2437, 41 L.Ed.2d 341 (1974).

JUSTICE REHNQUIST delivered the opinion of the Court.

[Like many other states, the North Carolina appellate system is multitiered, providing for both an intermediate Court of Appeals and a Supreme Court. North Carolina authorizes appointment of counsel for a convicted defendant appealing to the intermediate court of appeals, but not for a defendant who seeks either discretionary review in the state supreme court or a writ of certiorari in the U.S. Supreme Court. In one case, the Mecklenburg County forgery conviction, respondent sought appointed counsel for discretionary review in the state supreme court. In another case, the Guilford County forgery conviction, respondent was represented by the public defender in the state supreme court, but sought court-appointed counsel to prepare a writ of certiorari to the U.S. Supreme Court. On federal habeas corpus, a unanimous panel of the U.S. Court of Appeals for the Fourth Circuit, per Haynsworth, C.J., held that the *Douglas* rationale required appointment of counsel in both instances.]

[*Griffin* and succeeding cases, such as *Burns v. Ohio* and *Smith v. Bennett* (the filing fee cases summarized at p. 99),] stand for the proposition that a State cannot arbitrarily cut off appeal rights for indigents while leaving open avenues of appeal for more affluent persons. In *Douglas,* however, [the] Court departed somewhat from the limited doctrine of [these] cases [and] held that the State must go further and provide counsel for the indigent on his first appeal as of right. It is this decision we are asked to extend today.

[The] precise rationale for the *Griffin* and *Douglas* lines of cases has never been explicitly stated, some support being derived from the Equal Protection Clause of the Fourteenth Amendment, and some from the Due Process Clause of that Amendment. Neither clause by itself provides an entirely satisfactory basis for the result reached, each depending on a different inquiry which emphasizes different factors. "Due process" emphasizes fairness between the State and the individual dealing with the State, regardless of how other individuals in the same situation may be treated. "Equal protection," on the other hand, emphasizes disparity in treatment by a State between classes of individuals whose situations are arguably indistinguishable. We will address these issues separately in the succeeding sections.

Recognition of the due process rationale in *Douglas* is found both in the Court's opinion and in the dissenting opinion of Mr. Justice Harlan. [Indeed,] Mr. Justice Harlan thought that the due process issue in *Douglas* was the only one worthy of extended consideration. * * *

We do not believe that the Due Process Clause requires North Carolina to provide respondent with counsel on his discretionary appeal to the State Supreme Court. At the trial stage of a criminal proceeding, the right of an indigent defendant to counsel [is] fundamental and binding upon the States by virtue of the Sixth and Fourteenth Amendments. But there are significant differences between the trial and appellate stages of a criminal proceeding. The purpose of the trial stage from the State's point of view is to convert a criminal defendant from a person presumed innocent to one found guilty beyond a reasonable doubt.

[By] contrast, it is ordinarily the defendant, rather than the State, who initiates the appellate process, seeking not to fend off the efforts of the State's

---

defines the Sixth Amendment right to appointed counsel, is unsatisfactory under the equal protection clause?

prosecutor but rather to overturn a finding of guilt made by a judge or jury below. The defendant needs an attorney on appeal not as a shield to protect him against being "haled into court" by the State and stripped of his presumption of innocence, but rather as a sword to upset the prior determination of guilt. This difference is significant for, while no one would agree that the State may simply dispense with the trial stage of proceedings without a criminal defendant's consent, it is clear that the State need not provide any appeal at all. *McKane v. Durston.* The fact that an appeal *has* been provided does not automatically mean that a State then acts unfairly by refusing to provide counsel to indigent defendants at every stage of the way. Unfairness results only if indigents are singled out by the State and denied meaningful access to that system because of their poverty. That question is more profitably considered under an equal protection analysis.

[The] Fourteenth Amendment "does not require absolute equality or precisely equal advantages," nor does it require the State to "equalize economic conditions." *Griffin* (Frankfurter, J., concurring). It does require [that] indigents have an adequate opportunity to present their claims fairly within the adversarial system. [The] question is not one of absolutes, but one of degrees. In this case we do not believe that the Equal Protection Clause [requires] North Carolina to provide free counsel for indigent defendants seeking to take discretionary appeals to the North Carolina Supreme Court, or to file petitions for certiorari in this Court.

[The] facts show that respondent, in connection with his Mecklenburg County conviction, received the benefit of counsel in examining the record of his trial and in preparing an appellate brief on his behalf for the state Court of Appeals. Thus, prior to his seeking discretionary review in the State Supreme Court, his claims "had once been presented by a lawyer and passed upon by an appellate court." *Douglas.* We do not believe that it can be said, therefore, that a defendant in respondent's circumstances is denied meaningful access to the North Carolina Supreme Court simply because the State does not appoint counsel to aid him in seeking review in that court. At that stage he will have, at the very least, a transcript or other record of trial proceedings, a brief on his behalf in the Court of Appeals setting forth his claims of error, and in many cases an opinion by the Court of Appeals disposing of his case. These materials, supplemented by whatever submission respondent may make *pro se,* would appear to provide the Supreme Court of North Carolina with an adequate basis on which to base its decision to grant or deny review.

We are fortified in this conclusion by our understanding of the function served by discretionary review in the North Carolina Supreme Court. The critical issue in that court, as we perceive it, is not whether there has been "a correct adjudication of guilt" in every individual case, but rather whether "the subject matter of the appeal has significant public interest," whether "the cause involves legal principles of major significance to the jurisprudence of the state," or whether the decision below is in probable conflict with a decision of the Supreme Court. The Supreme Court may deny certiorari even though it believes that the decision of the Court of Appeals was incorrect, since a decision which appears incorrect may nevertheless fail to satisfy any of the criteria discussed above. Once a defendant's claims of error are organized and presented in a lawyer-like fashion to the Court of Appeals, the justices of the Supreme Court of North Carolina who make the decision to grant or deny discretionary review should be able to ascertain whether his case satisfies the standards established by the legislature for such review.

This is not to say, of course, that a skilled lawyer, particularly one trained in the somewhat arcane art of preparing petitions for discretionary review, would not prove helpful to any litigant able to employ him. An indigent defendant seeking review in the Supreme Court of North Carolina is therefore somewhat handicapped in comparison with a wealthy defendant who has counsel assisting him in every conceivable manner at every stage in the proceeding. But both the opportunity to have counsel prepare an initial brief in the Court of Appeals and the nature of discretionary review in the Supreme Court of North Carolina make this relative handicap far less than the handicap borne by the indigent defendant denied counsel on his initial appeal as of right in *Douglas*. And the fact that a particular service might be of benefit to an indigent defendant does not mean that the service is constitutionally required. The duty of the State under our cases is not to duplicate the legal arsenal that may be privately retained by a criminal defendant in a continuing effort to reverse his conviction, but only to assure the indigent defendant an adequate opportunity to present his claims fairly in the context of the State's appellate process. We think respondent was given that opportunity under the existing North Carolina system.

Much of the discussion in the preceding section is equally relevant to the question of whether a State must provide counsel for a defendant seeking review of his conviction in this Court. North Carolina will have provided counsel for a convicted defendant's only appeal as of right, and the brief prepared by that counsel together with one and perhaps two North Carolina appellate opinions will be available to this Court in order that it may decide whether or not to grant certiorari. This Court's review, much like that of the Supreme Court of North Carolina, is discretionary and depends on numerous factors other than the perceived correctness of the judgment we are asked to review. * * *

JUSTICE DOUGLAS, with whom JUSTICE BRENNAN and JUSTICE MARSHALL concur, dissenting.

[In his opinion below] Chief Judge Haynsworth could find "no logical basis for differentiation between appeals of right and permissive review procedures in the context of the Constitution and the right to counsel." More familiar with the functioning of the North Carolina criminal justice system than are we, he concluded that "in the context of constitutional questions arising in criminal prosecutions, permissive review in the state's highest court may be predictably the most meaningful review the conviction will receive." The North Carolina Court of Appeals, for example, will be constrained in diverging from an earlier opinion of the State Supreme Court, even if subsequent developments have rendered the earlier Supreme Court decision suspect. "[T]he state's highest court remains the ultimate arbiter of the rights of its citizens."

Chief Judge Haynsworth also correctly observed that the indigent defendant proceeding without counsel is at a substantial disadvantage relative to wealthy defendants represented by counsel when he is forced to fend for himself in seeking discretionary review from the State Supreme Court or from this Court. It may well not be enough to allege error in the courts below in layman's terms; a more sophisticated approach may be demanded:

"An indigent defendant is as much in need of the assistance of a lawyer in preparing and filing a petition for certiorari as he is in the handling of an appeal as of right. In many appeals, an articulate defendant could file an effective brief by telling his story in simple language without legalisms, but the technical requirement for applications for writs of certiorari are hazards which one untrained in the law could hardly be expected to negotiate. * * * *"

ON THE MEANING OF *ROSS v. MOFFITT*

1. Is *Mayer v. Chicago* (p. 100) "good law" after *Ross?* Are *Long v. District Court, Gardner v. California, Roberts v. LaVallee,* and *Britt v. North Carolina* (all summarized at pp. 99–100) "good law" after *Ross?* Does the *Long-Gardner* line of cases (never mentioned by the *Ross* Court) constitute a significant "departure" from what the *Ross* Court calls the "limited doctrine" of *Griffin* and succeeding cases?

2. Consider Laurence H. Tribe, *American Constitutional Law* 1647 (2d ed.1988): "[The *Ross* Court] disengaged *Griffin* from *Douglas,* deftly rewove the *Griffin* transcript and filing fee decisions together as minimal access cases rather than equal protection cases, and neatly severed *Douglas* from this newly created body of law." See also Kamisar, *Poverty, Equality, and Criminal Procedure,* in National College of District Attorneys, *Constitutional Law Deskbook* 1–97 to 1–100 (1977).

3. *Does the Ross opinion's "equal protection analysis" closely resemble a "due process analysis"?* Indeed, now that *Ross* is on the books, does the "equality" principle *add anything* to what the indigent defendant or prisoner already has in his arsenal? Consider Kamisar, supra, at 1–101 to 1–108:

"[The *Ross* 'equal protection analysis'] seems to put to one side the admitted fact that an indigent seeking discretionary review is 'somewhat handicapped in comparison with a wealthy defendant who has counsel assisting him' and focuses instead on whether an indigent seeking discretionary review without counsel has a '*meaningful* opportunity' (emphasis added) to present his claims in the state supreme court—to provide the court 'with an *adequate* basis for its decision to grant or deny review' (emphasis added)—*regardless* of whether a wealthy defendant who has counsel at this stage has a *significantly better* opportunity to present his claims.

"[What *Ross*] really seems to be asking, and deciding, is whether an indigent in respondent's circumstances has a *fair chance*, a *fighting chance* (or the requisite *minimum* chance), to get the attention of the state supreme court. [This] is 'due process,' not 'equal protection' reasoning. * * *

"So long as the indigent defendant's 'brand of justice' satisfies certain minimal standards—passes government inspection, one might say—[*Ross* tells us that] *it need not be* the same brand of justice or the same 'choice' or 'prime' grade of justice as the wealthy man's. [In some phases of the criminal process an indigent will not have 'meaningful access' to the hearing body or an 'adequate opportunity' to present his claim], but in [such] cases 'fundamental fairness'—'due process'—will require the state to furnish counsel. In those cases where due process *does not* impose a duty on the state to provide counsel, *neither,* it seems, *will 'equal protection.'* "

4. *Is there a right to appointed counsel on discretionary appeal from a plea of guilty?* When appointed counsel is not provided for indigent defendants seeking first-tier discretionary appellate review of guilty pleas or *nolo contendere* pleas, which case governs, *Ross* or *Douglas?* The *Douglas* case does, a 6–3 majority of the Court told us in HALBERT v. MICHIGAN, 545 U.S. 605 (2005).

Under Michigan law, the intermediate Court of Appeals adjudicated appeals from criminal convictions as of right *except* that those convicted on guilty or *nolo contendere* pleas had to apply for leave to appeal. The Michigan Supreme Court held that nothing in the Constitution required that counsel be appointed for plea-convicted defendants seeking review in the Court of Appeals. The Court, per Ginsburg, J., disagreed:

"[Halbert's] case is framed by two prior decisions of this Court concerning state-funded appellate counsel, *Douglas* and *Ross*. [With] which of those decisions should the instant case be aligned? We hold that *Douglas* provides the controlling instruction. Two aspects of the Michigan Court of Appeals' process following plea-based convictions lead us to that conclusion. First, in determining how to dispose of an application for leave to appeal, Michigan's intermediate appellate court looks to the merits of the claims made in the application. Second, indigent defendants pursuing first-tier review in the Court of Appeals are generally ill equipped to represent themselves.

"[As] *Ross* emphasized, a defendant seeking State Supreme Court review following a first-tier appeal as of right earlier had the assistance of appellate counsel. [A] first-tier review applicant, forced to act *pro se*, will face a record unreviewed by appellate counsel, and will be equipped with no attorney's brief prepared for, or reasoned opinion by, a court of review. * * *

"Navigating the appellate process without a lawyer's assistance is a perilous endeavor for a layperson, and well beyond the competence of individuals, like Halbert, who have little education, learning disabilities, and mental impairments.

"While the State has a legitimate interest in reducing the workload of its judiciary, providing indigents with appellate counsel will yield applications easier to comprehend. Michigan's Court of Appeals would still have recourse to summary denials of leave applications in cases not warranting further review. And when a defendant's case presents no genuinely arguable issue, appointed counsel may so inform the court. See *Anders v. California* [p. 218 infra]."

Justice Thomas, joined by Scalia, J., and Rehnquist, C.J., dissented:

"[The majority] finds that all plea-convicted indigent defendants have the right to appellate counsel when seeking leave to appeal. The majority does not say where in the Constitution that right is located—the Due Process Clause, the Equal Protection Clause, or some purported confluence of the two. * * *

"Instead, the majority pins its hopes on a single case: *Douglas v. California*. *Douglas*, however, does not support extending the right to counsel to any form of discretionary review, as *Ross* and later cases make clear. Moreover, Michigan has not engaged in the sort of invidious discrimination against indigent defendants that *Douglas* condemns. Michigan has done no more than recognize the undeniable difference between defendants who plead guilty and those who maintain their innocence, in an attempt to divert resources from largely frivolous appeals to more meritorious ones. The majority substitutes its own policy preference for that of Michigan voters, and it does so based on an untenable reading of *Douglas*.

"[Far] from being an 'arbitrary' or 'unreasoned' distinction, Michigan's differentiation between defendants convicted at trial and defendants convicted by plea is sensible. [The] danger of wrongful convictions is less significant than in *Douglas*. In *Douglas*, California preliminarily denied counsel to all indigent defendants, regardless of whether they maintained their innocence at trial or conceded their guilt by plea. Here, Michigan preliminarily denies paid counsel only to indigent defendants who admit or do not contest their guilt. * * *

"Lacking support in this Court's cases, the majority effects a not-so subtle shift from whether the record is adequate to enable discretionary review to whether plea-convicted defendants are generally able to '[n]aviga[te] the appellate process without a lawyer's assistance.' This rationale lacks any stopping point. *Pro se* defendants may have difficulty navigating discretionary direct appeals and collateral proceedings, but this Court has never extended the right to counsel beyond first appeals as of right. The majority does not demonstrate that *pro se* defendants have any more difficulty filing leave applications before the Michigan courts than, say, filing petitions for certiorari before this Court."

SECTION 4. WAIVER OF THE RIGHT TO COUNSEL; THE RIGHT TO PROCEED *PRO SE*

FARETTA v. CALIFORNIA
422 U.S. 806, 95 S.Ct. 2525, 45 L.Ed.2d 562 (1975).

JUSTICE STEWART delivered the opinion of the Court.

[Well before the date of his trial, Faretta, charged with grand theft, requested that he be allowed to represent himself. Questioning by the trial judge revealed that Faretta had once before represented himself in a criminal prosecution, that he had a high school education, and that he did not want to be represented by the public defender because he thought that office had too heavy a caseload. The trial judge subsequently held a hearing to inquire into Faretta's ability to conduct his own defense. In the course of that hearing, the judge questioned Faretta as to his knowledge of the hearsay rule and the law governing the challenge of jurors. Taking account of Faretta's answers, the judge ruled that Faretta had not made an intelligent and knowing waiver of his right to counsel. The judge also ruled that Faretta had no constitutional right to conduct his own defense. The judge then appointed the public defender to represent Faretta. Throughout the subsequent trial, the judge required that Faretta's defense be conducted only through the appointed lawyer. Faretta was found guilty as charged and sentenced to prison. The appellate court affirmed his conviction.]

[The] right of self-representation finds support in the structure of the Sixth Amendment, as well as in the English and colonial experience from which the Amendment emerged.

[The] Sixth Amendment does not provide merely that a defense shall be made for the accused; it grants to the accused personally the right to make his defense. It is the accused, not counsel, who must be "informed of the nature and cause of the accusation," who must be "confronted with witnesses against him," and who must be accorded "compulsory process for obtaining witnesses in his favor." [T]he right to self-representation—to make one's defense personally—is thus necessarily implied by the structure of the Amendment. The right to defend is given directly to the accused; for it is he who suffers the consequences if the defense fails.

The counsel provision supplements this design. It speaks of the "assistance" of counsel, and an assistant, however expert, is still an assistant. The language and spirit of the Sixth Amendment contemplate that counsel, like the other defense tools guaranteed by the Amendment, shall be an aid to a willing defendant—not an organ of the State interposed between an unwilling defendant and his right to defend himself personally. To thrust counsel upon the accused, against his considered wish, thus violates the logic of the Amendment. [It] is true that when a defendant chooses to have a lawyer manage and present his case, law and tradition may allocate to the counsel the power to make binding decisions of trial strategy in many areas. This allocation can only be justified, however, by the defendant's consent, at the outset, to accept counsel as his representative. An unwanted counsel "represents" the defendant only through a tenuous and unacceptable legal fiction. Unless the accused has acquiesced in such representation, the defense presented is not the defense guaranteed by the Constitution, for, in a very real sense, it is not *his* defense.

The Sixth Amendment, when naturally read, thus implies a right of self-representation. This reading is reinforced by the Amendment's roots in English legal history. [After an extensive discussion of the right of self-representation in England and the American colonies, the Court concluded:]

In sum, there is no evidence that the colonists and the Framers ever doubted the right of self-representation, or imagined that this right might be considered inferior to the right of assistance of counsel. To the contrary, [they], as well as their English ancestors, always conceived of the right to counsel as an "assistance" for the accused, to be used at his option, in defending himself. The Framers selected in the Sixth Amendment a form of words that necessarily implies the right of self-representation. That conclusion is supported by centuries of history.

There can be no blinking the fact that the right of an accused to conduct his own defense seems to cut against the grain of this Court's decisions holding that the Constitution requires that no accused can be convicted and imprisoned unless he has been accorded the right to the assistance of counsel. For it is surely true that the basic thesis of those decisions is that the help of a lawyer is essential to assure the defendant a fair trial. And a strong argument can surely be made that the whole thrust of those decisions must inevitably lead to the conclusion that a State may constitutionally impose a lawyer upon even an unwilling defendant.

But it is one thing to hold that every [accused] has the right to the assistance of counsel, and quite another to say that a State may compel a defendant to accept a lawyer he does not want. The value of state-appointed counsel was not unappreciated by the Founders, yet the notion of compulsory counsel was utterly foreign to them. [To] force a lawyer on a defendant can only lead him to believe that the law contrives against him. Moreover, it is not inconceivable that in some rare instances, the defendant might in fact present his case more effectively by conducting his own defense. Personal liberties are not rooted in the law of averages. The right to defend is personal. The defendant, and not his lawyer or the State, will bear the personal consequences of a conviction. It is the defendant, therefore, who must be free personally to decide whether in his particular case counsel is to his advantage. And although he may conduct his own defense ultimately to his own detriment, his choice must be honored out of "that respect for the individual which is the lifeblood of the law."[46]

When an accused manages his own defense, he relinquishes, as a purely factual matter, many of the traditional benefits associated with the right to counsel. For this reason, in order to represent himself, the accused must "knowingly and intelligently" forego those relinquished benefits. *Johnson v. Zerbst*, 304 U.S. 458 (1938). Although a defendant need not himself have the skill and experience of a lawyer in order competently and intelligently to choose self-representation, he should be made aware of the dangers and disadvantages of self-representation, so that the record will establish that "he knows what he is doing

---

46. We are told that many criminal defendants representing themselves may use the courtroom for deliberate disruption of their trials. But the right of self-representation has been recognized from our beginnings by federal law and by most of the States, and no such result has thereby occurred. Moreover, the trial judge may terminate self-representation by a defendant who deliberately engages in serious and obstructionist misconduct. Of course, a State may—even over objection by the accused—appoint a "standby counsel" to aid the accused if and when the accused requests help, and to be available to represent the accused in the event that termination of the defendant's self-representation is necessary.

The right of self-representation is not a license to abuse the dignity of the courtroom. Neither is it a license not to comply with relevant rules of procedural and substantive law. Thus, whatever else may or may not be open to him on appeal, a defendant who elects to represent himself cannot thereafter complain that the quality of his own defense amounted to a denial of "effective assistance of counsel."

and his choice is made with eyes open." *Adams v. United States ex rel. McCann*, 317 U.S. 269 (1942).

Here, weeks before trial, Faretta clearly and unequivocally declared [that] he wanted to represent himself and did not want counsel. The record affirmatively shows that [defendant] was literate, competent, and understanding, and that he was voluntarily exercising his informed free will. The trial judge had warned [defendant] that he thought it was a mistake not to accept the assistance of counsel and that [defendant] would be required to follow all the "ground rules" of trial procedure. We need make no assessment of how well or poorly [defendant] had mastered the intricacies of the hearsay rule and the California code provisions that govern challenges of potential jurors on *voir dire* [matters about which the trial judge specifically questioned defendant before ruling that he had not made an intelligent and knowing waiver of his right to the assistance of counsel]. For [defendant's] technical legal knowledge, as such, was not relevant to an assessment of his knowing exercise of the right to defend himself.

CHIEF JUSTICE BURGER, with whom JUSTICE BLACKMUN and JUSTICE REHNQUIST join, dissenting.

[The goal of achieving justice] is ill-served, and the integrity of and public confidence in the system are undermined, when an easy conviction is obtained due to the defendant's ill-advised decision to waive counsel. [The criminal justice system] should not be available as an instrument of self-destruction. [B]oth the "spirit and the logic" of the Sixth Amendment are that every person accused of crime shall receive the fullest possible defense; in the vast majority of cases this command can be honored only by means of the expressly-guaranteed right to counsel, and the trial judge is in the best position to determine whether the accused is capable of conducting his defense. True freedom of choice and society's interest in seeing that justice is achieved can be vindicated only if the trial court retains discretion to reject any attempted waiver of counsel and insist that the accused be tried according to the Constitution. This discretion is as critical an element of basic fairness as a trial judge's discretion to decline to accept a plea of guilty.

JUSTICE BLACKMUN, with whom THE CHIEF JUSTICE and JUSTICE REHNQUIST join, dissenting.

I cannot agree that there is anything in the [Constitution] that requires the States to subordinate the solemn business of conducting a criminal prosecution to the whimsical—albeit voluntary—caprice of every accused who wishes to use his trial as a vehicle for personal or political self-gratification. [I] do not believe that any amount of *pro se* pleading can cure the injury to society of an unjust result, but I do believe that a just result should prove to be an effective balm for almost any frustrated *pro se* defendant.

[I] note briefly the procedural problems that, I suspect, today's decision will visit upon trial courts in the future. [Must] every defendant be advised of his right to proceed *pro se?* If so, when must that notice be given? Since the right to the assistance of counsel and the right to self-representation are mutually exclusive, how is the waiver of each right to be measured? If a defendant has elected to exercise his right to proceed *pro se,* does he still have a constitutional right to assistance of standby counsel? How soon in the criminal proceeding must a defendant decide between proceeding by counsel or *pro se?* Must he be allowed to switch in mid-trial? May a violation of the right to self-representation ever be harmless error? Must the trial court treat the *pro se* defendant differently than it would professional counsel? [The] procedural problems spawned by an absolute right to self-representation will far outweigh whatever tactical advantage the defendant may feel he has gained by electing to represent himself.

NOTES AND QUESTIONS

1. **Questioning and reaffirming Faretta.** Twenty-five years after *Faretta* was decided, Justice Stevens expressed doubts about the merits of the decision. In *Martinez v. Court of Appeal of California*, 528 U.S. 152 (2000) (discussed Note 3 infra), he wrote:

"The historical evidence relied upon by *Faretta* as identifying a right of self-representation is not always useful because it pertained to times when lawyers were scarce, often mistrusted, and not readily available to the average person accused of crime. For one who could not obtain a lawyer, self-representation was the only feasible alternative to asserting no defense at all. [But] an individual's decision to represent himself is no longer compelled by the necessity of choosing self-representation over incompetent or nonexistent representation. [Therefore,] while *Faretta* is correct in concluding that there is abundant support for the proposition that a right to self-representation has been recognized for centuries, the original reasons for protecting that right do not have the same force when the availability of competent counsel for every indigent defendant has displaced the need—although not always the desire—for self-representation. [No] one, including [the] *Faretta* majority, attempts to argue that as a rule *pro se* representation is wise, desirable or efficient. [Our] experience has taught us that a 'pro se defense is usually a bad defense, particularly when compared to a defense provided by an experienced criminal defense attorney.'"

Justice Scalia, however, did not share his colleague's "apparent skepticism:"

"I have no doubt that the Framers of our Constitution, who were suspicious enough of governmental power—including judicial power—that they insisted upon a citizen's right to be judged by an independent jury of private citizens, would not have found acceptable the compulsory assignment of counsel *by the government* to plead a criminal defendant's case. [While] I might have rested the [*Faretta*] decision upon the Due Process Clause rather than the Sixth Amendment, I believe it was correct. [That] asserting the right of self-representation may often, or even usually, work to the defendant's disadvantage is no more remarkable—and no more a basis for withdrawing the right—than is the fact that proceeding without counsel in custodial interrogation, or confessing to the crime, usually works to the defendant's disadvantage. Our system of laws generally presumes that the criminal defendant, after being fully informed, knows his own best interests and does not need them dictated by the State. Any other approach is unworthy of a free people."

Justice Breyer wrote separately to express his concern "that judges closer to the firing line have sometimes expressed dismay about the practical consequences" of *Faretta*. However, he added "without some strong factual basis for believing that *Faretta's* holding has proved counterproductive in practice, we are not in a position to reconsider the constitutional assumptions that underlie that case."

A subsequent empirical study examined the outcomes for *pro se* felony defendants in federal and states cases and found that those outcomes "were at least as good as, and perhaps even better than the outcomes for their represented counterparts." Erica J. Hashimoto, *Defending The Right of Self–Representation: An Empirical Look at the Pro Se Felony Defendant*, 85 N.C.L.Rev. 423 (2007). While the sample of *pro se* defendants going to trial was quite small (23 cases), the percentage of acquittals was identical to that for represented defendants, and *pro se* defendants had a higher percentage of jury convictions that were limited to lesser-included misdemeanors. In the federal sample, while the percentage of trial acquittals was lower, the author noted that, as to overall outcomes, *"pro se* felony defendants do not appear to have done significantly worse than federal court defendants who were represented by counsel." Id. Relying in part on this study, the Supreme Court, per Justice Breyer, declined a recent invitation to overrule *Faretta.* See *Indiana v. Edwards*, 554 U.S. 164 (2008), other aspects of which are discussed infra Note 1, p. 118.

2.   *Harmless error.* Nine years after *Faretta,* the Supreme Court answered one of Justice Blackmun's questions when it emphasized that a violation of the right to self-representation could never be harmless error. See *McKaskle v. Wiggins,* 465 U.S. 168, 178 n.8 (1984) ("Since the right of self-representation is a right that when exercised usually increases the likelihood of a trial outcome unfavorable to the defendant, its denial is not amenable to 'harmless error' analysis. The right is either respected or denied; its deprivation cannot be harmless.").

3.   *Does the principle of self-representation apply to appeals as well?* In MARTINEZ v. COURT OF APPEAL OF CALIFORNIA, 528 U.S. 152 (2000), defendant (who described himself as a self-taught paralegal with 25 years experience) was convicted of embezzlement after representing himself at trial. He sought to represent himself on appeal as well, but was rebuffed by the state appellate courts. The Supreme Court, per Stevens, J., held, without a dissent, that "neither the holding nor the reasoning in *Faretta* requires [a state] to recognize a constitutional right to self-representation on direct appeal from a criminal conviction." Justice Stevens reasoned:

"Appeals as of right in federal courts were nonexistent for the first century of our Nation, and appellate review of any sort was 'rarely allowed.' [Thus,] unlike the inquiry in *Faretta,* the historical evidence does not provide any support for an affirmative constitutional right to appellate self-representation. [The] *Faretta* majority's reliance on the structure of the Sixth Amendment is also not relevant. The Sixth Amendment identifies the basic rights that the accused shall enjoy in 'all criminal prosecutions.' [The] Sixth Amendment does not include any right to appeal. [It] necessarily follows that the Amendment itself does not provide any basis for finding a right to self-representation on appeal."

As for a right to self-representation based on a respect for individual autonomy grounded in the Due Process Clause, Justice Stevens noted:

"[W]e are entirely unpersuaded that the risk of either [counsel] disloyalty or suspicion of disloyalty is a sufficient concern to conclude that a constitutional right of self-representation is a necessary component of a fair appellate proceeding. [As] the *Faretta* opinion recognized, the right to self-representation is not absolute. [Even] at the trial level, therefore, the government's interest in ensuring the integrity and efficiency of the trial at times outweighs the defendant's interest in acting as his own lawyer. In the appellate context, the balance between the two competing interests surely tips in favor of the State. The status of the accused defendant, who retains a presumption of innocence throughout the trial process, changes dramatically when a jury returns a guilty verdict. [Considering] the change in position from defendant to appellant, the autonomy interests that survive a felony conviction are less compelling than those motivating the decision in *Faretta.* Yet the overriding state interest in the fair and efficient administration of justice remains as strong as at the trial level."

4.   *"Standby counsel."* McKASKLE v. WIGGINS, 465 U.S. 168 (1984), made explicit "what is already implicit in *Faretta:* a defendant's Sixth Amendment rights are not violated when a trial judge appoints standby counsel—even over the defendant's objection[m]—to relieve the judge of the need to explain and enforce basic rules of courtroom protocol or to assist the defendant in overcoming routine obstacles that stand in the way of the defendant's achievement of his own clearly indicated goals." In describing the role of stand-by counsel, Justice O'Connor, writing for the Court noted:

"[T]he right to speak for oneself entails more than the opportunity to add one's voice to a cacophony of others. [Thus,] the *Faretta* right must impose some limits on the extent of standby counsel's unsolicited participation.

"First, the *pro se* defendant is entitled to preserve actual control over the case he chooses to present to the jury. This is the core of the *Faretta* right. If standby counsel's participation over the defendant's objection effectively allows counsel to make or substantially interfere with any significant tactical decisions, or to control the questioning of witnesses, or to speak *instead* of the defendant on any matter of importance, the *Faretta* right is eroded.

"Second, participation by standby counsel without the defendant's consent should not be allowed to destroy the jury's perception that the defendant is representing himself. The defendant's appearance in the status of one conducting his own defense is important in a criminal trial, since the right to appear *pro se* exists to affirm the accused's individual dignity and autonomy.

"[Participation] by standby counsel outside the presence of the jury engages only the first of these two limitations. [The] appearance of a *pro se* defendant's self-representation will not be unacceptably undermined by counsel's participation outside the presence of the jury. [Thus,] *Faretta* rights are adequately vindicated in proceedings outside the presence of the jury if the *pro se* defendant is allowed to address the court freely on his own behalf and if disagreements between counsel and the *pro se* defendant are resolved in the defendant's favor whenever the matter is one that would normally be left to the discretion of counsel.

"[Participation] by standby counsel in the presence of the jury is more problematic. It is here that the defendant may legitimately claim that excessive involvement by counsel will destroy the appearance that the defendant is acting *pro se*. [Nonetheless,] we believe that a categorical bar on participation by standby counsel in the presence of the jury is unnecessary.

"[If] a defendant is given the opportunity and elects to have counsel appear before the court or jury, his complaints concerning counsel's subsequent unsolicited participation lose much of their force. A defendant does not have a constitutional right to choreograph special appearances by counsel. Once a *pro se* defendant invites or agrees to any substantial participation by counsel, subsequent appearances by counsel must be presumed to be with the defendant's acquiescence, at least until the defendant expressly and unambiguously renews his request that standby counsel be silenced."

Dissenting Justice White, joined by Brennan and Marshall, JJ., protested:

"[Under] the Court's new test, it is necessary to determine whether the *pro se* defendant retained 'actual control over the case he [chose] to present to the jury' and whether standby counsel's participation 'destroy[ed] the jury's perception that the defendant [was] representing himself.' Although this test purports to protect all of the values underlying our holding in *Faretta*, it is unclear whether it can achieve this result.

"As long as the *pro se* defendant is allowed his say, the first prong of the Court's test accords standby counsel at a bench trial or any proceeding outside the

---

m. Who should compensate the standby counsel in this situation? See Poulin, infra Note 5 ("no court has directly addressed how to compensate standby counsel forced upon a nonindigent defendant").

presence of a jury virtually untrammeled discretion to present any factual or legal argument to which the defendant does not object. The limits placed on counsel's participation in this context by the 'actual control' test are more apparent than real.

"[Although] the Court is more solicitous of a *pro se* defendant's interests when standby counsel intervenes before a jury, the test's second prong suffers from similar shortcomings. To the extent that trial and appellate courts can discern the point at which counsel's unsolicited participation substantially undermines a *pro se* defendant's appearance before the jury, a matter about which I harbor substantial doubts, their decisions will, to a certain extent, 'affirm the accused's individual dignity and autonomy.' But they will do so incompletely, for in focusing on how the jury views the defendant, the majority opinion ignores *Faretta's* emphasis on the defendant's own perception of the criminal justice [system.]"

5.　*Lower courts and standby counsel.* Anne Bowen Poulin, *The Role of Standby Counsel in Criminal Cases: In the Twilight Zone of The Criminal Justice System*, 76 N.Y.U. L. Rev. 676 (2000), notes that "judicial decisions addressing *pro se* defendants' complaints," reveal several "troubling patterns" in current practice. These include:

(1) Some courts are "actually hostile" to *pro se* defendants' request for standby counsel, as reflected by an appellate court suggestion that "the defendant be given the stark choice of self-representation (with no standby counsel) or the assistance of counsel"—thereby ensuring that the decision to proceed *pro se* will not be made "with the comforting knowledge" that a back-up is always available.

(2) A common scenario leading to *pro se* representation involves: (1) an indigent defendant seeks replacement of appointed counsel, (2) the trial judge determines that the defendant's complaints against counsel do not present the extreme situation needed for mandatory replacement (see Note 3, p. 208); (3) the defendant is told that he must choose between continued representation by appointed counsel or proceeding *pro se*; (4) the defendant chooses to proceed *pro se*; and (5) the court then appoints as standby counsel the "very attorney whose representation precipitated the defendant's complaint."

(3) "In cases where the defendant is not irretrievably estranged from standby counsel," defendants quite naturally will drift towards asking counsel to make presentations as "defendants often assume that standby counsel is not merely a resource but also someone available to act for the defendant." However, in such a situation, some courts refuse to allow standby counsel to assume this "larger role" (particularly at trial), insisting that the defendant choose between waiving his "*Faretta* rights" or utilizing counsel strictly as an advisor.

(4) Many standby counsel will not (a) take it upon themselves to explore "factual investigations and legal options that the defendant might overlook" and then bring their findings to the attention of the defendant, (b) raise legal objections on their own initiative, or (c) present mitigating evidence at sentencing on their own initiative—all actions advocated by the author. This failure to initiate assistance arguably is a product in part of various lower court opinions that characterize the role of standby counsel as simply "an observer, an attorney who attends the trial or other proceeding and who may offer advice, but who does not speak for the defendant or bear responsibility for his defense." *United States v. Taylor*, 933 F.2d 307 (5th Cir.1991).

To what extent does the acceptance of such practices follow from a "judicial perception that standby counsel serves the court's purpose rather than the defendant's"? Poulin, supra. Did the Court in *McKaskle* approve of an "active role" for standby counsel, in which counsel acts as "part of the defense team," subject to the "defendant's right to actual control of the case and to the appearance of control in the presence of the factfinder"? Id.

6. *Ineffective assistance of standby counsel.* Lower courts generally have rejected claims of ineffective assistance by standby counsel. They note that the *pro se* defendant cannot complain of his own ineffective performance, (see *Faretta*, fn.46) and the final decisions are being made by the defendant. They also note that ineffective assistance claims are tied to a constitutional right to counsel's assistance, and the defendant has no constitutional right to the assistance of standby counsel. See Poulin, supra. However, "some courts" have held that *pro se* defendants may claim ineffective assistance of standby counsel as to erroneous "legal advice." Id.

7. *Timing of an assertion.* In *Faretta*, the Court stressed that the defendant made his request to represent himself "well before the date of trial." Lower courts have held that the defendant's right to self-representation is conditioned on a timely assertion of that right, which ordinarily is satisfied by a request made before the scheduled trial date (provided the defendant does not insist upon a continuance as a condition of proceeding *pro se*). The trial court has "broad discretion to reject as untimely a request made during the course of trial." See CRIMPROC § 11.5(d).

8. *Notice of the right to self-representation.* The lower courts have uniformly held that, in the absence of a clear indication on the defendant's part that he wants to consider representing himself, the court has no constitutional obligation to inform the defendant of his right to proceed *pro se*. Notification of the right to proceed *pro se*, these courts emphasize, might undermine the "overriding constitutional policy" favoring the provision of counsel by suggesting that counsel is not needed. See CRIMPROC § 11.5(b) (collecting cases). As one circuit put it, "because the right to self-representation does not implicate constitutional fair trial considerations to the same extent as does an accused's right to counsel, it requires neither notice of the right's existence prior to legal proceedings nor a knowing and intelligent waiver." *Munkus v. Furlong*, 170 F.3d 980, 983 (10th Cir. 1999) (internal quotation omitted). But wouldn't notice of the right to self-representation solve some of the timing problems discussed supra Note 7?

Do you agree that the right to self-representation should be subordinate to the right to counsel? Could you imagine a system wherein the court would have to advise a defendant that he has the right to either represent himself or to proceed through counsel and then require the defendant to chose one and waive the other? What is wrong with that system? Should there be a preference for counsel given the empirical data discussed supra Note 1?

NOTES AND QUESTIONS ON WARNING REQUIREMENTS AND THE WAIVER OF THE RIGHT TO COUNSEL

The *Faretta* Court held that, before a defendant would be permitted to proceed *pro se*, he would have to "knowingly and intelligently" waive his right to counsel. See *Johnson v. Zerbst*, 304 U.S. 458 (1938). As part of that waiver process, the Court noted, "he should be made aware of the dangers and disadvantages of self-representation, so that the record will establish that 'he knows what he is doing and his choice is made with eyes open.' " What do these statements mean? Are certain, specific warnings required before an individual can waive the right to counsel? How extensive must the colloquy be? And how searching must the waiver inquiry be?

1. *State and federal practices after Faretta.* Relying on the above-quoted statements, several lower courts after *Faretta* concluded that the Sixth

Amendment requires reference to "specific disadvantages" of proceeding without counsel rather than a "vague, general admonishment." These courts have suggested that defendants should be informed "(1) that 'presenting a defense is not a simple matter of telling one's story,' but requires adherence to various 'technical' rules governing the conduct of a trial; (2) that a lawyer has substantial experience and training in trial procedure and that the prosecution will be represented by an experienced lawyer; (3) that a person unfamiliar with legal procedures may allow the prosecutor an advantage by failing to make objections to inadmissible evidence, may not make effective use of such rights as the *voir dire* of jurors, and may make tactical decisions that produce unintended consequences; (4) that there may be possible defenses and other rights of which counsel would be aware and if those are not timely asserted, they may be lost permanently; (5) that a defendant proceeding *pro se* will not be allowed to complain on appeal about the competency of his representation; and (6) 'that the effectiveness of his defense may well be diminished by his dual role as attorney and accused.'" CRIMPROC. § 11.5(c). According to these courts, once these warnings are given, the waiver inquiry should be "realistically 'designed to reveal [defendants'] understanding.'" The trial court should determine through a penetrating inquiry (which goes beyond requiring "yes" and "no" answers) that the defendant understands and appreciates those disadvantages and consequences. See id.

Other courts, however, "take the position that *Faretta* requires only that the defendant have been aware of the disadvantages of proceeding *pro se*, and that awareness can be established without regard to any admonitions or colloquies." See id. (collecting cases). Consider, for example, Judge Easterbrook's statements for the court in *United States v. Hill*, 252 F.3d 919 (7th Cir. 2001):

"Waiver does not depend on astute (or even rudimentary) understanding of how rights can be employed to best advantage. Defendants routinely plead guilty, waiving oodles of constitutional rights, in proceedings where rights are named but not explained. For example, the judge will tell the defendant that the plea waives the right to jury trial but will not describe how juries work, when they are apt to find a prosecutor's case insufficient, why the process of formulating and giving jury instructions creates issues for appeal, and so on. [The] contention that 'knowing and intelligent' means something different when a defendant elects self-representation than when the same defendant elects a bench trial (or waives another constitutional right) has its genesis in *Faretta*. [But] *Faretta* adopted the waiver standard of *Johnson v. Zerbst*, which noted that the determination 'whether there has been an intelligent waiver of the right to counsel must depend, in each case, upon the particular facts and circumstances surrounding the case, including the background, experience, and conduct of the accused.' That standard can be met without a demonstration that the accused has a deep understanding of how counsel could assist him."

2. *The Supreme Court's response.* In IOWA v. TOVAR, 541 U.S. 77 (2004), the Supreme Court rejected one state's interpretation of the Sixth Amendment as requiring specific warnings regarding the usefulness of an attorney before a *pro se* defendant could plead guilty. The two warnings at issue included a warning that "waiving the assistance of counsel in deciding whether to plead guilty [entails] the risk that a viable defense will be overlooked" and the warning "that by waiving his right to an attorney he will lose the opportunity to obtain an independent opinion on whether, under the facts and applicable law, it is wise to plead guilty." This "rigid and detailed admonishment," the Supreme Court held, is not mandated by the Sixth Amendment. Rather, "[t]he constitutional requirement is satisfied when the trial court informs the accused of the nature of the charges against him, of his right to be counseled regarding his plea, and of the range of allowable punishments attendant upon the entry of a guilty plea." Justice Ginsburg, writing for the Court, explained:

"We have described a waiver of counsel as intelligent when the defendant 'knows what he is doing and his choice is made with eyes open.' We have not, however, prescribed any formula or script to be read to a defendant who states that he elects to proceed without counsel. The information a defendant must possess in order to make an intelligent election, our decisions indicate, will depend on a range of case-specific factors, including the defendant's education or sophistication, the complex or easily grasped nature of the charge, and the stage of the proceeding. See *Johnson*. [Similarly,] the information a defendant must have to waive counsel intelligently will 'depend, in each case, upon the particular facts and circumstances surrounding that case.'

"[The] States are free to adopt by statute, rule, or decision any guides to the acceptance of an uncounseled plea they deem useful. See, e.g., Alaska Rule Crim. Proc. 39(a) (2003); Fla. Rule Crim. Proc. 3.111(d) (2003); Md. Ct. Rule 4–215 (2002); Minn. Rule Crim. Proc. 5.02 (2003); Pa. Rule Crim. Proc. 121, comment (2003). We hold only that the two admonitions the Iowa Supreme Court ordered are not required by the Federal Constitution."

Does *Tovar* hold open the possibility that, under some circumstances, the judge accepting a waiver of counsel in connection with the entry of a guilty plea must advise the defendant of the possible benefits of counsel's assistance in considering whether to plead guilty? If so, what circumstances might require such advice? Would such advice be required where an element of the offense charged called for an arguably subjective jury determination (e.g., what constitutes negligence) and the facts presented in establishing a factual basis for the guilty plea were sufficient to convince a jury on that element, but not overwhelmingly so?

3. *The importance of the stage of the proceeding.* Notice that the *Tovar* Court included "the stage of the proceeding" in its list of relevant factors that inform what warnings are required in a case. Justice Ginsburg elaborated on this factor later in her opinion for the Court:

"As to waiver of trial counsel, we have said that before a defendant may be allowed to proceed *pro se,* he must be warned specifically of the hazards ahead. *Faretta v. California.* [Later,] in *Patterson v. Illinois*, 487 U.S. 285 (1988), we elaborated on 'the dangers and disadvantages of self-representation' to which *Faretta* referred. '[A]t trial,' we observed, 'counsel is required to help even the most gifted layman adhere to the rules of procedure and evidence, comprehend the subtleties of *voir dire,* examine and cross-examine witnesses effectively[,] object to improper prosecution questions, and much more.' Warnings of the pitfalls of proceeding to trial without counsel, we therefore said, must be 'rigorous[ly]' conveyed. We clarified, however, that at earlier stages of the criminal process, a less searching or formal colloquy may suffice. *Patterson* concerned postindictment questioning by police and prosecutor. At that stage of the case, we held, the warnings required by *Miranda v. Arizona* adequately informed the defendant not only of his Fifth Amendment rights, but of his Sixth Amendment right to counsel as well. [*Patterson*] describes a 'pragmatic approach to the waiver question,' one that asks 'what purposes a lawyer can serve at the particular stage of the proceedings in question, and what assistance he could provide to an accused at that stage,' in order 'to determine the scope of the Sixth Amendment right to counsel, and the type of warnings and procedures that should be required before a waiver of that right will be recognized.' We require less rigorous warnings pretrial, *Patterson* explained, not because pretrial proceedings are 'less important' than trial, but because, at that stage, 'the full dangers and disadvantages of self-representation [are] less substantial and more obvious to an accused than they are at trial.' "

Does this mean that a court could give even fewer warnings than the Court deemed necessary in *Tovar* before obtaining a waiver of the right to counsel at an earlier stage than the guilty plea, where the consequences were less serious (e.g., waiver of counsel in connection with the waiver of a preliminary hearing)? What, if anything, does this dicta suggest about what warnings are required before a defendant is permitted to proceed *pro se* at trial?

4. *State law requirements.* As noted in *Tovar*, states often require more extensive advisements for the waiver of counsel as a matter of state law. Such state provisions commonly require, in addition to an explanation of the advantages that come with representation by counsel, the prerequisites set forth in Justice Black's opinion (for a four justice plurality) in *Von Moltke v. Gillies*, 332 U.S. 708 (1948): "To be valid such a waiver must be made with an apprehension of the nature of the charges, the statutory offenses included within them, the range of allowable punishments thereunder, possible defenses to the charges and circumstances in mitigation thereof and all other facts essential to a broad understanding of the whole matter." *Von Moltke*, like *Tovar*, involved a defendant who waived counsel in connection with the entry of a guilty plea.

5. *The competency standard and the standard for waiving the right to counsel.* In order to be deemed competent to stand trial, a criminal defendant must have "sufficient present ability to consult with his lawyer with a reasonable degree of rational understanding" and "a rational as well as functional understanding of the proceedings against him." *Dusky v. United States*, 362 U.S. 402 (1960). In GODINEZ v. MORAN, 509 U.S. 389 (1993) (a case in which a capital defendant discharged his attorneys, pled guilty, and was ultimately sentenced to death), a 7–2 majority rejected the notion that competency to plead guilty or to waive the right to counsel must be measured by a higher or different standard than the competency standard for standing trial. On the relationship between the competency standard and the standard for waiver of the right to counsel, Justice Thomas, writing for the Court, explained:

"[There] is no reason to believe that the decision to waive counsel requires an appreciably higher level of mental functioning than the decision to waive other constitutional rights. [The defendant] suggests that a higher competency standard is necessary because a defendant who represents himself ' "must have greater powers of comprehension, judgment, and reason than would be necessary to stand trial with the aid of an attorney." ' But this argument has a flawed premise; the competence that is required of a defendant seeking to waive his right to counsel is the competence to *waive the right,* not the competence to represent himself. [A] criminal defendant's ability to represent himself has no bearing upon his competence to *choose* self-representation."

The majority also warned, however, that a finding of competency to stand trial would not in itself establish the understanding needed for pleading guilty or waiving the right to counsel: "[A] trial court must satisfy itself that the waiver [of] constitutional rights is knowing and voluntary. In this sense, there is a 'heightened' standard for pleading guilty and for waiving the right to counsel, but it is not a heightened standard of *competence.*" The purpose of a competency inquiry, explained the Court, is to determine whether a defendant "has the *ability* to understand the proceedings," but "the purpose of the 'knowing and voluntary' inquiry [is] to determine whether the defendant actually *does* understand the significance and consequences of a particular decision and whether the decision is uncoerced."

NOTES ON THE LIMITS OF THE RIGHT
TO SELF–REPRESENTATION

1. *Denying the right of self-representation to mentally ill defendants.*
In INDIANA v. EDWARDS, 554 U.S. 164 (2008), the Supreme Court held that a
state has the authority to permit its trial courts to deny self-representation to
mentally ill defendants when those defendants "suffer from severe mental illness
to the point where they are not competent to conduct trial proceedings by
themselves." Justice BREYER, writing for the majority, explained:

"[We] assume that a criminal defendant has sufficient mental competence to
stand trial (*i.e.,* the defendant meets *Dusky's* standard) and that the defendant
insists on representing himself during that trial. We ask whether the Constitution
permits a State to limit that defendant's self-representation right by insisting
upon representation by counsel at trial—on the ground that the defendant lacks
the mental capacity to conduct his trial defense unless represented.

"Several considerations taken together lead us to conclude that the answer to
this question is yes. First, the Court's precedent, while not answering the
question, points slightly in the direction of our affirmative answer. *Godinez*
[simply] leaves the question open. But the Court's 'mental competency' cases set
forth a standard that focuses directly upon a defendant's 'present ability to
consult with his lawyer,' *Dusky.* [They] assume representation by counsel and
emphasize the importance of counsel. They thus suggest (though do not hold) that
an instance in which a defendant who would choose to forgo counsel at trial
presents a very different set of circumstances, which in our view, calls for a
different standard.

"At the same time *Faretta*, the foundational self-representation case, rested
its conclusion in part upon preexisting state law set forth in cases all of which are
consistent with, and at least two of which expressly adopt, a competency limitation on the self-representation right. See 422 U. S. at 813, and n. 9 (citing 16
state-court decisions and two secondary sources).

"[Second,] the nature of the problem before us cautions against the use of a
single mental competency standard for deciding both (1) whether a defendant who
is represented by counsel can proceed to trial and (2) whether a defendant who
goes to trial must be permitted to represent himself. Mental illness itself is not a
unitary concept. It varies in degree. It can vary over time. It interferes with an
individual's functioning at different times in different ways. [In] certain instances
an individual may well be able to satisfy *Dusky's* mental competence standard, for
he will be able to work with counsel at trial, yet at the same time he may be
unable to carry out the basic tasks needed to present his own defense without the
help of counsel.

"[The] American Psychiatric Association (APA) tells us [that] '[d]isorganized
thinking, deficits in sustaining attention and concentration, impaired expressive
abilities, anxiety, and other common symptoms of severe mental illnesses can
impair the defendant's ability to play the significantly expanded role required for
self-representation even if he can play the lesser role of represented defendant.'

"[Third,] in our view, a right of self-representation at trial will not 'affirm the
dignity' of a defendant who lacks the mental capacity to conduct his defense
without the assistance of counsel. *McKaskle.* [To] the contrary, given that defendant's uncertain mental state, the spectacle that could well result from his self-
representation at trial is at least as likely to prove humiliating as ennobling.
Moreover, insofar as a defendant's lack of capacity threatens an improper convic-

tion or sentence, self-representation in that exceptional context undercuts the most basic of the Constitution's criminal law objectives, providing a fair trial.

"[Fourth,] proceedings must not only be fair, they must 'appear fair to all who observe them.' [An] *amicus* brief reports one psychiatrist's reaction to having observed a patient (a patient who had satisfied *Dusky*) try to conduct his own defense: '[H]ow in the world can our legal system allow an insane man to defend himself?' [The] application of *Dusky's* basic mental competence standard can help in part to avoid this result. But given the different capacities needed to proceed to trial without counsel, there is little reason to believe that *Dusky* alone is sufficient. At the same time, the trial judge, particularly one such as the trial judge in this case, who presided over one of Edwards' competency hearings and his two trials, will often prove best able to make more fine-tuned mental capacity decisions, tailored to the individualized circumstances of a particular defendant.

"We consequently conclude that the Constitution permits judges to take realistic account of the particular defendant's mental capacities by asking whether a defendant who seeks to conduct his own defense at trial is mentally competent to do so. That is to say, the Constitution permits States to insist upon representation by counsel for those competent enough to stand trial under *Dusky* but who still suffer from severe mental illness to the point where they are not competent to conduct trial proceedings by themselves.

"Indiana has also asked us to adopt, as a measure of a defendant's ability to conduct a trial, a more specific standard that would 'deny a criminal defendant the right to represent himself at trial where the defendant cannot communicate coherently with the court or a jury.' We are sufficiently uncertain, however, as to how that particular standard would work in practice to refrain from endorsing it as a federal constitutional standard here. We need not now, and we do not, adopt it."

Justice SCALIA (joined by Justice THOMAS) dissented from the Court's decision:

"[The] Court is correct that this case presents a variation on *Godinez:* It presents the question not whether another constitutional requirement (in *Godinez,* the proposed higher degree of competence required for a waiver) limits a defendant's constitutional right to elect self-representation, but whether a State's view of fairness (or of other values) permits it to strip the defendant of this right. But that makes the question before us an easier one. While one constitutional requirement must yield to another in case of conflict, nothing permits a State, because of *its* view of what is fair, to deny a constitutional protection.

"[While] there is little doubt that preserving individual "dignity" (to which the Court refers) [is] paramount among [the] purposes [of the right to self-representation], there is equally little doubt that the loss of 'dignity' the right is designed to prevent is *not* the defendant's making a fool of himself by presenting an amateurish or even incoherent defense. Rather, the dignity at issue is the supreme human dignity of being master of one's fate rather than a ward of the State—the dignity of individual choice.

"A further purpose that the Court finds is advanced by denial of the right of self-representation is the purpose of assuring that trials 'appear fair to all who observe them.' To my knowledge we have never denied a defendant a right simply on the ground that it would make his trial appear less 'fair' to outside observers, and I would not inaugurate that principle here. But were I to do so, I would not apply it to deny a defendant the right to represent himself when he knowingly and voluntarily waives counsel.

"[In] singling out mentally ill defendants for this treatment, the Court's opinion does not even have the questionable virtue of being politically correct. At a time when all society is trying to mainstream the mentally impaired, the Court permits them to be deprived of a basic constitutional right—for their own good.

"Today's holding is extraordinarily vague. The Court does not accept Indiana's position that self-representation can be denied ' "where the defendant cannot communicate coherently with the court or a jury." ' [It] holds only that lack of mental competence can under some circumstances form a basis for denying the right to proceed *pro se*. We will presumably give some meaning to this holding in the future, but the indeterminacy makes a bad holding worse. Once the right of self-representation for the mentally ill is a sometime thing, trial judges will have every incentive to make their lives easier [by] appointing knowledgeable and literate counsel."

2. *A cynical view of Godinez and Edwards.* One commentator has suggested that, taken together, *Godinez* and *Edwards* effectively mean that mentally ill defendants who are nonetheless competent to stand trial should be allowed to plead without counsel, but those same defendants should not be permitted to go to trial without counsel. On this understanding, "[o]ne would not be churlish in concluding that the overriding objective of *Godinez* and *Edwards* is to ensure that the state can proceed as efficiently as possible in dealing with mentally ill people." See Christopher Slobogin, *Mental Illness and Self–Representation: Faretta, Godinez, and Edwards*, 7 Ohio St. J. Crim. L. 391 (2009). Do you agree?

3. *The need to preserve a fair trial.* The majority's focus in *Edwards* on the "appearance of fairness" and the potential for an "unfair trial" could have consequences that go far beyond denying mentally ill defendants a right to self-representation. Even before *Edwards*, some lower courts viewed *Faretta* as leaving open the possibility of denying self-representation, notwithstanding a waiver of the right to counsel that is both knowing and voluntary, where the trial court views representation by counsel as absolutely necessary to ensure a fair trial—in particular, where a physical disability (e.g., a speech impediment) or educational deficiency "may significantly affect [defendant's] ability to communicate a possible defense to the jury." *Pickens v. State*, 292 N.W.2d 601 (Wis.1980); see CRIMPROC § 11.5(d) (collecting cases). What standard should lower courts use to determine whether a defendant is capable of representing himself at trial? When should the state's interest in ensuring a fair trial trump the defendant's autonomy interest in self-representation?

4. *Reconciling the state's interest in fair proceedings and the defendant's autonomy interest.* Consider Slobogin, supra: "First, the [*Edwards*] Court could have reaffirmed, rather than ignored, *Godinez*'s (and *Faretta*'s) holding that the key issue is competency to choose, not competency to represent oneself. Second, contra to *Godinez*, it could have recognized that one needs greater capacity to choose to waive counsel than to surrender other rights, which would have better protected both the defendant's autonomy interest and the state's interest in fair proceedings. Third, it could have further protected those interests by requiring an inquiry that *Godinez* did not consider: an investigation of the reasons the defendant wants to proceed *pro se*. If those reasons are delusional or non-existent, then the autonomy that gives rise to a right to self-representation does not exist. But otherwise the defendant who understands the risks of waiving the right to counsel should be allowed to represent himself; no competency-to-represent-oneself test, a la *Edwards*, should be required. [These] prescriptions more properly balance the interests identified in *Faretta, Godinez* and *Edwards*. They also achieve another goal [—namely,] the de-stigmatization and dignification of people with mental illness."

5. *Forfeiture of the right to counsel.* A series of lower court cases have held that misconduct by the defendant can produce a forfeiture of the right to assistance of counsel, requiring defendant thereafter to proceed *pro se.* Two settings have most frequently led to findings of forfeiture: (1) defendant assaulted or threatened counsel, who then asked to withdraw; (2) defendant was given ample time to obtain counsel, and after assuring the court that he would obtain counsel by the date of the trial, appeared on that date without counsel and without a reasonable excuse for failing to have obtained counsel. See CRIMPROC §§ 11.3(c), 11.4(d). Other courts have refused to accept the concept of forfeiture in such situations, but will force the defendant to proceed *pro se* on the basis of a "waiver by conduct." They require that the defendant previously has been made aware that the misconduct at issue would result in the loss of his right to counsel. Id. But see *State v. Carruthers*, 35 S.W.3d 516 (Tenn.2000) (reviewing the cases that have "attempted" to distinguish the concepts of "implicit waiver by conduct" and "forfeiture," finding the distinction "slight," and concluding that the right to counsel may be forfeited by interactions with counsel (here threats) that seek to "manipulate, delay, or disrupt trial proceedings").

SECTION 5. THE RIGHT TO "COUNSEL OF CHOICE"

Although the Supreme Court has recognized that "the right to select and be represented by one's preferred attorney is comprehended by the Sixth Amendment," *Wheat v. United States*, 486 U.S. 153 (1988) [p. 202], it has also emphasized that "the essential aim of the Amendment is to guarantee an effective advocate for each criminal defendant rather than to ensure that a defendant will inexorably be represented by the lawyer whom he prefers." Id. As a result, "[t]he Sixth Amendment right to choose one's own counsel is circumscribed in several important respects. Regardless of his persuasive powers, an advocate who is not a member of the bar may not represent clients (other than himself) in court. Similarly, a defendant may not insist on representation by an attorney he cannot afford or who for other reasons declines to represent the defendant. Nor may a defendant insist on the counsel of an attorney who has a previous or ongoing relationship with an opposing party, even when the opposing party is the Government. [Finally,] where a court justifiably finds an actual conflict of interest, [it may] insist that defendants be separately represented." Id.

If one of the above-listed limitations on the right to counsel of choice does not exist, what is a defendant's remedy if his right to counsel of choice is violated? The Supreme Court addressed that question in the case that follows.

UNITED STATES v. GONZALEZ–LOPEZ
548 U.S. 140, 126 S.Ct. 2557, 165 L.Ed.2d 409 (2006).

JUSTICE SCALIA delivered the opinion of the Court.

We must decide whether a trial court's erroneous deprivation of a criminal defendant's choice of counsel entitles him to reversal of his conviction.

Respondent Cuauhtemoc Gonzalez–Lopez was charged in the Eastern District of Missouri with conspiracy to distribute more than 100 kilograms of marijuana. His family hired attorney John Fahle to represent him. After the arraignment, respondent called a California attorney, Joseph Low, to discuss whether Low would represent him, either in addition to or instead of Fahle. Low flew from California to meet with respondent, who hired him.

The following week, respondent informed Fahle that he wanted Low to be his only attorney. Low then filed an application for admission *pro hac vice*. The District Court denied his application without comment. A month later, Low filed a second application, which the District Court again denied without explanation.

The case proceeded to trial, and Dickhaus represented respondent. Low again moved for admission and was again denied. The court also denied Dickhaus's request to have Low at counsel table with him and ordered Low to sit in the audience and to have no contact with Dickhaus during the proceedings. [Respondent] was unable to meet with Low throughout the trial, except for once on the last night. The jury found respondent guilty.

Respondent appealed, and the Eighth Circuit vacated the conviction. The Court [held] that the District Court erred in [denying Low's] motions [and] violated respondent's Sixth Amendment right to paid counsel of his choosing. The [Eighth Circuit] then concluded that this Sixth Amendment violation was not subject to harmless-error review. We granted certiorari.

The Government here agrees, as it has previously, that the Sixth Amendment guarantees the defendant the right to be represented by an otherwise qualified attorney whom that defendant can afford to hire, or who is willing to represent the defendant even though he is without funds. To be sure, the right to counsel of choice "is circumscribed in several important respects." *Wheat.* But the Government does not dispute the Eighth Circuit's conclusion in this case that the District Court erroneously deprived respondent of his counsel of choice.

The Government contends, however, that the Sixth Amendment violation is not "complete" unless the defendant can show that substitute counsel was ineffective within the meaning of *Strickland v. Washington*–i.e., that substitute counsel's performance was deficient and the defendant was prejudiced by it. In the alternative, the Government contends that the defendant must at least demonstrate that his counsel of choice would have pursued a different strategy that would have created a "reasonable probability that [the] result of the proceedings would have been different,"—in other words, that he was prejudiced within the meaning of *Strickland* by the denial of his counsel of choice even if substitute counsel's performance was not constitutionally deficient.[1] To support these propositions, the Government points to our prior cases, which note that the right to counsel "has been [accorded] not for its own sake, but because of the effect it has on the ability of the accused to receive a fair trial." *Mickens v. Taylor* [p. 191]. A trial is not unfair and thus the Sixth Amendment is not violated, the Government reasons, unless a defendant has been prejudiced.

Stated as broadly as this, the Government's argument in effect reads the Sixth Amendment as a more detailed version of the Due Process Clause—and then proceeds to give no effect to the details. It is true enough that the purpose of the rights set forth in that Amendment is to ensure a fair trial; but it does not follow that the rights can be disregarded so long as the trial is, on the whole, fair.

[The] Sixth Amendment right to counsel of choice [commands,] not that a trial be fair, but that a particular guarantee of fairness be provided-to wit, that the accused be defended by the counsel he believes to be best. "The Constitution guarantees a fair trial through the Due Process Clauses, but it defines the basic

---

1. The dissent proposes yet a third standard-viz., that the defendant must show "an identifiable difference in the quality of representation between the disqualified counsel and the attorney who represents the defendant at trial." That proposal suffers from the same infirmities (outlined later in text) that beset the Government's positions. In addition, however, it greatly impairs the clarity of the law. How is a lower-court judge to know what an identifiable difference consists of? Whereas the Government at least appeals to *Strickland* and the case law under it, the most the dissent can claim by way of precedential support for its rule is that it is consistent with cases that never discussed the issue of prejudice.

elements of a fair trial largely through the several provisions of the Sixth Amendment, including the Counsel Clause." *Strickland*. In sum, the right at stake here is the right to counsel of choice, not the right to a fair trial; and that right was violated because the deprivation of counsel was erroneous. No additional showing of prejudice is required to make the violation complete.

The cases the Government relies on involve the right to the effective assistance of counsel, the violation of which generally requires a defendant to establish prejudice. The earliest case generally cited for the proposition that "the right to counsel is the right to the effective assistance of counsel," was based on the Due Process Clause rather than on the Sixth Amendment, see *Powell* [*v. Alabama*, p. 70]. And even our recognition of the right to effective counsel within the Sixth Amendment was a consequence of our perception that representation by counsel "is critical to the ability of the adversarial system to produce just results." *Strickland*. Having derived the right to effective representation from the purpose of ensuring a fair trial, we have, logically enough, also derived the limits of that right from that same purpose. The requirement that a defendant show prejudice in effective representation cases arises from the very nature of the specific element of the right to counsel at issue there—*effective* (not mistake-free) representation. Counsel cannot be "ineffective" unless his mistakes have harmed the defense (or, at least, unless it is reasonably likely that they have). Thus, a violation of the Sixth Amendment right to *effective* representation is not "complete" until the defendant is prejudiced.

The right to select counsel of one's choice, by contrast, has never been derived from the Sixth Amendment's purpose of ensuring a fair trial.[3] It has been regarded as the root meaning of the constitutional guarantee. Where the right to be assisted by counsel of one's choice is wrongly denied, therefore, it is unnecessary to conduct an ineffectiveness or prejudice inquiry to establish a Sixth Amendment violation. Deprivation of the right is "complete" when the defendant is erroneously prevented from being represented by the lawyer he wants, regardless of the quality of the representation he received. To argue otherwise is to confuse the right to counsel of choice—which is the right to a particular lawyer regardless of comparative effectiveness—with the right to effective counsel—which imposes a baseline requirement of competence on whatever lawyer is chosen or appointed.

Having concluded, in light of the Government's concession of erroneous deprivation, that the trial court violated respondent's Sixth Amendment right to counsel of choice, we must consider whether this error is subject to review for harmlessness. In *Arizona v. Fulminante*, 499 U.S. 279 (1991) [p. 1562], we divided constitutional errors into two classes. The first we called "trial error," because the errors "occurred during presentation of the case to the jury" and their effect may "be quantitatively assessed in the context of other evidence presented in order to determine whether [they were] harmless beyond a reasonable doubt." These include "most constitutional errors." The second class of constitutional error we called "structural defects." These "defy analysis by 'harmless-error' standards" because they "affec[t] the framework within which the trial proceeds," and are not "simply an error in the trial process itself." Such errors include the denial of counsel, *Gideon* [p. 73,] [and] the denial of the right of self-representation, *McKaskle v. Wiggins* [fn. 8, p. 111].

---

3. In *Wheat v. United States*, 486 U.S. 153 (1988) [p. 202], where we formulated the right to counsel of choice and discussed some of the limitations upon it, we took note of the overarching purpose of fair trial in holding that the trial court has discretion to disallow a first choice of counsel that would create serious risk of conflict of interest. * * * It is one thing to conclude that the right to counsel of choice may be limited by the need for fair trial, but quite another to say that the right does not exist unless its denial renders the trial unfair.

We have little trouble concluding that erroneous deprivation of the right to counsel of choice, "with consequences that are necessarily unquantifiable and indeterminate, unquestionably qualifies as 'structural error.'" Different attorneys will pursue different strategies with regard to investigation and discovery, development of the theory of defense, selection of the jury, presentation of the witnesses, and style of witness examination and jury argument. And the choice of attorney will affect whether and on what terms the defendant cooperates with the prosecution, plea bargains, or decides instead to go to trial. In light of these myriad aspects of representation, the erroneous denial of counsel bears directly on the "framework within which the trial proceeds," *Fulminante*—or indeed on whether it proceeds at all. It is impossible to know what different choices the rejected counsel would have made, and then to quantify the impact of those different choices on the outcome of the proceedings. Many counseled decisions, including those involving plea bargains and cooperation with the government, do not even concern the conduct of the trial at all. Harmless-error analysis in such a context would be a speculative inquiry into what might have occurred in an alternate universe.

The Government acknowledges that the deprivation of choice of counsel pervades the entire trial, but points out that counsel's ineffectiveness may also do so and yet we do not allow reversal of a conviction for that reason without a showing of prejudice. But the requirement of showing prejudice in ineffectiveness claims stems from the very definition of the right at issue; it is not a matter of showing that the violation was harmless, but of showing that a violation of the right to effective representation *occurred*. A choice-of-counsel violation occurs *whenever* the defendant's choice is wrongfully denied. Moreover, if and when counsel's ineffectiveness "pervades" a trial, it does so (to the extent we can detect it) through identifiable mistakes. We can assess how those mistakes affected the outcome. To determine the effect of wrongful denial of choice of counsel, however, we would not be looking for mistakes committed by the actual counsel, but for differences in the defense that would have been made by the rejected counsel—in matters ranging from questions asked on *voir dire* and cross-examination to such intangibles as argument style and relationship with the prosecutors. We would have to speculate upon what matters the rejected counsel would have handled differently—or indeed, would have handled the same but with the benefit of a more jury-pleasing courtroom style or a longstanding relationship of trust with the prosecutors. And then we would have to speculate upon what effect those different choices or different intangibles might have had. The difficulties of conducting the two assessments of prejudice are not remotely comparable.

Nothing we have said today casts any doubt or places any qualification upon our previous holdings that limit the right to counsel of choice and recognize the authority of trial courts to establish criteria for admitting lawyers to argue before them. As the dissent too discusses, the right to counsel of choice does not extend to defendants who require counsel to be appointed for them. Nor may a defendant insist on representation by a person who is not a member of the bar, or demand that a court honor his waiver of conflict-free representation. See *Wheat* [fn.3]. We have recognized a trial court's wide latitude in balancing the right to counsel of choice against the needs of fairness, *Wheat*, and against the demands of its calendar. The court has, moreover, an "independent interest in ensuring that criminal trials are conducted within the ethical standards of the profession and that legal proceedings appear fair to all who observe them." *Wheat*. None of these limitations on the right to choose one's counsel is relevant here. This is not a case about a court's power to enforce rules or adhere to practices that determine which attorneys may appear before it, or to make scheduling and other decisions that effectively exclude a defendant's first choice of counsel. However broad a court's discretion may be, the Government has conceded that the District Court here erred when it denied respondent his choice of counsel. Accepting that premise, we hold that the error violated respondent's Sixth Amendment right to counsel of choice and that this violation is not subject to harmless-error analysis.

JUSTICE ALITO, with whom THE CHIEF JUSTICE, JUSTICE KENNEDY, and JUSTICE THOMAS join, dissenting.

I disagree with the Court's conclusion that a criminal conviction must automatically be reversed whenever a trial court errs in applying its rules regarding *pro hac vice* admissions and as a result prevents a defendant from being represented at trial by the defendant's first-choice attorney. Instead, a defendant should be required to make at least *some* showing that the trial court's erroneous ruling adversely affected the quality of assistance that the defendant received. In my view, the majority's contrary holding is based on an incorrect interpretation of the Sixth Amendment and a misapplication of harmless-error principles. I respectfully dissent.

The majority makes a subtle but important mistake at the outset in its characterization of what the Sixth Amendment guarantees. The majority states that the Sixth Amendment protects "the right of a defendant who does not require appointed counsel to choose who will represent him." What the Sixth Amendment actually protects, however, is the right to have *the assistance* that the defendant's counsel of choice is able to provide. It follows that if the erroneous disqualification of a defendant's counsel of choice does not impair the assistance that a defendant receives at trial, there is no violation of the Sixth Amendment.

The language of the Sixth Amendment supports this interpretation. The Assistance of Counsel Clause focuses on what a defendant is entitled to receive ("Assistance"), rather than on the identity of the provider. The background of the adoption of the Sixth Amendment points in the same direction. The specific evil against which the Assistance of Counsel Clause was aimed was the English common-law rule severely limiting a felony defendant's ability to be assisted by counsel.

There is no doubt, of course, that the right "to have the Assistance of Counsel" carries with it a limited right to be represented by counsel of choice. At the time of the adoption of the Bill of Rights, when the availability of appointed counsel was generally limited, that is how the right inevitably played out: A defendant's right to have the assistance of counsel necessarily meant the right to have the assistance of whatever counsel the defendant was able to secure. But from the beginning, the right to counsel of choice has been circumscribed.

For one thing, a defendant's choice of counsel has always been restricted by the rules governing admission to practice before the court in question.

The right to counsel of choice is also limited by conflict-of-interest rules.

Similarly, the right to be represented by counsel of choice can be limited by mundane case-management considerations. If a trial judge schedules a trial to begin on a particular date and defendant's counsel of choice is already committed for other trials until some time thereafter, the trial judge has discretion under appropriate circumstances to refuse to postpone the trial date and thereby, in effect, to force the defendant to forgo counsel of choice.

These limitations on the right to counsel of choice are tolerable because the focus of the right is the quality of the representation that the defendant receives, not the identity of the attorney who provides the representation. Limiting a defendant to those attorneys who are willing, available, and eligible to represent the defendant still leaves a defendant with a pool of attorneys to choose from-and, in most jurisdictions today, a large and diverse pool. Thus, these restrictions generally have no adverse effect on a defendant's ability to secure the best assistance that the defendant's circumstances permit.

Because the Sixth Amendment focuses on the quality of the assistance that counsel of choice would have provided, I would hold that the erroneous disqualification of counsel does not violate the Sixth Amendment unless the ruling diminishes the quality of assistance that the defendant would have otherwise received. This would not require a defendant to show that the second-choice attorney was constitutionally ineffective within the meaning of *Strickland v. Washington*. Rather, the defendant would be entitled to a new trial if the defendant could show "an identifiable difference in the quality of representation between the disqualified counsel and the attorney who represents the defendant at trial."

But even accepting, as the majority holds, that the erroneous disqualification of counsel of choice always violates the Sixth Amendment, it still would not follow that reversal is required in all cases. * * * [In *Neder v. United States*, 527 U.S. 1 (1999) [p. 1562], the Court applied harmless error analysis after rejecting] the argument that the omission of an element of a crime in a jury instruction "necessarily render[s] a criminal trial fundamentally unfair or an unreliable vehicle for determining guilt or innocence." In fact, in that case, "quite the opposite [was] true: Neder was tried before an impartial judge, under the correct standard of proof and with the assistance of counsel; a fairly selected, impartial jury was instructed to consider all of the evidence and argument in respect to Neder's defense. . . ." *Id.*

Neder's situation—with an impartial judge, the correct standard of proof, assistance of counsel, and a fair jury—is much like respondent's. Fundamental unfairness does not inexorably follow from the denial of first-choice counsel. The "decision to retain a particular lawyer" is "often uninformed;" a defendant's second-choice lawyer may thus turn out to be better than the defendant's first-choice lawyer. More often, a defendant's first-and second-choice lawyers may be simply indistinguishable. These possibilities would not justify violating the right to choice of counsel, but they do make me hard put to characterize the violation as "*always* render[ing] a trial unfair."

Either of the two courses outlined above—requiring at least some showing of prejudice, or engaging in harmless-error review—would avoid the anomalous and unjustifiable consequences that follow from the majority's two-part rule of error without prejudice followed by automatic reversal.

Under the majority's holding, a defendant who is erroneously required to go to trial with a second-choice attorney is automatically entitled to a new trial even if this attorney performed brilliantly.

Under the majority's holding, a trial court may adopt rules severely restricting *pro hac vice* admissions, but if it adopts a generous rule and then errs in interpreting or applying it, the error automatically requires reversal of any conviction, regardless of whether the erroneous ruling had any effect on the defendant.

Under the majority's holding, some defendants will be awarded new trials even though it is clear that the erroneous disqualification of their first-choice counsel did not prejudice them in the least. Suppose, for example, that a defendant is initially represented by an attorney who previously represented the defendant in civil matters and who has little criminal experience. Suppose that this attorney is erroneously disqualified and that the defendant is then able to secure the services of a nationally acclaimed and highly experienced criminal defense attorney who secures a surprisingly favorable result at trial—for instance, acquittal on most but not all counts. Under the majority's holding, the trial court's erroneous ruling automatically means that the Sixth Amendment was violated—even if the defendant makes no attempt to argue that the disqualified attorney would have done a better job. In fact, the defendant would still be entitled to a new trial on the counts of conviction even if the defendant publicly proclaimed after the verdict that the second attorney had provided better representation than any other attorney in the country could have possibly done.

NOTES AND QUESTIONS

1. ***Admission pro hac vice.*** The Supreme Court has not ruled on the extent to which a defendant's right to representation by "counsel of choice" restricts a trial court's authority to deny admission *pro hac vice* when that attorney is licensed in another jurisdiction.[n] Lower courts have suggested that a "court cannot peremptorily refuse to permit representation by out-of-state counsel[, but] it can insist upon special prerequisites to ensure 'ethical and orderly administration of justice,' taking account of possible scheduling difficulties, ease of exchanges between opposing counsel, and past behavior of counsel suggesting a lack of responsibility." CRIMPROC § 11.4(c).

2. ***Scheduling considerations.*** As the *Gonzalez-Lopez* majority notes, a trial court is given "wide latitude in balancing the right to counsel of choice [against] the demands of [the court's] calendar." See also the dissent ("[T]he right to be represented by counsel of choice can be limited by mundane case-management considerations."). Appellate decisions reviewing trial court denials of scheduling accommodations sought by defendants to facilitate representation by counsel of choice typically involve requests for continuances in order to replace current counsel with new counsel. Those decisions agree that trial courts cannot give scheduling concerns per se priority in that situation, but must engage in case-by-case balancing. The leading Supreme Court ruling on the subject noted: "The matter of a continuance is traditionally within the trial court's discretion.... There are no mechanical tests for deciding when a denial of a continuance is so arbitrary as to violate [defendant's constitutional right]. The answer must be found in the circumstances present in every case, particularly the reasons presented to the trial judge at the time the request is denied." *Ungar v. Sarafite*, 376 U.S. 575 (1964).

As noted in CRIMPROC. § 11.4(c), "while the appellate courts frequently note that they will give considerable leeway to the trial court in its determination not to grant a continuance, a substantial body of cases have found abuses of discretion resulting in a denial of defendants' constitutional rights." Among the factors weighed are whether the request came at a point sufficiently in advance of trial to permit the trial court to readily adjust its calendar, whether the continuance would carry the trial beyond the period specified in the speedy trial act, whether the continuance would inconvenience witnesses, and whether the defendant had some legitimate cause for dissatisfaction with counsel, even though it fell short of the "good cause" that automatically justifies replacement.

---

n. In *Leis v. Flynt*, 439 U.S. 438 (1979), the Court majority rejected the claim of out-of-state attorneys that the state court's refusal to permit them to represent the defendant in an obscenity prosecution violated the attorneys' constitutional rights. The Court held that the interest of an out-of-state attorney in being allowed to appear *pro hac vice* did not rise to the level of a "cognizable property or liberty interest within the terms of the Fourteenth Amendment." The Court noted that it was not ruling on whether the constitutional rights of the defendant might be violated since that claim was not before it. Three dissenting justices rejected "the notion that a state trial judge has arbitrary and unlimited power to refuse a nonresident lawyer permission to appear in his courtroom," noting that "the client's interest in representation by out-of-state counsel [surely] is entitled to some measure of constitutional protection."

3. _Replacing appointed counsel_. As both the _Gonzalez-Lopez_ majority and dissent note, "the right to counsel of choice does not extend to defendants who require counsel to be appointed for them." Thus, even where the state's practice is to appoint private attorneys to represent indigent defendants, the court has no constitutional obligation to give any weight to a defendant's request for a particular attorney who is both qualified and willing to accept appointment. But see CRIMPROC § 11.4(a) (noting that "at least two states have departed from [this] traditional position," and require the appointing court to weigh any special factors supporting defendant's preference against countervailing administrative considerations).

Relatedly, indigent defendants have no right to replace appointed counsel with an alternate counsel who is available and willing to accept appointment apart from certain extreme situations that produce "good cause" for replacing counsel. See infra Note 10, p. 217. Does it follow that the court can replace appointed counsel, notwithstanding defendant's preference to stay with that counsel, even where retention of current counsel requires only a relatively minor disruption in the court's schedule? Consider, in this connection, the situation presented in MORRIS v. SLAPPY, 461 U.S. 1 (1983).

In _Slappy_, the public defender initially assigned to defendant had represented defendant at the preliminary hearing (where defendant was bound over on charges of rape, robbery, and burglary), and had conducted an extensive investigation, before he was hospitalized for emergency surgery shortly before trial. An experienced attorney in the same office was assigned as a replacement, and six days later the trial started as scheduled. After the trial was under way, defendant Slappy, on his own initiative, asked for a continuance, arguing that the replacement attorney had insufficient time to prepare. After the attorney assured the trial court that he was "ready," the continuance was denied. On the third day of trial, Slappy again asked for a continuance, stating that he wanted to be represented by his original attorney and viewed himself as currently unrepresented. When that motion was denied, Slappy announced that he would no longer cooperate with the replacement attorney or participate in the trial. The trial continued and Slappy was convicted on several counts.

On subsequent federal habeas review, the Ninth Circuit overturned the convictions, concluding that the trial court had violated the Sixth Amendment when it failed to take into consideration defendant's interest in continued representation by the original attorney (it had not even inquired into the probable length of that attorney's absence). In reaching this conclusion, the Ninth Circuit noted that the Sixth Amendment "would be without substance if it did not include the right to a meaningful attorney-client relationship," and stated that the trial court had erred in ignoring Slappy's right to a "meaningful attorney-client relationship."

The Supreme Court, per Burger, C.J., overturned the Ninth Circuit ruling. The Court initially found no merit in the claim that a continuance had been needed to allow the replacement counsel to prepare for trial. It also concluded that Slappy's motion on the third day of trial, for a continuance and a return to representation by original counsel, had been untimely. Chief Justice Burger also rejected the Ninth Circuit's vision of the Sixth Amendment:

"[The] Court of Appeals' conclusion that the Sixth Amendment right to counsel 'would be without substance if it did not include the right to a _meaningful attorney-client relationship_' (emphasis added) is without basis in the law. [No] court could possibly guarantee that a defendant will develop the kind of rapport with his attorney—privately retained or provided by the public—that the Court of Appeals thought part of the Sixth Amendment guarantee of counsel. Accordingly, we reject the claim that the Sixth Amendment guarantees a 'meaningful relationship' between an accused and his counsel.''

Although he concurred in the result (because he agreed with the Court that Slappy did not make a timely motion for a continuance based on the original attorney's unavailability), Justice Brennan, joined by Marshall, J., disagreed with the thrust of the Court's reasoning. He noted:

''[In] light of the importance of a defendant's relationship with his attorney to his Sixth Amendment right to counsel, recognizing a qualified right to continue that relationship is eminently sensible. The Court of Appeals simply held that where a defendant expresses a desire to continue to be represented by counsel who already has been appointed for him by moving for a continuance until that attorney again will be available, the trial judge has an obligation to inquire into the length of counsel's expected unavailability and to balance the defendant's interest against the public's interest in the efficient and expeditious administration of criminal justice. Contrary to the Court's suggestion, this does not require a trial court 'to guarantee' attorney-defendant 'rapport.' [The] defendant's interest in preserving his relationship with a particular attorney is not afforded absolute protection. If the attorney is likely to be unavailable for an extended period, or if other factors exist that tip the balance in favor of proceeding in spite of a particular attorney's absence, the defendant's motion for a continuance clearly may be denied. Such denials would be subject to review under the traditional 'abuse of discretion' standard. As the Court of Appeals suggested, however, the balancing is critical. In the absence of a balancing inquiry a trial court cannot discharge its 'duty to preserve the fundamental rights of an accused.' ''

4. *Is there a right to counsel of choice on appeal?* Given that a defendant has no right to proceed *pro se* on appeal and thus can be forced to accept counsel against his will, see *Martinez v. Court of Appeal of California* (discussed supra Section 4, Note 3, p. 111), at least one lower court has held that there is no Sixth Amendment right to counsel of choice on appeal. See, e.g., *Tamalini v. Stewart*, 249 F.3d 895 (9th Cir. 2001). But see *State v. Peterson*, 757 N.W.2d 834 (Wis. 2008) (suggesting that there is a limited constitutional right to counsel of choice at a postconviction hearing). Even if such a right exists in theory, some lower courts have recognized that there is a potential conflict of interest in having the same lawyer at trial and on appeal, because defendants often raise the ineffectiveness of their trial counsel as a claim for relief on appeal, and an attorney cannot be expected to raise his own ineffectiveness. See, e.g., Adam Liptak, *Longtime Death Case Lawyer Appeals Ouster*, N.Y. Times (Mar. 24, 2003) (describing one such case); see also Eve Brensike Primus, *Structural Reform in Criminal Defense: Relocating Ineffective Assistance of Counsel Claims*, 92 Cornell L. Rev. 679, 724–27 (2007) (arguing that new counsel should be required for all criminal defendants on appeal for this reason).

5. *Forfeiture statutes and the right to counsel of choice*. In CAPLIN & DRYSDALE, CHARTERED v. UNITED STATES, 491 U.S. 617 (1989), a law firm sued the United States government to recover legal fees that it did not receive after defending Charles Reckmeyer on charges of running an illegal drug operation. The law firm had not received its fees, because the government had seized Reckmeyer's funds in accordance with a federal statute providing that a person convicted of specified drug violations forfeits all property ''constituting or derived from'' the proceeds of those violations. This federal statute, the law firm argued, effectively denies defendants convicted of the qualifying drug offenses of their Sixth Amendment rights to counsel of choice. The Supreme Court, in a 5–4 decision written by Justice White, disagreed, noting that a ''defendant has no Sixth Amendment right to spend another person's money for services rendered by an attorney, even if those funds are the only way that defendant will be able to retain the counsel of his choice." The majority also noted that "there is a strong governmental interest in obtaining full recovery of all forfeitable assets, an interest that overrides any Sixth Amendment interest in permitting criminals to use assets adjudged forfeitable to pay for their defense." Justice White elaborated on the governmental interests as follows:

"First, the Government has a pecuniary interest in forfeiture that goes beyond merely separating a criminal from his ill-gotten gains; that legitimate interest extends to recovering all forfeitable assets, for such assets are deposited in a Fund that supports law-enforcement efforts in a variety of important and useful ways. [Second,] the statute permits 'rightful owners' of forfeited assets to make claims for forfeited assets before they are retained by the government. The Government's interest in winning undiminished forfeiture thus includes the objective of returning property, in full, to those wrongfully deprived or defrauded of it. [Finally,] a major purpose motivating [these] forfeiture provisions has been the desire to lessen the economic power of organized crime and drug enterprises."

The petitioner in *Caplin & Drysdale* also contended that the forfeiture statute "upset the balance of forces between the accused and accuser" by allowing the prosecution, through its discretion as to the utilization of the forfeiture remedy, to exercise what the dissenters described as "an intolerable degree of power over any private attorney who takes on the task of representing a defendant in a forfeiture case." As Justice Blackmun, writing for the dissenters, explained it, "the Government will be ever tempted to use the forfeiture weapon against a defense attorney who is particularly talented or aggressive on the client's behalf—the attorney who is better than what, in the Government's view, the defendant deserves. The spectre of the Government's selectively excluding only the most talented defense counsel is a serious threat to the equality of forces necessary for the adversarial system to perform at its best." Although the majority recognized this potential for abuse, it noted that "[c]ases involving particular abuses can be dealt with by lower courts, when (and if) [they] arise."

CHAPTER 5

THE PERFORMANCE OF COUNSEL

■ ■ ■

SECTION 1. THE INEFFECTIVE ASSISTANCE OF COUNSEL (IAC) CLAIM: BASIC FEATURES

1. *Supreme Court recognition.* The Supreme Court's seminal ruling in *Powell v. Alabama* (1932) is known primarily as being the first Supreme Court ruling to establish a constitutional right to the appointment of counsel to assist an indigent defendant (see p. 70). *Powell*, however, also laid the foundation for the IAC claim. *Powell* noted that "the state's [due process] duty [to provide appointed counsel] is not discharged by an appointment at such time or under such circumstances as to preclude the giving of effective aid in preparation of the trial of the case," and it concluded that the appointment in the case before it suffered from that flaw (see Note 2, p. 172). Between *Powell* and the *Gideon* ruling in 1963 (holding the Sixth Amendment right to counsel applicable to the states, see p. 73), the Court acknowledged in various contexts that the right to appointed counsel, under either the due process clause (in state cases) or the Sixth Amendment (in federal cases), encompassed an element of appropriate performance by that appointed counsel. A failure in the "representation rendered," the Court noted, could "convert the appointment of counsel * * * [into a] sham." Only one case, *Glasser v. United States,* Note 1, p. 186, found a Sixth Amendment violation, and that was based on the trial court having taken action that prevented defendant's counsel from providing the "effective assistance of counsel." It was not until several years after *Gideon* that the Court began to refer to a defense right to challenge a conviction based solely on counsel's inadequate performance—described as an "ineffective assistance of counsel claim" (a description today commonly shortened in commentary and judicial opinions to the "IAC claim"). That claim was said to have its roots in the earliest Supreme Court discussions of the constitutional right to counsel's assistance, starting with *Powell.*

2. *Retained v. appointed counsel.* Prior to CUYLER v. SULLIVAN, 446 U.S. 335 (1980), many lower courts utilized different standards in reviewing ineffective assistance claims as to trial counsel, distinguishing between privately retained and appointed counsel. The distinction was based on the state-action requirement of the Fourteenth Amendment. A constitutional violation, it was argued, required state participation at a sufficient level to render the state responsible for counsel's inadequacies. That responsibility was seen as arising automatically from the trial court's selection of appointed counsel. As for retained counsel, the state bore responsibility for counsel's inadequacies only where they were so obvious that they should have been apparent to the trial court.

Cuyler put an end to drawing such a distinction. At issue there was alleged ineffectiveness by retained attorneys who failed to take certain actions because of the potential harm to codefendants also represented by the attorneys. The state argued that the attorneys had not been ineffective, but in any event, "the alleged failings of * * * retained counsel cannot provide a basis for a [constitutional violation] because the conduct of retained counsel does not involve state action." Rejecting that contention, the Court (per Powell, J.) noted:

"A proper respect for the Sixth Amendment disarms [the prosecution's] contention that defendants who retain their own lawyers are entitled to less protection than defendants for whom the State appoints counsel. * * * The vital guarantee of the Sixth Amendment would stand for little if the often uninformed decision to retain a particular lawyer could reduce or forfeit the defendant's entitlement to constitutional protection. Since the State's conduct of a criminal trial itself implicates the State in the defendant's conviction, we see no basis for drawing a distinction between retained and appointed counsel that would deny equal justice to defendants who must choose their own lawyers."

   3. *The prerequisite constitutional right.* In *Evitts v. Lucey*, 469 U.S. 387 (1985), the defendant raised an IAC claim as to representation by retained counsel on a first appeal as of right. The original IAC cases had dealt with ineffective assistance at trial. After *Douglas v. California* (p. 100) recognized a constitutional right to appointed counsel on first appeal of right (relying on equal protection and due process), the Court noted that an IAC claim similarly could be based on appointed counsel's performance at that stage. The *Evitts* Court concluded that the IAC claim also applied to retained counsel's performance on first appeal as of right, but only after first finding that the due process grounding noted in *Douglas* also established a constitutional right to representation by retained counsel at the first appeal of right. Where a constitutional guarantee establishes a constitutional right to representation by counsel at a particular stage, whether by retained or appointed counsel, ineffective assistance by that counsel would violate that constitutional right.

   Evitts and the other IAC rulings involving retained counsel all presented stages at which the Constitution guaranteed assistance by both an assigned counsel (for the indigent) and retained counsel (for the non-indigent). Commentators have suggested, however, that in judicial proceedings as to which the indigent defendant has no right to appointed counsel, due process may recognize the individual's interest in "defending himself in whatever manner he deems best, using every legitimate resource at his command," *People v. Crovedi*, 417 P.2d 868 (Cal. 1966), and therefore prohibit the state from precluding representation by retained counsel (absent some overriding state interest in precluding participation by attorneys on both sides). See CRIMPROC § 11.1(b). Assuming arguendo that there is such a right to representation by retained counsel at a stage not requiring the appointment of counsel, would due process also guarantee the effective assistance of retained counsel at that stage?

   Wainwright v. Torna, 455 U.S. 586 (1982), flatly rejected an effective assistance right in one such possible situation. There, respondent Torna's felony convictions had been affirmed by an intermediate state appellate court. His subsequent application for a writ of certiorari was dismissed by the state supreme court because it had not been filed timely. Respondent contended that he had been denied the effective assistance of counsel by the failure of his retained counsel to file that application in time. Summarily reversing a federal habeas ruling that had sustained respondent's contention, the Court majority (per curiam) held that respondent had no constitutional right to retain counsel's effective assistance. It noted: "*Ross v. Moffitt* [p. 102] held that a criminal defendant does not have a constitutional right to counsel to pursue discretionary state appeals or applications for review in this Court. [Since] respondent had no constitutional right to counsel, he could not be deprived of the effective assistance of counsel by his retained counsel's failure to file the application timely."

Torna's reference to the absence of a "constitutional right to counsel" centered on a constitutional right that encompasses the appointment of counsel for the indigent (the claim rejected in *Ross v. Moffitt*). It is not read as suggesting that the state constitutionally could have precluded Torna's use of retained counsel in filing an application for review, but simply as holding that, at that stage, the client must "bear the consequences of his unwise choice of counsel." CRIMPROC § 11.7a.

4. Would the result in *Torna* have been different if the counsel there had been chosen and provided by the state? *Pennsylvania v. Finley*, 481 U.S. 551 (1987), arguably indicates that factor would be irrelevant. *Finley* involved counsel appointed to represent an indigent prisoner in challenging her conviction through a state postconviction procedure. The appointed counsel advised the habeas court that the prisoner's claim was totally without merit, which resulted in the court-approved withdrawal of counsel and the dismissal of the petition for postconviction relief. Counsel's action had been inconsistent with the withdrawal safeguards prescribed in *Anders v. California* (Note 2, p. 218) to ensure that appellate counsel appointed pursuant to the constitutional mandate of *Douglas v. California* effectively represent their clients. *Finley* held, however, that the *Anders* safeguards were not constitutionally required in a postconviction proceeding because the state had no constitutional obligation to appoint counsel in such a proceeding. The *Finley* opinion contained language that arguably limited the Court's ruling (the Court noting that the *Anders* safeguards were "prophylactic" and that the procedures followed by counsel had "fully comported with 'fundamental fairness'"). However, a later case, *Coleman v. Thompson*, 501 U.S. 722 (1991), recognized no such limitation in its analysis of *Finley*, and concluded that *Finley* rejects ineffective-assistance claims as a general matter for all proceedings in which there is no constitutional obligation to provide appointed counsel. Such a claim may be allowed, however, under state law. Various state courts have read statutory provisions directing that appointed counsel be provided at a particular stage in the process as implicitly including a state statutory right to effective assistance, which is to be assessed, under state law, by reference to the Sixth Amendment performance standard. See CRIMPROC § 11.7(a).

5. In *Torna*, Justice Marshall, in dissent, concluded that, "where a defendant can show that he reasonably relied on his attorney's promise to seek discretionary review [in a timely fashion], due process requires the state [high court] to consider his application even where the application is untimely." Would a similar due process contention tied to a state proceeding's reliance on counsel's deficient performance be more likely to prevail where the defendant has an independently recognized due process right to fairness in the particular proceeding? Consider the analysis of CRIMPROC § 11.7(a): "Both *Torna* and *Finley* involved a proceeding that the state had no constitutional obligation to provide. Where the state has a constitutional obligation to provide a particular process, but that obligation does not include a duty to appoint counsel, the ineffective performance of counsel, whether retained or appointed, might be successfully challenged by reference to the adequacy of that process. Such a possibility would be presented, for example, by the ineffective assistance of retained counsel at a misdemeanor trial which resulted in the imposition only of a fine [and thus was a proceeding in which defendant was not constitutionally entitled to appointed counsel, see *Scott v. Illinois*, p. 81]. The defendant could argue here that ineffectiveness of counsel resulted in a proceeding in which defendant was so deprived of his ability to make use of the procedural rights constitutionally guaranteed to him in such a trial that the proceeding itself did not comport with due process."

6. *The adversarial process benchmark.* It was not until 1984, in the companion rulings of *United States v. Cronic* and *Strickland v. Washington*, that the Court "articulat[ed] a comprehensive conception of ineffective assistance of counsel." CRIMPROC § 11.7(c). As *Strickland* noted, previous rulings largely had involved judicial restrictions upon counsel's performance and the Court had no occasion "to elaborate on the meaning of the constitutional requirement of effective assistance * * * in cases presenting claims of 'actual ineffectiveness' "— i.e., where "counsel * * * deprive[d] a defendant of the right to effective assistance * * * simply by failing to render 'adequate legal assistance.' " In both *Cronic* and *Strickland*, the Court stressed that the actual performance of counsel was to be evaluated in light of the underlying purpose of the constitutional right to counsel—providing what *Strickland* described as an adversarial process "benchmark" (p. 139). See also Note 3, p. 149 (discussing commentator criticism of the grounding for that benchmark, as it was explained in *Cronic* (below) and *Strickland*).

UNITED STATES v. CRONIC, 466 U.S. 648 (1984), the first announced of the two cases, did not require the Court to apply its performance benchmark. As discussed in Note 2, p. 173, the lower court there had concluded that the circumstances faced by appointed counsel justified presuming that counsel's performance had been constitutionally deficient. A unanimous Supreme Court rejected that reasoning, and remanded for consideration of the adequacy of counsel's actual performance. The function of the counsel guarantee, it reasoned, required looking to counsel's actual performance, rather than presuming inadequacy, absent special situations that were not present in this case. The Court (per Stevens, J.) offered the following description, of that function and its shaping of the IAC claim.

"The substance of the Constitution's guarantee of the effective-assistance of counsel is illuminated by reference to its underlying purpose. '[T]ruth,' Lord Eldon said, 'is best discovered by powerful statements on both sides of the question.' * * * The very premise of our adversary system of criminal justice is that partisan advocacy on both sides of a case will best promote the ultimate objective that the guilty be convicted and the innocent go free. * * * Unless the accused receives the effective assistance of counsel, a serious risk of injustice infects the trial itself. * * * Thus, the adversarial process protected by the Sixth Amendment requires that the accused have, 'counsel acting in the role of an advocate'. The right to the effective assistance of counsel is * * * the right of the accused to require the prosecution's case to survive the crucible of meaningful adversarial testing. When a true adversarial criminal trial has been conducted— even if defense counsel may have made demonstrable errors—the kind of testing envisioned by the Sixth Amendment has occurred. But if the process loses its character as a confrontation between adversaries, the constitutional guarantee is violated.

"The Court of Appeals * * * [here] did not indicated that there had been an actual breakdown of the adversarial process during the trial of this case, * * * [but] instead * * * [adopted] an inference that counsel was unable to discharge his duties. In our evaluation of this conclusion, we begin by recognizing that the right to effective counsel is recognized not for its own sake, but because of the effect it has on the ability of the accused to receive a fair trial. Absent some effect of challenged conduct on the reliability of the trial process, the Sixth Amendment guarantee is generally not implicated."

7. *Raising an ineffectiveness claim.* Three major obstacles restrict raising an ineffective assistance claim on direct appeal from a conviction: (1) very often, the attorney on appeal is the trial counsel or an appellate specialist in the same office, and those attorneys not only are unlikely to look to their own (or their colleague's) ineptitude in developing grounds for appeal, but if they do look there, they face the ethical restrictions imposed on an attorney challenging his own (or his colleague's) representation; (2) many IAC claims are based on actions or omissions that are not revealed in the trial court record (e.g., a failure to investigate); and (3) even where the claim is based on an action by counsel reflected in the trial record, and the trial record suggests no explanation for that action other than incompetence, an off-record explanation could cast that action in an entirely different light, providing a reasonable strategic justification for the action. Because of these obstacles, most jurisdictions prefer that ineffective assistance claims be presented on collateral attack (where both sides have the opportunity to present evidence that goes beyond the trial record and the defendant can raise the claim *pro se* or with a different attorney). Some jurisdictions have concluded that so few ineffective assistance claims can be resolved on the trial record that all claims must be presented on collateral attack; they find greater benefit in ensuring that all aspects of potentially ineffective assistance are considered together than in allowing the few exceptions to be raised on direct appeal. Other jurisdictions allow ineffective assistance claims to be raised on appeal where the grounding for the claim arguably appears in the trial court record. They warn the defendant, however, that the limitations of that record may impact review of the claim. As noted in *United States v. Taglia*, 922 F.2d 413 (7th Cir.1991): "When the only record on which a claim of ineffective assistance is based is the trial record, every indulgence will be given to the possibility that a seeming lapse or error by defense counsel was in fact a tactical move flawed only in hindsight." Thus, the defendant must establish that there could be no explanation for counsel's performance other than counsel's ineptitude, and if the defendant fails to make that showing on the trial record, there will be no possibility of expanding the record on collateral attack, as rejection of a claim on appeal ordinarily precludes reconsideration on collateral attack.

Commentators and courts have recognized that deferring all (or most) IAC claims to collateral attack has its drawbacks for both the judiciary and the defendant. The state judiciary can readily be subjected to the wasteful use of limited resources: (1) in having bifurcated review of a single conviction (the initial appellate review and the subsequent postconviction proceeding on the IAC claim, with another appeal possible from that proceeding); (2) in dealing with frivolous or borderline frivolous appeals (or appellate counsel motions to withdraw because the appeal would be frivolous) where trial counsel's ineffective assistance leaves a trial record devoid of any significant issues; and (3) where trial counsel failed to object to possible trial errors, requiring the appellate court to first address whether those errors should be reviewable, notwithstanding the lack of objection, under the "plain error" doctrine, even through a court on collateral attack will subsequently consider whether that lack of objection establishes the ineffective assistance of counsel. The drawbacks for the defendant stem primarily from delay and procedural obstacles that accompany collateral review in many states. State postconviction proceedings follow the exhaustion of appellate review, which typically will take at least a few years (and in some jurisdictions as much as 4 or 5 years). At that point, the time gap makes investigation more difficult, both in establishing what trial counsel failed to do and what would have been uncovered if counsel had done more. The delay also may operate to preclude collateral-attack IAC claims by the many defendants who have served their prison sentences or completed their probationary terms, as many jurisdictions allow collateral attacks only by convicted persons who remain in custody. Another procedural obstacle in many jurisdictions is the absence of a right to appointed counsel on collateral attack. See Note 4, p. 1572.

These drawbacks have led commentators to urge that the challenge procedure be restructured to facilitate raising IAC claims at the trial court level, prior to pursuing an appeal, rather than on collateral attack. See Eve Brensike Primus,

Structural Reform in Criminal Defense: Relocating Ineffective Assistance of Counsel Claims, 92 Cornell L.Rev. 679 (2007) (presenting the most complete restructuring proposal, which would include: (1) requiring, as to appointed and retained counsel, that appellate counsel be different from trial counsel; (2) giving appellate counsel at least six months to investigate the possibility that trial counsel was ineffective; (3) extending time limits for new trial motions to cover this period and thereby allow the new counsel to supplement the record and raise an IAC claim in the trial court.) A small group of states have moved partially in this direction. Thus, several states allow appellate counsel to request a remand to the trial court to pursue an evidentiary hearing on an IAC claim. However, such procedures often impose "unrealistic time limits," do not guarantee an opportunity for an evidentiary hearing, and do not provide for new appellate counsel. See Primus, supra. No state, in particular, has been willing to require that retained trial counsel be replaced with new appellate counsel. See Note 4, p. 129.

8. Counsel's testimony. When an ineffective assistance claim is presented on collateral attack or a new trial motion, an evidentiary hearing permits the defendant to establish what occurred in counsel's pretrial preparation, what communications occurred between defendant and counsel, and what might have occurred if counsel had taken other actions (e.g., what further investigation would have revealed). In this connection, the defendant (or the prosecution) may require the trial counsel to testify. Moreover, that testimony may reveal conversations between the client and the lawyer, as the challenge to counsel's performance constitutes an implicit waiver of the lawyer-client privilege. See *Bittaker v. Woodford*, 331 F.3d 715 (9th Cir.2003) (viewing that waiver as limited to the adjudication of the ineffectiveness claim, so testimony as to such communications cannot be used in any subsequent proceedings): *Commonwealth v. Chmiel*, 738 A.2d 406 (Pa.1999) (viewing waiver as not so limited). Consider also *Binney v. State*, 683 S.E 2d 478 (S.C. 2009)(waiver allowed prosecution to review defense counsel's "entire trial file"); ABA Standing Committee on Ethics and Professional Responsibility, Formal Opinion 10–456 (7/14/2010) (former client's ineffective assistance claim does not authorize attorney to unilaterally furnish confidential information about the defense presentation to the prosecutor, in contrast to revealing that information in a "court-supervised response, by way of testimony or otherwise"). See also Notes 2–4, pp. 164–65 (addressing the judicial treatment of counsel's testimony).

SECTION 2. THE *STRICKLAND* STANDARDS

1. Pre-*Strickland*. Prior to the Supreme Court's ruling in *Strickland*, infra, lower courts had divided on several aspects of the IAC claim. Initially, there was division in their description of the level of performance that would be so deficient as to constitute ineffective assistance. For many years, the prevailing test had been whether counsel's performance was so poor "as to reduce the trial to a 'farce' or render it a mockery of justice." Courts varied in their interpretation of this vague standard, but some clearly required lawyering so inept as to fail completely to challenge the prosecution's case. However, many courts had moved to a standard that asked whether counsel's performance reflected the skills and diligence generally expected from criminal defense attorneys. In applying that performance standard, most courts looked to the totality of the performance under the circumstances of the particular case—an approach commonly characterized as "judgmental." See *United States v. Decoster*, 624 F.2d 196 (D.C.Cir.1976) (Leventhal, J.). However, several lower court judges had called for adoption of a "categorical approach," which measured performance against a checklist of minimum duties owed to the client (typically duties noted in the *ABA Standards*

Relating to the Defense Function). See e.g., *United States v. Decoster*, supra (Bazelon, J. dissenting).

Lower courts also were divided on the needed showing as to the impact of counsel's deficient performance. Opinions promoting a categorical approach argued that no such showing should be necessary, but all but a few courts concluded that some showing of "prejudice" was needed to establish the ineffective assistance of counsel. There was considerable variation, however, in the description of that showing. Some courts focused simply on whether there would otherwise have been a substantial difference in the thrust of the representation, while others looked to the likelihood of a difference in the outcome of the prosecution (with those courts then differing as to the needed degree of likelihood).

In *Strickland*, the en banc Court of Appeals had referred to these divisions, and was itself divided both on the use of a quasi-categorical approach and the appropriate standard of prejudice. The Supreme Court opinion in *Strickland* responded not only to the specific rulings below, but to the various divisions among lower courts in their basic conception of the IAC claim.

STRICKLAND v. WASHINGTON
466 U.S. 668, 104 S.Ct. 2052, 80 L.Ed.2d 674 (1984).

JUSTICE O'CONNOR delivered the opinion of the Court. * * *

During a 10–day period * * *, respondent [Washington] planned and committed three groups of crimes, which included three brutal stabbing murders, torture, kidnaping, severe assaults, attempted murders, attempted extortion, and theft. After his two accomplices were arrested, respondent surrendered to police and voluntarily gave a lengthy statement confessing to the third of the criminal episodes. [He was indicted and the state court] * * * appointed an experienced criminal lawyer to represent him.

Counsel actively pursued pretrial motions and discovery. He cut his efforts short, however, and he experienced a sense of hopelessness about the case, when he learned that, against his specific advice, respondent had also confessed to the first two murders. By the date set for trial, respondent was subject to indictment for three counts of first-degree murder and multiple counts of robbery, kidnaping for ransom, breaking and entering and assault, attempted murder, and conspiracy to commit robbery. Respondent waived his right to a jury trial, again acting against counsel's advice, and pleaded guilty to all charges, including the three capital murder charges.

In the plea colloquy, respondent told the trial judge that, although he had committed a string of burglaries, he had no significant prior criminal record and that at the time of his criminal spree he was under extreme stress caused by his inability to support his family. He also stated, however, that he accepted responsibility for the crimes. The trial judge told respondent that he had "a great deal of respect for people who are willing to step forward and admit their responsibility" but that he was making no statement at all about his likely sentencing decision. * * * Counsel advised respondent to invoke his right under Florida law to an advisory jury at his capital sentencing hearing. Respondent rejected the advice and waived the right. He chose instead to be sentenced by the trial judge without a jury recommendation.

In preparing for the sentencing hearing, counsel spoke with respondent about his background. He also spoke on the telephone with respondent's wife and mother, though he did not follow up on the one unsuccessful effort to meet with them. He did not otherwise seek out character witnesses for respondent. Nor did he request a psychiatric examination, since his conversations with his client gave no indication that respondent had psychological problems. * * * [Counsel's decision] not to present and hence not to look further for evidence concerning respondent's character and emotional state * * * reflected counsel's sense of hopelessness about overcoming the evidentiary effect of respondent's confessions to the gruesome crimes. It also reflected the judgment that it was advisable to rely on the plea colloquy for evidence about respondent's background and about his claim of emotional stress: the plea colloquy communicated sufficient information about these subjects, and by forgoing the opportunity to present new evidence on these subjects, counsel prevented the State from cross-examining respondent on his claim and from putting on psychiatric evidence of its own.

Counsel also excluded from the sentencing hearing other evidence he thought was potentially damaging. He successfully moved to exclude respondent's "rap sheet." Because he judged that a presentence report might prove more detrimental than helpful, as it would have included respondent's criminal history and thereby would have undermined the claim of no significant history of criminal activity, he did not request that one be prepared.

At the sentencing hearing, counsel's strategy was based primarily on the trial judge's remarks at the plea colloquy as well as on his reputation as a sentencing judge who thought it important for a convicted defendant to own up to his crime. Counsel argued that respondent's remorse and acceptance of responsibility justified sparing him from the death penalty. Counsel also argued that respondent had no history of criminal activity and that respondent committed the crimes under extreme mental or emotional disturbance, thus coming within the statutory list of mitigating circumstances. He further argued that respondent should be spared death because he had surrendered, confessed, and offered to testify against a codefendant and because respondent was fundamentally a good person who had briefly gone badly wrong in extremely stressful circumstances. The State put on evidence and witnesses largely for the purpose of describing the details of the crimes. * * *

[T]he trial judge found numerous aggravating circumstances and no (or a single comparatively insignificant) mitigating circumstance. With respect to each of the three convictions for capital murder, the trial judge concluded: "A careful consideration of all matters presented to the court impels the conclusion that there are insufficient mitigating circumstances . . . to outweigh the aggravating circumstances." He therefore sentenced respondent to death on each of the three counts of murder and to prison terms for the other crimes. The Florida Supreme Court upheld the convictions and sentences on direct appeal. * * *

[Washington subsequently sought collateral relief in state court. In support of his claim of ineffective assistance of counsel, Washington submitted 14 affidavits from "friends, neighbors, and relatives" stating that they would have provided favorable character evidence if asked. He also submitted "one psychiatric report and one psychological report stating that respondent, though not under the influence of extreme emotional disturbance, was 'chronically frustrated and depressed because of his economic dilemma.' " In denying the ineffectiveness claim, the state court noted that counsel could reasonably have decided not to seek psychiatric reports, as a previous psychiatric examination, conducted by state order soon after Washington's arraignment, had stated that there was no indication of major medical illness, and the two reports now submitted by Washington similarly failed to establish the extreme mental or emotional disturbance that constituted a mitigating circumstance. Relying on the plea colloquy and thereby cutting off the state's use of psychiatric rebuttal testimony was a reasonable strategy. The state court also concluded that, "in any event, the aggravating circumstances were so overwhelming that no substantial prejudice resulted from the absence at sentencing of the psychiatric evidence offered in the collateral attack." It then "rejected the challenge to counsel's failure to develop and to present character evidence for much the same reasons."

[Washington subsequently sought federal habeas relief, claiming ineffective assistance on essentially the same grounds presented in the state collateral proceedings. Although conducting an evidentiary hearing, the district court "disputed none of the state court's factual findings concerning trial counsel's assistance and made findings of its own that [were] consistent with the state court findings." The district court "concluded that, although trial counsel made errors in judgment in failing to investigate nonstatutory mitigating evidence further * * *, no prejudice resulted." On review, the Court of Appeals, sitting en banc, developed a special "framework" for analyzing ineffective assistance claims based on the failure to investigate, and remanded the case "for new factfinding under the newly announced standards." The Court of Appeals majority drew a distinction between a failure to investigate where "there is only one plausible line of defense" and "where there is more than one plausible line," the former requiring substantial investigation and the latter allowing counsel at some point to make a strategic decision not to pursue (and hence not to further investigate) a certain line of defense. As to both situations, the en banc majority outlined in some detail the factors to be considered in determining whether counsel fulfilled the duty to investigate. The majority also concluded that, as to prejudice, it was sufficient to show that counsel's violation of that duty "resulted in actual and substantial disadvantage"; it "expressly rejected the prejudice standard articulated * * * in [the] plurality opinion in * * * *Decoster* [Note 1, p. 136] * * * requir[ing] a showing that specified deficient conduct of counsel was likely to have affected the outcome of the proceeding."]

* * * [This] Court has recognized that "the right to counsel is the right to the effective assistance of counsel." *McMann v. Richardson*, 397 U.S. 759 (1970). Government violates the right to effective counsel when it interferes in certain ways with the ability of counsel to make independent decisions about how to conduct the defense [citing the cases discussed in Note 5, p. 176]. Counsel, however, can also deprive a defendant of the right to effective legal assistance, simply by failing to render "adequate legal assistance" * * *. The Court has not elaborated on the meaning of the constitutional requirement of effective assistance in the latter class of cases—that is, those presenting claims of "actual ineffectiveness." In giving meaning to the requirement, however, we must take its purpose—to ensure a fair trial—as the guide. The benchmark for judging any claim of ineffectiveness must be whether counsel's conduct so undermined the proper functioning of the adversarial process that the trial cannot be relied on as having produced a just result.

The same principle applies to a capital sentencing proceeding such as that provided by Florida law. We need not consider the role of counsel in an ordinary sentencing, which may involve informal proceedings and standardless discretion in the sentencer, and hence may require a different approach to the definition of constitutionally effective assistance. A capital sentencing proceeding like the one involved in this case, however, is sufficiently like a trial in its adversarial format and in the existence of standards for decision that counsel's role in the proceeding is comparable to counsel's role at trial—to ensure that the adversarial testing process works to produce a just result under the standards governing decision. For purposes of describing counsel's duties, therefore, Florida's capital sentencing proceeding need not be distinguished from an ordinary trial.

A convicted defendant's claim that counsel's assistance was so defective as to require reversal of a conviction or death sentence has two components. First, the defendant must show that counsel's performance was deficient. This requires showing that counsel made errors so serious that counsel was not functioning as the "counsel" guaranteed the defendant by the Sixth Amendment. Second, the defendant must show that the deficient performance prejudiced the defense. This requires showing that counsel's errors were so serious as to deprive the defendant of a fair trial, a trial whose result is reliable. Unless a defendant makes both showings, it cannot be said that the conviction or death sentence resulted from a breakdown in the adversary process that renders the result unreliable.

As all the Federal Courts of Appeals have now held, the proper standard for attorney performance is that of reasonably effective assistance. The Court indirectly recognized as much when it stated in *McMann*, supra, that a guilty plea cannot be attacked as based on inadequate legal advice unless counsel was not "a reasonably competent attorney" and the advice was not "within the range of competence demanded of attorneys in criminal cases." When a convicted defendant complains of the ineffectiveness of counsel's assistance, the defendant must show that counsel's representation fell below an objective standard of reasonableness.

More specific guidelines are not appropriate. The Sixth Amendment refers simply to "counsel," not specifying particular requirements of effective assistance. It relies instead on the legal profession's maintenance of standards sufficient to justify the law's presumption that counsel will fulfill the role in the adversary process that the Amendment envisions. The proper measure of attorney performance remains simply reasonableness under prevailing professional norms.

Representation of a criminal defendant entails certain basic duties. Counsel's function is to assist the defendant, and hence counsel owes the client a duty of loyalty, a duty to avoid conflicts of interest. From counsel's function as assistant to the defendant derive the overarching duty to advocate the defendant's cause and the more particular duties to consult with the defendant on important decisions and to keep the defendant informed of important developments in the course of the prosecution. Counsel also has a duty to bring to bear such skill and knowledge as will render the trial a reliable adversarial testing process.

These basic duties neither exhaustively define the obligations of counsel nor form a checklist for judicial evaluation of attorney performance. In any case presenting an ineffectiveness claim, the performance inquiry must be whether counsel's assistance was reasonable considering all the circumstances. Prevailing norms of practice as reflected in American Bar Association standards and the like are guides to determining what is reasonable, but they are only guides. No particular set of detailed rules for counsel's conduct can satisfactorily take account of the variety of circumstances faced by defense counsel or the range of legitimate decisions regarding how best to represent a criminal defendant. Any such set of rules would interfere with the constitutionally protected independence of counsel and restrict the wide latitude counsel must have in making tactical decisions. See *United States v. Decoster* [Note 1, p. 136]. Indeed, the existence of detailed guidelines for representation could distract counsel from the overriding mission of vigorous advocacy of the defendant's cause. Moreover, the purpose of the effective assistance guarantee of the Sixth Amendment is not to improve the quality of legal representation, although that is a goal of considerable importance to the legal system. The purpose is simply to ensure that criminal defendants receive a fair trial.

Judicial scrutiny of counsel's performance must be highly deferential. It is all too tempting for a defendant to second-guess counsel's assistance after conviction or adverse sentence, and it is all too easy for a court, examining counsel's defense after it has proved unsuccessful, to conclude that a particular act or omission of counsel was unreasonable. A fair assessment of attorney performance requires that every effort be made to eliminate the distorting effects of hindsight, to reconstruct the circumstances of counsel's challenged conduct, and to evaluate the conduct from counsel's perspective at the time. Because of the difficulties inherent in making the evaluation, a court must indulge a strong presumption that counsel's conduct falls within the wide range of reasonable professional assistance; that is, the defendant must overcome the presumption that, under the circumstances, the challenged action "might be considered sound trial strategy." There are countless ways to provide effective assistance in any given case. Even the best criminal defense attorneys would not defend a particular client in the same way.

The availability of intrusive post-trial inquiry into attorney performance or of detailed guidelines for its evaluation would encourage the proliferation of ineffectiveness challenges. Criminal trials resolved unfavorably to the defendant would increasingly come to be followed by a second trial, this one of counsel's unsuccessful defense. Counsel's performance and even willingness to serve could be adversely affected. * * *

Thus, a court deciding an actual ineffectiveness claim must judge the reasonableness of counsel's challenged conduct on the facts of the particular case, viewed as of the time of counsel's conduct. A convicted defendant making a claim of ineffective assistance must identify the acts or omissions of counsel that are alleged not to have been the result of reasonable professional judgment. The court must then determine whether, in light of all the circumstances, the identified acts or omissions were outside the wide range of professionally competent assistance. In making that determination, the court should keep in mind that counsel's function, as elaborated in prevailing professional norms, is to make the adversarial testing process work in the particular case. At the same time, the court should recognize that counsel is strongly presumed to have rendered adequate assistance and made all significant decisions in the exercise of reasonable professional judgment.

These standards require no special amplification in order to define counsel's duty to investigate, the duty at issue in this case. As the Court of Appeals concluded, strategic choices made after thorough investigation of law and facts relevant to plausible options are virtually unchallengeable; and strategic choices made after less than complete investigation are reasonable precisely to the extent that reasonable professional judgments support the limitations on investigation. In other words, counsel has a duty to make a reasonable investigation or to make a reasonable decision that makes particular investigations unnecessary. In any ineffectiveness case, a particular decision not to investigate must be directly assessed for reasonableness in all the circumstances, applying a heavy measure of deference to counsel's judgments.

The reasonableness of counsel's actions may be determined or substantially influenced by the defendant's own statements or actions. Counsel's actions are usually based, quite properly, on informed strategic choices made by the defendant and on information supplied by the defendant. In particular, what investigation decisions are reasonable depends critically on such information. For example, when the facts that support a certain potential line of defense are generally known to counsel because of what the defendant has said, the need for further investigation may be considerably diminished or eliminated altogether. And when a defendant has given counsel reason to believe that pursuing certain investigations would be fruitless or even harmful, counsel's failure to pursue those investigations may not later be challenged as unreasonable. In short, inquiry into counsel's conversations with the defendant may be critical to a proper assessment of counsel's investigation decisions, just as it may be critical to a proper assessment of counsel's other litigation decisions.

An error by counsel, even if professionally unreasonable, does not warrant setting aside the judgment of a criminal proceeding if the error had no effect on the judgment. The purpose of the Sixth Amendment guarantee of counsel is to ensure that a defendant has the assistance necessary to justify reliance on the outcome of the proceeding. Accordingly, any deficiencies in counsel's performance must be prejudicial to the defense in order to constitute ineffective assistance under the Constitution.

In certain Sixth Amendment contexts, prejudice is presumed. Actual or constructive denial of the assistance of counsel altogether is legally presumed to result in prejudice. So are various kinds of state interference with counsel's assistance. *United States v. Cronic*, fn. 25 [see p. 174]. Prejudice in these circumstances is so likely that case by case inquiry into prejudice is not worth the cost. Moreover, such circumstances involve impairments of the Sixth Amendment right that are easy to identify and, for that reason and because the prosecution is directly responsible, easy for the government to prevent.

One type of actual ineffectiveness claim warrants a similar, though more limited, presumption of prejudice. In *Cuyler v. Sullivan* [see fn. c, p. 193], the Court held that prejudice is presumed when counsel is burdened by an actual conflict of interest. In those circumstances, counsel breaches the duty of loyalty, perhaps the most basic of counsel's duties. Moreover, it is difficult to measure the precise effect on the defense of representation corrupted by conflicting interest. Given the obligation of counsel to avoid conflicts of interest and the ability of trial courts to make early inquiry in certain situations likely to give rise to conflicts, see e.g., Fed.R.Crim.P. 44(c), it is reasonable for the criminal justice system to maintain a fairly rigid rule of presumed prejudice for conflicts of interest. Even so, the rule is not quite the *per se* rule of prejudice that exists for the Sixth Amendment claims mentioned above. Prejudice is presumed only if the defendant demonstrates that counsel "actively represented conflicting interests" and "that an actual conflict of interest adversely affected his lawyer's performance." *Cuyler v. Sullivan.*

Conflict of interest claims aside, actual ineffectiveness claims alleging a deficiency in attorney performance are subject to a general requirement that the defendant affirmatively prove prejudice. The government is not responsible for, and hence not able to prevent, attorney errors that will result in reversal of a conviction or sentence. Attorney errors cannot be classified according to likelihood of causing prejudice. Nor can they be defined with sufficient precision to inform defense attorneys correctly just what conduct to avoid. Representation is an art, and an act or omission that is unprofessional in one case may be sound or even brilliant in another. Even if a defendant shows that particular errors of counsel were unreasonable, therefore, the defendant must show that they actually had an adverse effect on the defense.

It is not enough for the defendant to show that the errors had some conceivable effect on the outcome of the proceeding. Virtually every act or omission of counsel would meet that test, and not every error that conceivably could have influenced the outcome undermines the reliability of the result of the proceeding. Respondent suggests requiring a showing that the errors "impaired the presentation of the defense." That standard, however, provides no workable principle. Since any error, if it is indeed an error, "impairs" the presentation of the defense, the proposed standard [provides] no way of deciding what impairments are sufficiently serious to warrant setting aside the outcome of the proceeding.

On the other hand, we believe that a defendant need not show that counsel's deficient conduct more likely than not altered the outcome in the case. * * *

[While this standard] * * * is widely used for assessing motions for new trial based on newly discovered evidence * * *, it is not quite appropriate. * * * The high standard for newly discovered evidence claims presupposes that all essential elements of a presumptively accurate and fair proceeding were present in the proceeding whose result is challenged. An ineffective assistance claim asserts the absence of one of the crucial assurances * * *, so finality concerns are somewhat weaker and the appropriate standard of prejudice should be somewhat lower. * * * Accordingly, the appropriate test for prejudice finds its roots in the test for materiality of exculpatory information not disclosed to the defense by the prosecution, *United States v. Agurs*, 427 U.S. 97 (1976), and in the test for materiality of testimony made unavailable to the defense by Government deportation of a witness, *United States v. Valenzuela–Bernal*, 458 U.S. 858 (1982). The defendant must show that there is a reasonable probability that, but for counsel's unprofessional errors, the result of the proceeding would have been different. A reasonable probability is a probability sufficient to undermine confidence in the outcome.

In making [this] determination, [a] court should presume, absent challenge to the judgment on grounds of evidentiary insufficiency, that the judge or jury acted according to law. An assessment of the likelihood of a result more favorable to the defendant must exclude the possibility of arbitrariness, whimsy, caprice, "nullification," and the like. A defendant has no entitlement to the luck of a lawless decisionmaker, even if a lawless decision cannot be reviewed. The assessment of prejudice should proceed on the assumption that the decisionmaker is reasonably, conscientiously, and impartially applying the standards that govern the decision. It should not depend on the idiosyncracies of the particular decisionmaker, such as unusual propensities toward harshness or leniency. Although these factors may actually have entered into counsel's selection of strategies and, to that limited extent, may thus affect the performance inquiry, they are irrelevant to the prejudice inquiry. Thus, evidence about the actual process of decision, if not part of the record of the proceeding under review, and evidence about, for example, a particular judge's sentencing practices, should not be considered in the prejudice determination.

The governing legal standard plays a critical role in defining the question to be asked in assessing the prejudice from counsel's errors. When a defendant challenges a conviction, the question is whether there is a reasonable probability that, absent the errors, the factfinder would have had a reasonable doubt respecting guilt. When a defendant challenges a death sentence such as the one at issue in this case, the question is whether there is a reasonable probability that, absent the errors, the sentencer—including an appellate court, to the extent it independently reweighs the evidence—would have concluded that the balance of aggravating and mitigating circumstances did not warrant death.

In making this determination, a court hearing an ineffectiveness claim must consider the totality of the evidence before the judge or jury. Some of the factual findings will have been unaffected by the errors, and factual findings that were affected will have been affected in different ways. Some errors will have had a pervasive effect on the inferences to be drawn from the evidence, altering the entire evidentiary picture, and some will have had an isolated, trivial effect. Moreover, a verdict or conclusion only weakly supported by the record is more likely to have been affected by errors than one with overwhelming record support. Taking the unaffected findings as given, and taking due account of the effect of the errors on the remaining findings, a court making the prejudice inquiry must ask if the defendant has met the burden of showing that the decision reached would reasonably likely have been different absent the errors.

A number of practical considerations are important for the application of the standards we have outlined. Most important, in adjudicating a claim of actual ineffectiveness of counsel, a court should keep in mind that the principles we have stated do not establish mechanical rules. Although those principles should guide the process of decision, the ultimate focus of inquiry must be on the fundamental fairness of the proceeding whose result is being challenged. In every case the court should be concerned with whether, despite the strong presumption of reliability, the result of the particular proceeding is unreliable because of a breakdown in the adversarial process that our system counts on to produce just results.

To the extent that this has already been the guiding inquiry in the lower courts, the standards articulated today do not require reconsideration of ineffectiveness claims rejected under different standards. Cf. *Trapnell v. United States*, 725 F.2d 149 (2d Cir.1983) (in several years of applying "farce and mockery" standard along with "reasonable competence" standard, court "never found that the result of a case hinged on the choice of a particular standard"). In particular, the minor differences in the lower courts' precise formulations of the performance standard are insignificant: the different formulations are mere variations of the overarching reasonableness standard. With regard to the prejudice inquiry, only the strict outcome-determinative test, among the standards articulated in the lower courts, imposes a heavier burden on defendants than the tests laid down today. The difference, however, should alter the merit of an ineffectiveness claim only in the rarest case.

Although we have discussed the performance component of an ineffectiveness claim prior to the prejudice component, there is no reason for a court deciding an ineffective assistance claim to approach the inquiry in the same order or even to address both components of the inquiry if the defendant makes an insufficient showing on one. In particular, a court need not determine whether counsel's performance was deficient before examining the prejudice suffered by the defendant as a result of the alleged deficiencies. The object of an ineffectiveness claim is not to grade counsel's performance. If it is easier to dispose of an ineffectiveness claim on the ground of lack of sufficient prejudice, which we expect will often be so, that course should be followed. Courts should strive to ensure that ineffectiveness claims not become so burdensome to defense counsel that the entire criminal justice system suffers as a result. * * *

Having articulated general standards for judging ineffectiveness claims, we think it useful to apply those standards to the facts of this case in order to illustrate the meaning of the general principles. The record makes it possible to do so. * * * The facts make clear that the conduct of respondent's counsel at and before respondent's sentencing proceeding cannot be found unreasonable. They also make clear that, even assuming the challenged conduct of counsel was unreasonable, respondent suffered insufficient prejudice to warrant setting aside his death sentence.

With respect to the performance component, the record shows that respondent's counsel made a strategic choice to argue for the extreme emotional distress mitigating circumstance and to rely as fully as possible on respondent's acceptance of responsibility for his crimes. Although counsel understandably felt hopeless about respondent's prospects, nothing in the record indicates [that] counsel's sense of hopelessness distorted his professional judgment. Counsel's strategy choice was well within the range of professionally reasonable judgments, and the decision not to seek more character or psychological evidence than was already in hand was likewise reasonable.

The trial judge's views on the importance of owning up to one's crimes were well known to counsel. The aggravating circumstances were utterly overwhelming. Trial counsel could reasonably surmise from his conversations with respondent that character and psychological evidence would be of little help. Respondent had already been able to mention at the plea colloquy the substance of what there was to know about his financial and emotional troubles. Restricting testimony on respondent's character to what had come in at the plea colloquy ensured that contrary character and psychological evidence and respondent's criminal history, which counsel has successfully moved to exclude, would not come in. On these facts, there can be little question, even without application of the presumption of adequate performance, that trial counsel's defense, though unsuccessful, was the result of reasonable professional judgment.

With respect to the prejudice component, the lack of merit of respondent's claim is even more stark. The evidence that respondent says his trial counsel should have offered at the sentencing hearing would barely have altered the sentencing profile presented to the sentencing judge. As the state courts and District Court found, at most this evidence shows that numerous people who knew respondent thought he was generally a good person and that a psychiatrist and a psychologist believed he was under considerable emotional stress that did not rise to the level of extreme disturbance. Given the overwhelming aggravating factors, there is no reasonable probability that the omitted evidence would have changed the conclusion that the aggravating circumstances outweighed the mitigating circumstances and, hence, the sentence imposed. * * *

Failure to make the required showing of either deficient performance or sufficient prejudice defeats the ineffectiveness claim. Here there is a double failure. More generally, respondent has made no showing that the justice of his sentence was rendered unreliable by a breakdown in the adversary process caused by deficiencies in counsel's assistance. * * * We conclude, therefore, that the District Court properly declined to issue a writ of habeas corpus. * * * a

JUSTICE MARSHALL, dissenting.

[The] opinion of the Court revolves around two holdings. First, the majority ties the constitutional minima of attorney performance to a simple "standard of reasonableness." Second, the majority holds that only an error of counsel that has sufficient impact on a trial to "undermine confidence in the outcome" is grounds for overturning a conviction. I disagree with both of these rulings.

My objection to the performance standard adopted by the Court is that it is so malleable that, in practice, it will either have no grip at all or will yield excessive variation in the manner in which the Sixth Amendment is interpreted and applied by different courts. To tell lawyers and the lower courts that counsel for a criminal defendant must behave "reasonably" and must act like "a reasonably competent attorney" is to tell them almost nothing. * * * The debilitating ambiguity of an "objective standard of reasonableness" in this context is illustrated by the majority's failure to address important issues concerning the quality of representation mandated by the Constitution. It is an unfortunate but undeniable fact that a person of means, by selecting a lawyer and paying him enough to ensure he prepares thoroughly, usually can obtain better representation than that available to an indigent defendant, who must rely on appointed counsel, who, in turn, has limited time and resources to devote to a given case. Is a "reasonably competent attorney" a reasonably competent adequately paid retained lawyer or a reasonably competent appointed attorney? It is also a fact that the quality of representation available to ordinary defendants in different parts of the country varies significantly. Should the standard of performance mandated by the Sixth

---

a. Justice Brennan's separate opinion, concurring in part and dissenting in part, is omitted. Justice Brennan dissented from the judgment based on his view that capital punishment was unconstitutional. He joined the Court's opinion as to the IAC claim, but added that "the standards announced today can and should be applied with concern for the special considerations that must attend counsel's performance in a capital sentencing proceeding."

Amendment vary by locale? The majority offers no clues as to the proper responses to these questions.

* * * I agree that counsel must be afforded "wide latitude" when making "tactical decisions" regarding trial strategy, but many aspects of the job of a criminal defense attorney are more amenable to judicial oversight [than the majority indicates]. For example, much of the work involved in preparing for a trial, applying for bail, conferring with one's client, making timely objections to significant, arguably erroneous rulings of the trial judge, and filing a notice of appeal if there are colorable grounds therefor could profitably be made the subject of uniform standards. * * * The opinion of the Court of Appeals in this case represents one sound attempt to develop particularized standards designed to ensure that all defendants receive effective legal assistance. For other generally consistent efforts, see [citing several lower court decisions, and adding in a footnote reference that "many of these rely heavily on the standards developed by the American Bar Association"] * * *. By refusing to address the merits of these proposals, and indeed suggesting that no such effort is worthwhile, the opinion of the Court, I fear, will stunt the development of the constitutional doctrine in this area.

I object to the prejudice standard adopted by the Court for two independent reasons. First, it is often very difficult to tell whether a defendant convicted after a trial in which he was ineffectively represented would have fared better if his lawyer had been competent. Seemingly impregnable cases can sometimes be dismantled by good defense counsel. On the basis of a cold record, it may be impossible for a reviewing court confidently to ascertain how the government's evidence and arguments would have stood up against rebuttal and cross-examination by a shrewd, well prepared lawyer. The difficulties of estimating prejudice after the fact are exacerbated by the possibility that evidence of injury to the defendant may be missing from the record precisely because of the incompetence of defense counsel. In view of all these impediments to a fair evaluation of the probability that the outcome of a trial was affected by ineffectiveness of counsel, it seems to me senseless to impose on a defendant whose lawyer has been shown to have been incompetent the burden of demonstrating prejudice.

Second and more fundamentally, the assumption on which the Court's holding rests is that the only purpose of the constitutional guarantee of effective assistance of counsel is to reduce the chance that innocent persons will be convicted. In my view, the guarantee also functions to ensure that convictions are obtained only through fundamentally fair procedures. * * * A proceeding in which the defendant does not receive meaningful assistance in meeting the forces of the state does not, in my opinion, constitute due process. * * * We [have held] * * * that certain constitutional rights are "so basic to a fair trial that their infraction can never be treated as harmless error." Among these rights is the right to counsel. In my view, the right to *effective* assistance of counsel is entailed by the right to counsel, and abridgment of the former is equivalent to abridgment of the latter. I would thus hold that a showing that the performance of a defendant's lawyer departed from constitutionally prescribed standards requires a new trial regardless of whether the defendant suffered demonstrable prejudice thereby.

Even if I were inclined to join the majority's two central holdings, I could not abide the manner in which the majority elaborates upon its rulings. Particularly regrettable are the majority's discussion of the "presumption" of reasonableness to be accorded lawyers' decisions and its attempt to prejudge the merits of claims previously rejected by lower courts using different legal standards. * * * The adjectives "strong" [in describing the presumption] and "heavy" [in describing "the deference due to counsel's judgments"] might be read as imposing upon the defendant an unusually weighty burden of persuasion. * * * The majority's comments [on the lower court division on the performance standard, including use of "the forgiving 'farce and mockery' standard"] * * * seems to be prompted principally by a reluctance to acknowledge that today's decision will require a reassessment of many previously rejected ineffective-assistance-of-counsel claims," * * * [requiring] lower courts that hitherto having been using standards more tolerant of ineffectual advocacy * * * to scrutinize all claims, old as well as new, under the principles laid down today.* * *

[The] majority suggests that, "[f]or purposes of describing counsel's duties," a capital sentencing proceeding "need not be distinguished from an ordinary trial." I cannot agree. The Court has repeatedly acknowledged that the Constitution requires stricter adherence to procedural safeguards in a capital case than in other cases. * * *

The [above] views * * * oblige me to dissent from the majority's disposition of the case before us. It is undisputed that respondent's trial counsel made virtually no investigation of the possibility of obtaining testimony from respondent's relatives, friends, or former employers pertaining to respondent's character or background. Had counsel done so, he would have found several persons willing and able to testify that, in their experience, respondent was a responsible, nonviolent man, devoted to his family, and active in the affairs of his church. Respondent contends that his lawyer could have and should have used that testimony to "humanize" respondent, to counteract the impression conveyed by the trial that he was little more than a cold-blooded killer. Had this evidence been admitted, respondent argues, his chances of obtaining a life sentence would have been significantly better.

Measured against the standards outlined above, respondent's contentions are substantial. Experienced members of the death-penalty bar have long recognized the crucial importance of adducing evidence at a sentencing proceeding that establishes the defendant's social and familial connections. * * * The State makes a colorable—though in my view not compelling—argument that defense counsel in this case might have made a reasonable "strategic" decision not to present such evidence at the sentencing hearing on the assumption that an unadorned acknowledgment of respondent's responsibility for his crimes would be more likely to appeal to the trial judge, who was reputed to respect persons who accepted responsibility for their actions. But however justifiable such a choice might have been after counsel had fairly assessed the potential strength of the mitigating evidence available to him, counsel's failure to make any significant effort to find out what evidence might be garnered from respondent's relatives and acquaintances surely cannot be described as "reasonable." Counsel's failure to investigate is particularly suspicious in light of his candid admission that respondent's confession and conduct in the course of the trial gave him a feeling of "hopelessness" regarding the possibility of saving respondent's life. * * *

NOTES AND QUESTIONS

1. **Strickland in other settings.** As discussed in *Strickland* (p. 142) and in § 4 infra, certain types of claims relating to performance are not governed by the two-pronged *Strickland* test. *Strickland* does provide, however, the basic standards for assessing incompetent performance claims in most settings. In *Smith v. Murray*, 477 U.S. 527 (1986), the Court held that the "test of *Strickland v. Washington*" was not limited to trial counsel, but also applied to the alleged ineffective assistance of appellate counsel on a first appeal of right. *Hill v. Lockhart*, 474 U.S. 52 (1985), concluded that past precedent on counsel's ineffective assistance in a guilty plea case converted into the application of the *Strick-*

land standards. Lower courts have held *Strickland* to apply to counsel's performance not only in capital sentencing, but in sentencing generally.

2. *Commentator criticism.* Commentators have been nearly unanimous in their criticism of the *Strickland* standards and the *Strickland* majority opinion. See CRIMPROC. § 11.10(a) (collecting citations). Their criticism typically proceeds from two basic premises: (1) deficient performance by criminal defense attorneys at the trial level is widespread[b] and (2) the application of the lax *Strickland* standards (along with the deference prescribed in the *Strickland* opinion) has largely failed to correct that widespread inadequate performance,[c] a result that should have been predicted from the outset, given the prevailing judicial attitude on the limits of *ex ante* judicial review of counsel's performance.[d]

---

b. Commentators have stressed two sources in supporting this premise. First, they note the open acknowledgment of widespread counsel inadequacy by judges. For example, Judge Bazelon of the D.C. Circuit, who favored the adoption of a "categorical approach" in a pre-*Strickland* ruling (see Note 1, p. 136), stated in 1973: "I have often been told that if my court were to reverse every case in which there was inadequate counsel, we would send back half of the convictions in my jurisdiction." Also cited is the 1973 comment of Chief Justice Burger, who later joined *Strickland*: "[F]rom one-third to one-half of the lawyers who appear the serious cases are not really qualified to render fully adequate representation."

While commentators emphasize judicial statements made prior to *Strickland* (thereby evidencing the Supreme Court's failure in *Strickland* to acknowledge what was recognized at the time to be a "serious problem"), a similar perspective is reflected in later remarks by some very prominent judges. See e.g., fn. d infra and fn. g, p. 168. Compare, however, the results of the 2008 survey of state and federal judges conducted by Judge Posner (quoted in fn. d) and Professor Yoon. That survey used a scale of 1 (for poor) to 5 (for excellent), with 4 being "good" and 3 being "fair". Federal trial judges ranked public defenders above prosecutors, with both above 4, with court-appointed attorneys and privately retained attorneys ranked lower, but above 3.5. State trial judges had somewhat lower scores, but also above 3.5 (3.8 for prosecutors, 3.6 for public defenders, 3.6 for court-appointed attorneys, and 3.99 for privately retained attorneys). See Richard A. Posner & Albert H. Yoon, What Judges Think of the Quality of Representation, 63 Stan.L.Rev. 317 (2011).

Second, commentators point to widespread "structural deficiencies" in indigent defender systems (e.g., heavy caseloads, lack of adequate staffing, compensation caps for assigned counsel). See Note 1, p. 176. They argue that those deficiencies invariably preclude defense counsel from providing adequate representation in a significant portion of their cases. Limited resources forces a rationing of effort, leading counsel to do less than they feel should be done to provide full representation, at least in those cases given lower priority.

c. In support of this conclusion, commentators commonly cited three factors. First, they point to a variety of studies (typically limited to particular jurisdictions) showing that only a small percentage of IAC claims are successful (10% at best and typically much lower). Second they note that IAC claims have been rejected notwithstanding egregious circumstances. See. e.g., David Cole, No Equal Justice 78–79 (1999). ("[T]he [*Strickland*] test has proved impossible to meet. Courts have declined to find ineffective assistance where defense counsel slept during portions of thet trial, where counsel used heroin and cocaine throughout the trial, where counsel allowed his client to wear the same sweatshirt and shoes in court that the perpetrator was alleged to have worn on the day of the crime, where counsel stated prior to trial that he was not prepared on the law or the facts of the case, and where counsel appointed in a capital case could not name a single Supreme Court decision on the death penalty.") Third, they point to many cases in which delaying permissible challenges, by requiring that the challenge be raised on collateral attack, has either prevented defendants from bringing IAC claims or eliminated their incentive to bring such claims. See Note 7, p. 134.

d. Commentators contend that a standard as "lax" as *Strickland* presents an open invitation to limit conviction reversals to the most extreme situations. They add that this invitation was also implicit in various aspects of the *Strickland* opinion (e.g., the suggestion that it may be "easier to dispose of an ineffectiveness claim on the ground of lack of sufficient prejudice") (p. 144), and the reference to the possibility that "intrusive post-trial inquiry" could "adversely affect" counsel's "willingness to serve" (p. 141).

Many commentators also argue that the vast majority of trial judges, for a variety of reasons, are inclined to accept that invitation, and that inclination had been well documented prior to the adoption of *Strickland*, particularly in the writings of Judge Bazelon. Courts, he noted, were unwilling to give "the Sixth Amendment real bite" because "that would [require them] to swallow the bitter pill of reversing an uncomfortably large number of convictions." For many

Proceeding from these premises, the commentators commonly echo the criticisms of Justice Marshall's dissent, stressing, in particular, his challenge to the Court's insistence upon a showing of prejudice, and his recognition of the value of particularized standards of competent performance. The commentators also find the *Strickland* opinion lacking for its failure to recognize the possible role of the trial judge in ensuring that counsel is prepared to offer adequate representation and its failure to address the impact of structural impediments to providing adequate assistance (although *Cronic* is viewed as the primary culprit in this regard).

While the Court has sometimes been sharply divided in its application of *Strickland,* it has shown no inclination to revise *Strickland* or (as many commentators have urged) to start anew in defining ineffective assistance. As discussed in the notes that follow, the Court may, or may not, have added content somewhat different from what would have been anticipated immediately after *Strickland.* The Court's opinions, however, have always looked first to what was said in *Strickland* about the particular issue, and they have frequently reminded lower courts of the need to interpret "the *Strickland* standards" in light of the "guiding considerations" set forth in the *Strickland* opinion.

3. *Due process and the adversarial process benchmark.* *Strickland* looks to an adversary system "benchmark" (p. 139), a feature explored at greater length in the *Cronic* decision (see Note 6, p. 133). Commentators have argued that the analysis supporting this benchmark, in treating counsel's performance as a means to achieving a fair trial, rather than as a constitutionally mandated end in itself, and in looking to whether the process could achieve a "just result," treats the effective assistance of counsel as an element of due process, rather than as an aspect of the Sixth Amendment right guaranteed in *Gideon. United States v. Gonzalez–Lopez* (p. 121) later characterized the right to effective assistance of counsel as derived from *Powell v. Alabama* (see Note 1, p. 131), which "was based on the Due Process Clause rather than the Sixth Amendment" (p. 123). The *Gonzalez-Lopez* discussion focused on the "prejudice component" of the IAC claim. Does the Court's reliance on an adversary system benchmark, particularly in its reference to a "breakdown in the adversarial process," also bear upon the performance prong of *Strickland*? The majority opinion has been criticized for failing to explain what bearing, if any, this benchmark has in applying *Strickland's* performance prong.

4. *Reasonableness and attorney practice.* While commentators found persuasive Justice Marshall's criticism of the "debilitating ambiguity" of *Strickland's* description of its performance prong, some questioned his reading of that prong as possibly defined by the actual practice patterns in a particular locale or by differences in the representation provided by "adequately paid retained lawyers" and the state-funded attorneys provided the indigent. The majority, opinion,

---

judges, there was the additional concern that such reversals would be a wasted gesture, as reversals would not lead to additional government funding and retrials would almost always produce the same result due to the strength of the evidence, even with better representation. See Bazelon, The Defective Assistance of Counsel, 42. U.Cin.L.Rev. 1 (1973).

As to the judiciary's willingness to accept, under *Strickland,* the limitations flowing from typical structural impediments to providing better quality representation, consider the perspective advanced by Judge Richard Posner of the 7th Circuit, as quoted in Abbe Smith, *The Difference in Criminal Defense and the Difference It Makes*, 11 Wash.U.J.L. & Pol'y. 83, 129 (2003): "I can confirm from my own experience as a judge that criminal defendants are generally poorly represented. But if we are to be hardheaded, we must recognize that this may not be an entirely bad thing. The lawyers who represent indigent criminal defendants seem to be good enough to reduce the probability of convicting an innocent person to a very low level. If they were much better, either many guilty people would be acquitted or society would have to devote much greater resources to the prosecution of criminal cases. A bare-bones system for defense of indigent criminal defendants may be optimal."

it was noted, had in no way suggested that "reasonableness was to be judged by reference to any empirical survey of attorney practices." CRIMPROC § 11.10(b). The Court had referred to "professional norms of practice" but it had added that these were "only guides." The majority, it was argued, had described the perform-ance standard in terms that ultimately required reference to the function of the counsel guarantee. The Court had spoken of the "competence demanded of attorneys in criminal cases" and the requirement that counsel "bring to bear such skill and knowledge as will render the trial a reliable adversarial testing process." Such language "clearly rejected a measurement based solely on a comparison of counsel with his or her peers." CRIMPROC § 11.7(c). Cf. *Rogers v. Zant*, 13 F.3d 384 (11th Cir.1994) ("Even if many reasonable lawyers would have not have done as defense counsel did at trial, no relief can be granted on ineffectiveness grounds unless it is shown that no reasonable lawyer in the circumstances would have done so.") Consider also *Harrington v. Richter*, p. 155 ("The question is whether an attorney's representation amounted to incompetence under prevailing profes-sional norms, not whether it deviates from best practices or *most common custom*") (emphasis added).

In two of its post-*Strickland* rulings, the Court did point to the standard practice of defense lawyers at the time of representation in the state of defen-dant's conviction. In *Wiggins v. Smith*, Note 2, p. 167, the Court noted that the defense counsel's failure to obtain a social history report for use in capital sentencing was "contrary to standard practice in Maryland * * * at the time" (where the Public Defender Office provided funding for such a report). In *Cullen v. Pinholster*, Note 4, p. 172, the Court noted that the family mitigation defense that defense counsel had employed as an alternative to a standard mitigation defense was "known to the defense Bar in California at the time and had been used by other attorneys." The Court added that the dissent did not contest this characterization and had "cit[ed] no evidence that such an approach would have been inconsistent with the standard of professional competence in capital cases that prevailed in Los Angeles in 1984."

In both *Wiggins* and *Cullen*, the reference to local practice was combined with other sources (e.g., the ABA standards) in assessing "prevailing professional norms." Might that suggest that local practice has no greater significance than national practice, except insofar as it suggests a unique practice environment in a particular jurisdiction, tied to local law or local logistical considerations (e.g., the available funding in *Wiggins*). Consider also *Padilla v. Kentucky*, Note 5 infra. In discussing "professional norms," the *Padilla* Court looked only to national norms, not to the practice in Kentucky. In concluding, that the "weight of prevailing professional norms" requires counsel to advise the defendant of the "deportation risk" of conviction, it referred to the common practice of public defender organiza-tions, to standards issued by national professional organizations, and to treatises and law review articles viewing such advice as essential.

So far, the Court, in looking to professional norms, has not referred to any distinction in the practice of retained attorneys as opposed to state-funded attorneys. Of course, retained attorneys as a group include far more than that small slice of the defense bar that Justice Marshall may have had in mind (those paid enough to prepare in the most thorough fashion). Studies comparing the performance of retained attorneys and public defenders indicate that their out-comes are largely the same for similar offenses. See CRIMPROC § 11.8(c) (studies also noting less favorable outcomes for assigned counsel).

5. *The guidance of ABA Standards*. *Strickland* notes that the "prevailing norms of practice as reflected in American Bar Association Standards and the like" can be used only as "guides to determining what is reasonable" (p. 140). In several of the Court's rulings considering "counsel's failure to fully investigate possible mitigating circumstances in capital cases (e.g., *Wiggins v. Smith*, Note 2, p. 167, and *Rompilla v. Beard*, Note 3, p. 168), the Court's finding of ineffective assistance relied in part on counsel having failed to fulfill an obligation prescribed in the ABA Standards. Those rulings led some lower courts to treat the ABA Standards as a critical evaluative measure of competent performance, although other courts discounted the Standards as too often prescribing the kind of particularized requirements that *Strickland* had warned against. *Bobby v. Van Hook* responded to the former position, and *Padilla v. Kentucky* arguably responded to the latter. Commentators have suggested, however, that the message sent, as to appropriate treatment of the Standards, was not entirely consistent.

In BOBBY v. VAN HOOK, 130 S.Ct. 13 (2009), a unanimous Court held that the Sixth Circuit had erred in finding that counsel provided ineffective assistance when he failed to further investigate and present potential mitigating evidence in a capital sentencing proceeding. The Sixth Circuit reasoned that counsel's investigation fell short of the directives of the ABA Guidelines for the Appointment and Performance of Defense Counsel in Death Penalty Cases (compliance in this case would have required contacting a much broader range of relatives as well as a psychiatrist who was familiar with defendant's childhood experiences). That conclusion, the Court noted, ignored *Strickland's* warning that professional standards could be useful " 'guides' as to what reasonableness entails * * * only to the extent they describe the professional norms prevailing when the professional representation took place." The ABA Guidelines on Death Penalty Cases had been "announced 18 years after Van Hook went to trial," were far more detailed than the ABA Standards in effect in 1985, and were erroneously treated by the Sixth Circuit as "inexorable commands with which all capital defense counsel 'must fully comply'." The Court's *per curiam* opinion added in a footnote: "The narrow grounds for our opinion should not be regarded as accepting the legitimacy of a less categorical use of the [Death Penalty] Guidelines to evaluate post–2003 representation. For that to be proper, the Guidelines must reflect '[p]revailing norms of practice,' *Strickland*, and 'standard practice,' *Wiggins*, and must not be so detailed that they would 'interfere with the constitutionally protected independence of counsel and restrict the wide latitude counsel must have in making tactical decisions,' *Strickland*. We express no views on whether the 2003 Guidelines meet these criteria."

Justice Alito, concurring, added: "I join the Court's *per curiam* opinion but emphasize my understanding that the opinion in no way suggests that the American Bar Association's Guidelines for the Appointment and Performance of Defense Counsel in Death Penalty Cases * * * have special relevance in determining whether an attorney's performance meets the standard required by the Sixth Amendment. * * * The views of the association's members, not to mention the views of the members of the advisory committee that formulated the 2003 Guidelines, do not necessarily reflect the views of the American Bar as a whole. It is the responsibility of the courts to determine the nature of the work that a defense attorney must do in a capital case in order to meet the obligations imposed by the Constitution, and I see no reason why the ABA Guidelines should be given a privileged position in making that determination."

In PADILLA v. KENTUCKY, 130 S.Ct. 1473 (2010), the Court majority described two sets of ABA Standards (along with other sources, see Note 4 supra) as reflecting "prevailing professional norms" that established a very specific responsibility of defense counsel—informing a non-citizen client of the risk of deportation on entry of a guilty plea (see Note 11, p. 1315). After citing the discussion of the ABA standards in both *Strickland* and *Bobby v. Van Hook*, the Court majority stated that such professional standards (here also including National Legal Aid & Defender Office standards) "may be valuable measures of the prevailing professional norms of effective representation, especially as those standards have been adapted to deal with the intersection of modern criminal prosecutions and immigration laws." However, in establishing those norms, the Court also looked to descriptions of practice (see Note 4 supra), and in assessing what *Strickland*'s performance prong required, it looked to additional factors relating to the functions of counsel in advising on a guilty plea (see also Note 2, p. 1310).

Justice Alito's concurring opinion in *Padilla* advanced an advice-obligation more limited than that required by the majority. See fn. c, p. 1316. In this connection, he questioned both the majority's analysis and its reliance upon "professional norms". He noted: (1) while prevailing professional norms are a "relevant consideration," "ascertaining the level of professional competence required by the Sixth Amendment is ultimately the task for the courts"; (2) "we must recognize [also] that such standards [as the ABA standards] may represent only the aspirations of a bar group rather than an empirical assessment of actual practice"; and (3) "it is hard to see how [the] norms [cited by the majority] can support the duty the Court today imposes on defense counsel * * * [as] many criminal defense attorneys have little understanding of immigration law * * * [and] the Court's opinion [goes beyond] * * * just requir[ing] defense counsel to warn the client of a general risk of removal."

6. Prejudice and "just results." *Strickland* advises lower courts, in applying the *Strickland* standards, to ask whether "the result of the particular proceeding is unreliable because of a breakdown in the adversarial process that our system counts on to produce just results." See p. 144. *Cronic* describes that adversarial process as designed to achieve accuracy of verdict—that the "guilty be convicted and the innocent go free" (see Note 6, p. 134). In KIMMELMAN v. MORRISON, 477 U.S. 365 (1986), Justice Powell suggested that the prejudice prong of *Strickland* had to be read in light of those objectives, and not simply by reference to the probability of a different outcome.

In *Kimmelman*, counsel's ineffective performance consisted of his failure in a rape prosecution to gain exclusion of incriminatory evidence (a sheet seized from his bed and expert testimony concerning stains and hair found on the sheet) as the product of a Fourth Amendment violation. The state claimed that such ineffectiveness could not be considered in defendant's federal habeas challenge to his conviction because *Stone v. Powell* (p. 1576) had held that Fourth Amendment exclusionary rule claims were not cognizable in federal habeas proceedings. The defendant's ineffective assistance claim, the state argued, was simply an exclusionary rule claim cast in a different form. Rejecting that argument, the Court (per Brennan, J.) noted

"In determining that federal courts should withhold habeas review where the State has provided an opportunity for full and fair litigation of a Fourth Amendment claim, [*Stone*] found it crucial that the remedy for Fourth Amendment violations provided by the exclusionary rule 'is not a personal constitutional right.' [The] right of an accused to counsel is beyond question a fundamental [and personal] right. * * * Without counsel, the right to a fair trial itself would be of little consequence, for it is through counsel that the accused secures his other rights. * * * We also reject the suggestion that criminal defendants should not be allowed to vindicate through federal habeas corpus their right to effective assistance of counsel where counsel's primary error is [failing to gain] exclusion of illegally seized evidence—evidence which [*Stone* described as] 'typically reliable and often the most probative information bearing on the guilt or innocence * * *'. [W]e have never intimated that the right to counsel is conditioned upon actual innocence. The constitutional rights of criminal defendants are granted to the innocent and the guilty alike. Consequently, we decline to hold either that the guarantee of effective assistance of counsel belongs solely to the innocent or that it attaches only to matters affecting the determination of actual guilt.''

Having found the Morrison's claim to be cognizable and his attorney's performance to have been deficient under *Strickland*, the Court remanded to the lower court to determine whether the impact of the lack of exclusion was sufficient to meet the prejudice requirement of *Strickland*. That remand led to a concurring opinion by Justice Powell (joined by Burger, C.J., and Rehnquist, J.). Justice Powell "agree[d] that *Stone* does not bar consideration of respondent's ineffective assistance of counsel claim on federal habeas corpus," but doubted whether "the admission of illegally seized but reliable evidence can ever constitute 'prejudice' under *Strickland*". Since the state had not raised that issue, Justice Powell was willing to concur in the remand, but he thought it clear that the prejudice prong of *Strickland* should not be tied solely to a likely impact on the outcome. He noted:

"[The reasoning of *Strickland*] strongly suggests that only errors that call into question the basic justice of the defendant's conviction suffice to establish prejudice under [that case]. The question, in sum, must be whether the particular harm suffered by the defendant due to counsel's incompetence rendered the defendant's trial fundamentally unfair. [The] admission of illegally seized but reliable evidence does not lead to an unjust or fundamentally unfair result. [Thus,] the harm suffered by respondent in this case is not the denial of a fair and reliable adjudication of his guilty, but rather the absence of a windfall. * * * As we emphasized only last Term '[the] very premise of our adversary system of criminal justice is that partisan advocacy on both sides of a case will best promote the ultimate objective that the guilty be convicted and the innocent go free.' * * * The right to effective assistance of counsel flows logically from this premise. But it would shake that right loose from its constitutional moorings to hold that the Sixth Amendment protects criminal defendants against errors that merely deny those defendants a windfall."

Although Justice Brennan's opinion for the Court did not respond specifically to Justice Powell's concurring opinion, numerous lower courts have concluded that Justice Brennan's reasoning in rejecting the state's reliance on *Stone* implicitly rejected Justice Powell's reading of *Strickland*'s prejudice prong. In LOCK-HART v. FRETWELL, 506 U.S. 364 (1993), the Court majority agreed that the reference to a "just result" required more than simply looking to whether, but for counsel's deficient performance, a different result would have been reached. In *Lockhart*, the ineffective assistance claim rested on counsel's failure to object to the capital sentence being based on an aggravating factor that duplicated an element of an underlying felony. At the time, an Eighth Circuit ruling prohibited use of such an aggravating factor, but that Eighth Circuit ruling had subsequently been overruled, and use of that aggravating factor would have been permissible at the time that defendant's federal habeas claim was decided.

The *Lockhart* majority (per Rehnquist, C.J.) reasoned that *Strickland* "focuses on the question of whether a counsel's deficient performance renders the result of the trial unreliable or the proceeding fundamentally unfair." Here "the result of the sentencing proceeding is neither unfair nor unreliable" as the ineffectiveness "does not deprive the defendant of any substantive or procedural right to which the law entitles him." *Strickland* had noted that "a defendant has no entitlement to the luck of a lawless decisionmaker." Building on that point, the Court in *Nix v. Whiteside*, 475 U.S. 157 (1986), held that defendant could not be prejudiced by claimed incompetence (through counsel's allegedly improper threat of withdrawal) where that incompetence operated only to preclude the use of perjured testimony that might have produced a different verdict. Here also, as in

Nix, prejudice cannot be based on counsel error that would have "grant[ed] the defendant a windfall to which the law does not entitle him."

The two *Lockhart* dissenter (Stevens, J., jointed by Blackmun, J.) responded: "The Court's aversion to windfalls seems to disappear * * * when the state is the favored recipient. For the end result of this case is that the State, through the coincidence of inadequate representation and fortuitous timing, may carry out a death sentence that was invalid when imposed."

In *Williams (Terry) v. Taylor,* 529 U.S. 362 (2000), the court overturned a state ruling that read *Lockhart's* discussion of unfairness as extending broadly beyond the unusual *Lockhart* fact situation. The state court there had found that incompetency in a capital sentencing proceeding did not meet the prejudice requirement where, notwithstanding the requisite probability of a different outcome, the reviewing court could not also say that the sentencing proceeding was so lacking as to produce "fundamental unfairness." In *Glover v. United States,* 531 U.S. 198 (2001), the Court rejected a lower court ruling that had relied on *Lockhart's* reference to a fundamental fairness to hold that counsel's deficient performance did not violate the Sixth Amendment where the only consequence was to increase a prison sentence from 6 to 21 months. As the Court noted: "Although the amount by which a defendant's sentence is increased by a particular decision may be a factor to consider in determining whether counsel's performance in failing to argue the point constituted ineffective assistance, under a determinate system of constrained discretion * * *, it cannot serve as a bar to a showing of prejudice."

SECTION 3.   *STRICKLAND* APPLIED

1. *An immense body of precedent.* Apart from one or two search-and-seizure issues, no criminal process issue has more often been addressed in appellate opinions than the question of what constitutes ineffective assistance of counsel under the *Strickland* standards. Such rulings cover almost every action that could be taken by defense counsel, with the challenges sometimes based on what counsel failed to do and sometimes based on what counsel actually did. The body of precedent is immense, with hundreds of opinion added each year. As might be expected with such a large body of precedent, "the rulings are hardly consistent in their treatment of even roughly similar fact situations." CRIMPROC § 11.10.

The number of issues considered in this immense body of precedent is far too great to permit review here, even in a summary fashion. Indeed the post-*Strickland* Supreme Court rulings on IAC claims (over two dozen rulings) cover more issues that can be treated here. Apart from the paragraphs setting forth the two prongs of the *Strickland* standard, perhaps the most frequently discussed paragraphs in *Strickland* are those discussing strategic choices and their relationship to counsel's investigation (see p. 141). The cases included in this section focus on the Court's subsequent application of the principles stated there, read in light of other aspects of the *Strickland* opinion. The section includes only cases that ended in trial convictions. As to the application of *Strickland* in consideration of guilty pleas, see Ch. 22, §§ 3 and 5.

2. *Federal habeas review of state claims.* Although the Supreme Court occasionally considers a state defendant's IAC claim on a direct review of a state court ruling affirming defendant's conviction, IAC claims usually are considered by the Court on review of a federal habeas corpus challenge to the defendant's state conviction.[a] Prior to 1996, where a state court rejected an ineffective assistance claim and the defendant subsequently presented that claim in a federal habeas challenge, federal courts treated the issue as involving a mixed question of law and fact and therefore subject to de novo review. Thus, *Strickland* noted that its two-pronged test, and the principles governing application of that test, were applicable on federal habeas review of a state court rejection of an IAC claim, just as in the initial state court consideration of the IAC claim, notwithstanding that the "presumption of finality * * * is at its strongest on collateral attacks." In 1996, however, Congress adopted the Antiterrorism and Effective Death Penalty Act (AEDPA), which adopted a special review standard for federal habeas cases where the state court had considered and rejected on the merits the constitutional claim at issue. The review standard was no longer whether the state court had correctly interpreted federal constitutional law in rejecting the claim, but whether the state court's application of governing Supreme Court precedent was "objectively unreasonable." See § 2254(d)(1) (also allowing habeas relief where the state court ruling is "contrary to" that federal precedent, a review standard that typically would apply to an IAC claim only where the state court applied a test "contrary to" *Strickland*).

The bearing of this § 2254(d)(1) standard is discussed in *Harrington v. Richter,* infra. See also Ch. 29, § 6 (which includes a portion of the *Richter* opinion, not reproduced below, discussing the function of § 2254(d) as it relates to habeas review generally). Not all of the post 1996 Supreme Court rulings have involved application of the AEDPA standard. De novo review was applied where the habeas petition had been filed pre-AEDPA, and for post-AEDPA petitions, where the state court had not ruled on the particular prong of the *Strickland* test (e.g., where the state court had rejected the claim on a failure to show prejudice and had not considered the performance prong).

HARRINGTON v. RICHTER

___ U.S. ___, 131 S.Ct. 770, 178 L.Ed.2d 624 (2011).

JUSTICE KENNEDY delivered the opinion of the Court.

* * * It is necessary to begin by discussing the details of a crime committed more than a decade and a half ago. * * * Sometime after midnight on December 20, 1994, sheriff's deputies in Sacramento County, California, arrived at the home of a drug dealer named Joshua Johnson. Hours before, Johnson had been smoking marijuana in the company of Richter and two other men, Christian Branscombe and Patrick Klein. When the deputies arrived, however, they found only Johnson and Klein. Johnson was hysterical and covered in blood. Klein was lying on a couch in Johnson's living room, unconscious and bleeding. Klein and Johnson each had been shot twice. Johnson recovered; Klein died of his wounds.

Johnson gave investigators this account: After falling asleep, he awoke to find Richter and Branscombe in his bedroom, at which point Branscombe shot him. Johnson heard more gunfire in the living room and the sound of his assailants leaving. He got up, found Klein bleeding on the living room couch, and called 911. A gun safe, a pistol, and $6,000 cash, all of which had been in the bedroom, were missing. * * * Evidence at the scene corroborated Johnson's account. Investiga-

---

a. IAC claims are a mainstay of almost 20,000 federal habeas petitions filed by state prisoners each year. Roughly 50% of the petitions in non-capital cases and 80% in capital cases include IAC claims. See King, et. al, p. 1571, at 51–52, 89. The percentage of successful IAC claims in non-capital cases is less than one percent, see King, p. 1604 (Table 4), although not all rejections are based on the merits, as a substantial portion of petitions fail on such grounds as failure to exhaust state remedies and procedural default in state cases. See Ch. 29, § 1. As to the much higher success ratio in capital cases, see fn. g, p. 166.

tors found spent shell casings in the bedroom (where Johnson said he had been shot) and in the living room (where Johnson indicated Klein had been shot). In the living room there were two casings, a .32 caliber and a .22 caliber. One of the bullets recovered from Klein's body was a .32 and the other was a .22. In the bedroom there were two more casings, both .32 caliber. In addition detectives found blood spatter near the living room couch and bloodstains in the bedroom. Pools of blood had collected in the kitchen and the doorway to Johnson's bedroom. Investigators took only a few blood samples from the crime scene. One was from a blood splash on the wall near the bedroom doorway, but no sample was taken from the doorway blood pool itself.

Investigators searched Richter's residence and found Johnson's gun safe, two boxes of .22–caliber ammunition, and a gun magazine loaded with cartridges of the same brand and type as the boxes. A ballistics expert later concluded the .22–caliber bullet that struck Klein and the .22–caliber shell found in the living room matched the ammunition found in Richter's home and bore markings consistent with the model of gun for which the magazine was designed.

Richter and Branscombe were arrested. At first Richter denied involvement. He would later admit taking Johnson's pistol and disposing of it and of the .32–caliber weapon Branscombe used to shoot Johnson and Klein. Richter's counsel produced Johnson's missing pistol, but neither of the guns used to shoot Johnson and Klein was found.

Branscombe and Richter were tried together on charges of murder, attempted murder, burglary, and robbery. Only Richter's case is presented here. * * * The prosecution built its case on Johnson's testimony and on circumstantial evidence. Its opening statement took note of the shell casings found at the crime scene and the ammunition and gun safe found at Richter's residence. Defense counsel offered explanations for the circumstantial evidence and derided Johnson as a drug dealer, a paranoid, and a trigger-happy gun fanatic who had drawn a pistol on Branscombe and Richter the last time he had seen them. And there were inconsistencies in Johnson's story. In his 911 call, for instance, Johnson first said there were four or five men who had broken into his house, not two; and in the call he did not identify Richter and Branscombe among the intruders.

Blood evidence does not appear to have been part of the prosecution's planned case prior to trial, and investigators had not analyzed the few blood samples taken from the crime scene. But the opening statement from the defense led the prosecution to alter its approach. Richter's attorney outlined the theory that Branscombe had fired on Johnson in self-defense and that Klein had been killed not on the living room couch but in the crossfire in the bedroom doorway. Defense counsel stressed deficiencies in the investigation, including the absence of forensic support for the prosecution's version of events.

The prosecution took steps to adjust to the counterattack now disclosed. Without advance notice and over the objection of Richter's attorney, one of the detectives who investigated the shootings testified for the prosecution as an expert in blood pattern evidence. He concluded it was unlikely Klein had been shot outside the living room and then moved to the couch, given the patterns of blood on Klein's face, as well as other evidence including "high velocity" blood spatter near the couch consistent with the location of a shooting. The prosecution also offered testimony from a serologist. She testified the blood sample taken near the pool by the bedroom door could be Johnson's but not Klein's.

Defense counsel's cross-examination probed weaknesses in the testimony of these two witnesses. The detective who testified on blood patterns acknowledged that his inferences were imprecise, that it was unlikely Klein had been lying down on the couch when shot, and that he could not say the blood in the living room was from either of Klein's wounds. Defense counsel elicited from the serologist a concession that she had not tested the bedroom blood sample for cross-contamination. She said that if the year-old sample had degraded, it would be difficult to tell whether blood of Klein's type was also present in the sample.

For the defense, Richter's attorney called seven witnesses. Prominent among these was Richter himself. Richter testified he and Branscombe returned to Johnson's house just before the shootings in order to deliver something to one of Johnson's roommates. By Richter's account, Branscombe entered the house alone while Richter waited in the driveway; but after hearing screams and gunshots, Richter followed inside. There he saw Klein lying not on the couch but in the bedroom doorway, with Johnson on the bed and Branscombe standing in the middle of the room. According to Richter, Branscombe said he shot at Johnson and Klein after they attacked him. Other defense witnesses provided some corroboration for Richter's story. His former girlfriend, for instance, said she saw the gun safe at Richter's house shortly before the shootings.

The jury returned a verdict of guilty on all charges. Richter was sentenced to life without parole. On appeal, his conviction was affirmed [by the California Court of Appeals]. * * * The California Supreme Court denied a petition for review, and Richter did not file a petition for certiorari with this Court. His conviction became final.

Richter later petitioned the California Supreme Court for a writ of habeas corpus.[b] He asserted a number of grounds for relief, including ineffective assistance of counsel. As relevant here, he claimed his counsel was deficient for failing to present expert testimony on serology, pathology, and blood spatter patterns, testimony that, he argued, would disclose the source of the blood pool in the bedroom doorway. This, he contended, would bolster his theory that Johnson had moved Klein to the couch. * * * He offered affidavits from three types of forensic experts. First, he provided statements from two blood serologists who said there was a possibility Klein's blood was intermixed with blood of Johnson's type in the sample taken from near the pool in the bedroom doorway. Second, he provided a statement from a pathologist who said the blood pool was too large to have come from Johnson given the nature of his wounds and his own account of his actions while waiting for the police. Third, he provided a statement from an expert in bloodstain analysis who said the absence of "a large number of satellite droplets" in photographs of the area around the blood in the bedroom doorway was inconsistent with the blood pool coming from Johnson as he stood in the doorway. Richter argued this evidence established the possibility that the blood in the bedroom doorway came from Klein, not Johnson. If that were true, he argued, it would confirm his account, not Johnson's.

The California Supreme Court denied Richter's petition in a one-sentence summary order. * * * Richter [then] filed a petition for habeas corpus in United States District Court. He reasserted the claims in his state petition. The District Court denied his petition, and a three-judge panel of the Court of Appeals for the Ninth Circuit affirmed. [However], the Court of Appeals [then] granted rehearing en banc and reversed the District Court's decision. * * * As a preliminary matter, the Court of Appeals questioned whether 28 U.S.C. § 2254(d) [of the federal

---

b. California allows the state habeas petitioner to bypass lower courts and file directly with the California Supreme Court. The petition must state fully and particularly the facts establishing the grounds for relief, supported by "available documentary evidence * * * including trial transcripts and affidavits or declarations." If a prima facie case is established and the state's response establishes a factual dispute, an evidentiary hearing by a lower court will be ordered. However, if a prima facie case in not established (reading against the defendant all gaps, ambiguities, and inconsistencies in the alleged facts and accompanying documentary evidence), the petition is denied, typically in a summary ruling. See CRIMPROC § 11.10 (a).

habeas statute] was applicable to Richter's petition, since the California Supreme Court issued only a summary denial when it rejected his *Strickland* claims; but it determined the California decision was unreasonable in any event and that Richter was entitled to relief. The court held Richter's trial counsel was deficient for failing to consult experts on blood evidence in determining and pursuing a trial strategy and in preparing to rebut expert evidence the prosecution might—and later did—offer. Four judges dissented from the en banc decision. * * *

The statutory authority of federal courts to issue habeas corpus relief for persons in state custody is provided by 28 U.S.C. § 2254, as amended by the Antiterrorism and Effective Death Penalty Act of 1996 (AEDPA). * * * As an initial matter, it is necessary to decide whether § 2254(d) applies when a state court's order is unaccompanied by an opinion explaining the reasons relief has been denied. [The Court here examined and rejected various arguments advanced by Richter for viewing § 2254(d) as implicitly excluding summary rulings, or viewing the summary order here as resting on grounds other than the merits. See pp. 1601–02]. * * * [Since] Richter has failed to show that the California Supreme Court's decision did not involve a determination of the merits of his claim. Section 2254(d) applies to his petition.

Federal habeas relief may not be granted for claims subject to § 2254(d) unless it is shown that the earlier state court's decision "was contrary to" federal law then clearly established in the holdings of this Court, § 2254(d)(1); or that it "involved an unreasonable application of" such law, § 2254(d)(1); or that it "was based on an unreasonable determination of the facts" in light of the record before the state court, § 2254(d)(2). The Court of Appeals relied on the second of these exceptions to § 2254(d)'s relitigation bar, the exception in § 2254(d)(1) permitting relitigation where the earlier state decision resulted from an "unreasonable application of" clearly established federal law. In the view of the Court of Appeals, the California Supreme Court's decision on Richter's ineffective-assistance claim unreasonably applied the holding in *Strickland*. The Court of Appeals' lengthy opinion, however, discloses an improper understanding of § 2254(d)'s unreasonableness standard and of its operation in the context of a *Strickland* claim.

The pivotal question is whether the state court's application of the *Strickland* standard was unreasonable. This is different from asking whether defense counsel's performance fell below *Strickland*'s standard. Were that the inquiry, the analysis would be no different than if, for example, this Court were adjudicating a *Strickland* claim on direct review of a criminal conviction in a United States district court. Under AEDPA, though, it is a necessary premise that the two questions are different. For purposes of § 2254(d)(1), "an *unreasonable* application of federal law is different from an *incorrect* application of federal law." * * * A state court must be granted a deference and latitude that are not in operation when the case involves review under the *Strickland* standard itself. * * * A state court's determination that a claim lacks merit precludes federal habeas relief so long as "fairminded jurists could disagree" on the correctness of the state court's decision. * * *. [Also,] as this Court has explained, "[E]valuating whether a rule application was unreasonable requires considering the rule's specificity. The more general the rule, the more leeway courts have in reaching outcomes in case-by-case determinations." "[I]t is not an unreasonable application of clearly established Federal law for a state court to decline to apply a specific legal rule that has not been squarely established by this Court." *Knowles v. Mirzayance*, 556 U.S. 111 (2009).

Here it is not apparent how the Court of Appeals' analysis would have been any different without AEDPA. The court explicitly conducted a *de novo* review; and after finding a *Strickland* violation, it declared, without further explanation, that the "state court's decision to the contrary constituted an unreasonable application of *Strickland*." AEDPA demands more. Under § 2254(d), a habeas court must determine what arguments or theories supported or, as here, could have supported, the state court's decision; and then it must ask whether it is possible fairminded jurists could disagree that those arguments or theories are inconsistent with the holding in a prior decision of this Court. The opinion of the Court of Appeals all but ignored * * * [this] question* * *. Because [it] had little doubt that Richter's *Strickland* claim had merit, the Court of Appeals concluded the state court must have been unreasonable in rejecting it. * * *

The conclusion of the Court of Appeals that Richter demonstrated an unreasonable application by the state court of the *Strickland* standard now must be discussed. * * * "Surmounting *Strickland*'s high bar is never an easy task." *Padilla v. Kentucky*, [Note 11, p 1315]. An ineffective-assistance claim can function as a way to escape rules of waiver and forfeiture and raise issues not presented at trial, and so the *Strickland* standard must be applied with scrupulous care, lest "intrusive post-trial inquiry" threaten the integrity of the very adversary process the right to counsel is meant to serve. *Strickland*. Even under *de novo* review, the standard for judging counsel's representation is a most deferential one. Unlike a later reviewing court, the attorney observed the relevant proceedings, knew of materials outside the record, and interacted with the client, with opposing counsel, and with the judge. It is "all too tempting" to "second-guess counsel's assistance after conviction or adverse sentence." Ibid. * * *

Establishing that a state court's application of *Strickland* was unreasonable under § 2254(d) is all the more difficult. The standards created by *Strickland* and § 2254(d) are both "highly deferential," and when the two apply in tandem, review is "doubly" so, *Knowles*. The *Strickland* standard is a general one, so the range of reasonable applications is substantial. Federal habeas courts must guard against the danger of equating unreasonableness under *Strickland* with unreasonableness under § 2254(d). When § 2254(d) applies, the question is not whether counsel's actions were reasonable. The question is whether there is any reasonable argument that counsel satisfied *Strickland*'s deferential standard. * * *

The Court of Appeals first held that Richter's attorney rendered constitutionally deficient service because he did not consult blood evidence experts in developing the basic strategy for Richter's defense or offer their testimony as part of the principal case for the defense. *Strickland*, however, permits counsel to "make a reasonable decision that makes particular investigations unnecessary." It was at least arguable that a reasonable attorney could decide to forgo inquiry into the blood evidence in the circumstances here.

Criminal cases will arise where the only reasonable and available defense strategy requires consultation with experts or introduction of expert evidence, whether pretrial, at trial, or both. There are, however, "countless ways to provide effective assistance in any given case. Even the best criminal defense attorneys would not defend a particular client in the same way." *Strickland*. Rare are the situations in which the "wide latitude counsel must have in making tactical decisions" will be limited to any one technique or approach. Ibid. It can be assumed that in some cases counsel would be deemed ineffective for failing to consult or rely on experts, but even that formulation is sufficiently general that state courts would have wide latitude in applying it. Here it would be well within the bounds of a reasonable judicial determination for the state court to conclude that defense counsel could follow a strategy that did not require the use of experts regarding the pool in the doorway to Johnson's bedroom.

From the perspective of Richter's defense counsel when he was preparing Richter's defense, there were any number of hypothetical experts—specialists in psychiatry, psychology, ballistics, fingerprints, tire treads, physiology, or numerous other disciplines and subdisciplines—whose insight might possibly have been useful. An attorney can avoid activities that appear "distractive from more important duties." *Bobby v. Van Hook,* [Note 5, p. 151]. Counsel was entitled to formulate a strategy that was reasonable at the time and to balance limited resources in accord with effective trial tactics and strategies. * * *

In concluding otherwise the Court of Appeals failed to "reconstruct the circumstances of counsel's challenged conduct" and "evaluate the conduct from counsel's perspective at the time." *Strickland.* In its view Klein's location was "the single most critical issue in the case" given the differing theories of the prosecution and the defense, and the source of the blood in the doorway was therefore of central concern. But it was far from a necessary conclusion that this was evident at the time of the trial. There were many factual differences between prosecution and defense versions of the events on the night of the shootings. It is only because forensic evidence has emerged concerning the source of the blood pool that the issue could with any plausibility be said to stand apart. Reliance on "the harsh light of hindsight" to cast doubt on a trial that took place now more than 15 years ago is precisely what *Strickland* and AEDPA seek to prevent. * * *

Even if it had been apparent that expert blood testimony could support Richter's defense, it would be reasonable to conclude that a competent attorney might elect not to use it. The Court of Appeals opinion for the en banc majority rests in large part on a hypothesis that reasonably could have been rejected. The hypothesis is that without jeopardizing Richter's defense, an expert could have testified that the blood in Johnson's doorway could not have come from Johnson and could have come from Klein, thus suggesting that Richter's version of the shooting was correct and Johnson's a fabrication. This theory overlooks the fact that concentrating on the blood pool carried its own serious risks. If serological analysis or other forensic evidence demonstrated that the blood came from Johnson alone, Richter's story would be exposed as an invention. An attorney need not pursue an investigation that would be fruitless, much less one that might be harmful to the defense. Here Richter's attorney had reason to question the truth of his client's account, given, for instance, Richter's initial denial of involvement and the subsequent production of Johnson's missing pistol.

It would have been altogether reasonable to conclude that this concern justified the course Richter's counsel pursued. Indeed, the Court of Appeals recognized this risk insofar as it pertained to the suggestion that counsel should have had the blood evidence tested. 578 F.3d, at 956, n. 9.[c] But the court failed to recognize that making a central issue out of blood evidence would have increased

---

c. In the cited footnote, the Ninth Circuit majority reasoned: "We agree with the dissent that counsel's decision not to ask the prosecution to *test* the blood sample before trial in order to determine blood type was not unreasonable, as such a test might have eliminated existing ambiguities that were useful to the defense and instead have produced definitive results that were damaging. However, there could have been no negative consequence to *consulting* a blood spatter expert or a serology expert prior to trial. An adequate pretrial investigation would not have alerted the State to counsel's strategy, or somehow 'cooked his own client.' Dissent at 969. Had counsel consulted a blood spatter expert, the State would have been unaware that he had done so until the point at which counsel presented expert testimony at trial, and then only if he made an informed decision that doing so would be helpful to the defense. Had counsel consulted a serology expert, the State would similarly have been unaware of such pretrial consultations unless and until counsel made an informed decision to ask the expert to test the blood type, or until he presented the expert as a witness to counter the testimony of the State's serology expert. Such consultations would not, therefore, have posed any risk."

The Ninth Circuit dissent responded that an investigatory consultation at best would have led to testing and "very well could have (and in this case would have) aided the State in producing inculpatory evidence against his client." Counsel could assume that the defense was better off without testing, and "if the state decided independently to test the blood samples and found potentially exculpatory evidence it was required by law to disclose the result to defense counsel. *Brady v. Maryland* [p. 1247]." Consider also fn. a, p. 185.

the likelihood of the prosecution's producing its own evidence on the blood pool's origins and composition; and once matters proceeded on this course, there was a serious risk that expert evidence could destroy Richter's case. Even apart from this danger, there was the possibility that expert testimony could shift attention to esoteric matters of forensic science, distract the jury from whether Johnson was telling the truth, or transform the case into a battle of the experts. * * * True, it appears that defense counsel's opening statement itself inspired the prosecution to introduce expert forensic evidence. But the prosecution's evidence may well have been weakened by the fact that it was assembled late in the process; and in any event the prosecution's response shows merely that the defense strategy did not work out as well as counsel had hoped, not that counsel was incompetent.

To support a defense argument that the prosecution has not proved its case it sometimes is better to try to cast pervasive suspicion of doubt than to strive to prove a certainty that exonerates. All that happened here is that counsel pursued a course that conformed to the first option. If this case presented a *de novo* review of *Strickland,* the foregoing might well suffice to reject the claim of inadequate counsel, but that is an unnecessary step. The Court of Appeals must be reversed if there was a reasonable justification for the state court's decision. In light of the record here there was no basis to rule that the state court's determination was unreasonable.

The Court of Appeals erred in dismissing strategic considerations like these as an inaccurate account of counsel's actual thinking. Although courts may not indulge *"post hoc* rationalization" for counsel's decisionmaking that contradicts the available evidence of counsel's actions, *Wiggins v. Smith* [Note 2, p. 167],[d] neither may they insist counsel confirm every aspect of the strategic basis for his or her actions. There is a "strong presumption" that counsel's attention to certain issues to the exclusion of others reflects trial tactics rather than "sheer neglect." *Yarborough v. Gentry,* 540 U.S. 1, 8 (2003).[e] After an adverse verdict at trial even the most experienced counsel may find it difficult to resist asking whether a different strategy might have been better, and, in the course of that reflection, to magnify their own responsibility for an unfavorable outcome. *Strickland,* however,

---

d. The Ninth Circuit majority concluded that the defense strategy posed by the Ninth Circuit dissenters (basically that set forth in the Supreme Court's opinion) was nothing more than a "post hoc rationalization," as evidenced by counsel's deposition (which was part of the record before the California Supreme Court, see fn. a supra). In that deposition, the Ninth Circuit majority noted: "Counsel was unable to provide any reasoned explanation for failing to consult forensic experts or to seek expert testimony in order to corroborate his client's testimony or prepare to rebut the prosecution's case," as his explanation was simply that his strategy "was to pit his client's credibility against Johnson and to attack the evidentiary gaps in the police investigation of the crime scene." Indeed, "counsel acknowledged that he missed crucial information when conducting his cross-examination" and that with the assistance of experts, "you don't make those mistakes like I made."

e. *Yarborough v. Gentry* presented an IAC claim based upon claimed deficiencies in counsel's closing argument. The Ninth Circuit, in finding a Sixth Amendment violation, stressed that counsel had pointed to certain exculpatory aspects of the evidence but had failed to "highlight various other potentially exculpatory pieces of evidence." In reversing that ruling, a unanimous Supreme Court noted:

"When counsel focuses on some issues to the exclusion of others, there is a strong presumption that he did so for tactical reasons rather than through sheer neglect. That presumption has particular force where a petitioner bases his ineffective-assistance claim solely on the trial record, creating a situation in which a court may have no way of knowing whether a seemingly unusual or misguided action by counsel had a sound strategic motive. Moreover, even if an omission is inadvertent, relief is not automatic. The Sixth Amendment guarantees reasonable competence, not perfect advocacy judged with the benefit of hindsight. To recall the words of Justice (and former Solicitor General) Jackson: 'I made three arguments of every case. First came the one that I planned—as I thought, logical coherent, complete. Second, was the one actually presented—interrupted, incoherent, disjointed, disappointing. The third was the utterly devastating argument that I thought of after going to bed that night.'"

calls for an inquiry into the objective reasonableness of counsel's performance, not counsel's subjective state of mind.

The Court of Appeals also found that Richter's attorney was constitutionally deficient because he had not expected the prosecution to offer expert testimony and therefore was unable to offer expert testimony of his own in response. * * * The Court of Appeals erred in suggesting counsel had to be prepared for "any contingency." *Strickland* does not guarantee perfect representation, only a " 'reasonably competent attorney.' " * * * Representation is constitutionally ineffective only if it "so undermined the proper functioning of the adversarial process" that the defendant was denied a fair trial. *Strickland*. Just as there is no expectation that competent counsel will be a flawless strategist or tactician, an attorney may not be faulted for a reasonable miscalculation or lack of foresight or for failing to prepare for what appear to be remote possibilities.

Here, Richter's attorney was mistaken in thinking the prosecution would not present forensic testimony. But the prosecution itself did not expect to make that presentation and had made no preparations for doing so on the eve of trial. For this reason alone, it is at least debatable whether counsel's error was so fundamental as to call the fairness of the trial into doubt.

Even if counsel should have foreseen that the prosecution would offer expert evidence, Richter would still need to show it was indisputable that *Strickland* required his attorney to act upon that knowledge. Attempting to establish this, the Court of Appeals held that defense counsel should have offered expert testimony to rebut the evidence from the prosecution. But *Strickland* does not enact Newton's third law for the presentation of evidence, requiring for every prosecution expert an equal and opposite expert from the defense.

In many instances cross-examination will be sufficient to expose defects in an expert's presentation. When defense counsel does not have a solid case, the best strategy can be to say that there is too much doubt about the State's theory for a jury to convict. And while in some instances "even an isolated error" can support an ineffective-assistance claim if it is "sufficiently egregious and prejudicial," *Murray v. Carrier*, 477 U.S. 478 (1986), it is difficult to establish ineffective assistance when counsel's overall performance indicates active and capable advocacy. Here Richter's attorney represented him with vigor and conducted a skillful cross-examination. As noted, defense counsel elicited concessions from the State's experts and was able to draw attention to weaknesses in their conclusions stemming from the fact that their analyses were conducted long after investigators had left the crime scene. For all of these reasons, it would have been reasonable to find that Richter had not shown his attorney was deficient under *Strickland*.

The Court of Appeals further concluded that Richter had established prejudice under *Strickland* given the expert evidence his attorney could have introduced. It held that the California Supreme Court would have been unreasonable in concluding otherwise. This too was error. * * * In assessing prejudice under *Strickland,* the question is not whether a court can be certain counsel's performance had no effect on the outcome or whether it is possible a reasonable doubt might have been established if counsel acted differently. * * * Instead, *Strickland* asks whether it is "reasonably likely" the result would have been different. This does not require a showing that counsel's actions "more likely than not altered the outcome," but the difference between *Strickland*'s prejudice standard and a more-probable-than-not standard is slight and matters "only in the rarest case." Id. The likelihood of a different result must be substantial, not just conceivable.

It would not have been unreasonable for the California Supreme Court to conclude Richter's evidence of prejudice fell short of this standard. His expert serology evidence established nothing more than a theoretical possibility that, in addition to blood of Johnson's type, Klein's blood may also have been present in a blood sample taken near the bedroom doorway pool. At trial, defense counsel extracted a concession along these lines from the prosecution's expert. The pathology expert's claim about the size of the blood pool could be taken to suggest only that the wounded and hysterical Johnson erred in his assessment of time or that he bled more profusely than estimated. And the analysis of the purported blood pattern expert indicated no more than that Johnson was not standing up when the blood pool formed.

It was also reasonable to find Richter had not established prejudice given that he offered no evidence directly challenging other conclusions reached by the prosecution's experts. For example, there was no dispute that the blood sample taken near the doorway pool matched Johnson's blood type. * * * Nor did Richter provide any direct refutation of the State's expert testimony describing how blood spatter near the couch suggested a shooting in the living room and how the blood patterns on Klein's face were inconsistent with Richter's theory that Klein had been killed in the bedroom doorway and moved to the couch.

There was, furthermore, sufficient conventional circumstantial evidence pointing to Richter's guilt. It included the gun safe and ammunition found at his home; his flight from the crime scene; his disposal of the .32–caliber gun and of Johnson's pistol; his shifting story concerning his involvement; the disappearance prior to the arrival of the law enforcement officers of the .22–caliber weapon that killed Klein; the improbability of Branscombe's not being wounded in the shootout that resulted in a combined four bullet wounds to Johnson and Klein; and the difficulties the intoxicated and twice-shot Johnson would have had in carrying the body of a dying man from bedroom doorway to living room couch, not to mention the lack of any obvious reason for him to do so. There was ample basis for the California Supreme Court to think any real possibility of Richter's being acquitted was eclipsed by the remaining evidence pointing to guilt. * * *

The California Supreme Court's decision on the merits of Richter's *Strickland* claim required more deference than it received. Richter was not entitled to the relief ordered by the Court of Appeals. The judgment is reversed, and the case is remanded for further proceedings consistent with this opinion.

Justice KAGAN took no part in the consideration or decision of this case.

JUSTICE GINSBURG, concurring in the judgment.

In failing even to consult blood experts in preparation for the murder trial, Richter's counsel, I agree with the Court of Appeals, "was not functioning as the 'counsel' guaranteed the defendant by the Sixth Amendment." *Strickland v. Washington*. The strong force of the prosecution's case, however, was not significantly reduced by the affidavits offered in support of Richter's habeas petition. I would therefore not rank counsel's lapse "so serious as to deprive [Richter] of a fair trial, a trial whose result is reliable." Ibid. For that reason, I concur in the Court's judgment.

NOTES AND QUESTIONS

1. *Section 2254(d)(1) deference.* CRIMPROC § 11.10(c) notes that, over the last decade the Supreme Court reversed (often without dissent) seven Ninth Circuit IAC rulings, finding in each that the Ninth erred in concluding that a state court had unreasonably applied *Strickland* in its rejection of an IAC claim. CRIMPROC adds that, while these Supreme Court decisions were based on § 2254(d)(1) and its "additional layers of deference," they may, in some respects, be viewed as binding on state courts in their interpretation of *Strickland*. That is because "the Court often has pointed to flaws in the Ninth Circuit analysis that seemingly also would be flaws in a de novo application of *Strickland.*" Does that characterization apply to *Harrington v. Richter*?

2. *Establishing "counsel's actual thinking".* In its rejection of the Court of Appeals conclusion as to "counsel's actual thinking," the Supreme Court addressed a recurring issue in lower court IAC rulings—what weight should be given to what defense counsel does or does not say in the collateral attack proceedings raising the IAC claim? As discussed in Note 8, p. 136, the raising of the claim allows counsel to testify, and very often either the defense or the prosecution will require that counsel testify and produce any supporting documentary evidence in the case file as to counsel's efforts and reasoning. The Ninth Circuit, in a pre-*Strickland* ruling, warned against courts in habeas proceedings insisting on counsel's testimony and thereby placing counsel "in the unenviable position where, if he can recall his reasons, and they are good, he is hurting his former client, and if he can't recall his reasons or they are bad, or not very good, he is impugning his professional competence." Kuhl v. United States, 370 F.2d 20 (9th Cir. 1966). However, courts considering IAC claims in post conviction proceedings have since become accustomed to hearing counsel's testimony and weighing such considerations in evaluating that testimony.[f]

3. *Supreme Court rulings.* *Harrington v. Richter* was not the first Supreme Court ruling to address the weight given to counsel's explanation. In *Burger v. Kemp*, as discussed in Note 2, p. 201, the Court majority stressed that the habeas court had heard counsel's testimony and accepted his explanation as to his strategic thinking, and that finding had been "twice sustained by the Court of Appeals." In *Wiggins v. Smith*, discussed in Note 2, p. 167, one of the defense counsel had testified that both counsel had decided to focus their sentencing hearing presentation on "disputing Wiggins direct responsibility for the murder," but the Court majority concluded that the "record of the actual sentencing proceeding" indicated that counsel "had never abandoned the strategy of presenting a mitigation offence" (indeed, they had presented "a half hearted mitigation case"). Thus, it appeared that their failure to investigate more thoroughly and seek a social history report "resulted from inattention." In describing counsel's inaction as the product of a "reasoned strategic judgment," the state court had relied on a "*post hoc* rationalization."

In another case decided during the same term as *Richter, Cullen v. Pinhoster,* Note 4, p. 172, the Court again rejected a Ninth Circuit conclusion that a particular strategy was no more than a "*post hoc* rationalization" Here, the question was whether the state court could reasonably have found that counsel gave serious consideration to presenting a traditional mitigation defense in capital sentencing, but concluded that the better strategy was to rely on a more limited "family sympathy mitigation defense." The issue arose in a procedural setting identical to *Harrington* (on a summary denial by the California Supreme Court), and the Supreme Court was divided 5–3 as to whether the record would have

---

f. See CRIMPROC § 11.7(a), n. 87 (in considering counsel's personal stake in testifying so as to avoid a finding of incompetent performance, potential for malpractice action or bar disciple may be treated as too remote to be of significance; malpractice liability in most jurisdictions is conditioned on defendant's "actual innocence," and "while ineffective assistance will often violate an ethics provision * * *, states do not make active use of the disciplinary process against defense attorneys found to have rendered ineffective assistance"); CRIMPROC § 11.10(c) (whether defense counsel acknowledges inattention or claims strategic justifications, courts will look for corroboration in other aspects of counsel's actions); *Edwards v. Lamarque,* 475 F.3d 1121 (9th Cir. 2007) (en banc) (majority concludes that state trial judge "was in a unique position to observe counsel's actions" and therefore conclude that questioning leading to waiver of marital privilege was not "a mistake" as counsel claimed, but a tactical decision; five dissenters disagree, concluding that counsel's decision obviously was based on a mistaken view of the law of waiver).

allowed the state court reasonably to conclude that counsel had actually explored the possibility of a traditional mitigation defense. The dissenters, like the Ninth Circuit, relied heavily on a statement that defense counsel had made to the trial court, supplemented, in particular, by an affidavit of one of defendant's co-counsel. Defense counsel had move to preclude the state from presenting aggravation witnesses, arguing that the required notice had not been provided, and stating that they accordingly "had not prepared any evidence by way of mitigation." The dissent viewed this as "the best available evidence" of counsel's treatment of mitigation, but the majority concluded that this statement was simply designed to reinforce the claim as to lack of notice. Other evidence in the record would support a conclusion that defense counsel expected all along that their notice objection might fail and had spent "considerable time and effort investigating mitigation." The dissent noted that the one counsel had stated in his affidavit that he could not recall any extensive exploration of mitigation issues, but the majority noted that the affidavit also acknowledged that the other counsel (now deceased) was primarily responsible for that area and the affidavit was made seven years after trial.

In rejecting the Ninth Circuit's conclusion as to *"post hoc* rationalizations," neither *Harrington* nor *Pinholster* referred to the limitations imposed by § 2254(d)(2), which authorizes the habeas court to grant relief on a claim adjudicated on the merits in state court proceedings where that adjudication "was based on an unreasonable determination of facts in light of the evidence presented in the state court proceeding." *Wood v. Allen*, 130 S.Ct. 841 (2010), held that a finding that defense counsel made a strategic determination not to pursue a particular action was a factual determination subject to § 2254(d)(2) (or possibly the "even more deferential" § 2254(e)(1)). Was the Court thereby indicating in these cases that the state court's reasonable application of *Strickland* was not necessarily tied to whether counsel in fact considered the particular strategy supporting her actions? Consider Note 4 infra.

4. ***Counsel's "actual thought" and "objective reasonableness."*** The *Richter* opinion notes that *"Strickland* * * * calls for an inquiry into the objective reasonableness of counsel's performance, not counsel's subjective state of mind." That point was also made in *Pinholster* in connection with Court majority's discussion of the Ninth Circuit's *post hoc* rationalization analysis. Is the Court referring simply to discounting the type of inadvertence cited in *Yarborough*, fn. e, p. 161? Does the objective reasonableness standard also support the reasoning in *Hammond v. Hall,* 586 F.3d 1289 (11th Cir. 2009)? Defense counsel there obtained a jury instruction to disregard the prosecutor's comments after the prosecutor made an inappropriate reference to the defendant's parole eligibility. At a postconviction hearing on defendant's IAC claim, defense counsel acknowledged that he did not consider a mistrial because he did not recognize that state law entitled defendant to an automatic mistrial. Rejecting the IAC claim, the Court of Appeals reasoned that "the question is not why Hammond's counsel failed to move for a mistrial * * *, but whether a competent attorney could have decided not to move for one." Competency of performance under *Strickland* was to be determined by asking whether "a hypothetical competent counsel reasonably could have taken action at trial identical to actual trial counsel." That standard sustained counsel's performance here as there were substantial strategic reasons for preferring a curative instruction over a mistrial.

5. ***The isolated error.*** As *Richter* notes (p. 162), findings of incompetent performance typically are based on counsel's overall performance, but an "isolated error" may be sufficient. Numerous cases have been based on such errors, with commentators noting that this is an area in which the separate prongs of *Strickland* tend to merge. See e.g., CRIMPROC § 11.10(c) ("The potential prejudicial impact of the subject dealt with by counsel reaches over into the competency determination, as that impact obviously relates to the care and effort expected from a competent adversary"). The Eleventh Circuit has suggested that where a performance challenge is based on counsel's failure to object to a trial error, that failure must "at least" relate to an error that, if raised for the first time on appeal, would "satisfy the standard of prejudice we employ for plain error." *Gordon v. United States*, 518 F.3d 1291 (11th Cir. 2008). Plain error, as discussed in Ch. 28, § 4 requires a defense showing that (1) the error "affects the outcome" (i.e., would not be a harmless error) and (2) results in a "miscarriage of justice." (i.e., "seriously affects" the "fairness, integrity, or public reputation of judicial proceedings").

6. *The limits of tactical decision making.* Apart from requiring that the tactical decision be based on adequate investigation of the law and facts, what other limits apply to the "wide latitude counsel must have in making tactical decisions" (p. 159)? Consider *State v. Davis*, 872 So.2d 250 (Fla. 2004). There, defense counsel, representing an African–American defendant accused of murdering a white woman, informed the jury on voir dire that he did not like black people, that he was ashamed of his prejudice, but it sometimes did make him "mad towards black people because they're black." He urged the jury, which was entirely white, to live up to its word not to let race become a factor, stressing the need, as he well knew, to be especially vigilant against some feelings they may have "deep down," as he did.

On direct appeal from defendant's conviction, the Florida Supreme Court held that counsel's remarks to the jury brought his assistance below the level required by *Strickland*. The court reasoned that counsel's statements as to his own racial prejudice simply was not a "legitimate tactical approach," for "whether or not counsel is in fact a racist, his expressions of prejudice against African–Americans cannot be tolerated." The "manner in which counsel approached the subject [of racial prejudice] unnecessarily tended either to alienate jurors who did not share his animus against African–Americans * * *, or to legitimizing racial prejudice without accomplishing counsel's stated objective of bringing latent bias out into the open."

MITIGATING EVIDENCE AND CAPITAL SENTENCING

1. *Investigation in capital cases.* Since *Strickland,* the Supreme Court has returned to the issue presented there—application of the *Strickland* standards to defense counsel's investigation and presentation of mitigating evidence in a capital sentencing hearing—in a long line of cases. See CRIMPROC § 10.10(c), n. 132.1 (citing eleven post-*Strickland* rulings). All involved habeas review of state convictions and most of the Court's rulings reversed Court of Appeals decisions as having erroneously either sustained or rejected state court rulings that denied IAC claims. In some, the IAC claim was reviewed de novo, and in others, § 2254(d)(1) applied.

Where the Court concluded that the IAC claim should have been sustained, it did so by distinguishing its past precedent that had rejected IAC claims (including *Strickland* itself). Nonetheless, many commentators and several lower courts have viewed those decisions, particularly *Wiggins v. Smith* and *Rompilla v. Beard* (described below), as having moved to a more rigorous scrutiny of counsel's performance in capital sentencing investigations, and a less stringent view of the showing needed to establish prejudice.[g] Others derive a quite different lesson from

---

g. Commentators point to several factors that may have influenced that shift, apart from a partial change in the Court's composition. First, studies of federal habeas cases show a much

these rulings, particularly when considered along with later rulings, such as *Cullen v. Pinholster* (described below). They maintain that the capital sentencing cases that have produced sharp divisions in the Court simply indicate that there is sufficiently flexibility in the governing law for differences in judicial perspective to govern the outcome—either through different readings of the record or differences in assessing application of *Strickland* principles at the edges. Still, they argue, the guiding principles remain the same and their basic content remains stable, as evidence by unanimous or near-unanimous Supreme Court rulings reversing federal circuits that appeared to disregard those principles in rejecting or sustaining IAC claims. See CRIMPROC § 11.10(c) (noting the variation among the circuits in their application of *Strickland* in capital sentencing cases, and the Court's response in per curiam reversals). Although the differing characterizations are based upon an analysis of the total body of the Court's capital sentencing rulings, the three cases described below clearly have attracted the most attention.

    2. In WIGGINS v. SMITH, 539 U.S. 510 (2003), a 7–2 majority, per O'Connor, J., held that a state prisoner was entitled to federal habeas relief, as the state court had rendered an "unreasonable application of *Strickland*" in rejecting the defendant's claim of ineffective assistance at a capital sentencing hearing. After the trial court rejected a defense motion to bifurcate the sentencing hearing and thereby separate the issue of defendant's direct responsibility for the murder from the issue of mitigation, defense counsel (two experienced public defenders), apart from an opening statement reference to defendant's "difficult life" and "clean record," concentrated entirely on the direct responsibility issue. The state court concluded that counsel had made a reasonable strategic decision not to present any evidence of defendant's personal history. The Supreme Court majority found that determination unreasonable in light of the inadequacy of the investigation that led to counsels' decision. As the Supreme Court majority read the state court's decision (in contrast to the reading of dissenting Justices Scalia and Thomas), defense counsel were deemed to have satisfied their investigative responsibilities when they first examined two sources (a presentence investigative report [PSI] and Department of Social Service [DSS] records) that provided "rudimentary knowledge" of the harsh circumstances of the defendant's youth, and then decided (as they later testified) to focus their presentation entirely on disputing the defendant's direct responsibility for the killing. Rejecting that determination, the Court majority noted both that the trial court record strongly suggested that counsels' "failure to investigate thoroughly [defendant's personal history] resulted from inattention, not reasoned strategic judgment" (see Note 3, p. 164), and that "counsels' decision not to expand their investigation beyond the PSI and the DSS records fell short of the professional standards that prevailed in

---

higher success rate in capital cases, with a prime factor being successful IAC challenges to representation at capital sentencing hearings. See King, et. al., p. 1604 (noting an earlier study reporting a 40% reversal rate and finding a 15% reversal rate in post AEDPA petitions). Second, there had been "a steady stream of highly publicized DNA exonerations in capital cases," with ineffective counsel often cited as contributing to the erroneous conviction, see pp. 57–63. Third, the American Bar Association urged capital punishment states to adopt a death penalty moratorium until the state was able to achieve various reforms (including upgrading representation) that had produced a system flawed in both litigation of guilt and assignment of capital sentences. Fourth, various justices had taken note of the special bearing of the quality of representation upon the assignment of the death penalty. An Associated Press Report, Death Moratorium Backed, April 10, 2001, quoted Justice Ginsberg as having stated: "I have yet to see a death case among the dozens coming to the Supreme Court on eve-of-execution stay applications in which the defendant was well represented at trial. . . . People who are well represented do not get the death penalty." Justice Blackmun, dissenting from a denial of certiorari in *McFarland v. Scott,* 512 U.S. 1256 (1994), denounced key capital punishment states for failing to appoint qualified attorneys in death cases. Justice O'Connor in a 2001 speech noted that, "perhaps, it is time to look at minimum standards for appointed counsel in death cases." Lack of Lawyers Hinders Appeals in Death Cases, N.Y. Times, July 5, 2001.

Maryland [at the time of the trial]." In support of the latter determination, the majority noted that: (1) the two sources examined by counsel suggested a significant potential for mitigation in defendant's personal history; (2) those sources did not suggest offsetting aggravating factors, and thus did not present "the double edge we found to justify limited investigations in other cases, cf. *Burger v. Kemp* 483 U.S. 776 (1987)"[h]; (3) "standard practice in Maryland in capital cases at the time * * * included the preparation of a social history report" (a step also required by the ABA Guidelines for death penalty representation); and (4) Public Defender funding had been available to obtain such a report.

    3. In ROMPILLA v. BEARD, 545 U.S. 374 (2005), Rompilla's "evidence in mitigation consisted of relatively brief testimony: five of his family members argued in effect for residual doubt, and beseeched the jury for mercy" and Rompilla's 14 year-old-son "testified that he loved his father and would visit him in prison." However, state postconviction counsel produced significant mitigating evidence that trial counsel had failed to uncover relating to Rompilla's childhood, mental capacity, health, and alcoholism. The state court rejected the IAC claim, and the Third Circuit majority, applying the AEDPA, concluded that the state court's application of *Strickland* had been reasonable, "given defense counsel's efforts to uncover mitigation material, which included interviewing Rompilla and certain family members, as well as consultation with three mental health experts." A dissenting judge found otherwise, "concluding that counsels' failure to obtain relevant records on Rompilla's background was owing to the lawyers' unreasonable reliance on family members and medical experts to tell them what records might be useful." The Court majority (per Souter, J.) did not resolve this issue, finding ineffective representation based on a different failure in counsels' investigation. It noted:

    "Counsel knew that the Commonwealth intended to seek the death penalty by proving Rompilla had a significant history of felony convictions indicating the use or threat of violence, an aggravator under state law. Counsel further knew that the Commonwealth would attempt to establish this history by proving Rompilla's prior conviction for rape and assault, and would emphasize his violent character by introducing a transcript of the rape victim's testimony given in that earlier trial. * * * It is clear, however, that defense counsel did not look at any part of that file, including the transcript, until warned by the prosecution a second time, [in] a colloquy the day before the evidentiary sentencing phase began, [that] the prosecutor * * * would present the transcript of the victim's testimony to establish the prior conviction. * * * [C]rucially, even after obtaining the transcript of the victim's testimony on the eve of the sentencing hearing, counsel apparently examined none of the other material in the file.

    "With every effort to view the facts as a defense lawyer would have done at the time, it is difficult to see how counsel could have failed to realize that without examining the readily available file they were seriously compromising their opportunity to respond to a case for aggravation. * * * Without making reasonable efforts to review the file, defense counsel could have had no hope of knowing

---

    h. In *Burger*, the Court majority, in a 5–4 decision, concluded that while counsel "could well have made a more thorough investigation" as to mitigating background evidence, the decision to limit that investigation and focus on other issues reflected a "reasonable professional judgment," taking account of the substantial drawbacks suggested by the initial investigation. Counsel had expressed concern that: (1) evidence of defendant's unhappy childhood would come primarily from defendant's mother, but her testimony also would reveal that the defendant "had committed at least one petty offense" (while, "as the record [otherwise] stood, there was absolutely no evidence that petitioner had any prior criminal record of any kind"); (2) the psychologist's testimony would suggest that petitioner "never expressed any remorse about his crime"; and (3) the psychologist's report indicated that placing the defendant on the stand was risky as defendant "might even have bragged about [the] crime."

whether the prosecution was quoting selectively from the transcript, or whether there were circumstances extenuating the behavior described by the victim. The obligation to get the file was particularly pressing here owing to the similarity of the violent prior offense to the crime charged and Rompilla's sentencing strategy stressing residual doubt.

"The notion that defense counsel must obtain information that the State has and will use against the defendant is not simply a matter of common sense. As the District Court points out, the American Bar Association Standards for Criminal Justice in circulation at the time of Rompilla's trial describes the obligation in terms no one could misunderstand in the circumstances of a case like this one:

'It is the duty of the lawyer to conduct a prompt investigation of the circumstances of the case and to explore all avenues leading to facts relevant to the merits of the case and the penalty in the event of conviction. The investigation should always include efforts to secure information in the possession of the prosecution and law enforcement authorities. The duty to investigate exists regardless of the accused's admissions or statements to the lawyer of facts constituting guilt or the accused's stated desire to plead guilty.' 1 *ABA Standards for Criminal Justice* 4–4.1 (2d ed. 1982 Supp.). * * *

[W]e long have referred [to these ABA Standards] as 'guides to determining what is reasonable.' *Wiggins v. Smith*, (quoting *Strickland v. Washington*), and the Commonwealth has come up with no reason to think the quoted standard impertinent here.

"The dissent thinks [our] analysis creates a 'rigid, *per se*' rule that requires defense counsel to do a complete review of the file on any prior conviction introduced; but that is a mistake. Counsel fell short here because they failed to make reasonable efforts to review the prior conviction file, despite knowing that the prosecution intended to introduce Rompilla's prior conviction not merely by entering a notice of conviction into evidence but by quoting damaging testimony of the rape victim in that case. The unreasonableness of attempting no more than they did was heightened by the easy availability of the file at the trial courthouse, and the great risk that testimony about a similar violent crime would hamstring counsel's chosen defense of residual doubt. It is owing to these circumstances that the state courts were objectively unreasonable in concluding that counsel could reasonably decline to make any effort to review the file. Other situations, where a defense lawyer is not charged with knowledge that the prosecutor intends to use a prior conviction in this way, might well warrant a different assessment.

"Since counsel's failure to look at the file fell below the line of reasonable practice, there is a further question about prejudice, that is, whether 'there is a reasonable probability that, but for counsel's unprofessional errors, the result of the proceeding would have been different.' *Strickland.* * * * If the defense lawyers had looked in the file on Rompilla's prior conviction, it is uncontested they would have found a range of mitigation leads that no other source had opened up. In the same file with the transcript of the prior trial were the records of Rompilla's imprisonment on the earlier conviction, which defense counsel testified she had never seen. The prison files pictured Rompilla's childhood and mental health very differently from anything defense counsel had seen or heard. An evaluation by a corrections counselor states that Rompilla was 'reared in the slum environment of Allentown, Pa. vicinity. He early came to the attention of juvenile authorities, quit school at 16, [and] started a series of incarcerations in and out Penna. often of assaultive nature and commonly related to over-indulgence in alcoholic beverages.' The same file discloses test results that the defense's mental health experts would have viewed as pointing to schizophrenia and other disorders, and test scores showing a third grade level of cognition after nine years of schooling.[8]

"The accumulated entries would have destroyed the benign conception of Rompilla's upbringing and mental capacity defense counsel had formed from talking with Rompilla himself and some of his family members, and from the reports of the mental health experts. With this information, counsel would have become skeptical of the impression given by the five family members and would unquestionably have gone further to build a mitigation case. Further effort would presumably have unearthed much of the material postconviction counsel found, including testimony from several members of Rompilla's family, whom trial counsel did not interview. * * * This evidence adds up to a mitigation case that bears no relation to the few naked pleas for mercy actually put before the jury, and although we suppose it is possible that a jury could have heard it all and still have decided on the death penalty, that is not the test. It goes without saying that the undiscovered mitigating evidence, taken as a whole, 'might well have influenced the jury's appraisal' of [Rompilla's] culpability,' *Wiggins,* and the likelihood of a different result if the evidence had gone in is 'sufficient to undermine confidence in the outcome' actually reached at sentencing, *Strickland.*"

Justice Kennedy's dissent (joined by Chief Justice Rehnquist, and Justices Scalia and Thomas), responded, in part:

"A *per se* rule requiring counsel in every case to review the records of prior convictions used by the State as aggravation evidence is a radical departure from *Strickland* and its progeny. We have warned in the past against the creation of 'specific guidelines' or 'checklist[s] for judicial evaluation of attorney performance.' *Strickland.* * * * [So too, while] we have referred to the ABA Standards for Criminal Justice as a useful point of reference, we have been careful to say these standards 'are only guides' and do not establish the constitutional baseline for effective assistance of counsel. The majority, by parsing the guidelines as if they were binding statutory text, ignores this admonition. * * * The Court's opinion makes clear it has imposed on counsel a broad obligation to review prior conviction case files where those priors are used in aggravation—and to review every document in those files if not every single page of every document, regardless of the prosecution's proposed use for the prior conviction. * * * One member of the majority tries to limit the Court's new rule by arguing that counsel's decision here was 'not the result of an informed tactical decision,' (O'Connor, J., concurring), but the record gives no support for this notion. [i]

---

8. The dissent would ignore the opportunity to find this evidence on the ground that its discovery (and the consequent analysis of prejudice) "rests on serendipity." But once counsel had an obligation to examine the file, counsel had to make reasonable efforts to learn its contents; and once having done so, they could not reasonably have ignored mitigation evidence or red flags simply because they were unexpected. The dissent, however, assumes that counsel could reasonably decline even to read what was in the file, (if counsel had reviewed the case file for mitigating evidence, "[t]here would have been no reason for counsel to read, or even to skim, this obscure document"). While that could well have been true if counsel had been faced with a large amount of possible evidence, there is no indication that examining the case file in question here would have required significant labor. Indeed, Pennsylvania has conspicuously failed to contest Rompilla's claim that because the information was located in the prior conviction file, reasonable efforts would have led counsel to this information.

i. Justice O'Connor joined the opinion of the Court, but also wrote separately. Defense attorney Dantos testified at the postconviction hearing that she had examined some files regarding the prior conviction (see dissent infra), but offered no explanation of why she had not looked at the entire file. Justice O'Connor concluded that the decision not to examine the entire file "was not the result of an informed tactical decision about how the lawyers' time would best be spent" (as the dissent suggested). Their failure would "not necessarily have been deficient" if based on such a "careful exercise of judgment," as where they determined, for example, "that the file was inaccessible or so large that examining it would necessarily divert them from other trial-

"The majority also disregards the sound strategic calculation supporting the decisions made by Rompilla's attorneys. Charles and Dantos were 'aware of [Rompilla's] priors' and 'aware of the circumstances' surrounding these convictions. At the postconviction hearing, Dantos also indicated that she had reviewed documents relating to the prior conviction. Based on this information, as well as their numerous conversations with Rompilla and his family, Charles and Dantos reasonably could conclude that reviewing the full prior conviction case file was not the best allocation of resources. * * *

"In imposing this new rule, the Court states that counsel in this case could review the 'entire file' with 'ease.' There is simply no support in the record for this assumption. Case files often comprise numerous boxes. The file may contain, among other things, witness statements, forensic evidence, arrest reports, grand jury transcripts, testimony and exhibits relating to any pretrial suppression hearings, trial transcripts, trial exhibits, post-trial motions and presentence reports. Full review of even a single prior conviction case file could be time consuming, and many of the documents in a file are duplicative or irrelevant. * * * Today's decision will not increase the resources committed to capital defense. (At the time of Rompilla's trial, the Lehigh County Public Defender's Office had two investigators for 2,000 cases.) If defense attorneys dutifully comply with the Court's new rule, they will have to divert resources from other tasks. The net effect of today's holding in many cases—instances where trial counsel reasonably can conclude that reviewing old case files is not an effective use of time—will be to diminish the quality of representation. * * *

"Even accepting the Court's misguided analysis of the adequacy of representation by Rompilla's trial counsel, Rompilla is still not entitled to habeas relief. *Strickland* assigns the defendant the burden of demonstrating prejudice. Rompilla cannot satisfy this standard, and only through a remarkable leap can the Court conclude otherwise. * * * The Court's theory of prejudice rests on serendipity. Nothing in the old case file diminishes the aggravating nature of the prior conviction. * * * The Court, recognizing this problem, instead finds prejudice through chance. If Rompilla's attorneys had reviewed the case file of his prior rape and burglary conviction, the Court says, they would have stumbled across 'a range of mitigation leads.' The range of leads to which the Court refers is in fact a handful of notations within a single 10–page document. The document, an 'Initial Transfer Petition,' appears to have been prepared by the Pennsylvania Department of Corrections after Rompilla's conviction to facilitate his initial assignment to one of the Commonwealth's maximum-security prisons. * * * [N]othing in the record indicates that Rompilla's trial attorneys would have discovered the transfer petition, or the clues contained in it, if they had reviewed the old file. The majority faults Rompilla's attorneys for failing to 'learn what the Commonwealth knew about the crime,' 'discover any mitigating evidence the Commonwealth would downplay,' and 'anticipate the details of the aggravating evidence the Commonwealth would emphasize.' Yet if Rompilla's attorneys had reviewed the case file with these purposes in mind, they almost surely would have attributed no significance to the transfer petition following only a cursory review. * * * The Court claims that the transfer petition would have been discovered because it was in the 'same file' with the transcript, but this characterization is misleading and the conclusion the Court draws from it is accordingly fallacious. The record indicates only that the transfer petition was a part of the same case file, but Rompilla provides no indication of the size of the file, which for all we know originally comprised several boxes of documents."

---

preparation tasks they thought more promising." Here, however, the failure was "the result of inattention" and thus could not be justified under *Strickland*.

4. In CULLEN v. PINHOLSTER, 131 S.Ct. 1388 (2011), the Ninth Circuit had found that the state court unreasonably applied *Strickland* in summarily denying an IAC claim alleging counsel's failure to adequately investigate and present mitigating evidence in a capital sentencing proceeding. A divided Supreme Court reversed (5–3, with Justice Breyer not reaching the merits of the claim). Justice Thomas's opinion for the Court and Justice Sotomayor's dissent (joined by Justices Ginsburg and Kagan) agreed as to the standards of § 2254(d) review, but disagreed as to a reasonable reading of the record and the validity of the Ninth Circuit's reasoning.

The majority found that the record supported the state court having reasonably concluded that counsel had followed the strategic path outlined in the Ninth Circuit dissent. That path had the following elements: (1) counsel were fully aware of the need to deal with the mitigation issue; (2) counsel had in fact spent "considerable time and effort on investigating mitigation," interviewing defendant Pinholster's mother and brother, (who provided information on possible brain injuries, school placement in an "educationally handicapped class," time spent in a state hospital for emotionally handicapped children, and treatment for epilepsy), and consulting a psychiatrist (who reviewed Pinholster's personality traits and offered a diagnosis limited to an "antisocial personality disorder"); (3) counsel recognized that "they represented a psychotic client whose performance at trial hardly endeared him to the jury," presenting a substantial impediment to a successful mitigation strategy; and (4) counsel therefore adopted the strategy of "presenting only Pinholster's mother in the penalty phase to create sympathy not for Pinholster, but for his mother" (such a family-sympathy mitigation defense "at the time of the trial [was a strategy that] the defense bar in California had been using").[j]

The majority concluded that the Ninth Circuit had failed to give proper weight to this "reasonable tactical basis" for counsels' actions because it erroneously "attribut[ed] strict rules to this Court's recent case law." Those cases (including *Wiggins* and *Rompilla*) were described by the Ninth Circuit as establishing "a constitutional duty to investigate" the issue of mitigation, rendering "it * * * prima facie ineffective assistance * * * to abandon * * * [that investigation] after acquiring only rudimentary knowledge * * * from a narrow set of sources." Thus, the Ninth Circuit noted, it could not "lightly disregard, a failure to introduce evidence of 'excruciating life history' or 'nightmarish childhood'." This approach, the majority countered, ignored both *Strickland's* rejection of the use of "specific guidelines," and *Strickland's* recognition that "there comes a point where a defense attorney will reasonably decide that another strategy is in order, thus mak[ing] particular investigation unnecessary." The Court quoted in this connection a passage from Judge Kozinski's dissent below: "The current infatuation with 'humanizing' the defendant as the be-all and end-all of mitigation disregards the possibility that this may be the wrong tactic in some cases because experienced lawyers conclude that the jury won't buy it." Such decisions by counsel, the majority noted, "are due a heavy measure of deference."

---

j. As discussed in Note 3, p. 164, the dissent argued that the record presented a quite different picture of counsels' consideration of a mitigation defense. The majority and dissent similarly disagreed in their reading of the record as it related to the prejudice prong of *Strickland*. The majority concluded that the mitigation evidence presented by Pinholster's state habeas counsel "largely duplicated" the evidence presented at trial through his mother's testimony, and some of the new testimony "would likely have undercut the mitigating value of the testimony by Pinholster's mother." Thus, "the new material was not so significant that * * * it was necessarily unreasonable for the California Supreme Court to conclude that Pinholster had failed to show a substantial likelihood of a different sentence." The dissent responded that the prosecutor had largely undermined the mother's testimony. The new material, in contrast, provided "objective evidence" and developed a mitigation case that "bears no relation to [the mother's] unsubstantiated testimony."

The dissent concluded that acceptance of such a strategy as reasonably competent performance constituted an unreasonable application of *Strickland* under § 2254(d). The dissent reasoned that counsel's investigation of mitigation was far too limited to abandon that strategy in favor of a family-sympathy mitigation defense. The dissent cited the skimpy information given to the psychiatrist, the mother's natural interest in painting a more favorable picture of the family situation than actually existed, and the ready availability of other sources, such as schooling and medical records, and various health care providers who had treated Pinholster. Although Pinholster was an unsympathetic client, "that fact," the dissent noted, "compounds, rather than excused, counsel's deficiency in ignoring the glaring avenues of investigation that could explain why Pinholster was the way he was."

SECTION 4. THE *CRONIC* EXCEPTIONS AND OTHER POSSIBLE PER SE VIOLATIONS

1. ***Recognizing exceptions.*** *Strickland* presents the dominant standards for resolving ineffective assistance claims, but as *Strickland* itself noted, those standards are not universal. Thus *Strickland* distinguished (p. 142) two settings in which the Court departs from the *Strickland* two-pronged test: (1) where the trial court had prevented counsel from utilizing certain adversarial procedures (commonly described as the "interference cases") (Note 5, p. 176); and (2) where counsel had been "burdened by an actual conflict of interest," as in *Cuyler v. Sullivan* (Note 1, p. 200). The Court's opinion in *United States v. Cronic*, Note 2 infra, recognized additional exceptions while stressing the general applicability of the *Strickland* standards. The Notes that follow discuss the scope of those additional exceptions, and the Court's rejection of still broader exceptions.

2. ***Rejection of a broad inferential exception.*** In UNITED STATES v. CRONIC, 466 U.S. 648 (1984), decided on the same day as *Strickland*, the Court rejected an attempt to create a broad exception to the *Strickland* approach.

Respondent Cronic and two associates were indicted on mail fraud charges involving a "check kiting" scheme. When, shortly before the scheduled trial date, respondent's trial counsel withdrew, the district court appointed a young lawyer with a real estate practice who had never participated in a jury trial to represent respondent. Appointed counsel was allowed only 25 days for pretrial preparation, although it had taken the government over four and a half years to investigate the case and it had reviewed thousands of documents during that investigation. Without referring to any specific error or inadequacy in appointed counsel's performance, the Tenth Circuit reversed respondent's conviction, inferring from the circumstances surrounding the representation of respondent that his right to the effective assistance of counsel had been violated. The Tenth Ciruit based this conclusion on five factors: (1) the limited time afforded counsel for investigation and preparation; (2) counsel's inexperience; (3) the gravity of the charge; (4) the complexity of possible defenses; and (5) the inaccessibility of witnesses to counsel.

The Supreme Court (per Stevens, J.) rejected the "inferred incompetence" approach of the Tenth Circuit. Citing the underlying function of the right to counsel in protecting the adversary process (see Note 6, p. 133), the Court reasoned that a determination that counsel failed to fulfill that function ordinarily requires some showing of an adverse effect on that process. The Tenth Circuit had not pointed to anything in the actual conduct of the trial "indicating a breakdown in the adversarial process." The five factors it cited were "relevant to an evaluation of a lawyer's ineffectiveness in a particular case, * * * but neither separately nor in combination [did] they provide a basis for concluding that competent counsel was not able to provide the guiding hand that the Constitution guarantees." The Court had indicated as much in earlier rulings recognizing that not every refusal to give counsel more time to prepare results in ineffective assistance. The additional circumstances here did not present "surrounding circumstances that justify a presumption of ineffectiveness * * * without inquiry into counsel's actual performance at trial."

The *Cronic* opinion noted, however, that the Court previously had recognized exceptions to this general rule "requiring inquiry into counsel's actual perform-ance." These situations presented "circumstances that are so likely to prejudice the accused that the cost of litigating their effect in a particular case is unjusti-fied." The opinion included a brief, frequently quoted, description of those situations:

"Most obvious, of course, is the complete denial of counsel. The presumption that counsel's assistance is essential requires us to conclude that a trial is unfair if the accused is denied counsel at a critical stage of his trial.[25] Similarly, if counsel entirely fails to subject the prosecution's case to meaningful adversarial testing, then there has been a denial of Sixth Amendment rights that makes the adversary process itself presumptively unreliable. * * * Circumstances of that magnitude also may be present on some occasions when, although counsel is available to assist the accused during trial, the likelihood that any lawyer, even a fully competent one, could provide effective assistance is so small that a presumption of prejudice is appropriate without inquiry into the actual conduct of the trial. *Powell v. Alabama* [Note 1, p. 131] was such a case.

"The defendants [in *Powell*] had been indicted for a highly publicized capital offense. Six days before trial, the trial judge appointed 'all the members of the bar' for purposes of arraignment. 'Whether they would represent the defendants thereafter if no counsel appeared in their behalf, was a matter of speculation only, or, as the judge indicated, of mere anticipation on the part of the court.' On the day of trial, a lawyer from Tennessee appeared on behalf of persons 'interested' in the defendants, but stated that he had not had an opportunity to prepare the case or to familiarize himself with local procedure, and therefore was unwilling to represent the defendants on such short notice. The problem was resolved when the court decided that the Tennessee lawyer would represent the defendants, with whatever help the local bar could provide. * * * This Court held that 'such designation of counsel as was attempted was either so indefinite or so close upon the trial as to amount to a denial of effective and substantial aid in that regard.' * * * "

3. *The constructive denial of counsel.* Relying on both *Cronic*'s discus-sion of *Powell* and its reference to a counsel who "entirely fails to subject the prosecution's case to meaningful adversary testing," lower courts developed a doctrine of "constructive denial of counsel" (a phrase first used in *Strickland*, see p. 142). Those cases held that where counsel's absence at a critical proceeding or lack of effort was so extensive as to produce a "complete failure" of representa-tion, a presumption of prejudice was justified. BELL v. CONE, 535 U.S. 685 (2002), presented a typical lower court ruling of this type.

At respondent's trial the prosecution provided overwhelming evidence that he had killed an elderly couple in brutal fashion. Respondent's defense was that he was not guilty by reason of insanity due to substance abuse and posttraumatic

---

25. The Court has uniformly found constitutional error without any showing of prejudice when counsel was either totally absent or prevented from assisting the accused during a critical stage of the proceeding. [The Court here cited the "interference" cases discussed in Note 5, p. 176, and cases such as *Hamilton v. Alabama*, Note 2, p. 73, where the state failed to provide counsel at an arraignment deemed a critical stage].

stress disorder related to his Vietnam military service. The jury found respondent guilty of the murders, and a sentencing hearing followed. The prosecution introduced evidence of aggravating factors and the defense called the jury's attention to the mitigating evidence already before it. The defense also cross-examined prosecution witnesses, but called no witnesses of its own. After the junior prosecutor made a closing argument, defense counsel waived final argument, which prevented the lead prosecutor from arguing in rebuttal. The jury found four aggravating factors and no mitigating factors. Under state law, these findings required the death penalty.

The Sixth Circuit granted federal habeas relief, concluding that counsel's failures at the sentencing hearing amounted to a constructive denial of counsel and that justified a presumption of prejudice under the analysis of *Cronic*. But an 8–1 majority, per Rehnquist, C.J., held that the lower court's reliance on *Cronic* was misplaced:

"When we spoke in *Cronic* of the possibility of presuming prejudice based on an attorney's failure to test the prosecutor's case, we indicated that the attorney's failure must be complete. [Here] respondent's argument is not that his counsel failed to oppose the prosecution throughout the sentencing proceeding as a whole, but that his counsel failed to do so at specific points. For purposes of distinguishing between the rule of *Strickland* and that of *Cronic*, this difference is not of degree but of kind. The aspects of counsel's performance challenged by respondent—the failure to adduce mitigating evidence and the waiver of closing argument—are plainly of the same ilk as other specific attorney errors we have held subject to *Strickland*'s performance and prejudice components."

4. Does *Bell v. Cone* require reconsideration of a series of pre-*Bell* rulings that applied the constructive denial doctrine to situations in which counsel was absent from an arguably critical portion of the criminal justice process but otherwise participated in the proceedings leading to conviction? One such situation was that in which counsel fell asleep at different times during the trial. See e.g., *Burdine v. Johnson*, 262 F.3d 336 (5th Cir.2001) (en banc) (majority refuses to adopt a "per se rule that any dozing by defense counsel during trial merits a presumption of prejudice," but will presume prejudice based on "repeated unconsciousness of * * * counsel through not insubstantial portions of the critical guilty-innocence phase of Burdine's murder trial"; dissent concludes that the only specific factual finding is that counsel dozed during unidentified portions of the trial, with precise reconstruction impossible due to the passage of time, and these circumstances do not distinguish situations where the Circuit previously had insisted on a *Strickland* showing of specific prejudice, such as where counsel's capacity was allegedly restricted by alcohol use or a mental condition). Another is the situation in which the trial court conducted part of the trial or a pretrial proceeding in the absence of counsel, either because of counsel's tardiness or some misunderstanding relating to counsel's presence. See e.g., French v. Jones, 282 F.3d 893 (6th Cir.2002), reaffirmed after remand for reconsideration in light of *Cone*, 332 F.3d 430 (6th Cir.2003) (counsel not present when trial judge gave supplemental jury instruction to deadlocked jury).

As noted in CRIMPROC § 11.10(d): "Several post-*Cone* lower court rulings have continued to [apply the *Cronic* presumption] to such absences. They read *Cronic's* reference to 'counsel totally absent or prevented from assisting * * * during a critical stage' to encompass not only the state's failure to provide counsel (or its restriction of counsel's representation [see Note 5 infra]), but also an appointed counsel's failure to represent the defendant during a critical stage. *Bell v. Cone* is distinguished as involving a separate category for presuming prejudice (the total failure to subject the prosecution's case to adversarial testing)." The contrary position is that the *Bell* ruling suggests no such limitation. The *Cronic* reference in fn. 25 to counsel's absence during a critical stage clearly does not apply, as that footnote was discussing only situations in which the judiciary is responsible for the absence, by denying the appointment of counsel or precluding counsel from participation, as indicated by the cases fn. 25 cited.

5. *The interference cases.* As noted in fn. 25 of *Cronic* and in *Strickland* (see p. 142), the Court has found per se violations of the Sixth Amendment in what have come to be known as the "state interference" cases. The leading interference cases, as described in *Strickland*, are: "*Geders v. United States*, 425 U.S. 80 (1976) (bar on attorney-client consultation during overnight recess); *Herring v. New York*, 422 U.S. 853 (1975) (bar on summation at bench trial); *Brooks v. Tennessee*, 406 U.S. 605 (1972) (requirement that defendant be first defense witness); *Ferguson v. Georgia*, 365 U.S. 570 (1961) (bar on direct examination of defendant)."

The reasoning of the interference rulings is summarized in CRIMPROC § 11.8(a): "The 'right to the assistance of counsel,' the Supreme Court noted in *Herring v. New York*, 'has been understood to mean that there can be no restrictions upon the function of counsel in defending a criminal prosecution in accord with the traditions of the adversary factfinding process.' Accordingly, state action, whether by statute or trial court ruling, that prohibits counsel from making full use of traditional trial procedures may be viewed as denying defendant the effective assistance of counsel. In considering the constitutionality of such 'state interference,' courts are directed to look whether the interference denied counsel 'the opportunity to participate fully and fairly in the adversary factfinding process.' If the interference had that effect, then both the overall performance of counsel apart from the interference and the lack of any showing of actual outcome prejudice become irrelevant."

CHALLENGES TO THE DEFENSE DELIVERY SYSTEM DEFICIENCIES

1. Commentators have long contended that the various state delivery systems for providing state-funded counsel (see Notes 5-6, pp. 77–78) are woefully lacking in funding and quality controls, and therefore institutionally incapable of providing adequate representation of indigent defendants on a regular basis. They recognize that *Cronic* precludes overturning a conviction based on conditions of representation, but argue that challenges brought prospectively and tied to systemic deficiencies that produce "structural ineffectiveness" present a quite different legal issue. As discussed in CRIMPROF 11.8(c), the initial prospective challenges to alleged systemic deficiencies were presented in the course of criminal litigation (e.g., in a pretrial motion by defense counsel claiming that a heavy caseload or inadequate compensation would preclude effective representation). Most courts rejected such challenges as inconsistent with *Cronic* and *Strickland*, which were seen as requiring a review, after trial, as to whether counsel's performance actually failed to meet the *Strickland* standards. Prospective relief was granted in some cases (e.g., lifting the cap on compensation of the appointed attorney), but those rulings were generally based on grounds other than the Sixth Amendment. In the most prominent successful challenge, State v. Peart, 621 So.2d 780 (La. 1993), the Louisiana court recognized a rebuttable presumption that a heavily overloaded defender office "would provide assistance not sufficiently effective to meet constitutionally required standards," but never discussed *Cronic*.

The general lack of success for challenges raised pretrial in criminal cases led to a shift to a new form of systemic challenge. Civil class actions were brought, typically on behalf of accused persons, alleging that systemic deficiencies present a substantial risk of irreparable injury through specific flaws in representation, and seeking either injunctive relief relating to the alleged deficiencies or an appropriate declaratory judgment. This litigation has been grounded in part on the Sixth Amendment and state counterparts to the Sixth Amendment, but other sources of judicial authority have also been considered. The results have been mixed. Where the suits have survived a motion to dismiss, they often have resulted in settlements. See CRIMPROC § 11.8, fn. 69.1. In New York the litigation produced a high court ruling tied to the Sixth Amendment issues.

HURRELL-HARRING v. STATE OF NEW YORK
15 N.Y.3d 8, 904 N.Y.S.2d 296, 930 N.E.2d 217 (2010).

LIPPMAN, CHIEF JUDGE.

* * * In New York, the Legislature has left the performance of the State's obligation under *Gideon* to the counties, where it is discharged, for the most part, with county resources and according to local rules and practices. Plaintiffs in this action, defendants in various criminal prosecutions ongoing at the time of the action's commencement in Washington, Onondaga, Ontario, Schuyler and Suffolk counties, contend that this arrangement, involving what is in essence a costly, largely unfunded and politically unpopular mandate upon local government, has functioned to deprive them and other similarly situated indigent defendants in the aforementioned counties of constitutionally and statutorily guaranteed representational rights. [In a suit against the state and the governor,] they seek a declaration that their rights and those of the class they seek to represent are being violated and an injunction to avert further abridgment of their right to counsel; they do not seek relief within the criminal cases out of which their claims arise.

This appeal results from dispositions of defendants' motion * * * to dismiss the action as nonjusticiable. [I]n the decision and order now before us, the sought relief was granted by the Appellate Division. * * * We now reinstate the action, albeit with some substantial qualifications upon its scope.

Defendant's claim that the action is not justiciable [rests] principally on two theories: first, that there is no cognizable claim for ineffective assistance of counsel apart from one seeking relief from a conviction, and second, that recognition of a claim for systemic relief of the sort plaintiffs seek will involve the courts in the performance of properly legislative functions, most notably determining how public resources are to be allocated.

The first of these theories is rooted in case law conditioning relief for constitutionally ineffective assistance upon findings that attorney performance, when viewed in its total, case specific aspect, has both fallen below the standard of objective, and resulted in prejudice * * *. Defendants reason that the prescribed, deferential and highly context sensitive inquiry into the adequacy and particular effect of counsel's performance cannot occur until a prosecution has concluded in a conviction, and that, once there is a conviction, the appropriate avenues of relief are direct appeals and the various other established means of challenging a conviction * * *. [T]hey argue that a finding of constitutionally deficient performance—one necessarily rooted in the particular circumstances of an individual case—cannot serve as a predicate for systemic relief. Indeed, they remind us that the Supreme Court in *Strickland* has noted pointedly that "the purpose of the effective assistance guarantee of the Sixth Amendment is not to improve the quality of legal representation, although that is a goal of considerable importance to the legal system[,] . . . [but rather] to ensure that criminal defendants receive a fair trial."

These arguments possess a measure of merit. A fair reading of *Strickland* and our relevant state precedents supports defendants' contention that effective assistance is a judicial construct designed to do no more than protect an individual defendant's right to a fair adjudication; it is not a concept capable of expansive application to remediate systemic deficiencies. The cases in which the concept has been explicated are in this connection notable for their intentional omission of any broadly applicable defining performance standards. Indeed, *Strickland* is clear that articulation of any standard more specific than that of objective reasonableness is neither warranted by the Sixth Amendment nor compatible with its objectives. * * *

Having said this, however, we would add the very important caveat that *Strickland's* approach is expressly premised on the supposition that the fundamental underlying right to representation under *Gideon* has been enabled by the State in a manner that would justify the presumption that the standard of objective reasonableness will ordinarily be satisfied. The questions properly raised in this Sixth Amendment-grounded action, we think, go not to whether ineffectiveness has assumed systemic dimensions, but rather to whether the State has met its foundational obligation under *Gideon* to provide legal representation.

* * * While it is defendants' position, and was evidently that of the Appellate Division majority, that the complaint contains only performance-based claims for ineffective assistance, our examination of the pleading leads us to a different conclusion. According to the complaint, 10 of the 20 plaintiffs—two from Washington, two from Onondaga, two from Ontario and four from Schuyler County—were altogether without representation at the arraignments held in their underlying criminal proceedings. Eight of these unrepresented plaintiffs were jailed after bail had been set in amounts they could not afford. It is alleged that the experience of these plaintiffs is illustrative of what is a fairly common practice in the aforementioned counties of arraigning defendants without counsel and leaving them, particularly when accused of relatively low level offenses, unrepresented in subsequent proceedings where pleas are taken and other critically important legal transactions take place. * * *

In addition to the foregoing allegations of outright nonrepresentation, the complaint contains allegations to the effect that although lawyers were eventually nominally appointed for plaintiffs, they were unavailable to their clients—that they conferred with them little, if at all, were often completely unresponsive to their urgent inquiries and requests from jail, sometimes for months on end, waived important rights without consulting them, and ultimately appeared to do little more on their behalf than act as conduits for plea offers, some of which purportedly were highly unfavorable. It is repeatedly alleged that counsel missed court appearances, and that when they did appear they were not prepared to proceed, often because they were entirely new to the case, the matters having previously been handled by other similarly unprepared counsel. There are also allegations that the counsel appointed for at least one of the plaintiffs was seriously conflicted and thus unqualified to undertake the representation.

The allegations of the complaint must at this stage of the litigation be deemed true and construed in plaintiffs' favor, affording them the benefit of every reasonable inference, the very limited object being to ascertain whether any cognizable claim for relief is made out. * * * The above summarized allegations, in our view, state cognizable Sixth Amendment claims.

It is clear that a criminal defendant, regardless of wherewithal, is entitled to " 'the guiding hand of counsel at every step in the proceedings against him' " * * * The right attaches at arraignment (*see Rothgery v. Gillespie County* [p. 85]) and entails the presence of counsel at each subsequent "critical" stage of the proceedings. As is here relevant, arraignment itself must under the circumstances alleged be deemed a critical stage since, even if guilty pleas were not then elicited from the presently named plaintiffs, * * * plaintiffs' pretrial liberty interests were on that occasion regularly adjudicated, with most serious consequences, both direct and collateral, including the loss of employment and housing, and inability to support and care for particularly needy dependents. There is no question that "a bail hearing is a critical stage of the State's criminal process." * * * The cases cited by the dissent in which the allegedly consequential event at arraignment was the entry of a not guilty plea * * * do not stand for the proposition that counsel, as a general matter, is optional at arraignment. The cited cases rather stand for the very limited proposition that where it happens that what occurs at arraignment does not affect a defendant's ultimate adjudication, a defendant is not on the ground of nonrepresentation entitled to a reversal of his or her conviction. Plaintiffs here do not seek that relief.

Also "critical" for Sixth Amendment purposes is the period between arraignment and trial when a case must be factually developed and researched, decisions respecting grand jury testimony made, plea negotiations conducted, and pretrial motions filed. Indeed, it is clear that "to deprive a person of counsel during the period prior to trial may be more damaging than denial of counsel during the trial itself." * * * This complaint contains numerous plain allegations that in specific cases counsel simply was not provided at critical stages of the proceedings. * * * These allegations state a claim, not for ineffective assistance under *Strickland,* but for basic denial of the right to counsel under *Gideon.*

Similarly, while variously interpretable, the numerous allegations to the effect that counsel, although appointed, were uncommunicative, made virtually no efforts on their nominal clients' behalf during the very critical period subsequent to arraignment, and, indeed, waived important rights without authorization from their clients, may be reasonably understood to allege nonrepresentation rather than ineffective representation. Actual representation assumes a certain basic representational relationship. The allegations here, however, raise serious questions as to whether any such relationship may be really said to have existed between many of the plaintiffs and their putative attorneys and cumulatively may be understood to raise the distinct possibility that merely nominal attorney-client pairings occur in the subject counties with a fair degree of regularity, allegedly because of inadequate funding and staffing of indigent defense providers. * * *

While it may turn out after further factual development that what is really at issue is whether the representation afforded was effective—a subject not properly litigated in this civil action—at this juncture, construing the allegations before us as we must, in the light most favorable to plaintiffs, the complaint states a claim for constructive denial of the right to counsel by reason of insufficient compliance with the constitutional mandate of *Gideon.* The dissent's conclusion that these allegations assert only performance based claims, and not claims for nonrepresentation, seems to us premature. The picture which emerges from a fair and procedurally appropriate reading of the complaint is that defendants are with some regularity going unrepresented at arraignment and subsequent critical stages. * * *

Collateral preconviction claims seeking prospective relief for absolute, core denials of the right to the assistance of counsel cannot be understood to be incompatible with *Strickland.* These are not the sort of contextually sensitive claims that are typically involved when ineffectiveness is alleged. The basic, unadorned question presented by such claims where, as here, the defendant-claimants are poor, is whether the State has met its obligation to provide counsel, not whether under all the circumstances counsel's performance was inadequate or prejudicial. Indeed, in cases of outright denial of the right to counsel prejudice is presumed. *Strickland* itself, of course, recognizes the critical distinction [when it distinguished the "actual or constructive denial of counsel," as recognized in *United States* v. *Cronic* (see p. 142)]. * * * It is true, as the dissent points out, that claims, even within this category, have been most frequently litigated postconviction, but it does not follow from this circumstance that they are not cognizable apart from the postconviction context. * * *

Although defendants contend otherwise, we perceive no real danger that allowing these claims to proceed would impede the orderly progress of plaintiffs' underlying criminal actions. Those actions have, for the most part, been concluded, and we have, in any event, removed from the action the issue of ineffective assistance, thus eliminating any possibility that the collateral adjudication of generalized claims of ineffective assistance might be used to obtain relief from individual judgments of conviction. * * * Here we emphasize that our recognition that plaintiffs may have claims for constructive denial of counsel should not be viewed as a back door for what would be nonjusticiable assertions of ineffective assistance seeking remedies specifically addressed to attorney performance, such as uniform hiring, training and practice standards. * * *

* * * It is, of course, possible that a remedy in this action would necessitate the appropriation of funds and perhaps, particularly in a time of scarcity, some reordering of legislative priorities. But this does not amount to an argument upon which a court might be relieved of its essential obligation to provide a remedy for violation of a fundamental constitutional right. * * * We have consistently held that enforcement of a clear constitutional or statutory mandate is the proper work of the courts, and it would be odd if we made an exception in the case of a mandate as well-established and as essential to our institutional integrity as the one requiring the State to provide legal representation to indigent criminal defendants at all critical stages of the proceedings against them.

PIGOTT, J. (dissenting).

There is no doubt that there are inadequacies in the delivery of indigent legal services in this state, as pointed out by the New York State Commission on the Future of Indigent Defense Services, convened by former Chief Judge Kaye. I respectfully dissent, however, because, despite this, in my view, the complaint here fails to state a claim, either under the theories proffered by plaintiffs— ineffective assistance of counsel and deprivation of the right to counsel at a critical stage (arraignment)—or under the "constructive denial" theory read into the complaint by the majority.

The majority rightly rejects plaintiffs' ineffective assistance cause of action; such claims are limited to a case-by-case analysis and cannot be redressed in a civil proceeding. Rather than dismissing that claim, however, the majority replaces it with a "constructive denial" cause of action that, in my view, is nothing more than an ineffective assistance claim under another name. * * * In support of this ["constructive denial"] rationale, the majority relies on *United States v. Cronic*, which recognizes a "narrow exception" to *Strickland's* requirement that a defendant asserting an ineffective assistance of counsel claim must demonstrate a deficient performance and prejudice. In other words, *Cronic*, too, is an ineffective assistance of counsel case—decided on the same day as *Strickland*—but one that allows the courts to find a Sixth Amendment violation " 'without inquiring into counsel's actual performance or requiring the defendant to show the effect it had on the trial,' when 'circumstances [exist] that are so likely to prejudice the accused that the cost of litigating their effect in a particular case is unjustified.' " * * *

Constructive denial of counsel is a branch from the *Strickland* tree, with *Cronic* applying only when the appointed attorney's representation is so egregious that it's as if defendant had no attorney at all. Therefore, whether a defendant received ineffective assistance of counsel under *Strickland* or is entitled to a presumption of prejudice under *Cronic* is a determination that can only be made *after* the criminal proceeding has ended; neither approach lends itself to a proceeding like the one at bar where plaintiffs allege prospective violations of their Sixth Amendment rights.* * *

That is not to say that a claim of constructive denial could never apply to a class where the State effectively deprives indigent defendants of their right to counsel, only that the various claims asserted by plaintiffs here do not rise to that level. Here, plaintiffs' complaint raises basic ineffective assistance of counsel claims in the nature of *Strickland* (i.e., counsel was unresponsive, waived important rights, failed to appear at hearings, and was unprepared at court proceedings) and not the egregious type of conduct found in *Cronic*. Plaintiffs' mere lumping together of 20 generic ineffective assistance of counsel claims into one civil pleading does not ipso facto transform it into one alleging a systemic denial of the right to counsel.

Addressing plaintiffs' second theory—deprivation of the right to counsel at the arraignment—the majority posits that plaintiffs have stated a cognizable claim because 10 of them were arraigned without counsel, and eight of those remained in custody because they could not meet the bail that was set. * * * It is undisputed that a criminal defendant "requires the guiding hand of counsel at every step in the proceedings against him." But the majority's bare conclusion that any arraignment conducted without the presence of counsel renders the proceedings a violation of the Sixth Amendment flies in the face of reality. * * * [T]here is no allegation that the failure to have counsel at one's first court appearance had an adverse effect on the criminal proceedings. Where a criminal defendant is arraigned without the presence of counsel and pleads not guilty—or the court enters a not guilty plea on his behalf—there is no Sixth Amendment violation. The explanation as to why this is so is simple: "Under New York law, a defendant suffers no ... prejudice [by the imposition of a not guilty plea on arraignment without benefit of counsel], for whatever counsel could have done upon arraignment on defendant's behalf, counsel were free to do thereafter. There is nothing in New York law which in any way prevents counsel's later taking advantage of every opportunity or defense which was originally available to a defendant upon his initial arraignment." *People v. Combs*, 19 A.D.2d 639 (1963). * * *

As pleaded, none of the 10 plaintiffs arraigned without counsel entered guilty pleas and, indeed, in compliance with the strictures of CPL 180.10, all met with counsel shortly after the arraignment. Nor is there any claim that the absence of counsel prejudiced these plaintiffs. * * * [But] the majority implies that the complaint pleads a *Gideon* violation because certain of the plaintiffs were not represented when the court arranged for the imposition of bail at the arraignment. Quite often this initial appearance inures to the benefit of defendant who may be released on his own recognizance or on manageable bail within hours of arrest. The only substantive allegations plaintiffs make relative to bail is that assigned counsel failed to advocate for lower bail at the arraignment or move for a bail reduction post-arraignment. If anything, the complaint alleges a claim for ineffective assistance of counsel under the federal or state standard, but the majority has rejected such a claim in this litigation.

JUDGES CIPARICK, GRAFFEO and JONES concur with CHIEF JUDGE LIPPMAN; JUDGE PIGOTT dissents and votes to affirm in a separate opinion in which JUDGES READ and SMITH concur.

NOTES AND QUESTIONS

1. Strickland and systemic challenges. State courts have divided as to whether a pre-conviction civil challenge to systemic deficiencies can be grounded on the Sixth Amendment right to effective representation by counsel. *Hurrel-Harring* sets forth one line of reasoning commonly advanced in rejecting such challenges. Other courts reach the same result by looking to the standard prerequisites for injunctive relief—a risk of substantial and immediate irreparable injury and no adequate remedy at law. They acknowledge that a risk of injury (i.e., ineffective assistance by counsel) can be established pre-litigation, and therefore *Strickland's* requirement of a showing of actual prejudice is not a ban. However, the availability of post conviction relief under *Strickland* establishes that the injury is not irreparable and there is an adequate remedy at law. See CRIMPROC § 11.8(c).

Courts sustaining pre-conviction civil challenges argue that *Strickland* and *Cronic* are rulings limited to the postconviction context. They conclude that sufficient systemic deficiencies may present the prerequisites of irreparable injury and inadequate legal remedies. Consider, e.g., the reasoning of the court majority in DUNCAN v. STATE, 284 Mich.App. 246, 774 N.W.2d 89 (2009), order denying summary disposition affirmed, 2010 WL 5186037 (2010), reconsideration denied, 488 Mich. 906, 791 N.W.2d 713 (2010):

"A simple hypothetical illustrates the inappropriateness of applying, solely, the two-part *Strickland* test and in taking a position that the only avenue of relief is a criminal appeal. Imagine that, in 100 percent of indigent criminal cases being handled by court-appointed counsel, it could be proven that the proceedings were continuously infected with instances of deficient performance by counsel, yet the trial verdicts were all deemed reliable, assuming all cases went to trial. * * * In our scenario, under defendants' and the dissent's reasoning, court intervention in a class action suit such as the one filed here would not be permitted on justiciability grounds despite the constitutionally egregious circumstances. This is akin to taking a position that indigent defendants who are ostensibly guilty are unworthy or not deserving of counsel who will perform at or above an objective standard of reasonableness. * * * Even though a criminal appeal may occasionally result in a new trial, it has no bearing on eradication of continuing systemic constitutional deficiencies. Thus, contrary to defendants' argument and the dissent's position, there is no adequate legal remedy for the harm that plaintiffs are attempting to prevent.

"We additionally find that defendants' and the dissent's position ignores the reality that harm can take many shapes and forms. Consistently with the concept of prejudice as employed in criminal appeals we would agree that justiciable injury or harm is certainly indicated by a showing that there existed a reasonable probability that, but for an error by counsel, the result of a criminal proceeding would have been different. But injury or harm also occurs when there are instances of deficient performance by counsel at critical stages in the criminal proceedings that are detrimental to an indigent defendant in some relevant and meaningful fashion, even without neatly wrapping the justiciable harm around a verdict and trial. Such harm arises, for example, when there is an unnecessarily prolonged pretrial detention, a failure to file a dispositive motion, entry of a factually unwarranted guilty plea, or a legally unacceptable pretrial delay. And as indicated earlier in this opinion, simply being deprived of the constitutional right to effective representation at a critical stage in the proceedings, in and of itself, gives rise to harm."

2. *Compensation for appointed attorneys.* Does the reasoning of *Hurrel-Harrington* or rulings allowing systemic challenges based on likely ineffective representation extend to challenging fee caps and hourly rates for appointed attorneys? Successful challenges often have been based on judicial authority other than fulfilling the command of the Sixth Amendment. See e.g., *State v. Lynch*, 796 P.2d 1150 (1990) (relying on the court's "constitutional responsibilities relating to the managerial and superintending control of the district courts"). As to the argument that totally inadequate compensation will lead to ineffective representation, consider the response of *Ex Parte Grayson*, 479 So.2d 76 (Ala. 1985) (rejecting a challenge to a $1000 cap for a capital case): "These contentions are made on the premise that lawyers will not provide effective assistance unless paid a certain amount of money. But the legal profession requires its members to give their best efforts in 'advancing the undivided interests of [their] client[s].' * * * We reaffirm this belief that attorneys appointed to defend capital clients will serve them as directed by their consciences and the ethical rules enforced by the state bar association."

How different is the challenge that fees are so low that few lawyers will accept appointments, resulting in significant delays in providing appointed counsel? *Lavallee v. Justices in the Hampden Superior Court*, 442 Mass. 228, 812 N.E.2d 895 (2004), concluded that, in such a situation, there was a high likelihood that the petitioners would not receive the effective assistance of counsel (in part because of lost opportunities for prompt pretrial investigation). Since the defendants, being without counsel, were in no position to show that they were being prejudiced, the court had an obligation to fashion prospective protection of the constitutional right, avoiding a harm that would be "irremediable . . . if not corrected." Accordingly, it would order "the Attorney General to appear before the single justice to explain (1) why any petitioner held in lieu of bail for more than seven days without counsel should not be ordered released from confinement forthwith; and (2) why, with respect to any petitioner facing a felony charge for more than thirty days without counsel, * * * an order should not issue dismissing all such charges without prejudice until counsel is made available to provide representation to that petitioner."

3. *Lawyer withdrawal.* If the public defenders in *Hurrel-Harring* actually were representing defendants under the circumstances alleged, did they have an ethical duty to withdraw? In 2006, the ABA Standing Committee on Ethics and Professional Responsibility issued Formal Ethics Opinion No. 06–441, advising lawyers who represent indigents in criminal cases to refuse new cases or withdraw from current cases when excessive caseloads prevented them from providing "competent and diligent representation" to their clients. The opinion relied not only on the general ethical obligation to provide such representation, but also on rules imposing specific duties unlikely to be fulfilled where caseloads are excessive (e.g., keeping the client reasonably informed). Public defender offices in several states have been allowed to refuse to carry their caseload beyond a certain limit (typically one set by a state commission, see Note 6, p. 78).

THE RIGHT TO THE ASSISTANCE OF EXPERTS

1. *The Ake ruling.* In AKE v. OKLAHOMA, 470 U.S. 68 (1985), the defendant Ake, an indigent, was charged with first-degree murder. At his arraignment, Ake's behavior was so bizarre that the trial judge ordered that he be examined by a psychiatrist. The examining psychiatrist found Ake incompetent to stand trial, but Ake later was found to be competent to stand trial as long as he continued to be sedated with an antipsychotic drug. Ake's attorney informed the court that he would raise an insanity defense, but his motion for a psychiatric evaluation at state expense was denied. The jury rejected the insanity defense and Ake was convicted of first-degree murder. At the capital sentencing proceeding, the state asked for the death penalty, relying on a psychiatrist's testimony to establish the likelihood of Ake's future dangerousness. Ake had no expert witness to rebut this testimony or to give evidence in mitigation of his punishment, and he was sentenced to death. The Supreme Court (8–1) reversed. The majority opinion, per Marshall, J., reasoned:

"This Court has long recognized that when a State brings its judicial power to bear on an indigent defendant in a criminal proceeding, it must take steps to assure that the defendant has a fair opportunity to present his defense. This elementary principle, grounded in significant part in the Fourteenth Amendment's due process guarantee of fundamental fairness, derives from the belief that justice cannot be equal where, simply as a result of his poverty, a defendant is denied the opportunity to participate meaningfully in a judicial proceeding in which his liberty is at stake. * * * [A] criminal trial is fundamentally unfair if the State proceeds against an individual defendant without making certain that he has access to the raw materials integral to the building of an effective defense. Thus, while the Court has not held that a State must purchase for the indigent defendant all the assistance that his wealthier counterpart might buy, see *Ross v. Moffitt* [p. 164], it has often reaffirmed that fundamental fairness entitles indigent defendants to 'an adequate opportunity to present their claims fairly within the adversary system,' id. To implement this principle, we have focused on identifying the 'basic tools of an adequate defense or appeal,' and we have required that such tools be provided to those defendants who cannot afford to pay for them.

"[W]ithout the assistance of a psychiatrist to conduct a professional examination on issues relevant to the defense, to help determine whether the insanity defense is viable to present testimony, and to assist in preparing the cross-examination of a State's psychiatric witnesses, the risk of an inaccurate resolution of sanity issues is extremely high. With such assistance, the defendant is fairly able to present at least enough information to the jury, in a meaningful manner, as to permit it to make a sensible determination.

"A defendant's mental condition is not necessarily at issue in every criminal proceeding, however, and it is unlikely that psychiatric assistance of the kind we have described would be of probable value in cases where it is not. The risk of error, from denial of such assistance * * * is most predictably at its height when the defendant's mental condition is seriously in question. When the defendant is able to make an ex parte threshold showing to the trial court that his sanity is likely to be a significant factor in his defense, the need for the assistance of a psychiatrist is readily apparent. It is in such cases that a defense may be devastated by the absence of a psychiatric examination and testimony; with such assistance, the defendant might have a reasonable chance of success. In such a circumstance, where the potential accuracy of the jury's determination is so dramatically enhanced, and where the interests of the individual and the State in an accurate proceeding are substantial, the State's interest in its fisc must yield.

"[This] is not to say, of course, that the indigent defendant has a constitutional right to choose a psychiatrist of his personal liking or to receive funds to hire his own. Our concern is that the indigent defendant have access to a competent psychiatrist for the purpose we have discussed, and as in the case of provision of counsel we leave to the State the decision on how to implement this right.

"Ake also was denied the means of presenting evidence to rebut the State's evidence of his future dangerousness. The foregoing discussion compels a similar conclusion in the context of a capital sentencing proceeding, when the State presents psychiatric evidence of the defendant's future dangerousness. * * *

[W]here the consequence of error is so great, the relevance of responsive psychiatric testimony so evident, and the burden on the State so slim, due process requires access to a psychiatric examination on relevant issues, to the testimony of the psychiatrist, and to assistance in preparation at the sentencing phase."

2. *The Sixth Amendment vs. Fourteenth Amendment due process.* Although one might maintain that a right to a court-appointed psychiatrist under certain circumstances is implicit in the right to counsel or implements or effectuates that right, *Ake* is not written that way. It is a free-standing procedural due process decision (Note 4, p. 32)—one that applies "the Fourteenth Amendment's due process guarantee of fundamental fairness." (The *Ake* Court added in a footnote: "Because we conclude that the Due Process Clause guaranteed to Ake the assistance he requested and was denied, we have no occasion to consider the applicability of the Equal Protection Clause, or the Sixth Amendment, in this context.")

Does the reliance on due process clause provide a stronger foundation for limiting the scope of the "fair opportunity" principle? Does it provide a barrier against extension beyond experts to encompass the general resources often utilized by a defense attorney, including supporting personnel, and, in turn, to evaluating such factors as caseloads and compensation? Consider A.B.A. Standards § 5–1.4(a) (2d ed., 1980) (commentary): "Quality legal representation, * * * cannot be rendered either by defenders or by assigned counsel unless the lawyers have available for their use adequate supporting services. These [include] expert witnesses * * *, personnel skilled in social work and related disciplines to provide assistance at pretrial release hearings and at sentencing, and trained investigators to interview witnesses and to assemble demonstrative evidence. * * * If the defense attorney must personally conduct factual investigations, the financial cost to the justice system is likely to be greater. Moreover, when an attorney personally interviews witnesses, [the attorney] may be placed in the untenable position of either taking the stand to challenge their credibility if their testimony conflicts with statements previously given or withdrawing from the case."

3. *Other basic tools.* In *Caldwell v. Mississippi*, 472 U.S. 320 (1985), the Court found it unnecessary to rule on the extension of *Ake*. The defendant there argued that due process had been denied when the trial judge refused to grant appointed counsel's request for "the appointment of a criminal investigator, a fingerprint expert, and a ballistics expert." The Court responded (in a footnote): "Given that petitioner offered little more than undeveloped assertions that the requested assistance would be beneficial, we find no deprivation of due process in the trial judge's decision. Cf. *Ake v. Oklahoma*, 470 U.S. 68, 82–83 (1985) (discussing showing that would entitle defendant to psychiatric assistance as matter of federal constitutional law). We therefore have no need to determine as a matter of federal constitutional law what if any showing would have entitled a defendant to assistance of the type here sought."

Only a handful of lower courts have concluded that psychiatric expertise is so unique that the due process reasoning of *Ake* should not extend to other assistance. Most courts addressing the issue have concluded that due process may require appointment of other types of scientific experts and some have suggested that providing defense investigators with special expertise might also be required. These courts uniformly stress that the defense showing of need must set forth in detail "what assistance is being requested and why it is needed" (and not all will permit that filing to be made ex parte[a]). They vary considerably, however, in

---

a. Some jurisdictions give the judge discretion to choose between an ex parte proceeding and an adversary proceeding in which the prosecution may participate, with the judge also determining how much information the prosecutor will be given as to the defense's explanation of why its

describing the level of need that must be met by this particularized showing—both as to the importance of the issue on which the expert's assistance is sought and as to the need for an expert's assistance in contesting that issue. In particular, where the scientific methodology is well established and its application is viewed as largely mechanical, the defense often carries a special burden in convincing the court that a defense expert might assist in a successful challenge to the state's evidence. Fundamental fairness, lower courts have noted, does not demand that the defense be given an offsetting expert whenever the prosecution will use an expert in establishing a critical element of its case.

4. *Local law alternatives.* In many jurisdictions, expert assistance can be obtained without relying on the constitutional right recognized in *Ake.* Many jurisdiction have statutes granting indigent defendants funding for a broad range of experts under standards less rigorous than the constitutional standards discussed above. The federal statute, for example, employs a "private attorney standard, which directs the district court to authorize defense services under circumstances in which a reasonable attorney would engage such services for a client having the independent means to pay." CRIMPROC § 11.2(e). Where a public defender office's budget includes an allocation for retaining experts, there will be no need to use the constitutional or statutory right if that allocation is sufficient to cover all cases in which the defender office desires the assistance of experts.

5. *Reversible error.* Upon finding that the defendant had made a showing that "entitled [him] to the assistance of a psychiatrist and that the denial of that assistance deprived him of due process," the *Ake* Court reversed the defendant's conviction. The Court did not stop to examine how well the defense has done at trial and in the sentencing proceeding without that assistance. An occasional lower court ruling has viewed that performance as relevant to the conclusion that fundamental fairness was denied. See e.g., *Conklin v. Schofield*, 366 F.3d 1191 (11th Cir.2004) (trial court acted unreasonably in denying indigent's motion for funds for expert assistance after the defense made an appropriate showing, but fundamental fairness was not denied since defense expert's testimony would have undermined state's position that stab wounds occurred before death, but prosecution expert conceded on cross-examination that the wounds could have been inflicted shortly after death, and defense expert's additional support "would not have likely altered the jury's decision"). Most courts, however, reason that the due process violation occurs when the court denies assistance notwithstanding a defense showing that meets the *Ake* prerequisites. On the other hand, many of those courts also have concluded that the violation is subject to a state showing of "harmless error," although others disagree. See CRIMPROC § 27.6(c) at fn. 143 (courts rejecting harmless error view the violation as "structural" since it "eliminates a basic tool of an adequate defense," while others view it as akin to errors of the improper admission or exclusion of evidence, which are subject to harmless error analysis).

SECTION 5. CONFLICTS OF INTEREST

A. POTENTIAL CONFLICTS AND THE DUTY TO INQUIRE

1. *Range of Conflicts.* The Supreme Court first held, in *Glasser v. United States*, 315 U.S. 60 (1942), that the right to the assistance of counsel is not

---

case presents the need for an expert (and how it will use the expert). See CRIMPROC § 11.2(e). Of course, even if the funding for an expert is granted ex parte, the prosecutor will be made aware of the defense's use of an expert if that expert must examine physical evidence in the possession of the state. As to the possible prosecution discovery of the report of an expert that the defense will not use at trial, see Note 4, p. 1228.

satisfied by a counsel whose actions are influenced by a conflict of interest. The conflict in *Glasser* arose out of an attorney's joint representation of codefendants in the same trial. While that is the paradigm conflict setting, many other settings may also produce an "actual conflict of interest"—i.e., a situation in which action or inaction by defense counsel which would be favorable to the defendant would also be contrary to an obligation that counsel owes to another person or to counsel's self-interest. Those other settings include: (1) defense counsel simultaneously representing another defendant who will be tried separately for the same offense (either because charged separately or jointly charged and granted a severance); (2) defense counsel has previously represented, or is currently representing, in another matter or the same matter, a victim of the alleged offense; (3) defense counsel has previously represented, or is currently representing, in another matter or the same matter, a likely prosecution witness; (4) a third party with some interest in the case is paying defense counsel's fee; (5) a fee arrangement that creates a possible conflict between counsel's financial interests and the defendant's interests (e.g., a compensation agreement under which counsel has an interest in royalties received from a movie or book relating to the trial); (6) counsel faces a potential liability that might be impacted by choices made in representing the defendant, e.g., where counsel (i) was involved in the alleged crime and fears possible criminal prosecution, (ii) is under investigation or being actively prosecuted by the same prosecutor's office as to another matter, or (iii) is facing possible criminal or disciplinary consequences as a result of questionable behavior in representing the defendant; (7) counsel has delivered, or has an obligation to deliver, to the police physical evidence that can be used against the defendant; and (8) counsel is to be called as a prosecution witness.[a]

2. *Conflicts and professional responsibility standards.* While the various settings noted above each carry a significant potential for presenting an actual conflict in the course of representation, that result is not inevitable—even in the case of joint representation of codefendants in the same trial. Moreover, if that actual conflict should arise, ABA's Model Rules of Professional Conduct, Rule 1.7 provides a route for continued representation; where a defense counsel has another client whose interests are "directly adverse" to the defendant, the lawyer may nonetheless represent the defendant if the lawyer "reasonably believes that [he or she] will be able to provide competent and diligent representation to each affected client," and each client consents after full disclosure. So too, Rule 1.8 states that a lawyer is not prohibited from representing a client where the representation of that client "will be materially limited by the lawyer's responsibilities to another client, a former client, * * * or by a personal interest of the lawyer" if the lawyer believes the representation will be competent and diligent and there is adequate consultation and consent.

The profession's willingness to tolerate arrangements that create a high potential for dividing the attorney's loyalty is not based simply upon the fact that

---

a. In many of the above situations, conflicts also arise where the potentially conflicting representation is by another attorney in the same law firm as the defendant's counsel. Under ethics codes, conflicts generally are vicariously imputed to all members of a law firm. While the Supreme Court has not ruled directly on this approach, *Burger v. Kemp* (Note 2, p. 201) "assumed without deciding that two law partners are considered as one attorney" in analyzing the conflict potential of representing codefendants. Some states treat the lawyers in a public defender office in much the same manner. Many other jurisdictions, however, hold the "same firm" principle generally inapplicable to public defenders, in part because "the salaried government employee does not have the financial interest in the success of the departmental representation that is inherent in private practice." In these jurisdictions, where the defender office's potential conflict stems from confidential information received from a past client now a prosecution witness, the common solution is to utilize an internal ethical wall of separation which keeps that information away from the attorney representing the defendant. That device tends not to be viewed as sufficient, however, as to codefendants. See Note 3, infra.

those arrangements may not, in the end, result in an actual conflict. Its decision not to absolutely prohibit such arrangements is also based in part on the potential value of many of these arrangements to the client. Initially, they may permit the client to obtain the services of the one lawyer that he wants to represent him. Some defendants put their trust in a particular lawyer and would want that lawyer even though she may have previously represented one of the prosecution's witnesses or even the victim. Some would prefer a privately retained lawyer and can afford one only if their employer, a codefendant, or some other interested person will pay that lawyer. Joint representation of codefendants, in particular, may have strategic advantages. Thus the Supreme Court has noted: "Joint representation is a means of ensuring against reciprocal recrimination. A common defense often gives strength against a common attack." Holloway v. Arkansas, Note 5, infra.

3. *Prohibiting representation in potential-conflict situations.* As one might anticipate, neither courts nor legislatures have been willing to adopt prophylactic rules that ban defense arrangements which create a potential conflict where the profession has been unwilling to do so in its regulations. See CRIM-PROC § 11.9(b) (describing state law). In many jurisdictions, public defender offices are prohibited from representing multiple defendants charged with the same offense (typically by an internal policy, with judicial approval). No jurisdiction, however, has applied a similar absolute prohibition to joint representation by retained counsel. A few states have taken a partial step in this direction by viewing joint representation of codefendants as "inherently prejudicial," and therefore allowed only with an appropriate waiver by each defendant. Several other jurisdictions require a judicial inquiry when jointly charged defendants are represented by the same attorney, and as discussed infra (see Note 4, and *Wheat v. United States*), that inquiry may lead to a judicial preclusion of joint representation even where each defendant waives—but disqualification is not mandated.

4. *Non-constitutional requirements of judicial inquiry.* Federal Rule 44 requires the trial court to conduct an inquiry whenever defendants have been jointly charged under Rule 8(b) or joined for trial under Rule 13 and are represented by "the same counsel or counsel who are associated in the practice of law." The trial court is directed to "promptly inquire about the propriety of the joint representation," and to "personally advise each defendant of the right to the effective assistance of counsel, including separate representation." Moreover, "unless there is good cause to believe that no conflict of interest is likely to arise," the trial court "must take appropriate measures to protect each defendant's right to counsel." Several states impose similar obligations on their trial courts. The Advisory Committee Notes to Rule 44(c) clearly indicates that the failure to comply with Rule 44(c) should not in itself constitute a per se reversible error. Accordingly, on review after a conviction, appellate courts will look to whether the reversal is required under the Sixth Amendment. See Pt. B infra.

5. *The initial recognition of a constitutional duty of inquiry.* The Supreme Court first recognized a constitutional duty to inquire into a potential conflict in HOLLOWAY v. ARKANSAS, 435 U.S. 475 (1978). In that case, an appointed counsel representing three codefendants in a joint trial requested pretrial that the trial court appoint separate counsel for each defendant (counsel noting that confidential information revealed to him by the different defendants could place him in an actual conflict in addressing their testimony). The trial court denied the request without conducting an inquiry, and when the issue arose again, directed counsel to have each defendant give unguided direct testimony. The Supreme Court majority (per Burger, C.J.) reversed the convictions of all three defendants. *Glasser* (Note 1 supra), the majority noted, had established that "joint representation * * * is not per se violative of constitutional guarantees of effective counsel," and subsequent lower court rulings on joint representation had diverged as to: (1) what showing was needed postconviction to establish that an actual conflict had existed and had resulted in a denial of effective assistance; and (2) "the scope and nature of the affirmative duty of the trial judge to assure that criminal defendants are not deprived of their right to the effective assistance of counsel by joint representation of conflicting interests." However, there was no need here "to resolve these two issues," as this case presented a situation in which trial counsel's motion pretrial had given the trial court notice of the "probable risk of a conflict of interests." In that setting, the Court concluded, the judge's inadequate response was itself grounds for reversal of the convictions. It noted: "The judge * * * failed either to appoint separate counsel or to take adequate steps to ascertain whether the risk was too remote to warrant separate counsel. We hold that the failure, in the face of the representations made by counsel weeks before trial and again before the jury was impaneled, deprived petitioners of the guarantee of 'assistance of counsel.' "

The three dissenters in *Holloway* agreed that under the special circumstances presented there, the trial court "should have held an appropriate hearing on defense motion," but argued that this failure should do no more than shift to the prosecution the burden of showing the "improbability of conflict or prejudice." The majority rejected this approach, noting that Glasser had held that "whenever a trial court improperly requires joint representation over timely objection reversal is automatic" (see fn. c, p. 193).

Two years after *Holloway*, in *Cuyler v. Sullivan*, the Court addressed the two issues that *Holloway* found unnecessary to decide. Its response on the first issue, establishing a postconviction review standard where there was no duty to inquire, is discussed in *Mickens v. Taylor* (p. 191). Its response on the duty to inquire outside of the special situation presented in *Holloway* is discussed in Note 6 below.

6. *Defining the scope of the duty.* In CUYLER v. SULLIVAN,[b] 446 U.S. 335 (1980), defendant Sullivan had been indicted, along with two codefendants, for the first degree murders of two victims. Sullivan accepted representation from the two lawyers retained by his codefendants because he could not afford to retain a lawyer. Sullivan came to trial first and counsel challenged the prosecution's case, but did not put on any defense evidence. The jury found Sullivan guilty and set his sentence at life imprisonment. Sullivan's two codefendants were later acquitted in separate trials. Sullivan then sought collateral relief under state law, raising for the first time a claim that his counsel had represented conflicting interests. Although the Third Circuit, on federal habeas review, held that there had been an actual conflict of interest, the Supreme Court initially considered the contention that Sullivan was entitled to a reversal of his conviction, without examining whether an actual conflict had occurred, because, as in *Holloway*, the trial court had violated a constitutional duty to conduct an inquiry into the possibility of a conflict. The Court majority (per Powell, J.) rejected that contention:

"*Holloway* requires state trial courts to investigate timely [defense counsel] objections to multiple representation. But nothing in our precedents suggests that the Sixth Amendment requires state courts themselves to initiate inquiries into the propriety of multiple representation in every case. Defense counsel have an ethical obligation to avoid conflicting representations and to advise the court promptly when a conflict of interest arises during the course of trial. Absent special circumstances, therefore, trial courts may assume either that multiple

---

b. Since appellant Cuyler was the prison warden, also involved in many other reported cases, the case is often referred to as *Sullivan*, although some judges prefer *Cuyler*. See e.g., the different opinions in *Mickens v. Taylor,* infra.

representation entails no conflict or that the lawyer and his clients knowingly accept such risk of conflict as may exist. Indeed, as the Court noted in *Holloway,* trial courts necessarily rely in large measure upon the good faith and good judgment of defense counsel. 'An attorney representing two defendants in a criminal matter is in the best position professionally and ethically to determine when a conflict of interests exists or will probably develop at trial.' Id. Unless the trial court knows or reasonably should know that a particular conflict exists, the court need not initiate an inquiry.

"Nothing in the circumstances of this case indicates that the trial court had a duty to inquire whether there was a conflict of interest. The provision of separate trials for Sullivan and his codefendants significantly reduced the potential for a divergence in their interests. No participant in Sullivan's trial ever objected to the multiple representation. [Counsel's] opening argument for Sullivan outlined a defense compatible with the view that none of the defendants was connected with the murders. The opening arguments also suggested that counsel was not afraid to call witnesses whose testimony might be needed at the trials of Sullivan's codefendants. Finally counsel's critical decision to rest Sullivan's defense was on its face a reasonable tactical response to the weakness of the circumstantial evidence presented by the prosecutor. On these facts, we conclude that the Sixth Amendment imposed upon the trial court no affirmative duty to inquire into the propriety of multiple representation."

Justices Brennan and Marshall, in separate concurring opinions, disagreed with the Court's analysis on this issue. Justice Brennan noted: "[As the Court observes], 'a possible conflict inheres in almost every instance of multiple representation.' Therefore, upon discovery of joint representation, the duty of the trial court is to ensure that the defendants have not unwittingly given up their constitutional right to effective counsel. * * * [T]he trial court cannot safely assume that silence indicates a knowledgeable choice to proceed jointly. The court must at least affirmatively advise the defendants that joint representation creates potential hazards which the defendants should consider before proceeding with the representation. * * * *"

7. ***The "reasonably should know" standard.*** What circumstance present a situation in which the trial court "reasonably should know" that a conflict exists and therefore conduct an inquiry? In light of *Sullivan's* explanation of why the multiple representation presented there did not present such a situation, would an inquiry be required where counsel representing codefendants did not advise the court of any conflict, but began to present a united defense that clearly would favor one defendant over the other? See State v. Weese, 424 A.2d 705 (Me.1981) (united defense favored father over son). CRIMPROC. § 11.9(b) notes that the "reasonably should know" standard generally has been applied only to situations in which "actual conflicts were obvious," such as "where the record established that the defense counsel had previously represented a [prosecution] witness in connection with the same or a related matter [or] that the defense counsel was facing a disciplinary complaint in connection to this case." The courts have held it not to apply "where indicators were ambiguous, or suggested no more than a potential conflict." Is this approach consistent with the Supreme Court's ruling in *Wood v. Georgia,* Note 8 infra? Consider also *Mickens v. Taylor,* p. 191.

8. Although the Court's ruling was far from clear, *Wood v. Georgia,* 450 U.S. 261 (1981), appeared to conclude that the trial court reasonably should have known of a conflict (and the case was so interpreted in the subsequent decision of *Mickens v. Taylor,* p. 191). The Supreme Court granted certiorari in *Wood* to determine whether a state could constitutionally revoke the probation of defendants who were unable to pay fines imposed for a previous conviction. The case was remanded, however, for an evidentiary hearing on a conflict issue raised by the Court sua sponte. The defendants had been charged with an offense committed in the course of their employment and their counsel had been provided by their employer. They had been sentenced to pay substantial fines on the assumption that the employer would provide them with the necessary funds. When the employer refused to give them the funds, counsel did not immediately move for modification of the fines or ask for leniency. Instead, he pressed the argument that a probation revocation for the failure to pay fines that were beyond a defendant's means was unconstitutional, a contention which, if accepted, would work to the long range benefit of the employer. The Supreme Court (per Powell, J.) noted that the record of the revocation proceedings was not sufficiently complete for it to determine whether a conflict actually existed. "Nevertheless," it noted, "the record does demonstrate that the possibility of a conflict of interest was sufficiently apparent at the time of the revocation hearing to impose upon the [state] court a duty to inquire further." All of the relevant facts relating to the employer's retention of counsel, the employer's failure to pay the fines, and "counsel's insistence upon pressing a constitutional attack" were known to the state court. Moreover, "any doubt as to whether th[at] court should have been aware of the problem [was] dispelled by the fact that the [prosecutor] had raised the conflict problem."

9. Scope of the inquiry. Appellate courts note that where an inquiry is required under *Sullivan*, that inquiry should not be "perfunctory," but should include "probing and specific questions" regarding the apparent conflict. They also note, however, that the trial court is "entitled to rely on the attorney's representations" as to the "underlying facts." If the trial court determines that a potential or actual conflict exists, but disqualification is not needed (see pt. C), it has an obligation to explain the situation to the defendant and obtain a waiver. See CRIMPROC § 11.9(b). As to waivers, see Note 4, p. 208.

B. POSTCONVICTION REVIEW
MICKENS v. TAYLOR
535 U.S. 162, 122 S.Ct. 1237, 152 L.Ed.2d 291 (2002).

JUSTICE SCALIA delivered the opinion of the Court.

The question presented in this case is what a defendant must show in order to demonstrate a Sixth Amendment violation where the trial court fails to inquire into a potential conflict of interest about which it knew or reasonably should have known.

I

[A Virginia jury convicted Mickens of the murder and sexual assault of Timothy Hall and sentenced him to death. On a federal habeas corpus challenge to the conviction, Mickens alleged that he was denied the effective assistance of counsel because one of his court-appointed trial attorneys, Bryan Saunders, had been representing the murder victim Hall on assault and concealed weapons charges prior to Hall's death. The same juvenile court judge who had dismissed the charges against Hall upon his death three weeks later appointed Sanders to represent Mickens. Sanders had not disclosed his prior representation of Hall to the trial judge, his co-counsel, or Mickens.]

[Relying on *Cuyler v. Sullivan* [Note 6, p. 189], the U.S. Court of Appeals for the Fourth Circuit, sitting en banc, held that a defendant must show "both an actual conflict of interest and an adverse effect even if the trial court failed to inquire into a potential conflict about which it reasonably should have known."

Concluding that Mickens had not demonstrated an adverse effect, the court affirmed the denial of habeas relief.]

II

* * * As a general matter, a defendant alleging a Sixth Amendment violation must demonstrate "a reasonable probability that, but for counsel's unprofessional errors, the result of the proceeding would have been different." *Strickland.* There is an exception to this general rule. We have spared the defendant the need of showing probable effect upon the outcome, and have simply presumed such effect, where assistance of counsel has been denied entirely or during a critical stage of the proceeding. When that has occurred, the likelihood that the verdict is unreliable is so high that a case-by-case inquiry is unnecessary. But only in "circumstances of that magnitude" do we forgo individual inquiry into whether counsel's inadequate performance undermined the reliability of the verdict.

We have held in several cases that "circumstances of that magnitude" may also arise when the defendant's attorney actively represented conflicting interests. The nub of the question before us is whether the principle established by these cases provides an exception to the general rule of *Strickland* under the circumstances of the present case. To answer that question, we must examine those cases in some detail.[1]

Holloway [Note 5, p. 188] * * * creates an automatic reversal rule only where defense counsel is forced to represent codefendants over his timely objection, unless the trial court has determined that there is no conflict. * * * In *Sullivan,* the respondent was one of three defendants * * * tried separately, represented by the same counsel. Neither counsel nor anyone else objected to the multiple representation, and counsel's opening argument at Sullivan's trial suggested that the interests of the defendants were aligned. We declined to extend *Holloway*'s automatic reversal rule to this situation, and held that, absent objection, a defendant must demonstrate that "a conflict of interest actually affected the adequacy of his representation." In addition to describing the defendant's burden of proof, *Sullivan* addressed separately a trial court's duty to inquire into the propriety of a multiple representation, construing *Holloway* to require inquiry only when "the trial court knows or reasonably should know that a particular conflict exists"[2]—which is not to be confused with when the trial court is aware of a vague, unspecified possibility of conflict, such as that which "inheres in almost every instance of multiple representation." In *Sullivan,* no "special circumstances" triggered the trial court's duty to inquire.

---

1.   * * * [Those cases,] *Holloway, Sullivan,* and *Wood,* establish the framework that they do precisely because that framework is thought to identify the situations in which the conviction will reasonably not be regarded as fundamentally fair. We believe it eminently performs that function in the case at hand, and that Justice Breyer is mistaken to think otherwise. But if he does think otherwise, a proper regard for the judicial function—and especially for the function of this Court, which must lay down rules that can be followed in the innumerable cases we are unable to review—would counsel that he propose some other "sensible and coherent framework," rather than merely saying that prior representation of the victim, plus the capital nature of the case, plus judicial appointment of the counsel, strikes him as producing a result that will not be regarded as fundamentally fair. This is not a rule of law but expression of an ad hoc "fairness" judgment (with which we disagree).

2.   In order to circumvent *Sullivan*'s clear language, Justice Stevens suggests that a trial court must scrutinize representation by appointed counsel more closely than representation by retained counsel. But we have already rejected the notion that the Sixth Amendment draws such a distinction. "A proper respect for the Sixth Amendment disarms [the] contention that defendants who retain their own lawyers are entitled to less protection than defendants for whom the State appoints counsel. [The] vital guarantee of the Sixth Amendment would stand for little if the often uninformed decision to retain a particular lawyer could reduce or forfeit the defendant's entitlement to constitutional protection." *Cuyler v. Sullivan.* [Note 2, p. 131]

Finally, in *Wood v. Georgia* [Note 8, p. 190], [we concluded that] the possibility that counsel was actively representing the conflicting interests of employers and defendants "was sufficiently apparent at the time of the revocation hearing to impose upon the court a duty to inquire further." Because "[o]n the record before us, we [could not] be sure whether counsel was influenced in his basic strategic decisions by the interests of the employer who hired him," we remanded for the trial court "to determine whether the conflict of interest that this record strongly suggests actually existed."

Petitioner argues that the remand instruction in *Wood* established an "unambiguous rule" that where the trial judge neglects a duty to inquire into a potential conflict, the defendant, to obtain reversal of the judgment, need only show that his lawyer was subject to a conflict of interest, and need not show that the conflict adversely affected counsel's performance.[3] He relies upon the language in the remand instruction directing the trial court to grant a new revocation hearing if it determines that "an actual conflict of interest existed," without requiring a further determination that the conflict adversely affected counsel's performance. As used in the remand instruction, however, we think "an actual conflict of interest" meant precisely a conflict *that affected counsel's performance*—as opposed to a mere theoretical division of loyalties. It was shorthand for the statement in *Sullivan* that "a defendant who shows that a conflict of interest *actually affected the adequacy of his representation* need not demonstrate prejudice in order to obtain relief" (emphasis added).[c]

Petitioner's proposed rule of automatic reversal when there existed a conflict that did not affect counsel's performance, but the trial judge failed to make the *Sullivan*-mandated inquiry, makes little policy sense. As discussed, the rule applied when the trial judge is not aware of the conflict (and thus not obligated to inquire) is that prejudice will be presumed only if the conflict has significantly affected counsel's performance—thereby rendering the verdict unreliable, even though *Strickland* prejudice cannot be shown. The trial court's awareness of a

---

3. Petitioner no longer argues, as he did below and as Justice Souter does now, that the Sixth Amendment requires reversal of his conviction without further inquiry into whether the potential conflict that the judge should have investigated was real. * * * Justice Souter labors to suggest that the *Wood* remand order is part of "a coherent scheme," in which automatic reversal is required when the trial judge fails to inquire into a potential conflict that was apparent before the proceeding was "held or completed," but a defendant must demonstrate adverse effect when the judge fails to inquire into a conflict that was not apparent before the end of the proceeding. The problem with this carefully concealed "coherent scheme" (no case has ever mentioned it) is that in *Wood* itself the court did not decree automatic reversal, even though it found that "the *possibility* of a conflict of interest was sufficiently apparent *at the time of* the revocation hearing to impose upon the court a duty to inquire further" (second emphasis added). Indeed, the State had actually notified the judge of a potential conflict of interest " '[d]uring the probation revocation hearing.' " * * *

c. Relying on an earlier ruling, *Glasser v. United States*, 315 U.S. 60 (1942), the *Sullivan* Court stated that "unconstitutional multiple representation is never harmless error." In *Glasser*, *Sullivan* noted, "once the Court concluded that Glasser's lawyer had an actual conflict of interest [counsel failed to cross-examine a key witness and failed to object to "arguably inadmissible" evidence because of his desire to diminish the jury's perception of guilt as to a codefendant also represented by counsel], it "refused to indulge in nice calculations as to the amount of prejudice attributable to the conflict. The conflict itself demonstrated a denial of the 'right to have the effective assistance of counsel.' "

In *Strickland* (p. 141), the Court referred to this doctrine as presuming prejudice—a presumption justified because "counsel breaches the duty of loyalty, perhaps the most basic of duties" and "it is difficult to measure the precise effect on the defense of representation corrupted by conflicting interests." *Strickland* added (p. 141) that the *Sullivan* rule "is not quite the *per se* rule of prejudice that exists for the Sixth Amendment claims mentioned above [the interference cases]. Prejudice is presumed only if the defendant demonstrates that counsel 'actively represented conflicting interests' and an actual conflict of interest adversely affected his lawyer's performance' *Cuyler v. Sullivan*."

potential conflict neither renders it more likely that counsel's performance was significantly affected nor in any other way renders the verdict unreliable. Nor does the trial judge's failure to make the *Sullivan*-mandated inquiry often make it harder for reviewing courts to determine conflict and effect, particularly since those courts may rely on evidence and testimony whose importance only becomes established at the trial.

Nor, finally, is automatic reversal simply an appropriate means of enforcing *Sullivan*'s mandate of inquiry. Despite Justice Souter's belief that there must be a threat of sanction (to-wit, the risk of conferring a windfall upon the defendant) in order to induce "resolutely obdurate" trial judges to follow the law, we do not presume that judges are as careless or as partial as those police officers who need the incentive of the exclusionary rule.* * * And in any event, the *Sullivan* standard, which requires proof of effect upon representation but (once such effect is shown) presumes prejudice, already creates an "incentive" to inquire into a potential conflict. * * *

Since this was not a case in which (as in *Holloway*) counsel protested his inability simultaneously to represent multiple defendants; and since the trial court's failure to make the *Sullivan*-mandated inquiry does not reduce the petitioner's burden of proof; it was at least necessary, to void the conviction, for petitioner to establish that the conflict of interest adversely affected his counsel's performance. The Court of Appeals having found no such effect, the denial of habeas relief must be affirmed.

III

Lest today's holding be misconstrued, we note that the only question presented was the effect of a trial court's failure to inquire into a potential conflict upon the *Sullivan* rule that deficient performance of counsel must be shown. The case was presented and argued on the assumption that (absent some exception for failure to inquire) *Sullivan* would be applicable—requiring a showing of defective performance, but *not* requiring in addition (as *Strickland* does in other ineffectiveness-of-counsel cases), a showing of probable effect upon the outcome of trial. That assumption was not unreasonable in light of the holdings of Courts of Appeals, which have applied *Sullivan* "unblinkingly" to "all kinds of alleged attorney ethical conflicts," *Beets v. Scott*, 65 F.3d 1258, 1266 (CA5 1995) (en banc).[d] They have invoked the *Sullivan* standard not only when (as here) there is a conflict rooted in counsel's obligations to *former* clients, but even when representation of the defendant somehow implicates counsel's personal or financial interests, including a book deal, * * * a job with the prosecutor's office, * * * the teaching of classes to Internal Revenue Service agents, * * * a romantic "entanglement" with the prosecutor, * * * or fear of antagonizing the trial judge.

It must be said, however, that the language of *Sullivan* itself does not clearly establish, or indeed even support, such expansive application. "[U]ntil," it said, "a defendant shows that his counsel *actively represented* conflicting interests, he has

---

d. In *Beets*, a closely divided Fifth Circuit concluded that *Cuyler v. Sullivan*'s prejudice presumption should apply only to conflicts presented by "multiple representation" situations (i.e., defense counsel represented codefendants or represented the defendant and witnesses or other interested parties), as opposed to conflicts arising from some self-interest of the attorney. In the latter situation, a claim of ineffective assistance based on a conflict should be treated no differently than any other ineffective assistance claim, with the court applying the *Strickland* standard, which requires a showing of prejudicial impact upon the outcome. The *Beets* majority reasoned that attorney ethical conflicts that do not result from obligations owed to current or former clients simply reflect another form of incompetent performance. To allow a "recharacterization of ineffectiveness claims to duty of loyalty claims," thereby importing "*Cuyler*'s lesser standard of prejudice" was to "blu[r] the *Strickland* standard" and undercut its role as the "uniform standard of constitutional ineffectiveness."

not established the constitutional predicate for his claim of ineffective assistance" (emphasis added). Both *Sullivan* itself and *Holloway* stressed the high probability of prejudice arising from multiple concurrent representation, and the difficulty of proving that prejudice. Not all attorney conflicts present comparable difficulties. Thus, the Federal Rules of Criminal Procedure treat concurrent representation and prior representation differently, requiring a trial court to inquire into the likelihood of conflict whenever jointly charged defendants are represented by a single attorney (Rule 44(c)), but not when counsel previously represented another defendant in a substantially related matter, even where the trial court is aware of the prior representation.

This is not to suggest that one ethical duty is more or less important than another. The purpose of our *Holloway* and *Sullivan* exceptions from the ordinary requirements of *Strickland*, however, is not to enforce the Canons of Legal Ethics, but to apply needed prophylaxis in situations where *Strickland* itself is evidently inadequate to assure vindication of the defendant's Sixth Amendment right to counsel. [In] resolving this case on the grounds on which it was presented to us, we do not rule upon the need for the *Sullivan* prophylaxis in cases of successive representation. Whether *Sullivan* should be extended to such cases remains, as far as the jurisprudence of this Court is concerned, an open question. * * *

JUSTICE KENNEDY, with whom JUSTICE O'CONNOR joins, concurring.

In its comprehensive analysis the Court has said all that is necessary to address the issues raised by the question presented, and I join the opinion in full. The trial judge's failure to inquire into a suspected conflict is not the kind of error requiring a presumption of prejudice. We did not grant certiorari on a second question presented by petitioner: whether, if we rejected his proposed presumption, he had nonetheless established that a conflict of interest adversely affected his representation. I write separately to emphasize that the facts of this case well illustrate why a wooden rule requiring reversal is inappropriate for cases like this one.

At petitioner's request, the District Court conducted an evidentiary hearing on the conflict claim and issued a thorough opinion, which found that counsel's brief representation of the victim had no effect whatsoever on the course of petitioner's trial. The District Court's findings depend upon credibility judgments made after hearing the testimony of petitioner's counsel, Bryan Saunders, and other witnesses. As a reviewing court, our role is not to speculate about counsel's motives or about the plausibility of alternative litigation strategies. Our role is to defer to the District Court's factual findings unless we can conclude they are clearly erroneous. [The] District Court found that Saunders did not believe he had any obligation to his former client, Timothy Hall, that would interfere with the litigation. [Although] the District Court concluded that Saunders probably did learn some matters that were confidential, it found that nothing the attorney learned was relevant to the subsequent murder case. * * * Indeed, even if Saunders had learned relevant information, the District Court found that he labored under the impression he had no continuing duty at all to his deceased client. [While] Saunders' belief may have been mistaken, it establishes that the prior representation did not influence the choices he made during the course of the trial. This conclusion is a good example of why a case-by-case inquiry is required, rather than simply adopting an automatic rule of reversal.

Petitioner's description of roads not taken would entail two degrees of speculation. We would be required to assume that Saunders believed he had a continuing duty to the victim, and we then would be required to consider whether in this hypothetical case, the counsel would have been blocked from pursuing an alternative defense strategy. The District Court concluded that the prosecution's case, coupled with the defendant's insistence on testifying, foreclosed the strategies suggested by petitioner after the fact. According to the District Court, there was no plausible argument that the victim consented to sexual relations with his murderer, given the bruises on the victim's neck, blood marks showing the victim was stabbed before or during sexual intercourse, and, most important, petitioner's insistence on testifying at trial that he had never met the victim. [The] basic defense at the guilt phase was that petitioner was not at the scene; this is hardly consistent with the theory that there was a consensual encounter.

The District Court said the same for counsel's alleged dereliction at the sentencing phase. Saunder's failure to attack the character of the 17–year-old victim and his mother had nothing to do with the putative conflict of interest. This strategy was rejected as likely to backfire, not only by Saunders, but also by his co-counsel, who owed no duty to Hall. * * * These facts, and others relied upon by the District Court, provide compelling evidence that a theoretical conflict does not establish a constitutional violation, even when the conflict is one about which the trial judge should have known. * * *

JUSTICE STEVENS, dissenting.

This case raises three uniquely important questions about a fundamental component of our criminal justice system—the constitutional right of a person accused of a capital offense to have the effective assistance of counsel for his defense. The first is whether a capital defendant's attorney has a duty to disclose that he was representing the defendant's alleged victim at the time of the murder. Second, is whether, assuming disclosure of the prior representation, the capital defendant has a right to refuse the appointment of the conflicted attorney. Third, is whether the trial judge, who knows or should know of such prior representation, has a duty to obtain the defendant's consent before appointing that lawyer to represent him. Ultimately, the question presented by this case is whether, if these duties exist and if all of them are violated, there exist "circumstances that are so likely to prejudice the accused that the cost of litigating their effect in a particular case is unjustified." *United States v. Cronic* [p. 174].

The first critical stage in the defense of a capital case is the series of pretrial meetings between the accused and his counsel when they decide how the case should be defended. A lawyer cannot possibly determine how best to represent a new client unless that client is willing to provide the lawyer with a truthful account of the relevant facts. When an indigent defendant first meets his newly appointed counsel, he will often falsely maintain his complete innocence. Truthful disclosures of embarrassing or incriminating facts are contingent on the development of the client's confidence in the undivided loyalty of the lawyer. Quite obviously, knowledge that the lawyer represented the victim would be a substantial obstacle to the development of such confidence. * * * Saunders' concealment of essential information about his prior representation of the victim was a severe lapse in his professional duty. The lawyer's duty to disclose his representation of a client related to the instant charge is not only intuitively obvious, it is as old as the profession. * * *

If the defendant is found guilty of a capital offense, the ensuing proceedings that determine whether he will be put to death are critical in every sense of the word. At those proceedings, testimony about the impact of the crime on the victim, including testimony about the character of the victim, may have a critical effect on the jury's decision. Because a lawyer's fiduciary relationship with his deceased client survives the client's death, Saunders necessarily labored under conflicting obligations that were irreconcilable. He had a duty to protect the reputation and confidences of his deceased client, and a duty to impeach the impact evidence presented by the prosecutor. Saunders' conflicting obligations to his deceased client, on the one hand, and to his living client, on the other, were unquestionably sufficient to give Mickens the right to insist on different representation. * * *

[When] an indigent defendant is unable to retain his own lawyer, the trial judge's appointment of counsel is itself a critical stage of a criminal trial. At that point in the proceeding, by definition, the defendant has no lawyer to protect his interests and must rely entirely on the judge. For that reason it is "the solemn duty of [a] judge before whom a defendant appears without counsel to make a thorough inquiry and to take all steps necessary to insure the fullest protection of this constitutional right at every stage of the proceedings." *Von Moltke v. Gillies*, 332 U.S. 708 (1948). * * * This duty with respect to indigent defendants is far more imperative than the judge's duty to investigate the possibility of a conflict that arises when retained counsel represents either multiple or successive defendants. It is true that in a situation of retained counsel, "[u]nless the trial court knows or reasonably should know that a particular conflict exists, the court need not initiate an inquiry." *Sullivan*.[8] But when, as was true in this case, the judge is not merely reviewing the permissibility of the defendant's choice of counsel, but is responsible for making the choice herself, and when she knows or should know that a conflict does exist, the duty to make a thorough inquiry is manifest and unqualified. Indeed, under far less compelling circumstances, we squarely held that when a record discloses the possibility of a conflict between the interests of the defendants and the interests of the party paying their counsel's fees, the Constitution imposes a duty of inquiry on the state-court judge even when no objection was made. *Wood*.

Mickens had a constitutional right to the services of an attorney devoted solely to his interests. That right was violated. The lawyer who did represent him had a duty to disclose his prior representation of the victim to Mickens and to the trial judge. That duty was violated. When Mickens had no counsel, the trial judge had a duty to make a thorough inquiry and to take all steps necessary to insure the fullest protection of his right to counsel. *Von Moltke*. Despite knowledge of the lawyer's prior representation, she violated that duty.

We will never know whether Mickens would have received the death penalty if those violations had not occurred nor precisely what effect they had on Saunders' representation of Mickens. We do know that he did not receive the kind of representation that the Constitution guarantees. If Mickens had been represented by an attorney-impostor who never passed a bar examination, we might also be unable to determine whether the impostor's educational shortcomings "actually affected the adequacy of his representation" (emphasis deleted). We would, however, surely set aside his conviction if the person who had represented him was not a real lawyer. Four compelling reasons make setting aside the conviction the proper remedy in this case.

---

8. Part III of the Court's opinion is a foray into an issue that is not implicated by the question presented. In dicta, the Court states that *Sullivan* may not even apply in the first place to *successive* representations. Most Courts of Appeals, however, have applied *Sullivan* to claims of successive representation as well as to some insidious conflicts arising from a lawyer's self-interest. We have done the same. See *Wood* (applying *Sullivan* to a conflict stemming from a third-party payment arrangement). Neither we nor the Courts of Appeals have applied this standard "unblinkingly," as the Court accuses, but rather have relied upon principled reason. When a conflict of interest, whether multiple, successive, or otherwise, poses so substantial a risk that a lawyer's representation would be materially and adversely affected by diverging interests or loyalties and the trial court judge knows of this and yet fails to inquire, it is a "[c]ircumstanc[e] of [such] magnitude" that "the likelihood that any lawyer, even a fully competent one, could provide effective assistance is so small that a presumption of prejudice is appropriate without inquiry into the actual conduct of the trial." *Cronic*.

First, it is the remedy dictated by our holdings in *Holloway, Sullivan,* and *Wood.* * * * Second, it is the only remedy that responds to the real possibility that Mickens would not have received the death penalty if he had been represented by conflict-free counsel during the critical stage of the proceeding in which he first met with his lawyer. We should presume that the lawyer for the victim of a brutal homicide is incapable of establishing the kind of relationship with the defendant that is essential to effective representation. Third, it is the only remedy that is consistent with the legal profession's historic and universal condemnation of the representation of conflicting interests without the full disclosure and consent of all interested parties. The Court's novel and naive assumption that a lawyer's divided loyalties are acceptable unless it can be proved that they actually affected counsel's performance is demeaning to the profession. Finally, "justice must satisfy the appearance of justice." Setting aside Mickens' conviction is the only remedy that can maintain public confidence in the fairness of the procedures employed in capital cases. [A] rule that allows the State to foist a murder victim's lawyer onto his accused is not only capricious; it poisons the integrity of our adversary system of justice. * * *

JUSTICE SOUTER, dissenting.

* * * The Court today holds, * * * that Mickens should be denied * * * [conviction reversal and a new trial] because Saunders failed to employ a formal objection [as in *Holloway*] * * * as a means of bringing home to the appointing judge the risk of conflict. Without an objection, the majority holds, Mickens should get no relief absent a showing that the risk turned into an actual conflict with adverse effect on the representation provided to Mickens at trial. But why should an objection matter when even without an objection the state judge knew or should have known of the risk and was therefore obliged to enquire further? What would an objection have added to the obligation the state judge failed to honor? The majority says that in circumstances like those now before us, we have already held such an objection necessary for reversal, absent proof of actual conflict with adverse effect, so that this case calls simply for the application of precedent, albeit precedent not very clearly stated.

The majority's position is error, resting on a mistaken reading of our cases. * * * The different burdens [placed] on the *Holloway* and *Cuyler* defendants are consistent features of a coherent scheme for dealing with the problem of conflicted defense counsel; a prospective risk of conflict subject to judicial notice is treated differently from a retrospective claim that a completed proceeding was tainted by conflict, although the trial judge had not been derelict in any duty to guard against it. * * * [I]n this coherent scheme established by *Holloway* and *Cuyler,* there is nothing legally crucial about an objection by defense counsel to tell a trial judge that conflicting interests may impair the adequacy of counsel's representation. * * * Since the District Court in this case found that the state judge was on notice of a prospective potential conflict, this case calls for nothing more than the application of the prospective notice rule * * *.

But in the majority's eyes, this conclusion takes insufficient account of *Wood,* whatever may have been the sensible scheme staked out by *Holloway* and *Cuyler* * * *. *Wood* is not easy to read, and I believe the majority misreads it. * * * Careful attention to *Wood* shows that the case did not involve prospective notice of risk unrealized, and that it held nothing about the general rule to govern in such circumstances. What *Wood* did decide was how to deal with a possible conflict of interests that becomes known to the trial court only at the conclusion of the trial proceeding at which it may have occurred * * *. Treating the case more like *Cuyler* and remanding was the correct choice. *Wood* was not like *Holloway,* in which the judge was put on notice of a risk before trial. * * * It was rather, much closer to *Cuyler* since any notice to a court went to a conflict, if there was one, that had pervaded a completed trial proceeding extending over two years. * * *

* * * Since the majority will not leave the law as it is, however, the question is whether there is any merit in the rule it now adopts, of treating breaches of a judge's duty to enquire into prospective conflicts differently depending on whether defense counsel explicitly objected. There is not. The distinction is irrational on its face, it creates a scheme of incentives to judicial vigilance that is weakest in those cases presenting the greatest risk of conflict and unfair trial, and it reduces the so-called judicial duty to enquire into so many empty words.

The most obvious reason to reject the majority's rule starts with the accepted view that a trial judge placed on notice of a risk of prospective conflict has an obligation then and there to do something about it. The majority does not expressly repudiate that duty, which is too clear for cavil. It should go without saying that the best time to deal with a known threat to the basic guarantee of fair trial is before the trial has proceeded to become unfair. It would be absurd, after all, to suggest that a judge should sit quiescent in the face of an apparent risk that a lawyer's conflict will render representation illusory and the formal trial a waste of time, emotion, and a good deal of public money. And as if that were not bad enough, a failure to act early raises the specter, confronted by the *Holloway* Court, that failures on the part of conflicted counsel will elude demonstration after the fact, simply because they so often consist of what did not happen. While a defendant can fairly be saddled with the characteristically difficult burden of proving adverse effects of conflicted decisions after the fact when the judicial system was not to blame in tolerating the risk of conflict, the burden is indefensible when a judge was on notice of the risk but did nothing. * * *

The Court's rule makes no sense unless, that is, the real point of this case is to eliminate the judge's constitutional duty entirely in no-objection cases, for that is certainly the practical consequence of today's holding. The defendant has the same burden to prove adverse effect (and the prospect of reversal is the same) whether the judge has no reason to know of any risk or every reason to know about it short of explicit objection. In that latter case, the duty explicitly described in *Cuyler* and *Wood* becomes just a matter of words, devoid of sanction; it ceases to be any duty at all. * * *

JUSTICE BREYER, with whom JUSTICE GINSBURG joins, dissenting.

* * * The parties spend a great deal of time disputing how this Court's precedents of *Holloway*, *Cuyler*, and *Wood* resolve the case. * * * Although I express no view at this time about how our precedents should treat *most* ineffective-assistance-of-counsel claims involving an alleged conflict of interest (or, for that matter, whether *Holloway*, *Sullivan*, and *Wood* provide a sensible or coherent framework for dealing with those cases at all), I am convinced that *this* case is not governed by those precedents, for the following reasons.

First, this is the kind of representational incompatibility that is egregious on its face. Mickens was represented by the murder victim's lawyer; that lawyer had represented the victim on a criminal matter; and that lawyer's representation of the victim had continued until one business day before the lawyer was appointed to represent the defendant.

Second, the conflict is exacerbated by the fact that it occurred in a capital murder case. In a capital case, the evidence submitted by both sides regarding the victim's character may easily tip the scale of the jury's choice between life or death. Yet even with extensive investigation in post-trial proceedings, it will often prove difficult, if not impossible, to determine whether the prior representation affected defense counsel's decisions regarding, for example: which avenues to take when investigating the victim's background; which witnesses to call; what type of impeachment to undertake; which arguments to make to the jury; what language to use to characterize the victim; and, as a general matter, what basic strategy to adopt at the sentencing stage. Given the subtle forms that prejudice might take, the consequent difficulty of proving actual prejudice, and the significant likelihood that it will nonetheless occur when the same lawyer represents both accused killer and victim, the cost of litigating the existence of actual prejudice in a particular case cannot be easily justified. * * *

Third, the Commonwealth itself *created* the conflict in the first place. Indeed, it was the *same judge* who dismissed the case against the victim who then appointed the victim's lawyer to represent Mickens one business day later. In light of the judge's active role in bringing about the incompatible representation, I am not sure why the concept of a judge's "duty to inquire" is thought to be central to this case. No "inquiry" by the trial judge could have shed more light on the conflict than was obvious on the face of the matter, namely, that the lawyer who would represent Mickens today is the same lawyer who yesterday represented Mickens' alleged victim in a criminal case.

This kind of breakdown in the criminal justice system creates, at a minimum, the appearance that the proceeding will not " 'reliably serve its function as a vehicle for determination of guilt or innocence,' " and the resulting "criminal punishment" will not "be regarded as fundamentally fair." * * * This appearance, together with the likelihood of prejudice in the typical case, are serious enough to warrant a categorical rule—a rule that does not require proof of prejudice in the individual case.

NOTES AND QUESTIONS

1. *The "adverse impact" requirement.* Dissenting in *Sullivan*, Justice Marshall questioned the Court's requirement that the defendant not only show the presence of an actual conflict (i.e., a situation in which conflicting loyalties pointed in opposite directions), but also that the conflict "adversely affected counsel's performance" (i.e., that counsel proceeded to act against the defendant's interest, favoring the conflicting loyalty). Justice Marshall noted that the Court was willing to presume prejudice where the conflict adversely affected counsel's performance because determining the impact of the conflict upon the outcome of the case its too speculative (see fn. c, p. 193). Why, he asked, was not the same true of the impact of an actual conflict upon the counsel's performance?

Does the following explanation adequately respond to Justice Marshall's query? CRIMPROC. § 11.8(d) (describing the rationale suggested in various cases): "It would not be sufficient for reversal to show only that counsel had faced a situation in which action or inaction that might benefit his client would work to the detriment of another interest that divided counsel's loyalty. There would be no harm to the defendant if counsel actually pursued the route favoring his client, disregarding the conflicting interest. Moreover, even where counsel did not pursue that route, counsel's action or inaction may have been influenced solely by a reasonable determination that the route not taken was inferior to the alternative route, which was more beneficial to his client, putting aside any concern for the conflicting interest. Having identified an actual conflict of interest, defendant should be able to establish as well precisely how counsel acted in response to that conflict. However, once it is shown that counsel was actually influenced by the conflict in one aspect of his performance, it would be inappropriate to measure the impact of that conflict solely by reference to that action or inaction. A court could not assume that counsel so motivated had not also been influenced by the conflict in various other aspects of his representation."

2. *Applying The "adverse impact" requirement.* The leading Supreme Court ruling on the application of the adverse impact standard is BURGER v. KEMP, 483 U.S. 776 (1987). In that case Burger and Stevens were indicted for murder, but tried separately. Each made a confession that emphasized the culpability of the other. Leaphart, described as an experienced and well-respected criminal lawyer, was appointed to represent Burger. Leaphart's law partner was appointed to represent Stevens in his later, separate trial. Leaphart, however, did assist his partner in the representation of Stevens. Moreover, he prepared the briefs for both defendants on their second appeal to the Georgia Supreme Court.

At their separate trials, each of the defendants sought to underscore the culpability of the other in order to avoid the death penalty. Although he had relied on Burger's lesser culpability as a trial defense, Leaphart did not make a "lesser culpability" argument in his appellate brief on behalf of Burger. In a subsequent federal habeas petition, defendant Burger argued that this omission, along with others, established Leaphart's incompetency under the *Sullivan* standard. Two lower federal courts rejected that claim, and a divided Supreme Court, per Stevens, J., affirmed:

"In an effort to identify an actual conflict of interest, petitioner points out that Leaphart prepared the briefs for both Burger and Stevens on their second appeal to the Georgia Supreme Court, and that Leaphart did not make a 'lesser culpability' argument in his appellate brief on behalf of Burger even though he had relied on Burger's lesser culpability as a trial defense. Given the fact that it was petitioner who actually killed Honeycutt [and] the further fact that the Georgia Supreme Court expressed the opinion that petitioner's actions were 'outrageously and wantonly vile and inhuman under any reasonable standard of human conduct,' [the] decision to forgo this omission had a sound strategic basis. * * *

"In addition, determining that there was an actual conflict of interest requires the attribution of Leaphart's motivation for not making the 'lesser culpability' argument to the fact that his partner was Stevens' lawyer, or to the further fact that he assisted his partner in that representation. The District Court obviously credited his testimony to the contrary, and its findings were twice sustained by the Court of Appeals. It would thus be most inappropriate, and factually unsupportable, for this Court to speculate that the drafting of a brief on appeal was tainted by a lawyer's improper motivation. Our duty to search for constitutional error with painstaking care is never more exacting than it is in a capital case. Nevertheless, when the lower courts have found that a lawyer has performed his or her solemn duties in such a case at or above the lower boundary of professional competence, both respect for the bar and deference to the shared conclusion of two reviewing courts prevent us from substituting speculation for their considered opinions. The district judge, who presumably is familiar with the legal talents and character of the lawyers who practice at the local bar and who saw and heard the witness testify, is in a far better position than we are to evaluate a charge of this kind, and the regional courts of appeals are in a far better position than we are to conduct appellate review of these heavily fact-based rulings."

In dissent, Justice Blackmun, joined by Justices Brennan and Marshall, responded: "It is difficult to imagine a more direct conflict than existed here, where counsel was preparing the appellate brief for petitioner at the same time that he was preparing the appellate brief for Stevens, and where the state statute specifies that one of the roles of that appellate process is to consider the comparative culpability and sentences of defendants involved in similar crimes. Counsel's abandonment of the lesser-culpability argument on appeal, the stage at which the two cases would be reviewed contemporaneously, is indicative of the 'struggle to serve two masters.' This record *compels* a finding that counsel's representation of the conflicting interests of petitioner and Stevens had an adverse effect on his performance as petitioner's counsel."

3. ***Presuming an adverse impact.*** Federal appellate rulings have held that an adverse impact on counsel's performance can be presumed in the instance of certain flagrant conflicts. See e.g., *United States v. Fulton*, 5 F.3d 605 (2d Cir.1993) (*per se* rule applies where the "attorney has engaged in the defendant's crimes," and also where a prosecution witness alleged that "he has direct knowledge of criminal conduct by defense counsel"; "the danger arising from a counsel who has been implicated in related criminal activity by a government witness is of a different order of magnitude"); Walberg v. Israel, 766 F.2d 1071 (7th Cir.1985) (adverse impact presumed where trial judge indicated to appointed counsel that approval of his fee and future appointments would depend upon counsel "pulling his punches"). Does *Mickens* require reexamination of such rulings?

4. ***Limiting the presumption of prejudice.*** Post *Mickens*, several circuits have recognized the possible restriction of the presumption of prejudice but have not ruled on the issue. See CRIMPROC § 11.9(d), fn. 173 (collecting cases). These cases have suggested that the Supreme Court may well find that *Strickland* rather than *Sullivan* applies to: (1) "cases of successive representation" (but not where that representation involved "substantial relatedness," as where counsel represented successively defendants on charges "arising from identical facts"); (2) a counsel who would be a defense witness (resulting in his disqualification) if counsel chooses to present an "advice of counsel" defense; and (3) "all ethical conflicts" of counsel other than "multiple or serial [representation] conflicts." Several state courts have held *Strickland* applicable in various conflict situations not involving multiple representation (e.g., prior representation of a witness on an unrelated matter). Ibid. Of course, state courts are free under state law to refuse to "dra[w] any distinctions between 'types' of conflict of interest that may form the basis of a claim of ineffective assistance." *Acosta v. State*, 233 S.W.3d 349 (Tex.Crim.App. 2007).

C. DISQUALIFICATION OF COUNSEL
WHEAT v. UNITED STATES
486 U.S. 153, 108 S.Ct. 1692, 100 L.Ed.2d 140 (1988).

CHIEF JUSTICE REHNQUIST delivered the opinion of the Court.

[Petitioner, along with numerous codefendants, including Gomez–Barajas and Bravo, was charged with participating in a far-flung drug conspiracy. Both Gomez–Barajas and Bravo were represented by attorney Eugene Iredale. Gomez–Barajas was tried first and was acquitted on drug charges overlapping with those against petitioner. To avoid a second trial on other charges, Gomez–Barajas offered to plead guilty to certain offenses stemming from the conspiracy. At the commencement of petitioner's trial, the district court had not yet accepted the plea of Gomez–Barajas; thus he was free to withdraw his plea and proceed to trial. Bravo had pled guilty.]

[At the conclusion of Bravo's guilty plea proceedings and two court days before his trial was to commence, petitioner moved for the substitution of Iredale as his counsel as well. The government objected on the ground that Iredale's representation of the two other codefendants created a serious conflict of interest: (1) In the event that Gomez–Barajas's plea and the sentencing arrangement negotiated between him and the government were rejected by the court, petitioner was likely to be called as a witness for the prosecution at Gomez–Barajas's trial.

This scenario would pose a conflict of interest for Iredale, who would be prevented from cross-examining petitioner and thereby from effectively representing Gomez–Barajas. (2) In the likely event that Bravo was called as a witness for the prosecution against petitioner, ethical proscriptions would prevent Iredale from cross-examining Bravo in any meaningful way. Thus, Iredale would be unable to provide petitioner with effective assistance of counsel.]

[In response, petitioner emphasized his right to have counsel of his own choosing and his willingness, and the willingness of the other codefendants, to waive the right to conflict-free counsel. Moreover, maintained petitioner, the circumstances posited by the government that would create a conflict of interest were highly speculative and bore no connection to the true relationship among the co-conspirators. If called to testify against petitioner, Bravo would simply say that he did not know petitioner and had had no dealings with him. In the unlikely event that Gomez–Barajas went to trial, petitioner's lack of involvement in his alleged crimes made his appearance as a witness highly improbable. According to petitioner, the government was "manufacturing implausible conflicts" in an attempt to disqualify Iredale, who had already proved extremely effective in representing the other codefendants.]

[The district court denied petitioner's request to substitute Iredale as his attorney, concluding, on the basis of the representation of the government, that it "really has no choice at this point other than to find that an irreconcilable conflict of interest exists." Petitioner proceeded to trial with his original counsel and was convicted of various drug offenses. The Court of Appeals for the Ninth Circuit affirmed.] * * *

[While] the right to select and be represented by one's preferred attorney is comprehended by the Sixth Amendment, the essential aim of the Amendment is to guarantee an effective advocate for each criminal defendant rather than to ensure that a defendant will inexorably be represented by the lawyer whom he prefers.[e] * * * The Sixth Amendment right to choose one's own counsel is circumscribed in several important respects. Regardless of his persuasive powers, an advocate who is not a member of the bar may not represent clients (other than himself) in court. Similarly, a defendant may not insist on representation by an attorney he cannot afford or who for other reasons declines to represent the defendant. Nor may a defendant insist on the counsel of an attorney who has a previous or ongoing relationship with an opposing party, even when the opposing party is the Government. The question raised in this case is the extent to which a criminal defendant's right under the Sixth Amendment to his chosen attorney is qualified by the fact that the attorney has represented other defendants charged in the same criminal conspiracy.

[Petitioner] insists that the provision of waivers by all affected defendants cures any problems created by the multiple representation. But no such flat rule can be deduced from the Sixth Amendment presumption in favor of counsel of choice. Federal courts have an independent interest in ensuring that criminal trials are conducted within the ethical standards of the profession and that legal proceedings appear fair to all who observe them. Both the American Bar Association's Model Code of Professional Responsibility and its Model Rules of Professional Conduct, as well as the rules of the California Bar Association (which governed the attorneys in this case), impose limitations on multiple representation of clients. Not only the interest of a criminal defendant but the institutional interest in the rendition of just verdicts in criminal cases may be jeopardized by unregulated multiple representation.

---

   e. As to this statement, see also fn. 3 of the Court's opinion in United States v. Gonzalez–Lopez, [p. 123].

For this reason, the Federal Rules of Criminal Procedure direct trial judges to investigate specially cases involving joint representation. In pertinent part, Rule 44(c) [requires an inquiry in cases of joint representation]. * * * Although Rule 44(c) does not specify what particular measures may be taken by a district court, one option suggested by the Notes of the Advisory Committee is an order by the court that the defendants be separately represented in subsequent proceedings in the case. This suggestion comports with our instructions in *Holloway* [Note 5, p. 188] and in *Glasser* [Note 1, p. 186] that the trial courts, when alerted by objection from one of the parties, have an independent duty to ensure that criminal defendants receive a trial that is fair and does not contravene the Sixth Amendment.

To be sure, this need to investigate potential conflicts arises in part from the legitimate wish of district courts that their judgments remain intact on appeal. As the Court of Appeals accurately pointed out, trial courts confronted with multiple representations face the prospect of being "whip-sawed" by assertions of error no matter which way they rule. If a district court agrees to the multiple representation, and the advocacy of counsel is thereafter impaired as a result, the defendant may well claim that he did not receive effective assistance. On the other hand, a district court's refusal to accede to the multiple representation may result in a challenge such as petitioner's in this case. Nor does a waiver by the defendant necessarily solve the problem, for we note, without passing judgment on, the apparent willingness of Courts of Appeals to entertain ineffective assistance claims from defendants who have specifically waived the right to conflict-free counsel.

Thus, where a court justifiably finds an actual conflict of interest, there can be no doubt that it may decline a proffer of waiver, and insist that defendants be separately represented. * * * Unfortunately for all concerned, a district court must pass on the issue of whether or not to allow a waiver of a conflict of interest by a criminal defendant not with the wisdom of hindsight after the trial has taken place, but the murkier pretrial context when relationships between parties are seen through a glass, darkly. The likelihood and dimensions of nascent conflicts of interest are notoriously hard to predict, even for those thoroughly familiar with criminal trials. It is a rare attorney who will be fortunate enough to learn the entire truth from his own client, much less be fully apprised before trial of what each of the Government's witnesses will say on the stand. A few bits of unforeseen testimony or a single previously unknown or unnoticed document may significantly shift the relationship between multiple defendants. These imponderables are difficult enough for a lawyer to assess, and even more difficult to convey by way of explanation to a criminal defendant untutored in the niceties of legal ethics. Nor is it amiss to observe that the willingness of an attorney to obtain such waivers from his clients may bear an inverse relation to the care with which he conveys all the necessary information to them.

For these reasons we think the District Court must be allowed substantial latitude in refusing waivers of conflicts of interest not only in those rare cases where an actual conflict may be demonstrated before trial, but in the more common cases where a potential for conflict exists which may or may not burgeon into an actual conflict as the trial progresses. In the circumstances of this case, with the motion for substitution of counsel made so close to the time of trial, the District Court relied on instinct and judgment based on experience in making its decision. We do not think it can be said that the court exceeded the broad latitude which must be accorded it in making this decision. Petitioner of course rightly points out that the government may seek to "manufacture" a conflict in order to prevent a defendant from having a particularly able defense counsel at his side; but trial courts are undoubtedly aware of this possibility, and must take it into consideration along with all of the other factors which inform this sort of a decision.

Here the District Court was confronted not simply with an attorney who wished to represent two coequal defendants in a straightforward criminal prosecution; rather, Iredale proposed to defend three conspirators of varying stature in a complex drug distribution scheme. The Government intended to call Bravo as a witness for the prosecution at petitioner's trial.[4] The Government might readily have tied certain deliveries of marijuana by Bravo to petitioner, necessitating vigorous cross-examination of Bravo by petitioner's counsel. Iredale, because of his prior representation of Bravo, would have been unable ethically to provide that cross-examination.

Iredale had also represented Gomez–Barajas, one of the alleged kingpins of the distribution ring, and had succeeded in obtaining a verdict of acquittal for him. Gomez–Barajas had agreed with the Government to plead guilty to other charges, but the District Court had not yet accepted the plea arrangement. If the agreement were rejected, petitioner's probable testimony at the resulting trial of Gomez–Barajas would create an ethical dilemma for Iredale from which one or the other of his clients would likely suffer.

Viewing the situation as it did before trial, we hold that the District Court's refusal to permit the substitution of counsel in this case was within its discretion and did not violate petitioner's Sixth Amendment rights. Other district courts might have reached differing or opposite conclusions with equal justification, but that does not mean that one conclusion was "right" and the other "wrong." The District Court must recognize a presumption in favor of petitioner's counsel of choice, but that presumption may be overcome not only by a demonstration of actual conflict but by a showing of a serious potential for conflict. The evaluation [of the] circumstances of each case under this standard must be left primarily to the informed judgment of the trial court. * * *

JUSTICE MARSHALL, with whom JUSTICE BRENNAN joins, dissenting.

[I] disagree [with] the Court's suggestion that the trial court's decision as to whether a potential conflict justifies rejection of a defendant's chosen counsel is entitled to some kind of special deference on appeal. The Court grants trial courts "broad latitude" over the decision to accept or reject a defendant's choice of counsel; although never explicitly endorsing a standard of appellate review, the Court appears to limit such review to determining whether an abuse of discretion has occurred. [This approach] accords neither with the nature of the trial court's decision nor with the importance of the interest at stake.

[The] interest at stake in this kind of decision is nothing less than a criminal defendant's Sixth Amendment right to counsel of his choice. The trial court simply does not have "broad latitude" to vitiate this right. In my view, a trial court that rejects a criminal defendant's chosen counsel on the ground of a potential conflict should make findings on the record to facilitate review, and an appellate court should scrutinize closely the basis for the trial court's decision. Only in this way can a criminal defendant's right to counsel of his choice be appropriately protected.

The Court's resolution of the instant case flows from its deferential approach to the District Court's denial of petitioner's motion to add or substitute counsel; absent deference, a decision upholding the District Court's ruling would be inconceivable. Indeed, I believe that even under the Court's deferential standard, reversal is in order.

---

4. Bravo was in fact called as a witness at petitioner's trial. His testimony was elicited to demonstrate the transportation of drugs that the prosecution hoped to link to petitioner.

[At] the time of petitioner's trial, Iredale's representation of Gomez–Barajas was effectively completed. * * * Gomez–Barajas was not scheduled to appear as a witness at petitioner's trial; thus, Iredale's conduct of that trial would not require him to question his former client. The only possible conflict this Court can divine from Iredale's representation of both petitioner and Gomez–Barajas rests on the premise that the trial court would reject the negotiated plea agreement and that Gomez–Barajas then would decide to go to trial. In this event, the Court tells us, "petitioner's probable testimony at the resulting trial of Gomez–Barajas would create an ethical dilemma for Iredale."

This argument rests on speculation of the most dubious kind. The Court offers no reason to think that the trial court would have rejected Gomez–Barajas's plea agreement; neither did the Government posit any such reason in its argument or brief before this Court. The most likely occurrence at the time petitioner moved to retain Iredale as his defense counsel was that the trial court would accept Gomez–Barajas's plea agreement, as the court in fact later did. Moreover, even if Gomez–Barajas had gone to trial, petitioner probably would not have testified. [The] only alleged connection between petitioner and Gomez–Barajas sprang from the conspiracy to distribute marijuana, and a jury already had acquitted Gomez–Barajas of that charge. It is therefore disingenuous to say that representation of both petitioner and Gomez–Barajas posed a serious potential for a conflict of interest.

Similarly, Iredale's prior representation of Bravo was not a cause for concern. * * * Contrary to the Court's inference, Bravo could not have testified about petitioner's involvement in the alleged marijuana distribution scheme. As all parties were aware at the time, Bravo did not know and could not identify petitioner; indeed, prior to the commencement of legal proceedings, the two men never had heard of each other. Bravo's eventual testimony at petitioner's trial related to a shipment of marijuana in which petitioner was not involved; the testimony contained not a single reference to petitioner. Petitioner's counsel did not cross-examine Bravo, and neither petitioner's counsel nor the prosecutor mentioned Bravo's testimony in closing argument. All of these developments were predictable when the District Court ruled on petitioner's request that Iredale serve as trial counsel; the contours of Bravo's testimony were clear at that time. Given the insignificance of this testimony to any matter that petitioner's counsel would dispute, the proposed joint representation of petitioner and Bravo did not threaten a conflict of interest.

Moreover, even assuming that Bravo's testimony might have "necessitat[ed] vigorous cross-examination," the District Court could have insured against the possibility of any conflict of interest without wholly depriving petitioner of his constitutional right to the counsel of his choice. Petitioner's motion requested that Iredale either be substituted for petitioner's current counsel or be added to petitioner's defense team. Had the District Court allowed the addition of Iredale and then ordered that he take no part in the cross-examination of Bravo, any possibility of a conflict would have been removed. Especially in light of the availability of this precautionary measure, the notion that Iredale's prior representation of Bravo might well have caused a conflict of interest at petitioner's trial is nothing short of ludicrous. * * *

JUSTICE STEVENS, with whom JUSTICE BLACKMUN joins, dissenting.

[The] Court gives inadequate weight to the informed and voluntary character of the clients' waiver of their right to conflict-free representation. Particularly, the Court virtually ignores the fact that the additional counsel representing petitioner had provided him with sound advice concerning the wisdom of a waiver and would have remained available during the trial to assist in the defense. Thus, [the] question before [the District Judge] was whether petitioner should be permitted to have *additional* counsel of his choice. I agree with Justice Marshall that the answer to that question is perfectly clear.

NOTES AND QUESTIONS

1. *Viewing Wheat from different perspectives.* Commentators have approached the issue of disqualification from quite diverse perspectives, producing equally diverse evaluations of the *Wheat* ruling. Consider:

(a) William J. Stuntz, *Waiving Rights in Criminal Procedure*, 75 Va. L. Rev. 761 (1989): "One might try to explain *Wheat* as nothing more than a paternalistic attempt to protect Iredale's clients against their own irrationality * * * [but] that approach to the case seems strained. * * *[Professor Stuntz notes that Wheat was involved in a large-scale conspiracy, where defendants often are more "sophisticated."] * * * There are two reasons why the coconspirators [in Wheat] might have wished to use Iredale as common counsel. The first, offered by the defendants, is unobjectionable: the defendants believed Iredale to be a very good attorney, better than the likely alternatives. But the second is troubling. If the three defendants in question were guilty, they may well have faced a classic prisoners' dilemma: it may have been in each individual's interest to 'sell out' to the government and implicate his colleagues, but may have been far better for all if all either lied or remained silent. Common counsel may have removed the dilemma by facilitating the enforcement of an agreement not to finger each other. Obtaining the testimony of one conspirator against others may require careful negotiation with the would-be witness. If all the conspirators have the same lawyer, the government is, in effect, able to deal with one defendant only by dealing with all. One cannot be absolutely certain whether the codefendants wanted a common lawyer for good reasons or bad, but there is a fairly good proxy for that determination. If an objective observer familiar with the local bar would have concluded that Iredale was not any better than the lawyers who might have taken his place, then the defendants' motive for retaining him seems suspect. The district judge was in a good position to make that judgment. The ability of district judges to make case-by-case assessments of defendants' counsel of choice may be why the Court left the matter in the district courts' discretion, rather than promulgate a blanket rule either barring or allowing waiver."

(b) Bruce A. Green, *"Through a Glass, Darkly": How the Court Sees Motions to Disqualify Criminal Defense Lawyers,* 89 Colum.L.Rev. 1201, 1215–16, 1221–22 (1989): "In light of the nature of the potential conflict in *Wheat* and the manner in which it is addressed by the prevailing ethical standards, the district judge in that case had no basis for concluding that, if Bravo were to be a government witness at Wheat's trial, Iredale's representation of Wheat would violate the prevailing ethical norms. * * * Even if Iredale were called upon to cross-examine Bravo, the client's consent to the potential conflict would have eliminated the ethical barrier to the representation, notwithstanding Iredale's possession of confidences that needed to be preserved. * * * Thus, the *Wheat* decision is bottomed on the Court's misunderstanding of the ethical rules. [The] Court upheld the denial of Wheat's choice of counsel in a case where the ethical rules plainly would have permitted that choice."

(c) Note, 102 Harv.L.Rev. 143 (1988). "By allowing the government successfully to oppose Wheat's attempted waiver on the basis of institutional concerns external to Wheat, the Court in effect vested the right to conflict-free defense counsel in the state as well as in Wheat. * * * Recognizing such a right transforms the Sixth Amendment, presumably a shield to help criminal defendants receive fair treatment in their battle against a more powerful adversary, into an additional weapon for their prosecutors to use against them. The state might now intentionally manufacture conflicts in order to disqualify a particularly formidable opposing attorney. Indeed, the relative insignificance of Bravo's testimony against Wheat, the late date at which the government expressed interest in that testimony, and the success of Iredale in representing Wheat's alleged coconspirators together suggest that Wheat's prosecutor succeeded in doing just that."

2. *"Manufactured conflicts."* Assume that the defense claims, in responding to a motion to disqualify, that the prosecution has "manufactured a conflict" based on: (i) a prosecution offer of a plea bargain (in exchange for testifying for the government) to one of several jointly represented codefendants; (ii) the prosecution's current investigation of defense counsel as to events relating to the charges against the client; or (iii) the prosecution's intent to call the defense counsel as a witness. What type of inquiry, if any, is needed to satisfy *Wheat*'s directive that the trial court "must take * * * into consideration" the possibility that the conflict was "manufactured" by the prosecution to "prevent a defendant from having a particularly able defense counsel at his side" (p. 204). Consider *United States v. Diozzi*, 807 F.2d 10 (1st Cir.1986) (to ensure against a "manufactured conflict," where conflict is based on prosecution's use of defense counsel as a witness, the trial court should seek to determine whether the testimony of counsel is truly needed or whether the same facts could be established through other means, but the government should not be forced "to settle for less than its best evidence").

3. *Disqualification in other conflict settings.* "Recognizing [*Wheat*'s acceptance of trial court] discretion and applying a deferential standard of review, appellate courts have sustained the disqualification of counsel not only in cases involving multiple representation of codefendants (as in *Wheat*), but also in a broad range of other settings that present a realistic potential for a conflict of interest. These include cases in which: (1) defense counsel currently was representing an anticipated prosecution witness on either a related or different matter; (2) defense counsel has previously represented a prosecution witness on a related matter; (3) co-defendants (or co-targets of an investigation) had separate counsel, but shared information under a joint defense agreement, and one of the participants 'flipped,' leaving the agreement and agreeing to testify for the government; (4) defense counsel was a potential witness for the prosecution; (5) defense counsel's participation in events that would be described before the jury could lead to calling him as a defense witness, and would make him an 'unsworn' witness for the defense even if he were not called to testify; (6) defense counsel was a former member of the prosecution's staff who had participated in the bringing of these charges or otherwise had access through that position to confidential information relevant to the prosecution; (7) defense counsel was alleged to have been involved in criminal activity or professional misconduct that would bear upon his representation of the defendant; and (8) defense counsel also represented the entity with which defendant was associated (with that entity having interests separate from the defendant)." CRIMPROC § 11.9(c). Do all of these situations present the justifications for broad judicial discretion that were cited in *Wheat*?

4. *Waivers.* Where the conflict creates the potential of giving the defendant an adversarial advantage (e.g., where defense counsel is a former prosecutor and acquired confidential information relating to the prosecution's case), disqualification in all courts is virtually automatic. Where, however, the primary concern is that the particular conflict will adversely impact the defendant (or the related "judicial integrity" concern that such representation will appear less than fair), many trial courts will refuse to disqualify if they can obtain a satisfactory waiver of the conflict. Although *Wheat* spoke of federal appellate decisions that appeared to allow a defendant to press a postconviction conflict of interest challenge

notwithstanding defendant's waiver of the right to conflict-free counsel, "post-*Wheat* circuit court rulings have established that a knowing and intelligent waiver precludes a subsequent competency challenge based on the conflict." CRIMPROC § 11.9(c).

Various appellate courts have offered fairly detailed instructions for advising defendants of potential and actual conflicts in the course of obtaining a waiver, and some courts also insist that a defendant consult with independent counsel before entering the waiver. *United States v. Newell*, 315 F.3d 510 (5th Cir.2002), indicates, however, that even such precautions may not provide a waiver that is an acceptable response to a postconviction challenge.

In *Newell*, the trial judge followed the detailed instructions for obtaining a waiver set forth in Fifth Circuit precedent, and allowed continued representation of codefendants after receiving the waiver. The Fifth Circuit held, however, that the waiver was flawed. When the waiver was accepted, neither the trial judge nor the defendant anticipated that counsel's strategy eventually would include implicating the defendant in order to exonerate the codefendant. When this conflict emerged at trial, the trial judge did not reopen the waiver issue and undertake further inquiry (which the Fifth Circuit described as the trial court's obligation under Rule 44). Finding the waiver invalid, the Fifth Circuit noted: "We do not suggest that a trial court cannot at the outset * * * obtain a waiver of the right to conflict-free counsel, * * * [but] such a waiver * * * will be valid [only] against conflicts that emerge at trial in cases that were sufficiently *foreseeable* that the judge can bring them home to the defendants in concrete terms."

5. The Second Circuit has held that, no matter how extensive the warnings and inquiry, a valid defense waiver cannot be obtained where defense counsel is alleged to have personally participated in the crime charged (or a related crime) because that conflict "so permeate[s] the defense that no meaningful waiver can be obtained." *United States v. Fulton*, 5 F.3d 605 (2d Cir.1993). Building upon that ruling, the Second Circuit later held that waivers were similarly invalid where "the attorney suffers from a severe conflict—such that no rational defendant would knowingly and intelligently desire the conflicted lawyer's representation." See e.g., *United States v. Schwarz*, 283 F.3d 76 (2d Cir.2002) (defense waiver invalid under this standard; defendant police officer was charged with violating the civil rights of arrestee Abner Louima in a case that attracted nationwide attention; defendant waived conflicts in accepting representation by a law firm that also represented police union, but the union's interests completely diverged from that of defendant; Louima in a civil suit had alleged that the union participated in a "coverup conspiracy," and the plausible defense strategy of implicating another officer, not pursued by defense counsel, would have worked against the union's interest in that suit).

SECTION 6. CLIENT CONTROL

1. *Self-representation vs. attorney control.* As the Supreme Court noted in *Faretta* (p. 107), a defendant who chooses to be represented by counsel thereby relinquishes to counsel the authority to make various decisions relating to the defense presentation. As to those decisions, commonly characterized as "strategic decisions," the client is bound by the attorney's exercise of competent professional judgment even if the attorney's actions or inactions amount to a "forfeiture" or "waiver" of a defense right. On the other hand, the Court also has noted in various cases that the defendant, rather than defense counsel, has control over other decisions, commonly characterized as so "fundamental" that they must rest in the personal control of the defendant. Here the right can be exercised or relinquished only with the approval of the defendant. The two foundational rulings focusing on this distinction are *Brookhart v. Janis*, 384 U.S. 1(1966) and *Jones v. Barnes*, 463 U.S. 745 (1983).

Brookhart held that due process was violated when the state trial court accepted defense counsel's agreement with the prosecutor that "all the state had to prove was a prima facie case, that he would not contest it, and there would be no cross-examination of witness." The agreement was the practical equivalent of a guilty plea, which could be entered only with the consent of the defendant, and the defendant had stated in open court that he was "in no way pleading guilty."

In *Jones v. Barnes*, the Court rejected the claim that appointed appellate counsel had provided ineffective assistance by refusing to include in the appellate brief a claim that the defendant desired to press. While the accused had the "ultimate authority" to make certain fundamental decisions, such as whether to appeal, structuring the appellate contentions did not fall in that category. Defense counsel did not have to include a nonfrivolous claim that the defendant wished to present if counsel believed that the better strategy was to limit her argument and brief to other issues. Counsel was free to follow the time-tested advice of countless advocates that the inclusion of "every colorable claim" will "dilute and weaken a good case and not save a bad one." Contrary to the dissent, the majority viewed neither *Faretta* nor decisions defining the obligation of appointed counsel as to withdrawals (see Note 2, p. 218) as having altered the traditional division of authority as to such strategic decisions.[a]

2. *Identifying "strategic" and "personal" decisions.* Prior to *Florida v. Nixon* (Note 3, infra), "[t]he Supreme Court has stated, in dictum or holding, that it is for the defendant to decide whether to take each of the following steps: plead guilty or take action tantamount to entering a guilty plea; waive the right to jury trial; waive his right to be present at trial; testify on his own behalf; or forgo an appeal. * * * On the other side, the Supreme Court has indicated, in dictum or holding, that counsel has the ultimate authority in deciding whether or not to advance the following defense rights: barring prosecution use of unconstitutionally obtained evidence; obtaining dismissal of an indictment on the ground of racial discrimination in the selection of the grand jury; wearing civilian clothes, rather

---

a. In dissent, Justice Brennan, joined by Justice Marshall, offered a much broader view of the scope of defendant's control. Justice Brenan noted: "The right to counsel as *Faretta* [p. 107] and *Anders* [Note 2, p. 218] conceive it is not an all-or-nothing right, under which a defendant must choose between forgoing the assistance of counsel altogether or relinquishing control over every aspect of his case beyond its most basic structure (*i.e.*, how to plead, whether to present a defense, whether to appeal). A defendant's interest in his case clearly extends to other matters. Absent exceptional circumstances, he is bound [in later proceedings] by the tactics used by his counsel at trial and on appeal. He may want to press the argument that he is innocent, even if other stratagems are more likely to result in the dismissal of charges or in a reduction of punishment. He may want to insist on certain arguments for political reasons. He may want to protect third parties. This is just as true on appeal as at trial, and the proper role of counsel is to *assist* him in these efforts, insofar as that is possible consistent with the lawyer's conscience, the law, and his duties to the court. * * * I cannot accept the notion that lawyers are one of the punishments a person receives merely for being accused of a crime. Clients, if they wish, are capable of making informed judgments about which issues to appeal, and when they exercise that prerogative their choices should be respected unless they would require lawyers to violate their consciences, the law, or their duties to the court."

Justice Brennan added, in a general discussion of the division of authority between defendant and counsel: "A constitutional rule that encourages lawyers to disregard their clients wishes without compelling need can only exacerbate the clients' suspicion of their lawyers. * * * [U]ntil his conviction becomes final and he has had an opportunity to appeal, any restrictions on individual autonomy and dignity should be limited to the minimum necessary to vindicate the State's interest in a speedy, effective prosecution. The role of the defense lawyer should be above all to function as the instrument and defender of the client's autonomy and dignity in all phases of the criminal process."

than prison garb, during the trial; striking an improper jury instruction; including a particular nonfrivolous claim among the issues briefed and argued on appeal; foregoing cross-examination; calling a possible witness (other than defendant) to testify; providing discovery to the prosecution (even where the failure to do so risks possible sanctions of exclusion); and being tried within the 180 day time period specified in the Interstate Agreement on Detainers." CRIMPROC § 11.6(a).

3. *The Nixon ruling.* In FLORIDA v. NIXON, 543 U.S. 175 (2004), defense counsel Corin was faced with the inevitability of going to trial on a capital charge (the prosecutor refused to recommend a lesser sentence, even on a guilty plea) with the state's evidence of guilt (which included defendant's confession) "not 'subject to any reasonable dispute.' " Experienced in capital defense, Corin feared that "denying [defendant] Nixon's commission * * * [of the crime] during the guilt phase would compromise Corin's ability to persuade the jury, during the penalty phase, that Nixon's conduct was the product of his mental illness." Corin therefore adopted a strategy of "conceding guilt during the guilt phase, thereby preserving his credibility in urging leniency during the penalty phase." Corin "attempted to explain this strategy to Nixon at least three times," but, although he had represented Nixon previously and "the two had a good relationship in Corin's estimation," Nixon was "generally unresponsive during their discussions," and "never verbally approved or protested Corin's proposed strategy." At trial, Corin acknowledged Nixon's guilt in the opening statement, and urged the jury to focus on the penalty phase. Nixon was not present during the trial as his disruptive behavior during jury selection led to his "voluntary waiver" of his right to be present. During the guilt phase of the trial, Corin simply "cross-examined * * * witnesses only when he felt their statements needed clarification," and objected to the introduction of crime scene photographs as unduly prejudicial. After the jury found the defendant guilty, in the penalty phase, Corin presented a variety of evidence designed to establish that Nixon was "not normal organically, intellectually, emotionally or educationally or in any other way," and advanced in his closing arguments a variety of reasons why the death penalty was inappropriate. That evidence and argument failed to convince the jury, as it sentenced Nixon to death.

The Florida Supreme Court subsequently reversed Nixon's conviction, holding that a defense attorney's concession that his client committed murder automatically constituted prejudicial ineffective assistance of counsel when that strategy was implemented without the "affirmative, explicit acceptance" of the defendant. A unanimous Supreme Court (per Ginsburg, J.) reversed. The Court reasoned:

"An attorney undoubtedly has a duty to consult with the client regarding 'important decisions,' including questions of overarching defense strategy. *Strickland v. Washington* [p. 140]. That obligation, however, does not require counsel to obtain the defendant's consent to 'every tactical decision.' *Taylor v. Illinois* [p. 1240] (an attorney has authority to manage most aspects of the defense without obtaining his client's approval). But certain decisions regarding the exercise or waiver of basic trial rights are of such moment that they cannot be made for the defendant by a surrogate. A defendant, this Court affirmed, has 'the ultimate authority' to determine 'whether to plead guilty, waive a jury, testify in his or her own behalf, or take an appeal.' *Jones v. Barnes* [Note 1, p. 209]. Concerning those decisions, an attorney must both consult with the defendant and obtain consent to the recommended course of action. * * *

"The Florida Supreme Court * * * required Nixon's 'affirmative, explicit acceptance' of Corin's strategy because it deemed Corin's statements to the jury 'the functional equivalent of a guilty plea.' We disagree with that assessment. * * * Despite Corin's concession, Nixon retained the rights accorded a defendant in a criminal trial. Cf. *Boykin v. Alabama*, 395 U.S. 238 (1969) (a guilty plea is 'more than a confession which admits that the accused did various acts,' it is a 'stipulation that no proof by the prosecution need be advanced'). The State was obliged to present during the guilt phase competent, admissible evidence establishing the essential elements of the crimes with which Nixon was charged. That aggressive evidence would thus be separated from the penalty phase, enabling the defense to concentrate that portion of the trial on mitigating factors. Further, the defense reserved the right to cross-examine witnesses for the prosecution and could endeavor, as Corin did, to exclude prejudicial evidence. In addition, in the event of errors in the trial or jury instructions, a concession of guilt would not hinder the defendant's right to appeal.

"Nixon nevertheless urges, relying on *Brookhart v. Janis* [Note 1, p. 209], that this Court has already extended the requirement of 'affirmative, explicit acceptance' to proceedings 'surrender[ing] the right to contest the prosecution's factual case on the issue of guilt or innocence.' Defense counsel in *Brookhart* had agreed [without defendants' "knowing and intelligent" concurrence] to a 'prima facie' bench trial at which the State would be relieved of its obligation to put on 'complete proof' of guilt or persuade a jury of the defendant's guilt beyond a reasonable doubt. In contrast to *Brookhart*, there was in Nixon's case no 'truncated' proceeding, shorn of the need to persuade the trier 'beyond a reasonable doubt,' and of the defendant's right to confront and cross-examine witnesses. While the 'prima facie' trial in *Brookhart* was fairly characterized as 'the equivalent of a guilty plea,' the full presentation to the jury in Nixon's case does not resemble that severely abbreviated proceeding. *Brookhart,* in short, does not carry the weight Nixon would place on it.

"Corin was obliged to, and in fact several times did, explain his proposed trial strategy to Nixon. Given Nixon's constant resistance to answering inquiries put to him by counsel and court, Corin was not additionally required to gain express consent before conceding Nixon's guilt. The two evidentiary hearings conducted by the Florida trial court demonstrate beyond doubt that Corin fulfilled his duty of consultation by informing Nixon of counsel's proposed strategy and its potential benefits. Nixon's characteristic silence each time information was conveyed to him, in sum, did not suffice to render unreasonable Corin's decision to concede guilt and to home in, instead, on the life or death penalty issue.

"The Florida Supreme Court's erroneous equation of Corin's concession strategy to a guilty plea led it to apply the wrong standard in determining whether counsel's performance ranked as ineffective assistance. * * * [The correct standard is the *Strickland* standard]. * * * [I]f counsel's strategy, given the evidence bearing on the defendant's guilt, satisfies the *Strickland* [performance] standard [of a 'reasonably competent attorney'], that is the end of the matter; no tenable claim of ineffective assistance would remain."

4. Nixon and personal decisions. Prior to *Nixon*, lower courts had divided as to whether the defendant's consent was needed to pursue a defense that challenges only the higher level of multiple charges or to adopt an "all or nothing approach" by waiving the right to a jury instruction to lesser included offenses that are not specified in the charging instrument. See CRIMPROC § 11.6(a). What, if anything, does *Nixon* suggest as to the proper characterization of such decisions? Consider CRIMPROC § 11.6(a): "*Nixon* might suggest reconsideration by lower courts that viewed * * * [these decisions] as decisions within the defendant's control. However, the issue before the Court in *Nixon* was not whether the strategy adopted by the attorney there was within the defendant's control, but whether it was so personal to the defendant that it required (as in the case of guilty plea) an explicit affirmative acceptance. The holding in *Nixon* leaves open the possibility that some decisions may be subject to the defendant's control, but also open to a decision by counsel when the defendant is consulted and refuses to make a decision."

5. *Nixon and consultation.* Does *Nixon* suggest a category of decision-making on which the defense counsel must consult, even though counsel need not abide by the defendant's decision? The Third Circuit has noted that consultation serves four important functions even where ultimate authority rests with the counsel. Consultation, the court noted, will: (1) ensure that counsel receives any factual information relevant to the issue that the defendant might have; (2) give the defendant the opportunity (depending on timing) to consider the possibility of seeking substitute counsel (see Note 2, p. 127) or proceeding *pro se*; (3) "promote and maintain a cooperative client-counsel relationship"; and (4) give to the attorney the opportunity to shape his or her decision in light of the client's views and desires concerning the best course to be followed. *Government of Virgin Islands v. Weatherwax*, 77 F.3d 1425 (3d Cir.1996).

6. *Ineffective assistance and acceptance of defendant's directions.* Even where the ultimate authority lies with counsel, can defense counsel invariably adopt the position that, "on balance, it is better to go against [your] best professional judgment, and [follow] [your] client's strongly felt views, than run the risk of a breakdown in lawyer-client communications that would be even more likely to preclude a successful defense"? CRIMPROC § 11.6(a). In applying *Strickland,* should a distinction be drawn between following the client's wishes (against the lawyer's best professional judgment) as to decisions that relate to the client's "personal values" and decisions that reflect no more than a disagreement as to "best strategy"? Justice Brennan's dissent in *Jones v. Barnes,* see fn. a, p. 210, has been characterized as stressing such personal-value decisions in arguing that the attorney should function as "the instrument and defender of the client's autonomy and dignity in all phases of the criminal process."

May a client's desire not to pursue a strategy that portrays him in a certain way justify the failure even to investigate the evidentiary strength of that strategy? The ABA Guidelines on Capital Representation provide that the investigation of a possible mitigation presentation in capital sentencing should be conducted "regardless of any initial assertion by the client that mitigation is not to be offered." Without such an investigation, it is noted, the defendant will not be able to make an informed decision. The Court majority in *Schriro v. Landrigan,* 550 U.S. 465 (2007), viewed the state court ruling there as having addressed such a situation (in contrast to the dissent's reading of the record). Among the several errors made by the Ninth Circuit on habeas review was that court's insistence that counsel should have explored "additional grounds for arguing mitigating evidence" notwithstanding defendant's instruction that a mitigation defense not be presented. The majority (per Thomas, J.) reasoned:

"The Court of Appeals held that, even if Landrigan did not want any mitigating evidence presented, the Arizona courts' determination that Landrigan's [ineffective assistance] claims were 'frivolous' and 'meritless' was an 'unreasonable application of United States Supreme Court precedent." This holding was founded on the belief, derived from *Wiggins v. Smith* [Note 2, p. 167], that 'Landrigan's apparently last-minute decision cannot excuse his counsel's failure to conduct an adequate investigation prior to the sentencing.' * * * Neither *Wiggins* nor *Strickland* addresses a situation in which a client interferes with counsel's efforts to present mitigating evidence to a sentencing court. * * * Indeed, we have never addressed a situation like this. * * * In short, at the time of the Arizona postconviction court's decision, it was not objectively unreasonable for that court to conclude that a defendant who refused to allow the presentation of any mitigating evidence could not establish *Strickland* prejudice based on his counsel's failure to investigate further possible mitigating evidence."

7. *The Gonzalez ruling.* In the latest case to consider the division of authority over defense decisions, GONZALEZ v. UNITED STATES, 553 U.S. 242 (2008), the Court reached a result that would have been anticipated under its prior precedent—the defense consent needed by statute to allow a federal magistrate to conduct *voir dire* and jury selection is satisfied by the express consent of counsel alone. However, the Court's opinion, unlike *Nixon*, did not suggest that there was a need for counsel to consult on that issue. Also, it cautioned that the Court did not have before it a situation in which the defendant objected to counsel's decision.

Under the Federal Magistrate's Act, as previously interpreted by the Court, the district court could assign to a magistrate judge the "additional duty" of presiding over *voir dire* and jury selection in a felony case "provid[ed] there is consent but not if there is an objection."[b] In *Gonzalez*, the Court considered "whether the consent can be given by counsel acting on behalf of the client but without the client's own express consent." Although the defendant had been present when counsel expressed consent in open court, counsel had noted that the defendant would need the assistance of an interpreter. The case accordingly was "decide[d] * * * on the assumption that the defendant did not hear, or did not understand, the waiver discussions."

The Court majority (per Kennedy, J.) noted that long-standing precedent recognized that "the lawyer has—and must have—full authority to manage the conduct of the trial." That position rested on several factors:

"Numerous choices affecting conduct of the trial including the objections to make, the witnesses to call, and the arguments to advance, depend not only upon what is permissible under the rules of evidence and procedure but also upon tactical considerations of the moment and the larger strategic plan for the trial. These matters can be difficult to explain to a layperson; and to require in all instances that they be approved by the client could risk compromising the efficiencies and fairness that the trial process is designed to promote. In exercising professional judgment, moreover, the attorney draws upon the expertise and experience that members of the bar should bring to the trial process. In most instances the attorney will have a better understanding of the procedural choices than the client; or at least the law should so assume."

The same considerations, the majority noted, applied to the decision at issue here: "[A]cceptance of a magistrate judge at the jury selection phase is a tactical decision that is well suited for the attorney's own decision. Under Rule 24 of the Federal Rules of Criminal Procedure, the presiding judge has significant discretion over the structure of *voir dire*. The judge may ask questions of the jury pool or, as in this case, allow the attorneys for the parties to do so. A magistrate judge's or a district judge's particular approach to *voir dire* both in substance—the questions asked—and in tone—formal or informal—may be relevant in light of the attorney's own approach. The attorney may decide whether to accept the magistrate judge based in part on these factors. As with other tactical decisions, requiring personal, on-the-record approval from the client could necessitate a lengthy explanation the client might not understand at the moment and that might distract from more pressing matters as the attorney seeks to prepare the best defense."

In light of these considerations, and the relevant statute's failure to establish a specific procedure for establishing consent, "express consent by counsel" would be deemed sufficient under that statute. The defense had argued that the cannon

---

b. Justice Thomas, the sole dissenter in *Gonzalez*, argued that this reading of the Act was erroneous, as the Act did not authorize the delegation of jury selection responsibilities even with the consent of the parties, and the earlier precedent should be overruled.

of avoiding a statutory interpretation that raises "serious concerns about [a] statute's constitutionality" should lead to an interpretation requiring the consent of the defendant. The Court concluded, however, that this cannon was inapplicable because accepting consent by counsel alone did not present any serious constitutional difficulties. "Precedents * * * holding that some basic trial choices are so important that an attorney must seek the client's consent * * * to waive" did not bear upon the tactical decision at issue here. As the defendants conceded, "[a] magistrate judge is capable of competent and impartial performance of the judicial tasks involved in jury examination and selection." Also, "the district judge—insulated by life tenure and unreducible salary—is waiting in the wings, fully able to correct errors." While "a criminal defendant may demand that an Article III judge preside over the selection of a jury, the choice to do so reflects considerations more significant to the realm of the attorney than to the accused."

The Court twice noted, however, that it was dealing only with a situation in which counsel's waiver decision was not opposed by the client. At the beginning of its discussion the Court noted: "It should be noted that we don't have before us an instance where a defendant instructs the lawyer or advises the Court in any explicit, timely way that he or she demands that a district judge preside in this preliminary phase." At the end, it added: "We do not have before us, and we do not address, an instance where the attorney states consent but the party by express and timely objection seeks to override his or her counsel. We need not decide, moreover, if consent may be inferred from a failure by a party and his or her attorney to object to the presiding by a magistrate judge. These issues are not presented here."

8. *Justice Scalia's Gonzalez opinion.* Concurring in the judgment in *Gonzalez*, Justice Scalia called for reexamination of the the distinction between strategic decisions and "fundamental right" (i.e., personal choice) decisions. He noted:

"It is important to bear in mind that we are not speaking here of action taken by counsel over his client's objection—which would have the effect of revoking the agency with respect to the action in question. See *Brookhart v. Janis* [Note 1, p. 210]. There is no suggestion of that. The issue is whether consent expressed by counsel alone is ineffective simply because the defendant himself did not express to the court his consent. * * * I think not. Our opinions have sometimes said in passing that, under the Constitution, certain "fundamental" or "basic" rights cannot be waived unless a defendant personally participates in the waiver. * * * We have even repeated the suggestion in cases that actually involved the question whether a criminal defendant's attorney could waive a certain right—but never in a case where the suggestion governed the disposition. * * *

"Since a formula repeated in dictum but never the basis for judgment is not owed *stare decisis* weight, * * * our precedents have not established the rule of decision applicable in this case. I would not adopt the tactical-vs.-fundamental approach, which is vague and derives from nothing more substantial than this Court's say-so. One respected authority has noted that the approach has a 'potential for uncertainty,' and that our precedents purporting to apply it 'have been brief and conclusionary.' 3 W. LaFave, J. Israel, N. King, & O. Kerr, *Criminal Procedure* §§ 11.6(a), (c), pp. 784, 796 (3d ed. 2007). That is surely an understatement. What makes a right tactical? Depending on the circumstances, waiving *any* right can be a tactical decision. Even pleading guilty, which waives the right to trial, is highly tactical, since it usually requires balancing the prosecutor's plea bargain against the prospect of better and worse outcomes at trial.

"Whether a right is 'fundamental' is equally mysterious. One would think that any right guaranteed by the Constitution would be fundamental. But I doubt many think that the Sixth Amendment right to confront witnesses cannot be waived by counsel. * * * Perhaps, then, specification in the Constitution is a necessary, but not sufficient, condition for 'fundamental' status. But if something more is necessary, I cannot imagine what it might be. Apart from constitutional guarantee, I know of no objective criterion for ranking rights. The Court concludes that the right to have an Article III judge oversee *voir dire* is not a fundamental right, * * * without answering whether it is even a constitutional right, and without explaining what makes a right fundamental in the first place. The essence of 'fundamental' rights continues to elude.

"I would therefore adopt the rule that, as a constitutional matter, all waivable rights (except, of course, the right to counsel) can be waived by counsel. There is no basis in the Constitution, or as far as I am aware in common-law practice, for distinguishing in this regard between a criminal defendant and his authorized representative. In fact, the very notion of representative litigation suggests that the Constitution draws no distinction between them. * * *

"It may well be desirable to require a defendant's personal waiver with regard to certain rights. * * * I do not contend that the Sixth Amendment's right to assistance of counsel prohibits such requirements of personal participation, at least where they do not impair counsel's expert assistance. * * * Even without such rules it is certainly prudent, to forestall later challenges to counsel's conduct, for a trial court to satisfy itself of the defendant's personal consent to certain actions, such as entry of a guilty plea or waiver of jury trial, for which objective norms require an attorney to seek his client's authorization. * * * But I know of no basis for saying that the *Constitution* automatically invalidates *any* trial action not taken by the defendant personally, though taken by his authorized counsel."

9. *Failing to consult and per se prejudice.* Where the choice is within defendant's control, and counsel failed to even consult, does that establish per se ineffective assistance of counsel? That situation was presented in ROE v. FLORES–ORTEGA, 528 U.S. 470 (2000), where counsel had failed to consult with the client as to the filing of an appeal and did not file an appeal. The Court majority, per O'Connor, J., concluded that these facts alone did not establish incompetency.

Justice O'Connor noted initially that since the appeal involved was a first appeal of right, defendant had a constitutional right to the effective assistance of counsel. The Court had previously held that counsel's failure to file such an appeal, when an appeal had been requested by the defendant, constituted per se ineffective assistance of counsel as it inherently met both prongs of the *Strickland* test—incompetent performance and prejudicial impact.[c] Where there was a failure to consult, however, neither prong inherently existed as the failure did not necessarily deny the defendant a right that counsel reasonably could have assumed to be of interest to the defendant, and that defendant would have exercised.

Justice O'Connor concluded that, to establish *Strickland's* first prong of professional unreasonableness based upon a failure to consult, it must be shown

---

c. Explaining these rulings, Justice O'Connor noted that the failure to comply with the client's instruction clearly was "professionally unreasonable"—the failure was not a "strategic decision," but simply "reflect[ed] inattention to the defendant's wishes" as to a decision on which the "accused has ultimate authority." As for prejudice, as the Court had noted in *Cronic*, Note 2, p. 173, "the complete denial of counsel during a critical stage of a judicial proceeding mandates a presumption of prejudice, * * * [and therefore] the even more serious denial of the entire judicial proceeding itself, which the defendant wanted at the time, and to which he had a right, similarly demands a presumption of prejudice."

either that (1) the circumstances of the case were such that a "rational defendant would [have] want[ed] to appeal," or (2) that "this particular defendant reasonably demonstrated to counsel that he was interested in appealing." Thus, a "highly relevant factor would be whether the conviction follows a trial or a guilty plea, both because a guilty plea reduces the scope of potentially appealable issues and because such a plea may indicate that the defendant seeks an end to judicial proceedings." Where a guilty plea was entered, the court therefore should look to surrounding circumstances, including "whether the defendant received the sentence bargained for" and whether the plea "expressly reserved or waived some or all appeal rights."

As for the *Strickland* element of prejudicial impact, Justice O'Connor concluded that the failure-to-consult was not inherently prejudicial. For even if "all the information counsel knew or should have known" establishes that the rational defendant would want to appeal or that this defendant demonstrated an interest in an appeal, that does not invariably establish that the failure to consult "actually caus[ed] the forfeiture of the appeal." To meet the prejudice prerequisite, the defendant must "demonstrate that there is a reasonable probability that, but for counsel's deficient failure to consult with him about an appeal, he would have timely appealed." Justice O'Connor acknowledged that this inquiry "is not wholly dissimilar from the inquiry into whether counsel performed deficiently" by failing to consult. Thus, where the defendant shows nonfrivolous grounds for appeal, that will establish both that a "rational defendant would [have] want[ed] to appeal" and a "reasonable probability" that this defendant would have chosen to appeal after consultation. On the other hand, where the failure to consult constituted deficient performance because defendant had "sufficiently demonstrated to counsel his interest in an appeal," the defendant must also be able to establish that after consultation (which might suggest an appeal was fruitless), he would have continued that interest and instructed his counsel to file the appeal.[d]

10. *Lawyer/client disagreements and the replacement of counsel.* Lower courts uniformly agree that the indigent defendant has a right to substitution of new counsel upon a showing of "good cause," but a lawyer's refusal to accept defendant's directions on strategy, where ultimate decisionmaking authority does not rest with the client, does not constitute "good cause". Rather, "good cause" is created by a conflict of interest (see § 4 infra) or a "complete breakdown in communication," and the latter cannot have been the product of defendant's abusive or uncooperative behavior (indeed, such behavior may lead the court to allow counsel to withdraw, leaving defendant to proceed *pro se*). See CRIMPROC § 11.4(b). A defendant with retained counsel similarly does not establish "good cause" simply by establishing a disagreement on strategic matters within counsel's control. However, since the defendant has a constitutionally protected interest in retaining "counsel of choice," the defendant with retained counsel will have a right to substitute new counsel if that substitution does not disrupt the court's schedule. See Note 2, p. 127.

---

d. Justice Breyer, who provided the sixth vote for the majority noted that the question presented to the Court concerned only the "filing of a notice of appeal following a guilty plea," and the opinion of the Court "in my view, makes clear that counsel 'almost always' has a constitutional duty to consult with a defendant about an appeal after a trial." Justice Ginsburg, dissenting in part, also described the majority ruling as quite narrow. She described the issue before the Court as "whether, after a defendant pleads guilty or is convicted, the Sixth Amendment permits the defense counsel to simply walk away, leaving defendant uncounseled about his appeal rights," and she characterized the majority's answer as "effectively respond[ing]: hardly ever." Justice Souter, in dissent, similarly described the issue, but characterized the majority's answer as being "sometimes," while "mine is 'almost always' in cases in which a plea of guilty has not obviously waived any claims of error."

APPOINTED COUNSEL AND THE FRIVOLOUS APPEALS

1. *Frivolous appeals & retained or appointed counsel.* The decision to appeal clearly belongs to the defendant, but the lawyer representing the defendant has an ethical obligation not to present a frivolous appeal.[e] Commentators contend that the practical realities of reconciling these conflicting interests are quite different depending on whether appellate counsel is retained or appointed. Initially, where counsel informs the client that the appeal is frivolous and undoubtedly will fail, the client with a retained lawyer will take into account the financial costs and is more likely to drop the appeal. The indigent defendant, it is argued, is in a "no-lose situation," and therefore more likely to continue the appeal even if he believes that "only a miracle" will produce success. Second, recognizing that the retained attorney is turning down a fee, the defendant with retained counsel is more likely to accept counsel's conclusion than the indigent defendant, who may feel that appointed counsel is merely turning down a case that will require more effort than others. Third, if the defendant with retained counsel rejects counsel's advice to drop the appeal, he does not typically face the prospect of proceeding without counsel; instead, defendant can "shop around" and is likely to find a lawyer who, "if he finds the money right," will conclude that the case may be very weak, but still is "arguable." A defendant with appointed appellate counsel, in contrast, loses representation, as the appointed counsel must obtain court approval to withdraw, and if the court agrees that the appeal is frivolous, it certainly will not appoint substitute counsel.

The third distinction noted above has largely shaped the opportunity for courts to address the relationship between the defendant's right to insist upon an appeal, assisted by counsel, and the counsel's obligation not to press a frivolous claim. The relevant caselaw almost entirely involves motions by appointed counsel to withdraw, and the Supreme Court precedent, discussed below, has focused on that withdrawal procedure as it bears upon the indigent defendant's constitutional right to appointed counsel on an initial appeal as of right.

2. *The Anders rules.* In ANDERS v. CALIFORNIA, 386 U.S. 738 (1967), the Court unanimously agreed that the constitutional right to appointed counsel on first appeal as of right did not preclude a state's appellate court's acceptance of appointed counsel's withdrawal where the appeal was "frivolous." The Court majority (6–3) held, however, that the withdrawal procedure utilized in California did not provide satisfactory safeguards against undermining the defendant's constitutional right to representation by counsel. The California procedure allowed counsel to withdraw after counsel sent a conclusory "no merit" letter to the appellate court and the appellate court, after reviewing the record, affirmed the judgment below on a finding of "lack of merit." There was no assurance that the counsel acted in the role of an advocate rather than "as *amicus curiae*" in filing the no-merit letter. In addition, there was confusion as to whether the appellate court's "no merit" ruling constituted a "finding of frivolity." But even if it clearly found frivolity, since there was no assurance that counsel's conclusion came after "diligent investigation" in seeking to "support his client's appeal to the best of his ability," the court's finding would lack the "full consideration * * * as is obtained" when counsel has "act[ed] in the role of an advocate."

Describing the kind of withdrawal procedure that would provide adequate safeguards of the constitutional right, the *Anders* majority set forth the basic

---

e. See ABA Model Rule of Professional Conduct, Rule 3.1, noting that a lawyer shall not assert a claim "unless there is a basis for doing so that is not frivolous." The Rule adds, as to the trial stage, that a "lawyer for a defendant in a criminal proceeding * * * may nevertheless so defend * * * as to require every element of the case be established."

elements of what was later described as the "*Anders* prophylactic framework for withdrawal": That framework had four elements: (1) after a "conscientious examination" of the appeal, counsel must determine that the appeal is "wholly frivolous" and "so advise the court and request permission to withdraw"; (2) "that request must be accompanied by a brief referring to anything in the record that might arguably support the appeal"; (3) "a copy of counsel's brief should be furnished [to] the indigent [defendant] and time allowed him to raise any points that he chooses"; and (4) the appellate court, "after a full examination of all the proceeding," must find that "the case is wholly frivolous."

3. *State responses to Anders.* Most states continue to allow withdrawals, and in several of these states withdrawals are quite common, see CRIMPROC § 11.2(c) (as high as 39% in one state). Approximately a dozen states have responded to *Anders* by prohibiting withdrawal by appointed counsel, insisting that counsel file a brief even though regarding the appeal as frivolous. Some oppose withdrawal as "inappropriately limiting representation in cases where the defendant with retained counsel would be receiving representation." Others see the *Anders* withdrawal procedure as not worth its costs. They cite the following reasons: "(1) a defendant is prejudiced by an improper motion to withdraw even if eventually rejected by the appellate court; (2) an improper motion requires a substitution of new counsel, which is costly; (3) 'as long as counsel must research and prepare an advocate's brief, he or she might as well submit it for the purposes of an ordinary appeal'; and (4) the avoidance of a double review in cases in which the appeal is not frivolous results in a savings of time and effort for the reviewing court."

A substantial majority of the states continuing to allow withdrawals utilize a procedure modeled on the prophylactic framework set forth in *Anders*. Several states, however, have departed significantly from that framework, leading to further litigation.

4. *The constitutionality of Anders alternatives.* Subsequent Supreme Court rulings have concluded that the *Anders* prophylactic framework was not mandated, but simply presented as an illustration of "one method of satisfying the requirements of the Constitution for indigent criminal appeals." The state has leeway to craft other methods that also guarantee a "fair opportunity to obtain an adjudication on the merits of the appeal," with that fairness judged in light of "the underlying goals that the procedure should serve to ensure that those indigents whose appeals are not frivolous receive the counsel and merits brief required by *Douglas*, and [to allow the state] to protect itself so that frivolous appeals are not subsidized and public moneys not needlessly spent." *Smith v. Robbins*, 528 U.S. 259 (2000).

In *Smith*, a closely divided Court upheld a procedure under which counsel initially informed the appellate court (and the client) that he had reviewed the record and found the appeal to be frivolous and attached a summary of the "procedural and factual history of the case with citations to the record." The appellate court then independently examined the record and required counsel to brief on the merits if it found any non-frivolous issues, and if not, affirmed the conviction. The Court noted that this procedure: (1) required a determination that the appeal was "frivolous" (as contrasted to rejected state procedures that had asked counsel or court to determine only that the appeal was unlikely to prevail); (2) provided "at least two tiers of review" (by counsel and court) of the frivolity issue; (3) precluded the possibility of counsel withdrawing and the appellate court then being required to rule on the merits of a non-frivolous issue without substantive briefing; and (4) did not allow counsel to file a "bare conclusion" statement of his analysis, but required a summary of the case's procedural and factual history, which "both ensures that a trained legal eye has searched the record for arguable issues and assists the reviewing court in its own evaluation of the case." See also *McCoy v. Court of Appeals of Wis.*, 486 U.S. 429 (1988) (withdrawal procedure that required counsel to cite in his withdrawal brief the precedent which led him to conclude the appeal would be frivolous was consistent with *Anders,* as the function of an *Anders* brief is not to be a "substitute for an advocate's brief," but to ensure "that counsel has been diligent in examining the record for meritorious issues").

PART 2

POLICE PRACTICES

■ ■ ■

CHAPTER 6

ARREST, SEARCH AND SEIZURE[a]

■ ■ ■

The Fourth Amendment (see Supp. App. A), dealing with seizure and search of persons, places and things, often comes into play in criminal prosecutions because evidence acquired in violation of the Amendment is usually subject to exclusion. The most pervasive issues arising in that context, all discussed in this Chapter, are: (1) What is the rationale and scope of this exclusionary rule? (2) What police conduct constitutes a "search" or "seizure," so as to be subject to the Amendment's limitations? (3) How much information is needed to meet the Amendment's "probable cause" test, ordinarily the prerequisite for a search or seizure? (4) How does the Amendment govern the manner in which warrants are to be issued and executed? (5) In what circumstances may a search or a seizure be conducted without first obtaining a warrant? (6) In what circumstances may a search or seizure be conducted even without probable cause?

SECTION 1. THE EXCLUSIONARY RULE[b]

WOLF v. COLORADO
338 U.S. 25, 69 S.Ct. 1359, 93 L.Ed. 1782 (1949).

JUSTICE FRANKFURTER delivered the opinion of the Court.

The precise question for consideration is this: Does a conviction by a State court for a State offense deny the "due process of law" required by the Fourteenth Amendment, solely because evidence that was admitted at the trial was obtained under circumstances which would have rendered it inadmissible in a prosecution for violation of a federal law in a court of the United States because there deemed to be an infraction of the Fourth Amendment as applied in *Weeks v. United States,* 232 U.S. 383 [1914]? * * *

The security of one's privacy against arbitrary intrusion by the police—which is at the core of the Fourth Amendment—is basic to a free society. It is therefore implicit in "the concept of ordered liberty" and as such enforceable against the States through the Due Process Clause. * * *

---

a. For detailed treatment of this subject and reference to other secondary sources, consult Wayne R. LaFave, *Search and Seizure: A Treatise on the Fourth Amendment* (6 vols., 4th ed.2004) [cited herein by its Westlaw database name SEARCHSZR].

b. The concern herein is with the exclusion of evidence obtained in violation of the Fourth Amendment. An arrest or search which passes Fourth Amendment muster may nonetheless violate state law, and the exclusionary sanction is also used when state constitutional provisions similar to the Fourth Amendment have been violated, though if a state chooses not to do so this does not violate federal due process. *California v. Greenwood,* p. 267. As for violations of statutes, court rules and administrative regulations, it is customary to require exclusion if the violation significantly affected the defendant's substantial rights.

Accordingly, we have no hesitation in saying that were a State affirmatively to sanction such police incursion into privacy it would run counter to the guaranty of the Fourteenth Amendment. But the ways of enforcing such a basic right raise questions of a different order. How such arbitrary conduct should be checked, what remedies against it should be afforded, the means by which the right should be made effective, are all questions that are not to be so dogmatically answered as to preclude the varying solutions which spring from an allowable range of judgment on issues not susceptible of quantitative solution.

In *Weeks v. United States,* this Court held that in a federal prosecution the Fourth Amendment barred the use of evidence secured through an illegal search and seizure. This ruling * * * was not derived from the explicit requirements of the Fourth Amendment; it was not based on legislation expressing Congressional policy in the enforcement of the Constitution. The decision was a matter of judicial implication. Since then it has been frequently applied and we stoutly adhere to it. But the immediate question is whether the basic right to protection against arbitrary intrusion by the police demands the exclusion of logically relevant evidence obtained by an unreasonable search and seizure because, in a federal prosecution for a federal crime, it would be excluded. As a matter of inherent reason, one would suppose this to be an issue as to which men with complete devotion to the protection of the right of privacy might give different answers. When we find that in fact most of the English-speaking world does not regard as vital to such protection the exclusion of evidence thus obtained, we must hesitate to treat this remedy as an essential ingredient of the right. The contrariety of views of the States is particularly impressive in view of the careful reconsideration which they have given the problem in the light of the *Weeks* decision.

* * * As of today 30 States reject the *Weeks* doctrine, 17 States are in agreement with it. * * * Of 10 jurisdictions within the United Kingdom and the British Commonwealth of Nations which have passed on the question, none has held evidence obtained by illegal search and seizure inadmissible. * * *

The jurisdictions which have rejected the *Weeks* doctrine have not left the right to privacy without other means of protection. Indeed, the exclusion of evidence is a remedy which directly serves only to protect those upon whose person or premises something incriminating has been found. We cannot, therefore, regard it as a departure from basic standards to remand such persons, together with those who emerge scatheless from a search, to the remedies of private action and such protection as the internal discipline of the police, under the eyes of an alert public opinion, may afford. Granting that in practice the exclusion of evidence may be an effective way of deterring unreasonable searches, it is not for this Court to condemn as falling below the minimal standards assured by the Due Process Clause a State's reliance upon other methods which, if consistently enforced, would be equally effective. * * * There are, moreover, reasons for excluding evidence unreasonably obtained by the federal police which are less compelling in the case of police under State or local authority. The public opinion of a community can far more effectively be exerted against oppressive conduct on the part of police directly responsible to the community itself than can local opinion, sporadically aroused, be brought to bear upon remote authority pervasively exerted throughout the country.

We hold, therefore, that in a prosecution in a State court for a State crime the Fourteenth Amendment does not forbid the admission of evidence obtained by an unreasonable search and seizure. * * *

JUSTICE BLACK, concurring.

* * * I agree with what appears to be a plain implication of the Court's opinion that the federal exclusionary rule is not a command of the Fourth Amendment but is a judicially created rule of evidence which Congress might negate. * * *

JUSTICE MURPHY, with whom JUSTICE RUTLEDGE joins, dissenting.

[T]here is but one alternative to the rule of exclusion. That is no sanction at all.

* * * Little need be said concerning the possibilities of criminal prosecution. Self-scrutiny is a lofty ideal, but its exaltation reaches new heights if we expect a District Attorney to prosecute himself or his associates for well-meaning violations of the search and seizure clause during a raid the District Attorney or his associates have ordered. But there is an appealing ring in another alternative. A trespass action for damages is a venerable means of securing reparation for unauthorized invasion of the home. Why not put the old writ to a new use? When the Court cites cases permitting the action, the remedy seems complete.

But what an illusory remedy this is, if by "remedy" we mean a positive deterrent to police and prosecutors tempted to violate the Fourth Amendment. The appealing ring softens when we recall that in a trespass action the measure of damages is simply the extent of the injury to physical property. If the officer searches with care, he can avoid all but nominal damages—a penny, or a dollar. Are punitive damages possible? Perhaps. But a few states permit none, whatever the circumstances. In those that do, the plaintiff must show the real ill will or malice of the defendant, and surely it is not unreasonable to assume that one in honest pursuit of crime bears no malice toward the search victim. If that burden is carried, recovery may yet be defeated by the rule that there must be physical damages before punitive damages may be awarded. In addition, some states limit punitive damages to the actual expenses of litigation. * * * Even assuming the ill will of the officer, his reasonable grounds for belief that the home he searched harbored evidence of crime is admissible in mitigation of punitive damages. * * * The bad reputation of the plaintiff is likewise admissible. * * * If the evidence seized was actually used at a trial, that fact has been held a complete justification of the search, and a defense against the trespass action. * * * And even if the plaintiff hurdles all these obstacles, and gains a substantial verdict, the individual officer's finances may well make the judgment useless—for the municipality, of course, is not liable without its consent. Is it surprising that there is so little in the books concerning trespass actions for violation of the search and seizure clause? * * *

JUSTICE DOUGLAS, dissenting.

* * * I agree with Justice Murphy that * * * in absence of [an exclusionary] rule of evidence the Amendment would have no effective sanction. * * *

MAPP v. OHIO
367 U.S. 643, 81 S.Ct. 1684, 6 L.Ed.2d 1081 (1961).

JUSTICE CLARK delivered the opinion of the Court. * * *

On May 23, 1957, three Cleveland police officers arrived at appellant's residence in that city pursuant to information that "a person [was] hiding out in the home who was wanted for questioning in connection with a recent bombing, and that there was a large amount of policy paraphernalia being hidden in the home." Miss Mapp and her daughter by a former marriage lived on the top floor of the two-family dwelling. Upon their arrival at that house, the officers knocked on the door and demanded entrance but appellant, after telephoning her attorney, refused to admit them without a search warrant. * * *

The officers again sought entrance some three hours later when four or more additional officers arrived on the scene. When Miss Mapp did not come to the door immediately, at least one of the several doors to the house was forcibly opened and the policemen gained admittance. Meanwhile Miss Mapp's attorney arrived, but the officers, having secured their own entry, and continuing in their defiance of the law, would permit him neither to see Miss Mapp nor to enter the house. [When the officers broke into the hall, Miss Mapp] demanded to see the search warrant. A paper, claimed to be a warrant, was held up by one of the officers. She grabbed the "warrant" and placed it in her bosom. A struggle ensued in which the officers recovered the piece of paper and as a result of which they handcuffed appellant because she had been "belligerent" in resisting their official rescue of the "warrant" from her person. * * * Appellant, in handcuffs, was then forcibly taken upstairs to her bedroom where the officers searched a dresser, a chest of drawers, a closet and some suitcases. * * * The search spread to the rest of the second floor * * *. The basement of the building and a trunk found therein were also searched. The obscene materials for possession of which she was ultimately convicted were discovered in the course of that widespread search.

At the trial no search warrant was produced by the prosecution, nor was the failure to produce one explained or accounted for. At best [as the Ohio Supreme Court, which affirmed the conviction, expressed it], "there is, in the record, considerable doubt as to whether there ever was any warrant for the search of defendant's home." * * *

The State says that even if the search were made without authority, or otherwise unreasonably, it is not prevented from using the unconstitutionally seized evidence at trial, citing *Wolf v. Colorado,* * * *. On this appeal, * * * it is urged once again that we review that holding. * * *

The Court in *Wolf* first stated that "[t]he contrariety of views of the States" on the adoption of the exclusionary rule of *Weeks* was "particularly impressive." * * * While in 1949, prior to the *Wolf* case, almost two-thirds of the States were opposed to the use of the exclusionary rule, now, despite the *Wolf* case, more than half of those since passing upon it, by their own legislative or judicial decision, have wholly or partly adopted or adhered to the *Weeks* rule. * * * Significantly, among those now following the rule is California which, according to its highest court, was "compelled to reach that conclusion because other remedies have completely failed to secure compliance with the constitutional provisions * * *." In connection with this California case, we note that the second basis elaborated in *Wolf* in support of its failure to enforce the exclusionary doctrine against the States was that "other means of protection" have been afforded "the right to privacy." The experience of California that such other remedies have been worthless and futile is buttressed by the experience of other States. * * *

It, therefore, plainly appears that the factual considerations supporting the failure of the *Wolf* Court to include the *Weeks* exclusionary rule when it recognized the enforceability of the right to privacy against the States in 1949, while not basically relevant to the constitutional consideration, could not, in any analysis, now be deemed controlling.

* * * Today we once again examine *Wolf's* constitutional documentation of the right to privacy free from unreasonable state intrusion, and, after its dozen years on our books, are led by it to close the only courtroom door remaining open to evidence secured by official lawlessness in flagrant abuse of that basic right, reserved to all persons as a specific guarantee against that very same unlawful conduct. We hold that all evidence obtained by searches and seizures in violation of the Constitution is, by that same authority, inadmissible in a state court.

Since the Fourth Amendment's right of privacy has been declared enforceable against the States through the Due Process Clause of the Fourteenth, it is enforceable against them by the same sanction of exclusion as is used against the Federal Government. Were it otherwise then just as without the *Weeks* rule the assurance against unreasonable federal searches and seizures would be "a form of words," valueless and undeserving of mention in a perpetual charter of inestimable human liberties, so too, without that rule the freedom from state invasions of privacy would be so ephemeral and so neatly severed from its conceptual nexus with the freedom from all brutish means of coercing evidence as not to merit this Court's high regard as a freedom "implicit in 'the concept of ordered liberty.'"

* * * [I]n extending the substantive protections of due process to all constitutionally unreasonable searches—state or federal—it was logically and constitutionally necessary that the exclusion doctrine—an essential part of the right to privacy—be also insisted upon as an essential ingredient of the right newly recognized by the *Wolf* case. In short, the admission of the new constitutional right by *Wolf* could not consistently tolerate denial of its most important constitutional privilege, namely, the exclusion of the evidence which an accused had been forced to give by reason of the unlawful seizure. To hold otherwise is to grant the right but in reality to withhold its privilege and enjoyment. Only last year the Court itself recognized that the purpose of the exclusionary rule "is to deter—to compel respect for the constitutional guaranty in the only effectively available way—by removing the incentive to disregard it."

Indeed, we are aware of no restraint, similar to that rejected today, conditioning the enforcement of any other basic constitutional right. The right to privacy, no less important than any other right carefully and particularly reserved to the people, would stand in marked contrast to all other rights declared as "basic to a free society." * * * [N]othing could be more certain than that when a coerced confession is involved, "the relevant rules of evidence" are overridden without regard to "the incidence of such conduct by the police," slight or frequent. Why should not the same rule apply to what is tantamount to coerced testimony by way of unconstitutional seizure of goods, papers, effects, documents, etc.? We find that, as to the Federal Government the Fourth and Fifth Amendments and, as to the States, the freedom from unconscionable invasions of privacy and the freedom from convictions based upon coerced confessions do enjoy an "intimate relation" in their perpetuation of "principles of humanity and civil liberty * * *." They express "supplementing phases of the same constitutional purpose—to maintain inviolate large areas of personal privacy." The philosophy of each Amendment and of each freedom is complementary to, although not dependent upon, that of the other in its sphere of influence—the very least that together they assure in either sphere is that no man is to be convicted on unconstitutional evidence.

Moreover, our holding * * * is not only the logical dictate of prior cases, but it also makes very good sense. There is no war between the Constitution and common sense. Presently, a federal prosecutor may make no use of evidence illegally seized, but a State's attorney across the street may, although he supposedly is operating under the enforceable prohibitions of the same Amendment. Thus the State, by admitting evidence unlawfully seized, serves to encourage disobedience to the Federal Constitution which it is bound to uphold. * * *

There are those who say, as did Justice (then Judge) Cardozo, that under our constitutional exclusionary doctrine "[t]he criminal is to go free because the constable has blundered." *People v. Defore*, 150 N.E. 585 (N.Y.1926). In some cases this will undoubtedly be the result. But, "there is another consideration—the imperative of judicial integrity." The criminal goes free, if he must, but it is the law that sets him free. Nothing can destroy a government more quickly than its failure to observe its own laws, or worse, its disregard of the charter of its own existence. As Justice Brandeis, dissenting, said in *Olmstead v. United States* [p. 505]: "Our government is the potent, the omnipresent teacher. For good or for ill, it teaches the whole people by its example. * * * If the government becomes a lawbreaker, it breeds contempt for law; it invites every man to become a law unto himself; it invites anarchy." Nor can it lightly be assumed that, as a practical matter, adoption of the exclusionary rule fetters law enforcement. Only last year this Court expressly considered that contention and found that "pragmatic evidence of a sort" to the contrary was not wanting. *Elkins v. United States*, 364 U.S. 206 (1960). * * * The Court noted that:

"The federal courts themselves have operated under the exclusionary rule of *Weeks* for almost half a century; yet it has not been suggested either that the Federal Bureau of Investigation has thereby been rendered ineffective, or that the administration of criminal justice in the federal courts has thereby been disrupted. Moreover, the experience of the states is impressive * * *. The movement toward the rule of exclusion has been halting but seemingly inexorable."

The ignoble shortcut to conviction left open to the State tends to destroy the entire system of constitutional restraints on which the liberties of the people rest. Having once recognized that the right to privacy embodied in the Fourth Amendment is enforceable against the States, and that the right to be secure against rude invasions of privacy by state officers is, therefore, constitutional in origin, we can no longer permit that right to remain an empty promise. Because it is enforceable in the same manner and to like effect as other basic rights secured by the Due Process Clause, we can no longer permit it to be revocable at the whim of any police officer who, in the name of law enforcement itself, chooses to suspend its enjoyment. Our decision, founded on reason and truth, gives to the individual no more than that which the Constitution guarantees him, to the police officer no less than that to which honest law enforcement is entitled, and, to the courts, that judicial integrity so necessary in the true administration of justice. * * *

Reversed and remanded.[a]

JUSTICE HARLAN, whom JUSTICE FRANKFURTER and JUSTICE WHITTAKER join, dissenting. * * *

I would not impose upon the States this federal exclusionary remedy. The reasons given by the majority for now suddenly turning its back on *Wolf* seem to me notably unconvincing.

First, it is said that "the factual grounds upon which *Wolf* was based" have since changed, in that more States now follow the *Weeks* exclusionary rule than was so at the time *Wolf* was decided. While that is true, a recent survey indicates that at present one half of the States still adhere to the common-law non-exclusionary rule, and one, Maryland, retains the rule as to felonies. * * * But in any case surely all this is beside the point, as the majority itself indeed seems to recognize. Our concern here, as it was in *Wolf*, is not with the desirability of that rule but only with the question whether the States are Constitutionally free to follow it or not as they may themselves determine, and the relevance of the disparity of views among the States on this point lies simply in the fact that the judgment involved is a debatable one. Moreover, the very fact on which the majority relies, instead of lending support to what is now being done, points away from the need of replacing voluntary state action with federal compulsion.

The preservation of a proper balance between state and federal responsibility in the administration of criminal justice demands patience on the part of those who might like to see things move faster among the States in this respect.

---

a. Concurring opinions by Black and Douglas, JJ., and a memorandum by Stewart, J., are omitted.

Problems of criminal law enforcement vary widely from State to State. One State, in considering the totality of its legal picture, may conclude that the need for embracing the *Weeks* rule is pressing because other remedies are unavailable or inadequate to secure compliance with the substantive Constitutional principle involved. Another, though equally solicitous of Constitutional rights, may choose to pursue one purpose at a time, allowing all evidence relevant to guilt to be brought into a criminal trial, and dealing with Constitutional infractions by other means. Still another may consider the exclusionary rule too rough and ready a remedy, in that it reaches only unconstitutional intrusions which eventuate in criminal prosecution of the victims. Further, a State after experimenting with the *Weeks* rule for a time may, because of unsatisfactory experience with it, decide to revert to a non-exclusionary rule. And so on. * * * For us the question remains, as it has always been, one of state power, not one of passing judgment on the wisdom of one state course or another. In my view this Court should continue to forbear from fettering the States with an adamant rule which may embarrass them in coping with their own peculiar problems in criminal law enforcement. * * *

* * * Our role in promulgating the *Weeks* rule and its extensions * * * was quite a different one than it is here. There, in implementing the Fourth Amendment, we occupied the position of a tribunal having the ultimate responsibility for developing the standards and procedures of judicial administration within the judicial system over which it presides. Here we review State procedures whose measure is to be taken not against the specific substantive commands of the Fourth Amendment but under the flexible contours of the Due Process Clause. I do not believe that the Fourteenth Amendment empowers this Court to mould state remedies effectuating the right to freedom from "arbitrary intrusion by the police" to suit its own notions of how things should be done * * *.

Finally, it is said that the overruling of *Wolf* is supported by the established doctrine that the admission in evidence of an involuntary confession renders a state conviction constitutionally invalid. Since such a confession may often be entirely reliable, and therefore of the greatest relevance to the issue of the trial, the argument continues, this doctrine is ample warrant in precedent that the way evidence was obtained and not just its relevance, is constitutionally significant to the fairness of a trial. I believe this analogy is not a true one. The "coerced confession" rule is certainly not a rule that any illegally obtained statements may not be used in evidence. I would suppose that a statement which is procured during a period of illegal detention is, as much as unlawfully seized evidence, illegally obtained, but this Court has consistently refused to reverse state convictions resting on the use of such statements. * * *

The point, then, must be that in requiring exclusion of an involuntary statement of an accused, we are concerned not with an appropriate remedy for what the police have done, but with something which is regarded as going to the heart of our concepts of fairness in judicial procedure. The operative assumption of our procedural system is that "ours is the accusatorial as opposed to the inquisitorial system. * * *." * * * The pressures brought to bear against an accused leading to a confession, unlike an unconstitutional violation of privacy, do not, apart from the use of the confession at trial, necessarily involve independent Constitutional violations. What is crucial is that the trial defense to which an accused is entitled should not be rendered an empty formality by reason of statements wrung from him, for then "a prisoner * * * [has been] made the deluded instrument of his own conviction." That this is a *procedural right,* and that its violation occurs at the time his improperly obtained statement is admitted at trial, is manifest.^b * * *

This, and not the disciplining of the police, as with illegally seized evidence, is surely the true basis for excluding a statement of the accused which was unconstitutionally obtained. In sum, I think the coerced confession analogy works strongly *against* what the Court does today. * * *

UNITED STATES v. LEON

468 U.S. 897, 104 S.Ct. 3405, 82 L.Ed.2d 677 (1984).

JUSTICE WHITE delivered the opinion of the Court. * * *

This case presents the question whether the Fourth Amendment exclusionary rule should be modified so as not to bar the use in the prosecution's case-in-chief of evidence obtained by officers acting in reasonable reliance on a search warrant issued by a detached and neutral magistrate but ultimately found to be unsupported by probable cause. * * *

The Fourth Amendment contains no provision expressly precluding the use of evidence obtained in violation of its commands, and an examination of its origin and purposes makes clear that the use of fruits of a past unlawful search or seizure "work[s] no new Fourth Amendment wrong." The wrong condemned by the Amendment is "fully accomplished" by the unlawful search or seizure itself, and the exclusionary rule is neither intended nor able to "cure the invasion of the defendant's rights which he has already suffered." The rule thus operates as "a judicially created remedy designed to safeguard Fourth Amendment rights generally through its deterrent effect, rather than a personal constitutional right of the person aggrieved."

Whether the exclusionary sanction is appropriately imposed in a particular case, our decisions make clear, is "an issue separate from the question whether the Fourth Amendment rights of the party seeking to invoke the rule were violated by police conduct." Only the former question is currently before us,^a and it must be resolved by weighing the costs and benefits of preventing the use in the prosecution's case-in-chief of inherently trustworthy tangible evidence obtained in reliance on a search warrant issued by a detached and neutral magistrate that ultimately is found to be defective.

The substantial social costs exacted by the exclusionary rule for the vindication of Fourth Amendment rights have long been a source of concern. "Our cases have consistently recognized that unbending application of the exclusionary sanction to enforce ideals of governmental rectitude would impede unacceptably the truth-finding functions of judge and jury." An objectionable collateral consequence of this interference with the criminal justice system's truth-finding function is that some guilty defendants may go free or receive reduced sentences as a result of favorable plea bargains.⁶ Particularly when law enforcement officers have acted

---

b. Is this so? Would such an argument have carried more force after the privilege against self-incrimination was held applicable in the police station? See *Chavez v. Martinez*, p. 690.

a. Large quantities of drugs were suppressed on the ground the warrant had not issued on probable cause, in that the affidavit reported only the allegations of an untested informant and limited corroboration by police surveillance of events themselves "as consistent with innocence as * * * with guilt." The Court earlier noted that whether this warrant would pass muster under the intervening and less demanding test of *Illinois v. Gates,* p. 295, "has not been briefed or argued," and thus chose "to take the case as it comes to us."

6. Researchers have only recently begun to study extensively the effects of the exclusionary rule on the disposition of felony arrests. One study suggests that the rule results in the nonprosecution or nonconviction of between 0.6% and 2.35% of individuals arrested for felonies. Davies, *A Hard Look at What We Know (and Still Need to Learn) About the "Costs" of the Exclusionary Rule: The NIJ Study and Other Studies of "Lost" Arrests,* 1983 A.B.F.Res.J. 611,

in objective good faith or their transgressions have been minor, the magnitude of the benefit conferred on such guilty defendants offends basic concepts of the criminal justice system. Indiscriminate application of the exclusionary rule, therefore, may well "generat[e] disrespect for the law and the administration of justice." Accordingly, "[a]s with any remedial device, the application of the rule has been restricted to those areas where its remedial objectives are thought most efficaciously served."

Close attention to those remedial objectives has characterized our recent decisions concerning the scope of the Fourth Amendment exclusionary rule. The Court has, to be sure, not seriously questioned, "in the absence of a more efficacious sanction, the continued application of the rule to suppress evidence from the [prosecution's] case where a Fourth Amendment violation has been substantial and deliberate * * *." Nevertheless, the balancing approach that has evolved in various contexts—including criminal trials—"forcefully suggest[s] that the exclusionary rule be more generally modified to permit the introduction of evidence obtained in the reasonable good-faith belief that a search or seizure was in accord with the Fourth Amendment."

In *Stone v. Powell*, 428 U.S. 465 (1976), the Court emphasized the costs of the exclusionary rule, expressed its view that limiting the circumstances under which Fourth Amendment claims could be raised in federal habeas corpus proceedings would not reduce the rule's deterrent effect, and held that a state prisoner who has been afforded a full and fair opportunity to litigate a Fourth Amendment claim may not obtain federal habeas relief on the ground that unlawfully obtained evidence had been introduced at his trial. Proposed extensions of the exclusionary rule to proceedings other than the criminal trial itself have been evaluated and rejected under the same analytic approach[, as in *United States v. Calandra*, p. 247, and *United States v. Janis*, p. 248.]

[C]ases considering the use of unlawfully obtained evidence in criminal trials themselves [also] make clear [that] it does not follow from the emphasis on the exclusionary rule's deterrent value that "anything which deters illegal searches is thereby commanded by the Fourth Amendment." *Alderman v. United States* [p. 880]. * * * Standing to invoke the rule has thus been limited to cases in which the prosecution seeks to use the fruits of an illegal search or seizure against the victim of police misconduct. *Rakas v. Illinois* [p. 884]. Even defendants with standing to challenge the introduction in their criminal trials of unlawfully obtained evidence cannot prevent every conceivable use of such evidence. Evidence obtained in violation of the Fourth Amendment and inadmissible in the prosecution's case in chief may be used to impeach a defendant's direct testimony. *Walder v. United States* [p. 910]. * * *

When considering the use of evidence obtained in violation of the Fourth Amendment in the prosecution's case in chief, moreover, we have declined to

---

621. The estimates are higher for particular crimes the prosecution of which depends heavily on physical evidence. Thus, the cumulative loss due to nonprosecution or nonconviction of individuals arrested on felony drug charges is probably in the range of 2.8% to 7.1%. Davies' analysis of California data suggests that screening by police and prosecutors results in the release because of illegal searches or seizures of as many as 1.4% of all felony arrestees, id., at 650, that 0.9% of felony arrestees are released because of illegal searches or seizures at the preliminary hearing or after trial, *id.,* at 653, and that roughly 0.5% of all felony arrestees benefit from reversals on appeal because of illegal searches. * * *

Many of these researchers have concluded that the impact of the exclusionary rule is insubstantial, but the small percentages with which they deal mask a large absolute number of felons who are released because the cases against them were based in part on illegal searches or seizures. * * * Because we find that the rule can have no substantial deterrent effect in the sorts of situations under consideration in this case, we conclude that it cannot pay its way in those situations.

adopt a *per se* or "but for" rule that would render inadmissible any evidence that came to light through a chain of causation that began with an illegal arrest. *Brown v. Illinois* [p. 895]; *Wong Sun v. United States* [p. 894]. We also have held that a witness' testimony may be admitted even when his identity was discovered in an unconstitutional search. *United States v. Ceccolini* [p. 903]. The perception underlying these decisions—that the connection between police misconduct and evidence of crime may be sufficiently attenuated to permit the use of that evidence at trial—is a product of considerations relating to the exclusionary rule and the constitutional principles it is designed to protect. * * * Not surprisingly in view of this purpose, an assessment of the flagrancy of the police misconduct constitutes an important step in the calculus. *Brown v. Illinois*, supra. * * *

As yet, we have not recognized any form of good-faith exception to the Fourth Amendment exclusionary rule. But the balancing approach that has evolved during the years of experience with the rule provides strong support for the modification currently urged upon us. As we discuss below, our evaluation of the costs and benefits of suppressing reliable physical evidence seized by officers reasonably relying on a warrant issued by a detached and neutral magistrate leads to the conclusion that such evidence should be admissible in the prosecution's case in chief. * * *

Only [when a warrant is grounded upon an affidavit knowingly or recklessly false] has the Court set forth a rationale for suppressing evidence obtained pursuant to a search warrant;[b] in the other areas, it has simply excluded such evidence without considering whether Fourth Amendment interests will be advanced. To the extent that proponents of exclusion rely on its behavioral effects on judges and magistrates in these areas, their reliance is misplaced. First, the exclusionary rule is designed to deter police misconduct rather than to punish the errors of judges and magistrates. Second, there exists no evidence suggesting that judges and magistrates are inclined to ignore or subvert the Fourth Amendment or that lawlessness among these actors requires application of the extreme sanction of exclusion.[14]

Third, and most important, we discern no basis, and are offered none, for believing that exclusion of evidence seized pursuant to a warrant will have a significant deterrent effect on the issuing judge or magistrate. Many of the factors that indicate that the exclusionary rule cannot provide an effective "special" or "general" deterrent for individual offending law enforcement officers apply as well to judges or magistrates. And, to the extent that the rule is thought to operate as a "systemic" deterrent on a wider audience, it clearly can have no such effect on individuals empowered to issue warrants. Judges and magistrates are not adjuncts to the law enforcement team; as neutral judicial officers, they have no stake in the outcome of particular criminal prosecutions. The threat of exclusion thus cannot be expected significantly to deter them. Imposition of the exclusionary sanction is not necessary meaningfully to inform judicial officers of their errors, and we cannot conclude that admitting evidence obtained pursuant to a warrant while at the same time declaring that the warrant was somehow defective will in any way reduce judicial officers' professional incentives to comply with the Fourth Amendment, encourage them to repeat their mistakes, or lead to the granting of all colorable warrant requests.[18]

---

b. The reference is to the *Franks* case, p. 307, where the Court declared "it would be an unthinkable imposition upon [the magistrate's] authority if a warrant affidavit, revealed after the fact to contain a deliberately or recklessly false statement, were to stand beyond impeachment."

14. Although there are assertions that some magistrates become rubber stamps for the police and others may be unable effectively to screen police conduct, we are not convinced that this is a problem of major proportions.

18. Limiting the application of the exclusionary sanction may well increase the care with which magistrates scrutinize warrant applications. We doubt that magistrates are more desirous

If exclusion of evidence obtained pursuant to a subsequently invalidated warrant is to have any deterrent effect, therefore, it must alter the behavior of individual law enforcement officers or the policies of their departments. One could argue that applying the exclusionary rule in cases where the police failed to demonstrate probable cause in the warrant application deters future inadequate presentations or "magistrate shopping" and thus promotes the ends of the Fourth Amendment. Suppressing evidence obtained pursuant to a technically defective warrant supported by probable cause also might encourage officers to scrutinize more closely the form of the warrant and to point out suspected judicial errors. We find such arguments speculative and conclude that suppression of evidence obtained pursuant to a warrant should be ordered only on a case-by-case basis and only in those unusual cases in which exclusion will further the purposes of the exclusionary rule.[19]

We have frequently questioned whether the exclusionary rule can have any deterrent effect when the offending officers acted in the objectively reasonable belief that their conduct did not violate the Fourth Amendment. "No empirical researcher, proponent or opponent of the rule, has yet been able to establish with any assurance whether the rule has a deterrent effect * * *." But even assuming that the rule effectively deters some police misconduct and provides incentives for the law enforcement profession as a whole to conduct itself in accord with the Fourth Amendment, it cannot be expected, and should not be applied, to deter objectively reasonable law enforcement activity. * * *[20]

This is particularly true, we believe, when an officer acting with objective good faith has obtained a search warrant from a judge or magistrate and acted within its scope. In most such cases, there is no police illegality and thus nothing to deter. It is the magistrate's responsibility to determine whether the officer's allegations establish probable cause and, if so, to issue a warrant comporting in form with the requirements of the Fourth Amendment. In the ordinary case, an officer cannot be expected to question the magistrate's probable-cause determination or his judgment that the form of the warrant is technically sufficient. "[O]nce

---

of avoiding the exclusion of evidence obtained pursuant to warrants they have issued than of avoiding invasions of privacy.

Federal magistrates, moreover, are subject to the direct supervision of district courts. They may be removed for "incompetency, misconduct, neglect of duty, or physical or mental disability." 28 U.S.C. § 631(i). If a magistrate serves merely as a "rubber stamp" for the police or is unable to exercise mature judgment, closer supervision or removal provides a more effective remedy than the exclusionary rule.

19. Our discussion of the deterrent effect of excluding evidence obtained in reasonable reliance on a subsequently invalidated warrant assumes, of course, that the officers properly executed the warrant and searched only those places and for those objects that it was reasonable to believe were covered by the warrant. * * *

20. We emphasize that the standard of reasonableness we adopt is an objective one. Many objections to a good-faith exception assume that the exception will turn on the subjective good faith of individual officers. "Grounding the modification in objective reasonableness, however, retains the value of the exclusionary rule as an incentive for the law enforcement profession as a whole to conduct themselves in accord with the Fourth Amendment." The objective standard we adopt, moreover, requires officers to have a reasonable knowledge of what the law prohibits. As Professor Jerold Israel has observed:

"The key to the [exclusionary] rule's effectiveness as a deterrent lies, I believe, in the impetus it has provided to police training programs that make officers aware of the limits imposed by the fourth amendment and emphasize the need to operate within those limits. [An objective good-faith exception] * * * is not likely to result in the elimination of such programs, which are now viewed as an important aspect of police professionalism. Neither is it likely to alter the tenor of those programs; the possibility that illegally obtained evidence may be admitted in borderline cases is unlikely to encourage police instructors to pay less attention to fourth amendment limitations. Finally, [it] * * * should not encourage officers to pay less attention to what they are taught, as the requirement that the officer act in 'good faith' is inconsistent with closing one's mind to the possibility of illegality."

the warrant issues, there is literally nothing more the policeman can do in seeking to comply with the law." Penalizing the officer for the magistrate's error, rather than his own, cannot logically contribute to the deterrence of Fourth Amendment violations.[22]

We conclude that the marginal or nonexistent benefits produced by suppressing evidence obtained in objectively reasonable reliance on a subsequently invalidated search warrant cannot justify the substantial costs of exclusion. We do not suggest, however, that exclusion is always inappropriate in cases where an officer has obtained a warrant and abided by its terms. [T]he officer's reliance on the magistrate's probable-cause determination and on the technical sufficiency of the warrant he issues must be objectively reasonable,[23] and it is clear that in some circumstances the officer[24] will have no reasonable grounds for believing that the warrant was properly issued.

Suppression therefore remains an appropriate remedy if the magistrate or judge in issuing a warrant was misled by information in an affidavit that the affiant knew was false or would have known was false except for his reckless disregard of the truth. The exception we recognize today will also not apply in cases where the issuing magistrate wholly abandoned his judicial role in the manner condemned in *Lo-Ji Sales, Inc. v. New York,* [p. 316 fn. a][c], in such circumstances, no reasonably well-trained officer should rely on the warrant. Nor would an officer manifest objective good faith in relying on a warrant based on an affidavit "so lacking in indicia of probable cause as to render official belief in its existence entirely unreasonable." Finally, depending on the circumstances of the particular case, a warrant may be so facially deficient—i.e., in failing to particularize the place to be searched or the things to be seized—that the executing officers cannot reasonably presume it to be valid.

* * * The good-faith exception for searches conducted pursuant to warrants is not intended to signal our unwillingness strictly to enforce the requirements of the Fourth Amendment, and we do not believe that it will have this effect. As we have already suggested, the good-faith exception, turning as it does on objective reasonableness, should not be difficult to apply in practice. When officers have acted pursuant to a warrant, the prosecution should ordinarily be able to establish objective good faith without a substantial expenditure of judicial time.

---

22. * * * Our cases establish that the question whether the use of illegally obtained evidence in judicial proceedings represents judicial participation in a Fourth Amendment violation and offends the integrity of the courts "is essentially the same as the inquiry into whether exclusion would serve a deterrent purpose." * * * Absent unusual circumstances, when a Fourth Amendment violation has occurred because the police have reasonably relied on a warrant issued by a detached and neutral magistrate but ultimately found to be defective, "the integrity of the courts is not implicated."

23. [O]ur good-faith inquiry is confined to the objectively ascertainable question whether a reasonably well-trained officer would have known that the search was illegal despite the magistrate's authorization. In making this determination, all of the circumstances—including whether the warrant application had previously been rejected by a different magistrate—may be considered.

24. References to "officer" throughout this opinion should not be read too narrowly. It is necessary to consider the objective reasonableness, not only of the officers who eventually executed a warrant, but also of the officers who originally obtained it or who provided information material to the probable-cause determination. Nothing in our opinion suggests, for example, that an officer could obtain a warrant on the basis of a "bare bones" affidavit and then rely on colleagues who are ignorant of the circumstances under which the warrant was obtained to conduct the search.

c. There the magistrate was held not to have "manifest[ed] that neutrality and detachment demanded of a judicial officer when presented with a warrant application," where he went to the scene and made judgments there about what should be seized as obscene, as he "allowed himself to become a member, if not the leader of the search party which was essentially a police operation."

Nor are we persuaded that application of a good-faith exception to searches conducted pursuant to warrants will preclude review of the constitutionality of the search or seizure, deny needed guidance from the courts, or freeze Fourth Amendment law in its present state.[25] There is no need for courts to adopt the inflexible practice of always deciding whether the officers' conduct manifested objective good faith before turning to the question whether the Fourth Amendment has been violated. Defendants seeking suppression of the fruits of allegedly unconstitutional searches or seizures undoubtedly raise live controversies which Article III empowers federal courts to adjudicate. * * *

If the resolution of a particular Fourth Amendment question is necessary to guide future action by law enforcement officers and magistrates, nothing will prevent reviewing courts from deciding that question before turning to the good-faith issue.[26] Indeed, it frequently will be difficult to determine whether the officers acted reasonably without resolving the Fourth Amendment issue. Even if the Fourth Amendment question is not one of broad import, reviewing courts could decide in particular cases that magistrates under their supervision need to be informed of their errors and so evaluate the officers' good faith only after finding a violation. In other circumstances, those courts could reject suppression motions posing no important Fourth Amendment questions by turning immediately to a consideration of the officers' good faith. We have no reason to believe that our Fourth Amendment jurisprudence would suffer by allowing reviewing courts to exercise an informed discretion in making this choice. * * *

In the absence of an allegation that the magistrate abandoned his detached and neutral role, suppression is appropriate only if the officers were dishonest or reckless in preparing their affidavit or could not have harbored an objectively reasonable belief in the existence of probable cause. Only respondent Leon has contended that no reasonably well-trained police officer could have believed that there existed probable cause to search his house; significantly, the other respondents advance no comparable argument. Officer Rombach's application for a warrant clearly was supported by much more than a ''bare bones'' affidavit. The affidavit related the results of an extensive investigation and, as the opinions of the divided panel of the Court of Appeals make clear, provided evidence sufficient to create disagreement among thoughtful and competent judges as to the existence of probable cause. Under these circumstances, the officers' reliance on the magistrate's determination of probable cause was objectively reasonable, and application of the extreme sanction of exclusion is inappropriate.

Accordingly, the judgment of the Court of Appeals is *reversed.*

JUSTICE BLACKMUN, concurring. * * *

What must be stressed * * * is that any empirical judgment about the effect of the exclusionary rule in a particular class of cases necessarily is a provisional one. * * * If it should emerge from experience that, contrary to our expectations, the good faith exception to the exclusionary rule results in a material change in police compliance with the Fourth Amendment, we shall have to reconsider what we have undertaken here. The logic of a decision that rests on untested predictions about police conduct demands no less. * * *

---

25. The argument that defendants will lose their incentive to litigate meritorious Fourth Amendment claims as a result of the good-faith exception we adopt today is unpersuasive. Although the exception might discourage presentation of insubstantial suppression motions, the magnitude of the benefit conferred on defendants by a successful motion makes it unlikely that litigation of colorable claims will be substantially diminished.

26. It has been suggested, in fact, that ''the recognition of a 'penumbral zone,' within which an inadvertent mistake would not call for exclusion, * * * will make it less tempting for judges to bend fourth amendment standards to avoid releasing a possibly dangerous criminal because of a minor and unintentional miscalculation by the police.''

JUSTICE BRENNAN, with whom JUSTICE MARSHALL joins, dissenting.

* * * Because seizures are executed principally to secure evidence, and because such evidence generally has utility in our legal system only in the context of a trial supervised by a judge, it is apparent that the admission of illegally obtained evidence implicates the same constitutional concerns as the initial seizure of that evidence. Indeed, by admitting unlawfully seized evidence, the judiciary becomes a part of what is in fact a single governmental action prohibited by the terms of the Amendment. Once that connection between the evidence-gathering role of the police and the evidence-admitting function of the courts is acknowledged, the plausibility of the Court's interpretation becomes more suspect. Certainly nothing in the language or history of the Fourth Amendment suggests that a recognition of this evidentiary link between the police and the courts was meant to be foreclosed. It is difficult to give any meaning at all to the limitations imposed by the Amendment if they are read to proscribe only certain conduct by the police but to allow other agents of the same government to take advantage of evidence secured by the police in violation of its requirements. The Amendment therefore must be read to condemn not only the initial unconstitutional invasion of privacy—which is done, after all, for the purpose of securing evidence—but also the subsequent use of any evidence so obtained. * * *

[T]he question whether the exclusion of evidence would deter future police misconduct was never considered a relevant concern in the early cases from *Weeks* to *Olmstead*. In those formative decisions, the Court plainly understood that the exclusion of illegally obtained evidence was compelled not by judicially fashioned remedial purposes, but rather by a direct constitutional command. * * *

* * * Indeed, no other explanation suffices to account for the Court's holding in *Mapp,* since the only possible predicate for the Court's conclusion that the States were bound by the Fourteenth Amendment to honor the *Weeks* doctrine is that the exclusionary rule was "part and parcel of the Fourth Amendment's limitation upon [governmental] encroachment of individual privacy."

Despite this clear pronouncement, however, the Court * * * has gradually pressed the deterrence rationale for the rule back to center stage. The various arguments advanced by the Court in this campaign have only strengthened my conviction that the deterrence theory is both misguided and unworkable. First, the Court has frequently bewailed the "cost" of excluding reliable evidence. In large part, this criticism rests upon a refusal to acknowledge the function of the Fourth Amendment itself. If nothing else, the Amendment plainly operates to disable the government from gathering information and securing evidence in certain ways. In practical terms, of course, this restriction of official power means that some incriminating evidence inevitably will go undetected if the government obeys these constitutional restraints. It is the loss of that evidence that is the "price" our society pays for enjoying the freedom and privacy safeguarded by the Fourth Amendment. Thus, some criminals will go free *not*, in Justice (then Judge) Cardozo's misleading epigram, "because the constable has blundered," but rather because official compliance with Fourth Amendment requirements makes it more difficult to catch criminals. Understood in this way, the Amendment directly contemplates that some reliable and incriminating evidence will be lost to the government; therefore, it is not the exclusionary rule, but the Amendment itself that has imposed this cost.

In addition, the Court's decisions over the past decade have made plain that the entire enterprise of attempting to assess the benefits and costs of the exclusionary rule in various contexts is a virtually impossible task for the judiciary to perform honestly or accurately. Although the Court's language in those cases suggests that some specific empirical basis may support its analyses, the reality is that the Court's opinions represent inherently unstable compounds of intuition, hunches, and occasional pieces of partial and often inconclusive data. * * * To the extent empirical data is available regarding the general costs and benefits of the exclusionary rule, it has shown, on the one hand, as the Court acknowledges today, that the costs are not as substantial as critics have asserted in the past, and, on the other hand, that while the exclusionary rule may well have certain deterrent effects, it is extremely difficult to determine with any degree of precision whether the incidence of unlawful conduct by police is now lower than it was prior to *Mapp*. The Court has sought to turn this uncertainty to its advantage by casting the burden of proof upon proponents of the rule. "Obviously," however, "the assignment of the burden of proof on an issue where evidence does not exist and cannot be obtained is outcome determinative. [The] assignment of the burden is merely a way of announcing a predetermined conclusion." * * *

Even if I were to accept the Court's general approach to the exclusionary rule, I could not agree with today's result. * * *

At the outset, the Court suggests that society has been asked to pay a high price—in terms either of setting guilty persons free or of impeding the proper functioning of trials—as a result of excluding relevant physical evidence in cases where the police, in conducting searches and seizing evidence, have made only an "objectively reasonable" mistake concerning the constitutionality of their actions. But what evidence is there to support such a claim?

Significantly, the Court points to none, and, indeed, as the Court acknowledges, recent studies have demonstrated that the "costs" of the exclusionary rule—calculated in terms of dropped prosecutions and lost convictions—are quite low. Contrary to the claims of the rule's critics that exclusion leads to "the release of countless guilty criminals," these studies have demonstrated that federal and state prosecutors very rarely drop cases because of potential search and seizure problems. For example, a 1979 study prepared at the request of Congress by the General Accounting Office reported that only 0.4% of all cases actually declined for prosecution by federal prosecutors were declined primarily because of illegal search problems. If the GAO data are restated as a percentage of *all* arrests, the study shows that only 0.2% of all felony arrests are declined for prosecution because of potential exclusionary rule problems. Of course, these data describe only the costs attributable to the exclusion of evidence in all cases; the costs due to the exclusion of evidence in the narrower category of cases where police have made objectively reasonable mistakes must necessarily be even smaller. The Court, however, ignores this distinction and mistakenly weighs the aggregated costs of exclusion in *all* cases, irrespective of the circumstances that led to exclusion, against the potential benefits associated with only those cases in which evidence is excluded because police reasonably but mistakenly believe that their conduct does not violate the Fourth Amendment. When such faulty scales are used, it is little wonder that the balance tips in favor of restricting the application of the rule.

What then supports the Court's insistence that this evidence be admitted? Apparently, the Court's only answer is that even though the costs of exclusion are not very substantial, the potential deterrent effect in these circumstances is so marginal that exclusion cannot be justified. The key to the Court's conclusion in this respect is its belief that the prospective deterrent effect of the exclusionary rule operates only in those situations in which police officers, when deciding whether to go forward with some particular search, have reason to know that their planned conduct will violate the requirements of the Fourth Amendment.

* * * But what the Court overlooks is that the deterrence rationale for the rule is not designed to be, nor should it be thought of as, a form of "punishment"

of individual police officers for their failures to obey the restraints imposed by the Fourth Amendment. Instead, the chief deterrent function of the rule is its tendency to promote institutional compliance with Fourth Amendment requirements on the part of law enforcement agencies generally. Thus, as the Court has previously recognized, "over the long term, [the] demonstration [provided by the exclusionary rule] that our society attaches serious consequences to violation of constitutional rights is thought to encourage those who formulate law enforcement policies, and the officers who implement them, to incorporate Fourth Amendment ideals into their value system." It is only through such an institution-wide mechanism that information concerning Fourth Amendment standards can be effectively communicated to rank and file officers.

If the overall educational effect of the exclusionary rule is considered, application of the rule to even those situations in which individual police officers have acted on the basis of a reasonable but mistaken belief that their conduct was authorized can still be expected to have a considerable long-term deterrent effect. If evidence is consistently excluded in these circumstances, police departments will surely be prompted to instruct their officers to devote greater care and attention to providing sufficient information to establish probable cause when applying for a warrant, and to review with some attention the form of the warrant that they have been issued, rather than automatically assuming that whatever document the magistrate has signed will necessarily comport with Fourth Amendment requirements.

After today's decision, however, that institutional incentive will be lost. Indeed, the Court's "reasonable mistake" exception to the exclusionary rule will tend to put a premium on police ignorance of the law. Armed with the assurance provided by today's decision that evidence will always be admissible whenever an officer has "reasonably" relied upon a warrant, police departments will be encouraged to train officers that if a warrant has simply been signed, it is reasonable, without more, to rely on it. Since in close cases there will no longer be any incentive to err on the side of constitutional behavior, police would have every reason to adopt a "let's-wait-until-its-decided" approach in situations in which there is a question about a warrant's validity or the basis for its issuance. * * *

Finally, even if one were to believe, as the Court apparently does, that police are hobbled by inflexible and hypertechnical warrant procedures, today's decision cannot be justified. This is because, given the relaxed standard for assessing probable cause established just last Term in *Illinois v. Gates*, the Court's newly fashioned good faith exception, when applied in the warrant context, will rarely, if ever, offer any greater flexibility for police than the *Gates* standard already supplies.[d] In *Gates*, the Court held that "the task of an issuing magistrate is simply to make a practical, common-sense decision whether, given all the circumstances set forth in the affidavit before him, * * * there is a fair probability that contraband or evidence of a crime will be found in a particular place." The task of a reviewing court is confined to determining whether "the magistrate had a 'substantial basis' for concluding that probable cause existed." Given such a relaxed standard, it is virtually inconceivable that a reviewing court, when faced with a defendant's motion to suppress, could first find that a warrant was invalid under the new *Gates* standard, but then, at the same time, find that a police

---

d. Thus Stevens, J., dissenting, objected: "It is probable, though admittedly not certain, that the Court of Appeals would now conclude that the warrant in *Leon* satisfied the Fourth Amendment if it were given the opportunity to reconsider the issue in the light of *Gates*. Adherence to our normal practice following the announcement of a new rule would therefore postpone, and probably obviate, the need for the promulgation of the broad new rule the Court announces today."

officer's reliance on such an invalid warrant was nevertheless "objectively reasonable" under the test announced today. * * *

NOTES AND QUESTIONS

1. Must (should) the Fourth Amendment be read, as dissenting Justice Brennan maintains, "to condemn not only the initial unconstitutional invasion of privacy" but "also the subsequent use of any evidence so obtained"? Consider Arnold H. Loewy, *Police-Obtained Evidence and the Constitution: Distinguishing Unconstitutionally Obtained Evidence from Unconstitutionally Used Evidence,* 87 Mich.L.Rev. 907, 909–11, 939 (1989):

"[F]reedom from unreasonable searches and seizures is a substantive protection available to all inhabitants of the United States, whether or not charged with crime. The right thus differs from protections under most of the fifth amendment and all of the sixth amendment, which refers to persons charged with crime or the 'accused.' * * * [Because] the fourth amendment, in language and origin, is clearly substantive [the] Court was correct in holding the exclusionary rule to be simply a remedial device designed to make the substantive right more meaningful, rather than an independent procedural right.

" * * * Procedural rights are supposed to exclude evidence. Substantive rights need not. Consequently, fourth amendment rights should be deemed different from, but not less important than, the procedural rights protected by the fifth, sixth and fourteenth amendments. By way of comparison, first and third amendment rights are substantive, but nobody would deem them second class. * * *

"Whether evidence is unconstitutionally obtained or unconstitutionally used makes a difference. If the only constitutional wrong inheres in using the evidence, the Court has no business considering concepts of deterrence. The Court should prohibit use of such evidence. Conversely, when obtaining evidence is the constitutional wrong, exclusion should be subjected to a cost/benefit analysis."

2. Which of the Supreme Court's express or implicit assumptions in *Mapp* and *Leon* regarding the behavior of police and judges are correct? Consider Myron W. Orfield, *Deterrence, Perjury, and the Heater Factor: An Exclusionary Rule in the Chicago Criminal Courts,* 63 U.Colo.L.Rev. 75, 82–83 (1992), summarizing the views of interviewed actors in the Chicago criminal justice system:

"Respondents in the Courts Study[e] report the same perceptions of the deterrent effect of the rule as the officers in the Police Study.[f] First, respondents uniformly believe that officers care about convictions and experience adverse personal reactions when they lose evidence. Respondents report that police change their behavior in response to the suppression of evidence. They also believe that suppression effectively educates officers in the law of search and seizure and that the law is not too complicated for police officers to do their jobs effectively.

"The Courts Study respondents believe even more strongly than the Police Study respondents that the exclusionary rule's deterrent effect is greater when officers are working on big or important cases. They also believe the exclusionary rule has a greater deterrent effect on officers in specialized units like the Narcotics Section.

---

e. 14 public defenders, 14 prosecutors and 13 judges, all assigned to the felony trial courtrooms in the Criminal Division of the Circuit Court of Cook County.

f. 26 police officers in the Narcotics Section of the Organized Crime Division, Chicago Police Department.

"Respondents also stated that the exclusionary rule fosters a closer working relationship between prosecutors and police. They note that prosecutors help police officers conduct proper searches and understand why evidence is suppressed. * * *

"Significantly, the Courts respondents outlined a pattern of pervasive police perjury intended to avoid the requirements of the Fourth Amendment. Dishonesty occurs in both the investigative process and the courtroom. The respondents report systematic fabrications in case reports and affidavits for search warrants, creating artificial probable cause which forms the basis of later testimony. Moreover, police keep dual sets of investigatory files; official files and 'street files.' Exculpatory material in the street files may be edited from the official record. Respondents, including prosecutors, estimate that police commit perjury between 20 and 50% of the time they testify on Fourth Amendment issues. This perjury may be tolerated, or even encouraged, by prosecutors at each step in the process in both direct and indirect ways.

"The Courts respondents, including judges, also believe that judges may purposefully ignore the law to prevent evidence from being suppressed, and even more often, knowingly accept police perjury as truthful. When the crime is serious, this judicial 'cheating' is more likely to occur due to three primary reasons; first, the judge's sense that it is unjust to suppress the evidence under the circumstances of a particular case, second, the judge's fear of adverse publicity, and third, the fear that the suppression will hurt their chances in judicial elections. In addition, serious cases in Chicago are diverted to judges who are more likely to convict the defendant.

"However, even in the face of persistent police perjury and judicial abdication of function, the Courts respondents, like the police respondents, believe that the exclusionary rule, although imperfect and often avoided, clearly leads to increased police professionalism and greater observance of the law of the Fourth Amendment. They do not believe that the rule causes significant harm to police work. Although the Courts respondents acknowledge that the rule can sometimes be unjust to crime victims, they believe that the rule's benefits to society equal or exceed its costs. Respondents report that there is no more effective remedy for Fourth Amendment violations, and that a tort remedy would be less effective. Finally, they believe the rule should be retained."

3. Does (should) *Leon* mean that "when the Court speaks of the good faith of the police, it is talking about their good faith *before going* to the magistrate and not about their good faith *after* they have received the warrant"? Craig M. Bradley, *The "Good Faith Exception" Cases: Reasonable Exercises in Futility*, 60 Ind.L.J. 287, 297 (1985). Consider *Malley v. Briggs,* p. 242, fn. h, which the majority explained involved application of "the same standard of objective reasonableness that we applied in the context of a suppression hearing in *Leon*."

4. Will (should) *Leon* be extended to warrantless arrests and searches? In *Lopez-Mendoza,* p. 249, involving a warrantless arrest, White, J., dissenting, asserted *Leon* was applicable, so that "if the agents neither knew nor should have known that they were acting contrary to the dictates of the Fourth Amendment, evidence will not be suppressed even if it is held that their conduct was illegal." If that is wrong, then does it follow, as concluded in *United States v. O'Neal,* 17 F.3d 239 (8th Cir.1994), that *Leon* cannot save a search warrant where it now appears that some of the facts essential to the probable cause showing in the affidavit were acquired in a prior illegal warrantless search?

5. In the companion case of *Massachusetts v. Sheppard,* 468 U.S. 981 (1984), a detective prepared an affidavit for a search warrant to search for specified evidence of a homicide but, because it was Sunday, could only find a warrant form for controlled substances. He presented his affidavit and that form to a judge and pointed out the problem to him, and the judge, unable to locate a more suitable form, told the detective that he would make the necessary changes to make it a proper warrant. He made some changes, but failed to change that part of the warrant which authorized a search only for controlled substances and related paraphernalia. The detective took the two documents and he and other officers then executed the warrant, seizing evidence of the homicide. That evidence was suppressed in the state court because the warrant failed to particularly describe the items to be seized, as required by the Fourth Amendment. The Supreme Court, per White, J., held this situation fell within *Leon* because "there was an objectively reasonable basis for the officers' mistaken belief" that "the warrant authorized the search that they conducted." As for defendant's objection that the detective knew when he went to the judge that the warrant was defective, the Court stated: "Whatever an officer may be required to do when he executes a warrant without knowing beforehand what items are to be seized,[6] we refuse to rule that an officer is required to disbelieve a judge who has just advised him, by word and by action, that the warrant he possesses authorizes him to conduct the search he has requested."

What if the detective who obtained the warrant had simply turned it over to another officer for execution and that officer, after a careful reading of the warrant, had made a search for and found drugs within an envelope, a place he would not have been entitled to look had he been aware that the warrant should have described certain larger items which could not be concealed in the envelope?

6. What result under *Leon* and *Sheppard* on the following facts, essentially those in *People v. Deitchman,* 695 P.2d 1146 (Colo.1985)? Four teenage girls were sexually assaulted in the same area over a 10–day span, and they gave a similar general description of their assailant. One said he wore distinctively marked shoes; one said he had a red bandana; and two said his car license was CN–4714. Those facts were put into a search warrant affidavit, along with a statement that investigation "revealed that CN–4714 lists to Jerry M. Deitchman of 1755 South Pecos Street." The affidavit asserted, without explanation, that there was "reason to believe" that the shoes and bandana were at 3300 West Ohio Avenue; the magistrate issued a warrant to search that location for the shoes and bandana, which were found there in execution of the warrant. Police had earlier been unable to locate Deitchman until his employer said he had moved to 3300 West Ohio, and police arrested him there prior to obtaining the warrant, but those facts were not reported to the magistrate.

7. In GROH v. RAMIREZ, 540 U.S. 551 (2004), the affiant, who was also the executing officer, correctly stated the items to be seized in the search warrant application and the supporting affidavit, but in the search warrant itself mistakenly entered in the space for that specification a description of the place to be searched. That error was not noticed by the magistrate who issued the warrant, and was not noticed by the affiant/executing officer until after the warrant was executed; he instructed his search team on the basis of the items listed in the application and affidavit. In this action under *Bivens,* p. 242 fn. h, applying the

---

6. Normally, when an officer who has not been involved in the application stage receives a warrant, he will read it in order to determine the object of the search. In this case, Detective O'Malley, the officer who directed the search, knew what items were listed in the affidavit presented to the judge, and he had good reason to believe that the warrant authorized the seizure of those items. Whether an officer who is less familiar with the warrant application or who has unalleviated concerns about the proper scope of the search would be justified in failing to notice a defect like the one in the warrant in this case is an issue we need not decide. We hold only that it was not unreasonable for the police in this case to rely on the judge's assurances that the warrant authorized the search they had requested.

same standard as used under the *Leon* "good faith" exception, the Court, 5–4, concluded per Stevens, J.:

"Given that the particularity requirement is set forth in the text of the Constitution, no reasonable officer could believe that a warrant that plainly did not comply with that requirement was valid. * * * Moreover, because petitioner himself prepared the invalid warrant, he may not argue that he reasonably relied on the Magistrate's assurance that the warrant contained an adequate description of the things to be seized and was therefore valid. Cf. *Sheppard* * * *. And even a cursory reading of the warrant in this case—perhaps just a simple glance—would have revealed a glaring deficiency that any reasonable police officer would have known was constitutionally fatal. * * *

"Petitioner contends that the search in this case was the product, at worst, of a lack of due care, and that our case law requires more than negligent behavior before depriving an official of qualified immunity. * * * But as we observed in [*Leon*], 'a warrant may be so facially deficient—i.e., in failing to particularize the place to be searched or the things to be seized—that the executing officers cannot reasonably presume it to be valid.' "

The two dissenting opinions, collectively, made these points: (i) The case involves "a straightforward mistake of fact," as "the officer simply made a clerical error when he filled out the proposed warrant." (ii) "Given the sheer number of warrants prepared and executed by officers each year," it "is inevitable that officers acting reasonably and entirely in good faith will occasionally make such errors." (iii) The officer's later "failure to recognize his clerical error on a warrant form can be a reasonable mistake," and such was the case here, for "where the officer is already fully aware of the scope of the intended search and the magistrate gives no reason to believe that he has authorized anything other than the requested search," there is nothing unreasonable in the officer's failure "to proofread the warrant." (iv) The majority's reliance upon the *Leon* quote is in error, for it has to do with "a mistake of law"; that is, the "issue in this case is whether an officer can reasonably fail to recognize a clerical error, not whether an officer who recognizes a clerical error can reasonably conclude that a defective warrant is legally valid."

8. Are there other "limitations" which might well be imposed upon the exclusionary rule? Consider the two proposals made in John Kaplan, *The Limits of the Exclusionary Rule,* 26 Stan.L.Rev. 1027 (1974): (1) that "the rule not apply in the most serious cases—treason, espionage, murder, armed robbery, and kidnapping by organized groups" (where exclusion would occur only under the *Rochin,* p. 28, test), because "the political costs of the rule, the possibility of releasing serious and dangerous offenders into the community, and the disproportion between the magnitude of the policeman's constitutional violation and the crime in which the evidence is to be suppressed are sufficient reasons to modify the rule"; and (2) "to hold the exclusionary rule inapplicable to cases where the police department in question has taken seriously its responsibility to adhere to the fourth amendment," as reflected by "a set of published regulations giving guidance to police officers as to proper behavior in situations such as the one under litigation, a training program calculated to make violations of the fourth amendment rights isolated occurrences, and, perhaps most importantly, a history of taking disciplinary action where such violations are brought to its attention."[g]

---

g. For strong criticism of Professor Kaplan's proposal that the exclusionary rule not apply in the most serious cases and of a similar proposal by James D. Cameron & Richard Lustiger, *The Exclusionary Rule: A Cost–Benefit Analysis,* 101 F.R.D. 109 (1984) that the rule apply neither in the most serious cases nor in any case where the reprehensibility of the defendant's crime is greater than the gravity of the officer's illegality, see Yale Kamisar, *"Comparative Reprehensibility" and the Fourth Amendment Exclusionary Rule,* 86 Mich.L.Rev. 1 (1987).

9. Should the Court instead abolish the exclusionary rule entirely on the ground that the deterrence function stressed in *Leon* is more generally not served by exclusion? Consider Burger, C.J., dissenting in *Bivens v. Six Unknown Named Agents,* p. 242 n. h, asserting a lack of deterrent efficacy because: (i) "The rule does not apply any direct sanction to the individual official whose illegal conduct results in the exclusion of evidence in a criminal trial." (ii) Police "have no * * * stake in successful prosecutions," and "the prosecutor who loses his case because of police misconduct is not an official in the police department; he can rarely set in motion any corrective action or administrative penalties." (iii) "Policemen do not have the time, inclination, or training to read and grasp the nuances of the appellate opinions that ultimately define the standards of conduct they are to follow." (iv) "[T]here are large areas of police activity which do not result in criminal prosecutions—hence the rule has virtually no applicability and no effect in such situations." Would such abolition be more palatable if, as the Chief Justice also suggested in *Bivens,* Congress were to "develop an administrative or quasi-judicial remedy against the government itself to afford compensation and restitution for persons whose Fourth Amendment rights have been violated"?[h] Consider also Richard A. Posner, *Excessive Sanctions for Governmental Misconduct in*

A variation on the Kaplan scheme is Professor Dripps' more recent "virtual deterrence" proposal: "If the court hearing a suppression motion found a violation of the Fourth Amendment, it might be required to consider the specific steps, undertaken by the police department and/or the prosecutor's office, by way of training and/or discipline, to prevent recurrence of the violation. If the court concluded that these measures were adequate and reasonable, it could admit the evidence." Donald A. Dripps, *The "New" Exclusionary Rule Debate: From "Still Preoccupied with 1985" to "Virtual Deterrence,"* 37 Fordham Urb.L.J. 743, 793 (2010).

h. As for existing federal remedies, 42 U.S.C. § 1983 provides: "Every person who, under color of any statute, ordinance, regulation, custom, or usage, of any State or Territory, subjects, or causes to be subjected, any citizen of the United States or other person within the jurisdiction thereof to the deprivation of any rights, privileges, or immunities secured by the Constitution and laws, shall be liable to the party injured in an action at law, suit in equity, or other proper proceeding for redress." State and local police officers thus may be sued for damages for violation of Fourth Amendment rights, but the officers have an objective good faith defense. This is so even with respect to a police officer's action in applying for an arrest warrant; notwithstanding the magistrate's issuance of the warrant, the question "is whether a reasonably well-trained officer in petitioner's position would have known that his affidavit failed to establish probable cause and that he should not have applied for the warrant." *Malley v. Briggs,* 475 U.S. 335 (1986). By comparison, a state prosecutor's appearance in court in support of an application for a search warrant and presentation of evidence at that hearing are protected by absolute immunity, but such immunity does not extend to a state prosecutor's giving of legal advise to police, as there is no "historical or common-law support for extending absolute immunity to such actions," which are not "intimately associated with the judicial phase of the criminal process." *Burns v. Reed,* 500 U.S. 478 (1991). *Monell v. New York City Dep't of Social Services,* 436 U.S. 658 (1978), cautioned that the statute did not "impose liability vicariously on governing bodies solely on the basis of the existence of an employer-employee relationship with a tortfeasor," and thus concluded "that a local government may not be sued for an injury inflicted solely by its employees or agents. Instead, it is when execution of a government's policy or custom, whether made by its lawmakers or by those whose edicts or acts may fairly be said to represent official policy, inflicts the injury that the government as an entity is responsible under § 1983."

Section 1983 applies only to persons acting under color of state law, thus excluding federal officers acting under color of their authority. In *Bivens v. Six Unknown Named Agents,* 403 U.S. 388 (1971), the Court held that, although Congress had not provided a tort remedy under such circumstances, a complaint alleging that the Fourth Amendment had been violated by federal agents acting under color of their authority gives rise to a federal cause of action for damages. Here as well, there is personal liability only in the absence of "objective legal reasonableness." *Anderson v. Creighton,* 483 U.S. 635 (1987). As for liability of the federal government, the Court in *Bivens* stated this issue was better left to Congress because "the federal purse was involved." In 1974 Congress amended the Federal Tort Claims Act to make it applicable "to acts or omissions of investigative or law enforcement officers of the United States Government" on any subsequent claim arising "out of assault, battery, false imprisonment, false arrest, abuse of process, or malicious prosecution. For the purpose of this subsection, 'investigative or law enforcement officer' means any officer of the United States who is empowered by law to execute searches, to seize evidence, or to make arrests for violations of Federal law." 28 U.S.C. § 2680(h).

Criminal Cases, 57 Wash.L.Rev. 635 (1982) (applying an economic analysis to the problem and concluding it should suffice if the government were required to compensate the victim of an illegal search for his "cleanup costs"); Donald Dripps, *The Case for the Contingent Exclusionary Rule,* 38 Am.Crim.L.Rev.1, 2 (2001) (proposing "that courts should begin to experiment with suppression orders that are contingent on the failure of the police department to pay damages set by the court [in an amount] equal to the expected governmental gain from the violation").

10. In *Michigan v. DeFillippo,* 443 U.S. 31 (1979), the Court reaffirmed its earlier holdings "that the exclusionary rule required suppression of evidence obtained in searches carried out pursuant to statutes" subsequently held unconstitutional when the statutes, "by their own terms, authorized searches under circumstances which did not satisfy the traditional warrant and probable cause requirements of the Fourth Amendment." But after *Leon* the Court concluded otherwise in the 5–4 decision in ILLINOIS v. KRULL, 480 U.S. 340 (1987), concerning an unconstitutional search made pursuant to a statute authorizing warrantless inspection of the records of licensed motor vehicle and vehicular parts sellers. The Court, per Blackmun, J., reasoned:

"The approach used in *Leon* is equally applicable to the present case. The application of the exclusionary rule to suppress evidence obtained by an officer acting in objectively reasonable reliance on a statute would have as little deterrent effect on the officer's actions as would the exclusion of evidence when an officer acts in objectively reasonable reliance on a warrant. Unless a statute is clearly unconstitutional, an officer cannot be expected to question the judgment of the legislature that passed the law. * * *

"Any difference between our holding in *Leon* and our holding in the instant case, therefore, must rest on a difference between the effect of the exclusion of evidence on judicial officers and the effect of the exclusion of evidence on legislators. Although these two groups clearly serve different functions in the criminal justice system, those differences are not controlling for purposes of this case. We noted in *Leon* as an initial matter that the exclusionary rule was aimed at deterring police misconduct. Thus, legislators, like judicial officers, are not the focus of the rule. Moreover, to the extent we consider the rule's effect on legislators, our initial inquiry, as set out in *Leon,* is whether there is evidence to suggest that legislators 'are inclined to ignore or subvert the Fourth Amendment.' * * *

"There is no evidence suggesting that Congress or state legislatures have enacted a significant number of statutes permitting warrantless administrative searches violative of the Fourth Amendment. * * * Thus, we are given no basis for believing that legislators are inclined to subvert their oaths and the Fourth Amendment and that 'lawlessness among these actors requires application of the extreme sanction of exclusion.' *United States v. Leon.*

"Even if we were to conclude that legislators are different in certain relevant respects from magistrates, because legislators are not officers of the judicial system, the next inquiry necessitated by *Leon* is whether exclusion of evidence seized pursuant to a statute subsequently declared unconstitutional will 'have a significant deterrent effect' on legislators enacting such statutes. Respondents have offered us no reason to believe that applying the exclusionary rule will have such an effect. Legislators enact statutes for broad, programmatic purposes, not for the purpose of procuring evidence in particular criminal investigations. Thus, it is logical to assume that the greatest deterrent to the enactment of unconstitutional statutes by a legislature is the power of the courts to invalidate such statutes. Invalidating a statute informs the legislature of its constitutional error, affects the admissibility of all evidence obtained subsequent to the constitutional ruling, and often results in the legislature's enacting a modified and constitutional version of the statute, as happened in this very case."

O'Connor, J., for the dissenters, emphasized: (1) "[B]oth the history of the Fourth Amendment and this Court's later interpretations of it, support application of the exclusionary rule to evidence gathered under the 20th century equivalent of the act authorizing the writ of assistance." (2) "The distinction drawn between the legislator and the judicial officer is sound" because "a legislature's unreasonable authorization of searches may affect thousands or millions" and thus "poses a greater threat to liberty." (3) "[L]egislators by virtue of their political role are more often subjected to the political pressures that may threaten Fourth Amendment values than are judicial officers." (4) "Providing legislatures a grace period during which the police may freely perform unreasonable searches in order to convict those who might have otherwise escaped creates a positive incentive to promulgate unconstitutional laws." (5) "The scope of the Court's good-faith exception is unclear," as "it is not apparent how much constitutional law the reasonable officer is expected to know. In contrast, *Leon* simply instructs courts that police officers may rely upon a facially valid search warrant. Each case is a fact-specific self-terminating episode. Courts need not inquire into the officer's probable understanding of the state of the law except in the extreme instance of a search warrant upon which no reasonable officer would rely. Under the decision today, however, courts are expected to determine at what point a reasonable officer should be held to know that a statute has, under evolving legal rules, become 'clearly' unconstitutional."

11. Sgt. Miller of the Greenville, Ala., Police Department made a routine traffic stop and then arrested the driver for driving under the influence and passenger Davis for giving a false name to police. After both were removed from the vehicle and secured, Miller searched the car and found a gun in a jacket belonging to Davis, resulting in his being charged in *federal* court with possession of a firearm by a convicted felon. Davis sought suppression of the gun without success, as 15 years preceding Miller's search a panel of the 11th Circuit Court of Appeals, sitting in Atlanta, had ruled in *United States v. Gonzalez*, arising in southern Florida, that a search in such circumstances conformed to the requirements of *New York v. Belton*, p. 398. While Davis's appeal was pending, the Supreme Court decided *Arizona v. Gant*, p. 398, construing *Belton* as allowing search of a vehicle incident to arrest "only when the arrestee is unsecured and within reaching distance of the passenger compartment at the time of the search." While under the Supreme Court's retroactivity doctrine, see ch. 29, § 5, *Gant* was applicable on Davis's appeal, his conviction was nonetheless affirmed.

In DAVIS v. UNITED STATES, 131 S.Ct. 2419 (2011), the Court, per Alito, J., stated: "The question here is whether to apply [the exclusionary] sanction when the police conduct a search in compliance with binding precedent that is later overruled. Because suppression would do nothing to deter police misconduct in these circumstances, and because it would come at a high cost to both the truth and the public safety, we hold that searches conducted in objectively reasonable reliance on binding appellate precedent are not subject to the exclusionary rule.

"[I]n 27 years of practice under *Leon*'s good-faith exception, we have 'never applied' the exclusionary rule to suppress evidence obtained as a result of nonculpable, innocent police conduct. If the police in this case had reasonably relied on a warrant in conducting their search, see *Leon* * * *, the exclusionary rule would not apply. And if Congress or the Alabama Legislature had enacted a statute codifying the precise holding of the [circuit precedent], we would swiftly conclude that ' "[p]enalizing the officer for the legislature's error ... cannot logically contribute to the deterrence of Fourth Amendment violations." ' See

Krull. The same should be true of Davis's attempt here to ' "[p]enaliz[e] the officer for the [appellate judges'] error." ' "

As for the contention "that applying the good-faith exception in this case is 'incompatible' with our retroactivity precedent," the Court responded: "Our retroactivity jurisprudence is concerned with whether, as a categorical matter, a new rule is available on direct review as a *potential* ground for relief," and "does not, however, determine what 'appropriate remedy' (if any) the defendant should obtain." As for the contention that applying the good-faith exception in this context would "stunt the development of Fourth Amendment law,"[i] the Court responded (1) that since "the *sole* purpose the exclusionary rule is to deter misconduct by law enforcement," "facilitating the overruling of precedent" is not "a relevant consideration"; (2) it suffices that meaningful review (i.e., including at least a chance of benefit via evidence suppression) is available to defendants in jurisdictions where a particular Fourth Amendment issue "remains open" because there was no "binding appellate precedent" supporting the challenged police conduct; and (3) this argument in any event only means that perhaps "the petitioner in a case that results in the overruling of one of this Court's Fourth Amendment precedents should be given the benefit of the victory by permitting the suppression of evidence in that one case," which the Court could do "in a future case, * * * if necessary."

Does *Davis* require "reliance" or merely "compliance"? If it is "reliance," in what sense can it be said that Sgt. Miller relied on the 11th Circuit precedent, given that nothing in the record suggests he had ever heard of the *Gonzalez* decision or, assuming he knew of it, that he had any reason to believe it was relevant to his search activities relating to state law enforcement?[j] As for the "binding appellate precedent" requirement, would the 11th Circuit precedent "count" if Miller had instead found the fruits of a burglary committed in a distant state and the evidence was used in a state prosecution there? If not, does that mean that Miller's good faith blossoms or withers depending upon whether that distant state, at the time of Miller's search, had an appellate precedent comparable to *Gonzalez*? Is a "binding appellate precedent" *always* required, or would it suffice, as the *Davis* dissenters ask, if Miller's search was approved by "a rule that all other jurisdictions, but not the defendant's jurisdiction, had previously accepted"?[k] On the other hand, is a "binding appellate precedent" always sufficient, or would *Davis* come out differently if *Gonzalez* was an outlier? Consider Sotomayor, J., concurring in *Davis*, who agreed that "application of the exclusionary rule cannot reasonably be expected to yield appreciable deterrence" in the instant case,

---

i. Consider Orin S. Kerr, *Good Faith, New Law, and the Scope of the Exclusionary Rule*, 99 Geo.L.J. 1077, 1082 (2011): "Recognizing a good faith exception for overturned law would introduce a systemic bias into Fourth Amendment litigation: it would encourage the prosecution to argue for changes in the law in its favor but discourage the same argument from the defense. The result would be a systematic skewing of constitutional arguments in the government's favor which would ensure the retention of erroneous precedents that allow practices that should be recognized as unconstitutional."

j. There was *state* appellate precedent broadly construing *Belton*, e.g., *State v. Skaggs*, 903 So.2d 180 (Ala.Crim.2004), but this is apparently irrelevant, since it was never mentioned by the Court. *Davis*-style analysis, reaching the *Davis* result, has been used where, again, the searching officer was a state official enforcing state law, even though there was *no* such state precedent but was "settled circuit precedent" in the federal court where the case ended up. *United States v. McCane*, 573 F.3d 1037 (10th Cir.2009). Query, does this mean that the Court in *Davis* should have characterized the beneficiaries of this new version of good faith as "lucky" instead of "nonculpable"?

k. If so, is this because (as the *Gant* majority says) *Belton* was "widely understood to allow a vehicle search" in circumstances like the *Davis* case, and (as the *Gant* dissenters note), that this version of the "*Belton* rule has been taught to police officers for more than a quarter century," so that it is "reliance" in the sense of this more general police understanding that counts?

"where 'binding appellate precedent specifically *authorize[d]* a particular police practice' * * * in accord with the holdings of nearly every other court in the country," but then noted: "This case does not present the markedly different question whether the exclusionary rule applies when the law governing the constitutionality of a particular search is unsettled. * * * Whether exclusion would deter Fourth Amendment violations where appellate precedent does not specifically authorize a certain practice and, if so, whether the benefits of exclusion would outweigh its costs are questions unanswered by our previous decisions.

"The dissent*l* suggests that today's decision essentially answers those questions, noting that an officer who conducts a search in the face of unsettled precedent 'is no more culpable than an officer who follows erroneous "binding precedent." ' The Court does not address this issue. In my view, whether an officer's conduct can be characterized as 'culpable' is not itself dispositive. We have never refused to apply the exclusionary rule where its application would appreciably deter Fourth Amendment violations on the mere ground that the officer's conduct could be characterized as nonculpable. Rather, an officer's culpability is relevant because it may inform the overarching inquiry whether exclusion would result in appreciable deterrence."

12. Should the fruits of constitutional but yet illegal arrests and searches be excluded? Reconsider fn. b, p. 222, and consider *United States v. Caceres*, 440 U.S. 741 (1979), holding that the failure of an IRS agent to follow IRS electronic surveillance regulations did not require suppression. Stevens, J., for the majority, could not "ignore the possibility that a rigid application of an exclusionary rule to every regulatory violation could have a serious deterrent impact on the formulation of additional standards to govern prosecutorial and police procedures. Here, the Executive itself has provided for internal sanctions in cases of knowing violations of the electronic surveillance regulations. To go beyond that, and require exclusion in every case, would take away from the Executive Department the primary responsibility for fashioning the appropriate remedy for the violation of its regulations. But since the content, and indeed the existence, of the regulations would remain within the Executive's sole authority, the result might well be fewer and less protective regulations. In the long run, it is far better to have rules like those contained in the IRS Manual, and to tolerate occasional erroneous administration of the kind displayed by this record, than either to have no rules except those mandated by statute, or to have them framed in a mere precatory form."

13. Although an illegal arrest or other unreasonable seizure of the person is itself a violation of the Fourth and Fourteenth Amendments, the exclusionary sanction comes into play only when the police have obtained evidence as a result of the unconstitutional seizure. It is no defense to a state or federal criminal prosecution that the defendant was illegally arrested or forcibly brought within the jurisdiction of the court. The trial of such a defendant violates neither Fifth nor Fourteenth Amendment Due Process nor any federal legislation. *Frisbie v. Collins,* 342 U.S. 519 (1952); *Ker v. Illinois,* 119 U.S. 436 (1886).**m** In *Gerstein v.*

---

l. The reference is to the dissent by Breyer, J., joined by Ginsberg, J., which goes on to say: "Thus, if the Court means what it now says, if it would place determinative weight upon the culpability of an individual officer's conduct, and if it would apply the exclusionary rule only where a Fourth Amendment violation was 'deliberate, reckless, or grossly negligent,' then the 'good faith' exception will swallow the exclusionary rule." See also the quotation from the dissent in Note 1, p. 262.

m. In *United States v. Alvarez–Machain,* 504 U.S. 655 (1992), the Court held that *Ker,* involving forcible abduction from a foreign country, was "fully applicable to this case" despite the fact that here the abduction was from Mexico, with whom the U.S. has an extradition treaty. "The Treaty says nothing about the obligations of the [parties] to refrain from forcible abductions

Pugh, p. 340, the Court declined to "retreat from the established rule that illegal arrest or detention does not void a subsequent conviction." See also *United States v. Crews*, p. 898, holding an illegally arrested defendant "is not himself a suppressible 'fruit' and the illegality of his detention cannot deprive the Government of the opportunity to prove his guilt through the introduction of evidence wholly untainted by the police misconduct."

NOTES ON THE "DIMENSIONS" OF
THE EXCLUSIONARY RULE

1. *Evidence obtained by government agents, used as basis for questions to grand jury witness.* In *United States v. Calandra*, 414 U.S. 338 (1974), the Court, per Powell, J., held that a grand jury witness may not refuse to answer questions on the ground that they are based on evidence obtained from him in an earlier unlawful search. After observing that a contrary holding would unduly interfere with the effective and expeditious discharge of the grand jury's duties [see p. 822], the Court asserted: "Whatever deterrence of police misconduct may result from the exclusion of illegally-seized evidence from criminal trials, it is unrealistic to assume that application of the rule to grand jury proceedings would significantly further that goal. Such an extension would deter only police investigation consciously directed toward the discovery of evidence solely for use in a grand jury investigation. The incentive to disregard the requirement of the Fourth Amendment solely to obtain an indictment from a grand jury is substantially negated by the inadmissibility of the illegally-seized evidence in a subsequent criminal prosecution of the search victim. For the most part, a prosecutor would be unlikely to request an indictment where a conviction could not be obtained. We therefore decline to embrace a view that would achieve a speculative and undoubtedly minimal advance in the deterrence of police misconduct at the expense of substantially impeding the role of the grand jury."

2. *Evidence obtained by government agents, used in criminal case after conviction.* Should illegally seized evidence be admissible after conviction for consideration by the judge in determining the sentence to be imposed? *Verdugo v. United States*, 402 F.2d 599 (9th Cir.1968), holding no, was distinguished in *United States v. Schipani*, 315 F.Supp. 253 (E.D.N.Y.1970), aff'd, 435 F.2d 26 (2d Cir.1970), in that the decision in *Verdugo* was "predicated upon the fact that the search which had produced the improper evidence was conducted outside the course of the regular criminal investigation. It was undertaken, not to obtain evidence to support an indictment and conviction, but to recover contraband and thus to enhance the possibility of a heavier sentence after the basic investigation had been completed. [Under these circumstances,] law enforcement officials would have little to lose, but much to gain, in violating the Fourth Amendment." That situation was not present in *Schipani*, and thus the court concluded that "no appreciable increment in deterrence would result from applying a second exclusion at sentencing after the rule has been applied at the trial itself."

In *Pennsylvania Board of Probation and Parole v. Scott*, 524 U.S. 357 (1998), parole officers made an illegal search of parolee Scott's residence and found weapons there, which were later admitted at his parole revocation hearing, resulting in Scott being recommitted to serve 36 months. Thereafter, the state supreme court, although following the prevailing general rule against application of the exclusionary rule at parole revocation hearings, carved out an exception for cases in which the officer who conducted the search was aware of the person's

---

of people from the territory of the other nation, or the consequences under the Treaty if such an abduction occurs."

parole status. The Supreme Court, in a 5–4 decision, disagreed. Thomas, J., for the majority, relying upon *Calandra*, supra, and *Janis* and *Lopez-Mendoza*, infra, declined "to extend the operation of the exclusionary rule beyond the criminal trial context" because "application of the exclusionary rule would both hinder the functioning of state parole systems and alter the traditionally flexible, administrative nature of parole revocation proceedings," but at the same time "would provide only minimal deterrence benefits in this context." On the matter of deterrence, the majority declared it would be "minimal" even in the special situation that concerned the state court, for if the searcher was a police officer he would be deterred by the risk of exclusion of evidence at a criminal trial and would be unaffected by what happened at the parole proceeding, which, in the words of *Janis*, "falls outside the offending officer's zone of primary interest." If the searcher was a parole officer, he will likewise be deterred by the risk of evidence exclusion at a criminal trial, and, in any event, is not "engaged in the often competitive enterprise of ferreting out crime" and thus can be sufficiently deterred by "departmental training and discipline and the threat of damages actions."

3. Evidence obtained by government agents, used in "quasi-criminal" or civil case. In *One 1958 Plymouth Sedan v. Pennsylvania*, 380 U.S. 693 (1965), a unanimous Court held that the *Weeks-Mapp* exclusionary rule applies to forfeiture proceedings. *Boyd v. United States*, p. 806 "the leading case on the subject of search and seizure * * * itself was not a criminal case," pointed out the majority, "but was a proceeding by the United States to forfeit 35 cases of plate glass which had allegedly been imported without payment of the customs duty * * *. [As] pointed out in *Boyd*, a forfeiture proceeding is quasi-criminal in character. Its object, like a criminal proceeding, is to penalize for the commission of an offense against the law. In this case * * * the driver and owner of the automobile was arrested and charged with a criminal offense against the Pennsylvania liquor laws. * * * In this forfeiture proceeding he was subject to the loss of his automobile, which at the time involved had an estimated value of approximately $1,000, a higher amount than the maximum fine in the criminal proceeding. It would be anomalous indeed, under these circumstances, to hold that in the criminal proceeding the illegally seized evidence is excludable, while in the forfeiture proceeding, requiring the determination that the criminal law has been violated, the same evidence would be admissible."

Los Angeles police seized wagering records and $4,940 in cash pursuant to a search warrant, and then notified the IRS, which made an assessment against Janis for wagering taxes and levied upon the seized cash in partial satisfaction. After Janis' motion to suppress was granted in the state criminal proceedings, he sued for refund of the money and to quash the assessment because it was based upon illegally seized evidence. The federal district court ruled for Janis, and the court of appeals affirmed. In *United States v. Janis*, 428 U.S. 433 (1976), the Court, per Blackmun, J., reversed: "Working, as we must, with the absence of convincing empirical data, common sense dictates that the deterrent effect of the exclusion of relevant evidence is highly attenuated when the 'punishment' imposed upon the offending criminal enforcement officer is the removal of that evidence from a civil suit by or against a different sovereign. In *Elkins* [p. 227] the Court indicated that the assumed interest of criminal law enforcement officers in the criminal proceedings of another sovereign counterbalanced this attenuation sufficiently to justify an exclusionary rule. Here, however, the attenuation is further augmented by the fact that the proceeding is one to enforce only the civil law of the other sovereign.

"This attenuation coupled with the existing deterrence effected by the denial of use of the evidence by either sovereign in the criminal trials with which the searching officer is concerned, creates a situation in which the imposition of the exclusionary rule sought in this case is unlikely to provide significant, much less substantial, additional deterrence. It falls outside the offending officer's zone of primary interest."

Utilizing the *Janis* cost-benefit approach, the Court held 5–4 in *I.N.S. v. Lopez–Mendoza*, 468 U.S. 1032 (1984), that the exclusionary rule is inapplicable in a civil deportation hearing. O'Connor, J., explained that the deterrent value of the exclusionary rule in this context was reduced because (i) "deportation will still be possible when evidence not derived directly from the arrest is sufficient to support deportation," (ii) INS agents know "that it is highly unlikely that any particular arrestee will end up challenging the lawfulness of his arrest," (iii) "the INS has its own comprehensive scheme for deterring Fourth Amendment violations" by training and discipline, and (iv) "alternative remedies" including the "possibility of declaratory relief" are available for institutional practices violating the Fourth Amendment. On the cost side, the Court continued, are these factors: (i) that application of the exclusionary rule "in proceedings that are intended not to punish past transgressions but to prevent their continuance or renewal would require courts to close their eyes to ongoing violations of the law," (ii) that invocation of the exclusionary rule at deportation hearings, where "neither the hearing officers nor the attorneys * * * are likely to be well versed in the intricacies of Fourth Amendment law," "might significantly change and compli-cate the character of these proceedings," and (iii) that because many INS arrests "occur in crowded and confused circumstances," application of the exclusionary rule "might well result in the suppression of large amounts of information that had been obtained entirely lawfully."

4. *Evidence obtained by private persons, used in criminal proceed-ings.* In *Burdeau v. McDowell*, 256 U.S. 465 (1921), the exclusionary rule was characterized "as a restraint upon the activities of sovereign authority and * * * not * * * a limitation upon other than governmental agencies," and on this basis courts have declined to exclude evidence in criminal cases when obtained by private persons. However, the Fourth Amendment *is* applicable "to private individuals who are acting as instruments or agents of the government. * * * Whether a private individual is an agent of the government is determined by a totality-of-the-circumstances test. Circumstances to be considered in this test include the motive of the private actor; any compensation or other benefit the private actor receives from the government; and the advice, direction, and level of participation given by the government. Using this test, if it is found that the private actor was sufficiently influenced and supported by the state, the exclusion-ary rule will apply to any evidence obtained by the private actor." Comment, 65 U.Cin.L.Rev. 665, 672 (1997). Private police have traditionally been treated as private persons, a conclusion recently questioned because today "private police participate in much of the police work that their public counterparts do." Elizabeth E. Joh, *The Paradox of Private Policing*, 95 J. Crim.L. & Criminology 49, 51 (2004).

One issue which frequently arises with respect to private person searches is whether, if that person then summons the police, police activity with respect to the same object is a separate "search" subject to Fourth Amendment constraints. For example, in *United States v. Jacobsen*, 466 U.S. 109 (1984), Federal Express employees opened a damaged box and found newspapers covering a tube which, when cut open, was found to contain plastic bags of white powder. Federal drug agents were summoned, but before their arrival the bags had been put back into the tube and the tube and newspapers back into the box, which was left open. A federal agent reopened the packaging to the extent necessary to expose the powder, which he field tested and found to be cocaine. The Court, per Stevens, J., concluded the agent's actions were not a significant expansion of the earlier private search and that consequently no warrant was required. "Respondents could have no privacy interest in the contents of the package, since it remained unsealed and since the Federal Express employees had just examined the package and had, of their own accord, invited the federal agent to their offices for the express purpose of viewing its contents. The agent's viewing of what a private party had freely made available for his inspection did not violate the Fourth Amendment.

"Similarly, the removal of the plastic bags from the tube and the agent's visual inspection of their contents enabled the agent to learn nothing that had not previously been learned during the private search. It infringed no legitimate expectation of privacy and hence was not a 'search' within the meaning of the Fourth Amendment."[a]

Three members of the Court rejected that reasoning. White, J., objected: "The majority opinion is particularly troubling when one considers its logical implications. I would be hard-pressed to distinguish this case, which involves a private search, from (1) one in which the private party's knowledge, later communicated to the government, that a particular container concealed contraband and nothing else arose from his presence at the time the container was sealed; (2) one in which the private party learned that a container concealed contraband and nothing else when it was previously opened in his presence; or (3) one in which the private party knew to a certainty that a container concealed contraband and nothing else as a result of conversations with its owner. In each of these cases, the approach adopted by the Court today would seem to suggest that the owner of the container has no legitimate expectation of privacy in its contents and that government agents opening that container without a warrant on the strength of information provided by the private party would not violate the Fourth Amendment."

5. *Evidence obtained by virtue of conduct of nonpolice government employee, used in criminal proceedings.* The *Burdeau* rule must be distinguished from that recognized in ARIZONA v. EVANS, 514 U.S. 1 (1995): some government searches covered by the Fourth Amendment are nonetheless inappropriate occasions for use of the exclusionary rule, considering the kind of government official who was at fault. After Evans was stopped for a traffic violation, the patrol car's computer indicated he had an outstanding arrest warrant, so Evans was arrested; incident thereto, the officer found marijuana. It was later learned that this warrant (issued because of Evans' nonappearance on several traffic violations) had been quashed upon Evans' voluntary appearance in court a few weeks earlier, but that apparently the court clerk had not thereafter followed the usual procedure of notifying the sheriff's department so that the warrant could be removed from the computer records. The state supreme court held this amounted to a violation of the Fourth Amendment and that consequently the evidence must be suppressed, but the Supreme Court, per Rehnquist, C.J., considering only the latter point, disagreed:

"This holding is contrary to the reasoning of *Leon,* [p. 229]; *Massachusetts v. Sheppard* [p. 239]; and *Krull* [p. 243]. If court employees were responsible for the erroneous computer record, the exclusion of evidence at trial would not sufficiently deter future errors so as to warrant such a severe sanction. First, as we noted in *Leon,* the exclusionary rule was historically designed as a means of deterring police misconduct, not mistakes by court employees. Second, respondent offers no evidence that court employees are inclined to ignore or subvert the Fourth Amendment or that lawlessness among these actors requires application of the extreme sanction of exclusion. To the contrary, the Chief Clerk of the Justice

---

a. As for the field test, see p. 278.

Court testified at the suppression hearing that this type of error occurred once every three or four years.

"Finally, and most important, there is no basis for believing that application of the exclusionary rule in these circumstances will have a significant effect on court employees responsible for informing the police that a warrant has been quashed. Because court clerks are not adjuncts to the law enforcement team engaged in the often competitive enterprise of ferreting out crime, they have no stake in the outcome of particular criminal prosecutions. The threat of exclusion of evidence could not be expected to deter such individuals from failing to inform police officials that a warrant had been quashed.

"If it were indeed a court clerk who was responsible for the erroneous entry on the police computer, application of the exclusionary rule also could not be expected to alter the behavior of the arresting officer. * * * There is no indication that the arresting officer was not acting objectively reasonably when he relied upon the police computer record. Application of the *Leon* framework supports a categorical exception to the exclusionary rule for clerical errors of court employees."

O'Connor, J., joined by Souter and Breyer, concurring, cautioned: "Surely it would not be reasonable for the police to rely, say, on a recordkeeping system, their own or some other agency's, that has no mechanism to ensure its accuracy over time and that routinely leads to false arrests, even years after the probable cause for any such arrest has ceased to exist (if it ever existed)."

Ginsburg, J., joined by Stevens, objected: "In this electronic age, particularly with respect to recordkeeping, court personnel and police officers are not neatly compartmentalized actors. Instead, they serve together to carry out the State's information-gathering objectives. Whether particular records are maintained by the police or the courts should not be dispositive where a single computer database can answer all calls. Not only is it artificial to distinguish between court clerk and police clerk slips; in practice, it may be difficult to pinpoint whether one official, e.g., a court employee, or another, e.g., a police officer, caused the error to exist or to persist."[b]

In *New Jersey v. T.L.O.*, p. 442, involving search of a student by a high school administrator, the Court reaffirmed that "the Fourth Amendment [is] applicable to the activities of civil as well as criminal authorities." However, because the search was found to be reasonable, the Court avoided expressing any opinion about the question that prompted the original grant of certiorari: whether the exclusionary rule is also applicable to searches by school authorities. In light of *Evans*, what is the answer to that question?

6. *Evidence obtained by foreign officials, used in domestic criminal proceedings.* Would any purpose be served by applying the exclusionary rule in such circumstances? What if American authorities requested or participated in the actions of the foreign police? Consider Note, 49 Colum.J.Transnat'l L. 411 (2011), concluding "that the risk of international terrorism and heightened transnational law enforcement cooperation demands to some extent a broad international silver platter doctrine and a narrow joint venture exception."

Even if there has been direct U.S. involvement in the foreign search, the Fourth Amendment may be inapplicable for yet another reason. In *United States v. Verdugo–Urquidez*, 494 U.S. 259 (1990), the opinion of the Court, per Rehnquist, C.J., declared that the phrase "the people" in the Fourth Amendment (and the First, Second, Ninth and Tenth Amendments) "refers to a class of persons

---

b. This language was noted by the majority in *Herring v. United States*, p. 285, in effect extending *Evans* accordingly.

who are part of a national community or who have otherwise developed sufficient connection with this community to be considered part of that community." The defendant in the instant case was deemed not to be such a person; he was a Mexican citizen and resident who, to be sure, just two days before the search of his residence in Mexico had been turned over to U.S. authorities by Mexican police, but "this sort of presence—lawful but involuntary—is not the sort to indicate any substantial connection with our country." (The Court added it was an open question whether even the illegal aliens in *Lopez–Mendoza*, p. 249, were such persons, though their situation was different from the defendant's here because they "were in the United States voluntarily and presumably had accepted some societal obligations.") The three dissenters agreed, as Blackmun, J., put it, "that when a foreign national is held accountable for purported violations of United States criminal laws, he has effectively been treated as one of 'the governed' and therefore is entitled to Fourth Amendment protections." Because the two concurring Justices placed great emphasis upon the inapplicability of the Fourth Amendment's warrant clause to the search in the instant case (Kennedy, J., stressing this was not a case in which "the full protections of the Fourth Amendment would apply" because of the "absence of local judges or magistrates available to issue warrants"; Stevens, J., noting that "American magistrates have no power to authorize such searches"), the application of *Verdugo–Urquidez* to a foreign search of an alien's property made even without probable cause is not entirely clear.

HUDSON v. MICHIGAN
547 U.S. 586, 126 S.Ct. 2159, 165 L.Ed.2d 56 (2006).

JUSTICE SCALIA delivered the opinion of the Court * * *.

[Police executing a warrant for drugs and firearms at Hudson's home announced their presence, but waited only "three to five seconds" before entering. Hudson moved to suppress the drugs and weapon found, arguing that the premature entry violated his Fourth Amendment rights (which the state conceded was the case). The trial court granted his motion, but the appellate court reversed on the ground that suppression is inappropriate for such a violation.]

* * * Suppression of evidence * * * has always been our last resort, not our first impulse. The exclusionary rule generates "substantial social costs," *United States v. Leon*, [p. 229], which sometimes include setting the guilty free and the dangerous at large. We have therefore been "cautio[us] against expanding" it, and "have repeatedly emphasized that the rule's 'costly toll' upon truth-seeking and law enforcement objectives presents a high obstacle for those urging [its] application," *Pennsylvania Bd. of Probation and Parole v. Scott*, [p. 247]. We have rejected "[i]ndiscriminate application" of the rule, *Leon*, and have held it to be applicable only "where its remedial objectives are thought most efficaciously served"—that is, "where its deterrence benefits outweigh its 'substantial social costs,'" *Scott* (quoting *Leon*).

We did not always speak so guardedly. Expansive dicta in *Mapp*, for example, suggested wide scope for the exclusionary rule. ("[A]ll evidence obtained by searches and seizures in violation of the Constitution is, by that same authority, inadmissible in a state court"). * * * But we have long since rejected that approach. [I]n *Leon*, * * * we explained that "[w]hether the exclusionary sanction is appropriately imposed in a particular case, ... is 'an issue separate from the question whether the Fourth Amendment rights of the party seeking to invoke the rule were violated by police conduct.'" * * *

Quite apart from the requirement of unattenuated causation,[a] the exclusionary rule has never been applied except "where its deterrence benefits outweigh its 'substantial social costs,'" *Scott*. The costs here are considerable. In addition to the grave adverse consequence that exclusion of relevant incriminating evidence always entails (viz., the risk of releasing dangerous criminals into society), imposing that massive remedy for a knock-and-announce violation would generate a constant flood of alleged failures to observe the rule, and claims that any asserted * * * justification for a no-knock entry, had inadequate support. The cost of entering this lottery would be small, but the jackpot enormous: suppression of all evidence, amounting in many cases to a get-out-of-jail-free card. Courts would experience as never before the reality that "[t]he exclusionary rule frequently requires extensive litigation to determine whether particular evidence must be excluded." *Scott*. Unlike the warrant or *Miranda* requirements, compliance with which is readily determined (either there was or was not a warrant; either the *Miranda* warning was given, or it was not), what constituted a "reasonable wait time" in a particular case (or, for that matter, how many seconds the police in fact waited), or whether there was "reasonable suspicion" of the sort that would invoke the *Richards* exceptions, is difficult for the trial court to determine and even more difficult for an appellate court to review.

Another consequence of the incongruent remedy Hudson proposes would be police officers' refraining from timely entry after knocking and announcing. As we have observed, the amount of time they must wait is necessarily uncertain. If the consequences of running afoul of the rule were so massive, officers would be inclined to wait longer than the law requires—producing preventable violence against officers in some cases, and the destruction of evidence in many others. We deemed these consequences severe enough to produce our unanimous agreement that a mere "reasonable suspicion" that knocking and announcing "under the particular circumstances, would be dangerous or futile, or that it would inhibit the effective investigation of the crime," will cause the requirement to yield. *Richards*.

Next to these "substantial social costs" we must consider the deterrence benefits, existence of which is a necessary condition for exclusion. * * * To begin with, the value of deterrence depends upon the strength of the incentive to commit the forbidden act. Viewed from this perspective, deterrence of knock-and-announce violations is not worth a lot. Violation of the warrant requirement sometimes produces incriminating evidence that could not otherwise be obtained. But ignoring knock-and-announce can realistically be expected to achieve absolutely nothing except the prevention of destruction of evidence and the avoidance of life-threatening resistance by occupants of the premises—dangers which, if there is even "reasonable suspicion" of their existence, suspend the knock-and-announce requirement anyway. Massive deterrence is hardly required.

It seems to us not even true, as Hudson contends, that without suppression there will be no deterrence of knock-and-announce violations at all. Of course even if this assertion were accurate, it would not necessarily justify suppression. Assuming (as the assertion must) that civil suit is not an effective deterrent, one can think of many forms of police misconduct that are similarly "undeterred." When, for example, a confessed suspect in the killing of a police officer, arrested (along with incriminating evidence) in a lawful warranted search, is subjected to physical abuse at the station house, would it seriously be suggested that the evidence must be excluded, since that is the only "effective deterrent"? And what, other than civil suit, is the "effective deterrent" of police violation of an already-confessed suspect's Sixth Amendment rights by denying him prompt access to

---

a. This is a reference to the fact that in an omitted part of the majority opinion the Court gave another reason for nonexclusion, namely, that the drugs and weapon seized were not a fruit of the Fourth Amendment violation. That branch of the case is discussed at p. 907.

counsel? Many would regard these violated rights as more significant than the right not to be intruded upon in one's nightclothes—and yet nothing but "ineffective" civil suit is available as a deterrent. And the police incentive for those violations is arguably greater than the incentive for disregarding the knock-and-announce rule.

We cannot assume that exclusion in this context is necessary deterrence simply because we found that it was necessary deterrence in different contexts and long ago. That would be forcing the public today to pay for the sins and inadequacies of a legal regime that existed almost half a century ago. Dollree Mapp could not turn to 42 U.S.C. § 1983 [p. 242 fn. h] for meaningful relief; *Monroe v. Pape*, 365 U.S. 167 (1961), which began the slow but steady expansion of that remedy, was decided the same Term as *Mapp*. It would be another 17 years before the § 1983 remedy was extended to reach the deep pocket of municipalities, *Monell v. Department of Social Servs. of City of New York*, [p. 242 fn. h]. Citizens whose Fourth Amendment rights were violated by federal officers could not bring suit until 10 years after *Mapp*, with this Court's decision in *Bivens v. Six Unknown Fed. Narcotics Agents*, [p. 242 fn. h].

Hudson complains that "it would be very hard to find a lawyer to take a case such as this," but 42 U.S.C. § 1988(b) answers this objection. Since some civil-rights violations would yield damages too small to justify the expense of litigation, Congress has authorized attorney's fees for civil-rights plaintiffs. This remedy was unavailable in the heydays of our exclusionary-rule jurisprudence, because it is tied to the availability of a cause of action. For years after *Mapp*, "very few lawyers would even consider representation of persons who had civil rights claims against the police," but now "much has changed. Citizens and lawyers are much more willing to seek relief in the courts for police misconduct."[b] The number of public-interest law firms and lawyers who specialize in civil-rights grievances has greatly expanded.

Hudson points out that few published decisions to date announce huge awards for knock-and-announce violations. But this is an unhelpful statistic. Even if we thought that only large damages would deter police misconduct (and that police somehow are deterred by "damages" but indifferent to the prospect of large § 1988 attorney's fees), we do not know how many claims have been settled, or indeed how many violations have occurred that produced anything more than nominal injury. It is clear, at least, that the lower courts are allowing colorable knock-and-announce suits to go forward, unimpeded by assertions of qualified immunity. As far as we know, civil liability is an effective deterrent here, as we have assumed it is in other contexts.

Another development over the past half-century that deters civil-rights violations is the increasing professionalism of police forces, including a new emphasis on internal police discipline. Even as long ago as 1980 we felt it proper to "assume" that unlawful police behavior would "be dealt with appropriately" by the authorities, but we now have increasing evidence that police forces across the United States take the constitutional rights of citizens seriously. There have been "wide-ranging reforms in the education, training, and supervision of police offi-

---

   b. Quoting Michael Avery, David Rudovsky & Karen Blum, *Police Misconduct: Law and Litigation* v. (3d ed.2005). However, "the book itself went on to lament on just the next page how the scope of the Fourth Amendment right as well as the procedural mechanisms to challenge police misconduct have been 'dramatically narrowed.' In fact, the authors asserted in a footnote to their most recent edition that Justice Scalia's citation to their analysis in support of eliminating the exclusionary rule was 'highly misleading.' " Robert M. Bloom & David H. Fentin, *"A More Majestic Conception": The Importance of Judicial Integrity in Preserving the Exclusionary Rule*, 13 U.Pa.J.Const.L. 47, 76–77 (2010).

cers.''[c] Numerous sources are now available to teach officers and their supervisors what is required of them under this Court's cases, how to respect constitutional guarantees in various situations, and how to craft an effective regime for internal discipline. Failure to teach and enforce constitutional requirements exposes municipalities to financial liability. Moreover, modern police forces are staffed with professionals; it is not credible to assert that internal discipline, which can limit successful careers, will not have a deterrent effect. There is also evidence that the increasing use of various forms of citizen review can enhance police accountability.

In sum, the social costs of applying the exclusionary rule to knock-and-announce violations are considerable; the incentive to such violations is minimal to begin with, and the extant deterrences against them are substantial—incomparably greater than the factors deterring warrantless entries when *Mapp* was decided. Resort to the massive remedy of suppressing evidence of guilt is unjustified. * * *

JUSTICE KENNEDY, concurring in part and concurring in the judgment.

Two points should be underscored with respect to today's decision. First, the knock-and-announce requirement protects rights and expectations linked to ancient principles in our constitutional order. The Court's decision should not be interpreted as suggesting that violations of the requirement are trivial or beyond the law's concern. Second, the continued operation of the exclusionary rule, as settled and defined by our precedents, is not in doubt. Today's decision determines only that in the specific context of the knock-and-announce requirement, a violation is not sufficiently related to the later discovery of evidence to justify suppression. * * *

JUSTICE BREYER, with whom JUSTICE STEVENS, JUSTICE SOUTER, and JUSTICE GINSBURG join, dissenting. * * *

Why is application of the exclusionary rule any the less necessary here? Without such a rule, as in *Mapp*, police know that they can ignore the Constitution's requirements without risking suppression of evidence discovered after an unreasonable entry. As in *Mapp*, some government officers will find it easier, or believe it less risky, to proceed with what they consider a necessary search immediately and without the requisite constitutional (say, warrant or knock-and-announce) compliance.

Of course, the State or the Federal Government may provide alternative remedies for knock-and-announce violations. But that circumstance was true of *Mapp* as well. What reason is there to believe that those remedies (such as private damages actions under 42 U.S.C. § 1983), which the Court found inadequate in *Mapp*, can adequately deter unconstitutional police behavior here? See Kamisar, In Defense of the Search and Seizure Exclusionary Rule, 26 Harv. J.L. & Pub. Pol'y 119, 126–129 (2003) (arguing that "five decades of post-*Weeks* 'freedom' from the inhibiting effect of the federal exclusionary rule failed to produce any meaningful alternative to the exclusionary rule in any jurisdiction" and that there is no evidence that "times have changed" post-*Mapp*).

The cases reporting knock-and-announce violations are legion. Indeed, these cases of reported violations seem sufficiently frequent and serious as to indicate "a widespread pattern." Yet the majority, like Michigan and the United States, has

---

c. Quoting Samuel Walker, *Taming the System: The Control of Discretion in Criminal Justice 1905-1990*, p. 51 (1993). "Following the publication of [*Hudson*], Samuel Walker authored an article in the Los Angeles Times clarifying that his main argument was 'twisted' by Scalia 'to reach a conclusion the exact opposite' of what he had argued. Rather than arguing that the improvements indicated that the exclusionary rule was no longer required, as Scalia implied, Walker actually argued that such improvements indicated its continuing importance." Bloom & Fentin, supra note b, at 67-68.

failed to cite a single reported case in which a plaintiff has collected more than nominal damages solely as a result of a knock-and-announce violation. Even Michigan concedes that, "in cases like the present one ..., damages may be virtually non-existent." And Michigan's amici further concede that civil immunities prevent tort law from being an effective substitute for the exclusionary rule at this time.

As Justice Stewart, the author of a number of significant Fourth Amendment opinions, explained, the deterrent effect of damage actions "can hardly be said to be great," as such actions are "expensive, time-consuming, not readily available, and rarely successful." The upshot is that the need for deterrence—the critical factor driving this Court's Fourth Amendment cases for close to a century— argues with at least comparable strength for evidentiary exclusion here.

To argue, as the majority does, that new remedies, such as 42 U.S.C. § 1983 actions or better trained police, make suppression unnecessary is to argue that *Wolf*, not *Mapp*, is now the law. * * * To argue that there may be few civil suits because violations may produce nothing "more than nominal injury" is to confirm, not to deny, the inability of civil suits to deter violations. And to argue without evidence (and despite myriad reported cases of violations, no reported case of civil damages, and Michigan's concession of their nonexistence) that civil suits may provide deterrence because claims may "have been settled" is, perhaps, to search in desperation for an argument. Rather, the majority, as it candidly admits, has simply "assumed" that, "[a]s far as [it] know[s], civil liability is an effective deterrent," a support-free assumption that *Mapp* and subsequent cases make clear does not embody the Court's normal approach to difficult questions of Fourth Amendment law. * * *

The Court has [previously] declined to apply the exclusionary rule only:

(1) where there is a specific reason to believe that application of the rule would "not result in appreciable deterrence," *United States v. Janis*, [p. 248]; see, e.g., *United States v. Leon* (exception where searching officer executes defective search warrant in "good faith"); *Arizona v. Evans*, [p. 250] (exception for clerical errors by court employees); *Walder v. United States*, [p. 910] (exception for impeachment purposes), or

(2) where admissibility in proceedings other than criminal trials was at issue, see, e.g., *Pennsylvania Bd. of Probation and Parole v. Scott* (exception for parole revocation proceedings); *INS v. Lopez–Mendoza*, [p. 249] (plurality opinion) (exception for deportation proceedings); *Janis*, (exception for civil tax proceedings); *United States v. Calandra*, [p. 247] (exception for grand jury proceedings); *Stone v. Powell*, [p. 230] (exception for federal habeas proceedings).

Neither of these two exceptions applies here. The second does not apply because this case is an ordinary criminal trial. The first does not apply because (1) officers who violate the rule are not acting "as a reasonable officer would and should act in similar circumstances," *Leon*, (2) this case does not involve government employees other than police, *Evans*, and (3), most importantly, the key rationale for any exception, "lack of deterrence," is missing, see *Pennsylvania Bd. of Probation* (noting that the rationale for not applying the rule in noncriminal cases has been that the deterrence achieved by having the rule apply in those contexts is "minimal" because "application of the rule in the criminal trial context already provides significant deterrence of unconstitutional searches"); *Michigan v. Tucker*, [p. 591] (noting that deterrence rationale would not be served if rule applied to police officers acting in good faith, as the "deterrent purpose of the exclusionary rule necessarily assumes that the police have engaged in willful, or at the very least negligent, conduct"). That critical latter rationale, which underlies every exception, does not apply here, as there is no reason to think that, in the case of knock-and-announce violations by the police, "the exclusion of evidence at trial would not sufficiently deter future errors," *Evans*, or " 'further the ends of the exclusionary rule in any appreciable way,' " *Leon*.

I am aware of no other basis for an exception. * * *

Neither can the majority justify its failure to respect the need for deterrence, as set forth consistently in the Court's prior case law, through its claim of "substantial social costs"—at least if it means that those "social costs" are somehow special here. The only costs it mentions are those that typically accompany any use of the Fourth Amendment's exclusionary principle: (1) that where the constable blunders, a guilty defendant may be set free (consider *Mapp* itself); (2) that defendants may assert claims where Fourth Amendment rights are uncertain (consider the Court's qualified immunity jurisprudence), and (3) that sometimes it is difficult to decide the merits of those uncertain claims. In fact, the "no-knock" warrants that are provided by many States, by diminishing uncertainty, may make application of the knock-and-announce principle less "cost[ly]" on the whole than application of comparable Fourth Amendment principles, such as determining whether a particular warrantless search was justified by exigency. The majority's "substantial social costs" argument is an argument against the Fourth Amendment's exclusionary principle itself. And it is an argument that this Court, until now, has consistently rejected * * *.

NOTES AND QUESTIONS

1. While the *Hudson* dissenters discuss mainly the § 1983 alternative touted by the majority, others have responded to the majority's police professionalism/self-discipline point. Blog correspondent Dan Jacobs asks: "Why would the police give stronger internal discipline than a slap on the wrist for a violation that results in no loss of criminal evidence?"

2. In *United States v. Ankeny*, 490 F.3d 744 (9th Cir.2007), police armed with a warrant entered the home of defendant, wanted for several assaults and known to have a handgun, at 5:30 a.m. A total of 44 officers participated in execution of the warrant, and 13 were assigned to enter the home. Police yelled "police, search warrant" and one second later used a battering ram to break open the door; defendant, who had been sleeping nearby, stood up, and police then fired a flash-bang device into the middle of the room which exploded near defendant and caused first and second-degree burns to his face and chest and second-degree burns to his upper arms. Officers stationed outside shot out all the second-story windows with rubber bullets, and officers securing the second level threw another flash-bang device into an open area, causing a bed in which a couple were sleeping to catch fire. Extensive damage was done to the house: the police shot out ten windows, kicked in many doors, burned carpet, and made holes in the walls and ceilings with rubber bullets. In a subsequent search, several weapons were found. Was the court correct in concluding that "we need not determine whether the entry was unreasonable" because, under *Hudson*, "suppression is not appropriate in any event"?

3. Officer *A*, armed with an arrest warrant to arrest *B* for sale of drugs, entered *B*'s house to make the arrest and seized *B* just inside the front door. Concerned because drug sellers sometimes have armed accomplices, *A* searched the rest of the house and found stolen computers in a back bedroom. The state now concedes that the officer lacked the reasonable suspicion needed to make a search for his own protection under *Maryland v. Buie*, p. 366. Given the frequency with which police are confronted with "difficult" *Buie* issues, and the possibility that police reluctance to make a search even when one would be allowed under *Buie* would "produc[e] preventable violence against officers in some cases," is this another situation in which *Hudson* is applicable? Do other situations also fall within *Hudson*? Was Justice Breyer right, then, when he commented during oral argument that if the Court took the position later adopted by the majority, "we'd let a kind of computer virus loose in the Fourth Amendment"?

4. Indeed, if one takes the *Hudson* majority's analysis seriously, is there anything left of *Mapp*? That is, if (i) exclusion of evidence "always entails" "grave adverse consequences," (ii) other newly effective remedies now provide deterrence "incomparably greater" than that existing when *Mapp* was decided, and (iii) the public today should not have to "pay for the sins and inadequacies of a legal regime that existed almost half a century ago," then is it ever true today that the deterrence benefits of "the massive remedy of suppressing evidence of guilt" can be deemed to outweigh its "substantial costs"?

HERRING v. UNITED STATES
555 U.S. 135, 129 S.Ct. 695, 172 L.Ed.2d 496 (2009).

CHIEF JUSTICE ROBERTS delivered the opinion of the Court. * * *

[Upon learning that Bennie Herring, no stranger to law enforcement, had driven to the sheriff's department to retrieve something from his impounded truck, Investigator Anderson checked with the county's warrant clerk about any outstanding warrants for Herring's arrest. When she indicated there were none, Anderson asked her to check with her counterpart in neighboring Dale County. The information obtained from that county's computer database, that there was an active arrest warrant for Herring's failure to appear on a felony charge, was communicated to Anderson, who with a deputy then arrested Herring and, in a search incident to arrest, found drugs and a gun (which, as a felon, Herring could not lawfully possess). Minutes later, Anderson was informed that the Dale County warrant clerk had now discovered that the warrant had been recalled five months earlier, a fact not appearing on the sheriff's computer database. Herring, charged in federal court, moved to suppress the evidence on the ground that his arrest was illegal, but his motion was denied. The court of appeals affirmed because the arresting officers "were entirely innocent of any wrongdoing or carelessness," while whoever failed to update the Dale County records, presumably "also a law enforcement official," was guilty only of "a negligent failure to act."]

Our cases establish that such suppression is not an automatic consequence of a Fourth Amendment violation. Instead, the question turns on the culpability of the police and the potential of exclusion to deter wrongful police conduct. Here the error was the result of isolated negligence attenuated from the arrest. We hold that in these circumstances the jury should not be barred from considering all the evidence. * * *

The fact that a Fourth Amendment violation occurred—*i.e.,* that a search or arrest was unreasonable—does not necessarily mean that the exclusionary rule applies. * * *

First, the exclusionary rule is not an individual right and applies only where it " 'result[s] in appreciable deterrence.' " *Leon.* We have repeatedly rejected the argument that exclusion is a necessary consequence of a Fourth Amendment violation. *Leon; Evans,* [p. 250]; *Pennsylvania Bd. of Probation and Parole v. Scott,* [p. 247]. Instead we have focused on the efficacy of the rule in deterring Fourth

Amendment violations in the future. See *Calandra,* [p. 247]; *Stone v. Powell,* [p. 230].[2]

In addition, the benefits of deterrence must outweigh the costs. *Leon.* "We have never suggested that the exclusionary rule must apply in every circumstance in which it might provide marginal deterrence." *Scott.* "[T]o the extent that application of the exclusionary rule could provide some incremental deterrent, that possible benefit must be weighed against [its] substantial social costs." *Illinois v. Krull,* [p. 243]. The principal cost of applying the rule is, of course, letting guilty and possibly dangerous defendants go free—something that "offends basic concepts of the criminal justice system." *Leon.* * * *

These principles are reflected in the holding of *Leon*: When police act under a warrant that is invalid for lack of probable cause, the exclusionary rule does not apply if the police acted "in objectively reasonable reliance" on the subsequently invalidated search warrant. We (perhaps confusingly) called this objectively reasonable reliance "good faith." In a companion case, *Massachusetts v. Sheppard,* [p. 239], we held that the exclusionary rule did not apply when a warrant was invalid because a judge forgot to make "clerical corrections" to it.

Shortly thereafter we extended these holdings to warrantless administrative searches performed in good-faith reliance on a statute later declared unconstitutional. *Krull.* Finally, in *Evans,* we applied this good-faith rule to police who reasonably relied on mistaken information in a court's database that an arrest warrant was outstanding. * * *

The extent to which the exclusionary rule is justified by these deterrence principles varies with the culpability of the law enforcement conduct. As we said in *Leon,* "an assessment of the flagrancy of the police misconduct constitutes an important step in the calculus" of applying the exclusionary rule. Similarly, in *Krull* we elaborated that "evidence should be suppressed 'only if it can be said that the law enforcement officer had knowledge, or may properly be charged with knowledge, that the search was unconstitutional under the Fourth Amendment.' "

Anticipating the good-faith exception to the exclusionary rule, Judge Friendly wrote that "[t]he beneficent aim of the exclusionary rule to deter police misconduct can be sufficiently accomplished by a practice . . . outlawing evidence obtained by flagrant or deliberate violation of rights." The Bill of Rights as a Code of Criminal Procedure, 53 Calif. L.Rev. 929, 953 (1965).

Indeed, the abuses that gave rise to the exclusionary rule featured intentional conduct that was patently unconstitutional. In *Weeks,* [p. 223], a foundational exclusionary rule case, the officers had broken into the defendant's home (using a key shown to them by a neighbor), confiscated incriminating papers, then returned again with a U.S. Marshal to confiscate even more. Not only did they have no search warrant, which the Court held was required, but they could not have gotten one had they tried. * * *

Equally flagrant conduct was at issue in *Mapp v. Ohio,* [p. 224], which * * * extended the exclusionary rule to the States. Officers forced open a door to Ms. Mapp's house, kept her lawyer from entering, brandished what the court concluded was a false warrant, then forced her into handcuffs and canvassed the house for obscenity. An error that arises from nonrecurring and attenuated negligence is thus far removed from the core concerns that led us to adopt the rule in the first place. And in fact since *Leon,* we have never applied the rule to exclude evidence

---

2. Justice Ginsburg's dissent champions what she describes as " 'a more majestic conception' of . . . the exclusionary rule," which would exclude evidence even where deterrence does not justify doing so. Majestic or not, our cases reject this conception, see, *e.g., United States v. Leon* * * *.

obtained in violation of the Fourth Amendment, where the police conduct was no more intentional or culpable than this.

To trigger the exclusionary rule, police conduct must be sufficiently deliberate that exclusion can meaningfully deter it, and sufficiently culpable that such deterrence is worth the price paid by the justice system. As laid out in our cases, the exclusionary rule serves to deter deliberate, reckless, or grossly negligent conduct, or in some circumstances recurring or systemic negligence. The error in this case does not rise to that level.[4]

Our decision in *Franks v. Delaware,* [p. 307], provides an analogy. In *Franks,* we held that police negligence in obtaining a warrant did not even rise to the level of a Fourth Amendment violation, let alone meet the more stringent test for triggering the exclusionary rule. We held that the Constitution allowed defendants, in some circumstances, "to challenge the truthfulness of factual statements made in an affidavit supporting the warrant," even after the warrant had issued. If those false statements were necessary to the Magistrate Judge's probable-cause determination, the warrant would be "voided." But we did not find all false statements relevant: "There must be allegations of deliberate falsehood or of reckless disregard for the truth," and "[a]llegations of negligence or innocent mistake are insufficient."

Both this case and *Franks* concern false information provided by police. Under *Franks,* negligent police miscommunications in the course of acquiring a warrant do not provide a basis to rescind a warrant and render a search or arrest invalid. Here, the miscommunications occurred in a different context—after the warrant had been issued and recalled—but that fact should not require excluding the evidence obtained.

The pertinent analysis of deterrence and culpability is objective, not an "inquiry into the subjective awareness of arresting officers," We have already held that "our good-faith inquiry is confined to the objectively ascertainable question whether a reasonably well trained officer would have known that the search was illegal" in light of "all of the circumstances." *Leon.* These circumstances frequently include a particular officer's knowledge and experience, but that does not make the test any more subjective than the one for probable cause, which looks to an officer's knowledge and experience, but not his subjective intent.

We do not suggest that all recordkeeping errors by the police are immune from the exclusionary rule. In this case, however, the conduct at issue was not so objectively culpable as to require exclusion. In *Leon* we held that "the marginal or nonexistent benefits produced by suppressing evidence obtained in objectively reasonable reliance on a subsequently invalidated search warrant cannot justify the substantial costs of exclusion." The same is true when evidence is obtained in objectively reasonable reliance on a subsequently recalled warrant.

If the police have been shown to be reckless in maintaining a warrant system, or to have knowingly made false entries to lay the groundwork for future false arrests, exclusion would certainly be justified under our cases should such misconduct cause a Fourth Amendment violation. * * *

The dissent also adverts to the possible unreliability of a number of databases not relevant to this case. In a case where systemic errors were demonstrated, it might be reckless for officers to rely on an unreliable warrant system. * * * But

---

4. We do not quarrel with Justice Ginsburg's claim that "liability for negligence . . . creates an incentive to act with greater care," and we do not suggest that the exclusion of this evidence could have *no* deterrent effect. But our cases require any deterrence to "be weighed against the 'substantial social costs exacted by the exclusionary rule,'" *Illinois v. Krull,* and here exclusion is not worth the cost.

there is no evidence that errors in Dale County's system are routine or wide-spread. * * *

The judgment of the Court of Appeals for the Eleventh Circuit is affirmed. * * *

JUSTICE GINSBURG, with whom JUSTICE STEVENS, JUSTICE SOUTER, and JUSTICE BREYER join, dissenting. * * *

Beyond doubt, a main objective of the rule "is to deter—to compel respect for the constitutional guaranty in the only effectively available way—by removing the incentive to disregard it." But the rule also serves other important purposes: It "enabl[es] the judiciary to avoid the taint of partnership in official lawlessness," and it "assur[es] the people—all potential victims of unlawful government conduct—that the government would not profit from its lawless behavior, thus minimizing the risk of seriously undermining popular trust in government."

The exclusionary rule, the Court suggests, is capable of only marginal deterrence when the misconduct at issue is merely careless, not intentional or reckless. The suggestion runs counter to a foundational premise of tort law—that liability for negligence, *i.e.,* lack of due care, creates an incentive to act with greater care. The Government so acknowledges.

That the mistake here involved the failure to make a computer entry hardly means that application of the exclusionary rule would have minimal value. "Just as the risk of *respondeat superior* liability encourages employers to supervise . . . their employees' conduct [more carefully], so the risk of exclusion of evidence encourages policymakers and systems managers to monitor the performance of the systems they install and the personnel employed to operate those systems."

Consider the potential impact of a decision applying the exclusionary rule in this case. As earlier observed, the record indicates that there is no electronic connection between the warrant database of the Dale County Sheriff's Department and that of the County Circuit Clerk's office, which is located in the basement of the same building. When a warrant is recalled, one of the "many different people that have access to th[e] warrants," must find the hard copy of the warrant in the "two or three different places" where the department houses warrants, return it to the Clerk's office, and manually update the Department's database. The record reflects no routine practice of checking the database for accuracy, and the failure to remove the entry for Herring's warrant was not discovered until Investigator Anderson sought to pursue Herring five months later. Is it not altogether obvious that the Department could take further precautions to ensure the integrity of its database? The Sheriff's Department "is in a position to remedy the situation and might well do so if the exclusionary rule is there to remove the incentive to do otherwise." 1 W. LaFave, Search and Seizure § 1.8(e), p. 313 (4th ed.2004).

Is the potential deterrence here worth the costs it imposes? In light of the paramount importance of accurate recordkeeping in law enforcement, I would answer yes, and next explain why, as I see it, Herring's motion presents a particularly strong case for suppression.

Electronic databases form the nervous system of contemporary criminal justice operations. In recent years, their breadth and influence have dramatically expanded. Police today can access databases that include not only the updated National Crime Information Center (NCIC), but also terrorist watchlists, the Federal Government's employee eligibility system, and various commercial databases. Moreover, States are actively expanding information sharing between jurisdictions. As a result, law enforcement has an increasing supply of information within its easy electronic reach.

The risk of error stemming from these databases is not slim. Herring's *amici* warn that law enforcement databases are insufficiently monitored and often out of date. Government reports describe, for example, flaws in NCIC databases, terrorist watchlist databases, and databases associated with the Federal Government's employment eligibility verification system.

Inaccuracies in expansive, interconnected collections of electronic information raise grave concerns for individual liberty. "The offense to the dignity of the citizen who is arrested, handcuffed, and searched on a public street simply because some bureaucrat has failed to maintain an accurate computer data base" is evocative of the use of general warrants that so outraged the authors of our Bill of Rights.

The Court assures that "exclusion would certainly be justified" if "the police have been shown to be reckless in maintaining a warrant system, or to have knowingly made false entries to lay the groundwork for future false arrests." This concession provides little comfort.

First, by restricting suppression to bookkeeping errors that are deliberate or reckless, the majority leaves Herring, and others like him, with no remedy for violations of their constitutional rights. There can be no serious assertion that relief is available under 42 U.S.C. § 1983. The arresting officer would be sheltered by qualified immunity, and the police department itself is not liable for the negligent acts of its employees. Moreover, identifying the department employee who committed the error may be impossible.

Second, I doubt that police forces already possess sufficient incentives to maintain up-to-date records. The Government argues that police have no desire to send officers out on arrests unnecessarily, because arrests consume resources and place officers in danger. The facts of this case do not fit that description of police motivation. Here the officer wanted to arrest Herring and consulted the Department's records to legitimate his predisposition.[6]

Third, even when deliberate or reckless conduct is afoot, the Court's assurance will often be an empty promise: How is an impecunious defendant to make the required showing? If the answer is that a defendant is entitled to discovery (and if necessary, an audit of police databases), then the Court has imposed a considerable administrative burden on courts and law enforcement.[7]

JUSTICE BREYER, with whom JUSTICE SOUTER joins, dissenting. * * *

Distinguishing between police recordkeeping errors and judicial ones not only is consistent with our precedent [in *Evans*], but also is far easier for courts to administer than The Chief Justice's case-by-case, multifactored inquiry into the degree of police culpability. I therefore would apply the exclusionary rule when police personnel are responsible for a recordkeeping error that results in a Fourth Amendment violation. * * *

NOTES AND QUESTIONS

1. To what extent, if at all, is it a fair criticism of *Herring* to say that it "is not simply wrong; it is wrong over and over again" because the majority opinion "(1) falsely claims that cost/benefit balancing is an established basis for selectively

---

6. It has been asserted that police departments have become sufficiently "professional" that they do not need external deterrence to avoid Fourth Amendment violations. But professionalism is a sign of the exclusionary rule's efficacy—not of its superfluity.

7. It is not clear how the Court squares its focus on deliberate conduct with its recognition that application of the exclusionary rule does not require inquiry into the mental state of the police.

applying the exclusionary rule at a criminal trial because of a police violation of the Fourth Amendment; (2) falsely represents that the Court's precedents support the proposition that the exclusionary rule may be selectively applied depending upon the degree of 'culpability' attending the Fourth Amendment violation; (3) asserts as a foregone conclusion, without an iota of supporting analysis or evidence, the proposition that application of the exclusionary rule in instances of a negligent violation of the Fourth Amendment has a reduced 'deterrent effect'; (4) purports to cabin the holding by the apparent afterthought that the negligence must also be 'attenuated,' but without any explanation of what attenuation means in the instant or any other case or why attenuation is relevant to the critical conclusion of reduced 'deterrent effect'; and (5) inflicts upon trial and appellate courts new and uniquely difficult tasks to be performed in adjudicating Fourth Amendment claims. It is thus apparent that this *Herring* is no mere herring; it is *surströmming*, which (as any Swede can tell you) is touted as a 'delicacy' but is actually attended by both a loathsome smell that 'grows progressively stronger' and a dangerous capacity to 'explode' beyond its existing boundaries." Wayne R. LaFave, *The Smell of* Herring: *A Critique of the Supreme Court's Latest Assault on the Exclusionary Rule*, 99 J.Crim.L. & Criminology 757, 758 (2009).

The cost/benefit balancing, no culpability/no exclusion theme of *Herring* was frequently quoted by the majority in *Davis v. United States*, p. 244, prompting the reaction by the concurrence and dissent noted there. The dissenters continued: "Indeed, our broad dicta in *Herring*—dicta the Court repeats and expands upon today—may already be leading lower courts in this direction. See *United States v. Julius*, 610 F.3d 60 (2d Cir.2010) (assuming warrantless search was unconstitutional and remanding for District Court to 'perform the cost/benefit analysis required by *Herring*' and to consider 'whether the degree of police culpability in this case rose beyond mere ... negligence' before ordering suppression); *United States v. Master*, 614 F.3d 236 (6th Cir.2010) ('[T]he *Herring* Court's emphasis seems weighed more toward preserving evidence for use in obtaining convictions, even if illegally seized ... unless the officers engage in "deliberate, reckless, or grossly negligent conduct" ' (quoting *Herring*)). Today's decision will doubtless accelerate this trend."

2. Under *Herring*, must the negligence be "attenuated"? Compare *United States v. Julius*, 610 F.3d 60 (2d Cir.2010) (remand for consideration of *Herring* notwithstanding acknowledged fact "the error here was made by the searching officer"); *People v. Robinson*, 224 P.3d 55 (Cal.2010) (attenuation "has no relevance" to application of *Herring*); with Craig Bradley, *Red* Herring *or the Death of the Exclusionary Rule?*, 45 Trial 52, 53 (April 2009) (important element in *Herring*, probably attributable "to the refusal of Justice Anthony Kennedy to go along with the broad reworking of the exclusionary rule desired by the other four justices in the majority of this 5–4 decision").

But what does that word mean in this context? Consider: "The word 'attenuated' in *Herring* conceivably refers to any number of things: (i) that the negligence was by someone other than the officer who made the arrest; (ii) that the negligence was an omission rather than an act; (iii) that the negligence occurred five months prior to the arrest; (iv) that the negligence was by a person in a different jurisdiction than the locale of arrest or prosecution, who for that reason is not as amenable to deterrence; (v) that the negligence had to do with the maintenance of police records, a subset of police activity not prone to error or in need of deterrence; or (vi) that while the negligence was by a law enforcement employee, that employee, by virtue of his or her assignment, is less in need of deterrence than the typical policeman. As to each of these alternatives, it must be asked (a) how likely it is that this is the *Herring* majority's perception of the qualifier 'attenuated,' and (b) whether it can be said that such a perception of

'attenuated' actually describes a class of conduct as to which the critical consequence of reduced 'benefits of deterrence' actually exists." LaFave, supra Note 1,
at 771–72.

3. Given the dissenters' description of the nature of the problem in the Dale
County Sheriff's office, was the majority correct in concluding the negligence in
the instant case was not "systemic"?

4. Do the *Herring* dissenters, in discussing a defendant's efforts "to make
the required showing" to escape the *Herring* rule, mean to suggest that the
burden of proof is on the defendant? Compare LaFave, supra Note 1, at 786,
asserting that "since *Herring*, like *Evans*, purports to be simply an extension of
the 'good faith' doctrine, the controlling consideration is the fact that in the past
courts have consistently ruled 'that the government has the burden to prove facts
warranting application of the good faith exception.'" If this is so, did the
government meet its burden with respect to the degree of culpability involved,
considering the government could not even identify the particular person responsible?

SECTION 2. PROTECTED AREAS
AND INTERESTS

KATZ v. UNITED STATES
389 U.S. 347, 88 S.Ct. 507, 19 L.Ed.2d 576 (1967).

JUSTICE STEWART delivered the opinion of the Court.

The petitioner was convicted [of] transmitting wagering information by
telephone from Los Angeles to Miami and Boston in violation of a federal statute.
At trial the Government was permitted, over the petitioner's objection, to introduce evidence of the petitioner's end of telephone conversations, overheard by FBI
agents who had attached an electronic listening and recording device to the
outside of the public telephone booth from which he had placed his calls. In
affirming his conviction, the Court of Appeals rejected the contention that the
recordings had been obtained in violation of the Fourth Amendment, because
"[t]here was no physical entrance into the area occupied by [the petitioner]." We
granted certiorari in order to consider the constitutional questions thus presented.

The petitioner has phrased those questions as follows:

"A. Whether a public telephone booth is a constitutionally protected
area so that evidence obtained by attaching an electronic listening recording
device to the top of such a booth is obtained in violation of the right to privacy
of the user of the booth.

"B. Whether physical penetration of a constitutionally protected area is
necessary before a search and seizure can be said to be violative of the Fourth
Amendment to the United States Constitution."

We decline to adopt this formulation of the issues. In the first place the
correct solution of Fourth Amendment problems is not necessarily promoted by
incantation of the phrase "constitutionally protected area." Secondly, the Fourth
Amendment cannot be translated into a general constitutional "right to privacy."
That Amendment protects individual privacy against certain kinds of governmental intrusion, but its protections go further, and often have nothing to do with
privacy at all. Other provisions of the Constitution protect personal privacy from
other forms of governmental invasion. But the protection of a person's *general*
right to privacy—his right to be let alone by other people—is, like the protection
of his property and of his very life, left largely to the law of the individual States.

Because of the misleading way the issues have been formulated, the parties have attached great significance to the characterization of the telephone booth from which the petitioner placed his calls. The petitioner has strenuously argued that the booth was a "constitutionally protected area." The Government has maintained with equal vigor that it was not. But this effort to decide whether or not a given "area," viewed in the abstract, is "constitutionally protected" deflects attention from the problem presented by this case. For the Fourth Amendment protects people, not places. What a person knowingly exposes to the public, even in his own home or office, is not a subject of Fourth Amendment protection. * * * But what he seeks to preserve as private, even in an area accessible to the public, may be constitutionally protected. * * *

The Government stresses the fact that the telephone booth from which the petitioner made his calls was constructed partly of glass, so that he was as visible after he entered it as he would have been if he had remained outside. But what he sought to exclude when he entered the booth was not the intruding eye—it was the uninvited ear. He did not shed his right to do so simply because he made his calls from a place where he might be seen. No less than an individual in a business office, in a friend's apartment, or in a taxicab, a person in a telephone booth may rely upon the protection of the Fourth Amendment. One who occupies it, shuts the door behind him, and pays the toll that permits him to place a call is surely entitled to assume that the words he utters into the mouthpiece will not be broadcast to the world. To read the Constitution more narrowly is to ignore the vital role that the public telephone has come to play in private communication.

The Government contends, however, that the activities of its agents in this case should not be tested by Fourth Amendment requirements, for the surveillance technique they employed involved no physical penetration of the telephone booth from which the petitioner placed his calls.

* * * [A]lthough a closely divided Court supposed in *Olmstead* [p. 505] that surveillance without any trespass and without the seizure of any material object fell outside the ambit of the Constitution, we have since departed from the narrow view on which that decision rested. Indeed, we have expressly held that the Fourth Amendment governs not only the seizure of tangible items, but extends as well to the recording of oral statements overheard without any "technical trespass under * * * local property law." *Silverman v. United States*, 365 U.S. 505 (1961). Once this much is acknowledged, and once it is recognized that the Fourth Amendment protects people—and not simply "areas"—against unreasonable searches and seizures it becomes clear that the reach of that Amendment cannot turn upon the presence or absence of a physical intrusion into any given enclosure.

We conclude that the underpinnings of *Olmstead* and *Goldman* [p. 523] have been so eroded by our subsequent decisions that the "trespass" doctrine there enunciated can no longer be regarded as controlling. The Government's activities in electronically listening to and recording the petitioner's words violated the privacy upon which he justifiably relied while using the telephone booth and thus constituted a "search and seizure" within the meaning of the Fourth Amendment. The fact that the electronic device employed to achieve that end did not happen to penetrate the wall of the booth can have no constitutional significance.

The question remaining for decision, then, is whether the search and seizure conducted in this case complied with constitutional standards. In that regard, the Government's position is that its agents acted in an entirely defensible manner: They did not begin their electronic surveillance until investigation of the petitioner's activities had established a strong probability that he was using the telephone in question to transmit gambling information to persons in other States, in violation of federal law. Moreover, the surveillance was limited, both in scope and in duration to the specific purpose of establishing the contents of the petitioner's unlawful telephonic communications. The agents confined their surveillance to the brief periods during which he used the telephone booth, and they took great care to overhear only the conversations of the petitioner himself.

Accepting this account of the Government's actions as accurate, it is clear that this surveillance was so narrowly circumscribed that a duly authorized magistrate, properly notified of the need for such investigation, specifically informed of the basis on which it was to proceed, and clearly apprised of the precise intrusion it would entail, could constitutionally have authorized, with appropriate safeguards, the very limited search and seizure that the Government asserts in fact took place. * * *

The Government * * * urges the creation of a new exception to cover this case. It argues that surveillance of a telephone booth should be exempted from the usual requirement of advance authorization by a magistrate upon a showing of probable cause. We cannot agree. Omission of such authorization "bypasses the safeguards provided by an objective predetermination of probable cause, and substitutes instead the far less reliable procedure of an after-the-event justification for the * * * search, too likely to be subtly influenced by the familiar shortcomings of hindsight judgment." And bypassing a neutral predetermination of the *scope* of a search leaves individuals secure from Fourth Amendment violations "only in the discretion of the police."

These considerations do not vanish when the search in question is transferred from the setting of a home, an office, or a hotel room, to that of a telephone booth. Wherever a man may be, he is entitled to know that he will remain free from unreasonable searches and seizures. The government agents here ignored "the procedure of antecedent justification * * * that is central to the Fourth Amendment," a procedure that we hold to be a constitutional precondition of the kind of electronic surveillance involved in this case. * * *

Judgment reversed.[a]

JUSTICE HARLAN, concurring. * * *

As the Court's opinion states, "The Fourth Amendment protects people, not places." The question, however, is what protection it affords to those people. Generally, as here, the answer to that question requires reference to a "place." My understanding of the rule that has emerged from prior decisions is that there is a twofold requirement, first that a person have exhibited an actual (subjective) expectation of privacy and, second, that the expectation be one that society is prepared to recognize as "reasonable."[b] Thus a man's home is, for most purposes, a place where he expects privacy, but objects, activities, or statements that he exposes to the "plain view" of outsiders are not "protected" because no intention to keep them to himself has been exhibited. On the other hand, conversations in the open would not be protected against being overheard, for the expectation of privacy under the circumstances would be unreasonable. * * *

---

a. Justice Marshall took no part in the case. Concurring opinions by Douglas, J., joined by Brennan, J., and by White, J., are omitted.

b. Consider Anthony Amsterdam, *Perspectives on the Fourth Amendment,* 58 Minn.L.Rev. 349, 384 (1974): "But Justice Harlan himself [dissenting in *United States v. White,* p. 474] later expressed second thoughts about this conception, and rightly so. An actual, subjective expectation of privacy obviously has no place in a statement of what *Katz* held or in a theory of what the fourth amendment protects. It can neither add to, nor can its absence detract from, an individual's claim to fourth amendment protection. If it could, the government could diminish each person's subjective expectation of privacy merely by announcing half-hourly on television * * * that we were all forthwith being placed under comprehensive electronic surveillance."

The critical fact in this case is that "[o]ne who occupies it, [a telephone booth] shuts the door behind him, and pays the toll that permits him to place a call, is surely entitled to assume" that his conversation is not being intercepted. The point is not that the booth is "accessible to the public" at other times, but that it is a temporarily private place whose momentary occupants' expectations of freedom from intrusion are recognized as reasonable. * * *

JUSTICE BLACK, dissenting. * * *

Tapping telephone wires, of course, was an unknown possibility at the time the Fourth Amendment was adopted. But eavesdropping (and wiretapping is nothing more than eavesdropping by telephone) was * * * "an ancient practice which at common law was condemned as a nuisance. In those days the eavesdropper listened by naked ear under the eaves of houses or their windows, or beyond their walls seeking out private discourse." There can be no doubt that the Framers were aware of this practice, and if they had desired to outlaw or restrict the use of evidence obtained by eavesdropping, I believe that they would have used the appropriate language to do so in the Fourth Amendment. They certainly would not have left such a task to the ingenuity of language-stretching judges. * * *

NOTES AND QUESTIONS

1. *Fourth Amendment interests.* In *Katz,* the Court held that the police conduct "constituted a 'search and seizure' within the meaning of the Fourth Amendment" because of the intrusion upon the defendant's privacy interest. But this does not mean that privacy is the *only* interest protected by the Fourth Amendment. The Fourth Amendment also protects the interests in possession of property and liberty of person, as in *United States v. Place,* p. 277 (detention of traveler's luggage 90 minutes was an unreasonable seizure in two respects, as it constituted a deprivation of defendant's "possessory interest in his luggage" and his "liberty interest in proceeding with his itinerary"). In *Soldal v. Cook County,* 506 U.S. 56 (1992), a § 1983 action commenced against sheriff's deputies who knowingly participated in an unlawful eviction that involved disconnecting the plaintiff's trailer home from its utilities and hauling it off the landlord's property, the Court held "that seizures of property are subject to Fourth Amendment scrutiny even though no search within the meaning of the Amendment has taken place."

2. *Garbage.* In CALIFORNIA v. GREENWOOD, 486 U.S. 35 (1988), police on two occasions had the neighborhood garbage collector pick up opaque plastic bags of garbage, which Greenwood had left at his curb for pick-up, and turn them over without mixing their contents with other garbage collected. On each occasion evidence of narcotics use was found, and each discovery served as the basis for a search warrant to search Greenwood's home which, upon execution, led to the discovery of narcotics. In reversing the state court's holding that these actions violated the Fourth Amendment, the Court, per White, J., reasoned:

"Here, we conclude that respondents exposed their garbage to the public sufficiently to defeat their claim to Fourth Amendment protection.[c] It is common knowledge that plastic garbage bags left on or at the side of a public street are readily accessible to animals, children, scavengers, snoops, and other members of the public. Moreover, respondents placed their refuse at the curb for the express

---

c. As for the respondents' reliance upon their right to privacy in garbage recognized by California law, the Court later stated: "Respondent's argument is no less than a suggestion that concepts of privacy under the laws of each State are to determine the reach of the Fourth Amendment. We do not accept this submission."

purpose of conveying it to a third party, the trash collector, who might himself have sorted through respondents' trash or permitted others, such as the police, to do so. Accordingly, having deposited their garbage 'in an area particularly suited for public inspection and, in a manner of speaking, public consumption, for the express purpose of having strangers take it,' respondents could have had no reasonable expectation of privacy in the inculpatory items that they discarded.

"Furthermore, as we have held, the police cannot reasonably be expected to avert their eyes from evidence of criminal activity that could have been observed by any member of the public. Hence, '[w]hat a person knowingly exposes to the public, even in his own home or office, is not a subject of Fourth Amendment protection.' *Katz.* We held in *Smith v. Maryland,* [p. 510], for example, that the police did not violate the Fourth Amendment by causing a pen register to be installed at the telephone company's offices to record the telephone numbers dialed by a criminal suspect. An individual has no legitimate expectation of privacy in the numbers dialed on his telephone, we reasoned, because he voluntarily conveys those numbers to the telephone company when he uses the telephone. Again, we observed that 'a person has no legitimate expectation of privacy in information he voluntarily turns over to third parties.'

"Similarly, we held in *California v. Ciraolo,* 476 U.S. 207 (1986) that the police were not required by the Fourth Amendment to obtain a warrant before conducting surveillance of the respondent's fenced backyard from a private plane flying at an altitude of 1,000 feet. We concluded that the respondent's expectation that his yard was protected from such surveillance was unreasonable because '[a]ny member of the public flying in this airspace who glanced down could have seen everything that these officers observed.'[d]"

Brennan, J., for the two dissenters, objected that a "trash bag, like any of the above-mentioned containers, 'is a common repository for one's personal effects' and, even more than many of them, is 'therefore . . . inevitably associated with the expectation of privacy.' A single bag of trash testifies eloquently to the eating, reading, and recreational habits of the person who produced it. A search of trash, like a search of the bedroom, can relate intimate details about sexual practices, health, and personal hygiene. Like rifling through desk drawers or intercepting phone calls, rummaging through trash can divulge the target's financial and professional status, political affiliations and inclinations, private thoughts, personal relationships, and romantic interests. It cannot be doubted that a sealed trash bag harbors telling evidence of the 'intimate activity associated with the "sanctity of a man's home and the privacies of life," ' which the Fourth Amendment is designed to protect. * * *

"Nor is it dispositive that 'respondents placed their refuse at the curb for the express purpose of conveying it to a third party, . . . who might himself have sorted through respondents' trash or permitted others, such as police, to do so.' In the first place, Greenwood can hardly be faulted for leaving trash on his curb when a county ordinance commanded him to do so, and prohibited him from disposing of it in any other way. More importantly, even the voluntary relinquishment of possession or control over an effect does not necessarily amount to a relinquishment of a privacy expectation in it. Were it otherwise, a letter or package would lose all Fourth Amendment protection when placed in a mail box or other depository with the 'express purpose' of entrusting it to the postal officer

---

d. *Ciraolo* was a 5–4 decision. The dissenters objected that "the actual risk to privacy from commercial or pleasure aircraft is virtually nonexistent. Travelers on commercial flights, as well as private planes used for business or personal reasons, normally obtain at most a fleeting, anonymous, and nondiscriminating glimpse of the landscape and buildings over which they pass. The risk that a passenger on such a plane might observe private activities, and might connect those activities with particular people, is simply too trivial to protect against."

or a private carrier; those bailees are just as likely as trash collectors (and certainly have greater incentive) to 'sor[t] through' the personal effects entrusted to them, 'or permi[t] others, such as police to do so.' Yet, it has been clear for at least 110 years that the possibility of such an intrusion does not justify a warrantless search by police in the first instance. See *Ex parte Jackson,* 96 U.S. (6 Otto) 727 (1878)."

Should *Greenwood* apply even when the defendant has resorted to rather extraordinary means to ensure that the incriminating character of his garbage is not perceived by others? Yes is the answer given in *United States v. Scott,* 975 F.2d 927 (1st Cir.1992), where IRS agents painstakingly reassembled documents which defendant shredded into ⁵⁄₃₂–inch strips before putting them in the garbage later placed outside his curtilage. The court offered this analogy: "A person who prepares incriminating documents in a secret code (or for that matter in some obscure foreign language), and thereafter blithely discards them as trash, relying on the premise or hope that they will not be deciphered [or translated] by the authorities could well be in for an unpleasant surprise if his code is 'broken' by the police [or a translator is found for the abstruse language], but he cannot make a valid claim that his subjective expectation in keeping the contents private by use of the secret code [or language] was reasonable in a constitutional sense."

3. *"Curtilage" vs. "open fields."* After *Greenwood,* what result as to garbage left for pickup in a can well within the curtilage, if (i) the police merely enter and take the garbage, or (ii) the police have the garbage collector pick up and segregate the garbage from that can? More generally, what lands are protected by the Fourth Amendment from what kinds of police intrusions? Consider:

(a) In OLIVER v. UNITED STATES, 466 U.S. 170 (1984), the Court, per Powell, J., held that the "open fields" doctrine of *Hester v. United States,* 265 U.S. 57 (1924), by which police entry and examination of a field is free of any Fourth Amendment restraints, had not been implicitly overruled by *Katz.* This was because the *Hester* rule "was founded upon the explicit language of the Fourth Amendment. That Amendment indicates with some precision the places and things encompassed by its protections. As Justice Holmes explained for the Court in his characteristically laconic style: '[T]he special protection accorded by the Fourth Amendment to the people in their "persons, houses, papers, and effects," is not extended to the open fields. The distinction between the latter and the house is as old as the common law.' "

The Court in *Oliver* reasoned that this interpretation of the Amendment was consistent with *Katz,* as "open fields do not provide the setting for those intimate activities that the Amendment is intended to shelter from government interference or surveillance. There is no societal interest in protecting the privacy of those activities, such as the cultivation of crops, that occur in open fields. Moreover, as a practical matter these lands usually are accessible to the public and the police in ways that a home, an office or commercial structure would not be. It is not generally true that fences or no trespassing signs effectively bar the public from viewing open fields in rural areas. And both petitioner Oliver and respondent Thornton concede that the public and police lawfully may survey lands from the air. For these reasons, the asserted expectation of privacy in open fields is not an expectation that 'society recognizes as reasonable.'

"The historical underpinnings of the 'open fields' doctrine also demonstrate that the doctrine is consistent with respect for 'reasonable expectations of privacy.' As Justice Holmes, writing for the Court, observed in *Hester,* the common law distinguished 'open fields' from the 'curtilage,' the land immediately surrounding and associated with the home. The distinction implies that only the curtilage, not the neighboring open fields, warrants the Fourth Amendment protections that attach to the home. At common law, the curtilage is the area to which extends the intimate activity associated with the 'sanctity of a man's home and the privacies of life,' and therefore has been considered part of home itself for Fourth Amendment purposes. Thus, courts have extended Fourth Amendment protection to the curtilage; and they have defined the curtilage, as did the common law, by reference to the factors that determine whether an individual reasonably may expect that an area immediately adjacent to the home will remain private.[e] Conversely, the common law implies, as we reaffirm today, that no expectation of privacy legitimately attaches to open fields."

As for the contention that the circumstances may sometimes show the existence of a reasonable expectation of privacy, the Court said it was answered by the "language of the Fourth Amendment," but added that such a case-by-case approach would in any event be unworkable because "police officers would have to guess before every search whether landowners had erected fences sufficiently high, posted a sufficient number of warning signs, or located contraband in an area sufficiently secluded to establish a right of privacy." The *Oliver* majority also asserted that it rejected "the suggestion that steps taken to protect privacy establish that expectations of privacy in an open field are legitimate. It is true, of course, that petitioner Oliver and respondent Thornton, in order to conceal their criminal activities, planted the marijuana upon secluded land and erected fences and no trespassing signs around the property. And it may be that because of such precautions, few members of the public stumbled upon the marijuana crops seized by the police. Neither of these suppositions demonstrates, however, that the expectation of privacy was *legitimate* in the sense required by the Fourth Amendment. The test of legitimacy is not whether the individual chooses to conceal assertedly 'private' activity. Rather, the correct inquiry is whether the government's intrusion infringes upon the personal and societal values protected by the Fourth Amendment. As we have explained, we find no basis for concluding that a police inspection of open fields accomplishes such an infringement."

Marshall, J., for the three dissenters, argued (1) that the Court's first ground could not be squared with earlier decisions, including *Katz* itself, for "neither a public telephone booth nor a conversation conducted therein can fairly be described as a person, house, paper, or effect"; and (2) that society *is* prepared to recognize as reasonable the expectations of Oliver and Thornton, which were supported by the law of criminal trespass, the private uses to which privately owned lands could be put, and the precautions which they had taken to manifest their privacy interest to others. From this the dissenters posited this "clear, easily administrable rule": "Private land marked in a fashion sufficient to render entry thereon a criminal trespass under the law of the state in which the land lies is protected by the Fourth Amendment's proscription of unreasonable searches and seizures."

(b) FLORIDA v. RILEY, 488 U.S. 445 (1989), presented the question: "Whether surveillance of the interior of a partially covered greenhouse in a residential backyard from the vantage point of a helicopter located 400 feet above

---

e. As the Court explained in *United States v. Dunn,* 480 U.S. 294 (1987), "curtilage questions should be resolved with particular reference to four factors: the proximity of the area claimed to be curtilage to the home, whether the area is included within an enclosure surrounding the home, the nature of the uses to which the area is put, and the steps taken by the resident to protect the area from observation by people passing by." Applying these factors, the Court then concluded the barn into which the police looked was not within the curtilage, as it was 60 yards from the house, was outside the area surrounding the house enclosed by a fence, did not appear to the police to be "used for intimate activities of the home," and the fences outside the barn were not of a kind "to prevent persons from observing what lay inside the enclosed area." The Court added that even assuming the barn was protected business premises, it still was no search to look into the open barn from an open fields vantage point.

the greenhouse constitutes a 'search' for which a warrant is required under the Fourth Amendment." White, J., for the 4–Justice plurality, concluded it did not "make a difference for Fourth Amendment purposes that the helicopter was flying at 400 feet when the officer saw what was growing in the greenhouse through the partially open roof and sides of the structure. We would have a different case if flying at that altitude had been contrary to law or regulation. But helicopters are not bound by the lower limits of the navigable airspace allowed to other aircraft. Any member of the public could legally have been flying over Riley's property in a helicopter at the altitude of 400 feet and could have observed Riley's greenhouse. The police officer did no more. This is not to say that an inspection of the curtilage of a house from an aircraft will always pass muster under the Fourth Amendment simply because the plane is within the navigable airspace specified by law. But it is of obvious importance that the helicopter in this case was *not* violating the law, and there is nothing in the record or before us to suggest that helicopters flying at 400 feet are sufficiently rare in this country to lend substance to respondent's claim that he reasonably anticipated that his greenhouse would not be subject to observation from that altitude. Neither is there any intimation here that the helicopter interfered with respondent's normal use of the greenhouse or of other parts of the curtilage. As far as this record reveals, no intimate details connected with the use of the home or curtilage were observed, and there was no undue noise, no wind, dust, or threat of injury. In these circumstances, there was no violation of the Fourth Amendment."

O'Connor, J., concurring only in the judgment because "the plurality's approach rests the scope of Fourth Amendment protection too heavily on compliance with FAA regulations whose purpose is to promote air safety, not to protect" Fourth Amendment rights, concluded: "Because there is reason to believe that there is considerable public use of airspace at altitudes of 400 feet and above, and because Riley introduced no evidence to the contrary before the Florida courts, I conclude that Riley's expectation that his curtilage was protected from naked-eye aerial observation from that altitude was not a reasonable one. However, public use of altitudes lower than that—particularly public observations from helicopters circling over the curtilage of a home—may be sufficiently rare that police surveillance from such altitudes would violate reasonable expectations of privacy, despite compliance with FAA air safety regulations."

Brennan, J., joined by Marshall and Stevens, JJ., dissenting, objected: "Under the plurality's exceedingly grudging Fourth Amendment theory, the expectation of privacy is defeated if a single member of the public could conceivably position herself to see into the area in question without doing anything illegal. It is defeated whatever the difficulty a person would have in so positioning herself, and however infrequently anyone would in fact do so. In taking this view the plurality ignores the very essence of *Katz.* * * * Finding determinative the fact that the officer was where he had a right to be, at bottom, an attempt to analogize surveillance from a helicopter to surveillance by a police officer standing on a public road and viewing evidence of crime through an open window or a gap in a fence. In such a situation, the occupant of the home may be said to lack any reasonable expectation of privacy in what can be seen from that road—even if, in fact, people rarely pass that way.

"The police officer positioned 400 feet above Riley's backyard was not, however, standing on a public road. The vantage point he enjoyed was not one any citizen could readily share. His ability to see over Riley's fence depended on his use of a very expensive and sophisticated piece of machinery to which few ordinary citizens have access. In such circumstances it makes no more sense to rely on the legality of the officer's position in the skies than it would to judge the constitutionality of the wiretap in *Katz* by the legality of the officer's position outside the telephone booth. The simple inquiry whether the police officer had the legal right to be in the position from which he made his observations cannot suffice, for we cannot assume that Riley's curtilage was so open to the observations of passersby in the skies that he retained little privacy or personal security to be lost to police surveillance. The question before us must be not whether the police were where they had a right to be, but whether public observation of Riley's curtilage was so commonplace that Riley's expectation of privacy in his backyard could not be considered reasonable."

Blackmun, J., dissenting, first concluded that "a majority of this Court" (himself, the other three dissenters and O'Connor, J.) agreed "that the reasonableness of Riley's expectation depends, in large measure, on the frequency of nonpolice helicopter flights at an altitude of 400 feet." As for how this factual issue should be decided, he noted Brennan "suggests that we may resolve it ourselves without any evidence in the record on this point," while O'Connor "would impose the burden of proof on Riley" but would not now "allow Riley an opportunity to meet this burden." Blackmun, on the other hand, would impose upon the prosecution the burden of proving those "facts necessary to show that Riley lacked a reasonable expectation of privacy" and, "because our prior cases gave the parties little guidance on the burden of proof issue," would "remand this case to allow the prosecution an opportunity to meet this burden."

4. *Other premises.* (a) *Business and commercial premises* are covered by the Fourth Amendment. As stated in *See v. City of Seattle,* 387 U.S. 541 (1967), "[t]he businessman, like the occupant of a residence, has a constitutional right to go about his business free from unreasonable official entries upon his private commercial property."

(b) *Private areas in public places.* What if a police officer, positioned at an overhead vent above a rest room, looks down into an individual closed stall and observes criminal conduct? See *State v. Bryant,* 177 N.W.2d 800 (Minn.1970) (is a search). What, however, if the stalls had no doors?

(c) *Detention facilities.* In *Hudson v. Palmer,* 468 U.S. 517 (1984), involving a § 1983 action brought by a state prison inmate who alleged a prison guard had conducted a "shakedown" search of his cell and had destroyed his noncontraband property for purposes of harassment, the Court held, 5–4, "that the Fourth Amendment has no applicability to a prison cell." The Chief Justice reasoned: "A right of privacy in traditional Fourth Amendment terms is fundamentally incompatible with the close and continual surveillance of inmates and their cells required to ensure institutional security and internal order. We are satisfied that society would insist that the prisoner's expectation of privacy always yield to what must be considered the paramount interest in institutional security. We believe that it is accepted by our society that '[l]oss of freedom of choice and privacy are inherent incidents of confinement.'" The Court added that for "the same reasons" the seizure and destruction of a prisoner's effects did not fall within the protections of the Fourth Amendment. It is unclear whether *Hudson* applies to the search of the person of a prisoner[f] or, in any event, to a pretrial detention facility.[g]

---

f. As the dissenters noted, the majority "appears to limit its holding to a prisoner's 'papers and effects' located in his cell" and apparently "believes that at least a prisoner's 'person' is secure from unreasonable search and seizure." In *Bell v. Wolfish,* 441 U.S. 520 (1979), where the Court declared that at best prisoners have a "reasonable expectation of privacy * * * of a diminished scope," it was held that neither strip searches nor body cavity inspections of pretrial detainees after contact visits with outsiders were unreasonable.

g. Much, but certainly not all, of the Court's analysis in *Hudson* has to do with circumstances existing in facilities housing those convicted of crime. But O'Connor, J., concurring, stated the

5. *Vehicles.* (a) In *Cardwell v. Lewis,* 417 U.S. 583 (1974), police seized a car from a public parking lot and later took a small paint sample off the car and matched the tire tread with tracks at a crime scene. The Court divided on the propriety of the seizure of the car, but the plurality opinion seemed to view the later activity as no search: "With the 'search' limited to the examination of the tire on the wheel and the taking of paint scraping from the exterior of the vehicle left in the public parking lot, we fail to comprehend what expectation of privacy was infringed."

(b) In *New York v. Class,* 475 U.S. 106 (1986), an officer stopped a car for traffic violations and then, after the driver exited the car, opened the door and reached in to move papers obscuring the dashboard Vehicle Identification Number, at which time he saw a gun inside the car. Noting that "federal law requires that the VIN be placed in the plain view of someone *outside* the automobile," the Court concluded "there was no reasonable expectation of privacy in the VIN," so that the "mere viewing of the formerly obscured VIN was not" a search. But the Court then concluded that because "a car's interior [is] subject to Fourth Amendment protection," the officer's action in reaching inside the car "constituted a 'search'" (albeit a reasonable one in the circumstances).[h]

6. *Effects.* During a lawful stop of a Greyhound bus, federal agents walked through the bus and squeezed the soft luggage passengers had placed in the overhead storage spaces. An agent noticed thereby that one bag contained a brick-like object; passenger Downs admitted the bag was his and allowed the agent to open it, revealing a brick of methamphetamine. In BOND v. UNITED STATES, 529 U.S. 334 (2000), the Court, per Rehnquist, C.J., preliminarily noted: (1) that a "traveler's personal luggage is clearly an 'effect' protected by the Fourth Amendment"; (2) that the government's reliance on such cases as *Riley* was misplaced because "[p]hysical invasive inspection is simply more intrusive than purely visual inspection"; and (3) that while Bond's "bag was not part of his person," "travelers are particularly concerned about their carry-on luggage; they generally use it to transport personal items that, for whatever reason, they prefer to keep close at hand." The Court then concluded: "When a bus passenger places a bag in an overhead bin, he expects that other passengers or bus employees may move it for one reason or another. Thus, a bus passenger clearly expects that his bag may be handled. He does not expect that other passengers or bus employees will, as a matter of course, feel the bag in an exploratory manner. But this is exactly what the agent did here. We therefore hold that the agent's physical manipulation of petitioner's bag violated the Fourth Amendment."

Breyer and Scalia, JJ., dissenting, objected: (1) that the squeezing did not "differ from the treatment that overhead luggage is likely to receive from strangers in a world of travel that is somewhat less gentle than it used to be"; (2) that whether "tactile manipulation * * * is more intrusive or less intrusive than visual observation * * * necessarily depends on the particular circumstances"; and (3) that "the decision will lead to a constitutional jurisprudence of 'squeezes,' thereby complicating further already complex Fourth Amendment law."

What is the significance of *Bond* with respect to tactile examination of the carry-on luggage of train and airplane passengers, and of the checked luggage of passengers on various forms of public transportation? Does *Bond* support the holding in *People v. Bartelt,* 948 N.E.2d 52 (Ill.2011), that police about to have a drug dog lawfully sniff a vehicle stopped for a traffic violation (see *Illinois v.*

---

broader proposition that the "fact of arrest and incarceration abates all legitimate Fourth Amendment privacy and possessory interests in personal effects."

h. See Tracey Maclin, *New York v. Class: A Little–Noticed Case With Disturbing Implications,* 78 J.Crim.L. & C. 1 (1987).

Caballes, p. 428) may order the driver to roll up her windows and turn on the vehicle's ventilator system blowers on high in order "to force air inside the vehicle out through the seams"?

7. ***Enhancing the senses.*** Generally speaking, it is fair to say that it is not a search for an officer, lawfully present at a certain place, to detect something by one of his natural senses. *United States v. Mankani*, 738 F.2d 538 (2d Cir.1984) (no search where conversations in adjoining motel room "were overheard by the naked human ear"). The result ordinarily is the same when common means of enhancing the senses, such as a flashlight or binoculars, are used.[i] As for use of more sophisticated or less common means, consider the following material.

8. ***Thermal imaging.*** In KYLLO v. UNITED STATES, 533 U.S. 27 (2001), federal agents, suspecting Kyllo was growing marijuana in his home, used a thermal imager[j] from the street to establish that the roof over the garage and a side wall were relatively hot as compared with the rest of the home and substantially warmer than neighboring residences, suggesting Kyllo was using halide lights to grow marijuana. Based on that and other information, a search warrant was issued and executed; over 100 marijuana plants were seized. Kyllo's suppression motion was denied; he was convicted, and the court of appeals affirmed. Scalia, J., for the majority, concluded:

"It would be foolish to contend that the degree of privacy secured to citizens by the Fourth Amendment has been entirely unaffected by the advance of technology. For example, * * * the technology enabling human flight has exposed to public view (and hence, we have said, to official observation) uncovered portions of the house and its curtilage that once were private. See *Ciraolo*, [p. 268]. The question we confront today is what limits there are upon this power of technology to shrink the realm of guaranteed privacy.

"The *Katz* test—whether the individual has an expectation of privacy that society is prepared to recognize as reasonable—has often been criticized as circular, and hence subjective and unpredictable. While it may be difficult to refine *Katz* when the search of areas such as telephone booths, automobiles, or even the curtilage and uncovered portions of residences are at issue, in the case of the search of the interior of homes—the prototypical and hence most commonly litigated area of protected privacy—there is a ready criterion, with roots deep in the common law, of the minimal expectation of privacy that exists, and that is acknowledged to be reasonable. To withdraw protection of this minimum expectation would be to permit police technology to erode the privacy guaranteed by the Fourth Amendment. We think that obtaining by sense-enhancing technology any information regarding the interior of the home that could not otherwise have been obtained without physical 'intrusion into a constitutionally protected area' constitutes a search—at least where (as here) the technology in question is not in general public use. This assures preservation of that degree of privacy against government that existed when the Fourth Amendment was adopted. On the basis

---

i. But consider *Raettig v. State,* 406 So.2d 1273 (Fla.App.1981) (use of flashlight to look into camper through half-inch wide crack a search, as "a minute crack on the surface of such area can hardly be regarded as an implied invitation to any curious passerby to take a look"); *State v. Ward,* 617 P.2d 568 (Hawaii 1980) (use of binoculars to see crap game in 7th story apartment from closest vantage point an eighth of a mile away a search, as "the constitution does not require that in all cases a person, in order to protect his privacy, must shut himself off from fresh air, sunlight and scenery").

j. As the Court later elaborated, "the District Court found that the Agema 210 'is a non-intrusive device which emits no rays or beams and shows a crude visual image of the heat being radiated from the outside of the house'; it 'did not show any people or activity within the walls of the structure'; '[t]he device used cannot penetrate walls or windows to reveal conversations or human activities'; and '[n]o intimate details of the home were observed.' "

of this criterion, the information obtained by the thermal imager in this case was the product of a search.[2]

"The Government maintains, however, that the thermal imaging must be upheld because it detected 'only heat radiating from the external surface of the house.' The dissent makes this its leading point, contending that there is a fundamental difference between what it calls 'off-the-wall' observations and 'through-the-wall surveillance.' But just as a thermal imager captures only heat emanating from a house, so also a powerful directional microphone picks up only sound emanating from a house—and a satellite capable of scanning from many miles away would pick up only visible light emanating from a house. We rejected such a mechanical interpretation of the Fourth Amendment in *Katz*, where the eavesdropping device picked up only sound waves that reached the exterior of the phone booth. Reversing that approach would leave the homeowner at the mercy of advancing technology—including imaging technology that could discern all human activity in the home. While the technology used in the present case was relatively crude, the rule we adopt must take account of more sophisticated systems that are already in use or in development.[3] * * *

"The Government also contends that the thermal imaging was constitutional because it did not "detect private activities occurring in private areas." * * * The Fourth Amendment's protection of the home has never been tied to measurement of the quality or quantity of information obtained. * * * In the home, our cases show, all details are intimate details, because the entire area is held safe from prying government eyes. Thus, in *Karo*, [p. 280], the only thing detected was a can of ether in the home; and in *Arizona v. Hicks*, [p. 368], the only thing detected by a physical search that went beyond what officers lawfully present could observe in 'plain view' was the registration number of a phonograph turntable. These were intimate details because they were details of the home, just as was the detail of how warm—or even how relatively warm—Kyllo was heating his residence.

"Limiting the prohibition of thermal imaging to 'intimate details' would not only be wrong in principle; it would be impractical in application, failing to provide 'a workable accommodation between the needs of law enforcement and the interests protected by the Fourth Amendment.'"

Stevens, J., for the four dissenters, responded:

"While the Court 'take[s] the long view' and decides this case based largely on the potential of yet-to-be-developed technology that might allow 'through-the-wall surveillance,' this case involves nothing more than off-the-wall surveillance by law enforcement officers to gather information exposed to the general public from the outside of petitioner's home. All that the infrared camera did in this case was passively measure heat emitted from the exterior surfaces of petitioner's home; all

---

2. The dissent's repeated assertion that the thermal imaging did not obtain information regarding the interior of the home is simply inaccurate. A thermal imager reveals the relative heat of various rooms in the home. The dissent may not find that information particularly private or important, but there is no basis for saying it is not information regarding the interior of the home. The dissent's comparison of the thermal imaging to various circumstances in which outside observers might be able to perceive, without technology, the heat of the home—for example, by observing snowmelt on the roof—is quite irrelevant. The fact that equivalent information could sometimes be obtained by other means does not make lawful the use of means that violate the Fourth Amendment. The police might, for example, learn how many people are in a particular house by setting up year-round surveillance; but that does not make breaking and entering to find out the same information lawful. In any event, on the night of January 16, 1992, no outside observer could have discerned the relative heat of Kyllo's home without thermal imaging.

3. The ability to "see" through walls and other opaque barriers is a clear, and scientifically feasible, goal of law enforcement research and development. * * * Some devices may emit low levels of radiation that travel "through-the-wall," but others, such as more sophisticated thermal imaging devices, are entirely passive, or "off-the-wall" as the dissent puts it.

that those measurements showed were relative differences in emission levels, vaguely indicating that some areas of the roof and outside walls were warmer than others. As still images from the infrared scans show, no details regarding the interior of petitioner's home were revealed. Unlike an x-ray scan, or other possible 'through-the-wall' techniques, the detection of infrared radiation emanating from the home did not accomplish 'an unauthorized physical penetration into the premises,' nor did it 'obtain information that it could not have obtained by observation from outside the curtilage of the house.' * * *

"Despite the Court's attempt to draw a line that is 'not only firm but also bright,' the contours of its new rule are uncertain because its protection apparently dissipates as soon as the relevant technology is 'in general public use.' Yet how much use is general public use is not even hinted at by the Court's opinion, which makes the somewhat doubtful assumption that the thermal imager used in this case does not satisfy that criterion.[5] In any event, putting aside its lack of clarity, this criterion is somewhat perverse because it seems likely that the threat to privacy will grow, rather than recede, as the use of intrusive equipment becomes more readily available. * * *

"The two reasons advanced by the Court as justifications for the adoption of its new rule are both unpersuasive. First, the Court suggests that its rule is compelled by our holding in *Katz*, because in that case, as in this, the surveillance consisted of nothing more than the monitoring of waves emanating from a private area into the public domain. Yet there are critical differences between the cases. In *Katz*, the electronic listening device attached to the outside of the phone booth allowed the officers to pick up the content of the conversation inside the booth, making them the functional equivalent of intruders because they gathered information that was otherwise available only to someone inside the private area; it would be as if, in this case, the thermal imager presented a view of the heat-generating activity inside petitioner's home. By contrast, the thermal imager here disclosed only the relative amounts of heat radiating from the house; it would be as if, in *Katz*, the listening device disclosed only the relative volume of sound leaving the booth, which presumably was discernible in the public domain. * * *

"Second, the Court argues that the permissibility of 'through-the-wall surveillance' cannot depend on a distinction between observing 'intimate details' such as 'the lady of the house [taking] her daily sauna and bath,' and noticing only 'the nonintimate rug on the vestibule floor' or 'objects no smaller than 36 by 36 inches.' This entire argument assumes, of course, that the thermal imager in this case could or did perform 'through-the-wall surveillance' that could identify any detail 'that would previously have been unknowable without physical intrusion.' In fact, the device could not and did not enable its user to identify either the lady of the house, the rug on the vestibule floor, or anything else inside the house, whether smaller or larger than 36 by 36 inches."

Is it a fair conclusion, as stated in Richard H. Seamon, *Kyllo v. United States and the Partial Ascendance of Justice Scalia's Fourth Amendment*, 79 Wash. U.L.Q. 1013, 1022 (2001), that "the *Kyllo* majority did not apply the *Katz* test to the case before it"? If so, has Justice Scalia thereby avoided the faults he attributed to that test in *Minnesota v. Carter*, p. 889, namely that it "has no plausible foundation in the text of the Fourth Amendment," is "notoriously

---

5. The record describes a device that numbers close to a thousand manufactured units; that has a predecessor numbering in the neighborhood of 4,000 to 5,000 units; that competes with a similar product numbering from 5,000 to 6,000 units; and that is "readily available to the public" for commercial, personal, or law enforcement purposes, and is just an 800–number away from being rented from "half a dozen national companies" by anyone who wants one. Since, by virtue of the Court's new rule, the issue is one of first impression, perhaps it should order an evidentiary hearing to determine whether these facts suffice to establish "general public use."

unhelpful" in identifying what government conduct constitutes a search, and is "self-indulgent" because it allows judges to decide what privacy expectations are "reasonable"?

9. *The canine nose.* In *United States v. Place*, 462 U.S. 696 (1983), dealing with a temporary seizure of luggage at an airport so that it could be brought into contact with a drug detection dog, the majority declared "that a person possesses a privacy interest in the contents of personal luggage that is protected by the Fourth Amendment. A 'canine sniff' by a well-trained narcotics detection dog, however, does not require opening the luggage. It does not expose noncontraband items that otherwise would remain hidden from public view, as does, for example, an officer's rummaging through the contents of the luggage. Thus, the manner in which information is obtained through this investigative technique is much less intrusive than a typical search. Moreover, the sniff discloses only the presence or absence of narcotics, a contraband item. Thus, despite the fact that the sniff tells the authorities something about the contents of the luggage, the information obtained is limited. This limited disclosure also ensures that the owner of the property is not subjected to the embarrassment and inconvenience entailed in less discriminate and more intrusive investigative methods.

"In these respects, the canine sniff is *sui generis*. We are aware of no other investigative procedure that is so limited both in the manner in which the information is obtained and in the content of the information revealed by the procedure. Therefore, we conclude that the particular course of investigation that the agents intended to pursue here—exposure of respondent's luggage, which was located in a public place, to a trained canine—did not constitute a 'search' within the meaning of the Fourth Amendment."[k]

In *Illinois v. Caballes*, p. 428, *Place* was reaffirmed and applied to a dog sniff of a vehicle during a traffic stop, but dissenting Justice Souter argued for a contrary conclusion because the drug dog's "supposed infallibility is belied by judicial opinions describing well-trained animals sniffing and alerting with less than perfect accuracy, whether owing to errors by their handlers, the limitations of the dogs themselves, or even the pervasive contamination of currency by cocaine": "Once the dog's fallibility is recognized, however, that ends the justification claimed in *Place* for treating the sniff as sui generis under the Fourth Amendment: the sniff alert does not necessarily signal hidden contraband, and opening the container or enclosed space whose emanations the dog has sensed will not necessarily reveal contraband or any other evidence of crime. This is not, of course, to deny that a dog's reaction may provide reasonable suspicion, or probable cause, to search the container or enclosure; the Fourth Amendment does not demand certainty of success to justify a search for evidence or contraband. The point is simply that the sniff and alert cannot claim the certainty that *Place* assumed, both in treating the deliberate use of sniffing dogs as sui generis and then taking that characterization as a reason to say they are not searches subject to Fourth Amendment scrutiny. And when that aura of uniqueness disappears, there is no basis in *Place*'s reasoning, and no good reason otherwise, to ignore the actual function that dog sniffs perform. They are conducted to obtain information about the contents of private spaces beyond anything that human senses could perceive, even when conventionally enhanced. The information is not provided by independent third parties beyond the reach of constitutional limitations, but

---

k. Brennan and Marshall, JJ., concurring in the result, objected that this issue, neither reached by the court of appeals nor briefed and argued in the Supreme Court, should not be decided in "a discussion unnecessary to the judgment." Blackmun, J., concurring separately, expressed the same concern and added: "While the Court has adopted one plausible analysis of the issue, there are others. For example, a dog sniff may be a search, but a minimally intrusive one that could be justified in this situation under *Terry* upon mere reasonable suspicion."

gathered by the government's own officers in order to justify searches of the traditional sort, which may or may not reveal evidence of crime but will disclose anything meant to be kept private in the area searched. Thus in practice the government's use of a trained narcotics dog functions as a limited search to reveal undisclosed facts about private enclosures, to be used to justify a further and complete search of the enclosed area. And given the fallibility of the dog, the sniff is the first step in a process that may disclose 'intimate details' without revealing contraband, just as a thermal-imaging device might do, as described in *Kyllo*.''

Place was relied upon in *United States v. Jacobsen,* p. 249, holding that where police lawfully came upon a white powder in a package originally opened by private parties, an on-the-spot chemical test of a trace of the powder that would reveal only whether or not it was cocaine was not a search. "Here, as in *Place,* the likelihood that official conduct of the kind disclosed by the record will actually compromise any legitimate interest in privacy seems much too remote to characterize the testing as a search subject to the Fourth Amendment." Brennan and Marshall, JJ., dissenting, objected that "under the Court's analysis in these cases, law enforcement officers could release a trained cocaine-sensitive dog * * * to roam the streets at random, alerting the officers to people carrying cocaine. Or, if a device were developed that, when aimed at a person, would detect instantaneously whether the person is carrying cocaine, there would be no Fourth Amendment bar, under the Court's approach, to the police setting up such a device on a street corner and scanning all passersby. In fact, the Court's analysis is so unbounded that if a device were developed that could detect, from the outside of a building, the presence of cocaine inside, there would be no constitutional obstacle to the police cruising through a residential neighborhood and using the device to identify all homes in which the drug is present.''[l]

   10. *Photographic magnification.* In DOW CHEMICAL CO. v. UNITED STATES, 476 U.S. 227 (1986), the Court, per Burger, C.J., held that aerial photography of a chemical company's industrial complex was not a Fourth Amendment "search": "It may well be, as the Government concedes, that surveillance of private property by using highly sophisticated surveillance equipment not generally available to the public, such as satellite technology, might be constitutionally proscribed absent a warrant. But the photographs here are not so revealing of intimate details as to raise constitutional concerns. Although they undoubtedly give EPA more detailed information than naked-eye views, they remain limited to an outline of the facility's buildings and equipment. The mere fact that human vision is enhanced somewhat, at least to the degree here, does not give rise to constitutional problems.[6] An electronic device to penetrate walls or windows so as to hear and record confidential discussions of chemical formulae or

---

   l. What if a dog were utilized for this purpose? Compare *United States v. Thomas,* 757 F.2d 1359 (2d Cir.1985) (reading *Place* with *United States v. Karo,* p. 280, and concluding such use of those dogs is a search); with *United States v. Colyer,* 878 F.2d 469 (D.C.Cir.1989) (questioning and distinguishing *Thomas* in holding there was no search where a drug dog in the public corridor of a train "alerted" to a particular sleeper compartment). Is *Kyllo* irrelevant on this issue because, as asserted in *State v. Bergmann,* 633 N.W.2d 328 (Iowa 2001), "a drug sniffing dog is not 'technology' of the type addressed in *Kyllo*"?

   6. The partial dissent emphasizes Dow's claim that under magnification power lines as small as ½–inch diameter can be observed. But a glance at the photographs in issue shows that those power lines are observable only because of their stark contrast with the snow-white background. No objects as small as ½–inch diameter such as a class ring, for example, are recognizable, nor are there any identifiable human faces or secret documents captured in such a fashion as to implicate more serious privacy concerns. Fourth Amendment cases must be decided on the facts of each case, not by extravagant generalizations. "[W]e have never held that potential, as opposed to actual, invasions of privacy constitute searches for purposes of the Fourth Amendment." *United States v. Karo,* [p. 280]. On these facts, nothing in these photographs suggests that any reasonable expectations of privacy have been infringed.

other trade secrets would raise very different and far more serious questions; other protections such as trade secret laws are available to protect commercial activities from private surveillance by competitors.

"We conclude that the open areas of an industrial plant complex with numerous plant structures spread over an area of 2,000 acres are not analogous to the 'curtilage' of a dwelling for purposes of aerial surveillance; such an industrial complex is more comparable to an open field and as such it is open to the view and observation of persons in aircraft lawfully in the public airspace immediately above or sufficiently near the area for the reach of cameras."

Powell, J., for the dissenters, objected that "Dow has taken every feasible step to protect information claimed to constitute trade secrets from the public and particularly from its competitors," and accordingly "has a reasonable expectation of privacy in its commercial facility in the sense required by the Fourth Amendment." Moreover, the rationale of *Ciraolo,* [p. 268], is inapplicable here, for "the camera used in this case was highly sophisticated in terms of its capability to reveal minute details of Dow's confidential technology and equipment. The District Court found that the photographs revealed details as 'small as ½ inch in diameter.' Satellite photography hardly could have been more informative about Dow's technology. Nor are 'members of the public' likely to purchase $22,000.00 cameras."

UNITED STATES v. JONES
565 U.S. ___, 132 S.Ct. 945, 181 L.Ed.2d 911 (2012)

JUSTICE SCALIA delivered the opinion of the Court.

[Government agents installed a GPS tracking device on the undercarriage of a Jeep used by Jones, suspected of trafficking in narcotics, while it was parked in a public parking lot. Over the next 28 days the government used the device to track the vehicle's movements; the device established the vehicle's location within 50 to 100 feet and communicated its location by cell phone to a government computer. It relayed more than 2,000 pages of data over a 4–week period. The court of appeals reversed Jones' conviction on the ground that the evidence obtained by warrantless use of the GPS device violated the Fourth Amendment.]

* * * We hold that the Government's installation of a GPS device on a target's vehicle, and its use of that device to monitor the vehicle's movements, constitutes a "search."

It is important to be clear about what occurred in this case: The Government physically occupied private property for the purpose of obtaining information. We have no doubt that such a physical intrusion would have been considered a search within the meaning of the Fourth Amendment when it was adopted. * * *

The text of the Fourth Amendment reflects its close connection to property, since otherwise it would have referred simply to "the right of the people to be secure against unreasonable searches and seizures"; the phrase "in their persons, houses, papers, and effects" would have been superfluous.

Consistent with this understanding, our Fourth Amendment jurisprudence was tied to common-law trespass, at least until the latter half of the 20th century. * * *

Our later cases, of course, [as in *Katz,*] have deviated from that exclusively property-based approach.* * *

The Government contends that the Harlan standard [in *Katz*] shows that no search occurred here, since Jones had no "reasonable expectation of privacy" in the area of the Jeep accessed by Government agents (its underbody) and in the locations of the Jeep on the public roads, which were visible to all. But we need not address the Government's contentions, because Jones's Fourth Amendment rights do not rise or fall with the *Katz* formulation. At bottom, we must "assur[e] preservation of that degree of privacy against government that existed when the Fourth Amendment was adopted." As explained, for most of our history the Fourth Amendment was understood to embody a particular concern for government trespass upon the areas ("persons, houses, papers, and effects") it enumerates.[3] *Katz* did not repudiate that understanding. Less than two years later the Court upheld defendants' contention that the Government could not introduce against them conversations between *other* people obtained by warrantless placement of electronic surveillance devices in their homes. The opinion rejected the dissent's contention that there was no Fourth Amendment violation unless the conversational privacy of the homeowner himself is invaded.[4] *Alderman v. United States*, [p. 880]. "[W]e [do not] believe that *Katz*, by holding that the Fourth Amendment protects persons and their private conversations, was intended to withdraw any of the protection which the Amendment extends to the home...."

More recently, in *Soldal v. Cook County*, [p. 267], the Court unanimously rejected the argument that although a "seizure" had occurred "in a 'technical' sense" when a trailer home was forcibly removed, no Fourth Amendment violation occurred because law enforcement had not "invade[d] the [individuals'] privacy." *Katz*, the Court explained, established that "property rights are not the sole measure of Fourth Amendment violations," but did not "snuf[f] out the previously recognized protection for property." * * * *Katz* did not narrow the Fourth Amendment's scope.[5]

The Government contends that several of our post-*Katz* cases foreclose the conclusion that what occurred here constituted a search. It relies principally on two cases in which we rejected Fourth Amendment challenges to "beepers," electronic tracking devices that represent another form of electronic monitoring. The first case, [*United States v.*] *Knotts*, [460 U.S. 276 (1983),] upheld against

---

3. Justice Alito's concurrence (hereinafter concurrence) doubts the wisdom of our approach because "it is almost impossible to think of late–18th–century situations that are analogous to what took place in this case." But in fact it posits a situation that is not far afield—a constable's concealing himself in the target's coach in order to track its movements. There is no doubt that the information gained by that trespassory activity would be the product of an unlawful search—whether that information consisted of the conversations occurring in the coach, or of the destinations to which the coach traveled.

In any case, it is quite irrelevant whether there was an 18th-century analog. Whatever new methods of investigation may be devised, our task, *at a minimum*, is to decide whether the action in question would have constituted a "search" within the original meaning of the Fourth Amendment. Where, as here, the Government obtains information by physically intruding on a constitutionally protected area, such a search has undoubtedly occurred.

4. Thus, the concurrence's attempt to recast *Alderman* as meaning that individuals have a "legitimate expectation of privacy in all conversations that [take] place under their roof" is foreclosed by the Court's opinion. The Court took as a given that the homeowner's "conversational privacy" had not been violated.

5. The concurrence notes that post-*Katz* we have explained " 'that an actual trespass is neither necessary *nor sufficient* to establish a constitutional violation.' " (quoting *United States v. Karo*, infra). That is undoubtedly true, and undoubtedly irrelevant. *Karo* was considering whether a seizure occurred, and as the concurrence explains, a seizure of property occurs, not when there is a trespass, but "when there is some meaningful interference with an individual's possessory interests in that property." Likewise with a search. Trespass alone does not qualify, but there must be conjoined with that what was present here: an attempt to find something or to obtain information.

Related to this, and similarly irrelevant, is the concurrence's point that, if analyzed separately, neither the installation of the device nor its use would constitute a Fourth Amendment search. Of course not. A trespass on "houses‘ or "effects," or a *Katz* invasion of privacy, is not alone a search unless it is done to obtain information; and the obtaining of information is not alone a search unless it is achieved by such a trespass or invasion of privacy.

Fourth Amendment challenge the use of a "beeper" that had been placed in a container of chloroform, allowing law enforcement to monitor the location of the container. We said that there had been no infringement of Knotts' reasonable expectation of privacy since the information obtained—the location of the automobile carrying the container on public roads, and the location of the off-loaded container in open fields near Knotts' cabin—had been voluntarily conveyed to the public.[6] But as we have discussed, the *Katz* reasonable-expectation-of-privacy test has been *added to,* not *substituted for,* the common-law trespassory test. The holding in *Knotts* addressed only the former, since the latter was not at issue. The beeper had been placed in the container before it came into Knotts' possession, with the consent of the then-owner. Knotts did not challenge that installation, and we specifically declined to consider its effect on the Fourth Amendment analysis. * * *

The second "beeper" case, *United States v. Karo,* 468 U.S. 705 (1984), does not suggest a different conclusion. There we addressed the question left open by *Knotts,* whether the installation of a beeper in a container amounted to a search or seizure. As in *Knotts,* at the time the beeper was installed the container belonged to a third party, and it did not come into possession of the defendant until later. Thus, the specific question we considered was whether the installation *"with the consent of the original owner* constitute[d] a search or seizure . . . when the container is delivered to a buyer having no knowledge of the presence of the beeper" (emphasis added). We held not. The Government, we said, came into physical contact with the container only before it belonged to the defendant Karo; and the transfer of the container with the unmonitored beeper inside did not convey any information and thus did not invade Karo's privacy.[a] That conclusion is perfectly consistent with the one we reach here. Karo accepted the container as it came to him, beeper and all, and was therefore not entitled to object to the beeper's presence, even though it was used to monitor the container's location. Jones, who possessed the Jeep at the time the Government trespassorily inserted the information-gathering device, is on much different footing. * * *

* * * The concurrence posits that relatively short-term monitoring of a person's movements on public streets is okay, but that "the use of longer term GPS monitoring in investigations *of most offenses"* is no good (emphasis added). That introduces yet another novelty into our jurisprudence. There is no precedent for the proposition that whether a search has occurred depends on the nature of the crime being investigated. And even accepting that novelty, it remains unexplained why a 4-week investigation is "surely" too long and why a drug-trafficking conspiracy involving substantial amounts of cash and narcotics is not an "extraor-

---

6. *Knotts* noted the "limited use which the government made of the signals from this particular beeper," and reserved the question whether "different constitutional principles may be applicable" to "dragnet-type law enforcement practices" of the type that GPS tracking made possible here.

a. The Court in *Karo* went on to hold, however, with respect to use of the "beeper" to determine the location of the container within particular premises, that this would be a search, an invasion of the rights of those having a privacy expectation in that place, if such monitoring "reveals information that could not have been obtained through visual surveillance," which is the case even "if visual surveillance has revealed that the article to which the beeper is attached has entered the house" where "the later monitoring not only verifies the officers' observations but also establishes that the article remains on the premises." Absent "truly exigent circumstances," the Court added, such use of the beeper would require resort to a search warrant.

In response to the government's claim that a warrant should not be required because of the difficulty in satisfying the particularity requirement of the Fourth Amendment, in that it is usually not known in advance to what place the container with the beeper in it will be taken, the Court concluded that it would suffice if the warrant were to describe the object into which the beeper is to be placed, the circumstances that led the agents to wish to install the beeper, and the length of time for which beeper surveillance is requested."

dinary offens[e]" which may permit longer observation. What of a 2day monitoring of a suspected purveyor of stolen electronics? Or of a 6-month monitoring of a
suspected terrorist? We may have to grapple with these "vexing problems" in
some future case where a classic trespassory search is not involved and resort
must be had to *Katz* analysis; but there is no reason for rushing forward to resolve
them here. * * *

JUSTICE SOTOMAYOR, concurring.

* * * When the Government physically invades personal property to gather
information, a search occurs. The reaffirmation of that principle suffices to decide
this case.

Nonetheless, as Justice Alito notes, physical intrusion is now unnecessary to
many forms of surveillance.* * *

In cases involving even short-term monitoring, some unique attributes of GPS
surveillance relevant to the *Katz* analysis will require particular attention. GPS
monitoring generates a precise, comprehensive record of a person's public movements that reflects a wealth of detail about her familial, political, professional,
religious, and sexual associations. The Government can store such records and
efficiently mine them for information years into the future. And because GPS
monitoring is cheap in comparison to conventional surveillance techniques and, by
design, proceeds surreptitiously, it evades the ordinary checks that constrain
abusive law enforcement practices: "limited police resources and community
hostility." * * *

I would take these attributes of GPS monitoring into account when considering the existence of a reasonable societal expectation of privacy in the sum of one's
public * * *

JUSTICE ALITO, with whom JUSTICE GINSBURG, JUSTICE BREYER, and JUSTICE KAGAN
join, concurring in the judgment. * * *

This holding, in my judgment, is unwise. It strains the language of the Fourth
Amendment; it has little if any support in current Fourth Amendment case law;
and it is highly artificial. * * *

The Fourth Amendment prohibits "unreasonable searches and seizures," and
the Court makes very little effort to explain how the attachment or use of the GPS
device fits within these terms. The Court does not contend that there was a
seizure. * * *

The Court does claim that the installation and use of the GPS constituted a
search, but this conclusion is dependent on the questionable proposition that
these two procedures cannot be separated for purposes of Fourth Amendment
analysis. If these two procedures are analyzed separately, it is not at all clear from
the Court's opinion why either should be regarded as a search. It is clear that the
attachment of the GPS device was not itself a search; if the device had not
functioned or if the officers had not used it, no information would have been
obtained. And the Court does not contend that the use of the device constituted a
search either. On the contrary, the Court accepts the holding in *United States v.
Knotts* that the use of a surreptitiously planted electronic device to monitor a
vehicle's movements on public roads did not amount to a search.

The Court argues—and I agree—that "we must 'assur[e] preservation of that
degree of privacy against government that existed when the Fourth Amendment
was adopted.' " But it is almost impossible to think of late 18th-century situations
that are analogous to what took place in this case. (Is it possible to imagine a case
in which a constable secreted himself somewhere in a coach and remained there

for a period of time in order to monitor the movements of the coach's owner?[3]) The Court's theory seems to be that the concept of a search, as originally understood, comprehended any technical trespass that led to the gathering of evidence, but we know that this is incorrect. At common law, any unauthorized intrusion on private property was actionable, but a trespass on open fields, as opposed to the "curtilage" of a home, does not fall within the scope of the Fourth Amendment because private property outside the curtilage is not part of a hous[e] within the meaning of the Fourth Amendment.

The Court's reasoning in this case is very similar to that in the Court's early decisions involving wiretapping and electronic eavesdropping, namely, that a technical trespass followed by the gathering of evidence constitutes a search. * * *

Katz v. United States finally did away with the old approach, holding that a trespass was not required for a Fourth Amendment violation. * * *

The majority suggests that two post-*Katz* decisions—*Soldal v. Cook County* and *Alderman v. United States*—show that a technical trespass is sufficient to establish the existence of a search, but they provide little support.

In *Soldal,* the Court held that towing away a trailer home without the owner's consent constituted a seizure even if this did not invade the occupants' personal privacy. But in the present case, the Court does not find that there was a seizure, and it is clear that none occurred.

In *Alderman,* the Court held that the Fourth Amendment rights of home-owners were implicated by the use of a surreptitiously planted listening device to monitor third-party conversations that occurred within their home. *Alderman* is best understood to mean that the homeowners had a legitimate expectation of privacy in all conversations that took place under their roof.

In sum, the majority is hard pressed to find support in post-*Katz* cases for its trespass-based theory.

Disharmony with a substantial body of existing case law is only one of the problems with the Court's approach in this case.

I will briefly note [some] others. First, the Court's reasoning largely disregards what is really important (the *use* of a GPS for the purpose of long-term tracking) and instead attaches great significance to something that most would view as relatively minor (attaching to the bottom of a car a small, light object that does not interfere in any way with the car's operation). Attaching such an object is generally regarded as so trivial that it does not provide a basis for recovery under modern tort law. * * *.

Second, the Court's approach leads to incongruous results. If the police attach a GPS device to a car and use the device to follow the car for even a brief time, under the Court's theory, the Fourth Amendment applies. But if the police follow the same car for a much longer period using unmarked cars and aerial assistance, this tracking is not subject to any Fourth Amendment constraints.

[Also], the Court's reliance on the law of trespass will present particularly vexing problems in cases involving surveillance that is carried out by making electronic, as opposed to physical, contact with the item to be tracked. For example, suppose that the officers in the present case had followed respondent by surreptitiously activating a stolen vehicle detection system that came with the car when it was purchased. Would the sending of a radio signal to activate this system

---

3. The Court suggests that something like this might have occurred in 1791, but this would have required either a gigantic coach, a very tiny constable, or both—not to mention a constable with incredible fortitude and patience.

constitute a trespass to chattels? Trespass to chattels has traditionally required a physical touching of the property. * * *

The *Katz* expectation-of-privacy test avoids the problems and complications noted above, but it is not without its own difficulties. [T]he *Katz* test rests on the assumption that this hypothetical reasonable person has a well-developed and stable set of privacy expectations. But technology can change those expectations. * * *

Recent years have seen the emergence of many new devices that permit the monitoring of a person's movements. In some locales, closed-circuit television video monitoring is becoming ubiquitous. On toll roads, automatic toll collection systems create a precise record of the movements of motorists who choose to make use of that convenience. Many motorists purchase cars that are equipped with devices that permit a central station to ascertain the car's location at any time so that roadside assistance may be provided if needed and the car may be found if it is stolen.

Perhaps most significant, cell phones and other wireless devices now permit wireless carriers to track and record the location of users—and as of June 2011, it has been reported, there were more than 322 million wireless devices in use in the United States. For older phones, the accuracy of the location information depends on the density of the tower network, but new "smart phones," which are equipped with a GPS device, permit more precise tracking. * * * The availability and use of these and other new devices will continue to shape the average person's expectations about the privacy of his or her daily movements.

* * * A legislative body is well situated to gauge changing public attitudes, to draw detailed lines, and to balance privacy and public safety in a comprehensive way.

To date, however, Congress and most States have not enacted statutes regulating the use of GPS tracking technology for law enforcement purposes. The best that we can do in this case is to apply existing Fourth Amendment doctrine and to ask whether the use of GPS tracking in a particular case involved a degree of intrusion that a reasonable person would not have anticipated.

Under this approach, relatively short-term monitoring of a person's movements on public streets accords with expectations of privacy that our society has recognized as reasonable. But the use of longer term GPS monitoring in investigations of most offenses impinges on expectations of privacy. For such offenses, society's expectation has been that law enforcement agents and others would not—and indeed, in the main, simply could not—secretly monitor and catalogue every single movement of an individual's car for a very long period. In this case, for four weeks, law enforcement agents tracked every movement that respondent made in the vehicle he was driving. We need not identify with precision the point at which the tracking of this vehicle became a search, for the line was surely crossed before the 4-week mark. Other cases may present more difficult questions. But where uncertainty exists with respect to whether a certain period of GPS surveillance is long enough to constitute a Fourth Amendment search, the police may always seek a warrant. We also need not consider whether prolonged GPS monitoring in the context of investigations involving extraordinary offenses would similarly intrude on a constitutionally protected sphere of privacy. In such cases, long-term tracking might have been mounted using previously available techniques. * * *

NOTES AND QUESTIONS

1. ALPR cameras. What then of the data collection aspect of ALPR (Automated License Plate Recognition) technology,[a] more benignly used to determine that a particular vehicle at a particular location is connected to past criminality? "[M]any departments across the country are using ALPR not just for observational comparison, but also for *indiscriminate data collection*. When used in this manner, ALPR systems not only flag passing cars that match a criminal database, but also record the exact time and location of *all passing cars* into a searchable database, regardless of any evidence of wrongdoing. This data can be kept on file indefinitely. In communities with extensive, integrated networks of ALPR cameras, this could potentially amount of mass surveillance of an entire community. * * * Theoretically, by mounting ALPR at every intersection and on every police car in a city, it is conceivable that the police could begin to compile thousands of discrete data points about an individual's public movements. As the number of these discrete data points increases, law enforcement can ultimately create an incredibly accurate and arguably pervasive record of a person's movements over months, or even years." Stephen Rushin, *The Judicial Response to Mass Police Surveillance*, http://www.jltp.uiuc/works/Rushin/index.htm (posted 3/16/11).

2. Data aggregation and mining. Nonstop technological surveillance via ubiquitous ALPR cameras, as discussed in Note 1, may be less like the one-trip surveillance in *Knotts* (or even the one-month surveillance in *Jones*) than it is like the other forms of extensive surveillance possible via data aggregation and data mining. In the post–9/11 era, the federal government has undertaken the collection and examination of an enormous amount of personal information, including that obtained directly from individuals, that obtained and supplied by cooperating states, and that held in the private sector and obtained by purchase or otherwise. Using highly sophisticated computer equipment, the government has undertaken data aggregation, by which all of this data has been integrated, and data mining, by which otherwise undiscoverable patterns and subtle relationships are uncovered through statistical analysis and modeling. While such activity raises privacy concerns, it is by no means apparent that it is subject to Fourth Amendment limitation, given the longstanding third-party doctrine (see, e.g., *United States v. Miller*, p. 517, applying to banking records the established rule that "the Fourth Amendment does not prohibit the obtaining of information revealed to a third party and conveyed by him to Government authorities, even if the information is revealed on the assumption that it will be used only for a limited purpose and the confidence of the third party will not be betrayed"). However, some commentators have suggested this new technology requires consideration of new questions, such as (i) whether aggregation should be deemed a search because such integration of previously distributed sources of information negates the "practical obscurity" the Supreme Court has otherwise deemed worthy of protection;[b] and (ii) whether

---

a. "Cameras mounted on top of patrol cars automatically photograph license aplates at the rate of hundreds per minute. The images are converted into letters and numbers and sent to a computer located in the trunk of the police vehicle. The computer compares the information to a database containing a list of license plates corresponding to cars that have been reported stolen, where registration or insurance coverage has lapsed, or other similar violations of law. * * * If a license plate read by the camera matches one in the database, an alarm sounds on the laptop computer mounted between the driver and passenger seats, alerting the officer to the nature of the crime or violation associated with the plate." *People v. Davila*, 901 N.Y.S.2d 787 (2010).

b. K. A. Taipale, *Data Mining and Domestic Security: Connecting the Dots to Make Sense of Data*, 5 Colum.Sci. & Tech.L.Rev. 2 (2003), referring to *Department of Justice v. Reporter's Committee for Freedom of the Press*, 489 U.S. 749 (1989) (denying reporter's FOIA request for a

mining should be deemed a search because it involves acquisition of new knowledge, which may deserve legal protection even if the underlying data does not.[c] See SEARCHSZR § 3.7(d–1).

———————

In *Gouled v. United States,* 255 U.S. 298 (1921), the Court held that search warrants "may not be used as a means of gaining access to a man's house or office and papers solely for the purpose of making search to secure evidence to be used against him in a criminal or penal proceeding." The Court derived from *Boyd v. United States,* p. 806, the proposition that warrants may be resorted to "only when a primary right to such search and seizure may be found in the interest which the public or the complainant may have in the property to be seized, or in the right to the possession of it, or when a valid exercise of the police power renders possession of the property by the accused unlawful and provides that it may be taken," that is, when the property is an instrumentality or fruit of crime or contraband. This "mere evidence" rule, as it came to be called, was finally repudiated in *Warden v. Hayden,* 387 U.S. 294 (1967). Stressing that "the principal object of the Fourth Amendment is the protection of privacy rather than property," the Court noted that "privacy 'would be just as well served by a restriction on search to the even-numbered days of the month. * * * And it would have the extra advantage of avoiding hair-splitting questions.' " The government need not have a property interest in the property to be seized, as "government has an interest in solving crime," and that interest and the protection of privacy are best accommodated, the Court reasoned, by merely requiring probable cause that "the evidence sought will aid in a particular apprehension or conviction." But the Court cautioned:

"The items of clothing involved in this case are not 'testimonial' or 'communicative' in nature, and their introduction therefore did not compel respondent to become a witness against himself in violation of the Fifth Amendment. This case thus does not require that we consider whether there are items of evidential value whose very nature precludes them from being the object of a reasonable search and seizure."

ANDRESEN v. MARYLAND
427 U.S. 463, 96 S.Ct. 2737, 49 L.Ed.2d 627 (1976).

JUSTICE BLACKMUN delivered the opinion of the Court.

[State authorities obtained search warrants to search petitioner's law office and also corporate offices for specified documents pertaining to a fraudulent sale of land. The papers found in the execution of the warrants were admitted against the petitioner at his trial, and he was convicted.]

The Fifth Amendment * * * provides that "[n]o person * * * shall be compelled in any criminal case to be a witness against himself." * * * The "historic function" of the privilege has been to protect a " 'natural individual from compulsory incrimination through his own testimony or personal records.' " There is no question that the records seized from petitioner's offices and intro-

———————

rap sheet that was a public record because the aggregation of public records in such a fashion would negate the "practical obscurity" that otherwise protected those records: "[T]here is a vast difference between the public records that might be found after a diligent search of courthouse files, county archives and local police stations throughout the country and a computerized summary located in a single clearinghouse of information.").

    c.   Joseph S. Fulda, *Data Mining and Privacy,* 11 Alb.L.J.Sci. & Tech. 105, 109 (2000).

duced against him were incriminating. Moreover, it is undisputed that some of these business records contain statements made by petitioner. The question, therefore, is whether the seizure of these business records, and their admission into evidence at his trial, compelled petitioner to testify against himself in violation of the Fifth Amendment. This question may be said to have been reserved in *Warden v. Hayden.*

Petitioner contends that "the Fifth Amendment prohibition against compulsory self-incrimination applies as well to personal business papers seized from his offices as it does to the same papers being required to be produced under a subpoena." He bases his argument, naturally, on dicta in a number of cases which imply, or state, that the search for and seizure of a person's private papers violate the privilege against self-incrimination. Thus, in *Boyd v. United States* [p. 806] the Court said: "[W]e have been unable to perceive that the seizure of a man's private books and papers to be used in evidence against him is substantially different from compelling him to be a witness against himself." And in *Hale v. Henkel* [p. 811], it was observed that "the substance of the offense is the compulsory production of private papers, whether under a search warrant or a *subpoena duces tecum,* against which the person * * * is entitled to protection."

We do not agree, however, that these broad statements compel suppression of this petitioner's business records as a violation of the Fifth Amendment. In the very recent case of *Fisher v. United States* [p. 856], the Court held that an attorney's production, pursuant to a lawful summons, of his client's tax records in his hands did not violate the Fifth Amendment privilege of the taxpayer "because enforcement against a taxpayer's lawyer would not 'compel' the taxpayer to do anything—and certainly would not compel him to be a 'witness' against himself." We recognized that the continued validity of the broad statements contained in some of the Court's earlier cases had been discredited by later opinions. In those earlier cases, the legal predicate for the inadmissibility of the evidence seized was a violation of the Fourth Amendment; the unlawfulness of the search and seizure was thought to supply the compulsion of the accused necessary to invoke the Fifth Amendment. Compulsion of the accused was also absent in *Couch v. United States,* 409 U.S. 322 (1973), where the Court held that a summons served on a taxpayer's accountant requiring him to produce the taxpayer's personal business records in his possession did not violate the taxpayer's Fifth Amendment rights.

Similarly, in this case, petitioner was not asked to say or to do anything. The records seized contained statements that petitioner had voluntarily committed to writing. The search for and seizure of these records were conducted by law enforcement personnel. Finally, when these records were introduced at trial, they were authenticated by a handwriting expert, not by petitioner. Any compulsion of petitioner to speak, other than the inherent psychological pressure to respond at trial to unfavorable evidence, was not present.

This case thus falls within the principle stated by Mr. Justice Holmes: "A party is privileged from producing the evidence but not from its production." * * * Thus, although the Fifth Amendment may protect an individual from complying with a subpoena for the production of his personal records in his possession because the very act of production may constitute a compulsory authentication of incriminating information, a seizure of the same materials by law enforcement officers differs in a crucial respect—the individual against whom the search is directed is not required to aid in the discovery, production, or authentication of incriminating evidence. * * *

Moreover, a contrary determination would prohibit the admission of evidence traditionally used in criminal cases and traditionally admissible despite the Fifth Amendment. For example, it would bar the admission of an accused's gambling records in a prosecution for gambling; a note given temporarily to a bank teller during a robbery and subsequently seized in the accused's automobile or home in a prosecution for bank robbery; and incriminating notes prepared, but not sent, by an accused in a kidnapping or blackmail prosecution. * * *

In this case, petitioner, at the time he recorded his communication, at the time of the search, and at the time the records were admitted at trial, was not subjected to "the cruel trilemma of self-accusation, perjury or contempt." Indeed, he was never required to say or to do anything under penalty of sanction. Similarly, permitting the admission of the records in question does not convert our accusatorial system of justice into an inquisitorial system. * * *

JUSTICE BRENNAN, dissenting. * * *

Until today, no decision by this Court had held that the seizure of testimonial evidence by legal process did not violate the Fifth Amendment. Indeed, with few exceptions, the indications were strongly to the contrary. * * * These cases all reflect the root understanding of *Boyd v. United States:* "It is not the breaking of his doors, and the rummaging of his drawers, that constitutes the essence of the offence [to the Fifth Amendment]; but it is the invasion of his indefeasible right of personal security, personal liberty and private property. * * * [A]ny forcible and compulsory extortion of a man's own testimony or his private papers to be used as evidence to convict him of crime * * *, is within the condemnation of [the Amendment]. In this regard the fourth and fifth amendments run almost into each other."[a]

NOTES AND QUESTIONS

1. If the item to be seized was a diary instead of the business records in *Andresen,* would there be a stronger Fourth Amendment[b] or Fifth Amendment[c] argument against permitting the seizure? Consider *Model Pre–Arraignment Code* § SS 210.3(2): "With the exception of handwriting samples, and other writings or recordings of evidentiary value for reasons other than their testimonial content, things subject to seizure * * * shall not include personal diaries, letters, or other writings or recordings, made solely for private use or communication to an individual occupying a family, personal, or other confidential relation, other than a relation in criminal enterprise, unless such things have served or are serving a substantial purpose in furtherance of a criminal enterprise."

2. In ZURCHER v. STANFORD DAILY, 436 U.S. 547 (1978), police obtained and executed a warrant to search the offices of the Stanford Daily for negatives, film and pictures relevant to identification of those who had injured nine policemen during a campus demonstration. The Daily later brought a civil action in federal district court, where declaratory relief was granted. That court held (i) that the Fourth Amendment forbade the issuance of a warrant to search for materials in the possession of one not suspected of crime except upon a showing of probable cause a subpoena *duces tecum* would be impracticable; and (ii) that the First Amendment bars search of newspaper offices except upon a clear

---

a. Marshall, J., dissented on other grounds and thus found it unnecessary to reach the Fifth Amendment issue.

b. In *Fisher,* relied upon in *Andresen,* the Court, after stating that the taxpayers "have not raised arguments of a Fourth Amendment nature * * * and could not be successful if they had," cautioned that the "[s]pecial problems of privacy which might be presented by subpoena of a personal diary * * * are not involved here." See also fn. 7 on p. 858.

c. "[I]t has been thought that a diary in which its author has recited his criminal conduct, seized in an otherwise lawful search, should not be used against him, just as any other kind of involuntary confession is unusable under the Fifth Amendment." *United States v. Boyette,* 299 F.2d 92 (4th Cir.1962).

showing that important materials would otherwise be destroyed or removed and that a restraining order would be futile.

The Supreme Court, per White, J., concluded that "it is untenable to conclude that property may not be searched unless its occupant is reasonably suspected of crime and is subject to arrest. * * * The Fourth Amendment has itself struck the balance between privacy and public need, and there is no occasion or justification for a court to revise the Amendment and strike a new balance by denying the search warrant in the circumstances present here and by insisting that the investigation proceed by subpoena *duces tecum,* whether on the theory that the latter is a less intrusive alternative, or otherwise. * * *

"In any event, the reasons presented by the District Court and adopted by the Court of Appeals for arriving at its remarkable conclusion do not withstand analysis. First, as we have said, it is apparent that whether the third-party occupant is suspect or not, the State's interest in enforcing the criminal law and recovering the evidence remains the same; and it is the seeming innocence of the property owner that the District Court relied on to foreclose the warrant to search. But as respondents themselves now concede, if the third party knows that contraband or other illegal materials are on his property, he is sufficiently culpable to justify the issuance of a search warrant. Similarly, if his ethical stance is the determining factor, it seems to us that whether or not he knows that the sought-after articles are secreted on his property and whether or not he knows that the articles are in fact the fruits, instrumentalities, or evidence of crime, he will be so informed when the search warrant is served, and it is doubtful that he should then be permitted to object to the search, to withhold, if it is there, the evidence of crime reasonably believed to be possessed by him or secreted on his property, and to forbid the search and insist that the officers serve him with a subpoena *duces tecum.*

"Second, we are unpersuaded that the District Court's new rule denying search warrants against third parties and insisting on subpoenas would substantially further privacy interests without seriously undermining law enforcement efforts. As the District Court understands it, denying third-party search warrants would not have substantial adverse effects on criminal investigations because the nonsuspect third party, once served with a subpoena, will preserve the evidence and ultimately, lawfully respond. The difficulty with this assumption is that search warrants are often employed early in an investigation, perhaps before the identity of any likely criminal and certainly before all the perpetrators are or could be known. The seemingly blameless third party in possession of the fruits or evidence may not be innocent at all; and if he is, he may nevertheless be so related to or so sympathetic with the culpable that he cannot be relied upon to retain and preserve the articles that may implicate his friends, or at least not to notify those who would be damaged by the evidence that the authorities are aware of its location. In any event, it is likely that the real culprits will have access to the property, and the delay involved in employing the subpoena *duces tecum,* offering as it does the opportunity to litigate its validity, could easily result in the disappearance of the evidence, whatever the good faith of the third party. * * *[8]

---

8. It is also far from clear, even apart from the dangers of destruction and removal, whether the use of the subpoena *duces tecum* under circumstances where there is probable cause to believe that a crime has been committed and that the materials sought constitute evidence of its commission will result in the production of evidence with sufficient regularity to satisfy the public interest in law enforcement. Unlike the individual whose privacy is invaded by a search, the recipient of a subpoena may assert the Fifth Amendment privilege against self-incrimination in response to a summons to produce evidence or give testimony. See *Maness v. Meyers,* 419 U.S. 449 (1975). This privilege is not restricted to suspects. We have construed it broadly as covering any individual who might be incriminated by the evidence in connection with which the privilege is asserted. *Hoffman v. United States,* 341 U.S. 479 (1951). The burden of overcoming an assertion

"We are also not convinced that the net gain to privacy interests by the District Court's new rule would be worth the candle.[9] In the normal course of events, search warrants are more difficult to obtain than subpoenas, since the latter do not involve the judiciary and do not require proof of probable cause. Where, in the real world, subpoenas would suffice, it can be expected that they will be employed by the rational prosecutor. On the other hand, when choice is available under local law and the prosecutor chooses to use the search warrant, it is unlikely that he has needlessly selected the more difficult course. His choice is more likely to be based on the solid belief, arrived at through experience but difficult, if not impossible, to sustain a specific case, that the warranted search is necessary to secure and to avoid the destruction of evidence.

"[The Framers] did not forbid warrants where the press was involved, did not require special showings that subpoenas would be impractical, and did not insist that the owner of the place to be searched, if connected with the press, must be shown to be implicated in the offense being investigated. Further, the prior cases do no more than insist that the courts apply the warrant requirements with particular exactitude when First Amendment interests would be endangered by the search.[d] As we see it, no more than this is required where the warrant requested is for the seizure of criminal evidence reasonably believed to be on the premises occupied by a newspaper. Properly administered, the pre-conditions for a warrant—probable cause, specificity with respect to the place to be searched and the things to be seized, and overall reasonableness—should afford sufficient protection against the harms that are assertedly threatened by warrants for searching newspaper offices."

Justices Stewart and Marshall, dissenting, raised a First Amendment objection because of the "serious burden on a free press imposed by an unannounced police search of a newspaper office: the possibility of disclosure of information received from confidential sources, or of the identity of the sources themselves. Protection of those sources is necessary to ensure that the press can fulfill its constitutionally designated function of informing the public, because important information can often be obtained only by an assurance that the source will not be revealed.

---

of the Fifth Amendment privilege, even if prompted by a desire not to cooperate rather than any real fear of self-incrimination, is one which prosecutors would rarely be able to meet in the early stages of an investigation despite the fact they did not regard the witness as a suspect. Even time spent litigating such matters could seriously impede criminal investigations.

9. We reject totally the reasoning of the District Court that additional protections are required to assure that the Fourth Amendment rights of third parties are not violated because of the unavailability of the exclusionary rule as a deterrent to improper searches of premises in the control of nonsuspects. * * * It is probably seldom that police during the investigatory stage when most searches occur will be so convinced that no potential defendant will have standing to exclude evidence on Fourth Amendment grounds that they will feel free to ignore constitutional restraints. * * *

d. This does *not* mean, the Court later held in *New York v. P.J. Video, Inc.,* 475 U.S. 868 (1986), that a higher probable cause standard applies in such cases. The Court deemed sufficient "the longstanding special protections" established in its earlier cases, namely: (a) "that the police may not rely on the 'exigency' exception to the Fourth Amendment's warrant requirement in conducting a seizure of allegedly obscene materials, under circumstances where such a seizure would effectively constitute a 'prior restraint'"; (b) "that the large-scale seizure of books or films constituting a 'prior restraint' must be preceded by an adversary hearing on the question of obscenity"; (c) "that, even where a seizure of allegedly obscene materials would not constitute a 'prior restraint,' but instead would merely preserve evidence for trial, the seizure must be made pursuant to a warrant and there must be an opportunity for a prompt post-seizure judicial determination of obscenity"; and (d) "that a warrant authorizing the seizure of materials presumptively protected by the First Amendment may not issue based solely on the conclusory allegations of a police officer that the sought-after materials are obscene."

Justice Stevens, dissenting, raised a Fourth Amendment objection, namely, that a "showing of probable cause that was adequate to justify the issuance of a warrant to search for stolen goods in the 18th century does not automatically satisfy the new dimensions of the Fourth Amendment in the post-*Hayden* era. * * * The only conceivable justification for an unannounced search of an innocent citizen is the fear that, if notice were given, he would conceal or destroy the object of the search. Probable cause to believe that the custodian is a criminal, or that he holds a criminal's weapons, spoils, or the like, justifies that fear, and therefore such a showing complies with the Clause. But if nothing said under oath in the warrant application demonstrates the need for an unannounced search by force, the probable cause requirement is not satisfied. In the absence of some other showing of reasonableness, the ensuing search violates the Fourth Amendment."

3. Compare *O'Connor v. Johnson*, 287 N.W.2d 400 (Minn.1979), involving a warrant issued for an attorney's office to search for and seize a certain client's business records: "Even the most particular warrant cannot adequately safeguard client confidentiality, the attorney-client privilege, the attorney's work product, and the criminal defendant's constitutional right to counsel of all of the attorney's clients. It is unreasonable, in any case, to permit law enforcement officers to peruse miscellaneous documents in an attorney's office while attempting to locate documents listed in a search warrant. Even if it were possible to meet the particularity requirement regarding the place to be searched, the file would still contain some confidential information that is immune from seizure under the attorney-client privilege or the work product doctrine. Once that information is revealed to the police, the privileges are lost, and the information cannot be erased from the minds of the police. * * *

"It will not unreasonably burden prosecutors' offices and effective law enforcement to require officers to proceed by subpoena duces tecum in seeking documents held by an attorney. Attorneys are required by statute, the Code of Professional Responsibility, and the oath of admission to the bar to preserve and protect the judicial process. Thus, attorneys must respond faithfully and promptly, while still being allowed the opportunity to assert applicable privileges by a motion to quash."

4. Consider *Model Pre–Arraignment Code* §§ 220.5(2) & (3) providing that if the documents to be seized "cannot be searched for or identified without examining the contents of other documents, or if they constitute items or entries in account books, diaries, or other documents containing matter not specified in the warrant, the executing officer shall not examine the documents but shall either impound them under appropriate protection where found, or seal and remove them for safekeeping pending further proceedings." At a later adversary judicial hearing, a motion may be made for return of the documents or for "specification of such conditions and limitations on the further search for the documents to be seized as may be appropriate to prevent unnecessary or unreasonable invasion of privacy." If return is not ordered, "the search shall proceed under such conditions and limitations as the order shall prescribe."

5. In *Tattered Cover, Inc. v. City of Thornton*, 44 P.3d 1044 (Colo.2002), a bookseller brought suit to restrain the police from executing a search warrant for records of the books purchased by a particular customer. The court first concluded that such a warrant "intrudes into areas protected by" the First Amendment, which "embraces the individual's right to purchase and read whatever books she wishes to, without fear that the government will take steps to discover which books she buys, reads, or intends to read." Then, acknowledging that "the import of *Zurcher*" arguably foreclosed such a holding under the federal Constitution, the court ruled as a matter of state constitutional law "that an innocent, third-party bookstore must be afforded an opportunity for a hearing prior to the execution of

any search warrant that seeks to obtain its customers' book-purchasing records";
and that at the hearing the court must "determine whether law enforcement
officials have a sufficiently compelling need for the book purchase record that
outweighs the harms associated with enforcement of the search warrant."

When soon after 9/11 the PATRIOT Act was adopted in 2001, one of the many
objections voiced concerning that legislation was that it authorized the FBI to
obtain a court order requiring production of "all of the circulation, purchasing and
other records of library users and bookstore customers on no stronger a claim
than an FBI official's statement that they are part of a terrorism investigation."[e]
Although there existed considerable disagreement concerning the frequency with
which required production of such material occurred (especially because of the
secrecy requirements attending use of this authority), such power was a continuing source of controversy. When the PATRIOT Act was revised and reauthorized
in 2006, the provision in question was amended to include "greater congressional
oversight, enhanced procedural protections, more elaborate application requirements, and a judicial review process."[f] Consider the current version of 50 U.S.C.A.
§ 1861, set out in App. B. and discussed at p. 541. Does it strike a fair balance
between privacy and security?

6. While "congressional offices are subject to the operation of the Fourth
Amendment and thus subject to a search pursuant to a search warrant" notwithstanding the Speech or Debate Clause,[g] that Clause is violated if a congressman is
"denied ** * any opportunity to identify and assert the privilege with respect to
legislative materials before their compelled disclosure to Executive agents." *United States v. Rayburn House Office Building, Room 2113,* 497 F.3d 654 (D.C.Cir.
2007). Thus the court concluded that in this first-ever execution of a search
warrant at a congressman's office, the safeguards followed (screening of documents by a 3–person "filter team" of executive agents not involved in the
investigation) were insufficient. Rather, the congressman must have an opportunity to assert the privilege as to specific items, with those claims subject to judicial
review if challenged.

SECTION 3. "PROBABLE CAUSE"

SPINELLI v. UNITED STATES
393 U.S. 410, 89 S.Ct. 584, 21 L.Ed.2d 637 (1969).

JUSTICE HARLAN delivered the opinion of the Court.

William Spinelli was convicted * * * of traveling to St. Louis, Missouri, from a
nearby Illinois suburb with the intention of conducting gambling activities proscribed by Missouri law. At every appropriate stage in the proceedings in the
lower courts, the petitioner challenged the constitutionality of the warrant which
authorized the FBI search that uncovered the evidence necessary for his conviction. * * * Believing it desirable that the principles of [*Aguilar v. Texas,* 378 U.S.
108 (1964)] should be further explicated, we granted certiorari * * *.

In *Aguilar,* a search warrant had issued upon an affidavit of police officers
who swore only that they had "received reliable information from a credible
person and do believe" that narcotics were being illegally stored on the described

---

e. Congressman Bernie Sanders, *Pulling FBI's Nose Out of Your Books,* http://bernie.house.
gov/documents/opleds/20030508100516.asp

f. Congressional Research Service, *USA PATRIOT Act Improvement and Reauthorization Act
of 2005: A Legal Analysis,* http://www.fas.org/sgp/crs/intel /RL33332.pdf

g. The Clause provides that "for any Speech or Debate in either House, [Members of
Congress] shall not be questioned in any other Place."

premises. While recognizing that the constitutional requirement of probable cause can be satisfied by hearsay information, this Court held the affidavit inadequate for two reasons. First, the application failed to set forth any of the "underlying circumstances" necessary to enable the magistrate independently to judge of the validity of the informant's conclusion that the narcotics were where he said they were. Second, the affiant-officers did not attempt to support their claim that their informant was " 'credible' or his information 'reliable.' " The Government is, however, quite right in saying that the FBI affidavit in the present case is more ample than that in *Aguilar*. Not only does it contain a report from an anonymous informant, but it also contains a report of an independent FBI investigation which is said to corroborate the informant's tip. We are, then, required to delineate the manner in which *Aguilar's* two-pronged test should be applied in these circumstances.

In essence, the affidavit * * * contained the following allegations:

1. The FBI had kept track of Spinelli's movements on five days during the month of August 1965. On four of these occasions, Spinelli was seen crossing one of two bridges leading from Illinois into St. Louis, Missouri, between 11 a.m. and 12:15 p.m. On four of the five days, Spinelli was also seen parking his car in a lot used by residents of an apartment house at 1108 Indian Circle Drive in St. Louis, between 3:30 p.m. and 4:45 p.m. On one day, Spinelli was followed further and seen to enter a particular apartment in the building.

2. An FBI check with the telephone company revealed that this apartment contained two telephones listed under the name of Grace P. Hagen, and carrying the numbers WYdown 4–0029 and WYdown 4–0136.

3. The application stated that "William Spinelli is known to this affiant and to federal law enforcement agents and local law enforcement agents as a bookmaker, an associate of bookmakers, a gambler, and an associate of gamblers."

4. Finally, it was stated that the FBI "has been informed by a confidential reliable informant that William Spinelli is operating a handbook and accepting wagers and disseminating wagering information by means of the telephones which have been assigned the numbers WYdown 4–0029 and WYdown 4–0136."

There can be no question that the last item mentioned, detailing the informant's tip, has a fundamental place in this warrant application. Without it, probable cause could not be established. The first two items reflect only innocent-seeming activity and data. Spinelli's travels to and from the apartment building and his entry into a particular apartment on one occasion could hardly be taken as bespeaking gambling activity; and there is surely nothing unusual about an apartment containing two separate telephones. Many a householder indulges himself in this petty luxury. Finally, the allegation that Spinelli was "known" to the affiant and to other federal and local law enforcement officers as a gambler and an associate of gamblers is but a bald and unilluminating assertion of suspicion that is entitled to no weight in appraising the magistrate's decision. *Nathanson v. United States,* 290 U.S. 41, 46 (1933).

So much indeed the Government does not deny. Rather, following the reasoning of the Court of Appeals, the Government claims that the informant's tip gives a suspicious color to the FBI's reports detailing Spinelli's innocent-seeming conduct and that, conversely, the FBI's surveillance corroborates the informant's tip, thereby entitling it to more weight. * * * We believe, however, that the "totality of circumstances" approach taken by the Court of Appeals paints with too broad a brush. Where, as here, the informer's tip is a necessary element in a finding of probable cause, its proper weight must be determined by a more precise analysis.

The informer's report must first be measured against *Aguilar's* standards so that its probative value can be assessed. If the tip is found inadequate under *Aguilar,* the other allegations which corroborate the information contained in the hearsay report should then be considered. At this stage as well, however, the standards enunciated in *Aguilar* must inform the magistrate's decision. He must ask: Can it fairly be said that the tip, even when certain parts of it have been corroborated by independent sources, is as trustworthy as a tip which would pass *Aguilar's* tests without independent corroboration? * * *

Applying these principles to the present case, we first consider the weight to be given the informer's tip when it is considered apart from the rest of the affidavit. It is clear that a Commissioner could not credit it without abdicating his constitutional function. Though the affiant swore that his confidant was "reliable," he offered the magistrate no reason in support of this conclusion. Perhaps even more important is the fact that *Aguilar's* other test has not been satisfied. The tip does not contain a sufficient statement of the underlying circumstances from which the informer concluded that Spinelli was running a bookmaking operation. We are not told how the FBI's source received his information—it is not alleged that the informant personally observed Spinelli at work or that he had ever placed a bet with him. Moreover, if the informant came by the information indirectly, he did not explain why his sources were reliable. In the absence of a statement detailing the manner in which the information was gathered, it is especially important that the tip describe the accused's criminal activity in sufficient detail that the magistrate may know that he is relying on something more substantial than a casual rumor circulating in the underworld or an accusation based merely on an individual's general reputation.

The detail provided by the informant in *Draper v. United States,* 358 U.S. 307 (1959), provides a suitable benchmark. While Hereford, the FBI's informer in that case, did not state the way in which he had obtained his information, he reported that Draper had gone to Chicago the day before by train and that he would return to Denver by train with three ounces of heroin on one of two specified mornings. Moreover, Hereford went on to describe, with minute particularity, the clothes that Draper would be wearing upon his arrival at the Denver station. A magistrate, when confronted with such detail, could reasonably infer that the informant had gained his information in a reliable way. Such an inference cannot be made in the present case. Here, the only facts supplied were that Spinelli was using two specified telephones and that these phones were being used in gambling operations. This meager report could easily have been obtained from an off-hand remark heard at a neighborhood bar.

Nor do we believe that the patent doubts *Aguilar* raises as to the report's reliability are adequately resolved by a consideration of the allegations detailing the FBI's independent investigative efforts. At most, these allegations indicated that Spinelli could have used the telephones specified by the informant for some purpose. This cannot by itself be said to support both the inference that the informer was generally trustworthy and that he had made his charge against Spinelli on the basis of information obtained in a reliable way. Once again, *Draper* provides a relevant comparison. Independent police work in that case corroborated much more than one small detail that had been provided by the informant. There, the police, upon greeting the inbound Denver train on the second morning specified by informer Hereford, saw a man whose dress corresponded precisely to Hereford's detailed description. It was then apparent that the informant had not been fabricating his report out of whole cloth; since the report was of the sort which in common experience may be recognized as having been obtained in a reliable way, it was perfectly clear that probable cause had been established.

We conclude, then, that in the present case the informant's tip—even when corroborated to the extent indicated—was not sufficient to provide the basis for a finding of probable cause. * * *

The judgment of the Court of Appeals is reversed * * *.

JUSTICE WHITE, concurring. * * *

The tension between *Draper* and the *Nathanson-Aguilar* line of cases is evident from the course followed by the majority opinion. * * * Since [the informant's] specific information about Spinelli using two phones with particular numbers had been verified, did not his allegation about gambling thereby become sufficiently more believable if the *Draper* principle is to be given any scope at all? I would think so, particularly since the information from the informant which was verified was not neutral, irrelevant information but was material to proving the gambling allegation: two phones with different numbers in an apartment used away from home indicates a business use in an operation, like bookmaking, where multiple phones are needed. The *Draper* approach would reasonably justify the issuance of a warrant in this case, particularly since the police had some awareness of Spinelli's past activities. The majority, however, while seemingly embracing *Draper,* confines that case to its own facts. Pending full scale reconsideration of that case, on the one hand, or of the *Nathanson-Aguilar* cases on the other, I join the opinion of the Court and the judgment of reversal especially since a vote to affirm would produce an equally divided Court.[a]

ILLINOIS v. GATES

462 U.S. 213, 103 S.Ct. 2317, 76 L.Ed.2d 527 (1983).

JUSTICE REHNQUIST delivered the opinion of the Court.

[Bloomingdale, Ill., police received an anonymous letter reading:

"This letter is to inform you that you have a couple in your town who strictly make their living on selling drugs. They are Sue and Lance Gates, they live on Greenway, off Bloomingdale Rd. in the condominiums. Most of their buys are done in Florida. Sue his wife drives their car to Florida, where she leaves it to be loaded up with drugs, then Lance flys down and drives it back. Sue flys back after she drops the car off in Florida. May 3 she is driving down there again and Lance will be flying down in a few days to drive it back. At the time Lance drives the car back he has the trunk loaded with over $100,000.00 in drugs. Presently they have over $100,000.00 worth of drugs in their basement.

"They brag about the fact they never have to work, and make their entire living on pushers.

"I guarantee if you watch them carefully you will make a big catch. They are friends with some big drugs dealers, who visit their house often. * * * "

Subsequent investigation established that, as the anonymous letter predicted, Lance Gates had flown from Chicago to West Palm Beach late in the afternoon of May 5th, had checked into a hotel room registered in the name of his wife, and, at 7:00 a.m. the following morning, had headed north, accompanied by an unidentified woman, out of West Palm Beach on an interstate highway used by travelers from South Florida to Chicago in an automobile bearing a license plate issued to him. A search warrant for Gates' vehicle and residence was obtained, and it was executed when Gates and his wife arrived back home 22 hours later, resulting in discovery of 350 lbs. of marijuana in their car and some marijuana, weapons and

---

a. Black, Fortas, and Stewart, JJ., dissented separately; Marshall, J., took no part in the case.

other contraband in the home. The trial judge's suppression of the evidence was upheld by the Illinois appellate court and supreme court on the ground that the affidavit, containing the above-recited information, did not meet the *Spinelli* two-pronged test.]

The Illinois court, alluding to an elaborate set of legal rules that have developed among various lower courts to enforce the "two-pronged test,"[4] found that the test had not been satisfied. First, the "veracity" prong was not satisfied because, "there was simply no basis [for] * * * conclud[ing] that the anonymous person [who wrote the letter to the Bloomingdale Police Department] was credible." The court indicated that corroboration by police of details contained in the letter might never satisfy the "veracity" prong, and in any event, could not do so if, as in the present case, only "innocent" details are corroborated. In addition, the letter gave no indication of the basis of its writer's knowledge of the Gates' activities. The Illinois court understood *Spinelli* as permitting the detail contained in a tip to be used to infer that the informant had a reliable basis for his statements, but it thought that the anonymous letter failed to provide sufficient detail to permit such an inference. Thus, it concluded that no showing of probable cause had been made.

We agree with the Illinois Supreme Court that an informant's "veracity," "reliability" and "basis of knowledge" are all highly relevant in determining the value of his report. We do not agree, however, that these elements should be understood as entirely separate and independent requirements to be rigidly exacted in every case, which the opinion of the Supreme Court of Illinois would imply. Rather, as detailed below, they should be understood simply as closely intertwined issues that may usefully illuminate the common sense, practical question whether there is "probable cause" to believe that contraband or evidence is located in a particular place.

This totality of the circumstances approach is far more consistent with our prior treatment of probable cause than is any rigid demand that specific "tests" be satisfied by every informant's tip. Perhaps the central teaching of our decisions bearing on the probable cause standard is that it is a "practical, nontechnical conception." *Brinegar v. United States,* 338 U.S. 160 (1949). "In dealing with probable cause, * * * as the very name implies, we deal with probabilities. These are not technical; they are the factual and practical considerations of everyday life on which reasonable and prudent men, not legal technicians, act." Our observation in *United States v. Cortez,* [p. 419], regarding "particularized suspicion," is also applicable to the probable cause standard:

The process does not deal with hard certainties, but with probabilities. Long before the law of probabilities was articulated as such, practical people formulated certain common-sense conclusions about human behavior; jurors as factfinders are permitted to do the same—and so are law enforcement officers. Finally, the evidence thus collected must be seen and weighed not in terms of library analysis by scholars, but as understood by those versed in the field of law enforcement.

---

4. In summary, these rules posit that the "veracity" prong of the *Spinelli* test has two "spurs"—the informant's "credibility" and the "reliability" of his information. Various interpretations are advanced for the meaning of the "reliability" spur of the "veracity" prong. Both the "basis of knowledge" prong and the "veracity" prong are treated as entirely separate requirements, which must be independently satisfied in every case in order to sustain a determination of probable cause. Some ancillary doctrines are relied on to satisfy certain of the foregoing requirements. For example, the "self-verifying detail" of a tip may satisfy the "basis of knowledge" requirement, although not the "credibility" spur of the "veracity" prong. Conversely, corroboration would seem not capable of supporting the "basis of knowledge" prong, but only the "veracity" prong. * * *

As these comments illustrate, probable cause is a fluid concept—turning on the assessment of probabilities in particular factual contexts—not readily, or even usefully, reduced to a neat set of legal rules. Informants' tips doubtless come in many shapes and sizes from many different types of persons. * * * Rigid legal rules are ill-suited to an area of such diversity. "One simple rule will not cover every situation."

Moreover, the "two-pronged test" directs analysis into two largely independent channels—the informant's "veracity" or "reliability" and his "basis of knowledge." There are persuasive arguments against according these two elements such independent status. Instead, they are better understood as relevant considerations in the totality of circumstances analysis that traditionally has guided probable cause determinations: a deficiency in one may be compensated for, in determining the overall reliability of a tip, by a strong showing as to the other, or by some other indicia of reliability.

If, for example, a particular informant is known for the unusual reliability of his predictions of certain types of criminal activities in a locality, his failure, in a particular case, to thoroughly set forth the basis of his knowledge surely should not serve as an absolute bar to a finding of probable cause based on his tip. Likewise, if an unquestionably honest citizen comes forward with a report of criminal activity—which if fabricated would subject him to criminal liability—we have found rigorous scrutiny of the basis of his knowledge unnecessary. Conversely, even if we entertain some doubt as to an informant's motives, his explicit and detailed description of alleged wrongdoing, along with a statement that the event was observed first-hand, entitles his tip to greater weight than might otherwise be the case. Unlike a totality of circumstances analysis, which permits a balanced assessment of the relative weights of all the various indicia of reliability (and unreliability) attending an informant's tip, the "two-pronged test" has encouraged an excessively technical dissection of informants' tips, with undue attention being focused on isolated issues that cannot sensibly be divorced from the other facts presented to the magistrate. * * *

We also have recognized that affidavits "are normally drafted by non-lawyers in the midst and haste of a criminal investigation. Technical requirements of elaborate specificity once exacted under common law pleading have no proper place in this area." Likewise, search and arrest warrants long have been issued by persons who are neither lawyers nor judges, and who certainly do not remain abreast of each judicial refinement of the nature of "probable cause." The rigorous inquiry into the *Spinelli* prongs and the complex superstructure of evidentiary and analytical rules that some have seen implicit in our *Spinelli* decision, cannot be reconciled with the fact that many warrants are—quite properly—issued on the basis of nontechnical, common-sense judgments of laymen applying a standard less demanding than those used in more formal legal proceedings. Likewise, given the informal, often hurried context in which it must be applied, the "built-in subtleties" of the "two-pronged test" are particularly unlikely to assist magistrates in determining probable cause.

Similarly, we have repeatedly said that after-the-fact scrutiny by courts of the sufficiency of an affidavit should not take the form of *de novo* review. A magistrate's "determination of probable cause should be paid great deference by reviewing courts." "A grudging or negative attitude by reviewing courts toward warrants" is inconsistent with the Fourth Amendment's strong preference for searches conducted pursuant to a warrants; "courts should not invalidate * * * warrant[s] by interpreting affidavit[s] in a hypertechnical, rather than a common-sense, manner."

If the affidavits submitted by police officers are subjected to the type of scrutiny some courts have deemed appropriate, police might well resort to warrantless searches, with the hope of relying on consent or some other exception to the warrant clause that might develop at the time of the search. In addition, the possession of a warrant by officers conducting an arrest or search greatly reduces the perception of unlawful or intrusive police conduct, by assuring "the individual whose property is searched or seized of the lawful authority of the executing officer, his need to search, and the limits of his power to search." Reflecting this preference for the warrant process, the traditional standard for review of an issuing magistrate's probable cause determination has been that so long as the magistrate had a "substantial basis for * * * conclud[ing]" that a search would uncover evidence of wrongdoing, the Fourth Amendment requires no more. We think reaffirmation of this standard better serves the purpose of encouraging recourse to the warrant procedure and is more consistent with our traditional deference to the probable cause determinations of magistrates than is the "two-pronged test."

Finally, the direction taken by decisions following *Spinelli* poorly serves "the most basic function of any government": "to provide for the security of the individual and of his property". The strictures that inevitably accompany the "two-pronged test" cannot avoid seriously impeding the task of law enforcement. If, as the Illinois Supreme Court apparently thought, that test must be rigorously applied in every case, [anonymous tips would be] of greatly diminished value in police work. Ordinary citizens, like ordinary witnesses, generally do not provide extensive recitations of the basis of their everyday observations. Likewise, as the Illinois Supreme Court observed in this case, the veracity of persons supplying anonymous tips is by hypothesis largely unknown, and unknowable. As a result, anonymous tips seldom could survive a rigorous application of either of the *Spinelli* prongs. Yet, such tips, particularly when supplemented by independent police investigation, frequently contribute to the solution of otherwise "perfect crimes." While a conscientious assessment of the basis for crediting such tips is required by the Fourth Amendment, a standard that leaves virtually no place for anonymous citizen informants is not.

For all these reasons, we conclude that it is wiser to abandon the "two-pronged test" established by our decisions in *Aguilar* and *Spinelli*.[11] In its place we reaffirm the totality of the circumstances analysis that traditionally has informed probable cause determinations. The task of the issuing magistrate is simply to make a practical, common-sense decision whether, given all the circumstances set forth in the affidavit before him, including the "veracity" and "basis of knowledge" of persons supplying hearsay information, there is a fair probability that contraband or evidence of a crime will be found in a particular place. And the duty of a reviewing court is simply to ensure that the magistrate had a "substantial basis for * * * conclud[ing]" that probable cause existed. We are convinced that this flexible, easily applied standard will better achieve the accommodation of public and private interests that the Fourth Amendment requires than does the approach that has developed from *Aguilar* and *Spinelli*.

Our earlier cases illustrate the limits beyond which a magistrate may not venture in issuing a warrant. A sworn statement of an affiant that "he has cause

---

11. * * * Whether the allegations submitted to the magistrate in *Spinelli* would, under the view we now take, have supported a finding of probable cause, we think it would not be profitable to decide. There are so many variables in the probable cause equation that one determination will seldom be a useful "precedent" for another. Suffice it to say that while we in no way abandon *Spinelli's* concern for the trustworthiness of informers and for the principle that it is the magistrate who must ultimately make a finding of probable cause, we reject the rigid categorization suggested by some of its language.

to suspect and does believe that" liquor illegally brought into the United States is located on certain premises will not do. *Nathanson v. United States.* An affidavit must provide the magistrate with a substantial basis for determining the existence of probable cause, and the wholly conclusory statement at issue in *Nathanson* failed to meet this requirement. An officer's statement that "affiants have received reliable information from a credible person and believe" that heroin is stored in a home, is likewise inadequate. *Aguilar v. Texas.* As in *Nathanson,* this is a mere conclusory statement that gives the magistrate virtually no basis at all for making a judgment regarding probable cause. Sufficient information must be presented to the magistrate to allow that official to determine probable cause; his action cannot be a mere ratification of the bare conclusions of others. In order to ensure that such an abdication of the magistrate's duty does not occur, courts must continue to conscientiously review the sufficiency of affidavits on which warrants are issued. But when we move beyond the "bare bones" affidavits present in cases such as *Nathanson* and *Aguilar,* this area simply does not lend itself to a prescribed set of rules, like that which had developed from *Spinelli.* Instead, the flexible, common-sense standard articulated in * * * *Brinegar* better served the purposes of the Fourth Amendment's probable cause requirement. * * *

Our decisions applying the totality of circumstances analysis outlined above have consistently recognized the value of corroboration of details of an informant's tip by independent police work.

Our decision in *Draper v. United States,* however, is the classic case on the value of corroborative efforts of police officials. There, an informant named Hereford reported that Draper would arrive in Denver on a train from Chicago on one of two days, and that he would be carrying a quantity of heroin. The informant also supplied a fairly detailed physical description of Draper, and predicted that he would be wearing a light colored raincoat, brown slacks and black shoes, and would be walking "real fast." Hereford gave no indication of the basis for his information.[12]

On one of the stated dates police officers observed a man matching this description exit a train arriving from Chicago; his attire and luggage matched Hereford's report and he was walking rapidly. We explained in *Draper* that, by this point in his investigation, the arresting officer "had personally verified every facet of the information given him by Hereford except whether petitioner had accomplished his mission and had the three ounces of heroin on his person or in his bag. And surely with every other bit of Hereford's information being thus personally verified, [the officer] had 'reasonable grounds' to believe that the remaining unverified bit of Hereford's information—that Draper would have the heroin with him—was likewise true."

The showing of probable cause in the present case was fully as compelling as that in *Draper.* Even standing alone, the facts obtained through the independent investigation of Mader and the DEA at least suggested that the Gates were involved in drug trafficking. In addition to being a popular vacation site, Florida is well-known as a source of narcotics and other illegal drugs. Lance Gates' flight to Palm Beach, his brief, overnight stay in a motel, and apparent immediate return

---

12. The tip in *Draper* might well not have survived the rigid application of the "two-pronged test" that developed following *Spinelli.* The only reference to Hereford's reliability was that he had "been engaged as a 'special employee' of the Bureau of Narcotics at Denver for about six months, and from time to time gave information to [the police] for small sums of money, and that [the officer] had always found the information given by Hereford to be accurate and reliable." Likewise, the tip gave no indication of how Hereford came by his information. At most, the detailed and accurate predictions in the tip indicated that, however Hereford obtained his information, it was reliable.

north to Chicago in the family car, conveniently awaiting him in West Palm Beach, is as suggestive of a prearranged drug run, as it is of an ordinary vacation trip.

In addition, the magistrate could rely on the anonymous letter, which had been corroborated in major part by Mader's efforts—just as had occurred in *Draper*.[13] The Supreme Court of Illinois reasoned that *Draper* involved an informant who had given reliable information on previous occasions, while the honesty and reliability of the anonymous informant in this case were unknown to the Bloomingdale police. While this distinction might be an apt one at the time the police department received the anonymous letter, it became far less significant after Mader's independent investigative work occurred. The corroboration of the letter's predictions that the Gates' car would be in Florida, that Lance Gates would fly to Florida in the next day or so, and that he would drive the car north toward Bloomingdale all indicated, albeit not with certainty, that the informant's other assertions also were true. "Because an informant is right about some things, he is more probably right about other facts," *Spinelli, supra* (White, J., concurring)—including the claim regarding the Gates' illegal activity. This may well not be the type of "reliability" or "veracity" necessary to satisfy some view of the "veracity prong" of *Spinelli,* but we think it suffices for the practical, common-sense judgment called for in making a probable cause determination. It is enough, for purposes of assessing probable cause, that "corroboration through other sources of information reduced the chances of a reckless or prevaricating tale," thus providing "a substantial basis for crediting the hearsay."

Finally, the anonymous letter contained a range of details relating not just to easily obtained facts and conditions existing at the time of the tip, but to future actions of third parties ordinarily not easily predicted. The letter writer's accurate information as to the travel plans of each of the Gates was of a character likely obtained only from the Gates themselves, or from someone familiar with their not entirely ordinary travel plans. If the informant had access to accurate information of this type a magistrate could properly conclude that it was not unlikely that he also had access to reliable information of the Gates' alleged illegal activities.[14] Of

---

13. The Illinois Supreme Court thought that the verification of details contained in the anonymous letter in this case amounted only to "the corroboration of innocent activity," and that this was insufficient to support a finding of probable cause. We are inclined to agree, however, with the observation of Justice Moran in his dissenting opinion that "In this case, just as in *Draper,* seemingly innocent activity became suspicious in the light of the initial tip." And it bears noting that *all* of the corroborating detail established in *Draper, supra,* was of entirely innocent activity * * *.

This is perfectly reasonable. As discussed previously, probable cause requires only a probability or substantial chance of criminal activity, not an actual showing of such activity. By hypothesis, therefore, innocent behavior frequently will provide the basis for a showing of probable cause; to require otherwise would be to *sub silentio* impose a drastically more rigorous definition of probable cause than the security of our citizens demands. We think the Illinois court attempted a too rigid classification of the types of conduct that may be relied upon in seeking to demonstrate probable cause. In making a determination of probable cause the relevant inquiry is not whether particular conduct is "innocent" or "guilty," but the degree of suspicion that attaches to particular types of non-criminal acts.

14. The dissent seizes on one inaccuracy in the anonymous informant's letter—its statement that Sue Gates would fly from Florida to Illinois, when in fact she drove—and argues that the probative value of the entire tip was undermined by this allegedly "material mistake." We have never required that informants used by the police be infallible, and can see no reason to impose such a requirement in this case. Probable cause, particularly when police have obtained a warrant, simply does not require the perfection the dissent finds necessary.

Likewise, there is no force to the dissent's argument that the Gates' action in leaving their home unguarded undercut the informant's claim that drugs were hidden there. Indeed, the line-by-line scrutiny that the dissent applies to the anonymous letter is akin to that we find inappropriate in reviewing magistrates' decisions. The dissent apparently attributes to the

course, the Gates' travel plans might have been learned from a talkative neighbor or travel agent; under the "two-pronged test" developed from *Spinelli,* the character of the details in the anonymous letter might well not permit a sufficiently clear inference regarding the letter writer's "basis of knowledge." But, as discussed previously, probable cause does not demand the certainty we associate with formal trials. It is enough that there was a fair probability that the writer of the anonymous letter had obtained his entire story either from the Gates or someone they trusted. And corroboration of major portions of the letter's predictions provides just this probability. It is apparent, therefore, that the judge issuing the warrant had a "substantial basis for * * * conclud[ing]" that probable cause to search the Gates' home and car existed. The judgment of the Supreme Court of Illinois therefore must be

Reversed.

JUSTICE WHITE, concurring in the judgment.[a]

* * * Although I agree that the warrant should be upheld, I reach this conclusion in accordance with the *Aguilar-Spinelli* framework.

For present purposes, the *Aguilar-Spinelli* rules can be summed up as follows. First, an affidavit based on an informer's tip, standing alone, cannot provide probable cause for issuance of a warrant unless the tip includes information that apprises the magistrate of the informant's basis for concluding that the contraband is where he claims it is (the "basis of knowledge" prong), *and* the affiant informs the magistrate of his basis for believing that the informant is credible (the "veracity" prong).[20] Second, if a tip fails under either or both of the two prongs, probable cause may yet be established by independent police investigatory work

---

magistrate who issued the warrant in this case the rather implausible notion that persons dealing in drugs always stay at home, apparently out of fear that to leave might risk intrusion by criminals. If accurate, one could not help sympathizing with the self-imposed isolation of people so situated. In reality, however, it is scarcely likely that the magistrate ever thought that the anonymous tip "kept one spouse" at home, much less that he relied on the theory advanced by the dissent. The letter simply says that Sue would fly from Florida to Illinois, without indicating whether the Gates' made the bitter choice of leaving the drugs in their house, or those in their car, unguarded. The magistrate's determination that there might be drugs or evidence of criminal activity in the Gates' home was well-supported by the less speculative theory, noted in text, that if the informant could predict with considerable accuracy the somewhat unusual travel plans of the Gates, he probably also had a reliable basis for his statements that the Gates' kept a large quantity of drugs in their home and frequently were visited by other drug traffickers there.

a. In an omitted portion of his opinion, Justice White argued for adoption of a "good-faith" exception to the exclusionary rule.

20. The "veracity" prong is satisfied by a recitation in the affidavit that the informant previously supplied accurate information to the police, see *McCray v. Illinois,* [p. 308], or by proof that the informant gave his information against his penal interest, see *United States v. Harris,* 403 U.S. 573 (1971) (plurality opinion). [Editor's Note: In *Harris,* the informant said that he had purchased illicit whiskey from defendant for two years, most recently within the past two weeks, and had often seen defendant get the whiskey for him and others from a certain building. The plurality opinion concluded that because "people do not lightly admit a crime and place critical evidence in the hands of the police in the form of their own admissions," such admissions "carry their own indicia of credibility—sufficient at least to support finding of probable cause to search" when, as here, the basis of knowledge is also indicated (as almost inevitably will be the case when there is such an admission). The four dissenters objected that "the effect of adopting such a rule would be to encourage the Government to prefer as informants participants in criminal enterprises rather than ordinary citizens, a goal the Government specifically eschews in its brief in this case upon the explicit premise that such persons are often less reliable than those who obey the law."] The "basis of knowledge" prong is satisfied by a statement from the informant that he personally observed the criminal activity, or, if he came by the information indirectly, by a satisfactory explanation of why his sources were reliable, or, in the absence of a statement detailing the manner in which the information was gathered, by a description of the accused's criminal activity in sufficient detail that the magistrate may infer that the informant is relying on something more substantial than casual rumor or an individual's general reputation. *Spinelli v. United States.*

that corroborates the tip to such an extent that it supports "both the inference that the informer was generally trustworthy and that he made his charge on the basis of information obtained in a reliable way." In instances where the officers rely on corroboration, the ultimate question is whether the corroborated tip "is as trustworthy as a tip which would pass *Aguilar's* tests without independent corroboration."

In the present case, it is undisputed that the anonymous tip, by itself, did not furnish probable cause. The question is whether those portions of the affidavit describing the results of the police investigation of the respondents, when considered in light of the tip, "would permit the suspicions engendered by the informant's report to ripen into a judgment that a crime was probably being committed." * * *

In my view, the lower court's characterization of the Gates' activity here as totally "innocent" is dubious. In fact, the behavior was quite suspicious. I agree with the Court that Lance Gates' flight to Palm Beach, an area known to be a source of narcotics, the brief overnight stay in a motel, and apparent immediate return North, suggest a pattern that trained law-enforcement officers have recognized as indicative of illicit drug-dealing activity.

Even, however, had the corroboration related only to completely innocuous activities, this fact alone would not preclude the issuance of a valid warrant. The critical issue is not whether the activities observed by the police are innocent or suspicious. Instead, the proper focus should be on whether the actions of the suspects, whatever their nature, give rise to an inference that the informant is credible and that he obtained his information in a reliable manner.

Thus, in *Draper v. United States* an informant stated on Sept. 7 that Draper would be carrying narcotics when he arrived by train in Denver on the morning of Sept. 8 or Sept. 9. The informant also provided the police with a detailed physical description of the clothes Draper would be wearing when he alighted from the train. The police observed Draper leaving a train on the morning of Sept. 9, and he was wearing the precise clothing described by the informant. The Court held that the police had probable cause to arrest Draper at this point, even though the police had seen nothing more than the totally innocent act of a man getting off a train carrying a briefcase. As we later explained in *Spinelli,* the important point was that the corroboration showed both that the informant was credible, *i.e.* that he "had not been fabricating his report out of whole cloth," and that he had an adequate basis of knowledge for his allegations, "since the report was of the sort which in common experience may be recognized as having been obtained in a reliable way." The fact that the informer was able to predict, two days in advance, the exact clothing Draper would be wearing dispelled the possibility that his tip was just based on rumor or "an off-hand remark heard at a neighborhood bar." Probably Draper had planned in advance to wear these specific clothes so that an accomplice could identify him. A clear inference could therefore be drawn that the informant was either involved in the criminal scheme himself or that he otherwise had access to reliable, inside information.[22]

---

22. Thus, as interpreted in *Spinelli,* the Court in *Draper* held that there was probable cause because "the kind of information related by the informant [was] not generally sent ahead of a person's arrival in a city except to those who are intimately connected with making careful arrangements for meeting him." *Spinelli* (White, J., concurring). As I said in *Spinelli,* the conclusion that *Draper* itself was based on this fact is far from inescapable. Prior to *Spinelli,* *Draper* was susceptible to the interpretation that it stood for the proposition that "the existence of the tenth and critical fact is made sufficiently probable to justify the issuance of a warrant by verifying nine other facts coming from the same source." *Spinelli* (White, J., concurring). But it now seems clear that the Court in *Spinelli* rejected this reading of *Draper.* * * *

As in *Draper,* the police investigation in the present case satisfactorily demonstrated that the informant's tip was as trustworthy as one that would alone satisfy the *Aguilar* tests. The tip predicted that Sue Gates would drive to Florida, that Lance Gates would fly there a few days after May 3, and that Lance would then drive the car back. After the police corroborated these facts, the magistrate could reasonably have inferred, as he apparently did, that the informant, who had specific knowledge of these unusual travel plans, did not make up his story and that he obtained his information in a reliable way. * * * I therefore conclude that the judgment of the Illinois Supreme Court invalidating the warrant must be reversed.

The Court agrees that the warrant was valid, but, in the process of reaching this conclusion, it overrules the *Aguilar-Spinelli* tests and replaces them with a "totality of the circumstances" standard. As shown above, it is not at all necessary to overrule *Aguilar-Spinelli* in order to reverse the judgment below. Therefore, because I am inclined to believe that, when applied properly, the *Aguilar-Spinelli* rules play an appropriate role in probable cause determinations, and because the Court's holding may foretell an evisceration of the probable cause standard, I do not join the Court's holding.

The Court reasons that the "veracity" and "basis of knowledge" tests are not independent, and that a deficiency as to one can be compensated for by a strong showing as to the other. Thus, a finding of probable cause may be based on a tip from an informant "known for the unusual reliability of his predictions" or from "an unquestionably honest citizen," even if the report fails thoroughly to set forth the basis upon which the information was obtained. If this is so, then it must follow *a fortiori* that "the affidavit of an officer, known by the magistrate to be honest and experienced, stating that [contraband] is located in a certain building" must be acceptable. It would be "quixotic" if a similar statement from an honest informant, but not one from an honest officer, could furnish probable cause. But we have repeatedly held that the unsupported assertion or belief of an officer does not satisfy the probable cause requirement. Thus, this portion of today's holding can be read as implicitly rejecting the teachings of these prior holdings.

The Court may not intend so drastic a result. Indeed, the Court expressly reaffirms the validity of cases such as *Nathanson* that have held that, no matter how reliable the affiant-officer may be, a warrant should not be issued unless the affidavit discloses supporting facts and circumstances. The Court limits these cases to situations involving affidavits containing only "bare conclusions" and holds that, if an affidavit contains anything more, it should be left to the issuing magistrate to decide, based solely on "practical[ity]" and "common-sense," wheth-er there is a fair probability that contraband will be found in a particular place.

Thus, as I read the majority opinion, it appears that the question whether the probable cause standard is to be diluted is left to the common-sense judgments of issuing magistrates. I am reluctant to approve any standard that does not expressly require, as a prerequisite to issuance of a warrant, some showing of facts from which an inference may be drawn that the informant is credible and that his information was obtained in a reliable way. * * * Hence, I do not join the Court's opinion rejecting the *Aguilar-Spinelli* rules.

JUSTICE BRENNAN, with whom JUSTICE MARSHALL joins, dissenting.

Although I join Justice Stevens' dissenting opinion and agree with him that the warrant is invalid even under the Court's newly announced "totality of the circumstances" test, I write separately to dissent from the Court's unjustified and ill-advised rejection of the two-prong test for evaluating the validity of a warrant based on hearsay announced in *Aguilar v. Texas,* and refined in *Spinelli v. United States.* * * *

JUSTICE STEVENS, with whom JUSTICE BRENNAN&S JOINS, DISSENTING.

* * * The informant had indicated that "Sue drives their car to Florida *where she leaves it to be loaded up with drugs * * *. Sue flies back after she drops the car off in Florida.*" (emphasis added). Yet Detective Mader's affidavit reported that she "left the West Palm Beach area driving the Mercury northbound."

The discrepancy between the informant's predictions and the facts known to Detective Mader is significant for three reasons. First, it cast doubt on the informant's hypothesis that the Gates already had "over $100,000 worth of drugs in their basement." The informant had predicted an itinerary that always kept one spouse in Bloomingdale, suggesting that the Gates did not want to leave their home unguarded because something valuable was hidden within. That inference obviously could not be drawn when it was known that the pair was actually together over a thousand miles from home.

Second, the discrepancy made the Gates' conduct seem substantially less unusual than the informant had predicted it would be. It would have been odd if, as predicted, Sue had driven down to Florida on Wednesday, left the car, and flown right back to Illinois. But the mere facts that Sue was in West Palm Beach with the car,[1] that she was joined by her husband at the Holiday Inn on Friday,[2] and that the couple drove north together the next morning[3] are neither unusual nor probative of criminal activity.

Third, the fact that the anonymous letter contained a material mistake undermines the reasonableness of relying on it as a basis for making a forcible entry into a private home.

Of course, the activities in this case did not stop when the magistrate issued the warrant. The Gates drove all night to Bloomingdale, the officers searched the car and found 400 pounds of marijuana, and then they searched the house. However, none of these subsequent events may be considered in evaluating the warrant, and the search of the house was legal only if the warrant was valid. I cannot accept the Court's casual conclusion that, *before the Gates arrived in Bloomingdale,* there was probable cause to justify a valid entry and search of a private home. No one knows who the informant in this case was, or what motivated him or her to write the note. Given that the note's predictions were faulty in one significant respect, and were corroborated by nothing except ordinary innocent activity, I must surmise that the Court's evaluation of the warrant's validity has been colored by subsequent events. * * *

NOTES AND QUESTIONS

1. In MASSACHUSETTS v. UPTON, 466 U.S. 727 (1984), police Lt. Beland assisted in the execution of a search warrant for a motel room reserved by one

---

1. The anonymous note suggested that she was going down on Wednesday, but for all the officers knew she had been in Florida for a month.

2. Lance does not appear to have behaved suspiciously in flying down to Florida. He made a reservation in his own name and gave an accurate home phone number to the airlines. And Detective Mader's affidavit does not report that he did any of the other things drug couriers are notorious for doing, such as paying for the ticket in cash, dressing casually, looking pale and nervous, improperly filling out baggage tags, carrying American Tourister luggage, not carrying any luggage, or changing airlines en route.

3. Detective Mader's affidavit hinted darkly that the couple had set out upon "that interstate highway commonly used by travelers to the Chicago area." But the same highway is also commonly used by travelers to Disney World, Sea World, and Ringling Brothers and Barnum and Bailey Circus World. It is also the road to Cocoa Beach, Cape Canaveral, and Washington, D.C. I would venture that each year dozens of perfectly innocent people fly to Florida, meet a waiting spouse, and drive off together in the family car.

Richard Kelleher, which produced several items of identification belonging to two persons whose homes had recently been burglarized. Other items taken in the burglaries, such as jewelry, silver and gold, were not found. A few hours later Beland received a call from an unidentified female who told him that there was "a motor home full of stolen stuff," including jewelry, silver and gold, at George Upton's premises. After verifying that a motor home was parked there, Beland prepared an application for a search warrant, to which he attached the police reports on the two prior burglaries, along with lists of the stolen property, and his affidavit with the above information and the following:

"She further stated that George Upton was going to move the motor home any time now because of the fact that Ricky Kelleher's motel room was raided and that George Upton had purchased these stolen items from Ricky Kelleher. This unidentified female stated that she had seen the stolen items but refused to identify herself because 'he'll kill me,' referring to George Upton. I then told this unidentified female that I knew who she was, giving her the name of Lynn Alberico, who I had met on May 16, 1980, at George Upton's repair shop off Summer St., in Yarmouthport. She was identified to me by George Upton as being his girlfriend, Lynn Alberico. The unidentified female admitted that she was the girl that I had named, stating that she was surprised that I knew who she was. She then told me that she'd broken up with George Upton and wanted to burn him. She also told me that she wouldn't give me her address or phone number but that she would contact me in the future, if need be."

A magistrate issued the warrant, and a subsequent search of the motor home produced the described items. The Supreme Court, per curiam, upheld the warrant:

"Examined in light of *Gates*, Lt. Beland's affidavit provides a substantial basis for the issuance of the warrant. No single piece of evidence in it is conclusive. But the pieces fit neatly together and, so viewed, support the magistrate's determination that there was 'a fair probability that contraband or evidence of crime' would be found in Upton's motor home. The informant claimed to have seen the stolen goods and gave a description of them which tallied with the items taken in recent burglaries. She knew of the raid on the motel room—which produced evidence connected to those burglaries—and that the room had been reserved by Kelleher. She explained the connection between Kelleher's motel room and the stolen goods in Upton's motor home. And she provided a motive both for her attempt at anonymity—fear of Upton's retaliation—and for furnishing the information—her recent breakup with Upton and her desire 'to burn him.' "[a]

2. While the Fourth Amendment expressly requires probable cause for a valid arrest warrant or search warrant, police are often permitted to make arrests and searches without first obtaining a warrant, in which case the Fourth Amendment's protection against "unreasonable searches and seizures" applies. But, because a "principal incentive" for the procurement of warrants would be destroyed if police needed less evidence when acting without a warrant, the requirements in such instances "surely cannot be less stringent" than when a warrant is obtained, *Wong Sun v. United States*, 371 U.S. 471 (1963), meaning probable cause is also required for warrantless arrests and searches.[b]

---

a. Brennan and Marshall, JJ., dissented from the summary disposition of the case and would have denied the petition for certiorari. After remand, *Commonwealth v. Upton*, 476 N.E.2d 548 (Mass.1985), held that *Aguilar* and *Spinelli* "provide a more appropriate structure for probable cause inquiries" under the *state* constitution, and concluded that the affidavit failed to establish probable cause.

b. However, as discussed in §§ 8, 9 of this chapter, certain kinds of searches and seizures, because they involve a lesser degree of intrusion or interference, are permitted upon less than the traditional amount of probable cause.

3. It is generally assumed that the same quantum of evidence is required whether one is concerned with probable cause to arrest or probable cause to search. However, probable cause for search requires a somewhat different kind of conclusion than probable cause for arrest. For arrest, there must be a substantial probability that a crime has been committed and that the person to be arrested committed it; for search, there must be a substantial probability that certain items are the fruits, instrumentalities or evidence of crime and that these items are presently to be found at a certain place.

Because the latter type of probable cause has to do with the *present* location of certain objects, it may be found to be lacking because the time of the facts relied upon is unknown or highly uncertain. Does this mean, as held in *Schmidt v. State*, 659 S.W.2d 420 (Tex.Crim.App.1983), that there was no probable cause to search defendant's car for drugs when the affidavit said defendant, "presently under medical attention," had been found in that vehicle in need of medical attention and had said then that he "had been sniffing cocaine," in that the only reference to time is ambiguous because it is not clear whether defendant had been under medical attention "for a few hours or a few months"? When the time of the facts is given probable cause will sometimes be lacking because that information has become "stale." See, e.g., *United States v. Steeves*, 525 F.2d 33 (8th Cir.1975) (warrant to search for clothing, ski mask, hand gun, money and money bag, all sought as evidence of bank robbery which occupant of premises participated in three months earlier; held, there was no probable cause the money or bag would still be there, but there was probable cause the other items would be there, as "a highly incriminating or consumable item of personal property is less likely to remain in one place as long as an item of property which is not consumable or which is innocuous in itself or not particularly incriminating"). Finally, even if no such problems are present, it must be remembered that to have probable cause to search there must be a sufficient connection of the items sought with a particular place. Thus, while a valid search warrant can sometimes issue even when the perpetrator of the crime is unknown, it does not necessarily follow that probable cause to arrest a person will likewise constitute probable cause to search that person's residence for evidence of that crime. See, e.g., *United States v. Lalor*, 996 F.2d 1578 (4th Cir.1993) (where informants gave information re defendant's drug sales at certain street corner, probable cause to search defendant's residence elsewhere lacking where affidavit does not "explain the geographic relationship between the area where the drug sales occurred" and defendant's residence).

4. Sometimes the objection is that the information is premature rather than "stale," as in UNITED STATES v. GRUBBS, 547 U.S. 90 (2006), where an "anticipatory" search warrant was issued upon an affidavit indicating that a controlled delivery of a package containing a videotape of child pornography would later be made to defendant's residence and that the warrant would thereafter be executed there (as it was). Grubbs sought to have the evidence suppressed on the ground that probable cause had not existed when the warrant was issued, but the Court, per SCALIA, J., responded that anticipatory warrants are "no different in principle from ordinary warrants. They require the magistrate to determine (1) that it is *now probable* that (2) contraband, evidence of a crime, or a fugitive *will be* on the described premises (3) when the warrant is executed. It should be noted, however, that where the anticipatory warrant places a condition[c] (other than the mere passage of time) upon its execution, the first of these determinations goes not merely to what will probably be found if the condition is met. (If that were the

---

c. Grubbs also objected that the search warrant was defective because it failed to specify the "triggering condition" stated in the affidavit (i.e., that the package was "physically taken into" the described premises), which the Court rejected on the authority of *Dalia v. United States*, p. 525.

extent of the probability determination, an anticipatory warrant could be issued for every house in the country, authorizing search and seizure *if* contraband should be delivered—though for any single location there is no likelihood that contraband will be delivered.) Rather, the probability determination for a conditioned anticipatory warrant looks also to the likelihood that the condition will occur, and thus that a proper object of seizure will be on the described premises. In other words, for a conditioned anticipatory warrant to comply with the Fourth Amendment's requirement of probable cause, two prerequisites of probability must be satisfied. It must be true not only that *if* the triggering condition occurs 'there is a fair probability that contraband or evidence of a crime will be found in a particular place,' but also that there is probable cause to believe the triggering condition *will occur.* The supporting affidavit must provide the magistrate with sufficient information to evaluate both aspects of the probable-cause determination."

In *State v. Morris,* 668 P.2d 857 (Alaska App.1983), after drug dogs alerted to a package being shipped by airline for pickup at the airport, the authorities obtained a search warrant to search "whoever picks up said package or the premises * * * wherever the described package is taken." Agents saw a man pick up the package and followed his vehicle to a certain residence, which the man then entered; when police could see that only the wrapping paper from the package remained in his car, they executed the warrant at that residence. How would/should the Supreme Court decide such a case? Cf. the warrant contemplated by the *Karo* case, described in fn. a, p. 280.

5. When the police act without a warrant, they initially make the probable cause decision themselves, although it is subject to after-the-fact review by a judicial officer upon a motion to suppress evidence found because of the arrest or search. When the police act with a warrant, the probable cause decision is made by a magistrate in the first instance, but his decision may likewise be challenged in an adversary setting upon a motion to suppress (except insofar as the question is avoided entirely by reliance on *United States v. Leon,* p. 229). In a warrant case, the issue upon the motion to suppress is usually cast in terms of whether the facts set out in the complaint or affidavit upon which the warrant was issued establish probable cause.[d] However, the dissenters in *Aguilar* suggested that a defective affidavit might be cured by what the judge was told at the time the warrant was sought, and they would also resuscitate the affidavit on the basis of the officer's subsequent testimony on the motion to suppress.

As to the first possibility, consider *United States v. Clyburn,* 24 F.3d 613 (4th Cir.1994) (the "Fourth Amendment does not require that the basis for probable cause be established in a written affidavit," and thus "magistrates may consider sworn, unrecorded oral testimony in making probable cause determinations during warrant proceedings," even though "presentation of written affidavits or recorded testimony provides a preferable way of securing a search warrant"). As to the second possibility, consider *Whiteley v. Warden,* 401 U.S. 560 (1971): "Under the cases of this Court, an otherwise insufficient affidavit cannot be rehabilitated by testimony concerning information possessed by the affiant when he sought the warrant but not disclosed to the issuing magistrate. * * * A contrary rule would, of course, render the warrant requirements of the Fourth Amendment meaningless."

6. Does it follow that the defendant may not challenge an affidavit which is sufficient on its face? No, the Court answered in FRANKS v. DELAWARE, 438

---

d. But consider *United States v. Marin–Buitrago,* 734 F.2d 889 (2d Cir.1984), holding that police are required "to report [to the magistrate who issued the warrant] any material changes in the facts contained in a warrant affidavit that occur before the warrant is executed."

U.S. 154 (1978). Reasoning that (i) "a flat ban on impeachment of veracity could denude the probable cause requirement of all real meaning," (ii) "the hearing before the magistrate not always will suffice to discourage lawless or reckless misconduct," (iii) "the alternative sanctions of a perjury prosecution, administrative discipline, contempt, or a civil suit are not likely to fill the gap," (iv) "allowing an evidentiary hearing, after a suitable preliminary proffer of material falsity, will not diminish the importance and solemnity of the warrant-issuing process," (v) "the claim that a post-search hearing will confuse the issue of the defendant's guilt with the issue of the State's possible misbehavior is footless," and (vi) allowing impeachment does not really extend the exclusionary rule "to a 'new' area," the Court, per BLACKMUN, J., held "that, where the defendant makes a substantial preliminary showing that a false statement knowingly and intentionally, or with reckless disregard for the truth, was included by the affiant in the warrant affidavit, and if the allegedly false statement is necessary to the finding of probable cause, the Fourth Amendment requires that a hearing be held at the defendant's request. In the event that at that hearing the allegation of perjury or reckless disregard is established by the defendant by a preponderance of the evidence, and, with the affidavit's false material set to one side, the affidavit's remaining content is insufficient to establish probable cause, the search warrant must be voided and the fruits of the search excluded to the same extent as if probable cause was lacking on the face of the affidavit."[e]

Shouldn't the same result obtain if the false statement was negligently made, as reasoned in *Theodor v. Superior Court,* 501 P.2d 234 (Cal.1972), given "the overriding principle of reasonableness which governs the application of the Fourth Amendment"? Shouldn't the same result follow even as to innocently made falsehoods, where "[a]n honestly-erring individual * * * has substituted his erroneous judgment for that of the magistrate," as argued in Comment, 19 U.C.L.A.L.Rev. 96, 140 (1971)? If there was a deliberate false statement, then why shouldn't this *always* invalidate the warrant because, as stated in *United States v. Carmichael,* 489 F.2d 983 (7th Cir.1973), "[t]he fullest deterrent sanctions of the exclusionary rule should be applied to such serious and deliberate government wrongdoing"? Should *Franks* apply where defendant's objection is that the police left out of the affidavit some additional information which would have put into question the probable cause shown by the information included? If so, what constitutes a material omission for this purpose, and what is the applicable mental state regarding the affiant's failure to include that information?

NOTES ON THE INFORMER'S PRIVILEGE

1. In McCRAY v. ILLINOIS, 386 U.S. 300 (1967), petitioner was arrested and found to have heroin on his person. At the suppression hearing, the arresting officers testified that an informant who had supplied reliable information in about 20 previous cases told them that he had observed McCray selling narcotics at a certain corner and then accompanied them to that corner and pointed him out. Both officers were asked for the name and address of the informant, but objections to these questions were sustained. Petitioner's motion was denied, and he was subsequently convicted. The Court, per Stewart, J., affirmed:

"When the issue is not guilt or innocence, but, as here, the question of probable cause for an arrest or search, the Illinois Supreme Court has held that police officers need not invariably be required to disclose an informant's identity if

---

e. Rehnquist, J., joined by the Chief Justice, dissenting, argued: "If the function of the warrant requirement is to obtain the determination of a neutral magistrate as to whether sufficient grounds have been urged to support the issuance of a warrant, that function is fulfilled at the time the magistrate concludes that the requirement has been met."

the trial judge is convinced, by evidence submitted in open court and subject to cross-examination, that the officers did rely in good faith upon credible information supplied by a reliable informant. This Illinois evidentiary rule is consistent with the law of many other States. * * *

"The reasoning of the Supreme Court of New Jersey in judicially adopting the same basic evidentiary rule was instructively expressed by Chief Justice Weintraub in *State v. Burnett*, 201 A.2d 39 [N.J.1964]:

" 'If a defendant may insist upon disclosure of the informant in order to test the truth of the officer's statement that there is an informant or as to what the informant related or as to the informant's reliability, we can be sure that every defendant will demand disclosure. He has nothing to lose and the prize may be the suppression of damaging evidence if the State cannot afford to reveal its source, as is so often the case. And since there is no way to test the good faith of a defendant who presses the demand, we must assume the routine demand would have to be routinely granted. The result would be that the State could use the informant's information only as a lead and could search only if it could gather adequate evidence of probable cause apart from the informant's data. Perhaps that approach would sharpen investigatorial techniques, but we doubt that there would be enough talent and time to cope with crime upon that basis. Rather we accept the premise that the informer is a vital part of society's defensive arsenal. The basic rule protecting his identity rests upon that belief. * * *

" 'We must remember also that we are not dealing with the trial of the criminal charge itself. There the need for a truthful verdict outweighs society's need for the informer privilege. Here, however, the accused seeks to avoid the truth. The very purpose of a motion to suppress is to escape the inculpatory thrust of evidence in hand, not because its probative force is diluted in the least by the mode of seizure, but rather as a sanction to compel enforcement officers to respect the constitutional security of all of us under the Fourth Amendment. * * * If the motion to suppress is denied, defendant will still be judged upon the untarnished truth. * * *

" 'The Fourth Amendment is served if a judicial mind passes upon the existence of probable cause. Where the issue is submitted upon an application for a warrant, the magistrate is trusted to evaluate the credibility of the affiant in an *ex parte* proceeding. As we have said, the magistrate is concerned, not with whether the informant lied, but with whether the affiant is truthful in his recitation of what he was told. If the magistrate doubts the credibility of the affiant, he may require that the informant be identified or even produced. It seems to us that the same approach is equally sufficient where the search was without a warrant, that is to say, that it should rest entirely with the judge who hears the motion to suppress to decide whether he needs such disclosure as to the informant in order to decide whether the officer is a believable witness.' * * *

"[W]e are now asked to hold that the Constitution somehow compels Illinois to abolish the informer's privilege from its law of evidence, and to require disclosure of the informer's identity in every such preliminary hearing where it appears that the officers made the arrest or search in reliance upon facts supplied by an informer they had reason to trust . . . * * *

"Nothing in the Due Process Clause of the Fourteenth Amendment requires a state court judge in every such hearing to assume the arresting officers are committing perjury."

Douglas, J., joined by The Chief Justice, and Justices Brennan and Fortas, dissenting, objected: "There is no way to determine the reliability of Old Reliable, the informer, unless he is produced, at the trial and cross-examined."

2. Consider Irving Younger, *The Perjury Routine,* The Nation, May 8, 1967, pp. 596–97: "[The *McCray* majority] said that 'nothing in the Due Process Clause of the Fourteenth Amendment requires a state court judge in every such hearing to assume the arresting officers are committing perjury.' Why not? Every lawyer who practices in the criminal courts knows that police perjury is commonplace.

"The reason is not hard to find. Policemen see themselves as fighting a two-front war—against criminals in the street and against 'liberal' rules of law in court. All's fair in this war, including the use of perjury to subvert 'liberal' rules of law that might free those who 'ought' to be jailed. * * *

"Far from adopting a presumption of perjury, the *McCray* case almost guarantees wholesale police perjury. When his conduct is challenged as constituting an unreasonable search and seizure, all the policeman need say is that an unnamed 'reliable informant' told him that the defendant was committing a crime. Henceforth, every policeman will have a genie-like informer to legalize his master's arrests."

3. Consider *People v. Darden,* 313 N.E.2d 49 (N.Y.1974), concluding it is "fair and wise, in a case such as this, where there is insufficient evidence to establish probable cause apart from the testimony of the arresting officer as to communications received from an informer, when the issue of identity of the informer is raised at the suppression hearing, for the suppression judge then to conduct an in camera inquiry. The prosecution should be required to make the informer available for interrogation before the Judge. The prosecutor may be present but not the defendant or his counsel. Opportunity should be afforded counsel for defendant to submit in writing any questions which he may desire the Judge to put to the informer. The Judge should take testimony, with recognition of the special need for protection of the interests of the absent defendant, and make a summary report as to the existence of the informer and with respect to the communications made by the informer to the police to which the police testify. That report should be made available to the defendant and to the People and the transcript of testimony should be sealed to be available to the appellate courts if the occasion arises." Contra: *State v. Richardson,* 529 A.2d 1236 (Conn.1987): "Requiring an informant to attend an in camera hearing involves a substantial risk that his identity will be discovered."

MARYLAND v. PRINGLE
540 U.S. 366, 124 S.Ct. 795, 157 L.Ed.2d 769 (2003).

CHIEF JUSTICE REHNQUIST delivered the opinion of the Court. * * *

At 3:16 a.m. on August 7, 1999, a Baltimore County Police officer stopped a Nissan Maxima for speeding. There were three occupants in the car: Donte Partlow, the driver and owner, respondent Pringle, the front-seat passenger, and Otis Smith, the back-seat passenger. The officer asked Partlow for his license and registration. When Partlow opened the glove compartment to retrieve the vehicle registration, the officer observed a large amount of rolled-up money in the glove compartment. The officer returned to his patrol car with Partlow's license and registration to check the computer system for outstanding violations. The computer check did not reveal any violations. The officer returned to the stopped car, had Partlow get out, and issued him an oral warning.

After a second patrol car arrived, the officer asked Partlow if he had any weapons or narcotics in the vehicle. Partlow indicated that he did not. Partlow then consented to a search of the vehicle. The search yielded $763 from the glove compartment and five plastic glassine baggies containing cocaine from behind the back-seat armrest. When the officer began the search the armrest was in the upright position flat against the rear seat. The officer pulled down the armrest and found the drugs, which had been placed between the armrest and the back seat of the car.

The officer questioned all three men about the ownership of the drugs and money, and told them that if no one admitted to ownership of the drugs he was going to arrest them all. The men offered no information regarding the ownership of the drugs or money. All three were placed under arrest and transported to the police station.

Later that morning, Pringle * * * gave an oral and written confession in which he acknowledged that the cocaine belonged to him, that he and his friends were going to a party, and that he intended to sell the cocaine or "[u]se it for sex." Pringle maintained that the other occupants of the car did not know about the drugs, and they were released.

The trial court denied Pringle's motion to suppress his confession as the fruit of an illegal arrest, holding that the officer had probable cause to arrest Pringle. A jury convicted Pringle of possession with intent to distribute cocaine and possession of cocaine. He was sentenced to 10 years' incarceration without the possibility of parole. * * *

The Court of Appeals of Maryland, by divided vote, reversed, holding that, absent specific facts tending to show Pringle's knowledge and dominion or control over the drugs, "the mere finding of cocaine in the back armrest when [Pringle] was a front seat passenger in a car being driven by its owner is insufficient to establish probable cause for an arrest for possession." * * *

It is uncontested in the present case that the officer, upon recovering the five plastic glassine baggies containing suspected cocaine, had probable cause to believe a felony had been committed. The sole question is whether the officer had probable cause to believe that Pringle committed that crime.[1] * * *

The probable-cause standard is incapable of precise definition or quantification into percentages because it deals with probabilities and depends on the totality of the circumstances. We have stated, however, that "[t]he substance of all the definitions of probable cause is a reasonable ground for belief of guilt," and that the belief of guilt must be particularized with respect to the person to be searched or seized. * * *

In this case, Pringle was one of three men riding in a Nissan Maxima at 3:16 a.m. There was $763 of rolled-up cash in the glove compartment directly in front of Pringle.[2] Five plastic glassine baggies of cocaine were behind the back-seat armrest and accessible to all three men. Upon questioning, the three men failed to offer any information with respect to the ownership of the cocaine or the money.

We think it an entirely reasonable inference from these facts that any or all three of the occupants had knowledge of, and exercised dominion and control over, the cocaine. Thus a reasonable officer could conclude that there was probable cause to believe Pringle committed the crime of possession of cocaine, either solely or jointly.

Pringle's attempt to characterize this case as a guilt-by-association case is unavailing. His reliance on *Ybarra v. Illinois*, [p. 324], and *United States v. Di Re*,

---

1. Maryland law defines "possession" as "the exercise of actual or constructive dominion or control over a thing by one or more persons."

2. The Court of Appeals of Maryland dismissed the $763 seized from the glove compartment as a factor in the probable-cause determination, stating that "[m]oney, without more, is innocuous." The court's consideration of the money in isolation, rather than as a factor in the totality of the circumstances, is mistaken in light of our precedents. * * * We think it is abundantly clear from the facts that this case involves more than money alone.

[p. 394], is misplaced. In *Ybarra*, police officers obtained a warrant to search a tavern and its bartender for evidence of possession of a controlled substance. Upon entering the tavern, the officers conducted patdown searches of the customers present in the tavern, including Ybarra. Inside a cigarette pack retrieved from Ybarra's pocket, an officer found six tinfoil packets containing heroin. We stated:

> "[A] person's mere propinquity to others independently suspected of criminal activity does not, without more, give rise to probable cause to search that person. Where the standard is probable cause, a search or seizure of a person must be supported by probable cause particularized with respect to that person. This requirement cannot be undercut or avoided by simply pointing to the fact that coincidentally there exists probable cause to search or seize another or to search the premises where the person may happen to be."

We held that the search warrant did not permit body searches of all of the tavern's patrons and that the police could not pat down the patrons for weapons, absent individualized suspicion.

This case is quite different from *Ybarra*. Pringle and his two companions were in a relatively small automobile, not a public tavern. In *Wyoming v. Houghton*, [p. 393], we noted that "a car passenger—unlike the unwitting tavern patron in *Ybarra*—will often be engaged in a common enterprise with the driver, and have the same interest in concealing the fruits or the evidence of their wrongdoing." Here we think it was reasonable for the officer to infer a common enterprise among the three men. The quantity of drugs and cash in the car indicated the likelihood of drug dealing, an enterprise to which a dealer would be unlikely to admit an innocent person with the potential to furnish evidence against him.

In *Di Re*, a federal investigator had been told by an informant, Reed, that he was to receive counterfeit gasoline ration coupons from a certain Buttitta at a particular place. The investigator went to the appointed place and saw Reed, the sole occupant of the rear seat of the car, holding gasoline ration coupons. There were two other occupants in the car: Buttitta in the driver's seat and Di Re in the front passenger's seat. Reed informed the investigator that Buttitta had given him counterfeit coupons. Thereupon, all three men were arrested and searched. After noting that the officers had no information implicating Di Re and no information pointing to Di Re's possession of coupons, unless presence in the car warranted that inference, we concluded that the officer lacked probable cause to believe that Di Re was involved in the crime. We said "[a]ny inference that everyone on the scene of a crime is a party to it must disappear if the Government informer singles out the guilty person." No such singling out occurred in this case; none of the three men provided information with respect to the ownership of the cocaine or money.

We hold that the officer had probable cause to believe that Pringle had committed the crime of possession of a controlled substance. Pringle's arrest therefore did not contravene the Fourth and Fourteenth Amendments. Accordingly, the judgment of the Court of Appeals of Maryland is reversed, and the case is remanded for further proceedings not inconsistent with this opinion. * * *

NOTES AND QUESTIONS

1. Note that the "any or all three" and "solely or jointly" language makes it apparent that the Court has accepted *both* of the following propositions: (i) there is probable cause that the three men were jointly in possession of the drugs; and (ii) there is probable cause that Pringle alone was in possession of the drugs. Are you convinced as to both, one or neither?

2. On what basis can an inference of *sole* possession by Pringle be drawn? Can such an inference be squared with the common assertion that the "person

who owns or exercises dominion and control over a motor vehicle in which contraband is concealed, is deemed to possess the contraband," *Leavell v. Commonwealth*, 737 S.W.2d 695 (Ky.1987)? Is this because Partlow consented to the search that uncovered the cocaine? Because, as the Court notes at one point, there "was $763 of rolled-up cash in the glove compartment directly in front of Pringle"? Because, as the Court also notes, the hidden cocaine was "accessible to all three men"?

3. If drawing an inference of sole possession by Pringle is otherwise problematical, may it be said then that the point of *Pringle* is that when the presence of drugs has been established beyond question and it is a virtual certainty that the possession was by one of the three men in the vehicle at the time it was stopped, none of whom admitted possession, so that there is no clear basis for selecting one of the three to the exclusion of the two others, there is consequently a 33 1/3% possibility as to each of them, which should be deemed sufficient to establish probable cause as to each of them?

Is this branch of *Pringle* supported by *State v. Thomas,* 421 S.E.2d 227 (W.Va.1992), where police, investigating a sexual assault-murder apparently committed by one person acting alone, obtained separate search warrants to search the homes and cars of Mosier and Thomas, each of whom was known to have had contact with the victim on the night of her death and to fit the FBI psychological profile of a possible perpetrator of such crimes. As the court recognized, such facts starkly present this issue: "If the same facts can be used to implicate more than one person in a crime that could have been committed by one of them, can probable cause be found to exist?" Relying on the *Gates* assertion that no "numerically precise degree of certainty" is required to show probable cause, the *Thomas* court answered in the affirmative and thus upheld the search warrant which resulted in discovery of a minute portion of the victim's type of blood in defendant's car. Does the *Pringle* Court's assertion that the probable cause standard "is incapable of precise definition or quantification into percentages" manifest an acceptance or rejection of the *Thomas* approach, considering that such a version of probable cause was both championed and condemned in the various briefs in *Pringle* and was questioned as to its limits during oral argument of the case (e.g., as to what the outcome then would be if there were, say, 5 or 10 occupants of the vehicle)?

4. What then of the Court's alternative conclusion in *Pringle*, namely, that there was probable cause that the three occupants of the vehicle were in joint possession of the cocaine: "it was reasonable for the officer to infer a common enterprise among the three men" because the "quantity of drugs and cash in the car indicated the likelihood of drug dealing, an enterprise to which a dealer would be unlikely to admit an innocent person with the potential to furnish evidence against him"? Is such an inference more readily drawn in *Pringle*, where the drugs were not in view and it was unknown whether the drug dealing would occur 10 minutes, 10 hours, or 10 days in the future, as compared to *Di Re*, where the driver brought Di Re with him to the very place and time of the prearranged sale of counterfeit rationing coupons, which were in plain view in the vehicle (albeit perhaps not readily recognizable as contraband)? Can *Di Re* be distinguished on the basis of what *Pringle* calls the "singling out" of the guilty party, considering that *Di Re* itself only says that "Reed, on being asked [about the ration coupons in his hand], said he obtained them from Buttitta" but said nothing one way or another about Di Re?

5. Given the Court's conclusion that an inference of a "common enterprise" was permissible in *Pringle,* in what other situations is such an inference likewise permissible? Does the Court's reliance on *Houghton* mean *Pringle* is only a vehicle case, or does it also apply when drugs and money are uncovered in an apartment where three persons are present? Does the inference apply only when there is a "relatively small automobile," as the Court characterized the situation in *Pringle,* or also to SUVs, vans, and buses? Does it apply only when large sums of money and substantial quantities of drugs are *both* present? Also, what if in *Pringle* (a) the vehicle had been a taxi; (b) the vehicle was private but Pringle asserted he was a hitchhiker, which the other occupants did not dispute; or (c) the vehicle was private but Pringle asserted, without contradiction, that he was being driven home?

NOTES ON OTHER SOURCES OF PROBABLE CAUSE

The probable cause decisions of the United States Supreme Court, mostly concerned with when information from an informant, with or without some corroborating facts, is sufficient for arrest or search, are not fairly representative of the full range of probable cause issues confronted by the police. Consider these situations:

1. *Information from an alleged victim of, or witness to, a crime.* A major distinction between the victim-witness cases and the informant cases is that prior reliability need not be shown as to the former. As explained in *State v. Paszek,* 184 N.W.2d 836 (Wis.1971), "an ordinary citizen who reports a crime which has been committed in his presence, or that a crime is being or will be committed, stands on much different ground than a police informer. He is a witness to criminal activity who acts with an intent to aid the police in law enforcement because of his concern for society or for his own safety. He does not expect any gain or concession in exchange for his information. An informer of this type usually would not have more than one opportunity to supply information to the police, thereby precluding proof of his reliability by pointing to previous accurate information which he has supplied."

In the victim-witness cases, the critical question usually is whether the general description given by the victim or witness is sufficient to justify the arrest of any one person. For example, in *Brown v. United States,* 365 F.2d 976 (D.C.Cir.1966), the police received a radio report at 4:30 a.m. of a recent armed robbery, and were told to be on the lookout for a heavily built black male driving a maroon 1954 Ford. Shortly thereafter, 20 blocks from the robbery scene, the police saw what they thought to be such a car (actually, it was a 1952 Ford), and radioed for details about the robber. They were told that the robber was about five feet five inches, and that he was wearing a brown jacket and cream-colored straw hat. The suspect was about five feet eleven inches, was wearing blue, and had only a felt hat, but he was nonetheless arrested. Held: "These discrepancies, which can be the result of the victim's excitement or poor visibility or of the suspect's changing clothes, did not destroy the ascertainment made on the basis of the accurate portion of the identification, which was by itself enough to constitute probable cause."

2. *Direct observations by police.* Most troublesome, because the situations are so varied, are those cases in which the probable cause determination must be made solely upon suspicious conduct observed by police. For example, in *Brooks v. United States,* 159 A.2d 876 (D.C.Mun.App.1960), an officer observed two men, both known to have prior convictions for larceny, carrying a console-type record player in the commercial area at 6:30 p.m. The officer noted that the player was new and still bore store tags. Upon questioning, one of the suspects said the machine belonged to his mother and that he was taking it in to be repaired. When the officer pointed out the tags, the suspect changed his story and said that the machine had been given to him by an unknown person, whom he was unable to describe. The officer then placed the two men under arrest. The court, noting that "the probabilities must be measured by the standards of the reasonable, cautious and prudent peace officer as he sees them, and not those of the casual passerby," held that the officer had acted on probable cause.

What if the officer had not known of the suspects' past records? What if the suspects had refused to answer any questions? Or, what if the suspect had not changed his first story? If the officer had been aware of the fact that larcenies were common in that area, would this be relevant?[a] What if the suspects had taken flight upon being stopped? Cf. Note 4, p. 421. What if they had engaged in "furtive gestures" upon seeing the police? To what extent, if at all, should account be taken of the expertise of the police in ascertaining what is probably criminal conduct?[b]

3. *Information and orders from official channels.* In *Whiteley v. Warden,* 401 U.S. 560 (1971), Laramie, Wyoming police arrested two men fitting a description given in a police bulletin emanating from the office of the Carbon County Sheriff and transmitted over the state police radio network, indicating that the two described men were wanted for breaking and entering and that a warrant had been issued for their arrest. Although the warrant had not issued on probable cause, the state claimed that the arrests made by the Laramie officers were nonetheless legal because "they reasonably assumed that whoever authorized the bulletin had probable cause to direct Whiteley's and Daley's arrest." The Court, per Justice Harlan, disagreed: "We do not of course question that the Laramie police were entitled to act on the strength of the radio bulletin. Certainly police officers called upon to aid other officers in executing arrest warrants are entitled to assume that the officers requesting aid offered the magistrate the information requisite to support an independent judicial assessment of probable cause. Where, however, the contrary turns out to be true, an otherwise illegal arrest cannot be insulated from challenge by the decision of the instigating officer to rely on fellow officers to make the arrest."

4. *Collective knowledge.* Under the "collective knowledge doctrine," some courts have held probable cause may be established based upon the facts individually known to several officers working together, e.g., *United States v. Banks,* 514 F.3d 769 (8th Cir.2008) (probable cause to search, as searching officer knew gun in defendant's case and companion officer knew defendant a convicted felon, which made such possession illegal). Compare *United States v. Massenburg,* 654 F.3d 480 (4th Cir.2011), holding that the collective knowledge doctrine "does not permit us to aggregate bits and pieces of information from among myriad officers," even if they are all on the scene, for then "the legality of the search would depend solely on whether, after the fact, it turns out that the disparate pieces of information held by different officers added up to * * * probable cause."

---

a. Consider *United States v. Davis,* 458 F.2d 819 (D.C.Cir.1972): "Although no presumption of guilt arises from the activities of inhabitants of an area in which the police know that narcotics offenses frequently occur, the syndrome of criminality in those areas cannot realistically go unnoticed by the judiciary. It too is a valid consideration when coupled with other reliable indicia or suspicious circumstances. We make this statement warily, for it is all too clear that few live in these areas by choice."

Compare Jerome H. Skolnick, *Justice Without Trial* 217–18 (1966): "If an honest citizen resides in a neighborhood heavily populated by criminals, just as the chances are high that he might be one, so too are the chances high that he might be mistaken for one. The probabilities, from the point of view of the individual, are always the same—either he is or is not culpable. Thus, behavior which seems 'reasonable' to the police because of the character of the neighborhood is seen by the honest citizen in it as irresponsible and unreasonable. About *him,* more errors will necessarily be made under a 'reasonableness' standard."

b. Consider *Commonwealth v. Dunlap,* 941 A.2d 671 (Pa.2007) ("police training and experience, *without more,* is not a fact to be added to the quantum of evidence to determine if probable cause exists, but rather a 'lens' through which courts view the quantum of evidence observed at the scene").

SECTION 4. SEARCH WARRANTS

A. ISSUANCE OF THE WARRANT

1. *The "neutral and detached magistrate" requirement.* Consider *Coolidge v. New Hampshire*, 403 U.S. 443 (1971) (where State Attorney General, authorized by state law to issue search warrants as a justice of the peace, issued search warrant for defendant's car in course of murder investigation of which he had taken personal charge and for which he later served as chief prosecutor at trial, this procedure "violated a fundamental premise of both the Fourth and Fourteenth Amendments" because "the state official who was the chief investigator and prosecutor in this case * * * was not the neutral and detached magistrate required by the Constitution"); *Connally v. Georgia*, 429 U.S. 245 (1977) (search warrant not issued by a "neutral and detached magistrate" where issuing justice of the peace was unsalaried and, so far as search warrants were concerned, was paid a fee of $5 if he issued a warrant but nothing if he denied the application); *Rooker v. Commonwealth*, 508 S.W.2d 570 (Ky.App.1974) (in ruling that evidence obtained in execution of a search warrant must be suppressed, court held that where "a judge issues a search warrant based upon an affidavit which he does not read, he makes no determination of probable cause but merely serves as a rubber stamp for the police. Such action is improper even though the affidavit actually shows probable cause for the issuance of the warrant").

Compare *Shadwick v. City of Tampa*, 407 U.S. 345 (1972), where a unanimous Court, per Powell, J., upheld a city charter provision authorizing municipal court clerks to issue *arrest* warrants for municipal ordinance violations. Rejecting the notion "that all warrant authority must reside exclusively in a lawyer or judge" (and noting that "even within the federal system warrants were until recently widely issued by nonlawyers"), the Court concluded that "an issuing magistrate must meet two tests. He must be neutral and detached, and he must be capable of determining whether probable cause exists for the requested arrest or search." The clerk possesses the requisite detachment, as he "is removed from prosecutor or police and works within the judicial branch subject to the supervision of the municipal court judge."[a] As to capacity: "We presume from the nature of the clerk's position that he would be able to deduce from the facts on an affidavit before him whether there was probable cause to believe a citizen guilty of impaired driving, breach of peace, drunkenness, trespass or the multiple other common offenses covered by a municipal code. There has been no showing that this is too difficult a task for a clerk to accomplish. Our legal system has long entrusted nonlawyers to evaluate more complex and significant factual data than that in the case at hand. Grand juries daily determine probable cause prior to rendering indictments, and trial juries assess whether guilt is proved beyond a reasonable doubt." On the basis of *Shadwick*, could court clerks be authorized to issue arrest warrants in all cases? To issue search warrants? If so, can *Shadwick* be reconciled with *Leon*, p. 229?

In *United States v. Master*, 614 F.3d 236 (6th Cir.2010), the court held that because the Tennessee state judge who signed the search warrant in question lacked authority under state law to issue the warrant to be executed in another county, the search pursuant to this warrant consequently violated the Fourth Amendment. Can this be squared with *Virginia v. Moore*, p. 351?

---

a. Is the magistrate sufficiently detached from the police if it is his practice to assist the police in the preparation of search warrant affidavits? See *United States v. Steed*, 465 F.2d 1310 (9th Cir.1972); *Albitez v. Beto*, 465 F.2d 954 (5th Cir.1972). If he assists the police in execution of the warrant? See *Lo-Ji Sales, Inc. v. New York*, summarized at p. 233 fn. c.

United States v. Davis, 346 F.Supp. 435 (S.D.Ill.1972), involved these facts: A Treasury agent, accompanied by an assistant U.S. attorney, went to Magistrate Ghiglieri and presented an affidavit for a search warrant. The agent did not swear to the affidavit, but the magistrate dated and signed the affidavit and indicated that it was denied. The following day the agent, again accompanied by the assistant, went to Magistrate Giffin and presented the same affidavit. Giffin, after being apprised of the proceedings before Ghiglieri, issued a search warrant. The court found this procedure to be "highly improper" and concluded: "Magistrate Ghiglieri's decision was final and binding, and his denial of the application * * * equitably estopped Magistrate Giffin from issuing a search warrant on the exact same showing." Is this a desirable result, in that it limits magistrate-shopping? If the first magistrate was in error, what recourse should be open to the affiant-officer?

2.   *Particular description of the place to be searched.* As for the Fourth Amendment requirement of particularity in the description of the place to be searched, it "is enough if the description is such that the officer with a search warrant can, with reasonable effort ascertain and identify the place intended." *Steele v. United States,* 267 U.S. 498 (1925). The common practice is to identify premises in an urban area by street address, which is sufficient. Less particularity is required for rural premises; for example, description of a farm by the name of the owner and general directions for reaching the farm is adequate.

Most of the problems which arise concerning the particularity of description occur not because the warrant description is facially vague, but rather because upon execution it proves to be not as certain as theretofore assumed. One possibility is that the description will turn out not to be sufficiently precise, as where the warrant refers to apartment 3 in a certain building but the officers find apartments with that number on each floor. In this kind of case, courts are receptive to a showing that the executing officers had other information (e.g., the occupant's name), via the affidavit or otherwise, which made it apparent which place was intended.

Another type of case is that in which the executing officers find that some but not all of the descriptive facts fit the same place. Illustrative is *State v. Blackburn,* 511 P.2d 381 (Or.1973), where the apartment in a particular building was said to be apartment number 2 with "the letters ECURB on the door," but the officer found one apartment with the numeral 2 on the door and another with no numeral but the letters ECURB on the door. In upholding the search of the latter apartment, the court held that "there could be no real doubt as to which of the premises was intended" because "[n]o one could have made a mistake or been confused about a word like ECURB, but anyone could easily have made a mistake about a numeral."

In the absence of a probable cause showing as to all the separate living units in a multiple-occupancy structure, the warrant for such a building must describe the particular unit to be searched. But, if the building in question from its outward appearance would be taken to be a single-occupancy structure and neither the affiant nor other investigating officers nor the executing officers knew or had reason to know otherwise until execution of the warrant was under way, then the warrant is not defective for failure to specify a unit within the building.

A similar situation was involved in *Maryland v. Garrison,* 480 U.S. 79 (1987), where police obtained a search warrant to search the person of one McWebb and "the premises known as 2036 Park Avenue third floor apartment," but discovered only after uncovering contraband during execution that they were in respondent's separate apartment. The Court, per Stevens, J., concluded: (i) that the search warrant authorized search of the entire third floor but yet "was valid when it

issued," for such validity "must be assessed on the basis of the information that
the officers disclosed, or had a duty to discover and to disclose, to the issuing
magistrate"; (ii) that the execution of the search warrant was valid because "the
officers' failure to realize the overbreadth of the warrant was objectively understandable and reasonable." Blackmun, J., for the three dissenters, objected: (i)
that the search warrant did not authorize search of the entire third floor, but only
the apartment on that floor belonging to McWebb; and (ii) that the police knew
the building was a multiple-occupancy structure and should have known before
obtaining the search warrant and did know before executing it that there were
seven apartments in the 3–story building, and thus unreasonably assumed the
third floor was but one apartment.

3. *Particular description of the things to be seized.* The Fourth
Amendment requirement of particularity in the description of the persons[b] or
things to be seized is intended to prevent general searches, to prevent the seizure
of objects on the mistaken assumption that they fall within the magistrate's
authorization, and to prevent "the issuance of warrants on loose, vague or
doubtful bases of fact." *Go-Bart Importing Co. v. United States,* 282 U.S. 344
(1931). As noted in SEARCHSZR § 4.6:

"Consistent with these three purposes are certain general principles which
may be distilled from the decided cases in this area. They are: (1) A greater degree
of ambiguity will be tolerated when the police have done the best that could be
expected under the circumstances, by acquiring all the descriptive facts which
reasonable investigation of this type of crime could be expected to uncover and by
ensuring that all of those facts were included in the warrant.[19] (2) A more general
type of description will be sufficient when the nature of the objects to be seized
are such that they could not be expected to have more specific characteristics.[20] (3)
A less precise description is required of property which is, because of its particular
character, contraband. (4) Failure to provide all of the available descriptive facts is
not a basis for questioning the adequacy of the description when the omitted facts
could not have been expected to be of assistance to the executing officer.[22] (5) An
error in the statement of certain descriptive facts is not a basis for questioning the
adequacy of the description if the executing officer was nonetheless able to
determine, from the other facts provided, that the object seized was that intended
by the description.[23] (6) Greater care in description is ordinarily called for when
the type of property sought is generally in lawful use in substantial quantities.[24]
(7) A more particular description than otherwise might be necessary is required
when other objects of the same general classification are likely to be found at the
particular place to be searched.[25] (8) The greatest care in description is required

b. Search warrants are usually issued to search for and seize evidence of crimes, but are
sometimes issued to seek "a person to be arrested [see *Steagald v. United States,* p. 382] or a
person who is unlawfully restrained." Fed.R.Crim.P. 41(c)(4).

19. * * * Compare * * *United States v. Blakeney,* 942 F.2d 1001 (6th Cir.1991) ("jewelry"
insufficient where inventory available of what taken in jewelry store robbery) * * *.

20. * * * *State v. Salsman,* 290 A.2d 618 (N.H.1972) (description of 42 sheets of plywood
sufficient, "considering the nature of these items"). * * *

22. * * * *United States v. Scharfman,* 448 F.2d 1352 (2d Cir.1971) (any effort to describe
more particularly which furs in fur stores were stolen "would have required a legion of fur
experts" to execute the warrant).

23. *United States v. Rytman,* 475 F.2d 192 (5th Cir.1973) (compressor of described brand and
with serial number approximating that stated in the warrant could be seized); * * *

24. * * * *People v. Prall,* 145 N.E. 610 (Ill.1924) (thus description of "certain automobile tires
and tubes" insufficient); * * *

25. * * * *United States v. Cook,* 657 F.2d 730 (5th Cir.1981) ("cassettes onto which * * *
copyrighted films * * * have been electronically transferred" insufficient as to place with many
other cassettes). * * *

when the consequences of a seizure of innocent articles by mistake is most substantial, as when the objects to be seized are books or films or indicia of membership in an association, or where the place to be searched is an attorney's office. (9) The mere fact that some items were admittedly improperly seized in execution of the warrant 'does not mean that the warrant was not sufficiently particular.' (10) The Fourth Amendment's particularity requirement does *not* 'require particularity with respect to the criminal activity suspected.' (11) Some leeway will be tolerated where it appears additional time could have resulted in a more particularized description, where there was 'some urgency to conduct a search * * * before the defendant had the opportunity to remove or destroy the evidence' sought.''

In UNITED STATES v. BRADLEY, 644 F.3d 1213 (11th Cir.2011), the defendants "moved the district court to suppress the search of Bio–Med's head-quarters on the ground that the search was conducted pursuant to a warrant that was overbroad and lacking in particularity, in that it allowed the agents to seize, effectively, all personal and business files relating to Bio–Med's wholesale business from 1997 through 2002. The district court denied their motions under the 'perva-sive fraud doctrine,' [per *United States v. Sawyer*, 799 F.2d 1494 (11th Cir.1986), where] we upheld a warrant authorizing a seizure of all of the business records of an enterprise where evidence of fraudulent conduct obtained from twenty-five of the enterprise's customers 'made it probable that [the company] used identical deceptive and misleading sales techniques with other investors.' This 'pervasive fraud' doctrine, as it has come to be known, accordingly demands that we uphold an 'all records' search warrant where the affidavit supporting it demonstrates a 'pattern of illegal conduct' that is likely to extend beyond the conduct already in evidence and infect the rest of the company's business.

"The [defendants'] position is that the 'pervasive fraud' doctrine is inapplica-ble unless the Government alleges that the business in question is engaged almost exclusively in fraudulent business practices. As there is no dispute that the fraud complained of here represented only a small fraction of Bio–Med's legitimate business, the [defendants] claim that the district court erroneously denied their motion to suppress and allowed the seized evidence to be introduced in evidence at trial.

"But this is too narrow a reading of the 'pervasive fraud' doctrine. The district court correctly [concluded] that 'pervasive fraud' does not refer to the percentage of a defendant's business that is fraudulent. In other words, the doctrine is not concerned with how deeply the fraud runs. Rather, the 'pervasive fraud' doctrine addresses the extent to which fraud has permeated the scope of the defendant's business. That is, the doctrine is concerned with the breadth of the alleged fraud—whether evidence of fraud is likely to be found in records related to a wide range of company business.

"Here, that standard is easily met, as the alleged fraud supposedly infected Bio–Med, its principals and officers, its suppliers, and numerous other individuals and businesses with whom it did or had done business. As such, even though the fraud amounted to a small percentage of Bio–Med's overall business, traces of that fraud were likely to be found spread out amongst the myriad of records in Bio–Med's possession. * * *[96]''

---

96. We address here the "pervasive fraud" doctrine *only* as it applies to the seizure of business records, that is, records contained in a business location outside of a home. An "all records" search conducted within a home—a home business, for example, or where a defendant is known to keep business papers within the home—could be subject to more searching scrutiny. See, e.g., *United States v. Falon*, 959 F.2d 1143, 1148 (1st Cir.1992) ("On the other hand, when an individual's allegedly fraudulent business activities are centered in his home ... the 'all records' doctrine must be applied with caution.").

4. *Particular description, reliance on affidavit.* Courts have frequently been confronted with the question of whether a particularity defect in a warrant can be overcome by a sufficient description in the supporting affidavit, and the Supreme Court had occasion to deal with a rather unusual fact situation in this regard in GROH v. RAMIREZ, described at p. 240. On whether there had been a valid with-warrant search, the Court concluded:

"The fact that the *application* adequately described the 'things to be seized' does not save the *warrant* from its facial invalidity. The Fourth Amendment by its terms requires particularity in the warrant, not in the supporting documents. * * * And for good reason: 'The presence of a search warrant served a high function,' * * * and that high function is not necessarily vindicated when some other document, somewhere, says something about the objects of the search, but the contents of that document are neither known to the person whose home is being searched nor available for her inspection. We do not say that the Fourth Amendment forbids a warrant from cross-referencing other documents. Indeed, most Courts of Appeals have held that a court may construe a warrant with reference to a supporting application or affidavit if the warrant uses appropriate words of incorporation, and if the supporting document accompanies the warrant. * * * But in this case the warrant did not incorporate other documents by reference, nor did either the affidavit or the application * * * accompany the warrant. Hence, we need not further explore the matter of incorporation."

The Court in *Groh* then turned to the question of whether petitioner Groh was correct in asserting that the case was one in which it could be concluded a reasonable warrantless search was made because the search "was functionally equivalent to a search authorized by a valid warrant," in that "the goals served by the particularity requirement are otherwise satisfied." In examining that premise, the Court first considered the assertion that because the executing officers acted upon the basis of the sufficient description in the supporting documents, "the scope of the search did not exceed the limits set forth in the application." As to this, the Court concluded: "But unless the particular items described in the affidavit are also set forth in the warrant itself (or at least incorporated by reference, and the affidavit present at the search), there can be no written assurance that the Magistrate actually found probable cause to search for, and to seize, every item mentioned in the affidavit. * * * In this case, for example, it is at least theoretically possible that the Magistrate was satisfied that the search for weapons and explosives was justified by the showing in the affidavit, but not convinced that any evidentiary basis existed for rummaging through respondents' files and papers for receipts pertaining to the purchase or manufacture of such items. * * * Or, conceivably, the Magistrate might have believed that some of the weapons mentioned in the affidavit could have been lawfully possessed and therefore should not be seized. * * * The mere fact that the Magistrate issued a warrant does not necessarily establish that he agreed that the scope of the search should be as broad as the affiant's request." Two Justices disagreed on this branch of the case because "the more reasonable inference is that the Magistrate intended to authorize everything in the warrant application, as he signed the application and did not make any written adjustments to the application or the warrant itself."

Groh is an atypical case, quite unlike the usual case of this genre, and the majority seized upon its unique character as the fundamental reason for rejecting the contention that the search "was functionally equivalent to a search authorized by a valid warrant." "We disagree," the majority unequivocally responded, because the warrant "did not simply omit a few items from a list of many to be seized, or misdescribe a few of several items," nor "did it make what fairly could be characterized as a mere technical mistake or typographical error," but instead "did not describe the items to be seized *at all*." *Groh* thus covers the latter situation only, and leaves open the possibility that at least some of the other situations mentioned may justify affiant/executing officer reliance upon elaborating language in an unincorporated, unaccompanying affidavit.

5. *Neutrality, particularity, and "good faith."* Consider the impact of *United States v. Leon,* p. 229, and *Massachusetts v. Sheppard,* p. 239, in this context.

B. EXECUTION OF THE WARRANT

1. *Time of execution.* Statutes and court rules commonly provide that a search warrant must be executed within a certain time, such as 10 days. Execution within that time is proper, "provided that the probable cause recited in the affidavit continues until the time of execution, giving consideration to the intervening knowledge of the officers and the passage of time." *United States v. Nepstead,* 424 F.2d 269 (9th Cir.1970) (execution of warrant, for seizure of equipment used to manufacture LSD, 6 days after issuance timely, as premises under daily surveillance and no activity noted until after first 5 days).[c] Compare *State v. Neely,* 862 P.2d 1109 (Mont.1993) (where probable cause for search warrant not stale when it issued, warrant may be lawfully executed any time within 10–day statutory period); and consider the somewhat reverse situation in *State v. Miller,* 429 N.W.2d 26 (S.D.1988) (where violation of statutory 10–day rule but probable cause had not dissipated, suppression not necessary, as "the letter, not the spirit, of the law was broken").

In *United States v. Jones,* p. 279, the GPS tracking case, the concurrence noted: "In this case, the agents obtained a warrant, but they did not comply with two of the warrant's restrictions. They did not install the GPS device within the 10–day period required by the terms of the warrant and by Fed.R.Crim.P. 41(e)(2)(B)(i), and they did not install the GPS device within the District of Columbia, as required by the terms of the warrant and by 18 U.S.C. § 3117(a) and Rule 41(b)(4). In the courts below the Government did not argue, and has not argued here, that the Fourth Amendment does not impose those precise restrictions and that the violation of these restrictions does not demand the suppression of evidence obtained using the tracking device." What if the government *had* made such an argument, relying upon the assertion in *United States v. Gerber,* 994 F.2d 1556 (11th Cir.1993), "that completing a search shortly after the expiration of a search warrant does not rise to the level of a constitutional violation and cannot be the basis for suppressing evidence seized, so long as probable cause continues to exist, and the government does not act in bad faith"?

Also, in many jurisdictions a search warrant may be served only in the daytime unless it expressly states to the contrary, and a warrant so stating often can be obtained only by meeting special requirements—e.g., obtaining the concurrence of two magistrates, showing that the property is definitely in the place to be searched, or showing some need for prompt action. In *Gooding v. United States,* 416 U.S. 430 (1974), holding that the federal statute relating to searches for controlled substances required no special showing for a nighttime search other than that the contraband is likely to be on the property at that time, Justice Marshall, joined by Douglas and Brennan, JJ., noted in dissent that while the "constitutional question is not presented in this case and need not be resolved here," the principle that nighttime searches "involve a greater intrusion than ordinary searches and therefore require a greater justification * * * may well be a constitutional imperative. It is by now established Fourth Amendment doctrine

---

c. See also *United States v. Marin–Buitrago,* fn. d at p. 307.

that increasingly severe standards of probable cause are necessary to justify increasingly intrusive searches [citing *Camara v. Municipal Court*, p. 439]. In some situations—and the search of a private home during nighttime would seem to be a paradigm example—this principle requires a showing of additional justification for a search over and above the ordinary showing of probable cause."

In *United States v. Gervato*, 474 F.2d 40 (3d Cir.1973), the court emphasized the various protections provided by Fed.R.Crim.P. 41 in rejecting the district court's holding "that a search warrant executed in the absence of the occupant constitutes an unreasonable search because there exists the possibility of a general search and 'pilferage by officers of the law.'" So-called "sneak-and-peak" search warrants, authorizing police to enter premises, look around (e.g., to determine the status of a clandestine drug lab) and then depart without leaving any notice of the search, are deliberately executed when it is known no one is present. Given the Fourth Amendment requirement of notice of a search absent "some showing of special facts," *Berger v. New York*, p. 507, courts have imposed two limitations on such warrants: (i) "the court should not allow the officers to dispense with advance or contemporaneous notice of the search unless they have made a showing of reasonable necessity for the delay"; and (ii) "the court should nonetheless require the officers to give the appropriate person notice of the search within a reasonable time of the covert entry." *United States v. Villegas*, 899 F.2d 1324 (2d Cir.1990). Consider the treatment of the delayed notice search warrant in the PATRIOT Act, as amended in 2006, 18 U.S.C.A. § 3103a, App. B.

2. *Gaining entry.* In *Wilson v. Arkansas*, 514 U.S. 927 (1995), a unanimous Court, per Thomas, J., proceeded "to resolve the conflict among the lower courts" by holding that the common law doctrine which "recognized a law enforcement officer's authority to break open the doors of a dwelling, but generally indicated that he first ought to announce his presence and authority," "forms a part of the reasonableness inquiry under the Fourth Amendment." The Court cautioned that the "Fourth Amendment's flexible requirement of reasonableness should not be read to mandate a rigid rule of announcement that ignores countervailing law enforcement interests," for "the common-law principle of announcement was never stated as an inflexible rule."

In RICHARDS v. WISCONSIN, 520 U.S. 385 (1997), a unanimous Court, per Stevens, J., rejected the state supreme court's holding that police officers are *never* required to knock and announce their presence when executing a search warrant in a felony drug investigation. The Court had "two serious concerns": (i) "the exception contains considerable overgeneralization," as "while drug investigation frequently does pose special risks to officer safety and the preservation of evidence, not every drug investigation will pose these risks to a substantial degree"; and (ii) "the reasons for creating an exception in one category can, relatively easily, be applied to others. Armed bank robbers, for example, are, by definition, likely to have weapons, and the fruits of their crime may be destroyed without too much difficulty."

"In order to justify a 'no-knock' entry, the police must have a reasonable suspicion that knocking and announcing their presence, under the particular circumstances, would be dangerous or futile, or that it would inhibit the effective investigation of the crime by, for example, allowing the destruction of evidence.[d] This standard—as opposed to a probable cause requirement—strikes the appropriate balance between the legitimate law enforcement concerns at issue in the execution of search warrants and the individual privacy interests affected by no-

---

d. In *United States v. Ramirez*, 523 U.S. 65 (1998), the Court, per Rehnquist, C.J., unanimously held that whether the *Richards* reasonable suspicion test has been met "depends in no way on whether police must destroy property in order to enter."

knock entries. * * * This showing is not high, but the police should be required to make it whenever the reasonableness of a no-knock entry is challenged."

The Court concluded with two additional points: (1) The trial judge had correctly concluded that the police were excused from the knock-and-announce requirement because of the facts of the particular case. The officer who knocked at the door of defendant's hotel room claimed to be a maintenance man, defendant opened the door slightly and upon seeing a uniformed officer slammed the door, at which the police kicked the door in and entered. As the Court explained, once "the officers reasonably believed that Richards knew who they were * * * it was reasonable for them to force entry immediately given the disposable nature of the drugs." (2) The refusal of the magistrate issuing the search warrant to issue a no-knock warrant[e] did not alter this conclusion, as "a magistrate's decision not to authorize a no-knock entry should not be interpreted to remove the officers authority to exercise independent judgment concerning the wisdom of a no-knock entry at the time the warrant is being executed."

In light of the test set out in *Richards*, which of the following bits of information would justify an unannounced entry to execute a search warrant for drugs: (a) that the small amount of narcotics was always kept near a toilet; (b) that there was but a small amount of drugs; (c) that there was an unknown quantity of drugs; (d) that the person who planned to sell the drugs was present; (e) that the person who used the drugs was present; (f) that a person whose relationship to the drugs was unknown was present?

In UNITED STATES v. BANKS, 540 U.S. 31 (2003), a unanimous Court, per Souter, J., decided two issues regarding the *Wilson* notice requirement: (i) how long a wait is necessary before the police may reasonably conclude they have been refused admittance; and (ii) what shorter wait will suffice because of what kind of exigent circumstances. As to the first, the Court declared that in the absence of exigent circumstances, the issue is simply whether the occupant's "failure to admit [the police] fairly suggested a refusal to let them in," which means the question would be whether it reasonably appeared to the police that "an occupant has had time to get to the door." This judgment, the Court emphasized, is to be made upon the facts known by the police at the time (so that it would not be relevant that, as in *Banks*, the occupant "was actually in the shower and did not hear the officers"). The amount of time needed would vary, the Court added, depending on "the size of the establishment," as it would take "perhaps five seconds to open a motel room door, or several minutes to move through a townhouse." But, the Court cautioned, "in the case with no reason to suspect an immediate risk of frustration or futility in waiting at all, the reasonable wait time may well be longer when police make a forced entry, since they ought to be more certain the occupant has had time to answer the door."

But, as to the second question, where "the police claim exigent need to enter" and such claim is deemed legitimate when assessed under essentially "the same criteria" that apply to whether announcement is excused under *Richards,* then the "crucial fact" is "not time to reach the door but the particularly exigency claimed." The risk in *Banks*, re execution of a search warrant at Banks's apartment for cocaine, was that once the police announced their authority and

---

e. Wisconsin is among those few jurisdictions specifically authorizing magistrates to issue such search warrants, allowing entry without prior announcement, upon a sufficient showing to the magistrate of a need to do so. A "reverse twist" on the *Richards* view regarding a magistrate's *refusal* to issue such a warrant is the position, stated in *Parsley v. Superior Court*, 513 P.2d 611 (Cal.1973), that a magistrate's *issuance* of such a warrant is of no effect because "unannounced entry is excused only on the basis of exigent circumstances existing at the time an officer approached a site to make an arrest or execute a warrant," and thus "can be judged only in light of circumstances of which the officer is aware at the latter moment."

purpose, the defendant would attempt to "flush away the easily disposable cocaine," which the Court concluded made it "reasonable to suspect imminent loss of evidence" after the 15–20 second wait. This was because such a lapse of time would suffice "for getting to the bathroom or the kitchen to start flushing cocaine down the drain," considering that "a prudent dealer will keep [the drugs] near a commode or kitchen sink," and also that the warrant was being executed "during the day, when anyone inside would probably have been up and around." The Court added that "since the bathroom and kitchen are usually in the interior of a dwelling, not the front hall, there is no reason generally to peg the travel time to the location of the door, and no reliable basis for giving the proprietor of a mansion a longer wait than the resident of a bungalow, or an apartment like Banks's." Moreover, once "the exigency had matured, * * * the officers were not bound to learn anything more or wait any longer before going in, even though their entry entailed some harm to the building."

3. **Search of persons on the premises.** On the basis of information from an informant that he had frequently and recently observed tinfoil packets of heroin behind the bar and on the person of the bartender of a certain tavern and that the bartender told him he would that day have heroin for sale, a warrant authorizing search of the tavern and bartender for heroin was issued. The warrant was executed during the late afternoon by 7–8 officers, who proceeded to pat down each of the 9–13 customers then present. A cigarette package was located and retrieved from customer Ybarra's pocket, and tinfoil packets of heroin were found therein. State courts held the heroin admissible because found in a search authorized by a statute[f] deemed constitutional as applied in the instant case. In YBARRA v. ILLINOIS, 444 U.S. 85 (1979), the Court, in a 6–3 decision, reversed. Stewart, J., for the majority, stated:

"There is no reason to suppose that, when the search warrant was issued on March 1, 1976, the authorities had probable cause to believe that any person found on the premises of the Aurora Tap Tavern, aside from [bartender] 'Greg,' would be violating the law. The Complaint for Search Warrant did not allege that the bar was frequented by persons illegally purchasing drugs. It did not state that the informant had ever seen a patron of the tavern purchase drugs from 'Greg' or from any other person. Nowhere, in fact, did the complaint even mention the patrons of the Aurora Tap Tavern.

"Not only was probable cause to search Ybarra absent at the time the warrant was issued; it was still absent when the police executed the warrant. Upon entering the tavern, the police did not recognize Ybarra and had no reason to believe that he had committed, was committing or was about to commit any offense under state or federal law. Ybarra made no gestures indicative of criminal conduct, made no movements that might suggest an attempt to conceal contraband, and said nothing of a suspicious nature to the police officers. * * *

"It is true that the police possessed a warrant based on probable cause to search the tavern in which Ybarra happened to be at the time the warrant was executed. But, a person's mere propinquity to others independently suspected of criminal activity does not, without more, give rise to probable cause to search that person. * * *[7]"

---

f. This statute, Ill.Comp.Stat. ch. 725, § 5/108–9, reads: "In the execution of the warrant the person executing the same may reasonably detain to search any person in the place at the time: (a) To protect himself from attack, or (b) To prevent the disposal or concealment of any instruments, articles or things particularly described in the warrant."

7. [W]e need not consider situations where the warrant itself authorizes the search of unnamed persons in a place and is supported by probable cause to believe that persons who will be in the place at the time of the search will be in possession of illegal drugs.

As for the state's claim "that the first patdown search of Ybarra constituted a reasonable frisk for weapons under the doctrine of *Terry v. Ohio*," p. 408, the Court responded that the frisk was "not supported by a reasonable belief that he was armed and presently dangerous, a belief which this Court has invariably held must form the predicate to a patdown of a person for weapons. * * * Upon seeing Ybarra, [the police] neither recognized him as a person with a criminal history nor had any particular reason to believe that he might be inclined to assault them. Moreover, as police agent Johnson later testified, Ybarra, whose hands were empty, gave no indication of possessing a weapon, made no gestures or other actions indicative of an intent to commit an assault, and acted generally in a manner that was not threatening."

Emphasizing "the ease with which the evidence of narcotics possession may be concealed or moved around from person to person," the State next contended that the *Terry* standard "should be made applicable to aid the evidence-gathering function of the search warrant." The Court answered: "The 'long prevailing' constitutional standard of probable cause embodies 'the best compromise that has been found for accommodating the [ ] often opposing interests' in 'safeguard[ing] citizens from rash and unreasonable interferences with privacy' and in 'seek[ing] to give fair leeway for enforcing the law in the community's protection.'"

Rehnquist, J., for the dissenters, reasoned that the *Terry* individualized suspicion standard, "important in the case of an on-the-street stop, where the officer must articulate some reason for singling the person out of the general population," was of "less significance in the present situation" for two reasons: (i) "in place of the requirement of 'individualized suspicion' as a guard against arbitrary exercise of authority, we have here the determination of a neutral and detached magistrate that a search was necessary"; and (ii) "the task performed by the officers executing a search warrant is inherently more perilous than is a momentary encounter on the street."

In *Los Angeles County v. Rettele*, 550 U.S. 609 (2007), police obtained two search warrants to search the persons and homes of four black suspects connected with a fraud and identity-theft crime ring, one of whom owned a registered handgun. In executing one of the warrants at 7:15 a.m., police found Rettele and his girlfriend Sadler (both white) in bed and, despite their objections that they were naked, required them to get out of bed and stand there one or two minutes before dressing. Police soon determined they had made a mistake, in that Rettele had recently purchased the home and was not connected with the suspects being sought. Regarding the § 1983 action brought as a consequence of the raid, the Supreme Court, per curiam, ruled: (1) that the court of appeals was in error in concluding the police should not have proceeded upon finding white occupants, as "it is not uncommon in our society for people of different races to live together" and such persons "might * * * engage in joint criminal activity"; and (2) that the "orders by the police to the occupants * * * were permissible, and perhaps necessary, to protect the safety of the deputies," as "[b]lankets and bedding can conceal a weapon, and one of the suspects was known to own a firearm," and the "deputies needed a moment to secure the room and ensure that other persons were not close by or did not present a danger," and thus "were not required to turn their backs to allow Rettele and Sadler to retrieve clothing or to cover themselves with the sheets."

4. *Detention of persons on the premises.* MICHIGAN v. SUMMERS, 452 U.S. 692 (1981), involved these facts: "As Detroit police officers were about to execute a warrant to search a house for narcotics, they encountered respondent descending the front steps. They requested his assistance in gaining entry and detained him while they searched the premises. After finding narcotics in the basement and ascertaining that respondent owned the house, the police arrested him, searched his person, and found in his coat pocket an envelope containing 8.5 grams of heroin." The Court, per Stevens, J., upheld the seizure on the basis of the principle derived from *Terry* and related cases, namely, that "some seizures * * * constitute such limited intrusions on the personal security of those detained and are justified by such substantial law enforcement interests that they may be made on less than probable cause, so long as police have an articulable basis for suspecting criminal activity":

"Of prime importance in assessing the intrusion is the fact that the police had obtained a warrant to search respondent's house for contraband. A neutral and detached magistrate had found probable cause to believe that the law was being violated in that house and had authorized a substantial invasion of the privacy of the persons who resided there. The detention of one of the residents while the premises were searched, although admittedly a significant restraint on his liberty, was surely less intrusive than the search itself. Indeed, we may safely assume that most citizens—unless they intend flight to avoid arrest—would elect to remain in order to observe the search of their possessions. Furthermore, the type of detention imposed here is not likely to be exploited by the officer or unduly prolonged in order to gain more information, because the information the officers seek normally will be obtained through the search and not through the detention. Moreover, because the detention in this case was in respondent's own residence, it could add only minimally to the public stigma associated with the search itself and would involve neither the inconvenience nor the indignity associated with a compelled visit to the police station. * * *

"In assessing the justification for the detention of an occupant of premises being searched for contraband pursuant to a valid warrant, both the law enforcement interest and the nature of the 'articulable facts' supporting the detention are relevant. Most obvious is the legitimate law enforcement interest in preventing flight in the event that incriminating evidence is found. Less obvious, but sometimes of greater importance, is the interest in minimizing the risk of harm to the officers. Although no special danger to the police is suggested by the evidence in this record, the execution of a warrant to search for narcotics is the kind of transaction that may give rise to sudden violence or frantic efforts to conceal or destroy evidence. The risk of harm to both the police and the occupants is minimized if the officers routinely exercise unquestioned command of the situation. Finally, the orderly completion of the search may be facilitated if the occupants of the premises are present. Their self-interest may induce them to open locked doors or locked containers to avoid the use of force that is not only damaging to property but may also delay the completion of the task at hand.

"It is also appropriate to consider the nature of the articulable and individualized suspicion on which the police base the detention of the occupant of a home subject to a search warrant. We have already noted that the detention represents only an incremental intrusion on personal liberty when the search of a home has been authorized by a valid warrant. The existence of a search warrant, however, also provides an objective justification for the detention. A judicial officer has determined that police have probable cause to believe that someone in the home is committing a crime. Thus a neutral magistrate rather than an officer in the field has made the critical determination that the police should be given a special authorization to thrust themselves into the privacy of a home. The connection of an occupant to that home gives the police officer an easily identifiable and certain basis for determining that suspicion of criminal activity justifies a detention of that occupant."

Stewart, J., joined by Brennan and Marshall, JJ., dissenting, objected that *Terry* and related cases required "some governmental interest independent of the ordinary interest in investigating crime and apprehending suspects," which was not present here, and also that the majority's "view that the detention here is of the limited, unintrusive sort" required under *Terry* was in error, as "a detention 'while a proper search is being conducted' can mean a detention of several hours."

In *Muehler v. Mena*, 544 U.S. 93 (2005), a § 1983 case involving execution of a search warrant for deadly weapons and evidence of gang membership at a home where police believed at least one member of a gang involved in a recent drive-by shooting lived, Ms. Mena and three other occupants were detained in handcuffs for the entire 2–3 hours of the search. The 5–Justice majority, per Rehnquist, C.J., though conceding that the handcuffing made the detention "more intrusive than that which we upheld in *Summers*," concluded that such action "was reasonable because the governmental interests outweighed the marginal intrusion," for in "such inherently dangerous situations, the use of handcuffs minimizes the risk of harm to both officers and occupants" and was "all the more reasonable" because of "the need to detain multiple occupants." One of the five, Kennedy, J., added two cautions in a separate concurrence: (1) "If the search extends to the point when the handcuffs can cause real pain or discomfort, provision must be made to alter the conditions of detention at least long enough to attend to the needs of the detainee"; and (2) the restraint should "be removed if, at any point during the search, it would be readily apparent to any objectively reasonable officer that removing the handcuffs would not compromise the officers' safety or risk interference or substantial delay in the execution of the search," not so in the instant case given that "the detainees outnumber[ed] those supervising them, and this situation could not be remedied without diverting officers from an extensive, complex, and time-consuming search." In a separate concurrence by the four other Justices (agreeing with the majority's other point, that under *Caballes*, p. 428, it was not objectionable that during the detention police questioned Ms. Mena on an unrelated matter, her immigration status), it was contended that the following considerations showed "that the jury could properly have found that this 5–foot–2–inch young lady posed no threat to the officers at the scene": "the cuffs kept [her] arms behind her for two to three hours" notwithstanding the fact that because they were "real uncomfortable" she had "asked the officers to remove them," "[n]o contraband was found in her room or on her person," there "were no indications * * * she was or ever had been a gang member," she "was unarmed" and "fully cooperated with the officers," she "was not suspected of any crime and was not a person targeted by the search warrant," and "lack of resources" was apparently not a problem since "there were 18 officers at the scene."

    5. *Intensity and duration of the search.* Although a search under a search warrant may extend to all parts of the premises described in the warrant, it does not follow that the executing officers may look everywhere within the described premises; they may only look where the items described in the warrant might be concealed. For example, if a search warrant indicated that the items sought were stolen television sets, the officer would not be authorized to rummage through desk drawers and other places too small to hold these items. Once the items named in the search warrant have been found, the search must cease.

    6. *Seizure of items not named in the search warrant.* In HORTON v. CALIFORNIA, 496 U.S. 128 (1990), a police officer's affidavit established probable cause to search defendant's home for the proceeds of a robbery (including three specified rings) and for the weapons used in that robbery, but the magistrate issued a warrant only for the proceeds. They were not found in execution of the warrant, but the guns were; they were seized. The defendant claimed this seizure did not come within Justice Stewart's plurality decision in *Coolidge v. New Hampshire*, 403 U.S. 443 (1971), that items found in "plain view" may be seized "where it is immediately apparent to the police that they have evidence before them," because he also required "that the discovery of evidence in plain view must be inadvertent." The Court in *Horton,* per Stevens, J., disagreed, finding "two flaws" in the reasoning underlying the latter requirement: "First, evenhanded law enforcement is best achieved by the application of objective standards of conduct, rather than standards that depend upon the subjective state of mind of the officer. The fact that an officer is interested in an item of evidence and fully expects to find it in the course of a search should not invalidate its seizure if the search is confined in area and duration by the terms of a warrant or a valid exception to the warrant requirement. If the officer has knowledge approaching certainty that the item will be found, we see no reason why he or she would deliberately omit a particular description of the item to be seized from the application for a search warrant. Specification of the additional item could only permit the officer to expand the scope of the search. On the other hand, if he or she has a valid warrant to search for one item and merely a suspicion concerning the second, whether or not it amounts to probable cause, we fail to see why that suspicion should immunize the second item from seizure if it is found during a lawful search for the first. * * *

"Second, the suggestion that the inadvertence requirement is necessary to prevent the police from conducting general searches, or from converting specific warrants into general warrants, is not persuasive because that interest is already served by the requirements that no warrant issue unless it 'particularly describ[es] the place to be searched and the persons or things to be seized,' and that a warrantless search be circumscribed by the exigencies which justify its initiation. Scrupulous adherence to these requirements serves the interests in limiting the area and duration of the search that the inadvertence requirement inadequately protects. Once those commands have been satisfied and the officer has a lawful right of access, however, no additional Fourth Amendment interest is furthered by requiring that the discovery of evidence be inadvertent. If the scope of the search exceeds that permitted by the terms of a validly issued warrant or the character of the relevant exception from the warrant requirement, the subsequent seizure is unconstitutional without more."

In determining whether the discovered article is incriminating in nature, how carefully may the police examine it? See *Stanley v. Georgia,* 394 U.S. 557 (1969) (obscene films suppressed where police found reels of film while searching for gambling paraphernalia and then viewed the film on a projector and screen found in another room); cf. *Arizona v. Hicks,* p. 368; and compare *State v. Ruscoe,* 563 A.2d 267 (Conn.1989) (where in executing warrant for silver "candlesticks, napkin holders and a silver mug" police moved a TV, 2 VCR's and a tape deck and noticed they without serial numbers, this a lawful discovery under *Hicks,* as "the police moved items in the course of searching for items listed in the warrant").

7. *Presence of third parties.* Police executing search warrants are sometimes accompanied by others. The most common situation was noted in *Wilson v. Layne,* 526 U.S. 603 (1999): "Where the police enter a home under the authority of a warrant to search for stolen property, the presence of third parties for the purpose of identifying the stolen property has long been approved by this Court and our common-law tradition." But in *Wilson,* which involved execution of an *arrest* warrant within premises, the police were accompanied by a reporter and a photographer from the Washington Post. Citing such cases as *Summers,* p. 325, and *Horton,* p. 327, in support of the proposition that the Fourth Amendment requires "that police actions in execution of a warrant be related to the objectives of the authorized intrusion," a unanimous Court concluded the presence of members of the media was unconstitutional because it "was not in aid of the execution of the warrant." Had the media representatives been present during execution of a *search* warrant, would any evidence first discovered by them be inadmissible? Would all the evidence found by the police be inadmissible? In

Wilson, which was a § 1983 case, the Court, speaking of the media presence, dropped this footnote: "Even though such actions might violate the Fourth Amendment, if the police are lawfully present, the violation of the Fourth Amendment is the presence of the media and not the presence of the police in the home. We have no occasion here to decide whether the exclusionary rule would apply to any evidence discovered or developed by the media representatives."

8. *Delivery of warrant.* Many jurisdictions have statutes or court rules declaring that an officer executing a search warrant must deliver a copy of the warrant at the place searched; see, e.g., Fed.R.Crim.P. 41(d), App. C. Although it had often been assumed that these provisions were not grounded in the Fourth Amendment, the Supreme Court in *Groh v. Ramirez*, p. 240, indicated otherwise. In rejecting Groh's claim that what had occurred was a reasonable warrantless search because the goals of the warrant process had been "otherwise satisfied," the Court gave as an added reason the fact that yet another purpose of the particularity requirement—that it "also 'assures the individual whose property is searched or seized of the lawful authority of the executing officer, his need to search, and the limits of his power to search' "—had not been met. The unstated conclusion in *Groh* apparently is that the Fourth Amendment was violated when the police handed over at the conclusion of the search[g] a copy of a warrant that did not in fact specify the things to be seized.

C. SPECIAL PROBLEMS: COMPUTER SEARCHES

1. Police are with increasing frequency using search warrants to seek information stored on computers, giving rise to special problems. For example, as noted in *State v. Evers*, 815 A.2d 432 (N.J.2003), computers "are in use in both homes and businesses, and, with the advent of the laptop, in almost every other conceivable place. Business people and students leave their homes with laptops, use them at other locations, and return home with them." To what extent does this affect what *place* has a sufficient nexus with the sought computer to be specified as the place to be searched for it? For example, in *Evers*, where a detective's search warrant affidavit indicated that after entering a child porn chat room he received an e-mail of child porn from a sender with a certain screen name, for which AOL provided the billing address, may a valid warrant issue for *that* address?

2. How should a warrant authorizing a computer search describe the things to be seized? Consider *United States v. Riccardi*, 405 F.3d 852 (10th Cir.2005), where, in executing a warrant at defendant's home for material relating to child pornography, police noted the presence of a computer and got a second warrant for the computer, listing the items to be seized as the target computer "and all electronic and magnetic media stored therein, together with all storage devises

---

g. The Court did say that the Fourth Amendment does *not* require "serving the warrant on the owner before commencing the search," but went on to caution that it was not decided whether "it would be unreasonable to refuse a request to furnish the warrant at the outset of the search when, as in this case, an occupant of the premises is present and poses no threat to the officers' safe and effective performance of their mission."

In *United States v. Grubbs*, p. 306, also concerning whether the "triggering condition" for an anticipatory warrant must be listed in the warrant so as to give notice to the occupant, the Court noted "[t]he absence of a constitutional requirement that the warrant be exhibited at the outset of the search, or indeed until the search has ended."

When property is seized pursuant to a warrant, there is also a *due process* requirement that police "take reasonable steps to give notice that the property has been taken so that the owner can pursue remedies for the return," which can be met when no one is present by leaving a "notice of service" with a list of the property seized attached. *City of West Covina v. Perkins,* 525 U.S. 234 (1999).

[sic], internal or external to the computer or computer system, * * * and all electronic media stored within such devices."

3. In *Riccardi*, could the computer's contents simply have been examined at the scene during execution of the *first* warrant, even though a computer was not mentioned in the warrant? Compare *United States v. Hudspeth*, 459 F.3d 922 (8th Cir.2006) (yes as to warrant authorizing search of business for "any and all" business records of various types but not specifying computer records, as "[i]n this computer age, a warrant to search business records logically and reasonably includes a search of computer data"). Or, could the computer (even if not itself recognized as an instrumentality or fruit of any crime) have been seized and removed from the scene for the purpose of having its contents more thoroughly examined elsewhere? See *People v. Gall*, 30 P.3d 145 (Colo.2001) ("not only authorized but preferred * * * where 'the sorting out of the described items from the intermingled undescribed items would take so long that it is less intrusive merely to take that entire group of items to another location and do the sorting there.' * * * In addition to the problems of volume and commingling, the sorting of technological documents may require a search to be performed at another location 'because that action requires a degree of expertise beyond that of the executing officers,' not only to find the documents but to avoid destruction or oversearching"). Assuming lawful seizure and removal of the computer, must it be searched in a timely fashion? Consider *United States v. Gregoire*, 638 F.3d 962 (8th Cir.2011) (1–year delay does not require suppression; "To the extent [defendant] complains of interference with his possessory interest in the laptop, Rule 41(g) of the Federal Rules of Criminal Procedure provides a remedy he did not invoke"); cf. *United States v. Johns*, p. 390.

4. In *Gall*, the police then obtained a second warrant before searching the computer. Was that step necessary, considering that the practice is not to get a second warrant when filing cabinets are seized for purposes of searching them elsewhere for the documents described in the search warrant, e.g., *United States v. Hargus*, 128 F.3d 1358 (10th Cir.1997)? Is the answer yes because "a computer is not truly analogous to a single closed container or conventional file cabinet, even a locked one," but instead "is the digital equivalent of its owner's home, capable of holding a universe of private information." *State v. Rupnick*, 125 P.3d 541 (Kan.2005). Or, is that conclusion inconsistent with the reason stated in *Gall* for permitting search of the computer in the first place?

5. Could the agents in *Riccardi* have avoided all those issues if, when they discovered the computer not named in the warrant, they simply copied the hard drive for later examination elsewhere, as is common practice? Does this constitute Fourth Amendment activity? Consider that in *Arizona v. Hicks*, p. 368, the Court declared that "the mere recording of the serial numbers did not constitute a seizure" because it "did not 'meaningfully interfere' with respondent's possessory interest," and presumably would have said the same thing about subsequent police reexamination of their copy of the serial numbers. Is *Hicks* distinguishable? Consider Orin S. Kerr, *Fourth Amendment Seizures of Computer Data*, 119 Yale L.J. 700, 709 (2010) ("electronic copying by the government ordinarily constitutes a Fourth Amendment seizure. The reason is that the Fourth Amendment power to seize is the power to freeze. That is, the seizure power is the power to hold the crime scene and control evidence. Generating an electronic copy of data freezes that data for future use just like taking physical property freezes it: it adds to the amount of evidence under the government's control"); Josh Goldfoot, *The Physical Computer and the Fourth Amendment*, 16 Berkeley J.Crim.L. 112, 113 (2011) ("views storage media as physical evidence. Under this perspective, a hard drive is an object not a place. It does not contain things; it is one thing. Like any other physical evidence, it is examined, not 'searched.' So long as a storage medium is lawfully seized, the Fourth Amendment does not restrict forensic examination'').

6. Given that execution of a search warrant must be limited in intensity according to the items named in the warrant, what does this mean in the context of a computer search? For example, is it proper for the search for specific textual files to go beyond use of the "key word" search technique? Compare *United States v. Comprehensive Drug Testing, Inc.*, 513 F.3d 1085 (9th Cir.2008), on rehearing, 621 F.3d 1162 (9th Cir.2010); with *Commonwealth v. McDermott*, 864 N.E.2d 471 (Mass.2007). Where the warrant authorizes search of computer files for specified documentary evidence, may the executing officer open files with a .jpg suffix? Compare *United States v. Carey*, 172 F.3d 1268 (10th Cir.1999); with *United States v. Gray*, 78 F.Supp.2d 524 (E.D.Va.1999). If so, doesn't this mean that the usual intensity limits on search warrant execution "offer less protection against invasive computer searches" and "allow warrants that are particular on their face to become general warrants in practice"? Orin Kerr, *Searches and Seizures in a Digital World*, 119 Harv.L.Rev. 531, 565 (2005).

Does this mean that computer search warrants must instruct *how* the search is to be conducted by, e.g., mandating that certain advanced technological search engines be used or that a specified search strategy be followed? Courts appear disinclined to require that computer search warrants contain a search protocol. See, e.g., *United States v. Brooks*, 427 F.3d 1246 (10th Cir.2005). Is this conclusion supported as a Fourth Amendment matter by *Dalia v. United States*, p. 525, and *United States v. Grubbs*, p. 306? Or simply by the fact that such a requirement is not feasible? See Orin Kerr, *Ex Ante Regulation of Computer Search and Seizure*, 96 Va.L.Rev. 1241, 1271, 1277 (2010).

Then is some other solution needed? Consider *United States v. Comprehensive Drug Testing, Inc.*, 579 F.3d 989 (9th Cir.2009), revised and superseded, 621 F.3d 1162 (9th Cir.2010), asserting that "[i]f the government can't be sure whether data may be concealed, compressed, erased or boobytrapped without carefully examining the contents of every file," so that "everything the government chooses to seize will, under this theory, automatically come into plain view," then "[t]o avoid this illogical result, the government should in future warrant applications, forswear reliance on the plain view doctrine or any similar doctrine that would allow it to retain data to which it has gained access only because it was required to segregate seizable from non-seizable data."

7. As noted in *United States v. Gourde*, 440 F.3d 1065 (9th Cir.2006), "if a computer had ever received or downloaded illegal images, the images would remain on the computer for an extended period," for "even if the user sent the images to 'recycle' and then deleted the files in the recycling bin, the files were not actually erased but were kept in the computer's 'slack space' until randomly overwritten, making even deleted files retrievable by computer forensic experts * * * long after the file had been viewed or downloaded and even after it had been deleted." Does this foreclose a "stale" probable cause claim? See p. 305, Note 3. Does the typical defendant's understandable belief that the supposedly "deleted" files are gone mean he has a heightened privacy expectation as to those files, so that they are consequently beyond government reach, at least under a warrant not specifically authorizing retrieval of such files? Compare *Commonwealth v. Copenhefer*, 587 A.2d 1353 (Pa.1991) (no, analogizing such files to "a diary recorded in a private code"). Or, on the other hand, can the defendant not prevail in any event as to the "deleted" files because they are only "trash" as to which he lacks a reasonable expectation of privacy per *Greenwood*, p. 207, and *Scott*, p. 269? Compare *United States v. Upham*, 168 F.3d 532 (1st Cir.1999) ("to compare deletion to putting one's trash on the street where it can be searched by every passer-by is to reason by false analogy").

D. THE "PREFERENCE" FOR WARRANTS

1. The Supreme Court has long expressed a strong preference for searches made pursuant to a search warrant, e.g., *United States v. Ventresca*, 380 U.S. 102 (1965), and on occasion has even asserted "that the police must, whenever practicable, obtain advance judicial approval of searches and seizures." *Terry v. Ohio*, p. 408. But this is far from being an accurate portrayal of current law or practice; the fact of the matter is that the great majority of police seizures and searches are made and upheld notwithstanding the absence of a warrant.

This is so because, as elaborated later in this Chapter, the Supreme Court has recognized a considerable variety of circumstances in which the police may lawfully make a search or a seizure without the prior approval of a magistrate. A warrant is excused in situations other than those in which there existed genuine exigent circumstances making it unfeasible for the police to utilize the often time-consuming warrant process. Sometimes this is explained by the Court on the ground that the police activity being permitted without a warrant intrudes only upon lesser Fourth Amendment values. Illustrative is *California v. Carney*, p. 383, allowing warrantless search of vehicles because of the "diminished expectation of privacy" in them. Sometimes warrant excusal is rationalized on the ground that the permitted police activity is merely "routine," as with the inventory allowed in *Colorado v. Bertine*, p. 407. On other occasions the Supreme Court has recognized an exception to the warrant requirement because of a purported need for "bright lines" in the rules governing police conduct. Illustrative is *United States v. Watson*, p. 332, holding a warrant is never needed to arrest in a public place because a contrary holding would "encumber criminal prosecutions with endless litigation with respect to the existence of exigent circumstances, whether it was practicable to get a warrant, whether the suspect was about to flee, and the like." The tension between these and other considerations has not always produced predictable or consistent results in the Court's decisions concerning what is permissible warrantless police action, as will be seen in Sections 5, 6, and 7.

2. The preference for the warrant process is commonly explained on the ground that it, more so than the post-search suppression process, *prevents* illegal searches. Compare William S. Stuntz, *Warrants and Fourth Amendment Remedies,* 77 Va.L.Rev. 881, 884 (1991), suggesting some other reasons—that "the exclusionary rule generates an additional pair of problems for fourth amendment law, problems that warrants might plausibly help solve. Exclusion * * * may bias judges' after-the-fact probable cause determinations by requiring that they be made in cases where the officer actually found incriminating evidence. Similarly, the lack of a credible opponent (the defendant has, after all, been found with incriminating evidence) invites the police to subvert the governing legal standard by testifying falsely at suppression hearings. Warrants can reduce both problems by forcing the necessary judicial decision to be made, and the police officer's account of the facts to be given, before the evidence is found."

SECTION 5. WARRANTLESS ARRESTS AND SEARCHES OF THE PERSON

UNITED STATES v. WATSON
423 U.S. 411, 96 S.Ct. 820, 46 L.Ed.2d 598 (1976).

JUSTICE WHITE delivered the opinion of the Court.

[Reliable informant Khoury told a federal postal inspector that Watson had supplied him with a stolen credit card and had agreed to furnish additional cards at their next meeting, scheduled for a few days later. At that meeting, which occurred in a restaurant, Khoury signaled the inspector that Watson had the cards, at which point the inspector arrested Watson without a warrant, as he was authorized to do under 18 U.S.C. § 3061 and applicable postal regulations. The court of appeals held the arrest unconstitutional because the inspector had failed to secure an arrest warrant although he concededly had time to do so, and this was a significant factor in the court's additional holding that Watson's consent to a search of his car was not voluntary.]

* * * Section 3061 represents a judgment by Congress that it is not unreasonable under the Fourth Amendment for postal inspectors to arrest without a warrant provided they have probable cause to do so. This was not an isolated or quixotic judgment of the legislative branch. Other federal law enforcement officers have been expressly authorized by statute for many years to make felony arrests on probable cause but without a warrant. * * *

Because there is a "strong presumption of constitutionality due to an Act of Congress, especially when it turns on what is 'reasonable,' * * * [o]bviously the Court should be reluctant to decide that a search thus authorized by Congress was unreasonable and that the Act was therefore unconstitutional." Moreover, there is nothing in the Court's prior cases indicating that under the Fourth Amendment a warrant is required to make a valid arrest for a felony. Indeed, the relevant prior decisions are uniformly to the contrary. * * *[a]

The cases construing the Fourth Amendment thus reflect the ancient common-law rule that a peace officer was permitted to arrest without a warrant for a misdemeanor or felony committed in his presence as well as for a felony not committed in his presence if there was reasonable grounds for making the arrest. This has also been the prevailing rule under state constitutions and statutes. * * *

Because the common-law rule authorizing arrests without warrant generally prevailed in the States, it is important for present purposes to note that in 1792 Congress invested United States Marshals and their deputies with "the same powers in executing the laws of the United States, as sheriffs and their deputies in their several states have by law, in executing the laws of their respective states." The Second Congress thus saw no inconsistency between the Fourth Amendment and giving United States Marshals the same power as local peace officers to arrest for a felony without a warrant.[8] * * *

The balance struck by the common law in generally authorizing felony arrests on probable cause, but without a warrant, has survived substantially intact. It appears in almost all of the States in the form of express statutory authorization. * * *

This is the rule Congress has long directed its principal law enforcement officers to follow. Congress has plainly decided against conditioning warrantless arrest power on proof of exigent circumstances. Law enforcement officers may find it wise to seek arrest warrants where practicable to do so, and their judgments about probable cause may be more readily accepted where backed by a warrant issued by a magistrate. But we decline to transform this judicial preference into a constitutional rule when the judgment of the Nation and Congress has for so long

---

a. The Court noted by way of footnote that because the arrest here was in a public place, it did not have to resolve the "still unsettled question" of whether a warrant is needed to enter private premises to make an arrest. This issue is considered at p. 376.

8. Of equal import is the rule recognized by this Court that even in the absence of a federal statute granting or restricting the authority of federal law enforcement officers, "the law of the state where an arrest without warrant takes place determines its validity." *United States v. Di Re*, 332 U.S. 581 (1948). * * *

been to authorize warrantless public arrests on probable cause rather than to encumber criminal prosecutions with endless litigation with respect to the existence of exigent circumstances, whether it was practicable to get a warrant, whether the suspect was about to flee, and the like. * * *

Reversed.

JUSTICE STEVENS took no part in the consideration or decision of this case.

JUSTICE POWELL, concurring. * * *

On its face, our decision today creates a certain anomaly. There is no more basic constitutional rule in the Fourth Amendment area than that which makes a warrantless search unreasonable except in a few "jealously and carefully drawn" exceptional circumstances. * * *.

Since the Fourth Amendment speaks equally to both searches and seizures, and since an arrest, the taking hold of one's person, is quintessentially a seizure, it would seem that the constitutional provision should impose the same limitations upon arrests that it does upon searches. Indeed, as an abstract matter an argument can be made that the restrictions upon arrest perhaps should be greater. A search may cause only annoyance and temporary inconvenience to the law-abiding citizen, assuming more serious dimension only when it turns up evidence of criminality. An arrest, however, is a serious personal intrusion regardless of whether the person seized is guilty or innocent. * * * Logic therefore would seem to dictate that arrests be subject to the warrant requirement at least to the same extent as searches.

But logic sometimes must defer to history and experience. The Court's opinion emphasizes the historical sanction accorded warrantless felony arrests. * * *

Moreover, a constitutional rule permitting felony arrests only with a warrant or in exigent circumstances could severely hamper effective law enforcement. Good police practice often requires postponing an arrest, even after probable cause has been established, in order to place the suspect under surveillance or otherwise develop further evidence necessary to prove guilt to a jury. Under the holding of the Court of Appeals such additional investigative work could imperil the entire prosecution. Should the officers fail to obtain a warrant initially, and later be required by unforeseen circumstances to arrest immediately with no chance to procure a last-minute warrant, they would risk a court decision that the subsequent exigency did not excuse their failure to get a warrant in the interim since they first developed probable cause. If the officers attempted to meet such a contingency by procuring a warrant as soon as they had probable cause and then merely held it during their subsequent investigation, they would risk a court decision that the warrant had grown stale by the time it was used.[5] Law enforcement personnel caught in this squeeze could ensure validity of their arrests only by obtaining a warrant and arresting as soon as probable cause existed, thereby foreclosing the possibility of gathering vital additional evidence from the suspect's continued actions. * * *

JUSTICE STEWART, concurring in the result. * * *

JUSTICE MARSHALL, with whom JUSTICE BRENNAN joins, dissenting. * * *

---

5. The probable cause to support issuance of an arrest warrant normally would not grow stale as easily as that which supports a warrant to search a particular place for particular objects. This is true because once there is probable cause to believe that someone is a felon the passage of time often will bring new supporting evidence. But in some cases the original grounds supporting the warrant could be disproved by subsequent investigation that at the same time turns up wholly new evidence supporting probable cause on a different theory. In those cases the warrant could be stale because based upon discredited information.

The signal of the reliable informant that Watson was in possession of stolen credit cards gave the postal inspectors probable cause to make the arrest. * * * When law enforcement officers have probable cause to believe that an offense is taking place in their presence and that the suspect is at that moment in possession of the evidence, exigent circumstances exist. Delay could cause the escape of the suspect or the destruction of the evidence. Accordingly, Watson's warrantless arrest was valid under the recognized exigent circumstances exception to the warrant requirement, and the Court has no occasion to consider whether a warrant would otherwise be necessary. * * *

* * * Only the most serious crimes were felonies at common law, and many crimes now classified as felonies under federal or state law were treated as misdemeanors. * * * To make an arrest for any of these crimes at common law, the police officer was required to obtain a warrant, unless the crime was committed in his presence. Since many of these same crimes are commonly classified as felonies today however, under the Court's holding a warrant is no longer needed to make such arrests, a result in contravention of the common law.

[T]he only clear lesson of history is contrary to the one the Court draws: the common law considered the arrest warrant far more important than today's decision leaves it. * * *

[W]e must now consider (1) whether the privacy of our citizens will be better protected by ordinarily requiring a warrant to be issued before they may be arrested; and (2) whether a warrant requirement would unduly burden legitimate governmental interests.

The first question is easily answered. Of course the privacy of our citizens will be better protected by a warrant requirement. * * *

The Government's assertion that a warrant requirement would impose an intolerable burden stems, in large part, from the specious supposition that procurement of an arrest warrant would be necessary as soon as probable cause ripens. There is no requirement that a search warrant be obtained the moment police have probable cause to search. The rule is only that present probable cause be shown and a warrant obtained before a search is undertaken. The same rule should obtain for arrest warrants, where it may even make more sense. Certainly, there is less need for prompt procurement of a warrant in the arrest situation. Unlike probable cause to search, probable cause to arrest, once formed will continue to exist for the indefinite future, at least if no intervening exculpatory facts come to light.

This sensible approach obviates most of the difficulties that have been suggested with an arrest warrant rule. Police would not have to cut their investigation short the moment they obtain probable cause to arrest, nor would undercover agents be forced suddenly to terminate their work and forfeit their covers. Moreover, if in the course of the continued police investigation exigent circumstances develop that demand an immediate arrest, the arrest may be made without fear of unconstitutionality, so long as the exigency was unanticipated and not used to avoid the arrest warrant requirement. Likewise, if in the course of the continued investigation police uncover evidence tying the suspect to another crime, they may immediately arrest him for that crime if exigency demands it, and still be in full conformity with the warrant rule. This is why the arrest in this case was not improper.[15] * * *

---

15. Although the postal inspectors here anticipated the occurrence of the second crime, they could not have obtained a warrant for Watson's arrest for that crime until probable cause formed, just moments before the arrest. A warrant based on anticipated facts is premature and void. *United States v. Roberts,* 333 F.Supp. 786 (E.D.Tenn.1971).

NOTES AND QUESTIONS

1. Consider SEARCHSZR § 5.1: "A study conducted for the President's Commission on Law Enforcement and Administration of Justice indicated that, while nearly fifty percent of all arrests are made within two hours of the crime as a result of a 'hot' search of the crime scene or a 'warm' search of the general vicinity of the crime, very few additional arrests occur immediately thereafter. Rather, there is a delay while further investigation is conducted; about 45 percent of all arrests occur more than a day after the crime, and nearly 35 percent of all arrests are made after the passage of over a week. In these latter instances, * * * the risk is negligible that the defendant will suddenly flee between the time the police solve the case and the time which would be required to obtain and serve an arrest warrant. Indeed, in such cases the need to arrest before an arrest warrant can be obtained is likely to be considerably less apparent than the need to search before a search warrant can be acquired and executed; the defendant is unlikely suddenly to decide to flee or go into hiding at that point, but he well might have reached the stage where he is about to dispose of the fruits of his crime or destroy or abandon items of physical evidence which might link him with the crime."

2. As for the *Watson* dissenters' conclusion that "the privacy of our citizens will be better protected by ordinarily requiring a warrant to be issued before they may be arrested," consider Edward Barrett, *Criminal Justice: The Problem of Mass Production,* in The American Assembly, Columbia University, The Courts, the Public, and the Law Explosion 85, 117–18 (H.W. Jones ed. 1965): "How can a magistrate be more than a 'rubber stamp' in signing warrants unless he devotes at least some minutes in each case to reading the affidavits submitted to him in support of the request for a warrant, and inquiring into the background of the conclusions stated therein? And where is the judicial time going to be found to make such inquiries in the generality of cases? The Los Angeles Municipal Court with annual filings of about 130,000 (excluding parking and traffic) *finds itself so pressed that in large areas of its caseload it averages but a minute per case in receiving pleas and imposing sentence.* How could it cope with the added burden that would be involved in the issuance of warrants to govern the approximately 200,000 arrests made per year in Los Angeles for offenses other than traffic"?

3. Is the "preference" for arrest warrants nonetheless justified on the ground that, at least the police must make a record before the event of the basis for their actions? Consider Jerome H. Skolnick, *Justice Without Trial* 214–15 (1966): "[T]he policeman perceives * * * the need to be able to reconstruct a set of complex happenings in such a way that, subsequent to the arrest, probable cause can be found according to appellate court standards. In this way, as one district attorney expressed it, 'the policeman fabricates probable cause.' By saying this, he did not mean to assert that the policeman is a liar, but rather that he finds it necessary to construct an *ex post facto* description of the preceding events so that these conform to legal arrest requirements, whether in fact the events actually did so or not at the time of the arrest. Thus, the policeman respects the necessity for 'complying' with the arrest laws. His 'compliance,' however, may take the form of *post hoc* manipulation of the facts rather than before-the-fact behavior."

4. Given the concern regarding "*post hoc* manipulation of the facts," should the arrest of a person stated at arrest to be for one offense or resulting in booking for that offense be upheld on the ground that the police actually had sufficient evidence of a quite different offense? Compare Chief Justice Warren, dissenting from the dismissal of the writ of certiorari in *Wainwright v. New Orleans,* 392 U.S. 598 (1968) ("I see no more justification for permitting the State to disregard its own booking record than for permitting any other administrative body to disregard its own records. * * * If the police in this case really believed that petitioner was the murder suspect, and if they had probable cause to so believe, all they had to do was to arrest and book him for murder"); with *Devenpeck v. Alford*, 543 U.S. 146 (2004) (unanimous Court, per Scalia, J., rejects court of appeals' position that probable cause can only be shown as to the offense stated at the time of arrest or as to another offense "closely related" to it, for that position is inconsistent with precedent in, e.g., *Whren v. United States*, p. 353, "that an arresting officer's state of mind (except for the facts that he knows) is irrelevant to the existence of probable cause"; moreover, a "closely related" limitation would not ensure "that officers will cease making sham arrests on the hope that such arrests will later be validated, but rather that officers will cease providing reasons for arrest" or "would simply give every reason for which probable cause could conceivably exist"). But consider *Rosenbaum v. Washoe County*, 654 F.3d 1001 (9th Cir.2011): "It cannot be that probable cause for a warrantless arrest exists so long as the facts may arguably give rise to probable cause under *any* criminal statute on the books—even if the crime is buried deep in a dust-covered tomb and never charged or prosecuted. If it were so, officers could arrest without a warrant under virtually any set of facts and later search the legal archives for a statute that might arguably justify it. Such a approach would be inconsistent with the Fourth Amendment's fundamental requirement that searches be cabined by the requirement of reasonableness."

5. Some but by no means all relevant authorities have described the common law warrantless arrest power of police regarding misdemeanors as having two limitations: (i) that the offense have occurred in the officer's presence; and (ii) that the offense constitute a "breach of the peace." These authorities were relied upon by the plaintiff in the § 1983 case of ATWATER v. CITY OF LAGO VISTA, 532 U.S. 318 (2001), involving these facts:

"In March 1997, Petitioner Gail Atwater was driving her pickup truck in Lago Vista, Texas, with her 3-year-old son and 5-year-old daughter in the front seat. None of them was wearing a seatbelt. Respondent Bart Turek, a Lago Vista police officer at the time, observed the seatbelt violations and pulled Atwater over. According to Atwater's complaint (the allegations of which we assume to be true for present purposes), Turek approached the truck and 'yell[ed]' something to the effect of '[w]e've met before' and '[y]ou're going to jail.'[1] He then called for backup and asked to see Atwater's driver's license and insurance documentation, which state law required her to carry. When Atwater told Turek that she did not have the papers because her purse had been stolen the day before, Turek said that he had 'heard that story two-hundred times.'

"Atwater asked to take her 'frightened, upset, and crying' children to a friend's house nearby, but Turek told her, '[y]ou're not going anywhere.' As it turned out, Atwater's friend learned what was going on and soon arrived to take charge of the children. Turek then handcuffed Atwater, placed her in his squad car, and drove her to the local police station, where booking officers had her remove her shoes, jewelry, and eyeglasses, and empty her pockets. Officers took Atwater's 'mug shot' and placed her, alone, in a jail cell for about one hour, after which she was taken before a magistrate and released on $310 bond.

"Atwater was charged with driving without her seatbelt fastened, failing to secure her children in seatbelts, driving without a license, and failing to provide

---

1. Turek had previously stopped Atwater for what he had thought was a seatbelt violation, but had realized that Atwater's son, although seated on the vehicle's armrest, was in fact belted in. Atwater acknowledged that her son's seating position was unsafe, and Turek issued a verbal warning.

proof of insurance. She ultimately pleaded no contest to the misdemeanor seatbelt offenses and paid a $50 fine; the other charges were dismissed."

Although Texas law at that time gave the officer total discretion to choose between a custodial arrest and issuance of a citation in such circumstances, Atwater claimed the arrest was contrary to common law and hence in violation of the Fourth Amendment. The Court, per Souter, J., agreed that the common law view was "obviously relevant, if not entirely dispositive," as to what the Fourth Amendment's framers thought was reasonable, but then concluded that her "historical argument * * * ultimately fails" because the English and American cases and commentators reached "divergent conclusions" regarding any breach-of-the-peace requirement. Moreover, the post-Amendment history "is of two centuries of uninterrupted (and largely unchallenged) state and federal practice permitting warrantless arrests for misdemeanors not amounting to or involving breach of the peace."[a]

6. *Atwater* is one of several recent cases in which the Supreme Court has made the principal criterion for identifying violations of the Fourth Amendment "whether a particular governmental action * * * was regarded as an unlawful search or seizure under the common law when the Amendment was framed," *Wyoming v. Houghton*, p. 393. This approach, which "departs dramatically from the largely ahistorical approach the Court has taken to the Fourth Amendment for most of the past thirty years," has been criticized as "find[ing] support neither in the constitutional text, nor in what we know of the intentions of the 'Framers,'" and as obscuring the fact "that the Fourth Amendment places on courts a burden of judgment, and that the burden cannot be relieved by the common law's sporadic, contradictory, and necessarily time-bound rules of search and seizure." David A. Sklansky, *The Fourth Amendment and Common Law,* 100 Colum.L.Rev. 1739, 1813–14 (2000). As for use of the technique in *Atwater*, a leading Fourth Amendment historian has concluded that Justice "Souter's claims bear little resemblance to authentic framing-era arrest doctrine," and "that his supposed historical analysis consisted almost entirely of rhetorical ploys and distortions of the historical sources. * * * A robust comparison of the analysis and holding in *Atwater* with the pertinent historical sources reveals that the Framers neither expected nor intended for officers to exercise the sort of unfettered arrest authority that *Atwater* permits." Thomas Y. Davies, *The Fictional Character of Law-and-Order Originalism: A Case Study of the Distortions and Evasions of Framing–Era Arrest Doctrine in Atwater v. Lago Vista,* 37 Wake Forest L.Rev. 239, 246–47 (2002).

7. The common law "in presence" requirement for a warrantless misdemeanor arrest has sometimes caused the courts difficulties. Consider *People v. Burdo,* 223 N.W.2d 358 (Mich.App.1974) (officer could not arrest for misdemeanor of driving under influence of liquor when he came on scene of auto accident and found defendant there, even though defendant obviously was intoxicated and admitted he had been driving); *People v. Dixon,* 222 N.W.2d 749 (Mich.1974) (after stopping noisy vehicle, officer could arrest driver for misdemeanor of driving without a license after being advised via police radio that defendant's license had been suspended).

8. Some states use the felony-arrest rule for *all* offenses, and when such provisions have been challenged as unconstitutional it has been held that the Fourth Amendment should not "be interpreted to prohibit warrantless arrests for misdemeanors committed outside an officer's presence." *Street v. Surdyka,* 492

a. Four members of the Court dissented on another branch of the case, discussed at p. 348, but as to the above matter agreed "that warrantless misdemeanor arrests were not the subject of a clear and consistently applied rule at common law."

F.2d 368 (4th Cir.1974). Is this so after *Atwater*? Consider that in *Atwater* the Court dropped this footnote: "We need not, and thus do not, speculate whether the Fourth Amendment entails an 'in the presence' requirement for purposes of misdemeanor arrests. Cf. *Welsh v. Wisconsin*, p. 381 (White, J., dissenting) ('[T]he requirement that a misdemeanor must have occurred in the officer's presence to justify a warrantless arrest is not grounded in the Fourth Amendment')."

9. Rejecting the contention that if the *Watson* probable cause "requirement is satisfied the Fourth Amendment has nothing to say about *how* that seizure is made," the Court in TENNESSEE v. GARNER, 471 U.S. 1 (1985), held that the use of deadly force to arrest a fleeing felon is sometimes unreasonable under the Fourth Amendment. White, J., stated for the majority:

"The use of deadly force to prevent the escape of all felony suspects, whatever the circumstances, is constitutionally unreasonable. It is not better that all felony suspects die than that they escape. Where the suspect poses no immediate threat to the officer and no threat to others, the harm resulting from failing to apprehend him does not justify the use of deadly force to do so. It is no doubt unfortunate when a suspect who is in sight escapes, but the fact that the police arrive a little late or are a little slower afoot does not always justify killing the suspect. A police officer may not seize an unarmed, nondangerous suspect by shooting him dead. The Tennessee statute is unconstitutional insofar as it authorizes the use of deadly force against such fleeing suspects.

"It is not, however, unconstitutional on its face. Where the officer has probable cause to believe that the suspect poses a threat of serious physical harm, either to the officer or to others, it is not constitutionally unreasonable to prevent escape by using deadly force. Thus, if the suspect threatens the officer with a weapon or there is probable cause to believe that he has committed a crime involving the infliction or threatened infliction of serious physical harm, deadly force may be used if necessary to prevent escape, and if, where feasible, some warning has been given. As applied in such circumstances, the Tennessee statute would pass constitutional muster."

O'Connor, J., joined by the Chief Justice and Rehnquist, J., dissenting, objected that "the reasonableness of Officer Hymon's conduct for purposes of the Fourth Amendment cannot be evaluated by what later appears to have been a preferable course of police action. The officer pursued a suspect in the darkened backyard of a house that from all indications had just been burglarized. The police officer was not certain whether the suspect was alone or unarmed; nor did he know what had transpired inside the house. He ordered the suspect to halt, and when the suspect refused to obey and attempted to flee into the night, the officer fired his weapon to prevent escape. The reasonableness of this action for purposes of the Fourth Amendment is not determined by the unfortunate nature of this particular case; instead, the question is whether it is constitutionally impermissible for police officers, as a last resort, to shoot a burglary suspect fleeing the scene of the crime."

The Fourth Amendment reasonableness standard, the Court later declared in *Graham v. Connor,* 490 U.S. 386 (1989), (1) applies to "*all* claims that law enforcement officers have used excessive force—deadly or not—in the course of an arrest, investigatory stop, or other 'seizure' of a free citizen";[b] (2) "requires careful attention to the facts and circumstances of each particular case, including the severity of the crime at issue, whether the suspect poses an immediate threat to the safety of the officers or others, and whether he is actively resisting arrest or

---

b. If the police conduct causing death or bodily harm was not a search or seizure, then the Fourteenth Amendment due process shocks-the-conscience test, rather than the Fourth Amendment reasonableness test, applies. See *County of Sacramento v. Lewis,* p. 31.

attempting to evade arrest by flight"; (3) "must embody allowance for the fact that police officers are often forced to make split-second judgments—in circumstances that are tense, uncertain, and rapidly evolving—about the amount of force that is necessary in a particular situation"; and (4) asks "whether the officers' actions are 'objectively reasonable' in light of the facts and circumstances confronting them, without regard to their underlying intent or motivation."

10. In SCOTT v. HARRIS, 127 S.Ct. 1769 (2007), a deputy signaled a motorist to stop for traveling 73 m.p.h. in a 55 m.p.h. zone, but the motorist instead sped away at speeds exceeding 85 m.p.h.; the vehicle's license number was broadcast to other officers, who joined the search; six minutes and 10 miles later, another deputy (Scott) applied his push bumper to the rear of the vehicle, and the motorist then "lost control of his vehicle, which left the roadway, ran down an embankment, overturned, and crashed," as a consequence of which the motorist (Harris) "was badly injured and was rendered a quadriplegic." Harris brought a § 1983 action against Scott, alleging excessive force in violation of the Fourth Amendment; the court of appeals affirmed the district court's denial of Scott's motion for summary judgment. The Supreme Court, per Scalia, J., after examining a videotape of the chase[c] that "closely resembles a Hollywood-style car chase of the most frightening sort, placing police officers and innocent bystanders alike at great risk of serious injury," concluded:

"* * * So how does a court go about weighing the perhaps lesser probability of injuring or killing numerous bystanders against the perhaps larger probability of injuring or killing a single person? We think it appropriate in this process to take into account not only the number of lives at risk, but also their relative culpability. It was respondent, after all, who intentionally placed himself and the public in danger by unlawfully engaging in the reckless, high-speed flight that ultimately produced the choice between two evils that Scott confronted. Multiple police cars, with blue lights flashing and sirens blaring, had been chasing respondent for nearly 10 miles, but he ignored their warning to stop. By contrast, those who might have been harmed had Scott not taken the action he did were entirely innocent. We have little difficulty in concluding it was reasonable for Scott to take the action that he did."

Stevens, J., the lone dissenter, objected that the majority had exaggerated the risks presented by Harris ("The Court's concern about the 'imminent threat to the lives of any pedestrians who might have been present' * * * should be discounted in a case involving a nighttime chase in an area where no pedestrians were present"), and minimized the benefits from abandoning the chase ("There is no evidentiary basis for an assumption that dangers caused by flight from a police pursuit will continue after the pursuit ends"; indeed, "countless police departments" have concluded otherwise by adopting policies declaring that "[w]hen the immediate danger to the public created by the pursuit is greater than the immediate or potential danger to the public should the suspect remain at large, then the pursuit should be discontinued").

11. In GERSTEIN v. PUGH, 420 U.S. 103 (1975), the Court, per Powell, J., held that a "policeman's on-the-scene assessment of probable cause provides legal justification for arresting a person suspected of crime, and for a brief period of detention to take the administrative steps incident to arrest. Once the suspect is in custody, however, the reasons that justify dispensing with the magistrate's neutral judgment evaporate. There no longer is any danger that the suspect will escape or commit further crimes while the police submit their evidence to a magistrate. And, while the State's reasons for taking summary action subside, the

---

c. Which you can also view at http://www.supremecourtus.gov/opinions/video/scott_v_harris. rmvb.

suspect's need for a neutral determination of probable cause increases significantly. The consequences of prolonged detention may be more serious than the interference occasioned by arrest. Pretrial confinement may imperil the suspect's job, interrupt his source of income, and impair his family relationships. Even pretrial release may be accompanied by burdensome conditions that effect a significant restraint on liberty. When the stakes are this high, the detached judgment of a neutral magistrate is essential if the Fourth Amendment is to furnish meaningful protection from unfounded interference with liberty. Accordingly, we hold that the Fourth Amendment requires a judicial determination of probable cause as a prerequisite to extended restraint on liberty following arrest.[d]

"This result has historical support in the common law that has guided interpretation of the Fourth Amendment. At common law it was customary, if not obligatory, for an arrested person to be brought before a justice of the peace shortly after arrest. The justice of the peace would 'examine' the prisoner and the witnesses to determine whether there was reason to believe the prisoner had committed a crime. If there was, the suspect would be committed to jail or bailed pending trial. If not, he would be discharged from custody. The initial determination of probable cause also could be reviewed by higher courts on a writ of habeas corpus. This practice furnished the model for criminal procedure in America immediately following the adoption of the Fourth Amendment, and there are indications that the Framers of the Bill of Rights regarded it as a model for a 'reasonable' seizure."

The Court then concluded the Court of Appeals had erred in holding "that the determination of probable cause must be accompanied by the full panoply of adversary safeguards—counsel, confrontation, cross-examination, and compulsory process for witnesses." The Court of Appeals had required that the state provide, in effect, a "full preliminary hearing * * * modeled after the procedure used in many States to determine whether the evidence justifies going to trial under an information or presenting the case to a grand jury." The Fourth Amendment, the Court noted, did not require such an adversary proceeding:

"The sole issue is whether there is probable cause for detaining the arrested person pending further proceedings. This issue can be determined reliably without an adversary hearing. That standard—probable cause to believe the suspect has committed a crime—traditionally has been decided by a magistrate in a nonadversary proceeding on hearsay and written testimony, and the Court has approved these informal modes of proof. * * * The use of an informal procedure is justified not only by the lesser consequences of a probable cause determination but also by the nature of the determination itself. It does not require the fine resolution of conflicting evidence that a reasonable-doubt or even a preponderance standard demands, and credibility determinations are seldom crucial in deciding whether the evidence supports a reasonable belief in guilt. This is not to say that confrontation and cross-examination might not enhance the reliability of probable cause determinations in some cases. In most cases, however, their value would be too slight to justify holding, as a matter of constitutional principle, that these formalities and safeguards designed for trial must also be employed in making the Fourth Amendment determination of probable cause."[e]

---

   d. In a subsequent footnote, the Court indicated that a grand jury determination to indict would provide such a "judicial determination." In distinguishing the prosecutor's determination that probable cause exists, the Court noted: "By contrast, the Court has held that an indictment, 'fair upon its face,' and returned by a 'properly constituted grand jury' conclusively determines the existence of probable cause and requires issuance of an arrest warrant without further inquiry. The willingness to let a grand jury judgment substitute for that of a neutral and detached magistrate is attributable to the grand jury's relationship to the courts and its historical role of protecting individuals from unjust prosecution."

   e. Stewart, J., joined by Douglas, Brennan and Marshall, JJ., refused to join this portion of the Court's opinion. Justice Stewart noted: "I see no need in this case for the Court to say that

" * * * There is no single preferred pretrial procedure, and the nature of the probable cause determination usually will be shaped to accord with a State's pretrial procedure viewed as a whole. * * * It may be found desirable, for example, to make the probable cause determination at the suspect's first appearance before a judicial officer,[24] the determination may be incorporated into the procedure for setting bail or fixing other conditions of pretrial release. * * * Whatever procedure a State may adopt, it must provide a fair and reliable determination of probable cause as a condition for any significant pretrial restraint on liberty,[26] and this determination must be made by a judicial officer either before or promptly after arrest.[27]"

12. In COUNTY OF RIVERSIDE v. McLAUGHLIN, 500 U.S. 44 (1991), the Court confronted the question of "what is 'prompt' under *Gerstein*" and concluded, 5–4, per O'Connor, J., that "it is important to provide some degree of certainty so that States and counties may establish procedures with confidence that they fall within constitutional bounds. Taking into account the competing interests articulated in *Gerstein,* we believe that a jurisdiction that provides judicial determinations of probable cause within 48 hours of arrest will, as a general matter, comply with the promptness requirement of *Gerstein*. For this reason, such jurisdictions will be immune from systemic challenges.

"This is not to say that the probable cause determination in a particular case passes constitutional muster simply because it is provided within 48 hours. Such a hearing may nonetheless violate *Gerstein* if the arrested individual can prove that

---

the Constitution extends less procedural protection to an imprisoned human being than is required to test the propriety of garnishing a commercial bank account, *North Georgia Finishing, Inc. v. Di–Chem, Inc.,* 419 U.S. 601 [(1975)], the custody of a refrigerator, *Mitchell v. W. T. Grant Co.,* 416 U.S. 600 [(1974)], the temporary suspension of a public school student, *Goss v. Lopez,* 419 U.S. 565 [(1975)], or the suspension of a driver's license, *Bell v. Burson,* 402 U.S. 535 [(1971)]. Although it may be true that the Fourth Amendment's 'balance between individual and public interests always has been thought to define the "process that is due" for seizures of person or property in criminal cases,' this case does not involve an initial arrest, but rather the continuing incarceration of a presumptively innocent person. Accordingly, I cannot join the Court's effort to foreclose any claim that the traditional requirements of constitutional due process are applicable in the context of pretrial detention."

24. Several States already authorize a determination of probable cause at this stage or immediately thereafter. This Court has interpreted the Federal Rules of Criminal Procedure to require a determination of probable cause at the first appearance.

26. Because the probable cause determination is not a constitutional prerequisite to the charging decision, it is required only for those suspects who suffer restraints on liberty other than the condition that they appear for trial. There are many kinds of pretrial release and many degrees of conditional liberty. We cannot define specifically those that would require a prior probable cause determination, but the key factor is significant restraint on liberty. [Editors' note: Consider *In re Walters,* 543 P.2d 607 (Cal.1975): "As the posting of bail may impose an unwarranted burden on an accused if probable cause to detain is lacking, the accused is entitled to have that determination made prior to electing to post or not to post bail."]

27. In his concurring opinion, Mr. Justice Stewart objects to the Court's choice of the Fourth Amendment as the rationale for decision and suggests that the Court offers less procedural protection to a person in jail than it requires in certain civil cases. Here we deal with the complex procedures of a criminal case and a threshold right guaranteed by the Fourth Amendment. The historical basis of the probable cause requirement is quite different from the relatively recent application of variable procedural due process in debtor-creditor disputes and termination of government-created benefits. The Fourth Amendment was tailored explicitly for the criminal justice system, and its balance between individual and public interests always has been thought to define the "process that is due" for seizures of person or property in criminal cases, including the detention of suspects pending trial. Moreover, the Fourth Amendment probable cause determination is in fact only the *first* stage of an elaborate system, unique in jurisprudence, designed to safeguard the rights of those accused of criminal conduct. The relatively simple civil procedures (e.g., prior interview with school principal before suspension) presented in the cases cited in the concurring opinion are inapposite and irrelevant in the wholly different context of the criminal justice system. * * *

his or her probable cause determination was delayed unreasonably. Examples of unreasonable delay are delays for the purpose of gathering additional evidence to justify the arrest, a delay motivated by ill will against the arrested individual, or delay for delay's sake. In evaluating whether the delay in a particular case is unreasonable, however, courts must allow a substantial degree of flexibility. Courts cannot ignore the often unavoidable delays in transporting arrested persons from one facility to another, handling late-night bookings where no magistrate is readily available, obtaining the presence of an arresting officer who may be busy processing other suspects or securing the premises of an arrest, and other practical realities.

"Where an arrested individual does not receive a probable cause determination within 48 hours, the calculus changes. In such a case, the arrested individual does not bear the burden of proving an unreasonable delay. Rather, the burden shifts to the government to demonstrate the existence of a bona fide emergency or other extraordinary circumstance. The fact that in a particular case it may take longer than 48 hours to consolidate pretrial proceedings does not qualify as an extraordinary circumstance. Nor, for that matter, do intervening weekends. A jurisdiction that chooses to offer combined proceedings must do so as soon as is reasonably feasible, but in no event later than 48 hours after arrest."

13. Assuming a *Gerstein* violation, what bearing should it have if the individual is later prosecuted? In *Powell v. Nevada,* 511 U.S. 79 (1994), holding *McLaughlin* retroactive to that case, the Court, per Ginsburg, J., noted: "It does not necessarily follow, however, that Powell must 'be set free' or gain other relief, for several questions remain open for decision on remand," including "the appropriate remedy for a delay in determining probable cause (an issue not resolved by *McLaughlin*)." In *Powell,* an untimely probable cause determination was made four days after defendant's arrest, shortly after he gave the police an incriminating statement. In declaring that "whether a suppression remedy applies in that setting remains an unresolved question," Justice Ginsburg took note of two arguably analogous rules pointing in opposite directions: (i) that an after-the-fact judicial determination of probable cause does not make admissible evidence obtained in a search in violation of the Fourth Amendment's search warrant requirement; and (ii) that under *Harris,* p. 899, suppression of a statement subsequently obtained elsewhere is not required because of defendant's warrantless arrest inside premises in violation of the Fourth Amendment.

UNITED STATES v. ROBINSON
414 U.S. 218, 94 S.Ct. 467, 38 L.Ed.2d 427 (1973).

JUSTICE REHNQUIST delivered the opinion of the Court. * * *

[Officer Jenks of the D.C. Police Department arrested Robinson on belief, based upon prior investigation, that he was driving after revocation of his operator's permit, an offense which carries a mandatory minimum jail term, a mandatory minimum fine, or both. Robinson concedes "that Jenks had probable cause to arrest * * *, and that he effected a full custody arrest." Pursuant to a Department S.O.P. instructing that incident to such an arrest, mandatory in such circumstances, the officer should make a full "field type search," Jenks patted down Robinson and, upon feeling an object in his breast pocket, removed it and found it was a crumpled up cigarette package, which appeared to contain something other than cigarettes. On inspection of the contents, Jenks found heroin. Jenks' conviction for possession of the heroin was overturned by the court of appeals on the ground that the evidence should have been suppressed.]

It is well settled that a search incident to a lawful arrest is a traditional exception to the warrant requirement of the Fourth Amendment. * * *

Virtually all of the statements of this Court affirming the existence of an unqualified authority to search incident to a lawful arrest are dicta. We would not therefore be foreclosed by principles of *stare decisis* from further examination into history and practice in order to see whether the sort of qualifications imposed by the Court of Appeals in this case were in fact intended by the Framers of the Fourth Amendment or recognized in cases decided prior to *Weeks*. Unfortunately such authorities as exist are sparse. * * *

While these earlier authorities are sketchy, they tend to support the broad statement of the authority to search incident to arrest found in the successive decisions of this Court, rather than the restrictive one which was applied by the Court of Appeals in this case. * * *

The Court of Appeals in effect determined that the *only* reason supporting the authority for a *full* search incident to lawful arrest was the possibility of discovery of evidence or fruits. Concluding that there could be no evidence or fruits in the case of an offense such as that with which respondent was charged, it held that any protective search would have to be limited by the conditions laid down in *Terry* [*v. Ohio*, p. 408] for a search upon less than probable cause to arrest. Quite apart from the fact that *Terry* clearly recognized the distinction between the two types of searches, and that a different rule governed one than governed the other, we find additional reason to disagree with the Court of Appeals.

The justification or reason for the authority to search incident to a lawful arrest rests quite as much on the need to disarm the suspect in order to take him into custody as it does on the need to preserve evidence on his person for later use at trial. The standards traditionally governing a search incident to lawful arrest are not, therefore, commuted to the stricter *Terry* standards by the absence of probable fruits or further evidence of the particular crime for which the arrest is made.

Nor are we inclined, on the basis of what seems to us to be a rather speculative judgment, to qualify the breadth of the general authority to search incident to a lawful custodial arrest on an assumption that persons arrested for the offense of driving while their license has been revoked are less likely to be possessed of dangerous weapons than are those arrested for other crimes.[5] It is scarcely open to doubt that the danger to an officer is far greater in the case of the extended exposure which follows the taking of a suspect into custody and transporting him to the police station than in the case of the relatively fleeting contact resulting from the typical *Terry*-type stop. This is an adequate basis for treating all custodial arrests alike for purposes of search justification.

But quite apart from these distinctions, our more fundamental disagreement with the Court of Appeals arises from its suggestion that there must be litigated in each case the issue of whether or not there was present one of the reasons supporting the authority for a search of the person incident to a lawful arrest. We do not think the long line of authorities of this Court dating back to *Weeks*, nor what we can glean from the history of practice in this country and in England,

---

5. Such an assumption appears at least questionable in light of the available statistical data concerning assaults on police officers who are in the course of making arrests. The danger to the police officer flows from the fact of the arrest, and its attendant proximity, stress and uncertainty, and not from the grounds for arrest. One study concludes that approximately 30% of the shootings of police officers occur when the officer approaches a person seated in a car. Bristow, *Police Officer Shootings—A Tactical Evaluation,* 54 J.Crim.L.C. & P.S. 93 (1963). The Government in its brief notes that the Uniform Crime Reports, prepared by the Federal Bureau of Investigation, indicate that a significant percentage of murders of police officers occurs when the officers are making traffic stops. Brief for the United States, at 23. Those reports indicate that during January–March, 1973, 35 police officers were murdered; 11 of those officers were killed while engaged in traffic stops. Ibid.

requires such a case by case adjudication. A police officer's determination as to how and where to search the person of a suspect whom he has arrested is necessarily a quick *ad hoc* judgment which the Fourth Amendment does not require to be broken down in each instance into an analysis of each step in the search. The authority to search the person incident to a lawful custodial arrest, while based upon the need to disarm and to discover evidence, does not depend on what a court may later decide was the probability in a particular arrest situation that weapons or evidence would in fact be found upon the person of the suspect. A custodial arrest of a suspect based on probable cause is a reasonable intrusion under the Fourth Amendment; that intrusion being lawful, a search incident to the arrest requires no additional justification. It is the fact of the lawful arrest which establishes the authority to search, and we hold that in the case of a lawful custodial arrest a full search of the person is not only an exception to the warrant requirement of the Fourth Amendment, but is also a "reasonable" search under that Amendment.

The search of respondent's person conducted by Officer Jenks in this case and the seizure from him of the heroin, were permissible under established Fourth Amendment law. * * * Since it is the fact of custodial arrest which gives rise to the authority to search, it is of no moment that Jenks did not indicate any subjective fear of the respondent or that he did not himself suspect that respondent was armed.[7] Having in the course of a lawful search come upon the crumpled package of cigarettes, he was entitled to inspect it; and when his inspection revealed the heroin capsules, he was entitled to seize them as "fruits, instrumentalities, or contraband" probative of criminal conduct. The judgment of the Court of Appeals holding otherwise is reversed.

Reversed.

JUSTICE MARSHALL, with whom JUSTICE DOUGLAS and JUSTICE BRENNAN join, dissenting. * * *

The majority's attempt to avoid case-by-case adjudication of Fourth Amendment issues is not only misguided as a matter of principle, but is also doomed to fail as a matter of practical application. As the majority itself is well aware, the powers granted the police in this case are strong ones, subject to potential abuse. Although, in this particular case, Officer Jenks was required by Police Department regulation to make an in-custody arrest rather than to issue a citation, in most jurisdictions and for most traffic offenses the determination of whether to issue a citation or effect a full arrest is discretionary with the officer. There is always the possibility that a police officer, lacking probable cause to obtain a search warrant, will use a traffic arrest as a pretext to conduct a search. I suggest this possibility not to impugn the integrity of our police, but merely to point out that case-by-case adjudication will always be necessary to determine whether a full arrest was effected for purely legitimate reasons or, rather, as a pretext for searching the arrestee. * * *

The Government does not now contend that the search of respondent's pocket can be justified by any need to find and seize evidence in order to prevent its concealment or destruction, for as the Court of Appeals found, there are no evidence or fruits of the offense with which respondent was charged. The only rationale for a search in this case, then, is the removal of weapons which the

---

7. The United States concedes that "in searching respondent, [Officer Jenks] was not motivated by a feeling of imminent danger and was not specifically looking for weapons." Brief for the United States. Officer Jenks testified, "I just searched him [Robinson]. I didn't think about what I was looking for. I just searched him." Officer Jenks also testified that upon removing the cigarette package from the respondent's custody, he was still unsure what was in the package, but that he knew it was not cigarettes.

arrestee might use to harm the officer and attempt an escape. This rationale, of course, is identical to the rationale of the search permitted in *Terry*. * * *

Since the underlying rationale of a *Terry* search and the search of a traffic violator are identical, the Court of Appeals held that the scope of the searches must be the same. * * *

The most obvious difference between the two contexts relates to whether the officer has cause to believe that the individual he is dealing with possesses weapons which might be used against him. *Terry* did not permit an officer to conduct a weapons frisk of anyone he lawfully stopped on the street, but rather, only where "he has reason to believe that he is dealing with an armed and dangerous individual. * * * " While the policeman who arrests a suspected rapist or robber may well have reason to believe he is dealing with an armed and dangerous person, certainly this does not hold true with equal force with respect to persons arrested for motor vehicle violations of the sort involved in this case.

Nor was there any particular reason in this case to believe that respondent was dangerous. He had not attempted to evade arrest, but had quickly complied with the police both in bringing his car to a stop after being signalled to do so and in producing the documents Officer Jenks requested. In fact, Jenks admitted that he searched respondent face-to-face rather than in spread-eagle fashion because he had no reason to believe respondent would be violent.

While this difference between the situation presented in *Terry* and the context presented in this case would tend to suggest a lesser authority to search here than was permitted in *Terry,* other distinctions between the two contexts suggest just the opposite. As the Court of Appeals noted, a crucial feature distinguishing the in-custody arrest from the *Terry* context "is not the greater likelihood that a person taken into custody is armed, but rather the increased likelihood of danger to the officer *if* in fact the person is armed." A *Terry* stop involves a momentary encounter between officer and suspect, while an in-custody arrest places the two in close proximity for a much longer period of time. If the individual happens to have a weapon on his person, he will certainly have much more opportunity to use it against the officer in the in-custody situation. The prolonged proximity also makes it more likely that the individual will be able to extricate any small hidden weapon which might go undetected in a weapons frisk, such as a safety pin or razor blade. In addition, a suspect taken into custody may feel more threatened by the serious restraint on his liberty than a person who is simply stopped by an officer for questioning, and may therefore be more likely to resort to force.

Thus, in some senses there is less need for a weapons search in the in-custody traffic arrest situation than in a *Terry* context, while in other ways, there is a greater need. Balancing these competing considerations in order to determine what is a reasonable warrantless search in the traffic arrest context is a difficult process, one for which there may be no easy analytical guideposts. We are dealing in factors not easily quantified and, therefore, not easily weighed one against the other. And the competing interests we are protecting—the individual's interest in remaining free from unnecessarily intrusive invasions of privacy and society's interest that police officers not take unnecessary risks in the performance of their duties—are each deserving of our most serious attention and do not themselves tip the balance in any particular direction. * * *

The majority opinion fails to recognize that the search conducted by Officer Jenks did not merely involve a search of respondent's person. It also included a separate search of effects found on his person. And even were we to assume, *arguendo,* that it was reasonable for Jenks to remove the object he felt in respondent's pocket, clearly there was no justification consistent with the Fourth Amendment which would authorize his opening the package and looking inside.

To begin with, after Jenks had the cigarette package in his hands, there is no indication that he had reason to believe or did in fact believe that the package contained a weapon. More importantly, even if the crumpled up cigarette package had in fact contained some sort of small weapon, it would have been impossible for respondent to have used it once the package was in the officer's hands. Opening the package therefore did not further the protective purpose of the search. * * *

It is suggested, however, that since the custodial arrest itself represents a significant intrusion into the privacy of the person, any additional intrusion by way of opening or examining effects found on the person is not worthy of constitutional protection. But such an approach was expressly rejected by the Court in *Chimel* [p. 363]. There it was suggested that since the police had lawfully entered petitioner's house to effect an arrest, the additional invasion of privacy stemming from an accompanying search of the entire house was inconsequential. The Court answered: "[W]e see no reason why, simply because some interference with an individual's privacy and freedom of movement has lawfully taken place, further intrusions should automatically be allowed despite the absence of a warrant that the Fourth Amendment would otherwise require." * * *

NOTES AND QUESTIONS

1. Is a *Robinson* search at the place of arrest sometimes unreasonable because, as cautioned in *Illinois v. Lafayette*, p. 407, "the interests supporting a search incident to arrest would hardly justify disrobing an arrestee on the street"? Consider *Paulino v. State*, 924 A.2d 308 (Md.2007) (where police lifted up defendant's shorts and then manipulated his buttocks to find drugs he was believed to be hiding there, search deemed unreasonable because "conducted in the very place in which he was arrested, a car wash," and police took no steps "to limit the public's access to the car wash or took any similar precaution that would limit the ability of the public or any casual observer from viewing the search of Paulino").

2. Is the nature of certain containers carried on the person such that a full search of them should be deemed so uniquely intrusive as to fall outside *Robinson*? That argument has been made with respect to such "containers" as pagers and cell phones, but usually without success, and thus call records and text messages found in such a search are deemed admissible in evidence. See, e.g., *United States v. Finley*, 477 F.3d 250 (5th Cir.2007). But search of more sophisticated devices, such as the iPhone, "a handheld wireless device that functions as a cell phone, BlackBerry, camera, music player, and video player, while simultaneously providing internet access," "capable of holding tens of thousands of pages of personal information," arguably is another matter, as extending *Robinson* to such devices would mean that incident to any arrest an officer, without a warrant and indeed without any reason to believe that evidence of crime would be found, would "be in a position to review incoming and outgoing call histories, scan contact lists, read thousands of emails, view nearly limitless numbers of color photographs and movies, listen to voicemail at the touch of a button, and view the internet websites that an arrestee has visited." Adam M. Gershowitz, *The iPhone Meets the Fourth Amendment*, 56 UCLA L.Rev. 27, 29, 44 (2008).

Compare *State v. Smith*, 920 N.E.2d 949 (Ohio 2009), holding that "because a person has a high expectation of privacy in a cell phone's contents, police must * * * obtain a warrant before intruding into the phone's contents." *Smith* is not limited to a so-called "smart phone"; the court reasoned "that in today's advanced technological age many 'standard' cell phones include a variety of features above and beyond the ability to place phone calls," such as "the ability to send text messages and take pictures," and that "it would not be helpful to create a rule that requires officers to discern the capabilities of a cell phone before acting accordingly." But if the officer merely seizes the phone incident to arrest, may he under some circumstances answer incoming calls, as in *State v. Carroll*, 778 N.W.2d 1 (Wis.2010)?

NOTES AND QUESTIONS ON UNNECESSARY, PRETEXTUAL, AND ARBITRARY ARRESTS

     1.   In the companion case of *Gustafson v. Florida*, 414 U.S. 260 (1973), marijuana cigarettes were found on petitioner's person in a search incident to his custodial arrest for failure to have his operator's license with him while driving. Petitioner contended his case was different from *Robinson* in that (a) the offense for which he was arrested was "benign or trivial in nature," carrying with it no mandatory minimum sentence; and (b) there were no police regulations which required the officer to take petitioner into custody[a] or which required full scale body searches upon arrest in the field. The Court did "not find these differences determinative of the constitutional issue," and thus upheld the search on the basis of *Robinson*. Stewart, J., concurring, stated "that a persuasive claim might have been made in this case that the custodial arrest of the petitioner for a minor traffic offense violated his rights under the Fourth and Fourteenth Amendments," but since petitioner had "fully conceded the constitutional validity of his custodial arrest," the search of his person should be accepted as incidental to that arrest.

     Nearly thirty years later, the issue noted by Justice Stewart was addressed in ATWATER v. CITY OF LAGO VISTA, p. 337, where the Court, per Souter, J., responded to plaintiff's second argument, "for a modern arrest rule, one not necessarily requiring violent breach of the peace, but nonetheless forbidding custodial arrest, even upon probable cause, when conviction could not ultimately carry any jail time and when the government shows no compelling need for immediate detention.

     "If we were to derive a rule exclusively to address the uncontested facts of this case, Atwater might well prevail. She was a known and established resident of Lago Vista with no place to hide and no incentive to flee, and common sense says she would almost certainly have buckled up as a condition of driving off with a citation. In her case, the physical incidents of arrest were merely gratuitous humiliations imposed by a police officer who was (at best) exercising extremely poor judgment. Atwater's claim to live free of pointless indignity and confinement clearly outweighs anything the City can raise against it specific to her case.

     "But we have traditionally recognized that a responsible Fourth Amendment balance is not well served by standards requiring sensitive, case-by-case determinations of government need, lest every discretionary judgment in the field be

---

     a.   Note, in this regard, the variation in state law governing traffic "arrests." Some states require that persons halted for violations of misdemeanor traffic laws be released upon issuance of a citation unless they fall within certain exceptions. The exceptions usually are divided into two categories: (1) persons who must be arrested and taken before a magistrate—usually those violating several specified laws (e.g., driving with a suspended license, or driving under the influence of alcohol); and (2) persons who may be released on citation or taken before a magistrate at the option of the police officer—e.g., those who have violated several other specified laws (e.g., reckless driving or failure to submit to vehicle inspection), who fail to have a license in their possession, or who fail to furnish satisfactory evidence of identification. Other states require that persons in certain categories be taken into custody, but grant the officer discretion as to whether to take other misdemeanor violators into custody or to release them upon issuance of a citation. Special requirements are often imposed for release of nonresident drivers.

converted into an occasion for constitutional review. See, e.g., *United States v. Robinson*, [p. 343]. Often enough, the Fourth Amendment has to be applied on the spur (and in the heat) of the moment, and the object in implementing its command of reasonableness is to draw standards sufficiently clear and simple to be applied with a fair prospect of surviving judicial second-guessing months and years after an arrest or search is made. Courts attempting to strike a reasonable Fourth Amendment balance thus credit the government's side with an essential interest in readily administrable rules.

"At first glance, Atwater's argument may seem to respect the values of clarity and simplicity, so far as she claims that the Fourth Amendment generally forbids warrantless arrests for minor crimes not accompanied by violence or some demonstrable threat of it (whether 'minor crime' be defined as a fine-only traffic offense, a fine-only offense more generally, or a misdemeanor). But the claim is not ultimately so simple, nor could it be, for complications arise the moment we begin to think about the possible applications of the several criteria Atwater proposes for drawing a line between minor crimes with limited arrest authority and others not so restricted.

"One line, she suggests, might be between 'jailable' and 'fine-only' offenses, between those for which conviction could result in commitment and those for which it could not. The trouble with this distinction, of course, is that an officer on the street might not be able to tell. It is not merely that we cannot expect every police officer to know the details of frequently complex penalty schemes, but that penalties for ostensibly identical conduct can vary on account of facts difficult (if not impossible) to know at the scene of an arrest. Is this the first offense or is the suspect a repeat offender? Is the weight of the marijuana a gram above or a gram below the fine-only line? Where conduct could implicate more than one criminal prohibition, which one will the district attorney ultimately decide to charge? And so on.

"But Atwater's refinements would not end there. She represents that if the line were drawn at nonjailable traffic offenses, her proposed limitation should be qualified by a proviso authorizing warrantless arrests where 'necessary for enforcement of the traffic laws or when [an] offense would otherwise continue and pose a danger to others on the road.' (Were the line drawn at misdemeanors generally, a comparable qualification would presumably apply.) The proviso only compounds the difficulties. Would, for instance, either exception apply to speeding? * * *

"There is no need for more examples to show that Atwater's general rule and limiting proviso promise very little in the way of administrability. It is no answer that the police routinely make judgments on grounds like risk of immediate repetition; they surely do and should. But there is a world of difference between making that judgment in choosing between the discretionary leniency of a summons in place of a clearly lawful arrest, and making the same judgment when the question is the lawfulness of the warrantless arrest itself. It is the difference between no basis for legal action challenging the discretionary judgment, on the one hand, and the prospect of evidentiary exclusion or (as here) personal § 1983 liability for the misapplication of a constitutional standard, on the other. Atwater's rule therefore would not only place police in an almost impossible spot but would guarantee increased litigation over many of the arrests that would occur. * * *

"One may ask, of course, why these difficulties may not be answered by a simple tie breaker for the police to follow in the field: if in doubt, do not arrest. The first answer is that in practice the tie breaker would boil down to something akin to a least-restrictive-alternative limitation, which is itself one of those 'ifs, ands, and buts' rules, generally thought inappropriate in working out Fourth Amendment protection. Beyond that, whatever help the tie breaker might give would come at the price of a systematic disincentive to arrest in situations where even Atwater concedes that arresting would serve an important societal interest. * * *

"Just how easily the costs could outweigh the benefits may be shown by asking, as one Member of this Court did at oral argument, 'how bad the problem is out there.' The very fact that the law has never jelled the way Atwater would have it leads one to wonder whether warrantless misdemeanor arrests need constitutional attention, and there is cause to think the answer is no. So far as such arrests might be thought to pose a threat to the probable-cause requirement, anyone arrested for a crime without formal process, whether for felony or misdemeanor, is entitled to a magistrate's review of probable cause within 48 hours, and there is no reason to think the procedure in this case atypical in giving the suspect a prompt opportunity to request release. Many jurisdictions, moreover, have chosen to impose more restrictive safeguards through statutes limiting warrantless arrests for minor offenses. It is of course easier to devise a minor-offense limitation by statute than to derive one through the Constitution, simply because the statute can let the arrest power turn on any sort of practical consideration without having to subsume it under a broader principle. It is, in fact, only natural that States should resort to this sort of legislative regulation, for * * * it is in the interest of the police to limit petty-offense arrests, which carry costs that are simply too great to incur without good reason. Finally, and significantly, under current doctrine the preference for categorical treatment of Fourth Amendment claims gives way to individualized review when a defendant makes a colorable argument that an arrest, with or without a warrant, was 'conducted in an extraordinary manner, unusually harmful to [his] privacy or even physical interests.' *Whren v. United States*, [p. 353].

"The upshot of all these influences, combined with the good sense (and, failing that, the political accountability) of most local lawmakers and law-enforcement officials, is a dearth of horribles demanding redress. Indeed, when Atwater's counsel was asked at oral argument for any indications of comparably foolish, warrantless misdemeanor arrests, he could offer only one. We are sure that there are others, but just as surely the country is not confronting anything like an epidemic of unnecessary minor-offense arrests. That fact caps the reasons for rejecting Atwater's request for the development of a new and distinct body of constitutional law."

O'Connor, J., for the four dissenters, responded: "A custodial arrest exacts an obvious toll on an individual's liberty and privacy, even when the period of custody is relatively brief. The arrestee is subject to a full search of her person and confiscation of her possessions. *United States v. Robinson*, supra. If the arrestee is the occupant of a car, the entire passenger compartment of the car, including packages therein, is subject to search as well. See *New York v. Belton*, [p. 398]. The arrestee may be detained for up to 48 hours without having a magistrate determine whether there in fact was probable cause for the arrest. See *County of Riverside v. McLaughlin*, [p. 342]. Because people arrested for all types of violent and nonviolent offenses may be housed together awaiting such review, this detention period is potentially dangerous. And once the period of custody is over, the fact of the arrest is a permanent part of the public record.

"We have said that 'the penalty that may attach to any particular offense seems to provide the clearest and most consistent indication of the State's interest in arresting individuals suspected of committing that offense.' *Welsh v. Wisconsin*, [p. 381]. If the State has decided that a fine, and not imprisonment, is the appropriate punishment for an offense, the State's interest in taking a person suspected of committing that offense into custody is surely limited, at best. This is not to say that the State will never have such an interest. A full custodial arrest may on occasion vindicate legitimate state interests, even if the crime is punishable only by fine. Arrest is the surest way to abate criminal conduct. It may also allow the police to verify the offender's identity and, if the offender poses a flight risk, to ensure her appearance at trial. But when such considerations are not present, a citation or summons may serve the State's remaining law enforcement interests every bit as effectively as an arrest.

"Because a full custodial arrest is such a severe intrusion on an individual's liberty, its reasonableness hinges on 'the degree to which it is needed for the promotion of legitimate governmental interests.' In light of the availability of citations to promote a State's interests when a fine-only offense has been committed, I cannot concur in a rule which deems a full custodial arrest to be reasonable in every circumstance. Giving police officers constitutional carte blanche to effect an arrest whenever there is probable cause to believe a fine-only misdemeanor has been committed is irreconcilable with the Fourth Amendment's command that seizures be reasonable. Instead, I would require that when there is probable cause to believe that a fine-only offense has been committed, the police officer should issue a citation unless the officer is 'able to point to specific and articulable facts which, taken together with rational inferences from those facts, reasonably warrant [the additional] intrusion' of a full custodial arrest.

"The majority insists that a bright-line rule focused on probable cause is necessary to vindicate the State's interest in easily administrable law enforcement rules. Probable cause itself, however, is not a model of precision. * * * The rule I propose—which merely requires a legitimate reason for the decision to escalate the seizure into a full custodial arrest—thus does not undermine an otherwise 'clear and simple' rule.

"While clarity is certainly a value worthy of consideration in our Fourth Amendment jurisprudence, it by no means trumps the values of liberty and privacy at the heart of the Amendment's protections. * * *

"* * * The majority takes comfort in the lack of evidence of 'an epidemic of unnecessary minor-offense arrests.' But the relatively small number of published cases dealing with such arrests proves little and should provide little solace. Indeed, as the recent debate over racial profiling demonstrates all too clearly, a relatively minor traffic infraction may often serve as an excuse for stopping and harassing an individual. After today, the arsenal available to any officer extends to a full arrest and the searches permissible concomitant to that arrest. An officer's subjective motivations for making a traffic stop are not relevant considerations in determining the reasonableness of the stop. See *Whren v. United States*, supra. But it is precisely because these motivations are beyond our purview that we must vigilantly ensure that officers' poststop actions—which are properly within our reach—comport with the Fourth Amendment's guarantee of reasonableness."

   2. Whether the result in *Atwater* would be different had there been a state law proscribing custodial arrest in the case of a seat belt violation was resolved in *Virginia v. Moore*, 553 U.S. 164 (2008), where defendant was arrested for driving on a suspended license although state law mandated that a summons be utilized in the circumstances of the case. The state court held evidence found in a search incident to that arrest had to be suppressed on Fourth Amendment grounds, but a unanimous Supreme Court, per Scalia, J., concluded that neither the arrest nor the search was unconstitutional. After finding "no historical indication that those who ratified the Fourth Amendment understood it as a redundant guarantee of whatever limits on search and seizure legislatures might have enacted," the Court turned to an examination of "traditional standards of reasonableness," whereby "[i]n a long line of cases, we have said that when an officer has probable cause to believe a person committed even a minor crime in his presence, the balancing of private and public interests is not in doubt." The Court could see no reason for "changing this calculus when a State chooses to protect privacy beyond the level that the Fourth Amendment requires," and several reasons for not doing so. A contrary result "would often frustrate rather than further state policy" (as illustrated by the instant case, where state law mandated use of a summons in minor cases but did not attach a state-law exclusionary sanction to violation of that mandate), "would produce a constitutional regime no less vague and unpredictable than the one we rejected in *Atwater*," and "would cause [Fourth Amendment protections] to 'vary from place to place and from time to time.'" As for Moore's separate argument that the search was unconstitutional even if the arrest was not because of *Robinson*'s "lawful custodial arrest" requirement, the Court responded that this term in *Robinson* was used "as shorthand for compliance with constitutional constraints."

On the other hand, what is *Atwater*'s application when an arrest was made because the law *forbids* the officer from exercising any discretion in favor of the citation alternative, as in *Hedgepeth v. Washington Metropolitan Area Transit Authority*, 386 F.3d 1148 (D.C.Cir.2004), where a 12-year-old was arrested for eating a single french fry in a transit authority station, due to the combined effect of the transit authority's "zero tolerance" policy and a provision of District of Columbia law that prevented officers from issuing citations to minors? Should the minor prevail on the argument that *Atwater* "can only be understood in terms of the Court's concern to avoid interfering with the discretion of police officers called upon to decide 'on the spur (and in the heat) of the moment' * * * whether to arrest or to issue a citation"?

3. Compare with *Atwater* the situation regarding arrest of a person as a material witness (a tactic used with some frequency in the investigation immediately following the 9/11/01 attack[b]). In *Bacon v. United States*, 449 F.2d 933 (9th Cir.1971), the court held that the power to arrest and detain a person as a material witness was "fairly inferable" from what is now 18 U.S.C. § 3144, App. B, but then relied upon the Fourth Amendment in concluding that such arrest was permissible only upon a need-for-custody showing. *Bacon* thus concluded that a material witness arrest warrant must be based upon probable cause, which must be tested by two criteria: (1) "that the testimony of a person is material," and (2) "that it may become impracticable to secure his presence by subpoena." The court's added observation that the first of these could be met by "a mere statement by a responsible official, such as the United States Attorney," was later subjected to a Fourth Amendment challenge on the ground that it "permits a much lower standard than that required for the issuance of a standard arrest warrant," *United States v. Oliver*, 683 F.2d 224 (7th Cir.1982), to which the court responded: "We believe requiring a materiality representation by a responsible official of the United States Attorney's Office strikes a proper and adequate balance between protecting the secrecy of the grand jury's investigation and subjecting an individual to an unjustified arrest."

In *United States v. Awadallah*, 349 F.3d 42 (2d Cir.2003), the district court had concluded that the affidavit for a material witness warrant did not pass the *Bacon/Oliver* two-pronged test because, as for the first prong, "the affidavit fails * * * because it was submitted by [FBI] Agent Plunkett based solely upon his personal knowledge," but "he could not have made an informed judgment about

---

b. At least 70 suspects were jailed indefinitely as material witnesses. See Eric Lichtlau, *Two Groups Charge Abuse of Witness Law*, N.Y. Times, June 27, 2005, p. A10 (Nat'l ed.); Adam Liptak, *New Scrutiny for Law on Detaining Witnesses*, N.Y. Times, Mar. 22, 2006, p. A18 (Nat'l ed.).

the materiality of Awadallah's testimony to the grand jury's investigation as he was never present in the grand jury." The court of appeals disagreed, concluding that while "the person preparing the affidavit" should "have had at least some personal knowledge of what had transpired," "an FBI agent who works closely with a prosecutor in a grand jury investigation may satisfy the 'personal knowledge' requirement," as was the case as to Plunkett.

In *Ashcroft v. al-Kidd*, p. 358, Kennedy, J., for four Justices, noted that the Court had no occasion to explore "when material witness arrests might be consistent with statutory and constitutional requirements," and then commented: "In considering these issues, it is important to bear in mind that the Material Witness Statute might not provide for the issuance of warrants within the meaning of the Fourth Amendment's Warrant Clause. The typical arrest warrant is based on probable cause that the arrestee has committed a crime; but that is not the standard for the issuance of warrants under the Material Witness Statute. * * * If material witness warrants do not qualify as 'Warrants' under the Fourth Amendment, the material witness arrests might still be governed by the Fourth Amendment's separate reasonableness requirement for seizures of the person."

It has been held that this reasonableness requirement involves a "balancing of various competing interests," the expected cost to the witness by being held as compared to the expected cost to the public if the witness is not detained, meaning that the length of the time before the trial at which the witness is to testify is an important consideration. *Schneyder v. Smith*, 653 F.3d 313 (3d Cir.2011) (thus "the Fourth Amendment * * * requires a prosecutor responsible for such a detention to inform the judge who ordered the witness's incarceration of any substantial change in the underlying circumstances," such as that the trial date "had been pushed back several months").

4. As for the pretext arrest issue raised by the *Robinson* dissenters, it was finally addressed by the Supreme Court in WHREN v. UNITED STATES, 517 U.S. 806 (1996). Plainclothes vice-squad officers patrolling a "high drug area" of the District of Columbia in an unmarked car became suspicious of a certain truck, and when they made a U-turn in order to head back toward the truck it turned right suddenly without signaling and then sped off at an unreasonable speed. The police caught up with the vehicle when it was stopped at a red light; one officer approached and told the driver to put the vehicle in park and then saw through the window that passenger Whren had in his hands two large plastic bags of what appeared to be crack cocaine. The occupants of the truck were arrested, and the illegal drugs retrieved from the vehicle led to their conviction notwithstanding the claim of a pretextual stop. Justice Scalia delivered the opinion of a unanimous Court: "As a general matter, the decision to stop an automobile is reasonable where the police have probable cause to believe that a traffic violation has occurred.

"Petitioners accept that Officer Soto had probable cause to believe that various provisions of the District of Columbia traffic code [regarding inattentive driving, speeding, and turning without signalling] had been violated. They argue, however, that 'in the unique context of civil traffic regulations' probable cause is not enough. Since, they contend, the use of automobiles is so heavily and minutely regulated that total compliance with traffic and safety rules is nearly impossible, a police officer will almost invariably be able to catch any given motorist in a technical violation. This creates the temptation to use traffic stops as a means of investigating other law violations, as to which no probable cause or even articulable suspicion exists. Petitioners, who are both black, further contend that police officers might decide which motorists to stop based on decidedly impermissible factors, such as the race of the car's occupants. To avoid this danger, they say, the Fourth Amendment test for traffic stops should be, not the normal one (applied by the Court of Appeals) of whether probable cause existed to justify the stop; but rather, whether a police officer, acting reasonably, would have made the stop for the reason given.

"Petitioners contend that the standard they propose is consistent with our past cases' disapproval of police attempts to use valid bases of action against citizens as pretexts for pursuing other investigatory agendas. We are reminded that in *Florida v. Wells*, [p. 408], we stated that 'an inventory search must not be used as a ruse for a general rummaging in order to discover incriminating evidence'; that in *Colorado v. Bertine*, [p. 407], in approving an inventory search, we apparently thought it significant that there had been 'no showing that the police, who were following standard procedures, acted in bad faith or for the sole purpose of investigation'; and that in *New York v. Burger*, [p. 440], we observed, in upholding the constitutionality of a warrantless administrative inspection, that the search did not appear to be 'a "pretext" for obtaining evidence of . . . violation of . . . penal laws.' But only an undiscerning reader would regard these cases as endorsing the principle that ulterior motives can invalidate police conduct that is justifiable on the basis of probable cause to believe that a violation of law has occurred. In each case we were addressing the validity of a search conducted in the absence of probable cause. Our quoted statements simply explain that the exemption from the need for probable cause (and warrant), which is accorded to searches made for the purpose of inventory or administrative regulation, is not accorded to searches that are not made for those purposes.

" * * * Not only have we never held, outside the context of inventory search or administrative inspection (discussed above), that an officer's motive invalidates objectively justifiable behavior under the Fourth Amendment; but we have repeatedly held and asserted the contrary. In *United States v. Villamonte–Marquez*, 462 U.S. 579 (1983), we held that an otherwise valid warrantless boarding of a vessel by customs officials was not rendered invalid 'because the customs officers were accompanied by a Louisiana state policeman, and were following an informant's tip that a vessel in the ship channel was thought to be carrying marihuana.' We flatly dismissed the idea that an ulterior motive might serve to strip the agents of their legal justification. In *United States v. Robinson*, [p. 343], we held that a traffic-violation arrest (of the sort here) would not be rendered invalid by the fact that it was 'a mere pretext for a narcotics search,' and that a lawful postarrest search of the person would not be rendered invalid by the fact that it was not motivated by the officer-safety concern that justifies such searches. And in *Scott v. United States*, 436 U.S. 128 (1978), in rejecting the contention that wiretap evidence was subject to exclusion because the agents conducting the tap had failed to make any effort to comply with the statutory requirement that unauthorized acquisitions be minimized, we said that '[s]ubjective intent alone . . . does not make otherwise lawful conduct illegal or unconstitutional.' We described *Robinson* as having established that 'the fact that the officer does not have the state of mind which is hypothecated by the reasons which provide the legal justification for the officer's action does not invalidate the action taken as long as the circumstances, viewed objectively, justify that action.'

"We think these cases foreclose any argument that the constitutional reasonableness of traffic stops depends on the actual motivations of the individual officers involved. We of course agree with petitioners that the Constitution prohibits selective enforcement of the law based on considerations such as race. But the constitutional basis for objecting to intentionally discriminatory application of laws is the Equal Protection Clause, not the Fourth Amendment. Subjective intentions play no role in ordinary, probable-cause Fourth Amendment analysis.

"Recognizing that we have been unwilling to entertain Fourth Amendment challenges based on the actual motivations of individual officers, petitioners disavow any intention to make the individual officer's subjective good faith the touchstone of 'reasonableness.' They insist that the standard they have put forward—whether the officer's conduct deviated materially from usual police practices, so that a reasonable officer in the same circumstances would not have made the stop for the reasons given—is an 'objective' one.

"But although framed in empirical terms, this approach is plainly and indisputably driven by subjective considerations. Its whole purpose is to prevent the police from doing under the guise of enforcing the traffic code what they would like to do for different reasons. Petitioners' proposed standard may not use the word 'pretext,' but it is designed to combat nothing other than the perceived 'danger' of the pretextual stop, albeit only indirectly and over the run of cases. Instead of asking whether the individual officer had the proper state of mind, the petitioners would have us ask, in effect, whether (based on general police practices) it is plausible to believe that the officer had the proper state of mind.

"Why one would frame a test designed to combat pretext in such fashion that the court cannot take into account actual and admitted pretext is a curiosity that can only be explained by the fact that our cases have foreclosed the more sensible option. If those cases were based only upon the evidentiary difficulty of establishing subjective intent, petitioners' attempt to root out subjective vices through objective means might make sense. But they were not based only upon that, or indeed even principally upon that. Their principal basis—which applies equally to attempts to reach subjective intent through ostensibly objective means—is simply that the Fourth Amendment's concern with 'reasonableness' allows certain actions to be taken in certain circumstances, whatever the subjective intent. See, e.g., *Robinson,* supra ('Since it is the fact of custodial arrest which gives rise to the authority to search, it is of no moment that [the officer] did not indicate any subjective fear of the [arrestee] or that he did not himself suspect that [the arrestee] was armed'). But even if our concern had been only an evidentiary one, petitioners' proposal would by no means assuage it. Indeed, it seems to us somewhat easier to figure out the intent of an individual officer than to plumb the collective consciousness of law enforcement in order to determine whether a 'reasonable officer' would have been moved to act upon the traffic violation. While police manuals and standard procedures may sometimes provide objective assistance, ordinarily one would be reduced to speculating about the hypothetical reaction of a hypothetical constable—an exercise that might be called virtual subjectivity. * * *

"It is of course true that in principle every Fourth Amendment case, since it turns upon a 'reasonableness' determination, involves a balancing of all relevant factors. With rare exceptions not applicable here, however, the result of that balancing is not in doubt where the search or seizure is based upon probable cause. * * *

"Where probable cause has existed, the only cases in which we have found it necessary actually to perform the 'balancing' analysis involved searches or seizures conducted in an extraordinary manner, unusually harmful to an individual's privacy or even physical interests—such as, for example, seizure by means of deadly force, see *Tennessee v. Garner,* [p. 339], unannounced entry into a home, see *Wilson v. Arkansas,* [p. 322], entry into a home without a warrant, see *Welsh v. Wisconsin,* [p. 381], or physical penetration of the body, see *Winston v. Lee,* [p. 360]. The making of a traffic stop out-of-uniform does not remotely qualify as such an extreme practice, and so is governed by the usual rule that probable cause to believe the law has been broken 'outbalances' private interest in avoiding police contact.

"Petitioners urge as an extraordinary factor in this case that the 'multitude of applicable traffic and equipment regulations' is so large and so difficult to obey perfectly that virtually everyone is guilty of violation, permitting the police to single out almost whomever they wish for a stop. But we are aware of no principle that would allow us to decide at what point a code of law becomes so expansive and so commonly violated that infraction itself can no longer be the ordinary measure of the lawfulness of enforcement. And even if we could identify such exorbitant codes, we do not know by what standard (or what right) we would decide, as petitioners would have us do, which particular provisions are sufficiently important to merit enforcement.

"For the run-of-the-mine case, which this surely is, we think there is no realistic alternative to the traditional common-law rule that probable cause justifies a search and seizure."

5. As the Supreme Court was advised in the briefs of the petitioners and amici, the tactic at issue in *Whren* is one which has been commonly employed by police in recent years in their "war against drugs." Both in urban areas and on the interstates, police are on the watch for "suspicious" travellers, and once one is spotted it is only a matter of time before some technical or trivial offense produces the necessary excuse for pulling him over. Perhaps because the offenses are so often insignificant, the driver is typically told at the outset that he will merely be given a warning. But then things often turn ugly. The driver and passengers are usually closely questioned about their identities, the reason for their travels, their intended destination, and the like. The subject of drugs comes up, and often the driver is induced to "consent" to a full search of the vehicle and all effects therein for drugs. If such consent is not forthcoming, another police vehicle with a drug-sniffing dog may appear on the scene. See, e.g., *United States v. Mesa,* 62 F.3d 159 (6th Cir.1995); *United States v. Roberson,* 6 F.3d 1088 (5th Cir.1993) (noting the trooper's "remarkable record" of turning traffic stops into drug arrests on 250 prior occasions); *State v. Dominguez–Martinez,* 895 P.2d 306 (Or.1995).[c]

6. Two illustrations from the many reported cases of this genre reveal how little it takes to supply grounds for a traffic stop acceptable to the courts. In one, a Texas state trooper passing a van noticed it had four black occupants, so the officer crested a hill, pulled onto the shoulder and doused his lights. When the van approached, the driver cautiously changed lanes to distance the van from the vehicle on the shoulder, but failed to signal—hardly surprising considering that the van was the only moving vehicle on that stretch of road. Yet the stop for an illegal lane change was upheld. *United States v. Roberson,* supra. In the other case, the stop occurred after a Utah deputy patrolling Interstate 70 saw an automobile driven by a black man straddle the center line for about one second before proceeding to the other lane of traffic. The stop was upheld on the grounds that the officer had sufficient suspicion the operator was driving while impaired. *United States v. Lee,* 73 F.3d 1034 (10th Cir.1996).

7. The dissent by Chief Judge Seymour in *United States v. Botero–Ospina,* 71 F.3d 783 (10th Cir.1995), a pre-*Whren* decision which squares with the *Whren* holding, provides an interesting contrast to the later Scalia opinion in *Whren.* That dissent states in part:

"In addition to producing the intrusion any individual experiences when subjected to a traffic stop, the majority's standard frees a police officer to target

---

c. A recent study estimates that in 2005 17.8 million persons were subjected to a traffic stop; that about 5% of the stops included a search of the driver, the vehicle or both; that 57.6% of those searches were by consent; and that black (9.5%) and Hispanic (8.8%) motorists were searched at higher rates than whites (3.6%). Matthew R. Durose et al., *Contacts between Police and the Public, 2005* (U.S. Dep't of Justice, 2007).

members of minority communities for the selective enforcement of otherwise unenforced statutes. The Supreme Court recognized in *Terry* [*v. Ohio*, p. 408] that the harassment of minority groups by certain elements of the police population does occur, and that 'the degree of community resentment aroused by particular practices is clearly relevant to an assessment of the quality of the intrusion upon reasonable expectations of personal security caused by those practices.' By refusing to examine either the arbitrariness with which a particular statute is enforced or the motivation underlying its enforcement in a particular case, the majority standard does nothing to curb the ugly reality that minority groups are sometimes targeted for selective enforcement.[d] As a result, the majority standard adds the onus of discrimination and resentment to the already significant burden imposed by traffic stops generally. * * *

"The Supreme Court held in *Terry* that to justify a particular intrusion, a 'police officer must be able to point to specific and articulable facts which, taken together with the rational inferences from those facts, reasonably warrant that intrusion.' It is difficult to justify a stop as reasonable, even if supported by an observed violation, if the undisputed facts indicate that the violation does not ordinarily result in a stop. Moreover, the Court in *Terry* described in detail the appropriate reasonableness inquiry in language that is utterly irreconcilable with the majority standard. The Court stated that in assessing the reasonableness of a particular stop 'it is imperative that the facts be judged against an objective standard: would the facts available to the officer at the moment of the seizure or the search "warrant a man of reasonable caution in the belief" that the action taken was appropriate?' It would hardly seem necessary to point out that the Court's mandate to determine what a reasonable officer would do in the circumstances cannot be fulfilled by merely ascertaining in a vacuum what a particular officer could do under state law.

"Given the 'multitude of applicable traffic and equipment regulations' in any jurisdiction, upholding a stop on the basis of a regulation seldom enforced opens the door to the arbitrary exercise of police discretion condemned in *Terry* and its progeny. 'Anything less [than the reasonable officer standard] would invite intrusions upon constitutionally guaranteed rights based on nothing more substantial than inarticulate hunches, a result this Court has consistently refused to sanction.' *Terry*."

8. Is Chief Judge Seymour's concern about harassment of minorities met by Justice Scalia's observation that selective enforcement based on race is barred by the Equal Protection Clause? How could the petitioners in *Whren* have proved such an equal protection violation? Does/should the "rigorous standard for discovery" against the government upon a defendant's claim of race-based selective prosecution, see *United States v. Armstrong*, Ch. 13, § 3, also apply in this setting? And even if the *Whren* petitioners *did* prove that the traffic stop was itself a violation of the Equal Protection Clause, would that bar prosecution on the *drug* charges? Would it require suppression of the drugs? Cf. *United States v. Jennings*,

---

d. "As part of the settlement of a civil rights lawsuit, the Maryland State Police tracked the race of drivers stopped since January 1995.

"Statistics released last November showed that 73 percent of drivers who were stopped and searched on Interstate 95 between Baltimore and Delaware were African–American. A corresponding American Civil Liberties Union study concluded that only 14 percent of drivers on the highway were black.

"And in central Florida, black drivers on the Florida Turnpike were 6.5 times more likely to be searched than white drivers, according to an analysis by the *Orlando Sentinel*, which studied more than 3,800 traffic stops between January 1996 and April 1997." Michael Higgins, *Looki· the Part*, 48 A.B.A.J. 48, 49 (Nov.1997). See also David A. Harris, *"Driving While Black" and Other Traffic Offenses: The Supreme Court and Pretextual Traffic Stops*, 87 J.Crim Criminology 544 (1997).

985 F.2d 562 (6th Cir.1993) (dictum by majority that if defendant had proved he had been selected for a consensual encounter solely because of his race, then the evidence obtained in a consent search during that encounter ought to be excluded, as "evidence seized in violation of the Equal Protection Clause should be suppressed"; concurring opinion notes that the case cited in support by the majority, *Elkins v. United States,* p. 227, "provides absolutely no support for the majority's position").

9. Does Justice Scalia ever respond directly to the *Whren* petitioners' argument that probable cause is not enough "in the unique context of civil traffic regulations" because it is possible for a police officer to catch any given motorist in a technical violation? Is the proper response, as Scalia says at one point, that the matter of police purpose is relevant only in situations represented by *Wells, Bertine* and *Burger,* where the search is allowed without probable cause? Is the risk of pretext greater or lesser in those situations, where the police must show they complied with "standard procedures" or "reasonable legislative or administrative standards," than as to traffic stops?

Where does *Whren* end and *Bertine* begin? Consider *State v. Sullivan,* 16 S.W.3d 551 (Ark.2000), where the Court declined "to sanction conduct where a police officer can trail a targeted vehicle with a driver merely suspected of criminal activity, wait for the driver to exceed the speed limit by one mile per hour, arrest the driver for speeding, and conduct a full-blown inventory search of the vehicle with impunity." The Supreme Court summarily reversed because of the Arkansas court's erroneous claim that it could "interpret[] the U.S. Constitution more broadly than the United States Supreme Court," and added that *Whren,* itself a traffic stop case, also applied to custodial arrests. *Arkansas v. Sullivan,* 532 U.S. 769 (2001). The four concurring Justices said the above quotation from the state court opinion manifested "a concern rooted in the Fourth Amendment," but then concluded that "such exercises of official discretion are unlimited by the Fourth Amendment" in light of *Whren.* Is that a correct reading of *Whren*?

10. *Whren* was revisited in *Ashcroft v. al-Kidd,* 131 S.Ct. 2074 (2011), where al-Kidd brought a *Bivens* action (see p. 242), alleging his Fourth Amendment rights were violated by a pretextual detention policy whereby, after 9/11, then Attorney General Ashcroft authorized federal officials to use the federal material witness law (see p. 352–53) to detain terrorist suspects. All eight participating Justices agreed that Ashcroft was entitled to qualified immunity because the purported right to nonpretextual application of the statute was not "clearly established" at the time of the challenged conduct. Scalia, J., for the 5–Justice majority, then appeared to address the merits of the Fourth Amendment claim. Characterizing the instant case as one involving "a validly obtained warrant" which was "based on individualized suspicion" (purportedly conceded by al-Kidd), it was thus deemed to be outside the "two limited exception[s]" to *Whren,* i.e., "special-needs and administrative-search cases." That is, "subjective intent" can come into play only in the case of warrantless action not based upon individualized suspicion, as in *City of Indianapolis v. Edmond,* p. 449. The other three Justices, concurring in the judgment, objected (1) "to the Court's disposition of al-Kidd's Fourth Amendment claim on the merits"; (2) to the "validly obtained warrant" assumption, in that "omissions and misrepresentations" in the affidavit could mean it was vulnerable under *Franks,* p. 307; (3) to the "individualized suspicion" assumption, because the "Court's decisions, until today, have uniformly used the term * * * to mean individualized suspicion *of wrongdoing*"; and (4) that *Whren* did not settle "whether an official's subjective intent matters" in the "novel context" of the instant case, involving "prolonged detention of an individual without probable cause to believe he had committed any criminal offense."

NOTES AND QUESTIONS ON OTHER
SEARCHES OF THE PERSON

1. Full searches of an arrested person and his carried personal effects are more typically made when that person has been delivered to the place of his forthcoming detention. These searches are typically upheld on two bases: (1) as a delayed *Robinson* search incident to arrest; and (2) as an inventory incident to booking to safeguard the property of the accused and to ensure that weapons and contraband are not introduced into the jail.[a] However, some jurisdictions have rejected the *Robinson* rule and have also limited the extent of permissible inventory, see, e.g., *State v. Kaluna,* 520 P.2d 51 (Hawaii 1974), and in some jurisdictions a search at the station is deemed unlawful if the defendant was not afforded a sufficient opportunity to gain his release, see, e.g., *Zehrung v. State,* 569 P.2d 189 (Alaska 1977).

2. *United States v. Edwards,* 415 U.S. 800 (1974), concerned the admissibility of paint chips obtained from defendant's clothing, taken from him without a warrant while he was in jail about 10 hours after his arrest for attempted breaking and entering. The clothing was seized because investigation subsequent to the arrest showed that paint had been chipped from a window when entry was attempted with a pry bar. The Court, per White, J., concluded "that once the defendant is lawfully arrested and is in custody, the effects in his possession at the place of detention that were subject to search at the time and place of his arrest may lawfully be searched and seized without a warrant even though a substantial period of time has elapsed between the arrest and subsequent administrative processing on the one hand and the taking of the property for use as evidence on the other. This is true where the clothing or effects are immediately seized upon arrival at the jail, held under the defendant's name in the 'property room' of the jail and at a later time searched and taken for use at the subsequent criminal trial. The result is the same where the property is not physically taken from the defendant until sometime after his incarceration."[b] The Court added it was not holding "that the warrant clause of the Fourth Amendment is never applicable to postarrest seizures of the effects of an arrestee," and by footnote to that caveat stated it was expressing no view "concerning those circumstances surrounding custodial searches incident to incarceration which might 'violate the dictates of reason either because of their number or their manner of perpetration.' "

Stewart, J., joined by Douglas, Brennan, and Marshall, JJ., dissented, arguing that they could "see no justification for dispensing with the warrant requirement here. The police had ample time to seek a warrant, and no exigent circumstances were present to excuse their failure to do so," as the government "has not even suggested that [the defendant] was aware of the presence of the paint chips on his clothing."

3. After *Robinson* and *Edwards,* is a person in custody following a lawful arrest "fair game" for a search for evidence of crimes other than the crime for which the arrest was made? Compare *People v. Trudeau,* 187 N.W.2d 890 (Mich.1971) (defendant was under arrest for breaking and entering, in recent attempted burglary with similar modus operandi watchman was killed and heel print was left at scene, police subsequently took defendant's shoe and matched it with heel print; held, seizure illegal because police "had no probable cause to believe that the seized shoes were evidence linked to the crime").

---

a. See *Illinois v. Lafayette,* discussed in *Colorado v. Bertine,* p. 407.

b. A search incident to arrest made at the station is deemed unlawful if the grounds for the arrest have dissipated prior to the time of the search. See *United States v. Coughlin,* 338 F.Supp. 1328 (E.D.Mich.1972).

4. In SCHMERBER v. CALIFORNIA, [the facts and other aspects of which are discussed at p. 30], the Court per Brennan, J., observed:

"Although the facts which established probable cause to arrest in this case also suggested the required relevance and likely success of a test of petitioner's blood for alcohol, the question remains whether the arresting officer was permitted to draw these inferences himself, or was required instead to procure a warrant before proceeding with the test. Search warrants are ordinarily required for searches of dwellings, and, absent an emergency, no less could be required where intrusions into the human body are concerned. * * *

"The officer in the present case, however, might reasonably have believed that he was confronted with an emergency, in which the delay necessary to obtain a warrant, under the circumstances, threatened 'the destruction of evidence' * * *. We are told that the percentage of alcohol in the blood begins to diminish shortly after drinking stops, as the body functions to eliminate it from the system. Particularly in a case such as this, where time had to be taken to bring the accused to a hospital and to investigate the scene of the accident, there was no time to seek out a magistrate and secure a warrant. Given these special facts, we conclude that the attempt to secure evidence of blood-alcohol content in this case was an appropriate incident to petitioner's arrest.'"[c]

5. Applying the *Schmerber* balancing test, the Court in *Winston v. Lee*, 470 U.S. 753 (1985), held that the proposed court-ordered surgery on defendant, for the purpose of removing a bullet expected to show that defendant was the robber hit by the victim's gunfire, would constitute an unreasonable search. "The reasonableness of surgical intrusions beneath the skin," the Court stated per Brennan, J., "depends on a case-by-case approach, in which the individual's interests in privacy and security are weighed against society's interests in conducting the procedure." Taking into account medical evidence that the operation would require a general anesthetic, might last over two hours, and could require probing of muscle tissue which might cause injury to the muscle as well as to nerves, blood vessels and other tissue, the Court concluded the "operation sought will intrude substantially on respondent's protected interests." Such an intrusion would not be reasonable, the Court then decided, given the state's failure "to demonstrate a compelling need for it." No such need was deemed to be present, as the state had considerable other evidence connecting defendant with the robbery, including a prompt identification of him by the victim and his location near the robbery shortly after it occurred.[d]

6. In light of *Schmerber* and *Winston*, what about other scientific tests and intrusions into the body after arrest? If a warrantless blood draw would be permissible under *Schmerber*, may the police opt for forced catheterization? Consider *Miller v. Idaho State Patrol*, 252 P.3d 1274 (Idaho 2011) (existing "legal uncertainty" on this point provides officers with "qualified immunity" in § 1983 suit). Or, consider *United States ex rel. Guy v. McCauley*, 385 F.Supp. 193 (E.D.Wis.1974), concerning a stationhouse search of the vagina of an incarcerated female which resulted in the discovery of a packet of narcotics. The court held the search violated due process because not conducted "by skilled medical technicians." But what if it had been so conducted? In *Guy*, the defendant also objected that the search was not made upon probable cause, but the court, while noting

---

c. Is it essential that this be characterized as a search incident to arrest? What if the defendant had not been arrested and the blood sample was taken while he was in the emergency room of the hospital for treatment of injuries he received in an accident in which he was involved, because it reasonably appeared to the police investigating the accident that he was intoxicated? Is this issue resolved by *Cupp v. Murphy*, discussed in Note 8 infra?

d. See Ronald J. Bacigal, *Dodging a Bullet, But Opening Old Wounds in Fourth Amendment Jurisprudence*, 16 Seton Hall L.Rev. 597 (1986).

that the search was apparently prompted by "vague information several years old that [she] was known to carry heroin in her vagina," asserted that this objection "missed the mark" in light of *Robinson* and *Edwards*. Is that so? What then of a stationhouse strip search? Compare *Powell v. Barrett*, 541 F.3d 1298 (11th Cir.2008) (upholding county jail practice of conducting full body visual strip searches on *all* jail detainees being booked into the general population for the first time, regardless of whether there reasonable suspicion and regardless of whether inmates arrested for minor offenses or misdemeanors); with *Jimenez v. Wood County*, 621 F.3d 372 (5th Cir.2010) (despite contra authority in some other circuits, court adheres to rule that "a strip search of an individual arrested for a minor offense must be premised on reasonable suspicion that the detainee is carrying weapons or contraband"). What then of other warrantless searches of the body of an arrestee which have been upheld, including "the placing of the arrestee's hands under an ultraviolet lamp; examining the arrestee's arms to determine the age of burn marks; swabbing the arrestee's hands with a chemical substance; taking scrapings from under the arrestee's fingernails; taking a small sample of hair from the arrestee's head; obtaining a urine sample from the arrestee; taking a saliva sample from the arrestee; giving the arrestee a breathalyzer examination; swabbing the arrestee's penis; taking dental impressions from the arrestee; or taking pubic hair combings from him." SEARCHSZR § 5.3(c). As for routinely taking a DNA sample from an arrestee, see Note 7, p. 453.

7. In *Knowles v. Iowa*, 525 U.S. 113 (1998), a policeman stopped Knowles for speeding and then, pursuant to a statute authorizing (but not requiring) him to issue a citation in lieu of arrest for most bailable offenses, issued Knowles a citation. The officer then made a full search of Knowles' car and found a bag of marijuana. That search was upheld by the state courts on the ground that because an Iowa statute declared that issuance of a citation in lieu of arrest "does not affect the officer's authority to conduct an otherwise lawful search," it sufficed here that the officer had probable cause to make a custodial arrest. A unanimous Supreme Court, per REHNQUIST, C.J., reversed. Looking at the two historical rationales for search incident to arrest discussed in *Robinson*, the Court reasoned: (i) The "threat to officer safety from issuing a traffic citation * * * is a good deal less than in the case of a custodial arrest," where (as it was put in *Robinson*) there is "the extended exposure which follows the taking of a suspect into custody and transporting him to the police station," and thus the "concern for officer safety" incident to a traffic stop is sufficiently met by the officer's authority to order the driver and passengers out of the car,[e] to "perform a 'patdown' of a driver and any passengers upon reasonable suspicion that they may be armed and dangerous,"[f] and to conduct a patdown "of the passenger compartment of a vehicle upon reasonable suspicion that an occupant is dangerous and may gain immediate control of a weapon."[g] (ii) The "need to discover and preserve evi-

---

e. In *Pennsylvania v. Mimms*, 434 U.S. 106 (1977), officers stopped a vehicle with an expired license plate for the purpose of issuing a traffic summons and then ordered the driver out of the car, which resulted in the observation of a large bulge under his pocket, and this prompted a frisk and discovery of a gun. Rejecting the state court's holding that the driver could be directed to get out of the car only upon a reasonable suspicion he "posed a threat to police safety," the Court reasoned that "this additional intrusion can only be described as de minimis" and was justified because it "reduces the likelihood that the officer will be the victim of an assault." In *Maryland v. Wilson*, 519 U.S. 408 (1997), the Court held "that an officer making a traffic stop may order passengers to get out of the car pending completion of the stop." The Court agreed that "there is not the same basis for ordering the passengers out of the car as there is for ordering the driver out," but yet deemed "the additional intrusion on the passenger" to be "minimal" and justified in light of the fact that "danger to an officer from a traffic stop is likely to be greater when there are passengers in addition to the driver in the stopped car."

f. As authorized by *Terry v. Ohio*, p. 408.

g. As authorized by *Michigan v. Long*, p. 436.

dence" does not exist here, as "no further evidence of excessive speed was going to be found either on the person of the offender or in the passenger compartment of the car," and any concern with destruction of evidence as to identity can be met by arresting the driver whenever the officer is not satisfied with his identification.

Considering that Knowles "did not argue * * * that the statute could never be lawfully applied" and that the Court only passed upon "the search at issue," are there circumstances in which a search made under this statute would be lawful? Consider *State v. Greenslit*, 559 A.2d 672 (Vt.1989) (upholding search of person incident to issuance of notice to appear for present use of marijuana). What if Iowa reformulated its statute to conform to language used in some other states, i.e., that if an officer makes an arrest, the lawfulness of a search incident thereto is not affected by a subsequent decision at the scene to issue a citation and release the arrestee? Or, even absent such reformulation, may Iowa police, given their broad statutory authority to elect either citation or arrest as they wish, merely delay that decision until after a search, and then justify productive searches under the principle of the *Rawlings* case, note h infra?

While *Knowles* involves a situation in which state law permits an arrest but no arrest was made, is it relevant as well in the reverse situation, where an arrest *was* made but state law forbids the arrest notwithstanding probable cause? No, the Supreme Court answered in *Virginia v. Moore,* p. 351, for the "state officers *arrested* Moore, and therefore faced the risks that are 'an adequate basis for treating all custodial arrests alike for purposes of search justification'" (quoting *Robinson*).

8. As for search of the person without any prior seizure, consider *Cupp v. Murphy*, 412 U.S. 291 (1973). The Court, per Stewart, J., held that where Murphy voluntarily appeared at the station for questioning concerning the strangulation of his wife, at which time the police noticed what appeared to be blood on his finger, and the police had probable cause to arrest him but did not formally place him under arrest,[h] the warrantless taking of scrapings from his fingernails "was constitutionally permissible." Noting that Murphy was aware of the police suspicion and tried to wipe his fingers clean, the Court concluded that "the rationale of *Chimel* [p. 363] justified the police in subjecting him to the very limited search necessary to preserve the highly evanescent evidence they found under his fingernails." But, because a person not under formal arrest "might well be less hostile to the police and less likely to take conspicuous, immediate steps to destroy incriminating evidence on his person," the Court emphasized it was *not* holding "that a full *Chimel* search would have been justified in this case without a formal arrest and without a warrant." Marshall, J., concurring, noted that the police could not have preserved the evidence by "close surveillance" and that detaining Murphy while a warrant was sought "would have been as much a seizure as detaining him while his fingernails were scraped." Douglas, J., dissenting, argued: "There was time to get a warrant; Murphy could have been detained while one was sought; and that detention would have preserved the perishable evidence the police sought."

---

h. Murphy was not arrested until over a month later, and thus the case is unlike those in which the arrest followed the search by a matter of minutes. The prevailing view is that a search "incident" to arrest may actually come before the formal making of an arrest if the police had grounds to arrest at the time the search was made. As stated in *Rawlings v. Kentucky* (other aspects of which are discussed at p. 885): "Where the formal arrest followed quickly on the heels of the challenged search of petitioner's person, we do not believe it particularly important that the search preceded the arrest rather than vice versa."

SECTION 6. WARRANTLESS ENTRIES AND SEARCHES OF PREMISES

CHIMEL v. CALIFORNIA
395 U.S. 752, 89 S.Ct. 2034, 23 L.Ed.2d 685 (1969).

JUSTICE STEWART delivered the opinion of the Court. * * *

[Police armed with an arrest warrant for Chimel for burglary of a coin shop, after being admitted into his residence, arrested him therein, and then looked through the entire three-bedroom house, including the attic, the garage, and a small workshop, and seized coins and similar objects thought to be the fruits of the burglary. That evidence was admitted against Chimel at trial over his objection that the evidence had been unconstitutionally seized.]

Without deciding the question, we proceed on the hypothesis that the California courts were correct in holding that the arrest of the petitioner was valid under the Constitution. This brings us directly to the question whether the warrantless search of the petitioner's entire house can be constitutionally justified as incident to that arrest. The decisions of this Court bearing upon that question have been far from consistent, as even the most cursory review makes evident.[a]

In 1950 * * * came *United States v. Rabinowitz,* 339 U.S. 56 (1950), the decision upon which California primarily relies in the case now before us. In *Rabinowitz,* federal authorities had been informed that the defendant was dealing in stamps bearing forged overprints. On the basis of that information they secured a warrant for his arrest, which they executed at his one-room business office. At the time of the arrest, the officers "searched the desk, safe, and file cabinets in the office for about an hour and a half," and seized 573 stamps with forged overprints. The stamps were admitted into evidence at the defendant's trial, and this Court affirmed his conviction, rejecting the contention that the warrantless search had been unlawful. The Court held that the search in its entirety fell within the principle giving law enforcement authorities "[t]he right 'to search the place where the arrest is made in order to find and seize things connected with the crime * * *.'" * * * The test, said the Court, "is not whether it is reasonable to procure a search warrant, but whether the search was reasonable."

Rabinowitz has come to stand for the proposition, inter alia, that a warrantless search "incident to a lawful arrest" may generally extend to the area that is considered to be in the "possession" or under the "control" of the person arrested. And it was on the basis of that proposition that the California courts upheld the search of the petitioner's entire house in this case. That doctrine, however, at least in the broad sense in which it was applied by the California courts in this case, can withstand neither historical nor rational analysis.

---

a. In an omitted portion of the opinion, the Court described how dictum on search incident to arrest broadened from search of the "person," *Weeks v. United States,* 232 U.S. 383 (1914), to search for what is "upon his person or in his control," *Carroll v. United States,* 267 U.S. 132 (1925), to search of "persons lawfully arrested" and "the place where the arrest is made," *Agnello v. United States,* 269 U.S. 20 (1925). Then, in *Marron v. United States,* 275 U.S. 192 (1927), concerning seizure of evidence at a place where illegal liquor sales were occurring, the Court held that because the police had made an arrest on the premises they "had a right without a warrant contemporaneously to search the place in order to find and seize the things used to carry on the criminal enterprise." But in *Go-Bart Importing Co. v. United States,* 282 U.S. 344 (1931), *Marron* was limited to where the items seized "were visible and accessible and in the offender's immediate custody" and there "was no threat of force or general search or rummaging of the place." This limitation was reiterated in *United States v. Lefkowitz,* 285 U.S. 452 (1932), which, like *Go-Bart,* held unlawful a search of a desk despite the fact the search had accompanied a lawful arrest, but was abandoned in *Harris v. United States,* 331 U.S. 145 (1947), upholding the search of a four-room apartment as "incident to arrest." But *Harris* was not followed in *Trupiano v. United States,* 334 U.S. 699 (1948), declaring that "law enforcement agents must secure and use search warrants wherever reasonably practicable."

Even limited to its own facts, the *Rabinowitz* decision was, as we have seen, hardly founded on an unimpeachable line of authority. * * *

Nor is the rationale by which the State seeks here to sustain the search of the petitioner's house supported by a reasoned view of the background and purpose of the Fourth Amendment. Justice Frankfurter wisely pointed out in his *Rabinowitz* dissent that the Amendment's proscription of "unreasonable searches and seizures" must be read in light of "the history that gave rise to the words"—a history of "abuses so deeply felt by the Colonies as to be one of the potent causes of the Revolution * * *." The Amendment was in large part a reaction to the general warrants and warrantless searches that had so alienated the colonists and had helped speed the movement for independence. In the scheme of the Amendment, therefore, the requirement that "no Warrants shall issue, but upon probable cause," plays a crucial part. * * * Even in the *Agnello* case the Court relied upon the rule that "[b]elief, however well founded, that an article sought is concealed in a dwelling house furnishes no justification for a search of that place without a warrant. And such searches are held unlawful notwithstanding facts unquestionably showing probable cause." Clearly, the general requirement that a search warrant be obtained is not lightly to be dispensed with, and "the burden is on those seeking [an] exemption [from the requirement] to show the need for it * * *."

* * * When an arrest is made, it is reasonable for the arresting officer to search the person arrested in order to remove any weapons that the latter might seek to use in order to resist arrest or effect his escape. Otherwise, the officer's safety might well be endangered, and the arrest itself frustrated. In addition, it is entirely reasonable for the arresting officer to search for and seize any evidence on the arrestee's person in order to prevent its concealment or destruction. And the area into which an arrestee might reach in order to grab a weapon or evidentiary items must, of course, be governed by a like rule. A gun on a table or in a drawer in front of one who is arrested can be as dangerous to the arresting officer as one concealed in the clothing of the person arrested. There is ample justification, therefore, for a search of the arrestee's person and the area "within his immediate control"—construing that phrase to mean the area from within which he might gain possession of a weapon or destructible evidence.

There is no comparable justification, however, for routinely searching rooms other than that in which an arrest occurs—or, for that matter, for searching through all the desk drawers or other closed or concealed areas in that room itself. Such searches, in the absence of well-recognized exceptions, may be made only under the authority of a search warrant. The "adherence to judicial processes" mandated by the Fourth Amendment requires no less. * * *

It is argued in the present case that it is "reasonable" to search a man's house when he is arrested in it. But that argument is founded on little more than a subjective view regarding the acceptability of certain sorts of police conduct, and not on considerations relevant to Fourth Amendment interests. Under such an unconfined analysis, Fourth Amendment protection in this area would approach the evaporation point. It is not easy to explain why, for instance, it is less subjectively "reasonable" to search a man's house when he is arrested on his front lawn—or just down the street—than it is when he happens to be in the house at the time of arrest. * * *

It would be possible, of course, to draw a line between *Rabinowitz* and *Harris* on the one hand, and this case on the other. For *Rabinowitz* involved a single room, and *Harris* a four-room apartment, while in the case before us an entire house was searched. But such a distinction would be highly artificial. The rationale that allowed the searches and seizures in *Rabinowitz* and *Harris* would allow the searches and seizures in this case. No consideration relevant to the Fourth Amendment suggests any point of rational limitation, once the search is allowed to go beyond the area from which the person arrested might obtain weapons or evidentiary items. The only reasoned distinction is one between a search of the person arrested and the area within his reach on the one hand, and more extensive searches on the other.[12]

The petitioner correctly points out that one result of decisions such as *Rabinowitz* and *Harris* is to give law enforcement officials the opportunity to engage in searches not justified by probable cause, by the simple expedient of arranging to arrest suspects at home rather than elsewhere. We do not suggest that the petitioner is necessarily correct in his assertion that such a strategy was utilized here, but the fact remains that had he been arrested earlier in the day, at his place of employment rather than at home, no search of his house could have been made without a search warrant. * * *

Rabinowitz and *Harris* have been the subject of critical commentary for many years, and have been relied upon less and less in our own decisions. It is time, for the reasons we have stated, to hold that on their own facts, and insofar as the principles they stand for are inconsistent with those that we have endorsed today, they are no longer to be followed.

* * * The scope of the search was, therefore, "unreasonable" under the Fourth and Fourteenth Amendments, and the petitioner's conviction cannot stand.[b]

NOTES AND QUESTIONS

1. Some of the cases which have applied the *Chimel* "immediate control" test seem to assume that defendants maintain control over a considerable area even after they have been arrested. See, e.g., *People v. Perry*, 266 N.E.2d 330 (Ill.1971) (4 officers broke into a 10 by 12 foot motel room, saw defendant place something in a dresser drawer, handcuffed him, and took him out into the corridor; their immediately subsequent search of the partially open dresser drawer and a purse on the bed was within *Chimel* rule, "since it was within the area from which defendant could have obtained a weapon or something that could have been used as evidence against him"). Are such cases best explained on the ground that *Chimel* should be construed so as to give the police a "bright line" rule which, as

---

12. It is argued in dissent that so long as there is probable cause to search the place where an arrest occurs, a search of that place would be permitted even though no search warrant has been obtained. This position seems to be based principally on two premises: first, that once an arrest has been made, the additional invasion of privacy stemming from the accompanying search is "relatively minor"; and second, that the victim of the search may "shortly thereafter" obtain a judicial determination of whether the search was justified by probable cause. With respect to the second premise, one may initially question whether all of the States in fact provide the speedy suppression procedures the dissent assumes. More fundamentally, however, we cannot accept the view that Fourth Amendment interests are vindicated so long as "the rights of the criminal" are "protect[ed] * * * against introduction of evidence seized without probable cause." The Amendment is designed to prevent, not simply to redress, unlawful police action. In any event, we cannot join in characterizing the invasion of privacy that results from a top-to-bottom search of a man's house as "minor." And we can see no reason why, simply because some interference with an individual's privacy and freedom of movement has lawfully taken place, further intrusions should automatically be allowed despite the absence of a warrant that the Fourth Amendment would otherwise require.

b. Justice White, with Justice Black, dissenting, put forward a "line of analysis" that "hinges on two assumptions": (i) that "the law generally permits" warrantless in-premises arrests; and (ii) that "the fact of arrest supplies an exigent circumstance" justifying a warrantless search of the place of arrest on probable cause. Later decisions, *Payton v. New York*, p. 376, and *Vale v. Louisiana*, p. 372, respectively, made it clear that neither of those assumptions is correct.

concluded in *People v. Hufnagel*, 745 P.2d 242 (Colo.1987), makes it irrelevant whether "the arrestee was physically able to reach the exact place searched at the exact second it was searched"?

Consider that in *Arizona v. Gant*, p. 398, the Court held "that the *Chimel* rationale authorizes police to search a vehicle incident to a recent occupant's arrest only when the arrestee is unsecured and within reaching distance of the passenger compartment *at the time of the search*" (emphasis added). Three of the *Gant* dissenters objected that "the *Chimel* Court intended that its new rule apply in cases in which the arrestee is handcuffed before the search is conducted," but that after *Gant* "there is no logical reason why the same rule should not apply to all arrestees."

2. *Chimel* also requires attention to the question of when, if ever, officers may look into other areas of the defendant's home *after* the defendant has been placed under arrest there. Consider:

(a) *When it is necessary for the arrestee to put on street clothes.* See, e.g., *Giacalone v. Lucas,* 445 F.2d 1238 (6th Cir.1971) (defendant arrested at front door went into bedroom to change into street clothes; held, police could look into dresser drawer defendant was about to open, and gun found therein admissible; dissent argues defendant initially told police he was ready to go immediately, thereby expressing "his desire to limit the officers' intrusion into the privacy of his home," and that he went to get dressed upon order of the police).

(b) *When the officers are acting for their own protection.* The question of when a "protective sweep" is permissible reached the Court in MARYLAND v. BUIE, 494 U.S. 325 (1990), where the state court had required full probable cause of a dangerous situation. By analogy to *Terry v. Ohio*, p. 408, and *Michigan v. Long*, p. 436, the Court opted for a less demanding reasonable suspicion test. The state had argued for a "bright-line rule" to the effect that "police should be permitted to conduct a protective sweep whenever they make an in-home arrest for a violent crime"; the Court responded that *Terry* requires individualized suspicion, but then adopted a two-part sweep rule which included another kind of bright line. Specifically, the Court (7–2), per White, J., concluded:

"We agree with the State, as did the court below, that a warrant was not required. We also hold that as an incident to the arrest the officers could, as a precautionary matter and without probable cause or reasonable suspicion, look in closets and other spaces immediately adjoining the place of arrest from which an attack could be immediately launched. Beyond that, however, we hold that there must be articulable facts which, taken together with the rational inferences from those facts, would warrant a reasonable prudent officer in believing that the area to be swept harbors an individual posing a danger to those on the arrest scene. * * *

"We should emphasize that such a protective sweep, aimed at protecting the arresting officers, if justified by the circumstances, is nevertheless not a full search of the premises, but may extend only to a cursory inspection of those spaces where a person may be found. The sweep lasts no longer than is necessary to dispel the reasonable suspicion of danger and in any event no longer than it takes to complete the arrest and depart the premises."

The Court remanded for application of this test. The facts, as stated in the Supreme Court opinions, are these: Two men (one wearing a red running suit) committed an armed robbery of a restaurant on Feb. 3; warrants for them (Buie and Allen) were issued that day, and Buie's home was immediately placed under surveillance. On Feb. 5, after a police department secretary called the residence and verified that Buie was there, 6 or 7 officers proceeded to the house and fanned out through the first and second floors. Officer Rozar said he would "freeze" the basement so that no one could come up; he drew his weapon and twice shouted into the basement for anyone there to come out, and Buie then emerged from the basement. He was arrested, searched and handcuffed by Rozar. Once Buie was outside the house, Officer Frolich entered the basement, noticed a red running suit in plain view and seized it. Rozar testified he was not worried about any possible danger when he arrested Buie; Frolich said he entered the basement "in case there was someone else" down there, though he "had no idea who lived there." What should the result be on remand?

(c) *When the officers are seeking other offenders.* See, e.g., *People v. Block,* 499 P.2d 961 (Cal.1971) (officers knocked on door to check out tip concerning narcotics suspect, when door was opened they detected smell of burning marijuana, five persons in living room and two in dining room with odor of marijuana on their breath were arrested, after which one of the officers went upstairs and looked into bedrooms, where he found marijuana; held, in view of "undetermined number of participants" and fact upstairs light was on, officers had "reasonable cause to believe" other participants might be present; dissent objects there was not probable cause here and distinguishes *Guevara v. Superior Court,* 86 Cal.Rptr. 657 (App.1970), where informant had told police confederates were probably present). If a "potential accomplice" is located, should the police then be allowed to search areas within *his* immediate control?

3. In some circumstances, the Court concluded in WASHINGTON v. CHRISMAN, 455 U.S. 1 (1982), a warrantless *entry* of premises will be permissible incident to and following an arrest elsewhere. There, a campus policeman arrested an apparently underage student as he left a campus dormitory carrying a half-gallon bottle of gin, accompanied the student back to his room so that he could obtain his identification, and there observed marijuana seeds and a marijuana pipe. The state court had held that the entry was unlawful, but the Supreme Court, per Burger, C.J., disagreed:

"Every arrest must be presumed to present a risk of danger to the arresting officer. Cf. *United States v. Robinson,* [p. 343], n. 5. There is no way for an officer to predict reliably how a particular subject will react to arrest or the degree of the potential danger. Moreover, the possibility that an arrested person will attempt to escape if not properly supervised is obvious. Although the Supreme Court of Washington found little likelihood that Overdahl could escape from his dormitory room, an arresting officer's custodial authority over an arrested person does not depend upon a reviewing court's after-the-fact assessment of the particular arrest situation.

"We hold, therefore, that it is not 'unreasonable' under the Fourth Amendment for a police officer, as a matter of routine, to monitor the movements of an arrested person, as his judgment dictates, following the arrest."[c]

4. If an officer is lawfully present within premises to make an arrest, he may observe certain items not within the "immediate control" of the arrestee which will nonetheless be subject to warrantless seizure under the so-called "plain view" doctrine. But, as cautioned in *Coolidge v. New Hampshire,* 403 U.S. 443 (1971), such "extension of the original justification is legitimate only where it is immediately apparent[d] to the police that they have evidence before them; the 'plain view'

---

c. White, Brennan and Marshall, JJ., dissenting, could "perceive no justification for what is in effect a per se rule that an officer in Daugherty's circumstances could always enter the room and stay at the arrestee's elbow."

d. In *Texas v. Brown,* p. 397, the plurality opinion asserted that this phrase "was very likely an unhappy choice of words, since it can be taken to imply that an unduly high degree of certainty as to the incriminating character of evidence is necessary for an application of the 'plain

doctrine may not be used to extend a general exploratory search from one object to another until something incriminating at last emerges."

5. In ARIZONA v. HICKS, 480 U.S. 321 (1987), police lawfully entered premises from which a weapon was fired, and within one officer "noticed two sets of expensive stereo components, which seemed out of place in the squalid and otherwise ill-appointed four-room apartment. Suspecting that they were stolen, he read and recorded their serial numbers—moving some of the components, including a Bang and Olufsen turntable, in order to do so—which he then reported by phone to his headquarters. On being advised that the turntable had been taken in an armed robbery, he seized it immediately. It was later determined that some of the other serial numbers matched those on other stereo equipment taken in the same armed robbery, and a warrant was obtained and executed to seize that equipment as well." Scalia, J., for a 6–3 majority, concluded the moving of the equipment was an unreasonable search, while the dissenters relied on the fact that "the overwhelming majority of both state and federal courts have held that probable cause is not required for a minimal inspection of an item in plain view." The majority responded:

"Justice O'Connor's dissent suggests that we uphold the action here on the ground that it was a cursory inspection rather than a full-blown search, and could therefore be justified by reasonable suspicion instead of probable cause. As already noted, a truly cursory inspection—one that involves merely looking at what is already exposed to view, without disturbing it—is not a 'search' for Fourth Amendment purposes, and therefore does not even require reasonable suspicion. We are unwilling to send police and judges into a new thicket of Fourth Amendment law, to seek a creature of uncertain description that is neither a plain-view inspection nor yet a full-blown search. Nothing in the prior opinions of this Court supports such a distinction * * *.

"Justice Powell's dissent reasonably asks what it is we would have had Officer Nelson do in these circumstances. The answer depends, of course, upon whether he had probable cause to conduct a search, a question that was not preserved in this case. If he had, then he should have done precisely what he did. If not, then he should have followed up his suspicions, if possible, by means other than a search—just as he would have had to do if, while walking along the street, he had noticed the same suspicious stereo equipment sitting inside a house a few feet away from him, beneath an open window. It may well be that, in such circumstances, no effective means short of a search exist. But there is nothing new in the realization that the Constitution sometimes insulates the criminality of a few in order to protect the privacy of us all. Our disagreement with the dissenters pertains to where the proper balance should be struck; we choose to adhere to the textual and traditional standard of probable cause."

KENTUCKY v. KING
—— U.S. ——, 131 S.Ct. 1849, 179 L.Ed.2d 865 (2011).

JUSTICE ALITO delivered the opinion of the Court.

[An undercover officer watching a controlled buy of crack cocaine radioed nearby uniformed officers to apprehend the suspect, who was moving quickly toward the breezeway of a nearby apartment building. As officers entered the breezeway they heard a door shut and detected a strong odor of burnt marijuana. The officers did not know which of the two apartments at the end of the breezeway the suspect had entered, but because they smelled marijuana smoke

---

view' doctrine," and then concluded it was intended to be merely a "statement of the rule * * * requiring probable cause for seizure in the ordinary case."

emanating from the apartment on the left they knocked on that door and announced their presence. They immediately "could hear people inside moving," as well as sounds as though "things were being moved inside the apartment," which, one officer later testified, "led the officers to believe that drug-related evidence was about to be destroyed." The officers then entered that apartment, occupied by King and others, and in a subsequent search found drugs, cash, and drug paraphernalia. (The original suspect was later found in the apartment to the right!) King was convicted on drug charges after the court denied his motion to suppress, ruling the search was (i) based on probable cause, and (ii) properly made without a search warrant given an important variety of exigent circumstances—as the Supreme Court has put it, the need "to prevent the imminent destruction of evidence." The Kentucky supreme court reversed, concluding police may not rely on exigent circumstances if "it was reasonably foreseeable that the investigative tactics employed by the police would create the exigent circumstances."]

Over the years, lower courts have developed an exception to the exigent circumstances rule, the so-called "police-created exigency" doctrine. Under this doctrine, police may not rely on the need to prevent destruction of evidence when that exigency was "created" or "manufactured" by the conduct of the police. * * *

[T]he lower courts have held that the police-created exigency doctrine requires more than simple causation, but the lower courts have not agreed on the test to be applied. * * *

Some lower courts have adopted a rule that is similar to the one that we recognize today. * * * But others, including the Kentucky Supreme Court, have imposed additional requirements that are unsound and that we now reject.

Bad faith. Some courts, including the Kentucky Supreme Court, ask whether law enforcement officers " 'deliberately created the exigent circumstances with the bad faith intent to avoid the warrant requirement.' "

This approach is fundamentally inconsistent with our Fourth Amendment jurisprudence. "Our cases have repeatedly rejected" a subjective approach, asking only whether "the circumstances, viewed *objectively*, justify the action." Indeed, we have never held, outside limited contexts such as an "inventory search or administrative inspection . . ., that an officer's motive invalidates objectively justifiable behavior under the Fourth Amendment." *Whren v. United States,* [p. 353].

The reasons for looking to objective factors, rather than subjective intent, are clear. Legal tests based on reasonableness are generally objective, and this Court has long taken the view that "evenhanded law enforcement is best achieved by the application of objective standards of conduct, rather than standards that depend upon the subjective state of mind of the officer."

Reasonable foreseeability. Some courts, again including the Kentucky Supreme Court, hold that police may not rely on an exigency if " 'it was reasonably foreseeable that the investigative tactics employed by the police would create the exigent circumstances.' " Courts applying this test have invalidated warrantless home searches on the ground that it was reasonably foreseeable that police officers, by knocking on the door and announcing their presence, would lead a drug suspect to destroy evidence.

Contrary to this reasoning, however, we have rejected the notion that police may seize evidence without a warrant only when they come across the evidence by happenstance. In *Horton,* [p. 327], we held that the police may seize evidence in plain view even though the officers may be "interested in an item of evidence and fully expec[t] to find it in the course of a search."

Adoption of a reasonable foreseeability test would also introduce an unacceptable degree of unpredictability. For example, whenever law enforcement officers knock on the door of premises occupied by a person who may be involved in the drug trade, there is *some* possibility that the occupants may possess drugs and may seek to destroy them. Under a reasonable foreseeability test, it would be necessary to quantify the degree of predictability that must be reached before the police-created exigency doctrine comes into play.

A simple example illustrates the difficulties that such an approach would produce. Suppose that the officers in the present case did not smell marijuana smoke and thus knew only that there was a 50% chance that the fleeing suspect had entered the apartment on the left rather than the apartment on the right. Under those circumstances, would it have been reasonably foreseeable that the occupants of the apartment on the left would seek to destroy evidence upon learning that the police were at the door? Or suppose that the officers knew only that the suspect had disappeared into one of the apartments on a floor with 3, 5, 10, or even 20 units? If the police chose a door at random and knocked for the purpose of asking the occupants if they knew a person who fit the description of the suspect, would it have been reasonably foreseeable that the occupants would seek to destroy evidence?

We have noted that "[t]he calculus of reasonableness must embody allowance for the fact that police officers are often forced to make split-second judgments— in circumstances that are tense, uncertain, and rapidly evolving." The reasonable foreseeability test would create unacceptable and unwarranted difficulties for law enforcement officers who must make quick decisions in the field, as well as for judges who would be required to determine after the fact whether the destruction of evidence in response to a knock on the door was reasonably foreseeable based on what the officers knew at the time.

Probable cause and time to secure a warrant. Some courts, in applying the police-created exigency doctrine, fault law enforcement officers if, after acquiring evidence that is sufficient to establish probable cause to search particular premises, the officers do not seek a warrant but instead knock on the door and seek either to speak with an occupant or to obtain consent to search.

This approach unjustifiably interferes with legitimate law enforcement strategies. There are many entirely proper reasons why police may not want to seek a search warrant as soon as the bare minimum of evidence needed to establish probable cause is acquired. Without attempting to provide a comprehensive list of these reasons, we note a few.

First, the police may wish to speak with the occupants of a dwelling before deciding whether it is worthwhile to seek authorization for a search. They may think that a short and simple conversation may obviate the need to apply for and execute a warrant. Second, the police may want to ask an occupant of the premises for consent to search because doing so is simpler, faster, and less burdensome than applying for a warrant. A consensual search also "may result in considerably less inconvenience" and embarrassment to the occupants than a search conducted pursuant to a warrant. Third, law enforcement officers may wish to obtain more evidence before submitting what might otherwise be considered a marginal warrant application. Fourth, prosecutors may wish to wait until they acquire evidence that can justify a search that is broader in scope than the search that a judicial officer is likely to authorize based on the evidence then available. And finally, in many cases, law enforcement may not want to execute a search that will disclose the existence of an investigation because doing so may interfere with the acquisition of additional evidence against those already under suspicion or evidence about additional but as yet unknown participants in a criminal scheme.

We have said that "[l]aw enforcement officers are under no constitutional duty to call a halt to criminal investigation the moment they have the minimum evidence to establish probable cause." Faulting the police for failing to apply for a search warrant at the earliest possible time after obtaining probable cause imposes a duty that is nowhere to be found in the Constitution.

Standard or good investigative tactics. Finally, some lower court cases suggest that law enforcement officers may be found to have created or manufactured an exigency if the court concludes that the course of their investigation was "contrary to standard or good law enforcement practices (or to the policies or practices of their jurisdictions)." This approach fails to provide clear guidance for law enforcement officers and authorizes courts to make judgments on matters that are the province of those who are responsible for federal and state law enforcement agencies.

Respondent argues for a rule that differs from those discussed above, but his rule is also flawed. Respondent contends that law enforcement officers impermissibly create an exigency when they "engage in conduct that would cause a reasonable person to believe that entry is imminent and inevitable." In respondent's view, relevant factors include the officers' tone of voice in announcing their presence and the forcefulness of their knocks. But the ability of law enforcement officers to respond to an exigency cannot turn on such subtleties. * * *

If respondent's test were adopted, it would be extremely difficult for police officers to know how loudly they may announce their presence or how forcefully they may knock on a door without running afoul of the police-created exigency rule. And in most cases, it would be nearly impossible for a court to determine whether that threshold had been passed. The Fourth Amendment does not require the nebulous and impractical test that respondent proposes.

For these reasons, we conclude that the exigent circumstances rule applies when the police do not gain entry to premises by means of an actual or threatened violation of the Fourth Amendment. This holding provides ample protection for the privacy rights that the Amendment protects.

When law enforcement officers who are not armed with a warrant knock on a door, they do no more than any private citizen might do. And whether the person who knocks on the door and requests the opportunity to speak is a police officer or a private citizen, the occupant has no obligation to open the door or to speak. When the police knock on a door but the occupants choose not to respond or to speak, "the investigation will have reached a conspicuously low point," and the occupants "will have the kind of warning that even the most elaborate security system cannot provide." And even if an occupant chooses to open the door and speak with the officers, the occupant need not allow the officers to enter the premises and may refuse to answer any questions at any time.

Occupants who choose not to stand on their constitutional rights but instead elect to attempt to destroy evidence have only themselves to blame for the warrantless exigent-circumstances search that may ensue. * * *

We need not decide whether exigent circumstances existed in this case. * * * The Kentucky Supreme Court "assum[ed] for the purpose of argument that exigent circumstances existed," and it held that the police had impermissibly manufactured the exigency.

We, too, assume for purposes of argument that an exigency existed. * * * Any question about whether an exigency actually existed is better addressed by the Kentucky Supreme Court on remand.

In this case, we see no evidence that the officers either violated the Fourth Amendment or threatened to do so prior to the point when they entered the apartment. Officer Cobb testified without contradiction that the officers "banged on the door as loud as [they] could" and announced either " 'Police, police, police' "or " 'This is the police.' " This conduct was entirely consistent with the Fourth Amendment, and we are aware of no other evidence that might show that the officers either violated the Fourth Amendment or threatened to do so (for example, by announcing that they would break down the door if the occupants did not open the door voluntarily). * * *

JUSTICE GINSBURG, dissenting. * * *

Under an appropriately reined-in "emergency" or "exigent circumstances" exception, the result in this case should not be in doubt. The target of the investigation's entry into the building, and the smell of marijuana seeping under the apartment door into the hallway, the Kentucky Supreme Court rightly determined, gave the police "probable cause ... sufficient ... to obtain a warrant to search the ... apartment." As that court observed, nothing made it impracticable for the police to post officers on the premises while proceeding to obtain a warrant authorizing their entry. Before this Court, Kentucky does not urge otherwise. * * *

NOTES AND QUESTIONS

1. In VALE v. LOUISIANA, 399 U.S. 30 (1970), officers possessing two warrants for Vale's arrest and having information that he was residing at a specified address set up a surveillance of the house in an unmarked car. After about 15 minutes they observed a car drive up and sound the horn twice. A man they recognized as Vale then came out of the house and walked up to the car, had a brief conversation with the driver, looked up and down the street and then returned to the house. A few minutes later he reappeared on the porch, looked cautiously up and down the street, and then proceeded to the car and leaned through the window. Convinced that a narcotics sale had just occurred, the officers approached. Vale retreated toward the house while the driver of the car began driving off. The police blocked the car and saw the driver, one Saucier, place something in his mouth. Vale was then arrested on his front steps and the police advised him they were going to search the house. An officer made a cursory inspection of the house to ascertain if anyone else was present, after which Vale's mother and brother entered the house and were told of the arrest and impending search. A quantity of narcotics were found in a rear bedroom. The Court, per Stewart, J., concluded:

"The Louisiana Supreme Court thought the search independently supportable because it involved narcotics, which are easily removed, hidden, or destroyed. It would be unreasonable, the Louisiana court concluded, 'to require the officers under the facts of the case to first secure a search warrant before searching the premises, as time is of the essence inasmuch as the officers never know whether there is anyone on the premises to be searched who could very easily destroy the evidence.' Such a rationale could not apply to the present case, since by their own account the arresting officers satisfied themselves that no one else was in the house when they first entered the premises. But entirely apart from that point, our past decisions make clear that only in 'a few specifically established and well-delineated' situations, may a warrantless search of a dwelling withstand constitutional scrutiny, even though the authorities have probable cause to conduct it. The burden rests on the State to show the existence of such an exceptional situation. And the record before us discloses none. * * *

"The officers were able to procure two warrants for the appellant's arrest. They also had information that he was residing at the address where they found him. There is thus no reason, so far as anything before us appears, to suppose that it was impracticable for them to obtain a search warrant as well. We decline to hold that an arrest on the street can provide its own 'exigent circumstance' so as to justify a warrantless search of the arrestee's house."

Justice Black, joined by The Chief Justice, dissented:

"[When Vale and Saucier were arrested,] the police had probable cause to believe that Vale was engaged in a narcotics transfer, and that a supply of narcotics would be found in the house, to which Vale had returned after his first conversation, from which he had emerged furtively bearing what the police could readily deduce was a supply of narcotics, and toward which he hurried after seeing the police. But the police did not know then who else might be in the house. Vale's arrest took place near the house, and anyone observing from inside would surely have been alerted to destroy the stocks of contraband which the police believed Vale had left there. The police had already seen Saucier, the narcotics addict, apparently swallow what Vale had given him. Believing that some evidence had already been destroyed and that other evidence might well be, the police were faced with the choice of risking the immediate destruction of evidence or entering the house and conducting a search. I cannot say that their decision to search was unreasonable. Delay in order to obtain a warrant would have given an accomplice just the time he needed.

"That the arresting officers did, in fact, believe that others might be in the house is attested to by their actions upon entering the door left open by Vale. The police at once checked the small house to determine if anyone else was present. Just as they discovered the house was empty, however, Vale's mother and brother arrived. Now what had been a suspicion became a certainty: Vale's relatives were in possession and knew of his arrest. To have abandoned the search at this point, and left the house with Vale, would not have been the action of reasonable police officers. * * *

"The Court asserts, however, that because the police obtained two warrants for Vale's arrest there is 'no reason * * * to suppose that it was impracticable for them to obtain a search warrant as well.' The difficulty is that the two arrest warrants on which the Court seems to rely so heavily were not issued because of any present misconduct of Vale's; they were issued because the bond had been increased for an earlier narcotics charge then pending against Vale. When the police came to arrest Vale, they knew only that his bond had been increased. There is nothing in the record to indicate that, absent the increased bond, there would have been probable cause for an arrest, much less a search. Probable cause for the search arose for the first time when the police observed the activity of Vale and Saucier in and around the house."

2. What *should* the officers have done in *Vale?* Consider *United States v. Grummel,* 542 F.2d 789 (9th Cir.1976) (defendant picked up package known to contain heroin at post office; 10 minutes after taking the package into his home he was arrested there; because his mother was home, agent gave her the option of leaving the premises or remaining inside with him while another agent left to get a search warrant; held, it was proper on these facts to "secure the premises to the extent necessary to prevent destruction of the evidence until a warrant could be obtained"). Consider, in assessing the reasonableness of this alternative, the possibility of obtaining a warrant very promptly via telephone, as authorized in some jurisdictions (see, e.g., Fed.R.Crim.P. 41(d)(3), (e)(3)).

In *Segura v. United States,* 468 U.S. 796 (1984), the police, upon confirming that they had in fact observed a drug sale by Colon and Segura, went to their apartment building. Segura was arrested in the lobby, and when Colon answered a knock on the door she was also arrested. Police made a warrantless entry of the apartment and remained there until a search warrant was issued, which occurred some 19 hours later because of "administrative delay." The Court held "that where officers, having probable cause, enter premises, and with probable cause, arrest the occupants who have legitimate possessory interests in its contents and take them into custody and, for no more than the period here involved, secure the premises from within to preserve the status quo while others, in good faith, are in the process of obtaining a warrant, they do not violate the Fourth Amendment's proscription against unreasonable seizures." The Court also held that the evidence first discovered in execution of the warrant was not a fruit of the illegal entry. (See p. 900.) The first holding was explicated in a portion of an opinion by Burger, C.J., in which only O'Connor, J., joined, stressing (i) that securing "of the premises from within * * * was no more an interference with the petitioners' possessory interests in the contents of the apartment than a perimeter 'stake-out,'" as "both an internal securing and a perimeter stakeout interfere to the same extent with the possessory interests of the owners"; and (ii) "Segura and Colon, whose possessory interests were interfered with by the occupation, were under arrest and in the custody of the police throughout the entire period the agents occupied the apartment," so that "the actual interference with their possessory interests in the apartment and its contents was, thus, virtually nonexistent." The four dissenters, per Stevens, J., argued that the occupation was an unreasonable seizure, involving exercise of "complete dominion and control over the apartment and its contents," because the Fourth Amendment protects possessory interests in a residence even when the occupants are in custody.

In *Illinois v. McArthur*, 531 U.S. 326 (2001), two police officers stood by outside to keep the peace while defendant's wife removed her effects from the family residence, a trailer. Upon exiting, she told the officers her husband had hidden marijuana under the couch, so the officers sought his permission to search the premises. When he refused, one officer left to obtain a search warrant, while another officer remained on the porch with defendant, who was told he could not reenter unless he was accompanied by the officer. A warrant was obtained and executed two hours later, but in the interim defendant entered the trailer two or three times, and on each occasion the officer stood just inside the door and observed his actions. The Court, per Breyer, J., concluded "that the restriction at issue was reasonable," considering (i) "the police had probable cause to believe that McArthur's trailer home contained evidence of a crime and contraband, namely, unlawful drugs"; (ii) "the police had good reason to fear that, unless restrained, McArthur would destroy the drugs before they could return with a warrant"; (iii) "the police made reasonable efforts to reconcile their law enforcement needs with the demands of personal privacy"; and (iv) "the police imposed the restraint for a limited period of time."

3. Although in *Vale* the Court noted in passing that "the goods ultimately seized were not in the process of destruction," many lower courts have not taken that language too seriously in light of the Court's assumption that not even a threat of destruction was present. In *United States v. Rubin,* 474 F.2d 262 (3d Cir.1973), the court upheld a warrantless search[a] pursuant to this test:

---

a. The facts in *Rubin* were as follows: Customs agents received reliable information that a bronze statute containing a large shipment of illicit drugs would be shipped to a hospital in a certain area. Agents were posted at the airport and waterfront, and finally a crate answering the general description given by the informant arrived at the airport from abroad. It was inspected and found to contain narcotics. Agents observed one Agnes pick up the crate and take it to a certain address, where it was unloaded at about 5 p.m. After one agent was dispatched to secure a search warrant, Agnes left the premises in his car but without the crate. He was tailed for a short distance, but when his evasive actions led agents to believe he was aware of the tail, they arrested

"When Government agents, however, have probable cause to believe contraband is present and, in addition, based on the surrounding circumstances or the information at hand, they reasonably conclude that the evidence will be destroyed or removed before they can secure a search warrant, a warrantless search is justified. The emergency circumstances will vary from case to case, and the inherent necessities of the situation at the time must be scrutinized. Circumstances which have seemed relevant to courts include (1) the degree of urgency involved and the amount of time necessary to obtain a warrant * * *; (2) reasonable belief that the contraband is about to be removed * * *; (3) the possibility of danger to police officers guarding the site of the contraband while a search warrant is sought * * *; (4) information indicating the possessors of the contraband are aware that the police are on their trail * * *; and (5) the ready destructibility of the contraband and the knowledge 'that efforts to dispose of narcotics and to escape are characteristic behavior of persons engaged in the narcotics traffic.' "

4. Assuming no such exigent circumstances, is it permissible for police to engage in a subterfuge which causes an occupant to remove the evidence to another place where warrantless search is permissible? See *State v. Hendrix,* 782 S.W.2d 833 (Tenn.1989) (proper for police to telephone residence with anonymous false "tip" that police were on their way there with search warrant, causing defendant to leave with drugs in car, which was then stopped and searched). What if the telephoning police had falsely reported a gas leak and likely explosion?

5. Although several courts had held that when the police are summoned to the scene of a homicide they may remain on those premises without a warrant (and, perhaps, return after a brief absence) to conduct a general investigation into the cause of the death, in *Mincey v. Arizona,* 437 U.S. 385 (1978), the Court, confronted with a rather broad variation of the so-called homicide scene exception to the warrant requirement (the criminal nature and perpetrator of the homicide were known from the outset, no occupant of the premises had summoned the police, and the searches upheld by the lower court continued for four days), "decline[d] to hold that the seriousness of the offense under investigation itself creates exigent circumstances of the kind that under the Fourth Amendment justify a warrantless search." *Mincey* was later applied in *Thompson v. Louisiana,* 469 U.S. 17 (1984), to invalidate a two-hour general search of premises to which police were summoned because of defendant's attempt to get medical assistance after shooting her husband. The Court noted the authorities, "while they were in petitioner's house to offer her assistance," could have seized evidence in plain view and could also have made a limited search for a suspect or for other victims.

In *Flippo v. West Virginia,* 528 U.S. 11 (1999), after defendant's 911 call that he and his wife had been attacked at a cabin in a state park, police arrived at the scene and found defendant outside wounded and his wife inside dead. The contents of a briefcase near the body, found upon a warrantless police reentry and search several hours later, were held admissible by the trial judge because found "within the crime scene area," a position the Court unanimously concluded "squarely conflicts with *Mincey.*" As for the state's contention "that the trial court's ruling is supportable on the theory that petitioner's direction of the police to the scene of the attack implied consent to search as they did," the Court expressed no opinion because this "factual" issue had not been raised below.

6. In *Brigham City v. Stuart,* 547 U.S. 398 (2006), a unanimous Court declared: "One exigency obviating the requirement of a warrant is the need to

him. When he was placed under arrest about six blocks from the house in question, he yelled to spectators to call his brother. At this point the agents, fearing disposal of the narcotics if they waited for the search warrant, entered the house and searched for and seized the narcotics.

assist persons who are seriously injured or threatened with such injury. * * * Accordingly, law enforcement officers may enter a home without a warrant to render emergency assistance to an injured occupant or to protect an occupant from imminent injury." The officers' entry in the instant case was lawful, for they had seen through a screen door and window that a juvenile being held back by several adults had broken loose and struck one of them sufficiently hard that the victim was spitting blood, and thus "had an objectively reasonable basis for believing both that the injured adult might need help and that the violence in the kitchen was just beginning." While the state court had suggested the "emergency aid doctrine" was inapplicable because the officer had entered not to assist the injured adult, but instead had acted "exclusively in their law enforcement capacity," the Supreme Court, citing *Whren*, p. 353, responded: "An action is 'reasonable' under the Fourth Amendment, regardless of the individual officer's state of mind, 'as long as the circumstances, viewed *objectively,* justify [the] action.' * * *It therefore does not matter here—even if their subjective motives could be so neatly unraveled—whether the officers entered the kitchen to arrest respondents and gather evidence against them or to assist the injured and prevent further violence."[b]

PAYTON v. NEW YORK
445 U.S. 573, 100 S.Ct. 1371, 63 L.Ed.2d 639 (1980).

JUSTICE STEVENS delivered the opinion of the Court. * * *

On January 14, 1970, after two days of intensive investigation, New York detectives had assembled evidence sufficient to establish probable cause to believe that Theodore Payton had murdered the manager of a gas station two days earlier. At about 7:30 a.m. on January 15, six officers went to Payton's apartment in the Bronx, intending to arrest him. They had not obtained a warrant. Although light and music emanated from the apartment, there was no response to their knock on the metal door. They summoned emergency assistance and, about 30 minutes later, used crowbars to break open the door and enter the apartment. No one was there. In plain view, however, was a 30-caliber shell casing that was seized and later admitted into evidence at Payton's murder trial. * * *

On March 14, 1974, Obie Riddick was arrested for the commission of two armed robberies that had occurred in 1971. He had been identified by the victims in June of 1973 and in January 1974 the police had learned his address. They did not obtain a warrant for his arrest. At about noon on March 14, a detective, accompanied by three other officers, knocked on the door of the Queens house where Riddick was living. When his young son opened the door, they could see Riddick sitting in bed covered by a sheet. They entered the house and placed him under arrest. Before permitting him to dress, they opened a chest of drawers two feet from the bed in search of weapons and found narcotics and related paraphernalia. Riddick was subsequently indicted on narcotics charges. * * *

The New York Court of Appeals, in a single opinion, affirmed the convictions of both Payton and Riddick. * * *[a]

---

b. Similarly, in *Michigan v. Fisher*, 130 S.Ct. 546 (2009), the Court rejected Fisher's argument "that the officers here could not have been motivated by a perceived need to provide medical assistance, since they never summoned emergency medical personnel," responding that "even if the failure to summon medical personnel conclusively established that [the officer] did not subjectively believe * * * that Fisher or someone else was seriously injured * * *, the test, as we have said, is not what [the officer] believed, but whether there was 'an objectively reasonable basis for believing' that medical assistance was needed, or persons were in danger."

a. At this point, the Court "put to one side other related problems that are *not* presented today": whether there were exigent circumstances justifying a warrantless entry; whether police

It is a "basic principle of Fourth Amendment law" that searches and seizures inside a home without a warrant are presumptively unreasonable. Yet it is also well-settled that objects such as weapons or contraband found in a public place may be seized by the police without a warrant. The seizure of property in plain view involves no invasion of privacy and is presumptively reasonable, assuming that there is probable cause to associate the property with criminal activity. * * *

As the late Judge Leventhal recognized, this distinction has equal force when the seizure of a person is involved. Writing on the constitutional issue now before us for the United States Court of Appeals for the District of Columbia Circuit sitting en banc, *Dorman v. United States,* 435 F.2d 385 (D.C.Cir.1970), Judge Leventhal first noted the settled rule that warrantless arrests in public places are valid. He immediately recognized, however, that

> "[a] greater burden is placed [ ] on officials who enter a home or dwelling without consent. Freedom from intrusion into the home or dwelling is the archetype of the privacy protection secured by the Fourth Amendment."

His analysis of this question then focused on the long-settled premise that, absent exigent circumstances, a warrantless entry to search for weapons or contraband is unconstitutional even when a felony has been committed and there is probable cause to believe that incriminating evidence will be found within. He reasoned that the constitutional protection afforded to the individual's interest in the privacy of his own home is equally applicable to a warrantless entry for the purpose of arresting a resident of the house; for it is inherent in such an entry that a search for the suspect may be required before he can be apprehended. Judge Leventhal concluded that an entry to arrest and an entry to search for and to seize property implicate the same interest in preserving the privacy and the sanctity of the home, and justify the same level of constitutional protection. * * * We find this reasoning to be persuasive and in accord with this Court's Fourth Amendment decisions.

The majority of the New York Court of Appeals, however, suggested that there is a substantial difference in the relative intrusiveness of an entry to search for property and an entry to search for a person. It is true that the area that may legally be searched is broader when executing a search warrant than when executing an arrest warrant in the home. See *Chimel v. California,* [p. 363]. This difference may be more theoretical than real, however, because the police may need to check the entire premises for safety reasons, and sometimes they ignore the restrictions on searches incident to arrest.

But the critical point is that any differences in the intrusiveness of entries to search and entries to arrest are merely ones of degree rather than kind. The two intrusions share this fundamental characteristic: the breach of the entrance to an individual's home. * * * In terms that apply equally to seizures of property and to seizures of persons, the Fourth Amendment has drawn a firm line at the entrance to the house. Absent exigent circumstances, that threshold may not reasonably be crossed without a warrant. * * *[b]

---

can "enter a third party's home to arrest a suspect"; whether "the police lacked probable cause to believe that the suspect was at home when they entered"; and whether the entry was consented to.

b. At this point, Stevens, J., observed that New York argued that "the reasons supporting the *Watson* [p. 332] holding require a similar result here. In *Watson* the Court relied on (a) the well-settled common-law rule that a warrantless arrest in a public place is valid if the arresting officer had probable cause to believe the suspect is a felon; (b) the clear consensus among the States adhering to that well-settled common-law rule; and (c) the expression of the judgment of Congress that such an arrest is 'reasonable.' We consider each of these reasons as it applies to a warrantless entry into a home for the purpose of making a routine felony arrest."

The parties have argued at some length about the practical consequences of a warrant requirement as a precondition to a felony arrest in the home. In the absence of any evidence that effective law enforcement has suffered in those States that already have such a requirement, we are inclined to view such arguments with skepticism. More fundamentally, however, such arguments of policy must give way to a constitutional command that we consider to be unequivocal.

Finally, we note the State's suggestion that only a search warrant based on probable cause to believe the suspect is at home at a given time can adequately protect the privacy interests at stake, and since such a warrant requirement is manifestly impractical, there need be no warrant of any kind. We find this ingenious argument unpersuasive. It is true that an arrest warrant requirement may afford less protection than a search warrant requirement, but it will suffice to interpose the magistrate's determination of probable cause between the zealous officer and the citizen. If there is sufficient evidence of a citizen's participation in a felony to persuade a judicial officer that his arrest is justified, it is constitutionally reasonable to require him to open his doors to the officers of the law. Thus, for Fourth Amendment purposes, an arrest warrant founded on probable cause implicitly carries with it the limited authority to enter a dwelling in which the suspect lives when there is reason to believe the suspect is within.

Because no arrest warrant was obtained in either of these cases, the judgments must be reversed * * *.

JUSTICE BLACKMUN, concurring. * * *

JUSTICE WHITE, with whom THE CHIEF JUSTICE and JUSTICE REHNQUIST join, dissenting. * * *

Today's decision ignores the carefully crafted restrictions on the common-law power of arrest entry and thereby overestimates the dangers inherent in that practice. At common law, absent exigent circumstances, entries to arrest could be made only for felony. Even in cases of felony, the officers were required to announce their presence, demand admission, and be refused entry before they were entitled to break doors. Further, it seems generally accepted that entries could be made only during daylight hours. And, in my view, the officer entering to arrest must have reasonable grounds to believe, not only that the arrestee has committed a crime, but also that the person suspected is present in the house at the time of the entry.[13]

These four restrictions on home arrests—felony, knock and announce, daytime, and stringent probable cause—constitute powerful and complementary protections for the privacy interests associated with the home. * * * In short, these requirements, taken together, permit an individual suspected of a serious crime to

---

In an extended analysis, the *Payton* majority concluded (a) that "the relevant common law does not provide the same guidance that was present in *Watson*," as there is "no direct authority supporting forcible entries into a home to make a routine arrest and the weight of the scholarly opinion is somewhat to the contrary"; (b) that presently 24 states permit such warrantless entries, 15 prohibit them, and 11 have taken no position, with "a significant decline during the last decade in the number of States permitting warrantless entries for arrest"; and (c) that "no congressional determination that warrantless entries into the home are 'reasonable' has been called to our attention." While the majority then concluded from this that "neither history nor this Nation's experience" lent support to the New York position, the *Payton* dissenters read essentially the same data as supporting their position.

13. I do not necessarily disagree with the Court's discussion of the quantum of probable cause necessary to make a valid home arrest. The Court indicates that only an arrest warrant, and not a search warrant, is required. To obtain the warrant, therefore, the officers need only show probable cause that a crime has been committed and that the suspect committed it. However, under today's decision, the officers apparently need an extra increment of probable cause when executing the arrest warrant, namely grounds to believe that the suspect is within the dwelling.

surrender at the front door of his dwelling and thereby avoid most of the humiliation and indignity that the Court seems to believe necessarily accompany a house arrest entry. Such a front door arrest, in my view, is no more intrusive on personal privacy than the public warrantless arrests which we found to pass constitutional muster in *Watson*.[14]

All of these limitations on warrantless arrest entries are satisfied on the facts of the present cases. * * * Today's decision, therefore, sweeps away any possibility that warrantless home entries might be permitted in some limited situations other than those in which exigent circumstances are present. The Court substitutes, in one sweeping decision, a rigid constitutional rule in place of the common-law approach, evolved over hundreds of years, which achieved a flexible accommodation between the demands of personal privacy and the legitimate needs of law enforcement.

A rule permitting warrantless arrest entries would not pose a danger that officers would use their entry power as a pretext to justify an otherwise invalid warrantless search. A search pursuant to a warrantless arrest entry will rarely, if ever, be as complete as one under authority of a search warrant. If the suspect surrenders at the door, the officers may not enter other rooms. Of course, the suspect may flee or hide, or may not be at home, but the officers cannot anticipate the first two of these possibilities and the last is unlikely given the requirement of probable cause to believe that the suspect is at home. Even when officers are justified in searching other rooms, they may seize only items within the arrestee's position [sic] or immediate control or items in plain view discovered during the course of a search reasonably directed at discovering a hiding suspect. Hence a warrantless home entry is likely to uncover far less evidence than a search conducted under authority of a search warrant. Furthermore, an arrest entry will inevitably tip off the suspects and likely result in destruction or removal of evidence not uncovered during the arrest. I therefore cannot believe that the police would take the risk of losing valuable evidence through a pretextual arrest entry rather than applying to a magistrate for a search warrant.

While exaggerating the invasion of personal privacy involved in home arrests, the Court fails to account for the danger that its rule will "severely hamper effective law enforcement." The policeman on his beat must now make subtle discriminations that perplex even judges in their chambers. As Justice Powell noted, concurring in *United States v. Watson,* police will sometimes delay making an arrest, even after probable cause is established, in order to be sure that they have enough evidence to convict. Then, if they suddenly have to arrest, they run the risk that the subsequent exigency will not excuse their prior failure to obtain a warrant. This problem cannot effectively be cured by obtaining a warrant as soon as probable cause is established because of the chance that the warrant will go stale before the arrest is made.

Further, police officers will often face the difficult task of deciding whether the circumstances are sufficiently exigent to justify their entry to arrest without a warrant. This is a decision that must be made quickly in the most trying of circumstances. If the officers mistakenly decide that the circumstances are exigent, the arrest will be invalid and any evidence seized incident to the arrest or in plain view will be excluded at trial. On the other hand, if the officers mistakenly determine that exigent circumstances are lacking, they may refrain from making the arrest, thus creating the possibility that a dangerous criminal will escape into the community. The police could reduce the likelihood of escape by staking out all

---

14. If the suspect flees or hides, of course, the intrusiveness of the entry will be somewhat greater; but the policeman's hands should not be tied merely because of the possibility that the suspect will fail to cooperate with legitimate actions by law enforcement personnel.

possible exits until the circumstances become clearly exigent or a warrant is obtained. But the costs of such a stakeout seem excessive in an era of rising crime and scarce police resources.

The uncertainty inherent in the exigent circumstances determination burdens the judicial system as well. In the case of searches, exigent circumstances are sufficiently unusual that this Court has determined that the benefits of a warrant outweigh the burdens imposed, including the burdens on the judicial system. In contrast, arrests recurringly involve exigent circumstances, and this Court has heretofore held that a warrant can be dispensed with without undue sacrifice in Fourth Amendment values. The situation should be no different with respect to arrests in the home. Under today's decision, whenever the police have made a warrantless home arrest there will be the possibility of "endless litigation with respect to the existence of exigent circumstances, whether it was practicable to get a warrant, whether the suspect was about to flee, and the like." * * *

NOTES AND QUESTIONS

1. The Supreme Court has approved of warrantless entries to arrest under some circumstances. In *Warden v. Hayden,* 387 U.S. 294 (1967), where police were reliably informed that an armed robbery had taken place and that the perpetrator had entered a certain house five minutes earlier, the Court concluded they "acted reasonably when they entered the house and began to search for a man of the description they had been given and for weapons which he had used in the robbery or might use against them.[a] The Fourth Amendment does not require police officers to delay in the course of an investigation if to do so would gravely endanger their lives or the lives of others." And in *United States v. Santana,* 427 U.S. 38 (1976), it was held that *United States v. Watson,* p. 332, permitted the police to attempt a warrantless arrest of the defendant when she was found "standing directly in the doorway—one step forward would have put her outside, one step backward would have put her in the vestibule of her residence." The Court reasoned that she "was in a public place," as she "was not merely visible to the public but was exposed to public view, speech, hearing and touch as if she had been standing completely outside her house." Thus, under the *Hayden* "hot pursuit" rule the police could pursue her without a warrant when she sought refuge within upon their approach. What then if the person to be arrested answers a knock on the door by the police but does not step onto or over the threshold? What if he does because of a police request or subterfuge which conceals their purpose in being there? Or, what if the arrest takes place *outside* the premises after defendant exited in response to a police "threat to send a police dog into the house unless Defendant promptly exited," as in *United States v. Creighton,* 639 F.3d 1281 (10th Cir.2011)?

2. In *Dorman,* relied upon in *Payton,* the court found that exceptional circumstances were present by assessing these considerations: (1) "that a grave offense is involved, particularly one that is a crime of violence"; (2) "that the suspect is reasonably believed to be armed"; (3) "that there exists not merely the minimum of probable cause, that is requisite even when a warrant has been issued, but beyond that a clear showing of probable cause, including 'reasonably trustworthy information,' to believe that the suspect committed the crime involved"; (4) "strong reason to believe that the suspect is in the premises being entered"; (5) "a likelihood that the suspect will escape if not swiftly apprehended"; (6) "the circumstance that the entry, though not consented, is made peaceably"; and (7) "time of entry—whether it is made at night," which however

---

a. Thus, the Court held admissible clothing found in a washing machine, where an officer looked for weapons "prior to or immediately contemporaneous with Hayden's arrest."

"works in more than one direction," as "the late hour may underscore the delay (and perhaps impracticability of) obtaining a warrant and hence serve to justify proceeding without one," while "the fact that an entry is made at night raises a particular concern over its reasonableness * * * and may elevate the degree of probable cause required, both as implicating the suspect, and as showing that he is in the place entered."

3. The Supreme Court focused upon the first *Dorman* factor in WELSH v. WISCONSIN, 466 U.S. 740 (1984), where Welsh was arrested within his own home minutes after a witness had seen him nearby driving erratically and then departing on foot in an apparently inebriated condition after driving off the road into a field. The Court, per Brennan, J., held "that an important factor to be considered when determining whether any exigency exists is the gravity of the underlying offense for which the arrest is being made. Moreover, although no exigency is created simply because there is probable cause to believe that a serious crime has been committed, see *Payton,* application of the exigent-circumstances exception in the context of a home entry should rarely be sanctioned when there is probable cause to believe that only a minor offense, such as the kind at issue in this case, has been committed.

"Application of this principle to the facts of the present case is relatively straightforward. The petitioner was arrested in the privacy of his own bedroom for a noncriminal, traffic offense. The State attempts to justify the arrest by relying on the hot-pursuit doctrine, on the threat to public safety, and on the need to preserve evidence of the petitioner's blood-alcohol level. On the facts of this case, however, the claim of hot pursuit is unconvincing because there was no immediate or continuous pursuit of the petitioner from the scene of a crime. Moreover, because the petitioner had already arrived home, and had abandoned his car at the scene of the accident, there was little remaining threat to the public safety. Hence, the only potential emergency claimed by the State was the need to ascertain the petitioner's blood-alcohol level.

"Even assuming, however, that the underlying facts would support a finding of this exigent circumstance, mere similarity to other cases involving the imminent destruction of evidence is not sufficient. The State of Wisconsin has chosen to classify the first offense for driving while intoxicated as a noncriminal, civil forfeiture offense for which no imprisonment is possible. This is the best indication of the state's interest in precipitating an arrest, and is one that can be easily identified both by the courts and by officers faced with a decision to arrest. Given this expression of the state's interest, a warrantless home arrest cannot be upheld simply because evidence of the petitioner's blood-alcohol level might have dissipated while the police obtained a warrant. To allow a warrantless home entry on these facts would be to approve unreasonable police behavior that the principles of the Fourth Amendment will not sanction."[b]

White, J., joined by Rehnquist, J., dissenting, agreed that the gravity of the offense is "a factor to be considered," but asserted that "if, under all the circumstances of a particular case, an officer has probable cause to believe that the delay involved in procuring an arrest warrant will gravely endanger the officer or other persons or will result in the suspect's escape, I perceive no reason to disregard those exigencies on the ground that the offense for which the suspect is sought is a 'minor' one." By like reasoning, they concluded that "nothing in our previous decisions suggests that the fact that a State has defined an offense as a misdemeanor for a variety of social, cultural, and political reasons necessarily

---

b. In *McArthur* p. 374, the Court distinguished *Welsh* because (a) the offense involved here was punishable by up to 30 days in jail, and (b) "the restriction at issue here is less serious." Justice Stevens dissented as to the applicability of the *Welsh* doctrine.

requires the conclusion that warrantless in-home arrests designed to prevent the imminent destruction or removal of evidence of that offense are always impermissible. * * * A test under which the existence of exigent circumstances turns on the perceived gravity of the crime would significantly hamper law enforcement and burden courts with pointless litigation concerning the nature and gradation of various crimes."

Would the result in *Welsh* have been different if the police were in immediate hot pursuit? See *State v. Bolte,* 560 A.2d 644 (N.J.1989) (rejecting state's argument answer is yes because "citizens should not be encouraged to elude arrest by retreating into their homes").

4. In STEAGALD v. UNITED STATES, 451 U.S. 204 (1981), police entered Steagald's home in an effort to find one Lyons, for whom they had an arrest warrant; they did not find Lyons but did find drugs in plain view, resulting in Steagald's prosecution and conviction. In reversing the conviction, the Court, per Marshall, J., reasoned that "whether the arrest warrant issued in this case adequately safeguarded the interests protected by the Fourth Amendment depends upon what the warrant authorized the agents to do. To be sure, the warrant embodied a judicial finding that there was probable cause to believe that Ricky Lyons had committed a felony, and the warrant therefore authorized the officers to seize Lyons. However, the agents sought to do more than use the warrant to arrest Lyons in a public place or in his home; instead, they relied on the warrant as legal authority to enter the home of a third person based on their belief that Ricky Lyons might be a guest there. Regardless of how reasonable this belief might have been, it was never subjected to the detached scrutiny of a judicial officer. Thus, while the warrant in this case may have protected Lyons from an unreasonable seizure, it did absolutely nothing to protect petitioner's privacy interest in being free from an unreasonable invasion and search of his home. Instead, petitioner's only protection from an illegal entry and search was the agent's personal determination of probable cause. In the absence of exigent circumstances, we have consistently held that such judicially untested determinations are not reliable enough to justify an entry into a person's home to arrest him without a warrant, or a search of a home for objects in the absence of a search warrant. We see no reason to depart from this settled course when the search of a home is for a person rather than an object.

"A contrary conclusion—that the police, acting alone and in the absence of exigent circumstances, may decide when there is sufficient justification for searching the home of a third party for the subject of an arrest warrant—would create a significant potential for abuse. Armed solely with an arrest warrant for a single person, the police could search all the homes of that individual's friends and acquaintances. See, e.g., *Lankford v. Gelston,* 364 F.2d 197 (C.A.4 1966) (enjoining police practice under which 300 homes searched pursuant to arrest warrants for two fugitives). Moreover, an arrest warrant may serve as the pretext for entering a home in which the police have a suspicion, but not probable cause to believe, that illegal activity is taking place."

Though the majority went on to conclude that this result was not contrary to common law precedent and "will not significantly impede effective law enforcement efforts," in that "the situations in which a search warrant will be necessary are few" and in those situations "the inconvenience incurred by the police is simply not that significant," Rehnquist and White, JJ., dissenting, argued that "the common law as it existed at the time of the framing of the Fourth Amendment" did not support such a result, and concluded:

"The genuinely unfortunate aspect of today's ruling is not that fewer fugitives will be brought to book, or fewer criminals apprehended, though both of these consequences will undoubtedly occur; the greater misfortune is the increased uncertainty imposed on police officers in the field, committing magistrates, and trial judges, who must confront variations and permutations of this factual situation on a day-to-day basis. They will, in their various capacities, have to weigh the time during which a suspect for whom there is an outstanding arrest warrant has been in the building, whether the dwelling is the suspect's home, how long he has lived there, whether he is likely to leave immediately, and a number of related and equally imponderable questions. Certainty and repose, as Justice Holmes said, may not be the destiny of man, but one might have hoped for a higher degree of certainty in this one narrow but important area of the law than is offered by today's decision."

5. An unannounced entry of premises to make an arrest therein is subject to Fourth Amendment limitations like those regarding unannounced entry to execute a search warrant, as set out in *Richards v. Wisconsin*, p. 332. See, e.g., *United States v. Fields*, 113 F.3d 313 (2d Cir.1997). State statutes declaring an officer may not enter to arrest unless he has been denied admittance after giving "notice of his office and purpose" have usually been interpreted as codifying the common law exception for "exigent circumstances" when there is a reasonable belief compliance "would increase his peril, frustrate an arrest, or permit the destruction of evidence." *People v. Rosales*, 437 P.2d 489 (Cal.1968).

SECTION 7. WARRANTLESS SEIZURES AND SEARCHES OF VEHICLES AND CONTAINERS

CALIFORNIA v. CARNEY
471 U.S. 386, 105 S.Ct. 2066, 85 L.Ed.2d 406 (1985).

CHIEF JUSTICE BURGER delivered the opinion of the Court.

[Police saw Carney and a youth enter a Dodge Mini Motor Home parked on a lot in downtown San Diego. When police questioned the youth upon his exit over an hour later, he said Carney had given him marijuana in exchange for sexual contacts. The youth knocked on the door of the motor home at police request, and Carney exited, at which an officer entered and saw marijuana and drug paraphernalia. Carney was arrested and the motor home was seized; a subsequent search of it at the police station revealed additional marijuana. Carney's conviction for possession of marijuana for sale was overturned by the state supreme court on the ground that the search was unreasonable because no warrant was obtained.]

* * * There are, of course, exceptions to the general rule that a warrant must be secured before a search is undertaken; one is the so-called "automobile exception" at issue in this case. This exception to the warrant requirement was first set forth by the Court 60 years ago in *Carroll v. United States*, 267 U.S. 132 (1925). There, the Court recognized that the privacy interests in an automobile are constitutionally protected; however, it held that the ready mobility of the automobile justifies a lesser degree of protection of those interests. The Court rested this exception on a long-recognized distinction between stationary structures and vehicles:

"[T]he guaranty of freedom from unreasonable searches and seizures by the Fourth Amendment has been construed, practically since the beginning of Government, as recognizing a necessary difference between a search of a store, dwelling house or other structure in respect of which a proper official warrant readily may be obtained, and a search of a ship, motor boat, wagon or automobile, for contraband goods, where it is not practicable to secure a warrant because the vehicle can be *quickly moved* out of the locality or jurisdiction in which the warrant must be sought."

The capacity to be "quickly moved" was clearly the basis of the holding in *Carroll,* and our cases have consistently recognized ready mobility[a] as one of the principal bases of the automobile exception. * * *

However, although ready mobility alone was perhaps the original justification for the vehicle exception, our later cases have made clear that ready mobility is not the only basis for the exception. The reasons for the vehicle exception, we have said, are twofold. "Besides the element of mobility, less rigorous warrant requirements govern because the expectation of privacy with respect to one's automobile is significantly less than that relating to one's home or office."

Even in cases where an automobile was not immediately mobile, the lesser expectation of privacy resulting from its use as a readily mobile vehicle justified application of the vehicular exception. In some cases, the configuration of the vehicle contributed to the lower expectations of privacy; for example, we held in *Cardwell v. Lewis,* 417 U.S. [583 (1974)], that, because the passenger compartment of a standard automobile is relatively open to plain view, there are lesser expectations of privacy. But even when enclosed "repository" areas have been involved, we have concluded that the lesser expectations of privacy warrant application of the exception. We have applied the exception in the context of a locked car trunk, *Cady v. Dombrowski,* 413 U.S. 433 (1973), a sealed package in a car trunk, *United States v. Ross,* [p. 388], a closed compartment under the dashboard, *Chambers v. Maroney,* [p. 388], the interior of a vehicle's upholstery, *Carroll, supra,* or sealed packages inside a covered pickup truck, *United States v. Johns,* [p. 390].

These reduced expectations of privacy derive not from the fact that the area to be searched is in plain view, but from the pervasive regulation of vehicles capable of traveling on the public highways. As we explained in *South Dakota v. Opperman,* 428 U.S. 364 (1976), an inventory search case:

"Automobiles, unlike homes, are subjected to pervasive and continuing governmental regulation and controls, including periodic inspection and licensing requirements. As an everyday occurrence, police stop and examine vehicles when license plates or inspection stickers have expired, or if other violations, such as exhaust fumes or excessive noise, are noted, or if headlights or other safety equipment are not in proper working order."

The public is fully aware that it is accorded less privacy in its automobiles because of this compelling governmental need for regulation. Historically, "individuals always [have] been on notice that movable vessels may be stopped and searched on facts giving rise to probable cause that the vehicle contains contra-

---

a. The Court's earlier cases make it clear that "ready mobility" does *not* refer to the actual likelihood that the vehicle would be moved if a search warrant were sought. *Chambers v. Maroney,* 399 U.S. 42 (1970) (police stopped station wagon on probable cause occupants had just committed a robbery; occupants were arrested and car was driven to police station, where thorough search revealed a revolver under dashboard; search upheld over dissent's reasoning that there was no need for a warrantless search because the car could have been held in police custody until a warrant was obtained); *Colorado v. Bannister,* 449 U.S. 1 (1980) (unanimous Court concludes that where probable cause to search developed after car stopped for a traffic violation, "it would be especially unreasonable to require a detour to a magistrate before the unanticipated evidence could be lawfully seized"); *Michigan v. Thomas,* 458 U.S. 259 (1982) ("the justification to conduct such a warrantless search does not vanish once the car has been immobilized; nor does it depend upon a reviewing court's assessment of the likelihood in each particular case that the car would have been driven away, or that its contents would have been tampered with, during the period required for the police to obtain a warrant"); *Florida v. Meyers,* 466 U.S. 380 (1984) (lower court erred in concluding warrantless search of car improper where, as here, the car had been impounded eight hours earlier and was presently stored in a secure area).

band, without the protection afforded by a magistrate's prior evaluation of those facts." In short, the pervasive schemes of regulation, which necessarily lead to reduced expectations of privacy, and the exigencies attendant to ready mobility justify searches without prior recourse to the authority of a magistrate so long as the overriding standard of probable cause is met.

When a vehicle is being used on the highways, or if it is readily capable of such use and is found stationary in a place not regularly used for residential purposes—temporary or otherwise—the two justifications for the vehicle exception come into play. First, the vehicle is obviously readily mobile by the turn of a switch key, if not actually moving. Second, there is a reduced expectation of privacy stemming from its use as a licensed motor vehicle subject to a range of police regulation inapplicable to a fixed dwelling. At least in these circumstances, the overriding societal interests in effective law enforcement justify an immediate search before the vehicle and its occupants become unavailable.

While it is true that respondent's vehicle possessed some, if not many of the attributes of a home, it is equally clear that the vehicle falls clearly within the scope of the exception laid down in *Carroll* and applied in succeeding cases. Like the automobile in *Carroll,* respondent's motor home was readily mobile. Absent the prompt search and seizure, it could readily have been moved beyond the reach of the police. Furthermore, the vehicle was licensed to "operate on public streets; [was] serviced in public places; * * * and [was] subject to extensive regulation and inspection." And the vehicle was so situated that an objective observer would conclude that it was being used not as a residence, but as a vehicle.

Respondent urges us to distinguish his vehicle from other vehicles within the exception because it was *capable of functioning as a home.* In our increasingly mobile society, many vehicles used for transportation can be and are being used not only for transportation but for shelter, i.e., as a "home" or "residence." To distinguish between respondent's motor home and an ordinary sedan for purposes of the vehicle exception would require that we apply the exception depending upon the size of the vehicle and the quality of its appointments. Moreover, to fail to apply the exception to vehicles such as a motor home ignores the fact that a motor home lends itself easily to use as an instrument of illicit drug traffic and other illegal activity. In *United States v. Ross,* we declined to distinguish between "worthy" and "unworthy" containers, noting that "the central purpose of the Fourth Amendment forecloses such a distinction." We decline today to distinguish between "worthy" and "unworthy" vehicles which are either on the public roads and highways, or situated such that it is reasonable to conclude that the vehicle is not being used as a residence.

Our application of the vehicle exception has never turned on the other uses to which a vehicle might be put. The exception has historically turned on the ready mobility of the vehicle, and on the presence of the vehicle in a setting that objectively indicates that the vehicle is being used for transportation.[3] These two requirements for application of the exception ensure that law enforcement officials are not unnecessarily hamstrung in their efforts to detect and prosecute criminal activity, and that the legitimate privacy interests of the public are protected. Applying the vehicle exception in these circumstances allows the essential purposes served by the exception to be fulfilled, while assuring that the exception will acknowledge legitimate privacy interests. * * *

---

3. We need not pass on the application of the vehicle exception to a motor home that is situated in a way or place that objectively indicates that it is being used as a residence. Among the factors that might be relevant in determining whether a warrant would be required in such a circumstance is its location, whether the vehicle is readily mobile or instead, for instance, elevated on blocks, whether the vehicle is licensed, whether it is connected to utilities, and whether it has convenient access to a public road.

This search was not unreasonable; it was plainly one that the magistrate could authorize if presented with these facts. * * *

JUSTICE STEVENS, with whom JUSTICE BRENNAN and JUSTICE MARSHALL join, dissenting. * * *

As we explained in *Ross,* the automobile exception * * * has been developed to ameliorate the practical problems associated with the search of vehicles that have been stopped on the streets or public highways because there was probable cause to believe they were transporting contraband. Until today, however, the Court has never decided whether the practical justifications that apply to a vehicle that is stopped in transit on a public way apply with the same force to a vehicle parked in a lot near a court house where it could easily be detained while a warrant is issued.[15]

In this case, the motor home was parked in an off-the-street lot only a few blocks from the courthouse in downtown San Diego where dozens of magistrates were available to entertain a warrant application.[16] The officers clearly had the element of surprise with them, and with curtains covering the windshield, the motor home offered no indication of any imminent departure. The officers plainly had probable cause to arrest the petitioner and search the motor home, and on this record, it is inexplicable why they eschewed the safe harbor of a warrant.

In the absence of any evidence of exigency in the circumstances of this case, the Court relies on the inherent mobility of the motor home to create a conclusive presumption of exigency. This Court, however, has squarely held that mobility of the place to be searched is not a sufficient justification for abandoning the warrant requirement. In *United States v. Chadwick,* 433 U.S. 1 (1977), the Court held that a warrantless search of a footlocker violated the Fourth Amendment even though there was ample probable cause to believe it contained contraband. The Government had argued that the rationale of the automobile exception applied to movable containers in general, and that the warrant requirement should be limited to searches of homes and other "core" areas of privacy. We categorically rejected the Government's argument observing that there are greater privacy interests associated with containers than with automobiles, and that there are less practical problems associated with the temporary detention of a container than with the detention of an automobile.

* * * It is perfectly obvious that the citizen has a much greater expectation of privacy concerning the interior of a mobile home than of a piece of luggage such as a footlocker. If "inherent mobility" does not justify warrantless searches of

---

15. In *Coolidge v. New Hampshire,* 403 U.S. 443 (1971), a plurality refused to apply the automobile exception to an automobile that was seized while parked in the driveway of the suspect's house, towed to a secure police compound, and later searched:

"The word 'automobile' is not a talisman in whose presence the Fourth Amendment fades away and disappears. And surely there is nothing in this case to invoke the meaning and purpose of the rule of *Carroll v. United States*—no alerted criminal bent on flight, no fleeting opportunity on an open highway after a hazardous chase, no contraband or stolen goods or weapons, no confederates waiting to move the evidence, not even the inconvenience of a special police detail to guard the immobilized automobile. In short, by no possible stretch of the legal imagination can this be made into a case where 'it is not practicable to secure a warrant,' and the 'automobile exception' despite its label, is simply irrelevant." (opinion of Stewart, J., joined by Douglas, Brennan and Marshall, JJ.).

In *Cardwell v. Lewis,* 417 U.S. 583 (1974), a different plurality approved the seizure of an automobile from a public parking lot, and a later examination of its exterior. (opinion of Blackmun, J.). Here, of course, we are concerned with the reasonableness of the search, not the seizure. Even if the diminished expectations of privacy associated with an automobile justify the warrantless search of a parked automobile notwithstanding the diminished exigency, the heightened expectations of privacy in the interior of motor home require a different result.

16. In addition, a telephonic warrant was only 20 cents and the nearest phone booth away.

containers, it cannot rationally provide a sufficient justification for the search of a person's dwelling place.

Unlike a brick bungalow or a frame Victorian, a motor home seldom serves as a permanent lifetime abode. The motor home in this case, however, was designed to accommodate a breadth of ordinary everyday living. Photographs in the record indicate that its height, length and beam provided substantial living space inside: stuffed chairs surround a table; cupboards provide room for storage of personal effects; bunk-beds provide sleeping space; and a refrigerator provides ample space for food and beverages. Moreover, curtains and large opaque walls inhibit viewing the activities inside from the exterior of the vehicle. The interior configuration of the motor home establishes that the vehicle's size, shape, and mode of construction should have indicated to the officers that it was a vehicle containing mobile living quarters.

The State contends that officers in the field will have an impossible task determining whether or not other vehicles contain mobile living quarters. It is not necessary for the Court to resolve every unanswered question in this area in a single case, but common English usage suggests that we already distinguish between a "motor home" which is "equipped as a self-contained traveling home," a "camper" which is only equipped for "casual travel and camping," and an automobile which is "designed for passenger transportation." Surely the exteriors of these vehicles contain clues about their different functions which could alert officers in the field to the necessity of a warrant.[21] * * *

In my opinion, searches of places that regularly accommodate a wide range of private human activity are fundamentally different from searches of automobiles which primarily serve a public transportation function. Although it may not be a castle, a motor home is usually the functional equivalent of a hotel room, a vacation and retirement home, or a hunting and fishing cabin. These places may be as spartan as a humble cottage when compared to the most majestic mansion, but the highest and most legitimate expectations of privacy associated with these temporary abodes should command the respect of this Court. In my opinion, a warrantless search of living quarters in a motor home is "presumptively unreasonable absent exigent circumstances." * * *

NOTES AND QUESTIONS

1. In *Maryland v. Dyson*, 527 U.S. 465 (1999), the Court, per curiam, summarily reversed a state court decision holding "that in order for the automobile exception to the warrant requirement to apply, there must not only be probable cause to believe that evidence of a crime is contained in the automobile, but also a separate finding of exigency precluding the police from obtaining a warrant." That holding, the Court declared, "rests upon an incorrect interpretation of the automobile exception to the Fourth Amendment's warrant requirement," which "does not have a separate exigency requirement."

2. In *Florida v. White*, 526 U.S. 559 (1999), upholding the warrantless *seizure* of a car under the state forfeiture law on probable cause that the vehicle was contraband, the Court took note of "the special considerations recognized in the context of movable items" in the *Carroll-Carney* line of cases, and then concluded the need was "equally weighty when the *automobile*, as opposed to its

---

21. In refusing to extend the California Supreme Court's decision in *Carney* beyond its context, the California Courts of Appeals have had no difficulty in distinguishing the motor home involved there from a Ford van and a cab-high camper shell on the back of a pick-up truck. There is no reason to believe that trained officers could not make similar distinctions between different vehicles, especially when state vehicle laws already require them to do so.

contents, is the contraband that the police seek to secure." The Court also emphasized that "our Fourth Amendment jurisprudence has consistently accorded law enforcement officials greater latitude in exercising their duties in public places," and deemed the instant case "nearly indistinguishable" in this respect from *G.M. Leasing Corp. v. United States*, 429 U.S. 338 (1977), upholding the warrantless seizure from a public area of automobiles in partial satisfaction of income tax assessments. Two dissenting Justices in *White* objected (i) that an exigent circumstances rationale has no application "when the seizure is based upon a belief that the automobile may have been used at some time in the past to assist in illegal activity and the owner is already in custody," and (ii) that a warrant requirement "is bolstered by the inherent risks of hindsight at post-seizure hearings and law enforcement agencies' pecuniary interest in the seizure of such property."

    3. In *Chambers v. Maroney*, 399 U.S. 42 (1970), the Court stated that what is required, even if no warrant need first be obtained, is "probable cause to search a particular auto for particular articles." This probable cause must be assessed in order to ascertain whether an otherwise lawful warrantless search of a vehicle was properly limited in scope and intensity, as is illustrated by *Maldonado v. State*, 528 S.W.2d 234 (Tex.Crim.1975) (truck searched on probable cause it was stolen, officers pulled up flooring and found false compartment containing 650 packages of marijuana; held, that part of search illegal because it "could not reasonably be expected that evidence of theft might be uncovered by these means"); *Wimberly v. Superior Court*, 547 P.2d 417 (Cal.1976) (after vehicle stopped for traffic violation, officer saw pipe and 12 marijuana seeds on floor and smelled odor of marijuana, passenger compartment was searched and bag with very small amount of marijuana was found in jacket pocket, trunk of car then searched and several pounds of marijuana found there; held, latter search illegal, as police had probable cause occupants of car were occasional users rather than dealers, and thus "it was not reasonable to infer that petitioners had additional contraband hidden in the trunk"). Compare *United States v. Loucks*, 806 F.2d 208 (10th Cir.1986) (such user-dealer distinction is "illogical and unreasonable").

    4. In *United States v. Jones*, p. 279, the GPS tracking case, the government "argue[d] in the alternative that even if the [warrantless] attachment and use of the device was a search, it was reasonable—and thus lawful—under the Fourth Amendment because 'officers had reasonable suspicion, and indeed probable cause, to believe that [Jones] was a dealer in a large-scale cocaine distribution conspiracy.'" Since that argument had not been raised before, the Court deemed "the argument forfeited." Had that not been the case, how should the Court have ruled?

CALIFORNIA v. ACEVEDO
500 U.S. 565, 111 S.Ct. 1982, 114 L.Ed.2d 619 (1991).

JUSTICE BLACKMUN delivered the opinion of the Court.

    [One Daza picked up from a Federal Express office a package the police knew contained marijuana and took it to his apartment. About two hours later, Acevedo entered that apartment and shortly thereafter left carrying a brown paper bag the size of one of the wrapped marijuana packages. He placed the bag in the trunk of his car and drove off; the police then stopped him, opened the trunk and bag, and found marijuana. The California Court of Appeal held the marijuana should have been suppressed, the state supreme court denied review, and the Supreme Court then granted certiorari.]

    In *United States v. Ross*, 456 U.S. 798, decided in 1982, we held that a warrantless search of an automobile under the *Carroll* doctrine could include a search of a container or package found inside the car when such a search was supported by probable cause. The warrantless search of Ross' car occurred after an informant told the police that he had seen Ross complete a drug transaction using drugs stored in the trunk of his car. The police stopped the car, searched it, and discovered in the trunk a brown paper bag containing drugs. We decided that the search of Ross' car was not unreasonable under the Fourth Amendment: "The scope of a warrantless search based on probable cause is no narrower—and no broader—than the scope of a search authorized by a warrant supported by probable cause." Thus, "[i]f probable cause justifies the search of a lawfully stopped vehicle, it justifies the search of every part of the vehicle and its contents that may conceal the object of the search." In *Ross,* therefore, we clarified the scope of the *Carroll* doctrine as properly including a "probing search" of compartments and containers within the automobile so long as the search is supported by probable cause.

In addition to this clarification, *Ross* distinguished the *Carroll* doctrine from the separate rule that governed the search of closed containers. The Court had announced this separate rule, unique to luggage and other closed packages, bags, and containers, in *United States v. Chadwick,* [p. 386]. In *Chadwick,* federal narcotics agents had probable cause to believe that a 200–pound double-locked footlocker contained marijuana. The agents tracked the locker as the defendants removed it from a train and carried it through the station to a waiting car. As soon as the defendants lifted the locker into the trunk of the car, the agents arrested them, seized the locker, and searched it. In this Court, the United States did not contend that the locker's brief contact with the automobile's trunk sufficed to make the *Carroll* doctrine applicable. Rather, the United States urged that the search of movable luggage could be considered analogous to the search of an automobile.

The Court rejected this argument because, it reasoned, a person expects more privacy in his luggage and personal effects than he does in his automobile. Moreover, it concluded that as "may often not be the case when automobiles are seized," secure storage facilities are usually available when the police seize luggage.

In *Arkansas v. Sanders,* 442 U.S. 753 (1979), the Court extended *Chadwick*'s rule to apply to a suitcase actually being transported in the trunk of a car. In *Sanders,* the police had probable cause to believe a suitcase contained marijuana. They watched as the defendant placed the suitcase in the trunk of a taxi and was driven away. The police pursued the taxi for several blocks, stopped it, found the suitcase in the trunk, and searched it. Although the Court had applied the *Carroll* doctrine to searches of integral parts of the automobile itself, (indeed, in *Carroll,* contraband whiskey was in the upholstery of the seats), it did not extend the doctrine to the warrantless search of personal luggage "merely because it was located in an automobile lawfully stopped by the police." Again, the *Sanders* majority stressed the heightened privacy expectation in personal luggage and concluded that the presence of luggage in an automobile did not diminish the owner's expectation of privacy in his personal items.

In *Ross,* the Court endeavored to distinguish between *Carroll,* which governed the *Ross* automobile search, and *Chadwick,* which governed the *Sanders* automobile search. It held that the *Carroll* doctrine covered searches of automobiles when the police had probable cause to search an entire vehicle but that the *Chadwick* doctrine governed searches of luggage when the officers had probable cause to search only a container within the vehicle. Thus, in a *Ross* situation, the police could conduct a reasonable search under the Fourth Amendment without obtaining a warrant, whereas in a *Sanders* situation, the police had to obtain a warrant before they searched.

The dissent is correct, of course, that *Ross* involved the scope of an automobile search. *Ross* held that closed containers encountered by the police during a warrantless search of a car pursuant to the automobile exception could also be searched. Thus, this Court in *Ross* took the critical step of saying that closed containers in cars could be searched without a warrant because of their presence within the automobile. Despite the protection that *Sanders* purported to extend to closed containers, the privacy interest in those closed containers yielded to the broad scope of an automobile search. * * *

This Court in *Ross* rejected *Chadwick*'s distinction between containers and cars. It concluded that the expectation of privacy in one's vehicle is equal to one's expectation of privacy in the container, and noted that "the privacy interests in a car's trunk or glove compartment may be no less than those in a movable container." It also recognized that it was arguable that the same exigent circumstances that permit a warrantless search of an automobile would justify the warrantless search of a movable container. In deference to the rule of *Chadwick* and *Sanders,* however, the Court put that question to one side. It concluded that the time and expense of the warrant process would be misdirected if the police could search every cubic inch of an automobile until they discovered a paper sack, at which point the Fourth Amendment required them to take the sack to a magistrate for permission to look inside. We now must decide the question deferred in *Ross:* whether the Fourth Amendment requires the police to obtain a warrant to open the sack in a movable vehicle simply because they lack probable cause to search the entire car. We conclude that it does not.

Dissenters in *Ross* asked why the suitcase in *Sanders* was "more private, less difficult for police to seize and store, or in any other relevant respect more properly subject to the warrant requirement, than a container that police discover in a probable-cause search of an entire automobile?" We now agree that a container found after a general search of the automobile and a container found in a car after a limited search for the container are equally easy for the police to store and for the suspect to hide or destroy. In fact, we see no principled distinction in terms of either the privacy expectation or the exigent circumstances between the paper bag found by the police in *Ross* and the paper bag found by the police here. Furthermore, by attempting to distinguish between a container for which the police are specifically searching and a container which they come across in a car, we have provided only minimal protection for privacy and have impeded effective law enforcement.

The line between probable cause to search a vehicle and probable cause to search a package in that vehicle is not always clear, and separate rules that govern the two objects to be searched may enable the police to broaden their power to make warrantless searches and disserve privacy interests. * * * At the moment when officers stop an automobile, it may be less than clear whether they suspect with a high degree of certainty that the vehicle contains drugs in a bag or simply contains drugs. If the police know that they may open a bag only if they are actually searching the entire car, they may search more extensively than they otherwise would in order to establish the general probable cause required by *Ross.*

Such a situation is not far fetched. In *United States v. Johns,* 469 U.S. 478 (1985), customs agents saw two trucks drive to a private airstrip and approach two small planes. The agents drew near the trucks, smelled marijuana, and then saw in the backs of the trucks packages wrapped in a manner that marijuana smugglers customarily employed. The agents took the trucks to headquarters and searched the packages without a warrant. Relying on *Chadwick,* the defendants argued that the search was unlawful. The defendants contended that *Ross* was inapplicable because the agents lacked probable cause to search anything but the packages themselves and supported this contention by noting that a search of the entire vehicle never occurred. We rejected that argument and found *Chadwick* and *Sanders* inapposite because the agents had probable cause to search the entire body of each truck, although they had chosen not to do so.[a] We cannot see the benefit of a rule that requires law enforcement officers to conduct a more intrusive search in order to justify a less intrusive one.

To the extent that the *Chadwick–Sanders* rule protects privacy, its protection is minimal. Law enforcement officers may seize a container and hold it until they obtain a search warrant. "Since the police, by hypothesis, have probable cause to seize the property, we can assume that a warrant will be routinely forthcoming in the overwhelming majority of cases." And the police often will be able to search containers without a warrant, despite the *Chadwick–Sanders* rule, as a search incident to a lawful arrest [under] *Belton* [p. 398]. * * *

Finally, the search of a paper bag intrudes far less on individual privacy than does the incursion sanctioned long ago in *Carroll*. In that case, prohibition agents slashed the upholstery of the automobile. This Court nonetheless found their search to be reasonable under the Fourth Amendment. If destroying the interior of an automobile is not unreasonable, we cannot conclude that looking inside a closed container is. In light of the minimal protection to privacy afforded by the *Chadwick–Sanders* rule, and our serious doubt whether that rule substantially serves privacy interests, we now hold that the Fourth Amendment does not compel separate treatment for an automobile search that extends only to a container within the vehicle.

The *Chadwick–Sanders* rule not only has failed to protect privacy but it has also confused courts and police officers and impeded effective law enforcement. * * *

The discrepancy between the two rules has led to confusion for law enforcement officers. For example, when an officer, who has developed probable cause to believe that a vehicle contains drugs, begins to search the vehicle and immediately discovers a closed container, which rule applies? The defendant will argue that the fact that the officer first chose to search the container indicates that his probable cause extended only to the container and that *Chadwick* and *Sanders* therefore require a warrant. On the other hand, the fact that the officer first chose to search in the most obvious location should not restrict the propriety of the search. The *Chadwick* rule, as applied in *Sanders,* has developed into an anomaly such that the more likely the police are to discover drugs in a container, the less authority they have to search it. * * *

The interpretation of the *Carroll* doctrine set forth in *Ross* now applies to all searches of containers found in an automobile. In other words, the police may search without a warrant if their search is supported by probable cause. * * * In the case before us, the police had probable cause to believe that the paper bag in the automobile's trunk contained marijuana. That probable cause now allows a warrantless search of the paper bag. The facts in the record reveal that the police

---

a. However, "the central issue" in *Johns* was whether the warrantless search was permissible in light of the fact that the packages were not opened until three days after they had been removed from the trucks. The majority answered in the affirmative:

"We do not suggest that police officers may indefinitely retain possession of a vehicle and its contents before they complete a vehicle search. Nor do we foreclose the possibility that the owner of a vehicle or its contents might attempt to prove that delay in the completion of a vehicle search was unreasonable because it adversely affected a privacy or possessory interest. We note that in this case there was probable cause to believe that the trucks contained contraband and there is no plausible argument that the object of the search could not have been concealed in the packages. Respondents do not challenge the legitimacy of the seizure of the trucks or the packages, and they never sought return of the property. Thus, respondents have not even alleged, much less proved, that the delay in the search of packages adversely affected legitimate interests protected by the Fourth Amendment."

did not have probable cause to believe that contraband was hidden in any other part of the automobile and a search of the entire vehicle would have been without probable cause and unreasonable under the Fourth Amendment. * * *

JUSTICE SCALIA, concurring in the judgment. * * *

In my view, the path out of this confusion should be sought by returning to the first principle that the "reasonableness" requirement of the Fourth Amendment affords the protection that the common law afforded. [T]he supposed "general rule" that a warrant is always required does not appear to have any basis in the common law, and confuses rather than facilitates any attempt to develop rules of reasonableness in light of changed legal circumstances, as the anomaly eliminated and the anomaly created by today's holding both demonstrate. * * *

I would reverse the judgment in the present case, not because a closed container carried inside a car becomes subject to the "automobile" exception to the general warrant requirement, but because the search of a closed container, outside a privately owned building, with probable cause to believe that the container contains contraband, and when it in fact does contain contraband, is not one of those searches whose Fourth Amendment reasonableness depends upon a warrant. For that reason I concur in the judgment of the Court.

JUSTICE WHITE, dissenting.

Agreeing as I do with most of Justice Stevens' opinion and with the result he reaches, I dissent and would affirm the judgment below.

JUSTICE STEVENS, with whom &sJustice Marshall&s joins, dissenting.

At the end of its opinion, the Court pays lip service to the proposition that should provide the basis for a correct analysis of the legal question presented by this case: It is " 'a cardinal principle that "searches conducted outside the judicial process, without prior approval by judge or magistrate, are *per se* unreasonable under the Fourth Amendment—subject only to a few specifically established and well-delineated exceptions." ' * * * "

[The warrant] requirement * * * reflects the sound policy judgment that, absent exceptional circumstances, the decision to invade the privacy of an individual's personal effects should be made by a neutral magistrate rather than an agent of the Executive. * * *

The Court does not attempt to identify any exigent circumstances that would justify its refusal to apply the general rule against warrantless searches. Instead, it advances these three arguments: First, the rules identified in the foregoing cases are confusing and anomalous. Second, the rules do not protect any significant interest in privacy. And, third, the rules impede effective law enforcement. None of these arguments withstands scrutiny. * * *

The Court summarizes the alleged "anomaly" created by the coexistence of *Ross*, *Chadwick*, and *Sanders* with the statement that "the more likely the police are to discover drugs in a container, the less authority they have to search it." This juxtaposition is only anomalous, however, if one accepts the flawed premise that the degree to which the police are likely to discover contraband is correlated with their authority to search *without a warrant*. Yet, even proof beyond a reasonable doubt will not justify a warrantless search that is not supported by one of the exceptions to the warrant requirement. And, even when the police have a warrant or an exception applies, once the police possess probable cause, the extent to which they are more or less certain of the contents of a container has no bearing on their authority to search it.

To the extent there was any "anomaly" in our prior jurisprudence, the Court has "cured" it at the expense of creating a more serious paradox. For, surely it is anomalous to prohibit a search of a briefcase while the owner is carrying it exposed on a public street yet to permit a search once the owner has placed the briefcase in the locked trunk of his car. One's privacy interest in one's luggage can certainly not be diminished by one's removing it from a public thoroughfare and placing it—out of sight—in a privately owned vehicle. Nor is the danger that evidence will escape increased if the luggage is in a car rather than on the street. In either location, if the police have probable cause, they are authorized to seize the luggage and to detain it until they obtain judicial approval for a search. Any line demarking an exception to the warrant requirement will appear blurred at the edges, but the Court has certainly erred if it believes that, by erasing one line and drawing another, it has drawn a clearer boundary.

The Court's statement that *Chadwick* and *Sanders* provide only "minimal protection to privacy" is also unpersuasive. Every citizen clearly has an interest in the privacy of the contents of his or her luggage, briefcase, handbag or any other container that conceals private papers and effects from public scrutiny. That privacy interest has been recognized repeatedly in cases spanning more than a century.

Under the Court's holding today, the privacy interest that protects the contents of a suitcase or a briefcase from a warrantless search when it is in public view simply vanishes when its owner climbs into a taxicab. Unquestionably the rejection of the *Sanders* line of cases by today's decision will result in a significant loss of individual privacy. * * *

NOTES AND QUESTIONS

1. The question of whether *Acevedo* is applicable to every sort of container was raised but not resolved in *United States v. Burgess*, 576 F.3d 1078 (10th Cir.2009), where in the course of a search of a motor home connected with sale of controlled substances the police seized a laptop computer and two external hard drives and later forensically examined them, including viewing of several hundred digital images in an effort to find so-called "trophy photos," which actually uncovered child pornography. In an effort to justify this as a warrantless search under *Acevedo*, the government constructed "this syllogism: 1) the expectation of privacy of computer contents has been likened to that of a suitcase or briefcase * * *; 2) the automobile exception to the warrant requirement permits, with probable cause, the search of containers found in the automobile—even locked suitcases and briefcases * * *; therefore 3) police may (with probable cause, but without a warrant) search computers and hard drives, found in automobiles * * *." Do you agree?

2. After police stopped a vehicle for speeding, the driver admitted that he had used the syringe visible in his shirt pocket to take drugs. The police then ordered the two female passengers out of the car and searched the passenger compartment for contraband. On the back seat they found a purse that passenger Houghton claimed as hers; the police searched it and found drugs and drug paraphernalia. Houghton was convicted after her efforts to have the drugs suppressed failed, but the state supreme court overturned the conviction, reasoning that the search violated the Fourth Amendment because the officer "knew or should have known that the purse did not belong to the driver, but to one of the passengers," and because "there was no probable cause to search the passengers' personal effects and no reason to believe that contraband had been placed within the purse." But in WYOMING v. HOUGHTON, 526 U.S. 295 (1999), the Supreme Court, per Scalia, J., reversed, reasoning that "neither *Ross* itself nor the

historical evidence it relied upon admits of a distinction among packages or containers based on ownership. When there is probable cause to search for contraband in a car, it is reasonable for police officers—like customs officials in the Founding era—to examine packages and containers without a showing of individualized probable cause for each one. A passenger's personal belongings, just like the driver's belongings or containers attached to the car like a glove compartment, are 'in' the car, and the officer has probable cause to search for contraband in the car.

"Even if the historical evidence, as described by *Ross*, were thought to be equivocal, we would find that the balancing of the relative interests weighs decidedly in favor of allowing searches of a passenger's belongings. Passengers, no less than drivers, possess a reduced expectation of privacy with regard to the property that they transport in cars, which 'trave[l] public thoroughfares,' 'seldom serv[e] as . . . the repository of personal effects,' are subjected to police stop and examination to enforce 'pervasive' governmental controls '[a]s an everyday occurrence,' and, finally, are exposed to traffic accidents that may render all their contents open to public scrutiny.

"In this regard—the degree of intrusiveness upon personal privacy and indeed even personal dignity—the two cases the Wyoming Supreme Court found dispositive differ substantially from the package search at issue here. *United States v. Di Re*, 332 U.S. 581 (1948), held that probable cause to search a car did not justify a body search of a passenger.[a] And *Ybarra v. Illinois*, [p. 324], held that a search warrant for a tavern and its bartender did not permit body searches of all the bar's patrons. These cases turned on the unique, significantly heightened protection afforded against searches of one's person. 'Even a limited search of the outer clothing . . . constitutes a severe, though brief, intrusion upon cherished personal security, and it must surely be an annoying, frightening, and perhaps humiliating experience.' Such traumatic consequences are not to be expected when the police examine an item of personal property found in a car.[34]

---

a. But consider, *Model Pre–Arraignment Code* § SS 260.3, providing otherwise (except as to passengers in a common carrier) if the officer has not found the items sought in the vehicle and has "reason to suspect that one or more of the occupants of the vehicle may have the things subject to seizure so concealed." The Reporters argue that "it seems absurd to say that the occupants can take the narcotics out of the glove compartment and stuff them in their pockets, and drive happily away after the vehicle has been fruitlessly searched."

34. The dissent begins its analysis with an assertion that this case is governed by our decision in *United States v. Di Re*, which held, as the dissent describes it, that the automobile exception to the warrant requirement did not justify "searches of the passenger's pockets and the space between his shirt and underwear." It attributes that holding to "the settled distinction between drivers and passengers," rather than to a distinction between search of the person and search of property, which the dissent claims is "newly minted" by today's opinion—a "new rule that is based on a distinction between property contained in clothing worn by a passenger and property contained in a passenger's briefcase or purse."

In its peroration, however, the dissent quotes extensively from Justice Jackson's opinion in *Di Re*, which makes it very clear that it is precisely this distinction between search of the person and search of property that the case relied upon: "The Government says it would not contend that, armed 'with a search warrant for a residence only, it could search all persons found in it. But an occupant of a house could be used to conceal this contraband on his person quite as readily as can an occupant of a car.' " Does the dissent really believe that Justice Jackson was saying that a house-search could not inspect property belonging to persons found in the house—say a large standing safe or violin case belonging to the owner's visiting godfather? Of course that is not what Justice Jackson meant at all. He was referring precisely to that "distinction between property contained in clothing worn by a passenger and property contained in a passenger's briefcase or purse" that the dissent disparages. This distinction between searches of the person and searches of property is assuredly not "newly minted." And if the dissent thinks "pockets" and "clothing" do not count as part of the person, it must believe that the only searches of the person are strip searches.

"Whereas the passenger's privacy expectations are, as we have described, considerably diminished, the governmental interests at stake are substantial. Effective law enforcement would be appreciably impaired without the ability to search a passenger's personal belongings when there is reason to believe contraband or evidence of criminal wrongdoing is hidden in the car. As in all car-search cases, the 'ready mobility' of an automobile creates a risk that the evidence or contraband will be permanently lost while a warrant is obtained. In addition, a car passenger—unlike the unwitting tavern patron in *Ybarra*—will often be engaged in a common enterprise with the driver, and have the same interest in concealing the fruits or the evidence of their wrongdoing. A criminal might be able to hide contraband in a passenger's belongings as readily as in other containers in the car—perhaps even surreptitiously, without the passenger's knowledge or permission. (This last possibility provided the basis for respondent's defense at trial; she testified that most of the seized contraband must have been placed in her purse by her traveling companions at one or another of various times, including the time she was 'half asleep' in the car.)

"To be sure, these factors favoring a search will not always be present, but the balancing of interests must be conducted with an eye to the generality of cases. To require that the investigating officer have positive reason to believe that the passenger and driver were engaged in a common enterprise, or positive reason to believe that the driver had time and occasion to conceal the item in the passenger's belongings, surreptitiously or with friendly permission, is to impose requirements so seldom met that a 'passenger's property' rule would dramatically reduce the ability to find and seize contraband and evidence of crime. Of course these requirements would not attach (under the Wyoming Supreme Court's rule) until the police officer knows or has reason to know that the container belongs to a passenger. But once a 'passenger's property' exception to car searches became widely known, one would expect passenger-confederates to claim everything as their own. And one would anticipate a bog of litigation—in the form of both civil lawsuits and motions to suppress in criminal trials—involving such questions as whether the officer should have believed a passenger's claim of ownership, whether he should have inferred ownership from various objective factors, whether he had probable cause to believe that the passenger was a confederate, or to believe that the driver might have introduced the contraband into the package with or without the passenger's knowledge.[35] When balancing the competing interests, our determinations of 'reasonableness' under the Fourth Amendment must take account of these practical realities. We think they militate in favor of the needs of law enforcement, and against a personal-privacy interest that is ordinarily weak."

Stevens, J., for the three dissenters, objected that in "all of our prior cases applying the automobile exception to the Fourth Amendment's warrant requirement, either the defendant was the operator of the vehicle and in custody of the object of the search, or no question was raised as to the defendant's ownership or

---

35. The dissent is "confident in a police officer's ability to apply a rule requiring a warrant or individualized probable cause to search belongings that are ... obviously owned by and in the custody of a passenger." If this is the dissent's strange criterion for warrant protection ("obviously owned by and in the custody of") its preceding paean to the importance of preserving passengers' privacy rings a little hollow on rehearing. Should it not be enough if the passenger says he owns the briefcase, and the officer has no concrete reason to believe otherwise? Or would the dissent consider that an example of "obvious" ownership? On reflection, it seems not at all obvious precisely what constitutes obviousness—and so even the dissent's on-the-cheap protection of passengers' privacy interest in their property turns out to be unclear, and hence unadministrable. But maybe the dissent does not mean to propose an obviously-owned-by-and-in-the-custody-of test after all, since a few sentences later it endorses, simpliciter, "a rule requiring a warrant or individualized probable cause to search passenger belongings." For the reasons described in text, that will not work.

custody. In the only automobile case confronting the search of a passenger defendant—*United States v. Di Re*—the Court held that the exception to the warrant requirement did not apply. In *Di Re*, as here, the information prompting the search directly implicated the driver, not the passenger. Today, instead of adhering to the settled distinction between drivers and passengers, the Court fashions a new rule that is based on a distinction between property contained in clothing worn by a passenger and property contained in a passenger's briefcase or purse. In cases on both sides of the Court's newly minted test, the property is in a 'container' (whether a pocket or a pouch) located in the vehicle. Moreover, unlike the Court, I think it quite plain that the search of a passenger's purse or briefcase involves an intrusion on privacy that may be just as serious as was the intrusion in *Di Re*. * * *b

"Nor am I persuaded that the mere spatial association between a passenger and a driver provides an acceptable basis for presuming that they are partners in crime or for ignoring privacy interests in a purse. Whether or not the Fourth Amendment required a warrant to search Houghton's purse, at the very least the trooper in this case had to have probable cause to believe that her purse contained contraband. The Wyoming Supreme Court concluded that he did not.

"Finally, in my view, the State's legitimate interest in effective law enforcement does not outweigh the privacy concerns at issue. I am as confident in a police officer's ability to apply a rule requiring a warrant or individualized probable cause to search belongings that are—as in this case—obviously owned by and in the custody of a passenger as is the Court in a 'passenger-confederate[']s' ability to circumvent the rule. Certainly the ostensible clarity of the Court's rule is attractive. But that virtue is insufficient justification for its adoption. Moreover, a rule requiring a warrant or individualized probable cause to search passenger belongings is every bit as simple as the Court's rule; it simply protects more privacy. * * *2"

3. Reassess the law and facts of *Chadwick*, p. 386 in light of *Acevedo*. Absent true exigent circumstances, is a search warrant still required for a container having no connection with a vehicle? If so, is there actually a sufficient container-vehicle connection in *Chadwick* to make the *Acevedo* no-warrant rule applicable?

4. If there *is* a general rule that absent exigent circumstances search warrants are needed for the search of containers not sufficiently connected with vehicles, are there exceptions? Consider:

(a) Fn. 13 in *Sanders:* "Not all containers and packages found by police during the course of a search will deserve the full protection of the Fourth Amendment. Thus, some containers (for example a kit of burglar tools or a gun

---

b. Compare Breyer, concurring: "Purses are special containers. They are repositories of especially personal items that people generally like to keep with them at all times. So I am tempted to say that a search of a purse involves an intrusion so similar to a search of one's person that the same rule should govern both. However, given this Court's prior cases, I cannot argue that the fact that the container was a purse automatically makes a legal difference, for the Court has warned against trying to make that kind of distinction. But I can say that it would matter if a woman's purse, like a man's billfold, were attached to her person. It might then amount to a kind of 'outer clothing' which under the Court's cases would properly receive increased protection. In this case, the purse was separate from the person, and no one has claimed that, under those circumstances, the type of container makes a difference. For that reason, I join the Court's opinion."

2. In response to this dissent the Court has crafted an imaginative footnote suggesting that the *Di Re* decision rested, not on Di Re's status as a mere occupant of the vehicle and the importance of individualized suspicion, but rather on the intrusive character of the search. That the search of a safe or violin case would be less intrusive than a strip search does not, however, persuade me that the *Di Re* case would have been decided differently if Di Re had been a woman and the gas coupons had been found in her purse. * * *

case) by their very nature cannot support any reasonable expectation of privacy because their contents can be inferred from their outward appearance. Similarly, in some cases the contents of a package will be open to 'plain view,' thereby obviating the need for a warrant."

(b) In *Texas v. Brown,* 460 U.S. 730 (1983), involving a warrantless search of a knotted opaque party balloon found with several plastic vials, a quantity of loose white powder, and a bag of balloons, Stevens, J., for three members of the Court, after characterizing the plurality's explanation for why no search warrant was needed to search the balloon as "incomplete," speculated that the balloon "could be one of those rare single-purpose containers which 'by their very nature cannot support any reasonable expectation of privacy because their contents can be inferred from their outward appearance.' Whereas a suitcase or a paper bag may contain an almost infinite variety of items, a balloon of this kind might be used only to transport drugs. Viewing it where he did could have given the officer a degree of certainty that is equivalent to the plain view of the heroin itself. If that be true, I would conclude that the plain view doctrine supports the search as well as the seizure even though the contents of the balloon were not actually visible to the officer.

"This reasoning leads me to the conclusion that the Fourth Amendment would not require exclusion of the balloon's contents in this case if, but only if, there was probable cause to search the entire vehicle or there was virtual certainty that the balloon contained a controlled substance.[5]"

(c) After customs agents found marijuana inside a table shipped into the country, it was repackaged and delivered to defendant by police posing as delivery men. Surveilling police saw defendant pull the container into his apartment, and when he reemerged with it 30 to 45 minutes later he was arrested and the package searched without a warrant. The state court, relying upon *Sanders* and *Chadwick,* held the marijuana inadmissible, but the Supreme Court, in ILLINOIS v. ANDREAS, 463 U.S. 765 (1983), disagreed. The Court, per Burger, C.J., first addressed the threshold question of "whether an individual has a legitimate expectation of privacy in the contents of a previously lawfully searched container. It is obvious that the privacy interest in the contents of a container diminishes with respect to a container that law enforcement authorities have already lawfully opened and found to contain illicit drugs. No protected privacy interest remains in contraband in a container once government officers lawfully have opened that container and identified its contents as illegal. The simple act of resealing the container to enable the police to make a controlled delivery does not operate to revive or restore the lawfully invaded privacy rights.

"This conclusion is supported by the reasoning underlying the 'plain view' doctrine. The plain view doctrine authorizes seizure of illegal or evidentiary items visible to a police officer whose access to the object has some prior Fourth Amendment justification and who has probable cause to suspect that the item is connected with criminal activity. The plain view doctrine is grounded on the proposition that once police are lawfully in a position to observe an item first-hand, its owner's privacy interest in that item is lost; the owner may retain the incidents of title and possession but not privacy. That rationale applies here; once a container has been found to a certainty to contain illicit drugs, the contraband becomes like objects physically within the plain view of the police, and the claim to

---

5. Sometimes there can be greater certainty about the identity of a substance within a container than about the identity of a substance that is actually visible. One might actually see a white powder without realizing that it is heroin, but be virtually certain a balloon contains such a substance in a particular context. It seems to me that in evaluating whether a person's privacy interests are infringed, "virtual certainty" is a more meaningful indicator than visibility.

privacy is lost. Consequently the subsequent opening is not a 'search' within the intendment of the Fourth Amendment."

The Court then noted that "perfect" controlled deliveries are often impossible, so that there may result "a gap in surveillance" during which "it is possible that the container will be put to other uses—for example, the contraband may be removed or other items may be placed inside." On the resulting question of "at what point after an interruption of control or surveillance, courts should recognize the individual's expectation of privacy in the container as a legitimate right protected by the Fourth Amendment," the Court adopted the "workable," "reasonable" and "objective" standard of "whether there is a substantial likelihood that the contents of the container have been changed during the gap in surveillance. We hold that absent a substantial likelihood that the contents have been changed, there is no legitimate expectation of privacy in the contents of a container previously opened under lawful authority." The Court then concluded there was no substantial likelihood in the instant case. "The unusual size of the container, its specialized purpose, and the relatively short break in surveillance, combine to make it substantially unlikely that the respondent removed the table or placed new items inside the container while it was in his apartment."

Brennan and Marshall, JJ., dissenting, objected that while after the customs search "any reasonable expectation respondent may have had that the existence of the contraband would remain secret was lost, and could not be regained," he still had a Fourth Amendment right "to be 'let alone'" which "is, at the very least, the right not to have one's repose and possessions disturbed" without a warrant. Moreover, "if a person has no reasonable expectation of privacy in a package whose contents are already legally known to the authorities, a reasonable expectation of privacy should reattach if the person has unobserved access to the package and any opportunity to change its contents." STEVENS, J., dissenting separately, would remand for reconsideration under his "virtual certainty" test in *Texas v. Brown.*

ARIZONA v. GANT

556 U.S. 332, 129 S.Ct. 1710, 173 L.Ed.2d 485 (2009).

JUSTICE STEVENS delivered the opinion of the Court.

After Rodney Gant was arrested for driving with a suspended license, handcuffed, and locked in the back of a patrol car, police officers searched his car and discovered cocaine in the pocket of a jacket on the backseat.[a] Because Gant could not have accessed his car to retrieve weapons or evidence at the time of the search, the Arizona Supreme Court held that the search-incident-to-arrest exception to the Fourth Amendment's warrant requirement, as defined in *Chimel v. California,* [p. 363], and applied to vehicle searches in *New York v. Belton,* 453 U.S. 454 (1981), did not justify the search in this case. We agree with that conclusion. * * *

In *Chimel,* we held that a search incident to arrest may only include "the arrestee's person and the area 'within his immediate control'—construing that phrase to mean the area from within which he might gain possession of a weapon or destructible evidence." That limitation, which continues to define the bound-

***

a. The background is this: On an anonymous tip drugs were being sold at a certain residence, police went there and knocked on the door; Gant answered, identified himself, and said the owner would return later. The police left and conducted a records check, revealing there was an outstanding warrant for Gant's arrest for driving with a suspended license. Police returned to the premises that evening, and arrested a man in the back yard for providing a false name and a woman in a car parked in front for possessing drug paraphernalia, at which point Gant was seen pulling into the driveway.

aries of the exception, ensures that the scope of a search incident to arrest is commensurate with its purposes of protecting arresting officers and safeguarding any evidence of the offense of arrest that an arrestee might conceal or destroy. * * *

In *Belton,* we considered *Chimel*'s application to the automobile context. A lone police officer in that case stopped a speeding car in which Belton was one of four occupants. While asking for the driver's license and registration, the officer smelled burnt marijuana and observed an envelope on the car floor marked "Supergold"—a name he associated with marijuana. Thus having probable cause to believe the occupants had committed a drug offense, the officer ordered them out of the vehicle, placed them under arrest, and patted them down. Without handcuffing the arrestees, the officer " 'split them up into four separate areas of the Thruway . . . so they would not be in physical touching area of each other' " and searched the vehicle, including the pocket of a jacket on the backseat, in which he found cocaine.

The New York Court of Appeals found the search unconstitutional, concluding that after the occupants were arrested the vehicle and its contents were "safely within the exclusive custody and control of the police." [But] we held that when an officer lawfully arrests "the occupant of an automobile, he may, as a contemporaneous incident of that arrest, search the passenger compartment of the automobile" and any containers therein. That holding was based in large part on our assumption "that articles inside the relatively narrow compass of the passenger compartment of an automobile are in fact generally, even if not inevitably, within 'the area into which an arrestee might reach.' " * * *

Despite the textual and evidentiary support for the Arizona Supreme Court's reading of *Belton,* our opinion has been widely understood to allow a vehicle search incident to the arrest of a recent occupant even if there is no possibility the arrestee could gain access to the vehicle at the time of the search. This reading may be attributable to Justice Brennan's dissent in *Belton,* in which he characterized the Court's holding as resting on the "fiction . . . that the interior of a car is *always* within the immediate control of an arrestee who has recently been in the car." Under the majority's approach, he argued, "the result would presumably be the same even if [the officer] had handcuffed Belton and his companions in the patrol car" before conducting the search.

Since we decided *Belton,* Courts of Appeals have given different answers to the question whether a vehicle must be within an arrestee's reach to justify a vehicle search incident to arrest, but Justice Brennan's reading of the Court's opinion has predominated. * * *

Under this broad reading of *Belton,* a vehicle search would be authorized incident to every arrest of a recent occupant[b] notwithstanding that in most cases the vehicle's passenger compartment will not be within the arrestee's reach at the time of the search. To read *Belton* as authorizing a vehicle search incident to every recent occupant's arrest would thus untether the rule from the justifications underlying the *Chimel* exception—a result clearly incompatible with our statement in *Belton* that it "in no way alters the fundamental principles established in the *Chimel* case regarding the basic scope of searches incident to lawful custodial arrests." Accordingly, we reject this reading of *Belton* and hold that the *Chimel* rationale authorizes police to search a vehicle incident to a recent occupant's

---

b. While the rule in *Belton* was stated in terms of "a lawful custodial arrest of the occupant of an automobile," in *Thornton v. United States,* 541 U.S. 615 (2004), it was applied as well to a "recent occupant" of the vehicle (arrested when he revealed illegal drugs on his person) because "the arrest of a suspect who is next to a vehicle presents identical concerns regarding officer safety and the destruction of evidence as the arrest of one who is inside the vehicle."

arrest only when the arrestee is unsecured and within reaching distance of the passenger compartment at the time of the search.[4]

Although it does not follow from *Chimel,* we also conclude that circumstances unique to the vehicle context justify a search incident to a lawful arrest when it is "reasonable to believe evidence relevant to the crime of arrest might be found in the vehicle." *Thornton* (Scalia, J., concurring in judgment). In many cases, as when a recent occupant is arrested for a traffic violation, there will be no reasonable basis to believe the vehicle contains relevant evidence. But in others, including *Belton* and *Thornton,* the offense of arrest will supply a basis for searching the passenger compartment of an arrestee's vehicle and any containers therein.

Neither the possibility of access nor the likelihood of discovering offense-related evidence authorized the search in this case. Unlike in *Belton,* which involved a single officer confronted with four unsecured arrestees, the five officers in this case outnumbered the three arrestees, all of whom had been handcuffed and secured in separate patrol cars before the officers searched Gant's car. Under those circumstances, Gant clearly was not within reaching distance of his car at the time of the search. An evidentiary basis for the search was also lacking in this case. Whereas Belton and Thornton were arrested for drug offenses, Gant was arrested for driving with a suspended license—an offense for which police could not expect to find evidence in the passenger compartment of Gant's car. Because police could not reasonably have believed either that Gant could have accessed his car at the time of the search or that evidence of the offense for which he was arrested might have been found therein, the search in this case was unreasonable.

The State does not seriously disagree with the Arizona Supreme Court's conclusion that Gant could not have accessed his vehicle at the time of the search, but it nevertheless asks us to uphold the search of his vehicle under the broad reading of *Belton* discussed above. The State argues that *Belton* searches are reasonable regardless of the possibility of access in a given case because that expansive rule correctly balances law enforcement interests, including the interest in a bright-line rule, with an arrestee's limited privacy interest in his vehicle.

For several reasons, we reject the State's argument. First, the State seriously undervalues the privacy interests at stake. Although we have recognized that a motorist's privacy interest in his vehicle is less substantial than in his home, the former interest is nevertheless important and deserving of constitutional protection. It is particularly significant that *Belton* searches authorize police officers to search not just the passenger compartment but every purse, briefcase, or other container within that space. A rule that gives police the power to conduct such a search whenever an individual is caught committing a traffic offense, when there is no basis for believing evidence of the offense might be found in the vehicle, creates a serious and recurring threat to the privacy of countless individuals. Indeed, the character of that threat implicates the central concern underlying the Fourth Amendment—the concern about giving police officers unbridled discretion to rummage at will among a person's private effects.[5]

---

4. Because officers have many means of ensuring the safe arrest of vehicle occupants, it will be the rare case in which an officer is unable to fully effectuate an arrest so that a real possibility of access to the arrestee's vehicle remains. Cf. 3 W. LaFave, Search and Seizure § 7.1(c), p. 525 (4th ed.2004) (hereinafter LaFave) (noting that the availability of protective measures "ensur[es] the nonexistence of circumstances in which the arrestee's 'control' of the car is in doubt"). But in such a case a search incident to arrest is reasonable under the Fourth Amendment.

5. Many have observed that a broad reading of *Belton* gives police limitless discretion to conduct exploratory searches. See 3 LaFave § 7.1(c), at 527 (observing that *Belton* creates the risk "that police will make custodial arrests which they otherwise would not make as a cover for a search which the Fourth Amendment otherwise prohibits") * * *.

At the same time as it undervalues these privacy concerns, the State exaggerates the clarity that its reading of *Belton* provides. Courts that have read *Belton* expansively are at odds regarding how close in time to the arrest and how proximate to the arrestee's vehicle an officer's first contact with the arrestee must be to bring the encounter within *Belton*'s purview and whether a search is reasonable when it commences or continues after the arrestee has been removed from the scene. The rule has thus generated a great deal of uncertainty, particularly for a rule touted as providing a "bright line."

Contrary to the State's suggestion, a broad reading of *Belton* is also unnecessary to protect law enforcement safety and evidentiary interests. Under our view, *Belton* and *Thornton* permit an officer to conduct a vehicle search when an arrestee is within reaching distance of the vehicle or it is reasonable to believe the vehicle contains evidence of the offense of arrest. Other established exceptions to the warrant requirement authorize a vehicle search under additional circumstances when safety or evidentiary concerns demand. For instance, *Michigan v. Long,* [p. 436], permits an officer to search a vehicle's passenger compartment when he has reasonable suspicion that an individual, whether or not the arrestee, is "dangerous" and might access the vehicle to "gain immediate control of weapons." If there is probable cause to believe a vehicle contains evidence of criminal activity, *United States v. Ross,* [p. 388], authorizes a search of any area of the vehicle in which the evidence might be found. Unlike the searches permitted by Justice Scalia's opinion concurring in the judgment in *Thornton,* which we conclude today are reasonable for purposes of the Fourth Amendment, *Ross* allows searches for evidence relevant to offenses other than the offense of arrest, and the scope of the search authorized is broader. Finally, there may be still other circumstances in which safety or evidentiary interests would justify a search. Cf. *Maryland v. Buie,* [p. 366] (holding that, incident to arrest, an officer may conduct a limited protective sweep of those areas of a house in which he reasonably suspects a dangerous person may be hiding).

These exceptions together ensure that officers may search a vehicle when genuine safety or evidentiary concerns encountered during the arrest of a vehicle's recent occupant justify a search. Construing *Belton* broadly to allow vehicle searches incident to any arrest would serve no purpose except to provide a police entitlement, and it is anathema to the Fourth Amendment to permit a warrantless search on that basis. For these reasons, we are unpersuaded by the State's arguments that a broad reading of *Belton* would meaningfully further law enforcement interests and justify a substantial intrusion on individuals' privacy.

Our dissenting colleagues argue that the doctrine of *stare decisis* requires adherence to a broad reading of *Belton* even though the justifications for searching a vehicle incident to arrest are in most cases absent. The doctrine of *stare decisis* is of course "essential to the respect accorded to the judgments of the Court and to the stability of the law," but it does not compel us to follow a past decision when its rationale no longer withstands "careful analysis." * * *

We have never relied on *stare decisis* to justify the continuance of an unconstitutional police practice. And we would be particularly loath to uphold an unconstitutional result in a case that is so easily distinguished from the decisions that arguably compel it. The safety and evidentiary interests that supported the search in *Belton* simply are not present in this case. Indeed, it is hard to imagine two cases that are factually more distinct, as *Belton* involved one officer confronted by four unsecured arrestees suspected of committing a drug offense and this case involves several officers confronted with a securely detained arrestee apprehended for driving with a suspended license. This case is also distinguishable from *Thornton,* in which the petitioner was arrested for a drug offense. It is thus unsurprising that Members of this Court who concurred in the judgments in *Belton* and *Thornton* also concur in the decision in this case.[10]

Police may search a vehicle incident to a recent occupant's arrest only if the arrestee is within reaching distance of the passenger compartment at the time of the search or it is reasonable to believe the vehicle contains evidence of the offense of arrest. When these justifications are absent, a search of an arrestee's vehicle will be unreasonable unless police obtain a warrant or show that another exception to the warrant requirement applies. The Arizona Supreme Court correctly held that this case involved an unreasonable search. Accordingly, the judgment of the State Supreme Court is affirmed. * * *

JUSTICE SCALIA, concurring. * * *

Justice Stevens acknowledges that an officer-safety rationale cannot justify all vehicle searches incident to arrest, but asserts that that is not the rule *Belton* and *Thornton* adopted. * * * Justice Stevens would therefore retain the application of *Chimel v. California* in the car-search context but would apply in the future what he believes our cases held in the past: that officers making a roadside stop may search the vehicle so long as the "arrestee is within reaching distance of the passenger compartment at the time of the search." I believe that this standard fails to provide the needed guidance to arresting officers and also leaves much room for manipulation, inviting officers to leave the scene unsecured (at least where dangerous suspects are not involved) in order to conduct a vehicle search. In my view we should simply abandon the *Belton-Thornton* charade of officer safety and overrule those cases. I would hold that a vehicle search incident to arrest is *ipso facto* "reasonable" only when the object of the search is evidence of the crime for which the arrest was made, or of another crime that the officer has probable cause to believe occurred. Because respondent was arrested for driving without a license (a crime for which no evidence could be expected to be found in the vehicle), I would hold in the present case that the search was unlawful. * * *

No other Justice, however, shares my view that application of *Chimel* in this context should be entirely abandoned. It seems to me unacceptable for the Court to come forth with a 4–to–1–to–4 opinion that leaves the governing rule uncertain. I am therefore confronted with the choice of either leaving the current understanding of *Belton* and *Thornton* in effect, or acceding to what seems to me the artificial narrowing of those cases adopted by Justice Stevens. The latter, as I have said, does not provide the degree of certainty I think desirable in this field; but the former opens the field to what I think are plainly unconstitutional searches— which is the greater evil. I therefore join the opinion of the Court. * * *

JUSTICE ALITO, with whom THE CHIEF JUSTICE and JUSTICE KENNEDY join, and with whom JUSTICE BREYER joins[c] except as to Part II–E, dissenting. * * *

I

Although the Court refuses to acknowledge that it is overruling *Belton* and *Thornton,* there can be no doubt that it does so.

---

10. Justice Stevens concurred in the judgment in *Belton* for the reasons stated in his dissenting opinion in *Robbins v. California*, 453 U.S. 420 (1981)[, namely, that the search was made on "probable cause to believe that the vehicle contained contraband"], Justice Thomas joined the Court's opinion in *Thornton*, and Justice Scalia and Justice Ginsburg concurred in the judgment in that case.

c. A separate dissent by Justice Breyer is omitted. Relying on stare decisis, he declared that "those who wish this Court to change a well established precedent—where as here there has been considerable reliance on the rule in question—bear a heavy burden," and concluded that burden had not been met.

The precise holding in *Belton* could not be clearer. The Court stated unequivocally: "[W]e hold that when a policeman has made a lawful custodial arrest of the occupant of an automobile, he may, as a contemporaneous incident of that arrest, search the passenger compartment of that automobile."

Despite this explicit statement, the opinion of the Court in the present case curiously suggests that *Belton* may reasonably be read as adopting a holding that is narrower than the one explicitly set out in the *Belton* opinion, namely, that an officer arresting a vehicle occupant may search the passenger compartment "*when the passenger compartment is within an arrestee's reaching distance.*" According to the Court, the broader reading of *Belton* that has gained wide acceptance "may be attributable to Justice Brennan's dissent."

Contrary to the Court's suggestion, however, Justice Brennan's *Belton* dissent did not mischaracterize the Court's holding in that case or cause that holding to be misinterpreted. As noted, the *Belton* Court explicitly stated precisely what it held. * * *.

II

Because the Court has substantially overruled *Belton* and *Thornton,* the Court must explain why its departure from the usual rule of *stare decisis* is justified. I recognize that stare decisis is not an "inexorable command," and applies less rigidly in constitutional cases. But the Court has said that a constitutional precedent should be followed unless there is a " 'special justification' " for its abandonment. Relevant factors identified in prior cases include whether the precedent has engendered reliance, whether there has been an important change in circumstances in the outside world, whether the precedent has proved to be unworkable, whether the precedent has been undermined by later decisions, and whether the decision was badly reasoned. These factors weigh in favor of retaining the rule established in *Belton.* * * *

C

Workability. The *Belton* rule has not proved to be unworkable. On the contrary, the rule was adopted for the express purpose of providing a test that would be relatively easy for police officers and judges to apply. The Court correctly notes that even the *Belton* rule is not perfectly clear in all situations. Specifically, it is sometimes debatable whether a search is or is not contemporaneous with an arrest, but that problem is small in comparison with the problems that the Court's new two-part rule will produce.

The first part of the Court's new rule—which permits the search of a vehicle's passenger compartment if it is within an arrestee's reach at the time of the search—reintroduces the same sort of case-by-case, fact-specific decisionmaking that the *Belton* rule was adopted to avoid. As the situation in *Belton* illustrated, there are cases in which it is unclear whether an arrestee could retrieve a weapon or evidence in the passenger compartment of a car.

Even more serious problems will also result from the second part of the Court's new rule, which requires officers making roadside arrests to determine whether there is reason to believe that the vehicle contains evidence of the crime of arrest. What this rule permits in a variety of situations is entirely unclear. * * *

E

Bad reasoning. The Court is harshly critical of *Belton*'s reasoning, but the problem that the Court perceives cannot be remedied simply by overruling *Belton.*

Belton represented only a modest—and quite defensible—extension of *Chimel,* as I understand that decision.

Prior to *Chimel,* the Court's precedents permitted an arresting officer to search the area within an arrestee's "possession" and "control" for the purpose of gathering evidence. Based on this "abstract doctrine," the Court had sustained searches that extended far beyond an arrestee's grabbing area. See *United States v. Rabinowitz,* 339 U.S. 56 (1950) (search of entire office); *Harris v. United States,* 331 U.S. 145 (1947) (search of entire apartment).

The *Chimel* Court, in an opinion written by Justice Stewart, overruled these cases. Concluding that there are only two justifications for a warrantless search incident to arrest—officer safety and the preservation of evidence—the Court stated that such a search must be confined to "the arrestee's person" and "the area from within which he might gain possession of a weapon or destructible evidence."

Unfortunately, *Chimel* did not say whether "the area from within which [an arrestee] might gain possession of a weapon or destructible evidence" is to be measured at the time of the arrest or at the time of the search, but unless the *Chimel* rule was meant to be a specialty rule, applicable to only a few unusual cases, the Court must have intended for this area to be measured at the time of arrest.

This is so because the Court can hardly have failed to appreciate the following two facts. First, in the great majority of cases, an officer making an arrest is able to handcuff the arrestee and remove him to a secure place before conducting a search incident to the arrest. Second, because it is safer for an arresting officer to secure an arrestee before searching, it is likely that this is what arresting officers do in the great majority of cases. (And it appears, not surprisingly, that this is in fact the prevailing practice.) Thus, if the area within an arrestee's reach were assessed, not at the time of arrest, but at the time of the search, the *Chimel* rule would rarely come into play.

Moreover, if the applicability of the *Chimel* rule turned on whether an arresting officer chooses to secure an arrestee prior to conducting a search, rather than searching first and securing the arrestee later, the rule would "create a perverse incentive for an arresting officer to prolong the period during which the arrestee is kept in an area where he could pose a danger to the officer." If this is the law, the D.C. Circuit observed, "the law would truly be, as Mr. Bumble said, 'a ass.'" * * *

I do not think that this is what the *Chimel* Court intended. Handcuffs were in use in 1969. The ability of arresting officers to secure arrestees before conducting a search—and their incentive to do so—are facts that can hardly have escaped the Court's attention. I therefore believe that the *Chimel* Court intended that its new rule apply in cases in which the arrestee is handcuffed before the search is conducted.

The *Belton* Court, in my view, proceeded on the basis of this interpretation of *Chimel.* Again speaking through Justice Stewart, the *Belton* Court reasoned that articles in the passenger compartment of a car are "generally, even if not inevitably" within an arrestee's reach. This is undoubtedly true at the time of the arrest of a person who is seated in a car but plainly not true when the person has been removed from the car and placed in handcuffs. Accordingly, the *Belton* Court must have proceeded on the assumption that the *Chimel* rule was to be applied at the time of arrest. And that is why the *Belton* Court was able to say that its decision "in no way alter[ed] the fundamental principles established in the *Chimel* case regarding the basic scope of searches incident to lawful custodial arrests." Viewing *Chimel* as having focused on the time of arrest, *Belton*'s only new step was to eliminate the need to decide on a case-by-case basis whether a particular person seated in a car actually could have reached the part of the passenger compartment where a weapon or evidence was hidden. For this reason, if we are going to reexamine *Belton,* we should also reexamine the reasoning in *Chimel* on which *Belton* rests.

F

The Court, however, does not reexamine *Chimel* and thus leaves the law relating to searches incident to arrest in a confused and unstable state. The first part of the Court's new two-part rule—which permits an arresting officer to search the area within an arrestee's reach at the time of the search—applies, at least for now, only to vehicle occupants and recent occupants, but there is no logical reason why the same rule should not apply to all arrestees.

The second part of the Court's new rule, which the Court takes uncritically from Justice Scalia's separate opinion in *Thornton,* raises doctrinal and practical problems that the Court makes no effort to address. Why, for example, is the standard for this type of evidence-gathering search "reason to believe" rather than probable cause? And why is this type of search restricted to evidence of the offense of arrest? It is true that an arrestee's vehicle is probably more likely to contain evidence of the crime of arrest than of some other crime, but if reason-to-believe is the governing standard for an evidence-gathering search incident to arrest, it is not easy to see why an officer should not be able to search when the officer has reason to believe that the vehicle in question possesses evidence of a crime other than the crime of arrest.

Nor is it easy to see why an evidence-gathering search incident to arrest should be restricted to the passenger compartment. The *Belton* rule was limited in this way because the passenger compartment was considered to be the area that vehicle occupants can generally reach, but since the second part of the new rule is not based on officer safety or the preservation of evidence, the ground for this limitation is obscure.[2] * * *

NOTES AND QUESTIONS

1. With respect to the first branch of the *Gant* holding, the "reaching distance" standard, should the Court have instead traded the *Belton* "bright-line" rule for another running the opposite direction, as Justice Scalia contended? If the "reaching distance" requirement *had* been met in *Gant,* then what? Does it follow that then the police could conduct a search of the dimensions allowed under *Belton* (which, as *Gant* notes, "authorizes police officers to search not just the passenger compartment but every purse, briefcase, or other container within that space"), or must the arrestee's ability to reach a particular area or container (e.g., into the jacket on the back seat) be factored in as well? Is it relevant whether there is anything to reach for (e.g., that there was no evidence of the crime of arrest, and that the crime of arrest does not suggest armed resistance)? If so, can the police take into account their suspicion that Gant was involved with drug dealing?

---

2. I do not understand the Court's decision to reach the following situations. First, it is not uncommon for an officer to arrest some but not all of the occupants of a vehicle. The Court's decision in this case does not address the question whether in such a situation a search of the passenger compartment may be justified on the ground that the occupants who are not arrested could gain access to the car and retrieve a weapon or destroy evidence. Second, there may be situations in which an arresting officer has cause to fear that persons who were not passengers in the car might attempt to retrieve a weapon or evidence from the car while the officer is still on the scene. The decision in this case, as I understand it, does not address that situation either.

2. With respect to the second branch of the *Gant* holding, what exactly is/should be the extent of the authority to search for evidence of the crime of arrest? Is it (i) when "it is reasonable to believe the vehicle contains" such evidence, as the majority says several times; (ii) when it is "reasonable to believe [such] evidence * * * might be in the vehicle," as stated in Scalia's *Thornton* concurrence, quoted and relied upon by the majority; or (iii) when "the object of the search is [such] evidence," as it is put in Scalia's concurrence in *Gant*? How are these different from one another?

Consider *People v. Chamberlain*, 229 P.3d 1054 (Colo.2010): "Unlike simple traffic infractions like failing to signal, the driving-under-restraint type of offense for which Gant was arrested necessarily requires proof of awareness, or at least constructive notice, of the particular restraint being violated, making documentary evidence in the form of official notice a possible object of a search. * * * Nevertheless, both the majority and concurring opinions had little difficulty in declaring the crime of arrest in *Gant* to be an offense for which the police could not expect to find evidence in the passenger compartment of his car. Some reasonable expectation beyond a mere possibility, whether arising solely from the nature of the crime or from the particular circumstances surrounding the arrest, is therefore clearly contemplated by the Court."

3. Assuming that the second branch of *Gant* allows vehicle searches for evidence when both (a) probable cause is lacking and (b) there is no chance the arrestee could destroy any evidence in the car, then what is the justification? Is this anything other than a vehicles-only resurrection of *Rabinowitz,* which the Court rejected in *Chimel*? Consider the relevant discussion in Justice Scalia's concurrence in *Thornton*:

"If *Belton* searches are justifiable, it is not because the arrestee might grab a weapon or evidentiary item from his car, but simply because the car might contain evidence relevant to the crime for which he was arrested. This more general sort of evidence-gathering search is not without antecedent. For example, in *United States v. Rabinowitz,* we upheld a search of the suspect's place of business after he was arrested there. We did not restrict the officers' search authority to 'the area into which [the] arrestee might reach in order to grab a weapon or evidentiary ite[m],' and we did not justify the search as a means to prevent concealment or destruction of evidence. Rather, we relied on a more general interest in gathering evidence relevant to the crime for which the suspect had been arrested.

"Numerous earlier authorities support this approach, referring to the general interest in gathering evidence related to the crime of arrest with no mention of the more specific interest in preventing its concealment or destruction. * * * Only in the years leading up to *Chimel* did we start consistently referring to the narrower interest in frustrating concealment or destruction of evidence.

"There is nothing irrational about broader police authority to search for evidence when and where the perpetrator of a crime is lawfully arrested. The fact of prior lawful arrest distinguishes the arrestee from society at large, and distinguishes a search for evidence of *his* crime from general rummaging. Moreover, it is not illogical to assume that evidence of a crime is most likely to be found where the suspect was apprehended.

"Nevertheless, *Chimel*'s narrower focus on concealment or destruction of evidence also has historical support. And some of the authorities supporting the broader rule address only searches of the arrestee's *person,* as to which *Chimel*'s limitation might fairly be implicit. Moreover, carried to its logical end, the broader rule is hard to reconcile with the influential case of *Entick v. Carrington,* 19 How. St. Tr. 1029, 1031, 1063–1074 (C.P. 1765) (disapproving search of plaintiff's private papers under general warrant, despite arrest).

"In short, both *Rabinowitz* and *Chimel* are plausible accounts of what the Constitution requires, and neither is so persuasive as to justify departing from settled law. But if we are going to continue to allow *Belton* searches on *stare decisis* grounds, we should at least be honest about why we are doing so. *Belton* cannot reasonably be explained as a mere application of *Chimel*. Rather, it is a return to the broader sort of search incident to arrest that we allowed before *Chimel*—limited, of course, to searches of motor vehicles, a category of 'effects' which give rise to a reduced expectation of privacy, see *Wyoming v. Houghton,* [p. 393], and heightened law enforcement needs."

4. May every search undertaken pursuant to the second branch of *Gant* be of the dimensions allowed under *Belton*? Even if the crime of arrest was theft of the Maltese Falcon (45 lbs., 12 inches tall)?

5. *Belton* says that the arrest and the search must be "contemporaneous," which resulted in holdings that the vehicle search must occur at the scene of arrest rather than at the police station, e.g., *United States v. Ramos–Oseguera,* 120 F.3d 1028 (9th Cir.1997), and that it must occur before the arrestee is removed from that scene, e.g., *United States v. Lugo,* 978 F.2d 631 (10th Cir.1992). Do these limitations apply to searches made under the second branch of *Gant*?

6. The search of a vehicle incident to arrest authorized by *Gant* must be distinguished from another type of search of a vehicle commonly conducted subsequent to arrest. As noted in COLORADO v. BERTINE, 479 U.S. 367 (1987) (where, following Bertine's arrest for driving under the influence and before arrival of a tow truck to take Bertine's van to an impound lot, an officer inventoried the contents and found drugs inside a closed backpack), "an inventory search may be 'reasonable' under the Fourth Amendment even though it is not conducted pursuant to warrant based upon probable cause. In [*South Dakota v.*] *Opperman,* [428 U.S. 364 (1976),] this Court assessed the reasonableness of an inventory search of the glove compartment in an abandoned automobile impounded by the police. We found that inventory procedures serve to protect an owner's property while it is in the custody of the police, to insure against claims of lost, stolen, or vandalized property, and to guard the police from danger. In light of these strong governmental interests and the diminished expectation of privacy in an automobile, we upheld the search. In reaching this decision, we observed that our cases accorded deference to police caretaking procedures designed to secure and protect vehicles and their contents within police custody.

"In our more recent decision, [*Illinois v.*] *Lafayette,* [462 U.S. 640 (1983),] a police officer conducted an inventory search of the contents of a shoulder bag in the possession of an individual being taken into custody. In deciding whether this search was reasonable, we recognized that the search served legitimate governmental interests similar to those identified in *Opperman*. We determined that those interests outweighed the individual's Fourth Amendment interests and upheld the search.

"In the present case, as in *Opperman* and *Lafayette,* there was no showing that the police, who were following standardized procedures, acted in bad faith or for the sole purpose of investigation. In addition, the governmental interests justifying the inventory searches in *Opperman* and *Lafayette* are nearly the same as those which obtain here. In each case, the police were potentially responsible for the property taken into their custody. By securing the property, the police protected the property from unauthorized interference. Knowledge of the precise nature of the property helped guard against claims of theft, vandalism, or negligence. Such knowledge also helped to avert any danger to police or others that may have been posed by the property.

" * * * We conclude that here, as in *Lafayette,* reasonable police regulations relating to inventory procedures administered in good faith satisfy the Fourth Amendment, even though courts might as a matter of hindsight be able to devise equally reasonable rules requiring a different procedure."

7. Evidence found in an otherwise lawful inventory must be suppressed if the prior impoundment of the vehicle was not justified. See, e.g., *Dyke v. Taylor Implement Mfg. Co.,* 391 U.S. 216 (1968) (search of car outside courthouse while driver, arrested for reckless driving, inside to post bond was improper, as "there is no indication that the police had purported to impound or to hold the car [or] that they were authorized by any state law to do so"); *State v. Simpson,* 622 P.2d 1199 (Wash.1980) (where defendant arrested at home, impoundment of his truck lawfully parked in front of house illegal).

8. In *Florida v. Wells,* 495 U.S. 1 (1990), all members of the Court agreed that the inventory of a locked suitcase found in an impounded vehicle was unlawful under *Bertine* because "the Florida Highway Patrol had no policy whatever with respect to the opening of closed containers encountered during an inventory search." The Chief Justice, for five members of the Court, went on to say that the state court erred in saying *Bertine* requires a policy either mandating or barring inventory of all containers:

"But in forbidding uncanalized discretion to police officers conducting inventory searches, there is no reason to insist that they be conducted in a totally mechanical 'all or nothing' fashion. * * * A police officer may be allowed sufficient latitude to determine whether a particular container should or should not be opened in light of the nature of the search and characteristics of the container itself. Thus, while policies of opening all containers or of opening no containers are unquestionably permissible, it would be equally permissible, for example, to allow the opening of closed containers whose contents officers determine they are unable to ascertain from examining the containers' exteriors. The allowance of the exercise of judgment based on concerns related to the purposes of an inventory search does not violate the Fourth Amendment."

Brennan and Marshall, JJ., concurring, declined to join the majority opinion because, in "pure dictum given the disposition of the case," it "goes on to suggest that a State may adopt an inventory policy that vests individual police officers with *some* discretion to decide whether to open such containers." Blackmun, J., concurring, agreed that the Fourth Amendment did not impose an "all or nothing" requirement, so that a state "probably could adopt a policy which requires the opening of all containers that are not locked, or a policy which requires the opening of all containers over or under a certain size, even though these policies do not call for the opening of all or no containers," but objected it was "an entirely different matter, however, to say, as this majority does, that an individual policeman may be afforded discretion in conducting an inventory search." Stevens, J., concurring separately, agreed with the Blackmun opinion.

SECTION 8. STOP AND FRISK

TERRY v. OHIO
392 U.S. 1, 88 S.Ct. 1868, 20 L.Ed.2d 889 (1968).

CHIEF JUSTICE WARREN delivered the opinion of the court.

[Officer McFadden, a Cleveland plainclothes detective, became suspicious of two men standing on a street corner in the downtown area at about 2:30 in the afternoon. One of the suspects walked up the street, peered into a store, walked on, started back, looked into the same store, and then joined and conferred with his companion. The other suspect repeated this ritual, and between them the two men went through this performance about a dozen times. They also talked with a third man, and then followed him up the street about ten minutes after his departure. The officer, thinking that the suspects were "casing" a stickup and might be armed, followed and confronted the three men as they were again conversing. He identified himself and asked the suspects for their names. The men only mumbled something, and the officer spun Terry around and patted his breast pocket. He felt a pistol, which he removed. A frisk of Terry's companion also uncovered a pistol; a frisk of the third man did not disclose that he was armed, and he was not searched further. Terry was charged with carrying a concealed weapon, and he moved to suppress the weapon as evidence. The motion was denied by the trial judge, who upheld the officer's actions on a stop-and-frisk theory. The Ohio court of appeals affirmed, and the state supreme court dismissed Terry's appeal.]

      * * * The State has characterized the issue here as "the right of a police officer * * * to make an on-the-street stop, interrogate and pat down for weapons (known in the street vernacular as 'stop and frisk')." But this is only partly accurate. For the issue is not the abstract propriety of the police conduct, but the admissibility against petitioner of the evidence uncovered by the search and seizure. * * * [I]n our system evidentiary rulings provide the context in which the judicial process of inclusion and exclusion approves some conduct as comporting with constitutional guarantees and disapproves other actions by state agents. A ruling admitting evidence in a criminal trial, we recognize, has the necessary effect of legitimizing the conduct which produced the evidence, while an application of the exclusionary rule withholds the constitutional imprimatur.

      The exclusionary rule has its limitations, however, as a tool of judicial control. It cannot properly be invoked to exclude the products of legitimate police investigative techniques on the ground that much conduct which is closely similar involves unwarranted intrusions upon constitutional protections. Moreover, in some contexts the rule is ineffective as a deterrent. Street encounters between citizens and police officers are incredibly rich in diversity. They range from wholly friendly exchanges of pleasantries or mutually useful information to hostile confrontations of armed men involving arrests, or injuries, or loss of life. Moreover, hostile confrontations are not all of a piece. Some of them begin in a friendly enough manner, only to take a different turn upon the injection of some unexpected element into the conversation. Encounters are initiated by the police for a wide variety of purposes, some of which are wholly unrelated to a desire to prosecute for crime. Doubtless some police "field interrogation" conduct violates the Fourth Amendment. But a stern refusal by this Court to condone such activity does not necessarily render it responsive to the exclusionary rule. Regardless of how effective the rule may be where obtaining convictions is an important objective of the police, it is powerless to deter invasions of constitutionally guaranteed rights where the police either have no interest in prosecuting or are willing to forego successful prosecution in the interest of serving some other goal.

      Proper adjudication of cases in which the exclusionary rule is invoked demands a constant awareness of these limitations. The wholesale harassment by certain elements of the police community, of which minority groups, particularly Negroes, frequently complain, will not be stopped by the exclusion of any evidence from any criminal trial. Yet a rigid and unthinking application of the exclusionary rule, in futile protest against practices which it can never be used effectively to control, may exact a high toll in human injury and frustration of efforts to prevent crime. No judicial opinion can comprehend the protean variety of the street encounter, and we can only judge the facts of the case before us. * * *

[W]e turn our attention to the quite narrow question posed by the facts before us: whether it is always unreasonable for a policeman to seize a person and subject him to a limited search for weapons unless there is probable cause for an arrest.

* * * It is quite plain that the Fourth Amendment governs "seizures" of the person which do not eventuate in a trip to the station house and prosecution for crime—"arrests" in traditional terminology. It must be recognized that whenever a police officer accosts an individual and restrains his freedom to walk away, he has "seized" that person. And it is nothing less than sheer torture of the English language to suggest that a careful exploration of the outer surfaces of a person's clothing all over his or her body in an attempt to find weapons is not a "search." Moreover, it is simply fantastic to urge that such a procedure performed in public by a policeman while the citizen stands helpless, perhaps facing a wall with his hands raised, is a "petty indignity."[13] It is a serious intrusion upon the sanctity of the person, which may inflict great indignity and arouse strong resentment, and it is not to be undertaken lightly.

* * * We therefore reject the notions that the Fourth Amendment does not come into play at all as a limitation upon police conduct if the officers stop short of something called a "technical arrest" or a "full-blown search."

In this case there can be no question, then, that Officer McFadden "seized" petitioner and subjected him to a "search" when he took hold of him and patted down the outer surfaces of his clothing. We must decide whether at that point it was reasonable for Officer McFadden to have interfered with petitioner's personal security as he did.[16] And in determining whether the seizure and search were "unreasonable" our inquiry is a dual one—whether the officer's action was justified at its inception, and whether it was reasonably related in scope to the circumstances which justified the interference in the first place.

If this case involved police conduct subject to the Warrant Clause of the Fourth Amendment, we would have to ascertain whether "probable cause" existed to justify the search and seizure which took place. However, that is not the case. We do not retreat from our holdings that the police must, whenever practicable, obtain advance judicial approval of searches and seizures through the warrant procedure, * * * or that in most instances failure to comply with the warrant requirement can only be excused by exigent circumstances. * * * But we deal here with an entire rubric of police conduct—necessarily swift action predicated upon the on-the-spot observations of the officer on the beat—which historically has not been, and as a practical matter could not be, subjected to the warrant procedure. Instead, the conduct involved in this case must be tested by the Fourth Amendment's general proscription against unreasonable searches and seizures.

---

13. Consider the following apt description:

"[T]he officer must feel with sensitive fingers every portion of the prisoner's body. A thorough search must be made of the prisoner's arms and armpits, waistline and back, the groin and area about the testicles, and entire surface of the legs down to the feet." Priar & Martin, *Searching and Disarming Criminals,* 45 J.Crim.L.C. & P.S. 481 (1954).

16. We thus decide nothing today concerning the constitutional propriety of an investigative "seizure" upon less than probable cause for purposes of "detention" and/or interrogation. Obviously, not all personal intercourse between policemen and citizens involves "seizures" of persons. Only when the officer, by means of physical force or show of authority, has in some way restrained the liberty of a citizen may we conclude that a "seizure" has occurred. We cannot tell with any certainty upon this record whether any such "seizure" took place here prior to Officer McFadden's initiation of physical contact for purposes of searching Terry for weapons, and we thus may assume that up to that point no intrusion upon constitutionally protected rights had occurred.

Nonetheless, the notions which underlie both the warrant procedure and the requirement of probable cause remain fully relevant in this context. In order to assess the reasonableness of Officer McFadden's conduct as a general proposition, it is necessary "first to focus upon the governmental interest which allegedly justifies official intrusion upon the constitutionally protected interests of the private citizen," for there is "no ready test for determining reasonableness other than by balancing the need to search [or seize] against the invasion which the search [or seizure] entails." *Camara v. Municipal Court* [p. 439]. And in justifying the particular intrusion the police officer must be able to point to specific and articulable facts which, taken together with rational inferences from those facts, reasonably warrant that intrusion. The scheme of the Fourth Amendment becomes meaningful only when it is assured that at some point the conduct of those charged with enforcing the laws can be subjected to the more detached, neutral scrutiny of a judge who must evaluate the reasonableness of a particular search or seizure in light of the particular circumstances. And in making that assessment it is imperative that the facts be judged against an objective standard: would the facts available to the officer at the moment of the seizure or the search "warrant a man of reasonable caution in the belief" that the action taken was appropriate? * * * Anything less would invite intrusions upon constitutionally guaranteed rights based on nothing more substantial than inarticulate hunches, a result this Court has consistently refused to sanction. * * *

Applying these principles to this case, we consider first the nature and extent of the governmental interests involved. One general interest is of course that of effective crime prevention and detection; it is this interest which underlies the recognition that a police officer may in appropriate circumstances and in an appropriate manner approach a person for purposes of investigating possibly criminal behavior even though there is no probable cause to make an arrest. It was this legitimate investigative function Officer McFadden was discharging when he decided to approach petitioner and his companions. He had observed Terry, Chilton, and Katz go through a series of acts, each of them perhaps innocent in itself, but which taken together warranted further investigation. There is nothing unusual in two men standing together on a street corner, perhaps waiting for someone. Nor is there anything suspicious about people in such circumstances strolling up and down the street, singly or in pairs. Store windows, moreover, are made to be looked in. But the story is quite different where, as here, two men hover about a street corner for an extended period of time, at the end of which it becomes apparent that they are not waiting for anyone or anything; where these men pace alternately along an identical route, pausing to stare in the same store window roughly 24 times; where each completion of this route is followed immediately by a conference between the two men on the corner; where they are joined in one of these conferences by a third man who leaves swiftly; and where the two men finally follow the third and rejoin him a couple of blocks away. It would have been poor police work indeed for an officer of 30 years' experience in the detection of thievery from stores in this same neighborhood to have failed to investigate this behavior further.

The crux of this case, however, is not the propriety of Officer McFadden's taking steps to investigate petitioner's suspicious behavior, but rather, whether there was justification for McFadden's invasion of Terry's personal security by searching him for weapons in the course of that investigation. We are now concerned with more than the governmental interest in investigating crime; in addition, there is the more immediate interest of the police officer in taking steps to assure himself that the person with whom he is dealing is not armed with a weapon that could unexpectedly and fatally be used against him. Certainly it would be unreasonable to require that police officers take unnecessary risks in the performance of their duties. American criminals have a long tradition of armed violence, and every year in this country many law enforcement officers are killed in the line of duty, and thousands more are wounded. Virtually all of these deaths and a substantial portion of the injuries are inflicted with guns and knives.

In view of these facts, we cannot blind ourselves to the need for law enforcement officers to protect themselves and other prospective victims of violence in situations where they may lack probable cause for an arrest. When an officer is justified in believing that the individual whose suspicious behavior he is investigating at close range is armed and presently dangerous to the officer or to others, it would appear to be clearly unreasonable to deny the officer the power to take necessary measures to determine whether the person is in fact carrying a weapon and to neutralize the threat of physical harm. * * *

Petitioner * * * does not say that an officer is always unjustified in searching a suspect to discover weapons. Rather, he says it is unreasonable for the policeman to take that step until such time as the situation evolves to a point where there is probable cause to make an arrest. * * *

There are two weaknesses in this line of reasoning however. First, it fails to take account of traditional limitations upon the scope of searches, and thus recognizes no distinction in purpose, character, and extent between a search incident to an arrest and a limited search for weapons. The former, although justified in part by the acknowledged necessity to protect the arresting officer from assault with a concealed weapon, is also justified on other grounds, and can therefore involve a relatively extensive exploration of the person. A search for weapons in the absence of probable cause to arrest, however, must, like any other search, be strictly circumscribed by the exigencies which justify its initiation. Thus it must be limited to that which is necessary for the discovery of weapons which might be used to harm the officer or others nearby, and may realistically be characterized as something less than a "full" search, even though it remains a serious intrusion.

A second, and related, objection to petitioner's argument is that it assumes that the law of arrest has already worked out the balance between the particular interests involved here—the neutralization of danger to the policeman in the investigative circumstance and the sanctity of the individual. But this is not so. An arrest is a wholly different kind of intrusion upon individual freedom from a limited search for weapons, and the interests each is designed to serve are likewise quite different. An arrest is the initial stage of a criminal prosecution. It is intended to vindicate society's interest in having its laws obeyed, and it is inevitably accompanied by future interference with the individual's freedom of movement, whether or not trial or conviction ultimately follows. The protective search for weapons, on the other hand, constitutes a brief, though far from inconsiderable intrusion upon the sanctity of the person. It does not follow that because an officer may lawfully arrest a person only when he is apprised of facts sufficient to warrant a belief that the person has committed or is committing a crime, the officer is equally unjustified, absent that kind of evidence, in making any intrusions short of an arrest. Moreover, a perfectly reasonable apprehension of danger may arise long before the officer is possessed of adequate information to justify taking a person into custody for the purpose of prosecuting him for a crime. * * *

Our evaluation of the proper balance that has to be struck in this type of case leads us to conclude that there must be a narrowly drawn authority to permit a reasonable search for weapons for the protection of the police officer, where he has reason to believe that he is dealing with an armed and dangerous individual, regardless of whether he has probable cause to arrest the individual for a crime.

The officer need not be absolutely certain that the individual is armed; the issue is whether a reasonably prudent man in the circumstances would be warranted in the belief that his safety or that of others was in danger. * * * And in determining whether the officer acted reasonably in such circumstances, due weight must be given, not to his inchoate and unparticularized suspicion or "hunch", but to the specific reasonable inferences which he is entitled to draw from the facts in light of his experience.

We must now examine the conduct of Officer McFadden in this case to determine whether his search and seizure of petitioner were reasonable, both at their inception and as conducted. He had observed Terry, together with Chilton and another man, acting in a manner he took to be preface to a "stick-up." We think on the facts and circumstances Officer McFadden detailed before the trial judge a reasonably prudent man would have been warranted in believing petitioner was armed and thus presented a threat to the officer's safety while he was investigating his suspicious behavior. The actions of Terry and Chilton were consistent with McFadden's hypothesis that these men were contemplating a daylight robbery—which, it is reasonable to assume, would be likely to involve the use of weapons—and nothing in their conduct from the time he first noticed them until the time he confronted them and identified himself as a police officer gave him sufficient reason to negate that hypothesis. Although the trio had departed the original scene, there was nothing to indicate abandonment of an intent to commit a robbery at some point. Thus, when Officer McFadden approached the three men gathered before the display window at Zucker's store he had observed enough to make it quite reasonable to fear that they were armed; and nothing in their response to his hailing them, identifying himself as a police officer, and asking their names served to dispel that reasonable belief. We cannot say his decision at that point to seize Terry and pat his clothing for weapons was the product of a volatile or inventive imagination, or was undertaken simply as an act of harassment; the record evidences the tempered act of a policeman who in the course of an investigation had to make a quick decision as to how to protect himself and others from possible danger, and took limited steps to do so.

The manner in which the seizure and search were conducted is, of course, as vital a part of the inquiry as whether they were warranted at all. The Fourth Amendment proceeds as much by limitations upon the scope of governmental action as by imposing preconditions upon its initiation. The entire deterrent purpose of the rule excluding evidence seized in violation of the Fourth Amendment rests on the assumption that "limitations upon the fruit to be gathered tend to limit the quest itself." * * * Thus, evidence may not be introduced if it was discovered by means of a seizure and search which were not reasonably related in scope to the justification for their initiation.

[A protective search for weapons,] unlike a search without a warrant incident to a lawful arrest, is not justified by any need to prevent the disappearance or destruction of evidence of crime. The sole justification of the search in the present situation is the protection of the police officer and others nearby, and it must therefore be confined in scope to an intrusion reasonably designed to discover guns, knives, clubs, or other hidden instruments for the assault of the police officer.

The scope of the search in this case presents no serious problem in light of these standards. Officer McFadden patted down the outer clothing of petitioner and his two companions. He did not place his hands in their pockets or under the outer surface of their garments until he had felt weapons, and then he merely reached for and removed the guns. He never did invade Katz's person beyond the outer surfaces of his clothes, since he discovered nothing in his pat down which might have been a weapon. Officer McFadden confined his search strictly to what was minimally necessary to learn whether the men were armed and to disarm them once he discovered the weapons. He did not conduct a general exploratory search for whatever evidence of criminal activity he might find.

* * * Each case of this sort will, of course, have to be decided on its own facts. We merely hold today that where a police officer observes unusual conduct which leads him reasonably to conclude in light of his experience that criminal activity may be afoot and that the persons with whom he is dealing may be armed and presently dangerous; where in the course of investigating this behavior he identifies himself as a policeman and makes reasonable inquiries; and where nothing in the initial stages of the encounter serves to dispel his reasonable fear for his own or others' safety, he is entitled for the protection of himself and others in the area to conduct a carefully limited search of the outer clothing of such persons in an attempt to discover weapons which might be used to assault him. Such a search is a reasonable search under the Fourth Amendment, and any weapons seized may properly be introduced in evidence against the person from whom they were taken.

Affirmed.

Justice Harlan, concurring.

* * * The holding has * * * two logical corollaries that I do not think the Court has fully expressed.

In the first place, if the frisk is justified in order to protect the officer during an encounter with a citizen, the officer must first have constitutional grounds to insist on an encounter, to make a *forcible* stop. Any person, including a policeman, is at liberty to avoid a person he considers dangerous. If and when a policeman has a right instead to disarm such a person for his own protection, he must first have a right not to avoid him but to be in his presence. That right must be more than the liberty (again, possessed by every citizen) to address questions to other persons, for ordinarily the person addressed has an equal right to ignore his interrogator and walk away; he certainly need not submit to a frisk for the questioner's protection. I would make it perfectly clear that the right to frisk in this case depends upon the reasonableness of a forcible stop to investigate a suspected crime.

Where such a stop is reasonable, however, the right to frisk must be immediate and automatic if the reason for the stop is, as here, an articulable suspicion of a crime of violence. Just as a full search incident to a lawful arrest requires no additional justification, a limited frisk incident to a lawful stop must often be rapid and routine. There is no reason why an officer, rightfully but forcibly confronting a person suspected of a serious crime, should have to ask one question and take the risk that the answer might be a bullet. * * *

Justice White, concurring.

* * * I think an additional word is in order concerning the matter of interrogation during an investigative stop. There is nothing in the Constitution which prevents a policeman from addressing questions to anyone on the streets. Absent special circumstances, the person approached may not be detained or frisked but may refuse to cooperate and go on his way. However, given the proper circumstances, such as those in this case, it seems to me the person may be briefly detained against his will while pertinent questions are directed to him. Of course, the person stopped is not obliged to answer, answers may not be compelled, and refusal to answer furnishes no basis for an arrest, although it may alert the officer to the need for continued observation. * * *

Justice Douglas, dissenting.

* * * Had a warrant been sought, a magistrate would * * * have been unauthorized to issue one, for he can act only if there is a showing of "probable cause." We hold today that the police have greater authority to make a "seizure" and conduct a "search" than a judge has to authorize such action. We have said precisely the opposite over and over again. * * *

THE SIGNIFICANCE OF THE STOP–AND–FRISK CASES

A. POLICE ACTION SHORT OF A SEIZURE

1. UNITED STATES v. DRAYTON, 536 U.S. 194 (2002), involved an instance of on-bus drug interdiction activity. During a scheduled stop, the driver turned the bus over to three police officers; one knelt on the driver's seat and faced back, a second stayed in the rear and faced forward, and the third worked his way from back to front, speaking with individual passengers without first advising them of their right to refuse to cooperate. Upon reaching the row in which Drayton and Brown were seated, the officer declared that the police were looking for drugs and weapons and asked if the two had any bags. Both pointed to a bag overhead, the officer asked if he could check it, Brown agreed, and the subsequent search revealed no contraband. The officer then asked Brown whether he minded if the officer checked his person, Brown agreed, and when a pat-down revealed hard objects similar to drug packages in both thigh areas Brown was arrested. The same procedure with the same results was followed as to Drayton, and a further search revealed that both men had taped cocaine between their shorts. The officer testified that passengers who declined to cooperate or who chose to exit the bus would have been allowed to do so, and that five or six times in the previous year passengers had done so.

Kennedy, J., for the majority, concluded there had been no seizure, as there "was no application of force, no intimidating movement, no overwhelming show of force, no brandishing of weapons, no blocking of exits, no threat, no command, not even an authoritative tone of voice. It is beyond question that had this encounter occurred on the street, it would be constitutional. The fact that an encounter takes place on a bus does not on its own transform standard police questioning of citizens into an illegal seizure. Indeed, because many fellow passengers are present to witness officers' conduct, a reasonable person may feel even more secure in his or her decision not to cooperate with police on a bus than in other circumstances. * * * Finally, the fact that in Officer Lang's experience only a few passengers have refused to cooperate does not suggest that a reasonable person would not feel free to terminate the bus encounter. [B]us passengers answer officers' questions and otherwise cooperate not because of coercion but because the passengers know that their participation enhances their own safety and the safety of those around them."

Souter, J., for the three dissenters, questioned the majority's assumption as to a comparable "on the street" situation, stating that if a pedestrian were similarly the object of attention by three officers in equally-confined space, say, a small alley, then "there is every reason to believe that the pedestrian would have understood, to his considerable discomfort, what Justice Stewart described as the 'threatening presence of several officers.' [which] may overbear a normal person's ability to act freely, even in the absence of explicit commands or the formalities of detention." Stressing that "the driver with the tickets entitling the passengers to travel had yielded his custody of the bus and its seated travelers to three police officers, whose authority apparently superseded the driver's own," the dissenters concluded: "The reasonable inference was that the 'interdiction' was not a consensual exercise, but one the police would carry out whatever the circumstances; that they would prefer 'cooperation' but would not let the lack of it stand in their way. There was no contrary indication that day, since no passenger had refused the cooperation requested, and there was no reason for any passenger to believe that the driver would return and the trip resume until the police were satisfied."

2. In CALIFORNIA v. HODARI D., 499 U.S. 621 (1991), Hodari fled upon seeing an approaching police car, only to be pursued on foot by Officer Pertoso, after which Hodari tossed away what appeared to be a small rock but which when retrieved by the police proved to be crack cocaine. The state court suppressed the cocaine as the fruit of a seizure made without reasonable suspicion, but the Supreme Court, per Scalia, J., reversed:

"To say [as the common law authorities do] that an arrest is effected by the slightest application of physical force, despite the arrestee's escape, is not to say that for Fourth Amendment purposes there is a *continuing* arrest during the period of fugitivity. If, for example, Pertoso had laid his hands upon Hodari to arrest him, but Hodari had broken away and had *then* cast away the cocaine, it would hardly be realistic to say that that disclosure had been made during the course of an arrest. Cf. *Thompson v. Whitman*, 18 Wall. 457, 471 (1874) ('A seizure is a single act, and not a continuous fact'). The present case, however, is even one step further removed. It does not involve the application of any physical force; Hodari was untouched by Officer Pertoso at the time he discarded the cocaine. His defense relies instead upon the proposition that a seizure occurs 'when the officer, by means of physical force *or show of authority,* has in some way restrained the liberty of a citizen.' *Terry v. Ohio,* [p. 408]. Hodari contends (and we accept as true for purposes of this decision) that Pertoso's pursuit qualified as a 'show of authority' calling upon Hodari to halt. The narrow question before us is whether, with respect to a show of authority as with respect to application of physical force, a seizure occurs even though the subject does not yield. We hold that it does not.

"The language of the Fourth Amendment, of course, cannot sustain respondent's contention. The word 'seizure' readily bears the meaning of a laying on of hands or application of physical force to restrain movement, even when it is ultimately unsuccessful. ('She seized the purse-snatcher, but he broke out of her grasp.') It does not remotely apply, however, to the prospect of a policeman yelling 'Stop, in the name of the law!' at a fleeing form that continues to flee. That is no seizure. Nor can the result respondent wishes to achieve be produced—indirectly, as it were—by suggesting that Pertoso's uncomplied-with show of authority was a common-law arrest, and then appealing to the principle that all common-law arrests are seizures. An arrest requires *either* physical force (as described above) *or,* where that is absent, *submission* to the assertion of authority. * * *

"We do not think it desirable, even as a policy matter, to stretch the Fourth Amendment beyond its words and beyond the meaning of arrest, as respondent urges. Street pursuits always place the public at some risk, and compliance with police orders to stop should therefore be encouraged. Only a few of those orders, we must presume, will be without adequate basis, and since the addressee has no ready means of identifying the deficient ones it almost invariably is the responsible course to comply. Unlawful orders will not be deterred, moreover, by sanctioning through the exclusionary rule those of them that are *not* obeyed. Since policemen do not command 'Stop!' expecting to be ignored, or give chase hoping to be outrun, it fully suffices to apply the deterrent to their genuine, successful seizures."[a]

---

a. After citing *Hodari D.* to support the conclusion "that a police pursuit in attempting to seize a person does not amount to a 'seizure' within the meaning of the Fourth Amendment," the Court in *County of Sacramento v. Lewis,* p. 31, also concluded "that no Fourth Amendment

Stevens, J., for the two dissenters, objected: "The deterrent purposes of the exclusionary rule focus on the conduct of law enforcement officers, and on discouraging improper behavior on their part, and not on the reaction of the citizen to the show of force. In the present case, if Officer Pertoso had succeeded in tackling respondent before he dropped the rock of cocaine, the rock unquestionably would have been excluded as the fruit of the officer's unlawful seizure. Instead, under the Court's logic-chopping analysis, the exclusionary rule has no application because an attempt to make an unconstitutional seizure is beyond the coverage of the Fourth Amendment, no matter how outrageous or unreasonable the officer's conduct may be.

"It is too early to know the consequences of the Court's holding. If carried to its logical conclusion, it will encourage unlawful displays of force that will frighten countless innocent citizens into surrendering whatever privacy rights they may still have. It is not too soon, however, to note the irony in the fact that the Court's own justification for its result is its analysis of the rules of the common law of arrest that antedated our decisions in *Katz* [p. 264] and *Terry*. Yet, even in those days the common law provided the citizen with protection against an attempt to make an unlawful arrest. The central message of *Katz* and *Terry* was that the protection the Fourth Amendment provides to the average citizen is not rigidly confined by ancient common-law precept."

3. What result would the Court have reached if, before Hodari threw away the cocaine, Officer Pertoso had (a) fired his pistol at Hodari, barely missing him; (b) fired his pistol at Hodari, causing a wound which slowed down but did not stop him; (c) cornered Hodari in a dead-end alley; or (d) grabbed the collar of Hodari's jacket, only to have him slip out of the garment? Compare *United States v. Lender,* 985 F.2d 151 (4th Cir.1993) (officer called defendant to stop, defendant responded "you don't want me" and continued walking, officer again called defendant to stop and defendant did stop, at which loaded pistol fell to the ground, which officer prevented defendant from picking up; no prior seizure of defendant, as court refuses "to characterize as capitulation conduct that is fully consistent with preparation to whirl and shoot the officers"); with *United States v. Wood,* 981 F.2d 536 (D.C.Cir.1992) (when officer ordered defendant to stop, defendant "froze in his tracks and immediately dropped the [theretofore unobserved] weapon between his feet," there was a prior seizure; court "cannot imagine a more submissive response"). Compare *Brooks v. Gaenzle,* 614 F.3d 1213 (10th Cir.2010) (where police shot Brooks as he climbing a fence, but he continued his flight and escaped, no seizure of Brooks, as the gunshot "did not terminate his movement or otherwise cause the government to have physical control over him"); with *State v. Garcia,* 217 P.3d 1032 (N.M.2009) ("[t]o ascertain whether the officer's application of pepper spray to Defendant's body was physical force sufficient to constitute a seizure, it is irrelevant whether Defendant's movement was restrained, affected or deterred").

4. In BRENDLIN v. CALIFORNIA, p. 887, the issue was whether an officer making a traffic stop seizes the passengers as well as the driver, which a unanimous Court resolved "by asking whether a reasonable person in [the passenger's] position when the car stopped would have believed himself free to 'terminate the encounter' between the police and himself. *Bostick.* We think that in these circumstances any reasonable passenger would have understood the police officers to be exercising control to the point that no one in the car was free to depart without police permission.

---

seizure would take place where a 'pursuing police car sought to stop the suspect only by the show of authority represented by flashing lights and continuing pursuit,' but accidentally stopped the suspect by crashing into him." This is because for a Fourth Amendment seizure there must be "a governmental termination of freedom of movement *through means intentionally applied.*"

"A traffic stop necessarily curtails the travel a passenger has chosen just as much as it halts the driver, diverting both from the stream of traffic to the side of the road, and the police activity that normally amounts to intrusion on 'privacy and personal security' does not normally (and did not here) distinguish between passenger and driver. An officer who orders one particular car to pull over acts with an implicit claim of right based on fault of some sort, and a sensible person would not expect a police officer to allow people to come and go freely from the physical focal point of an investigation into faulty behavior or wrongdoing. If the likely wrongdoing is not the driving, the passenger will reasonably feel subject to suspicion owing to close association; but even when the wrongdoing is only bad driving, the passenger will expect to be subject to some scrutiny, and his attempt to leave the scene would be so obviously likely to prompt an objection from the officer that no passenger would feel free to leave in the first place."

    5. In *United States v. Wilson,* 953 F.2d 116 (4th Cir.1991), involving an airport encounter between a DEA agent and a drug courier suspect, Wilson granted the agent's request to speak with him and submitted to questioning, produced identification upon request, and allowed the agent and an associate to search his bag and his person. But when the agent asked to search the two coats Wilson was carrying, Wilson angrily refused and walked away. The agent stayed with him, repeatedly requesting that Wilson consent to search of the coats and repeatedly asking Wilson to explain why he would not allow the search. Wilson continued walking through the terminal and then outside on the sidewalk, objecting the entire time to the harassment, but he finally consented to the search, which uncovered a bag of cocaine. If Wilson claims his consent to the search was the fruit of an illegal seizure, what result under *Bostick* and *Hodari D.?*

    6. In *Hodari D.* the defendant was black. Is that relevant? Consider Tracey Maclin, *"Black and Blue Encounters"—Some Preliminary Thoughts About Fourth Amendment Seizures: Should Race Matter?,* 26 Val.U.L.Rev. 243, 250 (1991): "I submit that the dynamics surrounding an encounter between a police officer and a black male are quite different from those that surround an encounter between an officer and the so-called average, reasonable person. My tentative proposal is that the Court should disregard the notion that there is an average, hypothetical, reasonable person out there by which to judge the constitutionality of police encounters. When assessing the coercive nature of an encounter, the Court should consider the race of the person confronted by the police, and how that person's race might have influenced his attitude toward the encounter."

    Cf. *In re J.M.,* 619 A.2d 497 (D.C.App.1992) (majority, applying objective standard, concludes 14–year–old bus passenger had not been seized during his on-bus interrogation which culminated in the youth's supposed consent to a search of his bag and pat-down of his person; two concurring judges argue it "consistent with the teaching of the Supreme Court opinions that specific, objectively observable characteristics of the person who is the object of police conduct be considered by a court in determining whether a seizure has occurred," so that issue here is "whether a reasonable person who is a child would have thought that he or she was free to leave under the circumstances"; another judge "would factor into the totality of the circumstances the relevant characteristics of age and race," and suggests "that no reasonable innocent black male (with any knowledge of American history) would feel free to ignore or walk away from a drug interdicting team"). For the Supreme Court's more recent treatment of a comparable issue under *Miranda,* see *J.D.B. v. North Carolina,* p. 603.

B. GROUNDS FOR TEMPORARY SEIZURE FOR INVESTIGATION

1. In UNITED STATES v. CORTEZ, 449 U.S. 411 (1981), the Court elaborated:

"Courts have used a variety of terms to capture the elusive concept of what cause is sufficient to authorize police to stop a person. Terms like 'articulable reasons' and 'founded suspicion' are not self-defining; they fall short of providing clear guidance dispositive of the myriad factual situations that arise. But the essence of all that has been written is that the totality of the circumstances—the whole picture—must be taken into account.[b] Based upon that whole picture the detaining officers must have a particularized and objective basis for suspecting the particular person stopped of criminal activity.[c]

"The idea that an assessment of the whole picture must yield a particularized suspicion contains two elements, each of which must be present before a stop is permissible. First, the assessment must be based upon all the circumstances. The analysis proceeds with various objective observations, information from police reports, if such are available, and consideration of the modes or patterns of operation of certain kinds of lawbreakers. From these data, a trained officer draws inferences and makes deductions—inferences and deductions that might well elude an untrained person.

"The process does not deal with hard certainties, but with probabilities. Long before the law of probabilities was articulated as such, practical people formulated certain common sense conclusions about human behavior; jurors as factfinders are permitted to do the same—and so are law enforcement officers. Finally, the evidence thus collected must be seen and weighed not in terms of library analysis by scholars, but as understood by those versed in the field of law enforcement.

"The second element contained in the idea that an assessment of the whole picture must yield a particularized suspicion is the concept that the process just described must raise a suspicion that the particular individual being stopped is engaged in wrongdoing."

2. Should the nature or seriousness of the offense be relevant on the question of whether a stop on reasonable suspicion is justified? In a companion case to *Terry*, *Sibron v. New York*, 392 U.S. 40 (1968), where the defendant was suspected of drug possession, but the majority concluded that the reasonable suspicion test was not met, Harlan, J., concurring, emphasized that in *Terry* the officer was acting to prevent "a violent crime," not so in the instant case. But lower courts have not imposed any sort of serious crime limitation with respect to suspected contemporary criminality; indeed, it is said that "a traffic stop is valid

---

b. Hence, in *United States v. Arvizu*, 534 U.S. 266 (2002), where the court of appeals, in examining the factors relied upon by the officer and district court, assessed them one-by-one, dismissed some as entitled to "no weight" because individually susceptible to an innocent explanation, and found those remaining insufficient to show a reasonable suspicion, a unanimous Supreme Court reversed, reasoning that the court of appeals' approach would "seriously undercut the 'totality of the circumstances' principle which governs the existence *vel non* of 'reasonable suspicion,'" and that such "divide-and-conquer analysis" was precluded by *Terry*, where a series of acts each "perhaps innocent in itself" was deemed to add up to reasonable suspicion.

c. Generally or particularly? Compare *Derichsweiler v. State*, 348 S.W.3d 906 (Tex.Crim.App. 2011) ("Unlike the case with probable cause to justify an arrest, it is not a *sine qua non* of reasonable suspicion that a detaining officer be able to pinpoint a particular penal infraction"); with *In re Herman S.*, 359 N.Y.S.2d 645 (N.Y.Misc.2d 1974) ("unless the suspect's preparations have ripened to such a stage that his conduct points to a particular crime, imminent criminality, justifying a preventive invasion of individual liberty, seems unlikely").

under the Fourth Amendment * * * if the police officer has reasonable articulable suspicion that a traffic or equipment violation has occurred or is occurring." *United States v. Botero–Ospina,* 71 F.3d 783 (10th Cir.1995). Compare *Commonwealth v. Chase,* 960 A.2d 108 (Pa.2008) (concluding that "if the officer has a legitimate expectation of investigatory results, the existence of reasonable suspicion will allow the stop—if the officer has no such expectations of learning additional relevant information concerning the suspected criminal activity, the stop cannot be constitutionally permitted on the basis of mere suspicion," and thus reasonable suspicion of driving under the influence suffices, "as a post-stop investigation is normally feasible," but reasonable suspicion would *not* suffice to justify a stop for driving at an unsafe speed).

Is the seriousness of the suspected offense more relevant when the stop is for suspected *past* criminality? In UNITED STATES v. HENSLEY, 469 U.S. 221 (1985), the Court, per O'Connor, J., held by analogy to *Whiteley v. Warden,* p. 315, "that, if a flyer or bulletin has been issued on the basis of articulable facts supporting a reasonable suspicion that the wanted person has committed an offense, then reliance on that flyer or bulletin justifies a stop to check identification, to pose questions to the person, or to detain the person briefly while attempting to obtain further information." But the Court first rejected the lower court's position that *Terry* is limited to ongoing criminal activity:

"The factors in the balance may be somewhat different when a stop to investigate past criminal activity is involved rather than a stop to investigate ongoing criminal conduct. This is because the governmental interest and the nature of the intrusions involved in the two situations may differ. As we noted in *Terry,* one general interest present in the context of ongoing or imminent criminal activity is 'that of effective crime prevention and detection.' A stop to investigate an already completed crime does not necessarily promote the interest of crime prevention as directly as a stop to investigate suspected ongoing criminal activity. Similarly, the exigent circumstances which require a police officer to step in before a crime is committed or completed are not necessarily as pressing long afterwards. Public safety may be less threatened by a suspect in a past crime who now appears to be going about his lawful business than it is by a suspect who is currently in the process of violating the law. Finally, officers making a stop to investigate past crimes may have a wider range of opportunity to choose the time and circumstances of the stop.

"Despite these differences, where police have been unable to locate a person suspected of involvement in a past crime, the ability to briefly stop that person, ask questions, or check identification in the absence of probable cause promotes the strong government interest in solving crimes and bringing offenders to justice. Restraining police action until after probable cause is obtained would not only hinder the investigation, but might also enable the suspect to flee in the interim and to remain at large. Particularly in the context of felonies or crimes involving a threat to public safety, it is in the public interest that the crime be solved and the suspect detained as promptly as possible. The law enforcement interests at stake in these circumstances outweigh the individual's interest to be free of a stop and detention that is no more extensive than permissible in the investigation of imminent or ongoing crimes.

"We need not and do not decide today whether *Terry* stops to investigate all past crimes, however serious, are permitted. It is enough to say that, if police have a reasonable suspicion, grounded in specific and articulable facts, that a person they encounter was involved in or is wanted in connection with a completed felony, then a *Terry* stop may be made to investigate that suspicion."

3. In *United States v. Sokolow*, 490 U.S. 1 (1989), the defendant was stopped at the Honolulu airport by agents who knew "that (1) he paid $2,100 for two airplane tickets from a roll of $20 bills; (2) he traveled under a name that did not match the name under which his telephone number was listed; (3) his original destination was Miami, a source city for illicit drugs; (4) he stayed in Miami for only 48 hours, even though a round-trip flight from Honolulu to Miami takes 20 hours; (5) he appeared nervous during his trip; and (6) he checked none of his luggage." The Court, per Rehnquist, C.J., held this amounted to reasonable suspicion (said to be a level of suspicion "considerably less than proof of wrongdoing by a preponderance of the evidence") defendant was a drug courier:

"We do not agree with respondent that our analysis is somehow changed by the agents' belief that his behavior was consistent with one of the DEA's 'drug courier profiles.' A court sitting to determine the existence of reasonable suspicion must require the agent to articulate the factors leading to that conclusion, but the fact that these factors may be set forth in a 'profile' does not somehow detract from their evidentiary significance as seen by a trained agent."

4. In ILLINOIS v. WARDLOW, 528 U.S. 119 (2000), a Chicago police officer in the last car of a 4–car caravan, which was converging on an area known for heavy narcotics trafficking in order to investigate drug transactions, saw defendant look in the direction of the officers and then run away; defendant was stopped and frisked and found to be carrying a handgun. The Court, per Rehnquist, C.J., held "that the officer's stop did not violate the Fourth Amendment," reasoning: "An individual's presence in an area of expected criminal activity, standing alone, is not enough to support a reasonable, particularized suspicion that the person is committing a crime. But officers are not required to ignore the relevant characteristics of a location in determining whether the circumstances are sufficiently suspicious to warrant further investigation. Accordingly, we have previously noted the fact that the stop occurred in a 'high crime area' among the relevant contextual considerations in a *Terry* analysis.

"In this case, moreover, it was not merely respondent's presence in an area of heavy narcotics trafficking that aroused the officers' suspicion but his unprovoked flight upon noticing the police. Our cases have also recognized that nervous, evasive behavior is a pertinent factor in determining reasonable suspicion. Headlong flight—wherever it occurs—is the consummate act of evasion; it is not necessarily indicative of wrongdoing, but it is certainly suggestive of such." The Court emphasized in addition that while it had previously held that "refusal to cooperate, without more, does not furnish the minimal level of objective justification needed for a detention or seizure," "unprovoked flight is simply not a mere refusal to cooperate"; and that while it "is undoubtedly true" that "there are innocent reasons for flight from police," *Terry* "recognized that the officers could detain the individuals to resolve the ambiguity."

Stevens, J., for the four Justices concurring in part and dissenting in part, first noted the majority had "wisely" not endorsed either the state's per se rule that flight at the sight of police is always grounds for a stop or the defendant's rule that such flight is never grounds for a stop, for the "inference we can reasonably draw about the motivation for a person's flight * * * will depend on a number of different circumstances. Factors such as the time of day, the number of people in the area, the character of the neighborhood, whether the officer was in uniform, the way the runner was dressed, the direction and speed of flight, and whether the person's behavior was otherwise unusual might be relevant in specific cases." (As for the State's claim "for a *per se* rule regarding 'unprovoked flight upon seeing a clearly identifiable police officer,' the four Justices responded that even this 'described a category of activity too broad and varied to permit a *per se* reasonable inference regarding the motivation for the activity.' ") Noting that instead "the totality of the circumstances, as always, must dictate the result," the dissenters found the record as a whole failed to establish reasonable suspicion, considering that it did not show whether any vehicles in the caravan were marked, whether any other officers in the group were in uniform, where the intended destination of the officers was in relation to where defendant was seen, whether the caravan had passed before defendant ran, etc., and then concluded:

"The State, along with the majority of the Court, relies as well on the assumption that this flight occurred in a high crime area. Even if that assumption is accurate, it is insufficient because even in a high crime neighborhood unprovoked flight does not invariably lead to reasonable suspicion. On the contrary, because many factors providing innocent motivations for unprovoked flight are concentrated in high crime area, the character of the neighborhood arguably makes an inference of guilt less appropriate, rather than more so.[d] Like unprovoked flight itself, presence in a high crime neighborhood is a fact too generic and susceptible to innocent explanation to satisfy the reasonable suspicion inquiry."

Consider Tracey L. Meares & Bernard E. Harcourt, *Transparent Adjudication and Social Science Research in Constitutional Criminal Procedure*, 90 J.Crim.L. & Criminology 733, 786–92 (2000), noting that a "pathbreaking study of street stops in New York City released on December 1, 1999, about six weeks before *Wardlow* was published, provides critical insight to the central question in *Wardlow*." The overall ratio of stops to arrests was 9:1 (i.e., there were 9 stops for every 1 eventual arrest), but the stop/arrest ratio for blacks was twice as high as for whites, "suggest[ing] that minority individuals have a relationship with the police that makes interpretation of flight extremely difficult." The stop/arrest ratio for all cases where the stop was undertaken because of the suspect's flight was 26:1, but as to stops in the more discrete category of flight to elude the police the ratio was 15.8:1, but if that category was narrowed down further by considering only such stops in a high crime area the ratio was 45:1, which "is suggestive that in high-crime urban communities where the population is disproportionately minority, flight from an identifiable police officer is a very poor indicator that crime is afoot."

5. In FLORIDA v. J.L., 529 U.S. 266 (2000), an anonymous caller reported to police than a young black male standing at a particular bus stop and wearing a plaid shirt was carrying a gun; officers went there and saw such a person but did not see a firearm or any unusual movements, and had no reason to suspect him apart from the tip. A frisk of the suspect, which produced a firearm, was held by the Court, per Ginsburg, J., to be unreasonable: "Unlike a tip from a known informant whose reputation can be assessed and who can be held responsible if her allegations turn out to be fabricated, 'an anonymous tip alone seldom demonstrates the informant's basis of knowledge or veracity,' *Alabama v. White*, [496 U.S. 325 (1990)]. As we have recognized, however, there are situations in which an anonymous tip, suitably corroborated, exhibits 'sufficient indicia of reliability to provide reasonable suspicion to make the investigatory stop.' The question we here confront is whether the tip pointing to J.L. had those indicia of reliability.

---

d. As the dissenters elsewhere stated: "Among some citizens, particularly minorities and those residing in high crime areas, there is also the possibility that the fleeing person is entirely innocent, but, with or without justification, believes that contact with the police can itself be dangerous, apart from any criminal activity associated with the officer's sudden presence. For such a person, unprovoked flight is neither 'aberrant' nor 'abnormal.' Moreover, these concerns and fears are known to the police officers themselves, and are validated by law enforcement investigations into their own practices. Accordingly the evidence supporting the reasonableness of these beliefs is too pervasive to be dismissed as random or rare, and too persuasive to be disparaged as inconclusive or insufficient."

"In *White*, the police received an anonymous tip asserting that a woman was carrying cocaine and predicting that she would leave an apartment building at a specified time, get into a car matching a particular description, and drive to a named motel. Standing alone, the tip would not have justified a *Terry* stop. Only after police observation showed that the informant had accurately predicted the woman's movements, we explained, did it become reasonable to think the tipster had inside knowledge about the suspect and therefore to credit his assertion about the cocaine. Although the Court held that the suspicion in *White* became reasonable after police surveillance, we regarded the case as borderline. Knowledge about a person's future movements indicates some familiarity with that person's affairs, but having such knowledge does not necessarily imply that the informant knows, in particular, whether that person is carrying hidden contraband. We accordingly classified *White* as a 'close case.'

"The tip in the instant case lacked the moderate indicia of reliability present in *White* and essential to the Court's decision in that case. The anonymous call concerning J.L. provided no predictive information and therefore left the police without means to test the informant's knowledge or credibility. That the allegation about the gun turned out to be correct does not suggest that the officers, prior to the frisks, had a reasonable basis for suspecting J.L. of engaging in unlawful conduct: The reasonableness of official suspicion must be measured by what the officers knew before they conducted their search. All the police had to go on in this case was the bare report of an unknown, unaccountable informant who neither explained how he knew about the gun nor supplied any basis for believing he had inside information about J.L. If *White* was a close case on the reliability of anonymous tips, this one surely falls on the other side of the line. * * *

"An accurate description of a subject's readily observable location and appearance is of course reliable in this limited sense: It will help the police correctly identify the person whom the tipster means to accuse. Such a tip, however, does not show that the tipster has knowledge of concealed criminal activity. The reasonable suspicion here at issue requires that a tip be reliable in its assertion of illegality, not just in its tendency to identify a determinate person. * * *

"Firearms are dangerous, and extraordinary dangers sometimes justify unusual precautions. Our decisions recognize the serious threat that armed criminals pose to public safety; *Terry*'s rule, which permits protective police searches on the basis of reasonable suspicion rather than demanding that officers meet the higher standard of probable cause, responds to this very concern. But an automatic firearm exception to our established reliability analysis [advanced by Florida and the United States as *amicus*] would rove too far. Such an exception would enable any person seeking to harass another to set in motion an intrusive, embarrassing police search of the targeted person simply by placing an anonymous call falsely reporting the target's unlawful carriage of a gun. Nor could one securely confine such an exception to allegations involving firearms. Several Courts of Appeals have held it per se foreseeable for people carrying significant amounts of illegal drugs to be carrying guns as well. If police officers may properly conduct *Terry* frisks on the basis of bare-boned tips about guns, it would be reasonable to maintain under the above-cited decisions that the police should similarly have discretion to frisk based on bare-boned tips about narcotics. * * *

"The facts of this case do not require us to speculate about the circumstances under which the danger alleged in an anonymous tip might be so great as to justify a search even without a showing of reliability. We do not say, for example, that a report of a person carrying a bomb need bear the indicia of reliability we demand for a report of a person carrying a firearm before the police can constitutionally conduct a frisk. Nor do we hold that public safety officials in quarters where the reasonable expectation of Fourth Amendment privacy is diminished, such as airports and schools, cannot conduct protective searches on the basis of information insufficient to justify searches elsewhere.

"Finally, the requirement that an anonymous tip bear standard indicia of reliability in order to justify a stop in no way diminishes a police officer's prerogative, in accord with *Terry*, to conduct a protective search of a person who has already been legitimately stopped. We speak in today's decision only of cases in which the officer's authority to make the initial stop is at issue. In that context, we hold that an anonymous tip lacking indicia of reliability of the kind contemplated in *Adams* [p. 435] and *White* does not justify a stop and frisk whenever and however it alleges the illegal possession of a firearm."

Justice Kennedy, joined by The Chief Justice, concurring., added: "It seems appropriate to observe that a tip might be anonymous in some sense yet have certain other features, either supporting reliability or narrowing the likely class of informants, so that the tip does provide the lawful basis for some police action. One such feature, as the Court recognizes, is that the tip predicts future conduct of the alleged criminal. There may be others. For example, if an unnamed caller with a voice which sounds the same each time tells police on two successive nights about criminal activity which in fact occurs each night, a similar call on the third night ought not be treated automatically like the tip in the case now before us. In the instance supposed, there would be a plausible argument that experience cures some of the uncertainty surrounding the anonymity, justifying a proportionate police response. In today's case, however, the State provides us with no data about the reliability of anonymous tips. Nor do we know whether the dispatcher or arresting officer had any objective reason to believe that this tip had some particular indicia of reliability.

"If an informant places his anonymity at risk, a court can consider this factor in weighing the reliability of the tip. An instance where a tip might be considered anonymous but nevertheless sufficiently reliable to justify a proportionate police response may be when an unnamed person driving a car the police officer later describes stops for a moment and, face to face, informs the police that criminal activity is occurring. This too seems to be different from the tip in the present case.

"Instant caller identification is widely available to police, and, if anonymous tips are proving unreliable and distracting to police, squad cars can be sent within seconds to the location of the telephone used by the informant. Voice recording of telephone tips might, in appropriate cases, be used by police to locate the caller. It is unlawful to make false reports to the police, and the ability of the police to trace the identity of anonymous telephone informants may be a factor which lends reliability to what, years earlier, might have been considered unreliable anonymous tips."

6. In *Virginia v. Harris*, 130 S.Ct. 10 (2009), Chief Justice Roberts and Justice Scalia, dissenting from denial of certiorari from a Virginia case holding insufficient an anonymous tip of drunken driving by the subsequently-stopped defendant, stated:

"In the absence of controlling precedent on point, a sharp disagreement has emerged among federal and state courts over how to apply the Fourth Amendment in this context. The majority of courts examining the question have upheld investigative stops of allegedly drunk or erratic drivers, even when the police did not personally witness any traffic violations before conducting the stops. These courts have typically distinguished *J.L.*'s general rule based on some combination of (1) the especially grave and imminent dangers posed by drunk driving; (2) the enhanced reliability of tips alleging illegal activity in public, to which the tipster was presumably an eyewitness; (3) the fact that traffic stops are typically less invasive than searches or seizures of individuals on foot; and (4) the diminished expectation of privacy enjoyed by individuals driving their cars on public roads. A minority of jurisdictions, meanwhile, take the same position as the Virginia Supreme Court, requiring that officers first confirm an anonymous tip of drunk or erratic driving through their own independent observation. This conflict has been expressly noted by the lower courts."

C. PERMISSIBLE EXTENT AND SCOPE OF TEMPORARY SEIZURE

1. When courts decide whether a *Terry* stop was sufficiently limited, sometimes (especially when the concern is with a threat or show of force in making the seizure or movement of the suspect from the scene thereafter) the focus may be upon whether, in light of such aggravating circumstances, the seizure was sufficiently distinguishable from a full-fledged custodial arrest. Usually, however, the focus is upon the declaration in *Terry* that the seizure "must be 'strictly tied to and justified by' the circumstances which rendered its initiation permissible," so that the inquiry is "whether it was reasonably related in scope to the circumstances which justified the interference in the first place." But the Supreme Court's later discussions of that requirement in, e.g., *Royer*, Note 2 infra, *Hensley*, p. 420, and *McArthur*, p. 374, indicate that "scope" in the broad sense actually includes two factors, one variously called "time," "duration" or "length," and the other variously called "scope" in a narrower sense or "intrusiveness." Despite the "in the first place" language in *Terry*, lower courts have understandably taken the position that in judging the length or intrusiveness of a *Terry* stop it is proper to take into account the offense reasonably suspected at the outset and also other offenses reasonably suspected as a result of information previously obtained lawfully during the stop. See, e.g., *Medrano v. State*, 914 P.2d 804 (Wyo.1996) (officer did not exceed scope of stop by inquiring if defendant possessed drugs, as while stop was on reasonable suspicion of robbery, there then developed reasonable suspicion of drug possession).

2. While a *Terry* stop may be rendered unlawful because the officer used a threat or show of force suggestive of the making of a full-fledged arrest, such as drawing a weapon, handcuffing the suspect, or placing him in a squad car, such tactics do not inevitably establish that the officer exceeded his authority under *Terry*. Although such tactics are hardly "standard procedures" for *Terry* stops, their use has been upheld when the facts of the particular case show that the decision to utilize them was reasonable. See, e.g., *Flowers v. Fiore*, 359 F.3d 24 (1st Cir.2004) (officers properly drew their guns, as they "were faced with a report of an armed threat"); *State v. Munson*, 594 N.W.2d 128 (Minn.1999) ("brief handcuffing" proper here, as stop was late at night, involved multiple suspects, and was on information vehicle carrying large amount of drugs and that occupants might be armed); *Commonwealth v. Gwynn*, 723 A.2d 143 (Pa.1998) ("placing appellant in the police car during this nighttime street encounter in a high-crime area while his identification was checked" proper).

Movement of the suspect to another location may also indicate that the officer has exceeded his *Terry* authority, especially if, as in *Dunaway*, p. 438, the suspect is taken to the police station and subjected to a detention "in important respects indistinguishable from a traditional arrest." In FLORIDA v. ROYER, 460 U.S. 491 (1983), detectives questioned Royer on an airport concourse and then asked him to accompany them to a small room about 40 feet away. His luggage was retrieved from the airline and brought to that room, and Royer was then asked to consent to a search of the suitcases, which he did. About 15 minutes had elapsed since the initial encounter. The *Royer* plurality then concluded "that at the time Royer produced the key to his suitcase, the detention to which he was then subjected was a more serious intrusion on his personal liberty than is allowable on mere suspicion of criminal activity." They stressed: (i) that the situation "had escalated into an investigatory procedure in a police interrogation room," so that "[a]s a practical matter, Royer was under arrest"; and (ii) that "the officers' conduct was more intrusive than necessary to effectuate an investigative detention otherwise authorized by the *Terry* line of cases," as while "there are undoubtedly reasons of safety and security that would justify moving a suspect from one location to another during an investigatory detention, such as from an airport concourse to a more private area," there was "no indication in this case that such reasons prompted the officers to transfer the site of the encounter from the concourse to the interrogation room. It appears, rather, that the primary interest of the officers was not in having an extended conversation with Royer but in the contents of his luggage, a matter which the officers did not pursue orally with Royer until after the encounter was relocated to the police room. The record does not reflect any facts which would support a finding that the legitimate law enforcement purposes which justified the detention in the first instance were furthered by removing Royer to the police room prior to the officer's attempt to gain his consent to a search of his luggage. As we have noted, had Royer consented to a search on the spot, the search could have been conducted with Royer present in the area where the bags were retrieved by Officer Johnson and any evidence recovered would have been admissible against him. If the search proved negative, Royer would have been free to go much earlier and with less likelihood of missing his flight, which in itself can be a very serious matter in a variety of circumstances."

What then if the suspect was transported to a nearby crime scene for possible identification as the perpetrator? Consider *People v. Harris*, 540 P.2d 632 (Cal. 1975) (such action "violated defendant's constitutional rights," as officers failed to pursue "less intrusive and more reasonable alternatives to pre-arrest transportation," such as "escort[ing] the witness to the detention scene for an immediate viewing of the suspect, or [making] arrangements * * * for a subsequent confrontation with the witness"); *People v. Bloyd,* 331 N.W.2d 447 (Mich.1982) (because transportation of suspect even a short distance more intrusive than a mere stop, it "should be dependent upon knowledge that a crime has been committed" and impermissible when the defendant's conduct was suspicious but "there has not been any report of a crime" recently in the vicinity).

3. As for the time limits on a *Terry* stop, consider UNITED STATES v. SHARPE, 470 U.S. 675 (1985). There, a federal drug agent, patrolling in an unmarked car in a highway area under surveillance for drug trafficking, saw an apparently overloaded camper truck traveling in tandem with a Pontiac. He radioed for assistance, and when a highway patrolman responded they attempted to stop the two vehicles. The Pontiac pulled over, but the truck continued on, pursued by the patrolman. Once the drug agent obtained identification from the driver of the Pontiac, he sought without success to reach the patrolman by radio. He then radioed for more assistance, and when local police appeared he left them with the Pontiac and drove ahead to where the patrolman had stopped the truck. After smelling the odor of marijuana coming from the vehicle, he opened it and saw bales of marijuana and then arrested the driver of the truck, one Savage. The Court of Appeals held that the 20–minute detention of Savage "failed to meet the [Fourth Amendment's] requirement of brevity," but the Supreme Court, per Burger, C.J., disagreed:

"In assessing whether a detention is too long in duration to be justified as an investigative stop, we consider it appropriate to examine whether the police diligently pursued a means of investigation that was likely to confirm or dispel their suspicions quickly, during which time it was necessary to detain the defendant. A court making this assessment should take care to consider whether the police are acting in a swiftly developing situation, and in such cases the court should not indulge in unrealistic second-guessing. A creative judge engaged in *post hoc* evaluation of police conduct can almost always imagine some alternative means by which the objectives of the police might have been accomplished. But '[t]he fact that the protection of the public might, in the abstract, have been accomplished by "less intrusive" means does not, in itself, render the search unreasonable.' The question is not simply whether some other alternative was available, but whether the police acted unreasonably in failing to recognize or to pursue it."

Stressing that the "delay in this case was attributable almost entirely to the evasive actions of Savage," that most of the 20 minutes was consumed by the agent trying to reach the patrolman and to obtain additional assistance, and that when the agent reached Savage "he proceeded expeditiously," the majority in *Sharpe* concluded the delay was not unreasonable. Marshall, J., though concurring because the "prolonged encounter" was attributable to "the evasive actions" of Savage, argued that "fidelity to the rationales that justify *Terry* stops require that the intrusiveness of the stop be measured independently of law enforcement needs. A stop must first be found not unduly intrusive, particularly in its length, before it is proper to consider whether law enforcement aims warrant limited investigation." Brennan, J., dissenting, objected that record did not clearly show that Savage had tried to elude the police, and that the government had not met its burden under *Royer* to "show at a minimum that the 'least intrusive means reasonably available' were used in carrying out the stop."

4. In *Hiibel v. Sixth Judicial District Court*, 542 U.S. 177 (2004), defendant was convicted of obstructing an officer in his duties for not complying with the command in Nevada's "stop and identify" statute that a person lawfully stopped under *Terry* "shall identify himself." The Court held, 5–4, that defendant's conviction did not violate either the Fourth Amendment or (see Note 10, p. 619) the Fifth Amendment's privilege against self-incrimination. On the Fourth Amendment issue, the majority declared Justice White's statement in *Terry* (p. 414) meant only that "the Fourth Amendment itself cannot require a suspect to answer questions," while the instant case posed the "different issue" of whether state law could impose such a requirement without violating the Fourth Amendment. Using a *Terry*-style balancing of interests, the Court answered the latter question in the affirmative, reasoning (i) that the "request for identity has an immediate relation to the purpose, rationale, and practical demands of a *Terry* stop"; (ii) that the "threat of criminal sanction helps ensure that the request for identity does not become a legal nullity"; and (iii) that such threat "does not alter the nature of the stop itself" provided (as is essential under *Terry*) that the "the request for identification was 'reasonably related in scope to the circumstances which justified' the stop." (The dissenters objected there was "no good reason now to reject" a "generation-old statement of law," the "strong dicta" in *Berkemer v. McCarty*, p. 602, that a *Terry* detainee "is not obliged to respond" to any questions.) Does the *Terry* scope limitation mean that sometimes a request for identity will be outside the scope of the stop? Consider *Carey v. Nevada Gaming Control Board*, 279 F.3d 873 (9th Cir.2002) (asking Carey, detained in a Nevada casino because he was suspected of cheating while gambling, for identification made the detention unlawful, as "Carey's name was not related to determining whether Carey had cheated").

Hiibel has limited Fourth Amendment significance; it does not affect when a *Terry* stop may be made or how a post-stop investigation may be conducted, and only approves a crime definition permitting arrest in the rare event a suspect refuses to give a name. *Hiibel* is so limited because the Court, relying upon a sentence in the state court decision asserting that the suspect is only required "to state his name," assumed that "the statute does not require a suspect to give the officer a driver's license or any other document," and thus limited its holding to the "question whether a State can compel a suspect to disclose his name during a *Terry* stop." But the facts of the case as recited by the Court appear to indicate that Hiibel was repeatedly asked "to produce a driver's license or some other form of written identification," which he repeatedly refused to do, but was never asked (and thus never refused) merely to state his name. Would/should the Court come out the same way had it focused upon those facts rather than the state court's representation? Is requiring production of written identification actually the preferred investigative technique during a *Terry* stop because of its greater reliability, or is that offset by the fact any written identification tendered is likely to reveal additional information about the suspect? A dissent in *Hiibel* asks: "Can a State, in addition to requiring a stopped individual to answer 'What's your name?' also require an answer to 'What's your license number?' or 'Where do you live?' "

5. Often relying upon the Supreme Court's statement in *Berkemer v. McCarty*, p. 602, that "the usual traffic stop is more analogous to a so-called '*Terry* stop' than to a formal arrest," defendants subjected to the pretext traffic stop tactic discussed in Notes 5–8, pp. 356–58, have often relied upon the temporal and scope limitations in the *Terry* line of cases as a basis for seeking to suppress evidence (usually narcotics) found by police employing various investigative techniques after a traffic stop. As a consequence, some courts have held certain investigative activities improper because conducted after all legitimate actions relating to the traffic stop had been completed, e.g., *Harris v. Commonwealth*, 581 S.E.2d 206 (Va.2003), or because they were directed at criminal activity for which reasonable suspicion was then lacking, e.g., *State v. Fort*, 660 N.W.2d 415 (Minn.2003), while other courts have been unwilling or less willing to do so (sometimes noting the *Berkemer* statement has a qualifying footnote: "We of course do not suggest that a traffic stop supported by probable cause may not exceed the bounds set by the Fourth Amendment on the scope of a *Terry* stop"). See Wayne R. LaFave, *The "Routine Traffic Stop" From Start to Finish: Too Much "Routine," Not Enough Fourth Amendment*, 102 Mich.L.Rev. 1843 (2004).

Then came ILLINOIS v. CABALLES, 543 U.S. 405 (2005), where defendant was stopped by a state trooper for doing 71 m.p.h. on an interstate highway with a posted speed limit of 65. Another trooper assigned to the Drug Interdiction Team heard a radio transmission reporting the stop and without any request immediately traveled to the scene and walked his drug dog around defendant's car while defendant was in the patrol car awaiting a warning ticket. The dog alerted, and in a subsequent search of the car's trunk marijuana was found. The state supreme court overturned defendant's conviction on the ground that use of the dog "unjustifiably enlarge[ed] the scope of a routine traffic stop into a drug investigation." The *total* response by the Supreme Court to that conclusion[e] was, per Stevens, J., as follows:

"Here, the initial seizure of respondent when he was stopped on the highway was based on probable cause, and was concededly lawful. It is nevertheless clear that a seizure that is lawful at its inception can violate the Fourth Amendment if its manner of execution unreasonably infringes interests protected by the Constitution. A seizure that is justified solely by the interest in issuing a warning ticket to the driver can become unlawful if it is prolonged beyond the time reasonably required to complete that mission. In an earlier case involving a dog sniff that

---

e. The Court devoted an equal amount of space to explaining why it was not abandoning its prior holdings to the effect that a drug dog sniff is not a Fourth Amendment search; see p. 277. The state court had never claimed otherwise, although counsel for Caballes did.

occurred during an unreasonably prolonged traffic stop, the Illinois Supreme Court held that use of the dog and the subsequent discovery of contraband were the product of an unconstitutional seizure. We may assume that a similar result would be warranted in this case if the dog sniff had been conducted while respondent was being unlawfully detained.

"In the state-court proceedings, however, the judges carefully reviewed the details of Officer Gillette's conversations with respondent and the precise timing of his radio transmissions to the dispatcher to determine whether he had improperly extended the duration of the stop to enable the dog sniff to occur. We have not recounted those details because we accept the state court's conclusion that the duration of the stop in this case was entirely justified by the traffic offense and the ordinary inquiries incident to such a stop.

"Despite this conclusion, the Illinois Supreme Court held that the initially lawful traffic stop became an unlawful seizure solely as a result of the canine sniff that occurred outside respondent's stopped car. That is, the court characterized the dog sniff as the cause rather than the consequence of a constitutional violation. In its view, the use of the dog converted the citizen-police encounter from a lawful traffic stop into a drug investigation, and because the shift in purpose was not supported by any reasonable suspicion that respondent possessed narcotics, it was unlawful. In our view, conducting a dog sniff would not change the character of a traffic stop that is lawful at its inception and otherwise executed in a reasonable manner, unless the dog sniff itself infringed respondent's constitutionally protected interest in privacy. Our cases hold that it did not."

In light of *Caballes*, what is the status of various other investigative techniques commonly utilized incident to traffic stops, theretofore challenged with varied results, see LaFave, supra, at 1874–98, such as running a warrant check on the driver, running a criminal history check on the driver, questioning the driver about whether there are narcotics in the vehicle, questioning the driver about whether there are weapons in the vehicle, questioning the driver in detail about his travels (beginning, destination, route, purpose, contacts, etc.), seeking consent from the driver to conduct a search of the vehicle, or doing any of the above with respect to a mere passenger in the vehicle? Are all of them unobjectionable because they too are not searches? Even assuming that is so, is their occurrence always irrelevant? What if in *Caballes* the defendant had spent more time in the squad car because of such investigative activities and only because of that was still being detained when the dog arrived? That is, does the conclusion a particular investigative technique is permissible during a traffic stop necessarily means it is a permissible basis for extending the length of that stop?

6. A unanimous Court in *Arizona v. Johnson*, p. 434, sought to supply an answer to that last question, stating: "An officer's inquiries into matters unrelated to the justification for the traffic stop * * * do not convert the encounter into something other than a lawful seizure, so long as those inquiries do not measurably extend the duration of the stop." In UNITED STATES v. EVERETT, 601 F.3d 484 (6th Cir.2010), the court noted that language might be taken "as establishing a bright-line 'no prolongation' rule, under which *any* extension of a traffic stop due to suspicionless extraneous questioning—no matter how brief—is per se unreasonable," a position the court acknowledged finds some support in the "legitimate concern" "that a strict 'no prolongation' rule is necessary to prevent abuse of the wide discretion to stop errant motorists that police officers already enjoy under *Whren*," p. 353. But the court then joined the "overwhelming weight of authority" rejecting such a bright line rule, a position deemed consistent with the language in *Johnson* because "another definition of the word 'measurable' is 'significant' or 'great enough to be worth consideration.' " Moreover, the court reasoned, a policeman could "easily evade" a "no prolongation" rule by "delegating the standard traffic-stop routine to a backup officer, leaving himself free to conduct unrelated questioning all the while, or simply by learning to write and ask questions at the same time."

The *Everett* court then proceeded to "a second important question" as to which earlier decisions "are silent," namely: "if some prolongation is permissible * * *, how much is too much?" An answer depending solely upon the stopwatch was immediately dismissed; "having just refused to set a bright line at *zero*, we cannot very well select *another* arbitrary quantity of time and proclaim that any prolongation less than that amount is categorically 'de minimis'—as convenient as such a rule might be." Instead, courts "must conduct a fact-bound context-dependent inquiry in each case" to determine "whether the 'totality of the circumstances surrounding the stop' indicates that the duration of *the stop as a whole*—including any prolongation due to suspicionless unrelated questioning— was reasonable." As to this, "the overarching consideration is *the officer's diligence*" in "ascertaining whether the suspected traffic violation occurred, and, if necessary, issuing a ticket," which in turn depends upon the quantity and subject matter of the extraneous questions, especially if "the officer, without reasonable suspicion, definitively abandoned the prosecution of the traffic stop and embarked on another sustained course of investigation."

Assess the *Everett* approach in light of a critique quoted by that court: "Once the rather clear *Terry* limit, tied to those activities defensible in terms of responding to the traffic infraction, is abandoned, there remains no other basis for making a judgment . . .—unless it is simply a matter of applying the 'horseshoes rule,' i.e., that just being close counts."

7. SEARCHSZR § 9.3(b) takes a dim view of *Caballes*: "For all one would conclude from the *Caballes* majority opinion,[51.7] the Illinois supreme court had fancied up out of whole cloth a concept so wanting in bona fides that it could be dismissed out of hand. But in actuality, the state court opinion, as with the state and federal cases in general accord cited earlier, was grounded in the straightforward proposition that the temporal and scope limitations adopted in *Terry* and its progeny are equally applicable to traffic stops. It is odd, to say the least, that the Supreme Court, in overturning the state court ruling, never even cited *Terry* or any of the post-*Terry* stop-and-frisk cases discussing those limitations, and, for that matter, *never cited any prior Supreme Court decision at all* to justify its holding!

"The abruptness of the Court's decision and the virtually total lack of analysis might appear even to raise some doubt as to what the basis of the decision actually is. But, * * * the *Caballes* decision seems to be grounded in nothing other than the bald assertion that only such conduct as itself constitutes a Fourth Amendment search can qualify as investigative activity amounting to a scope violation under the *Terry* line of cases. If this is so, then the Court's failure to cite a single precedent in support becomes quite understandable, for the Supreme Court's relevant prior decisions[f] consistently point in the other direction. * * *

"Had the Supreme Court in *Caballes* been true to these precedents, the Court would have held that use of the drug dog, albeit no search, was unreasonable

---

51.7 However, the dissent by Justice Ginsburg, joined by Justice Souter, clearly indicates the *Terry* groundings of the state court's decision and correctly concludes that the *Terry* limits deserve to be followed in the instant case.

f. E.g., *Illinois v. McArthur*, p. 374; *Hiibel v. Sixth Judicial District Court*, p. 427; *Hayes v. Florida*, p. 437.

because it was beyond the scope limitation of that traffic stop and constituted something more than the 'non-event' the petitioner claimed it was."[g]

8. If, as *Caballes* appears to acknowledge, the *Terry* temporal limitation has application in traffic cases, then it will be necessary in many instances to determine whether a traffic stop was extended or instead terminated at a certain point. Even if it is apparent to the defendant that the officer has completed writing up the ticket or warning, that does not terminate the stop if the officer continues to hold the defendant's license, vehicle registration, or other credentials. *United States v. Fernandez*, 18 F.3d 874 (10th Cir.1994). But if the officer *has* returned those credentials, does this mean that the seizure has terminated even if the officer then uses the Lt. Colombo gambit ("Oh, one more thing, . . .") in order to question the defendant about drugs, as concluded in *United States v. Werking*, 915 F.2d 1404 (10th Cir.1990)?

Consider OHIO v. ROBINETTE, 519 U.S. 33 (1996), which involved these facts: a sheriff's deputy on "drug interdiction patrol" stopped defendant for speeding. The deputy examined defendant's license, ran a computer check indicating no previous violations, issued a verbal warning and returned defendant's license, and then immediately asked defendant if he had drugs in the car; when defendant answered in the negative, the deputy asked to search the car and defendant consented, resulting in a search which uncovered a small amount of marijuana and a single pill which was a controlled substance. The state supreme court concluded the evidence must be suppressed, reasoning that the "right to be secure in one's person and property requires that citizens stopped for traffic offenses be clearly informed by the detaining officer when they are free to go after a valid detention, before an officer attempts to engage in a consensual interrogation." The Supreme Court, per Rehnquist, C.J., focused on the issue stated in the certiorari petition, whether such a warning is a prerequisite to a voluntary consent, and answered in the negative. The state court's per se rule was deemed inconsistent with the approach to Fourth Amendment issues by the Supreme Court, which has "consistently eschewed bright-line rules, instead emphasizing the fact-specific nature of the reasonableness inquiry." Moreover, the Court reasoned in *Robinette*, requiring such warnings would be just as impractical as the right-to-refuse-consent warnings held unnecessary by the Court in *Schneckloth v. Bustamonte* [p. 454].

Only Justice Stevens, dissenting, fully considered an alternative characterization of the state court's holding, namely, that (i) the officer's failure to tell defendant he was free to leave meant that a reasonable person would continue to

---

g. This last point is elaborated in SEARCHSZR § 9.3(f): "(1) The use of large dogs in the immediate proximity of persons has an intimidating character to it, whether it occurs in Abu Graib prison or alongside an interstate. * * * (2) Use of a drug dog on the vehicle of a motorist stopped for a traffic violation is an accusatory act, one which will be upsetting to the innocent motorist because it will appear that he has been singled out as a drug suspect for reasons about which he can only speculate. * * * (3) Use of a drug dog incident to a traffic stop is likely to be humiliating to the driver of the vehicle, for such use manifests police suspicion of the driver as a drug courier to all those who may pass by while the scenario is being played out on the side of an interstate highway or city street. * * * (4) Use of a drug dog on a vehicle stopped for a traffic violation will in many instances cause the driver and his passengers to be delayed in their journey longer than would have been the case absent this type of investigative activity[, as when] a dog and handler are being summoned to the scene of a traffic stop, the stopping officer is tempted to engage in stalling regarding his proper functions during the stop (e.g., checking registration and driver's license credentials, writing up a citation or warning notice) in order to give the appearance that the time for the stop has not expired in the interim. * * * (5) Use of drug dogs in wholesale fashion without individualized suspicion creates an unnecessary and unjustified risk that many motorists totally innocent of any wrongdoing regarding drugs will be subjected to an extended and exhaustive roadside search of their vehicles[, as d]rug dogs and drug handlers do make mistakes." For more on the fallibility of drug dogs, see Justice Souter's *Caballes* dissent at p. 277.

believe he was not free to leave, so that the seizure had not yet ended at the time the consent was obtained; (ii) the seizure by that time was illegal, as it had exceeded its lawful purpose, the giving of a warning about the traffic offense; and (iii) consequently the evidence obtained via the voluntary consent was a suppressible fruit of that poisonous tree. He concluded that the evidence in the case (including the fact that this deputy had used this tactic to make 786 consent searches in one year) supported that conclusion, so that the suppression of evidence by the state court was justified.

The *Robinette* majority was not totally silent regarding this theory. The defendant argued the Court could not reach the voluntariness issue because the state court decision set out a valid alternative ground in the following language: "When the motivation behind a police officer's continued detention of a person stopped for a traffic violation is not related to the purpose of the original, constitutional stop, and when that continued detention is not based on articulable facts giving rise to a suspicion of some separate illegal activity justifying an extension of the detention, the continued detention constitutes an illegal seizure." Relying on the *Whren* case, p. 353, the Chief Justice declared that the state court was in error because "the subjective intentions of the officer did not make the continued detention of respondent illegal under the Fourth Amendment." Is this a proper application of *Whren*? Does it mean that in applying the *Terry* scope limitation, the fact the officer decided only to give a warning instead of a ticket is irrelevant? Or, is Justice Stevens correct in concluding that the irrelevant subjective motivation was drug interdiction, but that the subjective purpose of giving a warning bears on the justification for the continued detention, so that by the time the consent was obtained "the lawful traffic stop had come to an end" because the defendant "had been given his warning"?

Is Justice Stevens' first point in his *Robinette* dissent confirmed by the Court's later reference in *Brendlin v. California*, p. 417, to "a societal expectation of 'unquestioned police command' at odds with any notion that a passenger would feel free to leave, or to terminate the personal encounter any other way, without advance permission," and by the application of *Brendlin* in *Arizona v. Johnson*, p. 434?

9. If a *Terry* stop does not result in an arrest, is the fact the person was stopped a matter of legitimate continuing law enforcement interest? Consider N.Y.Crim.Proc.Law § 140.50, providing, as to New York city only (where a half million people are stopped annually, 90% of whom are released without further legal action), that "information that establishes the personal identity of an individual who has been stopped, questioned and/or frisked by a police officer or a peace officer, such as the name, address or social security number of such person, shall not be recorded in a computerized or electronic database if that individual is released without further legal action."

D. TEMPORARY SEIZURE OF EFFECTS

1. In *United States v. Van Leeuwen*, 397 U.S. 249 (1970) a postal clerk in Mt. Vernon, Washington, advised a policeman that he was suspicious of two packages of coins just mailed. The policeman immediately noted that the return address was fictitious and that the individual who mailed the packages had Canadian license plates, and later investigation disclosed that the addressees (one in California, the other in Tennessee) were under investigation for trafficking in illegal coins. Upon this basis a search warrant for both packages was obtained, but not until the packages had been held for slightly more than a day. A unanimous Court, although acknowledging that "detention of mail could at some point become an unreasonable seizure of 'papers' or 'effects' within the meaning of the Fourth Amendment," cited *Terry* in upholding this "detention, without a warrant, while an investigation was made." The Court emphasized that the investigation was conducted promptly and that most of the delay was attributable to the fact that because of the time differential the Tennessee authorities could not be reached until the following day.

2. In UNITED STATES v. PLACE, 462 U.S. 696 (1983), federal agents stopped respondent, a suspected drug courier, at LaGuardia Airport, seized his luggage for the purported purpose of taking it to a judge while a warrant was sought, and then allowed respondent to go his way. They took the bags to Kennedy Airport, where a trained narcotics dog reacted positively to one of them and ambiguously to the other, but because it was late Friday afternoon held the bags until Monday morning, when a warrant was obtained for the first bag and cocaine was found in execution of the warrant. The Court, per O'Connor, J., first recognized "the reasonableness under the Fourth Amendment of warrantless seizures of personal luggage from the custody of the owner on the basis of less than probable cause for the purpose of pursuing a limited course of investigation, short of opening the luggage, that would quickly confirm or dispel the authorities' suspicion." Applying the *Terry* balancing of interests approach, the Court concluded that "the governmental interest in seizing the luggage briefly to pursue further investigation is substantial," and that because "seizures of property can vary in intrusiveness, some brief detentions of personal effects may be so minimally intrusive of Fourth Amendment interests that strong countervailing governmental interests will justify a seizure based only on specific articulable facts that the property contains contraband or evidence of a crime.

" * * * Particularly in the case of detention of luggage within the traveler's immediate possession, the police conduct intrudes on both the suspect's possessory interest in his luggage as well as his liberty interest in proceeding with his itinerary. The person whose luggage is detained is technically still free to continue his travels or carry out other personal activities pending release of the luggage. Moreover, he is not subjected to the coercive atmosphere of a custodial confinement or to the public indignity of being personally detained. Nevertheless, such a seizure can effectively restrain the person since he is subjected to the possible disruption of his travel plans in order to remain with his luggage or to arrange for its return.[8] Therefore, when the police seize luggage from the suspect's custody, we think the limitations applicable to investigative detentions of the person should define the permissible scope of an investigative detention of the person's luggage on less than probable cause. Under this standard, it is clear that the police conduct here exceeded the permissible limits of a *Terry*-type investigative stop.

"The length of the detention of respondent's luggage alone precludes the conclusion that the seizure was reasonable in the absence of probable cause. Although we have recognized the reasonableness of seizures longer than the momentary ones involved in *Terry,* the brevity of the invasion of the individual's Fourth Amendment interests is an important factor in determining whether the seizure is so minimally intrusive as to be justifiable on reasonable suspicion. Moreover, in assessing the effect of the length of the detention, we take into account whether the police diligently pursue their investigation. We note that here the New York agents knew the time of Place's scheduled arrival at LaGuardia, had ample time to arrange for their additional investigation at that location, and

---

8. "At least when the authorities do not make it absolutely clear how they plan to reunite the suspect and his possessions at some future time and place, seizure of the object is tantamount to seizure of the person. This is because that person must either remain on the scene or else seemingly surrender his effects permanently to the police." 3 W. LaFave, *Search and Seizure* § 9.6, p. 61 (1982 Supp.).

thereby could have minimized the intrusion on respondent's Fourth Amendment interests. Thus, although we decline to adopt any outside time limitation for a permissible *Terry* stop, we have never approved a seizure of the person for the prolonged 90–minute period involved here and cannot do so on the facts presented by this case.

"Although the 90–minute detention of respondent's luggage is sufficient to render the seizure unreasonable, the violation was exacerbated by the failure of the agents to accurately inform respondent of the place to which they were transporting his luggage, of the length of time he might be dispossessed, and of what arrangements would be made for return of the luggage if the investigation dispelled the suspicion."

E. PROTECTIVE SEARCH

1. In ARIZONA v. JOHNSON, 555 U.S. 323 (2009), three officers stopped a vehicle with three occupants after a license plate check revealed the vehicle's registration had been suspended, a civil infraction warranting a citation. One officer "attended to" back-seat passenger Johnson, who watched the police closely as they approached, was wearing gang clothing, was carrying a scanner, had no identification, and admitted serving time in prison for burglary. She asked him to get out of the car and then, suspecting he "might have a weapon on him," frisked Johnson and found a gun at his waist. The state court concluded that absent "reason to believe Johnson was involved in criminal activity," the officer "had no right to pat him down for weapons, even if she had reason to suspect he was armed and dangerous." A unanimous Supreme Court reversed. Noting that the *Terry* prerequisites for a frisk were (i) a lawful stop, there present because of reasonable suspicion of criminal activity, and (ii) grounds for a frisk, and that per *Brendlin*, p. 417, a traffic stop seized "everyone in the vehicle," the Court held that "in a traffic-stop setting, the first *Terry* condition—a lawful investigatory stop—is met whenever it is lawful for police to detain an automobile and its occupants pending inquiry into a vehicular violation. The police need not have, in addition, cause to believe any occupant of the vehicle is involved in criminal activity. To justify a patdown of the driver or a passenger during a traffic stop, however, just as in the case of a pedestrian reasonably suspected of criminal activity, the police must harbor reasonable suspicion that the person subjected to the frisk is armed and dangerous." In concluding that the stop of Johnson had not terminated before the frisk, the Court stated: "Nothing occurred in this case that would have conveyed to Johnson that, prior to the frisk, the traffic stop had ended or that he was otherwise free 'to depart without police permission.' [The officer] surely was not constitutionally required to give Johnson an opportunity to depart the scene after he exited the vehicle without first ensuring that, in so doing, she was not permitting a dangerous person to get behind her."

What should the result be on facts identical to those in *Johnson*, except that just as the license plate check was concluded the vehicle was parked and the three occupants exited and began walking down the street, and when police ordered the driver to stop all three of the men ceased walking? Is the danger to the police any different in this situation?

2. After *Terry,* what is the test for determining whether an officer may conduct a "frisk"? Consider *Sibron v. New York*, 392 U.S. 40 (1968), where the Court stated: "In the case of the self-protective search for weapons, [the officer] must be able to point to particular facts from which he reasonably inferred that the individual was armed and dangerous. Patrolman Martin's testimony reveals no such facts. The suspect's mere act of talking with a number of known narcotics addicts over an eight-hour period no more gives rise to reasonable fear of life or limb on the part of the police officer than it justifies an arrest for committing a crime. Nor did Patrolman Martin urge that when Sibron put his hand in his pocket, he feared that he was going for a weapon and acted in self-defense. His opening statement to Sibron—'You know what I am after'—made it abundantly clear that he sought narcotics, and his testimony at the hearing left no doubt that he thought there were narcotics in Sibron's pocket.''

Compare *Adams v. Williams,* 407 U.S. 143 (1972), where the majority concluded the officer "had ample reason to fear for his own safety"[h] upon being told by an informant that defendant, seated in a nearby car, was carrying narcotics and had a gun at his waist. Marshall, J., joined by Douglas, J., dissenting, objected: "The fact remains that Connecticut specifically authorizes persons to carry guns so long as they have a permit. Thus, there was no reason for the officer to infer from anything that the informant said that the respondent was dangerous.''

Is the quantum and reliability of information needed to support a frisk the same or less than that needed to support a stop? For example, what if the stop was made on a reliable informant's information the suspect possessed illegal gambling paraphernalia, and the officer had also received a report from an anonymous informant that this same person regularly carries a gun? Reconsider the final paragraph of Justice Ginsburg's opinion in *J. L.,* p. 422.

3. Consider David A. Harris, *Frisking Every Suspect: The Withering of Terry,* 28 U.C. Davis L.Rev. 1, 5, 43–44 (1994): "Perhaps as a result of the high-visibility use of frisks as a contemporary crime control device, or because of general public antipathy to crime, lower courts have stretched the law governing frisks to the point that the Supreme Court might find it unrecognizable. Lower courts have consistently expanded the *types of offenses* always considered violent regardless of the individual circumstances. At the same time, lower courts have also found that certain *types of persons and situations* always pose a danger of armed violence to police [e.g., those present in a high-crime or drug-involved location who engage in allegedly evasive behavior toward the police]. When confronted with these offenses, persons, or situations, police may *automatically* frisk, whether or not any individualized circumstances point to danger. * * *

" * * * African–Americans and Hispanic–Americans pay a higher personal price for [these] contemporary stop and frisk practices than whites do.''

4. As for the requisite search procedure, the Court in *Sibron* stated: "The search for weapons approved in *Terry* consisted solely of a limited patting of the outer clothing of the suspect for concealed objects which might be used as instruments of assault. Only when he discovered such objects did the officer in *Terry* place his hands in the pockets of the men he searched. In this case, with no attempt at an initial limited exploration for arms, Patrolman Martin thrust his hand into Sibron's pocket and took from him envelopes of heroin. His testimony shows that he was looking for narcotics, and he found them. The search was not reasonably limited in scope to the accomplishment of the only goal which might conceivably have justified its inception—the protection of the officer by disarming a potentially dangerous man.''

Compare *Adams v. Williams,* where the officer immediately reached into the car and removed a theretofore concealed gun from defendant's waistband. The

---

h. The Court footnoted that statement with the following: "Figures reported by the Federal Bureau of Investigation indicate that 125 policemen were murdered in 1971, with all but five of them having been killed by gunshot wounds. Federal Bureau of Investigation *Law Enforcement Bulletin,* February 1972, p. 33. According to one study, approximately 30% of police shootings occurred when a police officer approached a suspect seated in an automobile. Bristow, *Police Officer Shootings—A Tactical Evaluation,* 54 J.Crim.L.C. & P.S. 93 (1963).''

Court stated: "When Williams rolled down his window, rather than complying with the policeman's request to step out of the car so that his movements could more easily be seen, the revolver allegedly at Williams' waist became an even greater threat. Under these circumstances the policeman's action in reaching to the spot where the gun was thought to be hidden constituted a limited intrusion designed to insure his safety, and we conclude that it was reasonable."

5.   Assuming that there are grounds for a protective search, how extensive a "patting down" of the suspect is permissible? Consider the description quoted in note 13 of *Terry*. Is the right to make a protective search limited to the person of the suspect? What if the suspect is carrying an attache case, a shopping bag, a purse, or similar object?

In *Minnesota v. Dickerson*, 508 U.S. 366 (1993), the frisking officer felt a small lump in the suspect's front pocket and then, upon further tactile examination, concluded the lump was crack cocaine in a plastic or cellophane bag, which the officer removed from the suspect's pocket. Noting the state court's findings that the officer "determined that the lump was contraband only after 'squeezing, sliding and otherwise manipulating the outside of the defendant's pocket' " *after* the officer knew it contained no weapon, the Supreme Court held the state court "was correct in holding that the police officer in this case overstepped the bounds of the 'strictly circumscribed' search for weapons allowed under *Terry*."

6.   In MICHIGAN v. LONG, 463 U.S. 1032 (1983), two deputies saw a car swerve into a ditch and stopped to investigate. Long, the only occupant of the car, met the deputies at the rear of the car, supplied his driver's license upon demand, and started back toward the open door when asked for his vehicle registration. The officers saw a large hunting knife on the floorboard, so Long was frisked and one officer then entered the vehicle and found an open pouch of marijuana under an armrest. The Supreme Court, per O'Connor, J., held:

"Our past cases indicate then that protection of police and others can justify protective searches when police have a reasonable belief that the suspect poses a danger, that roadside encounters between police and suspects are especially hazardous, and that danger may arise from the possible presence of weapons in the area surrounding a suspect. These principles compel our conclusion that the search of the passenger compartment of an automobile, limited to those areas in which a weapon may be placed or hidden, is permissible if the police officer possesses a reasonable belief based on 'specific and articulable facts which, taken together with the rational inferences from those facts, reasonably warrant' the officers in believing that the suspect is dangerous and the suspect may gain immediate control of weapons. * * *

"The Michigan Supreme Court appeared to believe that it was not reasonable for the officers to fear that Long could injure them, because he was effectively under their control during the investigative stop and could not get access to any weapons that might have been located in the automobile. This reasoning is mistaken in several respects. * * * Just as a *Terry* suspect on the street may, despite being under the brief control of a police officer, reach into his clothing and retrieve a weapon, so might a *Terry* suspect in Long's position break away from police control and retrieve a weapon from his automobile. In addition, if the suspect is not placed under arrest, he will be permitted to reenter his automobile, and he will then have access to any weapons inside. Or, as here, the suspect may be permitted to reenter the vehicle before the *Terry* investigation is over, and again, may have access to weapons. In any event, we stress that a *Terry* investigation, such as the one that occurred here, involves a police investigation 'at close range,' when the officer remains particularly vulnerable in part *because* a full custodial arrest has not been effected, and the officer must make a 'quick decision as to how to protect himself and others from possible danger * * *.' In such circumstances, we have not required that officers adopt alternate means to ensure their safety in order to avoid the intrusion involved in a *Terry* encounter."

7. Can a limited search for any other reason ever be undertaken incident to a lawful stop? In *State v. Flynn,* 285 N.W.2d 710 (Wis.1979), one of two suspects lawfully stopped for investigation of a just-completed burglary admitted he had identification in his wallet but refused to identify himself, so the officer removed the wallet and examined it to the extent necessary to find the suspect's name and then arrested the suspect when a radio check revealed he was wanted for an earlier crime. Reasoning that "unless the officer is entitled to at least ascertain the identity of the suspect, the right to stop him can serve no useful purpose at all," that the search was a very limited one, and "that defendant could himself have substantially avoided the intrusion simply by producing the identification himself as his companion did," the court held the officer's actions reasonable under the *Terry* balancing test. Compare *People v. Williams,* 234 N.W.2d 541 (Mich.App.1975) (even though officer had good reason to believe lawfully stopped suspect was lying when he said he had no identification, looking in his wallet at driver's license violated the Fourth Amendment). Cf. *Arizona v. Hicks,* p. 368; and *Ybarra v. Illinois,* p. 324. Consider also the *Hiibel* case, Note 4, p. 427.

What then of on-the-scene fingerprinting? In *Hayes v. Florida,* 470 U.S. 811 (1985), the majority in dictum opined this would be permissible "if there is reasonable suspicion that the suspect has committed a criminal act, if there is a reasonable basis for believing that fingerprinting will establish or negate the suspect's connection with that crime, and if the procedure is carried out with dispatch." Brennan and Marshall, JJ., concurring, responded "that on-site finger-printing (apparently undertaken in full view of any passerby) would involve a singular intrusion on the suspect's privacy, an intrusion that would not be justifiable (as was the patdown in *Terry*) as necessary for the officer's protection."

F. OTHER BRIEF DETENTION FOR INVESTIGATION

1. In DAVIS v. MISSISSIPPI, 394 U.S. 721 (1969), petitioner and 24 other black youths were detained at the police station for questioning and fingerprinting in connection with a rape for which the only leads were a general description given by the victim and a set of fingerprints around the window through which the assailant entered. Petitioner's prints were found to match those at the scene of the crime, and this evidence was admitted at his trial. The Court, per Brennan, J., held that the prints should have been excluded as the fruits of a seizure of petitioner in violation of the Fourth Amendment, but intimated that a detention for such a purpose might sometimes be permissible on evidence insufficient for arrest:

"Detentions for the sole purpose of obtaining fingerprints are no less subject to the constraints of the Fourth Amendment. It is arguable, however, that because of the unique nature of the fingerprinting process, such detentions might, under narrowly defined circumstances, be found to comply with the Fourth Amendment even though there is no probable cause in the traditional sense. Detention for fingerprinting may constitute a much less serious intrusion upon personal security than other types of police searches and detentions. Fingerprinting involves none of the probing into an individual's private life and thoughts which marks an interrogation or search. Nor can fingerprint detention be employed repeatedly to harass any individual, since the police need only one set of each person's prints. Furthermore, fingerprinting is an inherently more reliable and effective crime-solving tool than eyewitness identifications or confessions and is not subject to such abuses as the improper line-up[i] and the 'third degree.' Finally, because there is no danger of destruction of fingerprints, the limited detention need not come unexpectedly or at an inconvenient time. For this same reason, the general requirement that the authorization of a judicial officer be obtained in advance of detention would seem not to admit of any exception in the fingerprinting context."[j]

2. *United States v. Dionisio,* p. 816, holds that the Fourth Amendment was not violated by subpoenaing witnesses to appear before a grand jury to give voice exemplars. No preliminary showing of "probable cause" or "reasonableness" is required in such a case, as: (a) "a subpoena to appear before a grand jury is not a 'seizure' in the Fourth Amendment sense," and thus "*Davis* is plainly inapposite"; and (b) the requirement that the witness give exemplars does not infringe upon Fourth Amendment rights, as "the physical characteristics of a person's voice, its tone and manner, as opposed to the content of a specific conversation, are constantly exposed to the public," so that "no person can have a reasonable expectation that others will not know the sound of his voice." *United States v. Mara,* p. 819 fn. e, reached the same result as to the subpoenaing of a witness to give handwriting exemplars.

3. In DUNAWAY v. NEW YORK, 442 U.S. 200 (1979), the police, lacking grounds to arrest petitioner but suspecting he was implicated in an attempted robbery and homicide, had him "picked up" for questioning. He was placed in an interrogation room at police headquarters, where he was questioned by officers after being given the *Miranda* warnings. Petitioner waived counsel and within an hour gave incriminating statements. His conviction following a trial at which those statements were admitted was affirmed by the state court on the ground that officers "may detain an individual upon reasonable suspicion for questioning for a reasonable and brief period of time under carefully controlled conditions which are ample to protect the individual's Fifth and Sixth Amendment Rights." The Supreme Court, per Brennan, J., reversed:

"In contrast to the brief and narrowly circumscribed intrusions involved in [*Terry* and its progeny], the detention of petitioner was in important respects indistinguishable from a traditional arrest. Petitioner was not questioned briefly where he was found. Instead, he was taken from a neighbor's home to a police car, transported to a police station, and placed in an interrogation room. He was never informed that he was 'free to go'; indeed, he would have been physically restrained if he had refused to accompany the officers or had tried to escape their custody. The application of the Fourth Amendment's requirement of probable cause does not depend on whether an intrusion of this magnitude is termed an 'arrest' under state law. The mere facts that petitioner was not told he was under arrest, was not 'booked,' and would not have had an arrest record if the

---

i. In *Wise v. Murphy,* 275 A.2d 205 (D.C.App.1971), the court noted the negative reference in *Davis* was only to an "improper line-up" and thus concluded that upon a proper showing, lacking in the instant case, a court could order a person to appear in a lineup even if grounds for arrest were lacking, at least for investigation of "serious felonies involving grave personal injuries."

j. *Davis* was reaffirmed in *Hayes v. Florida,* p. 437, where the Court again suggested "the Fourth Amendment might permit the judiciary to authorize the seizure of a person on less than probable cause and his removal to the police station for the purpose of fingerprinting."

A few jurisdictions have adopted statutes or rules of court which authorize brief detention at the station (usually pursuant to court order), on less than the grounds needed to arrest, for the purpose of conducting certain identification procedures. Such provisions have been upheld by the courts, and some other cases have upheld similar procedures even absent such a provision. See, e.g., *In re Fingerprinting of M.B.,* 309 A.2d 3 (N.J.Super.1973) (order requiring all 22 male members of eighth grade class to submit to fingerprinting affirmed where ring of that elementary school's graduating class found near body of homicide victim, and fingerprints other than those of victim found both inside and outside victim's vehicle).

interrogation had proved fruitless, * * * obviously do not make petitioner's seizure even roughly analogous to the narrowly defined intrusions involved in *Terry* and its progeny. Indeed, any 'exception' that could cover a seizure as intrusive as that in this case would threaten to swallow the general rule that Fourth Amendment seizures are 'reasonable' only if based on probable cause. * * *

"In effect, respondents urge us to adopt a multifactor balancing test of 'reasonable police conduct under the circumstances' to cover all seizures that do not amount to technical arrests. But the protections intended by the Framers could all too easily disappear in the consideration and balancing of the multifarious circumstances presented by different cases, especially when that balancing may be done in the first instance by police officers engaged in the 'often competitive enterprise of ferreting out crime.' A single, familiar standard is essential to guide police officers, who have only limited time and expertise to reflect on and balance the social and individual interests involved in the specific circumstances they confront. Indeed, our recognition of these dangers, and our consequent reluctance to depart from the proven protections afforded by the general rule, is reflected in the narrow limitations emphasized in the cases employing the balancing test. For all but those narrowly defined intrusions, the requisite 'balancing' has been performed in centuries of precedent and is embodied in the principle that seizures are 'reasonable' only if supported by probable cause."

SECTION 9.　ADMINISTRATIVE INSPECTIONS AND REGULATORY SEARCHES: MORE ON BALANCING THE NEED AGAINST THE INVASION OF PRIVACY

The Supreme Court has upheld a rather broad range of searches and seizures even when conducted without the traditional quantum of probable cause. These decisions manifest further application of the *Camara* balancing test, also used by the Court in *Terry,* p. 408, to assay the discrete police practice of stop-and-frisk. But *Camara* itself was an administrative inspection type of case, and thus it is not surprising that this balancing process has since been utilized most often regarding various other administrative inspections and regulatory searches, where the Court has often emphasized certain "special needs" beyond those present in the more typical law enforcement context.[a]

Collectively, the cases briefly summarized below reflect two kinds of departures from the traditional probable cause requirement. One, as in *Terry,* is to require individualized suspicion (typically referred to as reasonable suspicion) less compelling than is needed for the usual arrest or search. (In contrast to the rule in a regular law enforcement context, see *Ybarra,* p. 324, and *Hicks,* p. 368, such reasonable suspicion sometimes suffices even to search for incriminating evidence.) Another kind of departure is to require no individualized suspicion whatsoever, but instead to require that the seizure or search be conducted pursuant to some neutral criteria which guard against arbitrary selection of those subjected to such procedures (similar to the impoundment-inventory process approved in *Bertine,* p. 407). But in *Samson,* p. 444, neither reasonable suspicion nor neutral criteria were required!

1.　*Safety inspections*. In *Camara v. Municipal Court,* 387 U.S. 523 (1967), dealing with fire, health, and housing code inspection programs directed at

---

a. For a thoughtful assessment of the Supreme Court's decisions in this area, see Eve Brensike Primus, *Disentangling Administrative Searches,* 111 Colum.L.Rev. 254 (2011).

dwellings, the Court concluded that if an occupant did not consent to an inspection the authorities would ordinarily have to get a warrant,[b] but "that 'probable cause' to issue a warrant to inspect must exist if reasonable legislative or administrative standards for conducting an area inspection are satisfied with respect to a particular dwelling. Such standards, which will vary with the municipal program being enforced, may be based upon the passage of time, the nature of the building (e.g., a multi-family apartment house), or the condition of the entire area, but they will not necessarily depend upon specific knowledge of the condition of the particular dwelling." Among the "persuasive factors" identified by the Court "to support the reasonableness of area code-enforcement inspections" were (i) doubt "that any other canvassing technique would achieve acceptable results," and (ii) that the contemplated inspections "involve a relatively limited invasion of the urban citizen's privacy" as compared to execution of the more traditional search warrant.[c]

A *Camara*-type warrant "showing that a specific business has been chosen * * * on the basis of a general administrative plan * * * derived from neutral sources" also suffices for inspection of business premises. *Marshall v. Barlow's, Inc.,* 436 U.S. 307 (1978). But the Court has often upheld warrantless business inspections by emphasizing the "closely regulated" nature of the business and that the inspection permitted by statute or regulations is "carefully limited in time, place, and scope," as in *New York v. Burger,* 482 U.S. 691 (1987). In *Burger,* the Court upheld such warrantless inspections of junkyards even though the administrative scheme concerned a social problem (stolen property) also addressed in the penal law, police officers were allowed to make the inspections, and the inspections would often uncover evidence of crime.

2. Border searches. In *United States v. Ramsey,* 431 U.S. 606 (1977), upholding a customs inspection of mail entering the United States (which, by regulation, could not extend to reading of correspondence), the Court stressed (i) that the search was constitutional under the longstanding rule generally applicable to border searches, namely, that such searches are "considered to be 'reasonable' by the single fact that the person or item in question had entered into our country from outside"; and (ii) that the lower court was wrong in concluding a warrant would be needed as to mail, for "the 'border search' exception is not based on the doctrine of 'exigent circumstances' at all."

As for nonroutine border inspections, lower courts have generally held that "a real suspicion" is needed for a strip search, and the "clear indication" of *Schmerber,* p. 30, for a body cavity search. See, e.g., *Henderson v. United States,*

---

b. Three dissenters objected: "This boxcar warrant will be identical as to every dwelling in the area, save the street number itself. I daresay they will be printed up in pads of a thousand or more—with space for the street number to be inserted—and issued by magistrates in broadcast fashion as a matter of course."

c. Another type of safety inspection is that conducted after a fire. In *Michigan v. Clifford,* 464 U.S. 287 (1984), four Justices concluded that a burning building creates exigent circumstances justifying authorities to enter to fight the blaze and to remain a reasonable time to investigate the cause of the fire, but that later entries without consent require a warrant—an administrative warrant "to determine the cause and origin of a recent fire" on the showing "that a fire of undetermined origin has occurred on the premises, that the scope of the proposed search is reasonable and will not intrude unnecessarily on the fire victim's privacy, and that the search will be executed at a reasonable and convenient time"; or a conventional search warrant on probable cause if the "primary objective of the search is to gather evidence of criminal activity." A fifth Justice, concurring, opined that a "traditional criminal search warrant" should be required for any later entry without advance notice to the owner. The four dissenters agreed that a conventional warrant was required to search the balance of the home, but declared that a warrantless inspection of the fire scene was permissible because "the utility of requiring a magistrate to evaluate the grounds for a search following a fire is so limited that the incidental protection of an individual's privacy interests simply does not justify imposing a warrant requirement."

390 F.2d 805 (9th Cir.1967). In *United States v. Montoya de Hernandez,* 473 U.S. 531 (1985), the Court held that when customs agents "reasonably suspect that the traveler is smuggling contraband in her alimentary canal" she may be detained so long as is "necessary to either verify or dispel the suspicion" (i.e., if the suspect declines to submit to an x-ray, until a bowel movement occurs).

"But the reasons that might support a requirement of some level of suspicion in the case of highly intrusive searches of the person—dignity and privacy interests of the person being searched—simply do not carry over to vehicles," and thus removal and disassembling of a vehicle's gas tank does not require reasonable suspicion, though "it may be true that some searches of property are so destructive as to require a different result." *United States v. Flores–Montano,* 541 U.S. 149 (2004).

In light of *Flores-Montano,* what then of a customs search into electronic files in a laptop or other personal electronic storage device? This was the question in *United States v. Arnold,* 533 F.3d 1003 (9th Cir.2008), where the court held such searches may be conducted without reasonable suspicion. The defendant attempted to distinguish *Flores-Montano* "by distinguishing between one's privacy interest in a vehicle compared to a laptop," but the court responded that the Supreme Court's analysis in *Flores-Montano* "was not based on the unique characteristics of vehicles with respect to other property, but was based on the fact that a vehicle, as a piece of property, simply does not implicate the same 'dignity and privacy' concerns as 'highly intrusive searches of the person.' "

    3. *Vehicle checkpoints.* In a series of cases dealing with the stopping of vehicles away from the border to see if they were occupied by illegal aliens, the Court held that while roving patrols could stop and search vehicles for illegal aliens only on probable cause, *Almeida–Sanchez v. United States,* 413 U.S. 266 (1973), only *Terry*-type reasonable suspicion was needed for such patrols to engage in the more "modest" interference with Fourth Amendment interests which attends the stopping of motorists and inquiring briefly as to their residential status. Even at a permanent checkpoint away from the border, search of a vehicle for aliens is not permissible absent probable cause, *United States v. Ortiz,* 422 U.S. 891 (1975), but the brief questioning of vehicle occupants at such checkpoints is permissible without any individualized suspicion whatsoever. *United States v. Martinez–Fuerte,* 428 U.S. 543 (1976). As to the latter practice, the Court emphasized (i) that "the potential interference with legitimate traffic is minimal"; and (ii) that such checkpoint operations "involve less discretionary enforcement activity," as "the officer may stop only those cars passing the checkpoint," which "is not chosen by officers in the field, but by officials responsible for making overall decisions as to the most effective allocation of limited enforcement resources."[d] The Court in *Martinez–Fuerte* also concluded that if more than the briefest inquiry was needed in a particular instance the vehicle could be referred to a secondary inspection area "on the basis of criteria that would not sustain a roving-patrol stop."

    Consistent with those cases, the Court held in *Delaware v. Prouse,* 440 U.S. 648 (1979), that absent reasonable suspicion the police may not stop individual vehicles for the purpose of checking the driver's license and the registration of the automobile. But the Court stressed it was not precluding states "from developing methods for spot checks that involve less intrusion or that do not involve the

---

    d. The Court also rejected the argument "that routine stops at a checkpoint are permissible only if a warrant has given judicial authorization to the particular checkpoint location." As for defendant's reliance on *Camara* in this connection, the Court answered that there but not here a warrant was necessary to provide assurance to the individual involved that the government agent was acting under proper authorization.

unconstrained exercise of discretion," and gave as "one possible alternative" the "questioning of all oncoming traffic at roadblock-type stops."

Then came *Michigan Dep't of State Police v. Sitz*, 496 U.S. 444 (1990), upholding the sobriety checkpoint program there at issue. Important ingredients in that conclusion were: (i) the intrusion upon motorists is "slight"; (ii) the program sufficiently limited officers' discretion, as "checkpoints are selected pursuant to [established] guidelines, and uniformed police officers stop every approaching vehicle"; (iii) the program addressed the very serious "drunken driving problem"; and (iv) there was support in the record for the law enforcement judgment that such checkpoints were among the "reasonable alternatives" available for dealing with that problem. The Court emphasized it was addressing "only the initial stop of each motorist passing through a checkpoint and the associated preliminary questioning and observation by checkpoint officers," and cautioned that "detention of particular motorists for more extensive field sobriety testing may require satisfaction of an individualized suspicion standard."

4. *Terrorist checkpoints.* In the post–9/11 era, courts have upheld checkpoints involving searches directed at those using public facilities deemed likely terrorist targets, including the airport checkpoint system in which all passengers must present sufficient identification, *Gilmore v. Gonzales*, 435 F.3d 1125 (9th Cir.2006), passengers and luggage are subjected to routine x-ray and magnetometer checks and closer scrutiny under suspicious circumstances, *United States v. Hartwell*, 436 F.3d 174 (3d Cir.2006), and some passengers are randomly selected for more intense scrutiny, *United States v. Marquez*, 410 F.3d 612 (9th Cir.2005).

See also *MacWade v. Kelly*, 460 F.3d 260 (2d Cir.2006) (upholding search of backpacks and other containers large enough to hold explosive device carried by those entering New York City subway system, court balances these considerations: (1) the threat was "sufficiently immediate," considering "the thwarted plots to bomb New York City's subway system, its continued desirability as a target, and the recent bombing of public transportation systems" elsewhere; (2) a "subway rider has a full expectation of privacy in his containers"; (3) the searches are "minimally intrusive," considering the advance notice, the limited examination of containers that lasts only seconds and occurs "out in the open," with police exercising "no discretion in selecting whom to search," and (4) the program is "reasonably effective," as "the expert testimony established that terrorists seek predictable and vulnerable targets, and the Program generates uncertainty that frustrates that goal, which, in turn, deters an attack"); *Cassidy v. Chertoff*, 471 F.3d 67 (2d Cir.2006) (similar analysis used in upholding search of backpacks and vehicle trunks on large passenger/vehicle ferries; searches were "random" but not alleged to be carried out in "a discriminatory or arbitrary manner").

5. *Search of students.* Utilizing the *Camara* balancing test, the Court in *New Jersey v. T.L.O.*, 469 U.S. 325 (1985), struck "the balance between the school child's legitimate expectations of privacy and the school's equally legitimate needs to maintain an environment in which learning can take place" by holding: (i) "that school officials need not obtain a warrant before searching a student who is under their authority"; (ii) that ordinarily "a search of a student by a teacher or other school official will be 'justified at its inception' when there are reasonable grounds for suspecting that the search will turn up evidence that the student has violated or is violating either the law or the rules of the school"; and (iii) that such a search "will be permissible in its scope when the measures adopted are reasonably related to the objectives of the search and not excessively intrusive in light of the age and sex of the student and the nature of the infraction."

The "scope" limitation of *T.L.O.* was applied in *Safford Unified School District #1 v. Redding*, 129 S.Ct. 2633 (2009). A student told school officials she had received pain relief pills, banned under school rules, from her 13-year-old classmate Savana. This, the Court concluded, provided reasonable suspicion "that Savana was involved in pill distribution," which was "enough to justify a search of Savana's backpack and outer clothing," as "[i]f a student is reasonably suspected of giving out contraband pills, she is reasonably suspected of carrying them." When that search was unproductive, school officials undertook what the Court characterized as a "strip search" by requiring Savana "to remove her clothes down to her underwear, and then 'pull out' her bra and the elastic band on her underpants." which "necessarily exposed her breasts and pelvic area to some degree." Such a search, the Court concluded, was "categorically distinct, requiring distinct elements of justification" absent in the instant case because "the content of the suspicion failed to match the degree of intrusion." Specifically, "what was missing from the suspected facts * * * was any indication of danger to the students from the power of the drugs or their quantity, and any reason to suppose that Savana was carrying pills in her underwear." The "combination of these deficiencies was fatal to finding the search reasonable," as the *T.L.O.* scope requirement mandates that for a strip search there be "reasonable suspicion of danger or of resort to underwear for hiding evidence of wrongdoing." (Thomas, J., dissenting, objected that the majority had imposed "a vague and amorphous standard on school administrators.")

6. *Drug testing.* While lower courts have approved government-mandated drug testing of government or private employees upon individualized reasonable suspicion, two programs not requiring such suspicion have been upheld by the Supreme Court. In *National Treasury Employees Union v. Von Raab*, 489 U.S. 656 (1989), the Court held "that the suspicionless testing of employees who apply for promotion to positions directly involving the interdiction of illegal drugs, or to positions which require the incumbent to carry a firearm, is reasonable." The Court reasoned that because the testing program at issue "is not designed to serve the ordinary needs of law enforcement," a balancing process was proper, in which the "Government's compelling interests in preventing the promotion of drug users to positions where they might endanger the integrity of our Nation's borders or the life of the citizenry" outweighed the "diminished expectation of privacy" of "those who seek promotion to these positions."[e]

By similar balancing, the Court in *Skinner v. Railway Labor Executives' Ass'n,* 489 U.S. 602 (1989), upheld blood and urine testing of railroad employees following major train accidents or incidents and the breath and urine testing of railroad employees who violate certain safety rules. In allowing such testing even "in the absence of * * * reasonable suspicion that any particular employee may be impaired," the Court emphasized (i) the special danger presented by the performance of "certain sensitive tasks while under the influence"; (ii) the "diminished expectation of privacy that attaches to information pertaining to the fitness of covered employees"; and (iii) "the limited discretion" railroad employers had regarding who and when to test.[f]

---

e. Two Justices who joined the Court's decision in *Skinner* because of "the demonstrated frequency of drug and alcohol use by the targeted class of employees, and the demonstrated connection between such use and grave harm," dissented in *Von Raab* because the government was unable to cite "even a single instance" of such use or connection to harm.

f. Compare *Chandler v. Miller,* 520 U.S. 305 (1997), invalidating a Georgia statute requiring each candidate for public office to submit to drug testing, where the Court stated: "Georgia asserts no evidence of a drug problem among the State's elected officials, those officials typically do not perform high-risk, safety-sensitive tasks, and the required certification immediately aids no interdiction effort. The need revealed, in short, is symbolic, not 'special,' as that term draws meaning from our case law." As for the state's reliance on *Von Raab,* the Court noted that there the affected employees and their work product were not amenable to "day-to-day scrutiny," and then concluded: "Candidates for public office, in contrast, are subject to relentless scrutiny—by

In *Board of Education of Independent School District No. 92 of Pottawatomie County v. Earls,* 536 U.S. 822 (2002), the Court upheld, 5–4, a random testing policy applicable to middle and high school students participating in any extracurricular activity. The majority reasoned: (a) all students who "voluntarily subject themselves" to additional regulations by opting for extracurricular activities have as a consequence "a limited expectation of privacy"; (b) as for the "nature and immediacy of the government's concern," it suffices that "the nationwide epidemic makes the war against drugs a pressing concern in every school" and that, in addition, there was "specific evidence of drug use" at the schools; and (c) as for the efficacy of the policy in meeting the government's concerns, the policy in question "is a reasonably effective means of * * * preventing, deterring, and detecting drug use."

In *Earls,* the Court stressed the limited privacy intrusion under the challenged policy, which "allow[s] male students to produce their sample behind a closed stall." Compare *Norris v. Premier Integrity Solutions, Inc.,* 641 F.3d 695 (6th Cir.2011) (upholding direct-observation testing of pretrial releasees, as the "record shows that it is easy and widespread for people providing urine for drug testing to substitute false or inaccurate specimens and that only the direct observation method of obtaining such samples is fully effective 'to prevent cheating on drug tests' ").

7. Supervision of probationers and parolees; "special needs" vs. balancing of interests

SAMSON v. CALIFORNIA
843 U.S. 547, 126 S.Ct. 2193, 165 L.Ed.2d 250 (2006).

JUSTICE THOMAS delivered the opinion of the Court.

[Samson, on state parole in California following a conviction for being a felon in possession of a firearm, was observed by Officer Rohleder as he was walking down the street. Rohleder stopped him and asked whether he had an outstanding parole warrant; Samson said he did not, which Rohleder confirmed by radio dispatch. Nevertheless, pursuant to a state law providing that every prisoner released on parole "shall agree in writing to be subject to search or seizure by a parole officer or other peace officer at any time of the day or night, with or without a search warrant and with or without cause," and based solely on Samson's status as a parolee, Rohleder searched him and found methamphetamine on his person. At Samson's possession trial, his motion to suppress was denied; he was convicted and sentenced to seven years' imprisonment. The California Court of Appeal affirmed, holding that suspicionless searches of parolees are lawful under California law; that " '[s]uch a search is reasonable within the meaning of the Fourth Amendment as long as it is not arbitrary, capricious or harassing' "; and that the search in this case was not arbitrary, capricious, or harassing.]

We granted certiorari to answer a variation of the question this Court left open in *United States v. Knights,* 534 U.S. 112 (2001)—whether a condition of release can so diminish or eliminate a released prisoner's reasonable expectation of privacy that a suspicionless search by a law enforcement officer would not offend the Fourth Amendment. Answering that question in the affirmative today, we affirm the judgment of the California Court of Appeal.

"[U]nder our general Fourth Amendment approach" we "examin[e] the totality of the circumstances" to determine whether a search is reasonable within

---

their peers, the public, and the press. Their day-to-day conduct attracts attention notable beyond the norm in ordinary work environments."

the meaning of the Fourth Amendment. Whether a search is reasonable "is determined by assessing, on the one hand, the degree to which it intrudes upon an individual's privacy and, on the other, the degree to which it is needed for the promotion of legitimate governmental interests."

We recently applied this approach in *United States v. Knights*. In that case, California law required Knights, as a probationer, to " '[s]ubmit his ... person, property, place of residence, vehicle, personal effects, to search anytime, with or without a search warrant, warrant of arrest or reasonable cause by any probation officer or law enforcement officer.' " Several days after Knights had been placed on probation, police suspected that he had been involved in several incidents of arson and vandalism. Based upon that suspicion and pursuant to the search condition of his probation, a police officer conducted a warrantless search of Knights' apartment and found arson and drug paraphernalia.

We concluded that the search of Knights' apartment was reasonable. In evaluating the degree of intrusion into Knights' privacy, we found Knights' probationary status "salient,", observing that "[p]robation is 'one point ... on a continuum of possible punishments ranging from solitary confinement in a maximum-security facility to a few hours of mandatory community service.' (quoting *Griffin v. Wisconsin,* 483 U.S. 868 (1987)). Cf. *Hudson v. Palmer*, [p. 272] (holding that prisoners have no reasonable expectation of privacy). We further observed that, by virtue of their status alone, probationers 'do not enjoy "the absolute liberty to which every citizen is entitled," ' " (quoting *Griffin,* in turn quoting *Morrissey v. Brewer*, [p. 94]), justifying the "impos[ition] [of] reasonable conditions that deprive the offender of some freedoms enjoyed by law-abiding citizens." We also considered the facts that Knights' probation order clearly set out the probation search condition, and that Knights was clearly informed of the condition. We concluded that under these circumstances, Knights' expectation of privacy was significantly diminished. We also concluded that probation searches, such as the search of Knights' apartment, are necessary to the promotion of legitimate governmental interests. Noting the State's dual interest in integrating probationers back into the community and combating recidivism, we credited the "assumption" that, by virtue of his status, a probationer "is more likely than the ordinary citizen to violate the law." We further found that "probationers have even more of an incentive to conceal their criminal activities and quickly dispose of incriminating evidence than the ordinary criminal because probationers are aware that they may be subject to supervision and face revocation of probation, and possible incarceration, in proceedings in which the trial rights of a jury and proof beyond a reasonable doubt, among other things, do not apply." We explained that the State did not have to ignore the reality of recidivism or suppress its interests in "protecting potential victims of criminal enterprise" for fear of running afoul of the Fourth Amendment.

Balancing these interests, we held that "[w]hen an officer has reasonable suspicion that a probationer subject to a search condition is engaged in criminal activity, there is enough likelihood that criminal conduct is occurring that an intrusion on the probationer's significantly diminished privacy interests is reasonable." Because the search at issue in *Knights* was predicated on both the probation search condition and reasonable suspicion, we did not reach the question whether the search would have been reasonable under the Fourth Amendment had it been solely predicated upon the condition of probation. Our attention is directed to that question today, albeit in the context of a parolee search.

As we noted in *Knights,* parolees are on the "continuum" of state-imposed punishments. On this continuum, parolees have fewer expectations of privacy than probationers, because parole is more akin to imprisonment than probation is to imprisonment. As this Court has pointed out, "parole is an established variation on imprisonment of convicted criminals.... The essence of parole is release from prison, before the completion of sentence, on the condition that the prisoner abides by certain rules during the balance of the sentence." "In most cases, the State is willing to extend parole only because it is able to condition it upon compliance with certain requirements." *Pennsylvania Bd. of Probation and Parole v. Scott,* [p. 247].[2]

California's system of parole is consistent with these observations: A California inmate may serve his parole period either in physical custody, or elect to complete his sentence out of physical custody and subject to certain conditions. Under the latter option, an inmate-turned-parolee remains in the legal custody of the California Department of Corrections through the remainder of his term, and must comply with all of the terms and conditions of parole, including mandatory drug tests, restrictions on association with felons or gang members, and mandatory meetings with parole officers. General conditions of parole also require a parolee to report to his assigned parole officer immediately upon release, inform the parole officer within 72 hours of any change in employment status, request permission to travel a distance of more than 50 miles from the parolee's home, and refrain from criminal conduct and possession of firearms, specified weapons, or knives unrelated to employment. Parolees may also be subject to special conditions, including psychiatric treatment programs, mandatory abstinence from alcohol, residence approval, and "[a]ny other condition deemed necessary by the Board [of Parole Hearings] or the Department [of Corrections and Rehabilitation] due to unusual circumstances." The extent and reach of these conditions clearly demonstrate that parolees like petitioner have severely diminished expectations of privacy by virtue of their status alone.

Additionally, as we found "salient" in *Knights* with respect to the probation search condition, the parole search condition under California law—requiring inmates who opt for parole to submit to suspicionless searches by a parole officer or other peace officer "at any time," Cal.Penal Code Ann. § 3067(a)—was "clearly expressed" to petitioner. He signed an order submitting to the condition and thus was "unambiguously" aware of it. In *Knights,* we found that acceptance of a clear and unambiguous search condition "significantly diminished Knights' reasonable expectation of privacy." Examining the totality of the circumstances pertaining to petitioner's status as a parolee, "an established variation on imprisonment," including the plain terms of the parole search condition, we conclude that petitioner did not have an expectation of privacy that society would recognize as legitimate.[3]

---

2. Contrary to the dissent's contention, nothing in our recognition that parolees are more akin to prisoners than probationers is inconsistent with our precedents. Nor, as the dissent suggests, do we equate parolees with prisoners for the purpose of concluding that parolees, like prisoners, have no Fourth Amendment rights. That view misperceives our holding. If that were the basis of our holding, then this case would have been resolved solely under *Hudson v. Palmer,* and there would have been no cause to resort to Fourth Amendment analysis. Nor is our rationale inconsistent with *Morrissey v. Brewer.* In that case, the Court recognized that restrictions on a parolee's liberty are not unqualified. That statement, even if accepted as a truism, sheds no light on the extent to which a parolee's constitutional rights are indeed limited-and no one argues that a parolee's constitutional rights are not limited. *Morrissey* itself does not cast doubt on today's holding given that the liberty at issue in that case-the Fourteenth Amendment Due Process right to a hearing before revocation of parole-invokes wholly different analysis than the search at issue here.

3. Because we find that the search at issue here is reasonable under our general Fourth Amendment approach, we need not reach the issue whether "acceptance of the search condition constituted consent in the *Schneckloth* [*v. Bustamonte,* p. 454] sense of a complete waiver of his Fourth Amendment rights." * * *

The State's interests, by contrast, are substantial. This Court has repeatedly acknowledged that a State has an "overwhelming interest" in supervising parolees because "parolees ... are more likely to commit future criminal offenses." *Pennsylvania Bd. of Probation and Parole* (explaining that the interest in combating recidivism "is the very premise behind the system of close parole supervision"). Similarly, this Court has repeatedly acknowledged that a State's interests in reducing recidivism and thereby promoting reintegration and positive citizenship among probationers and parolees warrant privacy intrusions that would not otherwise be tolerated under the Fourth Amendment.

The empirical evidence presented in this case clearly demonstrates the significance of these interests to the State of California. As of November 30, 2005, California had over 130,000 released parolees. California's parolee population has a 68–to–70 percent recidivism rate. This Court has acknowledged the grave safety concerns that attend recidivism. See *Ewing v. California,* 538 U.S. 11 (2003) (plurality opinion) ("Recidivism is a serious public safety concern in California and throughout the Nation").

As we made clear in *Knights,* the Fourth Amendment does not render the States powerless to address these concerns *effectively.* Contrary to petitioner's contention, California's ability to conduct suspicionless searches of parolees serves its interest in reducing recidivism, in a manner that aids, rather than hinders, the reintegration of parolees into productive society.

In California, an eligible inmate serving a determinate sentence may elect parole when the actual days he has served plus statutory time credits equal the term imposed by the trial court, irrespective of whether the inmate is capable of integrating himself back into productive society. As the recidivism rate demonstrates, most parolees are ill prepared to handle the pressures of reintegration. Thus, most parolees require intense supervision. The California Legislature has concluded that, given the number of inmates the State paroles and its high recidivism rate, a requirement that searches be based on individualized suspicion would undermine the State's ability to effectively supervise parolees and protect the public from criminal acts by reoffenders. This conclusion makes eminent sense. Imposing a reasonable suspicion requirement, as urged by petitioner, would give parolees greater opportunity to anticipate searches and conceal criminality. This Court concluded that the incentive-to-conceal concern justified an "intensive" system for supervising probationers in *Griffin.* That concern applies with even greater force to a system of supervising parolees.

Petitioner observes that the majority of States and the Federal Government have been able to further similar interests in reducing recidivism and promoting re-integration, despite having systems that permit parolee searches based upon some level of suspicion. Thus, petitioner contends, California's system is constitutionally defective by comparison. Petitioner's reliance on the practices of jurisdictions other than California, however, is misplaced. That some States and the Federal Government require a level of individualized suspicion is of little relevance to our determination whether California's supervisory system is drawn to meet its needs and is reasonable, taking into account a parolee's substantially diminished expectation of privacy.[4]

Nor do we address whether California's parole search condition is justified as a special need under *Griffin v. Wisconsin,* because our holding under general Fourth Amendment principles renders such an examination unnecessary.

4. The dissent argues that, "once one acknowledges that parolees do have legitimate expectations of privacy beyond those of prisoners, our Fourth Amendment jurisprudence does not permit the conclusion, reached by the Court here for the first time, that a search supported by neither individualized suspicion nor 'special needs' is nonetheless 'reasonable.' " That simply is not the case. The touchstone of the Fourth Amendment is reasonableness, not individualized suspicion.

Nor is there merit to the argument that California's parole search law permits "a blanket grant of discretion untethered by any procedural safeguards" (Stevens, J., dissenting). The concern that California's suspicionless search system gives officers unbridled discretion to conduct searches, thereby inflicting dignitary harms that arouse strong resentment in parolees and undermine their ability to reintegrate into productive society, is belied by California's prohibition on "arbitrary, capricious or harassing" searches.[5] The dissent's claim that parolees under California law are subject to capricious searches conducted at the unchecked "whim" of law enforcement officers, ignores this prohibition. Likewise, petitioner's concern that California's suspicionless search law frustrates reintegration efforts by permitting intrusions into the privacy interests of third parties is also unavailing because that concern would arise under a suspicion-based regime as well.

Thus, we conclude that the Fourth Amendment does not prohibit a police officer from conducting a suspicionless search of a parolee. Accordingly, we affirm the judgment of the California Court of Appeal.

JUSTICE STEVENS, with whom JUSTICE SOUTER and JUSTICE BREYER join, dissenting.

Our prior cases have consistently assumed that the Fourth Amendment provides some degree of protection for probationers and parolees. The protection is not as robust as that afforded to ordinary citizens; we have held that probationers' lowered expectation of privacy may justify their warrantless search upon reasonable suspicion of wrongdoing, see *United States v. Knights*. We have also recognized that the supervisory responsibilities of probation officers, who are required to provide " 'individualized counseling' " and to monitor their charges' progress, *Griffin v. Wisconsin*, and who are in a unique position to judge "how close a supervision the probationer requires," *id.*, may give rise to special needs justifying departures from Fourth Amendment strictures. See *ibid.* ("Although a probation officer is not an impartial magistrate, neither is he the police officer who normally conducts searches against the ordinary citizen"). But neither *Knights* nor *Griffin* supports a regime of suspicionless searches, conducted pursuant to a blanket grant of discretion untethered by any procedural safeguards, by law enforcement personnel who have no special interest in the welfare of the parolee or probationer. * * *

The suspicionless search is the very evil the Fourth Amendment was intended to stamp out. The pre-Revolutionary "writs of assistance," which permitted roving searches for contraband, were reviled precisely because they "placed 'the liberty of every man in the hands of every petty officer.' " While individualized suspicion "is not an 'irreducible' component of reasonableness" under the Fourth Amendment, the requirement has been dispensed with only when programmatic searches were

---

Thus, while this Court's jurisprudence has often recognized that "to accommodate public and private interests some quantum of individualized suspicion is usually a prerequisite to a constitutional search or seizure," *United States v. Martinez–Fuerte*, [p. 441], we have also recognized that the "Fourth Amendment imposes no irreducible requirement of such suspicion," *id*. Therefore, although this Court has only sanctioned suspicionless searches in limited circumstances, namely programmatic and special needs searches, we have never held that these are the only limited circumstances in which searches absent individualized suspicion could be "reasonable" under the Fourth Amendment. In light of California's earnest concerns respecting recidivism, public safety, and reintegration of parolees into productive society, and because the object of the Fourth Amendment is *reasonableness,* our decision today is far from remarkable. Nor, given our prior precedents and caveats, is it "unprecedented."

5. Under California precedent, we note, an officer would not act reasonably in conducting a suspicionless search absent knowledge that the person stopped for the search is a parolee. See *People v. Sanders,* 73 P.3d 496, 505–506 (Cal.2003).

required to meet a " 'special need' . . . divorced from the State's general interest in law enforcement." *Ferguson v. Charleston,* 532 U.S. 67 (2001).[a]

Not surprisingly, the majority does not seek to justify the search of petitioner on "special needs" grounds. Although the Court has in the past relied on special needs to uphold warrantless searches of probationers, [*Griffin*], it has never gone so far as to hold that a probationer or parolee may be subjected to full search at the whim of any law enforcement officer he happens to encounter, whether or not the officer has reason to suspect him of wrongdoing. *Griffin,* after all, involved a search *by a probation officer* that was supported by *reasonable suspicion*. The special role of probation officers was critical to the analysis; "we deal with a situation," the Court explained, "in which there is an ongoing supervisory relationship—and one that is not, or at least not entirely, adversarial—between the object of the search and the decisionmaker." The State's interest or "special need," as articulated in *Griffin,* was an interest in supervising the wayward probationer's reintegration into society—not, or at least not principally, the general law enforcement goal of detecting crime.[1]

It is no accident, then, that when we later upheld the search of a probationer *by a law enforcement officer* (again, based on reasonable suspicion), we forwent any reliance on the special needs doctrine. See *Knights.* Even if the supervisory relationship between a probation officer and her charge may properly be characterized as one giving rise to needs "divorced from the State's general interest in law enforcement," *Ferguson,* the relationship between an ordinary law enforcement officer and a probationer unknown to him may not. "None of our special needs precedents has sanctioned the routine inclusion of law enforcement, both in the design of the policy and in using arrests, either threatened or real, to implement the system designed for the special needs objectives."

Ignoring just how "closely guarded" is that "category of constitutionally permissible suspicionless searches," the Court for the first time upholds an entirely suspicionless search unsupported by any special need. And it goes further: In special needs cases we have at least insisted upon programmatic safeguards designed to ensure evenhandedness in application; if individualized suspicion is to be jettisoned, it must be replaced with measures to protect against the state actor's unfettered discretion. Here, by contrast, there are no policies in place—no "standards, guidelines, or procedures"—to rein in officers and furnish a bulwark against the arbitrary exercise of discretion that is the height of unreasonableness.

The Court is able to make this unprecedented move only by making another. Coupling the dubious holding of *Hudson v. Palmer* with the bald statement that "parolees have fewer expectations of privacy than probationers," the Court two-

---

a. Similarly, in *City of Indianapolis v. Edmond,* 531 U.S. 32 (2000), the Court struck down the use of vehicle checkpoints to interdict unlawful drugs, distinguishing the checkpoint cases in Note 3, p. 441, because in none of them "did we indicate approval of a checkpoint program whose primary purpose was to detect evidence of ordinary criminal wrongdoing."

1. As we observed in *Ferguson v. Charleston, Griffin's* special needs rationale was cast into doubt by our later decision in *Skinner v. Railway Labor Executives' Assn.,* [p. 443], which reserved the question whether " 'routine use in criminal prosecutions of evidence obtained pursuant to the administrative scheme would give rise to an inference of pretext, or otherwise impugn the administrative nature of the . . . program.' " But at least the State in *Griffin* could in good faith contend that its warrantless searches were supported by a special need conceptually distinct from law enforcement goals generally. Indeed, that a State's interest in supervising its parolees and probationers to ensure their smooth reintegration may occasionally diverge from its general law enforcement aims is illustrated by this very case. Petitioner's possession of a small amount of illegal drugs would not have been grounds for revocation of his parole. See Cal.Penal Code Ann. § 3063.1(a). Presumably, the California Legislature determined that it is unnecessary and perhaps even counterproductive, as a means of furthering the goals of the parole system, to reincarcerate former prisoners for simple possession. The general law enforcement interests the State espouses, by contrast, call for reincarceration.

steps its way through a faulty syllogism and, thus, avoids the application of Fourth Amendment principles altogether. The logic, apparently, is this: Prisoners have no legitimate expectation of privacy; parolees are like prisoners; therefore, parolees have no legitimate expectation of privacy. The conclusion is remarkable not least because we have long embraced its opposite.[2] It also rests on false premises. First, it is simply not true that a parolee's status, vis-à-vis either the State or the Constitution, is tantamount to that of a prisoner or even materially distinct from that of a probationer. See *Morrissey v. Brewer* ("Though the State properly subjects [a parolee] to many restrictions not applicable to other citizens, his condition is very different from that of confinement in a prison"). A parolee, like a probationer, is set free in the world subject to restrictions intended to facilitate supervision and guard against antisocial behavior. As with probation, "the State is willing to extend parole only because it is able to condition it upon compliance with certain requirements." *Pennsylvania Bd. of Probation and Parole v. Scott.* Certainly, parole differs from probation insofar as parole is " 'meted out in addition to, not in lieu of, incarceration.' " And, certainly, parolees typically will have committed more serious crimes—ones warranting a prior term of imprisonment—than probationers. The latter distinction, perhaps, would support the conclusion that a State has a stronger interest in supervising parolees than it does in supervising probationers. But why either distinction should result in refusal to acknowledge as legitimate, when harbored by parolees, the same expectation of privacy that probationers reasonably may harbor is beyond fathom.

In any event, the notion that a parolee legitimately expects only so much privacy as a prisoner is utterly without foundation. *Hudson v. Palmer* does stand for the proposition that "[a] right of privacy in traditional Fourth Amendment terms" is denied individuals who are incarcerated. But this is because it "is necessary, as a practical matter, to accommodate a myriad of 'institutional needs and objectives' of prison facilities, ... chief among which is internal security."[3] These "institutional needs"—safety of inmates and guards, "internal order," and sanitation—manifestly do not apply to parolees. As discussed above and in *Griffin, other* state interests may warrant certain intrusions into a parolee's privacy, but *Hudson's* rationale cannot be mapped blindly onto the situation with which we are presented in this case.

Nor is it enough, in deciding whether someone's expectation of privacy is "legitimate," to rely on the existence of the offending condition or the individual's notice thereof. The Court's reasoning in this respect is entirely circular. The mere fact that a particular State refuses to acknowledge a parolee's privacy interest cannot mean that a parolee in that State has no expectation of privacy that society is willing to recognize as legitimate—specially when the measure that invades privacy is both the *subject* of the Fourth Amendment challenge and a clear outlier. With only one or two arguable exceptions, neither the Federal Government nor any other State subjects parolees to searches of the kind to which petitioner was subjected. And the fact of notice hardly cures the circularity; the loss of a subjective expectation of privacy would play "no meaningful role" in analyzing the legitimacy of expectations, for example, "if the Government were suddenly to announce on nationwide television that all homes henceforth would be subject to warrantless entry."[4] * * *

---

2. See *Morrissey v. Brewer* ("[T]he liberty of a parolee, although indeterminate, includes many of the core values of unqualified liberty"); *Griffin v. Wisconsin* (the "degree of impingement upon [a probationer's] privacy ... is not unlimited").

3. Particularly in view of Justice O'Connor's concurrence, which emphasized the prison's programmatic interests in conducting suspicionless searches, *Hudson* is probably best understood as a "special needs" case-not as standing for the blanket proposition that prisoners have no Fourth Amendment rights.

4. Likewise, the State's argument that a California parolee "consents" to the suspicionless search condition is sophistry. Whether or not a prisoner can choose to remain in prison rather

Had the State imposed as a condition of parole a requirement that petitioner submit to random searches by his parole officer, who is "supposed to have in mind the welfare of the [parolee]" and guide the parolee's transition back into society, *Griffin,* the condition might have been justified either under the special needs doctrine or because at least part of the requisite "reasonable suspicion" is supplied in this context by the individual-specific knowledge gained through the supervisory relationship. Likewise, this might have been a different case had a court or parole board imposed the condition at issue based on specific knowledge of the individual's criminal history and projected likelihood of reoffending, or if the State had had in place programmatic safeguards to ensure evenhandedness. Under either of those scenarios, the State would at least have gone some way toward averting the greatest mischief wrought by officials' unfettered discretion. But the search condition here is imposed on *all* parolees—whatever the nature of their crimes, whatever their likelihood of recidivism, and whatever their supervisory needs—without any programmatic procedural protections.[6] * * *

NOTES AND QUESTIONS

1. "In *Samson,* the Court suggested a distinction between parole and probation,* * * but did not indicate whether it would have used a different analysis if the defendant had not been a parolee." *United States v. Weikert,* 504 F.3d 1 (1st Cir.2007). Could/should *Samson* be deemed equally applicable to probationers?

To what extent is *Samson* readily "exportable"? That is, given the Court's balancing approach, to what extent (if at all) are California "facts" and California "law" essential to the outcome? Could a state which does not have a parolee recidivism rate anywhere near California's 68–70% opt for suspicionless searches? Could a state without California's statutory prohibition on "arbitrary, capricious or harassing" parolee searches do so? Or, to put the latter question a different way, is that prohibition actually a part of the Fourth Amendment requirement, a necessary condition whenever suspicionless searches are allowed? Consider the application of *Whren,* p. 353, as construed in *Ashcroft,* p. 358, in this context.

2. The *Samson* majority says the dissent is wrong in saying the Court is upholding "a blanket grant of discretion untethered by any procedural safeguards," because in fact officers lack "unbridled discretion" in light of the state prohibition on "arbitrary, capricious or harassing" searches. But just how much distance, if any, is there between a search made without suspicion (and without adherence to any neutral criteria) and one made in an arbitrary or capricious manner? What is the proper characterization of the *Samson* case itself, as described by the California court? The officer saw "two adults and a little baby walking down the street," recognized one of the adults as a parolee he had "heard" "might have a parolee at large warrant," checked and found there was no

---

than be released on parole, he has no "choice" concerning the search condition; he may either remain in prison, where he will be subjected to suspicionless searches, or he may exit prison and still be subject to suspicionless searches. Accordingly, "to speak of consent in this context is to resort to a manifest fiction, for the [parolee] who purportedly waives his rights by accepting such a condition has little genuine option to refuse." 5 W. LaFave, *Search and Seizure: A Treatise on the Fourth Amendment* § 10.10(b), pp. 440–441 (4th ed.2004).

6. The Court devotes a good portion of its analysis to the recidivism rates among parolees in California. One might question whether those statistics, which postdate the California Supreme Court's decision to allow the purportedly recidivism-reducing suspicionless searches at issue here, actually demonstrate that the State's interest is being served by the searches. Of course, one cannot deny that the interest itself is valid. That said, though, it has never been held sufficient to justify suspicionless searches. If high crime rates were grounds enough for disposing of Fourth Amendment protections, the Amendment long ago would have become a dead letter.

warrant, "but nevertheless 'conducted a parolee search' " for the "sole reason * * * that defendant was 'on parole.' He * * * testified that he does not search all parolees 'all the time,' but does conduct parole searches 'on a regular basis' unless he has 'other work to do' or already 'dealt with' the parolee."

Regarding whether the *Samson* search complied with state law, the California court stated: "A search is arbitrary 'when the motivation for the search is unrelated to rehabilitative, reformative or legitimate law enforcement purposes, or when the search is motivated by personal animosity toward the parolee.' A search is a form of harassment when its motivation is a mere whim or caprice." "It may be unreasonable 'if made too often, or at an unreasonable hour, or if unreasonably prolonged.' We find nothing arbitrary or capricious in the search. * * * The testimony by Officer Rohleder that he customarily searches identified parolees does not demonstrate arbitrariness, and indicates that the search was not conducted by the officer for the purpose of harassment or due to any personal animosity toward defendant. Finally, the record shows that the search was not unreasonable in duration or the circumstances of its execution." *People v. Samson*, 2004 WL 2307111 (Cal.App.2004).

3. Both the majority and dissent in *Samson* take note of the "California precedent" that "an officer would not act reasonably in conducting a suspicionless search absent knowledge that the person stopped for the search is a parolee." Is that a Fourth Amendment limitation on suspicionless parolee searches, or should it suffice that the officer reasonably but mistakenly believed Samson was a parolee? Consider p. 464, fn. b. Is this yet another issue where the answer depends upon whether a "special needs" or "totality of the circumstances" balancing of interests approach is taken? Consider *United States v. Herrera*, 444 F.3d 1238 (10th Cir.2006) (officer's reasonable but mistaken belief that truck was a "commercial vehicle" subject to stopping for inspection, where in fact "it weighted 10,000 pounds, one pound short of the definition of a commercial vehicle" under the applicable law, did not make the stop lawful, as the controlling determination is that the owner/operator "had never chosen to engage in a pervasively regulated business and so, of course, had no notice or understanding that he could be subject to random warrantless seizures and inspections.")

The "California precedent" referred to in *Samson* dealt instead with situations where the officer had no belief or suspicion that the person he was searching was a probationer or parolee, but it turned out that the person did in fact have such status. If *Herrera* is correct, then isn't the other side of the coin the notion accepted in yet another California case, *In re Tyrell J.*, 876 P.2d 519 (Cal.1994), namely, that a probationer who knows that he is subject to "a valid search condition" to his release consequently "does not have a *reasonable* expectation of privacy over his person or property" vis-a-vis any search by anyone, including a police officer unaware of his probation status?

4. As the *Samson* dissenters note, the Court had previously taken two approaches in the general area of administrative inspections and regulatory searches (and especially as to probationer/parolee searches), "special needs" and a "totality of circumstances" balancing of interests, represented respectively by *Griffin* and *Knights,* and had applied the *Ferguson* limitation—that the government interest being served must be "divorced from the State's general interest in law enforcement"— to the former but not the latter. How do the two theories apply regarding the issue presented in *United States v. Kincade*, 379 F.3d 813 (9th Cir.2004), concerning "whether the Fourth Amendment permits compulsory DNA profiling of certain conditionally-released federal offenders in the absence of individualized suspicion that they have committed additional crimes"? One group of judges, after "balanc[ing] the degree to which DNA profiling interferes with the privacy interests of qualified federal offenders against the significance of the public interests served by such profiling," concluded that "reliance on a totality of the circumstances analysis to uphold compulsory DNA profiling of convicted offenders both comports with the Supreme Court's recent precedents and resolves this appeal in concert with the requirements of the Fourth Amendment." Another group of judges, on the other hand, deemed it inappropriate "to apply a totality of the circumstances test to a suspicionless law enforcement search," and then concluded that because "the primary purpose of the DNA Act is to collect information for ordinary law enforcement purposes—to help law enforcement authorities determine whether specific individuals have committed particular crimes, the Act did not pass muster under the 'special needs' approach. Another judge provided the deciding vote; he agreed the 'special needs' approach applied, but concluded that here just as in *Griffin* the challenged activity 'serves the special needs of a supervised release system,' for the person who refused to supply a DNA sample had not completed his period of such release."

5. After *Samson*, has the concern stated by the second group of judges been obviated, so that the DNA Act clearly can now be upheld on a balancing-of-interests theory? If there is some doubt on this, can it be said that the limitation stated by the last judge is now unnecessary, given the intervening decision in *Illinois v. Lidster*, 540 U.S. 419 (2004)? (In *Lidster*, involving a highway checkpoint set up by police to seek information from motorists about a hit-and-run accident a week earlier the same time of night, the Court held that this checkpoint did not fall within the prohibited "general interest in crime control" category because the "stop's primary law enforcement purpose was *not* to determine whether a vehicle's occupants were committing a crime, but to ask vehicle occupants, as members of the public, for their help in providing information about a crime in all likelihood committed by others."[a]) Such was the conclusion in *Nicholas v. Goord*, 430 F.3d 652 (2d Cir.2005), reasoning that though the post-probation retention of DNA samples "may eventually help law enforcement identify the perpetrators of a crime, at the time of collection, the samples 'in fact provide no evidence in and of themselves of criminal wrongdoing,' and are not sought for the investigation of a specific crime."

6. Or, may it simply be said, as to the post-probation retention of a "genetic fingerprint," that even innocent individuals have no Fourth Amendment right to expunge government records of identity, and that accessing such information on some later occasion is not itself a search, as concluded in *Johnson v. Quander*, 440 F.3d 489 (D.C.Cir.2006)? Does it follow, then, that DNA testing statutes may encompass all those convicted of any crime, as concluded in *State v. O'Hagen*, 914 A.2d 267 (N.J.2007)?

7. May DNA testing statutes encompass persons merely *arrested* for a crime, as is now authorized by legislation at the federal level and in some states? Consider that in *O'Hagen*, Note 6 supra, the court stated that "the taking of a buccal cheek swab is a very minor physical intrusion upon the person," "no more intrusive than the fingerprint procedure and the taking of one's photograph that a person must already undergo as part of the normal arrest process," outweighed by "the State's compelling interest in maintaining a database that will permit accurate identification of persons at the scene of a crime."

8. Would a system of universal DNA testing likewise pass muster? Consider D. H. Kaye & Michael E. Smith, *DNA Identification Databases: Legality, Legitimacy, and the Case for Population—Wide Coverage*, 2003 Wis.L.Rev. 413, 444 (the "Court's opinions in *Edmond* and *Ferguson* are less of a barrier here than they

---

a. What result, then, in a situation "similar to the one in *Lidster*" where "the person challenging the roadblock * * * was actually implicated in the crime that prompted the roadblock," as in *Underwood v. State*, 252 P.3d 221 (Okla.Crim.App.2011)?

are to arrestee DNA databases"). Would a statute requiring universal DNA testing, carry with it a very strong presumption of constitutionality because, as stated in Note, 82 N.Y.U.L.Rev. 247, 274 (2007), such a provision "would not be enacted, or if enacted would not long survive, if most of the populace was materially dissatisfied with the privacy burdens it imposed."

9. After *Samson*, may the continuous wearing of a GPS monitoring device be made a standard condition for a parolee, a probationer, or a released sex offender under a lifetime obligation to register? See Note, 38 Hastings Const.L.Q. 1085 (2011), and compare *Commonwealth v. Goodwin*, 933 N.E.2d 925 (Mass. 2010), with *In re R.V.*, 89 Cal.Rptr.3d 702 (App.2009).

SECTION 10. CONSENT SEARCHES

Consent searches are frequently relied upon by the police because they involve no time-consuming paper work and offer an opportunity to search even when probable cause is lacking. Thus, the constitutional protection against unreasonable search and seizure widens or narrows, depending on the difficulty or ease with which the prosecution can establish that the defendant (or some other authorized person) has "consented" to what would otherwise be an unconstitutional invasion of his privacy.

A. THE NATURE OF "CONSENT"

SCHNECKLOTH v. BUSTAMONTE

412 U.S. 218, 93 S.Ct. 2041, 36 L.Ed.2d 854 (1973).

JUSTICE STEWART delivered the opinion of the Court. * * *

[A police officer stopped a car containing six men when he observed that one headlight and the license plate light were burned out. After the driver could not produce a license, the officer asked passenger Alcala, who claimed he was the vehicle owner's brother, if he could search the car, and Alcala replied, "Sure, go ahead." The driver "helped in the search of the car, by opening the trunk and glove compartment." Stolen checks were found under a seat, leading to charges against passenger Bustamonte, whose motion to suppress was denied. His conviction was affirmed on appeal; the federal district court denied his petition for a writ of habeas corpus, but the 9th Circuit court of appeals set aside the district court's order.]

The precise question in this case, then, is what must the state prove to demonstrate that a consent was "voluntarily" given. * * *

The most extensive judicial exposition of the meaning of "voluntariness" has been developed in those cases in which the Court has had to determine the "voluntariness" of a defendant's confession for purposes of the Fourteenth Amendment. * * * It is to that body of case law to which we turn for initial guidance on the meaning of "voluntariness" in the present context. * * *

The significant fact about all of these decisions is that none of them turned on the presence or absence of a single controlling criterion; each reflected a careful scrutiny of all the surrounding circumstances. In none of them did the Court rule that the Due Process Clause required the prosecution to prove as part of its initial burden that the defendant knew he had a right to refuse to answer the questions that were put. While the state of the accused's mind, and the failure of the police to advise the accused of his rights, were certainly factors to be evaluated in assessing the "voluntariness" of an accused's responses, they were not in and of themselves determinative.

Similar considerations lead us to agree with the courts of California that the question whether a consent to a search was in fact "voluntary" or was the product of duress or coercion, express or implied, is a question of fact to be determined from the totality of all the circumstances. While knowledge of the right to refuse consent is one factor to be taken into account, the government need not establish such knowledge as the *sine qua non* of an effective consent. As with police questioning, two competing concerns must be accommodated in determining the meaning of a "voluntary" consent—the legitimate need for such searches and the equally important requirement of assuring the absence of coercion.

In situations where the police have some evidence of illicit activity, but lack probable cause to arrest or search, a search authorized by a valid consent may be the only means of obtaining important and reliable evidence. In the present case for example, while the police had reason to stop the car for traffic violations, the State does not contend that there was probable cause to search the vehicle or that the search was incident to a valid arrest of any of the occupants. Yet, the search yielded tangible evidence that served as a basis for a prosecution, and provided some assurance that others, wholly innocent of the crime, were not mistakenly brought to trial. And in those cases where there is probable cause to arrest or search, but where the police lack a warrant, a consent search may still be valuable. If the search is conducted and proves fruitless, that in itself may convince the police that an arrest with its possible stigma and embarrassment is unnecessary, or that a far more extensive search pursuant to a warrant is not justified. In short a search pursuant to consent may result in considerably less inconvenience for the subject of the search, and, properly conducted, is a constitutionally permissible and wholly legitimate aspect of effective police activity.

But the Fourth and Fourteenth Amendments require that a consent not be coerced, by explicit or implicit means, by implied threat or covert force. For, no matter how subtly the coercion were applied, the resulting "consent" would be no more than a pretext for the unjustified police intrusion against which the Fourth Amendment is directed. * * *

The problem of reconciling the recognized legitimacy of consent searches with the requirement that they be free from any aspect of official coercion cannot be resolved by an infallible touchstone. To approve such searches without the most careful scrutiny would sanction the possibility of official coercion; to place artificial restrictions upon such searches would jeopardize their basic validity. Just as was true with confessions, the requirement of a "voluntary" consent reflects a fair accommodation of the constitutional requirements involved. In examining all the surrounding circumstances to determine if in fact the consent to search was coerced, account must be taken of subtly coercive police questions, as well as the possibly vulnerable subjective state of the person who consents. Those searches that are the product of police coercion can thus be filtered out without undermining the continuing validity of consent searches. In sum, there is no reason for us to depart in the area of consent searches, from the traditional definition of "voluntariness."

The approach of the Court of Appeals for the Ninth Circuit finds no support in any of our decisions that have attempted to define the meaning of "voluntariness." Its ruling, that the State must affirmatively prove that the subject of the search knew that he had a right to refuse consent, would, in practice, create serious doubt whether consent searches could continue to be conducted. * * *

The very object of the inquiry—the nature of a person's subjective understanding—underlines the difficulty of the prosecution's burden under the rule applied by the Court of Appeals in this case. Any defendant who was the subject of a search authorized solely by his consent could effectively frustrate the introduction into evidence of the fruits of that search by simply failing to testify that he in fact knew he could refuse to consent. And the near impossibility of meeting this prosecutorial burden suggests why this Court has never accepted any such litmus-paper test of voluntariness. * * *

One alternative that would go far towards proving that the subject of a search did know he had a right to refuse consent would be to advise him of that right before eliciting his consent. That, however, is a suggestion that has been almost universally repudiated by both federal and state courts, and, we think, rightly so. For it would be thoroughly impractical to impose on the normal consent search the detailed requirements of an effective warning.[a] Consent searches are part of the standard investigatory techniques of law enforcement agencies. They normally occur on the highway, or in a person's home or office, and under informal and unstructured conditions. The circumstances that prompt the initial request to search may develop quickly or be a logical extension of investigative police questioning. The police may seek to investigate further suspicious circumstances or to follow up leads developed in questioning persons at the scene of a crime. These situations are a far cry from the structured atmosphere of a trial where, assisted by counsel if he chooses, a defendant is informed of his trial rights. And, while surely a closer question, these situations are still immeasurably far removed from "custodial interrogation" where, in *Miranda v. Arizona* [p. 571], we found that the Constitution required certain now familiar warnings as a prerequisite to police interrogation. * * *

It is said, however, that a "consent" is a "waiver" of a person's rights under the Fourth and Fourteenth Amendments. The argument is that by allowing the police to conduct a search, a person "waives" whatever right he had to prevent the police from searching. It is argued that under the doctrine of *Johnson v. Zerbst,* 304 U.S. 458 (1938), to establish such a "waiver" the state must demonstrate "an intentional relinquishment or abandonment of a known right or privilege." * * *

Almost without exception the requirement of a knowing and intelligent waiver has been applied only to those rights which the Constitution guarantees to a criminal defendant in order to preserve a fair trial. Hence, and hardly surprisingly in view of the facts of *Johnson* itself, the standard of a knowing and intelligent waiver has most often been applied to test the validity of a waiver of counsel, either at trial, or upon a guilty plea. And the Court has also applied the *Johnson* criteria to assess the effectiveness of a waiver of other trial rights such as the right to confrontation, to a jury trial, and to a speedy trial, and the right to be free from twice being placed in jeopardy. * * *

The guarantees afforded a criminal defendant at trial also protect him at certain stages before the actual trial, and any alleged waiver must meet the strict standard of an intentional relinquishment of a "known" right. But the "trial" guarantees that have been applied to the "pretrial" stage of the criminal process are similarly designed to protect the fairness of the trial itself. * * *[b]

---

a. Relying upon this language, the Court later held in *Ohio v. Robinette,* 519 U.S. 33 (1996), that if a person has been lawfully seized, for example, because of commission of a traffic violation, and following the point at which the detainee would be free to go he consents to a search, that consent is not involuntary because the officer failed to specifically advise the detainee that he was free to go, as a requirement of such warnings would be equally "unrealistic."

b. At this point, the Court noted that "the standard of a knowing and intelligent waiver" applies to waiver of counsel at a lineup under *United States v. Wade,* p. 761, and *Gilbert v. California,* p. 761 fn. b, because counsel is provided to protect the right of cross-examination at trial; and that the same standard applies to waiver of counsel at custodial interrogation under *Miranda v. Arizona,* p. 571, because counsel is provided to ensure that the safeguards concerning the giving of testimony at trial do not "become empty formalities."

The standards of *Johnson* were, therefore, found to be a necessary prerequisite to a finding of a valid waiver.[29] * * *

The protections of the Fourth Amendment are of a wholly different order, and have nothing whatever to do with promoting the fair ascertainment of truth at a criminal trial. Rather, as Justice Frankfurter's opinion for the Court put it in *Wolf v. Colorado* [p. 222], the Fourth Amendment protects the "security of one's privacy against arbitrary intrusion by the police. . . ." * * *

Nor can it even be said that a search, as opposed to an eventual trial, is somehow "unfair" if a person consents to a search. While the Fourth and Fourteenth Amendments limit the circumstances under which the police can conduct a search, there is nothing constitutionally suspect in a person voluntarily allowing a search. The actual conduct of the search may be precisely the same as if the police had obtained a warrant. And, unlike those constitutional guarantees that protect a defendant at trial, it cannot be said every reasonable presumption ought to be indulged against voluntary relinquishment. We have only recently stated: "[I]t is no part of the policy underlying the Fourth and Fourteenth Amendments to discourage citizens from aiding to the utmost of their ability in the apprehension of criminals." *Coolidge v. New Hampshire,* [p. 316]. Rather the community has a real interest in encouraging consent, for the resulting search may yield necessary evidence for the solution and prosecution of crime, evidence that may insure that a wholly innocent person is not wrongly charged with a criminal offense.

Those cases that have dealt with the application of the *Johnson v. Zerbst* rule make clear that it would be next to impossible to apply to a consent search the standard of "an intentional relinquishment or abandonment of a known right or privilege." To be true to *Johnson* and its progeny, there must be examination into the knowing and understanding nature of the waiver, an examination that was designed for a trial judge in the structured atmosphere of a courtroom. * * * It would be unrealistic to expect that in the informal, unstructured context of a consent search, a policeman, upon pain of tainting the evidence obtained, could make the detailed type of examination demanded by *Johnson.* * * *

Similarly, a "waiver" approach to consent searches would be thoroughly inconsistent with our decisions that have approved "third party consents." In *Coolidge v. New Hampshire,* where a wife surrendered to the police guns and clothing belonging to her husband, we found nothing constitutionally impermissible in the admission of that evidence at trial since the wife had not been coerced. *Frazier v. Cupp,* [p. 467], held that evidence seized from the defendant's duffel bag in a search authorized by his cousin's consent was admissible at trial. We found that the defendant had assumed the risk that his cousin with whom he shared the bag would allow the police to search it. And in *Hill v. California,* 401 U.S. 797 (1971), we held that the police had validly seized evidence from the petitioner's apartment incident to the arrest of a third party, since the police had probable cause to arrest the petitioner and reasonably though mistakenly believed the man they had arrested was he. Yet it is inconceivable that the Constitution could countenance the waiver of a defendant's right to counsel by a third party, or that a waiver could be found because a trial judge reasonably though mistakenly believed a defendant had waived his right to plead not guilty. * * *

---

29. As we have already noted, *Miranda* itself involved interrogation of a suspect detained in custody and did not concern the investigatory procedures of the police in general on-the-scene questioning. By the same token, the present case does not require a determination of the proper standard to be applied in assessing the validity of a search authorized solely by an alleged consent that is obtained from a person after he has been placed in custody. We do note, however, that other courts have been particularly sensitive to the heightened possibilities for coercion when the "consent" to a search was given by a person in custody.

Much of what has already been said disposes of the argument that the Court's decision in the *Miranda* case requires the conclusion that knowledge of a right to refuse is an indispensable element of a valid consent. The considerations that informed the Court's holding in *Miranda* are simply inapplicable in the present case. In *Miranda* the Court found that the techniques of police questioning and the nature of custodial surroundings produce an inherently coercive situation. The Court concluded that "[u]nless adequate protective devices are employed to dispel the compulsion inherent in custodial surroundings, no statement obtained from the defendant can truly be the product of his free choice." And at another point the Court noted that "without proper safeguards the process of in-custody interrogation of persons suspected or accused of crime contains inherently compelling pressures which work to undermine the individual's will to resist and to compel him to speak where he would not otherwise do so freely."

In this case there is no evidence of any inherently coercive tactics—either from the nature of the police questioning or the environment in which it took place. Indeed, since consent searches will normally occur on a person's own familiar territory, the spectre of incommunicado police interrogation in some remote station house is simply inapposite. There is no reason to believe, under circumstances such as are present here, that the response to a policeman's question is presumptively coerced; and there is, therefore, no reason to reject the traditional test for determining the voluntariness of a person's response. *Miranda,* of course, did not reach investigative questioning of a person not in custody, which is most directly analogous to the situation of a consent search, and it assuredly did not indicate that such questioning ought to be deemed inherently coercive.

It is also argued that the failure to require the Government to establish knowledge as a prerequisite to a valid consent, will relegate the Fourth Amendment to the special province of "the sophisticated, the knowledgeable, and the privileged." We cannot agree. The traditional definition of voluntariness we accept today has always taken into account evidence of minimal schooling, low intelligence, and the lack of any effective warnings to a person of his rights; and the voluntariness of any statement taken under those conditions has been carefully scrutinized to determine whether it was in fact voluntarily given.

Our decision today is a narrow one. We hold only that when the subject of a search is not in custody and the State attempts to justify a search on the basis of his consent, the Fourth and Fourteenth Amendments require that it demonstrate that the consent was in fact voluntarily given, and not the result of duress or coercion, express or implied. Voluntariness is a question of fact to be determined from all the circumstances, and while the subject's knowledge of a right to refuse is a factor to be taken into account, the prosecution is not required to demonstrate such knowledge as a prerequisite to establishing a voluntary consent.[c]

Justice MARSHALL, dissenting. * * *

If consent to search means that a person has chosen to forego his right to exclude the police from the place they seek to search, it follows that his consent cannot be considered a meaningful choice unless he knew that he could in fact exclude the police. * * * I would therefore hold, at a minimum, that the prosecu-

---

c. Powell, J., joined by the Chief Justice and Rehnquist, J., concurred on the ground "that federal collateral review of a state prisoner's Fourth Amendment claims—claims which rarely bear on innocence—should be confined solely to the question of whether the petitioner was provided a fair opportunity to raise and have adjudicated the question in state courts." Blackmun, J., concurred to express substantial agreement with the Powell opinion. Douglas, J., dissenting, would have remanded for a determination of whether Alcala knew he had the right to refuse. Brennan, J., dissenting, declared: "It wholly escapes me how our citizens can meaningfully be said to have waived something as precious as a constitutional guarantee without ever being aware of its existence."

tion may not rely on a purported consent to search if the subject of the search did not know that he could refuse to give consent. Where the police claim authority to search yet in fact lack such authority, the subject does not know that he may permissibly refuse them entry, and it is this lack of knowledge that invalidates the consent. * * *

The Court contends that if an officer paused to inform the subject of his rights, the informality of the exchange would be destroyed. I doubt that a simple statement by an officer of an individual's right to refuse consent would do much to alter the informality of the exchange, except to alert the subject to a fact that he surely is entitled to know. It is not without significance that for many years the agents of the Federal Bureau of Investigation have routinely informed subjects of their right to refuse consent, when they request consent to search. * * *

NOTES ON THE RELEVANT FACTORS IN DETERMINING THE VALIDITY OF A CONSENT

1. *What is the issue?* Some courts, as did the court of appeals in *Busta- monte*, 448 F.2d 699 (9th Cir.1971), characterize a consent to search as "a waiver of a constitutional right" and thus focus upon the state of mind of the person allegedly giving the consent. Some other courts look instead to the state of mind of the officer seeking the consent; the question is said to be whether "the officers, as reasonable men, could conclude that defendant's consent was given," e.g., *People v. Henderson*, 210 N.E.2d 483 (Ill.1965). Does *Bustamonte* clearly indicate a choice of either of these theories? Cf. *Florida v. Jimeno*, p. 461, and *Illinois v. Rodriguez*, p. 462. An illustration of how the choice of one of these theories over the other might affect the outcome is provided by *United States v. Elrod*, 441 F.2d 353 (5th Cir.1971), holding: "No matter how genuine the belief of the officers is that the consenter is apparently of sound mind and deliberately acting, the search depending upon his consent fails if it is judicially determined that he lacked mental capacity. It is not that the actions of the officers were imprudent or unfounded. It is that the key to validity—consent—is lacking for want of mental capacity, no matter how much concealed."

2. *Claim or show of authority.* In *Bumper v. North Carolina*, 391 U.S. 543 (1968), defendant's grandmother allowed the police to search her house after one of them announced, "I have a search warrant to search your house." At the hearing on the motion to suppress the rifle found therein, the prosecutor did not rely upon a warrant to justify the search. The Supreme Court was advised that the officers did have a warrant, but none was ever returned and nothing was known about the conditions under which it was issued. The Court held, 7–2, per Stewart, J., that a search cannot be justified on the basis of consent "when that 'consent' has been given only after the official conducting the search has asserted that he possesses a warrant," as when "a law enforcement officer claims authority to search a home under a warrant, he announces in effect that the occupant has no right to resist the search. The situation is instinct with coercion—albeit colorably lawful coercion. Where there is coercion there cannot be consent."

What if the grandmother had responded to the police, "You don't need a search warrant, go ahead"? What if the officer in *Bumper* had merely threatened to obtain a search warrant? Consider *United States v. Boukater*, 409 F.2d 537 (5th Cir.1969) (coercive unless the officer actually had grounds to obtain a warrant or he merely said he would seek a search warrant). The "claim of lawful authority" referred to in *Bumper* need not involve mention of a search warrant; a flat assertion by the police that they have come to search will suffice. *Amos v. United States*, 255 U.S. 313 (1921).

3. *Threat of incarceration.* In *United States v. Knights*, p. 444, Knights signed the probation order containing the search condition and a declaration he agreed "to abide by same." "The Government, advocating the approach of the Supreme Court of California, * * * contends that the search satisfied the Fourth Amendment under the 'consent' rationale of * * * *Schneckloth* * * *. In the Government's view, Knights's acceptance of the search condition was voluntary because he had the option of rejecting probation and going to prison instead, which the Government argues is analogous to the voluntary decision defendants often make to waive their right to a trial and accept a plea bargain." Had the Court found it necessary to decide the consent issue,[a] what conclusion should it have reached?

4. *Prior illegal police action.* Under the "fruit of the poisonous tree" doctrine of *Wong Sun*, p. 894, a consent may be held ineffective because obtained in exploitation of a prior illegal arrest.

5. *Mental or emotional state of the person.* Compare *United States v. Elrod*, Note 1 supra; and *Commonwealth v. Angivoni*, 417 N.E.2d 422 (Mass.1981) (voluntary consent of defendant in hospital emergency room with dislocated hip not established, as "defendant's understanding and ability to reason reflectively may have been impaired by intoxication or as a result of his injuries or an emotional trauma attendant to his just having been in an accident"); with the Supreme Court's more recent application of the voluntariness test in *Colorado v. Connelly*, p. 728.

6. *Denial of guilt.* Doesn't the ready discovery of incriminating evidence pursuant to the "consent" of a person who has denied his guilt manifest that the consent must have been involuntary? Yes, concluded the court in *Higgins v. United States*, 209 F.2d 819 (D.C.Cir.1954): "No sane man who denies his guilt would actually be willing that policemen search his room for contraband which is certain to be discovered." But in *Florida v. Bostick*, 501 U.S. 429 (1991), in response to the defendant's contention that "no reasonable person would freely consent to a search of luggage that he or she knows contains drugs," the Court responded that such an "argument cannot prevail because the 'reasonable person' test presupposes an *innocent* person."

7. *Custody; Warning of Fourth Amendment rights.* In *United States v. Watson*, p. 332, the majority concluded that the failure to give the defendant Fourth Amendment warnings "is not to be given controlling significance" where, as there, the defendant "had been arrested and was in custody, but his consent was given while on a public street, not in the confines of the police station." Marshall and Brennan, JJ., dissenting, objected that the "lack of custody was of decisional importance in *Schneckloth*, which repeatedly distinguished the case before it from one involving a suspect in custody."

In *Gentile v. United States*, 419 U.S. 979 (1974), where consent was obtained from the defendant during stationhouse custodial interrogation after the giving of the *Miranda* warnings but without Fourth Amendment warnings, Douglas and Marshall, JJ., dissenting from the denial of certiorari, noted: "When a suspect is in custody the situation is in control of the police. The pace of events will not somehow deny them an opportunity to give a warning, as the [*Schneckloth*] Court apparently feared would happen in noncustodial settings. Moreover, the custodial setting will permit easy documentation of both the giving of a warning and the arrestee's response."

---

a. Which the Court did not in *Knights*, or for that matter, in the subsequent case of *Samson v. California*, p. 494 (see fn. 3 therein; but consider fn. 4 of the dissent).

8. *Warning of Fifth Amendment rights.* It has sometimes been held that a valid consent to search, given by a person in custody, must be preceded by *Miranda* warnings because "the request to search is a request that defendant be a witness against himself which he is privileged to refuse under the Fifth Amendment." *State v. Williams,* 432 P.2d 679 (Or.1967). But the prevailing view, as stated in *United States v. LaGrone,* 43 F.3d 332 (7th Cir.1994), is that "because requesting consent to search is not likely to elicit an incriminating statement, such questioning is not interrogation, and thus *Miranda* warnings are not required."

9. *Right to counsel.* In *Tidwell v. Superior Court,* 95 Cal.Rptr. 213 (App. 1971), the police asked petitioner, who was in jail, if they could search his car, which had been impounded. Petitioner allegedly replied, "Go ahead and search." The court held that petitioner's consent was ineffective since at the time he had been arraigned on a burglary charge and counsel had been appointed, yet the police had asked him to consent to the search without notifying his lawyer. Rejecting the argument that *Massiah* [p. 557] should apply only to "statements elicited and not to consents given," the court observed: "This distinction is very thin considering the incriminating effect a consent to search may have. The reasoning of [the cases protecting] defendants' right to effective aid of counsel applies equally to a consent given at the instigation of the police."

10. *"Consent" by deception.* In contrast to the type of deception allegedly used in *Bumper,* Note 2 supra, the police sometimes obtain evidence of criminal activity by acting in an undercover capacity and obtaining a "consent" which the defendant would not have given had he known the officer's true identity; see *Lewis v. United States,* 385 U.S. 206 (1966), upholding this practice upon the facts presented. A third situation is that in which the officer's true identity is known but he misleads the suspect as to his intentions. Compare *Krause v. Commonwealth,* 206 S.W.3d 922 (Ky.2006) (where police wishing to look for drugs in certain residence knocked on door at 4 a.m. and falsely told occupant that a young girl had just reported being raped by occupant's roommate and asked to be allowed to enter and look around to see if her description of the interior was accurate, consent to entry not voluntary); with *United States v. DiModica,* 468 F.3d 495 (7th Cir.2006) (where police had probable cause to arrest defendant but passed up ample opportunity to get a warrant, warrantless arrest inside residence upheld because of defendant's consent to police entry, obtained by police falsely telling defendant that his wife had been badly injured in a car accident and then asking to come inside to talk to him).

11. *Scope of consent.* The standard for measuring the scope of a suspect's consent, the Court concluded in *Florida v. Jimeno,* 500 U.S. 248 (1991), is neither the suspect's intent nor the officer's perception thereof but rather "that of 'objective' reasonableness—what would the typical reasonable person have understood by the exchange between the officer and the suspect?" Given the officer's statement in *Jimeno* that he would be looking for narcotics, "it was objectively reasonable for the police to conclude that the general consent to search respondent's car included consent to search containers within that car which might bear drugs." But, the nature of the container is also relevant. "It is very unreasonable to think that a suspect, by consenting to the search of his trunk, has agreed to the breaking open of a locked briefcase within the trunk, but it is otherwise with respect to a closed paper bag."

Does the *Jimeno* principle, that "the scope of the search is generally defined by its expressed object," suffice as to consent searches of the person? Consider *United States v. Rodney,* 956 F.2d 295 (D.C.Cir.1992) (sweeping motion over crotch area during consent search for drugs lawful, as it no more intrusive than a *Terry* frisk; court distinguishes *United States v. Blake,* 888 F.2d 795 (11th

Cir.1989), suppressing drugs found on person, as that case involved "a direct 'frontal touching' of the defendant's private parts").

Does a consent, voluntary when given, justify a second search of the same place at a later time after a fruitless first search? Compare *People v. Nawrocki,* 150 N.W.2d 516 (Mich.App.1967) (defendant's consent to search his car construed as "permission to search the car at any time," thus justifying second search hours later after the car was impounded and the defendant was in jail); with *State v. Brochu,* 237 A.2d 418 (Me.1967) (contra where passage of time was greater, second search involved re-entry of defendant's home, and defendant's status had changed from suspect to accused in interim).

12. *The proper place of consent searches in law enforcement.* Compare: (a) "In a society based on law, the concept of agreement and consent should be given a weight and dignity of its own. Police officers act in full accord with the law when they ask citizens for consent. It reinforces the rule of law for the citizen to advise the police of his or her wishes and for the police to act in reliance on that understanding. When this exchange takes place, it dispels inferences of coercion." *United States v. Drayton,* 536 U.S. 194 (2002).

(b) "Every year, I witness the same mass incredulity. Why, one hundred criminal procedure students jointly wonder, would someone 'voluntarily' consent to allow a police officer to search the trunk of his car, knowing that massive amounts of cocaine are easily visible there? The answer, I have come to believe, is that most people don't willingly consent to police searches. Yet, absent extraordinary circumstances, chances are that a court nonetheless will conclude that the consent was valid and the evidence admissible under the Fourth Amendment. * * *

"Eliminating consent would require a huge leap of faith, but a worthy one. * * * It would mean that the dignity of the individual is not overpowered by the authority and power of the police officer. It would mean that the Fourth Amendment's concern for the privacy of each citizen would be restored to its rightful place—to be interfered with only when the government has the proper justification for doing so." Marcy Strauss, *Reconstructing Consent,* 92 J.Crim.L. & Crimin. 211–12, 271–72 (2002).

(c) "Abolishing consent searches would deprive police of their most effective racial profiling tool. As police can approach anyone on the street to ask for consent and can ask any driver who is stopped for a traffic infraction for consent, police are presently free to use race, and only race, to decide when to ask for consent in a huge number of situations. * * * Abolishing consent searches would do far more to remedy racial profiling in the real world than all the equal protection laws or statutory remedies that can be imagined." George C. Thomas, *Terrorism, Race and a New Approach to Consent Searches,* 73 Miss.L.J. 525, 551–52 (2003).

B. THIRD PARTY CONSENT

ILLINOIS v. RODRIGUEZ

497 U.S. 177, 110 S.Ct. 2793, 111 L.Ed.2d 148 (1990).

JUSTICE SCALIA delivered the opinion of the Court. * * *

[Gail Fischer, who showed signs of a severe beating, told police that she had been assaulted by Rodriguez earlier that day in an apartment on South California. Fischer stated that Rodriguez was then asleep in the apartment, and she consented to travel there with the police in order to unlock the door with her key so that the officers could enter and arrest him. During this conversation, Fischer several times referred to the apartment on South California as "our" apartment, and said that she had clothes and furniture there. The police drove to the apartment accompanied by Fischer, who unlocked the door with her key and gave the officers permission to enter. Inside they observed in plain view drug paraphernalia and containers filled with cocaine. The officers arrested Rodriguez and seized the drugs and related paraphernalia. Rodriguez, charged with possession of a controlled substance with intent to deliver, moved to suppress all evidence seized at the time of his arrest. The court granted the motion, holding that at the time she consented to the entry Fischer did not have common authority over the apartment.]

The Fourth Amendment generally prohibits the warrantless entry of a person's home, whether to make an arrest or to search for specific objects. The prohibition does not apply, however, to situations in which voluntary consent has been obtained, either from the individual whose property is searched, or from a third party who possesses common authority over the premises, see *United States v. Matlock,* [415 U.S. 164 (1974)]. The State of Illinois contends that that exception applies in the present case.

As we stated in *Matlock,* "[c]ommon authority" rests "on mutual use of the property by persons generally having joint access or control for most purposes."[a] The burden of establishing that common authority rests upon the State. On the basis of this record, it is clear that burden was not sustained. The evidence showed that although Fischer, with her two small children, had lived with Rodriguez beginning in December 1984, she had moved out on July 1, 1985, almost a month before the search at issue here, and had gone to live with her mother. She took her and her children's clothing with her, though leaving behind some furniture and household effects. During the period after July 1 she sometimes spent the night at Rodriguez's apartment, but never invited her friends there, and never went there herself when he was not home. Her name was not on the lease nor did she contribute to the rent. She had a key to the apartment, which she said at trial she had taken without Rodriguez's knowledge (though she testified at the preliminary hearing that Rodriguez had given her the key). On these facts the State has not established that, with respect to the South California apartment, Fischer had "joint access or control for most purposes." To the contrary, the Appellate Court's determination of no common authority over the apartment was obviously correct.

[R]espondent asserts that permitting a reasonable belief of common authority to validate an entry would cause a defendant's Fourth Amendment rights to be "vicariously waived." We disagree.

We have been unyielding in our insistence that a defendant's waiver of his trial rights cannot be given effect unless it is "knowing" and "intelligent." We would assuredly not permit, therefore, evidence seized in violation of the Fourth Amendment to be introduced on the basis of a trial court's mere "reasonable belief"—derived from statements by unauthorized persons—that the defendant has waived his objection. But one must make a distinction between, on the one hand, trial rights that *derive* from the violation of constitutional guarantees and, on the other hand, the nature of those constitutional guarantees themselves. * * *

What Rodriguez is assured by the trial right of the exclusionary rule, where it applies, is that no evidence seized in violation of the Fourth Amendment will be introduced at his trial unless he consents. What he is assured by the Fourth Amendment itself, however, is not that no government search of his house will

---

a. Where there is such "common authority," the Court went on to say in *Matlock,* "it is reasonable to recognize that any of the co-inhabitants has the right to permit the inspection in his own right and that the others have assumed the risk that one of their number might permit the common area to be searched."

occur unless he consents; but that no such search will occur that is "unreasonable." There are various elements, of course, that can make a search of a person's house "reasonable"—one of which is the consent of the person or his cotenant. The essence of respondent's argument is that we should impose upon this element a requirement that we have not imposed upon other elements that regularly compel government officers to exercise judgment regarding the facts: namely, the requirement that their judgment be not only responsible but correct.[b]

[I]n order to satisfy the "reasonableness" requirement of the Fourth Amendment, what is generally demanded of the many factual determinations that must regularly be made by agents of the government—whether the magistrate issuing a warrant, the police officer executing a warrant, or the police officer conducting a search or seizure under one of the exceptions to the warrant requirement—is not that they always be correct, but that they always be reasonable. As we put it in *Brinegar v. United States,* [p. 296]:

> "Because many situations which confront officers in the course of executing their duties are more or less ambiguous, room must be allowed for some mistakes on their part. But the mistakes must be those of reasonable men, acting on facts leading sensibly to their conclusions of probability."

We see no reason to depart from this general rule with respect to facts bearing upon the authority to consent to a search. Whether the basis for such authority exists is the sort of recurring factual question to which law enforcement officials must be expected to apply their judgment; and all the Fourth Amendment requires is that they answer it reasonably. The Constitution is no more violated when officers enter without a warrant because they reasonably (though erroneously) believe that the person who has consented to their entry is a resident of the premises, than it is violated when they enter without a warrant because they reasonably (though erroneously) believe they are in pursuit of a violent felon who is about to escape.

Stoner v. California, [p. 466] is in our view not to the contrary. There, in holding that police had improperly entered the defendant's hotel room based on the consent of a hotel clerk, we stated that "the rights protected by the Fourth Amendment are not to be eroded ... by unrealistic doctrines of 'apparent authority.' " It is ambiguous, of course, whether the word "unrealistic" is descriptive or limiting—that is, whether we were condemning as unrealistic all reliance upon apparent authority, or whether we were condemning only such reliance upon apparent authority as is unrealistic. Similarly ambiguous is the opinion's earlier statement that "there [is no] substance to the claim that the search was reasonable because the police, relying upon the night clerk's expressions of consent, had a reasonable basis for the belief that the clerk had authority to consent to the search." Was there no substance to it because it failed as a matter of law, or because the facts could not possibly support it? At one point the opinion does seem to speak clearly:

> "It is important to bear in mind that it was the petitioner's constitutional right which was at stake here, and not the night clerk's nor the hotel's. It was a right, therefore, which only the petitioner could waive by word or deed, either directly or through an agent."

---

b. In an omitted portion of the opinion, illustrations were given: (i) the probable cause requirement for a warrant, as to which the magistrate may act on "seemingly reliable but factually inaccurate information"; (ii) the warrant requirement, as to which the officer may be reasonably mistaken as to the warrant's scope, *Maryland v. Garrison,* p. 317; and (iii) the search incident to arrest doctrine, where the officer may be reasonably mistaken as to the person to be arrested, *Hill v. California,* p. 457.

But as we have discussed, what is at issue when a claim of apparent consent is raised is not whether the right to be free of searches has been *waived,* but whether the right to be free of *unreasonable* searches has been *violated.* Even if one does not think the *Stoner* opinion had this subtlety in mind, the supposed clarity of its foregoing statement is immediately compromised, as follows:

> "It is true that the night clerk clearly and unambiguously consented to the search. But there is nothing in the record to indicate that *the police had any basis whatsoever to believe that* the night clerk had been authorized by the petitioner to permit the police to search the petitioner's room."

The italicized language should have been deleted, of course, if the statement two sentences earlier meant that an appearance of authority could never validate a search. In the last analysis, one must admit that the rationale of *Stoner* was ambiguous—and perhaps deliberately so. It is at least a reasonable reading of the case, and perhaps a preferable one, that the police could not rely upon the obtained consent because they knew it came from a hotel clerk, knew that the room was rented and exclusively occupied by the defendant, and could not reasonably have believed that the former had general access to or control over the latter. * * *

As *Stoner* demonstrates, what we hold today does not suggest that law enforcement officers may always accept a person's invitation to enter premises. Even when the invitation is accompanied by an explicit assertion that the person lives there, the surrounding circumstances could conceivably be such that a reasonable person would doubt its truth and not act upon it without further inquiry. As with other factual determinations bearing upon search and seizure, determination of consent to enter must "be judged against an objective standard: would the facts available to the officer at the moment ... 'warrant a man of reasonable caution in the belief'" that the consenting party had authority over the premises? If not, then warrantless entry without further inquiry is unlawful unless authority actually exists. But if so, the search is valid.

In the present case, the Appellate Court found it unnecessary to determine whether the officers reasonably believed that Fischer had the authority to consent, because it ruled as a matter of law that a reasonable belief could not validate the entry. Since we find that ruling to be in error, we remand for consideration of that question. * * *

NOTE

In actual/apparent authority cases involving co-occupants of premises, the question often comes down to whether police are entitled to make certain assumptions about co-occupants' usual privacy expectations and about whether those expectations exist in the instant case, in lieu of asking questions to clarify the situations. Consider what the result should be on these facts, taken from *United States v. Andrus,* 483 F.3d 711 (10th Cir.2007). Federal agents learned that a subscription to a child porn website had been paid with a credit card belonging to Ray Andrus at a certain address and that the e-mail address provided, "bandrus@kc.rr.com," was associated with Dr. Bailey Andrus at that address. Agents went there and knocked on the door and were admitted by 91-year-old Dr. Andrus, who explained that Ray did not pay rent but lived there to care for his aging parents, and that Ray lived in the center bedroom, to which Dr. Andrus said he had access. Dr. Andrus signed a consent to a premises and computer search, and led the agents to Ray's bedroom, where the computer was in plain view. One agent used EnCase forensic software to examine the contents of the computer's hard drive without determining whether a user name or password were needed, and in about five minutes located child pornography. As it turned out, absent such equipment a person would need Ray Andrus' user name and password to access those files, Dr. Andrus did not know how to use the computer, had never used it, and did not know Ray's user name or password. Neither side has presented any evidence tending to establish either the truth or falsity of the proposition "that password protection of home computers is so common that a reasonable officer ought to know password protection is likely."

NOTES ON WHO MAY CONSENT

1. *Husband-wife.* In *United States v. Duran,* 957 F.2d 499 (7th Cir.1992), holding defendant's wife could consent to search of a separate building on their farm which he used as a gym, the court concluded the requisite access was established by the wife's testimony that she could have entered that building at any time, though the wife had not theretofore done so and had none of her personal effects there. This is not to say, the court cautioned, that there is "a per se rule that common spousal authority extends to every square inch of property upon which a couple's residence is built"; such an approach "presumes that spouses, in forging a marital bond, remove any and all boundaries between them," which "does not reflect reality, either in practice or in the eyes of the law." The *Duran* court thus opted for this position: "In the context of a more intimate marital relationship [as compared to other co-occupants], the burden upon the government should be lighter. We hold that a spouse presumptively has authority to consent to a search of all areas of the homestead; the nonconsenting spouse may rebut this presumption only by showing that the consenting spouse was denied access to the particular area searched." Query, what is the effect of the rebuttal in light of *Rodriguez?*

2. *Parent-child.* If a child is living at the home of his parents, the courts are in agreement that the head of the household may give consent to a search of the child's living quarters. A contrary result is sometimes reached if the "child" living with his parents has reached adulthood. A child may not give consent to a full search of the parent's house. However, where it is not unusual or unauthorized for the child to admit visitors into the home, the mere entry of police on the premises with the consent of the child is not improper.

3. *Landlord-tenant; co-tenants.* A landlord may not consent to a search of his tenant's premises (as compared to areas of common usage), and this is so even though the landlord may have some right of entry for purposes of inspecting or cleaning the premises. *Chapman v. United States,* 365 U.S. 610 (1961). Hotel employees may not consent to the search of a particular room during the period in which it has been rented by a guest. *Stoner v. California,* 376 U.S. 483 (1964). But "where two or more persons occupy a dwelling place jointly, the general rule is that a joint tenant can consent to police entry and search of the entire house or apartment, even though they occupy separate bedrooms." *State v. Thibodeau,* 317 A.2d 172 (Me.1974).

4. *Employer-employee.* As to consent by defendant's employer, compare *Gillard v. Schmidt,* 579 F.2d 825 (3d Cir.1978) (consent invalid as to search of defendant's desk; protection of the Fourth Amendment "does not turn on the nature of the property interest in the searched premises, but on the reasonableness of the person's privacy expectation," and defendant had a high expectation concerning his desk because he worked "in an office secured by a locked door and a desk containing psychological profiles and other confidential student records"); with *Commonwealth v. Glover,* 405 A.2d 945 (Pa.Super.1979) (factory owner could consent to search of items on top of work bench, as it not an area assigned to defendant or used exclusively by him).

Whether an employee can give a valid consent to a search of his employer's premises depends upon the scope of his authority. Generally, the courts have been of the view that the average employee, such as a clerk, janitor, driver, or other person temporarily in charge, may not give consent. However, if the employee is a manager or other person of considerable authority who is left in complete charge for a substantial period of time, then the prevailing view is that such a person can waive his employer's rights.

5. *Bailor-bailee.* In *Frazier v. Cupp,* 394 U.S. 731 (1969), the Court concluded that one of petitioner's contentions, namely, that the police illegally searched and seized clothing from his duffel bag, could "be dismissed rather quickly" where the "bag was being used jointly by petitioner and his cousin Rawls and * * * had been left in Rawls' home. The police, while arresting Rawls, asked him if they could have his clothing. They were directed to the duffel bag and both Rawls and his mother consented to its search. During this search, the officers came upon petitioner's clothing and it was seized as well. Since Rawls was a joint user of the bag, he clearly had authority to consent to its search. The officers therefore found evidence against petitioner while in the course of an otherwise lawful search. * * * Petitioner argues that Rawls only had actual permission to use one compartment of the bag and that he had no authority to consent to a search of the other compartments. We will not, however, engage in such metaphysical subleties in judging the efficacy of Rawls' consent. Petitioner, in allowing Rawls to use the bag and in leaving it in his house, must be taken to have assumed the risk that Rawls would allow someone else to look inside."

NOTES ON LIMITS ON THIRD–PARTY CONSENT

Even if the consent was given by a third party who, at least in some circumstances, could give effective consent, it may still be questioned whether other circumstances of the particular case made that person's consent ineffective vis-a-vis the defendant. Consider:

1. *Antagonism.* What if, for example, a wife calls the police into the house and points out incriminating evidence because she is angry at her husband? Compare *State v. Gonzalez–Valle,* 385 So.2d 681 (Fla.App.1980) (where "the motive of the defendant's wife in consenting to the search was clearly one of spite," she "had no right to waive her husband's protection against unreasonable searches and seizures"); with *Commonwealth v. Martin,* 264 N.E.2d 366 (Mass. 1970) ("while they are both living in the premises the equal authority does not lapse and revive with the lapse and revival of amicable relations between the spouses").

2. *Defendant's instructions.* If the defendant had previously instructed the third party not to allow a search, should those instructions be controlling? In *People v. Fry,* 76 Cal.Rptr. 718 (App.1969), the court held: "When the officers solicited consent of the wife to enter for the purpose of seizing property they knew her husband had instructed her not to consent and, under these circumstances, were not entitled to rely upon her consent as justification for their conduct" in searching the family home. *Fry* was distinguished in *People v. Reynolds,* 127 Cal.Rptr. 561 (App.1976), because in the later case the police were unaware of the husband's instructions to his wife. Is the *Matlock* test relevant on this issue?

3. *Defendant's refusal or failure to consent.* In GEORGIA v. RANDOLPH, 547 U.S. 103 (2006), police summoned to the Randolph residence were told by defendant's wife that he was a drug user and that there were "items of drug evidence" in the house. Police asked him to consent to a search of the house, but he "unequivocally refused," at which the police turned to the wife for consent, which she "readily gave" and then led an officer to an upstairs bedroom where drug paraphernalia was seen in plain view, after which a warrant was obtained to search the house. The Supreme Court, per Souter, J., affirmed the state court decision that the evidence obtained in execution of that warrant was the fruit of an invalid consent search. Asserting that the "common element in assessing Fourth Amendment reasonableness in the consent cases * * * is the great significance given to widely shared social expectations," the Court deemed it "fair to say that a caller standing at the door of shared premises would have no confidence that one occupant's invitation was a sufficiently good reason to enter when a fellow tenant stood there saying, 'stay out.' Without some very good reason, no sensible person would go inside under those conditions. Fear for the safety of the occupant issuing the invitation, or of someone else inside, would be thought to justify entry, but the justification then would be the personal risk, the threats to life or limb, not the disputed invitation.

"The visitor's reticence without some such good reason would show not timidity but a realization that when people living together disagree over the use of their common quarters, a resolution must come through voluntary accommodation, not by appeals to authority. Unless the people living together fall within some recognized hierarchy, like a household of parent and child or barracks housing military personnel of different grades, there is no societal understanding of superior and inferior, a fact reflected in a standard formulation of domestic property law, that '[e]ach cotenant has the right to use and enjoy the entire property as if he or she were the sole owner, limited only by the same right in the other cotenants.' * * *

"Since the co-tenant wishing to open the door to a third party has no recognized authority in law or social practice to prevail over a present and objecting co-tenant, his disputed invitation, without more, gives a police officer no better claim to reasonableness in entering than the officer would have in the absence of any consent at all."

As for "the consenting tenant's interest as a citizen in bringing criminal activity to light" and "a co-tenant's legitimate self-interest in siding with the police to deflect suspicion raised by sharing quarters with a criminal," the majority noted they could be served in other ways, such as by that tenant delivering evidence to the police on her own initiative or by delivering information to the police that would support issuance of a search warrant. Moreover, the police may "enter a dwelling to protect a resident from domestic violence, so long as they have good reason to believe such a threat exists."

The court then turned to "the significance of *Matlock* [p. 463] and *Rodriguez* [p. 462] after today's decision. Although the *Matlock* defendant was not present with the opportunity to object, he was in a squad car not far away; the *Rodriguez* defendant was actually asleep in the apartment, and the police might have roused him with a knock on the door before they entered with only the consent of an apparent co-tenant. If those cases are not to be undercut by today's holding, we have to admit that we are drawing a fine line; if a potential defendant with self-interest in objecting is in fact at the door and objects, the co-tenant's permission does not suffice for a reasonable search, whereas the potential objector, nearby but not invited to take part in the threshold colloquy, loses out.

"This is the line we draw, and we think the formalism is justified. So long as there is no evidence that the police have removed the potentially objecting tenant from the entrance for the sake of avoiding a possible objection, there is practical value in the simple clarity of complementary rules, one recognizing the co-tenant's permission when there is no fellow occupant on hand, the other according dispositive weight to the fellow occupant's contrary indication when he expresses it. [I]t would needlessly limit the capacity of the police to respond to ostensibly legitimate opportunities in the field if we were to hold that reasonableness required the police to take affirmative steps to find a potentially objecting co-tenant before acting on the permission they had already received."

Roberts, C.J., joined by Scalia, J., dissenting, objected: "Rather than draw such random and happenstance lines—and pretend that the Constitution decreed them—the more reasonable approach is to adopt a rule acknowledging that shared living space entails a limited yielding of privacy to others, and that the law historically permits those to whom we have yielded our privacy to in turn cooperate with the government." Thomas, J., dissenting separately, deemed it unnecessary to resolve the issue dividing the other Justices, for he believed this was a case of evidence obtained by a private person [see p. 249], just as held in *Coolidge v. New Hampshire*, 403 U.S. 443 (1971), where the police likewise accompanied the wife to the bedroom, albeit in response to her declaration that she would get her husband's guns for the police.

On which side of the "fine line" drawn by the Court in *Randolph* do the following situations, also involving husband and wife (H & W), belong? (1) H is arrested in the front yard and placed in a squad car parked at the curb, where he declines to consent to search of the house, but police then go to the front door and obtain consent from W. (2) H is approached by police at his place of employment and asked for consent to search his house, which he refuses, after which police go to the house and obtain consent from W. (3) Police knock on the door and H and W come to the door together, police ask for and obtain consent to search the house from W, and then enter without soliciting H's view of the matter. (4) Same as (3), except that immediately upon obtaining W's consent, the police order H to step out of the doorway so that they can enter. (5) W goes to the precinct station and then rides back home with police, but she remains in the squad car after giving consent to search the house, after which police then knock on the door and when H answers they order him to step aside and then enter and search. (6) Same as (5), except that police do not knock on the door but simply enter, using the key provided by W, and find drugs before they are confronted by H and ordered to leave.

CHAPTER 7

UNDERCOVER INVESTIGATIONS

■ ■ ■

Undercover investigations are an important tool of modern police work. The commission of crime often involves covertly sharing evidence with others. Members of a conspiracy may meet to share notes or discuss plans. A seller of narcotics may meet with a buyer. A prostitute may meet with a customer. In all of these cases, the commission of crime involves exposure of wrongdoing to another. In an undercover investigation, a state actor pretends to be a friend, colleague, or customer of the target in order to trick the target into divulging evidence that can be used for further investigation or at trial.

There are two basic categories of undercover individuals. The first type is an undercover law enforcement officer. The second type is a confidential informant, a private citizen who has agreed to work for the police. By working on behalf of the police, the confidential informant becomes a Fourth Amendment state actor just like an undercover police officer.

This chapter considers the legal limits placed on the use of undercover officers and confidential informants. It starts by studying the Fourth Amendment limits on such techniques, and then it considers the role of the entrapment defense.

SECTION 1. SECRET AGENTS AND THE FOURTH AMENDMENT

HOFFA v. UNITED STATES
385 U.S. 293, 87 S.Ct. 408, 17 L.Ed.2d 374 (1966).

Mr. Justice Stewart delivered the opinion of the Court.

Over a period of several weeks in the late autumn of 1962 there took place in a federal court in Nashville, Tennessee, a trial by jury in which James Hoffa was charged with violating a provision of the Taft–Hartley Act. That trial, known in the present record as the Test Fleet trial, ended with a hung jury. The petitioners now before us—James Hoffa, Thomas Parks, Larry Campbell, and Ewing King— were tried and convicted in 1964 for endeavoring to bribe members of that jury. The convictions were affirmed by the Court of Appeals. A substantial element in the Government's proof that led to the convictions of these four petitioners was contributed by a witness named Edward Partin, who testified to several incriminating statements which he said petitioners Hoffa and King had made in his presence during the course of the Test Fleet trial.

James Hoffa was president of the International Brotherhood of Teamsters. During the course of the trial he occupied a three-room suite in the Andrew Jackson Hotel in Nashville. One of his constant companions throughout the trial was the petitioner King, president of the Nashville local of the Teamsters Union. Edward Partin, a resident of Baton Rouge, Louisiana, and a local Teamsters Union official there, made repeated visits to Nashville during the period of the trial. On these visits he frequented the Hoffa hotel suite, and was continually in the company of Hoffa and his associates, including King, in and around the hotel suite, the hotel lobby, the courthouse, and elsewhere in Nashville. During this period Partin made frequent reports to a federal agent named Sheridan concerning conversations he said Hoffa and King had had with him and with each other, disclosing endeavors to bribe members of the Test Fleet jury. Partin's reports and his subsequent testimony at the petitioners' trial unquestionably contributed, directly or indirectly, to the convictions of all four of the petitioners.

The chain of circumstances which led Partin to be in Nashville during the Test Fleet trial extended back at least to September of 1962. At that time Partin was in jail in Baton Rouge on a state criminal charge. He was also under a federal indictment for embezzling union funds, and other indictments for state offenses were pending against him. Between that time and Partin's initial visit to Nashville on October 22 he was released on bail on the state criminal charge, and proceedings under the federal indictment were postponed. On October 8, Partin telephoned Hoffa in Washington, D.C., to discuss local union matters and Partin's difficulties with the authorities. In the course of this conversation Partin asked if he could see Hoffa to confer about these problems, and Hoffa acquiesced. Partin again called Hoffa on October 18 and arranged to meet him in Nashville. During this period Partin also consulted on several occasions with federal law enforcement agents, who told him that Hoffa might attempt to tamper with the Test Fleet jury, and asked him to be on the lookout in Nashville for such attempts and to report to the federal authorities any evidence of wrongdoing that he discovered. Partin agreed to do so.

After the Test Fleet trial was completed, Partin's wife received four monthly installment payments of $300 from government funds, and the state and federal charges against Partin were either dropped or not actively pursued. We proceed upon the premise that Partin was a government informer from the time he first arrived in Nashville on October 22, and that the Government compensated him for his services as such. It is upon that premise that we consider the constitutional issues presented.

It is contended that only by violating the petitioner's rights under the Fourth Amendment was Partin able to hear the petitioner's incriminating statements in the hotel suite, and that Partin's testimony was therefore inadmissible under the exclusionary rule of *Weeks v. United States*, 232 U.S. 383 (1914). The argument is that Partin's failure to disclose his role as a government informer vitiated the consent that the petitioner gave to Partin's repeated entries into the suite, and that by listening to the petitioner's statements Partin conducted an illegal 'search' for verbal evidence.

The preliminary steps of this argument are on solid ground. A hotel room can clearly be the object of Fourth Amendment protection as much as a home or an office. *United States v. Jeffers*, 342 U.S. 48 (1951). The Fourth Amendment can certainly be violated by guileful as well as by forcible intrusions into a constitutionally protected area. *Gouled v. United States*, 255 U.S. 298 (1921). And the protections of the Fourth Amendment are surely not limited to tangibles, but can extend as well to oral statements. *Silverman v. United States*, 365 U.S. 505 (1961). Where the argument falls is in its misapprehension of the fundamental nature and scope of Fourth Amendment protection. What the Fourth Amendment protects is the security a man relies upon when he places himself or his property within a constitutionally protected area, be it his home or his office, his hotel room or his automobile. There he is protected from unwarranted governmental intrusion. And when he puts something in his filing cabinet, in his desk drawer, or in his pocket, he has the right to know it will be secure from an unreasonable search or an unreasonable seizure.

In the present case, however, it is evident that no interest legitimately protected by the Fourth Amendment is involved. It is obvious that the petitioner was not relying on the security of his hotel suite when he made the incriminating statements to Partin or in Partin's presence. Partin did not enter the suite by force or by stealth. He was not a surreptitious eavesdropper. Partin was in the suite by invitation, and every conversation which he heard was either directed to him or knowingly carried on in his presence. The petitioner, in a word, was not relying on the security of the hotel room; he was relying upon his misplaced confidence that Partin would not reveal his wrongdoing. As counsel for the petitioner himself points out, some of the communications with Partin did not take place in the suite at all, but in the hall of the hotel, in the Andrew Jackson Hotel lobby, and at the courthouse.

Neither this Court nor any member of it has ever expressed the view that the Fourth Amendment protects a wrongdoer's misplaced belief that a person to whom he voluntarily confides his wrongdoing will not reveal it. Indeed, the Court unanimously rejected that very contention less than four years ago in *Lopez v. United States*, 373 US. 427 (1963). In that case the petitioner had been convicted of attempted bribery of an internal revenue agent named Davis. The Court was divided with regard to the admissibility in evidence of a surreptitious electronic recording of an incriminating conversation Lopez had had in his private office with Davis. But there was no dissent from the view that testimony about the conversation by Davis himself was clearly admissible.

As the Court put it, "Davis was not guilty of an unlawful invasion of petitioner's office simply because his apparent willingness to accept a bribe was not real. He was in the office with petitioner's consent, and while there he did not violate the privacy of the office by seizing something surreptitiously without petitioner's knowledge. The only evidence obtained consisted of statements made by Lopez to Davis, statements which Lopez knew full well could be used against him by Davis if he wished." In the words of the dissenting opinion in *Lopez*, "The risk of being overheard by an eavesdropper or betrayed by an informer or deceived as to the identity of one with whom one deals is probably inherent in the conditions of human society. It is the kind of risk we necessarily assume whenever we speak."

Adhering to these views, we hold that no right protected by the Fourth Amendment was violated in the present case.

Finally, the petitioner claims that even if there was no violation * * * of the Fourth Amendment, * * * the judgment of conviction must nonetheless be reversed. The argument is based upon the Due Process Clause of the Fifth Amendment. The totality of the Government's conduct during the Test Fleet trial operated, it is said, to "offend those canons of decency and fairness which express the notions of justice of English-speaking peoples even toward those charged with the most heinous offenses." *Rochin v. California*, p. 28.

The argument boils down to a general attack upon the use of a government informer as 'a shabby thing in any case,' and to the claim that in the circumstances of this particular case the risk that Partin's testimony might be perjurious was very high. Insofar as the general attack upon the use of informers is based upon historic 'notions' of 'English-speaking peoples,' it is without historical foundation. In the words of Judge Learned Hand, "Courts have countenanced the use of informers from time immemorial; in cases of conspiracy, or in other cases when the crime consists of preparing for another crime, it is usually necessary to rely upon them or upon accomplices because the criminals will almost certainly proceed covertly." *United States v. Dennis*, 183 F.2d 201, 224 (2d Cir. 1950).

The petitioner is quite correct in the contention that Partin, perhaps even more than most informers, may have had motives to lie. But it does not follow that his testimony was untrue, nor does it follow that his testimony was constitutionally inadmissible. The established safeguards of the Anglo–American legal system leave the veracity of a witness to be tested by cross-examination, and the credibility of his testimony to be determined by a properly instructed jury.

Affirmed.

MR. CHIEF JUSTICE WARREN, dissenting.

At this late date in the annals of law enforcement, it seems to me that we cannot say either that every use of informers and undercover agents is proper or, on the other hand, that no uses are. There are some situations where the law could not adequately be enforced without the employment of some guile or misrepresentation of identity. A law enforcement officer performing his official duties cannot be required always to be in uniform or to wear his badge of authority on the lapel of his civilian clothing. Nor need he be required in all situations to proclaim himself an arm of the law. It blinks the realities of sophisticated, modern-day criminal activity and legitimate law enforcement practices to argue the contrary. However, one of the important duties of this Court is to give careful scrutiny to practices of government agents when they are challenged in cases before us, in order to insure that the protections of the Constitution are respected and to maintain the integrity of federal law enforcement.

Here, Edward Partin, a jailbird languishing in a Louisiana jail under indictments for such state and federal crimes as embezzlement, kidnapping, and manslaughter (and soon to be charged with perjury and assault), contacted federal authorities and told them he was willing to become, and would be useful as, an informer against Hoffa who was then about to be tried in the Test Fleet case. A motive for his doing this is immediately apparent—namely, his strong desire to work his way out of jail and out of his various legal entanglements with the State and Federal Governments. And it is interesting to note that, if this was his motive, he has been uniquely successful in satisfying it. In the four years since he first volunteered to be an informer against Hoffa he has not been prosecuted on any of the serious federal charges for which he was at that time jailed, and the state charges have apparently vanished into thin air.

Shortly after Partin made contact with the federal authorities and told them of his position in the Baton Rouge Local of the Teamsters Union and of his acquaintance with Hoffa, his bail was suddenly reduced from $50,000 to $5,000 and he was released from jail. He immediately telephoned Hoffa, who was then in New Jersey, and, by collaborating with a state law enforcement official, surreptitiously made a tape recording of the conversation. A copy of the recording was furnished to federal authorities. Again on a pretext of wanting to talk with Hoffa regarding Partin's legal difficulties, Partin telephoned Hoffa a few weeks later and succeeded in making a date to meet in Nashville where Hoffa and his attorneys were then preparing for the Test Fleet trial. Unknown to Hoffa, this call was also recorded and again federal authorities were informed as to the details.

Upon his arrival in Nashville, Partin manifested his 'friendship' and made himself useful to Hoffa, thereby worming his way into Hoffa's hotel suite and becoming part and parcel of Hoffa's entourage. As the 'faithful' servant and factotum of the defense camp which he became, he was in a position to overhear conversations not directed to him, many of which were between attorneys and either their or prospective defense witnesses. Pursuant to the general instructions he received from federal authorities to report 'any attempts at witness intimidation or tampering with the jury,' anything 'illegal,' or even 'anything of interest,' Partin became the equivalent of a bugging device which moved with Hoffa wherever he went. Everything Partin saw or heard was reported to federal authorities and much of it was ultimately the subject matter of his testimony in this case. For his services he was well paid by the Government, both through devious and secret support payments to his wife and, it may be inferred, by executed promises not to pursue the indictments under which he was charged at the time he became an informer.

This type of informer and the uses to which he was put in this case evidence a serious potential for undermining the integrity of the truth-finding process in the federal courts. Given the incentives and background of Partin, no conviction should be allowed to stand when based heavily on his testimony. And that is exactly the quicksand upon which these convictions rest, because without Partin, who was the principal government witness, there would probably have been no convictions here. Thus, although petitioners make their main arguments on constitutional grounds and raise serious Fourth ... Amendment questions, it should not even be necessary for the Court to reach those questions. For the affront to the quality and fairness of federal law enforcement which this case presents is sufficient to require an exercise of our supervisory powers.

Here the Government reaches into the jailhouse to employ a man who was himself facing indictments far more serious (and later including one for perjury) than the one confronting the man against whom he offered to inform. It employed him not for the purpose of testifying to something that had already happened, but rather for the purpose of infiltration to see if crimes would in the future be committed. The Government in its zeal even assisted him in gaining a position from which he could be a witness to the confidential relationship of attorney and client engaged in the preparation of a criminal defense. And, for the dubious evidence thus obtained, the Government paid an enormous price. Certainly if a criminal defendant insinuated his informer into the prosecution's camp in this manner he would be guilty of obstructing justice. I cannot agree that what happened in this case is in keeping with the standards of justice in our federal system and I must, therefore, dissent.

NOTES AND QUESTIONS

1. *United States v. White and the "reasonable expectation of privacy" test.* The *Hoffa* case was decided one year before *Katz v. United States*, p. 264, and it therefore predates the "reasonable expectation of privacy" test first articulated in Justice Harlan's *Katz* concurrence. Following *Katz*, the Supreme Court reaffirmed the holding of *Hoffa* in UNITED STATES v. WHITE, 401 U.S. 745 (1971). Justice White's plurality opinion concluded that "[w]e see no indication in *Katz* that the Court meant to disturb that understanding of the Fourth Amendment," and added, "nor are we now inclined to overturn this view of the Fourth Amendment."

"*Hoffa v. United States*, which was left undisturbed by *Katz*, held that however strongly a defendant may trust an apparent colleague, his expectations in this respect are not protected by the Fourth Amendment when it turns out that the colleague is a government agent regularly communicating with the authorities. In these circumstances, no interest legitimately protected by the Fourth Amendment is involved, for that amendment affords no protection to 'a wrongdoer's misplaced belief that a person to whom he voluntarily confides his wrongdoing will not reveal it.' " (quoting *Hoffa*). According to Justice White, the switch to the reasonable expectation of privacy test made no difference:

"Our problem is not what the privacy expectations of particular defendants in particular situations may be or the extent to which they may in fact have relied on the discretion of their companions. Very probably, individual defendants neither know nor suspect that their colleagues have gone or will go to the police or are carrying recorders or transmitters. Otherwise, conversation would cease and our problem with these encounters would be nonexistent or far different from those now before us. Our problem, in terms of the principles announced in *Katz*, is what expectations of privacy are constitutionally 'justifiable'—what expectations the Fourth Amendment will protect in the absence of a warrant. * * *

"Inescapably, one contemplating illegal activities must realize and risk that his companions may be reporting to the police. If he sufficiently doubts their trustworthiness, the association will very probably end or never materialize. But if he has no doubts, or allays them, or risks what doubt he has, the risk is his."

Do you agree? The question appears to hinge on what the Fourth Amendment protects. According to the *Hoffa* majority, echoed in *White*, the Fourth Amendment protects expectations that the police will not enter constitutionally protected areas. The use of a secret agent involves a different kind of expectation, that a confidant will not disclose evidence of crime to the police. Are you persuaded that they are different?

2. Are cases such as *Hoffa* and *White* better explained as consent cases rather than cases on whether use of a secret agent is a search that implicates a reasonable expectation of privacy? Consider the facts of *Hoffa*. Hoffa had a reasonable expectation of privacy in his hotel room, and he knowingly consented to Partin entering his hotel room and listening to his discussions about the Test Fleet trial. From that perspective, the key question is whether Partin's secret intent to help the government invalidated Hoffa's consent. If this is a more persuasive approach, do you think the *Hoffa* case was correctly decided?

3. *Undercover agents and recording devices.* It is common for undercover agents or confidential informants to wear audio recording devices (a "wire") that record their conversations. In UNITED STATES v. WHITE, *supra*, Justice White's plurality opinion reaffirmed earlier Supreme Court precedents holding that undercover use of recording equipment does not make the agent's conduct a Fourth Amendment search. Justice White reasoned that there could be no constitutional difference between use of an undercover agent without a recording device and another undercover agent with such a device: "If the conduct and revelations of an agent operating without electronic equipment do not invade the defendant's constitutionally justifiable expectations of privacy, neither does a simultaneous recording of the same conversations made by the agent or by others from transmissions received from the agent to whom the defendant is talking and whose trustworthiness the defendant necessarily risks. * * * At least there is no persuasive evidence that the difference in this respect between the electronically equipped and the unequipped agent is substantial enough to require discrete constitutional recognition, particularly under the Fourth Amendment which is ruled by fluid concepts of 'reasonableness.'

"Nor should we be too ready to erect constitutional barriers to relevant and probative evidence which is also accurate and reliable. An electronic recording will many times produce a more reliable rendition of what a defendant has said than will the unaided memory of a police agent. It may also be that with the recording in existence it is less likely that the informant will change his mind, less chance that threat or injury will suppress unfavorable evidence and less chance that cross-examination will confound the testimony. Considerations like these obviously do not favor the defendant, but we are not prepared to hold that a defendant who has no constitutional right to exclude the informer's unaided testimony nevertheless has a Fourth Amendment privilege against a more accurate version of the events in question."

Justice Harlan dissented. According to Justice Harlan, the existence of recording equipment made a constitutional difference: "Since it is the task of the law to form and project, as well as mirror and reflect, we should not, as judges, merely recite the expectations and risks without examining the desirability of saddling them upon society. The critical question, therefore, is whether under our system of government, as reflected in the Constitution, we should impose on our citizens the risks of the electronic listener or observer without at least the protection of a warrant requirement.

"This question must, in my view, be answered by assessing the nature of a particular practice and the likely extent of its impact on the individual's sense of security balanced against the utility of the conduct as a technique of law enforcement. For those more extensive intrusions that significantly jeopardize the sense of security which is the paramount concern of Fourth Amendment liberties, I am of the view that more than self-restraint by law enforcement officials is required and at the least warrants should be necessary.

"The impact of the practice of third-party bugging, must, I think, be considered such as to undermine that confidence and sense of security in dealing with one another that is characteristic of individual relationships between citizens in a free society. It goes beyond the impact on privacy occasioned by the ordinary type of 'informer' investigation upheld in * * * *Hoffa*. The argument of the plurality opinion, to the effect that it is irrelevant whether secrets are revealed by the mere tattletale or the transistor, ignores the differences occasioned by third-party monitoring and recording which insures full and accurate disclosure of all that is said, free of the possibility of error and oversight that inheres in human reporting.

"Authority is hardly required to support the proposition that words would be measured a good deal more carefully and communication inhibited if one suspected his conversations were being transmitted and transcribed. Were third-party bugging a prevalent practice, it might well smother that spontaneity—reflected in frivolous, impetuous, sacrilegious, and defiant discourse—that liberates daily life. Much offhand exchange is easily forgotten and one may count on the obscurity of his remarks, protected by the very fact of a limited audience, and the likelihood that the listener will either overlook or forget what is said, as well as the listener's inability to reformulate a conversation without having to contend with a documented record. All these values are sacrificed by a rule of law that permits official monitoring of private discourse limited only by the need to locate a willing assistant."

4. In *United States v. Longoria*, 177 F.3d 1179 (10th Cir. 1999), members of a narcotics conspiracy smuggled drugs from Mexico to Kansas and used a tire shop in Kansas as a storage site. The smugglers all spoke both English and Spanish, but the owner of the tire shop only spoke English. Figuring that the tire shop owner could not understand them, the smugglers occasionally discussed their plans in Spanish in the presence of the shop owner. Unbeknownst to them, the shop owner was a confidential informant who recorded the Spanish conversations and gave the recordings to the FBI. The FBI translated the recordings into English and used them against the drug smugglers at trial. One smuggler, Longoria, argued that the use of the recording device violated his reasonable expectation of privacy because he spoke in a language the informant did not understand.

The Tenth Circuit disagreed: "[W]e find no precedent recognizing expectations of privacy based on a listener's ability to comprehend a foreign language and decline to find such an expectation in this case for several reasons. First, comprehension is a malleable concept not easily measured by either the defendant or the court. Attempting to delineate a standard based on subjective evaluations of linguistic capabilities would be unworkable to say the least. More important, we do not find such an expectation to be objectively reasonable. In our increasingly multilingual society, one exposing conversations to others must necessarily assume the risk his statements will be overheard and understood. Although Mr. Longoria contends he knew the informant could not understand Spanish, the informant very well may have concealed his ability to speak Spanish the same as he concealed the recording equipment and his allegiance with law enforcement. Mr. Longoria exposed his statements by speaking in a manner clearly audible by the informant. His hope that the informant would not fully understand the contents of the conversation is not an expectation society is prepared to recognize as 'reasonable.' "

5. Imagine that *Hoffa* had come out the other way, and that the Court had held that use of an undercover agent was a search that required a warrant. When would the government use undercover agents? To obtain a warrant, the government would need to establish probable cause that discussions with the target would be likely to reveal evidence of a crime. In most cases, the government would not have this degree of certainty until it was reasonably certain the defendant was guilty. If the government had this certainty, however, why would the police use undercover agents instead of simply arresting the target and charging him with the crime? How would such a rule change the enforcement of vice crimes and conspiracies?

6. *Undercover operations and the supervisory power.* In his dissent in *Hoffa*, Chief Justice Warren suggests an alternative approach to regulating undercover agents outside the Fourth Amendment. According to Warren, undercover agents should be regulated by the federal courts' "supervisory power" discussed on pages 34–37. Under this view, the Supreme Court has the power to craft standards of what evidence is admissible in federal court to maintain the integrity of the judicial system. Chief Justice Warren argues that Hoffa's conviction should not stand because Partin was himself a criminal who turned against Hoffa to help himself. According to Warren, "[t]his type of informer and the uses to which he was put in this case evidence a serious potential for undermining the integrity of the truth-finding process in the federal courts."

What exactly is wrong with using an informant in such circumstances? One concern may be that such informants are unreliable: A person facing conviction may be eager to lie about others if he thinks he will get a break in his own case. On the other hand, there are ways of dealing with this concern. The informant could be made to wear a recording device so the government need not rely on his oral testimony. Further, as Justice Stewart's majority opinion notes, counsel for the defendant will have full opportunity to cross-examine the informant at trial to demonstrate the witness's bias. Do these possibilities respond adequately to Chief Justice Warren's concerns? Or is the real problem that, as a practical matter, criminals like Hoffa only share secrets with other criminals like Partin—and that criminals like Partin only testify against criminals like Hoffa when they are facing serious jail time themselves?

7. *Government infiltration of groups engaged in First Amendment activities.* Lower courts have held that the First Amendment imposes a good faith requirement on government infiltration of groups that engage in First Amendment activities. For example, in *United States v. Mayer*, 503 F.3d 740 (9th Cir. 2007), an undercover FBI agent infiltrated the North American Man/Boy Love Association (NAMBLA). NAMBLA claims to be "a political, civil rights and educational organization" opposed to age-of-consent laws. After becoming an active member of the group, the undercover agent encountered several discussions of illegal activity. One group member named Mayer expressed in frustration that "NAMBLA kept up pretenses of trying to change society when in fact its members only wanted to travel to meet boys." The undercover agent then set up a fake trip for NAMBLA members to "meet boys," and Mayer signed up to go on the trip. When Mayer arrived at the trip destination, he was arrested for traveling in interstate commerce with intent to engage in illegal sexual activities. He then claimed that the undercover agent had violated his First and Fourth Amendment rights by infiltrating the NAMBLA group. The Ninth Circuit disagreed. The court reasoned that "an investigation threatening First Amendment rights" is permitted when it was "justified by a legitimate law enforcement purpose that outweighs any harm to First Amendment interests." The court found this requirement satisfied by reports of illegal activity the police had received relating to members of the NAMBLA group.

8.   *The Attorney General's Guidelines on the Use of Confidential Informants*. The use of confidential informants is often regulated closely by policy within law enforcement offices. For example, the U.S. Department of Justice has promulgated *The Attorney General's Guidelines Regarding The Use Of Confidential Informants*, a publicly-released document binding on federal law enforcement agencies. The Guidelines require case agents to submit applications seeking to use individual confidential informants. The applications are then reviewed by management within the agency based on the need for the informant, his likely reliability, and his background. The guidelines also impose limits on how informants can be used and how they can be paid.

9.   *Undercover agents and the scope of consent*. Under *Hoffa* and *White*, an undercover agent does not violate the Fourth Amendment if he is invited into a target's home and observes criminal activity exposed to him. Importantly, this does not mean that undercover agents are not regulated by the Fourth Amendment. Undercover agents and confidential informants are still state actors, and they must confine themselves to the scope of consent that they have been granted.

This principle was first enunciated in GOULED v. UNITED STATES, 255 U.S. 298 (1921), a case investigating government contract fraud. A government agent who was a friend of the suspect gained admission to the suspect's office by "pretending to make a friendly call." When the suspect was temporarily absent, the agent gathered incriminating documents in the suspect's office and took them away from the office and into the eager arms of the local federal prosecutor. Some of the documents were used at trial to establish the suspect's guilt. The Supreme Court ruled that the agent violated the Fourth Amendment by exceeding the scope of consent he had been granted:

"The prohibition of the Fourth Amendment is against all unreasonable searches and seizures, and if for a government officer to obtain entrance to a man's house or office by force or by an illegal threat or show of force, amounting to coercion, and then to search for and seize his private papers would be an unreasonable, and therefore a prohibited search and seizure, as it certainly would be, it is impossible to successfully contend that a like search and seizure would be a reasonable one if only admission were obtained by stealth, instead of by force or coercion. The security and privacy of the home or office and of the papers of the owner would be as much invaded and the search and seizure would be as much against his will in the one case as in the other, and it must therefore be regarded as equally in violation of his constitutional rights.

"Without discussing them, we cannot doubt that such decisions as there are in conflict with this conclusion are unsound, and that, whether entrance to the home or office of a person suspected of crime be obtained by a representative of any branch or subdivision of the government of the United States by stealth, or through social acquaintance, or in the guise of a business call, and whether the owner be present or not when he enters, any search and seizure subsequently and secretly made in his absence, falls within the scope of the prohibition of the Fourth Amendment[.]''

SECTION 2. THE ENTRAPMENT DEFENSE

A. INTRODUCTION

Entrapment law limits use of undercover agents to encourage a target to engage in criminal activity. Entrapment is a criminal law defense rather than a constitutional claim. The entrapment defense did not exist at common law. If an undercover government agent encouraged or induced a person to commit a crime, the government's conduct did not provide a defense. Courts reasoned that the public interest in punishing criminal activity existed regardless of the government's behavior. The result was that, as one court put it, "[t]he courts do not look to see who held out the bait, but to see who took it." *People v. Mills*, 18 N.Y.Crim.R. 269, 70 N.E. 786 (1904).

The first important decision recognizing an entrapment defense was SORRELLS v. UNITED STATES, 287 U.S. 435 (1932). An undercover Prohibition agent befriended Sorrells based on their shared experiences as soldiers in World War I. While at Sorrells' home, the agent twice asked Sorrells if he had any liquor (which under Prohibition was illegal to possess). Both times, Sorrells responded that he did not. Finally, the agent asked Sorrells if he could go out and buy some liquor for him. Sorrells agreed, and he returned a few minutes later with a half-gallon of whiskey that he sold to his fellow veteran for five dollars. Sorrells was then convicted of possessing and selling alcohol in violation of the National Prohibition Act. When the case reached the Supreme Court, however, the Supreme Court reversed the conviction. The Court reasoned that Congress could not have intended to prohibit possession and distribution of alcohol in such unusual circumstances. The "criminal design" had originated with the undercover agent, who had "implant[ed] in the mind of an innocent person the disposition to commit the alleged offense and induce[d] its commission in order that they may prosecute." The Court thus read the statute to implicitly exclude Sorrells' conduct.

Because *Sorrells* was based on an interpretation of the statute rather than the Constitution, the entrapment defense has developed as a statutory criminal law defense that varies depending on the jurisdiction. Courts and legislatures have devised two basic approaches to the entrapment defense: the "subjective" approach and the "objective" approach. The subjective approach is the approach seen in *Sorrells*, and it is the majority approach; it has been adopted by the federal courts and by most states, either by statute or judicial construction. In contrast, the objective approach is the minority view. It has been adopted by about a dozen states and also is embraced by the American Law Institute's Model Penal Code.

Under the subjective approach, entrapment focuses on whether the government's conduct actually caused that particular defendant to commit the crime. The basic idea is that a law-abiding person will not commit a crime if merely given the opportunity. However, if the government actively encourages a person to commit the offense and that person is not otherwise predisposed to commit it, the government's conduct may be the cause of the defendant's conduct and the entrapment defense should apply. On the other hand, if the government does not actively encourage the criminal act or the defendant is predisposed to commit it, then the defendant's own predisposition is the cause of the criminal act and the entrapment defense should not be available.

In jurisdictions that adopt the subjective approach, entrapment is a factual question for the jury rather than a legal question for the judge. Because the legislature is presumed not to have wished to prohibit certain conduct, whether the government's conduct brought the defendant's act outside the statute becomes a question for the jury. Appellate decisions on the entrapment defense therefore take on a narrow role. In jurisdictions that adopt the subjective approach to entrapment, appellate review of entrapment claims generally is limited to the accuracy of jury instructions and whether adequate evidence supports jury findings.

The objective approach is different. Under the objective approach, courts focus solely on the government's conduct and whether it 'goes too far' to be acceptable. The characteristics of the particular defendant are irrelevant. This inquiry raises a question of social policy rather than fact. The basic idea is that the entrapment defense deters government overreaching, and courts must monitor government behavior to identify practices that should not be permitted. In most (but not all) jurisdictions, entrapment becomes a question of law for the court rather than a question of fact for the jury.

Importantly, it is possible for the objective test to resemble the subjective test. For example, the Model Penal Code's objective approach permits the defense when the government agent "induces or encourages" another person to engage in criminal conduct in ways that "create a substantial risk that such an offense will be committed by persons other than those who are ready to commit it." MPC § 2.13(1). Like the subjective test, this objective approach looks at the government's inducement and considers the response of those predisposed to commit the offense. Unlike the subjective test, however, the question of predisposition is general rather than specific. The objective test asks whether the government's conduct creates a substantial risk that a hypothetical person who is not predisposed will nonetheless commit the crime. In contrast, the subjective approach looks at evidence that the particular defendant who has been charged was actually predisposed to commit the crime.

B. INDUCEMENT

To be entitled to an entrapment defense, the defendant must ordinarily show that the government's conduct "induced" the defendant to commit the crime. The following case considers the meaning of inducement, as well as the difference between inducement under the subjective approach and inducement under the objective approach.

SHERMAN v. UNITED STATES

356 U.S. 369, 78 S.Ct. 819, 2 L.Ed.2d 848 (1958).

MR. CHIEF JUSTICE WARREN delivered the opinion of the Court.

The issue before us is whether petitioner's conviction should be set aside on the ground that as a matter of law the defense of entrapment was established.

In late August 1951, Kalchinian, a government informer, first met petitioner at a doctor's office where apparently both were being treated to be cured of narcotics addition. Several accidental meetings followed, either at the doctor's office or at the pharmacy where both filled their prescriptions from the doctor. From mere greetings, conversation progressed to a discussion of mutual experiences and problems, including their attempts to overcome addiction to narcotics. Finally Kalchinian asked petitioner if he knew of a good source of narcotics. He asked petitioner to supply him with a source because he was not responding to treatment. From the first, petitioner tried to avoid the issue. Not until after a number of repetitions of the request, predicated on Kalchinian's presumed suffering, did petitioner finally acquiesce. Several times thereafter he obtained a quantity of narcotics which he shared with Kalchinian. Each time petitioner told Kalchinian that the total cost of narcotics he obtained was twenty-five dollars and that Kalchinian owed him fifteen dollars. The informer thus bore the cost of his share of the narcotics plus the taxi and other expenses necessary to obtain the drug. After several such sales Kalchinian informed agents of the Bureau of Narcotics that he had another seller for them. On three occasions during November 1951, Government agents observed petitioner give narcotics to Kalchinian in return for money supplied by the Government.

At the trial the factual issue was whether the informer had convinced an otherwise unwilling person to commit a criminal act or whether petitioner was already predisposed to commit the act and exhibited only the natural hesitancy of one acquainted with the narcotics trade. The issue of entrapment went to the jury, and a conviction resulted. Petitioner was sentenced to imprisonment for ten years. The Court of Appeals for the Second Circuit affirmed. We granted certiorari.

In *Sorrells v. United States*, [p. 479], this Court firmly recognized the defense of entrapment in the federal courts. The intervening years have in no way detracted from the principles underlying that decision. The function of law enforcement is the prevention of crime and the apprehension of criminals. Manifestly, that function does not include the manufacturing of crime. Criminal activity is such that stealth and strategy are necessary weapons in the arsenal of the police officer. However, 'A different question is presented when the criminal design originates with the officials of the government, and they implant in the mind of an innocent person the disposition to commit the alleged offense and induce its commission in order that they may prosecute.' The stealth and strategy become as objectionable police methods as the coerced confession and the unlawful search. Congress could not have intended that its statutes were to be enforced by tempting innocent persons into violations.

However, the fact that government agents merely afford opportunities or facilities for the commission of the offense does not constitute entrapment. Entrapment occurs only when the criminal conduct was 'the product of the creative activity' of law-enforcement officials. To determine whether entrapment has been established, a line must be drawn between the trap for the unwary innocent and the trap for the unwary criminal. The principles by which the courts are to make this determination were outlined in *Sorrells*. On the one hand, at trial the accused may examine the conduct of the government agent; and on the other hand, the accused will be subjected to an appropriate and searching inquiry into his own conduct and predisposition as bearing on his claim of innocence.

We conclude from the evidence that entrapment was established as a matter of law. In so holding, we are not choosing between conflicting witnesses, nor judging credibility. Aside from recalling Kalchinian, who was the Government's witness, the defense called no witnesses. We reach our conclusion from the undisputed testimony of the prosecution's witnesses.

It is patently clear that petitioner was induced by Kalchinian. The informer himself testified that, believing petitioner to be undergoing a cure for narcotics addiction, he nonetheless sought to persuade petitioner to obtain for him a source of narcotics. In Kalchinian's own words we are told of the accidental, yet recurring, meetings, the ensuing conversations concerning mutual experiences in regard to narcotics addiction, and then of Kalchinian's resort to sympathy. One request was not enough, for Kalchinian tells us that additional ones were necessary to overcome, first, petitioner's refusal, then has evasiveness, and then his hesitancy in order to achieve capitulation. Kalchinian not only procured a source of narcotics but apparently also induced petitioner to return to the habit. Finally, assured of a catch, Kalchinian informed the authorities so that they could close the net. The Government cannot disown Kalchinian and insist it is not responsible for his actions. Although he was not being paid, Kalchinian was an active government informer who had but recently been the instigator of at least two other prosecutions. Undoubtedly the impetus for such achievements was the fact that in 1951 Kalchinian was himself under criminal charges for illegally selling narcotics and had not yet been sentenced. It makes no difference that the sales for which petitioner was convicted occurred after a series of sales. They were not independent acts subsequent to the inducement but part of a course of conduct which was the product of the inducement.

The Government sought to overcome the defense of entrapment by claiming that petitioner evinced a 'ready complaisance' to accede to Kalchinian's request. Aside from a record of past convictions, which we discuss in the following paragraph, the Government's case is unsupported. There is no evidence that petitioner himself was in the trade. When his apartment was searched after arrest, no narcotics were found. There is no significant evidence that petitioner even made a profit on any sale to Kalchinian. The Government's characterization of petitioner's hesitancy to Kalchinian's request as the natural wariness of the criminal cannot fill the evidentiary void.

The Government's additional evidence in the second trial to show that petitioner was ready and willing to sell narcotics should the opportunity present itself was petitioner's record of two past narcotics convictions. In 1942 petitioner was convicted of illegally selling narcotics; in 1946 he was convicted of illegally possessing them. However, a nine-year-old sales conviction and a five-year-old possession conviction are insufficient to prove petitioner had a readiness to sell narcotics at the time Kalchinian approached him, particularly when we must assume from the record he was trying to overcome the narcotics habit at the time.

The case at bar illustrates an evil which the defense of entrapment is designed to overcome. The government informer entices someone attempting to avoid narcotics not only into carrying out an illegal sale but also into returning to the habit of use. Selecting the proper time, the informer then tells the government agent. The set-up is accepted by the agent without even a question as to the manner in which the informer encountered the seller. Thus the Government plays on the weaknesses of an innocent party and beguiles him into committing crimes which he otherwise would not have attempted. Law enforcement does not require methods such as this.

The judgment of the Court of Appeals is reversed and the case is remanded to the District Court with instructions to dismiss the indictment.

Mr. Justice Frankfurter, whom Mr. Justice Douglas, Mr. Justice Harlan, and Mr. Justice Brennan join, concurring in the result.

Although agreeing with the Court that the undisputed facts show entrapment as a matter of law, I reach this result by a route different from the Court's.

It is surely sheer fiction to suggest that a conviction cannot be had when a defendant has been entrapped by government officers or informers because 'Congress could not have intended that its statutes were to be enforced by tempting innocent persons into violations.' In these cases raising claims of entrapment, the only legislative intention that can with any show of reason be extracted from the statute is the intention to make criminal precisely the conduct in which the defendant has engaged. That conduct includes all the elements necessary to constitute criminality. Without compulsion and 'knowingly,' where that is requisite, the defendant has violated the statutory command. If he is to be relieved from the usual punitive consequences, it is on no account because he is innocent of the offense described. In these circumstances, conduct is not less criminal because the result of temptation, whether the tempter is a private person or government agent or informer.

The courts refuse to convict an entrapped defendant, not because his conduct falls outside the proscription of the statute, but because, even if his guilt be admitted, the methods employed on behalf of the Government to bring about conviction cannot be countenanced. * * * Insofar as they are used as instrumentalities in the administration of criminal justice, the federal courts have an obligation to set their face against enforcement of the law by lawless means or means that violate rationally vindicated standards of justice, and to refuse to sustain such methods by effectuating them. They do this in the exercise of a recognized jurisdiction to formulate and apply "proper standards for the enforcement of the federal criminal law in the federal courts," *McNabb v. United States*, [p. 34], an obligation that goes beyond the conviction of the particular defendant before the court. Public confidence in the fair and honorable administration of justice, upon which ultimately depends the rule of law, is the transcending value at stake.

The formulation of these standards does not in any way conflict with the statute the defendant has violated, or involve the initiation of a judicial policy disregarding or qualifying that framed by Congress. A false choice is put when it is said that either the defendant's conduct does not fall within the statute or he must be convicted. The statute is wholly directed to defining and prohibiting the substantive offense concerned and expresses no purpose, either permissive or prohibitory, regarding the police conduct that will be tolerated in the detection of crime. A statute prohibiting the sale of narcotics is as silent on the question of entrapment as it is on the admissibility of illegally obtained evidence. It is enacted, however, on the basis of certain presuppositions concerning the established legal order and the role of the courts within that system in formulating standards for the administration of criminal justice when Congress itself has not specifically legislated to that end. Specific statutes are to be fitted into an antecedent legal system.

It might be thought that it is largely an academic question whether the court's finding a bar to conviction derives from the statute or from a supervisory jurisdiction over the administration of criminal justice; under either theory substantially the same considerations will determine whether the defense of entrapment is sustained. But to look to a statute for guidance in the application of a policy not remotely within the contemplation of Congress at the time of its enactment is to distort analysis. It is to run the risk, furthermore, that the court will shirk the responsibility that is necessarily in its keeping, if Congress is truly silent, to accommodate the dangers of overzealous law enforcement and civilized methods adequate to counter the ingenuity of modern criminals. The reasons that actually underlie the defense of entrapment can too easily be lost sight of in the pursuit of a wholly fictitious congressional intent.

The crucial question, not easy of answer, to which the court must direct itself is whether the police conduct revealed in the particular case falls below standards, to which common feelings respond, for the proper use of governmental power. For answer it is wholly irrelevant to ask if the 'intention' to commit the crime originated with the defendant or government officers, or if the criminal conduct was the product of 'the creative activity' of law-enforcement officials. Yet in the present case the Court repeats and purports to apply these unrevealing tests. Of course in every case of this kind the intention that the particular crime be committed originates with the police, and without their inducement the crime would not have occurred. But it is perfectly clear from such decisions * * * that this is not enough to enable the defendant to escape conviction.

The intention referred to, therefore, must be a general intention or predisposition to commit, whenever the opportunity should arise, crimes of the kind solicited, and in proof of such a predisposition evidence has often been admitted to show the defendant's reputation, criminal activities, and prior disposition. The danger of prejudice in such a situation, particularly if the issue of entrapment must be submitted to the jury and disposed of by a general verdict of guilty or innocent, is evident. The defendant must either forego the claim of entrapment or run the substantial risk that, in spite of instructions, the jury will allow a criminal record or bad reputation to weigh in its determination of guilt of the specific offense of which he stands charged. Furthermore, a test that looks to the character and predisposition of the defendant rather than the conduct of the police loses sight of the underlying reason for the defense of entrapment. No matter what the defendant's past record and present inclinations to criminality, or the depths to which he has sunk in the estimation of society, certain police conduct to ensnare him into further crime is not to be tolerated by an advanced society.

In the present case it is clear that the Court in fact reverses the conviction because of the conduct of the informer Kalchinian, and not because the Government has failed to draw a convincing picture of petitioner's past criminal conduct. Permissible police activity does not vary according to the particular defendant concerned; surely if two suspects have been solicited at the same time in the same manner, one should not go to jail simply because he has been convicted before and is said to have a criminal disposition. No more does it vary according to the suspicions, reasonable or unreasonable, of the police concerning the defendant's activities. Appeals to sympathy, friendship, the possibility of exorbitant gain, and so forth, can no more be tolerated when directed against a past offender than against an ordinary law-abiding citizen. A contrary view runs afoul of fundamental principles of equality under law, and would espouse the notion that when dealing with the criminal classes anything goes. The possibility that no matter what his past crimes and general disposition the defendant might not have committed the particular crime unless confronted with inordinate inducements, must not be ignored. Past crimes do not forever outlaw the criminal and open him to police practices, aimed at securing his repeated conviction, from which the ordinary citizen is protected. The whole ameliorative hopes of modern penology and prison administration strongly counsel against such a view.

This does not mean that the police may not act so as to detect those engaged in criminal conduct and ready and willing to commit further crimes should the occasion arise. Such indeed is their obligation. It does mean that in holding out inducements they should act in such a manner as is likely to induce to the commission of crime only these persons and not others who would normally avoid crime and through self-struggle resist ordinary temptations. This test shifts attention from the record and predisposition of the particular defendant to the conduct of the police and the likelihood, objectively considered, that it would entrap only those ready and willing to commit crime. It is as objective a test as the subject matter permits, and will give guidance in regulating police conduct that is lacking when the reasonableness of police suspicions must be judged or the criminal disposition of the defendant retrospectively appraised. It draws directly on the fundamental intuition that led in the first instance to the outlawing of 'entrapment' as a prosecutorial instrument. The power of government is abused and directed to an end for which it was not constituted when employed to promote rather than detect crime and to bring about the downfall of those who, left to themselves, might well have obeyed the law. Human nature is weak enough and sufficiently beset by temptations without government adding to them and generating crime.

What police conduct is to be condemned, because likely to induce those not otherwise ready and willing to commit crime, must be picked out from case to case as new situations arise involving different crimes and new methods of detection. The *Sorrells* case [p. 479] involved persistent solicitation in the face of obvious reluctance, and appeals to sentiments aroused by reminiscences of experiences as companions in arms in the World War. Particularly reprehensible in the present case was the use of repeated requests to overcome petitioner's hesitancy, coupled with appeals to sympathy based on mutual experiences with narcotics addiction. Evidence of the setting in which the inducement took place is of course highly relevant in judging its likely effect, and the court should also consider the nature of the crime involved, its secrecy and difficulty of detection, and the manner in which the particular criminal business is usually carried on.

Such a judgment, aimed at blocking off areas of impermissible police conduct, is appropriate for the court and not the jury. The protection of its own functions and the preservation of the purity of its own temple belongs only to the court. It is the province of the court and of the court alone to protect itself and the government from such prostitution of the criminal law. The violation of the principles of justice by the entrapment of the unwary into crime should be dealt with by the court no matter by whom or at what stage of the proceedings the facts are brought to its attention. Equally important is the consideration that a jury verdict, although it may settle the issue of entrapment in the particular case, cannot give significant guidance for official conduct for the future. Only the court, through the gradual evolution of explicit standards in accumulated precedents, can do this with the degree of certainty that the wise administration of criminal justice demands.

NOTES AND QUESTIONS

1. *The meaning of "inducement."* The government does not entrap a defendant merely by affording opportunities or facilities for the commission of the offense. For the entrapment defense to be available, the government must "implant in the mind of an innocent person the disposition to commit the alleged offense and induce its commission." In what circumstances does government conduct "implant" such ideas and "induce" an otherwise innocent person to commit a crime?

Shortly before being nominated to the Supreme Court, then-Judge Stephen Breyer described the federal caselaw interpreting "inducement" in UNITED STATES v. GENDRON, 18 F.3d 955, 961–62 (1st Cir. 1994) (citations and quotations omitted):

"An inducement consists of an opportunity plus something else—typically, excessive pressure by the government upon the defendant or the government's taking advantage of an alternative, non-criminal type of motive. A sting that combines an ordinary opportunity with these extra elements runs the risk of catching in the law enforcement net not only those who might well have committed the crime elsewhere (in the absence of the sting), but also those who (in its absence) likely would never have done so. Insofar as the net catches the latter, it stretches beyond its basic law enforcement purpose.

"Some examples of improper inducement may help. Courts have found a basis for sending the entrapment issue to the jury (or finding entrapment established as a matter of law) where government officials: (1) used intimidation and threats against a defendant's family; (2) called every day, began threatening the defendant, and were belligerent; (3) engaged in forceful solicitation and dogged insistence until defendant capitulated; (4) played upon defendant's sympathy for informant's common narcotics experience and withdrawal symptoms; (5) played upon sentiment of one former war buddy for another to get liquor (during prohibition); (6) used repeated suggestions which succeeded only when defendant had lost his job and needed money for his family's food and rent; [and] (7) told defendant that she (the agent) was suicidal and in desperate need of money."

    2. Consider Ronald J. Allen, Melissa Luttrell & Anne Kreeger, *Clarifying Entrapment*, 89 J. Crim. L. & Criminology 407, 413 (1999): "We assume that there are a few people who would not commit any criminal acts no matter what the provocation or enticement. We will not refer further to such saintly or misguided individuals. Everyone else, we assume, has a price. That price may be quite high, for example because a person puts a high value on her good name, but it exists. * * * The only salient question is whether a person's price has been met, not whether he has one, since by hypothesis everyone but the saintly does. * * * [T]he person who does not take the bait almost surely would take a higher, even if greatly higher, bait."

    If this is correct, then the inducement requirement limits entrapment defenses to cases when a defendant has a high price. Does that make sense? Are defendants with a low price who will commit a crime without encouragement more culpable than those who have a high price and will only commit crimes when strongly encouraged to do so?

    3. *Subjective versus objective approaches*. In *Sherman*, all nine justices agreed that Sherman had a valid entrapment defense. The Justices divided sharply on the rationale. Chief Justice Warren's majority opinion applied a subjective approach, while Justice Frankfurter's concurring opinion applied an objective approach. Which approach is more persuasive? Do you agree with Chief Justice Warren that it was "patently clear" as a matter of fact that Kalchinian induced the crime? Do you agree with Justice Frankfurter's view that Kalchinian's conduct fell "below standards, to which common feelings respond, for the proper use of governmental power"? How different are these inquiries?

    Justice Frankfurter's concurrence in *Sherman* provides an extended argument against the subjective approach. Consider this criticism of the objective approach, Roger Park, *The Entrapment Controversy*, 60 Minn. L. Rev. 163, 270–71 (1976):

    "The principal goal of the [objective approach] is to control the conduct of police and informers. There are many reasons to doubt that it can succeed in doing so. Because of the nature of undercover work, courts will probably never develop a set of rules simple yet specific enough to provide clear guidance to police agents. Standardized procedures cannot govern the sundry and unpredictable events that occur during encounters between target and temptor. Moreover, even if such procedures could be formulated and somehow taught to the army of addicts and criminals used by police to set up controlled offenses, it is doubtful that they would be followed—particularly since the rules would inevitably become known to targets as well as police agents.

    "The doubtful preventive effect of the hypothetical-person defense would be purchased at a price. The defense creates a risk that dangerous chronic offenders will be acquitted because they were offered inducements that might have tempted a hypothetical law-abiding person. More subtly, it creates a danger that persons will be convicted who do not deserve punishment. This danger stems from its attempts to evaluate the quality of government conduct without considering the defendant's culpability. The notion that sauce for the wolf is sauce for the lamb leads to unhappy consequences, since the sauce will be brewed with wolves in mind. Because many targets are professional criminals, judges will be reluctant to rule that entrapment has occurred simply because an agent found it necessary to appeal to friendship, make multiple requests, or offer a substantial profit. Yet approval of such conduct would lead to unfair results in cases where the target was law-abiding but ductile. For example, conviction of someone who has been solicited by a friend may be fair enough in the general run of cases, but unfair if the target was a nondisposed person who would not have committed the type of crime charged but for a request from that particular friend."

4.   *United States v. Russell.* In UNITED STATES v. RUSSELL, 411 U.S. 423 (1973), an undercover agent named Shapiro attempted to locate a laboratory where the illegal drug methamphetamine was being manufactured. Shapiro met with Russell and the Connolly brothers (the defendants) and pretended to represent a large organization that wished to control the methamphetamine market in the area. The defendants had been manufacturing methamphetamine for some time in a laboratory of their own.

Shapiro offered the defendants a deal. He would provide them with the chemical phenyl–2–propanone, a chemical needed to manufacture the drug, in exchange for half of the manufactured drug. The chemical phenyl–2–propanone was legal to possess but difficult to find because the federal narcotics officials had urged suppliers not to sell the chemical given its use in the drug trade. Shapiro conditioned his offer on one requirement: The defendants would first need to show him their laboratory, and they would need to give him a sample of the methamphetamine they had recently manufactured. The defendants agreed, and they showed Shapiro their lab and demonstrated to him how they manufactured the drug. Shapiro later provided the chemical to the defendants, and they made methamphetamine using it. The defendants were eventually convicted of manufacturing and distributing methamphetamine based on what they had made using the chemical Shapiro provided.

On appeal following conviction, the Ninth Circuit reversed the defendants' convictions on the ground that providing the defendants with an essential ingredient in the manufacture of methamphetamine amounted to "an intolerable degree of governmental participation in the criminal enterprise." The Supreme Court granted certiorari, and the defendants argued to the Justices that the Due Process clause forbade any conviction when government agents "supplied an indispensable means to the commission of the crime that could not have been obtained otherwise, through legal or illegal channels."

In an opinion by Justice Rehnquist, the Supreme Court reversed the Ninth Circuit and held that the Due Process clause was no bar to conviction: "While we may some day be presented with a situation in which the conduct of law enforcement agents is so outrageous that due process principles would absolutely bar the government from invoking judicial processes to obtain a conviction, *cf. Rochin v. California*, [p. 28], the instant case is distinctly not of that breed. Shapiro's contribution of propanone to the criminal enterprise already in process was scarcely objectionable. The chemical is by itself a harmless substance and its possession is legal. While the Government may have been seeking to make it more difficult for drug rings, such as that of which respondent was a member, to obtain the chemical, the evidence described above shows that it nonetheless was obtainable. The law enforcement conduct here stops far short of violating that 'fundamental fairness, shocking to the universal sense of justice,' mandated by the Due Process Clause of the Fifth Amendment.

"The illicit manufacture of drugs is not a sporadic, isolated criminal incident, but a continuing, though illegal, business enterprise. In order to obtain convictions for illegally manufacturing drugs, the gathering of evidence of past unlawful conduct frequently proves to be an all but impossible task. Thus in drug-related offenses law enforcement personnel have turned to one of the only practicable means of detection: the infiltration of drug rings and a limited participation in their unlawful present practices. Such infiltration is a recognized and permissible means of investigation; if that be so, then the supply of some item of value that the drug ring requires must, as a general rule, also be permissible. For an agent will not be taken into the confidence of the illegal entrepreneurs unless he has something of value to offer them. Law enforcement tactics such as this can hardly be said to violate 'fundamental fairness' or 'shocking to the universal sense of justice.'

"Several decisions of the United States district courts and courts of appeals have undoubtedly gone beyond this Court's opinions in *Sorrells* and *Sherman* in order to bar prosecutions because of what they thought to be, for want of a better term, 'overzealous law enforcement.' But the defense of entrapment enunciated in those opinions was not intended to give the federal judiciary a 'chancellor's foot' veto over law enforcement practices of which it did not approve. The execution of the federal laws under our Constitution is confided primarily to the Executive Branch of the Government, subject to applicable constitutional and statutory limitations and to judicially fashioned rules to enforce those limitations. We think that the decision of the Court of Appeals in this case quite unnecessarily introduces an unmanageably subjective standard which is contrary to the holdings of this Court in *Sorrells* and *Sherman*.

"Those cases establish that entrapment is a relatively limited defense. It is rooted, not in any authority of the Judicial Branch to dismiss prosecutions for what it feels to have been 'overzealous law enforcement,' but instead in the notion that Congress could not have intended criminal punishment for a defendant who has committed all the elements of a proscribed offense, but was induced to commit them by the Government.

"Respondent's concession in the Court of Appeals that the jury finding as to predisposition was supported by the evidence is, therefore, fatal to his claim of entrapment. He was an active participant in an illegal drug manufacturing enterprise which began before the Government agent appeared on the scene, and continued after the Government agent had left the scene. He was, in the words of *Sherman, supra,* not an 'unwary innocent' but an 'unwary criminal.' The Court of Appeals was wrong, we believe, when it sought to broaden the principle laid down in *Sorrells* and *Sherman*."

Justices Douglas, Brennan, Marshall, and Stewart dissented. They reasoned that the Supreme Court should jettison the subjective standard to entrapment applied in *Sorrells* and *Sherman* and should instead adopt an objective approach that focused entirely on the government's conduct. According to these Justices, the government's conduct went 'too far' and should have provided the defendants with an entrapment defense.

Justice Stewart offered the following argument for this result in his dissent: "It is undisputed that phenyl-2-propanone is an essential ingredient in the manufacture of methamphetamine; that it is not used for any other purpose; and that, while its sale is not illegal, it is difficult to obtain, because a manufacturer's license is needed to purchase it, and because many suppliers, at the request of the Federal Bureau of Narcotics and Dangerous Drugs, do not sell it at all. It is also undisputed that the methamphetamine which the respondent was prosecuted for manufacturing and selling was all produced on [one day], and that all the phenyl-2-propanone used in the manufacture of that batch of the drug was provided by the government agent. In these circumstances, the agent's undertaking to supply this ingredient to the respondent, thus making it possible for the Government to prosecute him for manufacturing an illicit drug with it, was, I think, precisely the type of governmental conduct that the entrapment defense is meant to prevent.

"It cannot be doubted that if phenyl–2–propanone had been wholly unobtainable from other sources, the agent's undercover offer to supply it to the respondent in return for part of the illicit methamphetamine produced therewith—an offer initiated and carried out by the agent for the purpose of prosecuting the respondent for producing methamphetamine—would be precisely the type of governmental conduct that constitutes entrapment under any definition. For the agent's conduct in that situation would make possible the commission of an otherwise totally impossible crime, and, I should suppose, would thus be a textbook example of instigating the commission of a criminal offense in order to prosecute someone for committing it."

5. *The Fourth Amendment versus the entrapment defense.* Consider how entrapment doctrine regulates undercover investigations compared to how such investigations might have been regulated under the Fourth Amendment. The Fourth Amendment prohibits unreasonable searches and seizures; if use of a secret agent had been deemed a search, the Fourth Amendment would have regulated when secret agents could be used. It might have required a search warrant, or perhaps it would have required that secret agents be used only when circumstances made it "reasonable." In contrast, entrapment law focuses downstream. It regulates *how* the police use secret agents rather than *whether* or *when* they do so. Which is the better approach?

6. *A common myth about entrapment.* Some members of the public believe that defendants have a valid entrapment defense when an undercover police officer falsely claims not to be a member of law enforcement. According to the website *Snopes.com*, the belief is particularly common among working prostitutes: "It has long been accepted hooker lore that a working girl could render herself arrest-proof by asking a prospective john if he were a policeman before anyone's clothes came off. This belief in protection rested on the notion that even if the client did turn out to be a cop, his not being truthful about it would get the arrest thrown on the grounds of entrapment." www.snopes.com/risque/hookers/cop.asp.

Of course, this common belief is false. No undercover investigations could succeed if undercover officers had to admit their status when asked. More broadly, as the Supreme Court stated in *Lopez v. United States*, 373 U.S. 427, 434 (1963), "[t]he conduct with which the defense of entrapment is concerned is the manufacturing of crime by law enforcement officials and their agents. Such conduct, of course, is far different from the permissible stratagems involved in the detection and prevention of crime." Nonetheless, this myth persists: Targets of undercover investigations often ask officers if they are "cops," and undercover officers always say no.

C. PREDISPOSITION

Jurisdictions that adopt the subjective approach to entrapment supplement the inducement test with an inquiry into the target's predisposition. In the federal system, for example, entrapment doctrine works in the following way. First, the defendant bears the initial burden of making a showing to the trial judge that the government induced the defendant to commit the crime. If the defendant makes that showing, the burden shifts to the government. Specifically, the government must then prove to the jury beyond a reasonable doubt either that in fact there was no inducement or that the defendant was predisposed to commit the offense. *See generally United States v. Tom*, 330 F.3d 83, 89–90 (1st Cir. 2003).

The jurors must acquit the defendant if they have reasonable doubts both that he was induced and that he was predisposed. On the other hand, if the jurors agree beyond a reasonable doubt either that the defendant was predisposed or that he was not induced, the jury must reject the entrapment defense. If the jury acquits, the case is over; further proceedings are barred under the Double Jeopardy clause. If the jury convicts, the defendant may appeal the jury's conclusion that he was not entrapped. Judicial review of the jury's verdict following conviction is highly deferential. The defendant will obtain relief only if he can persuade an appellate court that, viewing the evidence in the light most favorable to the prosecution, no rational jury could have found beyond a reasonable doubt either that the defendant was predisposed or that he was not induced.

JACOBSON v. UNITED STATES
503 U.S. 540, 112 S.Ct. 1535, 118 L.Ed.2d 174 (1992).

JUSTICE WHITE delivered the opinion of the Court.

On September 24, 1987, petitioner Keith Jacobson was indicted for violating a provision of the Child Protection Act of 1984 which criminalizes the knowing receipt through the mails of a visual depiction that involves the use of a minor engaging in sexually explicit conduct. Petitioner defended on the ground that the Government entrapped him into committing the crime through a series of communications from undercover agents that spanned the 26 months preceding his arrest. Petitioner was found guilty after a jury trial. The Court of Appeals affirmed his conviction, holding that the Government had carried its burden of proving beyond reasonable doubt that petitioner was predisposed to break the law and hence was not entrapped.

Because the Government overstepped the line between setting a trap for the unwary innocent and the unwary criminal, and as a matter of law failed to establish that petitioner was independently predisposed to commit the crime for which he was arrested, we reverse the Court of Appeals' judgment affirming his conviction.

In February 1984, petitioner, a 56-year-old veteran-turned-farmer who supported his elderly father in Nebraska, ordered two magazines and a brochure from a California adult bookstore. The magazines, entitled Bare Boys I and Bare Boys II, contained photographs of nude preteen and teenage boys. The contents of the magazines startled petitioner, who testified that he had expected to receive photographs of "young men 18 years or older." * * *

The young men depicted in the magazines were not engaged in sexual activity, and petitioner's receipt of the magazines was legal under both federal and Nebraska law. Within three months, the law with respect to child pornography changed; Congress passed the Act illegalizing the receipt through the mails of sexually explicit depictions of children. In the very month that the new provision became law, postal inspectors found petitioner's name on the mailing list of the California bookstore that had mailed him Bare Boys I and II. There followed over the next 2 1/2 years repeated efforts by two Government agencies, through five fictitious organizations and a bogus pen pal, to explore petitioner's willingness to break the new law by ordering sexually explicit photographs of children through the mail.

The Government began its efforts in January 1985 when a postal inspector sent petitioner a letter supposedly from the American Hedonist Society, which in fact was a fictitious organization. The letter included a membership application and stated the Society's doctrine: that members had the "right to read what we desire, the right to discuss similar interests with those who share our philosophy, and finally that we have the right to seek pleasure without restrictions being placed on us by outdated puritan morality." Petitioner enrolled in the organization and returned a sexual attitude questionnaire that asked him to rank on a scale of one to four his enjoyment of various sexual materials, with one being "really enjoy," two being "enjoy," three being "somewhat enjoy," and four being "do not enjoy." Petitioner ranked the entry "pre-teen sex" as a two, but indicated that he was opposed to pedophilia.

For a time, the Government left petitioner alone. But then a new "prohibited mailing specialist" in the Postal Service found petitioner's name in a file, and in May 1986, petitioner received a solicitation from a second fictitious consumer research company, "Midlands Data Research," seeking a response from those who "believe in the joys of sex and the complete awareness of those lusty and youthful lads and lasses of the neophite [sic] age." The letter never explained whether "neophite" referred to minors or young adults. Petitioner responded: "Please feel free to send me more information, I am interested in teenage sexuality. Please keep my name confidential."

Petitioner then heard from yet another Government creation, "Heartland Institute for a New Tomorrow" (HINT), which proclaimed that it was "an organization founded to protect and promote sexual freedom and freedom of choice. We believe that arbitrarily imposed legislative sanctions restricting your sexual freedom should be rescinded through the legislative process." The letter also enclosed a second survey. Petitioner indicated that his interest in "preteen sex-homosexual" material was above average, but not high. In response to another question, petitioner wrote: "Not only sexual expression but freedom of the press is under attack. We must be ever vigilant to counter attack right wing fundamentalists who are determined to curtail our freedoms."

HINT replied, portraying itself as a lobbying organization seeking to repeal "all statutes which regulate sexual activities, except those laws which deal with violent behavior, such as rape. HINT is also lobbying to eliminate any legal definition of 'the age of consent.'" These lobbying efforts were to be funded by sales from a catalog to be published in the future "offering the sale of various items which we believe you will find to be both interesting and stimulating." HINT also provided computer matching of group members with similar survey responses; and, although petitioner was supplied with a list of potential "pen pals," he did not initiate any correspondence.

Nevertheless, the Government's "prohibited mailing specialist" began writing to petitioner, using the pseudonym "Carl Long." The letters employed a tactic known as "mirroring," which the inspector described as "reflecting whatever the interests are of the person we are writing to." Petitioner responded at first, indicating that his interest was primarily in "male-male items." Inspector "Long" wrote back:

> "My interests too are primarily male-male items. Are you satisfied with the type of VCR tapes available? Personally, I like the amateur stuff better if its [sic] well produced as it can get more kinky and also seems more real. I think the actors enjoy it more."

Petitioner responded:

> "As far as my likes are concerned, I like good looking young guys (in their late teens and early 20's) doing their thing together."

Petitioner's letters to "Long" made no reference to child pornography. After writing two letters, petitioner discontinued the correspondence.

By March 1987, 34 months had passed since the Government obtained petitioner's name from the mailing list of the California bookstore, and 26 months had passed since the Postal Service had commenced its mailings to petitioner. Although petitioner had responded to surveys and letters, the Government had no evidence that petitioner had ever intentionally possessed or been exposed to child pornography. The Postal Service had not checked petitioner's mail to determine whether he was receiving questionable mailings from persons—other than the Government—involved in the child pornography industry.

At this point, a second Government agency, the Customs Service, included petitioner in its own child pornography sting, "Operation Borderline," after receiving his name on lists submitted by the Postal Service. Using the name of a fictitious Canadian company called "Produit Outaouais," the Customs Service mailed petitioner a brochure advertising photographs of young boys engaging in sex. Petitioner placed an order that was never filled.

The Postal Service also continued its efforts in the Jacobson case, writing to petitioner as the "Far Eastern Trading Company Ltd." The letter began:

"As many of you know, much hysterical nonsense has appeared in the American media concerning 'pornography' and what must be done to stop it from coming across your borders. This brief letter does not allow us to give much comments; however, why is your government spending millions of dollars to exercise international censorship while tons of drugs, which makes yours the world's most crime ridden country are passed through easily."

The letter went on to say:

"We have devised a method of getting these to you without prying eyes of U.S. Customs seizing your mail. After consultations with American solicitors, we have been advised that once we have posted our material through your system, it cannot be opened for any inspection without authorization of a judge."

The letter invited petitioner to send for more information. It also asked petitioner to sign an affirmation that he was "not a law enforcement officer or agent of the U.S. Government acting in an undercover capacity for the purpose of entrapping Far Eastern Trading Company, its agents or customers." Petitioner responded. A catalog was sent, and petitioner ordered Boys Who Love Boys, a pornographic magazine depicting young boys engaged in various sexual activities. Petitioner was arrested after a controlled delivery of a photocopy of the magazine.

When petitioner was asked at trial why he placed such an order, he explained that the Government had succeeded in piquing his curiosity:

"Well, the statement was made of all the trouble and the hysteria over pornography and I wanted to see what the material was. It didn't describe the—I didn't know for sure what kind of sexual action they were referring to in the Canadian letter."

In petitioner's home, the Government found the Bare Boys magazines and materials that the Government had sent to him in the course of its protracted investigation, but no other materials that would indicate that petitioner collected, or was actively interested in, child pornography.

Petitioner was indicted for violating 18 U.S.C. § 2252(a)(2)(A). The trial court instructed the jury on the petitioner's entrapment defense, petitioner was convicted, and a divided Court of Appeals for the Eighth Circuit, sitting en banc, affirmed, concluding that Jacobson was not entrapped as a matter of law. We granted certiorari.

There can be no dispute about the evils of child pornography or the difficulties that laws and law enforcement have encountered in eliminating it. Likewise, there can be no dispute that the Government may use undercover agents to enforce the law. "It is well settled that the fact that officers or employees of the Government merely afford opportunities or facilities for the commission of the offense does not defeat the prosecution. Artifice and stratagem may be employed to catch those engaged in criminal enterprises." *Sorrells v. United States*, [p. 479].

In their zeal to enforce the law, however, Government agents may not originate a criminal design, implant in an innocent person's mind the disposition to commit a criminal act, and then induce commission of the crime so that the Government may prosecute. *Sorrells, supra; Sherman*, [p. 480], *supra*. Where the Government has induced an individual to break the law and the defense of entrapment is at issue, as it was in this case, the prosecution must prove beyond reasonable doubt that the defendant was disposed to commit the criminal act prior to first being approached by Government agents.[2]

Thus, an agent deployed to stop the traffic in illegal drugs may offer the opportunity to buy or sell drugs and, if the offer is accepted, make an arrest on the spot or later. In such a typical case, or in a more elaborate "sting" operation involving government-sponsored fencing where the defendant is simply provided with the opportunity to commit a crime, the entrapment defense is of little use because the ready commission of the criminal act amply demonstrates the defendant's predisposition. Had the agents in this case simply offered petitioner the opportunity to order child pornography through the mails, and petitioner—who must be presumed to know the law—had promptly availed himself of this criminal opportunity, it is unlikely that his entrapment defense would have warranted a jury instruction.

But that is not what happened here. By the time petitioner finally placed his order, he had already been the target of 26 months of repeated mailings and communications from Government agents and fictitious organizations. Therefore, although he had become predisposed to break the law by May 1987, it is our view that the Government did not prove that this predisposition was independent and not the product of the attention that the Government had directed at petitioner since January 1985.

The prosecution's evidence of predisposition falls into two categories: evidence developed prior to the Postal Service's mail campaign, and that developed during the course of the investigation. The sole piece of preinvestigation evidence is petitioner's 1984 order and receipt of the Bare Boys magazines. But this is scant if any proof of petitioner's predisposition to commit an illegal act, the criminal character of which a defendant is presumed to know. It may indicate a predisposition to view sexually oriented photographs that are responsive to his sexual tastes; but evidence that merely indicates a generic inclination to act within a broad range, not all of which is criminal, is of little probative value in establishing predisposition.

Furthermore, petitioner was acting within the law at the time he received these magazines. Receipt through the mails of sexually explicit depictions of children for noncommercial use did not become illegal under federal law until May 1984, and Nebraska had no law that forbade petitioner's possession of such material until 1988. Evidence of predisposition to do what once was lawful is not, by itself, sufficient to show predisposition to do what is now illegal, for there is a common understanding that most people obey the law even when they disapprove of it. This obedience may reflect a generalized respect for legality or the fear of prosecution, but for whatever reason, the law's prohibitions are matters of consequence. Hence, the fact that petitioner legally ordered and received the Bare Boys magazines does little to further the Government's burden of proving that

---

2. Inducement is not at issue in this case. The Government does not dispute that it induced petitioner to commit the crime.

petitioner was predisposed to commit a criminal act. This is particularly true given petitioner's unchallenged testimony that he did not know until they arrived that the magazines would depict minors.

The prosecution's evidence gathered during the investigation also fails to carry the Government's burden. Petitioner's responses to the many communications prior to the ultimate criminal act were at most indicative of certain personal inclinations, including a predisposition to view photographs of preteen sex and a willingness to promote a given agenda by supporting lobbying organizations. Even so, petitioner's responses hardly support an inference that he would commit the crime of receiving child pornography through the mails.[3] Furthermore, a person's inclinations and fantasies are his own and beyond the reach of government [under the First Amendment].

Petitioner's ready response to [the Government's] solicitations cannot be enough to establish beyond reasonable doubt that he was predisposed, prior to the Government acts intended to create predisposition, to commit the crime of receiving child pornography through the mails. The evidence that petitioner was ready and willing to commit the offense came only after the Government had devoted 2 1/2 years to convincing him that he had or should have the right to engage in the very behavior proscribed by law. Rational jurors could not say beyond a reasonable doubt that petitioner possessed the requisite predisposition prior to the Government's investigation and that it existed independent of the Government's many and varied approaches to petitioner.

Because we conclude that * * * the prosecution failed, as a matter of law, to adduce evidence to support the jury verdict that petitioner was predisposed, independent of the Government's acts and beyond a reasonable doubt, to violate the law by receiving child pornography through the mails, we reverse the Court of Appeals' judgment affirming the conviction of Keith Jacobson.

Justice O'CONNOR, with whom THE CHIEF JUSTICE and Justice KENNEDY join, and with whom Justice SCALIA joins [in part], dissenting.

Keith Jacobson was offered only two opportunities to buy child pornography through the mail. Both times, he ordered. Both times, he asked for opportunities to buy more. He needed no Government agent to coax, threaten, or persuade him; no one played on his sympathies, friendship, or suggested that his committing the crime would further a greater good. In fact, no Government agent even contacted him face to face. The Government contends that from the enthusiasm with which Mr. Jacobson responded to the chance to commit a crime, a reasonable jury could permissibly infer beyond a reasonable doubt that he was predisposed to commit the crime. I agree.

The Court, however, concludes that a reasonable jury could not have found Mr. Jacobson to be predisposed beyond a reasonable doubt on the basis of his responses to the Government's catalogs, even though it admits that, by that time, he was predisposed to commit the crime. The Government, the Court holds, failed to provide evidence that Mr. Jacobson's obvious predisposition at the time of the crime "was independent and not the product of the attention that the Government had directed at petitioner." In so holding, I believe the Court fails to acknowledge the reasonableness of the jury's inference from the evidence, redefines "predisposition," and introduces a new requirement that Government sting

---

3. We do not hold, as the dissent suggests, that the Government was required to prove that petitioner knowingly violated the law. We simply conclude that proof that petitioner engaged in legal conduct and possessed certain generalized personal inclinations is not sufficient evidence to prove beyond a reasonable doubt that he would have been predisposed to commit the crime charged independent of the Government's coaxing.

operations have a reasonable suspicion of illegal activity before contacting a suspect.

This Court has held previously that a defendant's predisposition is to be assessed as of the time the Government agent first suggested the crime, not when the Government agent first became involved. *Sherman v. United States*, [p. 480]. Until the Government actually makes a suggestion of criminal conduct, it could not be said to have "implant[ed] in the mind of an innocent person the disposition to commit the alleged offense and induce its commission. . . ." *Sorrells v. United States*, [p. 479]. Even in *Sherman v. United States*, *supra*, in which the Court held that the defendant had been entrapped as a matter of law, the Government agent had repeatedly and unsuccessfully coaxed the defendant to buy drugs, ultimately succeeding only by playing on the defendant's sympathy. The Court found lack of predisposition based on the Government's numerous unsuccessful attempts to induce the crime, not on the basis of preliminary contacts with the defendant.

Today, the Court holds that Government conduct may be considered to create a predisposition to commit a crime, even before any Government action to induce the commission of the crime. In my view, this holding changes entrapment doctrine. Generally, the inquiry is whether a suspect is predisposed before the Government induces the commission of the crime, not before the Government makes initial contact with him. There is no dispute here that the Government's questionnaires and letters were not sufficient to establish inducement; they did not even suggest that Mr. Jacobson should engage in any illegal activity. If all the Government had done was to send these materials, Mr. Jacobson's entrapment defense would fail. Yet the Court holds that the Government must prove not only that a suspect was predisposed to commit the crime before the opportunity to commit it arose, but also before the Government came on the scene.

The rule that preliminary Government contact can create a predisposition has the potential to be misread by lower courts as well as criminal investigators as requiring that the Government must have sufficient evidence of a defendant's predisposition before it ever seeks to contact him. Surely the Court cannot intend to impose such a requirement, for it would mean that the Government must have a reasonable suspicion of criminal activity before it begins an investigation, a condition that we have never before imposed. * * *

The second puzzling thing about the Court's opinion is its redefinition of predisposition. The Court acknowledges that "petitioner's responses to the many communications prior to the ultimate criminal act were . . . indicative of certain personal inclinations, including a predisposition to view photographs of preteen sex." If true, this should have settled the matter; Mr. Jacobson was predisposed to engage in the illegal conduct. Yet, the Court concludes, "petitioner's responses hardly support an inference that he would commit the crime of receiving child pornography through the mails."

The Court seems to add something new to the burden of proving predisposition. Not only must the Government show that a defendant was predisposed to engage in the illegal conduct, here, receiving photographs of minors engaged in sex, but also that the defendant was predisposed to break the law knowingly in order to do so. The statute violated here, however, does not require proof of specific intent to break the law; it requires only knowing receipt of visual depictions produced by using minors engaged in sexually explicit conduct. *See* 18 U.S.C. § 2252(a)(2). Under the Court's analysis, however, the Government must prove more to show predisposition than it need prove in order to convict.

The crux of the Court's concern in this case is that the Government went too far and "abused" the "processes of detection and enforcement" by luring an innocent person to violate the law. Consequently, the Court holds that the

Government failed to prove beyond a reasonable doubt that Mr. Jacobson was predisposed to commit the crime. It was, however, the jury's task, as the conscience of the community, to decide whether Mr. Jacobson was a willing participant in the criminal activity here or an innocent dupe. * * * There is no dispute that the jury in this case was fully and accurately instructed on the law of entrapment, and nonetheless found Mr. Jacobson guilty. Because I believe there was sufficient evidence to uphold the jury's verdict, I respectfully dissent.

NOTES AND QUESTIONS

1. *How much predisposition is enough?* Predisposition has been defined as a "state of mind which readily responds to the opportunity furnished by the officer or his agent to commit the forbidden act." *United States v. Burkley*, 591 F.2d 903, 916 (D.C. Cir. 1978). Determining that state of mind can be difficult. In some cases, the defendant will clearly indicate his interest in committing the offense before any inducement occurs. In other cases, however, the evidence of predisposition can be mixed, uncertain, or remote in time. Reasonable observers will differ as to whether the evidence proves disposition. In these circumstances, the burden of proof is particularly important. To convict, the government must prove beyond a reasonable doubt that the defendant was predisposed. If the defendant is convicted, the question on appeal becomes whether, viewing the evidence in the light most favorable to the prosecution, a rational jury could find beyond a reasonable doubt that the defendant was predisposed.

2. *What does predisposition measure?* After *Jacobson*, does predisposition hinge on the likelihood that the target would have committed the crime without the government present? Or is the issue whether the target would have likely committed the crime without the government's unusual amount of inducement? Lower courts have divided on the answer.

In *United States v. Gendron*, 18 F.3d 955 (1st Cir.1994), then Judge (now Supreme Court Justice) Breyer offered the following interpretation of the test for predisposition under *Jacobson*: "[The] right way to ask the question, it seems to us, is to abstract from—to assume away—the present circumstances *insofar as they reveal government overreaching*. That is to say, we should ask how the defendant likely would have reacted to an *ordinary* opportunity to commit the crime. By using the word 'ordinary,' we mean an opportunity that lacked those special features of the government's conduct that made of it an 'inducement,' or an 'overreaching.' Was the defendant 'predisposed' to respond affirmatively to a *proper*, not to an *improper*, lure?"

In *United States v. Thickstun*, 110 F.3d 1394 (9th Cir. 1997), the Ninth Circuit agreed with the First Circuit's approach: "We read *Jacobson* not as creating a requirement of positional readiness but as applying settled entrapment law. The inference that the government's methods had persuaded an otherwise law-abiding citizen to break the law, coupled with the absence of evidence of predisposition, established entrapment as a matter of law under the existing two-part test. It was not necessary for the court to expand the entrapment defense, nor is there language in the opinion indicating that it did so."

On the other hand, in *United States v. Hollingsworth*, 27 F.3d 1196 (7th Cir.1994) (en banc), Judge Posner offered a slightly different interpretation of the *Jacobson* test: "Predisposition is not a purely mental state, the state of being willing to swallow the government's bait. It has positional as well as dispositional force. [The] defendant must be so situated by reason of previous training or experience or occupation or acquaintances that it is likely that if the government had not induced him to commit the crime some criminal would have done so; only then does a sting or other arranged crime take a dangerous person out of circulation. A public official is in a position to take bribes; a drug addict to deal drugs; a gun dealer to engage in illegal gun sales. For these and other traditional targets of stings all that must be shown to establish the predisposition and thus defeat the defense of entrapment is willingness to violate the law without extraordinary inducements[.]''

In *United States v. Knox*, 112 F.3d 802 (5th Cir.1997), the Fifth Circuit agreed with the Seventh Circuit's approach: "[W]e are persuaded that the Seventh Circuit's *Hollingsworth* decision is correct. *See* Paul Marcus, *Presenting Back From the [Almost] Dead, the Entrapment Defense*, 47 Fla. L. Rev. 205, 233–34 (1995) (arguing *Hollingsworth* is the proper approach to entrapment law). The Supreme Court instructs that in determining predisposition we are to ask what the defendant would have done absent government involvement. To give effect to that command, we must look not only to the defendant's mental state (his 'disposition'), but also to whether the defendant was able and likely, based on experience, training, and contacts, to actually commit the crime (his 'position')."

Which approach offers the more persuasive interpretation of *Jacobson*? Which approach is preferable as a matter of policy?

3. ***The timing of predisposition evidence.*** In her dissent in *Jacobson*, Justice O'Connor expresses concern that lower courts may interpret the case as requiring that the Government "must have sufficient evidence of a defendant's predisposition before it ever seeks to contact him." Notably, however, predisposition evidence often derives from sources collected after the government's contact that relates to conduct occurring before the contact. For example, the government may only learn of a target's criminal record after the target's arrest. In that case, the criminal record can be used to show predisposition even though it was not known until after the government induced the crime and then arrested the target.

4. Consider the perspective of Judge Posner concurring in *United States v. Kaminski,* 703 F.2d 1004, 1010 (7th Cir.1983): "If the police entice someone to commit a crime who would not have done so without their blandishments, and then arrest him and he is prosecuted, convicted, and punished, law enforcement resources are squandered in the following sense: resources that could and should have been used in an effort to reduce the nation's unacceptably high crime rate are used instead in the entirely sterile activity of first inciting and then punishing a crime. However, if the police are just inducing someone to commit sooner a crime he would have committed eventually, but to do so in controlled circumstances where the costs to the criminal justice system of apprehension and conviction are minimized, the police are economizing on resources. It is particularly difficult to catch arsonists, so if all the police were doing here was making it easier to catch an arsonist—not inducing someone to become an arsonist—they were using law enforcement resources properly and there is no occasion for judicial intervention." * * *

"Thus in my view 'entrapment' is merely the name we give to a particularly unproductive use of law enforcement resources, which our system properly condemns. If this is right, the implementing concept of 'predisposition to crime' calls less for psychological conjecture than for a common-sense assessment of whether it is likely that the defendant would have committed the crime anyway—without the blandishments the police used on him—but at a time and place where it would have been more difficult for them to apprehend him and the state to convict him, or whether the police used threats or promises so powerful that a law-abiding individual was induced to commit a crime. If the latter is the case, the police tactics do not merely affect the timing and location of a crime; they cause crime."

5. *Private entrapment, vicarious entrapment, and derivative entrapment*. The entrapment defense does not apply to conduct by non-governmental actors; there is no private entrapment defense. "Only a government official or agent can entrap a defendant." *United States v. Thickstun*, 110 F.3d 1394, 1398 (9th Cir. 1997). On the other hand, if a private party is knowingly acting as an agent of the state, that private party is a state actor and the usual government entrapment rules apply. For example, a confidential informant acting on behalf of the government can trigger the entrapment defense. *See, e.g., Sherman v. United States*, p. 480.

Courts have divided on some of the possible combinations between these two categories. For example, sometimes government entrapment leads to "vicarious entrapment." In vicarious entrapment cases, the government induces a private party to act, and that private party then seeks out other private individuals, tells them of the inducements, and persuades them to join in the criminal act. Alternatively, consider the possibility of "derivative entrapment." In derivative entrapment cases, an undercover government agent persuades a private party to induce another private party to commit the crime. Should defendants be able to raise "vicarious" or "derivative" entrapment claims?

A typical vicarious entrapment case is *United States v. Valencia*, 645 F.2d 1158 (2d Cir. 1980). William Valencia and his wife Olga Valencia sold cocaine. The husband, William, played only a minor role because he had been injured in an automobile accident. An undercover officer and a confidential informant arranged to purchase cocaine from the Valencias, and worked primarily with Olga in arranging the deals. At trial, the district court permitted Olga to raise an entrapment defense but sharply limited William's entrapment defense. The trial court reasoned that Olga had worked directly with the government agents while William had only heard about the deal from Olga.

On appeal, the Second Circuit reversed. "If a person is brought into a criminal scheme after being informed indirectly of conduct or statements by a government agent which could amount to inducement, then that person should be able to avail himself of the defense of entrapment just as may the person who received the inducement directly." Although Olga had been unsuccessful in her effort to raise an entrapment defense, this did not mean that William could not succeed with the claim: "If there is sufficient evidence of inducement by a government agent to permit the case to go to the jury, then the question of entrapment turns on the individual propensity of each defendant who may have been induced. Thus, the jury might well have convicted Olga because it found that she had the propensity to commit the offense. That does not mean, however, that the jury would necessarily find that William also had such a propensity."

Next consider a derivative entrapment case, *United States v. Luisi*, 482 F.3d 43 (1st Cir. 2007). The FBI learned that Robert C. Luisi, Jr., was a captain in the "La Cosa Nostra" (LCN) crime family in Philadelphia. To obtain evidence against Luisi, the FBI directed another LCN captain named Previte, who was a cooperating witness working for the FBI, to approach Luisi with proposals for various illegal deals. When it looked unclear whether Luisi would go through a particular cocaine deal, Previte contacted Luisi's boss in the LCN family, Merlino, and urged Merlino to persuade Luisi to go forward with it. Merlino agreed to speak with Luisi, and he told Luisi to go ahead with the deal. Luisi complied soon after and was eventually charged with his role in the transaction.

The First Circuit ruled that Luisi was entitled to a jury instruction permitting the jury to find entrapment if Merlino's conduct had induced Luisi to commit the offense. The Court noted that "several circuits categorically deny the entrapment defense in *all* third-party situations where the middleman is unaware that he is helping the government." Not so in the First Circuit, however: "[I]n a case where the government agent specifically targets the defendant, and then causes the middleman to take a specifically contemplated action (that is arguably improper pressure) with the goal of ensnaring the defendant, the government's role is hardly attenuated" and can support an entrapment defense. The court therefore vacated the conviction and remanded for a new trial.

6. *"To Catch A Predator" and Internet entrapment.* The television program Dateline NBC has a regular feature, "To Catch A Predator," hosted by Chris Hansen. In these shows, volunteers working for a private organization called "Perverted Justice" enter Internet chat rooms posing as children and young teens. When a person contacts the undercover volunteer and tries to set up a sexual contact with what he thinks is a minor, the volunteer directs the person to visit a suburban home where Dateline NBC has set up video cameras that record the entire visit.

In most of the segments, the man arrives at the home expecting to find a young girl. A young actress makes a very brief appearance and then asks the man to wait for a few minutes until she returns. After the man has waited for a minute or so, TV host Chris Hansen enters the room and begins asking the man why he is there and what he plans to do. Some men confess to Hansen that they intended to engage in sexual activities with the young girl. Others contend that they came to the house just to talk or to play video games (a response sure to draw a raised eyebrow and further questioning from Hansen). After a few minutes, Hansen identifies himself and the camera crew comes out into the open. Most of the men then leave the home and are immediately arrested by local police.

Do the men caught on "To Catch A Predator" have a valid entrapment claim? To answer this, consider a few features of the entrapment defense. First, entrapment requires state action: a defendant cannot claim entrapment based on the conduct of a private party acting without police involvement. At the same time, the entrapment defense may be available if the government encouraged the private party conduct. See note 5, *supra*.

Second, it is relatively easy for an undercover agent in a chat room to avoid crossing the line and inducing criminal activity. The undercover agent can be passive and allow the defendant to take the lead in discussing sexual activity and arranging a meeting. Further, the entire exchange will be logged by the undercover agent's computer, making the facts of the exchange easy to reconstruct.

Third, the circumstances in which the defendant contacts the undercover agent can provide ready evidence of predisposition. Consider *United States v. Brand*, 467 F.3d 179 (2d Cir. 2006), in which the defendant entered an America Online chat room called "I Love Older Men" and contacted what he believed were two young girls, Sara and Julie. In the course of rejecting the defendant's entrapment defense, the court explained how the means of contact helped establish predisposition:

"[T]he manner in which Brand contacted both 'Sara' and 'Julie'—specifically, in an Internet chat room entitled 'I Love Older Men'—does bear on Brand's predisposition. He did not encounter them until he had chosen to log onto a chat room with a very suggestive name. Once in the chat room, Brand believed that 'Sara' was a thirteen-year-old girl from her screen profile and that 'Julie' was a thirteen-year-old girl from her screen name, 'julie13nyc.' Indeed, Brand confessed to using his ... screen name to chat over the Internet with other girls as young as ten years old and to engaging in sexual and explicit communications with those girls.... All of these events occurred *prior* to, and were *independent* of, any contact by government agents, as required under *Jacobson*. Based on these circumstances, the jury could rationally find that Brand was predisposed to commit the crimes charged."

Commenting on the difficulty of successfully asserting an entrapment defense in an Internet sting case, one court stated in *People v. Grizzle*, 140 P.3d 224, 227 (Colo. App. 2006): "We are aware that the Internet sting operations of the type used here are common and are used in many jurisdictions. They are relatively inexpensive and easy to do, lack substantial risk to law enforcement personnel, and are directed to very serious offenses with respect to which there is considerable public concern. . . . We are also aware that, because of the nature of the Internet, these sting operations approach a large general population, not an individual. It is, perhaps, inevitable that such an operation will ensnare an otherwise law-abiding citizen with sexual fantasies—involving conduct which is illegal, immoral, taboo, or all three—upon which he or she would not otherwise act were the opportunity not presented to them. However, merely providing an opportunity does not implicate the affirmative defense of entrapment."

CHAPTER 8

NETWORK SURVEILLANCE

■ ■ ■

Communications networks are a common feature of modern life. In a typical day, a person might make phone calls, send letters, receive e-mails, surf the Internet, and both receive and send text messages. All of these everyday occurrences involve communications networks that permit users to transmit, receive, or store information. This chapter considers the rules of criminal procedure that apply when the government seeks evidence of crime from a communications network. The materials begin with the Fourth Amendment and then turn to the statutory rules that regulate network surveillance and evidence collection.

SECTION 1.   THE FOURTH AMENDMENT

When individuals use communications networks, they send and receive communications to and from other users. The Fourth Amendment rules that regulate network evidence collection answer two primary questions. First, do the users of communications networks have Fourth Amendment rights in the contents of the communications sent and received over the network? And second, do the users of communications networks have Fourth Amendment rights in non-content information used by the network to deliver the communications? The materials start with the Fourth Amendment rules for contents, and then turn to the rules for non-content information.

A.   RIGHTS IN CONTENT INFORMATION
UNITED STATES v. WARSHAK
631 F.3d 266 (6th Cir. 2010).

BOGGS, CIRCUIT JUDGE.

Berkeley Premium Nutraceuticals was an incredibly profitable company that served as the distributor of Enzyte, an herbal supplement purported to enhance male sexual performance. In this appeal, defendants Steven Warshak, Harriet Warshak, and TCI Media, Inc., challenge their convictions stemming from a massive scheme to defraud Berkeley's customers.

Steven Warshak owned and operated Berkeley Premium Nutraceuticals, Inc. In the latter half of 2001, Berkeley launched Enzyte, its flagship product. At the time of its launch, Enzyte was purported to increase the size of a man's erection. The product proved tremendously popular, and business rose sharply. By 2004, demand for Berkeley's products had grown so dramatically that the company employed 1500 people, and the call center remained open throughout the night, taking orders at breakneck speed.

The popularity of Enzyte appears to have been due in large part to Berkeley's aggressive advertising campaigns. The vast majority of the advertising—approximately 98%—was conducted through television spots. Around 2004, network television was saturated with Enzyte advertisements featuring a character called "Smilin' Bob," whose trademark exaggerated smile was presumably the result of Enzyte's efficacy. The "Smilin' Bob" commercials were rife with innuendo and implied that users of Enzyte would become the envy of the neighborhood.

In 2001, just after Enzyte's premiere, advertisements appeared in a number of men's interest magazines. At Warshak's direction, those advertisements cited a 2001 independent customer study, which purported to show that, over a three-month period, 100 English-speaking men who took Enzyte experienced a 12 to 31% increase in the size of their penises. [Former employee] James Teegarden later testified that the survey was bogus. A number of advertisements also indicated that Enzyte boasted a 96% customer satisfaction rating. Teegarden testified that that statistic, too, was totally spurious.

II.

Email was a critical form of communication among Berkeley personnel. As a consequence, Warshak had a number of email accounts with various ISPs, including an account with NuVox Communications. In October 2004, the government formally requested that NuVox prospectively preserve the contents of any emails to or from Warshak's email account. The request was made pursuant to 18 U.S.C. § 2703(f) and it instructed NuVox to preserve all future messages. NuVox acceded to the government's request and began preserving copies of Warshak's incoming and outgoing emails—copies that would not have existed absent the prospective preservation request. Per the government's instructions, Warshak was not informed that his messages were being archived.

In January 2005, the government obtained a subpoena under § 2703(b) and compelled NuVox to turn over the emails that it had begun preserving the previous year. In May 2005, the government served NuVox with an *ex parte* court order under § 2703(d) that required NuVox to surrender any additional email messages in Warshak's account. In all, the government compelled NuVox to reveal the contents of approximately 27,000 emails. Warshak did not receive notice of either the subpoena or the order until May 2006.

III.

The Fourth Amendment's protections hinge on the occurrence of a 'search,' a legal term of art whose history is riddled with complexity. A 'search' occurs when the government infringes upon an expectation of privacy that society is prepared to consider reasonable. This standard breaks down into two discrete inquiries: first, has the target of the investigation manifested a subjective expectation of privacy in the object of the challenged search? Second, is society willing to recognize that expectation as reasonable?

Turning first to the subjective component of the test, we find that Warshak plainly manifested an expectation that his emails would be shielded from outside scrutiny. As he notes in his brief, his "entire business and personal life was contained within the emails seized." Appellant's Br. at 39–40. Given the often sensitive and sometimes damning substance of his emails, we think it highly unlikely that Warshak expected them to be made public, for people seldom unfurl their dirty laundry in plain view.

The next question is whether society is prepared to recognize that expectation as reasonable. This question is one of grave import and enduring consequence, given the prominent role that email has assumed in modern communication. Since the advent of email, the telephone call and the letter have waned in importance, and an explosion of Internet-based communication has taken place. People are now able to send sensitive and intimate information, instantaneously, to friends, family, and colleagues half a world away. Lovers exchange sweet nothings, and businessmen swap ambitious plans, all with the click of a mouse button.

Commerce has also taken hold in email. Online purchases are often documented in email accounts, and email is frequently used to remind patients and clients of imminent appointments. In short, "account" is an apt word for the conglomeration of stored messages that comprises an email account, as it provides an account of its owner's life. By obtaining access to someone's email, government agents gain the ability to peer deeply into his activities. Much hinges, therefore, on whether the government is permitted to request that a commercial ISP turn over the contents of a subscriber's emails without triggering the machinery of the Fourth Amendment.

In confronting this question, we take note of two bedrock principles. First, the very fact that information is being passed through a communications network is a paramount Fourth Amendment consideration. Second, the Fourth Amendment must keep pace with the inexorable march of technological progress, or its guarantees will wither and perish.

With those principles in mind, we begin our analysis by considering the manner in which the Fourth Amendment protects traditional forms of communication. In *Katz,* the Supreme Court was asked to determine how the Fourth Amendment applied in the context of the telephone. There, government agents had affixed an electronic listening device to the exterior of a public phone booth, and had used the device to intercept and record several phone conversations. The Supreme Court held that this constituted a search under the Fourth Amendment, notwithstanding the fact that the telephone company had the capacity to monitor and record the calls. In the eyes of the Court, the caller was "surely entitled to assume that the words he uttered into the mouthpiece would not be broadcast to the world." *Katz,* 389 U.S. at 352. The Court's holding in *Katz* has since come to stand for the broad proposition that, in many contexts, the government infringes a reasonable expectation of privacy when it surreptitiously intercepts a telephone call through electronic means.

Letters receive similar protection. *Ex Parte Jackson,* 96 U.S. 727, 733 (1877). While a letter is in the mail, the police may not intercept it and examine its contents unless they first obtain a warrant based on probable cause. This is true despite the fact that sealed letters are handed over to perhaps dozens of mail carriers, any one of whom could tear open the thin paper envelopes that separate the private words from the world outside. Put another way, trusting a letter to an intermediary does not necessarily defeat a reasonable expectation that the letter will remain private.

Given the fundamental similarities between email and traditional forms of communication, it would defy common sense to afford emails lesser Fourth Amendment protection. Email is the technological scion of tangible mail, and it plays an indispensable part in the Information Age. Over the last decade, email has become so pervasive that some persons may consider it to be an essential means or necessary instrument for self-expression, even self-identification. It follows that email requires strong protection under the Fourth Amendment; otherwise, the Fourth Amendment would prove an ineffective guardian of private communication, an essential purpose it has long been recognized to serve. As some forms of communication begin to diminish, the Fourth Amendment must recognize and protect nascent ones that arise.

If we accept that an email is analogous to a letter or a phone call, it is manifest that agents of the government cannot compel a commercial ISP to turn over the contents of an email without triggering the Fourth Amendment. An ISP is the intermediary that makes email communication possible. Emails must pass through an ISP's servers to reach their intended recipient. Thus, the ISP is the functional equivalent of a post office or a telephone company. As we have discussed above, the police may not storm the post office and intercept a letter, and they are likewise forbidden from using the phone system to make a clandestine recording of a telephone call—unless they get a warrant, that is. It only stands to reason that, if government agents compel an ISP to surrender the contents of a subscriber's emails, those agents have thereby conducted a Fourth Amendment search, which necessitates compliance with the warrant requirement absent some exception.

We recognize that our conclusion may be attacked in light of the Supreme Court's decision in *United States v. Miller,* 425 U.S. 435 (1976). In *Miller,* the Supreme Court held that a bank depositor does not have a reasonable expectation of privacy in the contents of bank records, checks, and deposit slips. The Court's holding in *Miller* was based on the fact that bank documents, including financial statements and deposit slips, contain only information voluntarily conveyed to the banks and exposed to their employees in the ordinary course of business. The Court noted: "The depositor takes the risk, in revealing his affairs to another, that the information will be conveyed by that person to the Government. The Fourth Amendment does not prohibit the obtaining of information revealed to a third party and conveyed by him to Government authorities, even if the information is revealed on the assumption that it will be used only for a limited purpose and the confidence placed in the third party will not be betrayed."

But *Miller* is distinguishable. First, *Miller* involved simple business records, as opposed to the potentially unlimited variety of "confidential communications" at issue here. Second, the bank depositor in *Miller* conveyed information to the bank so that the bank could put the information to use "in the ordinary course of business." By contrast, Warshak received his emails through NuVox. NuVox was an *intermediary,* not the intended recipient of the emails. Thus, *Miller* is not controlling.

Accordingly, we hold that a subscriber enjoys a reasonable expectation of privacy in the contents of emails that are stored with, or sent or received through, a commercial ISP. The government may not compel a commercial ISP to turn over the contents of a subscriber's emails without first obtaining a warrant based on probable cause. Therefore, because they did not obtain a warrant, the government agents violated the Fourth Amendment when they obtained the contents of Warshak's emails.

NOTES AND QUESTIONS

1. Compare *Warshak* to the Eleventh Circuit's decision in *Rehberg v. Paulk,* 598 F.3d 1268 (11th Cir. 2010), *vacated,* 611 F.3d 828 (11th Cir. 2010). In *Rehberg,* government investigators issued subpoenas to a criminal suspect's Internet service provider ordering the ISP to provide them with the suspect's stored e-mails. The ISP complied. The suspect later sued, and alleged that compelling his private e-mails with less process than a warrant violated his Fourth Amendment rights. The Eleventh Circuit disagreed on the ground that the suspect had no reasonable expectation of privacy in the stored e-mails:

"Rehberg's voluntary delivery of emails to third parties constituted a voluntary relinquishment of the right to privacy in that information. Rehberg does not allege [that the government] illegally searched his home computer for emails, but alleges [government officials] subpoenaed the emails directly from the third-party Internet service provider to which Rehberg transmitted the messages. Lacking a valid expectation of privacy in that email information, Rehberg fails to state a Fourth Amendment violation for the subpoenas for his Internet records."

Which is more persuasive: *Warshak* or *Rehberg*?

2. ***Postal mail privacy.*** The Supreme Court explained how the Fourth Amendment applies to postal mail in one of the earliest Fourth Amendment decisions, EX PARTE JACKSON, 96 U.S. 727 (1877):

"A distinction is to be made between different kinds of mail matter—between what is intended to be kept free from inspection, such as letters, and sealed packages subject to letter postage; and what is open to inspection, such as newspapers, magazines, pamphlets, and other printed matter, purposely left in a condition to be examined. Letters and sealed packages of this kind in the mail are as fully guarded from examination and inspection, except as to their outward form and weight, as if they were retained by the parties forwarding them in their own domiciles. The constitutional guaranty of the right of the people to be secure in their papers against unreasonable searches and seizures extends to their papers, thus closed against inspection, wherever they may be. Whilst in the mail, they can only be opened and examined under like warrant, issued upon similar oath or affirmation, particularly describing the thing to be seized, as is required when papers are subjected to search in one's own household. No law of Congress can place in the hands of officials connected with the postal service any authority to invade the secrecy of letters and such sealed packages in the mail; and all regulations adopted as to mail matter of this kind must be in subordination to the great principle embodied in the fourth amendment of the Constitution."

These basic principles remain true today. The contents of sealed packages are protected by the Fourth Amendment during transmission. However, the outside of packages is open to inspection by carriers or the Postal Service and is not protected by the Fourth Amendment. Similarly, forms of mail that the Post Office may open are also not protected by the Fourth Amendment. For example, in *United States v. Riley*, 554 F.2d 1282 (4th Cir. 1977), Riley sent a package that contained hashish through the mail. Riley sent the package by fourth class mail instead of first class mail, and a postal employee smelled hashish from the package and opened it without a warrant. The Fourth Circuit held that opening the package did not violate Riley's Fourth Amendment rights. Postal regulations stated that "[m]ailing of sealed parcels at the fourth-class rates of postage is considered consent by the sender to postal inspection of the contents." As a result, "[c]onsignment of the package to fourth class service plainly conferred consent to inspection of its contents," and no Fourth Amendment rights were violated.

3. ***The history of telephone privacy.*** The first case to raise the constitutionality of telephone wiretapping was OLMSTEAD v. UNITED STATES, 277 U.S. 438 (1928). Roy Olmstead was the leader of a massive Prohibition-era conspiracy to import illegal alcohol into the United States. Agents tapped the telephone lines to Olmstead's house and offices and then listened in on the calls to gather evidence against him. The Supreme Court ruled 5–4 that this wiretapping did not constitute a Fourth Amendment search. The Court, per Taft, C.J., rejected the analogy between telephone calls and sealed letters:

"The Fourth Amendment may have proper application to a sealed letter in the mail, because of the constitutional provision for the Postoffice Department and the relations between the government and those who pay to secure protection of their sealed letters. * * * It is plainly within the words of the amendment to say that the unlawful rifling by a government agent of a sealed letter is a search and seizure of the sender's papers of effects. The letter is a paper, an effect, and in the custody of a government that forbids carriage, except under its protection.

"The United States takes no such care of telegraph or telephone messages as of mailed sealed letters. The amendment does not forbid what was done here. There was no searching. There was no seizure. The evidence was secured by the use of the sense of hearing and that only. There was no entry of the houses or offices of the defendants.

"By the invention of the telephone 50 years ago, and its application for the purpose of extending communications, one can talk with another at a far distant place.

"The language of the amendment cannot be extended and expanded to include telephone wires, reaching to the whole world from the defendant's house or office. The intervening wires are not part of his house or office, any more than are the highways along which they are stretched."

According to the Court, sending a telephone call was akin to shouting a message out into the world: "The reasonable view is that one who installs in his house a telephone instrument with connecting wires intends to project his voice to those quite outside, and that the wires beyond his house, and messages while passing over them, are not within the protection of the Fourth Amendment. Here those who intercepted the projected voices were not in the house of either party to the conversation."

In a famous dissent, Justice Brandeis presented a very different picture of the Fourth Amendment and the role of wiretapping:

"When the Fourth and Fifth Amendments were adopted, the form that evil had theretofore taken had been necessarily simple. Force and violence were then the only means known to man by which a government could directly effect self-incrimination. It could compel the individual to testify—a compulsion effected, if need be, by torture. It could secure possession of his papers and other articles incident to his private life-a seizure effected, if need be, by breaking and entry. Protection against such invasion of 'the sanctities of a man's home and the privacies of life' was provided in the Fourth and Fifth Amendments by specific language. But time works changes, brings into existence new conditions and purposes. Subtler and more far-reaching means of invading privacy have become available to the government. Discovery and invention have made it possible for the government, by means far more effective than stretching upon the rack, to obtain disclosure in court of what is whispered in the closet.

"Moreover, in the application of a Constitution, our contemplation cannot be only of what has been, but of what may be. The progress of science in furnishing the government with means of espionage is not likely to stop with wire tapping. Ways may some day be developed by which the government, without removing papers from secret drawers, can reproduce them in court, and by which it will be enabled to expose to a jury the most intimate occurrences of the home. Advances in the psychic and related sciences may bring means of exploring unexpressed beliefs, thoughts and emotions. 'That places the liberty of every man in the hands of every petty officer' was said by James Otis of much lesser intrusions than these. To Lord Camden a far slighter intrusion seemed 'subversive of all the comforts of society.' Can it be that the Constitution affords no protection against such invasions of individual security?

"In *Ex parte Jackson*, it was held that a sealed letter entrusted to the mail is protected by the amendments. The mail is a public service furnished by the government. The telephone is a public service furnished by its authority. There is, in essence, no difference between the sealed letter and the private telephone message. As Judge Rudkin said below: 'True, the one is visible, the other invisible; the one is tangible, the other intangible; the one is sealed, and the other unsealed; but these are distinctions without a difference.'

"The evil incident to invasion of the privacy of the telephone is far greater than that involved in tampering with the mails. Whenever a telephone line is tapped, the privacy of the persons at both ends of the line is invaded, and all conversations between them upon any subject, and although proper, confidential, and privileged, may be overheard. Moreover, the tapping of one man's telephone line involves the tapping of the telephone of every other person whom he may call, or who may call him. As a means of espionage, writs of assistance and general warrants are but puny instruments of tyranny and oppression when compared with wire tapping.

* * * "The makers of our Constitution undertook to secure conditions favorable to the pursuit of happiness. They recognized the significance of man's spiritual nature, of his feelings and of his intellect. They knew that only a part of the pain, pleasure and satisfactions of life are to be found in material things. They sought to protect Americans in their beliefs, their thoughts, their emotions and their sensations. They conferred, as against the government, the right to be let alone—the most comprehensive of rights and the right most valued by civilized men. To protect, that right, every unjustifiable intrusion by the government upon the privacy of the individual, whatever the means employed, must be deemed a violation of the Fourth Amendment."

The Supreme Court effectively overruled *Olmstead* in two cases, BERGER v. NEW YORK, 388 U.S. 41 (1967), and KATZ v. UNITED STATES, 389 U.S. 347 (1967), see p. 264. *Berger* invalidated a New York state wiretapping law on the ground that it did not provide sufficient Fourth Amendment safeguards. The majority opinion did not directly hold that the wiretapping violated the rights of the person whose phone was tapped. Instead, the opinion took the opportunity to articulate general Fourth Amendment requirements for wiretapping statutes.

Unlike *Berger, Katz* was not a wiretapping case. *Katz* involved a microphone taped to a public phone booth, not the intercept of any calls. However, a passage in the majority opinion announced the end of the *Olmstead* regime: "It is true that the absence of [physical] penetration was at one time thought to foreclose further Fourth Amendment inquiry, for that Amendment was thought to limit only searches and seizures of tangible property. But the premise that property interests control the right of the Government to search and seize has been discredited. Thus, although a closely divided Court supposed in *Olmstead* that surveillance without any trespass and without the seizure of any material object fell outside the ambit of the Constitution, we have since departed from the narrow view on which that decision rested. * * * We conclude that the underpinnings of *Olmstead* * * * have been so eroded by our subsequent decisions that the trespass doctrine there enunciated can no longer be regarded as controlling."

Thus, after *Katz* and *Berger*, the warrantless interception of telephone calls normally will violate the Fourth Amendment absent special circumstances such as consent to monitoring. In addition, note that if one party is conversing with a second party, and the first party decides to record the call, the monitoring does not violate the Fourth Amendment rights of the second party under *Hoffa v. United States*, p. 470.

4. Cordless telephone privacy. In the 1980s, cordless telephones became available to the public. Cordless telephones work by broadcasting FM radio signals between the base of the phone and the handset. Each phone has two radio transmitters that work at the same time: the base transmits the incoming call signal to the handset, and the handset transmits the outgoing call signal to the base. Today's cordless phones use encrypted signals that are difficult to intercept. Before the mid–1990s, however, cordless phones generally used analog FM signals that were easily intercepted. Government agents would occasionally listen in on the cordless telephone calls of suspects without a warrant by intercepting the signals using widely available FM radio scanners.

Courts held that intercepting the cordless telephone calls that are broadcast over the FM radiowaves does not violate the reasonable expectation of privacy of either the cordless phone user or of those who spoke with him. *United States v. McNulty*, 47 F.3d 100, 104–106 (4th Cir. 1995); *Tyler v. Berodt*, 877 F.2d 705, 707 (8th Cir. 1989); *Price v. Turner*, 260 F.3d 1144, 1149 (9th Cir. 2001). According to one court, talking on the phone with a person using a cordless phone is akin to speaking with a confidential informant: "To be sure, there are differences between an informant and a cordless phone user at the other end of a communication. There exists, however, a crucial similarity between them for purposes of determining the existence of valid Fourth Amendment interests. The common characteristic of the government informant and the cordless phone user is that they are both unreliable recipients of the communicated information: one because he repeats the conversation to law enforcement officers and the other because he broadcasts the conversation over radio waves to all within range who wish to overhear." *McNulty*, 47 F.3d at 105.

Although such cases were relatively common in the 1990s, they are no longer common today. This is true for two reasons. First, Congress amended the statutory Wiretap Act in 1994 so that it now covers cordless and cell phone calls. The Wiretap Act, covered later in this chapter, extends statutory protections that are in many ways significantly stronger than any possible Fourth Amendment protection. Second, modern cordless and cell phone communications are encrypted, making interception very difficult, so that cases are much less likely to arise. Do you think encryption should change the constitutional analysis, creating a reasonable expectation of privacy? See Orin S. Kerr, *The Fourth Amendment in Cyberspace: Can Encryption Create A Reasonable Expectation of Privacy?*, 33 Conn. L. Rev. 503 (2001) (arguing "no").

5. Even if a network user can have a reasonable expectation of privacy in contents stored on the network, specific conduct can eliminate that expectation of privacy in some circumstances. In *United States v. King*, 509 F.3d 1338 (11th Cir. 2007), a civilian contractor worked at a U.S. Air Force base in Saudi Arabia. He often connected to the base network using his personal laptop computer. Unbeknownst to him, his laptop was configured to "share" its contents with the entire network. One day, an enlisted man at the base was searching the base network for music files when his search revealed the contents of King's computer. The discovery led to criminal charges against King for storing child pornography on his computer. King moved to suppress the evidence on the ground that he had a reasonable expectation of privacy in the contents of his computer that he believed were secure. The Eleventh Circuit disagreed:

"King has not shown a legitimate expectation of privacy in his computer files. His experience with computer security and the affirmative steps he took to install security settings demonstrate a subjective expectation of privacy in the files, so the question becomes whether society is prepared to accept King's subjective expectation of privacy as objectively reasonable.

"It is undisputed that King's files were 'shared' over the entire base network, and that everyone on the network had access to all of his files and could observe them in exactly the same manner as the computer specialist did. As the district court observed, rather than analyzing the military official's actions as a search of

King's personal computer in his private dorm room, it is more accurate to say that the authorities conducted a search of the military network, and King's computer files were a part of that network. King's files were exposed to thousands of individuals with network access, and the military authorities encountered the files without employing any special means or intruding into any area which King could reasonably expect would remain private."

6. *The private search doctrine.* *Warshak* and *King* suggest that if a network user successfully places a password gate or other security setting that blocks others from accessing materials on his computer, the user will have a reasonable expectation of privacy in those materials. If a government actor hacks in, that intrusion will be a Fourth Amendment search. On the other hand, note that the result will be different if a private party hacks in to the user's machine. The Fourth Amendment only regulates government actors and their agents, so an intrusion by a private party will not count as a Fourth Amendment search.

This has occurred often in Internet-related cases. For example, both *United States v. Jarrettt*, 338 F.3d 339 (4th Cir. 2003), and *United States v. Steiger*, 318 F.3d 1039 (11th Cir. 2003), involved an anonymous individual who went by the moniker "Unknownuser" and claimed to be from Istanbul, Turkey. Unknownuser posted files of child pornography on Internet message boards that were embedded with a "Trojan horse" program, a backdoor that allowed Unknownuser to access the computers of individuals who downloaded the file. Unknownuser would then access the computers of those who had downloaded the image; if he found evidence of sexual abuse crimes on their machines, he would e-mail the information to the FBI in the United States.

In both *Steiger* and *Jarrett*, the FBI used the information to obtain warrants authorizing the search of the homes of the individuals who had downloaded the files. In both cases, the courts ruled that the initial searches by Unknownuser did not violate the Fourth Amendment because there was no evidence that "Unknownuser" was a government actor.

7. *Materials posted on the World Wide Web.* In *United States v. Gines–Perez*, 214 F.Supp.2d 205 (D.P.R. 2002), the police suspected that a computer store manager was also a major heroin smuggler. Investigators found a website for the store and noticed that the defendant had posted a group portrait of the store employees. Investigators used the picture to identify the defendant and to follow him. A traffic stop and search of the car he was driving led to the discovery of 1.4 kilos of heroin and $5,000 in cash hidden in the car. The district court rejected the defendant's view that he had a reasonable expectation of privacy in the photograph posted on the World Wide Web:

"[I]t strikes the Court as obvious that a claim to privacy is unavailable to someone who places information on an indisputably, public medium, such as the Internet, without taking any measures to protect the information. * * * The Court finds that this society is simply not prepared to recognize as 'reasonable' a claim that a picture on the Internet is 'private' in nature, such that the Government cannot access it. In fact, the Court believes that our society would recognize the opposite; that a person who places a photograph on the Internet precisely intends to forsake and renounce all privacy rights to such imagery, particularly under circumstances such as here, where the Defendant did not employ protective measures or devices that would have controlled access to the Web page or the photograph itself."

B. RIGHTS IN NON–CONTENT INFORMATION

Although the purpose of every communications network is to send and receive the contents of communications, the delivery of those contents requires the creation and use of non-content addressing information. To send a letter through the mail, you must write the destination address on the envelope; to make a telephone call, you need to enter in the phone number to be called. Is this non-content addressing information protected by the Fourth Amendment?

SMITH v. MARYLAND
442 U.S. 735, 99 S.Ct. 2577, 61 L.Ed.2d 220 (1979).

MR. JUSTICE BLACKMUN delivered the opinion of the Court.

This case presents the question whether the installation and use of a pen register[1] constitutes a "search" within the meaning of the Fourth Amendment, made applicable to the States through the Fourteenth Amendment.

On March 5, 1976, in Baltimore, Md., Patricia McDonough was robbed. She gave the police a description of the robber and of a 1975 Monte Carlo automobile she had observed near the scene of the crime. After the robbery, McDonough began receiving threatening and obscene phone calls from a man identifying himself as the robber. On one occasion, the caller asked that she step out on her front porch; she did so, and saw the 1975 Monte Carlo she had earlier described to police moving slowly past her home. On March 16, police spotted a man who met McDonough's description driving a 1975 Monte Carlo in her neighborhood. By tracing the license plate number, police learned that the car was registered in the name of petitioner, Michael Lee Smith.

The next day, the telephone company, at police request, installed a pen register at its central offices to record the numbers dialed from the telephone at petitioner's home. The police did not get a warrant or court order before having the pen register installed. The register revealed that on March 17 a call was placed from petitioner's home to McDonough's phone. On the basis of this and other evidence, the police obtained a warrant to search petitioner's residence. The search revealed that a page in petitioner's phone book was turned down to the name and number of Patricia McDonough; the phone book was seized. Petitioner was arrested, and a six-man lineup was held on March 19. McDonough identified petitioner as the man who had robbed her.

Petitioner was indicted in the Criminal Court of Baltimore for robbery. By pretrial motion, he sought to suppress all fruits derived from the pen register on the ground that the police had failed to secure a warrant prior to its installation. The trial court denied the suppression motion, holding that the warrantless installation of the pen register did not violate the Fourth Amendment. Petitioner then waived a jury, and the case was submitted to the court on an agreed statement of facts. The pen register tape (evidencing the fact that a phone call had been made from petitioner's phone to McDonough's phone) and the phone book seized in the search of petitioner's residence were admitted into evidence against him. Petitioner was convicted, and was sentenced to six years. He appealed to the Maryland Court of Special Appeals, but the Court of Appeals of Maryland issued a

---

1. A pen register is a mechanical device that records the numbers dialed on a telephone by monitoring the electrical impulses caused when the dial on the telephone is released. It does not overhear oral communications and does not indicate whether calls are actually completed. A pen register is usually installed at a central telephone facility and records on a paper tape all numbers dialed from the line to which it is attached.

writ of certiorari to the intermediate court in advance of its decision in order to consider whether the pen register evidence had been properly admitted at petitioner's trial.

The Fourth Amendment guarantees "the right of the people to be secure in their persons, houses, papers, and effects, against unreasonable searches and seizures." In determining whether a particular form of government-initiated electronic surveillance is a "search" within the meaning of the Fourth Amendment,[4] our lodestar is *Katz v. United States*, [p. 264]. In *Katz*, Government agents had intercepted the contents of a telephone conversation by attaching an electronic listening device to the outside of a public phone booth. The Court rejected the argument that a "search" can occur only when there has been a "physical intrusion" into a "constitutionally protected area," noting that the Fourth Amendment "protects people, not places." Because the Government's monitoring of Katz' conversation "violated the privacy upon which he justifiably relied while using the telephone booth," the Court held that it "constituted a 'search and seizure' within the meaning of the Fourth Amendment."

Consistently with *Katz*, this Court uniformly has held that the application of the Fourth Amendment depends on whether the person invoking its protection can claim a "justifiable," a "reasonable," or a "legitimate expectation of privacy" that has been invaded by government action * * * . This inquiry, as Mr. Justice Harlan aptly noted in his *Katz* concurrence, normally embraces two discrete questions. The first is whether the individual, by his conduct, has exhibited an actual (subjective) expectation of privacy—whether, in the words of the *Katz* majority, the individual has shown that he seeks to preserve something as private. The second question is whether the individual's subjective expectation of privacy is one that society is prepared to recognize as reasonable—whether, in the words of the *Katz* majority, the individual's expectation, viewed objectively, is justifiable under the circumstances.[5]

In applying the *Katz* analysis to this case, it is important to begin by specifying precisely the nature of the state activity that is challenged. The activity here took the form of installing and using a pen register. Since the pen register was installed on telephone company property at the telephone company's central offices, petitioner obviously cannot claim that his property was invaded or that police intruded into a constitutionally protected area. Petitioner's claim, rather, is that, notwithstanding the absence of a trespass, the State, as did the Government in *Katz*, infringed a legitimate expectation of privacy that petitioner held. Yet a pen register differs significantly from the listening device employed in *Katz*, for pen registers do not acquire the *contents* of communications. This Court recently

---

4. In this case, the pen register was installed, and the numbers dialed were recorded, by the telephone company. The telephone company, however, acted at police request. In view of this, respondent appears to concede that the company is to be deemed an "agent" of the police for purposes of this case, so as to render the installation and use of the pen register "state action" under the Fourth and Fourteenth Amendments. We may assume that "state action" was present here.

5. Situations can be imagined, of course, in which *Katz*'s two-pronged inquiry would provide an inadequate index of Fourth Amendment protection. For example, if the Government were suddenly to announce on nationwide television that all homes henceforth would be subject to warrantless entry, individuals thereafter might not in fact entertain any actual expectation or privacy regarding their homes, papers, and effects. Similarly, if a refugee from a totalitarian country, unaware of this Nation's traditions, erroneously assumed that police were continuously monitoring his telephone conversations, a subjective expectation of privacy regarding the contents of his calls might be lacking as well. In such circumstances, where an individual's subjective expectations had been "conditioned" by influences alien to well-recognized Fourth Amendment freedoms, those subjective expectations obviously could play no meaningful role in ascertaining what the scope of Fourth Amendment protection was. In determining whether a "legitimate expectation of privacy" existed in such cases, a normative inquiry would be proper.

noted: "Indeed, a law enforcement official could not even determine from the use of a pen register whether a communication existed. These devices do not hear sound. They disclose only the telephone numbers that have been dialed—a means of establishing communication. Neither the purport of any communication between the caller and the recipient of the call, their identities, nor whether the call was even completed is disclosed by pen registers." *United States v. New York Tel. Co.,* 434 U.S. 159, 167 (1977).

Given a pen register's limited capabilities, therefore, petitioner's argument that its installation and use constituted a "search" necessarily rests upon a claim that he had a legitimate expectation of privacy regarding the numbers he dialed on his phone.

This claim must be rejected. First, we doubt that people in general entertain any actual expectation of privacy in the numbers they dial. All telephone users realize that they must "convey" phone numbers to the telephone company, since it is through telephone company switching equipment that their calls are completed. All subscribers realize, moreover, that the phone company has facilities for making permanent records of the numbers they dial, for they see a list of their long-distance (toll) calls on their monthly bills. In fact, pen registers and similar devices are routinely used by telephone companies for the purposes of checking billing operations, detecting fraud and preventing violations of law. Electronic equipment is used not only to keep billing records of toll calls, but also to keep a record of all calls dialed from a telephone which is subject to a special rate structure. Pen registers are regularly employed to determine whether a home phone is being used to conduct a business, to check for a defective dial, or to check for overbilling.

Although most people may be oblivious to a pen register's esoteric functions, they presumably have some awareness of one common use: to aid in the identification of persons making annoying or obscene calls. See, *e. g., Von Lusch v. C & P Telephone Co.,* 457 F. Supp. 814, 816 (Md.1978); Claerhout, The Pen Register, 20 Drake L. Rev. 108, 110–111 (1970). Most phone books tell subscribers, on a page entitled "Consumer Information," that the company "can frequently help in identifying to the authorities the origin of unwelcome and troublesome calls." *E.g.,* Baltimore Telephone Directory 21 (1978); District of Columbia Telephone Directory 13 (1978). Telephone users, in sum, typically know that they must convey numerical information to the phone company; that the phone company has facilities for recording this information; and that the phone company does in fact record this information for a variety of legitimate business purposes. Although subjective expectations cannot be scientifically gauged, it is too much to believe that telephone subscribers, under these circumstances, harbor any general expectation that the numbers they dial will remain secret.

Petitioner argues, however, that, whatever the expectations of telephone users in general, he demonstrated an expectation of privacy by his own conduct here, since he "used the telephone *in his house* to the exclusion of all others." Brief for Petitioner 6 (emphasis added). But the site of the call is immaterial for purposes of analysis in this case. Although petitioner's conduct may have been calculated to keep the *contents* of his conversation private, his conduct was not and could not have been calculated to preserve the privacy of the number he dialed. Regardless of his location, petitioner had to convey that number to the telephone company in precisely the same way if he wished to complete his call. The fact that he dialed the number on his home phone rather than on some other phone could make no conceivable difference, nor could any subscriber rationally think that it would.

Second, even if petitioner did harbor some subjective expectation that the phone numbers he dialed would remain private, this expectation is not "one that society is prepared to recognize as reasonable. " This Court consistently has held that a person has no legitimate expectation of privacy in information he voluntarily turns over to third parties. *E.g., United States v. Miller,* 425 U.S. 435, 442–4 (1976); *Hoffa v. United States,* [p. 470]. In *Miller,* for example, the Court held that a bank depositor has no legitimate expectation of privacy in financial information voluntarily conveyed to * * * banks and exposed to their employees in the ordinary course of business. The Court explained:

"The depositor takes the risk, in revealing his affairs to another, that the information will be conveyed by that person to the Government.... This Court has held repeatedly that the Fourth Amendment does not prohibit the obtaining of information revealed to a third party and conveyed by him to Government authorities, even if the information is revealed on the assumption that it will be used only for a limited purpose and the confidence placed in the third party will not be betrayed." Because the depositor "assumed the risk" of disclosure, the Court held that it would be unreasonable for him to expect his financial records to remain private.

This analysis dictates that petitioner can claim no legitimate expectation of privacy here. When he used his phone, petitioner voluntarily conveyed numerical information to the telephone company and "exposed" that information to its equipment in the ordinary course of business. In so doing, petitioner assumed the risk that the company would reveal to police the numbers he dialed. The switching equipment that processed those numbers is merely the modern counterpart of the operator who, in an earlier day, personally completed calls for the subscriber. Petitioner concedes that if he had placed his calls through an operator, he could claim no legitimate expectation of privacy. We are not inclined to hold that a different constitutional result is required because the telephone company has decided to automate.

Petitioner argues, however, that automatic switching equipment differs from a live operator in one pertinent respect. An operator, in theory at least, is capable of remembering every number that is conveyed to him by callers. Electronic equipment, by contrast, can "remember" only those numbers it is programmed to record, and telephone companies, in view of their present billing practices, usually do not record local calls. Since petitioner, in calling McDonough, was making a local call, his expectation of privacy as to her number, on this theory, would be "legitimate."

This argument does not withstand scrutiny. The fortuity of whether or not the phone company in fact elects to make a quasi-permanent record of a particular number dialed does not in our view, make any constitutional difference. Regardless of the phone company's election, petitioner voluntarily conveyed to it information that it had facilities for recording and that it was free to record. In these circumstances, petitioner assumed the risk that the information would be divulged to police. Under petitioner's theory, Fourth Amendment protection would exist, or not, depending on how the telephone company chose to define local-dialing zones, and depending on how it chose to bill its customers for local calls. Calls placed across town, or dialed directly, would be protected; calls placed across the river, or dialed with operator assistance, might not be. We are not inclined to make a crazy quilt of the Fourth Amendment, especially in circumstances where (as here) the pattern of protection would be dictated by billing practices of a private corporation.

We therefore conclude that petitioner in all probability entertained no actual expectation of privacy in the phone numbers he dialed, and that, even if he did, his expectation was not legitimate. The installation and use of a pen register, consequently, was not a "search," and no warrant was required.

MR. JUSTICE MARSHALL, with whom MR. JUSTICE BRENNAN joins, dissenting.

The crux of the Court's holding * * * is that whatever expectation of privacy petitioner may in fact have entertained regarding his calls, it is not one "society is prepared to recognize as 'reasonable'." In so ruling, the Court determines that individuals who convey information to third parties have "assumed the risk" of disclosure to the government. This analysis is misconceived in two critical respects.

Implicit in the concept of assumption of risk is some notion of choice. At least in the third-party consensual surveillance cases, which first incorporated risk analysis into Fourth Amendment doctrine, the defendant presumably had exercised some discretion in deciding who should enjoy his confidential communications. By contrast here, unless a person is prepared to forgo use of what for many has become a personal or professional necessity, he cannot help but accept the risk of surveillance. It is idle to speak of "assuming" risks in contexts where, as a practical matter, individuals have no realistic alternative.

More fundamentally, to make risk analysis dispositive in assessing the reasonableness of privacy expectations would allow the government to define the scope of Fourth Amendment protections. For example, law enforcement officials, simply by announcing their intent to monitor the content of random samples of first-class mail or private phone conversations, could put the public on notice of the risks they would thereafter assume in such communications. *See* Amsterdam, Perspectives on the Fourth Amendment, 58 Minn. L. Rev. 349, 384, 407 (1974). Yet, although acknowledging this implication of its analysis, the Court is willing to concede only that, in some circumstances, a further "normative inquiry would be proper." No meaningful effort is made to explain what those circumstances might be, or why this case is not among them.

In my view, whether privacy expectations are legitimate within the meaning of *Katz* depends not on the risks an individual can be presumed to accept when imparting information to third parties, but on the risks he should be forced to assume in a free and open society. * * *

The use of pen registers, I believe, constitutes such an extensive intrusion. To hold otherwise ignores the vital role telephonic communication plays in our personal and professional relationships as well as the First and Fourth Amendment interests implicated by unfettered official surveillance. Privacy in placing calls is of value not only to those engaged in criminal activity. The prospect of unregulated governmental monitoring will undoubtedly prove disturbing even to those with nothing illicit to hide. Many individuals, including members of unpopular political organizations or journalists with confidential sources, may legitimately wish to avoid disclosure of their personal contacts. Permitting governmental access to telephone records on less than probable cause may thus impede certain forms of political affiliation and journalistic endeavor that are the hallmark of a truly free society. Particularly given the Government's previous reliance on warrantless telephonic surveillance to trace reporters' sources and monitor protected political activity, I am unwilling to insulate use of pen registers from independent judicial review.

Just as one who enters a public telephone booth is "entitled to assume that the words he utters into the mouthpiece will not be broadcast to the world," *Katz v. United States,* [p. 264], so too, he should be entitled to assume that the numbers he dials in the privacy of his home will be recorded, if at all, solely for the phone company's business purposes. Accordingly, I would require law enforcement officials to obtain a warrant before they enlist telephone companies to secure information otherwise beyond the government's reach.

NOTES AND QUESTIONS

1. The opinions in *Smith v. Maryland* offer competing approaches to applying the Fourth Amendment to a network. Justice Blackmun focuses on the facts of how the network works and draws analogies to prior cases, whereas Justice Marshall focuses on the policy question of what is consistent with "a free and open society." Which is the better approach? Does your answer depend on whether you have a normative policy preference for requiring warrants before the police can install pen registers? If you prefer Justice Marshall's approach, how can the judiciary determine the needs of a free and open society? Are the needs of a free and open society different today in a world of "Caller ID" than they were in the 1970s when Caller ID did not exist? Why not leave such policy questions to Congress and state legislatures?

2. *Mail covers and postal mail privacy.* The exterior of letters and packages is not entitled to Fourth Amendment protection. Because the exterior appearance, size, and weight of a letter or package is exposed to the carrier, it cannot support a reasonable expectation of privacy. This permits the government to utilize a "mail cover," defined in 39 C.F.R. § 233.3 as a "process by which a nonconsensual record is made of any data appearing on the outside cover of any sealed or unsealed class of mail matter, or by which a record is made of the contents of any unsealed class of mail matter as allowed by law." As the Fifth Circuit has stated, "[b]oth before and after *Katz* * * * , the courts uniformly have upheld the constitutionality of mail covers. * * * There is no reasonable expectation of privacy in information placed on the exterior of mailed items and open to view and specifically intended to be viewed by others." *United States v. Huie*, 593 F.2d 14, 15 (5th Cir. 1979).

3. *Internet addresses.* In UNITED STATES v. FORRESTER, 512 F.3d 500 (9th Cir. 2008), Forrester and his co-defendant Alba were under investigation for manufacturing the drug Ecstasy. The government obtained a pen register order to allow monitoring of Alba's Internet usage on his home personal computer. The order was served on Alba's ISP Pacbell Internet, and PacBell installed a "mirror port" at its connection facility. The mirror port enabled the government to learn the to/from addresses of Alba's e-mail messages, the IP addresses of the websites that Alba visited, and the total volume of information sent to or from his account. The Ninth Circuit held that this surveillance was not a search because the surveillance was closely analogous to the use of a pen register in *Smith v. Maryland*:

"We conclude that the surveillance techniques the government employed here are constitutionally indistinguishable from the use of a pen register that the Court approved in *Smith*. First, e-mail and Internet users, like the telephone users in *Smith*, rely on third-party equipment in order to engage in communication. *Smith* based its holding that telephone users have no expectation of privacy in the numbers they dial on the users' imputed knowledge that their calls are completed through telephone company switching equipment. Analogously, e-mail and Internet users have no expectation of privacy in the to/from addresses of their messages or the IP addresses of the websites they visit because they should know that this information is provided to and used by Internet service providers for the specific purpose of directing the routing of information. Like telephone numbers, which provide instructions to the 'switching equipment that processed those numbers,' e-mail to/from addresses and IP addresses are not merely passively conveyed through third party equipment, but rather are voluntarily turned over in order to direct the third party's servers.

"Second, e-mail to/from addresses and IP addresses constitute addressing information and do not necessarily reveal any more about the underlying contents of communication than do phone numbers. When the government obtains the to/from addresses of a person's e-mails or the IP addresses of websites visited, it does not find out the contents of the messages or know the particular pages on the websites the person viewed. At best, the government may make educated guesses about what was said in the messages or viewed on the websites based on its knowledge of the e-mail to/from addresses and IP addresses—but this is no different from speculation about the contents of a phone conversation on the basis of the identity of the person or entity that was dialed. Like IP addresses, certain phone numbers may strongly indicate the underlying contents of the communication; for example, the government would know that a person who dialed the phone number of a chemicals company or a gun shop was likely seeking information about chemicals or firearms. Further, when an individual dials a pre-recorded information or subject-specific line, such as sports scores, lottery results or phone sex lines, the phone number may even show that the caller had access to specific content information. Nonetheless, the Court in *Smith* and *Katz* drew a clear line between unprotected addressing information and protected content information that the government did not cross here.

"The government's surveillance of e-mail addresses also may be technologically sophisticated, but it is conceptually indistinguishable from government surveillance of physical mail. In a line of cases dating back to the nineteenth century, the Supreme Court has held that the government cannot engage in a warrantless search of the contents of sealed mail, but can observe whatever information people put on the outside of mail, because that information is voluntarily transmitted to third parties. E-mail, like physical mail, has an outside address 'visible' to the third-party carriers that transmit it to its intended location, and also a package of content that the sender presumes will be read only by the intended recipient. The privacy interests in these two forms of communication are identical. The contents may deserve Fourth Amendment protection, but the address and size of the package do not."

In a footnote, the Ninth Circuit noted the uncertainty as to how this distinction would apply for other types of Internet communications: "Surveillance techniques that enable the government to determine not only the IP addresses that a person accesses but also the uniform resource locators ('URL') of the pages visited might be more constitutionally problematic. A URL, unlike an IP address, identifies the particular document within a website that a person views and thus reveals much more information about the person's Internet activity. For instance, a surveillance technique that captures IP addresses would show only that a person visited the New York Times' website at http://www.nytimes.com, whereas a technique that captures URLs would also divulge the particular articles the person viewed."

Do you think URLs count as contents that the Fourth Amendment likely protects or non-content information that it does not protect? Does that depend on the URL? How about a URL such as "www.facebook.com"? How about "www.google.com/search?ie==1&q=how+to+dispose+dead+body"?

4. *Fourth Amendment protection for stored account records.* Under *Smith v. Maryland*, communications network users lack a reasonable expectation of privacy in the fact that they have a network account as well as non-content information as to how that account has been used. The government can obtain the records of how an account was used without triggering the warrant requirement.

See, e.g., *United States v. Fregoso*, 60 F.3d 1314, 1321 (8th Cir. 1995) (telephone account); *In re Grand Jury Proceedings*, 827 F.2d 301, 302–03 (8th Cir. 1987) (Western Union money transfer account).

Does this rule give the government too much power? Does it permit the government to know where people are and what they have done without any legal cause? Consider the overall amount of privacy a person has in communications sent over networks relative to the overall amount of privacy a person has in open physical space. In a world without communications networks, individuals wishing to communicate would need to leave their homes and venture out into the open spaces where no Fourth Amendment protection exists. When in the open, the fact that they had left home and traveled to a meeting with someone else could be observed by the police without a warrant. Communications networks can eliminate this public aspect of communication, as a person can send an e-mail or make a phone call from home. Does the rule that non-content addressing information receives no Fourth Amendment protection create an analogous set of Fourth Amendment protections for communications sent over remote networks that already apply to communications that occur in person?

    5. *State constitutional protections.* Some state courts have rejected *Smith v. Maryland* under state constitutions. *See generally* Stephen E. Henderson, *Learning From All Fifty States: How To Apply The Fourth Amendment And Its State Analogs To Protect Third Party Information From Unreasonable Search*, 55 Cath. U. L. Rev. 373 (2006). Notably, state constitutional rules are binding on state officials but not on federal investigators. Under the Supremacy Clause, federal investigators are bound by the Fourth Amendment but not by state constitutions.

    6. *Third-party objections.* In UNITED STATES v. MILLER, 425 U.S. 435 (1976), respondent Miller sought to raise a Fourth Amendment challenge to the government's acquisition of bank records through a grand jury subpoena. In the course of an investigation of Miller's alleged involvement in a bootlegging conspiracy, federal agents served upon two banks grand jury subpoenas directing production of "all records of accounts, i.e., savings, checking loan or otherwise, in the name of Mitch Miller." Without informing Miller of the subpoena, the banks complied by making the records available to the agents for inspection and allowing the agents to make copies. After *Miller* was indicted, he moved to suppress all evidence derived from the information contained in the bank records. The Supreme Court majority, per Powell, J., ruled that the respondent had no protected Fourth Amendment interest in the bank records. The Court reasoned:

    "Even if we direct our attention to the original checks and deposit slips, rather than to the microfilm copies actually viewed and obtained by means of the subpoena, we perceive no legitimate 'expectation of privacy' in their contents. The checks are not confidential communications but negotiable instruments to be used in commercial transactions. All of the documents obtained, including financial statements and deposit slips, contain only information voluntarily conveyed to the banks and exposed to their employees in the ordinary course of business. The lack of any legitimate expectation of privacy concerning the information kept in bank records was assumed by Congress in enacting the Bank Secrecy Act, the expressed purpose of which is to require records to be maintained because they 'have a high degree of usefulness in criminal tax, and regulatory investigations and proceedings.' 12 U.S.C. § 1829b(a)(1). * * *

    "The depositor takes the risk, in revealing his affairs to another, that the information will be conveyed by that person to the Government. This Court has held repeatedly that the Fourth Amendment does not prohibit the obtaining of information revealed to a third party and conveyed by him to Government authorities, even if the information is revealed on the assumption that it will be used only for a limited purpose and the confidence placed in the third party will not be betrayed. * * * This analysis is not changed by the mandate of the Bank Secrecy Act that records of depositors' transactions be maintained by banks. In *California Bankers Assn. v. Shultz*, 416 U.S. 21 (1974), we rejected the contention that banks, when keeping records of their depositors' transactions pursuant to the Act, are acting solely as agents of the Government. But, even if the banks could be said to have been acting solely as Government agents in transcribing the necessary information and complying without protest with the requirements of the subpoenas, there would be no intrusion upon the depositors' Fourth Amendment rights. * * * Since no Fourth Amendment interests of the depositor are implicated here, this case is governed by the general rule that the issuance of a subpoena to a third party to obtain the records of that party does not violate the rights of a defendant, even if a criminal prosecution is contemplated at the time * * * the subpoena is issued."

Justices Brennan and Marshall each issued a separate dissent in *Miller*. Justice Brennan relied on the contrary reasoning in *Burrows v. Superior Court*, 529 P.2d 590 (Cal.1974), which concluded that the customer should be recognized as having a reasonable expectation of privacy in records of bank transactions, as the "totality of bank records provides a virtual current biography" which is given to the bank only because "it is impossible to participate in the economic life of contemporary society without maintaining a bank account."

SECTION 2. STATUTORY PRIVACY LAWS

A. INTRODUCTION

Fourth Amendment protections for network evidence collection are supplemented by a comprehensive framework of statutory privacy laws. The history of these statutory laws reveals frequent changes in light of Constitutional decisions, changing social attitudes, and technological advances.

The first permanent federal wiretapping statute was enacted in 1934 as part of the Communications Act. Codified at 47 U.S.C. § 605, the provision stated that "no person not being authorized by the sender shall intercept any communication and divulge or publish the existence, contents, substance, purport, effect, or meaning of such intercepted communication to any person." Section 605 did a poor job of regulating telephone wiretapping. The statute did not provide an exception permitting the government to monitor and use the evidence with a valid search warrant. Further, the statute prohibited only the combination of "intercepting" and "divulging" communications, which the Justice Department interpreted as permitting wiretapping so long as the government never disclosed the monitoring. As a result, J. Edgar Hoover's FBI could wiretap without restriction in secret, but the government could not obtain warrants permitting wiretapping evidence in criminal prosecutions even in the most compelling case. Finally, the law only regulated the admissibility of wiretapping evidence in federal court; it had no application in state court. *See Schwartz v. Texas*, 344 U.S. 199 (1952).

In 1968, Congress revisited the wiretapping laws and passed the Federal Wiretap Act, codified at 18 U.S.C. §§ 2510–22. The Wiretap Act is also known as "Title III," because it was passed as the third title of the Omnibus Crime Control and Safe Streets Act, Pub. L. No. 90–351 (1968). The Wiretap Act addresses two privacy-invading practices. The first is 'bugging,' the use of a secret recording device in a room or physical space, as addressed in *Katz v. United States*, 389 U.S. 347 (1967), p. 264. The second is wiretapping, the interception of private telephone calls, addressed by the Supreme Court in *Berger v. New York*, 388 U.S. 41 (1967). Unlike the Fourth Amendment, the Wiretap Act regulates both government actors and private parties. It imposes strict limitations on the use of devices to intercept "oral communications" (installing a bug to listen in on private conversations) or "wire communications" (tapping a telephone line to listen in on a private call). It also allows the government to obtain court orders permitting interception when investigators have probable cause and can satisfy a number of additional requirements.

In the 1980s, it became clear that additional privacy laws were necessary. This was true for two reasons. First, the Supreme Court's decision in *Smith v. Maryland*, p. 510, held that the Fourth Amendment did not regulate the use of pen registers. Second, the Wiretap Act was specifically tailored to telephone calls, and was unprepared to handle computer and Internet communications. In 1986, Congress passed the Electronic Communications Privacy Act, Pub. L. No. 99–508 (1986) ("ECPA"), to correct the gaps in existing legislation and respond to the new computer network technologies. ECPA includes three basic parts. The first part expanded the Wiretap Act to include a new category of protected communications, "electronic communications," which broadly includes computer communications. The second part created a new statute regulating access to stored electronic communications, known as the Stored Communications Act, codified at 18 U.S.C. §§ 2701–11. Finally, the third part created a new statute, generally known as the Pen Register Statute, 18 U.S.C. §§ 3121–27, which regulates the use of pen registers.

The basic framework created by ECPA remains in place today, although Congress has amended it in various ways at regular intervals. For example, in 2001 Congress passed the "Uniting and Strengthening America by Providing Appropriate Tools Required to Intercept and Obstruct Terrorism Act" of 2001, Pub. L.107–56, popularly known by its acronym as the Patriot Act. Title II of the Patriot Act included many provisions that amended ECPA. For example, Section 210 expanded the types of information that could be compelled from ISPs with a subpoena; Section 209 required a warrant for the government to compel voicemail from third party providers; and Section 216 applied the privacy protections of the Pen Register statute to the Internet.

The statutory surveillance laws reflect two major distinctions: prospective surveillance versus retrospective surveillance and the contents of communications versus non-content information. The distinction between contents and non-content information was seen in the Fourth Amendment materials earlier in this chapter, and it tends to be fairly intuitive. The contrast between prospective and retrospective surveillance is somewhat more complex. Prospective surveillance refers to obtaining communications still in the course of transmission, typically by installing a monitoring device at a particular point in the network and scanning the traffic as it passes by that point. The monitoring is prospective because the communication has not yet reached the place where the surveillance device is installed. For example, a traditional wiretapping device taps into the conversation while it is happening; any communication sent over the line will be tapped. In contrast, retrospective surveillance refers to access to stored communications that may be kept in the ordinary course of business by a third party provider. The privacy statutes reflect these two distinctions. The Wiretap Act regulates prospective content surveillance; the Pen Register statute regulates prospective non-content surveillance; and the Stored Communications Act regulates retrospective surveillance for both content and non-content information. The basic framework looks like this:

	Prospective	**Retrospective**
Contents	Wiretap Act 18 U.S.C. §§ 2510-22	Stored Communications Act 18 U.S.C. §§ 2701-11
Non-content	Pen Register Statute 18 U.S.C. §§ 3121-27	Stored Communications Act 18 U.S.C. §§ 2701-11

B. THE WIRETAP ACT ("TITLE III")

The basic structure of the Wiretap Act is simple. The statute envisions a network user who is exchanging communications with another. The statute makes it a crime for someone who is not a party to the communication to use an intercepting device to intentionally access the private communications in "real time" during transmission without the consent of a party to the communication.

UNITED STATES v. TURK
526 F.2d 654 (5th Cir. 1976).

GOLDBERG, CIRCUIT JUDGE:

Frederick Joseph Turk was convicted of committing perjury in his testimony before a federal grand jury. Most of the issues in this appeal relate to the manner in which law enforcement officials became privy to a telephone conversation between Turk and an acquaintance.

On July 13, 1973, officers of the Dade County Public Safety Department received a tip that two individuals would soon leave a specified Miami residence in a silver sports car containing cocaine and firearms. The officers stopped the car, discovered these illicit contents, and arrested the two individuals, Charles Kabbaby and Glenn Roblin. At that time the officers removed from the car, among other objects, a box containing a cassette tape recorder-player and two cassette tapes. Kabbaby told them that 'nothing' was on the tapes. The officers then proceeded to play the tapes at the stationhouse, without Kabbaby's permission and without attempting to obtain a warrant. They soon realized that they were listening, on one of the tapes, to a recording of a private telephone conversation between Kabbaby and someone called 'Freddy.' The officers continued to listen out of 'curiosity.'

In the course of the recorded conversation, Freddy mentioned his telephone number, which the authorities were able to use to locate him. Freddy was, of course, Frederick Turk, the appellant. Turk was then subpoenaed to appear before a federal grand jury that was investigating possible violations of federal narcotics laws. He initially invoked his fifth amendment privilege not to testify. After he was granted immunity from prosecution, * * * he returned to testify before the grand jury on November 27 and December 11 of 1973. During Turk's testimony, the following colloquy, and others like it, took place between government counsel (Q.) and Turk (A.):

Q. Let me ask you one final question, Mr. Turk. Have you ever at anytime been engaged in buying, selling, or otherwise trafficking in marijuana or any other narcotic substance?

A. No, sir.

Turk was subsequently indicted on two counts of making 'irreconcilably contradictory statements' and two counts of obstruction of justice. A superseding indictment, dated July 10, 1974, added two counts of perjury. In a jury trial in September, 1974, Turk was found guilty on one count of perjury, for having denied any involvement in marijuana trafficking. Over Turk's objections and motions to suppress, the tape seized from Kabbaby's car was played both at the grand jury before which he is alleged to have perjured himself, and at his perjury trial. The Government's other evidence at the trial consisted primarily of the testimony of Glenn Roblin and two other individuals who purported to have some personal knowledge relating to Turk's involvement in the importation of marijuana.

Title III of the 1968 'Omnibus Crime Control and Safe Streets Act,' codified at 18 U.S.C. §§ 2510–2520, proscribes generally the interception or disclosure of wire or oral communications, and provides a procedure through which law enforcement officials can be authorized to intercept such communications in certain limited circumstances. Turk argues that the action of the officers in listening to the cassette tape seized from Kabbaby's car constituted an impermissible 'interception' of Turk's oral communication, as defined in 18 U.S.C. § 2510(4). If this argument is valid, then the introduction of the tape into evidence at the grand jury proceeding and at Turk's trial might have been barred by 18 U.S.C. § 2515, a statutory exclusionary rule.

§ 2510(4) provides: " 'intercept' means the aural acquisition of the contents of any wire or oral communication through the use of any electronic, mechanical, or other device."

Kabbaby's action in recording his conversation with Turk was clearly an interception under this definition. This interception was not violative of the Act, however, because § 2511(2)(d) specifically exempts situations in which one party to the conversation is himself the interceptor.[1]

Whether the seizure and replaying of the cassette tape by the officers was also an 'interception' depends on the definition to be given 'aural acquisition.' Under one conceivable reading, an 'aural acquisition' could be said to occur whenever someone physically hears the contents of a communication, and thus the use of the tape player by the officers to hear the previously recorded conversation might fall within the definition set out above. No explicit limitation of coverage to contemporaneous 'acquisitions' appears in the Act.

We believe that a different interpretation—one which would exclude from the definition of 'intercept' the replaying of a previously recorded conversation—has a much firmer basis in the language of § 2510(4) and in logic, and corresponds more closely to the policies reflected in the legislative history. The words 'acquisition . . . through the use of any . . . device' suggest that the central concern is with the activity engaged in at the time of the oral communication which causes such communication to be overheard by uninvited listeners. If a person secrets a recorder in a room and thereby records a conversation between two others, an 'acquisition' occurs at the time the recording is made. This acquisition itself might be said to be 'aural' because the contents of the conversation are preserved in a form which permits the later aural disclosure of the contents.[2] Alternatively, a

---

1. The party exemption is inapplicable only if the interception is 'for the purpose of committing any criminal or tortious act.' The exemption applies, then, even if the purpose of the conversation is criminal, as long as the purpose of the recording is not.

2. In a forest devoid of living listeners, a tree falls. Is there a sound? The answer is yes, if an active tape recorder is present, and the sound might be thought of as 'aurally acquired' at (almost) the instant the action causing it occurred. For § 2510(4) purposes, the recorder can be the agent of the ear.

court facing the issue might conclude that an 'aural acquisition' is accomplished only when two steps are completed—the initial acquisition by the device and the hearing of the communication by the person or persons responsible for the recording. Either of these definitions would require participation by the one charged with an 'interception' in the contemporaneous acquisition of the communication through the use of the device. The argument that a new and different 'aural acquisition' occurs each time a recording of an oral communication is replayed is unpersuasive. That would mean that innumerable 'interceptions,' and thus violations of the Act, could follow from a single recording.

Appellant concedes that he reads the definition sections of the Act 'rather broadly,' but argues that such a reading is buttressed by the legislative history. We disagree. While Congress clearly was concerned with the protection of individual's privacy interests against unjustified intrusions, it did not attempt through Title III to deal with all such intrusions. The specific focus of Title III is reflected in the many references in the legislative history to the problem being dealt with as 'wiretapping and electronic surveillance.' The Senate Report, in explicating § 2510, contains the following: "Paragraph (4) defines 'intercept' to include the aural acquisition of the contents of any wire or oral communication by any electronic, mechanical, or other device. Other forms of surveillance are not within the proposed legislation."

This passage indicates that the act of surveillance and not the literal 'aural acquisition' (i.e., the hearing), which might be contemporaneous with the surveillance, or might follow therefrom, was at the center of congressional concern. 'Aural acquisition' seems to have been used by the Congress neither as a term of art nor as a term of technology. Whatever the precise temporal parameters under Title III of an 'aural acquisition' (and thus of an interception), we conclude that no new and distinct interception occurs when the contents of a communication are revealed through the replaying of a previous recording.

NOTES AND QUESTIONS

1. *Interception of wire, oral, and electronic communications.* The Wiretap Act prohibits the "intercept" of a wire, oral or electronic communication. Each of these terms has a very specific meaning. 18 U.S.C. § 2510(4), as amended in 1986, defines "intercept" as "the aural or other acquisition of the contents of any wire, electronic, or oral communication through the use of any electronic, mechanical, or other device." As the *Turk* court suggests, courts have held that the "acquisition" requirement refers to acquisition contemporaneous with transmission. That is, the acquisition must be made when the communication is 'in flight' in real-time, during prospective surveillance of an ongoing communication. *Konop v. Hawaiian Airlines, Inc.*, 302 F.3d 868 (9th Cir. 2002). Wire communications are communications that contain the human voice and that are sent over a wire, such as telephone calls. 18 U.S.C. § 2510(1); 18 U.S.C. § 2510(18). Oral communications are "in person" recordings of the human voice that can be picked up by a bugging device or microphone when the person recorded has a reasonable expectation of privacy. 18 U.S.C. § 2510(2). Electronic communications are communications that do not contain the human voice, such as most computer communications. 18 U.S.C. § 2510(12). Putting these pieces together, the Wiretap Act prohibits both bugging and real-time wiretapping of private conversations, telephone calls, and the contents of Internet communications unless an exception to the statute applies.

2. *Contents and non-content information.* The Wiretap Act applies only to the acquisition of "contents" because the definition of "intercept" limits intercepts to acquisition of content information. 18 U.S.C. § 2510(4). Contents are

defined somewhat awkwardly in 18 U.S.C. § 2510(8): " 'contents', when used with respect to any wire, oral, or electronic communication, includes any information concerning the substance, purport, or meaning of that communication." The scope of "contents" under the Wiretap Act is clear in some cases. In the case of a bugging device, the content of the communication is the human speech recorded. In the case of a telephone call, it is the call itself. In the case of an e-mail, it is the e-mail message and the subject lines of the e-mail. *See* In re Application of United States for an Order Authorizing Use of A Pen Register, 396 F.Supp.2d 45, 48 (D. Mass. 2005) (stating that e-mail subject lines are contents). Other cases are less clear. Consider the status of "Uniform Resource Locators," also known as URLs, the address lines commonly used to retrieve information on the World Wide Web. Do you think a URL entered into a web browser contains contents?

3. ***The beginning and end of the Wiretap Act.*** In the case of telephone calls and computer communications, the Wiretap Act only regulates access to the contents of information over the network itself. Collection of evidence that will be or has been sent over a network does not trigger the statute. For example, in *Goldman v. United States*, 316 U.S. 129 (1942), the defendants were attorneys engaged in a conspiracy relating to a bankruptcy scheme. Federal agents entered the room next door to one attorney's office and used a type of microphone placed against the wall to amplify the sound from the other room. They then recorded the defendant's speech while he was talking on the telephone. The defendant claimed that the use of the microphone from the adjoining room had "intercepted" the "communication" of his telephone call as those terms were used in 47 U.S.C. § 605 of the 1934 Communications Act, the predecessor to the Wiretap Act.

The Supreme Court rejected the defendant's argument: "What is protected is the message itself throughout the course of its transmission by the instrumentality or agency of transmission. Words written by a person and intended ultimately to be carried as so written to a telegraph office do not constitute a communication within the terms of the Act until they are handed to an agent of the telegraph company. Words spoken in a room in the presence of another into a telephone receiver do not constitute a communication by wire within the meaning of the section. Letters deposited in the Post Office are protected from examination by federal statute, but it could not rightly be claimed that the office carbon of such letter, or indeed the letter itself before it has left the office of the sender, comes within the protection of the statute."

What is the e-mail equivalent of handing a message to an agent of the telegraph company? Pressing "send"?

4. ***Bugging and oral communications.*** The Wiretap Act regulates the use of bugging equipment largely through the definition of "oral communication" in 18 U.S.C. § 2510(2). An oral communication is defined somewhat circularly as "any oral communication uttered by a person exhibiting an expectation that such communication is not subject to interception under circumstances justifying such expectation, but such term does not include any electronic communication." Courts have interpreted this as raising a constitutional question: Would the use of bugging equipment to overhear a "live" conversation violate a person's reasonable expectation of privacy under the Fourth Amendment? If so, the use of the bugging device intercepts an oral communication. *Kee v. City of Rowlett*, 247 F.3d 206, 211 n.7 (5th Cir. 2001). While the Fourth Amendment already regulates such conduct, the protections of the Wiretap Act expand considerably on the constitutional protections. For example, the government must obtain a statutory Title III order instead of a mere search warrant to install the bug. In addition, the Wiretap Act regulates both state actors and private parties, whereas the Fourth Amendment regulates only state actors.

5. *The Wiretap Act and interstate communications*. The Wiretap Act is powerful in part because it applies to essentially all communications sent over interstate networks either involving the human voice or data in whole or in part through a wire. This broad scope is a result of the broad definition of wire communication and electronic communication in 18 U.S.C. § 2510. For example, the definition of electronic communication generally includes "any transfer of signs, signals, writing, images, sounds, data, or intelligence of any nature transmitted in whole or in part by a wire, radio, electromagnetic, photoelectronic or photooptical system that affects interstate or foreign commerce." 18 U.S.C. § 2510(12). The communication does not need to be interstate; rather, the communication merely needs to be transmitted in whole or in part over a system that affects interstate or foreign commerce.

The meaning of this definition was at issue in *United States v. Ropp*, 347 F.Supp.2d 831 (C.D. Cal. 2004). Ropp installed a keystroke monitoring device called a "KeyKatcher" on the workplace computer of Karen Beck. The KeyKatcher connected to the cable between Beck's keyboard and computer and recorded all of Beck's keystrokes. After Ropp was charged with a criminal violation of the Wiretap Act, the district court dismissed the indictment: "[T]he Court concludes that the communication in question is not an 'electronic communication' within the meaning of the statute because it is not transmitted by a system that affects interstate or foreign commerce. The 'system' involved consists of the local computer's hardware—the Central Processing Unit, hard drive and peripherals (including the keyboard)—and one or more software programs including the computer's operating system (most likely some version of Microsoft Windows although other possibilities exist), and either an e-mail or other communications program being used to compose messages. Although this system is connected to a larger system—the network—which affects interstate or foreign commerce, the transmission in issue did not involve that system. The network connection is irrelevant to the transmissions, which could have been made on a stand-alone computer that had no link at all to the internet or any other external network. Thus, although defendant engaged in a gross invasion of privacy by his installation of the KeyKatcher on Ms. Beck's computer, his conduct did not violate the Wiretap Act."

Do you agree? Did the monitoring involve "the larger system" or only the "local" hardware? How can you tell?

6. *Obtaining wiretap orders.* The process for obtaining Title III wiretap orders is complex and time-consuming. Whereas any magistrate judge can issue a search warrant, and the police officer need not first clear the warrant application with a prosecutor, the process for obtaining a Title III order is heavily paper-intensive and requires extensive work beyond that required for a normal warrant. For example, federal applications must be approved by a high-level Justice Department official; in the case of wire and oral communications, can be obtained only in a case involving one or more of particular criminal offenses; and all applications must establish that normal investigative procedures have been tried and have failed or reasonably appear to be unlikely to succeed if tried or to be too dangerous. *See generally* CRIMPROC § 4.6(c).

7. *Number of wiretap orders and types of investigations.* In 2010, a total of 3,194 wiretap orders were authorized by federal or state judges around the United States. Most of the orders were obtained in just a handful of jurisdictions. The federal government obtained 1,207 orders; the state of California, 657 orders; the state of New York, 480 orders; and New Jersey, 215 orders. Together, these jurisdictions accounted for about 80% of the wiretap orders obtained nationwide.

The great majority of wiretap orders are obtained in narcotics cases. In 2010, narcotics investigations accounted for about 84% of the total number of wiretap orders. Although wiretap orders can be obtained to intercept wire, oral, and/or electronic communications, 96% of wiretap orders executed in 2010 were for wire communications (telephone calls). About 1% authorized the interception of oral communications, 1% permitted the interception of electronic communications, and about 2% were for combinations of wire, oral, and electronic communications. *See* Administrative Office of the United States Courts, 2010 Wiretap Report.

    8. *Covert entry.* To use a bugging device, agents may first need to enter homes in secret in order to install the devices. Does Title III permit this covert entry, and if so, does covert entry satisfy the Fourth Amendment? In *Dalia v. United States*, 441 U.S. 238 (1979), the Supreme Court answered both questions in the affirmative. According to the Court, covert entry was implicitly authorized as a statutory matter: "Those considering the surveillance legislation understood that, by authorizing electronic interception of oral communications in addition to wire communications, they were necessarily authorizing surreptitious entries." Covert entry was consistent with the Fourth Amendment, moreover, because warrants need not "include a specification of the precise manner in which they are to be executed. On the contrary, it is generally left to the discretion of the executing officers to determine the details of how best to proceed with the performance of a search authorized by warrant—subject of course to the general Fourth Amendment protection 'against unreasonable searches and seizures.'" The Court added that it "would promote empty formalism ... to require magistrates to make explicit what unquestionably is implicit in bugging authorizations: that a covert entry, with its attendant interference with Fourth Amendment interests, may be necessary for the installation of the surveillance equipment."

    9. *Use and disclosure of intercepted information.* In addition to prohibiting the interception of a wire, electronic, or oral communication, the Wiretap Act also prohibits the "use" or "disclosure" of information when the person knows or has reason to know "that the information was obtained through the interception of a wire, oral, or electronic communication" in violation of the Wiretap Act. 18 U.S.C. § 2511(1)(c),(d). The prohibition on the disclosure of information obtained through unlawful interception can raise difficult First Amendment questions. In BARTNICKI v. VOPPER, 532 U.S. 514 (2001), an unidentified person intercepted a private cell phone conversation between two union officials, Bartnicki and Kane, concerning a controversial union strike. The person who intercepted the call anonymously placed a tape recording of it in the mailbox of a union opponent. The union opponent then gave the recording to Vopper, a local radio commentator who also opposed the union. When Vopper broadcast the recording of the intercepted call on his public affairs radio program, Bartnicki and Kane sued Vopper under the Wiretap Act. They argued that although Vopper did not himself intercept the phone call, he disclosed the contents of the call and he knew or had reason to know that it had been unlawfully intercepted.

    The Supreme Court, per Justice Stevens, ruled that the First Amendment did not permit the Wiretap Act to be used to punish Vopper's disclosure. According to Justice Stevens, the constitutionality of prohibiting the disclosure of intercepted communications depended on whether the privacy interests served by the Wiretap Act could justify its restrictions on speech given the specific facts of the case: "[I]t seems to us that there are important interests to be considered on both sides of the constitutional calculus. In considering that balance, we acknowledge that some intrusions on privacy are more offensive than others, and that the disclosure of the contents of a private conversation can be an even greater intrusion on privacy than the interception itself. As a result, there is a valid independent justification for prohibiting such disclosures by persons who lawfully obtained access to the contents of an illegally intercepted message, even if that prohibition does not play a significant role in preventing such interceptions from occurring in the first place.

"We need not decide whether that interest is strong enough to justify the application of § 2511(c) to disclosures of trade secrets or domestic gossip or other information of purely private concern. In other words, the outcome of the case does not turn on whether § 2511(1)(c) may be enforced with respect to most violations of the statute without offending the First Amendment. The enforcement of that provision in this case, however, implicates the core purposes of the First Amendment because it imposes sanctions on the publication of truthful information of public concern.

"In this case, privacy concerns give way when balanced against the interest in publishing matters of public importance. As Warren and Brandeis stated in their classic law review article: 'The right of privacy does not prohibit any publication of matter which is of public or general interest.' The Right to Privacy, 4 Harv. L. Rev. 193, 214 (1890). One of the costs associated with participation in public affairs is an attendant loss of privacy."

   10. *Remedies for violations of the Wiretap Act.* Violations of the Wiretap Act can lead to a range of different remedies. First, a person who violates the Act can be subject to a civil suit. *See, e.g.,* 18 U.S.C. § 2520. Second, such a person can be criminally prosecuted. 18 U.S.C. § 2511(4). Third, the Wiretap Act provides for statutory suppression of evidence in some settings. 18 U.S.C. §§ 2515, 2518(10)(a).

Importantly, the statutory suppression remedy under the Wiretap Act is somewhat different from the Fourth Amendment's suppression remedy. First, the suppression remedy generally applies to interception both by private parties and the government. See, e.g., *United States v. Vest,* 813 F.2d 477, 481 (1st Cir. 1987). Second, the suppression remedy is permitted only in cases involving wire and oral communications. The Act does not provide a statutory suppression remedy for violations involving electronic communications (that is, most computer communications). The reason for the different treatment of electronic communications is largely historical. Congress added the category of "electronic communication" in 1986, when most Americans had not even heard of the Internet or e-mail. Michael S. Leib, *E-mail and the Wiretap Laws: Why Congress Should Add Electronic Communication To Title III's Statutory Exclusionary Rule and Expressly Reject A "Good Faith" Exception,* 34 Harv. J. on Legis. 393 (1997). At that time, it seemed plausible to treat computer communications as less deserving of privacy than telephone calls. The distinction no longer makes sense more than two decades later, but Congress has not yet amended the law to provide for a statutory suppression remedy in the case of electronic communications.

   11. *Exceptions to the Wiretap Act.* Although the prohibitions of the Wiretap Act are broad, the statute contains many exceptions that substantially limit its application. The statute has so many exceptions that one court complained that interpreting the statute requires "travers[ing] a fog of inclusions and exclusions." *Briggs v. American Air Filter Co.,* 630 F.2d 414, 415 (5th Cir. 1980). One exception arose in *United States v. Turk, supra,* at p. ___: the Fifth Circuit held that Kabbaby had lawfully recorded his conversation with Turk "because § 2511(2)(d) specifically exempts situations in which one party to the conversation is himself the interceptor." The following civil case considers this exception in more depth, together with another important exception to the Wiretap Act.

DEAL v. SPEARS

980 F.2d 1153 (8th Cir. 1992).

BOWMAN, CIRCUIT JUDGE.

   This civil action is based on Title III of the Omnibus Crime Control and Safe Streets Act of 1968, 18 U.S.C. §§ 2510–2520. Plaintiffs Sibbie Deal and Calvin

Lucas seek damages against Deal's former employers, defendants Newell and Juanita Spears, doing business as the White Oak Package Store, for the intentional interception and disclosure of plaintiffs' telephone conversations.

Newell and Juanita Spears have owned and operated the White Oak Package Store near Camden, Arkansas, for about twenty years. The Spearses live in a mobile home adjacent to the store. The telephone in the store has an extension in the home, and is the only phone line into either location. The same phone line thus is used for both the residential and the business phones.

Sibbie Deal was an employee at the store from December 1988 until she was fired in August 1990. The store was burglarized in April 1990 and approximately $16,000 was stolen. The Spearses believed that it was an inside job and suspected that Deal was involved. Hoping to catch the suspect in an unguarded admission, Newell Spears purchased and installed a recording device on the extension phone in the mobile home. When turned on, the machine would automatically record all conversations made or received on either phone, with no indication to the parties using the phone that their conversation was being recorded. Before purchasing the recorder, Newell Spears told a sheriff's department investigator that he was considering this surreptitious monitoring and the investigator told Spears that he did not "see anything wrong with that."

Calls were taped from June 27, 1990, through August 13, 1990. During that period, Sibbie Deal, who was married to Mike Deal at the time, was having an extramarital affair with Calvin Lucas, then married to Pam Lucas. Deal and Lucas spoke on the telephone at the store frequently and for long periods of time while Deal was at work. (Lucas was on 100% disability so he was at home all day.) Based on the trial testimony, the District Court concluded that much of the conversation between the two was "sexually provocative." Deal also made or received numerous other personal telephone calls during her workday. Even before Newell Spears purchased the recorder, Deal was asked by her employers to cut down on her use of the phone for personal calls, and the Spearses told her they might resort to monitoring calls or installing a pay phone in order to curtail the abuse.

Newell Spears listened to virtually all twenty-two hours of the tapes he recorded, regardless of the nature of the calls or the content of the conversations, and Juanita Spears listened to some of them. Although there was nothing in the record to indicate that they learned anything about the burglary, they did learn, among other things, that Deal sold Lucas a keg of beer at cost, in violation of store policy. On August 13, 1990, when Deal came in to work the evening shift, Newell Spears played a few seconds of the incriminating tape for Deal and then fired her. Deal and Lucas filed this action on August 29, 1990, and the tapes and recorder were seized by a United States deputy marshal pursuant to court order on September 3, 1990.

Mike Deal testified that Juanita Spears told him about the tapes, and that she divulged the general nature of the tapes to him. Pam Lucas testified that Juanita Spears intimated the contents of the tapes to her but only after Pam asked about them, and she also testified that Juanita told her to tell Sibbie to drop a workers compensation claim she had made against the store or "things could get ugly." Pam Lucas also testified that Juanita Spears "never told me what was on the tapes." Juanita testified that she discussed the tapes and the nature of them, but only in general terms.

The elements of a violation of the wire and electronic communications interception provisions (Title III) of the Omnibus Crime Control and Safe Streets Act of 1968 are set forth in the section that makes such interceptions a criminal offense. 18 U.S.C. § 2511. Under the relevant provisions of the statute, criminal liability attaches and a federal civil cause of action arises when a person intentionally intercepts a wire or electronic communication or intentionally discloses the contents of the interception.

The Spearses first claim they are exempt from civil liability because Sibbie Deal consented to the interception of calls that she made from and received at the store. Under the statute, it is not unlawful "to intercept a wire, oral, or electronic communication . . . where one of the parties to the communication has given prior consent to such interception," 18 U.S.C. § 2511(2)(d), and thus no civil liability is incurred. The Spearses contend that Deal's consent may be implied because Newell Spears had mentioned that he might be forced to monitor calls or restrict telephone privileges if abuse of the store's telephone for personal calls continued. They further argue that the extension in their home gave actual notice to Deal that her calls could be overheard, and that this notice resulted in her implied consent to interception. We find these arguments unpersuasive.

There is no evidence of express consent here. Although constructive consent is inadequate, actual consent may be implied from the circumstances. Nevertheless, consent under Title III is not to be cavalierly implied. Knowledge of the capability of monitoring alone cannot be considered implied consent.

We do not believe that Deal's consent may be implied from the circumstances relied upon in the Spearses' arguments. The Spearses did not inform Deal that they were monitoring the phone, but only told her they might do so in order to cut down on personal calls. Moreover, it seems clear that the couple anticipated Deal would not suspect that they were intercepting her calls, since they hoped to catch her making an admission about the burglary, an outcome they would not expect if she knew her calls were being recorded. As for listening in via the extension, Deal testified that she knew when someone picked up the extension in the residence while she was on the store phone, as there was an audible "click" on the line.

Given these circumstances, we hold as a matter of law that the Spearses have failed to show Deal's consent to the interception and recording of her conversations.

The Spearses also argue that they are immune from liability under what has become known as an exemption for business use of a telephone extension. The exception is actually a restrictive definition. Under Title III, a party becomes criminally and civilly liable when he or she "intercepts" wire communications. " 'Intercept' means the aural or other acquisition of the contents of any wire, electronic, or oral communication through the use of any electronic, mechanical, or other device." 18 U.S.C. § 2510(4). Such a device is "any device or apparatus which can be used to intercept a wire, oral, or electronic communication" except when that device is a

> telephone . . . instrument, equipment or facility, or any component thereof, (i) furnished to the subscriber or user by a provider of wire or electronic communication service in the ordinary course of its business and being used by the subscriber or user in the ordinary course of its business or furnished by such subscriber or user for connection to the facilities of such service and used in the ordinary course of its business.

Id. § 2510(5)(a)(i).

We do not quarrel with the contention that the Spearses had a legitimate business reason for listening in: they suspected Deal's involvement in a burglary of the store and hoped she would incriminate herself in a conversation on the phone. Moreover, Deal was abusing her privileges by using the phone for numerous personal calls even, by her own admission, when there were customers in the store. The Spearses might legitimately have monitored Deal's calls to the extent necessary to determine that the calls were personal and made or received in violation of store policy.

But the Spearses recorded twenty-two hours of calls, and Newell Spears listened to all of them without regard to their relation to his business interests. Granted, Deal might have mentioned the burglary at any time during the conversations, but we do not believe that the Spearses' suspicions justified the extent of the intrusion. We conclude that the scope of the interception in this case takes us well beyond the boundaries of the ordinary course of business.

For the reasons we have indicated, the Spearses cannot avail themselves of the telephone extension/business use exemption of Title III.

NOTES AND QUESTIONS

1. *The consent exception*. The Wiretap Act's consent exceptions are found in 18 U.S.C. § 2511(2)(c) and 2511(2)(d). The two exceptions share a common root: They both permit a party of the communication to intercept the communication or to consent to others intercepting the communication. In the *Turk* case, p. 520, one of the parties to the communication performed the interception: Kabbaby recorded the conversation with defendant Turk. In *Deal v. Spears*, in contrast, the question was whether Deal (a party to the communication) had consented to the Spearses intercepting the communication.

The consent provisions of the Wiretap Act are designed to mirror Fourth Amendment precedents. Recall that under *Hoffa v. United States*, p. 470, and *United States v. White*, p. 474, a secret agent can record a communication to which he is a party. Similarly, under *Schneckloth v. Bustamonte*, p. 454, a person can voluntarily consent to a law enforcement search. The Wiretap Act codifies these standards: A party to the communication can conduct monitoring and can consent to allow others to monitor his communications. The consent of one party to the communication makes the monitoring legal.

The Wiretap Act applies to monitoring both by private parties and state actors, and the consent exception for individuals who are not state actors is narrower than that of state actors. Under 18 U.S.C. § 2511(2)(d), consent of a party is insufficient if the communication is intercepted "for the purpose of committing any criminal or tortuous act in violation of the Constitution or laws of the United States or of any State."

2. *All-party consent statutes.* Title III, the federal Wiretap Act, is a one-party consent statute: The consent of any one party authorizes the interception of the communication to all parties. Some state wiretapping statutes offer broader privacy protections by requiring the consent of all parties to the communication before the communication can be recorded. In these states, the right not to be recorded is a personal right. You may have had the experience of calling a national customer service number and hearing that the call "may be monitored for quality assurance." These warnings are made just in case you placed your call from a state that has an all-party consent wiretap statute. By proceeding after being warned of the monitoring, you are deemed to have consented to monitoring under state wiretap statutes.

Which is preferable as a matter of policy: One-party consent or all-party consent? Note that in a state with an all-party consent statute, secret recordings are unlawful even if the person recorded is engaging in wrongdoing. For example, in *Commonwealth v. Hyde*, 434 Mass. 594, 750 N.E.2d 963 (2001), police officers stopped Hyde in his white Porsche for having an unusually loud exhaust system. The traffic stop turned confrontational, and the officers ended up screaming at Hyde and acting unprofessionally. After a few minutes, the officers ended the traffic stop without writing a ticket. Unbeknownst to the officers, Hyde had a tape recorder in his car that he had turned on when he was pulled over. A few days after the traffic stop, Hyde filed a formal complaint against the police officers and included a copy of the recording to bolster his claims. The state responded by bringing criminal charges against Hyde under the Massachusetts state wiretap act for having secretly recorded the police officers without their prior consent.

The Massachusetts Supreme Judicial Court agreed with the government that Hyde had violated the state statute: "The defendant argues that his prosecution was tantamount to holding him criminally liable for exercising his constitutional rights to petition the government for redress of his grievances and to hold police officers accountable for their behavior. This argument has no merit. * * * The defendant was not prosecuted for making the recording; he was prosecuted for doing so secretly.

"The problem here could have been avoided if, at the outset of the traffic stop, the defendant had simply informed the police of his intention to tape record the encounter, or even held the tape recorder in plain sight. Had he done so, his recording would not have been secret, and so would not have violated [the state wiretap statute]. Secret tape recording by private individuals has been unequivocally banned, and, unless and until the Legislature changes the statute, what was done here cannot be done lawfully."

3. *The extension telephone exception.* 18 U.S.C. § 2510(5)(a)(i) is often referred to as the "extension telephone" exception; it exempts from the definition of a "device" that could be used to intercept communications those telephones furnished and used in "the ordinary course of business." This exception is a holdover from *Rathbun v. United States*, 355 U.S. 107 (1957), an early wiretapping case decided under the Communications Act of 1934 in the era before the Wiretap Act. In *Rathbun*, the defendant placed a call to Sparks at his home and threatened to kill him. Unbeknownst to the defendant, Sparks had been tipped off to the threat and had asked local police officers to listen to the call. When the defendant placed the call, the police were listening in on a second telephone in the Sparks home. The defendant was charged with sending an interstate threat, and he moved to suppress the testimony of the officers who heard the threat on the ground that they had unlawfully intercepted his call in violation of the Communications Act, 47 U.S.C. § 605.

In an opinion by Chief Justice Warren, the Court held that use of an extension telephone in the ordinary course of business could not be an intercept: "It has been conceded by those who believe the conduct here violates Section 605 that either party may record the conversation and publish it. The conduct of the party would differ in no way if instead of repeating the message he held out his handset so that another could hear out of it. We see no distinction between that sort of action and permitting an outsider to use an extension telephone for the same purpose. * * * For example, it follows from petitioner's argument that every secretary who listens to a business conversation at her employer's direction in order to record it would be marked as a potential federal criminal. It is unreasonable to believe that Congress meant to extend criminal liability to conduct which is wholly innocent and ordinary.

"Common experience tells us that a call to a particular telephone number may cause the bell to ring in more than one ordinarily used instrument. Each party to a telephone conversation takes the risk that the other party may have an extension telephone and may allow another to overhear the conversation. When such takes place there has been no violation of any privacy of which the parties may complain. Consequently, one element of Section 605, interception, has not occurred."

When Congress enacted the Wiretap Act in 1968, it codified *Rathbun* in the extension telephone exception even though Congress also enacted a consent exception. The scope of the extension telephone exception has long been a source of confusion, however, owing largely to the difficulty of identifying the "ordinary course of business" of a person who is not engaging in business activities. For example, if a person believes that his spouse is cheating, can he listen in on his spouse's telephone calls from another telephone in the house? Courts have divided on such questions, although the more recent decisions suggest that the answer is "no." *See Glanzer v. Glanzer*, 347 F.3d 1212 (11th Cir. 2003) (en banc) (overturning circuit precedent from 1974 that had found an exception for interspousal wiretapping).

4. *The provider exception.* The provider exception, codified at 18 U.S.C. § 2511(2)(a)(i), is another important exception to the Wiretap Act. The exception permits "an operator of a switchboard, or an officer, employee, or agent of a provider of wire or electronic communication service, whose facilities are used in the transmission of a wire or electronic communication, to intercept, disclose, or use that communication in the normal course of his employment while engaged in any activity which is a necessary incident to the rendition of his service or to the protection of the rights or property of the provider of that service[.]" This exception permits communications service providers to conduct reasonable work-related monitoring of the contents of calls when needed to protect the network or ensure it is operating properly. For example, if a person is using an illegal "cloned" cellular phone that is billed to a different subscriber, allowing the cloned phone owner to place unlimited calls for free, the phone company can listen in on limited parts of the call to identify the individual placing the illegal calls. *See United States v. Pervaz*, 118 F.3d 1 (1st Cir. 1997).

5. *Packet sniffers and "Carnivore."* Internet communications ordinarily are sent and received using discrete "packets" of data. The packet is a stream of data that begins with a "header," the addressing information for the packet, and then is followed by the "payload," the message that the packet delivers. A long Internet communication might consist of a string of packets that are sent individually and then reassembled together into the original communication at its destination. When a private party or the government wishes to intercept Internet communications, one common tool for doing so is known as a "packet sniffer." A packet sniffer is a filter that scans traffic over a specific Internet connection. *See generally* David McPhie, *Almost Private: Pen Registers, Packet Sniffers, and Privacy at the Margin*, 2005 Stan. Tech. L. Rev. 1. The sniffer must be programmed to look for specific types of communications, and when those communications pass through the filter the sniffer can copy the packets and store them for later analysis. Whether the sniffer "intercepts" communications depends on how the filter is set; a filter set to collect contents will intercept communications, whereas a filter setting that does not collect contents will not intercept communications and therefore will not implicate the Wiretap Act.

In the late 1990s, the FBI's "Carnivore" surveillance tool received a great deal of critical attention. Carnivore, later renamed "DCS–1000," was a packet sniffer with an unusually sophisticated filter designed specifically to comply with court orders. The Carnivore system presented the user with a graphic user interface set for "content" or "non-content" monitoring, with the type of monitoring depending on the legal authority, and adjusted the filter automatically. By

2003, improvements in commercial packet sniffer design led to a phase-out of Carnivore/DCS–1000.

C. THE PEN REGISTER STATUTE

The Pen Registers and Trap and Trace Devices statute, commonly known as the Pen Register statute, is codified at 18 U.S.C. §§ 3121–27. The Pen Register statute was designed as a legislative response to *Smith v. Maryland*, p. 510. Under *Smith* and its progeny, the Fourth Amendment does not regulate the use of pen registers and other collection of non-content information. The Pen Register statute imposes a modest degree of regulation of pen registers and more modern analogs on communications networks.

18 U.S.C. § 3121(a) prohibits the installation or use of pen registers and trap and trace devices without a court order unless a statutory exception applies. In the 1960s and 1970s, pen registers were devices that could be installed to record the numbers dialed from a telephone line, and "trap and trace" devices could be used to record the incoming numbers dialed into a phone line. When the Pen Register statute was first enacted in 1986, the basic prohibition effectively regulated the tools that were used to collect "to" and "from" information for telephone calls.

The expansion of the Wiretap Act to encompass electronic communications in addition to wire communications (that is, Internet communications in addition to phone calls) required an expansion of the statute to account for the Internet equivalent of pen registers. Instead of eliminating the technology-specific language found in the statute, Congress changed the definitions of "pen register" and "trap and trace device" in 18 U.S.C. § 3127(3)–(4). Section 216 of the USA Patriot Act of 2001 replaced the telephone-focused language of the 1986 Act with more general language that covers non-content addressing information for both telephone calls and Internet communications.

Specifically, a pen register is defined as "a device or process which records or decodes dialing, routing, addressing, or signaling information transmitted by an instrument or facility from which a wire or electronic communication is transmitted, provided, however, that such information shall not include the contents of any communication." 18 U.S.C. § 3127(3). A trap and trace device is defined as "a device or process which captures the incoming electronic or other impulses which identify the originating number or other dialing, routing, addressing, and signaling information reasonably likely to identify the source of a wire or electronic communication, provided, however, that such information shall not include the contents of any communication." 18 U.S.C. § 3127(4).

Putting the new definitions into the old statutory text yields a statute that regulates the collection of non-content "dialing, routing, addressing, or signaling information" for both telephone calls and Internet communications. For example, if investigators or providers install a sniffer device that collects only non-content addressing information such as IP headers, the sniffer device acts as both a pen register (when it collects "from" information) and a trap and trace device (when it collects "to" information).

The privacy protections of the Pen Register statute are much more modest than those of the Wiretap Act. First, an order requiring a telecommunications service provider to install a pen register or trap and trace device does not require probable cause, or even reasonable suspicion. To obtain such an order, a government lawyer simply must certify (without articulating the basis for this belief) that he believes that the "information likely to be obtained * * * is relevant to an ongoing criminal investigation." 18 U.S.C. § 3123(a)(1). Second, violations of the

Pen Register statute do not lead to suppression of the evidence on statutory grounds, and the statute similarly does not support a civil remedy. The sole remedy for violations is a potential criminal prosecution. *See* 18 U.S.C. § 3121(d). Third, the Pen Register statute has broad exceptions from liability that mirror and expand upon the exceptions of the Wiretap Act. *See* 18 U.S.C. § 3121(b).

NOTES AND QUESTIONS

1. *Caller ID services.* Many telephone users have Caller ID services that automatically report the telephone number of an incoming call. Caller ID services do not violate the Pen Register statute thanks to the consent exception found in 18 U.S.C. § 3121(b)(3). That exception permits the installation of a pen register or trap and trace device "where the consent of the user of that service has been obtained."

2. *Telephone bills.* Telephone company bills may provide a list of calls that a user made during the billing period. This is permitted by an exception to the definition of "pen register" in 18 U.S.C. § 3127(3), which states that a pen register does not include "any device or process used by a provider or customer of a wire or electronic communication service for billing, or recording as an incident to billing[.]"

3. *Cell site data.* Cellular telephones are able to send and receive communications because they send out regular communications to nearby cell towers to let the towers know that the phone is close. Those signals inform the cell provider of the phone's location so it can route calls to that phone through the nearest tower. When a cell phone is turned on, it tries to touch base with local towers; as the phone moves, it loses connection to the towers that have become far away and establishes contact with the new towers nearby. If the phone company records the list of cell towers to which a particular phone is communicating, it generates a log of the rough physical location of the phone when it is turned on. Criminal investigators may seek access to these so-called "cell site" records in real time; because most people keep their cell phones with them, the telephone location information can be used as a type of tracking device.

Does the Pen Register statute permit the government to order the phone company to record cell-site information and give the records to the government? Consider this argument that the answer is "no," from In re Application for Pen Register and Trap/Trace Device with Cell Site Location Authority, 396 F.Supp.2d 747, 761–62 (S.D. Tex. 2005): "The traditional pen register was triggered only when the user dialed a telephone number; no information was recorded by the device unless the user attempted to make a call. The Patriot Act clarified that a pen register could also record 'routing, addressing, and signaling information,' as well as numbers dialed. But the expanded definition also indicates that this 'routing, addressing, and signaling' information is generated by, and incidental to, the transmission of 'a wire or electronic communication.' 18 U.S.C. § 3127(3). In other words, today's pen register must still be tied to an actual or attempted phone call. [However,] much cell site data is transmitted even when the user is not making or receiving a call, *i.e.*, when no wire or electronic communication is transmitted."

4. *Packet sniffers, once again.* Recall from Note 5 on p. 531 that if an Internet packet sniffer is configured to collect the contents of communications, then the device is regulated under the Wiretap Act. Conversely, if a packet sniffer is configured to collect only dialing, routing, addressing, and signaling information, then the device is regulated only under the Pen Register statute. If the

device is configured to collect both contents and non-content addressing information, then the device must be used in a way that satisfies both statutes.

   5. *State constitutional and statutory protections.* Recall from Note 5 on p. 517 that some state constitutions have been interpreted to reject *Smith v. Maryland*, p. 510. In these states, use of a pen register is a "search" under state constitutions. Even in the absence of state constitutional provisions, state statutory surveillance laws can impose stricter standards for the use and installation of pen registers and trap and trace devices than does the federal statute. Under the Supremacy Clause, however, federal investigators need not comply with state law restrictions and instead need only satisfy the federal Pen Register statute. The result is a bifurcated system, with federal investigators operating under the low federal standard and state investigators sometimes operating under higher state standards.

D. THE STORED COMMUNICATIONS ACT

   Both the Wiretap Act and the Pen Register statute deal with prospective surveillance. That is, they both regulate accessing communications and non-content information in "real time," as the communications are being sent and received. Congress has also enacted a statute to regulate access to stored communications. This law, known as the Stored Communications Act, is codified at 18 U.S.C. §§ 2701–11. The Stored Communications Act regulates efforts of the government to obtain stored account records and the contents of stored communications. The law also limits when account providers can voluntarily disclose such records to the police.

   Unlike the Wiretap Act and the Pen Register statute, the Stored Communications Act is limited to two specific types of providers. They are the only entities regulated by the statute. The first type of provider regulated under the Stored Communications Act is a provider of "electronic communications service" (ECS). The statute defines ECS as "any service which provides to users thereof the ability to send or receive wire or electronic communications," 18 U.S.C.A. § 2510(15). In other words, an ECS is a provider of connectivity like the telephone company or an Internet service provider.

   The second type of provider regulated under the Stored Communications Act is a provider of "remote computing service" (RCS). The statute defines RCS as "the provision to the public of computer storage or processing services by means of an electronic communications system." 18 U.S.C.A. § 2711(2). This means that an RCS is a computer service available to the public that permits users to store or process their files remotely. Although the concept may be somewhat outdated today, such services were common in 1986 when the Stored Communications Act was passed. The limited storage and functionality of computers at that time led many users to store their files with remote services and to send out files for processing (work that today would be performed by spreadsheets or payroll software).

   The core of the Stored Communications Act consists of the rules for when the government can access communications held by these two types of providers. Codified in 18 U.S.C. § 2703, the rules impose different legal thresholds for compelling different types of information. The lowest protection is given to basic subscriber information such as the name, address, and records of session times of subscribers. The government can compel a provider of either "electronic communications service" (ECS) or "remote computing service" (RCS) to disclose such information using a federal or state grand jury subpoena, trial subpoena, or administrative subpoena. *See* 18 U.S.C. § 2703(c)(2). To obtain other non-content information relating to the account, the government must normally obtain a special court order based on the standards of *Terry v. Ohio* p. 408. *See* 18 U.S.C. § 2703(c)(2). This court order can be issued when the government establishes "specific and articulable facts" to believe that the information to be obtained will be "relevant and material to an ongoing criminal investigation." *See* 18 U.S.C. § 2703(d).

The Stored Communications Act's rules for compelling contents of communications are found in 18 U.S.C. § 2703(a)-(b). According to the statutory text, contents held by an ECS for 180 days or less can be obtained only with a search warrant. 18 U.S.C. § 2703(a). On the other hand, contents that are held by an ECS for more than 180 days or contents that are held by an RCS are given lower protections: These contents can be obtained either with a warrant, or with the combination of prior notice to the subscriber and either a *Terry* order under § 2703(d) or a subpoena. 18 U.S.C. § 2703(b). Translating these rules into a practical set of directions for how the Stored Communications Act works turns out to be surprisingly difficult: Courts have divided on how modern communications fit into the framework of contents held by providers of ECS and RCS. The disagreement involves a difficult question of statutory interpretation and is explored in detail in Note 2 below.

The Stored Communications Act also contains rules that limit when providers can disclose account records. *See* 18 U.S.C. § 2702. These rules apply only to providers that provide services to the public, such as commercial Internet service providers or remote storage services. In general, providers to the public cannot disclose contents of communications unless an exception applies. Further, they cannot disclose non-content records to a governmental entity unless an exception applies. 18 U.S.C. § 2702(a). The exceptions that permit disclosure are largely modeled on the Fourth Amendment's exceptions to the warrant requirement. The different provisions largely mirror well-known Fourth Amendment exceptions such as consent, exigent circumstances, and plain view. *See* 18 U.S.C. § 2702(b)-(c).

The remedies for violations of the Stored Communications Act are notably limited. A statutory suppression remedy does not exist. Instead, the remedy for a statutory violation is a civil damages action. *See* 18 U.S.C. §§ 2707–08.

NOTES AND QUESTIONS

1. *Entities regulated by the Stored Communications Act.* The Stored Communications Act only regulates two types of providers, providers of ECS and RCS. This means that there are many third-party services that the SCA does not regulate at all. Consider *In re Jetblue Airways Corp. Privacy Litigation*, 379 F.Supp.2d 299 (E.D.N.Y. 2005). In this case, the airline JetBlue had disclosed data from the JetBlue Passenger Reservation System computer to a company that had contracted with the government to explore data mining techniques. The plaintiffs, a class of JetBlue customers, claimed that the disclosure of customer data violated the voluntary disclosure provisions of 18 U.S.C. § 2702. The district court rejected this claim on the ground that JetBlue was not a provider covered by the Stored Communications Act:

"The term 'electronic communication service,' as defined, refers to a service that provides users with capacity to transmit electronic communications. Although JetBlue operates a website that receives and transmits data to and from its customers, it is undisputed that it is not the provider of the electronic communication service that allows such data to be transmitted over the Internet. Rather, JetBlue is more appropriately characterized as a provider of air travel services and a consumer of electronic communication services. The website that it operates, like a telephone, enables the company to communicate with its customers in the regular course of business. Mere operation of the website, however, does not transform JetBlue into a provider of internet access, just as the use of a telephone to accept telephone reservations does not transform the company into a provider of telephone service. Thus, a company such as JetBlue does not become an 'electronic communication service' provider simply because it maintains a website that allows for the transmission of electronic communications between itself and its customers. * * *

"Plaintiffs have also failed to establish that JetBlue is a remote computing service. Plaintiffs simply make the allegation without providing any legal or factual support for such a claim. As discussed, the term 'remote computing service' is defined in the ECPA as 'the provision to the public of computer storage or processing services by means of an electronic communication system.' 18 U.S.C. § 2711(2). The statute's legislative history explains that such services exist to provide sophisticated and convenient data processing services to subscribers and customers, such as hospitals and banks, from remote facilities. *See* S. Rep. No. 99–541 (1986), *reprinted in* 1986 U.S.C.C.A.N. 3555, 3564. By supplying the necessary equipment, remote computing services alleviate the need for users of computer technology to process data in-house. Customers or subscribers may enter into time-sharing arrangements with the remote computing service, or data processing may be accomplished by the service provider on the basis of information supplied by the subscriber or customer. Although plaintiffs allege that JetBlue operates a website and computer servers, no facts alleged indicate that JetBlue provides either computer processing services or computer storage to the public. As such, under the plain meaning of the statute, JetBlue is not a remote computing service."

Under this reasoning, are search terms sent to Internet search engines such as Google protected under the Stored Communications Act? Is the search engine acting as a provider of RCS?

2. A difficult question of statutory interpretation: The rules for compelling opened e-mail. Under *United States v. Warshak*, p. 501, the Fourth Amendment generally requires a warrant to compel an Internet service provider to disclose the contents of an e-mail account. Notably, however, the Stored Communications Act suggests a narrower reading of privacy protections. Although 18 U.S.C. § 2703(a) requires a warrant to compel an ISP to disclose contents, 18 U.S.C. § 2703(b) does not. To the extent § 2703(b) is constitutional, its scope implicates a difficult question of statutory interpretation. Specifically, courts and commentators have divided on how the Stored Communications Act regulates access to opened e-mail stored for less than 180 days. The question is this: Are opened e-mails considered contents held in electronic storage by an ECS and protected under the search warrant protections of 18 U.S.C. § 2703(a), or are they stored communications held by an RCS and therefore protected only under the less protective rules of 18 U.S.C. § 2703(b)?

The source of the difficulty is the narrow definition of "electronic storage" in 18 U.S.C. § 2510(17). This definition is critical because contents in "electronic storage" are the only types of contents held by providers of ECS. As a result, only contents in "electronic storage" receive the privacy protections of a full search warrant found in 18 U.S.C. § 2703(a). 18 U.S.C. § 2510(17) defines "electronic storage" as: "(A) any temporary, intermediate storage of a wire or electronic communication incidental to the electronic transmission thereof; and (B) any storage of such communication by an electronic communication service for purposes of backup protection of such communication."

Note that this statutory definition is much narrower than the broad term "electronic storage" suggests. It refers only to a particular type of electronic storage rather than all electronic storage. Specifically, § 2510(17)(A) reflects the very specific function of ECS providers: servers may make temporary copies of e-mails in the course of transmission, and § 2510(17)(A) protects these temporary copies made pending transmission of communications. For example, unopened e-mail in a user's in-box is in "electronic storage," as it is awaiting the user's retrieval of the message. Before the user has read the e-mail, the copy stored on the server is a temporary, intermediate copy stored incident to the transmission of the message to the user.

How does this framework apply to opened e-mail? Two different interpretations exist. Under one interpretation, adopted by the Justice Department and accepted by several district courts, the status of an opened e-mail is different from the status of an unopened e-mail. When a user reads an e-mail and decides not to delete it, and instead wants to store it on the ISP's servers, that copy is no longer temporary or intermediate. Rather, the opened e-mail is stored permanently on the ISP's server. The ISP is now acting like an RCS, not an ECS, and it should therefore be covered by the RCS rules found in 18 U.S.C. § 2703(b). *See, e.g.*, United States Department of Justice, Searching and Seizing Computers and Obtaining Electronic Evidence in Criminal Investigations, Chapter III, Part B (2002), available at http://www.usdoj.gov/criminal/cybercrime/s & smanual2002.htm#_IIIB_; *Fraser v. Nationwide Mut. Ins.*, 135 F.Supp.2d 623 (E.D. Pa. 2001), *affirmed on other grounds*, 352 F.3d 107 (3d. Cir. 2003); *In re DoubleClick, Inc. Privacy Litig.*, 154 F.Supp.2d 497, 511–12 (S.D.N.Y.2001). *See also* H.R. Rep. No. 99–647, at 64–65 (1986).

The alternative view, adopted by the Ninth Circuit, is that opened e-mails are treated just like unopened e-mails because opened e-mails are copies stored for "backup protection" under § 2510(17)(B). Under this view, a user who leaves an opened copy of an e-mail on a server is leaving that copy for "back up protection." Opening the e-mail merely shifts the protection from the electronic storage provision of § 2510(17)(A) to that of § 2510(17)(B). As a result, the warrant requirement of 18 U.S.C. § 2703(a) applies to all unopened e-mail and any opened e-mail that a user intended to leave as a backup copy that has been in storage for 180 days or less. *See Theofel v. Farey–Jones*, 359 F.3d 1066 (9th Cir. 2004).

3. Why does the Stored Communications Act have lower protections for remote computing services and for storage for more than 180 days? Consider the explanation in Orin S. Kerr, *A User's Guide to the Stored Communications Act—and a Legislator's Guide to Amending It*, 72 Geo. Wash. L. Rev. 1208, 1234 (2004) (hereinafter, Kerr, *A User's Guide*): "The apparent thinking behind the lower thresholds for government access of both permanently stored files and unretrieved files stored for more than 180 days is that the lower thresholds track Supreme Court precedents interpreting the Fourth Amendment. For example, in *Couch v. United States*, 409 U.S. 322 (1973), a defendant handed over records to her accountant so her accountant could process the data and complete the defendant's tax returns. The Court held that by giving her records to the accountant, Couch had relinquished her reasonable expectation of privacy. A provider acting as an RCS likely falls under this precedent: a person uses an RCS for outsourcing much like Couch used her accountant. Similarly, the strange '180 day rule' dividing § 2703(a) from § 2703(b) may reflect the Fourth Amendment abandonment doctrine at work. Individuals lose the Fourth Amendment protection in property if they abandon the property, and the SCA's drafters may have figured that unretrieved files not accessed after 180 days have been abandoned."

Assuming this explains what the statute's drafters had in mind, does that explanation make sense today? Do users "abandon" e-mail left on the server for more than 180 days? If not, is § 2703(b) unconstitutional?

4. *The meaning of providers "to the public."* The Stored Communications Act occasionally distinguishes rules for providers "to the public" from other providers. The meaning of providing services "to the public" was explored in *Andersen Consulting LLP v. UOP*, 991 F.Supp. 1041 (N.D. Ill. 1998). UOP hired Andersen for consulting work and provided Andersen consultants with UOP internal e-mail accounts. After the relationship soured, UOP disclosed the contents of e-mails from the UOP e-mail accounts used by Andersen consultants to the Wall Street Journal. Andersen sued under 18 U.S.C. § 2702, but the district court ruled that the disclosure did not violate the Stored Communications Act because UOP did not provide e-mail services to the public:

"The statute does not define 'public.' The word 'public,' however, is unambiguous. Public means the 'aggregate of the citizens' or 'everybody' or 'the people at large' or 'the community at large.' *Black's Law Dictionary* 1227 (6th ed.1990). Thus, the statute covers any entity that provides electronic communication service (e.g., e-mail) to the community at large.

"Andersen claims that UOP provides an electronic communication service to the public. However, giving Andersen access to its e-mail system is not equivalent to providing e-mail to the public. Andersen was hired by UOP to do a project and as such, was given access to UOP's e-mail system similar to UOP employees. Andersen was not any member of the community at large, but a hired contractor. Further, the fact that Andersen could communicate to third-parties over the internet and that third-parties could communicate with it did not mean that UOP provided an electronic communication service to the public. UOP's internal e-mail system is separate from the internet. UOP must purchase internet access from an electronic communication service provider like any other consumer; it does not independently provide internet services."

5. *Why does the Stored Communications Act limit voluntary disclosure only for services available to the public?* Consider Kerr, *A User's Guide*, at 1226–27: "[T]he law may afford less protection to accounts with nonpublic providers because nonpublic accounts may exist more for the benefit of providers than for the benefit of users. For example, companies often provide e-mail accounts to employees for work-related purposes; the U.S. military often provides accounts to service members for official government business. These nonpublic providers generally have a legitimate interest in controlling and accessing the accounts they provide to users. Plus, their users tend to recognize that the providers will view those provider interests as more important than the privacy interests of users.

"In contrast, an individual who contracts with a commercial ISP available to the public usually does so solely for his own benefit. The account belongs to the user, not the provider. As a result, the user may understandably rely more heavily on the privacy of the commercial account from the public provider rather than another account with a nonpublic provider. Many Internet users have experienced this dynamic. When an e-mail exchange using a work account turns to private matters, it is common for a user to move the discussion to a commercial account. 'I don't want my boss to read this,' a user might note, 'I'll e-mail you from my personal account later.' The law recognizes this distinction by drawing a line between accounts held with public and nonpublic providers. In practice, the public/nonpublic line often acts as a proxy for the distinction between a user's private account and one assigned to him by his employer."

6. *Notice under the Stored Communications Act.* The Stored Communications Act provides subscribers with limited rights to receive notice that their communications have been accessed. As a statutory matter, notice to the customer or subscriber is required only when the government obtains contents of communications with less process than a search warrant under 18 U.S.C. § 2703(b)(1)(B). Further, notice can be delayed pursuant to 18 U.S.C. § 2705. If the government obtains a search warrant, or if the government compels only non-content records, no statutory notice is required.

NOTE ON NATIONAL SECURITY MONITORING AND THE FOREIGN INTELLIGENCE SURVEILLANCE ACT

The materials in this chapter have considered the constitutional and statutory rules that regulate network surveillance in the context of criminal investigations. A parallel set of rules exists in the case of national security investigations. The national security interests in network surveillance are different from the interests arising in criminal cases. In the national security setting, the goal is collecting intelligence to help protect the country rather than bringing criminal prosecutions to deter and punish criminal wrongdoing. Although a detailed discussion of the law in national security cases is beyond the scope of these materials,[b] a few highlights can be noted here.

Under the Fourth Amendment, a warrant is required to wiretap the communications of domestic groups for national security reasons. In *United States v. United States District Court*, 407 U.S. 297 (1972), the Supreme Court held that a warrant was required in these settings: "Fourth Amendment freedoms cannot properly be guaranteed if domestic security surveillances may be conducted solely within the discretion of the Executive Branch. The Fourth Amendment does not contemplate the executive officers of Government as neutral and disinterested magistrates. Their duty and responsibility are to enforce the laws, to investigate, and to prosecute. But those charged with this investigative and prosecutorial duty should not be the sole judges of when to utilize constitutionally sensitive means in pursuing their tasks. The historical judgment, which the Fourth Amendment accepts, is that unreviewed executive discretion may yield too readily to pressures to obtain incriminating evidence and overlook potential invasions of privacy and protected speech."

At the same time, lower courts have held that no warrant is required to wiretap communications of agents of foreign powers inside the United States. *See, e.g., United States v. Truong Dinh Hung*, 629 F.2d 908, 915 (4th Cir. 1980) (holding that "the government should be relieved of seeking a warrant only when the object of the search or the surveillance is a foreign power, its agent or collaborators" and "surveillance is conducted primarily for foreign intelligence reasons."). Further, the Fourth Amendment does not apply at all to the monitoring of individuals outside the United States who have no voluntary contacts with the United States. *See United States v. Verdugo–Urquidez*, 494 U.S. 259 (1990). Under *Verdugo–Urquidez*, intelligence monitoring of individuals outside the United States who have no voluntary contacts with the United States are not regulated by the Fourth Amendment: "Situations threatening to important American interests may arise half-way around the globe, situations which in the view of the political branches of our Government require an American response with armed force. If there are to be restrictions on searches and seizures which occur incident to such American action, they must be imposed by the political branches through diplomatic understanding, treaty, or legislation." United States citizens abroad

---

b. Readers wishing to understand this area in detail should consult David S. Kris & J. Douglas Wilson, National Security Investigations and Prosecutions (2007).

retain their Fourth Amendment rights, but exactly what rules must apply to monitoring of their communications by the United States remains largely unclear. *See United States v. Bin Laden*, 126 F.Supp.2d 264 (S.D.N.Y. 2000).

The Fourth Amendment limits in national security investigations are supplemented by important statutory protections. In 1978, Congress enacted the Foreign Intelligence Surveillance Act, Pub. L. 95–511, 92 Stat. 1783 (1978), often known by its acronym "FISA" (rhymes with Eliza). As amended, FISA creates a set of statutory laws that parallel the criminal law protections of the Wiretap Act, the Pen Register statute, and the Stored Communications Act. The FISA equivalent of the Wiretap Act is found at 50 U.S.C. §§ 1801–11. Instead of regulating the interception of contents of wire and electronic communications, FISA regulates engaging in "electronic surveillance."

"Electronic surveillance" is defined in a complicated way by 50 U.S.C. § 1801(f). In a nutshell, the definition requires the government to obtain a FISA court order to intercept the contents of known United States persons inside the United States if a Title III order would be required in an analogous criminal case; to collect communications sent over a wire if the interception occurs inside the United States; to collect the contents of communications sent over the airwaves if all parties are inside the United States and a Title III order would be required in an analogous case; and also to install a surreptitious listening "bug" if a Title III order would be required in an analogous case. FISA court orders are roughly equivalent to Title III orders, although the standards are tailored to national security cases and the orders are reviewed and signed by District Court judges specially assigned to the Foreign Intelligence Surveillance Court. *See generally In re Sealed Case*, 310 F.3d 717, 737–41 (Foreign Int. Surv. Ct. Rev. 2002) (comparing the process of obtaining FISA orders and Title III orders).

FISA also contains an analogous provision to the Pen Register statute, codified at 50 U.S.C. §§ 1841–46. FISA's version borrows the Pen Register statute's definition of "pen register" and "trap and trace device," and it permits such a device to be installed when the government submits a certification "that the information likely to be obtained is foreign intelligence information not concerning a United States person or is relevant to an ongoing investigation to protect against international terrorism or clandestine intelligence activities, provided that such investigation of a United States person is not conducted solely upon the basis of activities protected by the first amendment to the Constitution." 50 U.S.C.A. § 1842(c)(2).

FISA's version of the Stored Communications Act can be constructed by pulling together several different statutes. Although FISA does not have a provision specifically addressing access to the contents of e-mails by an ISP, it seems likely that e-mail is compelled under the probable cause standard of 50 U.S.C. §§ 1821–29. These provisions of FISA regulate "physical searches," defined as "any physical intrusion within the United States into premises or property (including examination of the interior of property by technical means) that is intended to result in a seizure, reproduction, inspection, or alteration of information, material, or property, under circumstances in which a person has a reasonable expectation of privacy and a warrant would be required for law enforcement purposes."

There are two different and parallel authorities that the government can use to compel non-content account information from ISPs, telephone companies, and other network providers. The first and most important is the "National Security Letter" provision in the Stored Communications Act, 18 U.S.C. § 2709. An NSL is something like an administrative subpoena. Like an administrative subpoena, it does not require an order signed by a judge or issued by a court. Instead, high-ranking FBI officials can request information from ISPs via written letters. According to § 2709, a "wire or electronic communication service provider shall comply with a request for subscriber information and toll billing records information, or electronic communication transactional records in its custody or possession" from appropriate authorities within the FBI. The records sought must be "relevant to an authorized investigation to protect against international terrorism or clandestine intelligence activities, provided that such an investigation of a United States person is not conducted solely on the basis of activities protected by the first amendment to the Constitution of the United States."

The National Security Letter provision in Section 2709 is only one of five different National Security Letter authorities,[c] although it is used by far more often than the others, which generally can be used to obtain bank records and consumer credit records. In 2005, for example, the FBI issued National Security Letters 47,000 times. *See* Office of the Inspector General, A Review of the Federal Bureau of Investigation's Use of National Security Letters xvi (2007). The "overwhelming majority" of these were obtained from telephone companies and ISPs under Section 2709. *Id.* at xvii.

In addition to the NSL authority, FISA contains a provision allowing the government to obtain court orders to compel "tangible things (including books, records, papers, documents, and other items)." 50 U.S.C. § 1861(a)(1). Such orders are commonly referred to as "Section 215" orders, as this authority was expanded by Section 215 of the USA Patriot Act. Section 215 orders are roughly equivalent to grand jury subpoenas, although the government must apply for an order by submitting an application before a judge. The authority has been controversial because of public concern that it could be used by the government to obtain library records. Despite (or perhaps because of) the public controversy over this power, it has been rarely used. According to a report by the Justice Department's Inspector General, the government's first application for a Section 215 order did not occur until 2004, and in 2004 the government obtained only seven orders during the entire calendar year. None of these seven orders involved libraries. *See* Office of the Inspector General, A Review of the Federal Bureau of Investigation's Use of Section 215 Orders for Business Records 17 (2007).

To obtain a Section 215 order, the government must present "reasonable grounds to believe that the tangible things sought are relevant to an authorized investigation ... to obtain foreign intelligence information not concerning a United States person or to protect against international terrorism or clandestine intelligence activities, such things being presumptively relevant to an authorized investigation if the applicant shows in the statement of the facts that they pertain to—(i) a foreign power or an agent of a foreign power; (ii) the activities of a suspected agent of a foreign power who is the subject of such authorized investigation; or (iii) an individual in contact with, or known to, a suspected agent of a foreign power who is the subject of such authorized investigation[.]"

In 2008, Congress passed a new amendment to the Foreign Intelligence Surveillance Act, H.R. 6304, known as the FISA Amendments Act of 2008. The amendment builds on the approach of the Protect America Act of 2007, Pub. L. 110–55, in creating a framework for the foreign intelligence surveillance of individuals located outside the United States from wiretaps located inside the United States.

The legal rules for monitoring individuals outside the United States have become an important issue under FISA because many foreign Internet and telephone communications are now routed through the United States in the

---

c. The other provisions are found at 12 U.S.C. § 3414; 15 U.S.C. § 1681u; 15 U.S.C. § 1581v(a); and 50 U.S.C. § 436.

course of delivery. For example, a person in Pakistan who calls another person in Pakistan might have the call routed through New York. This creates an opportunity for monitoring of that communication from inside the network of the provider located in New York.

The legal question is, what kinds of rules should govern monitoring directed at targets overseas from surveillance points inside the United States? Should an individualized warrant be required? Should a type of "blanket order" be required? Or should such monitoring be left to the Constitution and not regulated at all by statute?

The Protect America Act of 2007 required the Executive to submit proposals for monitoring individuals overseas to the Foreign Intelligence Surveillance Court (FISC). The FISC would then determine whether the monitoring proposals were "directed at a person reasonably believed to be located outside of the United States." So long as it was not "clearly erroneous" that the proposals were "reasonably" so directed, the FISC would approve the monitoring. The monitoring could occur for one year. *See* 50 U.S.C. § 1805B (2007). The Protect America Act sunset after six months, however, requiring new legislation to be passed if Congress wished to authorize such surveillance in the future.

The new legislation continues the basic approach of the Protect America Act, although it significantly strengthens the scope of judicial review. In particular, statutory review by the FISC is now de novo rather than under a clearly erroneous standard: The court assesses de novo whether the protocols are reasonably designed to be limited to those outside the U.S. and that the minimization procedures satisfy traditional statutory standards. *See* § 702(i)(2)-(3). In addition, the FISC must make an independent constitutional analysis: The court can only sign the order if it finds that the surveillance plan is "consistent with the ... Fourth Amendment to the Constitution of the United States." § 702(i)(3)(A). The new law also brings under FISA the surveillance of U.S. citizens abroad. In the past, this was left to executive order: The government was trusted to comply with the Fourth Amendment and only monitor U.S. citizens abroad in ways that satisfied the Fourth Amendment. In contrast, the new law imposes a statutory warrant requirement for surveillance of U.S. persons abroad. *See* § 704.

CHAPTER 9

POLICE INTERROGATION AND CONFESSIONS

■ ■ ■

"As a symbolic matter, police interrogation is a microcosm for some of our most fundamental conflicts about the appropriate relationship between the state and the individual about the norms that should guide state conduct, particularly manipulative, deceptive, and coercive conduct in the modern era. In short, police interrogation and confession-taking go to the heart of our conceptions of procedural fairness and substantive justice and raise questions about the kind of criminal justice system and society we wish to have."

—Richard A. Leo, *Police Interrogation and American Justice* 1 (2008).

———

"Triers of fact accord confessions such heavy weight in their determinations that 'the introduction of a confession makes the other aspects of a trial in court superfluous, and the real trial, for all practical purposes, occurs when the confession is obtained.' * * * No other class of evidence is so profoundly prejudicial. * * * 'Thus the decision to confess before trial amounts in effect to a waiver of the right to require the state at trial to meet its heavy burden of proof.'"

—Brennan, J., dissenting in *Colorado v. Connelly*, 479 U.S. 157, 182 (1986).

———

SECTION 1. HISTORICAL BACKGROUND[a]

A. THE THIRD DEGREE (AND TORTURE)

The heyday of what came to be known in American culture as the "third degree"—the infliction of physical pain or mental suffering to obtain information about a crime—was the first third of the twentieth century.[a] See RICHARD A.

---

a. For a much more detailed treatment of the subject matter of this Note, see Mark Berger, Taking the Fifth 99–124 (1980); Joseph D. Grano, Confessions, Truth, and the Law 59–172 (1993); Otis Stephens, The Supreme Court and Confessions of Guilt 17–119 (1973); 3 Wigmore, Evidence §§ 817–26 (Chadbourn rev. 1970); Anthony G. Amsterdam, The Supreme Court and the Rights of Suspects in Criminal Cases, 45 N.Y.U. L.Rev. 785, 803–10 (1970); Laurence A. Benner, Requiem for Miranda: The Rehnquist Court's Voluntariness Doctrine in Historical Perspective, 67 Wash. U.L.Q. 59 (1989); Gerald M. Caplan, Questioning Miranda, 38 Vand.L.Rev. 1417, 1427–43 (1985); Catherine Hancock, Due Process before Miranda, 70 Tul.L.Rev. 2195 (1996); Yale Kamisar, What is an *"Involuntary"* Confession?, 17 Rutgers L.Rev. 728 (1963); Welsh S. White, *What is an Involuntary Confession Now?*, 50 Rutgers L.Rev. 2001 (1998).

a. The term "third degree" appears to have originally referred to the test necessary to reach the master rank in free masonry. It subsequently came to signify in police folklore the third stage of the criminal process, following arrest and custodial confinement.

LEO, *Police Interrogation and American Justice* 69 (2008) (hereinafter Leo). (It is noteworthy that when the Wickersham Commission Report was published in 1931–detailing the widespread use of the third degree—according to one of the authors of the Report, Zechariah Chaffee, "it was greeted by the police with two answers which they regarded as conclusive: first, there wasn't any third degree; and second, they couldn't do their work without it." Leo 70). (Compare the responses of defenders of harsh interrogation tactics by the CIA after 9/11.)

The most common form of coercive interrogation was prolonged incommunicado questioning, during which time suspects were subjected to extreme psychological pressure. In order to obtain a confession, the police considered it essential to hide suspects from their friends and family and—especially—from their attorneys and the courts. See id. at 51. A frequent practice during incommunicado questioning was to "grill" or "sweat" suspects in prolonged relay questioning that often involved severe verbal bullying of the suspect. Common tactics were to shine a bright, blinding light continuously on a suspect's face, or to turn the light on and off or to require a suspect to remain standing for many hours, slapping or jolting him when he started to fall asleep. Id. A common police practice was known as "losing" the suspect—not recording his arrest on the police blotter so that no attorney could locate him. The police might also mislead defense counsel or friends as to the suspect's whereabouts by charging him with a different felony every forty-eight hours or by booking him on "vagrancy" or "open" charges. Id. at 52.

Because the police were well aware that visible marks of physically abusive interrogation methods might arouse the sympathy of judges and juries, they were attracted to abusive methods that left no marks. The most infamous and probably the most common tactic was the use of a rubber hose, which did not break the skin. Another tactic was the use of a blackjack soaked in water and wrapped in a handkerchief. The Chicago police made an interesting discovery: the local phone book, weighing several pounds, could knock a suspect down if hit against his ear, yet would leave no marks because it was soft. Id. at 48–49.

During the era of the third degree, police interrogators used tactics quite similar to those used by the CIA (at least for a while) after 9/11. The police used the "water cure," which closely resembled "waterboarding,"a technique used by the CIA, to extract information from a detainee by strapping him to a board, covering his face with cloth and pouring water over the cloth to produce a feeling of imminent drowning. The "water cure" involved holding a suspect's head in water until he almost drowned or putting a water hose into his mouth or even down his throat. Sometimes the police forced a suspect to lie on his back and poured water into his nostrils. See Leo 50. As did the CIA after 9/11(at least for a while), city police during the era of the third degree also staged mock executions. A suspect might hear screams or the thud of falling bodies coming from an adjacent room. The message was clear: the suspect would get the same treatment as his neighbor if he did not confess. See id. at 53–54.[b]

---

b. The police used the third degree not only to extract the initial admission of guilt, but to obtain a post-admission narrative that fit their theory of the crime, one which would be helpful to them both in plea bargaining and at trial. Once the police obtained the narrative, they often inserted the following words in the suspect's signed statement: "This statement is made freely and voluntarily and is not made by me as the result of any form or threat or inducement." Leo 59.

In *Miranda*, p. 571 infra, the defendant was not advised of any of his rights before he confessed orally, but when Miranda's statement was written up and signed by him it contained a typed paragraph stating that the confession was made voluntarily, without any threats or promises, and "with full knowledge of my legal rights, understanding any statements I make may be used against me." The *Miranda* majority dismissed the typed paragraph, observing that the "mere

"From the hindsight of more than seventy years," observes Professor Richard Leo, "it is clear that the third degree was, in essence, a totalitarian practice. That is, it was not simply the infliction of pain or suffering to extract incriminating information [the definition the Wickersham Commission gave the term], but the creation of an environment in which police could inflict punishment and terror virtually *without* restraint. * * * Because there was no effective mechanism of restraint on police power inside the interrogation room, the third degree was fundamentally lawless." Id. at 46.

B. POLICE PROFESSIONALISM AND THE RISE OF THE POLICE INTERROGATION MANUAL

The Wickersham Report and other widely publicized accounts of the third degree led to a fundamental distrust of the police—an attitude that made it very difficult to obtain convictions. Although some of their colleagues hotly disputed the findings of the Wickersham Commission, police reformers realized that the third degree "had become a black mark on the image of policing" (Leo 78) and that they had to abolish it.

Police reformers and progressive elites managed to mobilize public opinion against the third degree in a short time, but the two groups had different agendas. The police reformers, observes Leo 73, "were not interested in changing the structure of interrogation so much as sanitizing its content. By replacing the third degree with so-called scientific methods, interrogation could remain police-dominated and secretive and more effectively serve the goals of incrimination, case-building, and conviction."

The signal event in the development of a modern psychology of interrogation was the rise of the police interrogation manual. Since the early 1940s, these manuals have taught generations of police interrogators the techniques and strategies of psychological interrogation and "defined [the] culture of American police interrogation." Leo 81. According to Leo 109, the early interrogation manuals "were, in effect, an attempt by police reformers to assert ownership and control over the public problem of interrogation. Drawing on the rhetoric, symbols and cultural authority of science, they sought to further the goal of professionalizing interrogation so as to insulate it from outside review or control."

By educating detectives and police officers about morally appropriate and inappropriate tactics, the manuals defined professional standards of interrogation. The manuals asserted that the psychological methods they recommended were much more effective in obtaining truthful statements than the traditional physical methods these new techniques sought to replace. They also maintained that the psychological methods they spelled out could not induce an innocent person to confess falsely. (According to Leo 111, however, in recent years that claim has been disproven by considerable research.)

A former police lieutenant, W.R. Kidd, published the first American interrogation training manual in 1940. He urged the police never to use the third degree because it did not produce the truth. Moreover, knowledge of its use "shattered" public confidence in the police.

Lt. Kidd equated the third degree with torture and summed up the case against third degree or torture as follows (Kidd, *Police Interrogation* 47 (1940)):

"Under [the] third degree, only three things can happen to the suspect:

"1. He will tell anything desired.

---

fact" that the defendant had signed a statement containing that paragraph "does not approach the knowing and intelligent waiver required to relinquish constitutional rights."

"2.   He will go insane if the torture is severe enough.

"3.   He will die."

Two years later, Fred Inbau, the former director of the Scientific Crime Detection Laboratory in Chicago and then a professor of law at Northwestern University, published the first edition of what would become, in subsequent editions, the most widely read and best known police interrogation manual in American history.

Professor Inbau, too, made clear his opposition to the third degree. As did other authors of interrogation manuals at the time, he offered an alternative, what were called "psychological methods." See, e.g., Fred E. Inbau, *Police Interrogation—A Practical Necessity*, 52 J.CRIM.L.C. & P.S. 16 (1961). These methods included deceiving, cajoling, manipulating and pressuring suspects to stop denying the crimes the police "knew" they had committed and to start confessing.

At one point, in a 1953 police manual Inbau co-authored, the reader was told that "the interrogator's task is somewhat akin to that of a hunter stalking his game. [In] the same manner that the hunter may lose his game by a noisy dash through the bush, can the interrogator fail by not exercising the proper degree of patience." Fred Inbau & John Reid, *Lie Detection and Criminal Interrogation* 185 (3d ed. 1953). In a later edition, Inbau and his co-author instructed that "once the subject's attention is called to a particular piece of incriminating evidence the interrogator must be on guard to cut off immediately any explanation the subject may start to offer at that time." He must do so because "permit[ing] the subject to offer an explanation of the incriminating evidence will serve to bolster his confidence, for then he is putting the interrogator on the defensive and this should never be permitted to occur." Fred Inbau & John Reid, *Criminal Interrogation and Confessions* 27 (1962).

What if, in the years before *Miranda*, a suspect insisted on his right to remain silent or expressed a desire to see a lawyer? An interrogator who had read a pre-*Miranda* interrogation manual would know how to respond. He would pretend to concede the person the right to remain silent (impressing him with his apparent fairness) and, after some more "psychological conditioning," ask him some "innocuous questions that have no bearing whatever on the matter under investigation," and then gradually resume questioning about the offense. Id. at 111–12. As for the suspect who asks for a lawyer, the interrogator was told to "suggest that the subject save himself or his family the expense of any such professional service, particularly if he is innocent." The interrogator might add, "I'm only looking for the truth. * * * You can handle this by yourself." Id. at 112.

The pre-*Miranda* Inbau manuals (as well as other police interrogation manuals of that era) were regarded by reformers as a significant advance at the time. See Leo 108. But in 1966 the *Miranda* Court quoted extensively from Inbau's manual and others—which they called "the most enlightened and effective means presently used to obtain statements through custodial interrogation"—to conclude: "It is obvious that [the] interrogation environment is created for no purpose other than to subjugate the individual to the will of his examiner. This atmosphere carries its own badge of intimidation. To be sure, this is not physical intimidation, but it is equally destructive of human dignity. The current practice of incommunicado interrogation is at odds with one of our Nation's most cherished principles—that the individual may not be compelled to incriminate himself. Unless adequate protective devices are employed to dispel the compulsion inherent in custodial surroundings, no statement obtained from the defendant can truly be the product of his free choice." (See Casebook at p. 572–73 infra.)

C. THE INTERESTS PROTECTED BY THE DUE PROCESS "VOLUNTARINESS" OR "TOTALITY OF CIRCUMSTANCES" TEST FOR ADMITTING CONFESSIONS

Since they first appeared in the 1940s, the police interrogation training materials have been "the medium through which investigators acquire their working knowledge of the constitutional law of criminal procedure, the primary source of constitutional restraint on their interrogation practices." Leo 109. Until the so-called revolution in American criminal procedure in the 1960s, the manuals "focused almost exclusively on the development of the Supreme Court's case-by-case 'voluntariness' standard." Id.

The first rules governing the admissibility of confessions were laid down in the eighteenth and nineteenth centuries, a time when illegal police methods were relevant only insofar as they affected the trustworthiness of the evidence. Whatever the meaning of the elusive terms "involuntary" and "coerced" confessions since 1940, for centuries the rule that a confession was admissible so long as it was "voluntary" was more or less an alternative statement of the rule that a confession was admissible so long as it was free of influence which made it untrustworthy or "probably untrue." See generally Charles T. McCormick, *Evidence* 226 (1954); 3 John Henry Wigmore, *Evidence* § 822 (3d ed. 1940).

Indeed, Dean Wigmore condemned the use of the "voluntary" terminology for the reason that "there is nothing in the mere circumstance of compulsion to speak in general * * * which create any risk of untruth." 3 Wigmore, § 843. But the courts' continued reference to the term "voluntariness" in enunciating the requisites for the admissibility of a confession under the due process clause was defended by Dean McCormick, who suggested that it might be prompted "not only by a liking for its convenient brevity, but also by a recognition that there is an interest here to be protected closely akin to the interest of a witness or of an accused person which is protected by the privilege against compulsory self-incrimination." Charles McCormick, *The Scope of Privilege in the Law of Evidence,* 16 Texas L.Rev. 447, 453 (1938).

The due process "voluntariness" test was also called the "totality of circumstances" test because it took into account almost every factor involved in the case (e.g., the intelligence, physical health and emotional characteristics of the particular suspect; his age, education and prior criminal record; whether he was deprived of sleep, how long the police questioning lasted, and whether the suspect's request for a lawyer had been denied.) "Under the 'totality of the circumstances' approach," observed Lawrence Herman, *The Supreme Court, the Attorney General, and the Good Old Days of Police Interrogation,* 48 Ohio State L.J. 733, 745 (1987), "virtually everything is relevant and nothing is determinative. If you place a premium on clarity, this is not a good sign."

At least in its advanced stage (the early 1960s), the "due process" or "voluntariness" or "totality of circumstances" test (as it was variously called) appeared to have *three* underlying values or goals. It barred the use of confessions (a) which were of doubtful reliability because of the police methods used to obtain them;[b] (b) which were produced by offensive methods even though the reliability of the confession was not in question; and (c) which were involuntary *in fact* (e.g.,

---

b. But see *Colorado v. Connelly* (1986) (p. 728), viewing the unreliability of a confession as "a matter to be governed by the evidentiary laws of the forum and not by the Due Process Clause."

obtained from a drugged person) even though the confession was entirely trust-worthy and not the product of any conscious police wrongdoing.[c]

At the outset, however, the primary (and perhaps the exclusive) basis for excluding confessions under the due process "voluntariness" test was the "un-trustworthiness" rationale, the view that the confession rule was designed merely to protect the integrity of the fact-finding process. This rationale sufficed in *Brown v. Mississippi*, 297 U.S. 278 (1936), a case decided only five years after the Wickersham Commission Report had publicized the wide-spread use of the "third degree" and a case that marked the first time the Court used the Due Process Clause of the Fourteenth Amendment to hold a confession in a state case inadmissible. (In *Brown*, the deputy who had presided over the beating of the defendants conceded that one prisoner had been whipped but "not too much for a Negro; not as much as I would have done if it were left to me".) This rationale also sufficed for the cases which immediately followed for they, too, were pervaded by threats of, or outright, physical violence. "But when cases involving the more subtle 'psychological' pressures began to appear—usually instances of prolonged interrogation [it] was no longer possible easily to assume that the confessions exacted were unreliable as evidence of guilt. [In *Ashcraft v. Tennessee*, 322 U.S. 143 (1944)] a conviction was reversed where a confession had been obtained after some thirty-six hours of continuous interrogation of the defendant by the police. In effect, the Court ruled that the extended questioning raised a conclusive presumption of 'coercion.' Considering the facts as revealed in the record of the *Ashcraft* case, it is fair to suggest that the result reached by the Court reflected less a concern with the reliability of the confession as evidence of guilt in the particular case than disapproval of police methods which a majority of the Court conceived as generally dangerous and subject to serious abuse." Francis Allen, *The Supreme Court, Federalism, and State Systems of Criminal Justice*, 8 DePaul L.Rev. 213, 235 (1959). See also Monrad Paulsen, *The Fourteenth Amendment and the Third Degree*, 6 Stan.L.Rev. 411, 418–19 (1954).

As Professor Catherine Hancock has recently observed, *Due Process Before Miranda*, 70 Tul. 2195, 2226 (1996), "*Ashcraft* was a milestone because it prefigured *Miranda*'s recognition of the coercion inherent in all custodial interro-gations. [In] a prophetic dictum, [dissenting Justice Jackson] declared that 'even one hour' of interrogation would be inherently coercive, and so there could be no stopping point to the *Ashcraft* doctrine. However, more than twenty years elapsed before this prophecy came to pass in the form of *Miranda*'s presumption that even a few moments of custodial interrogation are inherently coercive."

Consider, too, George C. Thomas III & Richard A. Leo, *Confessions of Guilt* 304–06 (2012).

"Though the *Miranda* opinion claimed it was relying on *Bram v. United States* [1897] [discussed at p. 565, 575 infra], that truly odd nineteenth century case will not bear the weight that the Court placed on it * * *. It is *Ashcraft*, not *Bram*, that is the true ancestor of *Miranda*. [In *Ashcraft*, the Court, per Justice Black,] analogized the situation of a suspect to that of a criminal defendant on the witness stand[:]

---

c. As for the third underlying value, see *Townsend v. Sain*, 372 U.S. 293 (1963), excluding a confession obtained from one given a drug with the properties of a truth serum, even though the police were unaware of the drug's effect and had engaged in no conscious wrongdoing (although they may have been negligent), and even though the confession was apparently reliable. "Any questioning by police officers which *in fact* produces a confession which is not the product of free intellect," observed the Court, "renders the confession inadmissible."

However, in *Colorado v. Connelly* (1986) (p. 728), the Court looked back at *Townsend* as a case that "presented [an] instance of police wrongdoing."

It is inconceivable that any court [in] the land [would] permit prosecutors serving in relays to keep a [defense] witness under continuous cross-examination for thirty-six hours without rest or sleep in an effort to extract a voluntary confession. Nor can we, consistently with Constitutional due process of law, hold voluntary a confession where prosecutors do the same thing away from the restraining influence of a public trial in an open court room.

"[The] courtroom analogy in *Ashcraft* raised the specter that any police questioning of a suspect in custody might be coercive. [Moreover,] the Court began to view police interrogation as itself deviant. Unlike [some of the older cases] there were no drag-net arrests and detention of many suspects in *Ashcraft*. Unlike Brown [v. Mississippi (1936)], there was no torture."

In *Watts v. Indiana,* 338 U.S. 49 (1949) and the companion cases of *Harris v. South Carolina,* 338 U.S. 68 (1949) and *Turner v. Pennsylvania,* 338 U.S. 62 (1949), the Court reversed three convictions resting on coerced confessions without disputing the accuracy of Justice Jackson's observation (concurring in *Watts* and dissenting in the other cases) that "checked with external evidence they [the confessions in each case] are inherently believable and were not shaken as to truth by anything that occurred at the trial."

The majority, per Frankfurter, J., commented: "In holding that the Due Process Clause *bars police procedure* which violates the basic notions of our accusatorial mode of prosecuting crime and vitiates a conviction based on the fruits of such procedure, we apply the Due Process Clause to its historic function of *assuring appropriate procedure* before liberty is curtailed or life is taken." (Emphasis added.) And three years later, in the famous "stomach-pumping" case of *Rochin v. California,* p. 28, the Court, again speaking through Justice Frankfurter, viewed the coerced confession cases as "only instances of the general requirement that States in their prosecutions respect certain decencies of civilized conduct," pointing out: "Use of involuntary verbal confessions in State criminal trials is constitutionally obnoxious not only because of their unreliability. They are inadmissible under the Due Process Clause even though statements contained in them may be independently established as true. Coerced confessions offend the community's sense of fair play and decency."

That the Court was applying a "police methods"—as well as a "trustworthiness"—test was made clear by *Spano v. New York,* 360 U.S. 315 (1959); *Blackburn v. Alabama,* 361 U.S. 199 (1960) and *Rogers v. Richmond,* 365 U.S. 534 (1961). Thus, the Court, per Warren, C.J., pointed out in *Spano* that the ban against "involuntary" confessions turns not only on their reliability but on the notion that "*the police must obey the law while enforcing the law.*" And the Court, again speaking through the Chief Justice, acknowledged in *Blackburn* that "a *complex of values* underlies the strictures against use by the state of confessions which, by way of *convenient shorthand,* this Court terms involuntary." (Emphasis added.)

Perhaps the most emphatic statement of the point that the untrustworthiness of a confession was not (or no longer) the principal reason for excluding it appears in one of Justice Frankfurter's last opinions on the subject. Writing for the Court in *Rogers,* he observed: "Our decisions under [the Fourteenth Amendment] have made clear that convictions following the admission into evidence of [involuntary confessions] cannot stand * * * not so much because such confessions are unlikely to be true but because the methods used to extract them offend an underlying principle in the enforcement of our criminal law: that ours is an accusatorial and not an inquisitorial system. * * * Indeed, in many of the cases [reversing] state convictions involving the use of confessions obtained by impermissible methods, independent corroborating evidence left little doubt of the truth of what the defendant had confessed."[d]

On the eve of *Miranda*, as Illinois Supreme Court Justice Walter Schaefer noted at the time, although the concern about unreliability "still exerted some influence" in confession cases, "it had ceased to be the dominant consideration." Walter Schaefer, *The Suspect and Society* 10 (1967) (based on a lecture delivered before *Miranda* was decided).

Although, theoretically, the "police methods" and "trustworthiness" standards for admitting confessions are to be applied independently of each other, in practice they often overlap. Even though it might be conclusively demonstrated that "offensive" police interrogation methods did not produce an "untrustworthy" confession *in the particular case* before the Court, the continued use of such methods is likely to create a substantial risk that other suspects subjected to similar tactics would falsely confess. See Kamisar, *What is an "Involuntary" Confession?*, 17 Rutgers L.Rev. 728, 754–55 (1963), reprinted in Kamisar, Police Interrogation and Confessions 1, 20–22 (1980) (hereinafter referred to as Kamisar Essays).

What *are* the objectionable police methods which render a resulting confession "involuntary"? In the advanced stages of the test, at least, the use or threatened use of physical violence or the kind of protracted relay interrogation that occurred in *Ashcraft, supra,* rendered any resulting confession inadmissible *per se.* In the main, however, it is difficult to isolate any particular interrogation tactic and say that, standing alone, it is so "coercive" or so "offensive" that it requires the exclusion of any resulting confession. For the significant fact about the great bulk of the "involuntary confessions" cases is that "none of them turned on the presence or absence of a single controlling criterion; each reflected a careful scrutiny of all the surrounding circumstances" *Schneckloth v. Bustamonte* (p. 454). And the totality of the surrounding circumstances included "both the characteristics of the accused [many of whom were uneducated, of low mentality or emotionally unstable] and the details of the interrogation." Ibid.

Nevertheless, the pre-*Escobedo,* pre-*Miranda* cases reveal numerous police practices which, if not impermissible *per se,* certainly militate heavily against the "voluntariness" of any resulting confession: stripping off defendant's clothes and keeping him naked for several hours, *Malinski v. New York,* 324 U.S. 401 (1945); informing defendant that state financial aid for her infant children would be cut off, and her children taken from her, if she failed to "cooperate" with police, *Lynumn v. Illinois,* 372 U.S. 528 (1963); after defendant persisted in his denial of guilt, pretending to "bring in" defendant's wife (who suffered from arthritis) for questioning, *Rogers v. Richmond, supra;* repeatedly rejecting defendant's requests to phone his wife and repeatedly informing him that he would not be able to call her or anyone else unless and until he gave the police a statement, *Haynes v. Washington,* 373 U.S. 503 (1963); removing defendant from jail to a distant place in order to thwart the efforts of his friends or relatives to secure his release, or at least to contact him, *Ward v. Texas,* 316 U.S. 547 (1942); utilization of a state-employed psychiatrist, with considerable knowledge of hypnosis, who posed as a "general practitioner" who would provide defendant with the medical relief he needed and succeeded in obtaining a confession from defendant by skillful and suggestive questioning, *Leyra v. Denno,* 347 U.S. 556 (1954); utilization of defen-

---

d. In admitting the confession, the *Rogers* trial court had found that the interrogation tactics "had no tendency to produce a confession that was not in accord with the truth." The Supreme Court did not consider the finding *unwarranted,* but *irrelevant.* The admissibility of the confession had been decided "by reference to a legal standard which took into account the circumstance of probable truth or falsity"—"and this is not a permissible standard under the Due Process Clause." See Stephen J. Schulhofer, *Confessions and the Court,* 79 Mich.L.Rev. 865, 867 (1981).

dant's "childhood friend," then a fledgling police officer, who, pursuant to his superiors' instructions, pretended that defendant's phone call had gotten his "friend" "in a lot of trouble," so much so that his "friend's" job was in jeopardy, and loss of his job would prove disastrous to his "friend's" wife and children, *Spano,* supra.

Consider Albert Alschuler, *Constraint and Confessions*, 74 Denv.U.L.Rev. 957 (1997): "The Court should define the term coerced confession to mean a confession caused by offensive governmental conduct, period. * * * Shifting their attention almost entirely from the minds of suspects to the conduct of government officers, courts should abandon the search for 'overborne wills' and attempts to assess the quality of individual choices."

D. THE SHORTCOMINGS OF THE "VOLUNTARINESS" TEST

Although the Supreme Court customarily used the terms "voluntariness" and "involuntariness" in explaining and applying the due process test for the admissibility of confessions, the "voluntariness" concept seems to be at once too wide and too narrow. In one sense, in the sense of wanting to confess, or doing so in a completely spontaneous manner, "in the sense of a confession to a priest merely to rid one's soul of a sense of guilt" (Jackson, J., dissenting in *Ashcraft v. Tennessee*), few criminal confessions reviewed by the courts, if any, had been "voluntary." On the other hand, in the sense that the situation always presents a "choice" between two alternatives, either one disagreeable, to be sure, *all* confessions are "voluntary." See 3 Wigmore, § 824.

Moreover, as the rationales for the Court's coerced confession cases evolved, it became increasingly doubtful that terms such as "voluntariness," "coercion," and "breaking the will" were very helpful in resolving the issue. For such terms do not focus directly on either the risk of untrue confessions or the offensiveness of police interrogation methods employed in eliciting the confession. See Paulsen, supra, at 429–30.

As the Court, per O'Connor, J., observed in *Miller v. Fenton*, 474 U.S. 104 (1985) (holding that the "voluntariness" of a confession is not a "factual issue" but "a legal question meriting independent consideration in a federal habeas corpus proceeding"): "[T]he admissibility of a confession turns as much on whether the techniques for extracting the statements, as applied to *this* suspect, are compatible with a system that presumes innocence and assures that a conviction will not be secured by inquisitorial means as on whether the defendant's will was in fact overborne. [The] hybrid quality of the voluntariness inquiry, subsuming, as it does, a 'complex of values,' *Blackburn,* itself militates against treating the question as one of simple historical fact." As the *Miller* Court also noted, "[t]he voluntariness rubric has been variously condemned as 'useless,' 'perplexing,' and 'legal 'double-talk.' "[a]

Nor was "the elusive, measureless standard of psychological coercion heretofore developed in this Court by accretion on almost an ad hoc, case-by-case basis," as Justice Clark described it, dissenting in *Reck v. Pate*, 367 U.S. 433 (1961); a test which seemed to permit constitutionally permissible police interrogation to vary widely according to how dull or alert or soft or tough the particular suspect, see e.g., Maguire, *Evidence of Guilt* 134 fn. 5 (1959); likely to guide or to shape police conduct very much, if at all. Moreover, as pointed out in Schulhofer, fn. d supra, at 869–70, because of its ambiguity and "its subtle mixture of factual and legal elements," the "voluntariness" test "virtually invited [trial judges] to give weight to their subjective preferences" and "discouraged review even by the most

---

a. See also Notes 3 & 4 following *Colorado v. Connelly*, p. 732.

conscientious appellate judges." See also Kamisar Essays at 12–25, 69–76; CRIM-PROC § 6.2(d); Geoffrey R. Stone, *The Miranda Doctrine in the Burger Court,* 1977 Sup.Ct.Rev. 99, 102–03; Welsh White, *Defending Miranda: A Reply to Professor Caplan,* 39 Vand.L.Rev. 1, 7–9, 11–16 (1986).[b]

In his *Miranda* dissent, Justice Harlan stoutly defended the due process/totality of the circumstances/voluntariness test. See 384 U.S. at 508. But even Harlan recognized that "synopses of the cases [applying the voluntariness test] would serve little use because the overall gauge has been steadily changing, usually in the direction of restricting admissibility." Id. Moreover, the values underlying the "voluntariness" and "coercion" rhetoric kept changing, as did the weight given to the various factors making up the "totality of circumstances." What made matters worse, "the Court usually never overruled a Due Process precedent"; it "simply ignored inconsistent cases, or distinguished them when necessary or convenient." Catherine Hancock, *Due Process Before Miranda,* 70 Tulane L.Rev. 2195, 2237 (1996).

As police interrogators made greater use of "psychological" techniques over the years, the always difficult problems of proof confronting the alleged victims of improper interrogation practices became increasingly arduous. Disputes over whether physical violence occurred are not always easy to resolve, but evidence of "mental" or "psychological" coercion is especially elusive. Frequently, the defendant was inarticulate, which aggravated the difficulties of recreating the tenor and atmosphere of the police questioning or the *manner* in which the appropriate advice about the suspect's rights might have been given or, if properly given, subsequently undermined.

Moreover, the local courts almost always resolved the almost inevitable "swearing contest" over what happened behind the closed doors in favor of the police, perhaps for the reasons suggested by Walter Schaefer, *Federalism and State Criminal Procedure,* 70 Harv.L.Rev. 1, 7 (1956): "In the field of criminal procedure [a] strong local interest competes only against an ideal. Local interest is concerned with the particular case and with the guilt or innocence of the particular individual. * * * While it is hard indeed for any judge to set apart the question of the guilt or innocence of a particular defendant and focus solely upon the procedural aspect of the case, it becomes easier [in] a reviewing court where the impact of the evidence is diluted. The more remote the court, the easier it is to consider the case in terms of a hypothetical defendant accused of crime, instead of a particular man whose guilt has been established."[c]

---

b. But consider Gerald Caplan, *Questioning Miranda,* 38 Vand.L.Rev. 1417, 1433–34 (1985): "[The voluntariness test] allowed the Court to move carefully, to feel its way, and to make its judgments without fear of prematurely constitutionalizing interrogation practices. [The] Court's failure to state the basis for a particular decision or its blurring of a holding in the veiled attire of the 'totality of the circumstances' can be seen as shrewd and responsible pragmatism. Pragmatism may have been preferable to principles at a time when there was little general agreement on the principles to be applied. [If] the development of the voluntariness test had not come to a near end with the advent of *Miranda,* perhaps the test would have continued to achieve definition and improved serviceability."

c. This may help to explain the strikingly different reactions of the state courts and the U.S. Supreme Court to the situation in *Mincey v. Arizona,* 437 U.S. 385 (1978) (other aspects of which are discussed at pp. 693, 917). Just a few hours before the interrogation occurred, Mincey had been seriously wounded during a narcotics raid which resulted in the death of a police officer. According to the attending physician, Mincey had arrived at the hospital "depressed almost to the point of coma." At the time Detective Hust questioned him, Mincey's condition was still sufficiently serious that he was in the intensive care unit. Lying on his back on a hospital bed, encumbered by tubes, needles and breathing apparatus, Mincey (according to the Supreme Court) clearly and repeatedly expressed his wish not to be interrogated, but Hust continued to question him. Unable to speak because of the tube in his mouth, Mincey responded to Hust's questions by writing answers on pieces of paper provided by the hospital, at one point writing: "This is all I

Under the old case-by-case approach, however, the defendant could not often avail himself of the "remoteness" of the U.S. Supreme Court. In the thirty years since *Brown v. Mississippi,* the Court had taken an average of about one state confession case per year and *two-thirds of these* had been "death penalty" cases. Indeed, the Court's workload was so great that it even denied a hearing in most "death penalty" cases. See Kamisar Essays 75. Almost no garden-variety criminal defendant who cried "coerced confession" but lost the "swearing contest" below was likely to survive the winnowing process above. Not surprisingly, Justice Black remarked in the course of the oral arguments in *Miranda:* "[I]f you are going to determine [the admissibility of the confession] each time on the circumstances, [if] this Court will take them one by one [it] is more than we are capable of doing."

Consider Louis Michael Seidman, *Brown and Miranda,* 80 Calif.L.Rev. 673, 730, 732–33 (1992):

"Frankfurter addressed the confession problem for the last time [at] the very end of his long and brilliant career in CULOMBE v. CONNECTICUT [367 U.S. 568 (1961)]. In sixty-seven pages of elegantly written prose, he purported to systematize, rationalize, and defend the quarter century of work that had gone before. [Yet the opinion] is riven with contradiction from beginning to end and leaves the effort to justify and systematize the Court's role in shambles. * * * Frankfurter hoped that the Court's common-law method would gradually clarify the law of confessions. But in fact, the method's substantive emptiness left the Court free in every case to strike the balance in any fashion it chose. * * *

"The total futility of Frankfurter's efforts is illustrated by the *Culombe* opinion itself. Despite his herculean effort to clarify the law of confessions, he succeeded in attracting only one other Justice to his opinion [Stewart]. Writing for the Court's liberal wing, Chief Justice Warren concurred in the result, but openly mocked Frankfurter's efforts to bring unity to the Court's confession jurisprudence. In an ironic invocation of Frankfurtian insistence on judicial restraint—an invocation that became more ironic still in light of his subsequent *Miranda* opinion—Warren chastised Frankfurter for departing from the Court's custom of deciding only the case that came before it. * * *

"Frankfurter's pretensions to precision and objectivity were also mocked, although less intentionally, in Justice Harlan's dissenting opinion. Harlan, unlike Warren, purported to understand and agree with Frankfurter's voluntariness approach. Yet his opinion read the same facts that Frankfurter thought clearly established coercion as showing that Culombe's confession was the 'product of a

---

can say without a lawyer." (In a written report dated about a week later, Hust transcribed Mincey's answers and added the questions he believed he had asked.)

Under these circumstances, the trial court found "with unmistakable clarity" that Mincey's statements were "voluntary" and thus, despite being obtained in violation of *Miranda,* admissible for impeachment purposes. (On this point, see p. 911). The state supreme court unanimously affirmed. On the basis of its independent evaluation of the record, the Court, per Stewart, J., reversed. It noted, inter alia, that "the reliability of Hust's report [reconstructing the interrogation] is uncertain." It concluded that "the undisputed evidence makes clear that Mincey wanted *not* to answer Detective Hust" but that—"weakened by pain and shock, isolated from family, friends and legal counsel, and barely conscious"—Mincey's "will was simply overborne."

Rehnquist, J., dissented from the holding that Mincey's statements were involuntary and—as was true of so many of the older "involuntariness" cases—disputed the Court's reading of the record: "[The Court] ignores entirely some evidence of voluntariness and distinguishes away yet other testimony. * * * Despite the contrary impression given by the Court, [the state supreme court's] opinion casts no doubt on the testimony or report of Detective Hust. The Court is thus left solely with its own conclusions as to the reliability of various witnesses based on a re-examination of the record on appeal. * * * I believe that the trial court was entitled to conclude that, notwithstanding Mincey's medical condition, his statements in the intensive care unit were admissible. [T]hat the same court might have been equally entitled to reach the opposite conclusion does not justify this Court's adopting the opposite conclusion."

deliberate choice.' Thus, the Justices who concurred on an analytical framework for resolving the problem disagreed on the result produced by that framework, while the Justices who concurred on the result disagreed on the analytic framework producing that result.

"In short, the *Culombe* opinion was a total disaster. The Court had managed to produce a veritable treatise on the law of confessions with no majority opinion, no agreement on the appropriate standard, no agreement on how the standard endorsed by the plurality should be applied, and no prospect of enforcing that or any other standard in the courts below or in police departments across the country."

Although the 1964 *Massiah* and *Escobedo* cases and the 1966 *Miranda* case (all discussed infra) were to catch heavy criticism, "[g]iven the Court's inability to articulate a clear and predictable definition of 'voluntariness,' the apparent persistence of state courts in utilizing the ambiguity of the concept to validate confessions of doubtful constitutionality, and the resultant burden on its own workload, it seemed inevitable that the Court would seek 'some automatic device by which the potential evils of incommunicado interrogation [could] be controlled.' " Geoffrey R. Stone, *The Miranda Doctrine in the Burger Court*, 1977 Sup.Ct.Rev. 102–03 (quoting from Schaefer, *The Suspect and Society* 10 (1967)).[d]

E. THE *McNABB–MALLORY* RULE: SUPERVISORY AUTHORITY OVER FEDERAL CRIMINAL JUSTICE vs. FOURTEENTH AMENDMENT DUE PROCESS

As Justice FRANKFURTER pointed out for the majority in the famous case of McNABB v. UNITED STATES, 318 U.S. 332 (1943), while the power of the Court to upset *state* convictions is limited to the enforcement of fourteenth amendment due process, the standards of *federal* criminal justice "are not satisfied merely by observance of those minimal historic safeguards." Rather, the Court can, and has, formulated rules of evidence in the exercise of its "supervisory authority" over the administration of federal criminal justice which go well beyond due process requirements.[a] A good example was the significance given to the fact that incriminating statements were obtained during illegal detention, i.e.,

---

d. *The continued vitality of the pre-Miranda voluntariness test.* Since the landmark *Miranda* case, the police must give a suspect the now familiar warnings and obtain a waiver of his rights before subjecting him to "custodial interrogation." However, the "old" due process-voluntariness test is still important in a number of situations, e.g., when the police question a suspect not in "custody"; when the police question a suspect who waives his rights and agrees to talk, but denies any involvement in the crime. See generally pp. 717–34. Moreover, the distinction between an "involuntary" confession and one obtained only in violation of *Miranda* is important in a number of procedural contexts, e.g., use of the confession for impeachment purposes. See generally pp. 910–22.

Thus, "[c]areful attention to the voluntariness issue remains an imperative, though sometimes overlooked, obligation of court and counsel," Schulhofer, supra, at 878. To illustrate his point, Professor Schulhofer refers to *United States v. Mesa*, discussed at pp. 602 n. a., 624. The *Mesa* court's rejection of a *Miranda* challenge, observes Schulhofer, id. at 878 n. 58, was "based on particularities of *Miranda's* rationale and therefore by no means preclude a voluntariness claim. Yet the defense never argued, and so the [Third Circuit] never considered, whether the statements made by this psychologically distraught suspect, on the verge of suicide, [who had barricaded himself in a motel room and threatened that he would not surrender peacefully], in the course of a three-and-one-half-hour conversation [with an FBI crisis negotiator] under highly charged circumstances, were admissible under the due process test."

a. For a long, hard look at the federal courts' exercise of "supervisory powers" over the administration of federal criminal justice generally and a look back at *McNabb*, regarded by many as the first supervisory power decision, see Sara Sun Beale, *Reconsidering Supervisory Power in Criminal Cases: Constitutional and Statutory Limits on the Authority of the Federal Courts*, 84 Colum.L.Rev. 1433 (1984). Extracts from Professor Beale's article appear at pp. 34–35.

while the suspect was held in violation of federal statutory requirements that he be promptly taken before a committing magistrate to ascertain whether good cause exists to hold him for trial. Although, during this period, an otherwise voluntary confession was not rendered inadmissible in a *state* prosecution solely because it was elicited during prolonged and hence illegal precommitment detention (this was only *one* of many factors in determining whether a confession was voluntary), the 1943 *McNabb* case, although hardly free from ambiguity, seemed to hold that such a confession had to be excluded from *federal* prosecutions.

The *McNabb* rule was heavily criticized by law enforcement spokesmen and many members of Congress and begrudgingly interpreted by most lower federal courts. See generally James E. Hogan & Joseph M. Snee, *The McNabb–Mallory Rule: Its Rise, Rationale and Rescue,* 47 Geo.L.J. 1 (1958). However, it was emphatically reaffirmed in MALLORY v. UNITED STATES, 354 U.S. 449 (1957), where, speaking for a unanimous Court, Justice FRANKFURTER observed:

"We cannot sanction this extended delay [some seven hours], resulting in confession, without subordinating [Fed.R.Crim.P. 5(a), requiring that an arrestee be taken 'without unnecessary delay' to the nearest available committing officer] to the discretion of arresting officers in finding exceptional circumstances for its disregard. [There is no escape] from the constraint laid upon the police by that Rule in that two other suspects were involved for the same crime. Presumably, whomever the police arrest they must arrest on 'probable cause.' It is not the function of the police to arrest, as it were, at large and to use an interrogating process at police headquarters in order to determine whom they should charge before a committing magistrate on 'probable cause.'"

Only a handful of states adopted the *McNabb–Mallory* rule or its equivalent on their own initiative.[b] But many hoped (and many others feared) that some day the Court would apply the rule to the states as a matter of fourteenth amendment due process. The Court never did. Instead, in the years since the 1957 *Mallory* decision, the last of the *McNabb* line of cases, the Court closed in on the state confession problem by making increasing resort to the right to counsel and the privilege against self-incrimination. By such means the state confession rules were eventually to *go beyond* the *McNabb–Mallory* doctrine in a number of respects.[c]

---

b. It was not until 1960 that the states' unanimity in refusing to follow the Supreme Court's lead in the *McNabb–Mallory* line of cases was broken. See *People v. Hamilton,* 102 N.W.2d 738, 741–43 (Mich.1960); Rothblatt & Rothblatt, *Police Interrogation: The Right to Counsel and to Prompt Arraignment,* 27 Brooklyn L.Rev. 24, 40–44 (1960). On the eve of *Miranda,* two more states adopted an equivalent of the rule, Delaware, see *Webster v. State,* 213 A.2d 298, 301 (Del.1965); and Connecticut, by legislation, see *State v. Vollhardt,* 244 A.2d 601, 607 (Conn.1968) (subsequent case construing statute). In recent years at least three more state courts—Maryland, Montana, and Pennsylvania—adopted some equivalent of the rule. See *Johnson v. State,* 384 A.2d 709, 714–18 (Md.1978); *State v. Benbo,* 570 P.2d 894, 899–900 (Mont.1977); *Commonwealth v. Davenport,* 370 A.2d 301, 306 (Pa.1977); *Commonwealth v. Futch,* 290 A.2d 417, 418–19 (Pa. 1972).

The life of Maryland's version of the *McNabb–Mallory* rule, adopted in the 1978 *Johnson* case, "was short and unhappy." Donald E. Wilkes, *The New Federalism in Criminal Procedure in 1984: Death of the Phoenix?,* in Developments in State Constitutional Law 166, 170 (B. McGraw ed. 1985). The *Johnson* rule was usually interpreted begrudgingly and—in a "legislative blow to the new federalism"—repealed by statute in 1981. See id. at 169–171.

For a close examination and strong criticism of the "state court revival" *McNabb–Mallory* rule, see Note, 72 J.Crim.L. & C. 204 (1981). The Note maintains, id. at 241, that "current constitutional law addresses many of the original concerns underlying delay statutes, obviating the need for reliance on a doctrine of implied statutory exclusion."

c. A provision of the Omnibus Crime Control and Safe Street Act of 1968, § 3501 (c) (quoted at p. 676 of the Casebook), seemed to overrule the *McNabb-Mallory* rule. But in *Corley v. United States,* 556 U.S. 303 (2009), a 5–4 majority, per Souter, J., held that the provision "modified *McNabb-Mallory* without supplanting it. Under the rule as revised by § 3501 (c), a district court with a suppression claim must find whether the defendant confessed within six hours of arrest

F. THE RIGHT TO COUNSEL AND THE ANALOGY TO THE ACCUSATORIAL, ADVERSARY TRIAL

CROOKER v. CALIFORNIA, 357 U.S. 433 (1958), involved a petitioner who attended one year of law school, during which time he studied criminal law, and who indicated in his dealings with the police that he was fully aware of his right to remain silent. On the basis of a challenged confession, he was convicted of murder of his paramour and sentenced to death. He contended that by persisting in interrogating him after denying his specific request to contact his lawyer the police violated his due process right to legal representation and advice and that therefore use of any confession obtained from him under these circumstances should be barred even though "freely" and "voluntarily" made under traditional standards. Such a rule retorted the Court, per CLARK, J., "would have [a] devastating effect on enforcement of criminal law, for it would effectively preclude police questioning—*fair as well as unfair*—until the accused was afforded opportunity to call his attorney. Due process, a concept 'less rigid and more fluid than those envisaged in other specific and particular provisions of the Bill of Rights,' *Betts v. Brady,* demands no such rule."

In his dissenting opinion, Justice DOUGLAS, with whom Warren, C.J., and Black and Brennan, JJ., joined, insisted: "The right to have counsel at the pretrial stage is often necessary to give meaning and protection to the right to be heard at the trial itself. It may also be necessary as a restraint on the coercive power of the police. [The] demands of our civilization expressed in the Due Process Clause require that the accused who wants a counsel should have one at any time after the moment of arrest."

In the companion case of CICENIA v. LA GAY, 357 U.S. 504 (1958), not only did petitioner unsuccessfully ask to see his lawyer while he was being questioned by the police, but his lawyer, who arrived at the police station while petitioner was being interrogated, repeatedly (and unsuccessfully) asked to see his client. Moreover, petitioner was not well educated as was Crooker. Nevertheless, the Court affirmed the murder conviction (which led to a life sentence), disposing of petitioner's contention that he had a constitutional right to confer with counsel on the authority of *Crooker*. With the exception of Justice Brennan, who took no part in the case, the Court split along the same lines it had in *Crooker*.

The following year, however, by virtue of SPANO v. NEW YORK, it appeared that the Court had reached the view that once a person was *formally charged* by indictment or information his constitutional right to counsel had "begun"—at least his right to the assistance of counsel he himself had retained. Four concurring Justices took this position in *Spano:* Justices Black, Douglas and Brennan, all of whom had dissented in *Crooker;* and newly appointed Justice Stewart, who had replaced Justice Burton.

In separate concurring opinions both Justice Douglas (joined by Black and Brennan, JJ.) and Justice Stewart (joined by Douglas and Brennan, JJ.) stressed

---

(unless a longer delay was 'reasonable considering the means of transportation and the distance to be traveled to the nearest available [magistrate]'). [If] the confession came within that period, it is admissible [subject to other evidentiary rules] so long as it was 'made voluntarily and [the weight to be given [it] is left to the jury.]' If the confession occurred before presentment and beyond six hours, however, the court must decide whether delaying that long was unreasonable or unnecessary under the *McNabb-Mallory* cases, and if it was, the confession is to be suppressed."

Dissenting Justice Alito, joined by Roberts, C.J., and Scalia and Thomas, JJ., maintained that "[u]nless the unambiguous language of § 3501 (a) is ignored petitioner's confession may not be suppressed." Section 3501 (a) states in any criminal prosecution brought by the United States "a confession [shall] be admissible in evidence if it is voluntarily given."

that *Spano* was not a case where the police were questioning a suspect in the course of investigating an unsolved crime but one where the subject of interrogation was already under indictment for murder when he surrendered to the authorities. Both concurring opinions also measured the proceedings in the "interrogation" room against the standard of a public trial and formal judicial proceedings. Thus Justice STEWART observed: "Under our system of justice an indictment is supposed to be followed by an arraignment and a trial. * * * What followed the petitioner's surrender in this case was not arraignment in a court of law, but an all-night inquisition in a prosecutor's office, a police station, and an automobile. * * * Our Constitution guarantees the assistance of counsel to a man on trial for his life in an orderly courtroom, presided over by a judge, open to the public, and protected by all the procedural safeguards of the law. Surely a Constitution which promises that much can vouchsafe no less to the same man under midnight inquisition in the squad room of a police station."

As we have already seen, a majority of the *Spano* Court did not go off on "right to counsel" grounds, finding the confession inadmissible on straight "coerced confession" grounds, but the Chief Justice, who wrote the majority opinion, had taken the position, a year earlier in *Crooker,* that the right to counsel should "begin" even earlier than at the point of indictment. Thus, counting heads, it appeared that by 1959 the view of the concurring Justices in *Spano* commanded a majority of the Court.

G. *MASSIAH AND ESCOBEDO*: THE COURT CLOSES IN ON THE "CONFESSION PROBLEM"

"There is a case in the Supreme Court now from Illinois, *People v. Escobedo,* that involves this very issue [of when the right to counsel begins] and I am scared that the Court is going to hold that this right exists from the time of arrest—if a person asks for counsel and he is not given counsel, anything you get from him after that has to be excluded."

—Fred E. Inbau, *A Forum on the Interrogation of the Accused,* 49 Corn.L.Q. 382, 401 (January 31, 1964).

Five years after *Spano,* in MASSIAH v. UNITED STATES, 377 U.S. 201 (1964), a 6–3 majority (consisting of the four concurring Justices in *Spano,* Chief Justice Warren, and newly appointed Justice Goldberg) adopted the view advanced in the *Spano* concurring opinions. *Massiah* arose as follows: After he had been indicted for federal narcotics violations, Massiah retained a lawyer, pled not guilty, and was released on bail. A codefendant, Colson, invited him to discuss the pending case in Colson's car, parked on a city street. Unknown to Massiah, Colson had decided to cooperate with federal agents in their continuing investigation of the case. A radio transmitter was installed under the front seat of Colson's car, enabling a nearby agent (Murphy), who was equipped with a recording device, to overhear the Massiah–Colson conversation. As expected, Massiah made several damaging admissions.

It is hardly surprising that the *Massiah* dissenters considered the facts of the case a "peculiarly inappropriate" setting for a major breakthrough on the "police interrogation"-"confession" front. Even if the *Spano* concurring opinions had come to represent the majority view, argued then Solicitor General Archibald Cox, Massiah's statements should still be admissible because at the time he made them he was neither in "custody"—not even in the loosest sense—nor undergoing "police interrogation." He was under no "official pressure" to answer questions or even to engage in conversation; his conversation "was not affected by even that degree of constraint which may result from a suspect's knowledge that he is talking to a law enforcement officer.''[a] Moreover, Colson, a layman unskilled in the art of interrogation, did not and probably could not utilize any of the standard techniques to induce Massiah to incriminate himself.[b]

Nevertheless, as the *Massiah* majority, per STEWART, J., saw it, the decisive feature of the case was that after he had been indicted—"and therefore at a time when he was clearly entitled to a lawyer's help" and at a time when he was awaiting trial "in an orderly courtroom, presided over by a judge, open to the public, and protected by all the procedural safeguards of the law"—Massiah had been subjected to a "completely extrajudicial" police-orchestrated proceeding designed to obtain incriminating statements from him. Besides, if in one respect— the lack of an inherently or potentially "coercive atmosphere"—Massiah had been less seriously imposed upon than the average "confession" defendant, he was more seriously imposed upon in another respect—he did not, and could not be expected to, keep his guard up because he was not even aware that he was dealing with a government agent[c]: "We hold that the petitioner was denied the basic protections of [the right to counsel] when there was used against him at his trial evidence of his own incriminating words, which federal agents had deliberately elicited from him after he had been indicted and in the absence of his counsel. It is true that in the *Spano* case the defendant was interrogated in a police station, while here the damaging testimony was elicited from [him] without his knowledge while he was free on bail. But, as Judge Hays pointed out in his dissent in the [Second Circuit], 'if such a rule is to have any efficacy it must apply to indirect and surreptitious interrogations as well as those conducted in the jailhouse. In this case, Massiah was more seriously imposed upon * * * because he did not even know that he was under interrogation by a government agent.' * * *

"We do not question that in this case, as in many cases, it was entirely proper to continue an investigation of the suspected criminal activities of the defendant and his alleged confederates, even though the defendant had already been indicted. All that we hold is that the defendant's own incriminating statements, obtained by federal agents under the circumstances here disclosed, could not constitutionally be used by the prosecution as evidence against *him* at his trial."

Dissenting Justice WHITE, joined by Clark and Harlan, JJ., protested: "[H]ere there was no substitution of brutality for brains, no inherent danger of police coercion justifying the prophylactic effect of another exclusionary rule. Massiah was not being interrogated in a police station, was not surrounded by numerous officers or questioned in relays, and was not forbidden access to others. Law enforcement may have the elements of a contest about it, but it is not a game."

The dissenters were "unable to see how this case presents an unconstitutional interference with Massiah's right to counsel. Massiah was not prevented from consulting with counsel as often as he wished. No meetings with counsel were

---

a. Extensive extracts from the Government's brief and oral argument in *Massiah* appear in Kamisar Essays 171–73.

b. The Massiah–Colson conversation was not only broadcast to a nearby federal agent, but secretly tape-recorded by Colson. In the district court, however, Massiah successfully objected to the admission of these tapes on the ground that they implicated other defendants and contained privileged matters. The Government maintained that the recording confirmed the testimony of Agent Murphy that Colson did not coerce Massiah into making any incriminating statements or even induce him by appeals to talk in the guise of friendship and filed the recording with the clerk of the Court. Colson did not testify himself. Massiah did not testify either or otherwise contradict Murphy's testimony about the meeting. See Kamisar Essays at 278 fn. 202.

c. Massiah's unawareness that he was, in effect, talking to the police, and thus his inability to protect himself, "was a nice point (or counterpoint), but it was hardly the decisive one." Kamisar Essays 174. Any doubts that the *Massiah* doctrine also applies when the suspect realizes he is in the presence of the police were removed in *Brewer v. Williams* (1977), p. 739.

disturbed or spied upon. Preparation for trial was in no way obstructed. It is only a sterile syllogism—an unsound one besides—to say that because Massiah had a right to counsel's aid before and during the trial, his out-of-court conversations and admissions must be excluded if obtained without counsel's consent or presence."

"This case," maintained the dissenters, "cannot be analogized to [Canon 9 of the ABA's Canons of Professional Ethics] forbidding an attorney to talk to the opposing party litigant outside the presence of his counsel.[d] Aside from the fact that [the canons] are not of constitutional dimensions, [Canon 9] deals with the conduct of lawyers and not with the conduct of investigators.[e] Lawyers are forbidden to interview the opposing party because of the supposed imbalance of legal skill and acumen between the lawyer and the party litigant; the reason for the rule does not apply to nonlawyers and certainly not to Colson, Massiah's codefendant."

Were the *Massiah* dissenters right when they observed that "the reason given for the result here—the admissions were obtained in the absence of counsel— would seem equally pertinent to statements obtained at any time after the right to counsel attaches, whether there has been an indictment or not"? Does a suspect who has not yet been indicted need "a lawyer's help" every bit as much as one who has been formally charged? By drawing the line at the initiation of formal judicial proceedings, had Justice Stewart (author of *Massiah,* but a dissenter in *Escobedo,* infra) "painted himself into a corner [from] which he could extricate himself only by a highly formalistic reading of the Sixth Amendment"? See Lawrence Herman, *The Supreme Court and Restrictions on Police Interrogation,* 25 Ohio St.L.J. 449, 491 (1964).

As made plain a short five weeks later in the same Term, ESCOBEDO v. ILLINOIS, 378 U.S. 478 (1964), a majority of the Court was not about to give the Sixth Amendment a formalistic reading. Escobedo's interrogation had occurred before "judicial" or "adversary" proceedings had commenced against him, but, as dissenting Justice Stewart characterized the *Escobedo* majority's reasoning, "[t]he Court disregards this basic difference between the present case and Massiah's, with the bland assertion that 'that fact should make no difference.' "

Escobedo arose as follows: On the night of January 19, petitioner's brother-in-law was fatally shot. A few hours later petitioner was taken into custody for questioning, but he made no statement and was released the following afternoon pursuant to a writ of habeas corpus obtained by his retained counsel. On January 30, one Di Gerlando, who was then in police custody and who was later indicted for the murder along with petitioner, stated that petitioner had fired the shots which killed his brother-in-law. That evening petitioner was again arrested and taken to police headquarters. En route to the police station he was told that Di Gerlando had named him as the one who fired the fatal shots and that he might as well admit it, but petitioner replied (probably because his attorney had obtained his release from police custody only 11 days earlier or because he had consulted with his attorney in the meantime): "I am sorry but I would like to have advice from my lawyer." Shortly after petitioner reached police headquarters, his retained lawyer arrived and spent the next several hours trying unsuccessfully to

---

d. Does (should) this ethical rule apply to criminal proceedings?

e. But consider Breitel, C.J., in *People v. Hobson,* 348 N.E.2d 894, 898 (N.Y.1976): "[I]t would not be rational, logical, moral or realistic to make any distinction between a lawyer acting for the State who [by seeking a waiver of the right to counsel from a suspect in the absence of, and without notification to, his lawyer] violates [the Code of Professional Responsibility] directly and one who indirectly uses the admissions improperly obtained by a police officer, who is the badged and uniformed representative of the State." See also *United States v. Springer,* 460 F.2d 1344, 1354–55 (7th Cir.1972) (Judge (now Justice) Stevens, dissenting).

speak to his client. He talked to every officer he could find, but was repeatedly told that he could not see his client and that he would have to get a writ of habeas corpus. In the meantime, petitioner repeatedly but unsuccessfully asked to speak to his lawyer. Instead, the police arranged a confrontation between petitioner and Di Gerlando. Petitioner denied that he had fired the fatal shots, claiming that Di Gerlando had done so, but thereby implicated himself in the murder plot. Petitioner's subsequent statement, to an assistant prosecutor who asked carefully framed questions, was admitted into evidence and he was convicted of murder. The Supreme Court of Illinois affirmed.

When certiorari was granted, the lawyers involved realized, as did close students of the problem, that *Escobedo* might be a momentous case. Bernard Weisberg, author of an important article on police interrogation, *Police Interrogation of Arrested Persons: A Skeptical View,* 52 J.Crim.L. & P.S. 21 (1961) (also quoted at p. 628 infra), argued the case for the ACLU, as *amicus curiae.* Because he thought it "playing Hamlet without the ghost to discuss police questioning without knowing what such questioning is really like," in his article Weisberg had made very extensive use of the interrogation manuals. He did the same in his *Escobedo* brief, maintaining that these books "are invaluable because they vividly describe the kind of interrogation practices which are accepted as lawful and proper under the best current standards of professional police work." What these manuals reveal, argued Weisberg, "is that 'fair and reasonable' and 'effective interrogation' is basically unfair and inherently coercive."[f]

Former Northwestern University law professor James Thompson (who later became Governor of Illinois) argued the *Escobedo* case for the state. He warned the U.S. Supreme Court: "[A decision that the right to counsel begins at the moment of arrest] means the end of confessions as a tool of law enforcement. [For] once this petitioner's claim with Illinois is settled, the inevitable progression of the law must follow:

"*First,* if the right to counsel attaches at the moment of arrest [as the dissent in *Crooker* maintained], then it can hardly be denied that this right must be available to the poor as well as to the rich. * * *

"*Second,* if indigent criminal defendants are entitled to counsel from the moment of arrest, then already established law makes it clear that such a right does not depend upon a request. [N]ot only must the state furnish counsel to the indigent defendant at this stage of the criminal proceeding, it must make sure that he does not waive the right through ignorance of its existence. * * * "[g]

Added Thompson: "Criminal defendants, rich as well as poor, enjoy more protection from unjust conviction today than at any time in our history. 'The

---

f. Weisberg's article on confessions, apparently the first to make extensive use of the interrogation manuals, and his *Escobedo* brief set the fashion for civil libertarians. The ACLU brief in *Miranda,* primarily the work of Professors Anthony Amsterdam and Paul Mishkin, reprinted a full chapter from one interrogation manual. In turn, Chief Justice Warren's opinion for the Court in *Miranda,* infra, devoted six full pages to extracts from various police manuals and texts "document[ing] procedures employed with success in the past, [and] recommend[ing] various other effective tactics." Many of the examples selected by the *Miranda* Court in 1966 were the same ones Weisberg used in his 1961 article and his 1964 *Escobedo* brief.

g. Thompson's discussion of "the inevitable progression of the law" was, of course, the statement of an advocate; Illinois deemed it advantageous to underscore the extent to which the rule espoused by its adversaries would "cripple" law enforcement. But Escobedo's lawyers were advocates, too, and they could not, or at least did not try to, minimize the impact of the rule they sought. Neither the ACLU brief nor the brief filed by Escobedo's own lawyers ever cited *Gideon, Douglas, Griffin,* or *Carnley.*

Moreover, shortly after *Escobedo* was decided, Thompson continued to view the case essentially the same way, now not as an advocate, but as assistant director of the Northwestern University Law School's Criminal Law Program. See fn. i infra.

terrible engine' of the criminal law has been repeatedly braked by this Court, by state courts and legislatures and by fair and honest administration of the law by prosecutors and police. We need to guard against its derailment. * * * "

A 5–4 majority of the Court, per GOLDBERG, J., struck down Escobedo's confession, but, until *Miranda* moved *Escobedo* off center stage two years later, the scope and meaning of the decision was a matter of strong and widespread disagreement. In large part this was due to the accordion-like quality of the *Escobedo* opinion. At some places the opinion launched so broad an attack on the use of confessions in general and rejected the arguments for an "effective interrogation opportunity" so forcefully that it threatened (or promised) to eliminate virtually all police interrogation. At other places, however, the language of the opinion was so narrow and confining that it arguably limited the case to its special facts:

"The interrogation here was conducted before petitioner was formally indicted. But in the context of this case, that fact should make no difference. When petitioner requested, and was denied, an opportunity to consult with his lawyer, the investigation had ceased to be a general investigation of 'an unsolved crime.' Petitioner had become the accused, and the purpose of the interrogation was to 'get him' to confess his guilt despite his constitutional right not to do so. At the time of his arrest and throughout the course of the interrogation, the police told petitioner that they had convincing evidence that he had fired the fatal shots. Without informing him of his absolute right to remain silent in the face of this accusation, the police urged him to make a statement. * * *

"Petitioner, a layman, was undoubtedly unaware that under Illinois law an admission of 'mere' complicity in the murder plot was legally as damaging as an admission of firing of the fatal shots. The 'guiding hand of counsel' was essential to advise petitioner of his rights in this delicate situation. This was the 'stage when legal aid and advice' were most critical to petitioner. *Massiah*.

"[It] is argued that if the right to counsel is afforded prior to indictment, the number of confessions obtained by the police will diminish significantly, because most confessions are obtained during the period between arrest and indictment, and 'any lawyer worth his salt will tell the suspect in no uncertain terms to make no statement to police under any circumstances.' This argument, of course, cuts two ways. The fact that many confessions are obtained during this period points up its critical nature as a 'stage when legal aid and advice' are surely needed. *Massiah*. The right to counsel would indeed be hollow if it began at a period when few confessions were obtained. * * *

"We have learned the lesson of history, ancient and modern, that a system of criminal law enforcement which comes to depend on the 'confession' will, in the long run, be less reliable and more subject to abuses than a system which depends on extrinsic evidence independently secured through skillful investigation. * * *

"We have also learned the companion lesson of history that no system of criminal justice can, or should, survive if it comes to depend for its continued effectiveness on the citizens' abdication through unawareness of their constitutional rights. No system worth preserving should have to *fear* that if an accused is permitted to consult with a lawyer, he will become aware of, and exercise, these rights. If the exercise of constitutional rights will thwart the effectiveness of a system of law enforcement, then there is something very wrong with that system."[h]

---

h. But consider Gerald Caplan, *Questioning Miranda,* 38 Vand.L.Rev. 1417, 1440 (1985): "This statement is misleading because the right that the Court was defending, far from being of long standing, was newly discovered, indeed created, in this very opinion. What may have been 'very wrong' was not the extant 'system,' but the right the Court just announced."

"We hold, therefore, that where, as here, the investigation is no longer a general inquiry into an unsolved crime but has begun to focus on a particular suspect, the suspect has been taken into police custody, the police carry out a process of interrogations that lends itself to eliciting incriminating statements, the suspect has requested and been denied an opportunity to consult with his lawyer, and the police have not effectively warned him of his absolute constitutional right to remain silent, the accused has been denied 'the Assistance of Counsel' in violation of the Sixth Amendment to the Constitution as 'made obligatory upon the States by the Fourteenth Amendment,' *Gideon,* and that no statement elicited by the police during the interrogation may be used against him at a criminal trial. * * *

"Nothing we have said today affects the power of the police to investigate 'an unsolved crime' by gathering information from witnesses and by other 'proper investigative efforts.' We hold only that when the process shifts from investigatory to accusatory—when its focus is on the accused and its purpose is to elicit a confession—our adversary system begins to operate, and, under the circumstances here, the accused must be permitted to consult with his lawyer."[i]

Dissenting Justice STEWART protested:

"*Massiah* is not in point here. * * * Putting to one side the fact that the case now before us is not a federal case, the vital fact remains that this case does not involve the deliberate interrogation of a defendant after the initiation of judicial proceedings against him. The Court disregards this basic difference between the present case and Massiah's, with the bland assertion that "that fact should make no difference."

"It is 'that fact,' I submit, which makes all the difference. Under our system of criminal justice the institution of formal, meaningful judicial proceedings, by way of indictment, information, or arraignment, marks the point at which a criminal investigation has ended and adversary litigative proceedings have commenced. It is at this point that the constitutional guarantees attach which pertain to a criminal trial."

In a separate dissent, Justice WHITE, joined by Stewart and Clark, JJ., observed:

"[*Massiah*] held that as of the date of the indictment the prosecution is disentitled to secure admissions from the accused. The Court now moves that date back to the time when the prosecution begins to 'focus' on the accused. Although the opinion purports to be limited to the facts of this case, it would be naive to think that the new constitutional right announced will depend upon whether the accused has retained his own counsel, or has asked to consult with counsel in the course of interrogation. At the very least the Court holds that once the accused

---

i. As to whether *Escobedo* extended the constitutional role of counsel to the preindictment stage "when the process shifts from investigatory to accusatory—when its focus is on the accused and its purpose is to elicit a confession"—or when the process so shifts *and* one or some combination or all of the limiting facts in *Escobedo* are also present, see the summary of the wide disagreement over the probable meaning of the case in Kamisar Essays at 161 fn. 26.

Although many lower courts construed *Escobedo* quite narrowly, James Thompson, who had the distinction of making the losing argument in the case, read it quite broadly. He told a group of prosecuting attorneys attending a criminal law program that "in all cases where the police desire to obtain a confession from a suspect under circumstances like those in *Escobedo* [and] the suspect does not have retained counsel and does not request counsel, the police should, before interrogation, (a) inform him of his right not to say anything; and (b) inform him that anything he does say might be used against him." He also observed: "[I]n dealing with [a suspect who, unlike Danny Escobedo,] has not expressly indicated that he is aware of his right to counsel, absolute compliance with the *Escobedo* rule may well require a warning of the right to counsel along with the warning of the privilege against self-incrimination." See the extensive extracts from Thompson's analysis of *Escobedo* in Kamisar Essays, at 66–68.

becomes a suspect and, presumably, is arrested, any admission made to the police thereafter is inadmissible in evidence unless the accused has waived his right to counsel. * * *

"It is incongruous to assume that the provision for counsel in the Sixth Amendment was meant to amend or supersede the self-incrimination provision of the Fifth Amendment, which is now applicable to the States. That amendment addresses itself to the very issue of incriminating admissions of an accused and resolves it by proscribing only compelled statements.

"[The] Court chooses [to] rely on the virtues and morality of a system of criminal law enforcement which does not depend on the 'confession.' No such judgment is to be found in the Constitution. The only 'inquisitions' the Constitution forbids are those which compel incrimination. Escobedo's statements were not compelled and the Court does not hold that they were. * * *

"[The] Court may be concerned with a narrower matter: the unknowing defendant who responds to police questioning because he mistakenly believes that he must and that his admissions will not be used against him. But this worry hardly calls for the broadside the Court has now fired. [If] an accused is told he must answer and did not know better, it would be very doubtful that the resulting admissions could be used against him. When the accused has not been informed of his rights at all the Court characteristically and properly looks very closely at the surrounding circumstances. I would continue to do so. But, in this case Danny Escobedo knew full well that he need not answer and knew full well that his lawyer had advised him not to answer."[j]

ON THE MEANING OF *ESCOBEDO*

1. **What right comes into play?** Once the investigation has ceased to be "a general inquiry of an unsolved crime but has begun to focus on a particular suspect," what right comes into play? The right of the suspect to consult with his lawyer before resuming the interrogation or the right to enjoy his attorney's *continued presence* and *constant advice* from that point on, as a protection in the face of any further police interrogation? Cf. *Massiah*.

2. **The role of counsel.** Consider Gerald Caplan, *Questioning Miranda,* 38 Vand.L.Rev. 1417, 1440–41 (1985): "Danny Escobedo's lawyer had advised him not to say anything to the police. If the homicide detectives had granted Escobedo's request to see his attorney again, there would have been nothing additional for his attorney to communicate. Escobedo had already been given all the assistance his counsel could provide without actually being present to assist his client on a question-by-question basis. Was Escobedo's attorney seeking the right to be present during the interrogation? Probably not. His intent in seeking entry to the homicide bureau was most likely to bring the interrogation to a close. Given that a defense attorney's usual objective is to stop the interrogation, it is hard to understand why the Court was so certain that 'no system worth preserving should have to fear that if an accused person is permitted to consult with a lawyer, he will become aware of, and exercise [his] rights,' unless the Court simply believed that there was no social utility in police interrogation. The *Escobedo* opinion contains no hint of anxiety that harm may accrue from a right to counsel: that there may be fewer confessions, and more crime."

3. **The "right to remain silent."** As we have seen, *Escobedo* refers to a suspect's "absolute constitutional right to remain silent." Where does this right

---

j. In a brief separate dissent, Justice Harlan agreed with Justice White that "the rule announced today is most ill-conceived and that it seriously and unjustifiably fetters perfectly legitimate methods of criminal law enforcement."

come from? Does the privilege against self-incrimination confer (or was it intended to confer) a right to remain silent or a right to refuse to respond to incriminating questions or only the right to be free of compulsion? See Albert W. Alschuler, *A Peculiar Privilege in Historical Perspective: The Right to Remain Silent*, 94 Mich.L.Rev. 2625, 2630–32 (1996); Joseph D. Grano, *Confessions, Truth, and the Law* 141–43 (1993).

Does the Court simply mean that since the police lack legislative authorization to compel answers, a suspect is not required to provide any? Does the Court mean more—that the Constitution would prevent a legislature from investing police with the power to compel non-incriminating answers? Or does the Court mean that since a layperson cannot be expected to know what statements may be incriminating, if *in the absence of counsel,* she chooses not to incriminate herself, the only practical way she can assure that she will not do so is to remain completely silent?

H. A LATE ARRIVAL ON THE SCENE: THE PRIVILEGE AGAINST SELF–INCRIMINATION

"[Despite] a great deal of emotional writing which elevates the privilege against self-incrimination to 'one of the great landmarks in man's struggle to make himself civilized,' [the] most abundant proof [that it does not prohibit pretrial interrogation] is to be found in the United States. There the privilege is in the Federal Constitution and in [forty-eight state constitutions]. But in none of the forty-nine jurisdictions does it apply to what happens in the police station. The police interrogate freely, sometimes for seven to eight hours on end. The statements thus extracted are given in evidence. [O]nly statements made voluntarily may be given in evidence, but that seems to be interpreted rather liberally, judged by our standards."

—Judge V.G. Hiemstra of the Supreme Court of South Africa, *Abolition of the Right Not to be Questioned,* 80 South African L.J. 187, 194–95 (1963).

As long ago as 1931, Ernest Hopkins, a member of the Wickersham Commission staff, forcefully argued that the "third degree"—indeed, all secret police interrogation as typically practiced—was fundamentally in violation of the privilege against self-incrimination. Ernest Hopkins, *Our Lawless Police* 193–95 (1931). As we have seen, however, the concurring justice in *Spano* and the majorities in *Massiah* and *Escobedo* relied primarily on the right to counsel, not the privilege against self-incrimination—the other essential mainstay of the accusatorial, adversary system. But the "prime suspect"-"focal point"-"accusatory state" test(s) of *Escobedo* threatened the admissibility of even "volunteered" statements. There was reason to think that the Court might be in the process of shaping "a novel right not to confess except knowingly and with the tactical assistance of counsel," Arnold Enker & Sheldon Elsen, *Counsel for the Suspect: Massiah v. United States and Escobedo v. Illinois,* 49 Minn.L.Rev. 47, 60–61, 69, 83 (1964). Thus *critics* of *Escobedo* turned to the privilege against self-incrimination as a less restrictive alternative. Dissenting in *Escobedo,* Justice White, joined by Clark and Stewart, JJ., observed:

"It is incongruous to assume that the provision for counsel in the Sixth Amendment was meant to amend or supersede the self-incrimination provision of the Fifth Amendment which is now applicable to the States. [*Malloy v. Hogan,* infra.] That amendment addresses itself to the very issue of incriminating admissions and resolves it by proscribing only compelled statements. [That amendment provides no support] for the idea that an accused has an absolute constitutional right not to answer even in the absence of compulsion, [no support for the view that he has] the constitutional right not to incriminate himself by making voluntary disclosures."

Even as Justice White spoke, there was reason to think that, at long last, the privilege against self-incrimination was knocking on the door of the interrogation room. Only a few months before *Escobedo* had been decided, the Court, in MALLOY v. HOGAN, 378 U.S. 1 (1964) (per Brennan, J.), had performed "what might have seemed to some a shotgun wedding of the privilege [against self-incrimination] to the confession rule," Lawrence Herman, *The Supreme Court and Restrictions on Police Interrogation,* 25 Ohio St.L.J. 449, 465 (1965), by declaring that "today the admissibility of a confession in a state criminal prosecution is tested by the same standard applied in federal prosecutions since 1897, when in *Bram v. United States,* 168 U.S. 532, the Court held that '[i]n criminal trials, in the courts of the United States, wherever a question arises whether a confession is incompetent because not voluntary, the issue is controlled by [the self-incrimination] portion of the Fifth Amendment.' "[a]

Whether or not this approach to police interrogation and confessions makes good sense it constitutes very questionable history—at least since *Brown v. Mississippi* (1936). The old *Bram* case might well have furnished a steppingstone to the standard advanced in *Malloy,* but until *Escobedo,* at any rate, it only seemed to amount to an early excursion from the prevailing multifactor or "totality of circumstances" approach. In none of the dozens of federal *or* state confession cases decided by the Court in the 1930's, 1940's and 1950's had the privilege against self-incrimination, certainly not as it applied to judicial proceedings, been the basis for judgment (although it had occasionally been mentioned in an opinion). If the privilege against self-incrimination had been the way to resolve the confession problem, then all the state courts and lower federal courts that had admitted confessions would have been reversed *per curiam.* For it was plain that law enforcement officers could, and without hesitation did, resort to methods they would never consider utilizing at the trial, that they had much greater power over a suspect or defendant away from the restraining influence of a public trial in an open courtroom.

Although certain factors, such as the length of pre-arraignment detention, had been taking on increasing significance, as Justice Frankfurter described the situation in *Culombe v. Connecticut* (1961), neither the privilege against self-incrimination nor any other "single litmus-paper test for constitutionally impermissible interrogation [had] been evolved: neither extensive cross-questioning-deprecated by the English judges; nor undue delay in arraignment-proscribed by *McNabb;* nor failure to caution a prisoner—enjoined by the [English] Judges' Rules; nor refusal to permit communication with friends and legal counsel at stages in the proceedings when the prisoner is still only a suspect—prohibited by several state statutes." That was why, as Justice Goldberg put it for a majority in *Haynes v. Washington,* 373 U.S. 503 (1963) (only a year before he wrote the opinion of the Court in *Escobedo*), "the line between proper and permissible police conduct and techniques and methods offensive to due process is, at best, a difficult one to draw, particularly in cases such as this where it is necessary to make fine judgments as to the effect of psychologically coercive pressures and inducements on the mind and will of an accused."

---

a. Until the 1960's *Bram* had become a largely forgotten case, but in recent years it has been the subject of close analysis and spirited debate. Compare Lawrence A. Benner, *Requiem for Miranda: The Rehnquist Court's Voluntariness Doctrine in Historical Perspective,* 67 Wash.U.L.Q. 59, 107–11 (1989) and Stephen A. Saltzburg, *Miranda v. Arizona Revisited: Constitutional Law or Judicial Fiat,* 26 Washburn L.J. 1, 4–14 (1986) with Joseph D. Grano, *Confessions, Truth, and the Law* 123–31 (1993).

Why had the privilege against self-incrimination been excluded from the stationhouse all these years? The legal reasoning was that compulsion to testify meant *legal* compulsion. Since he is threatened neither with perjury for testifying falsely nor contempt for refusing to testify at all, it cannot be said, ran the argument, that the subject of police interrogation is being "compelled" to be "a witness against himself" within the meaning of the privilege—even though he may assume or be led to believe that there *are* legal (or extralegal) sanctions for contumacy. Since the police have no *legal right* to make a suspect answer, there is no legal obligation to answer to which a privilege in the technical sense can apply. For an appraisal of this argument, see Lewis Mayers, *Shall We Amend the Fifth Amendment?*, 82–83, 223–33 (1959); Walter Schaefer, *The Suspect and Society* 16–18 (1967); 8 John Henry Wigmore, *Evidence* 329 fn. 27 (McNaughton rev. 1961). Consider, too, Note 1, p. 838, and Note 5, p. 842.

It has been suggested that the reasoning above "had a great deal more to commend it than merely the inherent force of its 'logic' or the self-restraint and tenderness of the exempted class of interrogators," Kamisar Essays 59–60; and that among the forces at work were *"necessity"*—the conviction that police interrogation without advising the suspect of his rights was "indispensable" in law enforcement—and the *invisibility* of the process, which made it easy for society to be complacent about what was really going on and to readily accept police-prosecution "sanitized" versions of what was going on. Id. at 60–63.

How the *Malloy* opinion looked back, however, was not as important as how it looked forward. Whatever one thought of the manner in which *Malloy* had recorded the recent past, one could not treat lightly the way it anticipated the near future.

SECTION 2.   THE *MIRANDA* "REVOLUTION"

ORAL ARGUMENTS IN *MIRANDA* AND COMPANION CASES

* * *

MR. DUANE R. NEDRUD, on behalf of the National District Attorneys Association, *Amicus Curiae*. * * *

THE CHIEF JUSTICE: May I ask you this, please, Mr. Nedrud: if you agree on the facts that *Escobedo* should not be overruled, what would you say as to the man who did not have a lawyer, but who said he wanted a lawyer before he talked?

MR. NEDRUD: If he asked for a lawyer, and he does not waive his right to counsel, I think that he should have a lawyer. [I] would go so far as to say that I think the state should appoint a lawyer if he asks for a lawyer. I do not think, however, that we should in effect encourage him to have a lawyer.

THE CHIEF JUSTICE: Why do you say we should not encourage him to have a lawyer? Are lawyers a menace? * * *

MR. NEDRUD: I think [a lawyer] is not a menace at the trial level. He is not a menace, per se, but he is, in doing his duty, going to prevent a confession from being obtained. * * *

JUSTICE DOUGLAS: * * * [A lawyer] needs time to prepare for the trial, so the appointment must be at some point anterior to the trial. Our question here is how far anterior. * * *

MR. NEDRUD: The question comes down I think, Mr. Justice Douglas, to whether or not we are going to allow the trial court to determine guilt or innocence or the defense counsel. If the defense counsel comes in at the arrest stage, he will, as he should, prevent the defendant from confessing to his crime, and you will have fewer convictions. If this is what is wanted, this is what will occur.

JUSTICE BLACK: I guess there is no doubt, is there, as to the effect of the provision which provides for protection against compelling him to give testimony. Is it not fewer convictions?

MR. NEDRUD: [I believe] there is a point of diminishing returns and at some stage the police must be in a position to protect us.

JUSTICE BLACK: * * * Can you think of any time when [a person] needs a lawyer more than [at] the point of detention?

MR. NEDRUD: Mr. Justice Black, again, the question is are we interested in convicting the defendant, or are we interested in protecting or acquitting him? This is the only point that I can, in effect, make, if you say that this defendant needs counsel at this time.

For example, if I may use this illustration, I worked when I was a professor of law, which I was prior to taking this position, I worked on the defense project for the American Bar Association. In the questionnaire there was a statement, "When is the ideal time for counsel to be appointed for the defendant?"

Actually, the question is, "When is the ideal time for whom, the people or the defendant?" If it is for the defendant, then it is the earliest possible opportunity; if it is for the people, it should not be until a critical stage. * * *

JUSTICE BLACK: I have found out over many years a very critical stage is when a person is taken to the police headquarters. * * *

A person is taken to police headquarters and placed under arrest or detention. He can't leave, if he wants to, unless they let him. Would you call that voluntary for him, then, for [the police] to have him there in that situation and probe him about probable conviction of crime? Would you think of that as voluntary?

MR. NEDRUD: As being voluntarily in the police station, no. * * *

MR. VICTOR M. EARLE, III on behalf of the petitioner in VIGNERA v. NEW YORK. * * *

JUSTICE FORTAS: [Are you saying] that when the point of time comes where it appears that the police have enough information to satisfy themselves that the fellow really did the act, then the right to arrange for counsel or to give the warning attaches?

MR. EARLE: I think that is correct, although we don't have to look into the mind of the police necessarily to be able to determine that. * * * If in doubt, push it out on the other side of the warning. That is why I don't see that it should pose so much of a problem. I think the FBI Agents give warnings on this proceeding.

JUSTICE STEWART: What should this warning contain? What should this warning be?

MR. EARLE: The Chief of Police in the District of Columbia last August promulgated a warning which, I understand, is now being given by all police officials in the District. It goes something like this: You have been placed under arrest. You are not required to say anything to us any time or to answer any questions. Anything you say may be used as evidence in court. You may call a lawyer or a relative or a friend. Your lawyer may be present here, and you may talk with him. If you cannot obtain a lawyer, one will be appointed for you when your case first goes to court.

I might have a little quibble with that third point, because it suggests a little bit that you might not be able to get a lawyer now.

JUSTICE FORTAS: Much more than a little bit of quibble on the basis of what you have argued so far—that he has an absolute right for a lawyer to be appointed for him at that point, unless he waives it.

MR. EARLE: Yes, sir, unless he waives it. The question might come up of how do the police, or what do the police do when the fellow says, "Thanks. I would like a lawyer now that you mention it, but I don't happen to have any money." They have a choice. They can give him ten cents and the number of a legal aid society.

They have another alternative—just stop interrogating. That alternative was never mentioned. * * *

JUSTICE WHITE: They give him the warning, and he nods his head, yes. (laughter)

JUSTICE WHITE: What happens?

MR. EARLE: It takes a conscious relinquishing of his known rights, those rights I have been telling you about, Justice White.

JUSTICE WHITE: I thought that is what you would say. What happens then if the fellow just nods his head and just looks at him?

MR. EARLE: If we can believe he nodded his head, it is possible that he waives it. I would be very reluctant to come to that conclusion on [that] hypothesis.

JUSTICE WHITE: What else besides giving a warning and right to counsel?

MR. EARLE: I think if he writes down in his own handwriting, "I have been warned, I understand that I have a right to a lawyer now, to talk to him this minute, if I want to, or the right to say nothing if I want to. I understand that. I would like to go ahead and cooperate with the police. Signed: Michael Vignera." That would be enough.

JUSTICE WHITE: That is just barely the first stage.

MR. EARLE: That is what the police have to say.

JUSTICE WHITE: Sure, but if they want to rely on a waiver at any time, is this the only ground that you would accept for a lawyer not being present, a written waiver? Isn't that right?

MR. EARLE: I think that is right. It should be definitely recorded.

JUSTICE WHITE: It should be a written waiver?

MR. EARLE: Absolutely. It shouldn't be something he is conned into giving.
* * *

JUSTICE WHITE: What if he doesn't waive? He says, "I do want counsel," and the state says, "Fine. Here is a dime, and there is the legal aid number," and the fellow calls him. He talks to the lawyer, and he comes back and sits down, and you ask him some questions, and he answers them.

MR. EARLE: Without his lawyer being present, for example?

JUSTICE WHITE: Yes.

MR. EARLE: I take it that would be a decision made by his lawyer, and the lawyer can waive rights for his client.

JUSTICE WHITE: Is that a waiver in your book? What is it, a waiver of the right to consult counsel or a waiver of the right to have counsel present?

MR. EARLE: I think it is a waiver to have a counsel in all the ways it is meant. The lawyer can make the determination of whether he should be present or not. Lawyers have waived many rights, like not filing the 30th day and the notice of appeal and the like * * *

JUSTICE WHITE: My question is really going to what you think the scope of the right is. You think the scope of the right is to have counsel present and that you must waive not only the right to consult counsel, but the right to have counsel present?

MR. EARLE: I think that is right, Mr. Justice White. I want to elaborate on it, if I might. In a deposition in a civil case, for example, customarily, the plaintiff and the defendant can have counsel present. I can certainly conceive that one lawyer will not be present. The client, through him, would, therefore, waive that right. It would seem that the only way we could distinguish this case from *Escobedo* is the fact that Vignera did not make a request. What we have been talking about is doing that.

Obviously, it wasn't the request of the individual that made the right attach. The significance of the request, I think, in *Escobedo* was that it was a subjective piece of evidence to show that a stage had been reached. * * *

JUSTICE STEWART: How can there be a waiver, if these are Constitutional rights and are important? How can anybody waive them without the consent of counsel or without the advice of counsel? Doesn't he need a lawyer before he can waive them, if you are right?

MR. EARLE: You are entitled to waive in other situations. It is true in court when they want to plead guilty, for example, the judge will decline assignment of counsel, and the judge will, typically, interrogate him to some length to realize the significance of his act, and that is a lot more advisable a situation than—and more conducive to our being receptive to the idea of a waiver than the police station. I agree that is the worst place for waiver. The party alleging waiver has control of the party alleged to have waived.

JUSTICE STEWART: It seems to follow that he needs a lawyer before he can waive his right to a lawyer.

MR. EARLE: I wouldn't be unhappy to have lawyers in the police station.

JUSTICE STEWART: It follows naturally.

MR. EARLE: It doesn't follow naturally, because a majority of the court in *Escobedo* said these rights can be waived. I think we do have to recognize some of the realities of law enforcement. They do have to investigate. They do have the public duty of—if crimes are being committed by the minute, they do have to operate out of the police station. * * *

JUSTICE HARLAN: Is there a claim that the confession was coerced?

MR. EARLE: In no sense. I don't think it was coerced at all. Mr. Justice White asked yesterday a question about compelling someone to give up his Fifth Amendment privilege. I think there is a substantial difference between that and coercing a confession. I mean, it wasn't until 1964 that the Fifth Amendment privilege applied to the states, and so * * * all through until the 1960's, really, state convictions were overturned only by looking to the generality of the totality of the circumstances under the due process clause.

Now, we have specific Constitutional guarantees that are applied in branch to the states, of both the Fifth and Sixth Amendment rights. It is true that the word "compel" is used in the Fifth Amendment with respect to the privilege, but it is quite different to say that the privilege is cut down and impaired by detention and to say a man's will has been so overborne a confession is forced from him. * * *

I hate to sound cynical, but if we go back to the totality of circumstances, that means this Court will sit all by itself as it has so many years to overturn the few confessions it can take, necessarily, by the bulk of the work. The lower courts won't do their job. We need some specific guidelines as *Escobedo* to help them along the way. * * *

MR. WILLIAM I. SIEGEL, on behalf of the respondent in VIGNERA v. NEW YORK. * * *

JUSTICE FORTAS: Mr. Siegel, [the problem presented by these cases] really affects the basic relationship of the individual and the state. It really goes beyond the administration of justice, and that has been the history of mankind. * * *

MR. SIEGEL: [T]here is an immediate objective, also, and the immediate objective is to protect society; because, if society isn't protected, it, in one degree or another, lapses into anarchy because of crime and then the opportunity to reach this beautiful ideal is gone. It is the function of the police—

JUSTICE FORTAS: (Interrupting) * * * The problem is to reconcile a good many objectives that are not totally consonant.

I am a little troubled, I must say, when I sit here and hear so much reference to this problem as if it were merely a pragmatic problem of convicting people who did a crime, because there are many more dimensions, I suggest, to the problem than just that simple statement.

MR. SIEGEL: * * * The problem that is before this Court, it seems to me, is just how to keep the balance between the ultimate necessity of the civilized, peaceful society and the constitutional rights of a specific defendant.

JUSTICE BLACK: Don't you think that the Bill of Rights has something to do with making that balance?

MR. SIEGEL: Yes, sir.

JUSTICE BLACK: There is not any doubt, is there, that no person should be convicted on evidence he has been compelled to give? Why do we have to get into a discussion of society or the beauties of the ideal civilization when that is the issue before us?

MR. SIEGEL: Because the Bill of Rights only says that [one] shall not be compelled, but the word "compelled" is not self-defining. We, for many, many years, were told [by] a great majority of Your Honors' predecessors, that compelled meant that which couldn't make a man talk by the exercise of process.

JUSTICE BLACK: By what?

MR. SIEGEL: By the exercise of process. You couldn't subpoena him into a court and, under pain of punishment, make him talk. * * *

SOLICITOR GENERAL THURGOOD MARSHALL, on behalf of the government in WESTOVER v. UNITED STATES. * * *

JUSTICE BLACK: [As] I understand you to say, of course, any person that has a lawyer or has the money to get a lawyer could get one immediately. This man has no lawyer and has no money to get one. The only reason he doesn't have a lawyer is for that reason. Does that raise any principles as to what an indigent is entitled to? He is certainly not getting treated like a man who has the money to get a lawyer.

MR. MARSHALL: He is not being denied anything. The state is not affirmatively denying anything. The state is just not furnishing him anything. * * *

JUSTICE BLACK: I understood you to say if he had the money he would have the right to have the lawyer but the man that has no money has no chance to. That is the situation that we had in *Griffin*.

MR. MARSHALL: *Griffin* was a different point. You can't equalize the whole thing. I don't believe that we can. * * *

"I was introduced for my accomplishments primarily as being of counsel in *Miranda,* and consistently I must disabuse everyone of the accomplishment * * *. When certiorari was granted and we were asked by the ACLU to prepare and file the brief, we had a meeting in our law office in which we agreed that the briefs should be written with the entire focus on the Sixth Amendment [right to counsel] because that is where the Court was headed after *Escobedo,* and, as you are all aware, in the very first paragraph [of the *Miranda* opinion] Chief Justice Warren said, 'It is the Fifth Amendment to the Constitution that is at issue today.' That was Miranda's effective use of counsel."

—John J. Flynn, *Panel Discussion on the Exclusionary Rule,* 61 F.R.D. 259, 278 (1972).

MIRANDA v. ARIZONA (NO. 759)*
384 U.S. 436, 86 S.Ct. 1602, 16 L.Ed.2d 694 (1966).

CHIEF JUSTICE WARREN delivered the opinion of the Court.

The cases before us raise questions which go to the roots of American criminal jurisprudence: the restraints society must observe [in] prosecuting individuals for crime. More specifically, we deal with the admissibility of statements obtained from an individual who is subjected to custodial police interrogation and the necessity for procedures which assure that the individual is accorded his privilege under the Fifth Amendment to the Constitution not to be compelled to incriminate himself. * * *

We start here, as we did in *Escobedo* with the premise that our holding is not an innovation in our jurisprudence, but is an application of principles long recognized and applied in other settings. We have undertaken a thorough re-examination of the *Escobedo* decision and the principles it announced, and we reaffirm it. That case was but an explication of basic rights that are enshrined in our Constitution—that "No person * * * shall be compelled in any criminal case to be a witness against himself," and that "the accused [shall] have the Assistance of Counsel"—rights which were put in jeopardy in that case through official overbearing. * * *

Our holding will be spelled out with some specificity in the pages which follow but briefly stated it is this: the prosecution may not use statements, whether exculpatory or inculpatory, stemming from custodial interrogation of the defendant unless it demonstrates the use of procedural safeguards effective to secure the privilege against self-incrimination. By custodial interrogation, we mean questioning initiated by law enforcement officers after a person has been taken into custody or otherwise deprived of his freedom of action in any significant way.[4] As for the procedural safeguards to be employed, unless other fully effective

---

* Together with No. 760, *Vignera v. New York* [and] No. 761, *Westover v. United States* [and] No. 584, *California v. Stewart* * * *.

4. This is what we meant in *Escobedo* when we spoke of an investigation which had focused on an accused.

means are devised to inform accused persons of their right of silence and to assure a continuous opportunity to exercise it, the following measures are required. Prior to any questioning, the person must be warned that he has a right to remain silent, that any statement he does make may be used as evidence against him, and that he has a right to the presence of an attorney, either retained or appointed. The defendant may waive effectuation of these rights, provided the waiver is made voluntarily, knowingly and intelligently. If, however, he indicates in any manner and at any stage of the process that he wishes to consult with an attorney before speaking there can be no questioning. Likewise, if the individual is alone and indicates in any manner that he does not wish to be interrogated, the police may not question him. The mere fact that he may have answered some questions or volunteered some statements on his own does not deprive him of the right to refrain from answering any further inquiries until he has consulted with an attorney and thereafter consents to be questioned.

The constitutional issue we decide in each of these cases is the admissibility of statements obtained from a defendant questioned while in custody and deprived of his freedom of action in any significant way. In each, the defendant was questioned by police officers, detectives, or a prosecuting attorney in a room in which he was cut off from the outside world. In none of these cases was the defendant given a full and effective warning of his rights at the outset of the interrogation process. In all the cases, the questioning elicited oral admissions, and in three of them, signed statements as well which were admitted at their trials. They all thus share salient features—incommunicado interrogation of individuals in a police-dominated atmosphere, resulting in self-incriminating statements without full warnings of constitutional rights. * * *

Again we stress that the modern practice of in-custody interrogation is psychologically rather than physically oriented. * * * Interrogation still takes place in privacy. Privacy results in secrecy and this in turn results in a gap in our knowledge as to what in fact goes on in the interrogation rooms. A valuable source of information about present police practices, however, may be found in various police manuals and texts which document procedures employed with success in the past, and which recommend various other effective tactics. These texts are used by law enforcement agencies themselves as guides.[9]

It should be noted that these texts professedly present the most enlightened and effective means presently used to obtain statements through custodial interrogation. By considering these texts and other data, it is possible to describe procedures observed and noted around the country. * * *

To highlight the isolation and unfamiliar surroundings, the manuals instruct the police to display an air of confidence in the suspect's guilt and from outward appearance to maintain only an interest in confirming certain details. The guilt of the subject is to be posited as a fact. The interrogator should direct his comments toward the reasons why the subject committed the act, rather than court failure by asking the subject whether he did it. Like other men, perhaps the subject has had a bad family life, had an unhappy childhood, had too much to drink, had an

---

9. The methods described in Inbau and Reid, *Criminal Interrogation and Confessions* (1962), are a revision and enlargement of material presented in three prior editions of a predecessor text, *Lie Detection and Criminal Interrogation* (3d ed. 1953). The authors and their associates are officers of the Chicago Police Scientific Crime–Detection Laboratory and have had extensive experience in writing, lecturing and speaking to law enforcement authorities over a 20–year period. They say that the techniques portrayed in their manuals reflect their experiences and are the most effective psychological stratagems to employ during interrogations. Similarly, the techniques described in O'Hara, *Fundamentals of Criminal Investigation* (1959), were gleaned from long service as observer, lecturer in police science, and work as a federal criminal investigator. All these texts have had rather extensive use among law enforcement agencies and among students of police science, with total sales and circulation of over 44,000.

unrequited desire for women. The officers are instructed to minimize the moral seriousness of the offense, to cast blame on the victim or on society. These tactics are designed to put the subject in a psychological state where his story is but an elaboration of what the police purport to know already—that he is guilty. Explanations to the contrary are dismissed and discouraged.

The texts thus stress that the major qualities an interrogator should possess are patience and perseverance. * * *

[When other techniques] prove unavailing, the texts recommend they be alternated with a show of some hostility. One ploy often used has been termed the "friendly-unfriendly" or the "Mutt and Jeff" act:

"[In] this technique, two agents are employed. Mutt, the relentless investigator, who knows the subject is guilty and is not going to waste any time. He's sent a dozen men away for this crime and he's going to send the subject away for the full term. Jeff, on the other hand, is obviously a kindhearted man. He has a family himself. He has a brother who was involved in a little scrape like this. He disapproves of Mutt and his tactics and will arrange to get him off the case if the subject will cooperate. He can't hold Mutt off for very long. The subject would be wise to make a quick decision. The technique is applied by having both investigators present while Mutt acts out his role. Jeff may stand by quietly and demur at some of Mutt's tactics. When Jeff makes his plea for cooperation, Mutt is not present in the room."

The interrogators sometimes are instructed to induce a confession out of trickery. The technique here is quite effective in crimes which require identification or which run in series. In the identification situation, the interrogator may take a break in his questioning to place the subject among a group of men in a line-up. "The witness or complainant (previously coached, if necessary) studies the line-up and confidently points out the subject as the guilty party." Then the questioning resumes "as though there were now no doubt about the guilt of the subject." A variation on this technique is called the "reverse line-up":

"The accused is placed in a line-up, but this time he is identified by several fictitious witnesses or victims who associated him with different offenses. It is expected that the subject will become desperate and confess to the offense under investigation in order to escape from the false accusations."

The manuals also contain instructions for police on how to handle the individual who refuses to discuss the matter entirely, or who asks for an attorney or relatives. The examiner is to concede him the right to remain silent. "This usually has a very undermining effect. First of all, he is disappointed in his expectation of an unfavorable reaction on the part of the interrogator. Secondly, a concession of this right to remain silent impresses the subject with the apparent fairness of his interrogator." After this psychological conditioning, however, the officer is told to point out the incriminating significance of the suspect's refusal to talk * * *.

From these representative samples of interrogation techniques, the setting prescribed by the manuals and observed in practice becomes clear. In essence, it is this: To be alone with the subject is essential to prevent distraction and to deprive him of any outside support. The aura of confidence in his guilt undermines his will to resist. He merely confirms the preconceived story the police seek to have him describe. Patience and persistence, at times relentless questioning, are employed. To obtain a confession, the interrogator must "patiently maneuver himself or his quarry into a position from which the desired object may be obtained." When normal procedures fail to produce the needed result, the police may resort to deceptive stratagems such as giving false legal advice. It is important to keep the subject off balance, for example, by trading on his insecurity about himself or his surroundings. The police then persuade, trick, or cajole him out of exercising his constitutional rights.

Even without employing brutality, the "third degree" or the specific stratagems described above, the very fact of custodial interrogation exacts a heavy toll on individual liberty and trades on the weakness of individuals.

In the cases before us today, given this background, we concern ourselves primarily with this interrogation atmosphere and the evils it can bring. In *Miranda v. Arizona,* the police arrested the defendant and took him to a special interrogation room where they secured a confession. In *Vignera v. New York,* the defendant made oral admissions to the police after interrogation in the afternoon, and then signed an inculpatory statement upon being questioned by an assistant district attorney later the same evening. In *Westover v. United States,* the defendant was handed over to the Federal Bureau of Investigation by local authorities after they had detained and interrogated him for a lengthy period, both at night and the following morning. After some two hours of questioning, the federal officers had obtained signed statements from the defendant. Lastly, in *California v. Stewart,* the local police held the defendant five days in the station and interrogated him on nine separate occasions before they secured his inculpatory statement.

In these cases, we might not find the defendants' statements to have been involuntary in traditional terms. Our concern for adequate safeguards to protect precious Fifth Amendment rights is, of course, not lessened in the slightest. In each of the cases, the defendant was thrust into an unfamiliar atmosphere and run through menacing police interrogation procedures. The potentiality for compulsion is forcefully apparent, for example, in *Miranda,* where the indigent Mexican defendant was a seriously disturbed individual with pronounced sexual fantasies, and in *Stewart,* in which the defendant was an indigent Los Angeles Negro who had dropped out of school in the sixth grade. To be sure, the records do not evince overt physical coercion or patented psychological ploys. The fact remains that in none of these cases did the officers undertake to afford appropriate safeguards at the outset of the interrogation to insure that the statements were truly the product of free choice.

It is obvious that such an interrogation environment is created for no purpose other than to subjugate the individual to the will of his examiner. This atmosphere carries its own badge of intimidation. To be sure, this is not physical intimidation, but it is equally destructive of human dignity. The current practice of incommunicado interrogation is at odds with one of our Nation's most cherished principles—that the individual may not be compelled to incriminate himself. Unless adequate protective devices are employed to dispel the compulsion inherent in custodial surroundings, no statement obtained from the defendant can truly be the product of his free choice.

From the foregoing, we can readily perceive an intimate connection between the privilege against self-incrimination and police custodial questioning. It is fitting to turn to history and precedent underlying the Self–Incrimination Clause to determine its applicability in this situation.

We sometimes forget how long it has taken to establish the privilege against self-incrimination, the sources from which it came and the fervor with which it was defended. Its roots go back into ancient times.[27] * * *

---

27. Thirteenth century commentators found an analogue to the privilege grounded in the Bible. * * * [See generally Irene Rosenberg & Yale Rosenberg, *In the Beginning: The Talmudic Rule Against Self–Incrimination,* 63 N.Y.U.L.Rev. 955 (1988) and the authorities discussed therein].

[W]e may view the historical development of the privilege as one which groped for the proper scope of governmental power over the citizen. As a "noble principle often transcends its origins," the privilege has come rightfully to be recognized in part as an individual's substantive right, a "right to a private enclave where he may lead a private life. That right is the hallmark of our democracy." We have recently noted that the privilege against self-incrimination—the essential mainstay of our adversary system—is founded on a complex of values. *Murphy v. Waterfront Comm'n* [fn. d, p. 840.] All these policies point to one overriding thought: the constitutional foundation underlying the privilege is the respect a government—state or federal—must accord to the dignity and integrity of its citizens. To maintain a "fair state-individual balance," to require the government "to shoulder the entire load," 8 Wigmore, *Evidence* (McNaughton rev., 1961), to respect the inviolability of the human personality, our accusatory system of criminal justice demands that the government seeking to punish an individual produce the evidence against him by its own independent labors, rather than by the cruel, simple expedient of compelling it from his own mouth. In sum, the privilege is fulfilled only when the person is guaranteed the right "to remain silent unless he chooses to speak in the unfettered exercise of his own will." *Malloy v. Hogan* [p. 565].

* * * We are satisfied that all the principles embodied in the privilege apply to informal compulsion exerted by law-enforcement officers during in-custody questioning. An individual swept from familiar surroundings into police custody, surrounded by antagonistic forces, and subjected to the techniques of persuasion described above cannot be otherwise than under compulsion to speak. As a practical matter, the compulsion to speak in the isolated setting of the police station may well be greater than in courts or other official investigations, where there are often impartial observers to guard against intimidation or trickery.

This question in fact could have been taken as settled in federal courts almost seventy years ago [by] *Bram v. United States* (1897) [discussed at p. 565]. Because of the adoption by Congress of Rule 5(a) of the Federal Rules of Criminal Procedure, and this Court's effectuation of that Rule in *McNabb* and *Mallory,* we have had little occasion in the past quarter century to reach the constitutional issues in dealing with federal interrogations. These supervisory rules, requiring production of an arrested person before a commissioner "without unnecessary delay" and excluding evidence obtained in default of that statutory obligation, were nonetheless responsive to the same considerations of Fifth Amendment policy that unavoidably face us now as to the States. In [the *McNabb* and *Mallory* cases] we recognized both the dangers of interrogation and the appropriateness of prophylaxis stemming from the very fact of interrogation itself.[32]

Our decision in *Malloy v. Hogan* necessitates an examination of the scope of the privilege in state cases as well. In *Malloy,* we squarely held the privilege applicable to the States, and held that the substantive standards underlying the privilege applied with full force to state court proceedings. The implications [of *Malloy*] were elaborated in our decision in *Escobedo,* decided one week after *Malloy* applied the privilege to the States. * * *[35]

Today [there] can be no doubt that the Fifth Amendment privilege is available outside of criminal court proceedings and serves to protect persons in all settings

---

32. Our decision today does not indicate in any manner, of course, that these rules can be disregarded. When federal officials arrest an individual, they must as always comply with the dictates of the congressional legislation and cases thereunder. * * *

35. [In *Escobedo,* the] police also prevented the attorney from consulting with his client. Independent of any other constitutional proscription, this action constitutes a violation of the Sixth Amendment right to the assistance of counsel and excludes any statement obtained in its wake. See *People v. Donovan,* 193 N.E.2d 628 (N.Y.1963) (Fuld, J.).

in which their freedom of action is curtailed from being compelled to incriminate themselves. We have concluded that without proper safeguards the process of in-custody interrogation of persons suspected or accused of crime contains inherently compelling pressures which work to undermine the individual's will to resist and to compel him to speak where he would not otherwise do so freely. In order to combat these pressures and to permit a full opportunity to exercise the privilege against self-incrimination, the accused must be adequately and effectively apprised of his rights and the exercise of those rights must be fully honored.

It is impossible for us to foresee the potential alternatives for protecting the privilege which might be devised by Congress or the States in the exercise of their creative rule-making capacities. Therefore we cannot say that the Constitution necessarily requires adherence to any particular solution for the inherent compulsions of the interrogation process as it is presently conducted. Our decision in no way creates a constitutional straitjacket which will handicap sound efforts at reform, nor is it intended to have this effect. We encourage Congress and the States to continue their laudable search for increasingly effective ways of protecting the rights of the individual while promoting efficient enforcement of our criminal laws. However, unless we are shown other procedures which are at least as effective in apprising accused persons of their right of silence and in assuring a continuous opportunity to exercise it, the following safeguards must be observed.[a]

At the outset, if a person in custody is to be subjected to interrogation, he must first be informed in clear and unequivocal terms that he has the right to remain silent. For those unaware of the privilege, the warning is needed simply to make them aware of it—the threshold requirement for an intelligent decision as to its exercise. More important, such a warning is an absolute prerequisite in overcoming the inherent pressures of the interrogation atmosphere. It is not just the subnormal or woefully ignorant who succumb to an interrogator's imprecations, whether implied or expressly stated, that the interrogation will continue until a confession is obtained or that silence in the face of accusation is itself damning and will bode ill when presented to a jury.[37] Further, the warning will show the individual that his interrogators are prepared to recognize his privilege should he choose to exercise it.

The Fifth Amendment privilege is so fundamental to our system of constitutional rule and the expedient of giving an adequate warning as to the availability of the privilege so simple, we will not pause to inquire in individual cases whether the defendant was aware of his rights without a warning being given. Assessments of the knowledge the defendant possessed, based on information as to his age, education, intelligence, or prior contact with authorities, can never be more than speculation;[38] a warning is a clearcut fact. More important, whatever the back-

---

a. Ed. Note—Chief Justice Warren inserted the language in this paragraph at the suggestion of Justice Brennan, who wrote a lengthy memorandum to Warren, commenting on an early draft of the *Miranda* opinion. Brennan "agree[d] that, largely for the reasons you have stated, all four cases must be reversed for lack of any safeguards against denial of the right [against self-incrimination]. [But] should we not leave Congress and the States latitude to devise other means (if they can) which might also create an interrogation climate which has the similar effect of preventing the fettering of a person's own will?" Ironically, the language that Chief Justice Warren used at Brennan's suggestion was seized upon by Justice Rehnquist in *Michigan v. Tucker* (1974) (p. 591) as evidence that *Miranda* was not a constitutional decision.

For a discussion of, and substantial extracts from, Justice Brennan's memorandum to Chief Justice Warren, see Charles D. Weisselberg, *Saving Miranda*, 84 Cornell L.Rev. 109, 123–25 (1998).

37. [In] accord with this decision, it is impermissible to penalize an individual for exercising his Fifth Amendment privilege when he is under police custodial interrogation. The prosecution may not, therefore, use at trial the fact that he stood mute or claimed his privilege in the face of accusation.

38. Cf. *Betts v. Brady,* and the recurrent inquiry into special circumstances it necessitated.
* * *

ground of the person interrogated, a warning at the time of the interrogation is indispensable to overcome its pressures and to insure that the individual knows he is free to exercise the privilege at that point in time.

The warning of the right to remain silent must be accompanied by the explanation that anything said can and will be used against the individual in court. This warning is needed in order to make him aware not only of the privilege, but also of the consequences of forgoing it. It is only through an awareness of these consequences that there can be any assurance of real understanding and intelligent exercise of the privilege. Moreover, this warning may serve to make the individual more acutely aware that he is faced with a phase of the adversary system—that he is not in the presence of persons acting solely in his interest.

The circumstances surrounding in-custody interrogation can operate very quickly to overbear the will of one merely made aware of his privilege by his interrogators. Therefore, the right to have counsel present at the interrogation is indispensable to the protection of the Fifth Amendment privilege under the system we delineate today. Our aim is to assure that the individual's right to choose between silence and speech remains unfettered throughout the interrogation process. A once-stated warning, delivered by those who will conduct the interrogation, cannot itself suffice to that end among those who most require knowledge of their rights. A mere warning given by the interrogators is not alone sufficient to accomplish that end. Prosecutors themselves claim that the admonishment of the right to remain silent without more "will benefit only the recidivist and the professional." Brief for the National District Attorneys Association as *amicus curiae*. Even preliminary advice given to the accused by his own attorney can be swiftly overcome by the secret interrogation process. Thus, the need for counsel to protect the Fifth Amendment privilege comprehends not merely a right to consult with counsel prior to questioning but also to have counsel present during any questioning if the defendant so desires.

The presence of counsel at the interrogation may serve several significant subsidiary functions as well. If the accused decides to talk to his interrogators, the assistance of counsel can mitigate the dangers of untrustworthiness. With a lawyer present the likelihood that the police will practice coercion is reduced, and if coercion is nevertheless exercised the lawyer can testify to it in court. The presence of a lawyer can also help to guarantee that the accused gives a fully accurate statement to the police and that the statement is rightly reported by the prosecution at trial.

An individual need not make a preinterrogation request for a lawyer. While such request affirmatively secures his right to have one, his failure to ask for a lawyer does not constitute a waiver. No effective waiver of the right to counsel during interrogation can be recognized unless specifically made after the warnings we here delineate have been given. The accused who does not know his rights and therefore does not make a request may be the person who most needs counsel.
* * *

Accordingly we hold that an individual held for interrogation must be clearly informed that he has the right to consult with a lawyer and to have the lawyer with him during interrogation under the system for protecting the privilege we delineate today. As with the warnings of the right to remain silent and that anything stated can be used in evidence against him, this warning is an absolute prerequisite to interrogation. No amount of circumstantial evidence that the person may have been aware of this right will suffice to stand in its stead. Only through such a warning is there ascertainable assurance that the accused was aware of this right.

If an individual indicates that he wishes the assistance of counsel before any interrogation occurs, the authorities cannot rationally ignore or deny his request on the basis that the individual does not have or cannot afford a retained attorney. The financial ability of the individual has no relationship to the scope of the rights involved here. The privilege against self-incrimination secured by the Constitution applies to all individuals. The need for counsel in order to protect the privilege exists for the indigent as well as the affluent. In fact, were we to limit these constitutional rights to those who can retain an attorney, our decisions today would be of little significance. The cases before us as well as the vast majority of confession cases with which we have dealt in the past involve those unable to retain counsel. While authorities are not required to relieve the accused of his poverty, they have the obligation not to take advantage of indigence in the administration of justice.[41] Denial of counsel to the indigent at the time of interrogation while allowing an attorney to those who can afford one would be no more supportable by reason or logic than the similar situation at trial and on appeal struck down in *Gideon* and *Douglas v. California.*

In order fully to apprise a person interrogated of the extent of his rights under this system then, it is necessary to warn him not only that he has the right to consult with an attorney, but also that if he is indigent a lawyer will be appointed to represent him. Without this additional warning, the admonition of the right to consult with counsel would often be understood as meaning only that he can consult with a lawyer if he has one or has the funds to obtain one. The warning of a right to counsel would be hollow if not couched in terms that would convey to the indigent—the person most often subjected to interrogation—the knowledge that he too has a right to have counsel present. As with the warnings of the right to remain silent and of the general right to counsel, only by effective and express explanation to the indigent of this right can there be assurance that he was truly in a position to exercise it.[43]

Once warnings have been given, the subsequent procedure is clear. If the individual indicates in any manner, at any time prior to or during questioning, that he wishes to remain silent, the interrogation must cease.[44] At this point he has shown that he intends to exercise his Fifth Amendment privilege; any statement taken after the person invokes his privilege cannot be other than the product of compulsion, subtle or otherwise. Without the right to cut off questioning, the setting of in-custody interrogation operates on the individual to overcome free choice in producing a statement after the privilege has been once invoked. If the individual states that he wants an attorney, the interrogation must cease until an attorney is present. At that time, the individual must have an opportunity to confer with the attorney and to have him present during any subsequent questioning. If the individual cannot obtain an attorney and he indicates that he wants one before speaking to police, they must respect his decision to remain silent.

This does not mean, as some have suggested, that each police station must have a "station house lawyer" present at all times to advise prisoners. It does

---

41. See Kamisar, *Equal Justice in the Gatehouses and Mansions of American Criminal Procedure,* in Criminal Justice in Our Time (1965), 64–81; * * * Report of the Attorney General's Committee on *Poverty and the Administration of Federal Criminal Justice* (1963), p. 9 * * *.

43. While a warning that the indigent may have counsel appointed need not be given to the person who is known to have an attorney or is known to have ample funds to secure one, the expedient of giving a warning is too simple and the rights involved too important to engage in *ex post facto* inquiries into financial ability when there is any doubt at all on that score.

44. If an individual indicates his desire to remain silent, but has an attorney present, there may be some circumstances in which further questioning would be permissible. In the absence of evidence of overbearing, statements then made in the presence of counsel might be free of the compelling influence of the interrogation process and might fairly be construed as a waiver of the privilege for purposes of these statements.

mean, however, that if police propose to interrogate a person they
known to him that he is entitled to a lawyer and that if he cannot
lawyer will be provided for him prior to any interrogation. If authori
that they will not provide counsel during a reasonable period of tir
investigation in the field is carried out, they may do so without v
person's Fifth Amendment privilege so long as they do not question
that time.

If the interrogation continues without the presence of an attorney and a
statement is taken, a heavy burden rests on the Government to demonstrate that
the defendant knowingly and intelligently waived his privilege against self-
incrimination and his right to retained or appointed counsel. This Court has
always set high standards of proof for the waiver of constitutional rights, *Johnson
v. Zerbst,* and we reassert these standards as applied to in-custody interrogation.
Since the State is responsible for establishing the isolated circumstances under
which the interrogation takes place and has the only means of making available
corroborated evidence of warnings given during incommunicado interrogation, the
burden is rightly on its shoulders.

An express statement that the individual is willing to make a statement and
does not want an attorney followed closely by a statement could constitute a
waiver. But a valid waiver will not be presumed simply from the silence of the
accused after warnings are given or simply from the fact that a confession was in
fact eventually obtained [referring to *Carnley v. Cochran,* 369 U.S. 506 (1962)].

* * * Moreover, where in-custody interrogation is involved, there is no room
for the contention that the privilege is waived if the individual answers some
questions or gives some information on his own prior to invoking his right to
remain silent when interrogated.[45]

Whatever the testimony of the authorities as to waiver of rights by an
accused, the fact of lengthy interrogation or incommunicado incarceration before a
statement is made is strong evidence that the accused did not validly waive his
rights. In these circumstances the fact that the individual eventually made a
statement is consistent with the conclusion that the compelling influence of the
interrogation finally forced him to do so. It is inconsistent with any notion of a
voluntary relinquishment of the privilege. Moreover, any evidence that the accused was threatened, tricked, or cajoled into a waiver will, of course, show that
the defendant did not voluntarily waive his privilege. The requirement of warnings and waiver of rights is a fundamental with respect to the Fifth Amendment
privilege and not simply a preliminary ritual to existing methods of interrogation.

The warnings required and the waiver necessary in accordance with our
opinion today are, in the absence of a fully effective equivalent, prerequisites to
the admissibility of any statement made by a defendant. No distinction can be
drawn between statements which are direct confessions and statements which
amount to "admissions" of part or all of an offense. The privilege against self-
incrimination protects the individual from being compelled to incriminate himself
in any manner; it does not distinguish degrees of incrimination. Similarly, for
precisely the same reason, no distinction may be drawn between inculpatory
statements and statements alleged to be merely "exculpatory." If a statement
made were in fact truly exculpatory it would, of course, never be used by the
prosecution. In fact, statements merely intended to be exculpatory by the defen-

---

45. Although this Court held in *Rogers v. United States,* [discussed in Note 4, p. 841] over
strong dissent, that a witness before a grand jury may not in certain circumstances decide to
answer some questions and then refuse to answer others that decision has no application to the
interrogation situation we deal with today. No legislative or judicial fact-finding authority is
involved here, nor is there a possibility that the individual might make self-serving statements of
which he could make use at trial while refusing to answer incriminating statements.

dant are often used to impeach his testimony at trial or to demonstrate untruths in the statement given under interrogation and thus to prove guilt by implication. These statements are incriminating in any meaningful sense of the word and may not be used without the full warnings and effective waiver required for any other statement. In *Escobedo* itself, the defendant fully intended his accusation of another as the slayer to be exculpatory as to himself.

The principles announced today deal with the protection which must be given to the privilege against self-incrimination when the individual is first subjected to police interrogation while in custody at the station or otherwise deprived of his freedom of action in any significant way. It is at this point that our adversary system of criminal proceedings commences, distinguishing itself at the outset from the inquisitorial system recognized in some countries. Under the system of warnings we delineate today or under any other system which may be devised and found effective, the safeguards to be erected about the privilege must come into play at this point.

Our decision is not intended to hamper the traditional function of police officers in investigating crime. When an individual is in custody on probable cause, the police may, of course, seek out evidence in the field to be used at trial against him. Such investigation may include inquiry of persons not under restraint. General on-the-scene questioning as to facts surrounding a crime or other general questioning of citizens in the fact-finding process is not affected by our holding. It is an act of responsible citizenship for individuals to give whatever information they may have to aid in law enforcement. In such situations the compelling atmosphere inherent in the process of in-custody interrogation is not necessarily present.[46]

[To] summarize, we hold that when an individual is taken into custody or otherwise deprived of his freedom by the authorities in any significant way and is subjected to questioning, the privilege against self-incrimination is jeopardized. Procedural safeguards must be employed to protect the privilege, and unless other fully effective means are adopted to notify the person of his right of silence and to assure that the exercise of the right will be scrupulously honored, the following measures are required. He must be warned prior to any questioning that he has the right to remain silent, that anything he says can be used against him in a court of law, that he has the right to the presence of an attorney, and that if he cannot afford an attorney one will be appointed for him prior to any questioning if he so desires. Opportunity to exercise these rights must be afforded to him throughout the interrogation. After such warnings have been given, and such opportunity afforded him, the individual may knowingly and intelligently waive these rights and agree to answer questions or make a statement. But unless and until such warnings and waiver are demonstrated by the prosecution at trial, no evidence obtained as a result of interrogation can be used against him. * * *

If the individual desires to exercise his privilege, he has the right to do so. This is not for the authorities to decide. An attorney may advise his client not to talk to police until he has had an opportunity to investigate the case, or he may wish to be present with his client during any police questioning. In doing so an attorney is merely exercising the good professional judgment he has been taught. This is not cause for considering the attorney a menace to law enforcement. He is

---

46. The distinction and its significance has been aptly described in the opinion of a Scottish court:

"In former times such questioning, if undertaken, would be conducted by police officers visiting the house or place of business of the suspect and there questioning him, probably in the presence of a relation or friend. However convenient the modern practice may be, it must normally create a situation very unfavorable to the suspect." *Chalmers v. H.M. Advocate,* [1954] Sess.Cas. 66, 78 (J.C.).

merely carrying out what he is sworn to do under his oath—to protect to the extent of his ability the rights of his client. In fulfilling this responsibility the attorney plays a vital role in the administration of criminal justice under our Constitution.

[The] experience in some other countries * * * suggests that the danger to law enforcement in curbs on interrogation is overplayed. The English procedure since 1912 under the Judges' Rules is significant. As recently strengthened, the Rules require that a cautionary warning be given an accused by a police officer as soon as he has evidence that affords reasonable grounds for suspicion; they also require that any statement made be given by the accused without questioning by police.[b] The right of the individual to consult with an attorney during this period is expressly recognized. * * *

Because of the nature of the problem and because of its recurrent significance in numerous cases, we have to this point discussed the relationship of the Fifth Amendment privilege to police interrogation without specific concentration on the facts of the cases before us. We turn now to these facts to consider the application to these cases of the constitutional principles discussed above. In each instance, we have concluded that statements were obtained from the defendant under circumstances that did not meet constitutional standards for protection of the privilege.

No. 759. *Miranda v. Arizona.*

On March 13, 1963, petitioner, Ernesto Miranda, was arrested at his home and taken in custody to a Phoenix police station. He was there identified by the complaining witness. The police then took him to "Interrogation Room No. 2" of the detective bureau. There he was questioned by two police officers. The officers admitted at trial that Miranda was not advised that he had a right to have an attorney present. Two hours later, the officers emerged from the interrogation room with a written confession signed by Miranda. At the top of the statement was a typed paragraph stating that the confession was made voluntarily, without threats or promises of immunity and "with full knowledge of my legal rights, understanding any statement I make may be used against me."[67]

[Miranda] was found guilty of kidnapping and rape. [On] appeal, the Supreme Court of Arizona held that Miranda's constitutional rights were not violated in obtaining the confession and affirmed the conviction. In reaching its decision, the court emphasized heavily the fact that Miranda did not specifically request counsel.

We reverse. From the testimony of the officers and by the admission of respondent, it is clear that Miranda was not in any way apprised of his right to consult with an attorney and to have one present during the interrogation, nor was his right not to be compelled to incriminate himself effectively protected in any other manner. Without these warnings the statements were inadmissible. The mere fact that he signed a statement which contained a typed-in clause stating that he had "full knowledge" of his legal rights does not approach the knowing and intelligent waiver required to relinquish constitutional rights. * * *[c]

---

b. **Ed. Note**—*England curtails the right to silence.* In the fall of 1994, the British Parliament adopted various restrictions on the right to silence, effective March 1, 1995, which permit judges and jurors to draw adverse inferences when, during interrogation, suspects do not tell the police any fact subsequently relied upon in their defense at trial, if under the circumstances, the suspects would have "been 'reasonably expected' to mention that fact to the police.

67. One of the officers testified that he read this paragraph to Miranda. Apparently, however, he did not do so until after Miranda had confessed orally.

c. On retrial, *Miranda* was again convicted of kidnapping and rape. The conviction was affirmed in *State v. Miranda*, 450 P.2d 364 (Ariz.1969). For a rich narrative of *Miranda* from arrest to reconviction, see L. Baker, *Miranda: Crime, Law & Politics* (1983).

[The Court also reversed the convictions in two companion cases, *Vignera* and *Westover*, and affirmed the reversal of the conviction in a third companion case, *California v. Stewart.*[d]]

JUSTICE CLARK, dissenting in [*Miranda, Vignera,* and *Westover,* and concurring in the result in *Stewart.*]

[I cannot] agree with the Court's characterization of the present practices of police and investigatory agencies as to custodial interrogation. The materials referred to as "police manuals" are not shown by the record here to be the official manuals of any police department, much less in universal use in crime detection. Moreover, the examples of police brutality mentioned by the Court are rare exceptions to the thousands of cases that appear every year in the law reports. * * *

[The Court's] strict constitutional specific inserted at the nerve center of crime detection may well kill the patient. Since there is at this time a paucity of information and an almost total lack of empirical knowledge on the practical operation of requirements truly comparable to those announced by the majority, I would be more restrained lest we go too far too fast. * * *

Rather than employing the arbitrary Fifth Amendment rule which the Court lays down I would follow the more pliable dictates of Due Process Clauses of the Fifth and Fourteenth Amendments which we are accustomed to administering and which we know from our cases are effective instruments in protecting persons in police custody. In this way we would not be acting in the dark nor in one full sweep changing the traditional rules of custodial interrogation which this Court has for so long recognized as a justifiable and proper tool in balancing individual rights against the rights of society. It will be soon enough to go further when we are able to appraise with somewhat better accuracy the effect of such a holding. * * *

JUSTICE HARLAN, whom JUSTICE STEWART and JUSTICE WHITE join, dissenting. * * *

While the fine points of [the Court's new constitutional code of rules for confessions] are far less clear than the Court admits, the tenor is quite apparent. The new rules are not designed to guard against police brutality or other unmistakably banned forms of coercion. Those who use third-degree tactics and deny them in court are equally able and destined to lie as skillfully about warnings and waivers. Rather, the thrust of the new rules is to negate all pressures, to reinforce the nervous or ignorant suspect, and ultimately to discourage any confession at all. The aim in short is toward "voluntariness" in a utopian sense, or to view it from a different angle, voluntariness with a vengeance.

[The] Court's asserted reliance on the Fifth Amendment [is] an approach which I frankly regard as a *trompe l'oeil.* The Court's opinion in my view reveals no adequate basis for extending the Fifth Amendment's privilege against self-incrimination to the police station. Far more important, it fails to show that the Court's new rules are well supported, let alone compelled, by Fifth Amendment precedents. Instead, the new rules actually derive from quotation and analogy drawn from precedents under the Sixth Amendment, which should properly have no bearing on police interrogation. * * *

Having decided that the Fifth Amendment privilege does apply in the police station, the Court reveals that the privilege imposes more exacting restrictions than does the Fourteenth Amendment's voluntariness test. It then emerges from a discussion of *Escobedo* that the Fifth Amendment requires for an admissible

---

d. A week later, the Court ruled that *Escobedo* and *Miranda* applied only to trials begun after the decisions were announced.

confession that it be given by one distinctly aware of his right not to speak and shielded from "the compelling atmosphere" of interrogation. From these key premises, the Court finally develops the safeguards of warning, counsel, and so forth. I do not believe these premises are sustained by precedents under the Fifth Amendment.[9]

The more important premise is that pressure on the suspect must be eliminated though it be only the subtle influence of the atmosphere and surroundings. The Fifth Amendment, however, has never been thought to forbid *all* pressure to incriminate one's self in the situations covered by it. * * *

A closing word must be said about the Assistance of Counsel Clause of the Sixth Amendment, which is never expressly relied on by the Court but whose judicial precedents turn out to be linchpins of the confession rules announced today.

[The] only attempt in this Court to carry the right to counsel into the station house occurred in *Escobedo,* the Court repeating several times that that stage was no less "critical" than trial itself. * * * This is hardly persuasive when we consider that a grand jury inquiry, the filing of a certiorari petition, and certainly the purchase of narcotics by an undercover agent from a prospective defendant may all be equally "critical" yet provision of counsel and advice on that score have never been thought compelled by the Constitution in such cases. The sound reason why this right is so freely extended for a criminal trial is the severe injustice risked by confronting an untrained defendant with a range of technical points of law, evidence, and tactics familiar to the prosecutor but not to himself. This danger shrinks markedly in the police station where indeed the lawyer in fulfilling his professional responsibilities of necessity may become an obstacle to truthfinding. See infra, n. 12.

[The] Court's new rules aim to offset [the] minor pressures and disadvantages intrinsic to any kind of police interrogation. The rules do not serve due process interests in preventing blatant coercion [since] they do nothing to contain the policeman who is prepared to lie from the start. The rules work for reliability in confessions almost only in the Pickwickian sense that they can prevent some from being given at all.[12] * * *

What the Court largely ignores is that its rules impair, if they will not eventually serve wholly to frustrate, an instrument of law enforcement that has long and quite reasonably been thought worth the price paid for it. There can be little doubt that the Court's new code would markedly decrease the number of confessions. To warn the suspect that he may remain silent and remind him that his confession may be used in court are minor obstructions. To require also an express waiver by the suspect and an end to questioning whenever he demurs must heavily handicap questioning. And to suggest or provide counsel for the suspect simply invites the end of the interrogation. See supra, n. 12. * * *

While passing over the costs and risks of its experiment, the Court portrays the evils of normal police questioning in terms which I think are exaggerated. Albeit stringently confined by the due process standards interrogation is no doubt often inconvenient and unpleasant for the suspect. However, it is no less so for a

---

9. I lay aside *Escobedo* itself; it contains no reasoning or even general conclusions addressed to the Fifth Amendment and indeed its citation in this regard seems surprising in view of *Escobedo's* primary reliance on the Sixth Amendment.

12. The Court's vision of a lawyer "mitigat[ing] the dangers of untrustworthiness" by witnessing coercion and assisting accuracy in the confession is largely a fancy; for if counsel arrives, there is rarely going to be a police station confession. *Watts v. Indiana* (separate opinion of Jackson, J.): "[A]ny lawyer worth his salt will tell the suspect in no uncertain terms to make no statement to police under any circumstances."

man to be arrested and jailed, to have his house searched, or to stand trial in court, yet all this may properly happen to the most innocent given probable cause, a warrant, or an indictment. Society has always paid a stiff price for law and order, and peaceful interrogation is not one of the dark moments of the law.

This brief statement of the competing considerations seems to me ample proof that the Court's preference is highly debatable at best and therefore not to be read into the Constitution. However, it may make the analysis more graphic to consider the actual facts of one of the four cases reversed by the Court. *Miranda* serves best, being neither the hardest nor easiest of the four under the Court's standards.[15]

On March 3, 1963, an 18-year-old girl was kidnapped and forcibly raped near Phoenix, Arizona. Ten days later, on the morning of March 13, petitioner Miranda was arrested and taken to the police station. At this time Miranda was 23 years old, indigent, and educated to the extent of completing half the ninth grade. He had "an emotional illness" of the schizophrenic type, according to the doctor who eventually examined him; the doctor's report also stated that Miranda was "alert and oriented as to time, place, and person", intelligent within normal limits, competent to stand trial, and sane within the legal definition. At the police station, the victim picked Miranda out of a lineup, and two officers then took him into a separate room to interrogate him, starting about 11:30 a.m. Though at first denying his guilt, within a short time Miranda gave a detailed oral confession and then wrote out in his own hand and signed a brief statement admitting and describing the crime. All this was accomplished in two hours or less without any force, threats or promises and—I will assume this though the record is uncertain * * *—without any effective warnings at all.

Miranda's oral and written confessions are now held inadmissible under the Court's new rules. One is entitled to feel astonished that the Constitution can be read to produce this result. These confessions were obtained during brief, daytime questioning conducted by two officers and unmarked by any of the traditional indicia of coercion. They assured a conviction for a brutal and unsettling crime, for which the police had and quite possibly could obtain little evidence other than the victim's identifications, evidence which is frequently unreliable. There was, in sum, a legitimate purpose, no perceptible unfairness, and certainly little risk of injustice in the interrogation. Yet the resulting confessions, and the responsible course of police practice they represent, are to be sacrificed to the Court's own finespun conception of fairness which I seriously doubt is shared by many thinking citizens in this country.

[It is] instructive to compare the attitude in this case of those responsible for law enforcement with the official views that existed when the Court undertook three major revisions of prosecutorial practice prior to this case, *Johnson v. Zerbst, Mapp,* and *Gideon.* In *Johnson,* which established that appointed counsel must be offered the indigent in federal criminal trials, the Federal Government all but conceded the basic issue, which had in fact been recently fixed as Department of Justice policy. In *Mapp,* which imposed the exclusionary rule on the States for Fourth Amendment violations, more than half of the States had themselves already adopted some such rule. In *Gideon,* which extended *Johnson v. Zerbst* to the States, an *amicus* brief was filed by 22 States and Commonwealths urging that course; only two States beside the respondent came forward to protest. By contrast, in this case new restrictions on police questioning have been opposed by the United States and in an *amicus* brief signed by 27 States and Common-

---

15. In *Westover,* a seasoned criminal was practically given the Court's full complement of warnings and did not heed them. The *Stewart* case, on the other hand, involves long detention and successive questioning. In *Vignera,* the facts are complicated and the record somewhat incomplete.

wealths, not including the three other States who are parties. No State in the country has urged this Court to impose the newly announced rules, nor has any State chosen to go nearly so far on its own.

[The] law of the foreign countries described by the [majority] reflects a more moderate conception of the rights of the accused as against those of society when other data is considered. Concededly, the English experience is most relevant. In that country, a caution as to silence but not counsel has long been mandated by the "Judges' Rules," which also place other somewhat imprecise limits on police cross-examination of suspects. However, in the court's discretion confessions can be and apparently quite frequently are admitted in evidence despite disregard of the Judges' Rules, so long as they are found voluntary under the common-law test. Moreover, the check that exists on the use of pretrial statements is counterbalanced by the evident admissibility of fruits of an illegal confession and by the judge's often-used authority to comment adversely on the defendant's failure to testify. * * *

[S]ome reference must be made to [the] ironic untimeliness [of these confession rules]. There is now in progress in this country a massive re-examination of criminal law enforcement procedures on a scale never before witnessed. Participants in this undertaking include a Special Committee of the American Bar Association, under the chairmanship of Chief Judge Lumbard of the Court of Appeals for the Second Circuit; a distinguished study group of the American Law Institute, headed by Professor Vorenberg of the Harvard Law School; and the President's Commission on Law Enforcement and Administration of Justice, under the leadership of the Attorney General of the United States. Studies are also being conducted by [other groups] equipped to do practical research.

[It] is no secret that concern has been expressed lest long-range and lasting reforms be frustrated by this Court's too rapid departure from existing constitutional standards. Despite the Court's disclaimer, the practical effect of the decision made today must inevitably be to handicap seriously sound efforts at reform, not least by removing options necessary to a just compromise of competing interests. [T]he legislative reforms when they came would have the vast advantage of empirical data and comprehensive study, they would allow experimentation and use of solutions not open to the courts, and they would restore the initiative in criminal law reform to those forums where it truly belongs. * * *

JUSTICE WHITE, with whom JUSTICE HARLAN and JUSTICE STEWART join, dissenting.

The proposition that the privilege against self-incrimination forbids in-custody interrogation without the warnings specified in the majority opinion and without a clear waiver of counsel has no significant support in the history of the privilege or in the language of the Fifth Amendment. As for the English authorities and the common-law history, the privilege, firmly established in the second half of the seventeenth century, was never applied except to prohibit compelled judicial interrogations. The rule excluding coerced confessions matured about 100 years later, "[b]ut there is nothing in the reports to suggest that the theory has its roots in the privilege against self-incrimination. And so far as the cases reveal, the privilege, as such, seems to have been given effect only in judicial proceedings, including the preliminary examinations by authorized magistrates." Morgan, *The Privilege Against Self–Incrimination*, 34 Minn.L.Rev. 1, 18 (1949).

[That] the Court's holding today is neither compelled nor even strongly suggested by the language of the Fifth Amendment, is at odds with American and English legal history, and involves a departure from a long line of precedent does not prove either that the Court has exceeded its powers or that the Court is wrong or unwise in its present reinterpretation of the Fifth Amendment. It does, however, underscore the obvious—that the Court has not discovered or found the law in making today's decision, nor has it derived it from some irrefutable sources; what it has done is to make new law and new public policy in much the same way that it has in the course of interpreting other great clauses of the Constitution. This is what the Court historically has done. Indeed, it is what it must do and will continue to do until and unless there is some fundamental change in the constitutional distribution of governmental powers.

But if the Court is here and now to announce new and fundamental policy to govern certain aspects of our affairs, it is wholly legitimate to examine the mode of this or any other constitutional decision in this Court and to inquire into the advisability of its end product in terms of the long-range interest of the country. At the very least the Court's text and reasoning should withstand analysis and be a fair exposition of the constitutional provision which its opinion interprets. Decisions like these cannot rest alone on syllogism, metaphysics or some ill-defined notions of natural justice, although each will perhaps play its part.

[The Court] extrapolates a picture of what it conceives to be the norm from police investigatorial manuals, published in 1959 and 1962 or earlier, without any attempt to allow for adjustments in police practices that may have occurred in the wake of more recent decisions of state appellate tribunals or this Court. But even if the relentless application of the described procedures could lead to involuntary confessions, it most assuredly does not follow that each and every case will disclose this kind of interrogation or this kind of consequence.[2]

Insofar as it appears from the Court's opinion, it has not examined a single transcript of any police interrogation, let alone the interrogation that took place in any one of these cases which it decides today. Judged by any of the standards for empirical investigation utilized in the social sciences the factual basis for the Court's premises is patently inadequate.

Although in the Court's view in-custody interrogation is inherently coercive, it says that the spontaneous product of the coercion of arrest and detention is still to be deemed voluntary. An accused, arrested on probable cause, may blurt out a confession which will be admissible despite the fact that he is alone and in custody, without any showing that he had any notion of his right to remain silent or of the consequences of his admission. Yet, under the Court's rule, if the police ask him a single question such as "Do you have anything to say?" or "Did you kill your wife?" his response, if there is one, has somehow been compelled, even if the accused has been clearly warned of his right to remain silent. Common sense informs us to the contrary. While one may say that the response was "involuntary" in the sense the question provoked or was the occasion for the response and thus the defendant was induced to speak out when he might have remained silent if not arrested and not questioned, it is patently unsound to say the response is compelled.

[If] the rule announced today were truly based on a conclusion that all confessions resulting from custodial interrogation are coerced, then it would simply have no rational foundation. * * * Even if one were to postulate that the Court's concern is not that all confessions induced by police interrogation are coerced but rather that some such confessions are coerced and present judicial procedures are believed to be inadequate to identify the confessions that are

---

2. In fact, the type of sustained interrogation described by the Court appears to be the exception rather than the rule. A survey of 399 cases in one city found that in almost half of the cases the interrogation lasted less than 30 minutes. Barrett, *Police Practices and the Law—From Arrest to Release or Charge*, 50 Calif.L.Rev. 11, 41–45 (1962). Questioning tends to be confused and sporadic and is usually concentrated on confrontations with witnesses or new items of evidence, as these are obtained by officers conducting the investigation. See generally LaFave, *Arrest: The Decision to Take a Suspect into Custody* 386 (1965); ALI, *Model Pre–Arraignment Procedure Code,* Commentary § 5.01, at 170, n. 4 (Tent.Draft No. 1, 1966).

coerced and those that are not, it would still not be essential to impose the rule that the Court has now fashioned. Transcripts or observers could be required, specific time limits, tailored to fit the cause, could be imposed, or other devices could be utilized to reduce the chances that otherwise indiscernible coercion will produce an inadmissible confession.

On the other hand, even if one assumed that there was an adequate factual basis for the conclusion that all confessions obtained during in-custody interrogation are the product of compulsion, the rule propounded by the Court would still be irrational, for, apparently, it is only if the accused is also warned of his right to counsel and waives both that right and the right against self-incrimination that the inherent compulsiveness of interrogation disappears. But if the defendant may not answer without a warning a question such as "Where were you last night?" without having his answer be a compelled one, how can the court ever accept his negative answer to the question of whether he wants to consult his retained counsel or counsel whom the court will appoint? And why if counsel is present and the accused nevertheless confesses, or counsel tells the accused to tell the truth, and that is what the accused does, is the situation any less coercive insofar as the accused is concerned? The court apparently realizes its dilemma of foreclosing questioning without the necessary warnings but at the same time permitting the accused, sitting in the same chair in front of the same policemen, to waive his right to consult an attorney. It expects, however, that not too many will waive the right; and if it is claimed that he has, the State faces a severe, if not impossible burden of proof.

All of this makes very little sense in terms of the compulsion which the Fifth Amendment proscribes. That amendment deals with compelling the accused himself. It is his free will that is involved. Confessions and incriminating admissions, as such, are not forbidden evidence; only those which are compelled are banned. I doubt that the Court observes these distinctions today. By considering any answers to any interrogation to be compelled regardless of the content and course of examination and by escalating the requirements to prove waiver, the Court not only prevents the use of compelled confessions but for all practical purposes forbids interrogation except in the presence of counsel. That is, instead of confining itself to protection of the right against compelled self-incrimination the Court has created a limited Fifth Amendment right to counsel—or, as the Court expresses it, a "right to counsel to protect the Fifth Amendment privilege * * *." The focus then is not on the will of the accused but on the will of counsel and how much influence he can have on the accused. Obviously there is no warrant in the Fifth Amendment for thus installing counsel as the arbiter of the privilege.

In sum, for all the Court's expounding on the menacing atmosphere of police interrogation procedures it has failed to supply any foundation for the conclusions it draws or the measures it adopts.

Criticism of the Court's opinion, however, cannot stop at a demonstration that the factual and textual bases for the rule it propounds are, at best, less than compelling. Equally relevant is an assessment of the rule's consequences measured against community values. The Court's duty to assess the consequences of its action is not satisfied by the utterance of the truth that a value of our system of criminal justice is "to respect the inviolability of the human personality" and to require government to produce the evidence against the accused by its own independent labors. More than the human dignity of the accused is involved; the human personality of others in the society must also be preserved. Thus the values reflected by the privilege are not the sole desideratum; society's interest in the general security is of equal weight.

The obvious underpinning of the Court's decision is a deep-seated distrust of all confessions. As the Court declares that the accused may not be interrogated without counsel present, absent a waiver of the right to counsel, and as the Court all but admonishes the lawyer to advise the accused to remain silent, the result adds up to a judicial judgment that evidence from the accused should not be used against him in any way, whether compelled or not. This is the not so subtle overtone of the opinion that it is inherently wrong for the police to gather evidence from the accused himself. And this is precisely the nub of this dissent. I see nothing wrong or immoral, and certainly nothing unconstitutional, with the police asking a suspect whom they have reasonable cause to arrest whether or not he killed his wife or with confronting him with the evidence on which the arrest was based, at least where he has been plainly advised that he may remain completely silent. * * * Particularly when corroborated, as where the police have confirmed the accused's disclosure of the hiding place of implements or fruits of the crime, such confessions have the highest reliability and significantly contribute to the certitude with which we may believe the accused is guilty. * * *

Much of the trouble with the Court's new rule is that it will operate indiscriminately in all criminal cases, regardless of the severity of the crime or the circumstances involved. It applies to every defendant whether the professional criminal or one committing a crime of momentary passion who is not part and parcel of organized crime. It will slow down the investigation and the apprehension of confederates in those cases where time is of the essence, such as kidnapping, [those] involving the national security, [and] some organized crime situations. In the latter context the lawyer who arrives may also be the lawyer for the defendants' colleagues and can be relied upon to insure that no breach of the organization's security takes place even though the accused may feel that the best thing he can do is to cooperate.

At the same time, the Court's *per se* approach may not be justified on the ground that it provides a "bright line" permitting the authorities to judge in advance whether interrogation may safely be pursued without jeopardizing the admissibility of any information obtained as a consequence. Nor can it be claimed that judicial time and effort, assuming that is a relevant consideration, will be conserved because of the ease of application of the new rule. Today's decision leaves open such questions as whether the accused was in custody, whether his statements were spontaneous or the product of interrogation, whether the accused has effectively waived his rights, and whether nontestimonial evidence introduced at trial is the fruit of statements made during a prohibited interrogation, all of which are certain to prove productive of uncertainty during investigation and litigation during prosecution. For all these reasons, if further restrictions on police interrogation are desirable at this time, a more flexible approach makes much more sense than the Court's constitutional strait-jacket which forecloses more discriminating treatment by legislative or rule-making pronouncements.

Justice Kennedy's Question About Miranda's Constitutional Status

During the oral arguments in *Dickerson v. United States* (p. 677), which took place 34 years after *Miranda*, U.S. Solicitor General Seth Waxman maintained that a 1968 federal statutory provision (discussed immediately below), which purported to replace *Miranda* with the pre-*Miranda* "voluntariness" test, was unconstitutional. He told the Court that Congress lacked the authority to "overrule" *Miranda* because *Miranda* was a constitutional rule. When reminded by Justice O'Connor that in the past the Department of Justice had taken the position that the *Miranda* warnings are not constitutionally required, Mr. Waxman agreed they are not. At this point Justice Kennedy interrupted: "You say the warnings are not constitutionally required, but the *Miranda* rule is constitutional. . . . I don't understand that."

How would you respond to Justice Kennedy?

CAN (DID) CONGRESS "REPEAL" *MIRANDA*? (AND WHY TREATMENT OF THIS ISSUE SHOULD BE POSTPONED)

A provision of Title II of the Omnibus Crime Control and Safe Streets Act of 1968, a provision usually called § 3501 (because of its designation under Title 18 of the U.S. Code), purports, in effect, to "repeal" or "overrule" *Miranda* and to reinstate the old "totality of circumstances"-"voluntariness" test.[a] At various places, the *Miranda* Court appears to say that it is interpreting the Fifth Amendment. At one point, for example, the *Miranda* Court states that application of "the constitutional principles" discussed in its opinion to the four cases before it leads to the conclusion that in each instance "statements were obtained under circumstances that did not meet constitutional standards for protection of the privilege." (See p. 581 supra.) Thus, it seems highly unlikely that the Court would have upheld § 3501 if it had considered its validity shortly after it was enacted.[b] But the Court did not do so. Indeed, it did not decide the fate of § 3501 until it handed down *Dickerson v. United States*—in the year 2000.[c]

In the thirty-four years between *Miranda* and *Dickerson* the Burger and Rehnquist Court's characterization of and comments about *Miranda* furnished good reason to believe that the Court's thinking about that famous case had changed dramatically since it was first decided—and therefore that § 3501's attempt to overturn *Miranda* might well succeed.

Although it was not an easy call, the editors of this book concluded that since a number of the post-*Miranda* cases seemed to downgrade and to "deconstitutionalize" that landmark decision, e.g., by referring to the *Miranda* warnings as "prophylactic" and "not themselves rights protected by the Constitution," it would be preferable to postpone discussion of § 3501 and *Dickerson* until the students had read and thought about (a) the many cases applying and explaining *Miranda* from 1966–2000 and (b) what various Justices had to say, in all that time, about the desirability, efficacy and legitimacy of *Miranda*.

Here as elsewhere, of course, reasonable people may differ. Those instructors who would rather discuss the constitutionality of § 3501 at this point in the course, not later, need only turn to pp. 677 to 690 to do so.

FORTY–SIX YEARS WITH *MIRANDA:* AN OVERVIEW

Because *Miranda* was the centerpiece of the Warren Court's "revolution in American criminal procedure" and the prime target of those who thought the

---

a. The text of § 3501 is set forth at p. 676.

b. Indeed, in *Orozco v. Texas*, 394 U.S. 324 (1969), the Court, per Black, J., told us that it was holding a confession inadmissible because obtaining it "in the absence of the required warnings was a flat violation of the Self–Incrimination Clause of the Fifth Amendment as construed in *Miranda*."

c. *Dickerson* is set forth at p. 677.

courts were "soft" on criminals, almost everyone expected the so-called Burger Court to treat *Miranda* unkindly. And it did. It did not help *Miranda* that Richard Nixon was elected President in 1968 and made four Supreme Court appointments in his first term: Warren Burger, Harry Blackmun, Lewis Powell, Jr., and William Rehnquist. The new president did his best to make sure none of his appointees were enamored of the Warren Court's "revolution" in criminal procedure. And none of them were.

As one commentator noted, Presidential candidate Richard Nixon reduced "the bewildering problems of crime in the United States" to "a war between the 'peace forces' and the 'criminal forces.'" Francis A. Allen, *The Judicial Quest for Penal Justice: The Warren Court and the Criminal Cases*, 1975 U.Ill.L.F. 518, 539 (referring to Mr. Nixon's position paper on crime, *Toward Freedom from Fear*, dated May 8, 1968).

A well-publicized 1967 speech by then-Judge Warren Burger caught the attention of future President Nixon. The speech deplored the high rate of crime and criticized America's ineffective legal system. If it sounded a good deal like a Nixon campaign speech it probably was—because Nixon referred to and quoted from the speech during his 1968 campaign. See John W. Dean, *The Rehnquist Choice* 13 (2001).

As for future Justice Rehnquist, in 1969, when he was in his new post as Assistant Attorney General, in charge of the Office of Legal Counsel, he wrote a memorandum to Associate Deputy Attorney General John W. Dean, proposing that the President appoint a Commission to reexamine such cases as *Escobedo* and *Miranda* "to determine whether the overriding public interest in law enforcement * * * requires a constitutional amendment." (Because Attorney General John Mitchell was not sure that the Nixon administration could control such a commission, Rehnquist's proposal never went beyond a Dean–Mitchell meeting about the matter.)

Warren Burger and William Rehnquist were among the most "police-friendly" Justices in Supreme Court history. Each played a prominent role in downsizing and dismantling *Miranda*. Chief Justice Burger administered the first blow to *Miranda* in *Harris v. New York*, 401 U.S. 222 (1971). Justice Rehnquist delivered the second blow in *Michigan v. Tucker*, 417 U.S. 433 (1974).

Harris held that statements preceded by defective warnings, and thus inadmissible to establish the prosecution's case-in-chief, could nevertheless be used to impeach the defendant's credibility if he chose to take the stand in his own defense.[a] The Chief Justice recognized, but seemed unperturbed by the fact, that some language in the *Miranda* opinion could be read as barring the use of *Miranda*-defective statements *for any purpose*. The Chief Justice brushed off the language by noting that discussion of the impeachment issue "was not at all necessary to the Court's holding and cannot be regarded as controlling."

As Geoffrey Stone has observed, however, *The Miranda Doctrine in the Burger Court*, 1977 Sup.Ct.Rev. 99, 107–08, "*Miranda* was deliberately structured

---

a. The Court went a step beyond *Harris* in *Oregon v. Hass* (1975) (p. 912). In *Hass*, after being advised of his rights, the defendant *asserted* them. Nevertheless, the police refused to honor his request for a lawyer and continued to question him. The Court ruled that in this situation, too, the resulting incriminating statements could be used for impeachment purposes. Since many suspects waive their rights and make incriminating statements even after the receipt of complete *Miranda* warnings, *Harris* might have been explained–and contained–on the ground that permitting impeachment use of statements acquired without complete warnings would not greatly encourage the police to violate *Miranda*. But now that *Hass* is on the books, when a suspect asserts his rights, it seems the police have virtually nothing to lose and much to gain by continuing to question him.

See also *Jenkins v. Anderson* (1980) and *Fletcher v. Weir* (1982), both discussed in Ch. 11, § 4.

to canvass a wide range of problems, many of which were not directly raised by the cases before the Court. This approach was thought necessary in order to give 'concrete guidelines for law enforcement agencies and courts to follow.' " To put it another way, a technical reading of *Miranda*, such as the one utilized by the Chief Justice in *Harris*, would lead to the conclusion that the great bulk of the 60–page majority opinion in *Miranda* was mere dictum and thus not "controlling."

After *Harris* came *Michigan v. Tucker* (1974). This was a very appealing case from the prosecution's point of view. First of all, the police questioning—which was not preceded by a complete set of warnings—occurred *before Miranda* was decided. However, the defendant's trial took place after *Miranda* was handed down. Thus, *Miranda* was barely applicable.[b] Second, *Tucker* did not deal with the admissibility of the defendant's own statements—they had been excluded–but only with the testimony of a witness whose identity had been discovered *as a result of* questioning the suspect without giving him a full set of warnings.

Justice Rehnquist's opinion for the Court, holding the witness's testimony admissible, can be read very narrowly. But the opinion contains a good deal of broad language—and, so far as defenders of *Miranda* are concerned, quite mischievous language.

At one point, Justice Rehnquist seemed to equate (a) "compulsion" within the meaning of the privilege against self-incrimination and (b) "coercion" under the "voluntariness" test. This is puzzling. "Compulsion" and "coercion" do have similar meanings when one turns to the dictionary. But they have different connotations when one takes into account their different constitutional bases, legal history and legal meaning.

It is hard to see how reading *Miranda* to say that the privilege is not violated unless and until the pressures on the custodial suspect are strong enough to render any statement obtained from him "coerced" under the "voluntariness" test makes sense. If *Miranda* were to be read this way, what would it have accomplished? The due process test for the admissibility of confessions *already* prohibited the use of coerced confessions. As Geoffrey Stone has observed, "Mr. Justice Rehnquist's conclusion that there is a violation of the Self–Incrimination Clause only if a statement is involuntary under traditional standards is an outright rejection of the core premise of *Miranda*" Stone, supra, at 118–10.

For *Miranda* supporters, the most troubling aspect of Justice Rehnquist's opinion in *Tucker* was his effort to drive a wedge between the privilege against self-incrimination and the *Miranda* rights. At various places in his opinion, Rehnquist called the *Miranda* rules "prophylactic rules," "prophylactic standards" and "procedural safeguards." Does this make the *Miranda* rights "second-class rights" (if they are constitutional rights at all)? At other places Justice Rehnquist called the *Miranda* rights or rules "protective *guidelines*" (emphasis added) and "*recommended* 'procedural safeguards' " (emphasis added). Does this mean that they are "third-class" rights?

Although this is not at all clear from Justice Rehnquist's discussion in his *Tucker* opinion, not once in his 60–page *Miranda* opinion did Chief Justice Warren call the *Miranda* rights prophylactic rules, procedural safeguards or protective guidelines. What is probably more significant, not once did any of the *Miranda* dissenters do so either. The *Miranda* dissenters did maintain that the *Miranda* decision was unwise and untimely. But not once did any of them complain that the majority opinion represented an "extraconstitutional" or "illegitimate" exercise of the Supreme Court's authority to review state-court judgments.

---

b. The Court held, that *Miranda* affected only those cases in which *the trial* began after that decision. *Johnson v. New Jersey*, 384 U.S. 719 (1966). The Court probably should have held that *Miranda* affected only *those confessions obtained* after the date of the decision.

Although language in *Miranda* could be read as establishing a *per se* rule against any further questioning of one who has asserted his "right to silence" (as opposed to his *right to counsel,* discussed below), *Michigan v. Mosley* (1975) (p. 635) held that under certain circumstances (and what they are is unclear), if they cease questioning on the spot, the police may "try again," and succeed at a later interrogation session. At the very least, it seems, the police must promptly terminate the original interrogation, resume questioning after the passage of a significant period of time, and give the suspect a fresh set of warnings at the outset of the second session. Whether *Mosley* requires more is a matter of dispute.

The Court has read "custody" or *"custodial* interrogation" rather narrowly. *Oregon v. Mathiason* (1977) (p. 602) and *California v. Beheler* (1983) (p. 602) illustrate that even *police station* questioning designed to produce incriminating statements is not necessarily "custodial interrogation." The result in *Mathiason* is more easily defensible because the suspect went down to the station house on his own after an officer had requested that he meet him there at a convenient time and he had agreed to do so. In *Beheler,* however, the suspect went to the station house in the company of the police. (He was said to have "voluntarily agreed" to accompany the police.)

Recently, however, a 5–4 majority, per newly appointed Justice Sotomayor, held that "the age of a child subjected to a police questioning is relevant to the custody analysis of *Miranda.*"[c] Rejecting the argument that a child's age has no place in the custody analysis, no matter how young the child is, the Court told us: "So long as the child's age was known to the officer at the time of the interview, or would have been objectively apparent to any reasonable officer, including age as part of the custody analysis requires officers neither to consider circumstances 'unknowable' to them, nor to 'anticipate the frailties or idiosyncrasies of the particular suspect whom they question.'"

Dissenting Justice Alito, joined by Chief Justice Roberts and Justices Scalia and Thomas, maintained that one of *Miranda*'s chief strengths has been "the ease and clarity of its application" and that "[a] key contributor to this clarity, at least up until now, has been *Miranda*'s objective reasonable-person test for determining custody." Justice Alito did not deny that many suspects under 18 are more susceptible to police pressure than the average adult, but he was quick to add that "many persons *over* the age of 18 are also more susceptible to police pressure than the hypothetical reasonable person. Yet the *Miranda* custody standard has never accounted for the personal characteristics of these or any other individual defendants." Alito failed to see why age is different from one's intelligence, education, or cultural background.

In *Brown v. Illinois* (1975) (p. 895), the Court declined an invitation to do serious damage to the Fourth Amendment by making the *Miranda* warnings, in effect, a "cure-all." The Court rejected the contention that the giving of the warnings should purge the taint of any preceding illegal arrest—a view that would have permitted the admissibility at trial of any resulting incriminating statements to be considered without regard to the illegal arrest and thus would have encouraged such arrests.[d]

---

c. The case involved a 13-year-old seventh grade student suspected of two home break-ins. He was taken out of his classroom by a uniformed police officer and brought to a closed-door conference room. There he was met by two school administrators and a second police officer, a juvenile officer with the local police force. Prior to the questioning, J.D.B. was given neither the *Miranda* warnings nor the opportunity to speak to his legal guardian. Nor was he told he was free to leave the room.

d. *Brown* was reaffirmed and fortified in *Dunaway v. New York* (1979) and *Taylor v. Alabama* (1982), discussed at p. 897.

In the early 1980's *Miranda* seemed to enjoy a "second honeymoon." Considering the alternatives (e.g., a mechanical approach to "interrogation," one limited to situations where the police directly address a suspect), the Court gave the key term "interrogation" a fairly generous reading in *Rhode Island v. Innis* (1980) (p. 608). Although the *Innis* case itself involved police "speech," the Court's definition of "interrogation" embraces interrogation techniques that do not. The following year, in *Edwards v. Arizona* (1981) (p. 636), the Court reinvigorated *Miranda* in an important respect. In effect, it added a "bright line" test to the "bright line" *Miranda* rules. Indeed, one might say that it established a new "prophylactic rule" that built on *Miranda*'s "prophylactic rules."

Sharply distinguishing *Michigan v. Mosley* (p. 635) (which dealt with a suspect who asserted his "right to remain silent"), the *Edwards* Court held that when a suspect asserts his right to counsel, the police *cannot* "try again." Under these circumstances, *Edwards* told us, a suspect cannot be questioned anew *"until* counsel has been made available to him, *unless* [he] himself *initiates* further communication, exchanges or conversations with the police" (emphasis added).

The Court has read *Edwards* quite expansively. In *Arizona v. Roberson* (1988) (p. 636), a 6–2 majority, per Stevens, J., held that once a suspect asserts his *Miranda-Edwards* right to counsel, the police cannot even initiate interrogation about crimes *other than* the one for which the suspect has invoked his right to counsel. In *Minnick v. Mississippi* (1990) (p. 637), the Court expanded the *Edwards* rule still further. It held–over a strong protest by dissenting Justice Scalia that this "is the latest stage of prophylaxis built upon prophylaxis"–that when counsel is requested, interrogation must cease and officials may not reinstate interrogation without counsel present, *whether or not* the accused has consulted with his attorney *in the meantime.*[e]

As a general matter, however, the post-Warren Courts' treatment of *Edwards* and its progeny was unusual. In the main, the Courts that followed the Warren Court have read *Miranda* narrowly and grudgingly. Moreover, the language in *Michigan v. Tucker* (1974) which seemed to "deconstitutionalize" *Miranda* began to reappear.

In *New York v. Quarles* (1984) (p. 621), a 6–3 majority, per Rehnquist, J., held that "a situation posing a threat to the public safety outweighs the need for the prophylactic rule protecting the Fifth Amendment privilege." A year later, the Court ruled in *Oregon v. Elstad* (1985) (p. 698) that the fact that the police had earlier obtained a statement from a custodial suspect (when they questioned him in his own home, without advising him of his *Miranda* rights), did not bar the admissibility of a subsequent statement (obtained at the stationhouse) when, this time, the police did comply with *Miranda*.

There is, emphasized Justice O'Connor for a 6–3 majority in *Elstad*, "a vast difference between the direct consequences flowing from coercion of a confession by physical violence [and] the uncertain consequences of disclosure of a 'guilty secret' freely given in response to an unwarned but noncoercive question as in this case." The *Elstad* case could plausibly be read as saying that a failure to comply with *Miranda* (as opposed to an "involuntary" or "coerced" confession) is not a violation of a *real* or *core* constitutional right (but only a prophylactic rule or rule of evidence designed to implement the privilege against self-incrimination). Therefore, a failure to satisfy *Miranda* is not entitled to, or worthy of, the "fruit of the

---

e. Speaking for a 7–2 majority, Justice Kennedy observed: "*Edwards* conserves judicial resources which would otherwise be expended in making difficult determinations of voluntariness, and implements the protections of *Miranda* in practical and straight forward terms. The rule provides 'clear and unequivocal' guidelines to the law enforcement profession."

Is this explanation and defense of *Edwards* an explanation and defense of *Miranda* as well?

poisonous tree" doctrine. Thus, unlike evidence obtained as the result of an unreasonable search or a coerced confession, secondary evidence derived from a failure to satisfy *Miranda* need not, and should not, be suppressed as the tainted fruit.

Tucker, Quarles and *Elstad* encouraged critics of *Miranda* to believe that some day the new Court would overrule that much-criticized case. Instead, in *Dickerson v. United States* (2000) (p. 677), in an opinion written by Chief Justice Rehnquist (!), the Court struck down a federal statute purporting to abolish *Miranda*, removing any doubt that "*Miranda* is a constitutional decision of this Court."[f]

Logically, *Dickerson* would seem to undermine those cases which viewed the *Miranda* rights as prophylactic rules. But in his opinion for the Court in *Dickerson*, Chief Justice Rehnquist did not repudiate any of these cases. Indeed, one might say he worked hard to avoid doing so.

A post-*Dickerson* case, *United States v. Patane* (2004) (p. 699), indicates that *Elstad* has survived *Dickerson* completely unscathed. In *Patane*, a detective questioned the defendant about the location of a Glock pistol he was supposed to own without administering a complete set of *Miranda* warnings. Mr. Patane told the detective where the weapon was and the police soon found it. A 5–4 majority of the Court held the pistol admissible.

There was no opinion of the Court. Justice Thomas announced the judgment of the Court and delivered the three-Justice plurality opinion he had written.[g] Since Justice Scalia and Thomas had both dissented in *Dickerson*, the fact that Scalia joined Thomas's plurality opinion in *Patane* is not surprising. But the fact that the Chief Justice did is. In a post-*Dickerson* confession case, the two strong dissenters in *Dickerson* and the author of the majority opinion in that case made strange bedfellows.

At no point in his *Dickerson* opinion did Justice Rehnquist contrast *Miranda* violations with a "core" violation of the Self–Incrimination Clause itself. Nowhere in *Dickerson* did he call the *Miranda* rules "prophylactic." However, in his *Patane* plurality opinion, the opinion which Rehnquist joined, Justice Thomas repeatedly characterized the *Miranda* rules as "prophylactic" and repeatedly contrasted these rules with "the core protection afforded by the Self–Incrimination Clause." Thomas also told us, in language very similar to that used in *Elstad*, that because prophylactic rules such as the *Miranda* rules "necessarily sweep beyond the actual protections of the Self–Incrimination Clause, any further extension of these rules must be justified by its necessity for the protection of the actual right against compelled self-incrimination."

Miranda supporters will find little to cheer about in Justice Kennedy's concurring opinion in *Patane*. He did not seem at all troubled by the fact that the Thomas plurality had repeated the old *Tucker-Quarles–Elstad* rhetoric about *Miranda* four years after *Dickerson*. Indeed, Kennedy gave no indication that he thought *Dickerson* had any bearing on the *Patane* case.

Justice Kennedy did mention *Dickerson* once in his concurring opinion—but only to say that he "agree[d] with the plurality" that *Dickerson* did *not* undermine such cases as *Elstad* and *Quarles*. Nor is that all. Kennedy went on to say that *Dickerson* had cited those cases "in support" of its opinion.[h]

---

f. For speculation about why Chief Justice Rehnquist, widely regarded as a long-time critic of *Miranda*, wrote the opinion of the Court reaffirming its constitutionality, see pp. 685 to 690, infra.

g. Justice Thomas's plurality opinion prevailed only because Justice Kennedy, joined by O'Connor, J., concurred in the result.

h. *Missouri v. Seibert* (2004), a companion case to *Patane*, is set forth at p. 702 infra and discussed in the Notes and Questions following this case.

Miranda suffered another blow in BERGHUIS v. THOMPKINS (2010) (p. 651), a case that underscores the distinction between the right to remain silent and the right not to be questioned. Defendant Thompkins, a murder suspect, was advised of his *Miranda* rights. He declined to sign a form indicating that he understood his rights. But neither did he explicitly assert any of his rights. Without specifically asking Thompkins whether he wanted to assert his rights, the police began to question him about the murder. He remained largely silent during the questioning, giving only a few very limited verbal responses such as "yeah" or "I don't know."

About 2 hours and 45 minutes into the interrogation, a detective asked Thompkins three questions: (1) "Do you believe in God?" (2) "Do you pray to God?" (3) "Do you pray to God to forgive you for shooting that boy down?" Thompkins answered "Yes" to all three questions. But he refused to make a written confession. The interrogation ended about 15 minutes later.

A 5–4 majority, per Kennedy, J., held that once the police have advised a custodial suspect of his *Miranda* rights, and the suspect has not asserted any of his rights, the police need not obtain a waiver of these rights before proceeding to interrogate him: "a suspect who has received and understood the *Miranda* warnings, and has not invoked his *Miranda* rights, waives the right to remain silent by making an uncoerced statement to the police." However, Thompkins refused to make a written confession and about 15 minutes later the interrogation ended.

Dissenting Justice Sotomayor, joined by Stevens, Ginsburg and Breyer, JJ., maintained that "even when warnings have been administered and a suspect has not affirmatively invoked his rights, statements made in custodial interrogation may not be admitted [in] the prosecution's case in chief 'unless and until' the prosecution demonstrates that an individual 'knowingly and intelligently waive[d] [his] rights.' *Miranda*." The dissenters failed to see how the prosecution "met its 'heavy burden' of proof [to establish waiver] on a record consisting of three one-word answers, following 2 hours and 45 minutes of silence punctuated by a few largely nonverbal responses to unidentified questions."

Cases like *Patane* and *Berghuis v. Thompkins* have led various commentators to say that *Miranda* is "a failure," "largely dead" or the victim of "stealth overruling." See Barry Friedman, *The Wages of Stealth Overruling (with Particular Attention to Miranda v. Arizona)*, 99 Geo.L.J. 1 (2010); Sandra Guerra Thompson, *Evading Miranda: How Seibert and Patane Failed to "Save" Miranda*, 40 Val.U.L.Rev. 645 (2006); Charles D. Weisselberg, *Mourning Miranda*, 96 Calif.L.Rev. 1519 (2008).

"There is one quite persuasive—perhaps even obvious—explanation [for] why Justices engage in stealth overruling," observes Professor Friedman, supra, at 33, and that is "avoiding the publicity attendant explicit overruling." The reaffirmation of *Miranda*'s constitutionality in *Dickerson* (2000) "occurred in the glare of publicity, and polls at the time showed extremely strong public support for *Miranda*." Id. at 33–34.

"But "[s]tealth overruling imposes its own costs. The least of these, though certainly of substance, is that it confuses the law, eliminating the traditional virtues of transparency and predictability. Somewhat graver is the blow taken to the Court's long-term authority as officials and lower courts are taught to treat precedents casually once given the wink from above. It is somewhat surprising the Justices cannot see this long-term threat to their authority. Most seriously, stealth overruling obscures the path of constitutional law from public view, allowing the Court to alter constitutional meaning without public supervision." Id. at 63.

APPLYING AND EXPLAINING *MIRANDA*

1. *"Exploiting a criminal's ignorance or stupidity"; "intelligent" waivers vs. "wise" ones.* Consider **STATE v. McKNIGHT**, 243 A.2d 240 (N.J.1968), per WEINTRAUB, C.J.:

"The Constitution is not at all offended when a guilty man stubs his toe. On the contrary, it is decent to hope that he will. [T]he Fifth Amendment does not say that a man shall not be permitted to incriminate himself, or that he shall not be persuaded to do so. It says no more than that a man shall not be 'compelled' to give evidence against himself. [It] is consonant with good morals, and the Constitution, to exploit a criminal's ignorance or stupidity in the detectional process. This must be so if Government is to succeed in its primary mission to live free from criminal attack.

" * * * Nowhere does *Miranda* suggest that the waiver of counsel at the detectional stage would not be 'knowing' or 'intelligent' if the suspect did not understand the law relating to the crime, the possible defenses, and the hazards of talking without the aid of counsel, or if the suspect was not able to protect his interests without such aid, [or] if it was not 'wise' of the prisoner to forego counsel or the right to silence. * * * However relevant to 'waiver' of the right to counsel at trial or in connection with a plea of guilty, those factors are foreign to the investigational scene where the detection of crime is the legitimate aim.

"Hence if a defendant has been given the *Miranda* warnings, if the coercion of custodial interrogation was thus dissipated, his 'waiver' was no less 'voluntary' and 'knowing' and 'intelligent' because he misconceived the inculpatory thrust of the facts he admitted, or because he thought that what he said could not be used because it was only oral or because he had his fingers crossed, or because he could well have used a lawyer. A man need not have the understanding of a lawyer to waive one."

See also *Collins v. Brierly,* 492 F.2d 735 (3d Cir.1974) (en banc): "*Miranda* speaks of 'intelligent' waiver [in the sense] that the individual must know of his available options before deciding what he thinks best suits his particular situation. In this context intelligence is not equated with wisdom." Consider, too, James J. Tomkovicz, *Standards for Invocation and Waiver of Counsel in Confession Contexts,* 71 Iowa L.Rev. 975, 1049 (1986): "The policies of the fifth amendment privilege do not demand rationality, intelligence, or knowledge, but only a voluntary choice not to remain silent." Is this (ought this be) so?

2. *Do the Miranda warnings actually induce some suspects to talk rather than to remain silent?* Consider Steven B. Duke, *Does Miranda Protect the Innocent or the Guilty?,* 10 Chapman L.Rev. 551, 558–60 (2007):

"The warnings implicitly suggest to the suspect that the police are respectful of the suspect's rights, that the police are not only law-abiding, but that they are also fair and objective. If delivered with the proper tone, the warnings could even suggest to the suspect that the investigators are sympathetic, naive or gullible. Surely Patrick Malone is right that '[s]killfully presented, the *Miranda* warnings themselves sound chords of fairness and sympathy at the outset of the interrogation. * * * ' If a cop tells the suspect he need not answer, that he can have an attorney if he wants, is that not reassuring? [The] warnings may also increase the suspect's bravado during the early stages of interrogation, which of course facilitates the interrogators. So, against the guilty who are induced *not* to talk by the warnings, we have to compare the guilty who *are* induced to talk. Which is the larger group? Nobody knows. It seems reasonable to speculate, however, that after four decades of living with *Miranda*, the small number of suspects who are induced to remain silent by the administration of the warnings is getting even smaller while the number encouraged to talk is at least remaining stable."

3. *Adequacy of warnings.* Consider DUCKWORTH v. EAGAN, 492 U.S. 195 (1989), which arose as follows: Respondent Eagan, suspected of murdering a woman, denied any involvement in the crime. He agreed to go to police headquarters for further questioning. At the stationhouse an officer read him a waiver form which provided, inter alia:

"You have a right to talk to a lawyer for advice before we ask you any questions, and to have him with you during questioning. You have the right to the advice and presence of a lawyer even if you cannot afford to hire one. *We have no way of giving you a lawyer, but one will be appointed for you, if you wish, if and when you go to court.* If you wish to answer questions now without a lawyer present, you have the right to stop answering questions at any time. You also have the right to stop answering at any time until you've talked to a lawyer." (Emphasis added.)

Eagan signed the waiver form, but again denied any involvement in the crime. He was then placed in the "lock up" at police headquarters. Some 29 hours later, the police met with Eagan again. Before questioning him, an officer read from a differently worded waiver form. Eagan signed it and then confessed to stabbing the woman. A 5–4 majority, per Rehnquist, C.J., concluded that the initial warnings given to Eagan at police headquarters "touched all of the bases required by *Miranda*":

"*Miranda* has not been limited to station-house questioning, and the officer in the field may not always have access to printed *Miranda* warnings, or he may inadvertently depart from routine practice, particularly if a suspect requests an elaboration of the warnings. *Michigan v. Tucker.* [Reviewing courts] need not examine *Miranda* warnings as if construing a will or defining the terms of an easement. The inquiry is simply whether the warnings reasonably 'convey[y] to [a suspect] his rights as required by *Miranda.*' *California v. Prysock*, 453 U.S. 355 (1981) (per curiam) [where, in the course of upholding the challenged warnings, the Supreme Court observed: "This Court has never indicated that the 'rigidity' of *Miranda* extends to the precise formulation of the warnings given a criminal defendant."]

"[On federal habeas corpus, the U.S. Court of Appeals for the Seventh Circuit thought that the] 'if and when you go to court' language suggested that 'only those accused who can afford an attorney have the right to have one present before answering any questions,' and 'implie[d] that if the accused does not 'go to court,' i.e., the government does not file charges, the accused is not entitled to [counsel] at all.'

"[This] instruction accurately described the procedure for the appointment of counsel in Indiana, [where] counsel is appointed at the defendant's initial appearance in court and formal charges must be filed at or before that hearing. We think it must be relatively commonplace for a suspect, after receiving *Miranda* warnings, to ask *when* he will obtain counsel. The 'if and when you go to court' advice simply anticipates that question. Second, *Miranda* does not require that attorneys be producible on call, but only that the suspect be informed, as here, that he has the right to an attorney before and during questioning, and that an attorney would be appointed for him if he could not afford one. [If] the police cannot provide appointed counsel, *Miranda* requires only that the police not question a suspect unless he waives his right to counsel. Here, respondent did just that. * * *."

Dissenting Justice Marshall, joined by Brennan, Blackmun and Stevens, JJ., maintained:

"[Upon] hearing the warnings given in this case, a suspect would likely conclude that no lawyer would be provided until trial. In common parlance, 'going to court' is synonymous with 'going to trial.' Furthermore, the negative implication of the caveat is that, if the suspect is never taken to court, he 'is not entitled to an attorney at all.' An unwitting suspect harboring uncertainty on this score is precisely the sort of person who may feel compelled to talk 'voluntarily' to the police, without the presence of counsel, in an effort to extricate himself from his predicament * * *."

NOTES AND QUESTIONS

(a) *Access to a Miranda card.* An officer "in the field," notes the Court, "may not always have access to printed *Miranda* warnings" or may "inadvertently depart from routine practice, particularly if a suspect requests an elaboration of the warnings." What bearing should this have on a case like *Duckworth v. Eagan,* where the suspect was questioned at police headquarters and never asked for an elaboration of the warnings? Moreover, would it be burdensome or unreasonable to require police officers always to carry a standard *Miranda* card?

(b) *Anticipating a suspect's questions.* Should it be the business of the police to "anticipate" a suspect's questions? Does this confuse the role of the police officer with that of the defense lawyer? "Anticipating" a question by Eagan, the police informed him that if he could not afford a lawyer "we have no way of giving you a lawyer" before or during questioning. What impact could that information have other than to make it *less likely* that Eagan would assert his right to appointed counsel? Should the police have "anticipated" *another* question: "If you cannot give me a lawyer now, what happens if I ask for one now?" Under *Edwards v. Arizona* (1981) (p. 636) would the truthful answer to that question have been: "Then, we would be very restricted as to how we could proceed. We would have to cease questioning on the spot. And we could not resume questioning at a later time. We could not talk to you any more about this case unless and until you yourself initiated further communication with us." What would the impact of that information be other than to make it *more likely* that Eagan would assert his right to appointed counsel?

Are the police (should the police be) free to "anticipate" those questions they would like to answer and free *not* to "anticipate" those questions they would rather not answer? Does *Duckworth* give them that freedom? See Kamisar, *Duckworth v. Eagan: A Little–Noticed Miranda Case that May Cause Much Mischief,* 25 Crim.L.Bull. 550 (1989).

(c) *Complying with Miranda.* According to *Miranda,* "if police propose to interrogate a person they must make known to him that he is entitled to a lawyer and that if he cannot afford one, a lawyer will be provided for him prior to any interrogation." Was Eagan told, in effect, that if he could not afford a lawyer, one would *not* be—and *could not* be—provided for him prior to (or during) any questioning?

(d) *"For or against you."* Suppose, instead of giving the second *Miranda* warning the way it is usually given, an officer advised a suspect: "Anything you say *can be used for or* against you." Isn't it true that sometimes something a suspect tells the police *might be* used *for* him? In light of *Duckworth v. Eagan,* would this version of the second warning constitute compliance with *Miranda?*[a]

---

a. Consider, too, *Florida v. Powell,* 130 S.Ct. 1195 (2010). Before making an incriminating statement, defendant was advised that he had "the right to talk to a lawyer before answering any of [the officers'] questions" and that he could invoke this right "at any time * * * during the interview." Rejecting the argument that the advice given was misleading because it could lead a

4. *Need for police admonitions in addition to the four Miranda warnings.*

(a) *The consequences of silence.* If, as *Miranda* points out, many suspects will assume that "silence in the face of accusation is itself damning and will bode ill when presented to a jury" (text at fn. 37), should the suspect be explicitly advised not only that any statement he makes may be used against him but that his silence may *not* be used against him? Isn't a suspect likely to ask himself most urgently: "How do I get out of this mess and avoid looking guilty?" Absent assurance on this point, are many suspects likely to assert their *Miranda* rights?

Convinced that a major reason Mirandized suspects talk to the police is that many of them "naturally believe, albeit incorrectly, that remaining silent will make them 'look guilty' and will be used against them as evidence of guilt," Mark A. Godsey, *Reformulating the Miranda Warnings in Light of Contemporary Law & Understandings*, 90 Minn.L.Rev. 781, 783, 793 (2006), proposes that the first two warnings "should be buttressed by a new 'right to silence' warning that provides something to the effect of: 'If you choose to remain silent, your silence will not be used against you as evidence to suggest that you committed a crime because you refused to speak.' "

An interrogator can truthfully tell a suspect that once the police advise him of his right to remain silent the prosecution may not comment at trial on his reliance on that right, but can he truthfully tell him that his silence will not be used against him *in any way?* For example, won't the suspect's silence affect the decision to investigate his involvement in the crime further? The decision to prosecute? See Sheldon Elsen & Arthur Rosett, *Protections for the Suspect under Miranda v. Arizona,* 67 Colum.L.Rev. 645, 654–55 (1967).

(b) *The right to be told that if he chooses to talk to the police at the outset, he may terminate the conversation at any time.* The suspect has the right to change his mind and cut off the questioning at any time. But should he be explicitly warned that he has such a right? Yes, maintains Godsey at 806–07, proposing that a suspect be warned: "If you choose to talk, you may change your mind and remain silent at any time, even if you have already spoken." The standard *Miranda* card used by the FBI, notes Godsey, contains a similar warning.

But would such a warning lead a suspect to lower his guard and start talking to the police? Once a suspect chooses to do so and is confronted with inconsistencies or contradictions in his story or assurances by the police that the crime he is suspected of committing is not nearly as serious as he believes, is he likely to bring the conversation to a halt?

(c) *The right to be made aware of the subject matter of the questioning.*

In COLORADO v. SPRING, 479 U.S. 564 (1987), a 7–2 majority, per POWELL, J., held that "a suspect's awareness of all the possible subjects of questioning in advance of interrogation is not relevant to determining whether the suspect

---

suspect to believe that he could only consult with a lawyer *before* questioning and was not entitled to a lawyer's presence *throughout* the interrogation, a 7–2 majority, per Ginsburg, J., concluded that the warning satisfied *Miranda*: "The first statement communicated that Powell could consult with a lawyer before answering any particular question, and the second statement confirmed that he could exercise that right while the interrogation was underway. In combination, the two warnings reasonably conveyed Powell's right to have an attorney present, not only at the outset of interrogation, but at all times."

Dissenting Justice Stevens, joined by Breyer, J., maintained that the warning "entirely failed" to inform the defendant of "the separate and distinct right 'to have counsel present during any questioning.' " According to the dissenters, the case marked "the first time the Court has approved a warning, which, if given its natural reading, entirely omitted an essential element of a suspect's rights."

voluntarily, knowingly, and intelligently waived his Fifth Amendment privilege." The case arose as follows:

An informant told agents of the Bureau of Alcohol, Tobacco and Firearms (ATF) that Spring (a) was engaged in the interstate shipment of stolen firearms and (b) had been involved in a Colorado killing. The ATF agents set up an undercover operation to purchase firearms from Spring. On March 30, ATF agents arrested Spring in Missouri during the undercover purchase. Spring was advised of his *Miranda* rights and signed a written waiver form.

The agents first questioned Spring about the firearms transactions that led to his arrest. They then asked him if he had ever shot anyone. Spring admitted that he had "shot [a] guy once." On May 26, Colorado officers visited Spring in jail and advised him of his *Miranda* rights. He again signed a written waiver form. The officers then informed Spring that they wanted to question him about the Colorado homicide. Spring confessed to the crime and was convicted of murder.

Spring contended that his waiver of *Miranda* rights before the March 30 statement was invalid because the ATF agents had not informed him that he would be questioned about the Colorado murder and that the May 26 confession was the illegal "fruit" of the March 30 admission. The Colorado Supreme Court agreed, but the U.S. Supreme Court reversed:

"[There] is no doubt that Spring's [March 30 waiver] was knowingly and intelligently made: that is, that Spring understood that he had the right to remain silent and that anything he said could be used as evidence against him. The Constitution does not require that a criminal suspect know and understand every possible consequence of a waiver of the Fifth Amendment privilege." Nor, the Court told us, does the failure to inform a suspect of the potential subjects of interrogation constitute the police trickery and deception condemned in *Miranda:*

"Once *Miranda* warnings are given, it is difficult to see how official silence could cause a suspect to misunderstand the nature of his constitutional right—'his right to refuse to answer any question which might incriminate him.' '[W]e have never read the Constitution to require that the police supply a suspect with a flow of information to help him calibrate his self-interest in deciding whether to speak or stand by his rights.' *Moran v. Burbine* [p. 665]. Here, the additional information could affect only the wisdom of a *Miranda* waiver, not its essentially voluntary and knowing nature."

MARSHALL, joined by Brennan, J., dissented:

"Spring could not have expected questions about the [murder case] when he agreed to waive his rights, as it occurred in a different state and was a violation of state law outside the normal investigative focus of federal [ATF] agents. [If] a suspect has signed a waiver form with the intention of making a statement regarding a specifically alleged crime, the Court today would hold this waiver valid with respect to questioning about any other crime, regardless of its relation to the charges the suspect believes he will be asked to address. Yet once this waiver is given and the intended statement made, the protections afforded by *Miranda* against the 'inherently compelling pressures' of the custodial interrogation have effectively dissipated. Additional questioning about entirely separate and more serious suspicions of criminal activity can take unfair advantage of the suspect's psychological state, as the unexpected questions cause the compulsive pressures suddenly to reappear. Given this technique of interrogation, a suspect's understanding of the topics planned for questioning is, therefore, at the very least 'relevant' to assessing whether his decision to talk to the officers was voluntarily, knowingly, and intelligently made."

NOTES AND QUESTIONS

(i) Should the *Spring* Court have given weight to the fact that the ATF agents had deprived defendant of information regarding the *more serious charge?* Since the agents had arrested Spring in the act of selling illegal firearms, is it likely that Spring decided to talk to the agents because he felt he had nothing more to lose? See Note, 30 Ariz.L.Rev. 551, 564 (1988).

(ii) Would the Court have reached the same result if Spring had asked the ATF agents what crimes they planned to question him about and the agents (a) had remained silent or (b) had replied that the firearms transactions were the only crimes under investigation? If so, why? If not, is it sound "to fashion a confession law doctrine which turns on the fortuity of a suspect asking the right questions"? See id. at 560–61.

5. ***"Custody" vs. "focus."*** After defining "custodial interrogation" in the text, the *Miranda* Court, as one commentator put it, Kenneth W. Graham, *What Is "Custodial Interrogation"?*, 14 U.C.L.A.Rev. 59, 114 (1966), dropped an "obfuscating footnote [4]": "This is what we meant in *Escobedo* when we spoke of an investigation which has focused on an accused." This footnote led some to think that "custody" and "focus" were alternative grounds for requiring the warnings, but these are different events and they have very different consequences.[a] The likely explanation for footnote 4 was the *Miranda* Court's understandable effort to maintain some continuity with a recent precedent. Despite that footnote, however, *Miranda* actually marked a fresh start in describing the circumstances under which constitutional protections first come into play.

The "focus" test, as it had generally been understood at the time of *Escobedo* was expressly rejected in BECKWITH v. UNITED STATES, 425 U.S. 341 (1976). Agents of the Intelligence Division of the IRS did not arrest petitioner, but met with him in a private home where he occasionally stayed. Petitioner argued that the "interview," which produced incriminating statements, should have been preceded by full *Miranda* warnings (instead of the modified *Miranda* warning which petitioner received) because the taxpayer is clearly the "focus" of a criminal investigation when a case is assigned to the Intelligence Division and such a confrontation "places the taxpayer under 'psychological restraints' which are the functional, and therefore, the legal equivalent of custody." The Court per BURGER, C.J., was "not impressed with this argument in the abstract nor as applied to the particular facts of [petitioner's] interrogation":

"[Although] the 'focus' of an investigation may indeed have been on [petitioner] at the time of the interview in the sense that it was his tax liability which was under scrutiny, he hardly found himself in the custodial situation described by the *Miranda* Court as the basis for its holding. *Miranda* specifically defined 'focus,' for its purposes, as 'questioning initiated by law enforcement officers *after* a person has been taken into custody or otherwise deprived of his freedom of action in any significant way.' "[b]

---

a. *Hoffa v. United States*, p. 470, emphasized, albeit not in a *Miranda* context, that "there is no constitutional right to be arrested" and that the police "are under no constitutional duty to call a halt to a criminal investigation the moment they have the minimum evidence to establish probable cause."

b. See also Chief Justice Burger's plurality opinion in *United States v. Mandujano*, p. 843, rejecting the argument that a "putative" or "virtual" defendant called before the grand jury is entitled to full *Miranda* warnings and stressing that the *Miranda* warnings "were aimed at the evils seen by the Court as endemic to police interrogation of a person in custody. [*Miranda*] recognized that many official investigations, such as grand jury questioning, take place in a setting wholly different from custodial police interrogation. [To] extend [*Miranda*] concepts to

In *Stansbury v. California*, 511 U.S. 318 (1994) (per curiam), the Court held, "not for the first time, that an officer's subjective and undisclosed view concerning whether the person being interrogated is a suspect is irrelevant to the assessment whether the person is in custody." Unless they are communicated to the person being questioned, emphasized the Court, "an officer's evolving but unarticulated suspicions do not affect the objective circumstances of an interrogation or interview, and thus cannot affect the *Miranda* custody inquiry."

6. *What constitutes "custody" or "custodial interrogation"?* According to Israel, *Criminal Procedure, the Burger Court and the Legacy of the Warren Court*, 75 Mich.L.Rev. 1320, 1383–84 (1977), "difficulties [with *Miranda*] have arisen primarily in situations involving questioning 'on the street.' [P]olice can easily identify what constitutes 'custodial interrogation' where that concept is limited to questioning at the police station or a similar setting." In the main, the concept has been so limited. Most courts have concluded that absent special circumstances (such as arresting a suspect at gunpoint or forcibly subduing him),[a] police questioning "on the street," in a public place or in a person's home or office is not "custodial." Indeed, whether the suspect goes to the stationhouse on his own, see *Oregon v. Mathiason*, 429 U.S. 492 (1977) (per curiam), or whether he "voluntarily" agrees to accompany the police to that site, see *California v. Beheler*, 463 U.S. 1121 (1983) (per curiam), even *police station* questioning designed to produce incriminating statements may not be "custodial interrogation."

Consider, too, *Berkemer v. McCarty*, 468 U.S. 420 (1984), where the Court, per Marshall, J., one of *Miranda*'s strongest supporters, held (without a dissent) that the "roadside questioning" of a motorist detained pursuant to a traffic stop is quite different from questioning at the stationhouse and thus should not be considered "custodial interrogation." *Cf. Schneckloth v. Bustamonte* (p. 454)

---

questioning before a grand jury inquiring into criminal activity under the guidance of a judge is an extravagant expansion [of that case]." But see Justice Brennan's concurring opinion in *Mandujano*.

a. See *Orozco v. Texas,* 394 U.S. 324 (1969) (applying *Miranda* to a situation where defendant was questioned in his bedroom by four police officers at 4:00 a.m., circumstances that produced a "potentiality for compulsion" equivalent to police station interrogation); *New York v. Quarles* (1984) (p. 621) (defendant in "custody" when questioned in a supermarket minutes after arrested at gunpoint, surrounded by four officers, "frisked" and handcuffed, but "public safety" exception to *Miranda* applied).

The "custodial interrogation" issue arose in a unique setting in *United States v. Mesa*, 638 F.2d 582 (3d Cir.1980). After shooting and wounding both his wife and daughter, Mesa barricaded himself in a motel room. FBI agents cleared the area and repeatedly called to him, through a bullhorn, to surrender. Mesa did not respond. Believing that Mesa was armed (he was) and not knowing whether he had hostages (he did not), the FBI brought in a "hostage negotiator." Mesa agreed to take a mobile phone into his room. Before Mesa finally surrendered peacefully, the negotiator and Mesa conversed over the mobile phone for three and a half hours. The conversation consisted mainly of long narrative monologues by Mesa, but in the course of his exchange of remarks with the negotiator Mesa did make some incriminating statements about the shootings. At no time was he given the *Miranda* warnings. A 2–1 majority of the Third Circuit held that Mesa's statements were admissible, but because one judge decided the case solely on the ground that the exchange between Mesa and the negotiator did not constitute "interrogation," there was no majority opinion on the "custody" issue.

Did the judges who addressed the "custody" issue in *Mesa* make the "logical error" of assuming that exclusion of the incriminating statements would somehow *require* the police to give *Miranda* warnings in such situations? Is the best resolution of "standoff situations" for the police "simply [to] decide, as they probably did here, that it [is] better to withhold the *Miranda* warnings and do without the evidence obtained during the conversation"? See Gibbons, J., dissenting from the denial of a petition for rehearing en banc in *Mesa*. See also Note, 91 Yale L.J. 344 (1981).

How would *Miranda* and a "hostage situation" be resolved if it arose today? See Note (a), p. 624.

(warning requirement need not be imposed on "normal consent searches" because they occur "under informal and unstructured conditions" "immeasurably far removed from 'custodial interrogations' ").[b]

The Court has often said that "custody" for *Miranda* purposes is an objective test—how would reasonable people in the suspect's situation have perceived their circumstances? As the next case illustrates, however, it is not always easy to apply this principle to the particular facts.

J.D.B. v. NORTH CAROLINA
___ U.S. ___, 131 S.Ct. 2394, 180 L.Ed.2d 310 (2011).

JUSTICE SOTOMAYOR delivered the opinion of the Court.

This case presents the question whether the age of a child subjected to a police questioning is relevant to the custody analysis of *Miranda*. It is beyond dispute that children will often feel bound to submit to police questioning when an adult in the same circumstances would feel free to leave. Seeing no reason for police officers or courts to blind themselves to that commonsense reality, we hold that a child's age properly informs the *Miranda* custody analysis. * * *

[Petitioner J.D.B., a 13–year–old, seventh grade student, was suspected of being involved in two home break-ins. He was taken out of his classroom by a uniformed police officer and brought to a closed-door conference room. There, he was met by two school administrators and a second police officer, a juvenile investigator with the local police force who had been assigned to this case.

[The juvenile investigator informed J.D.B. he was there to question him about the break-ins. In the presence of the others, J.D.B. was then questioned for the next 30 to 45 minutes. Prior to the questioning, J.D.B. was given neither *Miranda* warnings nor the opportunity to speak to his grandmother, his legal guardian. Nor was he told he was free to leave the room. Only after he confessed to his involvement in the break-ins was he told he could refuse to answer the investigator's questions and that he was free to leave the room. The trial court adjudicated J.D.B. delinquent and the North Carolina Supreme Court affirmed, ruling that J.D.B. was not in custody when he confessed and declining to "extend the test for custody" to include the age of the individual questioned by the police.]

[W]hether a suspect is "in custody" is an objective inquiry. [The] "subjective views harbored by either the interrogating officers or the person being questioned" are irrelevant. The test, in other words, involves no consideration of the "actual mindset" of the particular suspect subjected to police questioning. *Yarborough v. Alvarado*, 541 U.S. 652, 662 (2004). [By] limiting analysis to the objective circumstances of the interrogation, and asking how a reasonable person in the suspect's position would understand his freedom to terminate questioning and

---

b. Consider *Minnesota v. Murphy*, 465 U.S. 420 (1984). Murphy, a probationer, arranged to meet with his probation officer in her office as she had requested. He then admitted, in response to her questioning, that he had committed a rape and a murder a number of years earlier. Although the terms of his probation required Murphy to report to his probation officer periodically and to respond truthfully to all her questions, and although the officer had substantial reason to believe that Murphy's answers to her questions were likely to be incriminating, a 6–3 majority, per White, J., concluded that Murphy could not claim the "in custody" exception to the general rule that the privilege against self-incrimination is not self-executing:

"Custodial arrest is said to convey to the suspect a message that he has no choice but to submit to the officers' will and to confess. It is unlikely that a probation interview, arranged by appointment at a mutually convenient time, would give rise to a similar impression. [Since] Murphy was not physically restrained and could have left the office, any compulsion he might have felt from the possibility that terminating the meeting would have led to revocation of probation was not comparable to the pressure on a suspect who is painfully aware that he literally cannot escape a persistent custodial interrogator."

leave, the objective test avoids burdening police with the task of anticipating the idiosyncrasies of every individual suspect and divining how these particular traits affect each person's subjective state of mind.

[The] State [contends] that a child's age has no place in the custody analysis, no matter how young the child subjected to police questioning. We cannot agree. [A] reasonable child subjected to police questioning will sometimes feel pressured to submit when a reasonable adult will feel free to go. We think it clear that courts can account for that reality without doing any damage to the objective nature of the custody analysis.

[Even] where a "reasonable person" standard otherwise applies, the common law has reflected the reality that children are not adults. In negligence suits, for instance, where liability turns on what an objectively reasonable person would do in the circumstances, "[a]ll American jurisdictions accept the idea that a person's childhood in a relevant circumstance" to be considered. "[O]ur history is replete with laws and judicial recognition" that children cannot be viewed simply as miniature adults. We see no justification for taking a different course here. So long as the child's age was known to the officer at the time of the interview, or would have been objectively apparent to any reasonable officer, including age as part of the custody analysis requires officers neither to consider circumstances "unknowable" to them, nor to "anticipate the frailties or idiosyncrasies" of the particular suspect whom they question.

[In] many cases involving juvenile suspects, the custody analysis would be nonsensical absent some consideration of the suspect's age. This case is a prime example. Were the court precluded from taking J. D. B.'s youth into account, it would be forced to evaluate the circumstances present here through the eyes of a reasonable person of average years. In other words, how would a reasonable adult understand his situation, after being removed from a seventh-grade social studies class by a uniformed school resource officer; being encouraged by his assistant principal to "do the right thing"; and being warned by a police investigator of the prospect of juvenile detention and separation from his guardian and primary caretaker? To describe such an inquiry is to demonstrate its absurdity. [A] student—whose presence at school is compulsory and whose disobedience at school is cause for disciplinary action—is in a far different position than, say, a parent volunteer on school grounds to chaperone an event, or an adult from the community on school grounds to attend a basketball game. Without asking whether the person "questioned in school" is a "minor," the coercive effect of the schoolhouse setting is unknowable. * * *

Relying on our statements that the objective custody test is "designed to give clear guidance to the police," *Alvarado*, [the State] argues that a child's age must be excluded from the analysis in order to preserve clarity. Similarly, the dissent insists that the clarity of the custody analysis will be destroyed unless a "one-size-fits-all reasonable-person test" applies. In reality, however, ignoring a juvenile defendant's age will often make the inquiry more artificial, and thus only add confusion. And in any event, a child's age, when known or apparent, is hardly an obscure factor to assess. Though the State and the dissent worry about gradations among children of different ages, that concern cannot justify ignoring a child's age altogether. Just as police officers are competent to account for other objective circumstances that are a matter of degree such as the length of questioning or the number of officers present, so too are they competent to evaluate the effect of relative age. [The] same is true of judges, including those whose childhoods have long since passed. In short, officers and judges need no imaginative powers, knowledge of developmental psychology, training in cognitive science, or expertise in social and cultural anthropology to account for a child's age. They simply need the common sense to know that a 7–year–old is not a 13–year–old and neither is an adult. * * *

Finally, the State and the dissent suggest that excluding age from the custody analysis comes at no cost to juveniles' constitutional rights because the due process voluntariness test independently accounts for a child's youth. [But] *Miranda*'s procedural safeguards exist precisely because the voluntariness test is an inadequate barrier when custodial interrogation is at stake. [To] hold, as the State requests, that a child's age is never relevant to whether a suspect has been taken into custody—and thus to ignore the very real differences between children and adults—would be to deny children the full scope of the procedural safeguards that *Miranda* guarantees to adults.

* * *

The question remains whether J. D. B. was in custody when police interrogated him. We remand for the state courts to address that question, this time taking account of all of the relevant circumstances of the interrogation, including J. D. B.'s age at the time. * * *

JUSTICE ALITO, with whom THE CHIEF JUSTICE, JUSTICE SCALIA, and JUSTICE THOMAS join, dissenting.

The Court's decision in this case may seem on first consideration to be modest and sensible, but in truth it is neither. It is fundamentally inconsistent with one of the main justifications for the *Miranda* rule: the perceived need for a clear rule that can be easily applied in all cases. And today's holding is not needed to protect the constitutional rights of minors who are questioned by the police.

* * * Dissatisfied with the highly fact specific constitutional rule against the admission of in-voluntary confessions, the *Miranda* Court set down rigid standards that often require courts to ignore personal characteristics that may be highly relevant to a particular suspect's actual susceptibility to police pressure. This rigidity, however, has brought with it one of *Miranda*'s principal strengths— "the ease and clarity of its application" by law enforcement officials and courts. A key contributor to this clarity, at least up until now, has been *Miranda*'s objective reasonable-person test for determining custody. * * *

Many suspects, of course, will differ from this hypothetical reasonable person. Some, including those who have been hardened by past interrogations, may have no need for *Miranda* warnings at all. And for other suspects—those who are unusually sensitive to the pressures of police questioning—*Miranda* warnings may come too late to be of any use. That is a necessary consequence of *Miranda*'s rigid standards, but it does not mean that the constitutional rights of these especially sensitive suspects are left unprotected. A vulnerable defendant can still turn to the constitutional rule against *actual* coercion and contend that that his confession was extracted against his will.

Today's decision shifts the *Miranda* custody determination from a one-size-fits-all reasonable-person test into an inquiry that must account for at least one individualized characteristic—age—that is thought to correlate with susceptibility to coercive pressures. Age, however, is in no way the only personal characteristic that may correlate with pliability, and in future cases the Court will be forced to choose between two unpalatable alternatives. It may choose to limit today's decision by arbitrarily distinguishing a suspect's age from other personal characteristics—such as intelligence, education, occupation, or prior experience with law enforcement—that may also correlate with susceptibility to coercive pressures. Or, if the Court is unwilling to draw these arbitrary lines, it will be forced to effect a fundamental transformation of the *Miranda* custody test—from a clear, easily applied prophylactic rule into a highly fact-intensive standard resembling the voluntariness test that the *Miranda* Court found to be unsatisfactory.

For at least three reasons, there is no need to go down this road. First, many minors subjected to police interrogation are near the age of majority, and for these suspects the one-size-fits-all *Miranda* custody rule may not be a bad fit. Second, many of the difficulties in applying the *Miranda* custody rule to minors arise because of the unique circumstances present when the police conduct interrogations at school. The *Miranda* custody rule has always taken into account the setting in which questioning occurs, and accounting for the school setting in such cases will address many of these problems. Third, in cases like the one now before us, where the suspect is especially young, courts applying the constitutional voluntariness standard can take special care to ensure that incriminating statements were not obtained through coercion.

Safeguarding the constitutional rights of minors does not require the extreme makeover of *Miranda* that today's decision may portend.

[The] Court's rationale for importing age into the custody standard is that minors tend to lack adults' "capacity to exercise mature judgment" and that failing to account for that "reality" will leave some minors unprotected under *Miranda* in situations where they perceive themselves to be confined. I do not dispute that many suspects who are under 18 will be more susceptible to police pressure than the average adult. [It] is no less a "reality," however, that many persons *over* the age of 18 are also more susceptible to police pressure than the hypothetical reasonable person. Yet the *Miranda* custody standard has never accounted for the personal characteristics of these or any other individual defendants.

Indeed, it has always been the case under *Miranda* that the unusually meek or compliant are subject to the same fixed rules, including the same custody requirement, as those who are unusually resistant to police pressure. *Miranda*'s rigid standards are both overinclusive and underinclusive. They are overinclusive to the extent that they provide a windfall to the most hardened and savvy of suspects, who often have no need for *Miranda*'s protections. [And] *Miranda*'s requirements are underinclusive to the extent that they fail to account for "frailties," "idiosyncrasies," and other individualized considerations that might cause a person to bend more easily during a confrontation with the police.

[That] is undoubtedly why this Court's *Miranda* cases have never before mentioned "the suspect's age" or any other individualized consideration in applying the custody standard. And unless the *Miranda* custody rule is now to be radically transformed into one that takes into account the wide range of individual characteristics that are relevant in determining whether a confession is voluntary, the Court must shoulder the burden of explaining why age is different from these other personal characteristics.

Why, for example, is age different from intelligence? [How] about the suspect's cultural background? Suppose the police learn (or should have learned) that a suspect they wish to question is a recent immigrant from a country in which dire consequences often befall any person who dares to attempt to cut short any meeting with the police. Is this really less relevant than the fact that a suspect is a month or so away from his 18th birthday? The defendant's education is another personal characteristic that may generate "conclusions about behavior and perception." Under today's decision, why should police officers and courts "blind themselves," to the fact that a suspect has "only a fifth-grade education"? Alternatively, what if the police know or should know that the suspect is "a college-educated man with law school training"?

[In] time, the Court will have to confront these issues, and it will be faced with a difficult choice. It may choose to distinguish today's decision and adhere to the arbitrary proclamation that "age [is] different." Or it may choose to extend today's holding and, in doing so, further undermine the very rationale for the *Miranda* regime.

[The] Court holds that age must be taken into account when it "was known to the officer at the time of the interview," or when it "would have been objectively apparent" to a reasonable officer. The first half of this test overturns the rule that the "initial determination of custody" does not depend on the "subjective views harbored [by] interrogating officers." The second half will generate time-consuming satellite litigation over a reasonable officer's perceptions. When, as here, the interrogation takes place in school, the inquiry may be relatively simple. But not all police questioning of minors takes place in schools. In many cases, courts will presumably have to make findings as to whether a particular suspect had a sufficiently youthful look to alert a reasonable officer to the possibility that the suspect was under 18, or whether a reasonable officer would have recognized that a suspect's I. D. was a fake. The inquiry will be both "time-consuming and disruptive" for the police and the courts. * * *

Take a fairly typical case in which today's holding may make a difference. A 16½-year-old moves to suppress incriminating statements made prior to the administration of *Miranda* warnings. [The] judge will not have the luxury of merely saying: "It is common sense that a 16½-year-old is not an 18-year-old. Motion granted." Rather, the judge will be required to determine whether the differences between a typical 16½-year-old and a typical 18-year-old with respect to susceptibility to the pressures of interrogation are sufficient to change the outcome of the custody determination. Today's opinion contains not a word of actual guidance as to how judges are supposed to go about making that determination.

Petitioner and the Court attempt to show that this task is not unmanageable by pointing out that age is taken into account in other legal contexts. In particular, the Court relies on the fact that the age of a defendant is a relevant factor under the reasonable-person standard applicable in negligence suits. But negligence is generally a question for the jury, the members of which can draw on their varied experiences with persons of different ages. It also involves a *post hoc* determination, in the reflective atmosphere of a deliberation room, about whether the defendant conformed to a standard of care. The *Miranda* custody determination, by contrast, must be made in the first instance by police officers in the course of an investigation that may require quick decisionmaking.

[The] Court's decision greatly diminishes the clarity and administrability that have long been recognized as "principal advantages" of *Miranda*'s prophylactic requirements. But what is worse, the Court takes this step unnecessarily, as there are other, less disruptive tools available to ensure that minors are not coerced into confessing.

As an initial matter, the difficulties that the Court's standard introduces will likely yield little added protection for most juvenile defendants. Most juveniles who are subjected to police interrogation are teenagers nearing the age of majority. These defendants' reactions to police pressure are unlikely to be much different from the reaction of a typical 18–year-old in similar circumstances. A one-size-fits-all *Miranda* custody rule thus provides a roughly reasonable fit for these defendants.

In addition, many of the concerns that petitioner raises regarding the application of the *Miranda* custody rule to minors can be accommodated by considering the unique circumstances present when minors are questioned in school. * * *

Finally, in cases like the one now before us, where the suspect is much younger than the typical juvenile defendant, courts should be instructed to take particular care to ensure that incriminating statements were not obtained involuntarily. The voluntariness inquiry is flexible and accommodating by nature and the Court's precedents already make clear that "special care" must be exercised in applying the voluntariness test where the confession of a "mere child" is at issue. If *Miranda*'s rigid, one-size-fits-all standards fail to account for the unique needs of juveniles, the response should be to rigorously apply the constitutional rule against coercion to ensure that the rights of minors are protected. There is no need to run *Miranda* off the rails. * * *

NOTES AND QUESTIONS

(a) If J.D.B. had been confined to a wheelchair or had been on crutches, would Justice Alito have agreed that the trial judge should have taken these factors into account?

(b) In many instances will it be more obvious whether a custodial suspect is a child, a teenager or an adult than how intelligent he or she is or what her educational or cultural background is?

7. What constitutes interrogation within the meaning of Miranda?

RHODE ISLAND v. INNIS
446 U.S. 291, 100 S.Ct. 1682, 64 L.Ed.2d 297 (1980).

JUSTICE STEWART delivered the opinion of the Court.

[*Miranda*] held that, once a defendant in custody asks to speak with a lawyer, all interrogation must cease until a lawyer is present. The issue in this case is whether the respondent was "interrogated" in violation [of *Miranda*].[a]

[At approximately 4:30 a.m., a patrolman arrested respondent, suspected of robbing a taxicab driver and murdering him with a shotgun blast to the back of the head. Respondent was unarmed. He was advised of his rights. Within minutes a sergeant (who advised respondent of his rights) and then a captain arrived at the scene of the arrest. The captain also gave respondent the *Miranda* warnings, whereupon respondent asked to speak with a lawyer. The captain then directed that respondent be placed in a police vehicle with a wire screen mesh between the front and rear seats and be driven to the police station. Three officers were assigned to accompany the arrestee. Although the record is somewhat unclear, it appears that Patrolman Williams was in the back seat with respondent and that Patrolmen Gleckman and McKenna were in front.]

While enroute to the central station, Patrolman Gleckman initiated a conversation with Patrolman McKenna concerning the missing shotgun.[1] As Patrolman Gleckman later testified:

"A. At this point, I was talking back and forth with Patrolman McKenna stating that I frequent this area while on patrol and [that because a school for handicapped children is located nearby,] there's a lot of handicapped children

---

a. Why is *this* the issue? Since respondent asserted his right to counsel, why isn't the issue whether the police "scrupulously honored" the exercise of that right? Cf. *Michigan v. Mosley* (p. 635). Or why isn't the issue (a) whether the police impermissibly "prompted" respondent to change his mind after he invoked his right to counsel or (b) whether respondent "*himself initiate[d]* further communication, exchanges or conversations with the police," *Edwards v. Arizona* (p. 636) (emphasis added), after initially invoking his right to counsel?

1. Although there was conflicting testimony about the exact seating arrangements, it is clear that everyone in the vehicle heard the conversation.

running around in this area, and God forbid one of them might find a weapon with shells and they might hurt themselves."

Patrolman McKenna apparently shared his fellow officer's concern:

"A. I more or less concurred with him [Gleckman] that it was a safety factor and that we should, you know, continue to search for the weapon and try to find it."

[Respondent then interrupted the conversation, stating that he would show the officers where the gun was located. He told the police that he understood his rights, but "wanted to get the gun out of the way because of the kids in the area in the school." He then led the police to a nearby field, where he pointed out the shotgun under some rocks.]

[Respondent was convicted of murder. The trial judge admitted the shotgun and testimony related to its discovery. On appeal, the Rhode Island Supreme Court concluded that the police had "interrogated" respondent without a valid waiver of his right to counsel; the conversation in the police vehicle had constituted "subtle coercion" that was the equivalent of *Miranda* "interrogation."]

[In determining whether respondent had been "interrogated" in violation of *Miranda*] we first define the term "interrogation" under *Miranda* before turning to a consideration of the facts of this case. [The] concern of the Court in *Miranda* was that the "interrogation environment" created by the interplay of interrogation and custody would "subjugate the individual to the will of his examiner" and thereby undermine the privilege against compulsory self-incrimination. The police practices that evoked this concern included several that did not involve express questioning [such as] the so-called "reverse lineup" in which a defendant would be identified by coached witnesses as the perpetrator of a fictitious crime, [to induce] him to confess to the actual crime of which he was suspected in order to escape the false prosecution. [It] is clear that these techniques of persuasion, no less than express questioning, were thought, in a custodial setting, to amount to interrogation.[3]

This is not to say, however, that all statements obtained by the police after a person has been taken into custody are to be considered the product of interrogation. [The *Miranda* warnings] are required not where a suspect is simply taken into custody, but rather where a suspect in custody is subjected to interrogation. "Interrogation," as conceptualized [in *Miranda*], must reflect a measure of compulsion above and beyond that inherent in custody itself.[4]

We conclude that the *Miranda* safeguards come into play whenever a person in custody is subjected to either express questioning or its functional equivalent.

---

3. To limit the ambit of *Miranda* to express questioning would "place a premium on the ingenuity of the police to devise methods of indirect interrogation, rather than to implement the plain mandate of *Miranda*." *Commonwealth v. Hamilton*, 445 Pa. 292, 297, 285 A.2d 172, 175 [(1971)].

4. There is language in the opinion of the Rhode Island Supreme Court in this case suggesting that the definition of "interrogation" under *Miranda* is informed by this Court's decision in *Brewer v. Williams*, [p. 739, reaffirming and expansively interpreting the *Massiah* doctrine]. This suggestion is erroneous. Our decision in *Brewer* rested solely on the Sixth and Fourteenth Amendment right to counsel. That right, as we held in *Massiah*, prohibits law enforcement officers from "deliberately elicit[ing]" incriminating information from a defendant in the absence of counsel after a formal charge against the defendant has been filed. Custody in such a case is not controlling; indeed, the petitioner in *Massiah* was not in custody. By contrast, the right to counsel at issue in the present case is based not on the Sixth and Fourteenth Amendments, but rather on the Fifth and Fourteenth Amendments as interpreted in the *Miranda* opinion. The definitions of "interrogation" under the Fifth and Sixth Amendments, if indeed the term "interrogation" is even apt in the Sixth Amendment context, are not necessarily interchangeable, since the policies underlying the two constitutional protections are quite distinct. See Kamisar, *Brewer v. Williams, Massiah and Miranda: What is "Interrogation"? When Does it Matter?*, 67 Geo.L.J. 1, 41–55 (1978).

That is to say, the term "interrogation" under *Miranda* refers not only to express questioning, but also to any words or actions on the part of the police (other than those normally attendant to arrest and custody)[a] that the police should know are reasonably likely to elicit an incriminating response from the suspect. The latter portion of this definition focuses primarily upon the perceptions of the suspect, rather than the intent of the police. This focus reflects the fact that the *Miranda* safeguards were designed to vest a suspect in custody with an added measure of protection against coercive police practices, without regard to objective proof of the underlying intent of the police. A practice that the police should know is reasonably likely to evoke an incriminating response from a suspect thus amounts to interrogation.[7] But, since the police surely cannot be held accountable for the unforeseeable results of their words or actions, the definition of interrogation can extend only to words or actions on the part of police officers that they *should have known* were reasonably likely to elicit an incriminating response.[8]

Turning to the facts of the present case, we conclude that the respondent was not "interrogated" within the meaning of *Miranda*. It is undisputed that the first prong of the definition of "interrogation" was not satisfied, for the [Gleckman–McKenna conversation] included no express questioning of the respondent. [Moreover,] it cannot be fairly concluded that the respondent was subjected to the "functional equivalent" of questioning. It cannot be said [that the officers] should have known that their conversation was reasonably likely to elicit an incriminating response from the respondent. There is nothing in the record to suggest that the officers were aware that the respondent was peculiarly susceptible to an appeal to his conscience concerning the safety of handicapped children [or that] the police knew that the respondent was unusually disoriented or upset at the time of his arrest.[9]

[It] may be said, as the Rhode Island Supreme Court did say, that the respondent was subjected to "subtle compulsion." But that is not the end of the inquiry. It must also be established that a suspect's incriminating response was the product of words or actions on the part of the police that they should have known were reasonably likely to elicit an incriminating response.[10] This was not established in the present case. * * *

---

a. In *South Dakota v. Neville,* 459 U.S. 553 (1983), the Court noted (fn. 15) that "in the context of an arrest for driving while intoxicated, a police inquiry of whether the suspect will take a blood-alcohol test is not an interrogation within the meaning of *Miranda.*" Recalling that *Innis* had excluded "police words or actions 'normally attendant to arrest and custody'" from the definition of "interrogation," the *Neville* Court added: "The police inquiry here is highly regulated by state law, and is presented in virtually the same words to all suspects. It is similar to a police request to submit to fingerprinting or photography. Respondent's choice of refusal thus enjoys no prophylactic *Miranda* protection outside the basic Fifth Amendment protection. See generally Peter Arenella, *Schmerber and the Privilege Against Self–Incrimination: A Reappraisal,* 20 Am.Crim.L.Rev. 31, 56–58 (1982)."

7. This is not to say that the intent of the police is irrelevant, for it may well have a bearing on whether the police should have known that their words or actions were reasonably likely to evoke an incriminating response. In particular, where a police practice is designed to elicit an incriminating response from the accused, it is unlikely that the practice will not also be one which the police should have known was reasonably likely to have that effect.

8. Any knowledge the police may have had concerning the unusual susceptibility of a defendant to a particular form of persuasion might be an important factor in determining whether the police should have known that their words or actions were reasonably likely to elicit an incriminating response from the suspect.

9. The record in no way suggests that the officers' remarks were *designed* to elicit a response. It is significant that the trial judge, after hearing the officers' testimony, concluded that it was "entirely understandable that [the officers] would voice their concern [for the safety of the handicapped children] to each other."

10. By way of example, if the police had done no more than to drive past the site of the concealed weapon while taking the most direct route to the police station, and if the respondent,

CHIEF JUSTICE BURGER, concurring in the judgment.

Since the result is not inconsistent with *Miranda,* I concur in the judgment. The meaning of *Miranda* has become reasonably clear and law enforcement practices have adjusted to its strictures; I would neither overrule *Miranda,* disparage it, nor extend it at this late date. I fear, however, that [the Court's opinion] may introduce new elements of uncertainty; under the Court's test, a police officer, in the brief time available, apparently must evaluate the suggestibility and susceptibility of an accused. * * *

JUSTICE MARSHALL, with whom JUSTICE BRENNAN joins, dissenting.

I am substantially in agreement with the Court's definition of "interrogation" within the meaning of *Miranda.* In my view, the *Miranda* safeguards apply whenever police conduct is intended or likely to produce a response from a suspect in custody. As I read the Court's opinion, its definition of "interrogation" for *Miranda* purposes is equivalent, for practical purposes, to my formulation. [The] Court requires an objective inquiry into the likely effect of police conduct on a typical individual, taking into account any special susceptibility of the suspect to certain kinds of pressure of which the police know or have reason to know. I am utterly at a loss, however, to understand how this objective standard as applied to the facts before us can rationally lead to the conclusion that there was no interrogation. * * *

One can scarcely imagine a stronger appeal to the conscience of a suspect— *any* suspect—than the assertion that if the weapon is not found an innocent person will be hurt or killed. And not just any innocent person, but an innocent child—a little girl—a helpless, handicapped little girl on her way to school. [As] a matter of fact, the appeal to a suspect to confess for the sake of others, to "display some evidence of decency and honor," is a classic interrogation technique.

Gleckman's remarks would obviously have constituted interrogation if they had been explicitly directed to petitioner, and the result should not be different because they were nominally addressed to McKenna. [The officers] knew petitioner would hear and attend to their conversation, and they are chargeable with knowledge of and responsibility for the pressures to speak which they created. * * *

JUSTICE STEVENS, dissenting.

[In] my view any statement that would normally be understood by the average listener as calling for a response is the functional equivalent of a direct question, whether or not it is punctuated by a question mark. The Court, however, takes a much narrower view. It holds that police conduct is not the "functional equivalent" of direct questioning unless the police should have known that what they were saying or doing was likely to elicit an incriminating response from the suspect. This holding represents a plain departure from the principles set forth in *Miranda.*

[In] order to give full protection to a suspect's right to be free from any interrogation at all, the definition of "interrogation" must include any police statement or conduct that has the same purpose or effect as a direct question. Statements that appear to call for a response from the suspect, as well as those that are designed to do so, should be considered interrogation. By prohibiting only those relatively few statements or actions that a police officer should know are likely to elicit an incriminating response, the Court today accords a suspect

---

upon noticing for the first time the proximity of the school for handicapped children, had blurted out that he would show the officers where the gun was located, it could not seriously be argued that this "subtle compulsion" would have constituted "interrogation" within the meaning of the *Miranda* opinion.

considerably less protection. Indeed, since I suppose most suspects are unlikely to incriminate themselves even when questioned directly, this new definition will almost certainly exclude every statement that is not punctuated with a question mark from the concept of "interrogation."

The difference between the approach required by a faithful adherence to *Miranda* and the stinted test applied by the Court today can be illustrated by comparing three different ways in which Officer Gleckman could have communicated his fears about the possible dangers posed by the shotgun to handicapped children. He could have:

(1) directly asked Innis:

Will you please tell me where the shotgun is so we can protect handicapped schoolchildren from danger?

(2) announced to the other officers in the wagon:

If the man sitting in the back seat with me should decide to tell us where the gun is, we can protect handicapped children from danger.

or (3) stated to the other officers:

It would be too bad if a little handicapped girl would pick up the gun that this man left in the area and maybe kill herself.

In my opinion, all three of these statements should be considered interrogation because all three appear to be designed to elicit a response from anyone who in fact knew where the gun was located. Under the Court's test, on the other hand, the form of the statements would be critical. The third statement would not be interrogation because in the Court's view there was no reason for Officer Gleckman to believe that Innis was susceptible to this type of an implied appeal; therefore, the statement would not be reasonably likely to elicit an incriminating response. Assuming that this is true, then it seems to me that the first two statements, which would be just as unlikely to elicit such a response, should also not be considered interrogation. But, because the first statement is clearly an express question, it *would* be considered interrogation under the Court's test. The second statement, although just as clearly a deliberate appeal to Innis to reveal the location of the gun, would presumably not be interrogation because (a) it was not in form a direct question and (b) it does not fit within the "reasonably likely to elicit an incriminating response" category that applies to indirect interrogation.

As this example illustrates, the Court's test creates an incentive for police to ignore a suspect's invocation of his rights in order to make continued attempts to extract information from him. If a suspect does not appear to be susceptible to a particular type of psychological pressure, the police are apparently free to exert that pressure on him despite his request for counsel, so long as they are careful not to punctuate their statements with question marks. And if, contrary to all reasonable expectations, the suspect makes an incriminating statement, that statement can be used against him at trial. The Court thus turns *Miranda*'s unequivocal rule against any interrogation at all into a trap in which unwary suspects may be caught by police deception. * * *

NOTES AND QUESTIONS

(a) If Officer Gleckman's remarks had been explicitly directed to Innis, would they have constituted "interrogation" regardless of whether they were reasonably likely—or at all likely—to elicit an incriminating response? If so, why should words or actions that are the "functional equivalent" of express questioning have to satisfy a "reasonable likelihood" or "apparent probability" of success standard?

Why isn't it sufficient that the police speech or conduct—unlike "administrative questioning" (routine questions asked of all arrestees "booked" or otherwise processed) and unlike casual conversation in no way related to the case—would normally be understood as *calling for* a response about the merits of the case or be *likely to be viewed* as *having the same force and effect* as a question about the merits of the case? See Welsh White, *Interrogation without Questions,* 78 Mich. L.Rev. 1209, 1227–36 (1980); Jesse H. Choper, Yale Kamisar & Laurence H. Tribe, *The Supreme Court: Trends and Developments, 1979–80* at 88–89, 92–95 (1981) (remarks of Professor Kamisar).

(b) If Gleckman *had admitted* that his remarks to McKenna were *designed* to get Innis to make incriminating statements, would (should) they have constituted "interrogation" regardless of Gleckman's apparent likelihood of success? Why (not)? Did it (should it) matter whether the "Christian burial speech" delivered in *Brewer v. Williams,* p. 739, was reasonably likely to elicit an incriminating response from Williams? Why (not)?

(c) In ARIZONA v. MAURO, 481 U.S. 520 (1987), a 5–4 majority, per Powell, J., held that it was not "custodial interrogation" within the meaning of *Miranda* for the police to accede to the request of defendant's wife, also a suspect in the murder of their son, to speak with defendant (being held in a room at the station house) in the presence of a police officer (Detective Manson), who placed a tape recorder in plain sight on a desk. (Defendant had been given the *Miranda* warnings and had asserted his right to counsel.) Observed the Court:

"There is no evidence that the officers sent Mrs. Mauro in to see her husband for the purpose of eliciting incriminating statements. [T]he officers tried to discourage her from talking to her husband, but finally 'yielded to her insistent demands.' Nor was Detective Manson's presence improper. [There were] a number of legitimate reasons—not related to securing incriminating statements—for having a police officer present. Finally, the weakness of Mauro's claim that he was interrogated is underscored by examining the situation from his perspective. * * * We doubt that a suspect, told by officers that his wife will be allowed to speak to him, would feel that he was being coerced to incriminate himself in any way.

"[The state supreme court] was correct to note that there was a 'possibility' that Mauro would incriminate himself while talking to his wife [and] that the officers were aware of that possibility. [But] the actions in this case were far less questionable than the 'subtle compulsion' [held] *not* to be interrogation in *Innis.* Officers do not interrogate a suspect simply by hoping that he will incriminate himself. * * *

"[In] deciding whether particular police conduct is interrogation, we must remember the purpose behind [*Miranda*]: preventing government officials from using the coercive nature of confinement to extract confessions that would not be given in an unrestrained environment. The government actions in this case do not implicate the purpose in any way."

Dissenting Justice Stevens, joined by Brennan, Marshall and Blackmun, JJ., maintained:

"[The] facts compel the conclusion that the police took advantage of Mrs. Mauro's request to visit her husband, setting up a confrontation between them at a time when he manifestly desired to remain silent. Because they allowed [Mauro's] conversation with his wife to commence at a time when they knew it was reasonably likely to produce an incriminating statement, the police interrogated him.

"[The] intent of the detectives is clear from their own testimony. They both knew that if the conversation took place, incriminating statements were likely to be made. With that in mind, they decided to take in a tape recorder, sit near [Mauro] and his wife and allow the conversation to commence. * * *

"It is undisputed that a police decision to place two suspects in the same room and then to listen to or record their conversation may constitute a form of interrogation even if no questions are asked by any police officers.[a] That is exactly what happened here. [The Mauros] were both suspects in the murder of their son. Each of them had been interrogated separately before the officers decided to allow them to converse, an act that surely did not require a tape recorder or the presence of a police officer within hearing range. Under the circumstances, the police knew or should have known that [this encounter] was reasonably likely to produce an incriminating statement. * * *

"[Under] the circumstances, the mere fact that [Mrs. Mauro] made the initial request leading to the conversation does not alter [the fact that the police violated *Miranda*]. [They] exercised exclusive control over whether and when the suspects spoke with each other; the police knew that whatever Mauro wished to convey to his wife at that moment, he would have to say under the conditions unilaterally imposed by the officers. In brief, the police exploited the custodial situation and the understandable desire of Mrs. Mauro to speak with [her husband] to conduct an interrogation."

NOTES AND QUESTIONS

(i) *Likelihood of incrimination.* According to the *Mauro* majority, the meeting between Mauro and his wife did not "present a sufficient likelihood of incrimination" to satisfy the *Innis* standard [fn. 6]. What if it did? What if, as the dissenters maintained, the police did know or should have known that the meeting between Mauro and his wife was likely to produce an incriminating statement. Should this be decisive in a case like *Mauro?*

Should the *Innis* language defining police interrogation or its functional equivalent be taken literally? Did the *Innis* Court assume a basic factual setting— police conduct equivalent to direct police questioning in terms of its compulsion or pressure? Did the *Innis* Court have in mind conduct *by the police* and in *the presence of the suspect,* such as confronting the suspect with a report indicating that he "flunked" a lie detector exam or confronting him with the confession of an accomplice or bringing an effusive and accusing accomplice into the same room with the police and the suspect?[b]

(ii) *"Police blue" compulsion.* If a spouse or parent or friend meets with someone in custody, does that add significantly to the *official* compulsion, the *"police blue"* compulsion? If not, why should this conduct be considered the equivalent of "custodial *police* interrogation"?

(iii) *The purpose of the police.* The *Mauro* majority emphasizes the lack of any evidence that the police sent Mrs. Mauro to see her husband "for the purpose of eliciting incriminating statements." What if the detectives had asked Mrs. Mauro

---

a. Does Justice Stevens mean that this situation may constitute a form of interrogation within the meaning of *Miranda* even if the suspects are *unaware* that the police are listening to, or recording, their conversation? If so, why? Where is the "compulsion"? See the discussion following this case and the discussion in Note 8.

b. Although the *Innis* case involved police "speech," the Court's definition of "interrogation" embraces police tactics that do not. Thus, the Court seems to have repudiated the position taken by a number of courts prior to *Innis* that *confronting* a suspect with physical or documentary evidence (e.g., a ballistics report or a bank surveillance photograph) or *arranging a meeting in the presence of the police* between an arrestee and an accomplice who has already confessed is not "interrogation" because it does not involve verbal conduct on the part of the police. For criticism of these pre *Innis* cases, see Kamisar Essays at 156–58 n. 21.

to try to get her husband to confess and she had agreed to do so? Would she have become an "agent" of the police? Why does this matter for *Miranda* purposes? If defendant *were unaware* of his wife's or the detectives' purpose, how would that purpose render defendant's environment more "compelling" or make him more likely to feel that he was being "coerced" to incriminate himself? How would the undisclosed purpose of the police alter the situation *from the defendant's perspective?*

(iv) *The suspect's awareness that the police are present.* Is the key factor in a case like *Mauro* not the intent of the police but the suspect's awareness that the police are present, or listening, when he meets with a spouse or friend? If Detective Manson had not been physically present, but the police had *secretly recorded* defendant's meeting with his wife, would *Mauro* have been a much easier case? Why (not)? See next Note.

8. *The "jail plant" situation; "surreptitious interrogation."* Suppose a secret government agent, posing as a fellow-prisoner, is placed in the same cell or cellblock with an incarcerated suspect and induces him to discuss the crime for which he has been arrested. Does this constitute "custodial interrogation"? No, answered the Court in ILLINOIS v. PERKINS, 496 U.S. 292 (1990); "*Miranda* warnings are not required when the suspect is unaware that he is speaking to a law enforcement officer and gives a voluntary statement."

The case arose as follows: Respondent Perkins, who was suspected of committing the Stephenson murder, was incarcerated on charges unrelated to the murder. The police placed Charlton (who had been a fellow inmate of Perkins in another prison) and Parisi (an undercover officer) in the same cellblock with Perkins. The secret government agents were instructed to engage Perkins in casual conversation and to report anything he said about the Stephenson murder. The cellblock consisted of 12 separate cells that opened onto a common room. When Charlton met Perkins in the prison he introduced Parisi by his alias. Parisi suggested that the three of them escape. There was further conversation. Parisi asked Perkins if he had ever "done" anybody. Perkins replied that he had and proceeded to describe his involvement in the Stephenson murder in detail.

In an opinion joined by six other Justices, KENNEDY, J., explained why Perkins' statements were not barred by *Miranda:*

"The essential ingredients of a 'police-dominated atmosphere' and compulsion are not present when an incarcerated person speaks freely to someone that he believes to be a fellow inmate. Coercion is determined from the perspective of the suspect. [When] a suspect considers himself in the company of cellmates and not officers, the coercive atmosphere is lacking.

"[It] is the premise of *Miranda* that the danger of coercion results from the interaction of custody and official interrogation. We reject the argument that *Miranda* warnings are required whenever a suspect is in custody in a technical sense and converses with someone who happens to be a government agent. [When] the suspect has no reason to think that the listeners have official power over him, it should not be assumed that his words are motivated by the reaction he expects from his listeners. '[W]hen the agent carries neither badge nor gun and wears not "police blue," but the same prison gray' as the suspect, there is no '*interplay* between police interrogation and police custody.' Kamisar, *Brewer v. Williams, Massiah and Miranda: What is 'Interrogation?' When Does it Matter?,* 67 Geo.L.J. 1, 67, 63 (1978). [The] only difference between this case and *Hoffa* is that the suspect here was incarcerated, but detention, whether or not for the crime in question, does not warrant a presumption that the use of an undercover agent to speak with an incarcerated suspect makes any confession thus obtained involuntary. * * *

"[This] Court's Sixth Amendment decisions in [the *Massiah* line of cases] also do not avail respondent. [No] charges had been filed [against him] on the subject of the interrogation, and our Sixth Amendment precedents are not applicable."[a]

Only MARSHALL, J., dissented, maintaining that "[t]he conditions that require the police to apprise a defendant of his constitutional rights—custodial interrogation conducted by an agent of the police—were present in this case. Because [respondent] received no *Miranda* warnings before he was subjected to custodial interrogation, his confession was not admissible." Continued Justice Marshall:

"Because Perkins was interrogated by police while he was in custody, *Miranda* required that the officer inform him of his rights. In rejecting that conclusion, the Court finds that 'conversations' between undercover agents and suspects are devoid of the coercion inherent in stationhouse interrogations conducted by law enforcement officials who openly represent the State. *Miranda* was not, however, concerned solely with police *coercion*. It dealt with *any* police tactics that may operate to compel a suspect in custody to make incriminating statements without full awareness of his constitutional rights. [Thus,] when a law enforcement agent structures a custodial interrogation so that a suspect feels compelled to reveal incriminating information, he must inform the suspect of his constitutional rights and give him an opportunity to decide whether or not to talk. * * *

"[The] psychological pressures inherent in confinement increase the suspect's anxiety, making him likely to seek relief by talking with others. [The] inmate is thus more susceptible to efforts by undercover agents to elicit information from him. Similarly, where the suspect is incarcerated, the constant threat of physical danger peculiar to the prison environment may make him demonstrate his toughness to other inmates by recounting or inventing past violent acts. [In] this case, the police deceptively took advantage of Perkins' psychological vulnerability by including him in a sham escape plot, a situation in which he would feel compelled to demonstrate his willingness to shoot a prison guard by revealing his past involvement in a murder.

"[Thus,] the pressures unique to custody allow the police to use deceptive interrogation tactics to compel a suspect to make an incriminating statement. The compulsion is not eliminated by the suspect's ignorance of his interrogator's true identity. The Court therefore need not inquire past the bare facts of custody and interrogation to determine whether *Miranda* warnings are required. * * * *"

NOTES AND QUESTIONS

(a) Is *Perkins* a case where, as dissenting Justice Marshall maintains, "a law enforcement agent structures a custodial interrogation so that a suspect feels compelled to reveal incriminating information" or is it a case where a law enforcement agent structures a situation so that a suspect feels free to reveal incriminating information?

(b) Consider Fred Cohen, *Miranda and Police Deception in Interrogation*, 26 Crim.L.Bull. 534, 543–44 (1990): "Can it be that the *Miranda* rule was intended

a. Brennan, J., concurred in the judgment of the Court, "agree[ing] that when a suspect does not know that his questioner is a police agent, such questioning does not amount to 'interrogation' in an 'inherently coercive' environment so as to require application of *Miranda*"—"the only issue raised at this stage of the litigation." But he went on to say that "the deception and manipulation practiced on respondent raise a substantial claim that the confession was obtained in violation of the Due Process Clause." For "the deliberate use of deception and manipulation by the police appears to be incompatible 'with a system that presumes innocence and assures that a conviction will not be secured by inquisitional means' and raises serious concerns that respondent's will was overborne."

to be responsive only to force while leaving in place and indeed encouraging the refinement of other methods for achieving an *uninformed* confession? [If] *Miranda* was fashioned solely to ameliorate the inherent coercion associated with a police-dominated environment, then *Perkins* was correctly decided. If *Miranda* was concerned also with informational equivalency and with giving suspects an opportunity to obtain counsel and, in effect, barter information, instead of making an uninformed gift, then *Perkins* was wrongly decided."

9. PENNSYLVANIA v. MUNIZ, 496 U.S. 582 (1990). *What constitutes "testimonial" evidence? What questions fall within the "routine booking question" exception to Miranda? More on what amounts to "custodial interrogation" within the meaning of Miranda.* The *Muniz* case arose as follows:

Respondent Muniz was arrested for driving while intoxicated. Without advising him of his *Miranda* rights, Officer Hosterman asked Muniz to perform three standard field sobriety tests. Muniz performed poorly and then admitted that he had been drinking. Muniz was taken to a Booking Center. Following its routine practice for receiving persons suspected of driving under the influence, the Booking Center videotaped the ensuing proceedings. Muniz was told that his action and voice were being recorded, but again he was not advised of his *Miranda* rights. Officer Hosterman first asked Muniz his name, address, height, weight, eye color, date of birth, and current age (the "first seven questions" or the seven "booking" questions). Both the delivery and content of his answers were incriminating. Next the officer asked Muniz what the Court called "the sixth birthday question": "Do you know what the date was of your sixth birthday?" Muniz responded, "No, I don't."

The officer then requested Muniz to perform the same sobriety tests that he had been asked to do earlier during the initial roadside stop. While performing the tests, Muniz made several audible and incriminating statements. Finally, Muniz was asked to submit to a breathalyzer test. He refused. At this point, for the first time, Muniz was advised of his *Miranda* rights. Both the video and audio portions of the videotape were admitted into evidence, along with the arresting officer's testimony that Muniz failed the roadside sobriety tests and made incriminating statements at the time. Muniz was convicted of driving while intoxicated.

The Court excluded only Muniz's response to the "sixth birthday question" (by a 5–4 vote). Eight members of the Court agreed that the answers to the first seven questions or "booking" questions were admissible, but they differed as to the reason. BRENNAN, J., wrote the opinion of the Court, except as to the grounds for admitting Muniz's answers to the "booking" questions.

Extracts from Justice Brennan's opinion follow (under four headings provided by the editors):

(a) Why Muniz's responses to the questions he was asked at the Booking Center were admissible even though the slurred nature of his speech was incriminating.

"The physical inability to articulate words in a clear manner due to 'the lack of muscular coordination of his tongue and mouth' is not itself a testimonial component of Muniz's responses to Officer Hosterman's introductory questions.

"[Under] *Schmerber* [p. 30] and its progeny, [any] slurring of speech and other evidence of lack of muscular coordination revealed by Muniz's responses to Officer Hosterman's direct questions constitute nontestimonial components of those responses. * * *

(b) More on what constitutes "testimonial" evidence. Why the response to the "sixth birthday question" was testimonial.

"[Muniz's] answer to the sixth birthday question was incriminating, not just because of his delivery, but also because of his answer's *content*; the trier of fact could infer from Muniz's answer (that he did not *know* the proper date) that his mental state was confused. [The] question [is] whether the incriminating inference of mental confusion is drawn from a testimonial act or from physical evidence. In *Schmerber*, for example, we held that [compelling a suspect to provide a blood sample] was outside of the Fifth Amendment's protection [because] the evidence was *obtained* in a manner that did not entail any testimonial act on the part of the suspect. [In] contrast, had the police instead asked the suspect directly whether his blood contained a high concentration of alcohol, his affirmative response would have been testimonial even though it would have been used to draw the same inference concerning his physiology. [In] this case, the question is not whether a suspect's 'impaired mental faculties' can fairly be characterized as an aspect of his physiology, but rather whether Muniz's response to the sixth birthday question that gave rise to the inference of such an impairment was testimonial in nature. * * *

[The sixth birthday question] "required a testimonial response. When Officer Hosterman asked Muniz if he knew the date of his sixth birthday and Muniz, for whatever reason, could not remember or calculate that date, he was [placed in a predicament the self-incrimination clause was designed to prevent]. By hypothesis, the inherently coercive environment created by the custodial interrogation precluded the option of remaining silent. Muniz was left with the choice of incriminating himself by admitting that he did not then know the date of his sixth birthday, or answering untruthfully by reporting a date that he did not then believe to be accurate (an incorrect guess would be incriminating as well as untruthful). [The] incriminating inference of impaired mental facilities stemmed, not just from the fact that Muniz slurred his response, but also from a testimonial aspect of that response."[a]

(c) The "routine booking question" exception to Miranda: Why Muniz's answers to the first seven questions he was asked at the Booking Center are admissible even though the questions qualify as "custodial interrogation."

"We disagree with [the prosecution's] contention that Officer Hosterman's first seven questions [regarding Muniz's name, address, height, etc.] do not qualify as custodial interrogation * * * merely because the questions were not intended to elicit information for investigatory purposes. [But] Muniz's answers to these first seven questions are nonetheless admissible because the questions fall within a 'routine booking question' exception which exempts from *Miranda*'s coverage questions to secure the 'biographical data necessary to complete booking or pretrial services.'[b] [The] questions appear reasonably related to the police's

---

a. Justice Brennan spoke for only four Justices on this issue. Marshall, J., who concurred in the result on the issue, provided the fifth vote. Chief Justice Rehnquist, joined by White, Blackmun and Stevens, JJ., dissented, maintaining that the answer to this question also fell into the "real or physical evidence" category:

"[The] sixth birthday question here was an effort on the part of the police to check how well Muniz was able to do a simple mathematical exercise. Indeed, had the question related only to the date of his birth, it presumably would have come under the 'booking exception' to *Miranda*. [If] the police may require Muniz to use his body in order to demonstrate the level of his physical coordination, there is no reason why they should not be able to require him to speak or write in order to determine his mental condition. That was all that was sought here. Since it was permissible for the police to extract and examine a sample of Schmerber's blood to determine how much that part of his system had been affected by alcohol, I see no reason why they may not examine the functioning of Muniz's mental processes for the same purpose."

b. Cf. *Rhode Island v. Innis*: "[The] term 'interrogation' under *Miranda* refers not only to express questioning, but also to any words or actions on the part of the police (*other than those normally attendant to arrest and custody*) that the police should know are reasonably likely to elicit an incriminating response from the subject." (Emphasis added.)

administrative concerns. In this context, the first seven questions asked at the Booking Center fall outside the protection of *Miranda*.[c]

(d) More on what constitutes "custodial interrogation": Why Muniz's incriminating utterances during physical sobriety tests conducted by the police were admissible.

"During [the] videotaped proceedings, Officer Hosterman asked Muniz to perform the same three sobriety tests that he had earlier performed at roadside prior to his arrest [e.g., the "one leg stand" test]. While Muniz was attempting to comprehend [the officer's] instructions and then perform the requested sobriety tests, [he] made several audible and incriminating statements. * * *

"Officer Hosterman's dialogue with Muniz concerning [the] tests consisted primarily of carefully scripted instructions as to how the tests were to be performed. These instructions were not likely to be perceived as calling for any verbal responses and therefore were not "words or actions" constituting custodial interrogation * * *. Hence, Muniz's incriminating statements were 'voluntary' in the sense that they were not elicited in response to custodial interrogation. * * *

"Similarly, we conclude that *Miranda* does not require suppression of the statements Muniz made when asked to submit to a breathalyzer examination. [The officer who asked Muniz to take the test] carefully limited her role to providing Muniz with relevant information about [the] test and the Implied Consent Law. She questioned Muniz only as to whether he understood her instructions and wished to submit to the test. These limited and focused inquiries were necessarily 'attendant to' the legitimate police procedure [and] not likely to be perceived as calling for any incriminating response.'[d]

10. When does a response to an officer's question present a reasonable danger of incrimination? As discussed at p. 427, HIIBEL v. SIXTH JUDICIAL COURT, 542 U.S. 177 (2004), sustained against a Fourth Amendment challenge Nevada's "stop and identify" statute. The Court, per Kennedy, J., also rejected the defendant's self-incrimination challenge to the statute. The Court saw no need to decide whether, as the state argued, the privilege did not apply because a statement of identification was not "testimonial" because "even if those required actions [of self-identification] are testimonial * * * in this case disclosure of [petitioner's] name presented no reasonable danger of incrimination":

"[Petitioner's] refusal to disclose his name was not based on any articulated real and appreciable fear that his name would be used to incriminate him, or that it 'would furnish a link in the chain of evidence needed to prosecute' him. *Hoffman v. United States* [p. 839]. As best we can tell, petitioner refused to identify himself only because he thought his name was none of the officer's business. Even today, petitioner does not explain how the disclosure of his name could have been used against him in a criminal case. While we recognize petitioner's strong belief that he should not have to disclose his identity, the Fifth

---

c. On this issue Justice Brennan spoke only for four Justices. Four other members of the Court, Rehnquist, C.J., joined by White, Blackmun and Stevens, JJ., agreed that the responses to the booking questions should not be suppressed. However, because they believed that Muniz's responses to the "booking" questions were not testimonial, they deemed it unnecessary to decide whether the questions fell within the "routine booking question" exception.

Dissenting Justice Marshall balked at "creat[ing] yet another exception to *Miranda*," maintaining that such exceptions "undermine *Miranda*'s fundamental principle that the doctrine should be clear so that it can be easily applied by both police and courts."

d. Dissenting Justice Marshall would have suppressed the statements made in connection with the sobriety tests and the breathalyzer examination because "the circumstances of this case—in particular, Muniz's apparent intoxication—rendered the officers' words and actions the functional equivalent' of express questioning. [For] the police should have known that their conduct was 'reasonably likely to evoke an incriminating response.' *Innes*."

Amendment does not override the Nevada Legislature's judgment to the contrary absent a reasonable belief that the disclosure would tend to incriminate him.

"The narrow scope of the disclosure requirement is also important. One's identity is, by definition, unique; yet it is, in another sense, a universal characteristic. Answering a request to disclose a name is likely to be so insignificant in the scheme of things as to be incriminating only in unusual circumstances. See *Baltimore City Dept. of Social Servs. v. Bouknight*, [p. 869] (suggesting that "fact[s] the State could readily establish" may render "any testimony regarding existence or authenticity [of them] insufficiently incriminating"); Cf. *California v. Byers*, 402 U.S. 424 (1971)[a] (opinion of Burger, C.J.). In every criminal case, it is known and must be known who has been arrested and who is being tried. Cf. *Pennsylvania v. Muniz*. Even witnesses who plan to invoke the Fifth Amendment privilege answer when their names are called to take the stand. Still, a case may arise where there is a substantial allegation that furnishing identity at the time of a stop would have given the police a link in the chain of evidence needed to convict the individual of a separate offense. In that case, the court can then consider whether the privilege applies, and, if the Fifth Amendment has been violated, what remedy must follow. We need not resolve those questions here."

Justice Stevens, dissenting on the self-incrimination issue,[b] argued that "compelled statement at issue in this case is clearly testimonial" and would be "incriminating" under the standard set forth in *Hoffman* and other cases. As to the later point, the dissent reasoned:

"The Court reasons that we should not assume that the disclosure of petitioner's name would be used to incriminate him or that it would furnish a link in a chain of evidence needed to prosecute him. But why else would an officer ask for it? And why else would the Nevada Legislature require its disclosure only when circumstances 'reasonably indicate that the person has committed, is committing, or is about to commit a crime.' [A] person's identity obviously bears informational and incriminating worth, 'even if the [name] itself is not inculpatory.' *Hubbell* [p. 870]. A name can provide the key to a broad array of information about the person, particularly in the hands of a police officer with access to a range of law enforcement databases. And that information, in turn, can be tremendously useful in a criminal prosecution. It is therefore quite wrong to suggest that a person's identity provides a link in the chain to incriminating evidence 'only in unusual circumstances.' "

NOTES AND QUESTIONS

(a) Is the key to the lack of incriminatory potential in the *Hiibel* setting the fact that the information supplied (the individual's name) ordinarily provides only a link to evidence already possessed? See CRIMPROC § 8.10(a).

(b) Without the individual's name, it might be impossible to locate and arrest him at some subsequent time when investigation converted reasonable suspicion into probable cause. Moreover, being able to utilize a name, rather than simply a

---

a. *Byers* upheld a state "hit and run" statute which required the drive of a motor vehicle involved in an accident to stop at the scene and give his name and address. The Court noted that such statutes were regulatory measures, "not intended to facilitate criminal convictions" nor directed at all persons who drove automobiles. Moreover, there was no disclosure of inherently illegal activity as "most automobile accidents occur without creating criminal liability."

b. Justice Breyer's dissent, joined by Justices Souter and Ginsburg, concluded that the Fourth Amendment prohibited requiring responses to any police questions incident to a *Terry* stop. As to the self-incrimination issue, it did note: "There are sound reasons rooted in Fifth Amendment considerations for adhering to this Fourth Amendment legal condition circumscribing police authority * * *. See Stevens, J., dissenting."

description, might be critical in obtaining from various sources further information relating to suspicious activity. However, the same law enforcement advantages might flow from the self-identification in the booking process. Does *Hiibel* say, in effect, that the advantage of attaching a name to a face, even if it eventually leads to obtaining more evidence as to the offense under investigation, does not provide a sufficient nexus to incriminating evidence to meet the *Hoffman* standard? See *id*. Cf. *Byers*.

    11. *Questioning prompted by concern for "public safety."* Consider NEW YORK v. QUARLES, 467 U.S. 649 (1984), which arose as follows:

    At approximately 12:30 a.m., police apprehended respondent Quarles in the rear of a supermarket. He matched the description of the man who had just raped a woman. The woman had told the police that the rapist had just entered the supermarket and that he was carrying a gun. Apparently upon seeing Officer Kraft enter the store, respondent Quarles turned and ran toward the rear. Officer Kraft pursued him with a drawn gun and, upon regaining sight of him, ordered him to stop and put his hands over his head. Although several other officers had arrived at the scene by then, Kraft was the first to reach Quarles. He frisked him and discovered he was wearing an empty shoulder holster. After handcuffing him, the officer asked where the gun was. Quarles nodded in the direction of some empty cartons and responded, "the gun is over there." At that time, emphasized the New York Court of Appeals, Quarles was surrounded by four officers whose guns had been returned to their holsters because, as one testified, the situation was under control.

    The gun was not visible, but Officer Kraft reached into one of the cartons and retrieved a loaded revolver. Quarles was then formally placed under arrest and advised of his *Miranda* rights. He waived his rights. In response to questions, he then stated that he owned the revolver and had purchased it in Miami.

    In the subsequent prosecution of Quarles for criminal possession of a weapon (the record does not reveal why the state failed to pursue the rape charge), the New York courts suppressed the statement "the gun is over there" as well as the gun itself because they had been obtained in violation of Quarles's *Miranda* rights. His statements about his ownership of the gun and the place of purchase were also excluded as having been fatally tainted by the seizure of the gun and the prewarning response as to its location. A 6–3 majority per REHNQUIST, J., reversed:

    "[We] conclude that under the circumstances involved in this case, overriding considerations of public safety justify the officer's failure to provide *Miranda* warnings before he asked questions devoted to locating the abandoned weapon.

    "[We] have before us no claim that respondent's statements were actually compelled by police conduct which overcame his will to resist. Thus the only issue before us is whether Officer Kraft was justified in failing to make available to respondent the procedural safeguards associated with the privilege against compulsory self-incrimination since *Miranda*.[5]

    "[We] hold that on these facts there is a 'public safety' exception to the requirement that *Miranda* warnings be given before a suspect's answers may be admitted into evidence, and that the availability of that exception does not depend upon the motivation of the individual officers involved. In a kaleidoscopic situation

---

    5. The dissent curiously takes us to task for "endors[ing] the introduction of coerced self-incriminating statements in criminal prosecutions." [Of] course our decision today does nothing of the kind. [R]espondent is certainly free on remand to argue that his statement was coerced under traditional due process standards. Today we merely reject the only argument that respondent has raised to support the exclusion of his statement, that the statement must be *presumed* compelled because of Officer Kraft's failure to read him his *Miranda* warnings.

such as the one confronting these officers, where spontaneity rather than adherence to a police manual is necessarily the order of the day, the application of the exception which we recognize today should not be made to depend on *post hoc* findings at a suppression hearing concerning the subjective motivation of the arresting officer. Undoubtedly most police officers, if placed in Officer Kraft's position, would act out of a host of different, instinctive, and largely unverifiable motives—their own safety, the safety of others, and perhaps as well the desire to obtain incriminating evidence from the suspect.

"Whatever the motivation of individual officers in such a situation, we do not believe that the doctrinal underpinnings of *Miranda* require that it be applied in all its rigor to a situation in which police officers ask questions reasonably prompted by a concern for the public safety. [The] police in this case, in the very act of apprehending a suspect, were confronted with the immediate necessity of ascertaining the whereabouts of a gun which they had every reason to believe the suspect had just removed from his empty holster and discarded in the supermarket. So long as the gun was concealed somewhere in the supermarket, with its actual whereabouts unknown, it obviously posed more than one danger to the public safety: an accomplice might make use of it, a customer or employee might later come upon it.

"In such a situation, if the police are required to recite the familiar *Miranda* warnings before asking the whereabouts of the gun, suspects in Quarles' position might well be deterred from responding. Procedural safeguards which deter a suspect from responding were deemed acceptable in *Miranda* in order to protect the Fifth Amendment privilege; when the primary social cost of those added protections is the possibility of fewer convictions, the *Miranda* majority was willing to bear that cost. Here, had *Miranda* warnings deterred Quarles from responding to Officer Kraft's question about the whereabouts of the gun, the cost would have been something more than merely the failure to obtain evidence useful in convicting Quarles. Officer Kraft needed an answer to his question not simply to make his case against Quarles but to insure that further danger to the public did not result from the concealment of the gun in a public area.

"We conclude that the need for answers to questions in a situation posing a threat to the public safety outweighs the need for the prophylactic rule protecting the Fifth Amendment's privilege against self-incrimination. We decline to place officers such as Officer Kraft in the untenable position of having to consider, often in a matter of seconds, whether it best serves society for them to ask the necessary questions without the *Miranda* warnings and render whatever probative evidence they uncover inadmissible, or for them to give the warnings in order to preserve the admissibility of evidence they might uncover but possibly damage or destroy their ability to obtain that evidence and neutralize the volatile situation confronting them.[7] * * *

"We hold that the [court below] erred in excluding the statement, 'the gun is over there,' and the gun because of the officer's failure to read respondent his *Miranda* rights before attempting to locate the weapon. Accordingly [it] also erred in excluding the subsequent statements as illegal fruits of a *Miranda* violation.'"[9]

---

7. The dissent argues that a public safety exception to *Miranda* is unnecessary because in every case an officer can simply ask the necessary questions to protect himself or the public, and then the prosecution can decline to introduce any incriminating responses at a subsequent trial. But absent actual coercion by the officer, there is no constitutional imperative requiring the exclusion of the evidence that results from police inquiry of this kind; and we do not believe that the doctrinal underpinnings of *Miranda* require us to exclude the evidence, thus penalizing officers for asking the very questions which are the most crucial to their efforts to protect themselves and the public.

9. Because we hold that there is no violation of *Miranda* in this case, we have no occasion to [decide whether] the gun is admissible either because it is nontestimonial or because the police would inevitably have discovered it absent their questioning.

O'CONNOR J., concurred in part in the judgment and dissented in part. She would have suppressed Quarles's initial statement ("the gun is over there"), but not the gun itself—because "nothing in *Miranda* or the privilege itself requires exclusion of nontestimonial evidence derived from informal custodial interrogation." (Twenty years later, the Supreme Court addressed this issue in *United States v. Patane*, p. 699.)

Justice O'Connor would have excluded Quarles's initial statement because "a 'public safety' exception unnecessarily blurs the edges of the clear line heretofore established and makes *Miranda's* requirements more difficult to understand. In some cases, police will benefit because a reviewing court will find that an exigency excused their failure to administer the required warnings. But in other cases, police will suffer because a reviewing court will view the 'objective' circumstances differently [than they did]. The end result will be a finespun new doctrine on public safety exigencies incident to custodial interrogation, complete with the hair-splitting distinctions that currently plague our Fourth Amendment jurisprudence." She added:

"[*Miranda*] has never been read to prohibit the police from asking questions to secure the public safety. Rather, the critical question *Miranda* addresses is who shall bear the cost of securing the public safety when such questions are asked and answered: the defendant or the State. *Miranda,* for better or worse, found the resolution of that question implicit in the prohibition against compulsory self-incrimination and placed the burden on the State. When police ask custodial questions without administering the required warnings, *Miranda* quite clearly requires that the answers received be presumed compelled and that they be excluded from evidence at trial."

MARSHALL, J., joined by Brennan and Stevens, JJ., dissented:.

"The majority's entire analysis rests on the factual assumption that the public was at risk during Quarles' interrogation. This assumption is completely in conflict with the facts as found by New York's highest court. * * * Contrary to the majority's speculations, Quarles was not believed to have, nor did he in fact have, an accomplice to come to his rescue. When the questioning began, the arresting officers were sufficiently confident of their safety to put away their guns.

"[The] New York court's conclusion that neither Quarles nor his missing gun posed a threat to the public's safety is amply supported by the evidence presented at the suppression hearing. [Although] the supermarket was open to the public, Quarles' arrest took place during the middle of the night when the store was apparently deserted except for the clerks at the checkout counter. The police could easily have cordoned off the store and searched for the missing gun. Had they done so, they would have found the gun forthwith. The police were well aware that Quarles had discarded his weapon somewhere near the scene of the arrest.

"[Whether] society would be better off if the police warned suspects of their rights before beginning an interrogation or whether the advantages of giving such warnings would outweigh their costs did not inform the *Miranda* decision. On the contrary, the *Miranda* Court was concerned [with] whether the Self–Incrimination Clause permits the government to prosecute individuals based on statements made in the course of custodial interrogations.

[A year earlier, in *Nix v. Williams (Williams II)*, p. 903, the Court had held that the "fruit of the poisonous tree" doctrine did not bar the use of evidence derived from a constitutional violation if such evidence would "ultimately" or "inevitably" have been discovered even if the police had acted lawfully. The "fruits" doctrine, formulated initially in applying the Fourth Amendment exclusionary rule, prohibits the use of evidence derived from, and thus "tainted" by, a constitutional violation.]

"[The] majority's only contention is that police officers could more easily protect the public if *Miranda* did not apply to custodial interrogations concerning the public's safety. But *Miranda* was not a decision about public safety; it was a decision about coerced confessions. Without establishing that interrogations concerning the public's safety are less likely to be coercive than other interrogations, the majority cannot endorse the 'public-safety' exception and remain faithful to the logic of *Miranda*.

"[The] irony of the majority's decision is that the public's safety can be perfectly well protected without abridging the Fifth Amendment. If a bomb is about to explode or the public is otherwise imminently imperiled, the police are free to interrogate suspects without advising them of their constitutional rights. [N]othing in the Fifth Amendment or our decision in *Miranda* proscribes this sort of emergency questioning. All the Fifth Amendment forbids is the introduction of coerced statements at trial."

NOTES AND QUESTIONS

(a) If a case like *Innis* or *Mesa* (the "hostage negotiator" case) arose today, would the courts quickly dispose of it by invoking the "public safety" exception to *Miranda*? For a case that does just that, see *State v. Finch*, 975 P.2d 967 (Wash.1999).

(b) *Asking an arrestee whether he has drugs or needles on his person.* Defendant was arrested for a drug offense and taken to a detention facility. There, before giving him any *Miranda* warnings, an officer asked the defendant whether he had any drugs or needles on his person. "No," responded the defendant, "I don't use drugs, I sell them." Is the statement admissible under the "public safety" exception to *Miranda*?

Yes, concluded *United States v. Carrillo*, 16 F.3d 1046 (9th Cir.1994). The court noted that the officer had testified that in order to avoid contact with syringes (which have poked him in the past) and toxic substances (which have caused headaches and skin irritation in the past), he now routinely asks the questions he asked defendant. Would the Supreme Court have approved of this application of *Quarles*? Should the "public safety" exception apply when no member of the public is in danger? Should it apply when the police do not come upon the scene in hot pursuit?

(c) *Miranda and the privilege against self-incrimination*, By posing the issue as "whether [the police officer] was *justified* in failing to make available to respondent the procedural safeguards associated with the privilege against compulsory self-incrimination since *Miranda*" (emphasis added), did the *Quarles* majority miss the point? Yes, maintains Steven D. Clymer, *Are Police Free to Disregard Miranda?*, 112 Yale L.J. 447, 550 (2002): "Whether there is a pressing concern for public safety or only an effort to solve a crime, neither the privilege nor *Miranda* ever dictates whether police efforts to compel a statement, by failure to give *Miranda* warnings or otherwise, are 'justified.' Instead, they leave the decision whether to use compulsion to the officer, and determine only that any compelled statements are inadmissible." See generally *Chavez v. Martinez*, p. 690.

(d) *The "rescue doctrine."* Somewhat similar to the "public safety" exception is the "rescue doctrine." Should statements obtained in violation of *Miranda* be admissible if police interrogation of a suspected kidnapper is motivated primarily by a desire to save the victim's life? Yes, answer *People v. Dean*, 114 Cal.Rptr. 555 (Cal.App.1974) and *People v. Krom*, 461 N.E.2d 276 (N.Y.1984). See generally William T. Pizzi, *The Privilege Against Self–Incrimination in a Rescue Situation*, 76 J.Crim.L. & C. 657 (1985). It is unsound, maintains Professor Pizzi, id. at 595–

603, to approach the scope of the privilege against self-incrimination "solely from the defendant's point of view while totally ignoring the threat to the lives of others and the purpose and function of the police conduct"; the privilege and its attendant rules should not control "where the police are functioning in a situation which is primarily noninvestigative and where life is at stake."

Are there (should there be) any limits on what a police officer may do to a suspected kidnapper in order to get him to reveal the location of a kidnap victim? Cf. *Leon v. State*, 410 So.2d 201 (Fla.App.1982), holding, over a forceful dissent, that the use of police threats and physical violence at the scene of arrest in order to ascertain the kidnap victim's whereabouts "did not constitutionally infect the later confessions." Consider Pizzi, supra, at 606: "[T]here are [due process] limits on the conduct of the police in their treatment of suspects even in an emergency situation where life is at stake," but "[i]n determining those limits [the] traditional scope of police conduct permitted in a purely investigative context is only a starting point."

12. *Is the Quarles "public safety" exception to Miranda insufficient when it comes to dealing with suspected terrorists?* Recently Attorney General Eric Holder and other public official have indicated that in order to cope with suspected terrorists the "public safety" exception should be expanded. But see Amos N. Guiora, *Relearning Lessons of History: Miranda and Counterterrorism*, 71 Louisiana L.Rev. 1, 20 (2011): "Attorney General Holder's comments show that it is remarkably unclear how the Attorney General defines terrorism, much less a terrorist. [Even] if Congress [were] to legislate an exception to *Quarles*, the current reality of terrorism and counterterrorism in the U.S. is that there is no clarity regarding whether a just-detained individual is a terrorist to whom the new, expanded version applies, or a criminal to whom it would not."

Some who favor expanding *Quarles* in order to deal with terrorists "argue that *Miranda* protections [are] relevant *only* when an individual is prosecuted. In essence, they argue that if an individual is detained (whether lawfully or not) and subsequently interrogated (without having been 'Mirandized') but not prosecuted, then the confession would not be subject to admissibility standards and judicial scrutiny." Guiora, supra, at 24. Is this an argument for expanding *Quarles* or for *not* expanding it?

13. *When, if ever, should interrogators be allowed to use "torture" in order to obtain information from suspected terrorists?* Professor Alan Dershowitz, among others, has suggested that when lives are at stake interrogators should sometimes be allowed to torture suspects to obtain information. In such circumstances, suggests Dershowitz, judges should issue "torture warrants" so that interrogators could utilize torture in extraordinary cases within our legal system rather than "outside the law." See Alan M. Dershowitz, *Why Terrorism Works* 131–64 (2002). Under what circumstances, if any, and pursuant to what procedures, if any, should suspected terrorists be tortured? Consider the following:

MARCY STRAUSS, *Torture*, 48 N.Y. Law Sch.L.Rev. 203, 266–68, 271–74 (2004):

If torture can be utilized to save ten lives from a bomb, why not allow it to be used to save the lives of five children hidden by a crazed neighbor? Or, why not sanction torture to reveal the name of a madman who has killed a random, innocent person almost every day for a few weeks and shows no sign of stopping?

Even if we could determine the number of lives at risk that justifies the use of torture, and the level of certainty that a crime has occurred or is about to occur, and that the suspect in custody has critical information, how do we assess the level of exigency and the inability to obtain the information through traditional means? Must the bomb literally be ticking—what if the information pertains to a plot to plant a bomb within the month? A week? Of course, the longer the time period, the greater the chance that traditional methods of law enforcement will detect the plot. But where do we draw the line? And how do we decide that methods besides torture will not work in time?

The point is simply this: no matter how one tries to confine the use of torture to extreme, narrow circumstances, the temptation to broaden those circumstances is inevitable. Without an absolute prohibition on the use of torture, it is virtually impossible to ensure that "special cases" remain special. [As] Professor [Sanford] Kadish so eloquently concludes, "when torture is no longer unthinkable, it will be thought about." * * *

[A] warrant requirement would do little in providing oversight to the process of torturing. It is certain, that proceedings to obtain a warrant would be conducted in secret. After all, a torture warrant would presumably be sought only in extreme circumstances dictated by national security. Even now, much of what happens to the detainees at Camp X–Ray, in Guantanamo Bay, is shrouded in secrecy. Public disclosure of a desire to obtain a "torture warrant" because of concern that a weapon of mass destruction is hidden in a major city, simply, would not happen.

[In] sum, the warrant requirement would do nothing to rectify the evils of torture, and do little to restrict its use. Indeed, having a warrant process established might encourage police officers to seek the right to torture more often than they would engage in such behavior on their own. And, in the current climate of ever-present national emergency, a judge might very well issue a warrant permitting torture in circumstances that do not begin to resemble a "ticking bomb" scenario. Put simply, a warrant procedure likely would be an invitation to the increasing use of torture.

ALAN M. DERSHOWITZ, *The Torture Warrant: A Response to Professor Strauss*, 48 N.Y. Law Sch.L.Rev. 275, 289, 291–94 (2004):

I agree [that the United States should not become a nation whose police torture a small child in order to get his terrorist parent to confess]. But I believe we are more likely to become such a nation if we leave decisions of this kind to the uncontrolled discretion of those whose only job is to protect us from terrorism and who are paid to believe that the ends always justify the means. * * *

There is a difference in principle, as Bentham noted more than 200 years ago, between torturing the guilty to save the lives of the innocent, and torturing innocent people. A system which requires an articulated justification for the use of non-lethal torture and approval by a judge is more likely to honor that principle than a system that discreetly and without open accountability relegates these decisions to law enforcement agents whose only job is to protect the public from terrorism.

[In] a democracy governed by a rule of law, we should never want our soldiers or president to take any action which we deem wrong or illegal. A good test of whether an action should or should not be done is whether we are prepared to have it disclosed—perhaps not immediately, but certainly after some time has passed. No legal system operating under the rule of law should ever tolerate an "off-the-books" approach to necessity. Even the defense of necessity must be justified lawfully. The road to tyranny has always been paved with claims of necessity made by those responsible for the security of a nation. Our system of checks and balances requires that all presidential actions, like all legislative or military actions, be consistent with governing law. If it is necessary to torture in the ticking bomb case, then our governing laws must accommodate this practice. If we refuse to change our law to accommodate any particular action then our government should not take that action. Requiring that a controversial action be made openly and with accountability is one way of minimizing resort to unjustifiable means.

———

SETH F. KREIMER, *Too Close to the Rack and the Screw: Constitutional Constraints on Torture in the War on Terror*, 6 U.Pa.J.Const.L. 278, 319–22, 324–25 (2003):

* * * By Professor Dershowitz's hypothesis, officials would be willing to violate a prohibition of torture to achieve antiterrorist goals; one might suspect those same officials would be inclined to "sex up" applications for torture warrants. [Moreover judges,] like executive officials, would be subject to public pressure to do everything possible to prevent a recurrence of September 11.

Armed with a doctrine that requires them to "balance" the rights of suspects against the needs of the public, it seems entirely plausible to predict that judges would issue warrants in cases far short of the "ticking bomb." Each warrant granted would be the starting point for an argument that a subsequent warrant should be granted in circumstances just a little short of the exigencies of the prior case. * * *

Faced with a threat of mass devastation that can be avoided only through torture, could an American official believe, as a matter of morality and public policy, that she should choose the path of the torturer as the lesser evil? On this question, I am prepared to concede that there is room for debate, as there is room for debate as to whether under extraordinary circumstances a public official should choose to violate any provision of the Constitution. But on the question of whether scholars or courts should announce before the fact that the Constitution permits torture, the answer seems clearer: ours is not a Constitution that condones such actions. An official who proclaims fidelity to the Constitution cannot in the same breath claim the right to use methods "too close to the rack and the screw to permit of constitutional differentiation."

———

ALAN M. DERSHOWITZ, *Torture Without Visibility and Accountability Is Worse Than with It*, 6 U.Pa.J.Const.L. 326 (2003):

My own normative preference would be for the courts to declare all forms of torture unconstitutional, even if its fruits are not used against the defendant and even if it is not administered as "punishment." My own normative preference would also be for law enforcement officials to refrain from using torture, but my empirical conclusion is that they will, in fact, employ it in "ticking bomb" cases. My prediction of what the current courts "will do in fact" is different from Professor Kreimer's. I hope he is right, but I think I am right.

If he is right, he should support my proposal for some kind of legal structure that promotes visibility and accountability through a "torture warrant." In the absence of some such structure, it will be difficult to get a test case before the courts, since torture will continue to be administered beneath the radar screen and with the kind of "deniability" that currently shrouds the practice. The open authorization of limited torture warrants could, on the other hand, be challenged on its face, and we would soon learn whose prediction is more accurate. If he is right, all forms of torture would be declared unconstitutional. If I am right, there would, at least, be some accountability, visibility, and limitations on a dangerous practice that is currently shrouded in secrecy and deniability. * * *

JOHN T. PARRY & WELSH S. WHITE, *Interrogating Suspected Terrorists: Should Torture Be An Option?*, 63 U.Pitt.L.Rev. 743, 763 (2002):[b]

[The] best approach is to place the decision [to resort to torture] squarely on the shoulders of the individuals who order or carry out torture. Government agents should use torture only when it provides the last remaining chance to save lives that are in imminent peril. If interrogators know that they act at their peril, because the law provides no authority for torture under any circumstances, then they are likely to be deterred from acting except when the choice—however distasteful—seems obvious.

When a government agent uses torture to gain information that would avert a future terrorist act, the necessity defense should be available in any resulting criminal prosecution. A successful necessity claim requires proof that the defendant reasonably believed his harmful actions were necessary to avert a greater, imminent harm. * * *

Allowing the necessity defense in torture cases is consistent with providing strong deterrence against torture. [Even] if interrogators know that the necessity defense is available, they will not be able to predict with certainty before they act whether the defense would be successful, and the resulting uncertainty would also foster deterrence. The primary obstacle to deterrence is prosecutorial discretion. An interrogator might assume that the government will not prosecute if torture reveals critical information. For that reason, the Department of Justice should have a clear and public policy of prosecuting without exception any law enforcement official who uses torture. * * *

14. Meeting the "heavy burden" of demonstrating waiver: should tape recordings of the warnings and police questioning be required? As pointed out in Richard A. Leo, *Police Interrogation and American Justice* 293 (2008) (hereinafter Leo), "[the] first explicit call for tape-recording interrogations came not from legal reformers, [but] from police themselves. In the first interrogation manual ever published, W.R. Kidd [, a California police lieutenant,] called for the verbatim recording of interrogations, either through a sound recording if one was available or a stenographer if one was not." Lt. Kidd maintained that recording interrogations would "trap the suspect in lies" and assist police during and after the interrogation. Moreover, added Kidd, "[by] their very nature [sound recording] refute any implications that the third degree has been used."

The first law review article calling for the recording of custodial police interrogation from beginning to end (as opposed to merely recording the confession itself) did not appear until twenty-one years later (and five years before *Miranda*). In this article, *Police Interrogation of Arrested Persons: A Skeptical View*, 52 J.Crim.L. & P.S. 21, 48 (1961) (also discussed at p. 560 supra), Bernard Weisberg, an ACLU lawyer, attacked the secrecy surrounding police interrogation: "No other case comes to mind in which an administrative official is permitted the broad discretionary power assumed by the police interrogator, together with the power to prevent objective recordation of the facts. The absence of a record makes disputes inevitable about the conduct of the police and, sometimes, about what the prisoner has actually said. It is secrecy, not privacy, which accounts for the

---

b. In the article by Professors Parry and White that follows, the authors use "torture" to refer to any coercive interrogation practice that involves the inflection of pain or extreme discomfort.

absence of a reliable record of interrogation proceedings in a police station. If the need for some pre-judicial questioning is assumed, privacy may be defended on grounds of necessity; secrecy cannot be defended on this or any other ground."

At one point, the *Miranda* opinion (see p. 579) came to the very edge of requiring law enforcement officers to tape, where feasible, the warning, waiver and subsequent questioning and statements made in response: "If the interrogation continues without the presence of an attorney and a statement is taken, a heavy burden rests on the Government to demonstrate that the defendant knowingly and intelligently waived his [rights]. Since the State is responsible for establishing the isolated circumstances under which the interrogation takes place and *has the only means of making available corroborated evidence* of warnings given during incommunicado interrogation, the burden is rightly on its shoulders." (Emphasis added.) However, the *Miranda* Court fell short of imposing a tape recording requirement on police interrogators—perhaps because it was well aware that such a requirement would add much fuel to the criticism that it was exercising undue control over police practices—that it was "legislating."

Despite the references to "heavy burden" and "corroborated evidence" in the *Miranda* opinion and the strong support for video, or at least audio, taping in the literature, most state courts have held that—even when taping the proceedings in the interrogation room is feasible—the uncorroborated testimony of an officer that he gave complete *Miranda* warnings and obtained a waiver is sufficient. The exceptions are discussed below.

Since DNA testing became available in the late 1980s some 250 innocent people have been exonerated by postconviction DNA testing, including 22 people convicted of murder and 52 convicted of both murder and rape. See Brandon L. Garrett, *Convicting the Innocent* 5 (2011). Forty of these exonerees confessed to crimes they did not commit and almost all of these defendants made "contaminated" confession statements, i.e., confessed to details about the crime that only the killer or rapist could have known—details that must have been improperly disclosed to them, most likely by the police. See id. at pp. 5–8. (Typically, police and prosecutors then emphasized that the defendant must be guilty because only the guilty person would have known about the details.)

Despite the fact that video or audiotaping of the entire interrogation would simplify such issues as the delivery of the *Miranda* warnings, the voluntariness of a confession and the aforementioned "contamination" of the suspect's statements, and despite the fact that "the need for video and audiotaping is the one proposition that wins universal agreement in the *Miranda* literature," William J. Stuntz, *Miranda's Mistake*, 99 Mich.L.Rev. 975, 981 n. 19 (2001),[a] only eleven

---

a. See generally Joseph D. Grano, *Confessions, Truth and the Law* 116, 121 (1993); Yale Kamisar, *Police Interrogations and Confessions* 129–37 (1980); Richard A. Leo, *Police Interrogation and American Justice* 291–305 (2008); Stephen A. Drizin & Beth A. Colgan, *Let the Cameras Roll: Mandatory Videotaping of Interrogations Is the Solution to Illinois' Problem of False Confessions* 32 Loyola U.Chi.L.J. 337 (2001); William A. Geller, *Videotaping Interrogation and Confessions*, in *The Miranda Debate: Law, Justice and Policing* 303 (Richard A. Leo & George C. Thomas III eds. 1998).

Paul G. Cassell, *Miranda's Social Costs: An Empirical Reassessment*, 90 Nw.U.L.Rev. 387, 486–97 (1996), has forcefully argued that a recording requirement should be viewed as an *alternative* to *Miranda*. He maintains that a recording requirement furnishes a suspect much more protection than a system which requires a police officer to "mumble the *Miranda* warnings and have you waive your rights, all as reported by [the officer] in later testimony." Cassell's article evoked a response from Stephen J. Schulhofer, *Miranda's Practical Effect: Substantial Benefits and Vanishingly Small Social Costs*, 90 Nw.U.L.Rev. 556 (1996). Schulhofer agrees that videotaping is

states and the District of Columbia (and until 2003, only two states) "require or encourage electronic recording of at least some interrogations by statute." Garrett, supra, at 248. (However, "seven more state supreme courts have written opinions either requiring or encouraging the recording of interrogations," id.)

The Alaska Supreme Court was the first state supreme court to require its law enforcement officers to tape custodial police interrogation when feasible. It did so as a matter of due process under its state constitution. *Stephan v. State*, 711 P.2d 1156 (Alaska 1985). A decade later, the Minnesota Supreme Court followed, exercising its supervisory powers over state criminal justice. *State v. Scales*, 518 N.W.2d 587 (Minn. 1994).

The ILLINOIS GOVERNOR'S COMMISSION ON CAPITAL PUNISHMENT (2002) recommended that custodial interrogation of a homicide suspect should be videotaped. The following year, despite substantial resistance by some law enforcement groups, who voiced fear that a taping requirement would interfere with police work and provide another "loophole" for the guilty to escape punishment, Illinois became the first state to pass legislation requiring the electronic recording of police interrogation under certain circumstances (effective 2005).

According to Steven A. Drizin & Beth A. Colgan, *Let the Cameras Roll: Mandatory Videotaping of Interrogations is the Solution to Illinois' Problem of False Confessions*, 32 Loyola U. Chi. L. J. 337, 339 (2001), "the push" for the Illinois legislation "arose from a spate of false confession cases and questionable interrogations that have plagued Illinois law enforcement and undermined the general public's faith in the criminal justice system."

Even in jurisdictions which do not require electronic recording of police interrogations, there has been a significant movement among law enforcement agencies to record. Professor Garrett reports that "[a]t least 500 police departments now videotape interrogations." Id. at 248.

However, despite the appreciable surge in favor of electronic recording in recent years, "most police departments still do not record interrogations, and many of those who do tape selectively or only tape the admission. [A] majority of law enforcement agencies continue to oppose [the practice] altogether. [The FBI] still refuses to record interrogations as a matter of policy. Several major urban police departments, [have] also resisted recording requirements." Richard Leo, *Police Interrogation and American Justice* 296 (2008).

Electronic recording of police interrogations has a great many supporters, but few, if any, are more enthusiastic about it than Professor Richard Leo (id. at 297, 302):

"Taping creates an objective, comprehensive and reviewable record of an interrogation, making it unnecessary to rely on the incomplete, selective, and potentially biased accounts of the disputants over what occurred. The indisputable record it provides is 'law enforcement's version of instant replay' * * *

---

an extremely valuable tool—for both the police interrogator and the suspect—but maintains that "without clear substantive requirements against which to test the police behavior that the videotape will reveal, the objective record will lack any specific legal implications."

For the view that there are three constitutional grounds for requiring police interrogations to be taped, see Christopher Slobogin, *Towards Taping*, 1 Ohio State J.Crim.L. 309 (2003). Professor Slobogin argues that the only way the government can meet its due process obligation to preserve evidence that is exculpatory and the only way, in many instances, that the government can meet its need to prove by a preponderance of the evidence that the police gave, and the suspect understood, the warnings and the suspect has waived his rights voluntarily and intelligently is by taping the proceedings in the stationhouse. Slobogin also contends that, unless defense counsel is present at the interrogation, taping is necessary to effectuate the suspect's right to confront the witnesses against him. Cf. *United States v. Wade*, p. 761 infra.

"Electronic recording also promotes truth-finding by preventing false confessions and erroneous convictions. [It] opens up police practices to the possibility of external scrutiny, and thus interrogators are less likely to use impermissible or questionable techniques, including the psychologically coercive and improper ones that are the primary cause of false confessions.[a] * * *

"Electronic recording professionalizes the interrogation function by opening it up to greater external review. That improves the quality of interrogation and lends greater credibility to detective work—especially in urban communities where police may be distrusted by large segments of the populations—by demonstrating to prosecutors, judges, and juries the lawfulness of police methods and the confessions they obtain."

As for the argument that recording inhibits suspects from talking, "in most states, police are not required to notify suspects that they are recording and thus can do so surreptitiously. And even in those states where permission is required, most suspects consent and quickly forget about the recording (which need not be visible)." Leo at 303.

As for the argument that electronic recording is too costly, "[a]ny cost-benefit analysis must take into account the costs and benefits to the entire criminal justice system, not just to police. They include the savings in salary and court time by police, prosecutors, and judges in reconstructing and resolving disputed interrogation and confessions. The cost-benefit analysis must also take into account the costs and benefits to the criminal justice system that cannot be reduced to monetary value, such as the greater accuracy of prosecutorial charging decisions, judicial rulings, and jury verdicts." Id. at 303–04.

15. Implied waiver. Although a waiver is not established merely by showing that a defendant was given complete *Miranda* warnings and thereafter made an incriminating statement, *Tague v. Louisiana,* 444 U.S. 469 (1980), this does not mean that a waiver of *Miranda* rights will never be recognized unless "specifically made" after the warnings are given. As the Court, per Stewart, J., observed in NORTH CAROLINA v. BUTLER, 441 U.S. 369 (1979):

"The question is not one of form, but rather whether the defendant knowingly and voluntarily waived [his *Miranda* rights]. [Although] mere silence is not enough [that] does not mean that the defendant's silence, coupled with an understanding of his rights and a course of conduct indicating waiver, may never support a conclusion that a defendant has waived his rights. The courts must presume that a defendant did not waive his rights; the prosecution's burden is great; but in at least some cases waiver can be clearly inferred from the actions and words of the person interrogated."[b]

Dissenting Justice Brennan, joined by Marshall and Stevens, JJ., protested: "[The Court] shrouds in half-light the question of waiver, allowing courts to construct inferences from ambiguous word and gestures. But the very premise of *Miranda* requires that ambiguity be interpreted against the interrogator. [Under the conditions inherent in custodial interrogation], only the most explicit waiver of rights can be considered knowingly and freely given. [S]ince the Court agrees

---

a. For more on false confessions, see pp. 734–38 infra.

b. After reading the FBI's "Advice of Rights" form, defendant was asked whether he understood his rights. He replied that he did, but refused to sign the waiver at the bottom of the form. He was then told that he need neither speak nor sign the form, but that the agents would like him to talk to them. He replied, "I will talk to you but I am not signing any form." He then made incriminating statements. Because defendant had said nothing when advised of his right to counsel, and because the state supreme court read *Miranda* as requiring a specific waiver of each right, it concluded that defendant had not waived his right to counsel. The U.S. Supreme Court disagreed: "By creating an inflexible rule that no implicit waiver [of *Miranda* rights] can ever suffice, the [state court] has gone beyond the requirements of federal organic law."

that *Miranda* requires the police to obtain some kind of waiver—whether express or implied—the requirement of an express waiver would impose no burden on the police not imposed by the Court's interpretation. It would merely make that burden explicit. Had [the agent] simply elicited a clear answer to the question, 'Do you waive your right to a lawyer?' this journey through three courts would not have been necessary."

16. *Why do so many suspects waive their rights?* Approximately 80 percent of custodial suspects waive their rights. See Leo 280–81; Mark A. Godsey, *Reformulating the Miranda warnings in Light of Contemporary Law and Understanding*, 90 MINN. L. REV. 781, 792 (2006) (and authorities collected therein.)[1]

To what extent is the large percentage of waivers due to the fact that many suspects believe, incorrectly, that remaining silent will make them "look guilty"? See Note 4(a), p. 599 supra.

To what extent is it due to the fact that, as George C. Thomas III, *Stories about Miranda*, 102 Mich. L. Rev. 1959, 1998 (2004), has concluded, "at some level many suspects *want* to talk to police; [they] *want* to tell their story because they think they can skillfully navigate the shoals of police interrogation and arrive safely on the other shore. [As] long as suspects think they are better off trying to persuade police that they are not guilty, they will continue to talk to the police. *Miranda* provides knowledge that it *might* not be in a suspect's best interest to talk to police. But this knowledge is meaningless as long as suspects are willing to take the chance that it *is* in their best interest to talk. As that calculation is based on a suspect's entire life telling stories, the *Miranda* Court was naive if it thought that a set of formal warnings could change story-telling behavior."

To what extent is the high incidence of waiver of rights due to the widespread use of *pre*-waiver police tactics undermining *Miranda*? (According to David Simon a *Baltimore Sun* reporter who was granted unlimited access to the city's homicide unit for a full year), before giving a suspect the *Miranda* warnings, Baltimore detectives often "advise" a suspect that if he were to assert his rights he would deprive himself of the opportunity to "tell his side of the story" and prevent "his friend, the detective" from writing up the homicide as, say, manslaughter instead of murder—or even self-defense. See David Simon, *Homicide: A Year on the Killing Streets* 194–207 (1991). The academic writings of Richard Leo and Welsh White essentially corroborate Davis Simon's account and establish that these police tactics occur in other jurisdictions. See, e.g., Richard A. Leo & Welsh S. White, *Adapting to Miranda: Modern Interrogators' Strategies for Dealing with the Obstacles Pose by Miranda*, 84 Minn. L. Rev. 397 (1999).

When discussing the pre-waiver police tactics described above, the aforementioned writers often call them *"adapting"* to *Miranda*. But one commentator, Yale Kamisar, *On the Fortieth Anniversary of the Miranda Case*, 5 Ohio St. J. Crim. L. 163, 186 (2007), maintains that the more appropriate words are "evading" or "disregarding" *Miranda*. He continues, id. at 187–88' "According to Simon, Leo and White, in a significant number of instances, [the] police, in effect, are *talking the suspect out of asserting* his rights *before* the waiver of rights transaction ever takes place. There is no phase of the criminal process known as the 'pre-waiver of rights' stage, during which time custodial suspects are 'conditioned' or 'conned' into waiving their rights *before* being asked whether they want to assert them."

To what extent is the high incidence of waiver due to the ease with which courts find waiver? Consider George C. Thomas III, *Separated at Birth but Siblings Nonetheless: Miranda and the Due Process Cases* 99 Mich. L. Rev. 1081,

---

1. Moreover, adds Professor Leo, once a suspect has waived his rights, the police may engage in "deliberate, suggestive, or manipulative interrogation techniques. [And] very few suspects later invoke their rights after first waiving them."

1082 (2001). After studying hundreds of appellate opinions, Professor Thomas reported this "basic finding": "Once the prosecutor proves that the warnings were given in a language that the suspect understands, courts find waiver in almost every case. [The] waiver process bears little resemblance to waiver of the Fifth Amendment privilege at trial, where the prosecutor is not permitted to badger the defendant with requests that he take the witness stand. [The] *Miranda* version of the Fifth Amendment permits waiver to be made carelessly, inattentively and without counsel."

What about the "Silent Types"?

Although there is general agreement that the great majority of custodial suspects waive their *Miranda* rights, this is not the whole picture. As some critics of *Miranda* point out, various studies reveal that custodial suspects with felony records are three or four times more likely to invoke their rights than those with no prior records. Professor Stuntz calls custodial suspects who have felony records the "Silent Types." William J. Stuntz, *Miranda's Mistake*, 99 Mich.L.Rev. 975, 982 (2001).

According to Richard A. Leo & Welsh S. White, *Adapting to Miranda: Modern Interrogation Strategies for Dealing with the Obstacles Posed by Miranda*, 84 Minn.L.Rev. 397, 469 (1999), "even if *Miranda* were abolished" the police would be "unlikely" to loosen the tongues of the Silent Types: "Taken as a group, suspects who assert their *Miranda* rights may be unlikely to make incriminating statements to the police under any [acceptable or tolerable] circumstances because they have been hardened by exposure to the criminal justice system."

17. *"Qualified" or "conditional" waiver.* As *North Carolina v. Butler* itself illustrates (see fn. a supra), a suspect may refuse to sign a waiver but nonetheless indicate that he is willing to talk.[a] Or he may object to any notetaking by an officer but agree to talk about the case or indicate that he will talk only if a tape recorder is turned off. Are oral waivers effective in the face of such objections? A number of courts have held that they are. See, e.g., *United States v. Frazier,* 476 F.2d 891 (D.C.Cir.1973) (en banc) (*Frazier II*). But see CRIMPROC § 6.9(f) (in these situations defendant probably acted as he did "because of a mistaken impression that an oral confession which was not contemporaneously recorded could not be used against him"; therefore, police should be required to "clear up misunderstandings of this nature which are apparent to any reasonable observer").[b]

The Court addressed this general problem in CONNECTICUT v. BARRETT, 479 U.S. 523 (1987). While in custody, respondent, a suspect in a sexual assault case, was thrice advised of his *Miranda* rights. On each occasion, after signing an acknowledgment that he had been informed of his rights, respondent indicated that he would not make a written statement, but that he was willing to talk about the incident that led to his arrest. On the second and third such occasions, respondent added that he would not make a written statement outside the presence of counsel, and then orally admitted his involvement in the crime. An officer reduced to writing his recollection of respondent's last such statement, and the confession was admitted into evidence at respondent's trial. The Court, per

---

   a. The *Butler* Court did not hold that this constituted a valid waiver, but only rejected the state court's view that nothing short of an express waiver would satisfy *Miranda*.

   b. One study indicates that 45 percent of post-*Miranda* defendants mistakenly believed that oral statements could not be used against them. See Lawrence S. Leiken, *Police Interrogation in Colorado: The Implementation of Miranda,* 47 Denver L.J. 1, 15–16, 33 (1970). If so many people do not realize the significance of an oral statement, should the warning take this form: "You have a right to remain silent and anything you say, *orally or* in writing, may (will) be used against you"? *Unif.R.Crim.P.* 212(b) and 243 so provide.

Rehnquist, C.J., rejected the contention that respondent's expressed desire for counsel before making a written statement served as an invocation of the right for all purposes.

Brennan, J., concurred in the judgment. Although "Barrett's contemporaneous waiver of his right to silence and limited invocation of his right to counsel (for the purpose of making a written statement) suggested that he did not understand that anything he *said* could be used against him," he testified that "he understood his *Miranda* rights, i.e., he knew that he need not talk to the police without a lawyer and that anything he said could be used against him. Under these circumstances, the waiver of the right to silence and the limited invocation of the right to counsel were valid."

18. *What constitutes an invocation of Miranda rights?* In FARE v. MICHAEL C., 442 U.S. 707 (1979), after being fully advised of his *Miranda* rights, a juvenile, who had been taken into custody on suspicion of murder, asked, "Can I have my probation officer here?" The police officer replied that he was "not going to call [the probation officer] right now," then continued: "If you want to talk to us without an attorney present, you can. If you don't want to, you don't have to." The juvenile then agreed to talk to the police without an attorney being present and made incriminating statements. The Court, per Blackmun, J., held the statements admissible, deeming the request to see a probation officer not a *per se* invocation of *Miranda* rights—not the equivalent of asking for a lawyer. The admissibility of the statements on the basis of waiver turned on "the totality of the circumstance surrounding the interrogation" (e.g., evaluation of the juvenile's age, experience, background and intelligence).

"The *per se* aspect of *Miranda*," emphasized the Court, was "based on the unique role the lawyer plays in the adversarial system of criminal justice in this country. [A] probation officer is not in the same posture with regard to either the accused or the system of justice as a whole. * * * Moreover, [he] is the employee of the State which seeks to prosecute the alleged offender. He is a peace officer, and as such is allied, to a greater or lesser extent, with his fellow peace officers. [It is the] pivotal role of legal counsel [in the administration of criminal justice] that justifies the *per se* rule established in *Miranda* and that distinguishes the request for counsel from the request for a probation officer, a clergyman, or a close friend."

Justice Marshall, joined by Brennan and Stevens, JJ., dissented. Noting that the California Supreme Court had "determined that probation officers have a statutory duty to represent minors' interests and, indeed, are 'trusted guardian figure[s]' to whom a juvenile would likely turn for assistance," the dissenters maintained that "*Miranda* requires that interrogation cease whenever a juvenile requests an adult who is obligated to represent his interests." Such request "constitutes both an attempt to obtain advice and a general invocation of the right to silence. For, as the California Supreme Court recognized, 'it is fatuous to assume that a minor in custody will be in a position to call an attorney for assistance,' or that he will trust the police to obtain an attorney for him."[a]

Does *Fare v. Michael C.* stand for the broad proposition that a request by any suspect (with the possible exception of a young, inexperienced juvenile; Michael C. was an "experienced" 16½ year old) to see anyone *other than an attorney*, whether it be a parent, spouse or best friend, does not *per se* constitute an assertion or invocation of *Miranda* rights? If so, is this because neither parent, spouse or best friend has the "unique ability to protect the Fifth Amendment rights" of a suspect

---

a. Justice Powell wrote a separate dissent, "not satisfied that this particular 16–year-old boy, in this particular situation was subjected to a fair interrogation free from inherently coercive circumstances."

undergoing custodial interrogation? How much weight, if any, should be given to the fact that the mother, father or husband requested by the suspect plays a "unique role" in the life of the particular suspect?

19. *The scope of "second-level" Miranda safeguards—the procedures that must be followed when suspects do assert their rights—and the distinction between invoking the right to remain silent and the right to counsel.* In most *Miranda* cases, the issue is the need for the *Miranda* warnings or the adequacy of the warnings given or the suspect's alleged waiver in response to the warnings. But different issues arise when the suspect *asserts* his rights— thereby triggering what have been called "second level" *Miranda* safeguards. Although this development may have surprised the *Miranda* Court, it turns out that the procedures that must be followed when a suspect invokes his rights depends on whether he asserted the right to remain silent or the right to counsel.

The Court first addressed this issue in MICHIGAN v. MOSLEY, 423 U.S. 96 (1975). Mosley was arrested in connection with certain robberies. After being given *Miranda* warnings by a robbery detective, Mosley declined to talk about the robberies (but he did not request a lawyer). The detective promptly ceased questioning and made no effort to persuade Mosley to reconsider his position. Mosley was then taken to a cell block in the building. After a two-hour interval, a homicide detective brought Mosley from the cell block to the homicide bureau for questioning about "an unrelated holdup murder." Mosley was again advised of his rights. This time he waived them and made an incriminating statement. A 7–2 majority, per Stewart, J., held the statement admissible.

After studying the *Miranda* opinion, the Court concluded that "the admissibility of statements obtained after the person in custody has decided to remain silent depends [on] whether his 'right to cut off questioning' was 'scrupulously honored.' " After examining the facts, the Court concluded that Mosley's right had been honored. The questioning by the homicide detective, emphasized the Court, had "focused exclusively on [a] crime different in nature and in time and place by occurrence from the robberies for which Mosley had been arrested and interrogated by [the robbery detective]" and the subsequent questioning by another detective about an unrelated homicide was "quite consistent with a reasonable interpretation of Mosley's earlier refusal to answer any questions about the robberies." Therefore, "this is not a case [where] the police failed to honor a decision [to] cut off questioning, either by refusing to discontinue the interrogation upon request or by persisting in repeated efforts to wear down [the suspect's] resistance and make him change his mind. [The] police here immediately ceased the interrogation, resumed questioning only after the passage of a significant period of time and the provision of a fresh set of warnings, and restricted the second interrogation to a crime that had not been a subject of the earlier interrogation."

Concurring Justice White foreshadowed his opinion for the Court six years later in *Edwards v. Arizona,* below, by observing: "[The *Miranda* Court showed in its opinion] that when it wanted to create a *per se* rule against further interrogation after assertion of a right, it knew how to do so. The Court there said 'if the individual states that he wants an attorney, the interrogation must cease *until an attorney is present.*' [Emphasis added by White, J.]"

Three factors seem to be *minimal requirements* for the resumption of questioning once a suspect asserts his right to remain silent: (1) immediately ceasing the interrogation; (2) suspending questioning entirely for a significant period; (3)

giving a fresh set of *Miranda* warnings at the outset of the second interrogation. May these three circumstances also be *the only* critical factors? May *Mosley* mean that these three circumstances suffice without more to eliminate the coercion inherent in the continuing custody and the renewed questioning? How significant is it that a different officer resumed the questioning? That the second interrogation occurred at another location? That the second interrogation was limited to a separate and "unrelated" crime? Compare Geoffrey Stone, *The Miranda Doctrine in the Burger Court*, 1977 Sup.Ct.Rev. 99, 134 (last factor "seems critical") with Kamisar, *The Warren Court (Was It Really So Defense–Minded?), the Burger Court (Is It Really So Prosecution–Oriented?) and Police Investigatory Practices*, in The Burger Court: The Counter–Revolution That Wasn't 62, 83 & n. 133 (V. Blasi ed. 1983) (not at all clear that *Mosley* was meant to be or will be so limited).

Distinguishing the *Mosley* case, EDWARDS v. ARIZONA, 451 U.S. 477 (1981), held that once a suspect has invoked his right to counsel he may not be "subject[ed] to further interrogation [until] counsel has been made available to him unless [he] himself initiates further communication, exchanges or conversations with the police."

Edwards was arrested for burglary, robbery and murder and taken to the police station. He waived his rights and agreed to talk about these crimes. But some time later he asserted his right to counsel. At this point, questioning ceased and Edwards was taken to jail. The next morning, two detectives, colleagues of the officer who had questioned Edwards the previous day, came to the jail, met with Edwards and again informed him of his rights.[a] This time Edwards agreed to talk about the same crimes. He then made incriminating statements which led to his conviction for these crimes. The state supreme court held that although Edwards had asserted his right to counsel the day before, he waived this right the following day when he agreed to talk after again being given his *Miranda* warnings. The Court, per White, J., disagreed:

"[H]owever sound the conclusion of the state courts as to the voluntariness of Edwards' admission may be, [neither court] undertook to focus on whether Edwards understood his right to counsel and intelligently and knowingly relinquished it. It is thus apparent that the decision below misunderstood the requirement for finding a valid waiver of the right to counsel, once invoked.

"[A]dditional safeguards [for waiver] are necessary when the accused asks for counsel; and we now hold that when an [in-custody suspect does assert this right a valid waiver of it] cannot be established by showing only that he responded to further police-initiated custodial interrogation even if he has been advised of his rights. [An] accused, such as Edwards, having expressed his desire to deal with the police only through counsel, is not subject to further interrogation by the authorities until counsel has been made available to him, unless the accused himself initiates further communication, exchanges or conversations with the police."[b]

Clarification (or extension?) of the Edwards rule

In Arizona v. Roberson, 486 U.S. 675 (1988), a 6–2 majority, per Stevens, J., held that once a suspect effectively asserts his *Miranda–Edwards* right to counsel,

---

a. When a guard informed Edwards that two detectives wanted to talk to him, Edwards replied that he did not want to talk to anyone. But the guard told him "he had" to talk to the detectives and then took him to meet with them. The opinion of the Court, however, seems to be written without regard to these particular facts.

b. Chief Justice Burger and Justices Powell and Rehnquist concurred in the result.

the police cannot even initiate interrogation about crimes *other than* the one for which the suspect has invoked his right to counsel. Newly appointed Justice Kennedy, joined by Chief Justice Rehnquist, dissented, emphasizing that *"Edwards* is our rule, not a constitutional command; and it is our obligation to justify its expansion." According to dissenters, the majority's approach was not "consistent with the practical realities of suspects' rights and police investigations."

In *Minnick v. Mississippi*, 498 U.S. 146 (1990), a 7–2 majority, per Kennedy, J., ruled that *Edwards'* protection continues even after the suspect has consulted with a lawyer. The Court maintained that the proposed exception would "undermine the advantages flowing from *Edwards'* 'clear and unequivocal' character. Moreover, 'adopting the rule proposed would leave far from certain the sort of consultation required to displace *Edwards.*' "

Because he believed that the *Edwards* rule should not extend beyond the circumstances present in *Edwards* itself—"where the suspect in custody asked to consult an attorney, and was interrogated before that attorney had ever been provided"—Justice Scalia, joined by Rehnquist, C.J., dissented. "Today's extension of the *Edwards* prohibition," protested Scalia, "is the latest stage of prophylaxis built upon prophylaxis, providing a veritable fairyland castle of imagined constitutional restriction upon law enforcement. This newest tower, according to the Court, is needed to avoid 'inconsisten[cy] with [the] purpose' of *Edwards'* prophylactic rule, which was needed to protect *Miranda's* prophylactic rule, which was needed to protect *Miranda's* prophylactic right to have counsel present, which was needed to protect the right against *compelled self-incrimination* found (at last!) in the Constitution."

NOTES AND QUESTIONS

(a) *The need to prevent the police from "badgering" a suspect who has previously asserted his rights.* The *Minnick* majority reiterates that the *Edwards* rule is "designed to prevent police from badgering a defendant into waiving his previously asserted" *right to counsel* and to "ensure that any statement made in subsequent interrogation is not the result of coercive pressures." But why isn't there a comparable need for a rule designed to prevent the police from badgering or pressuring a suspect into waiving his previously asserted *right to remain silent?*

(b) Is there a "public safety" exception to *Edwards*? The Supreme Court has never addressed this question, but lower federal courts have answered in the affirmative. See *United States v. Mobley*, 40 F.3d 688 (4th Cir.1994); *United States v. DeSantis*, 870 F.2d 536 (9th Cir.1989). For the view that these courts have reached the right result, see M.K.B. Darmer, *Lessons from the Lindh Case: Public Safety and the Fifth Amendment*, 68 Brooklyn L.Rev. 241, 279 (2002).

20. When do the Edwards protections come to an end? What constitutes a "break in custody"?

MARYLAND v. SHATZER
___ U.S. ___, 130 S.Ct. 1213, 175 L.Ed.2d 1045 (2010).

JUSTICE SCALIA delivered the opinion of the Court.

[In August 2003, when defendant Shatzer was serving a sentence in a state correctional facility for an unrelated crime, a detective tried to question him about allegations that he had sexually assaulted his own son. However, when Shatzer invoked his right to counsel, the detective ended the meeting and Shatzer was then released back into the general prison population.

[Two and a half years later, on March 2, 2006, another detective obtained more information about the incident and decided to discuss the matter once more. (Shatzer was still serving time in a correctional facility and his meeting with the detectives took place in a small room, apart from the general prison population.) At this meeting Shatzer signed a written waiver of his *Miranda* rights. After 30 minutes of questioning, during which time Shatzer made an incriminating statement, he agreed to take a polygraph examination.

[Five days later, after again being advised of his rights and after again waiving his rights in writing, Shatzer took the polygraph examination. He was informed that he had failed the exam. He then made another incriminating statement.

[The trial court ruled that the *Edwards* protections did not apply because Shatzer had experienced a "break in custody" for *Miranda* purposes between the 2003 and 2006 interrogations. However, the Maryland Court of Appeals reversed, holding that the passing of time *alone* is insufficient to end the *Edwards* protections and that, even if a "break-in-custody" exception did exist, Shatzer's release into the general prison population did not constitute such an exception.]

We consider whether a break in custody ends the presumption of involuntariness established in *Edwards v. Arizona.* * * *

[The *Edwards* Court] determined that [the] traditional standard for waiver was not sufficient to protect a suspect's right to have counsel present at a subsequent interrogation if he had previously requested counsel; "additional safeguards" were necessary. The Court therefore superimposed a "second layer of prophylaxis" [describing *Edwards*].

A judicially crafted rule [such as *Edwards*] is "justified only by reference to its prophylactic purpose" and applies only where its benefits outweigh its costs. [*Edwards'*] fundamental purpose [is] to "[p]reserv[e] the integrity of an accused's choice to communicate with police only through counsel" by "prevent[ing] police from badgering a defendant into waiving his previously asserted *Miranda* rights." Thus, the benefits of the rule are measured by the number of coerced confessions it suppresses that otherwise would have been admitted.

It is easy to believe that a suspect may be coerced or badgered into abandoning his earlier refusal to be questioned without counsel in the paradigm *Edwards* case, [where] the suspect has been arrested for a particular crime and is held in uninterrupted pretrial custody while that crime is being actively investigated. After the initial interrogation, and up to and including the second one, he remains cut off from his normal life and companions, "thrust into" and isolated in an "unfamiliar," "police-dominated atmosphere," *Miranda*, where his captors "appear to control [his] fate." That was the situation confronted by the suspects in *Edwards*, *Roberson*, and *Minnick*, the three cases in which we have held the *Edwards* rule applicable.

[When,] unlike what happened in these three cases, a suspect has been released from his pretrial custody and has returned to his normal life for some time before the later attempted interrogation, there is little reason to think that his change of heart regarding interrogation without counsel has been coerced. He has no longer been isolated. He has likely been able to seek advice from an attorney, family members, and friends.[3] And he knows from his earlier experience

---

3. Justice Stevens points out (opinion concurring in judgment), that in *Minnick*, actual pre-reinterrogation consultation with an attorney during *continued* custody did not suffice to avoid application of *Edwards*. That does not mean that the ability to consult freely with attorneys and others does not reduce the level of coercion at all, or that it is "only questionably relevant" to whether termination of custody reduces the coercive pressure that is the basis for *Edwards'* super-prophylactic rule.

that he need only demand counsel to bring the interrogation to a halt; and that investigative custody does not last indefinitely. In these circumstances, it is far fetched to think that a police officer's asking the suspect whether he would like to waive his *Miranda* rights will any more "wear down the accused" than did the first such request at the original attempted interrogation—which is of course not deemed coercive. His change of heart is less likely attributable to "badgering" than it is to the fact that further deliberation in familiar surroundings has caused him to believe (rightly or wrongly) that cooperating with the investigation is in his interest.

[At] the same time that extending the *Edwards* rule yields diminished benefits, extending the rule also increases its costs: the in-fact voluntary confessions it excludes from trial, and the voluntary confessions it deters law enforcement officers from even trying to obtain. Voluntary confessions are not merely "a proper element in law enforcement," they are an "unmitigated good." * * *

[If] Shatzer's return to the general prison population qualified as a break in custody (a question we address *infra*), there is no doubt that it lasted long enough (2½ years) to meet that durational requirement. But what about a break that has lasted only one year? Or only one week? It is impractical to leave the answer to that question for clarification in future case-by-case adjudication; law enforcement officers need to know, with certainty and beforehand, when renewed interrogation is lawful. And while it is certainly unusual for this Court to set forth precise time limits governing police action, it is not unheard-of. In *County of Riverside* v. *McLaughlin* [p. 342], we specified 48 hours as the time within which the police must comply with the requirement of *Gerstein* v. *Pugh* [p. 340], that a person arrested without a warrant be brought before a magistrate to establish probable cause for continued detention.

* * * We think it appropriate to specify a period of time to avoid the consequence that continuation of the *Edwards* presumption "will not reach the correct result most of the time." It seems to us that period is 14 days. That provides plenty of time for the suspect to get reacclimated to his normal life, to consult with friends and counsel, and to shake off any residual coercive effects of his prior custody.

The 14–day limitation meets Shatzer's concern that a break-in-custody rule lends itself to police abuse. He envisions that once a suspect invokes his *Miranda* right to counsel, the police will release the suspect briefly (to end the *Edwards* presumption) and then promptly bring him back into custody for reinterrogation. But once the suspect has been out of custody long enough (14 days) to eliminate its coercive effect, there will be nothing to gain by such gamesmanship—nothing, that is, except the entirely appropriate gain of being able to interrogate a suspect who has made a valid waiver of his *Miranda* rights.[7]

Shatzer argues that ending the *Edwards* protections at a break in custody will undermine *Edwards'* purpose to conserve judicial resources. * * * Confessions obtained after a 2–week break in custody and a waiver of *Miranda* rights are most unlikely to be compelled, and hence are unreasonably excluded. In any case, a break-in-custody exception will dim only marginally, if at all, the bright-line nature of *Edwards*. * * *

[After] the 2003 interview, Shatzer was released back into the general prison population where he was serving an unrelated sentence. The issue is whether that

---

7. A defendant who experiences a 14–day break in custody after invoking the *Miranda* right to counsel is not left without protection. *Edwards* establishes a *presumption* that a suspect's waiver of *Miranda* rights is involuntary. Even without this "second layer of prophylaxis," a defendant is still free to claim the prophylactic protection of *Miranda*—arguing that his waiver of *Miranda* rights was in fact involuntary. * * *

constitutes a break in *Miranda* custody. * * * Without minimizing the harsh realities of incarceration, we think lawful imprisonment imposed upon conviction of a crime does not create the coercive pressures identified in *Miranda*.

Interrogated suspects who have previously been convicted of crime live in prison. When they are released back into the general prison population, they return to their accustomed surroundings and daily routine—they regain the degree of control they had over their lives prior to the interrogation. Sentenced prisoners, in contrast to the *Miranda* paradigm, are not isolated with their accusers. They live among other inmates, guards, and workers, and often can receive visitors and communicate with people on the outside by mail or telephone.

Their detention, moreover, is relatively disconnected from their prior unwillingness to cooperate in an investigation. The former interrogator has no power to increase the duration of incarceration, which was determined at sentencing. And even where the possibility of parole exists, the former interrogator has no apparent power to decrease the time served. This is in stark contrast to the circumstances faced by the defendants in *Edwards*, *Roberson*, and *Minnick*, whose continued detention as suspects rested with those controlling their interrogation, and who confronted the uncertainties of what final charges they would face, whether they would be convicted, and what sentence they would receive. * * *

A few words in response to Justice Stevens' concurrence: It claims we ignore that "[w]hen police tell an indigent suspect that he has the right to an attorney" and then "reinterrogate" him without providing a lawyer, "the suspect is likely to feel that the police lied to him and that he really does not have any right to a lawyer." The fallacy here is that we are not talking about "reinterrogating" the suspect; we are talking about *asking his permission* to be interrogated. An officer has in no sense lied to a suspect when, after advising, as *Miranda* requires, * * * he promptly ends the attempted interrogation because the suspect declines to speak without counsel present, and then, two weeks later, reapproaches the suspect and asks, "Are you now willing to speak without a lawyer present?" * * *

Contrary to the concurrence's conclusion, there is no reason to believe a suspect will view confession as " 'the only way to end his interrogation' " when, before the interrogation begins, he is told that he can avoid it by simply requesting that he not be interrogated without counsel present—an option that worked before. * * *

Because Shatzer experienced a break in *Miranda* custody lasting more than two weeks between the first and second attempts at interrogation, *Edwards* does not mandate suppression of his March 2006 statements. * * *

JUSTICE THOMAS, concurring in part and concurring in the judgment.

I join [the part] of the Court's opinion, [holding] that release into the general prison population constitutes a break in custody. I do not join the Court's decision to extend the presumption of involuntariness established in *Edwards* v. *Arizona*, [for] 14 days after custody ends.

It is not apparent to me that the presumption of involuntariness the Court recognized in *Edwards* is justifiable even in the custodial setting to which *Edwards* applies it. Accordingly, I would not extend the *Edwards* rule "beyond the circumstances present in *Edwards* itself." But even if one believes that the Court is obliged to apply *Edwards* to any case involving continuing custody, the Court's opinion today goes well beyond that. It extends the presumption of involuntariness *Edwards* applies in custodial settings to interrogations that occur after custody ends.

[As] the Court concedes, "clarity and certainty are not goals in themselves. They are valuable only when they reasonably further the achievement of some substantive end—here, the exclusion of compelled confessions" that the Fifth Amendment prohibits. The Court's arbitrary 14–day rule fails this test, even under the relatively permissive criteria set forth in our precedents. Accordingly, I do not join that portion of the Court's opinion.

JUSTICE STEVENS, concurring in the judgment.

While I agree that the presumption from *Edwards* is not "eternal" and does not mandate suppression of Shatzer's statement made after a 2½-year break in custody, I do not agree with the Court's newly announced rule: that *Edwards* *always* ceases to apply when there is a 14–day break in custody.

In conducting its "cost-benefit" analysis, the Court demeans *Edwards* as a " 'second layer' " of "judicially prescribed prophylaxis." [The] source of the holdings in the long line of cases that include both *Edwards* and *Miranda*, however, is the Fifth Amendment protection against compelled self-incrimination applied to the "compulsion inherent in custodial" interrogation, *Miranda* and the "significan[ce]" of "the assertion of the right to counsel," *Edwards*. The Court's analysis today is insufficiently sensitive to the concerns that motivated the *Edwards* line of cases.

The most troubling aspect of the Court's time-based rule is that it disregards the compulsion caused by a second (or third, or fourth) interrogation of an indigent suspect who was told that if he requests a lawyer, one will be provided for him. When police tell an indigent suspect that he has the right to an attorney, that he is not required to speak without an attorney present, and that an attorney will be provided to him at no cost before questioning, the police have made a significant promise. If they cease questioning and then reinterrogate the suspect 14 days later without providing him with a lawyer, the suspect is likely to feel that the police lied to him and that he really does not have any right to a lawyer.

[When] police have not honored an earlier commitment to provide a detainee with a lawyer, the detainee likely will "understan[d] his (expressed) wishes to have been ignored" and "may well see further objection as futile and confession (true or not) as the only way to end his interrogation." * * * Simply giving a "fresh se[t] of *Miranda* warnings" will not " 'reassure' a suspect who has been denied the counsel he has clearly requested that his rights have remained untrammeled."

[The] many problems with the Court's new rule are exacerbated in the very situation in this case: a suspect who is in prison. Even if, as the Court assumes, a trip to one's home significantly changes the *Edwards* calculus, a trip to one's prison cell is not the same. A prisoner's freedom is severely limited, and his entire life remains subject to government control. Such an environment is not conducive to "shak[ing] off any residual coercive effects of his prior custody." Nor can a prisoner easily "seek advice from an attorney, family members, and friends," especially not within 14 days; prisoners are frequently subject to restrictions on communications. Nor, in most cases, can he live comfortably knowing that he cannot be badgered by police; prison is not like a normal situation in which a suspect "is in control, and need only shut his door or walk away to avoid police badgering." Indeed, for a person whose every move is controlled by the State, it is likely that "his sense of dependence on, and trust in, counsel as the guardian of his interests in dealing with government officials intensified."[13] * * * The Court ignores these realities of prison, and instead rests its argument on the supposition that a prisoner's "detention [is] relatively disconnected from their prior unwillingness to cooperate in an investigation." But that is not necessarily the case.

---

13. Prison also presents a troubling set of incentives for police. First, because investigators know that their suspect is also a prisoner, there is no need formally to place him under arrest. Thus, police generally can interview prisoners even without probable cause to hold them.

Prisoners are uniquely vulnerable to the officials who control every aspect of their lives; prison guards may not look kindly upon a prisoner who refuses to cooperate with police. And cooperation frequently is relevant to whether the prisoner can obtain parole. Moreover, even if it is true as a factual matter that a prisoner's fate is not controlled by the police who come to interrogate him, how is the prisoner supposed to know that? As the Court itself admits, compulsion is likely when a suspect's "captors appear to control [his] fate." [But] when a guard informs a suspect that he must go speak with police, it will "appear" to the prisoner that the guard and police are not independent. "Questioning by captors, who *appear* to control the suspect's fate, may create mutually reinforcing pressures that the Court has assumed will weaken the suspect's will."

[An] indigent suspect who took police at their word that they would provide an attorney probably will feel that he has "been denied the counsel he has clearly requested" when police begin to question him, without a lawyer, only 14 days later. But, when a suspect has been left alone for a significant period of time, he is not as likely to draw such conclusions when the police interrogate him again. [In] the case before us [the] suspect was returned to the general prison population for 2½ years. I am convinced that this period of time is sufficient. I therefore concur in the judgment.

NOTES AND QUESTIONS

According to dissenting Justice Stevens, if the police inform a suspect that if he is indigent a lawyer will be appointed to represent him, the police *"promise"* to provide him with a lawyer–and to do so within a reasonable time. Is this so? At another point in his dissenting opinion, Stevens writes about the police "not honor[ing] an earlier commitment to provide a detainee with a lawyer." When did the police make this commitment? When they advised the detainee of his rights? *Miranda* states that if a suspect asserts his right to an attorney, "the interrogation must cease until an attorney is present" (Casebook at p. 578). Do the police have any obligation beyond this?

Recall that *Miranda* also tells us that if "the authorities conclude that they will not provide counsel during a reasonable period of time in which interrogation in the field is carried out, *they may do so* without violating the person's Fifth Amendment privilege *so long as they do not question him during that time*" (p. 579) (emphasis added). Moreover, *Miranda* rejected the idea that each police station must have "a station house lawyer present at all times to advise prisoners" (p. 578).

Recall, too, *Duckworth v. Eagan.* That case upheld a *Miranda* warning which told a custodial suspect: "We have no way of getting you a lawyer, but one will be appointed for you, if you wish, if and when you go to court." The dissenting Justices maintained that upon hearing this warning the average suspect would "likely conclude" that he would not be provided with a lawyer until trial. If the police are obliged to provide a lawyer for a custodial suspect, and to do so within a reasonable time, how could the warning in *Duckworth* be considered adequate?

21. What constitutes "initiating" further communication with the police? The *Edwards* rule was deemed inapplicable in OREGON v. BRADSHAW, 462 U.S. 1039 (1983). Bradshaw, suspected of causing the death of Reynolds, a minor, by drunken driving, was arrested for furnishing liquor to Reynolds. Bradshaw agreed to talk to an officer about the fatal crash, but when the officer suggested that Bradshaw had been behind the wheel of the truck when Reynolds died, Bradshaw denied his involvement and expressed a desire to talk to a lawyer. The officers immediately terminated the conversation.

A few minutes later, either while still at the police station or enroute to the jail, Bradshaw asked the officer: "Well, what is going to happen to me now?" In response, the officer said that Bradshaw didn't have to talk to him and, because he had requested a lawyer, he didn't want Bradshaw to talk to him unless he decided to do so as a matter of his "own free will." Bradshaw said he understood. General conversation followed, in the course of which there was a discussion about where Bradshaw was being taken and the crime(s) for which he would be charged. The officer reiterated his own theory of how Bradshaw had caused Reynolds' death and then suggested that Bradshaw take a lie detector test to "clean the matter up." Bradshaw agreed.[a]

The next day, just before he took the lie detector test, Bradshaw was given another set of *Miranda* warnings and he signed a written waiver of his rights. At the conclusion of the test, the polygraph examiner told Bradshaw that he had not been truthful in response to certain questions. Bradshaw then admitted that he had been driving the vehicle in which Reynolds was killed and that he had consumed a considerable amount of alcohol before passing out at the wheel.

The Supreme Court held that under the circumstances Bradshaw could not avail himself of the *Edwards* rule, but there was no opinion of the Court. Justice Rehnquist, joined by Burger, C.J., and White and O'Connor, JJ., observed:

"There are some inquiries, such as a request for a drink of water or a request to use a telephone that are so routine that they cannot be fairly said to represent a desire on the part of an accused to open up a more generalized discussion relating directly or indirectly to the investigation. Such inquiries or statements, by either an accused or a police officer, relating to routine incidents of the custodial relationship, will not generally 'initiate' a conversation in the sense in which that word was used in *Edwards*.

"Although ambiguous, the respondent's question in this case as to what was going to happen to him evinced a willingness and a desire for a generalized discussion about the investigation; it was not merely a necessary inquiry arising out of the incidents of the custodial relationship. It could reasonably have been interpreted by the officer as relating generally to the investigation. That the police

---

a. Should Bradshaw have been advised of his rights and a valid waiver obtained at this point (not the next day, just before Bradshaw took the lie-detector test)? Does the critical moment occur when a suspect *agrees* to take a lie detector test (or agrees to submit to further interrogation) regardless of whether the test is given (or further interrogation takes place) then or later? Compare *Bradshaw* with *Wyrick v. Fields*, 459 U.S. 42 (1982) (per curiam), which arose as follows: After discussing the matter with his private counsel and with a military attorney, Fields, a soldier charged with rape, requested a polygraph examination. Prior to undergoing the examination, Fields signed a waiver-of-rights form. He was also told: "If you are now going to discuss the offense under investigation, which is rape, with or without a lawyer present, you have a right to stop answering questions at any time or speak to a lawyer before answering further, even if you sign a waiver certificate. Do you want a lawyer at this time?" Fields answered: "No."

At the conclusion of the polygraph examination, which took less than two hours, a CID agent asked Fields if he could explain why his answers were bothering him. Fields then made some incriminating statements. On federal habeas corpus, the Eighth Circuit found that the State had failed to satisfy its burden of proving that Fields knowingly and intelligently waived his right to have counsel present at the *post*-test interrogation. The Supreme Court disagreed:

[The Eighth Circuit rule] certainly finds no support in *Edwards*, which emphasizes that the totality of the circumstances, including the fact that the suspect initiated the questioning, is controlling. Nor is the rule logical; the questions put to Fields after the examination would not have caused him to forget the rights of which he had been advised and which he had understood moments before. The rule is simply an unjustifiable restriction on reasonable police questioning.

Dissenting Justice Marshall underscored the distinction between "an agreement to submit to a polygraph examination" and "the initiation of an ordinary conversation with the authorities": "[A] polygraph examination is a discrete test. It has a readily identifiable beginning and end. An individual who submits to such an examination does not necessarily have any reason whatsoever to expect that he will be subjected to a post-examination interrogation."

officer so understood it is apparent from the fact that he immediately reminded the accused that 'you do not have to talk to me,' and only after the accused told him that he 'understood' did they have a generalized conversation. On these facts we believe that there was not a violation of the *Edwards* rule.

"[The next inquiry, therefore] was 'whether a valid waiver of [Bradshaw's rights] had occurred, that is, whether the purported waiver was knowing and intelligent and found to be so under the totality of the circumstances, including the necessary fact that the accused, not the police, reopened the dialogue with the authorities.' *Edwards*.

"[The] state trial court [found that a valid waiver of defendant's rights did occur and] we have no reason to dispute these conclusions * * *.'"

Concurring Justice Powell, whose vote was decisive, agreed that Bradshaw had knowingly and intelligently waived his right to counsel, but saw no need for a two-step analysis—whether the suspect "initiated" a conversation with the police, and if so, whether under the "totality of circumstances" a valid waiver of rights followed. According to Powell, J.: "Fragmenting the standard into a novel two-step analysis—if followed literally—often would frustrate justice as well as common sense. Courts should engage in more substantive inquiries than 'who said what first.' [The *Edwards* rule] cannot in my view fairly be reduced to this."

Marshall, J., joined by Brennan, Blackmun and Stevens, JJ., dissented, "agree[ing] with the plurality that, in order to constitute 'interrogation' under *Edwards,* an accused's inquiry must demonstrate a desire to discuss the subject matter of the criminal investigation," but expressing "baffle[ment] [at] the plurality's application of that standard to the facts of this case":

"The plurality asserts that respondent's question, 'What is going to happen to me now?', evinced both 'a willingness and a desire for a generalized discussion about the investigation.' If respondent's question had been posed by Jean–Paul Sartre before a class of philosophy students, it might well have evinced a desire for a 'generalized' discussion. But under the circumstances of this case, it is plain that respondent's only 'desire' was to find out where the police were going to take him."

"[To] hold that respondent's question in this case opened a dialogue with the authorities flies in the face of the basic purpose of the *Miranda* safeguards. When someone in custody asks, 'What is going to happen to me now?', he is surely responding to his custodial surroundings. The very essence of custody is the loss of control over one's freedom of movement. [To] allow the authorities to recommence an interrogation based on such a question is to permit them to capitalize on the custodial setting. Yet *Miranda's* procedural protections were adopted precisely in order 'to dispel the compulsion inherent in custodial surroundings.' "

NOTES AND QUESTIONS

(i) *Is the Edwards–Bradshaw test for "initiating" further communication with the police a satisfactory one?* Consider James Tomkovicz, *Standards for Invocation and Waiver of Counsel in Confession Contexts,* 74 Iowa L.Rev. 975, 1033–34 (1986), maintaining that the *Edwards-Bradshaw* test, "which at most demands evidence of a generalized desire or willingness to discuss the investigation" is too broad and too spongy because "it allows officers to recommence interrogation in many situations in which suspects may not have changed their minds [about desiring counsel]." According to Professor Tomkovicz, a definition of suspect initiation of further communication with the police "must describe conduct by the individual that revokes the earlier claim [of counsel] and conveys the message that the added support of counsel is not desired."

(ii) *The suspect's counterpart to "administrative questioning."* Should a "natural response" to arrest or transportation to a jail or police station be viewed as the suspect's counterpart to "administrative questioning"? Consider the remarks of Professor Kamisar in Choper, Kamisar & Tribe, *The Supreme Court: Trends and Developments 1982–83* (1984) at 165–66:

"When the [*Innis* Court defined 'police interrogation'] it *excluded* police words or actions 'normally attendant to arrest and custody' and properly so. Such statements, often called 'administrative questioning,' e.g., the routine questions asked of all persons 'booked' or otherwise processed, do not enhance the pressures and anxiety generated by arrest and detention. Thus, any incriminating statements in response to administrative questioning is, and should be, viewed as a 'volunteered' statement.

"The suspect's counterpart to 'administrative questioning' [is] an expression of fear, anxiety or confusion *normally attendant* to arrest, removal from the scene of arrest, or transportation to the stationhouse or jail. These expressions, such as, Where am I being taken? When can I call my lawyer? and, yes, What's going to happen to me? should not count as "initiation of dialogue" for *Edwards* purposes.

"Of course, if the officer *answers* one of the arrestee's questions about what's going to happen to him by *telling him* where he is being taken [or] when he will be able to meet with an attorney that should not count either. But when the officer's response to the suspect's expression of concern or confusion clearly goes beyond the scope of the suspect's question—when the officer exploits the situation, as he did in [*Bradshaw*]—that *should* count as 'police interrogation.' [Under] such circumstances, the suspect did not 'invite' or 'initiate' conversation about the merits of the case—the officer 'initiated' a *new* conversation."

22. *How direct, assertive and unambiguous must a suspect be in order to invoke the right to counsel?* A year before the decision in *Davis v. United States,* set forth immediately below, Professor Janet Ainsworth pointed out that sociolinguistic research indicates that certain discrete segments of the population (women and a majority of minority racial and ethnic groups) are far more likely than other groups to avoid strong, assertive means of expression and to use indirect and hedged speech patterns that give the impression of uncertainty or equivocality. See Janet E. Ainsworth, *In a Different Register: The Pragmatics of Powerlessness in Police Interrogation,* 103 Yale L.J. 259 (1993). However, observed Ainsworth, in determining whether a suspect had effectively invoked his or her right to counsel, a majority of the lower courts assumed that "direct and assertive speech—a mode of expression more characteristic of men than women—is or should be, the norm." This assumption not only manifests a "kind of gender bias"; it "does not serve the interests of the many speech communities whose discourse patterns deviate from the implicit norms in standard, 'male register' English."

Moreover, since the custodial police interrogation setting involves an imbalance of power between the suspect and his or her interrogator(s), such a setting increases the likelihood that a suspect will adopt an indirect or hedged—and thus ambiguous—means of expression. Even within speech communities whose members do not ordinarily use indirect modes of expression, one who is situationally powerless, that is, aware of the dominant power of the person he or she is addressing (and it is hard to think of a better example than a custodial suspect confronting one or more police interrogators), may also adopt a hedging or otherwise deferential speech register. According to Professor Ainsworth, only a *per se* invocation standard, a rule requiring all police questioning to cease upon any request for or reference to counsel, however equivocal or ambiguous, would provide "both assertive and deferential suspects with equivalent protection" and furnish "the powerless [the] same constitutional protections as the powerful."

However, in DAVIS v. UNITED STATES, 512 U.S. 452 (1994), Justice O'Connor, speaking for five members of the Court rejected the view that (a) the courts should not place a premium on suspects making direct, assertive unqualified invocations of the right to counsel and (b) all arguable references to counsel should be treated as valid invocations of the right. The *Davis* case arose as follows:

Davis, a member of the U.S. Navy, was suspected of murdering another sailor. When interviewed by agents of the Naval Investigative Service (NIS) at the NIS office, he initially waived his *Miranda* rights. About an hour and a half into the interview, he said: "Maybe I should talk to a lawyer." At this point, according to the uncontradicted testimony of one of the agents, "we made it very clear [that] we weren't going to pursue the matter unless we have it clarified is he asking for a lawyer or is he just making a comment about a lawyer" and Davis replied, "No, I'm not asking for a lawyer" and then said, "No, I don't want a lawyer."

After a short break, the agents then reminded Davis of his *Miranda* rights and the interview continued for another hour—until Davis said, "I think I want a lawyer before I say anything." At this point, questioning ceased. A military judge admitted Davis's statements and he was convicted of murder. The U.S. Court of Appeals affirmed the conviction—as did the U.S. Supreme Court:

"[To invoke the *Edwards* rule] the suspect must unambiguously request counsel. [Although] a suspect need not 'speak with the discrimination of an Oxford don' (Souter, J., concurring in judgment), he must articulate his desire to have counsel present sufficiently clearly that a reasonable police officer in the circumstances would understand the statement to be a request for an attorney. If the statement fails to meet the requisite level of clarity, *Edwards* does not require that the officers stop questioning the suspect. * * *

"We decline petitioner's invitation to extend *Edwards* and require law enforcement officers to cease questioning immediately upon the making of an ambiguous or equivocal reference to an attorney. [When] the officers conducting the questioning reasonably do not know whether or not the suspect wants a lawyer, a rule requiring the immediate cessation of questioning 'would transform the *Miranda* safeguards into wholly irrational obstacles to legitimate police investigative activity,' because it would needlessly prevent the police from questioning a suspect in the absence of counsel even if the suspect did not wish to have a lawyer present. * * *

"We recognize that requiring a clear assertion of the right to counsel might disadvantage some suspects who—because of fear, intimidation, lack of linguistic skills, or a variety of other reasons—will not clearly articulate their right to counsel although they actually want to have a lawyer present. But the primary protection afforded suspects subject to custodial interrogation is the *Miranda* warnings themselves. [A] suspect who knowingly and voluntarily waives his right to counsel after having that right explained to him has indicated his willingness to deal with the police unassisted. Although *Edwards* provides an additional protection—if a suspect subsequently requests an attorney, questioning must cease—it is one that must be affirmatively invoked by the suspect.

"[If] we were to require questioning to cease if a suspect makes a statement that *might* be a request for an attorney, [the *Edwards* Rule's] clarity and ease of application would be lost. [We] therefore hold that, after a knowing and voluntary waiver of the *Miranda* rights, law enforcement officers may continue questioning until and unless the suspect clearly requests an attorney.

"[To] recapitulate: We held in *Miranda* that a suspect is entitled to the assistance of counsel during custodial interrogation even though the Constitution does not provide for such assistance. We held in *Edwards* that if the suspect invokes the right to counsel at any time, the police must immediately cease questioning him until an attorney is present. But we are unwilling to create a third layer of prophylaxis to prevent police questioning when the suspect *might* want a lawyer. Unless the suspect actually requests an attorney, questioning may continue."

Justice Souter, joined by Blackmun, Stevens and Ginsburg, JJ., wrote a separate opinion. Although he concurred in the judgment affirming Davis's conviction, "resting partly on evidence of statements given after agents ascertained that he did not wish to deal with them through counsel," Justice Souter could not join the majority's "further conclusion that if the investigators here had been so inclined, they were at liberty to disregard Davis's reference to a lawyer entirely, in accordance with a general rule that interrogators have no legal obligation to discover what a custodial subject meant by an ambiguous statement that could reasonably be understood to express a desire to consult a lawyer":

"[For nearly three decades], two precepts have commanded broad assent: that the *Miranda* safeguards exist 'to assure that *the individual's right to choose* between speech and silence remains unfettered throughout the interrogation process,' and that the justification for *Miranda* rules, intended to operate in the real world, 'must be consistent [with] practical realities.' *Arizona v. Roberson* (Kennedy, J., dissenting). A rule barring government agents from further interrogation until they determine whether a suspect's ambiguous statement was meant as a request for counsel fulfills both ambitions. It assures that a suspect's choice whether or not to deal with police through counsel will be 'scrupulously honored' and it faces both the real-world reasons why misunderstandings arise between suspect and interrogator and the real-world limitations on the capacity of police and trial courts to apply fine distinctions and intricate rules.

"Tested against the same two principles, the approach the Court adopts does not fare so well. First, as the majority expressly acknowledges, criminal suspects who may (in *Miranda*'s words) be 'thrust into an unfamiliar atmosphere and run through menacing police interrogation procedures,' would seem an odd group to single out for the Court's demand of heightened linguistic care. A substantial percentage of them lack anything like a confident command of the English language, many are 'woefully ignorant,' and many more will be sufficiently intimidated by the interrogation process or overwhelmed by the uncertainty of their predicament that the ability to speak assertively will abandon them.[4] Indeed, the awareness of just these realities has, in the past, dissuaded the Court from placing any burden of clarity upon individuals in custody, but has led it instead to require that requests for counsel be 'give[n] a broad, rather than a narrow, interpretation' and that courts 'indulge every reasonable presumption,' *Johnson v. Zerbst,* that a suspect has not waived his right to counsel under *Miranda*.

"[Nor] may the standard governing waivers as expressed in these statements be deflected away by drawing a distinction between initial waivers of *Miranda* rights and subsequent decisions to reinvoke them, on the theory that so long as the burden to demonstrate waiver rests on the government, it is only fair to make the suspect shoulder a burden of showing a clear subsequent assertion. *Miranda* itself discredited the legitimacy of any such distinction. The opinion described the

---

4. Social science confirms what common sense would suggest, that individuals who feel intimidated or powerless are more likely to speak in equivocal or nonstandard terms when no ambiguity or equivocation is meant. Suspects in police interrogation are strong candidates for these effects. Even while resort by the police to the "third degree" has abated since *Miranda,* the basic forms of psychological pressure applied by police appear to have changed less. * * *

object of the warning as being to assure 'a continuous opportunity to exercise [the right of silence].' '[C]ontinuous opportunity' suggests an unvarying one, governed by a common standard of effectiveness. * * *

"Our cases are best respected by a rule that when a suspect under custodial interrogation makes an ambiguous statement that might reasonably be understood as expressing a wish that a lawyer be summoned (and questioning cease), interrogators' questions should be confined to verifying whether the individual meant to ask for a lawyer. While there is reason to expect that trial courts will apply today's ruling sensibly (without requiring criminal suspects to speak with the discrimination of an Oxford don) and that interrogators will continue to follow what the Court rightly calls 'good police practice' (compelled up to now by a substantial body of state and Circuit law), I believe that the case law under *Miranda* does not allow them to do otherwise."

NOTES AND QUESTIONS

(a) *How the Davis case works in practice.* After examining state and federal cases for the past twelve years, Marcy Strauss, *Understanding Davis v. United States*, 40 Loyola of L.A.L.Rev. 1011, 1047, 1055 (2007), reports that only 19 percent of all suspects' statements were found to constitute unambiguous requests for counsel. She observes, id. at 1057, 1060–62: "[T]here is clear evidence to support the proposition that women, minorities, and Caucasion males fail to demand an attorney in declarative, clear language. Instead, the use of questions, hedges and imprecise language in the custodial interrogation setting is very common among all suspects of any race or gender. * * * Not only do officers ignore ambiguous requests, but they frequently use them to subtly or overtly encourage suspects to waive their right to counsel. * * *

"[P]erhaps most disturbing, the evidence suggests gross inconsistencies in the approaches of the courts. Some courts deem seemingly clear demands as ambiguous. Yet in other cases, virtually identical language is treated differently in ways unexplicable by the context. It is drastically unfair that a suspect in one jurisdiction who says, 'I think I would like to talk to my attorney,' can be ignored, while a similar statement in another jurisdiction is treated as invoking *Edwards*."

(b) *How significant is it that Mr. Davis initially waived his Miranda rights?* When first advised of his rights, Davis waived them. An hour and a half later he made an ambiguous statement about wanting to talk to a lawyer. At one point in her majority opinion Justice O'Connor tells us that the Court is "hold[ing] that, *after a knowing and voluntary waiver* of the *Miranda* rights, law enforcement officers may continue questioning until and unless the suspect clearly requests an attorney" (emphasis added).

Moreover, in his four-Justice concurring opinion, Justice Souter observes: "[Nor] may the standard governing waivers * * * be deflected away by drawing a distinction between initial waivers of *Miranda* rights and subsequent decisions to reinvoke them, on the theory that so long as the burden to demonstrate waiver rests on the government, it is only fair to make the suspect shoulder a burden of showing a clear *subsequent assertion*" (emphasis added). However, as *Berghuis v. Thompkins*, set forth immediately below, demonstrates, when a majority of the Court reexamined waiver, it attached no significance at all to the fact that Mr. Davis had initially waived his rights.

23. *Another look at implied waiver: the distinction between the right to remain silent and the right not to be interrogated.*

The facts of *Berghuis v. Thompkins*

Detective Helgert and another police officer questioned defendant Thompkins about a shooting in which one person died. The interrogation was conducted in the early afternoon in a room 8 by 10 feet. Thompkins sat in a chair resembling a desk.

At no time during the interrogation did Thompkins say he wanted to remain silent or that he wanted a lawyer. Nor did he ever say that he did not want to talk to the police. However, he declined to sign a written acknowledgement that he had been advised of, and understood, his rights. During the interrogation, which lasted about three hours, Thompkins was "[l]argely" silent, but he did give a few "limited verbal responses," such as "yeah," "no," or "I don't know."

At the outset of the interrogation, Detective Helgert presented Thompkins with a form containing the four standard *Miranda* warnings and a fifth warning which read: "You have the right to decide at any time before or during questioning to use your right to remain silent and your right to talk with a lawyer while you are being questioned." At Helgert's request, Thompkins read the fifth warning out loud. The detective himself then read the four standard *Miranda* warnings out loud.

About 2 hours and 45 minutes into the interrogation, Helgert asked Thompkins whether he "believ[ed] in God." Thompkins replied that he did, his eyes "well[ing] up in tears." Helgert then asked: "Do you pray to God?" Again, Thompkins answered that he did. Finally, Helgert asked: "Do you pray to God to forgive you for shooting that boy down?" Thompkins answered that he did, looking away. About 15 minutes later, after Thompkins had refused to make a written confession, the interrogation ended.

The Michigan trial court refused to suppress Thompkins's statements. He was found guilty of murder and sentenced to life imprisonment without parole. The Michigan Court of Appeals affirmed. On habeas corpus, the federal district court denied relief. But a unanimous three-judge panel of the U.S. Court of Appeals for the Sixth Circuit reversed, concluding that the state courts had unreasonably applied clearly established law and based its decision on an unreasonable determination of the facts. Under the Antiterrorism and Effective Death Penalty Act of 1966 (AEDPA), a federal court cannot grant a petition for a writ of habeas corpus unless the state court's adjudication of the merits was "contrary to, or involved an unreasonable application of, clearly established Federal law."

The Sixth Circuit found that the state court unreasonably determined the facts because "the evidence demonstrates that Thompkins was silent for two hours and forty-five minutes." Moreover, concluded the Sixth Circuit, the defendant's "persistent silence for nearly three hours in response to questioning and repeated invitations to tell his side of the story offered a clear and unequivocal message to the officers: Thompkins did not wish to waive his rights."

Oral arguments in *Berghuis v. Thompkins*

MICHIGAN SOLICITOR GENERAL RESTUCCIA: I have to carefully delineate between waiver and invocation. So here the waiver occurs at the time that [the defendant] is asked the series of questions [about believing in God and praying to God].

JUSTICE BREYER: That happened about 2 hours and 15 minutes into the exercise, didn't it? * * *

MR. RESTUCCIA: [Well,] this Court in *Butler* didn't say that the waiver has to occur immediately.

JUSTICE BREYER: In *Butler* [the defendant] said: I will talk to you, but I am not signing any forms. [Is] there anything during the 2 hours and 15 minutes that could suggest a waiver?

MR. RESTUCCIA: [The] waiver occurs at the time that [the defendant] answered the question [about praying to God to forgive him].

JUSTICE BREYER: I thought *Miranda* held that you can't question a person unless he waives [the right to remain silent]. Is it clear law that once [a custodial suspect] says "I do not waive my right," the police cannot continue to question him? * * *

MR. RESTUCCIA: Mr. Thompkins didn't say he was unwilling to waive [his right to remain silent]. He's participating.

JUSTICE KENNEDY: You're saying there's a difference between a waiver and a failure to assert?

MR. RESTUCCIA: Yes, exactly. * * *

JUSTICE SCALIA: Why shouldn't we have a rule which simply says if you don't want to be interrogated, all you have to say is "I don't want to answer your questions"? * * * Is every failure to assert [one's rights] a waiver?

MR. RESTUCCIA: No, [the] point at which Mr. Thompkins waived [his rights] is when [his actions were] inconsistent with the exercise of his rights. When he answers questions knowing that he doesn't have to answer, that is the waiver.

JUSTICE KENNEDY: [Do] you read *Miranda* as saying that there cannot be questioning unless there is a waiver?

MS. SAHARSKY, ASSISTANT TO THE SOLICITOR GENERAL, DEPART-MENT OF JUSTICE, as *amicus curiae*: No. [After] the point that he gets his rights and understands them, the police can question him. You'd have to overrule *Butler* to say that there has to be a waiver before any questioning. [There is] language in *Miranda* [saying] that a waiver is a prerequisite to the admission of the evidence at trial. [But that] doesn't mean [a custodial suspect] has to make the decision to talk right away. He might want to listen to what the police have to say about the benefits of cooperation or [about the kind of] evidence they have in his case. * * *

JUSTICE KENNEDY: Why don't we tell the police [that] there must be a waiver before you can continue the interrogation?

MS. SAHARSKY: [That would] exact a substantial price on law enforcement, and that's the exact argument that Justice Brennan made in the *Butler* case–[an argument] that was rejected. * * *

JUSTICE SCALIA: [As you see it, a custodial suspect] has the right to terminate the whole thing by asserting his right [to remain silent]. If he neither asserts the right nor grants the waiver, the police can continue to try to obtain a statement from him?

MS. SAHARSKY: Right. * * *

JUSTICE SOTOMAYOR: * * * What's clear is that at no point did [Mr. Thompkins] answer [the police's] questions, because nothing about [Mr. Thompkins's] nods of the head or anything else showed a willingness to confess. * * * How does one infer a voluntary statement from a situation in which someone's really not talking? * * *

MS. SAHARSKY: [W]e say that the waiver occurred at the time [Mr. Thompkins] answered the questions about his belief in God. And it doesn't matter what he said in response to the earlier questions, as long as at the time he answered questions about God, his decision to talk was a knowing and intelligent and voluntary one. * * *

JUSTICE SCALIA: [It] seems to me [Ms. Jacobs] you're confusing [a waiver] of the right to remain silent with a waiver of the right not to be interrogated, which is the right that you are asserting here. [That's] the new right that you are asserting.

MS. JACOBS, on behalf of respondent Thompkins: * * * It's not a new right. The police cannot interrogate the defendant unless they read him his rights [and, as I understand *Miranda*, neither can they question him unless] they obtain a waiver of those rights.

Without obtaining the waiver, questioning cannot ensue, because then the rest of the questioning becomes trying to talk the defendant into waiving [his] rights, trying to talk [him] into confessing, and you have badgering * * * and you don't end up with a volitional waiver or a volitional statement.

BERGHUIS v. THOMPKINS

___ U.S. ___, 130 S.Ct. 2250, 176 L.Ed.2d 1098 (2010).

JUSTICE KENNEDY delivered the opinion of the Court. * * *

Thompkins [first] contends that he "invoke[d] his privilege" to remain silent by not saying anything for a sufficient period of time, so the interrogation should have "cease[d]" before he made his inculpatory statements.

[This] argument is unpersuasive. In the context of invoking the *Miranda* right to counsel, the Court in *Davis* v. *United States*, held that a suspect must do so "unambiguously." If an accused makes a statement concerning the right to counsel "that is ambiguous or equivocal" or makes no statement, the police are not required to end the interrogation or ask questions to clarify whether the accused wants to invoke his or her *Miranda* rights.

The Court has not yet stated whether an invocation of the right to remain silent can be ambiguous or equivocal, but there is no principled reason to adopt different standards for determining when an accused has invoked the *Miranda* right to remain silent and the *Miranda* right to counsel at issue in *Davis*. [There] is good reason to require an accused who wants to invoke his or her right to remain silent to do so unambiguously. A requirement of an unambiguous invocation of *Miranda* rights results in an objective inquiry that "avoid[s] difficulties of proof [and] provide[s] guidance to officers" on how to proceed in the face of ambiguity. *Davis*. [If] an ambiguous act, omission, or statement could require police to end the interrogation, police would be required to make difficult decisions about an accused's unclear intent and face the consequence of suppression "if they guess wrong." Suppression of a voluntary confession in these circumstances would place a significant burden on society's interest in prosecuting criminal activity. * * *

Thompkins did not say that he wanted to remain silent or that he did not want to talk with the police. Had he made either of these simple, unambiguous statements, he would have invoked his " 'right to cut off questioning.' " Here he did neither, so he did not invoke his right to remain silent.

We next consider whether Thompkins waived his right to remain silent. Even absent the accused's invocation of the right to remain silent, the accused's statement during a custodial interrogation is inadmissible at trial unless the prosecution can establish that the accused "in fact knowingly and voluntarily waived *[Miranda]* rights" when making the statement. The waiver inquiry "has two distinct dimensions": waiver must be "voluntary in the sense that it was the product of a free and deliberate choice rather than intimidation, coercion, or deception," and "made with a full awareness of both the nature of the right being abandoned and the consequences of the decision to abandon it."

Some language in *Miranda* could be read to indicate that waivers are difficult to establish absent an explicit written waiver or a formal, express oral statement. [But the] course of decisions since *Miranda*, informed by the application of *Miranda* warnings in the whole course of law enforcement, demonstrates that waivers can be established even absent formal or express statements of waiver that would be expected in, say, a judicial hearing to determine if a guilty plea has been properly entered. The main purpose of *Miranda* is to ensure that an accused is advised of and understands the right to remain silent and the right to counsel. Thus, "[i]f anything, our subsequent cases have reduced the impact of the *Miranda* rule on legitimate law enforcement while reaffirming the decision's core ruling that unwarned statements may not be used as evidence in the prosecution's case in chief." *Dickerson* v. *United States*, [p. 677].

One of the first cases to decide the meaning and import of *Miranda* with respect to the question of waiver was *North Carolina* v. *Butler*, 441 U.S. 369 (1979). [This case] interpreted the *Miranda* language concerning the "heavy burden" to show waiver in accord with usual principles of determining waiver, which can include waiver implied from all the circumstances. And in a later case, the Court stated that this "heavy burden" is not more than the burden to establish waiver by a preponderance of the evidence. *Colorado* v. *Connelly*, [p. 728].

The prosecution therefore does not need to show that a waiver of *Miranda* rights was express. [*Butler*] made clear that a waiver of *Miranda* rights may be implied through "the defendant's silence, coupled with an understanding of his rights and a course of conduct indicating waiver." [*Butler*] therefore "retreated" from the "language and tenor of the *Miranda* opinion," which "suggested that the Court would require that a waiver [be] 'specifically made.' "

If the State establishes that a *Miranda* warning was given and the accused made an uncoerced statement, this showing, standing alone, is insufficient to demonstrate "a valid waiver" of *Miranda* rights. The prosecution must make the additional showing that the accused understood these rights. [Where] the prosecution shows that a *Miranda* warning was given and that it was understood by the accused, an accused's uncoerced statement establishes an implied waiver of the right to remain silent.

[As] a general proposition, the law can presume that an individual who, with a full understanding of his or her rights, acts in a manner inconsistent with their exercise has made a deliberate choice to relinquish the protection those rights afford. [As] *Butler* recognized, *Miranda* rights can therefore be waived through means less formal than a typical waiver on the record in a courtroom, given the practical constraints and necessities of interrogation and the fact that *Miranda*'s main protection lies in advising defendants of their rights.

The record in this case shows that Thompkins waived his right to remain silent. There is no basis in this case to conclude that he did not understand his rights; and on these facts it follows that he chose not to invoke or rely on those rights when he did speak. [Thompkins] received a written copy of the *Miranda* warnings; Detective Helgert determined that Thompkins could read and understand English; and Thompkins was given time to read the warnings. Thompkins, furthermore, read aloud the fifth warning, which stated that "you have the right to decide at any time before or during questioning to use your right to remain silent and your right to talk with a lawyer while you are being questioned." He was thus aware that his right to remain silent would not dissipate after a certain amount of time and that police would have to honor his right to be silent and his right to counsel during the whole course of interrogation. Those rights, the warning made clear, could be asserted at any time. Helgert, moreover, read the warnings aloud.

Second, Thompkins's answer to Detective Helgert's question about whether Thompkins prayed to God for forgiveness for shooting the victim is a "course of conduct indicating waiver" of the right to remain silent. If Thompkins wanted to remain silent, he could have said nothing in response to Helgert's questions, or he could have unambiguously invoked his *Miranda* rights and ended the interrogation. The fact that Thompkins made a statement about three hours after receiving a *Miranda* warning does not overcome the fact that he engaged in a course of conduct indicating waiver. Police are not required to rewarn suspects from time to time. Thompkins's answer to Helgert's question about praying to God for forgiveness for shooting the victim was sufficient to show a course of conduct indicating waiver. This is confirmed by the fact that before then Thompkins had given sporadic answers to questions throughout the interrogation.

Third, there is no evidence that Thompkins's statement was coerced. Thompkins does not claim that police threatened or injured him during the interrogation or that he was in any way fearful. [The] fact that Helgert's question referred to Thompkins's religious beliefs also did not render Thompkins's statement involuntary. [In] these circumstances, Thompkins knowingly and voluntarily made a statement to police, so he waived his right to remain silent.

Thompkins next argues that, even if his answer to Detective Helgert could constitute a waiver of his right to remain silent, the police were not allowed to question him until they obtained a waiver first. *Butler* forecloses this argument. The *Butler* Court held that courts can infer a waiver of *Miranda* rights "from the actions and words of the person interrogated." This principle would be inconsistent with a rule that requires a waiver at the outset. The *Butler* Court thus rejected the rule proposed by the *Butler* dissent, which would have "requir[ed] the police to obtain an express waiver of [*Miranda* rights] before proceeding with interrogation." This holding also makes sense given that "the primary protection afforded suspects subject[ed] to custodial interrogation is the *Miranda* warnings themselves." The *Miranda* rule and its requirements are met if a suspect receives adequate *Miranda* warnings, understands them, and has an opportunity to invoke the rights before giving any answers or admissions. * * *

Interrogation provides the suspect with additional information that can put his or her decision to waive, or not to invoke, into perspective. As questioning commences and then continues, the suspect has the opportunity to consider the choices he or she faces and to make a more informed decision, either to insist on silence or to cooperate. When the suspect knows that *Miranda* rights can be invoked at any time, he or she has the opportunity to reassess his or her immediate and long-term interests. Cooperation with the police may result in more favorable treatment for the suspect; the apprehension of accomplices; the prevention of continuing injury and fear; beginning steps towards relief or solace for the victims; and the beginning of the suspect's own return to the law and the social order it seeks to protect.

[In] sum, a suspect who has received and understood the *Miranda* warnings, and has not invoked his *Miranda* rights, waives the right to remain silent by making an uncoerced statement to the police. Thompkins did not invoke his right to remain silent and stop the questioning. Understanding his rights in full, he waived his right to remain silent by making a voluntary statement to the police. The police, moreover, were not required to obtain a waiver of Thompkins's right to remain silent before interrogating him. The state court's decision rejecting Thompkins's *Miranda* claim was thus correct under *de novo* review and therefore

necessarily reasonable under the more deferential AEDPA standard of review.
* * *

JUSTICE SOTOMAYOR, with whom JUSTICE STEVENS, JUSTICE GINSBURG, and JUSTICE BREYER join, dissenting.

The Court concludes today that a criminal suspect waives his right to remain silent if, after sitting tacit and uncommunicative through nearly three hours of police interrogation, he utters a few one-word responses. The Court also concludes that a suspect who wishes to guard his right to remain silent against such a finding of "waiver" must, counterintuitively, speak—and must do so with sufficient precision to satisfy a clear-statement rule that construes ambiguity in favor of the police. Both propositions mark a substantial retreat from the protection against compelled self-incrimination that *Miranda* has long provided during custodial interrogation. The broad rules the Court announces today are also troubling because they are unnecessary to decide this case, which is governed by the deferential standard of review set forth in the AEDPA. Because I believe Thompkins is entitled to relief [on] the ground that his statements were admitted at trial without the prosecution having carried its burden to show that he waived his right to remain silent; because longstanding principles of judicial restraint counsel leaving for another day the questions of law the Court reaches out to decide; and because the Court's answers to those questions do not result from a faithful application of our prior decisions, I respectfully dissent.

[The] strength of Thompkins' *Miranda* claims depends in large part on the circumstances of the 3–hour interrogation, at the end of which he made inculpatory statements later introduced at trial. The Court's opinion downplays record evidence that Thompkins remained almost completely silent and unresponsive throughout that session. One of the interrogating officers, Detective Helgert, testified that although Thompkins was administered *Miranda* warnings, the last of which he read aloud, Thompkins expressly declined to sign a written acknowledgment that he had been advised of and understood his rights. There is conflicting evidence in the record about whether Thompkins ever verbally confirmed understanding his rights. The record contains no indication that the officers sought or obtained an express waiver.

As to the interrogation itself, Helgert candidly characterized it as "very, very one-sided" and "nearly a monologue." Thompkins was "[p]eculiar," "[s]ullen," and "[g]enerally quiet." Helgert and his partner "did most of the talking," as Thompkins was "not verbally communicative" and "[l]argely" remained silent. [After] proceeding in this fashion for approximately 2 hours and 45 minutes, Helgert asked Thompkins three questions relating to his faith in God. The prosecution relied at trial on Thompkins' one-word answers of "yes."

Thompkins' nonresponsiveness is particularly striking in the context of the officers' interview strategy, later explained as conveying to Thompkins that "this was his opportunity to explain his side [of the story]" because "[e]verybody else, including [his] co-[d]efendants, had given their version," and asking him "[w]ho is going to speak up for you if you don't speak up for yourself?" Yet, Helgert confirmed that the "*only* thing [Thompkins said] relative to his involvement [in the shooting]" occurred near the end of the interview—i.e., in response to the questions about God (emphasis added).

[The] question whether a suspect has validly waived his right is "entirely distinct" as a matter of law from whether he invoked that right. The questions are related, however, in terms of the practical effect on the exercise of a suspect's rights. A suspect may at any time revoke his prior waiver of rights—or, closer to the facts of this case, guard against the possibility of a future finding that he implicitly waived his rights—by invoking the rights and thereby requiring the police to cease questioning.

[This] Court's decisions subsequent to *Miranda* have emphasized the prosecution's "heavy burden" in proving waiver. We have also reaffirmed that a court may not presume waiver from a suspect's silence or from the mere fact that a confession was eventually obtained. See *Butler*.

Even in concluding that *Miranda* does not invariably require an express waiver of the right to silence or the right to counsel, *Butler* made clear that the prosecution bears a substantial burden in establishing an implied waiver. The FBI had obtained statements after advising Butler of his rights and confirming that he understood them. When presented with a written waiver-of-rights form, Butler told the agents, " 'I will talk to you but I am not signing any form.' " He then made inculpatory statements, which he later sought to suppress on the ground that he had not expressly waived his right to counsel. * * *

Rarely do this Court's precedents provide clearly established law so closely on point with the facts of a particular case. Together, *Miranda* and *Butler* establish that a court "must presume that a defendant did not waive his right[s]"; the prosecution bears a "heavy burden" in attempting to demonstrate waiver; the fact of a "lengthy interrogation" prior to obtaining statements is "strong evidence" against a finding of valid waiver; "mere silence" in response to questioning is "not enough"; and waiver may not be presumed "simply from the fact that a confession was in fact eventually obtained."

It is undisputed here that Thompkins never expressly waived his right to remain silent. His refusal to sign even an acknowledgment that he understood his *Miranda* rights evinces, if anything, an intent not to waive those rights. [That] Thompkins did not make the inculpatory statements at issue until after approximately 2 hours and 45 minutes of interrogation serves as "strong evidence" against waiver. *Miranda* and *Butler* expressly preclude the possibility that the inculpatory statements themselves are sufficient to establish waiver. * * *

Michigan and the United States concede that no waiver occurred in this case until Thompkins responded "yes" to the questions about God. I believe it is objectively unreasonable under our clearly established precedents to conclude the prosecution met its "heavy burden" of proof on a record consisting of three one-word answers, following 2 hours and 45 minutes of silence punctuated by a few largely nonverbal responses to unidentified questions.

Perhaps because our prior *Miranda* precedents so clearly favor Thompkins, the Court today goes beyond AEDPA's deferential standard of review and announces a new general principle of law. Any new rule, it must be emphasized, is unnecessary to the disposition of this case. If, in the Court's view, the Michigan court did not unreasonably apply our *Miranda* precedents in denying Thompkins relief, it should simply say so and reverse the Sixth Circuit's judgment on that ground.

[The] Court concludes that when *Miranda* warnings have been given and understood, "an accused's uncoerced statement establishes an implied waiver of the right to remain silent." More broadly still, the Court states that, "[a]s a general proposition, the law can presume that an individual who, with a full understanding of his or her rights, acts in a manner inconsistent with their exercise has made a deliberate choice to relinquish the protection those rights afford."

These principles flatly contradict our longstanding views that "a valid waiver will not be presumed * * * simply from the fact that a confession was in fact eventually obtained," *Miranda*, and that "[t]he courts must presume that a defendant did not waive his rights," *Butler*. [The] evidence of implied waiver in *Butler* was worlds apart from the evidence in this case, because Butler unequivocally said "I will talk to you" after having been read *Miranda* warnings. Thompkins, of course, made no such statement. * * *

Today's dilution of the prosecution's burden of proof to the bare fact that a suspect made inculpatory statements after *Miranda* warnings were given and understood takes an unprecedented step away from the "high standards of proof for the waiver of constitutional rights" this Court has long demanded. [When] waiver is to be inferred during a custodial interrogation, there are sound reasons to require evidence beyond inculpatory statements themselves. *Miranda* and our subsequent cases are premised on the idea that custodial interrogation is inherently coercive. * * *

Taken together with the Court's reformulation of the prosecution's burden of proof as to waiver, today's novel clear-statement rule for invocation invites police to question a suspect at length—notwithstanding his persistent refusal to answer questions—in the hope of eventually obtaining a single inculpatory response which will suffice to prove waiver of rights. Such a result bears little semblance to the "fully effective" prophylaxis [that] *Miranda* requires. * * *

Thompkins contends that in refusing to respond to questions he effectively invoked his right to remain silent, such that police were required to terminate the interrogation prior to his inculpatory statements. * * * Notwithstanding *Miranda*'s statement that "there can be no questioning" if a suspect "indicates in any manner [that] he wishes to consult with an attorney," the Court in *Davis* established a clear-statement rule for invoking the right to counsel. After a suspect has knowingly and voluntarily waived his *Miranda* rights, *Davis* held, police may continue questioning "until and unless the suspect *clearly* requests an attorney" (emphasis added).

Because this Court has never decided whether *Davis'* clear-statement rule applies to an invocation of the right to silence, Michigan contends, there was no clearly established federal law prohibiting the state court from requiring an unambiguous invocation. That the state court's decision was not objectively unreasonable is confirmed, in Michigan's view, by the number of federal Courts of Appeals to have applied *Davis* to invocation of the right to silence.

Under AEDPA's deferential standard of review, it is indeed difficult to conclude that the state court's application of our precedents was objectively unreasonable. Although the duration and consistency of Thompkins' refusal to answer questions throughout the 3–hour interrogation provide substantial evidence in support of his claim, Thompkins did not remain absolutely silent, and this Court has not previously addressed whether a suspect can invoke the right to silence by remaining uncooperative and nearly silent for 2 hours and 45 minutes.

The Court, however, eschews this narrow ground of decision, instead extending *Davis* to hold that police may continue questioning a suspect until he unambiguously invokes his right to remain silent. Because Thompkins neither said "he wanted to remain silent" nor said "he did not want to talk with the police," the Court concludes, he did not clearly invoke his right to silence.

I disagree with this novel application of *Davis*. Neither the rationale nor holding of that case compels today's result. *Davis* involved the right to counsel, not the right to silence. [The] different effects of invoking the rights are consistent with distinct standards for invocation. To the extent *Mosley* contemplates a more flexible form of prophylaxis than *Edwards*—and, in particular, does not categorically bar police from reapproaching a suspect who has invoked his right to remain silent—*Davis'* concern about " 'wholly irrational obstacles' " to police investigation applies with less force.

In addition, the suspect's equivocal reference to a lawyer in *Davis* occurred only *after* he had given express oral and written waivers of his rights. *Davis'* holding is explicitly predicated on that fact. [The] Court ignores this aspect of *Davis*, as well as the decisions of numerous federal and state courts declining to apply a clear-statement rule when a suspect has not previously given an express waiver of rights.

In my mind, a more appropriate standard for addressing a suspect's ambiguous invocation of the right to remain silent is the constraint *Mosley* places on questioning a suspect who has invoked that right: The suspect's " 'right to cut off questioning' " must be " 'scrupulously honored.' " Such a standard is necessarily precautionary and fact specific. * * * [8]

Davis' clear-statement rule is also a poor fit for the right to silence. Advising a suspect that he has a "right to remain silent" is unlikely to convey that he must speak (and must do so in some particular fashion) to ensure the right will be protected. [By] contrast, telling a suspect "he has the right to the presence of an attorney, and that if he cannot afford an attorney one will be appointed for him prior to any questioning if he so desires," *Miranda*, implies the need for speech to exercise that right. *Davis'* requirement that a suspect must "clearly reques[t] an attorney" to terminate questioning thus aligns with a suspect's likely understanding of the *Miranda* warnings in a way today's rule does not. The Court suggests Thompkins could have employed the "simple, unambiguous" means of saying "he wanted to remain silent" or "did not want to talk with the police." But the *Miranda* warnings give no hint that a suspect should use those magic words, and there is little reason to believe police—who have ample incentives to avoid invocation—will provide such guidance.

Conversely, the Court's concern that police will face "difficult decisions about an accused's unclear intent" and suffer the consequences of " 'guess[ing] wrong,' " [is] misplaced. If a suspect makes an ambiguous statement or engages in conduct that creates uncertainty about his intent to invoke his right, police can simply ask for clarification. It is hardly an unreasonable burden for police to ask a suspect, for instance, "Do you want to talk to us?" * * * Police may well prefer not to seek clarification of an ambiguous statement out of fear that a suspect will invoke his rights. But "our system of justice is not founded on a fear that a suspect will exercise his rights."

[In] the 16 years since *Davis* was decided, ample evidence has accrued that criminal suspects often use equivocal or colloquial language in attempting to invoke their right to silence. A number of lower courts that have (erroneously, in my view) imposed a clear-statement requirement for invocation of the right to silence have rejected as ambiguous an array of statements whose meaning might otherwise be thought plain. At a minimum, these decisions suggest that differentiating "clear" from "ambiguous" statements is often a subjective inquiry. Even if some of the cited decisions are themselves in tension with *Davis'* admonition that a suspect need not " 'speak with the discrimination of an Oxford don' " to invoke his rights, they demonstrate that today's decision will significantly burden the exercise of the right to silence.

[For] these reasons, I believe a precautionary requirement that police "scrupulously hono[r]" a suspect's right to cut off questioning is a more faithful

---

8. * * * Thompkins' *amici* collect a range of training materials that instruct police not to engage in prolonged interrogation after a suspect has failed to respond to initial questioning. One widely used police manual, for example, teaches that a suspect who "indicates," "even by silence itself," his unwillingness to answer questions "has obviously exercised his constitutional privilege against self-incrimination."

application of our precedents than the Court's awkward and needless extension of *Davis.* * * *

Today's decision turns *Miranda* upside down. Criminal suspects must now unambiguously invoke their right to remain silent—which, counterintuitively, requires them to speak. At the same time, suspects will be legally presumed to have waived their rights even if they have given no clear expression of their intent to do so. Those results, in my view, find no basis in *Miranda* or our subsequent cases and are inconsistent with the fair-trial principles on which those precedents are grounded. Today's broad new rules are all the more unfortunate because they are unnecessary to the disposition of the case before us. I respectfully dissent.

NOTES AND QUESTIONS

1. ***The standard for granting habeas corpus relief.*** Note that the four dissenters in *Berghuis v. Thompkins* not only believed the majority was wrong but maintained it was so wrong as to satisfy the exceedingly demanding standard for granting habeas relief under AEDPA—the dissenters maintained that the decision to admit the suspect's statement into evidence was "an unreasonable application of clearly established Federal law." On the other hand, the majority did not uphold the state court decision rejecting Thompkins' *Miranda* claim under the demanding standard for granting relief under the AEDPA, but on the ground that the state court's decision was correct under *de novo* review.

2. ***The right to remain silent vs. the right not to be questioned.*** The standard *Miranda* warnings do not tell suspects that they have a right not to be interrogated. However, the *Miranda* opinion does state that "the very fact of custodial interrogation exacts a heavy toll on individual liberty and trades on the weakness of individuals" (p. 574). The *Miranda* opinion also observes that "an interrogation environment is created for no purpose other than to subjugate the individual to the will of the examiner" (id) and that "the current practice of incommunicado interrogation" "is at odds with" the privilege against self incrimination (id). At still another point, the *Miranda* opinion states that "an individual swept from familiar surroundings into police custody" and "subjected to the techniques of persuasion described [in the interrogation manuals] cannot be otherwise than under compulsion to speak." (p. 575).

3. ***How important is the Thompkins case?*** Earlier this year, two of the nation's leading commentators said of *Thompkins*: "[I]n removing the last residue of the 'heavy burden' waiver language from *Miranda* doctrine, *Thompkins* is perhaps the most significant *Miranda* case yet decided." George C. Thomas III and Richard A. Leo, *Confessions of Guilt* 192 (2012).

4. ***What the leading police interrogation manual had to say about waiver of rights.*** Two years before *Berghuis v. Thompkins* was decided, Charles D. Weisselberg, *Mourning Miranda*, 96 Calif.L.Rev. 1519, 1528 (2008), observed: "Given the [*Miranda*] Court's extensive and critical discussion of the interrogation manuals, this could only mean that waivers could not be obtained while interrogators were applying the tactics advocated in the manuals. Inbau and Reid—whose training manual was heavily cited in *Miranda*—recognized this point, putting a somewhat optimistic spin on the decision in the next edition of their book. Published just one year after *Miranda* was decided, the new edition stated: 'As we interpret the June, 1966, five to four decision * * *, all but a very few of the interrogation tactics and techniques presented in our earlier publication are still valid if used *after* the recently prescribed *warnings have been given* to the suspect [and] *after he has waived* his self-incrimination privilege and his right to counsel' (emphasis added by Professor Weisselberg)."

5. If one reads Miranda as saying that a custodial suspect has a right not to be questioned, can that reading be reconciled with Chavez v. Martinez (p. 690)?

---

24. The Miranda–Edwards rule and the Sixth Amendment right to counsel compared and contrasted.

MONTEJO v. LOUISIANA

556 U.S. 778, 129 S.Ct. 2079, 173 L.Ed.2d 955 (2009).

JUSTICE SCALIA delivered the opinion of the Court.

We consider in this case the scope and continued viability of the rule announced by this Court in *Michigan v. Jackson*, 475 U.S. 625 (1986), forbidding police to initiate interrogation of a criminal defendant once he has requested counsel at an arraignment or similar proceeding.

[Petitioner Montejo, a murder suspect, waived his *Miranda* rights and was interrogated at the sheriff's office on September 6 and the morning of September 7. Three days later he was brought before a judge for what is known as a "72–hour hearing"—what the Supreme Court described as a "preliminary hearing required under state law." At this hearing the judge ordered that the Office of Indigent Defender be appointed to represent the defendant.

[Later that same day, two police detectives visited petitioner back at the prison and requested that he accompany them on an excursion to locate the murder weapon (which Montejo had earlier indicated he had thrown into a lake). He was again read his *Miranda* rights and agreed to accompany the detectives. During the trip, he wrote an inculpatory letter of apology to the victim's widow. Montejo did not meet his court-appointed attorney until his return.]

[At trial, the letter of apology was admitted over defense objection. Montejo was convicted of first-degree murder and sentenced to death. The Louisiana Supreme Court affirmed the conviction, rejecting petitioner's *Jackson* arguments on the ground that *Jackson*'s protection is not triggered unless and until the defendant has actually requested a lawyer or otherwise asserted his right to counsel. In the *Jackson* case, when brought before a magistrate during a pretrial appearance, the defendants had requested that counsel be appointed for them because they were indigent. In *Montejo*, however, petitioner had made no such request or assertion. He had simply stood mute. As the state supreme court saw it, therefore, the only issue presented in *Montejo* was whether petitioner had validly waived his right to have counsel present during the interaction with the police. Since Montejo had been read his *Miranda* rights and waived them, he had.]

[The rule adopted by the Louisiana Supreme Court] would apply well enough in States [such as Michigan, where the *Jackson* case arose,] that require indigent defendant formally to request counsel before any appointment is made, which usually occurs after the court has informed him that he will receive counsel if he asks for it. [But in] many States [the] appointment of counsel is automatic upon a finding of indigency, and in a number of others, appointment can be made either upon the defendant's request or *sua sponte* by the court. * * * Nothing in our *Jackson* opinion indicates whether we were then aware that not all States require that a defendant affirmatively request counsel before one is appointed; and of course we had no occasion there to decide how the rule we announced would apply to these other States. * * *

When this Court creates a prophylactic rule in order to protect a constitutional right, the relevant "reasoning" is the weighing of the rule's benefits against its costs. * * * We think that the marginal benefits of *Jackson* (viz., the number of confessions obtained coercively that are suppressed by its bright-line rule and would otherwise have been admitted) are dwarfed by its substantial costs (viz., hindering "society's compelling interest in finding, convicting, and punishing those who violate the law").

What does the *Jackson* rule actually achieve by way of preventing unconstitutional conduct? Recall that the purpose of the rule is to preclude the State from badgering defendants into waiving their previously asserted rights. The effect of this badgering might be to coerce a waiver, which would render the subsequent interrogation a violation of the Sixth Amendment. Even though involuntary waivers are invalid even apart from *Jackson*, mistakes are of course possible when courts conduct case-by-case voluntariness review. A bright-line rule like that adopted in *Jackson* ensures that no fruits of interrogations made possible by badgering-induced involuntary waivers are ever erroneously admitted at trial.

But without *Jackson*, how many would be? The answer is few if any. The principal reason is that the Court has already taken substantial other, overlapping measures toward the same end. Under *Miranda*'s prophylactic protection of the right against compelled self-incrimination, any suspect subject to custodial interrogation has the right to have a lawyer present if he so requests, and to be advised of that right. Under *Edwards*' prophylactic protection of the *Miranda* right, once such a defendant "has invoked his right to have counsel present," interrogation must stop. And under *Minnick*'s prophylactic protection of the *Edwards* right, no subsequent interrogation may take place until counsel is present, "whether or not the accused has consulted with his attorney."

These three layers of prophylaxis are sufficient. * * * It is true [that] the doctrine established by *Miranda* and *Edwards* is designed to protect Fifth Amendment, not Sixth Amendment, rights. But that is irrelevant. What matters is that these cases, like *Jackson,* protect the right to have counsel during custodial interrogation—which right happens to be guaranteed (once the adversary judicial process has begun) by *two* sources of law. Since the right under both sources is waived using the same procedure, doctrines ensuring voluntariness of the Fifth Amendment waiver simultaneously ensure the voluntariness of the Sixth Amendment waiver.

Montejo also correctly observes that the *Miranda-Edwards* regime is narrower than *Jackson* in one respect: The former applies only in the context of custodial interrogation. If the defendant is not in custody then those decisions do not apply; nor do they govern other, noninterrogative types of interactions between the defendant and the State (like pretrial lineups). However, those uncovered situations are the *least* likely to pose a risk of coerced waivers. When a defendant is not in custody, he is in control, and need only shut his door or walk away to avoid police badgering. And noninterrogative interactions with the State do not involve the "inherently compelling pressures," *Miranda*, that one might reasonably fear could lead to involuntary waivers.

Jackson was policy driven, and if that policy is being adequately served through other means, there is no reason to retain its rule. *Miranda* and the cases that elaborate upon it already guarantee not simply noncoercion in the traditional sense, but what Justice Harlan referred to as "voluntariness with a vengeance." There is no need to take *Jackson*'s further step of requiring voluntariness on stilts.

On the other side of the equation are the costs of adding the bright-line *Jackson* rule on top of *Edwards* and other extant protections. * * * *Jackson* not only "operates to invalidate a confession given by the free choice of suspects who have received proper advice of their *Miranda* rights but waived them nonetheless," but also deters law enforcement officers from even trying to obtain voluntary confessions. The "ready ability to obtain uncoerced confessions is not an evil but an unmitigated good." Without these confessions, crimes go unsolved and criminals unpunished. These are not negligible costs, and in our view the *Jackson* Court gave them too short shrift.

[When] the marginal benefits of the *Jackson* rule are weighed against its substantial costs to the truth-seeking process and the criminal justice system, we readily conclude that the rule does not "pay its way," *United States v. Leon.* *Michigan v. Jackson* should be and now is overruled.

Although our holding means that the Louisiana Supreme Court correctly rejected Montejo's claim under *Jackson*, we think that Montejo should be given an opportunity to contend that his letter of apology should still have been suppressed under the rule of *Edwards*. If Montejo made a clear assertion of the right to counsel when the officers approached him about accompanying them on the excursion for the murder weapon, then no interrogation should have taken place unless Montejo initiated it.

[Montejo] understandably did not pursue an *Edwards* objection, because *Jackson* served as the Sixth Amendment analogy to *Edwards* and offered broader protections. Our decision today, overruling *Jackson*, changes the legal landscape and does so in part based on the protections already provided by *Edwards*. Thus we think that a remand is appropriate so that Montejo can pursue this alternative avenue for relief. * * * a

JUSTICE STEVENS, joined by JUSTICES SOUTER and GINSBURG and, in large part, by JUSTICE BREYER, dissenting.b * * *

[The] majority's decision to overrule *Jackson* rests on its assumption that *Jackson*'s protective rule was intended to "prevent police from badgering defendants into changing their minds about their rights," just as the rule adopted in *Edwards* was designed to prevent police from coercing unindicted suspects into revoking their requests for counsel at interrogation. Operating on that limited understanding of the purpose behind *Jackson*'s protective rule, the Court concludes that *Jackson* provides no safeguard not already secured by this Court's Fifth Amendment jurisprudence.

[The] majority's analysis flagrantly misrepresents *Jackson*'s underlying rationale and the constitutional interests the decision sought to protect. While it is true that the rule adopted in *Jackson* was patterned after the rule in *Edwards*, the *Jackson* opinion does not even mention the anti-badgering considerations that provide the basis for the Court's decision today. Instead, *Jackson* relied primarily on cases discussing the broad protections guaranteed by the Sixth Amendment right to counsel—not its Fifth Amendment counterpart. * * * Underscoring that the commencement of criminal proceedings is a decisive event that transforms a suspect into an accused within the meaning of the Sixth Amendment, we concluded that arraigned defendants are entitled to "at least as much protection" during interrogation as the Fifth Amendment affords unindicted suspects. [Thus,] although the rules adopted in *Edwards* and *Jackson* are similar, *Jackson* did not rely on the reasoning of *Edwards* but remained firmly rooted in the unique protections afforded to the attorney-client relationship by the Sixth Amendment.

---

a. The concurring opinion of Justice Alito, joined by Kennedy, J., is omitted. The dissenting opinion of Justice Breyer is omitted.

b. Justice Stevens wrote the opinion of the Court in *Michigan v. Jackson*.

Once *Jackson* is placed in its proper Sixth Amendment context, the majority's justifications for overruling the decision crumble. * * *

First, and most central to the Court's decision to overrule *Jackson*, is its assertion that *Jackson*'s " 'reasoning' "—which the Court defines as "the weighing of the [protective] rule's benefits against its costs,"—does not justify continued application of the rule it created. The balancing test the Court performs, however, depends entirely on its misunderstanding of *Jackson* as a rule designed to prevent police badgering, rather than a rule designed to safeguard a defendant's right to rely on the assistance of counsel.

Next, in order to reach the conclusion that the *Jackson* rule is unworkable, the Court reframes the relevant inquiry, asking not whether the *Jackson* rule as applied for the past quarter century has proved easily administrable, but instead whether the Louisiana Supreme Court's cramped interpretation of that rule is practically workable. The answer to that question, of course, is no. When framed more broadly, however, the evidence is overwhelming that *Jackson*'s simple, bright-line rule has done more to advance effective law enforcement than to undermine it. In a supplemental brief submitted by lawyers and judges with extensive experience in law enforcement and prosecution, amici argue persuasively that *Jackson*'s bright-line rule has provided law enforcement officers with clear guidance, allowed prosecutors to quickly and easily assess whether confessions will be admissible in court, and assisted judges in determining whether a defendant's Sixth Amendment rights have been violated by police interrogation. [The amicus brief maintains] that "it is a rare case where this rule lets a guilty defendant go free." Notably, these representations are not contradicted by the State of Louisiana or other amici, including the United States.

A defendant's decision to forgo counsel's assistance and speak openly with police is a momentous one. Given the high stakes of making such a choice and the potential value of counsel's advice and mediation at that critical stage of the criminal proceedings, it is imperative that a defendant possess "a full awareness of both the nature of the right being abandoned and the consequences of the decision to abandon it." Because the administration of *Miranda* warnings was insufficient to ensure Montejo understood the Sixth Amendment right he was being asked to surrender, the record in this case provides no basis for concluding that Montejo validly waived his right to counsel, even in the absence of *Jackson*'s enhanced protections.

The Court's decision to overrule *Jackson* is unwarranted. Not only does it rest on a flawed doctrinal premise, but the dubious benefits it hopes to achieve are far outweighed by the damage it does to the rule of law and the integrity of the Sixth Amendment right to counsel. Moreover, even apart from the protections afforded by *Jackson*, the police interrogation in this case violated [petitioner's] Sixth Amendment right to counsel. * * *

NOTES AND QUESTIONS

The *Montejo* majority tells us it is "irrelevant" that the *Miranda-Edwards* rule is designed to protect the Fifth Amendment, not Sixth Amendment rights; the important matter is that the *Miranda-Edwards* rule adequately protects the right to have counsel during custodial interrogation. Should the Sixth Amendment play *any* role when the police are trying to obtain incriminating statements from a suspect?

In McNEIL v. WISCONSIN, 501 U.S. 171 (1991) (where a suspect asserted his Sixth Amendment right to counsel by his appearance with counsel at a bail hearing concerning an offense with which he had been charged), a 6–3 majority, per Scalia, J., made it clear that the Sixth Amendment right to counsel provides less protection than does the *Miranda–Edwards–Roberson* rule. Unlike the latter rule, which, when invoked, protects one from police-initiated interrogation with respect to *any* crime, the Sixth Amendment right is "offense-specific." Thus, even though a defendant invokes this right, the police can initiate questioning about crimes *other than* the one with which he was charged.

The case arose as follows: After his arrest for armed robbery McNeil was represented by a public defender at a bail hearing. A short time later, a deputy sheriff visited McNeil in jail. After McNeil waived his *Miranda* rights, the deputy questioned him about a murder and attempted murder *factually unrelated* to the armed robbery with which he had been charged.[a] McNeil's statements were admitted into evidence and he was convicted of murder and attempted murder. The Court, per Scalia, J., rejected his contention that his appearance at the bail hearing for the armed robbery constituted an invocation of the *Miranda–Edwards–Roberson* right to counsel:

"[To] invoke the Sixth Amendment interest is, as a matter of *fact, not* to invoke the *Miranda-Edwards* interest. One might be quite willing to speak to the police without counsel present concerning many matters, but not the matter under prosecution. It can be said, perhaps, that it is *likely* that one who has asked for counsel's assistance in defending against a prosecution would want counsel present for all custodial interrogation, even interrogation unrelated to the charge. [But] even if [that] were true, the *likelihood* that a suspect would wish counsel to be present is not the test for applicability of *Edwards*. [That rule] requires, at a minimum, some statement that can reasonably be construed to be expression of a desire for the assistance of an attorney *in dealing with custodial interrogation by the police*. Requesting the assistance of an attorney at a bail hearing does not bear that construction.

"[Petitioner's] proposed rule [would] seriously impede effective law enforcement. The Sixth Amendment right to counsel attaches at the first formal proceeding against an accused, and in most States, at least with respect to serious offenses, free counsel is made available at that time and ordinarily requested. Thus, if we were to adopt petitioner's rule, most persons in pretrial custody for serious offenses would be *unapproachable* by police officers suspecting them of involvement in other crimes, *even though they have never expressed any unwillingness to be questioned*. Since the ready ability to obtain uncoerced confessions is not an evil but an unmitigated good, society would be the loser."

25. *"Anticipatorily" invoking the Miranda–Edwards–Roberson right to counsel.*

Dissenting in *McNeil* (joined by Marshall and Blackmun, J.J.), Justice Stevens (author of *Michigan v. Jackson*) maintained that *McNeil* "demeans the importance of the right to counsel." But he took comfort in the fact that *McNeil* "probably will have only a slight impact on current custodial interrogation procedures":

"[If] petitioner in this case had made [a] statement indicating that he was invoking his Fifth Amendment right to counsel as well as his Sixth Amendment right to counsel, the entire offense-specific house of cards that the Court has

---

a. Once the right to counsel attaches to the offense charged, does (should) it also attach to any other offense "closely related to" or "inextricably intertwined with" the particular offense charged? See *Texas v. Cobb*, p. 754.

erected today would collapse, pursuant to our holding in *Roberson,* that a defendant who invokes the right to counsel for interrogation on one offense may not be reapproached regarding any offense unless counsel is present. In future preliminary hearings, competent counsel can be expected to make sure that they, or their clients, make a statement on the record that will obviate the consequences of today's holding. That is why I think this decision will have little, if any, practical effect on police practices."

But Justice Scalia replied:

"We have in fact never held that a person can invoke his *Miranda* rights anticipatorily, in a context other than 'custodial interrogation' which a preliminary hearing will not always or even usually involve. [If] the *Miranda* right to counsel can be invoked at a preliminary hearing, it could be argued, there is no logical reason why it could not be invoked by a letter prior to arrest, or indeed even prior to identification as a suspect. Most rights must be asserted when the government seeks to take the action they protect against. The fact that we have allowed the *Miranda* right to counsel, once asserted, to be effective with respect to future custodial interrogation does not necessarily mean that we will allow it to be asserted initially outside the context of custodial interrogation, with similar future effect."

Is Justice Scalia correct? Is even a person taken in to police custody *unable* to assert his *Miranda–Edwards–Roberson* right "in a context other than 'custodial interrogation' "? (Emphasis added.) Consider the following *alternative* hypothetical situations:

(1) A murder suspect is arrested in his apartment and told he is being taken to police headquarters where he will be questioned by the lieutenant in charge of the case. He tells the arresting officers: "Before I leave my apartment and go with you, I want to make one thing perfectly clear. When I get to the police station, I'm not talking to the lieutenant or anybody else unless my lawyer is present."

(2) Same facts as above except that the suspect says nothing until he arrives at the police station and is ushered into the office of the lieutenant in charge of the case. At this point, the suspect tells the lieutenant: "Before you ask me anything, I want you to know that I am well aware that I have a right to a lawyer and I want one at my side before I answer any questions."

(3) Same facts as above except that when the suspect enters the lieutenant's office, the lieutenant tells him: "I'm in charge of this case. I want you to know that I am going to treat you fairly and squarely. As soon as you take off your coat and sit down in that chair next to my desk I am going to advise you fully of your rights." The suspect, who has said nothing to any officer up to this point, remains standing and replies: "Don't bother to read me my rights. I know my rights and I want a lawyer right now. I'm not going to answer a single question without a lawyer being present."

Assume further that in each of these alternative hypothetical situations the lieutenant proceeds to give the suspect the *Miranda* warnings and in each instance the suspect *agrees* to talk to the police about his involvement in the murder when he is advised of his rights. In which instance, if any, has the suspect effectively invoked his *Miranda-Edwards* right to counsel?

The position taken by the lower courts. Relying heavily on footnote 3 to Justice Scalia's opinion in *McNeil,* most courts that have addressed the issue have balked at the notion that *Miranda-Edwards* protections can be triggered anticipatorily. However, they have left open the possibility that a suspect might be able to invoke the *Miranda-Edwards* right to counsel if custodial interrogation is about to begin or is "imminent." See, e.g., *United States v. Wyatt,* 179 F.3d 532 (7th Cir.1999);

United States v. Melgar, 139 F.3d 1005 (4th Cir.1998); *Alston v. Redman*, 34 F.3d 1237 (3d Cir.1994).

26. *If a suspect has not requested a lawyer but, unbeknownst to him, somebody else has retained one for him, does the failure to inform the suspect that a lawyer is trying to see him vitiate the waiver of his Miranda rights? If the police mislead the attorney about whether her client will be questioned or otherwise deceive an inquiring attorney, should the confession be excluded?*

MORAN v. BURBINE

475 U.S. 412, 106 S.Ct. 1135, 89 L.Ed.2d 410 (1986).

JUSTICE O'CONNOR delivered the opinion of the Court.

After being informed of his rights pursuant to *Miranda* and after executing a series of written waivers, respondent confessed to the murder of a young woman. At no point during the course of the interrogation, which occurred prior to arraignment, did he request an attorney. While he was in police custody, his sister attempted to retain a lawyer to represent him. The attorney telephoned the police station and received assurances that respondent would not be questioned further until the next day. In fact, the interrogation session that yielded the inculpatory statements began later that evening. The question presented is whether either the conduct of the police or respondent's ignorance of the attorney's efforts to reach him taints the validity of the waivers and therefore requires exclusion of the confessions.

[Several months after Mary Jo Hickey was beaten to death in Providence, Rhode Island, respondent Burbine and two others were arrested by Cranston, Rhode Island police for a local burglary. When the other burglary suspects implicated Burbine in Ms. Hickey's murder, a Cranston detective notified the Providence police. An hour later, early in the evening, three Providence officers arrived at Cranston police headquarters to question Burbine about the Providence murder.]

That same evening, at about 7:45 p.m., respondent's sister telephoned the Public Defender's Office to obtain legal assistance for her brother. Her sole concern was the breaking and entering charge, as she was unaware that respondent was then under suspicion for murder. [She tried to contact the attorney who was to represent her brother on the breaking and entering charge, but when unable to do so, wound up talking to another Assistant Public Defender (Ms. Munson) about her brother's situation. At 8:15 p.m. Ms. Munson phoned the Cranston police station, asked that her call be transferred to the detective division, and stated that she would act as Burbine's counsel in the event the police intended to put him in a lineup or question him. An unidentified person told her that neither act would occur and that the police were "through" with Burbine "for the night." Ms. Munson was told neither that the Providence police were at the stationhouse nor that Burbine was a suspect in Ms. Hickey's murder.]

At all relevant times, respondent was unaware of his sister's efforts to retain counsel and of the fact and contents of Ms. Munson's telephone conversation.

Less than an hour later, the police brought respondent to an interrogation room and conducted the first of a series of interviews concerning the murder. Prior to each session, respondent was informed of his *Miranda* rights, and on three separate occasions he signed a written form acknowledging that he understood his right to the presence of an attorney and explicitly indicating that he "[did] not want an attorney called or appointed for [him]" before he gave a statement. [At] least twice during the course of the evening, respondent was left in a room where he had access to a telephone, which he apparently declined to use. Eventually, respondent signed three written statements fully admitting to the murder.

[The trial judge denied respondent's motion to suppress the statements. The jury found respondent guilty of first degree murder. On federal habeas corpus, the First Circuit held that the police conduct had fatally tainted respondent's "otherwise valid" waiver. The U.S. Supreme Court reversed.]

Events occurring outside of the presence of the suspect and entirely unknown to him surely can have no bearing on the capacity to comprehend and knowingly relinquish a constitutional right. Under the analysis of the Court of Appeals, the same defendant, armed with the same information and confronted with precisely the same police conduct, would have knowingly waived his *Miranda* rights had a lawyer not telephoned the police station to inquire about his status. Nothing in any of our waiver decisions or in our understanding of the essential components of a valid waiver requires so incongruous a result. No doubt the additional information would have been useful to respondent; perhaps even it might have affected his decision to confess. But we have never read the Constitution to require that the police supply a suspect with a flow of information to help him calibrate his self interest in deciding whether to speak or stand by his rights. Once it is determined that a suspect's decision not to rely on his rights was uncoerced, that he at all times knew he could stand mute and request a lawyer, and that he was aware of the state's intention to use his statements to secure a conviction, the analysis is complete and the waiver is valid as a matter of law.

[Nor] do we believe that the level of the police's culpability in failing to inform respondent of the telephone call has any bearing on the validity of the waiver. [Although] highly inappropriate, even deliberate deception of an attorney could not possibly affect a suspect's decision to waive his *Miranda* rights unless he were at least aware of the incident. [Because] respondent's voluntary decision to speak was made with full awareness and comprehension of all the information *Miranda* requires the police to convey, the waivers were valid.

* * * Regardless of any issue of waiver, [contends respondent], the Fifth Amendment requires the reversal of a conviction if the police are less than forthright in their dealings with an attorney or if they fail to tell a suspect of a lawyer's unilateral efforts to contact him. Because the proposed modification ignores the underlying purposes of the *Miranda* rules and because we think that the decision as written strikes the proper balance between society's legitimate law enforcement interests and the protection of the defendant's Fifth Amendment rights, we decline the invitation to further extend *Miranda*'s reach.

At the outset, while we share respondent's distaste for the deliberate misleading of an officer of the court, reading *Miranda* to forbid police deception of an *attorney* "would cut [the decision] completely loose from its own explicitly stated rationale."

[The] purpose of the *Miranda* warnings * * * is to dissipate the compulsion inherent in custodial interrogation and, in so doing, guard against abridgment of the suspect's Fifth Amendment rights. Clearly, a rule that focuses on how the police treat an attorney—conduct that has no relevance at all to the degree of compulsion experienced by the defendant during interrogation—would ignore both *Miranda*'s mission and its only source of legitimacy.

Nor are we prepared to adopt a rule requiring that the police inform a suspect of an attorney's efforts to reach him. While such a rule might add marginally to *Miranda*'s goal of dispelling the compulsion inherent in custodial interrogation, overriding practical considerations counsel against its adoption. [We] have little doubt that the approach urged by respondent and endorsed by the Court of

Appeals would have the inevitable consequence of muddying *Miranda*'s otherwise relatively clear waters. The legal questions it would spawn are legion: To what extent should the police be held accountable for knowing that the accused has counsel? Is it enough that someone in the station house knows, or must the interrogating officer himself know, of counsel's efforts to contact the suspect? Do counsel's efforts to talk to the suspect concerning one criminal investigation trigger the obligation to inform the defendant before interrogation may proceed on a wholly separate matter?

[Moreover,] reading *Miranda* to require the police in each instance to inform a suspect of an attorney's efforts to reach him would work a substantial and, we think, inappropriate shift in the subtle balance struck in that decision. Custodial interrogations implicate two competing concerns. On the one hand, "the need for police questioning as a tool for effective enforcement of criminal laws" cannot be doubted. [On] the other hand, the Court has recognized that the interrogation process is "inherently coercive" and that, as a consequence, there exists a substantial risk that the police will inadvertently traverse the fine line between legitimate efforts to elicit admissions and constitutionally impermissible compulsion. *Miranda* attempted to reconcile these opposing concerns by giving the *defendant* the power to exert some control over the course of the interrogation. Declining to adopt the more extreme position that the actual presence of a lawyer was necessary to dispel the coercion inherent in custodial interrogation, the Court found that the suspect's Fifth Amendment rights could be adequately protected by less intrusive means. Police questioning, often an essential part of the investigatory process, could continue in its traditional form, the Court held, but only if the suspect clearly understood that, at any time, he could bring the proceeding to a halt or, short of that, call in an attorney to give advice and monitor the conduct of his interrogators.

The position urged by respondent would upset this carefully drawn approach in a manner that is both unnecessary for the protection of the Fifth Amendment privilege and injurious to legitimate law enforcement. Because, as *Miranda* holds, full comprehension of the rights to remain silent and request an attorney are sufficient to dispel whatever coercion is inherent in the interrogation process, a rule requiring the police to inform the suspect of an attorney's efforts to contact him would contribute to the protection of the Fifth Amendment privilege only incidentally, if at all. This minimal benefit, however, would come at a substantial cost to society's legitimate and substantial interest in securing admissions of guilt.

[Respondent] also contends that the Sixth Amendment requires exclusion of his three confessions. [The] difficulty for respondent is that the interrogation sessions that yielded the inculpatory statements took place *before* the initiation of "adversary judicial proceedings." He contends, however, that [the] right to noninterference with an attorney's dealings with a [suspect] arises the moment that the relationship is formed, or, at the very least, once the defendant is placed in custodial interrogation.

We are not persuaded. [Although] *Escobedo* was originally decided as a Sixth Amendment case, "the Court in retrospect perceived that the 'prime purpose' of *Escobedo* was not to vindicate the constitutional right to counsel as such, but, like *Miranda*, 'to guarantee full effectuation of the privilege against self-incrimination....'" *Kirby v. Illinois* [p. 769]. Clearly then, *Escobedo* provides no support for respondent's argument. Nor, of course, does *Miranda*, the holding of which rested exclusively on the Fifth Amendment.

[As] a practical matter, it makes little sense to say that the Sixth Amendment right to counsel attaches at different times depending on the fortuity of whether the suspect or his family happens to have retained counsel prior to interrogation.

More importantly, the suggestion that the existence of an attorney-client relationship itself triggers the protections of the Sixth Amendment misconceives the underlying purposes of the right to counsel. The Sixth Amendment's intended function is not to wrap a protective cloak around the attorney-client relationship for its own sake any more than it is to protect a suspect from the consequences of his own candor. [By] its very terms, [the Sixth Amendment] becomes applicable only when the government's role shifts from investigation to accusation. * * *[4]

JUSTICE STEVENS, with whom JUSTICE BRENNAN and JUSTICE MARSHALL join, dissenting.

[Until] today, incommunicado questioning has been viewed with the strictest scrutiny by this Court; today, incommunicado questioning is embraced as a societal goal of the highest order that justifies police deception of the shabbiest kind. * * * Police interference with communications between an attorney and his client is a recurrent problem. [The] near-consensus of state courts and the [ABA Standards of Criminal Justice] about this recurrent problem lends powerful support to the conclusion that police may not interfere with communications between an attorney and the client whom they are questioning. Indeed, at least two opinions from this Court seemed to express precisely that view.[20] The Court today flatly rejects that widely held view.

[*Miranda*] clearly condemns threats or trickery that cause a suspect to make an unwise waiver of his rights even though he fully understands those rights. In my opinion there can be no constitutional distinction—as the Court appears to draw—between a deceptive misstatement and the concealment by the police of the critical fact that an attorney retained by the accused or his family has offered assistance, either by telephone or in person.

[If,] as the Court asserts, "the analysis is at an end" as soon as the suspect is provided with enough information to have the *capacity* to understand and exercise his rights, I see no reason why the police should not be permitted to make the same kind of misstatements to the suspect that they are apparently allowed to make to his lawyer. *Miranda,* however, clearly establishes that both kinds of deception vitiate the suspect's waiver of his right to counsel. * * *

What is the cost of requiring the police to inform a suspect of his attorney's call? It would decrease the likelihood that custodial interrogation will enable the police to obtain a confession. This is certainly a real cost, but it is the same cost

---

4. [The] dissent's misreading of *Miranda* itself is breathtaking in its scope. For example, it reads *Miranda* as creating an undifferentiated right to the presence of an attorney that is triggered automatically by the initiation of the interrogation itself. [The] dissent condemns us for embracing "incommunicado questioning [as] a societal goal of the highest order that justifies police deception of the shabbiest kind." We, of course, do nothing of the kind. As any reading of *Miranda* reveals, the decision, rather than proceeding from the premise that the rights and needs of the defendant are paramount to all others, embodies a carefully crafted balance designed to fully protect *both* the defendant's and society's interests. The dissent may not share our view that the Fifth Amendment rights of the defendant are amply protected by application of *Miranda as written.* But the dissent is "simply wrong" in suggesting that exclusion of Burbine's three confessions follows perfunctorily from *Miranda*'s mandate. Y. Kamisar, *Police Interrogation and Confessions* 217–218, n. 94 (1980).

Quite understandably, the dissent is outraged by the very idea of police deception of a lawyer. Significantly less understandable is its willingness to misconstrue this Court's constitutional holdings in order to implement its subjective notions of sound policy.

20. See *Miranda* at n. 35 (in *Escobedo*, "[t]he police also prevented the attorney from consulting with his client. Independent of any other constitutional proscription, this action constitutes a violation of the Sixth Amendment right to the assistance of counsel and excludes any statement obtained in its wake"); *Escobedo* ("[I]t 'would be highly incongruous if our system of justice permitted the district attorney, the lawyer representing the State, to extract a confession from the accused while his own lawyer, seeking to speak with him, was kept from him by the police' ").

that this Court has repeatedly found necessary to preserve the character of our free society and our rejection of an inquisitorial system. [At] the time attorney Munson made her call to the Cranston Police Station, she was acting as Burbine's attorney. Under ordinary principles of agency law the deliberate deception of Munson was tantamount to deliberate deception of her client.

[The] possible reach of the Court's opinion is stunning. For the majority seems to suggest that police may deny counsel all access to a client who is being held. At least since *Escobedo,* it has been widely accepted that police may not simply deny attorneys access to their clients who are in custody. This view has survived the recasting of *Escobedo* from a Sixth Amendment to a Fifth Amendment case that the majority finds so critically important. [The] law enforcement profession has apparently believed, quite rightly in my view, that denying lawyers access to their clients is impermissible.

[This] case turns on a proper appraisal of the role of the lawyer in our society. If a lawyer is seen as a nettlesome obstacle to the pursuit of wrongdoers—as in an inquisitorial society—then the Court's decision today makes a good deal of sense. If a lawyer is seen as an aid to the understanding and protection of constitutional rights—as in an accusatorial society—then today's decision makes no sense at all.
* * *

NOTES AND QUESTIONS

(a) *"Incommunicado questioning."* What exactly is meant by "incommunicado" or "incommunicado questioning" (terms used frequently by dissenting Justice Stevens)? These terms may mean either (1) preventing a prisoner from communicating with or meeting with counsel; or (2) not informing the outside world of the prisoner's whereabouts; or (3) denying a prisoner's friends, relatives or lawyers access to him. In which sense, if any, was Burbine held "incommunicado"?

(b) *The Miranda warnings and the need for a lawyer's advice.* Consider Note, 100 Harv.L.Rev. 125, 133 (1986): "[T]o the extent that the population at large is unaware of its fifth and sixth amendment rights, the role of the lawyer—possibly the only one capable of safeguarding these rights—must be protected." Is *a suspect advised of his rights* (as opposed to "the population at large") unaware of his rights? If a lawyer is "the only one capable of safeguarding these rights," did the *Miranda* Court commit grievous error by not requiring that a suspect first consult with a lawyer or actually have a lawyer present in order for his waiver of rights to be effective?

(c) *The Burbine dissent's reliance on fn. 35 to Miranda.* In fn. 20 to his dissenting opinion, Justice Stevens maintains that the majority opinion cannot be reconciled with fn. 35 to *Miranda,* which, discussing *Escobedo,* states that "prevent[ing] [an] attorney from consulting with his client" violates the Sixth Amendment "independent of any other constitutional proscription." Should this statement be read in light of *Escobedo's* particular facts? Consider Kamisar, Essays 217 n. 94 (1980):

"It is hard to believe that in the course of writing a 60–page opinion *based on the premise* that police-issued warnings can adequately protect a suspect's rights the [*Miranda*] Court would say in the next breath that such warnings are insufficient when, but only when, a suspect's lawyer is not allowed to consult with him—that even though a suspect has been emphatically and unequivocally advised of his rights and insists on talking, what he says is inadmissible [when] a lawyer *whose services he has not requested* has, *unbeknown to him,* entered the picture.

"Although the police did not advise Escobedo of any of his rights, 'he repeatedly asked to speak to his lawyer.' * * * Indeed, [the *Escobedo*] opinion begins: 'The critical issue in this case is whether [the] refusal by the police to honor petitioner's request to consult with his lawyer during the course of an interrogation constitutes a denial of "the Assistance of Counsel." '[If the refusal of the police to let Escobedo's lawyer meet with him] has any relevance, it is only because Escobedo became *aware of the fact* that the police were preventing his lawyer from talking to him, and this realization may well have underscored the police domination of the situation and the gravity of his plight."

(d) *Should Burbine dishearten or encourage Miranda's defenders?* Consider Kamisar, *The "Police Practice" Phases of the Criminal Process and the Three Phases of the Burger Court,* in The Burger Years (Herman Schwartz ed. 1987) at 143, 150: "[The *Burbine* Court's view of *Miranda* as not 'proceeding from the premise that the rights and needs of the defendant are paramount to all others, [but as a case that] embodies a carefully crafted balance designed to fully protect *both* the defendant's and society's interests'] [see fn. 4 to the Court's opinion] is the way *Miranda*'s defenders—not its critics—have talked about the case for the past twenty years. [The *Burbine* Court's view of *Miranda* as a serious effort to strike a proper 'balance,' between, or to 'reconcile,' competing interests may turn out to be more important than its specific ruling.]" See also Kamisar, *Remembering the "Old World" of Criminal Procedure: A Reply to Professor Grano,* 23 U.Mich.J.L.Ref. 537, 575–84 (1990).

(e) *What result if, before being taken away by the police, a suspect asks a relative to contact a lawyer?* Would the result in *Burbine* have been different if, before being taken to the police station (a) the defendant had asked his sister to contact the Public Defender's Office and get somebody in the office to represent him; (b) his sister had done so; (c) the assistant public defender who had agreed to represent defendant had told the police she wanted to meet with her client immediately; but (d) the police had failed to inform defendant of this development? Why (not)? Cf. *People v. Griggs,* 604 N.E.2d 257 (Ill.1992).

27. *Use of a pretrial psychiatric examination at a capital sentencing proceeding.* ESTELLE v. SMITH, 451 U.S. 454 (1981), arose as follows: Respondent was indicted for murder in Texas. The state announced its intention to seek the death penalty. Thereafter, although defense counsel had not put into issue his client's competency to stand trial or his sanity at the time of the offense, a judge informally ordered the prosecution to arrange a psychiatric examination of respondent by Dr. Grigson to determine respondent's capacity to stand trial. After respondent was convicted of murder, the doctor also testified—on the basis of his pretrial examination of respondent—as to respondent's "future dangerousness," one of the critical issues to be resolved by a Texas jury at the capital sentencing proceeding. The jury answered the "future dangerousness" question and other requisite questions in the affirmative and, thus, under Texas law, the death penalty for respondent was mandatory.

Although respondent had not been warned before the pretrial psychiatric examination that anything he said during the examination could be used against him at the sentencing proceeding, the state argued that the privilege against self-incrimination was inapplicable because (a) Dr. Grigson's testimony was used only to determine punishment after conviction, not to establish guilt; and (b) respondent's communications to Dr. Grigson were "nontestimonial" in nature. Rejecting these contentions, the Court held, per Burger, C.J., that both respondent's Fifth and Sixth Amendment rights were violated by the use of Dr. Grigson's testimony at the penalty phase of the case:

"Just as the Fifth Amendment prevents a criminal defendant from being made 'the deluded instrument of his own conviction,' it protects him as well from being made the 'deluded instrument' of his own execution." As for the argument that respondent's communications to the examining psychiatrist were "nontestimonial" in nature, "Dr. Grigson's prognosis as to future dangerousness rested on statements respondent made and remarks he omitted in reciting the details of the crime. [Thus,] the State used as evidence against respondent the substance of his disclosures during the pretrial psychiatric examination."[a]

28. *Miranda and mentally retarded suspects: The Cloud–Shepherd– Barkoff–Shur study.* The results of an empirical study, Morgan Cloud, George B. Shepherd, Alison Nodwin Barkoff and Justin V. Shur, *Words Without Meaning: The Constitution, Confessions, and Mentally Retarded Suspects*, 69 U. Chi. L.Rev. 495 (2002) (hereinafter called the Cloud study) "indicate that mentally retarded people simply do not understand the *Miranda* warnings. Virtually all of the disabled subjects failed to understand the context in which the interrogation occurs, the legal consequences embedded in the rules or the significance of confessing, the meaning of the sentences that comprise the warnings, or even the individual operative words used to construct the warnings.[a] In contrast, comparably large percentages of the non-disabled control group did understand the individual words, the complete warnings, and their legal significance."

The results of the Cloud study support two additional conclusions about the validity of confessions obtained from mentally retarded suspects:

First, "the number of people to whom the *Miranda* warnings are meaningless [appears to be] much larger than previously acknowledged within the criminal justice system. [The warnings] also are incomprehensible to people whose mental retardation is classified as mild, as well as some people whose 'intelligence quotient' (IQ) scores exceed 70, the number typically used to demarcate mental retardation."

Second, the study raises "disquieting questions" about the capacity of current doctrine to "accommodate the special problems accompanying police interrogation of mentally retarded suspects": "When confronted with challenges to the validity of a mentally retarded suspect's waiver of the *Miranda* 'rights,' courts typically revert to a 'totality of the circumstances' analysis to determine whether the suspect was capable of understanding the *Miranda* warnings." But the results of the study "suggest that the 'totalities' analysis ... is incapable of identifying suspects competent to understand the *Miranda* warnings.... Multiple regression analysis demonstrates that variations in age, education and experience with the criminal justice system or the *Miranda* warnings do not compensate for a mentally retarded person's inability to comprehend the *Miranda* warnings. If mental retardation is present, then the disabled person will not understand the warnings, regardless of the presence of the other factors."

Another serious problem posed by mentally retarded persons' confessions is that it now seems indisputable that "mentally retarded suspects are likely to confess falsely, that is confess to crimes they did not commit, far more frequently

---

a. Because respondent had been indicted and assigned counsel before Dr. Grigson examined him and the examination had taken place without notice to respondent's counsel, Stewart, J., joined by Powell, J., concurred in the judgment on *Massiah* grounds without reaching the *Miranda* issue. Although he dissented, in effect, on the *Miranda* issue, Rehnquist, J., also concurred in the result of *Massiah* grounds. Thus, the Court's judgment that respondent's Sixth Amendment right to counsel had been violated was unanimous.

See also *Powell v. Texas*, 492 U.S. 680 (1989) (that defendant raised insanity defense "no basis for concluding" he waived Sixth Amendment right to counsel set out in *Estelle*).

a. According to the authors of the study, "the best available data suggests that at least forty-five thousand, and perhaps more than two hundred thousand mentally retarded people currently are imprisoned in the United States. Undoubtedly, these people have been arrested. Many, probably most, have been 'Mirandized' and interrogated while in custody. Some have waived their rights and made statements to investigators."

than do suspects of average and above average intelligence. Similarly, interrogation tactics generally believed to be acceptable with most suspects are more likely to produce false confessions from mentally retarded suspects."[b]

What is the solution? Should the courts take the position that *any* confession from a mentally retarded suspect is inadmissible in a criminal case? Should law enforcement officers be required to administer simplified warnings? Are the mentally retarded likely to understand warnings containing simplified synonyms for difficult words in the *Miranda* warnings much better than they do the original vocabulary of the warnings? See Part V. of the Cloud study.[c]

29. Juveniles. "Because juvenile suspects share many of the same characteristics as the developmentally disabled, notably their eagerness to comply with adult authority figures, impulsivity, immature judgment, and inability to recognize and weigh risks in decision-making and appear to be at greater risk of falsely confessing when subjected to psychological interrogation techniques," Steven A. Drizin & Richard A. Leo, *The Problem of False Confessions in the Post–DNA World*, 82 N.C.L.Rev. 891, 1005 (2004), maintain that "the same protections [which are given or ought to be given developmentally disabled suspects] should be afforded to juveniles." Professors Drizin and Leo analyzed 125 proven false confessions obtained in the post-*Miranda* era. Of these, forty were from suspects under the age of eighteen at the time they confessed. See id. at 968. (By contrast, "at least twenty-eight cases" in the Drizin–Leo data set involve mentally retarded defendants. See id. at 971.)[a]

As the result of several false confession cases in the Chicago area involving children and teenagers, note Drizin & Leo, Illinois passed a law requiring that all children under age thirteen be provided access to attorneys before being interrogated in murder and sex offense cases. See id. at 1005. Chicago's Juvenile Court Competency Commission, a panel of experts from many disciplines, would have gone even further. Among the reforms the Commission recommended were prohibiting the use of any uncounseled statements against children under seventeen in any proceeding where children might receive adult punishments, a requirement that the entire custodial interrogation of juveniles charged with felonies be videotaped, and better ways to assure that a minor's parent of guardian be present during police questioning. Id.[b]

30. Comparing and contrasting Miranda with (a) the prohibition against the use of involuntary or compelled statements and (b) the Fourth

---

b. See also Richard A. Leo, *Police Interrogation and American Justice* 232–33 (2008):

"[T]he mentally retarded are highly susceptible to leading, misleading, and erroneous information. It is therefore easy to get them to agree with and repeat back false or misleading statements, even incriminating ones. "Second, [the] mentally retarded are eager to please. They tend to have a high need for approval. They have adapted [by] learning to submit to and comply with the demands of others, especially authority figures. * * * Third, because of their cognitive disabilities and learned coping behavior, the mentally retarded are easily overwhelmed by stress."

c. See also the recent report by Samuel R. Gross et al., quoted at pp. 760–61: "[A study of exonerations of defendants convicted of serious crimes in the United States since 1989 discloses that] [f]alse confessions * * * played a large role in the murder convictions that led to exonerations, primarily among two particularly vulnerable groups of innocent defendants: juveniles, and those who are mentally retarded or mentally ill. Almost all the juvenile exonerees who falsely confessed are African American. In fact, one of our most startling findings is that 90% of all exonerated juvenile defendants are black or Hispanic, an extreme disparity that, sadly, is of a piece with racial disparities in our juvenile justice system in general."

a. As pointed out in George Thomas III, *Regulating Police Deception During Interrogation*, 39 Tex.Tech.L.Rev. 1293, 1310 (2007), of the five teenagers who falsely confessed to gang rape and assault in the Central Park jogger case (discussed at p. 734–36 infra), two were fourteen years old, two were fifteen, and the one who was sixteen years old had a second-grade reading level. Moreover, one of the fifteen-year-olds had an IQ of 87.

b. For more on false confessions, see pp. 734–38 infra.

Amendment exclusionary rule. In *Stone v. Powell* (p. 230), the Court held that when a state has provided a full and fair chance to litigate a Fourth Amendment claim, federal habeas review is not available to a state prisoner claiming that his conviction rests on evidence obtained through an unconstitutional search or seizure. However, in WITHROW v. WILLIAMS, 507 U.S. 680 (1993), a 5–4 majority per Souter, J., held that *Stone* "does not extend to a state prisoner's claim that his conviction rests on statements obtained in violation [of] *Miranda*":

"[The *Miranda* Court] acknowledged that, in barring introduction of a statement obtained without the required warnings, *Miranda* might exclude a confession that we would not condemn as 'involuntary in traditional terms,' and for this reason we have sometimes called the *Miranda* safeguards 'prophylactic' in nature. * * * Calling the *Miranda* safeguards 'prophylactic,' however, is a far cry from putting *Miranda* on all fours with *Mapp,* or from rendering *Miranda* subject to *Stone.*

"As we explained in *Stone,* the *Mapp* rule 'is not a personal constitutional right,' but serves to deter future constitutional violations; although it mitigates the juridical consequences of invading the defendant's privacy, the exclusion of evidence at trial can do nothing to remedy the completed and wholly extrajudicial Fourth Amendment violation. Nor can the *Mapp* rule be thought to enhance the soundness of the criminal process by improving the reliability of evidence introduced at trial. *Miranda* differs from *Mapp* in both respects. 'Prophylactic' though it may be, in protecting a defendant's Fifth Amendment privilege against self-incrimination *Miranda* safeguards 'a fundamental *trial* right.' [The privilege] reflects 'many of our fundamental values and most noble aspirations' [quoting *Murphy v. Waterfront Comm'n.*] Nor does the Fifth Amendment 'trial right' protected by *Miranda* serve some value necessarily divorced from the correct ascertainment of guilt. [By] bracing against 'the possibility of unreliable statements in every instance of in-custody interrogation,' *Miranda* serves to guard against 'the use of unreliable statements at trial.'

"Finally, and most importantly, eliminating review of *Miranda* claims would not significantly benefit the federal courts in their exercise of habeas jurisdiction, or advance the cause of federalism in any substantial way. [For it] would not prevent a state prisoner from simply converting his barred *Miranda* claim into a due process claim that his conviction rested on an involuntary confession. If that is so, the federal courts would certainly not have heard the last of *Miranda* on collateral review. Under the due process approach, [courts] look to the totality of circumstances to determine whether a confession was voluntary. Those potential circumstances include [the] failure of police to advise the defendant of his rights to remain silent and to have counsel present during custodial interrogation. * * * We could lock the front door against *Miranda,* but not the back.

"We thus fail to see how abdicating *Miranda*'s bright-line (or, at least, brighter-line) rules in favor of an exhaustive totality-of-circumstances approach on habeas would do much of anything to lighten the burdens placed on busy federal courts."

Justice O'Connor, with whom The Chief Justice joined, dissented "because the principles that inform our habeas jurisprudence—finality, federalism, and fairness—counsel decisively against the result the Court reaches * * *. Like the suppression of the fruits of an illegal search or seizure, the exclusion of statements obtained in violation of *Miranda* is not constitutionally required. This Court repeatedly has held that *Miranda*'s warning requirement is not a dictate of the Fifth Amendment itself, but a prophylactic rule. [Unlike] involuntary or compelled statements—which are of dubious reliability and are therefore inadmissible for any purpose—confessions obtained in violation of *Miranda* are not necessarily untrustworthy. In fact, because *voluntary* statements are 'trustworthy' even when obtained without proper warnings, their suppression actually *impairs* the pursuit of truth by concealing probative information from the trier of fact."

In a separate dissent, Justice Scalia, joined by Thomas, J., maintained:

"The issue in this case—whether the extraordinary remedy of federal habeas corpus should routinely be available for claimed violations of *Miranda* rights—involves not *jurisdiction* to issue the writ, but the *equity* of doing so. In my view, both the Court and Justice O'Connor disregard the most powerful equitable consideration: that Williams has already had full and fair opportunity to litigate this claim. [The] question at this stage is whether [a] federal habeas court should now reopen the issue and adjudicate the *Miranda* claim anew. The answer seems to me obvious: it should not. That would be the course followed by a federal habeas court reviewing a *federal* conviction; it mocks our federal system to accord state convictions less respect. * * * Prior opportunity to litigate an issue should be an important equitable consideration in *any* habeas case, and should ordinarily preclude the court from reaching the merits of a claim, unless it goes to the fairness of the trial process or to the accuracy of the ultimate result."

NOTES AND QUESTIONS

Does Withrow affirm that the Miranda rule contains a constitutional command? "If the Court had viewed *Miranda* as truly non-constitutional," comments Charles D. Weisselberg, *Saving Miranda*, 84 Cornell L.Rev. 109, 130–31 (1998), "then it had little reason to refuse *Withrow*'s invitation to take mere *Miranda* violations out of federal habeas corpus. The Court in *Withrow* thus kept the universe of *Miranda* claims within the Constitution." But see *Chavez v. Martinez*, p. 690 infra.

(b) *Do Fifth Amendment violations occur only at trial? Withrow* talks about "the Fifth Amendment 'trial right' " and about "*Miranda* safeguard[ing] 'a fundamental *trial* right.' " However, Weisselberg, supra at 180, observes that "a number of cases have found Fifth Amendment violations in circumstances in which witnesses suffered penalties for asserting the privilege against self-incrimination, even though they faced no criminal charges and had no criminal trial." [He refers to such cases as *Lefkowitz v. Cunningham*, 431 U.S. 801 (1977), holding that a grand jury witness cannot be divested of political office as a penalty for exercising his Fifth Amendment privilege; and *Gardner v. Broderick*, 392 U.S. 273 (1968), holding that a police officer cannot lose his job for asserting the privilege before a grand jury.] These cases are impossible to square with the notion that Fifth Amendment violations occur only at trial. But see *Chavez v. Martinez*, p. 690.

31. *Is the failure of the police to notify the consular post of a detainee's home country that he has been arrested, a notification required by the Vienna Convention, ground for suppressing the detainee's subsequent statements to the police?* Consider SANCHEZ–LLAMAS v. OREGON, 548 U.S. 331 (2006). Article 36 of the Vienna Convention, ratified by the United States in 1969, provides that if a national of one country is detained by authorities in another, and the detainee so requests, the authorities must promptly inform the consular post of the detainee's home country of his detention. The convention also provides that the authorities should promptly advise the detainee of this right. After being arrested for his involvement in a shootout with American police, petitioner was given his *Miranda* warnings in both English and Spanish. At no time, however, was he informed that he could have the Mexican Consulate notified of his detention. Petitioner waived his *Miranda* rights and made several incriminating statements to the police. A 6–3 majority of the Court, per ROBERTS, C.J., rejected the contention that the Vienna Convention violation furnished a basis for suppressing petitioner's statements:

"[The Convention] expressly leaves the implementation of Article 36 to domestic law. [Where] a treaty does not provide a particular remedy, either expressly or implicitly, it is not for the federal courts to impose one on the States through law making of their own. * * *

"The violation of the right to consular notification * * * is at best remotely connected to the gathering of evidence. Article 36 has nothing whatsoever to do with searches or interrogations. Indeed, Article 36 does not guarantee defendants any assistance at all. The provision secures only a right of foreign nationals to have their consulate informed of their arrest or detention—not to have their consulate intervene, or to have law enforcement authorities cease their investigation pending any such notice or intervention. [Moreover,] [s]uppression would be a vastly disproportionate remedy for an Article 36 violation."

BREYER, J., joined by Stevens and Souter, JJ. dissented:

"I agree with the majority insofar as it rejects the argument that the Convention creates a *Miranda*-style 'automatic exclusionary rule.' But I do not agree with the absolute nature of its statement. Rather, sometimes suppression could prove the only effective remedy. And, if that is so, then the Convention, which insists upon effective remedies, would require suppression in an appropriate case.

"[While] [concurring] Justice Ginsburg is correct that a defendant who is prejudiced under the Convention may be able to show that his confession is involuntary under *Miranda*, I am not persuaded that this will always be so. A person who fully understands his *Miranda* rights but does not fully understand the implications of these rights for our legal system may or may not be able to show that his confession was involuntary under *Miranda*, but he will certainly have a claim under the Vienna Convention. In such a case suppression of a confession may prove the only effective remedy. I would not rule out the existence of such cases in advance."

32. *Other Miranda problems discussed elsewhere in the book.* Is *Miranda*'s prohibition against police trickery and deception confined to their use in obtaining a waiver of rights or does it also bar such tactics *after* a person has validly waived his rights? See the next section.

If a defendant takes the stand in his own defense, may the prosecution impeach him by using statements obtained from him in violation of *Miranda*? See p. 911. May a defendant's *prior silence*, even his *post* arrest silence, be used to impeach his credibility when he chooses to testify at his trial? See p. 918 infra.

Suppose, after a suspect is illegally arrested, he is advised of his rights, waives them, and confesses? Do the *Miranda* warnings "cure" the illegality of the arrest? See p. 895.

Suppose, an hour after the police obtain an incriminating statement from a suspect in violation of the *Miranda* rules, they give him the complete warnings and the suspect waives his rights and confesses? Is the "second confession" admissible or is it "the fruit" of the first inadmissible statement? See *Missouri v. Seibert*, p. 702. Suppose, as the result of a statement obtained in violation of the *Miranda* rules, the police find the murder weapon. Is the murder weapon admissible? Or is it the "fruit of the poisonous tree"? See *United States v. Patane*, p. 699.

CAN (DID) CONGRESS "REPEAL" *MIRANDA?*

Consider *Title II of the Omnibus Crime Control and Safe Streets Act of 1968,*[a] which provides in relevant part:

"§ 3501. Admissibility of confessions

"(a) In any criminal prosecution brought by the United States or by the District of Columbia, a confession, as defined in subsection (e) hereof, shall be admissible in evidence if it is voluntarily given. Before such confession is received in evidence, the trial judge shall, out of the presence of the jury, determine any issue as to voluntariness. If the trial judge determines that the confession was voluntarily made it shall be admitted in evidence and the trial judge shall permit the jury to hear relevant evidence on the issue of voluntariness and shall instruct the jury to give such weight to the confession as the jury feels it deserves under all the circumstances.

"(b) The trial judge in determining the issue of voluntariness shall take into consideration all the circumstances surrounding the giving of the confession, including (1) the time elapsing between arrest and arraignment of the defendant making the confession, if it was made after arrest and before arraignment, (2) whether such defendant knew the nature of the offense with which he was charged or of which he was suspected at the time of making the confession, (3) whether or not such defendant was advised or knew that he was not required to make any statement and that any such statement could be used against him, (4) whether or not such defendant had been advised prior to questioning of his right to the assistance of counsel; and (5) whether or not such defendant was without the assistance of counsel when questioned and when giving such confession.

"The presence or absence of any of the above-mentioned factors to be taken into consideration by the judge need not be conclusive on the issue of voluntariness of the confession. * * *

"(d) Nothing contained in this section shall bar the admission in evidence of any confession made or given voluntarily by any person to any other person without interrogation by anyone, or at any time at which the person who made or gave such confession was not under arrest or other detention.

"(e) As used in this section, the term 'confession' means any confession of guilt of any criminal offense or any self-incriminating statement made or given orally or in writing."[b]

---

a. For the legislative history of Title II of the Crime Control Act, see Adam C. Breckenridge, *Congress Against the Court* (1970); Fred P. Graham, *The Self–Inflicted Wound* 305–32 (1970); Richard Harris, *The Fear of Crime* (1969); Yale Kamisar, *Can (Did) Congress "Overrule" Miranda?*, 85 Cornell L.Rev. 883, 887–906 (2000); Michael Edmund O'Neill, *Undoing Miranda,* 2000 BYU L.Rev. 185; Otis H. Stephens, Jr., *The Supreme Court and Confessions of Guilt*, 139–45, 163–66 (1973).

b. Another provision of § 3501, Part (c), is aimed squarely at a rule that law-enforcement officials strongly disliked, the *McNabb–Mallory* rule (p. 554). Part (c) provides that in any federal criminal prosecution a confession by a person under arrest or other detention "shall not be inadmissible solely because of delay in bringing such person before a commissioner * * * if such confession is found by the trial judge to have been voluntarily made [and] if such confession was made [within] six hours immediately following [the person's] arrest or other detention." Moreover, the six-hour time limitation does not apply where the delay in bringing such person before a commissioner beyond the six-hour period "is found by the trial judge to be reasonable considering the means of transportation and the distance to be traveled to the nearest available commissioner."

Some thirty years after § 3501 became law, *United States v. Dickerson*, 166 F.3d 667 (4th Cir.1999), held, against the express wishes of the Department of Justice, that the pre-*Miranda* due process-voluntariness test set forth in § 3501, rather than *Miranda*, governed the admissibility of confessions in the federal courts. Thus, concluded the Fourth Circuit, the district court had erred when it had excluded a voluntary confession simply because it was obtained in violation of *Miranda*. In upholding the constitutionality of § 3501, the Fourth Circuit relied heavily on the fact that the Burger and Rehnquist Courts had "consistently referred to the *Miranda* warnings as 'prophylactic' " and "not themselves rights protected by the Constitution."

When the Supreme Court granted certiorari, most experts thought the vote would be close. Most thought that Justices Stevens, Souter, Ginsburg and Breyer were almost certain to invalidate § 3501 and that the Chief Justice and Justices Scalia and Thomas were almost certain to uphold it. Most considered Justice O'Connor and Kennedy the "swing votes." But a number of *Miranda* supporters feared that, on the basis of her majority opinion in *Oregon v. Elstad* and her strong dissent in *Withrow v. Williams*, Justice O'Connor would vote to uphold § 3501. As it turned out, most experts were wide of the mark.

DICKERSON v. UNITED STATES
530 U.S. 428, 120 S.Ct. 2326, 147 L.Ed.2d 405 (2000).

CHIEF JUSTICE REHNQUIST delivered the opinion of the Court.

[In] the wake of [*Miranda*], Congress enacted 18 U.S.C. § 3501, which in essence laid down a rule that the admissibility of [a custodial suspect's] statements should turn only on whether or not they were voluntarily made. We hold that *Miranda*, being a constitutional decision of this Court, may not be in effect overruled by an Act of Congress, and we decline to overrule *Miranda* ourselves. We therefore hold that *Miranda* and its progeny in this Court govern the admissibility of statements made during custodial interrogation in both state and federal courts.

Petitioner Dickerson was indicted for bank robbery [and] conspiracy to commit bank robbery. [Before] trial, [he] moved to suppress a statement he had made at [an FBI] field office, on the grounds that he had not received "*Miranda* warnings" before being interrogated. The District Court granted his motion to suppress, and the Government took an interlocutory appeal to the United States Court of Appeals for the Fourth Circuit. That court [reversed.] It agreed [that] petitioner had not received *Miranda* warnings before making his statement. But it went on to hold that § 3501, which in effect makes the admissibility of statements such as Dickerson's turn solely on whether they were made voluntarily, was

---

Since the *McNabb–Mallory* rule was fashioned "quite apart from the Constitution," *McNabb*, and in the exercise of the Supreme Court's "supervisory authority over the administration of [federal] criminal justice," id., it *is* subject to repeal by Congress. However, it is unclear whether Congress has only seriously weakened the *McNabb–Mallory* rule or whether it has completely abolished it. In *United States v. Alvarez–Sanchez*, 511 U.S. 350, 114 S.Ct. 1599, 128 L.Ed.2d 319 (1994), the government argued that § 3501 repudiated the *McNabb–Mallory* rule in its entirety and that the admissibility of a confession obtained beyond the six-hour limit is controlled by § 3501 (a), which provides that a confession is admissible so long as "it is voluntarily given." But the Court saw no need to decide the question because "the terms of § 3501 (c) were never triggered in this case."

satisfied in this case. It then concluded that our decision in *Miranda* was not a constitutional holding, and that therefore Congress could by statute have the final say on the question of admissibility.

* * * Prior to *Miranda*, we evaluated the admissibility of a suspect's confession under a voluntariness test. [Over] time, our cases recognized two constitutional bases for the requirement that a confession be voluntary to be admitted into evidence: the Fifth Amendment right against self-incrimination and the Due Process Clause of the Fourteenth Amendment. See, *e.g.*, *Bram v. United States* (1897) (stating that the voluntariness test "is controlled by that portion of the Fifth Amendment ... commanding that no person 'shall be compelled in any criminal case to be a witness against himself' "); *Brown v. Mississippi* (1936) (reversing a criminal conviction under the Due Process Clause because it was based on a confession obtained by physical coercion).

While *Bram* was decided before *Brown* and its progeny, for the middle third of the 20th century our cases based the rule against admitting coerced confessions primarily, if not exclusively, on notions of due process. We applied the due process voluntariness test in "some 30 different cases decided during the era that intervened between *Brown* and *Escobedo v. Illinois*." Those cases refined the test into an inquiry that examines "whether a defendant's will was overborne" by the circumstances surrounding the giving of a confession. The due process test takes into consideration "the totality of all the surrounding circumstances—both the characteristics of the accused and the details of the interrogation." * * *

We have never abandoned this due process jurisprudence, and thus continue to exclude confessions that were obtained involuntarily. But our decisions in *Malloy* and *Miranda* changed the focus of much of the inquiry in determining the admissibility of suspects' incriminating statements. In *Malloy*, we held that the Fifth Amendment's Self–Incrimination Clause is incorporated in the Due Process Clause of the Fourteenth Amendment and thus applies to the States. We decided *Miranda* on the heels of *Malloy*.

In *Miranda*, [we] concluded that the coercion inherent in custodial interrogation blurs the line between voluntary and involuntary statements, and thus heightens the risk that an individual will not be "accorded his privilege under the Fifth Amendment ... not to be compelled to incriminate himself." Accordingly, we laid down "concrete constitutional guidelines for law enforcement agencies and courts to follow."

Two years after *Miranda* was decided, Congress enacted § 3501. * * *

Given § 3501's express designation of voluntariness as the touchstone of admissibility, its omission of any warning requirement, and the instruction for trial courts to consider a nonexclusive list of factors relevant to the circumstances of a confession, we agree with the Court of Appeals that Congress intended by its enactment to overrule *Miranda*. Because of the obvious conflict between our decision in *Miranda* and § 3501, we must address whether Congress has constitutional authority to thus supersede *Miranda*. If Congress has such authority, § 3501's totality-of-the-circumstances approach must prevail over *Miranda*'s requirement of warnings; if not, that section must yield to *Miranda*'s more specific requirements.

The law in this area is clear. This Court has supervisory authority over the federal courts, and we may use that authority to prescribe rules of evidence and procedure that are binding in those tribunals. However, the power to judicially create and enforce nonconstitutional "rules of procedure and evidence for the federal courts exists only in the absence of a relevant Act of Congress." Congress retains the ultimate authority to modify or set aside any judicially created rules of evidence and procedure that are not required by the Constitution.

But Congress may not legislatively supersede our decisions interpreting and applying the Constitution. This case therefore turns on whether the *Miranda* Court announced a constitutional rule or merely exercised its supervisory authority to regulate evidence in the absence of congressional direction. [Relying] on the fact that we have created several exceptions to *Miranda*'s warnings requirement and that we have repeatedly referred to the *Miranda* warnings as "prophylactic," *Quarles*, and "not themselves rights protected by the Constitution," *Tucker*, the Court of Appeals concluded that the protections announced in *Miranda* are not constitutionally required.

We disagree * * *, although we concede that there is language in some of our opinions that supports the view taken by that court. But first and foremost of the factors on the other side—that *Miranda* is a constitutional decision—is that both *Miranda* and two of its companion cases applied the rule to proceedings in state courts—to wit, Arizona, California, and New York. Since that time, we have consistently applied *Miranda*'s rule to prosecutions arising in state courts. It is beyond dispute that we do not hold a supervisory power over the courts of the several States. With respect to proceedings in state courts, our "authority is limited to enforcing the commands of the United States Constitution."

The *Miranda* opinion itself begins by stating that the Court granted certiorari "to explore some facets of the problems [of] applying the privilege against self-incrimination to in-custody interrogation, *and to give concrete constitutional guidelines for law enforcement agencies and courts to follow*." (emphasis added). In fact, the majority opinion is replete with statements indicating that the majority thought it was announcing a constitutional rule. Indeed, the Court's ultimate conclusion was that the unwarned confessions obtained in the four cases before the Court in *Miranda* "were obtained from the defendant under circumstances that did not meet constitutional standards for protection of the privilege."

Additional support for our conclusion that *Miranda* is constitutionally based is found in the *Miranda* Court's invitation for legislative action to protect the constitutional right against coerced self-incrimination. [The] Court emphasized that it could not foresee "the potential alternatives for protecting the privilege which might be devised by Congress or the States," and it accordingly opined that the Constitution would not preclude legislative solutions that differed from the prescribed *Miranda* warnings but which were "at least as effective in apprising accused persons of their right of silence and in assuring a continuous opportunity to exercise it."

The Court of Appeals also relied on the fact that we have, after our *Miranda* decision, made exceptions from its rule in cases such as *Quarles* and *Harris v. New York* [p. 911]. But we have also broadened the application of the *Miranda* doctrine in cases such as *Doyle v. Ohio,* [p. 918] and *Arizona v. Roberson* [p. 636]. These decisions illustrate the principle—not that *Miranda* is not a constitutional rule—but that no constitutional rule is immutable. No court laying down a general rule can possibly foresee the various circumstances in which counsel will seek to apply it, and the sort of modifications represented by these cases are as much a normal part of constitutional law as the original decision.

The Court of Appeals also noted that in *Elstad*, we stated that " 'the *Miranda* exclusionary rule . . . serves the Fifth Amendment and sweeps more broadly than the Fifth Amendment itself.' " Our decision in that case—refusing to apply the traditional "fruits" doctrine developed in Fourth Amendment cases—does not prove that *Miranda* is a nonconstitutional decision, but simply recognizes the fact that unreasonable searches under the Fourth Amendment are different from unwarned interrogation under the Fifth Amendment.

[T]he dissent argues that it is judicial overreaching for this Court to hold § 3501 unconstitutional unless we hold that the *Miranda* warnings are required by the Constitution, in the sense that nothing else will suffice to satisfy constitutional requirements. But we need not go farther than *Miranda* to decide this case. In *Miranda*, the Court noted that reliance on the traditional totality-of-the-circumstances test raised a risk of overlooking an involuntary custodial confession, a risk that the Court found unacceptably great when the confession is offered in the case in chief to prove guilt. The Court therefore concluded that something more than the totality test was necessary. Section 3501 reinstates the totality test as sufficient. [The statute] therefore cannot be sustained if *Miranda* is to remain the law.

Whether or not we would agree with *Miranda*'s reasoning and its resulting rule, were we addressing the issue in the first instance, the principles of *stare decisis* weigh heavily against overruling it now. [*Miranda*] has become embedded in routine police practice to the point where the warnings have become part of our national culture. [While] we have overruled our precedents when subsequent cases have undermined their doctrinal underpinnings, we do not believe that this has happened to the *Miranda* decision. If anything, our subsequent cases have reduced the impact of the *Miranda* rule on legitimate law enforcement while reaffirming the decision's core ruling that unwarned statements may not be used as evidence in the prosecution's case in chief.

The disadvantage of the *Miranda* rule is that statements which may be by no means involuntary, made by a defendant who is aware of his "rights," may nonetheless be excluded and a guilty defendant go free as a result. But experience suggests that the totality-of-the-circumstances test which § 3501 seeks to revive is more difficult than *Miranda* for law enforcement officers to conform to, and for courts to apply in a consistent manner. The requirement that *Miranda* warnings be given does not, of course, dispense with the voluntariness inquiry. But * * * "[c]ases in which a defendant can make a colorable argument that a self-incriminating statement was 'compelled' despite the fact that the law enforcement authorities adhered to the dictates of *Miranda* are rare."

In sum, we conclude that *Miranda* announced a constitutional rule that Congress may not supersede legislatively. Following the rule of *stare decisis*, we decline to overrule *Miranda* ourselves. * * *

JUSTICE SCALIA, with whom JUSTICE THOMAS joins, dissenting.

Those to whom judicial decisions are an unconnected series of judgments that produce either favored or disfavored results will doubtless greet today's decision as a paragon of moderation, since it declines to overrule *Miranda*. Those who understand the judicial process will appreciate that today's decision is not a reaffirmation of *Miranda*, but a radical revision of the most significant element of *Miranda* (as of all cases): the rationale that gives it a permanent place in our jurisprudence.

Marbury v. Madison held that an Act of Congress will not be enforced by the courts if what it prescribes violates the Constitution of the United States. That was the basis on which *Miranda* was decided. One will search today's opinion in vain, however, for a statement (surely simple enough to make) that what § 3501 prescribes—the use at trial of a voluntary confession, even when a *Miranda* warning or its equivalent has failed to be given—violates the Constitution. The reason the statement does not appear is not only (and perhaps not so much) that it would be absurd, inasmuch as § 3501 excludes from trial precisely what the Constitution excludes from trial, viz., compelled confessions; but also that Justices whose votes are needed to compose today's majority are on record as believing that a violation of *Miranda* is *not* a violation of the Constitution. And so, to justify today's agreed-upon result, the Court must adopt a significant *new*, if not entirely comprehensible, principle of constitutional law. As the Court chooses to describe that principle, statutes of Congress can be disregarded, not only when what they prescribe violates the Constitution, but when what they prescribe contradicts a decision of this Court that "announced a constitutional rule." As I shall discuss in some detail, the only thing that can possibly mean in the context of this case is that this Court has the power, not merely to apply the Constitution but to expand it, imposing what it regards as useful "prophylactic" restrictions upon Congress and the States. That is an immense and frightening antidemocratic power, and it does not exist.

It takes only a small step to bring today's opinion out of the realm of power-judging and into the mainstream of legal reasoning: The Court need only go beyond its carefully couched iterations that "*Miranda* is a constitutional decision," that "*Miranda* is constitutionally based," that *Miranda* has "constitutional underpinnings," and come out and say quite clearly: "We reaffirm today that custodial interrogation that is not preceded by *Miranda* warnings or their equivalent violates the Constitution of the United States." It cannot say that, because a majority of the Court does not believe it. The Court therefore acts in plain violation of the Constitution when it denies effect to this Act of Congress.

[It] was once possible to characterize the so-called *Miranda* rule as resting (however implausibly) upon the proposition that what the statute here before us permits—the admission at trial of un-*Mirandized* confessions—violates the Constitution. That is the fairest reading of the *Miranda* case itself. [At] least one case decided shortly after *Miranda* explicitly confirmed the view. See *Orozco v. Texas* [p. 589 n. b] ("The use of these admissions obtained in the absence of the required warnings was a flat violation of the Self–Incrimination Clause of the Fifth Amendment as construed in *Miranda*").

So understood, *Miranda* was objectionable for innumerable reasons, not least the fact that cases spanning more than 70 years had rejected its core premise that, absent the warnings and an effective waiver of the right to remain silent and of the (hitherto unknown) right to have an attorney present, a statement obtained pursuant to custodial interrogation was necessarily the product of compulsion. [Moreover,] history and precedent aside, the decision in *Miranda*, if read as an explication of what the Constitution *requires*, is preposterous. There is, for example, simply no basis in reason for concluding that a response to the very first question asked, by a suspect who already *knows* all of the rights described in the *Miranda* warning, is anything other than a volitional act. And even if one assumes that the elimination of compulsion absolutely requires informing even the most knowledgeable suspect of his right to remain silent, it cannot conceivably require the right to have *counsel* present. There is a world of difference, which the Court recognized under the traditional voluntariness test but ignored in *Miranda*, between compelling a suspect to incriminate himself and preventing him from foolishly doing so of his own accord. Only the latter (which is *not* required by the Constitution) could explain the Court's inclusion of a right to counsel and the requirement that it, too, be knowingly and intelligently waived. Counsel's presence is not required to tell the suspect that he *need* not speak; the interrogators can do that. The only good reason for having counsel there is that he can be counted on to advise the suspect that he *should* not speak. * * *

Preventing foolish (rather than compelled) confessions is likewise the only conceivable basis for the rules (suggested in *Miranda*) that courts must exclude any confession elicited by questioning conducted, without interruption, after the suspect has indicated a desire to stand on his right to remain silent, or initiated by police after the suspect has expressed a desire to have counsel present. Nonthreatening attempts to persuade the suspect to reconsider that initial decision are not, without more, enough to render a change of heart the product of anything other than the suspect's free will. Thus, what is most remarkable about the *Miranda* decision—and what made it unacceptable as a matter of straightforward constitutional interpretation in the *Marbury* tradition—is its palpable hostility toward the act of confession *per se*, rather than toward what the Constitution abhors, *compelled* confession.

[For] these reasons, and others more than adequately developed in the *Miranda* dissents and in the subsequent works of the decision's many critics, any conclusion that a violation of the *Miranda* rules *necessarily* amounts to a violation of the privilege against compelled self-incrimination can claim no support in history, precedent, or common sense, and as a result would at least presumptively be worth reconsidering even at this late date. But that is unnecessary, since the Court has (thankfully) long since abandoned the notion that failure to comply with *Miranda*'s rules is itself a violation of the Constitution.

As the Court today acknowledges, since *Miranda* we have explicitly, and repeatedly, interpreted that decision as having announced, not the circumstances in which custodial interrogation runs afoul of the Fifth or Fourteenth Amendment, but rather only "prophylactic" rules that go beyond the right against compelled self-incrimination. Of course the seeds of this "prophylactic" interpretation of *Miranda* were present in the decision itself. [In] subsequent cases, the seeds have sprouted and borne fruit: The Court has squarely concluded that it is possible—indeed not uncommon—for the police to violate *Miranda* without also violating the Constitution.

In light of [such cases as *Michigan v. Tucker* (p. 591), *New York v. Quarles* (pp. 593, 621, *Oregon v. Elstad* (pp. 621, 697) and *Oregon v. Hass* (pp. 590, 912)] and our statements to the same effect in others, it is simply no longer possible for the Court to conclude, even if it wanted to, that a violation of *Miranda*'s rules is a violation of the Constitution. [By] disregarding congressional action that concededly does not violate the Constitution, the Court flagrantly offends fundamental principles of separation of powers, and arrogates to itself prerogatives reserved to the representatives of the people.

The Court seeks to avoid this conclusion in two ways: First, by misdescribing these post-*Miranda* cases as mere dicta. [But it] is not a matter of *language*; it is a matter of *holdings*. The proposition that failure to comply with *Miranda*'s rules does not establish a constitutional violation was central to the *holdings* of *Tucker*, *Hass*, *Quarles*, and *Elstad*.

The second way the Court seeks to avoid the impact of these cases is simply to disclaim responsibility for reasoned decisionmaking. It says:

"These decisions illustrate the principle—not that *Miranda* is not a constitutional rule—but that no constitutional rule is immutable." * * *

[The] issue, however, is not whether court rules are "mutable"; they assuredly are. It is not whether, in the light of "various circumstances," they can be "modified"; they assuredly can. The issue is whether, *as mutated and modified*, they must *make sense*. The requirement that they do so is the only thing that prevents this Court from being some sort of nine-headed Caesar, giving thumbs-up or thumbs-down to whatever outcome, case by case, suits or offends its collective fancy. And if confessions procured in violation of *Miranda* are confessions "compelled" in violation of the Constitution, the post-*Miranda* decisions I have discussed do not make sense. The only reasoned basis for their outcome was that a violation of *Miranda* is *not* a violation of the Constitution. [To] say simply that "unreasonable searches under the Fourth Amendment are different from unwarned interrogation under the Fifth Amendment" is true but supremely unhelpful.

[There] was available to the Court a means of reconciling the established proposition that a violation of *Miranda* does not itself offend the Fifth Amendment with the Court's assertion of a right to ignore the present statute. That means of reconciliation was argued strenuously by both petitioner and the United States, who were evidently more concerned than the Court is with maintaining the coherence of our jurisprudence. It is not mentioned in the Court's opinion because, I assume, a majority of the Justices intent on reversing believes that incoherence is the lesser evil. They may be right.

Petitioner and the United States contend that there is nothing at all exceptional, much less unconstitutional, about the Court's adopting prophylactic rules to buttress constitutional rights, and enforcing them against Congress and the States. Indeed, the United States argues that "prophylactic rules are now and have been for many years a feature of this Court's constitutional adjudication." That statement is not wholly inaccurate, if by "many years" one means since the mid–1960's. However, in their zeal to validate what is in my view a lawless practice, the United States and petitioner greatly overstate the frequency with which we have engaged in it. * * *

Petitioner and the United States are right on target [in] characterizing the Court's actions in a case decided within a few years of *Miranda, North Carolina v. Pearce* [p. 1540]. There, the Court concluded that due process would be offended were a judge vindictively to resentence with added severity a defendant who had successfully appealed his original conviction. Rather than simply announce that vindictive sentencing violates the Due Process Clause, the Court went on to hold that "in order to assure the absence of such a [vindictive] motivation, [the] reasons for [imposing the increased sentence] must affirmatively appear" and must "be based upon objective information concerning identifiable conduct on the part of the defendant occurring after the time of the original sentencing proceeding." The Court later explicitly acknowledged *Pearce*'s prophylactic character, see *Michigan v. Payne* [412 U.S. 47 (1973)]. It is true, therefore, that the case exhibits the same fundamental flaw as does *Miranda* when deprived (as it has been) of its original (implausible) pretension to announcement of what the Constitution itself required. That is, although the Due Process Clause may well prohibit punishment based on judicial vindictiveness, the Constitution by no means vests in the courts "any general power to prescribe particular devices 'in order to assure the absence of such a motivation' " (Black, J., dissenting). Justice Black surely had the right idea when he derided the Court's requirement as "pure legislation if there ever was legislation," although in truth *Pearce*'s rule pales as a legislative achievement when compared to the detailed code promulgated in *Miranda*.

The foregoing demonstrates that, petitioner's and the United States' suggestions to the contrary notwithstanding, what the Court did in *Miranda* (assuming, as later cases hold, that *Miranda* went beyond what the Constitution actually requires) is in fact extraordinary. That the Court has, on rare and recent occasion, repeated the mistake does not transform error into truth, but illustrates the potential for future mischief that the error entails. * * *

I applaud, therefore, the refusal of the Justices in the majority to enunciate this boundless doctrine of judicial empowerment as a means of rendering today's decision rational. In nonetheless joining the Court's judgment, however, they overlook two truisms: that actions speak louder than silence, and that (in judge-made law at least) logic will out. Since there is in fact no other principle that can reconcile today's judgment with the post-*Miranda* cases that the Court refuses to abandon, what today's decision will stand for, whether the Justices can bring themselves to say it or not, is the power of the Supreme Court to write a prophylactic, extraconstitutional Constitution, binding on Congress and the States.[a]

Thus, while I agree with the Court that § 3501 cannot be upheld without also concluding that *Miranda* represents an illegitimate exercise of our authority to review state-court judgments, I do not share the Court's hesitation in reaching that conclusion. For while the Court is also correct that the doctrine of *stare decisis* demands some "special justification" for a departure from longstanding precedent—even precedent of the constitutional variety—that criterion is more than met here. * * *

Neither am I persuaded by the argument for retaining *Miranda* that touts its supposed workability as compared with the totality-of-the-circumstances test it purported to replace. *Miranda*'s proponents cite *ad nauseam* the fact that the Court was called upon to make difficult and subtle distinctions in applying the "voluntariness" test in some 30–odd due process "coerced confessions" cases in the 30 years between *Brown* and *Miranda*. It is not immediately apparent, however, that the judicial burden has been eased by the "bright-line" rules adopted in *Miranda*. In fact, in the 34 years since *Miranda* was decided, this Court has been called upon to decide nearly 60 cases involving a host of *Miranda* issues * * *.

Moreover, it is not clear why the Court thinks that the "totality-of-the-circumstances test [is] more difficult than *Miranda* for law enforcement officers to conform to, and for courts to apply in a consistent manner." [But] even were I to agree that the old totality-of-the-circumstances test was more cumbersome, it is simply not true that *Miranda* has banished it from the law and replaced it with a new test. Under the current regime, which the Court today retains in its entirety, courts are frequently called upon to undertake *both* inquiries. That is [because] voluntariness remains the *constitutional* standard, and as such continues to govern the admissibility for impeachment purposes of statements taken in violation of *Miranda*, the admissibility of the "fruits" of such statements, and the admissibility of statements challenged as unconstitutionally obtained *despite* the interrogator's compliance with *Miranda*.

Finally, I am not convinced by petitioner's argument that *Miranda* should be preserved because the decision occupies a special place in the "public's consciousness." As far as I am aware, the public is not under the illusion that we are infallible. I see little harm in admitting that we made a mistake in taking away from the people the ability to decide for themselves what protections (beyond those required by the Constitution) are reasonably affordable in the criminal investigatory process. * * *

Today's judgment converts *Miranda* from a milestone of judicial overreaching into the very Cheops' Pyramid (or perhaps the Sphinx would be a better analogue) of judicial arrogance. In imposing its Court-made code upon the States, the original opinion at least *asserted* that it was demanded by the Constitution. Today's decision does not pretend that it is—and yet *still* asserts the right to impose it against the will of the people's representatives in Congress. Far from believing that *stare decisis* compels this result, I believe we cannot allow to remain on the books even a celebrated decision—*especially* a celebrated decision—that has come to stand for the proposition that the Supreme Court has power to impose extraconstitutional constraints upon Congress and the States. This is not the

---

a. See the characterization of *Miranda* by Justice Thomas in his plurality opinion in *United States v. Patane*, p. 699. Justice Thomas was joined by Rehnquist, C.J., and Scalia, J. In *Patane*, did the *Dickerson* dissenters "fulfill their own prophecy" as to what *Dickerson* will come to mean? See Note, 118 Harv.L.Rev. 296, 301 (2004).

system that was established by the Framers, or that would be established by any sane supporter of government by the people.

I dissent from today's decision, and, until § 3501 is repealed, will continue to apply it in all cases where there has been a sustainable finding that the defendant's confession was voluntary.

NOTES AND QUESTIONS

1. *Reconciling the prophylactic-rule cases with Miranda.* Consider DONALD A. DRIPPS, *Constitutional Theory for Criminal Procedure: Miranda, Dickerson, and the Continuing Quest for Broad–But–Shallow*, 43 Wm. & Mary L.Rev. 1, 33 (2001): "Once the court granted [certiorari in *Dickerson*] courtwatchers knew the hour had come. At long last the Court would have to either repudiate *Miranda*, repudiate the prophylactic-rule cases [the cases viewing *Miranda's* requirements as not rights protected by the Constitution, but merely "prophylactic rules"] or offer some ingenious reconciliation of the two lines of precedent. The Supreme Court of the United States, however, doesn't " 'have to' do anything, as the decision in *Dickerson* again reminds us."

2. *Foolish confessions.* Does Miranda, as Justice Scalia maintains in his Dickerson dissent, prevent suspects from foolishly deciding to talk to the police? Don't most custodial suspects waive their Miranda rights? Are not almost all decisions by suspects to talk to the police about their cases before meeting with a lawyer foolish decisions?

3. *Why did Chief Justice Rehnquist come to the rescue of Miranda?* Did the Chief Justice decide to vote with the majority so that he could assign the opinion to himself rather than let it go to someone like Justice John Paul Stevens?[a] Did the Chief Justice conclude that the best resolution of *Dickerson* would be a compromise, one that "reaffirmed" *Miranda's* constitutional status, but preserved all the qualifications and exceptions the much-criticized case had acquired over three and a half decades? Did the Chief Justice regard *Dickerson* as an occasion for the Court to maintain its power against Congress?[b] Did he consider § 3501 "a slap at the Court"?[c] Was the Chief Justice interested in assuming an increasingly large leadership rule, as opposed to his more partisan days as Associate Justice?[d]

Was the Chief Justice concerned that the "overruling" of *Miranda* by legislation would have wiped out some 35 years of jurisprudence—nearly 60 cases? Why pay the price when, whatever their initial experience with *Miranda*, the police now seem to be living comfortably with it?[e] Did the Chief Justice know that the police obtain waiver of rights in the "overwhelming majority" of cases and that

---

a. See R. Ted Cruz, *In Memoriam: William H. Rehnquist*, 119 Harv.L.Rev. 10, 14–15 (2005); Daniel M. Katz, *Institutional Rules, Strategic Behavior, and the Legacy of Chief Justice Rehnquist: Setting the Record Straight in Dickerson v. United States*, 22 J.Law & Politics 303 (2006).

b. Consider Craig Bradley, *Behind the Dickerson Decision*, TRIAL, Oct. 2000, at 80.

c. Whether or not the Chief Justice did, some commentators did. See Michael C. Dorf & Barry Friedman, *Shared Constitutional Interpretation*, 2001 Sup.Ct.Rev. 61, 72: "[Section 3501] was a slap at the Court and if any Court was likely to slap back it was this one." See also Susan R. Klein, *Identifying and (Re)Formulating Prophylactic Rules, Safe Harbors, and Incidental Rights in Constitutional Criminal Procedure*, 99 Mich.L.Rev. 1030, 1057 (2001), calling § 3501 "an angry, disrespectful, and disingenuous attempt" to "overrule a decision [Congress] loathed."

d. Bradley, supra note b.

e. Richard A. Leo, *Questioning the Relevance of Miranda in the Twenty–First Century*, 99 Mich.L.Rev. 975, 1027 (2001), sums up the current situation as follows: "Once feared to be the equivalent of sand in the machinery of criminal justice, *Miranda* has now become a standard part of the machine."

once they do *"Miranda* offers very little, if any, meaningful protection"?[f] Was the Chief Justice aware that once the police have complied with *Miranda* and a suspect has waived his rights (as suspects usually do) "it is very difficult for a defendant to establish" that any resulting confession was "involuntary" in the pre-*Miranda* due process voluntariness sense?[g]

Would overruling *Miranda* be viewed by the police as a signal that they could return to the "old days" of police interrogation? Would overturning *Miranda* after all this time have caused much confusion? Would it have been easy to figure out what combination of circumstances satisfied the ever-changing voluntariness test in the twenty-first century? Would it have been easy to know exactly how the police should respond when persons *not warned* of their "rights" *asserted* what they thought were their rights on their own initiative or *asked the police* whether they had a right to a lawyer or a right to remain silent?[h]

4. *Does Dickerson leave Miranda incoherent?* Consider PAUL G. CAS-SELL, *The Paths Not Taken: The Supreme Court's Failures in Dickerson*, 99 Mich.L.Rev. 898, 901–04 (2001):

"[The *Dickerson* majority offers] no rationale for numerous results over the last twenty-five years. Why can the 'fruits' of *Miranda* violations be used against a defendant? The traditional rule excludes fruits of, for example, unconstitutional searches. * * * Similarly, in *New York v. Quarles* the Court carved out a 'public safety' exception to *Miranda*. The Fifth Amendment admits of no such public safety exception; the police cannot coerce an involuntary statement from a suspect and use it against him even if there are strong public safety reasons for doing so. The rationale *Quarles* gave, however, was that the *Miranda* rules were nonconstitutional rules subject to modification by the Court. * * * My thesis is that *Dickerson* could have been written coherently—that the Court could have crafted other resolutions that would have allowed it to harmonize its doctrine far more effectively than the skimpy, jerry-built opinion the Court announced. * * *[i]

"Perhaps the simplest way for the Court to reconcile its various pronouncements was to treat *Miranda* as a form of 'constitutional common law,' to use the phrase made famous [by Henry Monaghan].[26] Under this view, the *Miranda* rules are interim remedies not required by the Constitution, but designed in the absence of legislation to assist in protecting constitutional rights. [For] present purposes, the salient feature of constitutional common law is that it is subject to change—change by the Court and, in appropriate cases, by Congress. [The] touchstone for assessing the constitutionality of Congress's remedial regime [is] not whether it matched in every respect the judicially-devised regime for which it substituted. Rather, the touchstone [is] whether the congressional regime provid-

---

f. Id. To be sure, suspects who agree to talk to the police may still cut off questioning or invoke their right to have counsel—but they "almost never" do. William J. Stuntz, *Miranda's Mistake*, 99 Mich.L.Rev. 975, 977 (2001).

g. See Welsh S. White, *Miranda's Failure to Restrain Pernicious Interrogation Practices*, 99 Mich.L.Rev. 1211, 1219 (2001). See also Louis Michael Seidman, *Brown and Miranda*, 80 Calif.L.Rev. 673, 743–47 (1992).

h. See Yale Kamisar, *Miranda Thirty–Five Years Later: A Close Look at the Majority and Dissenting Opinions in Dickerson*, 33 Ariz.St.L.J. 387, 388–90 (2001).

i. Consider Cruz, supra note a: "[The] majority opinion in *Dickerson* is, in many respects, amusing to read. Its holding can be characterized as three-fold: First, *Miranda* is NOT required by the Constitution; it is merely prophylactic, and its exceptions remain good law. Second, 18 U.S.C. § 3501 is not good law. Third, do not ask why, and please, never, ever, ever cite this opinion for any reason." Cruz adds (fn.26) that although *Dickerson* described *Miranda* as a "constitutional rule," the Court "took pains to distinguish that characterization from the broader assertion that 'the *Miranda* warnings are required by the Constitution.' "

26. Henry P. Monaghan, *Foreword: Constitutional Common Law*, 89 Harv.L.Rev. 1, 42 (1975).

ed 'meaningful' protection for the constitutional right at issue. If it did, then its strength compared to the judicially-devised scheme was irrelevant."

5. *Is constitutional law filled with "prophylactic rules"? On the other hand, as Justice Scalia defines "prophylactic rules," is Miranda such a rule?* Chief Justice Rehnquist did not respond directly to Justice Scalia's attack on the Court's power to promulgate "prophylactic, extraconstitutional rules." (Indeed, the *Dickerson* opinion never characterizes *Miranda* as a "prophylactic rule.") How might the Chief Justice have responded? One way would be to say that constitutional law, and constitutional-criminal procedure especially, is filled with "prophylactic rules," i.e., much constitutional law is shaped to some extent (as was *Miranda*) by institutional judgments as to how constitutional goals can best be attained and how constitutional values can best be implemented. See David A. Strauss, *The Ubiquity of Prophylactic Rules*, 55 U.Chi.L.Rev. 190 (1988); David A. Strauss, *Miranda, the Constitution, and Congress*, 99 Mich.L.Rev. 958 (2001). See also Susan R. Klein, *Identifying and (Re)Formulating Prophylactic Rules, Safe Harbors, and Incidental Rights in Constitutional Criminal Procedure*, 99 Mich.L.Rev. 1030, 1037–44 (2001). Another way to respond to Scalia is to say that *Miranda* is *not* a prophylactic rule as Justice Scalia and other critics of *Miranda* have defined such a rule (a judge-made rule that "overenforces" or "overprotects" judge-interpreted constitutional meaning).[j] Consider MITCHELL N. BERMAN, *Constitutional Decision Rules*, 90 Va.L.Rev. 1, 154 (2004):

"The *Dickerson* majority (or some member thereof) could have replied to Justice Scalia's dissent as follows: (1) the *Miranda* warnings requirement was part of a constitutional decision rule [a rule directing how courts should adjudicate claimed violations of constitutional meaning] designed to minimize errors in adjudicating whether out-of-court statements had been compelled within the meaning of the Self–Incrimination Clause (as *Miranda* interpreted that particular constitutional provision); (2) constitutional decision rules are ineliminable, hence cannot be categorically illegitimate; (3) while the extent of the Court's constitutional authority to craft decision rules may be reasonably debated, the creation of decision rules to minimize adjudicating error has the strongest claim to legitimacy; (4) such a device is not a "prophylactic" rule in the Grano–Scalia sense because it does not *overenforce* constitutional meaning as measured against the appropriate baseline; rather it was adopted to *optimally* enforce constitutional meaning; (5) use of a conclusive presumption is common to constitutional decision rules * * * and is not incompatible with an interest in reducing adjudicatory error. None of this * * * is to extol *Miranda*. Like any other judicial product, it might have been wise or foolish. But, on the reading thus far developed, it is not susceptible to the charge of judicial usurpation."

6. *"The advantage of reactivism."* Consider STEPHEN F. SMITH, *Activism as Restraint: Lessons from Criminal Procedure*, 80 Texas L. Rev. 1056, 1110–12 (2002):

"Given all the Court has done in the decades since *Miranda*, in Rehnquist's wonderful, almost self-congratulatory euphemism, to 'reduce[] the impact of the *Miranda* rule on legitimate law enforcement' [*Dickerson*], it comes as no surprise that the Rehnquist Court ultimately saw no need to overrule *Miranda*. This is not to say that *Miranda* had been gutted; where it applied, *Miranda* still had teeth, and so the police had (and still have) incentives to comply with *Miranda* doctrine

---

j. As Berman, infra, points out, Justice Scalia's definition of "prophylactic rule" is similar to Professor Joseph Grano's. Grano maintained that *Miranda* was an "illegitimate" decision. His writings are cited in Justice Scalia *Dickerson* dissent.

in interrogating suspects. Even so, the adverse impact of *Miranda* had been blunted in fairly substantial ways long before *Dickerson* came to the Court.[212]

"The end result after decades of case-by-case refinement (and frequently revisionism) was a considerable change in *Miranda* doctrine, but not a complete evisceration of *Miranda*. Neither Warren nor Rehnquist got to have his first-best preference. What they did get was a second-best approach in which the suspect must be given basic information as to his rights and has the power, by making (and sticking to) an unequivocal request for counsel, to stop all questioning. Of course, the police have ample latitude to use persuasion or clever, noncoercive means to cause suspects not to exercise that power and, ultimately, to make incriminating statements that can be used against them at trial. After *Dickerson*, it would appear that *Miranda* law is finally at an equilibrium that almost all of the Justices—including supporters and critics of *Miranda*—can accept, as shown by the fact that seven of the nine Justices signed onto without comment an opinion reaffirming *both Miranda and* all of the limitations and exceptions adopted over the ensuing three decades. This is the advantage of reactivism—it provides an efficacious means by which a Court that fundamentally disagrees with earlier precedents, but is unwilling or unable to overrule them explicitly, can move the law (and, with it, actual case outcomes) back in what it believes to be the right direction. The legal system and the public thereby gain, to varying degrees, the benefits of the overruling. At the same time, reactivism allows risk-adverse Justices and the Court as an institution to avoid the unpleasant consequences of overruling that have historically made Justices so reluctant to overrule even the most indefensible decisions.[215] Thus, the law gets 'fixed' in a way that avoids sharp doctrinal shifts."

7. Why does the "right" seek to do away with Miranda's restrictions on police questioning? Why does the "left" (or center) seek to maintain them? Does Dickerson represent an opportunity missed? Consider WILLIAM J. STUNTZ, *Miranda's Mistake*, 99 Mich.L.Rev. 975, 976–77 (2001):

"*Miranda* imposes only the slightest of costs on the police, and its existence may well forestall more serious, and more successful, regulation of police questioning. The right should therefore be either indifferent to *Miranda* or supportive of it. Meanwhile, *Miranda* does nothing to protect suspects against abusive police tactics. The left should therefore be its enemy, and should rejoice at the prospect of seeing it fall, since anything that took its place would likely be an improvement. Another, better answer is that *Miranda* should attract support from neither right nor left. Its effects are probably small, perhaps vanishingly so. But what effects it has are probably perverse * * *. *Dickerson* represents not a bullet dodged but an opportunity missed. As things stand now, from almost any plausible set of premises, police interrogation is badly regulated. Because of *Dickerson*, it will continue to be badly regulated for a long time to come.

"The reason has to do with *Miranda*'s regulatory strategy. The essence of that strategy was to shift, from courts to suspects, the burden of separating good

---

212. In fact, so many limitations had been engrafted upon *Miranda* by the Burger Court (let alone the Rehnquist Court) that Albert Alschuler surmised back in 1987 that "a police training manual authored by Justice Holmes' 'bad man of the law' " might advise police officers, in many instances, that they should "*not* give [the suspect] the *Miranda* warnings." Albert W. Alschuler, *Failed Pragmatism: Reflections on the Burger Court*, 100 HARV. L. REV. 1436, 1442 (1987) (emphasis added).

215. In this sense, reactivism serves the same purposes as the Warren Court's retroactivity rules did. By making controversial, law-changing rulings like *Miranda* and *Mapp* prospective only—that is, applicable only in future prosecutions—the Warren Court was able to overrule scores of restrictive precedents in favor of vastly expanded rights of the accused yet avoid the need to reverse scores of past convictions obtained in compliance with the overruled precedents. * * *

police interrogation from bad. Instead of courts deciding based on all the circumstances (or at least all the circumstances disclosed during the suppression hearing) whether the suspect's confession was voluntary, *Miranda* left it for suspects to decide, by either agreeing to talk or by calling a halt to questioning and/or calling for the help of a lawyer, whether the police were behaving too coercively. A growing literature on the empirics of police questioning shows why that strategy has failed. Suspects do not, in fact, separate good questioning from bad; once suspects agree to talk to police, they almost never call a halt to questioning or invoke their right to have the assistance of counsel. Instead, suspects separate *themselves*, not the police, into two categories: talkative and quiet. The sorting says nothing at all about the police, because it happens before police questioning has begun, hence before any police coercion has begun. Rather, the sorting is a signal of the suspect's savvy and experience. Because of *Miranda*, sophisticated suspects have a right to be free from questioning altogether—not simply free from coercive questioning—while unsophisticated suspects have very nearly no protection at all. The first group receives more than it deserves, while the second receives less than it needs."

    8. *Is Congress still free to replace Miranda warnings with other procedures? Is it likely to do so?* Consider YALE KAMISAR, *Miranda Thirty-Five Years Later: A Close Look at the Majority and Dissenting Opinions in Dickerson*, 33 Ariz.St.L.J. 387, 425 (2001): "*Miranda* left the door open for Congress to replace the warnings with other safeguards that perform the same function. Unfortunately, Congress did not walk in the door. But the door remains open.

    "The alternative often mentioned is a system of audiotaping or videotaping police questioning *and* a modified set of warnings.[k] I think such a system would and should pass constitutional muster. (It seems clear, however, that, no matter

---

    k. See Note 14, p. 628. Consider, too judicial or judicially supervised questioning, another frequently mentioned alternative to police interrogation. Paul Kauper, *Judicial Examination of the Accused—A Remedy for the Third Degree*, 30 Mich.L.Rev. 1224 (1932), seems to be the first commentator to spell out the desirability of, and historical support, for judicial questioning. In the wake of *Miranda*, two eminent judges returned to the Kauper model and built upon it. See Walter Schaefer, *The Suspect and Society*, 76–81 (1967); Henry Friendly, *The Fifth Amendment Tomorrow: The Case for Constitutional Change*, 37 U.Cin.L.Rev. 671, 713–16 (1968). Under the "Kauper–Schaefer–Friendly" model, discussed at length in Kamisar, *Kauper's Judicial Examination of the Accused Forty Years Later—Some Comments on a Remarkable Article*, 73 Mich.L.Rev. 15 (1974), a suspect questioned either by or before a judicial officer would have the assistance of counsel and be informed that she need not answer any questions. But she would also be told that if subsequently prosecuted her refusal to answer questions at the earlier proceeding would be disclosed at trial.

    Does *Griffin v. California* (1965) (set forth at p. 1450,) which forbids comment on a defendant's failure to testify at trial, stand in the way of this proposal? As have many other commentators, both Judges Friendly and Schaefer assumed that their proposal could not be effectuated without a constitutional amendment. But Albert W. Alschuler, *A Peculiar Privilege in Historical Perspective: The Right to Remain Silent*, 94 Mich.L.Rev. 2625, 2670–72 (1996), and Marvin Frankel, *From Private Rights to Public Justice*, 51 N.Y.U.L.Rev. 516, 531 (1976), have forcefully argued to the contrary. They have maintained that such an alternative would probably promote accurate fact-finding (both when it would help the suspect and when it would hurt him) and sharply reduce the amount of truly compelled self-incrimination in our society.

    Recently, Akhil Reed Amar & Renée B. Lettow, *Fifth Amendment First Principles: The Self-Incrimination Clause*, 93 Mich.L.Rev. 857, 858, 898, 908 (1995), revisited and revised the "Kauper–Schaefer–Friendly" proposal. Under the Amar–Lettow version, the suspect at a judicially supervised pretrial hearing who failed to answer truthfully would be held in contempt. If he did answer, he would only be entitled to "testimonial immunity," i.e., his compelled *words* could not be introduced in a criminal trial, but the evidence derived from those words—such as the whereabouts of damaging physical evidence or a potential witness for the prosecution—would be admissible. For strong criticism of the Amar–Lettow proposal see Kamisar, *On the "Fruits of Miranda Violations," Coerced Confessions, and Compelled Testimony*, 93 Mich.L.Rev. 929, 932–33 (1995).

how fool-proof, a tape recording system that dispensed with all warnings would not be upheld.[212])

"If such a system replaced the four-fold *Miranda* warnings it would make clear that 'a decision may be *both* an interpretation of the Constitution *and* a principle that Congress may modify.'[213] However, I doubt that any legislature will enact any audiotaping or videotaping system that contains some warnings of rights or any other *effective* alternative to the *Miranda* regime. For any alternative that *is* equally effective is likely to be 'politically unacceptable for precisely the reason that saves it from being constitutionally unacceptable—it would be at least as protective of the suspect (and therefore at least as burdensome to investigators) as *Miranda* itself.'[214]

"I believe Stephen Schulhofer is quite right—'politically attractive alternatives to *Miranda* can't pass constitutional muster, and constitutional alternatives cannot attract political support.'[215] That is why the *Miranda* warnings will probably be with us for a long time."

9. *Unrepentant dissenters.* Recall that, dissenting in *Dickerson*, Justice Scalia vowed that, until § 3501 was repealed by Congress, he would "continue to apply it in all cases where there had been a sustainable finding that the defendant's confession was voluntary." Is this position defensible? Consider Dripps, Note 1, supra, at 65–66:

"Whatever the theory on which the doctrine of judicial supremacy rests, no justice can consistently maintain judicial supremacy while regarding herself as unobligated by decisions of the Court. This is not to say that civil disobedience is never justified. * * * Judicial civil disobedience, however, is especially hard to defend. Judges, unlike ordinary citizens, swear an oath to uphold the law. Unlike ordinary citizens, they claim the obedience of others to their decisions on the basis of a general obligation to obey the law."

SECTION 3. *MIRANDA*, THE PRIVILEGE AGAINST COMPELLED SELF–INCRIMINATION AND FOURTEENTH AMENDMENT DUE PROCESS: WHEN DOES A VIOLATION OF THESE SAFEGUARDS OCCUR?

CHAVEZ v. MARTINEZ
538 U.S. 760, 123 S.Ct. 1994, 155 L.Ed.2d 984 (2003).

JUSTICE THOMAS announced the judgment of the Court and delivered an opinion [joined by the CHIEF JUSTICE REHNQUIST in its entirety, by JUSTICE O'CONNOR with respect to Parts I and II—A, and by JUSTICE SCALIA with respect to Parts I and II].

[This case involves a § 1983 suit arising out of petitioner Ben Chavez's allegedly coercive interrogation of respondent Oliverio Martinez. The [Ninth

---

212. As the *Dickerson* Court told us, referring to very similar language in the *Miranda* opinion, "*Miranda* requires procedures that will warn a suspect in custody of his right to remain silent and which will assure the suspect that the exercise of that right will be honored."

213. David A. Strauss, *Miranda, The Constitution and Congress*, 99 Mich.L.Rev. 958, 960 (2001).

214. Stephen J. Schulhofer, *Miranda, Dickerson and the Puzzling Persistence of Fifth Amendment Exceptionalism*, 99 Mich.L.Rev. 941, 955 (2001).

215. Id.

Circuit] held that Chavez was not entitled to a defense of qualified immunity because he violated Martinez's clearly established constitutional rights. We conclude that Chavez did not deprive Martinez of a constitutional right.

I

[During an altercation with the police, an officer shot Martinez five times, causing severe injuries that left him partially blinded and paralyzed from the waist down. Chavez, a patrol supervisor who had arrived on the scene a few minutes after the shooting, accompanied Martinez to the hospital where he questioned him while he was receiving treatment from medical personnel. The questioning lasted a total of about 10 minutes over a 45–minute period, with Chavez leaving the emergency room from time to time to permit medical personnel to treat Martinez. At no point during the exchange between Martinez and Chavez was Martinez given the *Miranda* warnings.

[At first Martinez's responses to Chavez's questions about what had happened between him and the police were simply "I don't know," "I am choking" or "My leg hurts." Later, however, Martinez admitted that he had taken a pistol from an officer's holster and pointed the weapon at him. On seven different occasions, Martinez told the officer: "I am dying," "I am dying, please," or "I don't want to die, I don't want to die," but the questioning continued. At one point, Martinez told the officer: "I am not telling you anything until they [the doctors] treat me." But he continued to answer questions. According to a tape recording, toward the end of questioning, the following exchange between Chavez and Martinez occurred:

Chavez: [Do] you think you are going to die?

Martinez: Aren't you going to treat me or what?

Chavez: [That's] all I want to know, if you think you're going to die?

Martinez: My belly hurts, please treat me.

Chavez: Sir?

Martinez: If you treat me I tell you everything, if not, no.

Chavez: Sir, I want to know if you think you are going to die right now?

Martinez: I think so.

Chavez: You think so? Ok, look, the doctors are going to help you with all they can do, Ok? . . .

Martinez: Get moving, I am dying, can't you see me? Come on.

Chavez: Ah, huh, right now they are giving you medication.

[Although Martinez was never charged with a crime and his answers were never used against him in any criminal prosecution, he brought a § 1983 action, claiming that Chavez had violated both his Fifth Amendment right not to be "compelled in any criminal case to a be a witness against himself" and his Fourteenth Amendment due process right to be free from coercive questioning. The Ninth Circuit agreed with Martinez. It viewed the Fifth and Fourteenth Amendment rights asserted by Martinez clearly established by federal law, explaining that a reasonable police officer "would have known that persistent interrogation of the suspect despite repeated requests to stop violated the suspect's Fifth and Fourteenth Amendment right to be free from coercive interrogation."]

II

In deciding whether an officer is entitled to qualified immunity, we must first determine whether the officer's alleged conduct violated a constitutional right. If not, the officer is entitled to qualified immunity, and we need not consider whether the asserted right was "clearly established." We conclude that Martinez's allegations fail to state a violation of his constitutional rights.

A

The Fifth Amendment, made applicable to the States by the Fourteenth Amendment, requires that "[n]o person ... shall be compelled *in any criminal case* to be a *witness* against himself" (emphases added). We fail to see how, based on the text of the Fifth Amendment, Martinez can allege a violation of this right, since Martinez was never prosecuted for a crime, let alone compelled to be a witness against himself in a criminal case.

Although Martinez contends that the meaning of "criminal case" should encompass the entire criminal investigatory process, including police interrogations, we disagree. In our view, a "criminal case" at the very least requires the initiation of legal proceedings. * * * Statements compelled by police interrogations of course may not be used against a defendant at trial, but it is not until their use in a criminal case that a violation of the Self–Incrimination Clause occurs. "[Although] conduct by law enforcement officials prior to trial may ultimately impair that right, *a constitutional violation occurs only at trial*" (emphases added); *Withrow v. Williams*, (describing the Fifth Amendment as a "trial right"); id. (O'Connor, J., concurring in part and dissenting in part) (describing "true Fifth Amendment claims" as "the extraction and use of compelled testimony" (emphasis altered)).

Here, Martinez was never made to be a "witness" against himself in violation of the Fifth Amendment's Self–Incrimination Clause because his statements were never admitted as testimony against him in a criminal case. Nor was he ever placed under oath and exposed to " 'the cruel trilemma of self-accusation, perjury or contempt.' " [See fn. d, p. 840.] The text of the Self–Incrimination Clause simply cannot support the Ninth Circuit's view that the mere use of compulsive questioning, without more, violates the Constitution. * * *

We fail to see how Martinez was any more "compelled in any criminal case to be a witness against himself" than an immunized witness forced to testify on pain of contempt. One difference, perhaps, is that the immunized witness *knows* that his statements will not, and may not, be used against him, whereas Martinez likely did not. But this does not make the statements of the immunized witness any less "compelled" and lends no support to the Ninth Circuit's conclusion that coercive police interrogations, absent the use of the involuntary statements in a criminal case, violate the Fifth Amendment's Self–Incrimination Clause.

[In] the Fifth Amendment context, we have created prophylactic rules designed to safeguard the core constitutional right protected by the Self–Incrimination Clause. [Among] these rules is an evidentiary privilege that protects witnesses from being forced to give incriminating testimony, even in noncriminal cases, unless that testimony has been immunized from use and derivative use in a future criminal proceeding before it is compelled. [By] allowing a witness to insist on an immunity agreement *before* being compelled to give incriminating testimony in a noncriminal case, the privilege preserves the core Fifth Amendment right from invasion by the use of that compelled testimony in a subsequent criminal case. * * * Because the failure to assert the privilege will often forfeit the right to exclude the evidence in a subsequent "criminal case," [it] is necessary to allow assertion of the privilege prior to the commencement of a "criminal case" to safeguard the core Fifth Amendment trial right. If the privilege could not be asserted in such situations, testimony given in those judicial proceedings would be deemed "voluntary"; hence, insistence on a prior grant of immunity is essential to memorialize the fact that the testimony had indeed been compelled and therefore protected from use against the speaker in any "criminal case."

Rules designed to safeguard a constitutional right, however, do not extend the scope of the constitutional right itself, just as violations of judicially crafted prophylactic rules do not violate the constitutional rights of any person. * * * We have likewise established the *Miranda* exclusionary rule as a prophylactic measure to prevent violations of the right protected by the text of the Self–Incrimination Clause—the admission into evidence in criminal case of confessions obtained through coercive custodial questioning. [Accordingly,] Chavez's failure to read Miranda warnings to Martinez did not violate Martinez's constitutional rights and cannot be grounds for a § 1983 action. * * *

We are satisfied that Chavez's questioning did not violate Martinez's due process rights. Even assuming, *arguendo*, that the persistent questioning of Martinez somehow deprived him of a liberty interest, we cannot agree with Martinez's characterization of Chavez's behavior as "egregious" or "conscience shocking." [There] is no evidence that Chavez acted with a purpose to harm Martinez by intentionally interfering with his medical treatment. Medical personnel were able to treat Martinez throughout the interview and Chavez ceased his questioning to allow tests and other procedures to be performed. Nor is there evidence that Chavez's conduct exacerbated Martinez's injuries or prolonged his stay in the hospital. Moreover, the need to investigate whether there had been police misconduct constituted a justifiable government interest given the risk that key evidence would have been lost if Martinez had died without the authorities ever hearing his side of the story. * * *

JUSTICE SOUTER, delivered an opinion, Part II of which is the opinion of the Court, and Part I of which is an opinion concurring in the judgment. [Justice Breyer joined the opinion in its entirety and Justices Stevens, Kennedy and Ginsburg joined Part II of the opinion.]

I

Respondent Martinez's claim [under] § 1983 for violation of his privilege against compelled self-incrimination should be rejected and his case remanded for further proceedings. I write separately because I believe that our decision requires a degree of discretionary judgment greater than Justice Thomas acknowledges. As he points out, the text of the Fifth Amendment * * * focuses on courtroom use of a criminal defendant's compelled, self-incriminating testimony, and the core of the guarantee against compelled self-incrimination is the exclusion of any such evidence. Justice Ginsburg makes it clear that the present case is very close to *Mincey v. Arizona* [p. 552 n. c], and Martinez's testimony would clearly be inadmissible if offered in evidence against him. But Martinez claims more than evidentiary protection in asking this Court to hold that the questioning alone was a completed violation of the Fifth and Fourteenth Amendments subject to redress by an action for damages under § 1983. * * *

I do not [believe] that Martinez can make the "powerful showing," subject to a realistic assessment of costs and risks, necessary to expand protection of the privilege against compelled self-incrimination to the point of the civil liability he asks us to recognize here. The most obvious drawback inherent in Martinez's purely Fifth Amendment claim to damages is its risk of global application in every instance of interrogation producing a statement inadmissible under Fifth and Fourteenth Amendment principles, or violating one of the complementary rules we have accepted in aid of the privilege against evidentiary use. If obtaining Martinez's statement is to be treated as a stand-alone violation of the privilege subject to compensation, why should the same not be true whenever the police obtain any involuntary self-incriminating statement, or whenever the government so much as threatens a penalty in derogation of the right to immunity, or whenever the police fail to honor *Miranda*?[1] Martinez offers no limiting principle or reason to foresee a stopping place short of liability in all such cases. * * *

II

Whether Martinez may pursue a claim of liability for a substantive due process violation is thus an issue that should be addressed on remand, along with the scope and merits of any such action that may be found open to him.[a]

JUSTICE SCALIA, concurring in part in the judgment.

I agree with the Court's rejection of Martinez's Fifth Amendment claim, that is, his claim that Chavez violated his right not to be compelled in any criminal case to be a witness against himself. And without a violation of the right protected by the text of the Self–Incrimination Clause, (what the plurality and Justice Souter call the Fifth Amendment's "core"), Martinez's § 1983 action is doomed. Section 1983 does not provide remedies for violations of judicially created prophylactic rules, such as the rule of *Miranda*, as the Court today holds [referring to Justice Thomas's and Justice Kennedy's opinions]; nor is it concerned with "extensions" of constitutional provisions designed to safeguard actual constitutional rights [referring to Justice Souter's opinion]. Rather, a plaintiff seeking redress through § 1983 must establish the violation of a federal constitutional or statutory *right*. * * *

JUSTICE STEVENS, concurring in part and dissenting in part.

As a matter of fact, the interrogation of respondent was the functional equivalent of an attempt to obtain an involuntary confession from a prisoner by torturous methods. As a matter of law, that type of brutal police conduct constitutes an immediate deprivation of the prisoner's constitutionally protected interest in liberty. Because these propositions are so clear, the [courts below] correctly held that petitioner is not entitled to qualified immunity.

I

[Most of this part of Justice Steven's opinion consists of an English translation of substantial portions of the tape-recorded questioning of Martinez in Spanish that occurred in the emergency room. This part of his opinion is omitted. However, portions of the recorded questioning are set forth at p. 691.]

The sound recording of this interrogation, which has been lodged with the Court, vividly demonstrates that respondent was suffering severe pain and mental anguish throughout petitioner's persistent questioning. * * *

JUSTICE KENNEDY, with whom JUSTICE STEVENS joins, and with whom Justice Ginsburg joins as to Parts II and III, concurring in part and dissenting in part.

A single police interrogation now presents us with two issues: first, whether failure to give a required warning under *Miranda* was itself a completed constitutional violation actionable [under] § 1983; and second, whether an actionable violation arose at once under the Self–Incrimination Clause [when] the police,

---

1. The question whether the absence of *Miranda* warnings may be a basis for a § 1983 action under any circumstance is not before the Court.

a. Of the six opinions produced by *Chavez v. Martinez*, the only text that commanded a majority was Part II of Justice Souter's opinion.

after failing to warn, used severe compulsion or extraordinary pressure in an attempt to elicit a statement or confession.

I agree with Justice Thomas that failure to give a *Miranda* warning does not, without more, establish a completed violation when the unwarned interrogation ensues. As to the second aspect of the case, which does not involve the simple failure to give a *Miranda* warning, it is my respectful submission that Justice Souter and Justice Thomas are incorrect. They conclude that a violation of the Self–Incrimination Clause does not arise until a privileged statement is introduced at some later criminal proceeding.

A constitutional right is traduced the moment torture or its close equivalents are brought to bear. Constitutional protection for a tortured suspect is not held in abeyance until some later criminal proceeding takes place. These are the premises of this separate opinion.

II

Justice Souter and Justice Thomas are wrong, in my view, to maintain that in all instances a violation of the Self–Incrimination Clause simply does not occur unless and until a statement is introduced at trial, no matter how severe the pain or how direct and commanding the official compulsion used to extract it. * * *

[The] conclusion that the Self–Incrimination Clause is not violated until the government seeks to use a statement in some later criminal proceeding strips the Clause of an essential part of its force and meaning. This is no small matter. It should come as an unwelcome surprise to judges, attorneys, and the citizenry as a whole that if a legislative committee or a judge in a civil case demands incriminating testimony without offering immunity, and even imposes sanctions for failure to comply, that the witness and counsel cannot insist the right against compelled self-incrimination is applicable then and there. * * *

III

Had the officer inflicted the initial injuries sustained by Martinez (the gunshot wounds) for purposes of extracting a statement, there would be a clear and immediate violation of the Constitution, and no further inquiry would be needed. That is not what happened, however. The initial injuries and anguish suffered by the suspect were not inflicted to aid the interrogation.

[There are], however, actions police may not take if the prohibition against the use of coercion to elicit a statement is to be respected. The police may not prolong or increase a suspect's suffering against the suspect's will. [The] officers must not give the impression that severe pain will be alleviated only if the declarant cooperates, for that, too, uses pain to extract a statement. In a case like this one, recovery should be available under § 1983 if a complainant can demonstrate that an officer exploited his pain and suffering with the purpose and intent of securing an incriminating statement. That showing has been made here.

The transcript of the interrogation set out by Justice Stevens, and other evidence considered by the District Court demonstrate that the suspect thought his treatment would be delayed, and thus his pain and condition worsened, by refusal to answer questions.

* * * I would affirm the decision of the Court of Appeals that a cause of action under § 1983 has been stated. The other opinions filed today, however, reach different conclusions as to the correct disposition of the case. Were Justice Stevens, Justice Ginsburg, and I to adhere to our position, there would be no controlling judgment of the Court. In these circumstances, and because a ruling on substantive due process in this case could provide much of the essential

protection the Self–Incrimination Clause secures, I join Part II of Justice Souter's opinion and would remand the case for further consideration.

JUSTICE GINSBURG, concurring in part and dissenting in part.

I join Parts II and III of Justice Kennedy's opinion. For reasons well stated therein, I would hold that the Self–Incrimination Clause applies at the time and place police use severe compulsion to extract a statement from a suspect. * * * I write separately to state my view that, even if no finding were made concerning Martinez's belief that refusal to answer would delay his treatment, or Chavez's intent to create such an impression, the interrogation in this case would remain a clear instance of the kind of compulsion no reasonable officer would have thought constitutionally permissible. * * *

Convinced that Chavez's conduct violated Martinez's right to be spared from self-incriminating interrogation, I would affirm the judgment of the Court of Appeals. To assure a controlling judgment of the Court, however, * * * I join Part II of Justice Souter's opinion.

NOTES AND QUESTIONS

1. Consider Alan Dershowitz, *Is There a Right to Remain Silent?* xi (2008): "[In *Chavez v. Martinez*], the Supreme Court * * * told Americans, in effect, the following: " 'You may *believe* you have the right to remain silent. We may have *told you* that you have to right to remain silent. Policemen may have the *obligation to advise you* that you have the right to remain silent. But you *do not* have the right to remain silent. You do not even have the right not to be compelled or coerced into confessing your crimes. All you have is the right to *exclude* the fruits of compelled self-incrimination at your criminal trial—*if* you ever have a criminal trial. If the objective of the interrogation is to produce intelligence information rather than evidence to be used against you in your criminal trial—an increasingly common objective in the age of terrorism—you may have no constitutional rights at all.' "

2. *The recurring use of "prophylactic rule" terminology.* The *Dickerson* Court called *Miranda* "a constitutional decision," "constitutionally based" and a case that "announced a constitutional rule." Although it recognized that the Court had described *Miranda* as a "prophylactic" rule *in the past,* the *Dickerson* Court itself never referred to *Miranda* as a prophylactic rule—a point underscored by the *Dickerson* dissent (Scalia, J., joined by Thomas, J.). Is it consistent with his position in *Dickerson* for Justice Thomas, speaking for four Justices in *Chavez v. Martinez*, to call *Miranda* a "prophylactic measure" established "to prevent violations of the rights protected by the text of the Self–Incrimination Clause"?

3. *The meaning of "criminal case."* For strong criticism of Justice Thomas's view of the meaning of "criminal case" in the text of the Fifth Amendment, see Thomas Y. Davies, *Farther and Farther from the Original Fifth Amendment: The Recharacterization of the Right Against Self–Incrimination as a "Trial Right" in Chavez v. Martinez,* 70 Tenn.L.Rev. 987, 1009–18 (2003):

"[It] seems highly probable that the phrase 'in any criminal case' was added to the Fifth Amendment simply to clarify that the right against compelled self-incrimination did not extend to governmentally compelled interrogation, production of evidence, or oath-taking that might expose a person to only civil liability.

"[The] historical sources show that the right against self-accusation was understood to arise primarily in pretrial or preprosecution settings rather than in the context of a person's own criminal trial. Thus, a witness in the trial of another person could invoke the right to refuse to answer a potentially self-incriminating question. Again, as of the framing era, broadly applicable grants of immunity by which a person could be compelled to answer had not yet been invented."

SECTION 4. THE *PATANE* AND *SEIBERT* CASES: IS PHYSICAL EVIDENCE OR A "SECOND CONFESSION" DERIVED FROM A FAILURE TO COMPLY WITH THE *MIRANDA* RULES ADMISSIBLE? THE COURT'S ANSWERS SHED LIGHT ON *DICKERSON*

Background

For many years, courts have not only excluded evidence that is "direct" or "primary" in its relationship to the prior illegal arrest or search, but also "secondary" or "derivative" evidence that is tainted by the primary evidence, e.g., an otherwise "volunteered" confession obtained from an illegally arrested person or physical evidence found as the result of an illegal wiretap. To use a popular term, the courts have not only excluded the primary evidence that is illegally obtained, but the "fruit of the poisonous tree" as well. See generally pp. 893 to 910.

In OREGON v. ELSTAD, 470 U.S. 298 (1985), however, the Court declined to apply the "poisoned fruit" doctrine to a "second confession" following a confession obtained without giving defendant the *Miranda* warnings. The case arose as follows: When police questioned defendant in his own home about a recent burglary, he replied, "Yes, I was there." About an hour later, after he had been taken to the sheriff's office, the defendant was advised of his rights for the first time. He waived his rights and gave the police a statement detailing his participation in the burglary. The state conceded that the statement defendant made in his own home should be excluded (a questionable concession), but argued that the second confession should be admitted. The state court ruled *both* statements inadmissible.

The U.S. Supreme Court reversed. A 6–3 majority, per O'Connor, J., informed us that the state court had "misconstrued" the protections afforded by *Miranda* by assuming that "a failure to administer *Miranda* warnings necessarily breeds the same consequences as police infringement of a constitutional right, so that evidence uncovered following an unwarned statement must be suppressed as 'fruit of the poisonous tree.'" There is, Justice O'Connor emphasized, "a vast difference between the direct consequences flowing from coercion of a confession by physical violence [and] the uncertain consequences of disclosure of a 'guilty secret' freely given in response to an unwarned but noncoercive question as in this case." At one point she described a person whose *Miranda* rights had been violated, but whose statements had not actually been coerced, as someone "who has suffered no identifiable constitutional harm."

The *Elstad* Court seemed to say—it certainly could plausibly be read as saying—that because a violation of *Miranda* is not a violation of a *real* constitutional right (but only a rule of evidence designed to implement the privilege against self-incrimination), it is not entitled to, or worthy of, the "fruit of the poisonous tree" doctrine. Thus, unlike evidence obtained as the result of an unreasonable search or a coerced confession (which *are* real constitutional violations), secondary evidence derived from a *Miranda* violation need not, and should not, be suppressed as the tainted fruit.

Elstad was one of the post-Warren Court cases that encouraged critics of *Miranda* to believe that some day the new Court would overrule that much-criticized case. But that day never came. Instead, as we have seen, fifteen years later, in the *Dickerson* case, the Court struck down a federal statute purporting to abolish *Miranda*, removing any doubt that "*Miranda* is a constitutional decision of this Court."

What about *Oregon v. Elstad*? As we have also seen, somewhat surprisingly, the *Dickerson* Court had nothing negative to say about that case. As for the argument that *Elstad* rested largely on the premise that *Miranda* is not a constitutional decision, Chief Justice Rehnquist commented only that *Elstad* "simply recognizes the fact that unreasonable searches under the Fourth Amendment are different from unwarned interrogation under the Fifth Amendment."

However, in *Patane*, set forth below, the U.S. Court of Appeals for the Tenth Circuit, per Ebel, J., believed, understandably, that *Dickerson* had had a greater bearing on *Elstad* than the *Dickerson* Court had been prepared to spell out. According to the Tenth Circuit, the premise upon which cases like *Elstad* relied was "fundamentally altered" in *Dickerson*; that case "undermined the logic underlying" cases like *Elstad*. (The U.S. Supreme Court was to disagree.)

Oral Arguments in the Patane case

* * *

JUSTICE SCALIA: [Is *Miranda*] a Fifth Amendment right or not a Fifth Amendment right? [It] has to be based on something in the Constitution or we would have had to respect the statute enacted by Congress in *Dickerson*. * * *

DEPUTY SOLICITOR GENERAL DREEBEN: It's a Fifth Amendment right * * *. What the Court concluded in *Miranda* and then reaffirmed in *Dickerson* is that the traditional "totality of the circumstances" test for ascertaining whether a statement is voluntary or has been compelled is not adequate when the statements are taken in the inherently pressuring environment of custodial interrogation. And to provide an extra layer of protection [in order] to avoid the violation of the defendant's Fifth Amendment rights, the Court adopted a prophylactic warnings and waiver procedure.

JUSTICE SCALIA: Whether it's prophylactic or not, it is a constitutional right, is it not? * * *

MR. DREEBEN: [It] is a constitutional right that is distinct from the right not to have one's compelled statements used against oneself. * * *

JUSTICE STEVENS: Supposing that the Government used official powers, such as a grand jury subpoena or a congressional committee subpoena [to] get a confession out of a person under the threat of contempt of court [and] the person made an answer that revealed the existence of [a] gun. [Should] the gun be admissible [in] that scenario?

MR. DREEBEN: [The] gun would not be admissible, because this Court has defined a violation of the Fifth Amendment that involves actual compulsion as entailing two different evidentiary consequences. One [is] that the statements themselves may not be used. The other evidentiary consequence is that nothing derived from the statements may be used. But the critical feature of that hypothetical, and its distinction from *Miranda*, is it involves actual compulsion. * * *

JUSTICE GINSBURG: [The *Miranda* opinion] itself said, but unless and until [the *Miranda*] warnings and waivers are demonstrated by the prosecution at trial, no evidence obtained as a result of interrogation can be used against [the defendant], no evidence as a result of interrogation. That sounds like [a] derivative evidence rule to me.

MR. DREEBEN: It does [and] there are many things in the *Miranda* opinion that have not stood the test of later litigation in this Court.

UNITED STATES v. PATANE
542 U.S. 630, 124 S.Ct. 2620, 159 L.Ed.2d 667 (2004).

JUSTICE THOMAS announced the judgment of the Court and delivered an opinion, in which THE CHIEF JUSTICE and JUSTICE SCALIA join.

[Defendant Patane was arrested outside his home and handcuffed. A federal agent, who had been told that defendant, a convicted felon, illegally possessed a Glock pistol, began giving him the *Miranda* warnings, but defendant interrupted the agent, stating that he knew his rights. No further *Miranda* warnings were given (which the government conceded on appeal resulted in a violation of the *Miranda* rules).

[When the federal agent told defendant he wanted to know about a Glock pistol he possessed, defendant replied: "The Glock is in my bedroom on a shelf * * *." The agent found the pistol where defendant said it would be and seized it. Defendant was convicted of being a felon in possession of a firearm in violation of federal law.]

[The] *Miranda* rule is a prophylactic employed to protect against violations of the Self–Incrimination Clause. [That clause], however, is not implicated by the admission into evidence of the physical fruit of a voluntary statement. Accordingly, there is no justification for extending the *Miranda* rule to this context. [The] *Miranda* rule is not a code of police conduct, and police do not violate the Constitution (or even the *Miranda* rules for that matter) by mere failures to warn. For this reason, the exclusionary rule articulated in various [Fourth Amendment cases] does not apply.

[The] core protection afforded by the Self–Incrimination Clause is a prohibition on compelling a criminal defendant to testify against himself at trial. See, e.g., *Chavez v. Martinez* (plurality opinion). [The] Clause cannot be violated by the introduction of nontestimonial evidence obtained as a result of voluntary statements. See, e.g., *United States v. Hubbell* [p. 870] (noting that the word "witness" in the Self–Incrimination Clause "limits the relevant category of compelled incriminating statements to those that are 'testimonial' in character").

[Because such] prophylactic rules [as the *Miranda* rule] necessarily sweep beyond the actual protections of the Self–Incrimination Clause, any further extension of these rules must be justified by its necessity for the protection of the actual right against compelled self-incrimination, *Chavez* (opinion of Souter, J.). [Furthermore,] the Self–Incrimination Clause contains its own exclusionary rule. It provides that "[n]o person [shall] be compelled in any criminal case to be a witness against himself." [We] have repeatedly explained "that those subjected to coercive interrogations have an *automatic* protection from the use of their involuntary statements (or evidence derived from their statements) in any subsequent criminal trial," *Chavez* (plurality opinion). This explicit textual protection supports a strong presumption against expanding the *Miranda* rule any further.

Finally, nothing in *Dickerson*, including its characterization of *Miranda* as announcing a constitutional rule, changes any of these observations. Indeed, [*Dickerson*] specifically noted that the Court's "subsequent cases have reduced the impact of the *Miranda* rule on legitimate law enforcement while reaffirming [*Miranda*'s] core ruling that unwarned statements may not be used as evidence in the prosecution's case in chief." [The *Dickerson* Court's] reliance on our *Miranda* precedents [including *Elstad*, which read *Miranda* narrowly] further demonstrates the continuing validity of those decisions. In short, nothing in *Dickerson* calls into question our continued insistence that the closest possible fit be maintained between the Self–Incrimination Clause and any rule designed to protect it.

Our cases also make clear the related point that a mere failure to give *Miranda* warnings does not, by itself, violate a suspect's constitutional rights or even the *Miranda* rule. See *Chavez*. [This], of course, follows from the nature of the right protected by the Self–Incrimination Clause, which the *Miranda* rule, in turn protects. "It is a fundamental *trial* right." *Withrow v. Williams* [p. 673].

[It] follows that police do not violate a suspect's constitutional rights (or the *Miranda* rule) by negligent or even deliberate failures to provide the suspect with the full panoply of warnings prescribed by *Miranda*. Potential violations occur, if at all, only upon the admission of unwarned statements into evidence at trial. And, at that point, "the exclusion of unwarned statements [is] a complete and sufficient remedy" for any perceived *Miranda* violations. *Chavez*.

Thus, unlike unreasonable searches under the Fourth Amendment or actual violations of the Due Process Clause or the Self–Incrimination Clause, there is, with respect to mere failures to warn, nothing to deter. There is therefore no reason to apply the "fruit of the poisonous tree" doctrine [utilized in Fourth Amendment cases]. It is not for this Court to impose its preferred police practices on either federal law enforcement officials or their state counterparts.

[We] have held that "[t]he word 'witness' in the constitutional text limits the" scope of the Self–Incrimination Clause to testimonial evidence. *Hubbell*. The Constitution itself makes the distinction.[6] And although it is true that the Court requires the exclusion of the physical fruit of actually coerced confessions, it must be remembered that statements taken without sufficient *Miranda* warnings are presumed to have been coerced only for certain purposes and then only when necessary to protect the privilege against self-incrimination. [We] decline to extend that presumption further. * * *

JUSTICE KENNEDY, with whom JUSTICE O'CONNOR joins, concurring in the judgment.

[In such cases as *Elstad* and *Quarles*], evidence obtained following an unwarned interrogation was held admissible. The result was based in large part on our recognition that the concerns underlying the [*Miranda* rule] must be accommodated to other objectives of the criminal justice system. I agree with the plurality that *Dickerson* did not undermine these precedents and, in fact, cited them in support. [Unlike] the plurality, however, I find it unnecessary to decide whether the [federal agent's] failure to give Patane the full *Miranda* warnings should be characterized as a violation of the *Miranda* rule itself, or whether there is "[any]thing to deter" so long as the unwarned statements are not later introduced at trial.

JUSTICE SOUTER, with whom JUSTICE STEVENS and JUSTICE GINSBURG join, dissenting.

[The] issue actually presented today is whether courts should apply the fruit of the poisonous tree doctrine lest we create an incentive for the police to omit *Miranda* warnings before custodial interrogation. In closing their eyes to the consequences of giving an evidentiary advantage to those who ignore *Miranda*, the majority adds an important inducement for interrogators to ignore the rule in that case.

[There] is, of course, a price for excluding evidence, but the Fifth Amendment is worth a price, and in the absence of a very good reason, the logic of *Miranda*

---

6. While Fourth Amendment protections extend to "persons, houses, papers, and effects," the Self–Incrimination Clause prohibits only compelling a defendant to be a "witness against himself."

should be followed: a *Miranda* violation raises a presumption of coercion, and the Fifth Amendment privilege against compelled self-incrimination extends to the exclusion of derivative evidence, see *United States v. Hubbell* (recognizing "the Fifth Amendment's protection against the prosecutor's use of incriminating information derived directly or indirectly [from] [actually] compelled testimony"); *Kastigar v. United States* [p. 850]. That should be the end of this case.

[Of] course the premise of *Elstad* is not on point; although a failure to give *Miranda* warnings before one individual statement does not necessarily bar the admission of a subsequent statement given after adequate warnings, that rule obviously does not apply to physical evidence seized once and for all.

There is no way to read this case except as an unjustifiable invitation to law enforcement to flaunt *Miranda* when there may be physical evidence to be gained. The incentive is an odd one, coming from the Court on the same day it decides *Missouri v. Seibert* [the next main case].

Justice Breyer, dissenting.

For reasons similar to those set forth in Justice Souter's dissent and in my concurring opinion in *Seibert*, I would extend to this context the "fruit of the poisonous tree" approach, which I believe the Court has come close to adopting in *Seibert*. Under that approach, courts would exclude physical evidence derived from unwarned questioning unless the failure to provide *Miranda* warnings was in good faith. Because the courts below made no explicit finding as to good or bad faith, I would remand for such a determination.

NOTES AND QUESTIONS

1. Does the word "witness" in the text of the Self–Incrimination Clause prevent the exclusion of the pistol in a case like Patane? As we have seen from the oral arguments in *Patane* (p. 698), the prosecution conceded that physical evidence derived from actually compelled testimony would be excluded. The language of the Self–Incrimination Clause does not prevent such a result in this setting. Moreover, Justice Thomas recognized that physical evidence derived from a coerced confession would also be excluded. Ever since *Malloy v. Hogan* (p. 565) (holding that the privilege against self-incrimination applies to the states and that the safeguards surrounding the admissibility of confessions in state cases have come to reflect all the policies embedded in the privilege) and *Miranda* (which applied the privilege against self-incrimination to the police station) the Self–Incrimination Clause has been widely viewed as a basis for the ban against the use of coerced confessions. Yet Justice Thomas concedes that the wording of the Self–Incrimination Clause would not prevent the exclusion of a pistol derived from an actually coerced confession. Why, then, in the circumstances that took place in *Patane*, does Justice Thomas tell us that " '[t]he word "witness" in the constitutional text limits the' scope of the Self–Incrimination Clause to testimonial evidence'?" Why does the specific language of the Self–Incrimination Clause constitute an impenetrable barrier to the exclusion of physical evidence in Mr. Patane's circumstances but become inoperative when the question presented is the admissibility of the same kind of evidence derived from statements obtained under the other circumstances discussed in this Note. In all instances we are talking about the same Self–Incrimination Clause, are we not? See Kamisar, *Postscript: Another Look at Patane and Seibert, the 2004 Miranda "Poisoned Fruit" Cases*, 2 Ohio St.J.Crim.Law 97, 102 (2004).

2. Are some "voluntary" statements less voluntary than others? Justice Thomas repeatedly asserts that "the Self–Incrimination Clause is not implicated by the admission into evidence of the physical fruit of a voluntary statement." But consider Kamisar, supra Note 1, at 99:

"The question presented in *Patane* was whether, for purposes of the Fifth Amendment's ban against the use of evidence derived from compelled statements (or, if one prefers, for purposes of the 'poisoned fruit' doctrine), a statement obtained without giving the requisite warnings should be treated as a compelled statement [or a presumptively compelled statement] or a voluntary one. Once you *assume* that statements obtained as a result of a failure to comply with the *Miranda* rules are 'voluntary'—just as voluntary for derivative evidence or tainted fruit purposes as, for example, a statement *volunteered* by someone *not* in police custody—the analysis is over. You have *assumed* the answer to the question.

"But why lump together (a) statements obtained without satisfying the *Miranda* rules and (b) what might be called purely or completely voluntary statements? Instead of putting the *Miranda*-deficient statements under the heading 'Voluntary Statements,' why not classify them under the heading 'Compelled, Coerced and Presumptively Compelled Statements'?"

3. *The clear implication of Miranda.* Consider Note, 118 Harv.L.Rev. 296, 302 (2004): "Although it is true that '[t]he admission of [unwarned] fruit[s] presents no risk that a defendant's *coerced* statements ... *will be used* against him at a criminal trial' [Thomas, J., emphasis added], this focus ignores *Miranda*'s clear implication: the admission of the fruits of unwarned statements runs the constitutionally unacceptable risk that the fruits of coerced statements will be used at trial in violation of the Self–Incrimination Clause. In other words, excluding fruits is not an extension of *Miranda*'s prophylaxis; it is simply an application of it."

4. *Patane and Dickerson.* Consider the Harvard Note, supra, at 301: "The [*Patane*] plurality opinion characterized *Miranda* as a constitutionally based prophylactic rule. This representation is somewhat surprising because Justice Scalia and Thomas, when dissenting in *Dickerson*, had explicitly noted that the Court failed to embrace this approach despite the strenuous arguments made for it by both the petitioner and the United States. In fact, although the dissenters recognized that this approach might have rendered *Miranda* jurisprudence coherent, they rejoiced in the Court's failure to rely on it because, believing that such prophylaxis was an 'immense and frightening antidemocratic power that does not exist,' they suggested that 'incoherence [might be] the lesser evil.'"

MISSOURI v. SEIBERT
542 U.S. 600, 124 S.Ct. 2601, 159 L.Ed.2d 643 (2004).

JUSTICE SOUTER announced the judgment of the Court and delivered an opinion, in which JUSTICE STEVENS, JUSTICE GINSBURG, and JUSTICE BREYER join.

This case tests a police protocol for custodial interrogation that calls for giving no warnings of the rights to silence and counsel until interrogation has produced a confession. Although such a statement is generally inadmissible, since taken in violation of *Miranda*, the interrogating officer follows it with *Miranda* warnings and then leads the suspect to cover the same ground a second time. The question here is the admissibility of the repeated statement. Because this midstream recitation of warnings after interrogation and unwarned confession could not effectively comply with *Miranda*'s constitutional requirement, we hold that a statement repeated after a warning in such circumstances is inadmissible.

[Officer Hanrahan arranged for another officer to arrest Ms. Seibert, a murder suspect, specifically instructing the officer not to advise Seibert of her

Miranda rights. After Seibert had been taken to the police station and left alone in an "interview room" for 15 to 20 minutes, Hanrahan questioned her for 30 to 40 minutes. After she made an incriminating statement, she was given a 20–minute break. Hanrahan then resumed questioning, this time advising Seibert of her *Miranda* rights. After she waived her rights, Hanrahan confronted Seibert with the incriminating statement she had made at the prewarning questioning session. As Hanrahan acknowledged, Seibert's ultimate statement was "largely a repeat of information * * * obtained" prior to the *Miranda* warnings. The trial court excluded only the statement obtained during the first questioning session. A 4–3 majority of the state supreme court reversed, holding that the statement the defendant made after she had been given the *Miranda* warnings and waived her rights had to be suppressed as well.]

* * * *Miranda* conditioned the admissibility at trial of any custodial confession on warning a suspect of his rights: failure to give the prescribed warnings and obtain a waiver of rights before custodial questioning generally requires exclusion of any statements obtained. Conversely, giving the warnings and getting a waiver has generally produced a virtual ticket of admissibility; maintaining that a statement is involuntary even though given after warnings and voluntary waiver of rights requires unusual stamina, and litigation over voluntariness tends to end with the finding of a valid waiver. * * *

[The] technique of interrogating in successive, unwarned and warned phases raises a new challenge to *Miranda*. Although we have no statistics on the frequency of this practice, it is not confined to Rolla, Missouri. An officer of that police department testified that the strategy of withholding *Miranda* warnings until after interrogating and drawing out a confession was promoted not only by his own department, but by a national police training organization and other departments in which he had worked. [The] upshot of [various training programs'] advice is a question-first practice of some popularity, as one can see from the reported cases describing its use, sometimes in obedience to departmental policy.

[*Miranda*] addressed "interrogation practices [likely] to disable [an individual] from making a free and rational choice" about speaking and held that a suspect must be "adequately and effectively" advised of the choice the Constitution guarantees. The object of question-first is to render *Miranda* warnings ineffective by waiting for a particularly opportune time to give them, after the suspect has already confessed.

[The] threshold issue when interrogators question first and warn later is thus whether it would be reasonable to find that in these circumstances the warnings could function "effectively" as *Miranda* requires. Could the warnings effectively advise the suspect that he had a real choice about giving an admissible statement at that juncture? Could they reasonably convey that he could choose to stop talking even if he had talked earlier? For unless the warnings could place a suspect who has just been interrogated in a position to make such an informed choice, there is no practical justification for accepting the formal warnings as compliance with *Miranda,* or for treating the second stage of interrogation as distinct from the first, unwarned and inadmissible segment.[1]

---

1. Respondent Seibert argues that her second confession should be excluded from evidence under the doctrine known by the metaphor of the "fruit of the poisonous tree," developed in the Fourth Amendment context in *Wong Sun v. United States*; evidence otherwise admissible but discovered as a result of an earlier violation is excluded as tainted, lest the law encourage future violations. But the Court in *Elstad* rejected the *Wong Sun* fruits doctrine for analyzing the admissibility of a subsequent warned confession following "an initial failure [to] administer the warnings required by *Miranda*." * * * *Elstad* held that "a suspect who has once responded to unwarned yet uncoercive questioning is not thereby disabled from waiving his rights and

There is no doubt about the answer that proponents of question-first give to this question about the effectiveness of warnings given only after successful interrogation, and we think their answer is correct. By any objective measure, applied to circumstances exemplified here, it is likely that if the interrogators employ the technique of withholding warnings until after interrogation succeeds in eliciting a confession, the warnings will be ineffective in preparing the suspect for successive interrogation, close in time and similar in content. After all, the reason that question-first is catching on is as obvious as its manifest purpose, which is to get a confession the suspect would not make if he understood his rights at the outset; the sensible underlying assumption is that with one confession in hand before the warnings, the interrogator can count on getting its duplicate, with trifling additional trouble. Upon hearing warnings only in the aftermath of interrogation and just after making a confession, a suspect would hardly think he had a genuine right to remain silent, let alone persist in so believing once the police began to lead him over the same ground again.[2]

A more likely reaction on a suspect's part would be perplexity about the reason for discussing rights at that point, bewilderment being an unpromising frame of mind for knowledgeable decision. What is worse, telling a suspect that "anything you say can and will be used against you," without expressly excepting the statement just given, could lead to an entirely reasonable inference that what he has just said will be used, with subsequent silence being of no avail. * * *

Missouri argues that a confession repeated at the end of an interrogation sequence envisioned in a question-first strategy is admissible on the authority of *Elstad,* but the argument disfigures that case. In *Elstad,* the police went to the young suspect's house to take him into custody on a charge of burglary. Before the arrest, one officer spoke with the suspect's mother, while the other one joined the suspect in a "brief stop in the living room," where the officer said he "felt" the young man was involved in a burglary. The suspect acknowledged he had been at the scene. [The Court] took care to mention that the officer's initial failure to warn was an "oversight" that "may have been the result of confusion as to whether the brief exchange qualified as 'custodial interrogation' * * *." [At] the outset of a later and systematic station house interrogation going well beyond the scope of the laconic prior admission, the suspect was given *Miranda* warnings and made a full confession. [On] the facts of [the] case, the Court thought any causal connection between the first and second responses to the police was "speculative and attenuated." [It] is fair to read *Elstad* as treating the living room conversation as a good-faith *Miranda* mistake, not only open to correction by careful warnings before systematic questioning in that particular case, but posing no threat to warn-first practice generally.

[The] contrast between *Elstad* and this case reveals a series of relevant facts that bear on whether *Miranda* warnings delivered midstream could be effective enough to accomplish their object: the completeness and detail of the questions

---

confessing after he has been given the requisite *Miranda* warnings." In a sequential confession case, clarity is served if the later confession is approached by asking whether in the circumstances the *Miranda* warnings given could reasonably be found effective. If yes, a court can take up the standard issues of voluntary waiver and voluntary statement; if no, the subsequent statement is inadmissible for want of adequate *Miranda* warnings, because the earlier and later statements are realistically seen as parts of a single, unwarned sequence of questioning.

2. It bears emphasizing that the effectiveness *Miranda* assumes the warnings can have must potentially extend through the repeated interrogation, since a suspect has a right to stop at any time. It seems highly unlikely that a suspect could retain any such understanding when the interrogator leads him a second time through a line of questioning the suspect has already answered fully. The point is not that a later unknowing or involuntary confession cancels out an earlier, adequate warning; the point is that the warning is unlikely to be effective in the question-first sequence we have described.

and answers in the first round of interrogation, the overlapping content of the two statements, the timing and setting of the first and the second, the continuity of police personnel, and the degree to which the interrogator's questions treated the second round as continuous with the first. In *Elstad,* it was not unreasonable to see the occasion for questioning at the station house as presenting a markedly different experience from the short conversation at home; since a reasonable person in the suspect's shoes could have seen the station house questioning as a new and distinct experience, the *Miranda* warnings could have made sense as presenting a genuine choice whether to follow up on the earlier admission.

At the opposite extreme are the facts here, which by any objective measure reveal a police strategy adapted to undermine the *Miranda* warnings.[6] The unwarned interrogation was conducted in the station house, and the questioning was systematic, exhaustive, and managed with psychological skill. When the police were finished there was little, if anything, of incriminating potential left unsaid. The warned phase of questioning proceeded after a pause of only 15 to 20 minutes, in the same place as the unwarned segment. [In] particular, the police did not advise that her prior statement could not be used.[7] Nothing was said or done to dispel the oddity of warning about legal rights to silence and counsel right after the police had led her through a systematic interrogation * * *. [The] impression that the further questioning was a mere continuation of the earlier questions and responses was fostered by references back to the confession already given. It would have been reasonable to regard the two sessions as parts of a continuum, in which it would have been unnatural to refuse to repeat at the second stage what had been said before. These circumstances must be seen as challenging the comprehensibility and efficacy of the *Miranda* warnings to the point that a reasonable person in the suspect's shoes would not have understood them to convey a message that she retained a choice about continuing to talk.

Strategists dedicated to draining the substance out of *Miranda* cannot accomplish by training instructions what *Dickerson* held Congress could not do by statute. Because the question-first tactic effectively threatens to thwart *Miranda*'s purpose of reducing the risk that a coerced confession would be admitted, and because the facts here do not reasonably support a conclusion that the warnings given could have served their purpose, Seibert's postwarning statements are inadmissible.

JUSTICE BREYER, concurring.

In my view, the following simple rule should apply to the two-stage interrogation technique: Courts should exclude the "fruits" of the initial unwarned questioning unless the failure to warn was in good faith. I believe this is a sound and workable approach to the problem this case presents. Prosecutors and judges have long understood how to apply the "fruits" approach, which they use in other areas of law. And in the workaday world of criminal law enforcement the administrative simplicity of the familiar has significant advantages over a more complex exclusionary rule.

I believe the plurality's approach in practice will function as a "fruits" test. The truly "effective" *Miranda* warnings on which the plurality insists, will occur only when certain circumstances—a lapse in time, a change in location or

---

6. Because the intent of the officer will rarely be as candidly admitted as it was here (even as it is likely to determine the conduct of the interrogation), the focus is on facts apart from intent that show the question-first tactic at work.

7. We do not hold that a formal addendum warning that a previous statement could not be used would be sufficient to change the character of the question-first procedure to the point of rendering an ensuing statement admissible, but its absence is clearly a factor that blunts the efficacy of the warnings and points to a continuing, not a new, interrogation.

interrogating officer, or a shift in the focus of the questioning—intervene between the unwarned questioning and any postwarning statement.

I consequently join the plurality's opinion in full. I also agree with Justice Kennedy's opinion insofar as it is consistent with this approach and makes clear that a good-faith exception applies.

JUSTICE KENNEDY, concurring in the judgment.

The interrogation technique used in this case is designed to circumvent *Miranda*. It undermines the *Miranda* warning and obscures its meaning. The plurality opinion is correct to conclude that statements obtained through the use of this technique are inadmissible. Although I agree with much in the careful and convincing opinion for the plurality, my approach does differ in some respects, requiring this separate statement.

The *Miranda* rule has become an important and accepted element of the criminal justice system. At the same time, not every violation of the rule requires suppression of the evidence obtained. Evidence is admissible when the central concerns of *Miranda* are not likely to be implicated and when other objectives of the criminal justice system are best served by its introduction. Thus, we have held that statements obtained in violation of the rule can be used for impeachment; [that] there is an exception to protect countervailing concerns of public safety; and that physical evidence obtained in reliance on statements taken in violation of the rule is admissible, see *Patane*. These cases, in my view, are correct. They recognize that admission of evidence is proper when it would further important objectives without compromising *Miranda*'s central concerns.

[In] my view, *Elstad* was correct in its reasoning and its result. *Elstad* reflects a balanced and pragmatic approach to enforcement of the *Miranda* warning. An officer may not realize that a suspect is in custody and warnings are required. The officer may not plan to question the suspect or may be waiting for a more appropriate time. [In] light of these realities it would be extravagant to treat the presence of one statement that cannot be admitted under *Miranda* as sufficient reason to prohibit subsequent statements preceded by a proper warning.

[This] case presents different considerations. The police used a two-step questioning technique based on a deliberate violation of *Miranda*. [Further,] the interrogating officer here relied on the defendant's prewarning statement to obtain the postwarning statement used against her at trial. The postwarning interview resembled a cross-examination. The officer confronted the defendant with her inadmissible prewarning statements and pushed her to acknowledge them.

The technique used in this case distorts the meaning of *Miranda* and furthers no legitimate countervailing interest. The *Miranda* rule would be frustrated were we to allow police to undermine its meaning and effect. [When] an interrogator uses this deliberate, two-step strategy, predicated upon violating *Miranda* during an extended interview, postwarning statements that are related to the substance of prewarning statements must be excluded absent specific, curative steps.

The plurality concludes that whenever a two-stage interview occurs, admissibility of the postwarning statement should depend on "whether the *Miranda* warnings delivered midstream could have been effective enough to accomplish their object" given the specific facts of the case. This test envisions an objective inquiry from the perspective of the suspect, and applies in the case of both intentional and unintentional two-stage interrogations. In my view, this test cuts too broadly. *Miranda'* s clarity is one of its strengths, and a multifactor test that applies to every two-stage interrogation may serve to undermine that clarity. I would apply a narrower test applicable only in the infrequent case, such as we have here, in which the two-step interrogation technique was used in a calculated way to undermine the *Miranda* warning.

The admissibility of postwarning statements should continue to be governed by the principles of *Elstad* unless the deliberate two-step strategy was employed. If the deliberate two-step strategy has been used, postwarning statements that are related to the substance of prewarning statements must be excluded unless curative measures are taken before the postwarning statement is made. Curative measures should be designed to ensure that a reasonable person in the suspect's situation would understand the import and effect of the *Miranda* warning and of the *Miranda* waiver. For example, a substantial break in time and circumstances between the prewarning statement and the *Miranda* warning may suffice in most circumstances, as it allows the accused to distinguish the two contexts and appreciate that the interrogation has taken a new turn. Alternatively, an additional warning that explains the likely inadmissibility of the prewarning custodial statement may be sufficient. No curative steps were taken in this case, however, so the postwarning statements are inadmissible and the conviction cannot stand. * * *

JUSTICE O'CONNOR, with whom THE CHIEF JUSTICE, JUSTICE SCALIA, and JUSTICE THOMAS join, dissenting.

The plurality devours *Elstad* even as it accuses petitioner's argument of "disfigur[ing]" that decision. I believe that we are bound by *Elstad* to reach a different result, and I would vacate the judgment of the Supreme Court of Missouri.

On two preliminary questions I am in full agreement with the plurality. First, the plurality appropriately follows *Elstad* in concluding that Seibert's statement cannot be held inadmissible under a "fruit of the poisonous tree" theory. Second, the plurality correctly declines to focus its analysis on the subjective intent of the interrogating officer.

This Court has made clear that there simply is no place for a robust deterrence doctrine with regard to violations of *Miranda*. * * * Consistent with that view, the Court today refuses to apply the traditional "fruits" analysis to the physical fruit of a claimed *Miranda* violation. *Patane*. The plurality correctly refuses to apply a similar analysis to testimonial fruits.

Although the analysis the plurality ultimately espouses examines the same facts and circumstances that a "fruits" analysis would consider (such as the lapse of time between the two interrogations and change of questioner or location), it does so for entirely different reasons. The fruits analysis would examine those factors because they are relevant to the balance of deterrence value versus the "drastic and socially costly course" of excluding reliable evidence. The plurality, by contrast, looks to those factors to inform the *psychological* judgment regarding whether the suspect has been informed effectively of her right to remain silent. The analytical underpinnings of the two approaches are thus entirely distinct, and they should not be conflated just because they function similarly in practice.

The plurality's rejection of an intent-based test is also, in my view, correct. Freedom from compulsion lies at the heart of the Fifth Amendment, and requires us to assess whether a suspect's decision to speak truly was voluntary. Because voluntariness is a matter of the suspect's state of mind, we focus our analysis on the way in which suspects experience interrogation. * * *

Thoughts kept inside a police officer's head cannot affect that experience. [A] suspect who experienced the exact same interrogation as Seibert, save for a difference in the undivulged, subjective intent of the interrogating officer when he failed to give *Miranda* warnings, would not experience the interrogation any differently.

[Because] the isolated fact of Officer Hanrahan's intent could not have had any bearing on Seibert's "capacity to comprehend and knowingly relinquish" her right to remain silent, it could not by itself affect the voluntariness of her confession. Moreover, recognizing an exception to *Elstad* for intentional violations would require focusing constitutional analysis on a police officer's subjective intent, an unattractive proposition that we all but uniformly avoid. [This] case presents the uncommonly straightforward circumstance of an officer openly admitting that the violation was intentional. But the inquiry will be complicated in other situations probably more likely to occur.

[Thus], I believe that the approach espoused by Justice Kennedy is ill advised. Justice Kennedy would extend *Miranda's* exclusionary rule to any case in which the use of the "two-step interrogation technique" was "deliberate" or "calculated." This approach untethers the analysis from facts knowable to, and therefore having any potential directly to affect, the suspect. * * *

I would analyze the two-step interrogation procedure under the voluntariness standards central to the Fifth Amendment and reiterated in *Elstad*. *Elstad* commands that if Seibert's first statement is shown to have been involuntary, the court must examine whether the taint dissipated through the passing of time or a change in circumstances. [In] addition, Seibert's second statement should be suppressed if she showed that it was involuntary despite the *Miranda* warnings. * * *

Because I believe that the plurality gives insufficient deference to *Elstad* and that Justice Kennedy places improper weight on subjective intent, I respectfully dissent.

NOTES AND QUESTIONS

1. *Suppose a defendant had shot someone with a Glock pistol and been arrested for murder.* Suppose further the defendant had been subjected to the same deliberate two-step questioning technique utilized in the *Seibert* case and, as a result, had revealed where she had hidden the murder weapon. Even though the interrogation technique had been "designed to circumvent Miranda" and had "undermine[d] the Miranda warning" and "obscure[d] its meaning" (Kennedy, J., concurring in Seibert), would the Glock pistol still be admissible? Why (not)?

2. Suppose, a week after Seibert was decided, a deputy district attorney told a group of officers attending a police training session the following:

"Don't write off the interrogation tactics used in *Seibert*. You can continue to use the same deliberate two-step questioning technique used in that case and still get the postwarning statements admitted into evidence. All you have to do is make one of several changes in the *Seibert* facts: (1) call for a three or four-hour break between the first and second questioning session instead of the 20–minute break that took place in *Seibert* or (2) have a different police officer resume the questioning after the break instead of using the same officer who did the questioning in the prewarning session or (3) after resuming questioning, be careful not to confront the suspect with the same incriminating statement(s) she made at the first questioning session. Making any of these changes is likely to result in the admissibility of the postwarning statement(s). Making all these changes will undoubtedly do so."

Would the deputy district attorney be right? Why (not)?

3. *The Seibert case and the assertion of a right to counsel.* Suppose during the first stage of a two-stage interrogation, the suspect emphatically asserts his right to counsel. Would the administration of the *Miranda* warnings during the second stage of the interrogation (after a half-hour or hour-long recess) make a "second confession" admissible? Isn't this essentially the *Edwards* case (p. 636) all over again? But what result if the officer not only gives the suspect the *Miranda* warnings during the second stage, but assures him that the incriminating statement he made during the first stage (the statement made after the police paid no attention to the request for a lawyer), is not admissible in evidence?

4. *If the suspect is unaware of the nature of the police conduct, is the deliberate and flagrant nature of the police action relevant?* The four *Seibert* dissenters (O'Connor, J., joined by Rehnquist, C.J., and Scalia and Thomas, JJ.) answer in the negative. But in *Oregon v. Elstad* (p. 697), the first Supreme Court case to address the question whether the "poisoned fruit" doctrine applies to *Miranda*-deficient statements, the Court, per O'Connor, J., pointed out that the failure to give the warnings in the first instance (when Elstad was in his home) "may have been the result of confusion as to whether the brief exchange [in Elstad's home] qualified as 'custodial interrogation' or it may simply have reflected [the officer's] reluctance to initiate an alarming procedure [the recitation of the *Miranda* warnings] before [a second officer] had spoken with [Elstad's] mother." But why (according to Justice O'Connor's *Seibert* dissent) was any of this relevant? Mr. Elstad had no idea what was in the officer's head. He did not know, for example, that the officer was "confused" about whether the situation called for the *Miranda* warnings. If the technical or inadvertent nature of the failure to comply with *Miranda* is relevant for derivative evidence purposes, as it seemed to be in *Elstad,* why shouldn't the deliberate and flagrant nature of the failure to comply with *Miranda* be relevant for the same purposes?

SECTION 5. SOME FINAL COMMENTS ABOUT *MIRANDA*

A. WAS THE *MIRANDA* RULING A STRAIGHTFORWARD INTERPRETATION OF THE FIFTH AMENDMENT?

JUSTICE BYRON R. WHITE—RECENT DEVELOPMENTS IN CRIMINAL LAW

Address before the Conference of Chief Justices (Aug. 3, 1967) in Council of State Governments, Proceedings of the 19th Annual Meeting of the Conference of Chief Justices (1967).

Is the arrested suspect, alone with the police in the station house, being "compelled" to incriminate himself when he is interrogated without proper warnings? Reasonable men may differ about the answer to that question, but the question itself is a perfectly straightforward one under the Fifth Amendment and little different in kind from many others which arise under the Constitution and which must be decided by the courts. No ready answer to *Miranda* can be found by reference to the text of the Constitution alone. The answer lies in the purpose and history of the self-incrimination clause and in our accumulated experience.

This kind of judicial decision making is inherent in our present governmental structure. All of you know it is, for you too are faced with the identical provisions and must decide the same questions.

* * *

Of course, to say that the courts must decide a case like *Miranda* is one thing. The question of whether it is correctly or wisely decided is quite another. As a matter of constitutional interpretation, I disagreed with the result reached in that case and the reasons given for it and repeated my disagreement last term. But it is now the law and whatever its merits, it is plainly a derivative of *Malloy v. Hogan*, applying the Fifth Amendment to the States, and *Gideon v. Wainwright* which required counsel in most kinds of criminal cases. In terms of the function which the Court was performing, I see little difference between *Miranda* and the several other decisions, some old, some new, which have construed the Fifth Amendment in a manner in which it has never been construed before, or as in the case of *Miranda*, contrary to previous decisions of the Court and of other courts as well. Cases such as *Boyd v. United States*, 116 U.S. 616 [1886],[a] and *Counselman v. Hitchcock*, 142 U.S. 547 [1892],[b] immediately comes to mind. I likewise consider extremely important the two cases of last term, *Garrity v. New Jersey* [385 U.S. 493 (1967)],[c] and *Spevack v. Klein* [385 U.S. 511 (1967)]. In the first, *Garrity*, the Court held inadmissible, as compelled within the meaning of the Fifth Amendment, the statements of a city employee made in response to inquiries about his job performance and under threat of loss of employment. In *Spevack*, the Fifth Amendment was said to shield a lawyer from producing information at a disbarment hearing and to prevent his disbarment for such refusal.

B.   ARE THE *MIRANDA* WARNINGS OVERPLAYED? DOES *MIRANDA* CONTAIN THREE DIFFERENT HOLDINGS?

STEPHEN J. SCHULHOFER—RECONSIDERING *MIRANDA*
54 U.Chi.L.Rev. 435, 436–40, 446, 453–55 (1987).

Talk about "overruling *Miranda*" usually obscures the fact that *Miranda* contains not one holding but a complex series of holdings. They can be subdivided in various ways, but three conceptually distinct steps were involved in the Court's decision. First, the Court held that informal pressure to speak—that is, pressure

---

a. In *Boyd* [set forth at p. 806 infra] the Court first endorsed the concept of the exclusionary rule.

b. In *Counselman*, the Court (a) rejected the view that the self-incrimination clause only protects a person from being required to appear as a witness in her own criminal trial, emphasizing that the clause protects a person *in any proceeding* from giving testimony which will tend to incriminate her; and (b) invalidated an immunity grant that prohibited the use of the testimony given by a witness, but failed to protect the witness against the *derivative use* of the compelled testimony.

c. In *Garrity*, at an inquiry into a traffic ticket-fixing scheme conducted by the state attorney general, several police officers were told they would be fired if they invoked their right to remain silent. They confessed. Overturning the convictions based on these confessions, the Court condemned the tactics used by the state attorney general's office.

Commenting on cases like *Garrity*, Stephen J. Schulhofer, *Miranda, Dickerson, and the Puzzling Persistence of Fifth Amendment Exceptionalism*, 99 Mich.L.Rev. 941 (2001), observes: "[A] threat to discharge a public employee for a refusal to testify [is] impermissibly compelling per se. [The] Court has never suggested that the totality of the circumstances must be assessed to determine if such a threat is compelling in light of the particular employee's economic situation; the specific circumstances are irrelevant. [In] short, totality-of-circumstances analysis, so often touted as the only really pure and correct way to make Fifth Amendment judgments, is entirely foreign to the Court's Fifth Amendment jurisprudence, at least in settings other than the police station."

Consider, too, Mark A. Godsey, *Rethinking the Involuntary Confession Rule: Toward a Workable Test for Identifying Compelled Self-Incrimination*, 93 Calif.L.Rev. 465 (2005): "[*Garrity*] raises the following paramount question: If threatening a suspect with [loss of his job] violates the self-incrimination clause and renders a confession inadmissible as a matter of law when the threat occurs in a formal inquiry, why would this same sort of threat not render a confession inadmissible as a matter of law when it occurs in the stationhouse interrogation room?"

not backed by legal process or any formal sanction—can constitute "compulsion" within the meaning of the fifth amendment. Second, it held that this element of informal compulsion is present in *any* questioning of a suspect in custody, no matter how short the period of questioning may be. Third, the Court held that precisely specified warnings are required to dispel the compelling pressure of custodial interrogation. The third step, the series of particularized warnings, raises the concerns about judicial legislation that usually preoccupy *Miranda*'s critics. But the core of *Miranda* is located in the first two steps. * * *

I. INFORMAL COMPULSION

The Court's first holding was that compulsion, within the meaning of the fifth amendment, can include informal pressure to speak. Note first that there is not the slightest doubt about the legitimacy of settling this question by adjudication. The fifth amendment says that no person shall be "compelled" to be a witness against himself. According to one view, this word referred only to formal legal compulsion. But it is a normal act of interpretation for a court to consider whether "compulsion" was intended to cover informal pressures as well.

[In] holding the fifth amendment applicable to informal compulsion, *Miranda* rejected a long line of precedent. Nonetheless, this step in the *Miranda* analysis was not at odds with the original understanding of the fifth amendment. The early history of the privilege is clouded and ambiguous, but it seems clear that the privilege was intended to bar pretrial examination by magistrates, the only form of pretrial interrogation known at the time. The reasons for concern about that form of interrogation under formal process apply with even greater force to questioning under compelling informal pressures. * * *

Not only do policy and history suggest the implausibility of restricting the fifth amendment's protection to purely formal pressures, but the principles applied in contexts other than police interrogation make clear that no tenable line can be drawn between formal and informal compulsion. In fact, *Miranda*'s first holding was strongly foreshadowed by *Griffin v. California*, [380 U.S. 609 (1965), discussed at p. 1450], in which the Court held that prosecutorial comment upon a defendant's failure to testify at trial violated the privilege by making its assertion costly. The compulsion in *Griffin* did not flow from formal process or any legal obligation to speak. The problem was that the prosecutor's comment increased (indirectly) the chances of conviction. [What] mattered in *Griffin* were the real world consequences of the prosecutorial behavior, not whether the state had brought to bear any formal process or official sanction. * * *

II. INTERROGATION AS COMPULSION

Miranda's second major step was the holding that any custodial interrogation involves enough pressure to constitute "compulsion" within the meaning of the fifth amendment. Again, notice that there is no doubt about the legitimacy of settling this issue by judicial decision. The question of what pressures constitute "compulsion" unavoidably confronts the Court in cases involving loss of a job, a comment on silence, or the menacing look of a person in authority. There is nothing improper or even unusual about deciding such questions in the course of adjudication.

III. THE WARNINGS * * *

Do the [*Miranda*] warnings "handcuff" the police? [Their] function is precisely the opposite. If the Court was correct in the first two steps of its analysis, and I submit that it was, then far from handcuffing the police, the warnings work to *liberate* the police. *Miranda*'s much-maligned rules permit the officer to continue questioning his isolated suspect, the very process that the Court's first two holdings found to be a violation of the fifth amendment.

[The] notion that police-initiated warnings can "dispel" the compulsion [seems] dubious at best. But whether or not they went far enough, *Miranda*'s warnings unquestionably serve—and from the outset were designed to serve—the function of permitting custodial interrogation to continue. Indeed, the Court would have incurred far more police criticism if it had remained within a narrow conception of the judicial role, pronounced interrogation "inherently compelling," and then left law enforcement officials to guess about what countermeasures would keep police on the safe side of the constitutional line. * * *

C. THE "STEALTH OVERRULING" OF *MIRANDA*[a]

BARRY FRIEDMAN—THE WAGES OF STEALTH OVERRULING (WITH PARTICULAR ATTENTION TO *MIRANDA v. ARIZONA*)
99 Geo.L.J. 1, 60–62 (2010)

[S]tealth overruling successfully obscures what the Court is really about. It excuses the Justices from having to justify their actions. Readers of the media coverage of *Seibert* and *Patane* have the impression the Court was faithful to *Miranda* and coming down hard on cops who made an end run around it. What really happened, however, is that the Court deeply undermined *Miranda* and encouraged police to do the same–without explaining why.

* * * [I]t is clear the Justices do not like *Miranda*, but we do not know exactly why. We *did* know why the *Miranda* dissenters disliked the rule–and why the majority in that case preferred it nonetheless. They laid bare their reasoning, which rested firmly in the costs and benefits of providing warnings to criminal suspects. Since then, however, the entire merits discussion regarding *Miranda* has grown underground. Despite years of learning, and the existence of widely accepted data on the subject, there is virtually no discussion among the Justices of when custodial interrogation proves problematic or any recognition of how easy compliance with *Miranda* has been, let alone whether the costs of *Miranda* in lost convictions are appropriate. Rather, as the tortured opinions of *Seibert* and *Patane* made clear, the Justices prefer to rest on bald pronouncements about what the Fifth Amendment does or does not require and uncomfortable distinctions of precedents. * * *

The failure to discuss the underlying merits of police conduct is particularly disappointing given that *Miranda* now seems to supplant any meaningful examination in decided cases of the voluntariness of confessions. Perhaps (as one account would go) police forces have professionalized, and in the vast majority of case suspects are treated in a perfectly acceptable fashion, one that properly balances the needs of society and the rights of the suspect. Or perhaps police engage in deception and apply pressure in troubling ways, including denying people lawyers when they ask for them. No clear answer may emerge from a debate about where the line should properly be drawn. But this is the right debate to have.

* * * The public (within limits, one supposes) supports *Miranda*, which is indeed embedded in the national culture. Yet the Court tunnels under the rule without admitting what it is doing. Perhaps *Miranda* should be overruled.

---

a. For an earlier discussion of "stealth overruling," see p. 595 supra.

Certainly there are Justices that believe this. But if that is the case, then they should do that overtly and allow a national discussion to begin.

D. SHOULD WE RECOGNIZE THAT *MIRANDA* HAS TURNED OUT TO BE A FAILURE AND START OVER?

CHARLES D. WEISSELBERG–MOURNING *MIRANDA*
96 Calif.L.Rev. 1521, 1523, 1592–99 (2008).

[In] the more than four decades since *Miranda* was decided, the Supreme Court has effectively encouraged police practices that have gutted *Miranda*'s safeguards, to the extent those safeguards ever truly existed. The best evidence now shows that, as a protective device, *Miranda* is largely dead. It is time to 'pronounce the body' as they say on television and move on.

[The] system of warnings and waivers the Court prescribed as a solution in *Miranda* is now detrimental to our criminal justice system. It is bad enough that *Miranda*'s vaunted safeguards appear not to afford meaningful protection to suspects. But it turns out that following *Miranda*'s hollow ritual often forecloses a searching inquiry into the voluntariness of a statement. Further, it has frozen legislative and other efforts to regulate police interrogation practices. * * *

Some may ask whether a system of warnings and waivers can be made effective in protecting Fifth Amendment rights. Surely we should try to repair *Miranda* rather than abandon a decades-old precedent that has "become part of our national culture." A uniform repair would have to come from the Supreme Court and I do not believe there is a reasonable possibility of a meaningful fix, though some individual state courts may make some headway.

To begin with, the evidence no longer supports the per se aspect of *Miranda*'s safeguards. Standardized warnings simply do not work in large numbers of cases. If we are honest about this, we cannot avoid making individual assessments of voluntariness or of the validity of waivers.

[The] Court has issued decisions that tolerate tactics that diminish *Miranda*'s effectiveness, and officers have predictably been trained to use these tactics. [The] Supreme Court would have to refashion several lines of cases, including those that affect the timing and content of warnings, as well as the implied waiver and invocation doctrines. This is a tall order. I do not see any appetite on the Court for engaging in a wholesale revision of the *Miranda* doctrine, or even for restricting *Davis*. Nor, given the Justices' deep divisions and their quite tepid support for *Miranda*–as revealed most recently in *Seibert* and *Patane*–does there seem to be any consensus for any different circumstances.

[While] courts seem unlikely to retool *Miranda* directly, there is one way in which the judiciary may spark reform. A better understanding of interrogation practices and the realities of *Miranda* might cause judges to take claims disputing the voluntariness of a statement more seriously and lead to more robust litigation of the issue. If judges then become more willing to find statements involuntary under the Due Process clause, even after warnings are given and waivers obtained, there might be some enthusiasm for fixing *Miranda*.

[Since] the voluntariness doctrine theoretically exists alongside *Miranda*, the reason *Miranda* is advantageous [to the police] is that it has practically displaced voluntariness determinations. Former Solicitor General Charles Fried has written that police organizations have "learned to live with *Miranda*, and even to love it, to the extent that it provided them with a safe harbor: if they followed the rules, they had a fair assurance that a confession would be admissible and a conviction built on it would stick."[401]

* * * I am not against warnings and waivers per se, just the assumed effect of them. For me, the main problem with *Miranda* is the judiciary's unjustified confidence in *Miranda*'s safeguards. There is an almost religious belief that the warnings and waivers actually work, and an apparent deafness to claims that they do not. I am not the first to observe that *Miranda* can be an obstacle to the more important assessment of voluntariness * * *.[404]

We should also consider the possible role of state and federal legislatures. A legislative solution may seem problematic after *Dickerson*. I believe it is an open question, though there may be room for such a solution if it is based on legislative findings about the current operation of *Miranda*'s procedures.

[In 2000, the *Dickerson* Court] may well have viewed section 3501 [purporting to replace *Miranda* with the old voluntariness test] as a naked attack on *Miranda*'s holdings rather than a legitimate search for an effective alternative. * * * I suggest that a legislative solution based upon a rich factual record may be viewed differently, and we of course now have much more social science data than was available to Congress in 1968.

Imagine legislative hearings exploring the contemporary process of interrogation, with findings that only a moderate percentage of suspects understand form warnings. Imagine a legislature determining that many individuals in a position of powerlessness, such as those in a police station, assert their rights in tentative language because they are afraid. Imagine further findings that implied waivers are prevalent, and that many suspects do not feel free to assert their rights unless they are expressly asked if they wish to do so. What would be an appropriate legislative response? There are a number of interesting possibilities.

One possible outcome might be legislation that directly regulates the police and affords greater protection to suspects than *Miranda* currently provides. A legislature might, for example, require warnings in very simple language and instruct police to give them prior to any suspect interviews or interrogations. And most importantly, it might require videotaping, a movement that is gaining strength among the states. While a requirement of videotaping would not directly impact a suspect's decision to speak or not, it would foster transparency in the interrogation process, give police supervisors a greater ability to review the actions of investigating officers, and establish an accurate factual record for an assessment of voluntariness. These sorts of reforms may counter some of the signaling and police professionalism concerns associated with replacing *Miranda*. * * *[413]

Any of these legislative responses would at least begin a dialogue about interrogation practices, the value of the Fifth and Fourteenth Amendments, and the best ways to regulate the police. With *Miranda*'s current procedures in place, there is neither discussion nor experimentation. With courts doings the work of policing the police, there has been little incentive for legislators to act. * * *

---

401. Charles Fried, *Order and Law: Arguing the Reagan Revolution—A Firsthand Account* 45 (1991).

404. See Alfredo Garcia, *Is Miranda Dead, Was It Overruled, or Is It Irrelevant?*, 10 St. Thomas L.Rev. 461, 496–502 (1988) * * *.

413. For some discussions of alternatives to *Miranda*, see, for example, Paul G. Cassell, *The Statute that Time Forgot: 18 U.S.C. § 3501 and the Overhauling of Miranda*, 58 Iowa L.Rev. 175, 252–59 (1999); Morgan Cloud, et.al., *Words Without Meaning: The Constitution, Confessions, and Mentally Retarded Suspects*, 69 U.Chi.L.Rev. 495, 572–90 (2002); Stephen J. Schulhofer, *Miranda's Practical Effect: Substantial Benefits and Vanishingly Small Social Costs*, 90 Nw. U.L.Rev. 500, 556–61 (1996).

Perhaps the most positive outcome may be the resurrection or even the reshaping of the voluntariness doctrine. If *Miranda*'s procedures do not adequately advise suspects of their rights and provide them with opportunities to assert these rights, law enforcement would presumably lose *Miranda* as a "safe harbor." Courts would be required to assess the voluntariness of statements in light of all of the circumstances, including suspects' age, education, the existence of any mental disabilities or disorders, the application of sophisticated interrogation tactics, express and implied promises, and other factors, shorn of the unwarranted assumptions that all suspects somehow understand form warnings and are empowered thereby. * * *

[It] may turn out that courts, including the Supreme Court, will fail to facilitate the growth of the [voluntariness] doctrine. Trial court judges may continue to make superficial judgments about voluntariness. Without *Miranda*'s purportedly bright-line test, appellate courts may find it more difficult to review interrogation cases and give clear guidance to the lower courts. Nevertheless, there is at least a chance that we could see a voluntariness standard that looks carefully at the dynamics of police interrogation and asks whether a confession was elicited by offensive police conduct.[416] We might see a standard that places greater emphasis on reliability of a confession by looking at, among other things, the fit between the real facts of the offense and those contained in the suspect's post-admission narrative.[417] Given the few constraints on interrogation tactics after a *Miranda* waiver is obtained, that type of standard might do more to address concerns about false confessions. We would lose *Miranda*'s "bright lines" and courts would have to make many more individualized assessments of the voluntariness of a statement. But this surely is the right outcome.

E. WHAT IF *MIRANDA* WERE ABOLISHED?
YALE KAMISAR—ON THE FORTIETH ANNIVERSARY OF THE *MIRANDA* CASE
5 Ohio St.J.Crim.L. 163, 194–197 (2007).

[If *Miranda* were abolished], the failure to require the police to give any warnings[153] [would] not mean that a custodial suspect could not ask questions about her rights on her own initiative. (It would hardly be surprising if a person who had been watching TV detective shows for many years did so.)

Suppose a custodial suspect were to ask a police officer if he could (or would) *prevent her* from communicating with a lawyer until she answered his questions? How should he respond? Could he say he *would prevent her* without jeopardizing the admissibility of any resulting confession?

Or suppose a custodial suspect were to ask a police officer whether she *had to* answer his questions or whether the police officer had *a right* to an answer?

---

416. *See generally* Albert W. Alschuler, *Constraint and Confession*, 74 Denv.U.L.Rev. 957 (1997) (arguing for a test that focuses on offensive conduct, regardless of the reliability of a confession).

417. *See generally* Richard J. Ofshe & Richard A. Leo, *The Decision to Confess Falsely: Rational Choice and Irrational Action*, 74 Denv.U.L.Rev. 979, 1118 (1997).

153. Although no longer required to do so, some police departments (perhaps many) would continue to advise people of their rights because "[e]ven without *Miranda*, an important factor in determining whether a confession was voluntary would be whether the warnings had been given." Jerold H. Israel, *Criminal Procedure, the Burger Court, and the Legacy of the Warren Court*, 75 Mich.L.Rev. 1320, 1386 n.283 (1977). But the odds are high that they would not be *the same Miranda* warnings, but some abbreviated or diluted version. If so, this would probably only contribute to the general confusion.

Again, how should the officer respond? (Very carefully.) A good argument may be made that, as it had evolved by the time of *Miranda*, the "voluntariness" test would have barred the admissibility of any statements made by one who had been told by the police that she must answer their questions or that they had a right to an answer.

Dissenting in *Escobedo* (as he was to dissent in *Miranda*), Justice White recognized that under the due process-voluntariness test if a suspect "is told he must answer and does not know better, it would be very doubtful that the resulting admissions could be used against him."[154] Decades later, Professor Joseph Grano, the most prominent *Miranda* critic of his time, put it even more strongly than Justice White had: Because the police "may not deceive defendants about the nature or scope of their legal rights," "it would violate due process to tell suspects that they are obligated to answer questions."[155]

It is possible that in a world without *Miranda* the Court might permit the officer to respond: "I can't answer that question" or "I can't answer any of your questions." We can't be sure. Perhaps the only thing we can be fairly confident about is that the abolition of *Miranda* would cause a great deal of confusion and uncertainty—perhaps even more than *Miranda* did in the first place.

Of course, avoiding confusion is hardly the only reason, or even the primary one, for not abolishing *Miranda*. As Professor Leo has observed:

> *Miranda* has exerted a civilizing effect on police behavior and in so doing has professionalized the interrogation process in America.... [T]he *Miranda* decision has transformed the culture—the shared norms, values, and attitudes—of police detecting in America by fundamentally reframing how police talk about and think about the process of custodial interrogation....

> * * *

> In the world of modern policing, *Miranda* constitutes the moral and legal standard by which interrogators are judged and evaluated.... Indeed, virtually all police officers and detectives today have known no law other than *Miranda*.[156]

Even if a custodial suspect knows all his rights, he needs to know, as Professor Stephen Schulhofer has put it, "whether the *police* know his rights. And he needs to know whether the police are prepared to *respect* those rights."[157]

To many, "*Miranda* may seem like a mere symbol."[158] However, to quote Schulhofer again, "the symbolic effects of criminal procedural guarantees are important; they underscore our societal commitment to restraint in an area in which emotions easily run uncontrolled."[159] Even one of the landmark case's strongest critics recognizes that *Miranda* may be seen as "a question of government's willingness to treat the lowliest antagonist as worthy of respect and consideration."[160]

Abolishing *Miranda* would be symbolic, too. "And surely the symbolic message that such a decision would seem to send—that police can disregard constitu-

---

154. 378 U.S. at 499 (White, J., joined by Clark and Stewart, JJ., dissenting).

155. Joseph D. Grano, *Confessions, Truth and the Law* 114 (1993).

156. Richard A. Leo, *The Impact of Miranda Revisited*, 86 J. Criminal Law and Criminology 621, 670–71 (1996).

157. Stephen J. Schulhofer, *Reconsidering Miranda*, 54 U.Chi.L.Rev. 435, 447 (1987).

158. *Id.* at 460.

159. *Id.*

160. Gerald Caplan, *Questioning Miranda*, 38 Vand.L.Rev. 1417, 1471 (1985).

tional rights when interrogating criminal suspects—would cause a backlash of resentment against, and more distrust of, American police."[161]

It is noteworthy, I believe, that in a tribute to Professor Fred Inbau, for many years the great champion of police interrogation, Professor Ronald Allen, Inbau's former colleague, recalled that Inbau balked at explicitly overruling *Miranda*. As did Allen himself, Inbau "feared that [overruling *Miranda*] would be taken as a symbol by the police that, so to speak, all bets were off, and a return to the days of the third degree were acceptable."[162]

I began this section of the paper by asking: "*What good* does *Miranda* do?" Perhaps a more appropriate question would be: "At this point in time, what good would it do (and how much harm would it cause) to abolish *Miranda*?" * * *

SECTION 6. THE "DUE PROCESS"— "VOLUNTARINESS" TEST REVISITED

The Significance of the "Voluntariness" Test in the post-Miranda Era

Although one might say (and many commentators have) that *Miranda* displaced the due process-totality of circumstances-voluntariness test, in a number of important situations "the primary criterion of [confession] admissibility under current law is [still] the 'old' due process voluntariness test." Stephen J. Schulhofer, *Confessions and the Court*, 79 Mich.L.Rev. 865, 877 (1981). For one thing, empirical studies indicate that most suspects waive their rights and submit to police questioning. "Because the admissibility of statements given after a valid waiver of *Miranda* rights must be determined on the basis of the voluntariness test, that test remains vitally important." Welsh S. White, *What is an Involuntary Confession Now?*, 50 Rutgers L.Rev. 2001, 2004 (1998). Moreover, as Schulhofer, supra, points out, the voluntariness test is important when suspects not in custody are questioned by the police; when suspects in a custody-like situation are questioned (or threatened) by private citizens (e.g. *Commonwealth v. Mahnke*, 335 N.E.2d 660 (Mass.1975)); or when the prosecution seeks to use a confession to impeach a defendant's testimony at trial or to use the "fruits" of the confession (e.g., the murder weapon), but not the confession itself. As discussed in Ch. 12, §§ 2, 3, although statements obtained in violation of *Miranda* may be used for impeachment purposes, "coerced" or "involuntary" statements may not. Moreover, as we have just seen, the Court will usually permit the use of evidence derived from a *Miranda* violation but exclude the "fruits" of an "involuntary" confession.

ONE PROFESSOR'S CONCLUSIONS AFTER READING EVERY REPORTED STATE AND FEDERAL APPEALS DECISIONS ON VOLUNTARINESS FOR THE PAST TWENTY YEARS

"[The] clarity of the [due process/'voluntariness'/'totality of the circumstances'] test as stated is in sharp contrast to its application in practice. The reality is that few criteria stand out as especially significant, and even fewer appellate decisions can be viewed as establishing noteworthy precedents. The due process test offers almost no guidance for lawyers and judges.

---

161. Leo, supra note 156, at 680. * * *

162. Ronald J. Allen, *Tribute to Fred Inbau*, 89 J.Crim.L. & Criminology 1271, 1273 (1999).

" * * * One necessarily comes away with a feeling of being unclean and tainted by government activities that are not honorable even given the environment needed for interrogations. Many judges allow confessions into evidence in cases in which police interrogators lied and threatened defendants or played on the mental, emotional, or physical weaknesses of suspects. While judges write that they do not condone such conduct and find such practices repugnant, reprehensible, or deplorable, some of those same judges have upheld the admission of such confessions that result from those practices after applying the totality of circumstances test.

"I began by asking two questions: (1) How important are the due process rules today now that we have lived for almost forty years with *Miranda*?, and (2) Have these principles improved at all in practice from the muddled mess found prior to the Chief Justice's opinion there? The strong belief I have formed is that the rules are most important and are widely applied in the twenty-first century, [but that] they are just as poorly and inconsistently applied as they were in the 1950s and 1960s. In comparison, the imprecisely bright line rules of *Miranda* look very good."

— Paul Marcus, *It's Not Just About Miranda: Determining the Voluntariness of Confessions in Criminal Cases*, 40 Val.U.L.Rev. 601, 643–44 (2006).

A. *MILLER v. FENTON:* WHAT KINDS OF TRICKERY OR DECEPTION, IF ANY, MAY THE POLICE EMPLOY AFTER A SUSPECT HAS WAIVED HIS RIGHTS?

Is *Miranda*'s prohibition against police deception and trickery limited to their use in obtaining a waiver of *Miranda* rights or does it also bar such police techniques after a person has validly waived his rights? Suppose a suspect waives his rights and expresses a willingness to talk, but denies any involvement in the case. May the police then display apparent sympathy? Turn the suspect over to a friendly, gentle interrogator and then to a hostile, short-tempered one (the "Mutt and Jeff" routine)? Although such techniques seemed to have vented Chief Justice Warren's judicial ire in *Miranda*, that landmark case "did not condemn any specific techniques as such or hold that evidence obtained by use of them would be inadmissible. Reliance was placed on warning and counsel to protect the suspect." Sheldon Elsen & Arthur Rosett, *Protections for the Suspect under Miranda v. Arizona*, 67 Colum.L.Rev. 645, 667 (1967). More than three decades after *Miranda*, the issue has yet to be clearly resolved.[a]

A year after *Miranda*, Professor Fred Inbau and Mr. John Reid published a new edition of their leading interrogation manual and maintained that "all but a very few of the interrogation techniques presented in our earlier [pre-*Escobedo*, pre-*Miranda*] publication are still valid if used after the recently prescribed warnings have been given to the suspect under interrogation, and after he has waived his self-incriminating privilege and his right to counsel." See *Criminal Interrogation and Confessions*, (2d ed. 1967). See also Inbau, Reid & Buckley, *Criminal Interrogation and Confessions* 216 (3d ed. 1986), maintaining that, although the Court did not explicitly address the issue in *Frazier v. Cupp*, fn. a supra, that case "implicitly recognized" the essentiality of interrogation practices

---

a. Cf. *Frazier v. Cupp*, 394 U.S. 731 (1969) (admitting a confession in a pre-*Miranda* case although the police had falsely told the defendant that another had confessed and had also "sympathetically" suggested that the victim's homosexual advances may have started the fight). See also *Oregon v. Mathiason* (p. 602) (interrogator's false statement to defendant that his fingerprints were found at scene may have bearing on other issues in case, but "has nothing to do with whether [defendant] was in custody for [*Miranda*] purposes").

involving trickery or deceit, and approved of them. [Moreover,] there are many appellate court cases holding that a confession is admissible even when it was obtained by trickery and deceit, [provided that the trickery does not] " 'shock the conscience' [or is not] apt to induce a false confession."[b]

Welsh S. White, *Police Trickery in Inducing Confessions*, 127 U.Pa.L.Rev. 581–90, 599–600, 628–29 (1979), takes a very different view of police use of trickery in the post-*Miranda* era, maintaining that, because they are likely to render a resulting confession involuntary or because they distort the meaning or vitiate the effect of the *Miranda* warnings or because they "undermine [a] suspect's independent right to an attorney," "several widely employed interrogation tactics * * * should be absolutely prohibited." Among the techniques Professor White considers "impermissible per se" are deception that distorts the seriousness of the matter under investigation (e.g., falsely informing a murder suspect that the victim is still alive), the "assumption of non-adversary roles" by interrogating officers (e.g., assuming the role of a father figure or religious counselor), repeated assurances that the suspect is known to be guilty, and the "Mutt and Jeff" routine. See also Note, 40 Stan.L.Rev. 1593, 1612–15 (1988).

But police deception and trickery did not prevent the admissibility of the resulting confession in *Miller v. Fenton*, below. *Miller* is a dramatic illustration that the problems raised by the old "totality of the circumstances"—"due process"—"voluntariness" test have not disappeared in the post-*Miranda* era.

When he accompanied the police to a state police barracks, Miller, the prime suspect in the brutal murder of Ms. Margolin, was advised of his rights and signed "a *Miranda* card," waiving his rights.[a] Thus, the issue in MILLER v. FENTON, 796 F.2d 598 (3d Cir.1986), was the "voluntariness" of the defendant's murder confession.[b] A 2–1 majority, per BECKER, J. (joined by Seitz, J.), framed the issue in terms of whether the tactics of Detective Boyce during the 53–minute interrogation "were sufficiently manipulative to overbear the will of a person with [defendant's] characteristics" and viewed the limits of permissible interrogation as turning on "a weighing of the circumstances of pressure [applied by the police] against the power of resistance of the person confessing." After listening to Detective Boyce's questions and defendant Miller's responses (the police had taped

---

b. Although agreeing that a goodly number of lower courts have interpreted *Frazier* as "definitively ruling that police trickery is a mere factor to be included in a court's assessment of a confession's involuntariness under a totality of the circumstances analysis," Note, 40 Stan.L.Rev. 1593, 1607–08 (1988), maintains that "several factors make *Frazier* a particularly bad case for a definitive ruling on police trickery":

"First, the opinion does not recognize as trickery the detective's feigned sympathy in his suggestion that a homosexual advance was a reason for the fight. Also, Frazier was tried and decided before the *Miranda* decision, and so the Court's indictment of police misconduct in *Miranda* did not apply. * * * Third, apart from the one recognized and one unrecognized instances of police trickery, the interrogators' behavior was exemplary. The police gave coercive conduct a wide berth, questioning Frazier for only forty-five minutes immediately after he was brought to the police station. In addition, the interrogation was tape-recorded and the tape played for the trial judge, who subsequently concluded that the confession was voluntary. Last and most important, the police lie that [another person] had confessed, the only trickery recognized by the Court, does *not* seem to have induced Frazier's confession."

a. Several hours earlier, Miller had been questioned by the police for about 45 minutes at his place of employment, but had denied any involvement in the murder.

b. The case has a long procedural history. After a New Jersey trial court admitted his confession, Miller was convicted of murder. A three-judge panel of an intermediate state appellate court reversed, holding Miller's confession "involuntary." But a 4–3 majority of the New Jersey Supreme Court reinstated the conviction, deeming the confession "voluntary." On federal habeas corpus, the Third Circuit, deferring to the state court's finding of "voluntariness," upheld the admissibility of the confession. The U.S. Supreme Court reversed (see p. ___), holding that on federal habeas corpus the "voluntariness" of a confession is a matter for independent federal court determination, and remanding the case for a fuller analysis under the correct standard.

the interrogation), the majority concluded that "under the totality of circumstances of this case" Miller's confession was "voluntarily given":

"It is clear that Boyce made no threats and engaged in no physical coercion of Miller. To the contrary, throughout the interview, Detective Boyce assumed a friendly, understanding manner and spoke in a soft tone of voice. He repeatedly assured Miller that he was sympathetic to him and wanted to help him unburden his mind. [The detective's] statements of sympathy at times approached the maudlin. [E.g., 'This hurts me more than it hurts you because I love people * * * I'm on your side, Frank * * * I'm your brother, you and I are brothers, Frank [and] I want to help my brother.']

"Boyce also gave Miller certain factual information, some of which was untrue. At the beginning of the interrogation, for example, Boyce informed Miller that the victim was still alive; this was false. During the interview, Boyce told Miller that Ms. Margolin had just died, although in fact she had been found dead several hours earlier.

"Detective Boyce's major theme throughout the interrogation was that whoever had committed such a heinous crime had mental problems and was desperately in need of psychological treatment. [The] Detective stated several times that Miller was not a criminal who should be punished, but a sick individual who should receive help. * * *

"Boyce also appealed to Miller's conscience and described the importance of Miller's purging himself of the memories that must be haunting him. [E.g., 'First thing we have to do is let it all come out. Don't fight it because it's worse * * * It's hurting me because I feel it. I feel it wanting to come out, but it's hurting me, Frank. * * * I know how you feel inside, Frank, it's eating you up, am I right? * * * You've got to come forward. You've got to do it for yourself, for your family, for your father, this is what's important, the truth, Frank.']

"When Miller at last confessed [almost an hour after the interrogation session began], he collapsed in a state of shock. He slid off his chair and onto the floor with a blank stare on his face. The police officers sent for a first aid squad that took him to the hospital. * * *

"[Psychological] ploys may play a part in the suspect's decision to confess, but as long as that decision is a product of the suspect's own balancing of competing considerations, the confession is voluntary. The question we must answer [is] whether [the detective's] statements were so manipulative or coercive that they deprived Miller of his ability to make an unconstrained autonomous decision to confess. To that inquiry we now turn. * * *

"Miller is a mature adult, thirty-two years of age [and] has some high school education. Such a person is more resistant to interrogation than a person who is very young, uneducated or weak-minded. [Moreover,] Miller [had] served a jail sentence. Thus, he was aware of the consequences of confessing. [He had also] received Miranda warnings. Detective Boyce's interrogation of Miller lasted less than an hour. [I]t is thus distinguishable from the lengthy interrogations during incommunicado detention that have been held to result in involuntary confessions. * * *

"Boyce's supportive, encouraging manner was an interrogation tactic aimed at winning Miller's trust and making him feel comfortable about confessing. Excessive friendliness on the part of an interrogator can be deceptive. In some instances, in combination with other tactics, it might create an atmosphere in which a suspect forgets that his questioner is in an adversarial role, and thereby prompt admissions that the suspect would ordinarily make only to a friend, not to the police. [But] the 'good guy' approach is recognized as a permissible interrogation tactic.

"[While an officer's] lie [about] an important aspect of the case may affect the voluntariness of the confession, the effect of the lie must be analyzed in the context of all the circumstances of the interrogation. See, e.g., *Frazier v. Cupp*. [The] record suggests that this emotional reaction did not occur, for it appears that Miller was not affected at all by the news of the death. Indeed, he remained quite impassive. * * *

"Detective Boyce's statements that Miller was not a criminal, but rather a mentally ill individual not responsible for his actions, and Boyce's promises to help Miller raise a more serious question about the voluntariness of Miller's confession. By telling Miller that he was not responsible for anything he might have done, Boyce may have been understood to be making an implied promise to Miller that [he] would not be prosecuted, or that if he were prosecuted Boyce would aid him in presenting the insanity defense. Similarly, the promises of psychiatric help might have suggested to Miller that he would be treated, rather than prosecuted. If these promises, implicit and explicit, tricked Miller into confessing, his confession may have been involuntary. To determine whether Boyce's promises affected the voluntariness of Miller's confession, we must consider how manipulative these tactics in fact were.

"In *Bram v. United States* (1897) [pp. 565, 575] [the Court] endorsed the view that to be voluntary a confession must not have been 'extracted by any sort of threats or violence, nor obtained by any direct or implied promises, however slight.' [Emphasis added.] Although the Bram test has been reaffirmed [it] has not been interpreted as a per se proscription against promises made during interrogation.[c] Nor does the Supreme Court even use a but-for test when promises have been made during an interrogation.

"[At] no time did Detective Boyce state that Miller would not be prosecuted or that he could successfully avail himself of the insanity defense. * * * Indeed, Boyce's statements that Miller was 'not a criminal' need not be understood as assurances of leniency at all. Since [Boyce's] strategy was to present himself as a friend to whom Miller could unburden himself, he of course attempted throughout the interview to persuade Miller to trust him and confide in him. The statement at issue can be viewed as a means of convincing Miller that Boyce was sympathetic, no matter what the state's reaction might be. 'You are not responsible' and 'You are not a criminal' thus would mean 'In my eyes, you are not responsible or a criminal and therefore you should relieve your conscience by talking to me, who understands you.' * * * Detective Boyce never stated that anyone but he thought that Miller was 'not a criminal' nor did he state that he had any authority to affect the charges brought against Miller. Miller's confession may have been made in the hope of leniency, but that does not mean that it was made in response to a promise of leniency. * * *

"Moreover, throughout the interview, Miller made remarks that indicate that he knew that this was an ordinary police interrogation rather than an encounter with a compassionate friend, and that he was aware that a confession would result in criminal prosecution and possibly in conviction and sentence. Throughout the session, he appears to have retained a suspicious, guarded attitude. * * *

"We have little doubt that Detective Boyce's encouraging words, perhaps in contribution with the sad announcement that the victim had just died, helped Miller to reach his decision to unburden himself. However, the test for voluntari-

---

c. For a discussion of the significance of a promise not to prosecute and related matters, see Notes 4, 5 & 6 following this case.

ness is not a but-for test, but a question of whether the confession was a product of free choice. * * * Many criminals experience an urge during interrogation to own up to their crimes. * * * Boyce's manner and his statements may have stirred this urge in Miller, but, in our view, they did not produce psychological pressure strong enough to overbear the will of a mature, experienced man, who was suffering from no mental or physical illness and was interrogated for less than an hour at a police station close to his home.

"Detective Boyce's method of interrogation might have overborne the will of another detainee, for example, a young, inexperienced person of lower intelligence than Miller, or a person suffering from a painful physical ailment. It might have overcome the will of Miller himself if the interrogation had been longer or if Miller had been refused food, sleep, or contact with a person he wished to see. Moreover, if Miller had made remarks that indicated that he truly believed that the state would treat him leniently because he was 'not responsible' for what he had done or that he believed that he would receive psychiatric help rather than punishment, we might not find the confession voluntary. We hold simply that, under the totality of the circumstances of this case, the confession was voluntarily given."

Dissenting Judge GIBBONS protested:

"[As] the majority well knows the state police are not in the business of acting as religious or psychiatric counselors. Boyce was not sympathetic. He was no more interested in helping Miller 'unburden his inner tensions' than he was in any other aspect of Miller's health. Instead Boyce was determined and ultimately successful in obtaining from an unwilling defendant the one thing that was his purpose—a confession. * * *

[At one point, when the interrogation was well underway, the following occurred:]

BOYCE: Now listen to me Frank. This hurts me more than it hurts you, because I love people.

MILLER: It can't hurt you anymore than it hurts me. * * *

BOYCE: Okay, listen Frank. If I promise to, you know, do all I can with the psychiatrist and everything, and we get the proper help for you, and get the proper help for you, will you talk to me about it?

MILLER: I can't talk to you about something I'm not ...

BOYCE: Alright, listen Frank, alright, honest. I know, I know what's going on inside you, Frank. I want to help you, you know, between us right now. I know what going on inside you, Frank, you've got to come forward and tell me that you want to help yourself. You've got to talk to me about it. This is the only way we'll be able to work it out. I mean, you know, listen, I want to help you, because you are in my mind, you are not responsible. You are not responsible, Frank. Frank, what's the matter?

MILLER: I feel bad.

BOYCE: Frank, listen to me, honest to God, I'm I'm telling you, Frank (inaudible). I know, it's going to bother you, Frank, it's going to bother you. It's there, it's not going to go away, it's there. It's right in front of you, Frank. Am I right or wrong?

MILLER: Yeah.

BOYCE: You can see it Frank, you can feel it, you can feel it, but you are not responsible. This is what I'm trying to tell you, but you've got to come forward and tell me. Don't, don't, don't let it eat you up, don't, don't fight it. You've got to rectify it, Frank. We've got to get together on this thing, or I, I mean really, you need help, you need proper help and you know it, my God, you know, in God's name you, you, you know it. You are not a criminal, you are not a criminal.

MILLER: Alright. Yes, I was over there and I talked to her about the cow and left. I left in my car and I stopped up on the road where, you know, where the cow had been and she followed me in her car ...

"Thus, approximately thirty minutes into the second interrogation, Miller made his first incriminating statement. By far the largest part of that thirty minutes is comprised of lies and promises by Boyce * * * directed to the sole purpose of obtaining a confession. There is nothing in the record from which it can be inferred that Miller's abandonment of his self-interested denials of involvement in the homicide was the product of any other influence. The majority opinion describes Boyce's conduct as if he were a confessor, offering solace under the seal of the confessional, or a psychiatrist offering relief from anxiety under the shelter of a physician-patient privilege, rather than what he was—a wily interrogator determined to break down Miller's resistance by lies and false promises. The majority's treatment of the police tactics leading to Miller's collapse is about as fair as those tactics. Confession may be good for the soul, but it was Miller's freedom, not his soul, that was at stake, and it was his freedom, not his soul, that interested Boyce. * * *

"The reason why the state had to preserve and make use of the tape-recorded interrogation appears in Boyce's testimony at the suppression hearing:

Q. I gather that [a] statement was never taken, is that right?

A. It was not.

Q. Why was that, Officer?

A. Momentarily after terminating this particular interview Mr. Miller went into as I can best define it a state of shock.

Q. What do you mean by that, sir?

A. He was sitting on a chair? ... Mr. Miller had been sitting on a chair, had slid off the chair on the floor maintaining a blank stare on his face, staring straight ahead and we were unable to get any type of verbal response from him. * * *

"Incredibly, the only reference in the majority's opinion to Miller's collapse is the cryptic sentence [that] 'One hour into the interrogation, Miller confessed to the murder of Deborah Margolin, then passed out.' The majority does not even recognize Miller's collapse into a catatonic state and his transportation to a hospital as relevant circumstances in its totality of the circumstances analysis! This most telling of all indications as to the effect on Miller of Boyce's tactics is simply ignored. [The majority] ignores the fact that at the end of the interrogation Miller collapsed and was taken to a hospital. How can it be honestly represented that he was suffering from no mental or physical illness? And, unless the majority identifies some other reason for Miller's abrupt abandonment of his self-interested denials of guilt than the psychological coercion exercised by Boyce, what other cause is left? * * *

"Boyce's second interrogation cannot be read in pieces. Its effect was cumulative, as it was intended to be. From the moment he began it, Boyce put relentless psychological pressure on Miller. Boyce repeatedly assured Miller that he only wanted to help Miller, that Miller was not a criminal, that Miller was not responsible for his actions, and that Miller would not be punished. In addition to these express promises, Boyce confused Miller by lying to him about the time of Ms. Margolin's death and the strength of the evidence against Miller.

"The majority emphasizes that the key issue is whether, in the totality of the circumstances, Miller's will was overborne. While I agree with the majority's general focus, I disagree with the majority's method of analysis. In ascertaining the effects of Boyce's interrogation tactics on Miller, the majority attempts to place itself in Miller's position and thereby evaluate the impact of Boyce's promises and lies. Unfortunately, we cannot know what effects those promises and lies had on Miller's will. Instead what we can know is that when, as in this case, the record reveals a series of repeated promises of psychological help and assurances that the suspect will not be punished, *Bram* requires as a matter of law that we hold the resulting confession to be coerced. Any other rule leads to the kind of subjective speculation that the majority engages in. Thus applying the *Bram* rule within the totality of the circumstances of Miller's interrogation, the confession used to commit Miller must be declared inadmissible as a violation of Miller's fifth amendment right to remain silent."

NOTES AND QUESTIONS

1. ***The malleability of the "totality of circumstances" test.*** Does *Miller v. Fenton* support the view that "the totality of the circumstances approach allows a court to reach any conclusion it wishes by accentuating the evidence that points in the direction the court wishes to go and understating the evidence that points in the other direction?" See George C. Thomas III, *Regulating Police Deception During Interrogation*, 39 Tex.Tech.L.Rev. 1293, 1304 (2007).

2. ***Should "police trickery" in obtaining confessions be barred? What is "trickery" in the confession context?*** Consider Note, 40 Stan.L.Rev. 1593, 1594–95 (1988): "The courts have not clearly defined the term 'trickery' and 'trickery' has been used interchangeably with 'misrepresentation,' 'artifice,' 'deception,' 'fraud,' and 'subterfuge.' This note argues that the term trickery, when used in the confessions context, should be defined as police elicitation of a confession by deliberate distortion of material fact, by failure to disclose to the defendant a material fact, or by playing on a defendant's emotions or scruples. Police trickery should be viewed as a type of fraud, the use of which as an interrogation tool is inconsistent with our adversarial system of criminal justice because it allows the prosecution an unfair, indeed an unconstitutional, advantage at trial."

3. ***The relationship between Miller and Detective Boyce.*** At one point the Miller majority observes that Boyce's statements to Miller that he is "not a criminal" who should be punished, and "not responsible" for anything he might have done "need not be understood as assurances of leniency" but could be viewed as the expression of sympathy by "a friend"—"a means of convincing Miller that Boyce [personally] was sympathetic, no matter what the state's reaction might be." At another point, however, the majority opinion observes that Miller's responses indicated "he knew that this was an ordinary police interrogation, rather than an encounter with a compassionate friend." Which is it?

To avoid the prohibition against obtaining confessions by promises of leniency, one might say, as the majority does at one point, that Boyce's "interrogation strategy was to present himself as a friend to whom Miller would unburden," and that, as the majority suggests at several places, the detective's strategy succeeded. If so, however, doesn't this raise another problem? If Boyce led Miller to believe he was a sympathetic friend didn't Boyce cause Miller to forget that his questioner was in an adversarial role and thus negate the effect of the Miranda warnings?

4. ***Drawing a line between expressions of sympathy and implied promises of leniency.*** Compare the Stanford Note with Phillip Johnson, *A*

Statutory Replacement for the Miranda Doctrine, 24 Am.Crim.L.Rev. 303, 305 (1987), proposing that the police be forbidden to make "any statement which is intended to imply or may reasonably be understood as implying that the suspect will not be prosecuted or punished," but approving police expressions of sympathy and compassion, whether real or feigned; police appeals to the suspect's conscience, religious or otherwise; and police appeals to the suspect's sympathy for the victim or other affected persons.

Observes Professor Johnson, id. at 310–11: "Offers of leniency can be made later in the plea bargaining process, where the accused is represented by counsel and can properly evaluate what is being offered. Promises of leniency from the police during interrogation are too likely to be deceptive, and too likely to give even an innocent suspect the impression that confession is the only way to escape conviction or mitigate the punishment. [However, police expressions of sympathy and compassion should be permitted because] a pose of sympathy is not overbearing or coercive, nor is it likely by itself to encourage an innocent person to provide a confession. A difficulty in this area is that the difference between expressions of compassionate understanding on the one hand, and implied promises of leniency on the other, is at the margin sometimes a matter of emphasis and nuance." Did Detective Boyce cross the line in the Miller case? See id. at 311.

5. *Bram v. United States a century later.* As the *Miller v. Fenton* majority indicates, few courts today take literally the statement in *Bram* that, in order to be admissible, a confession "must not be . . . obtained by any direct or implied promises, however slight." "The modern view," observes Paul Marcus, *It's Not Just About Miranda: Determining the Voluntariness of Confessions in Criminal Prosecutions*, 40 Val.U.L.Rev. 601, 606–07 (2006), "is that threats and promises are to be taken seriously but that these are rarely determinative on their own. If such evidence is present, the court must view that inducement along with other key factors in determining if the resulting statement was given voluntarily. As explained by one court, the key question is whether the inducement is 'so attractive as to render a confession involuntary.' "

Have the courts been moving in the wrong direction? Are they giving insufficient weight to the effects of a promise of leniency on a suspect? Consider Richard A. Leo, *Police Interrogation and American Justice* 309, 311 (2008): "In the modern era, * * * promises of leniency and threats of punishment, whether implicit or explicit, are the primary causes of police-induced false confessions."

6. *Resisting "freeing a murder" because of a promise not to prosecute.* The great reluctance of some courts to "free a murderer" even when the police made a flat promise not to prosecute him if he confesses—without taking into account other factors such as the length of the questioning, the defendant's sophistication, and his understanding of his rights at the time of the questioning—is illustrated by UNITED STATES v. LeBRUN, 363 F.3d 715 (8th Cir.2004) (en banc). In upholding the admissibility of the confession, a 7–4 majority, per Hansen, J. observed:

"Even assuming that a reasonable person would view the Agents' statements as a promise, a promise made by law enforcement 'does not render a confession involuntary per se' [quoting an Eighth Circuit case]. [Our] polestar always must be to determine whether or not the authorities overbore the defendant's will and critically impaired his capacity for self-determination. * * *

"We place substantial weight on the fact that LeBrun confessed after a mere thirty-three minutes, [that he] testified that he had a subjective understanding of his *Miranda* rights at the time of the interview, [and that he had] attended five years of college and one year of law school and worked as a manager in a real estate office."

"[The] videotape of the interview demonstrates that LeBrun was composed and aware of his surroundings and the circumstances confronting him. [After] watching the videotape, it is apparent that LeBrun is an intelligent, calculating person who erroneously perceived a substantial loophole in the prosecution's case and tried to take advantage of it by confessing to 'spontaneous' murder. Whatever his motivation, it is clear to us that LeBrun's capacity for self-determination was not impaired. Thus, the district court erred in concluding that LeBrun's confession was involuntary."

Speaking for four judges, Judge Morris Arnold, J., dissented:

"[The] clear purport of what the agents said in this case was that Mr. LeBrun would not be prosecuted if he said what the agents wanted him to say, and they even assured [him that the victim's] family approved of the deal. Indeed, they said the family would not pursue civil remedies if he confessed and apologized. What the family wanted, the interrogators said, was simply to clear [the victim's] name. [We] need [to] consider the possibility that what lies at the bottom of these kinds of cases is not merely an aversion to something called coercion, but a general uneasiness about the fairness of admitting confessions that were induced by knowing, lurid falsehoods and unfulfilled promises, whether 'coercive' or not."

7. False verbal assertions by the police vs. the fabrication of scientific evidence. *State v. Cayward*, 552 So.2d 971 (Fla.App.1989), drew a line between police deception generally (which does not render a confession involuntary per se) and the "manufacturing" of false documents or scientific evidence by the police (which "has no place in our criminal justice system"). The case arose as follows: The police suspected defendant of sexually assaulting and killing his five-year-old niece. They intentionally fabricated laboratory reports indicating that a scientific test established that the semen stains on the victim's underwear came from defendant and showed the reports to him. He confessed soon after. In upholding the trial court's suppression of the confession, the District Court of Appeal of Florida observed:

"We think [that] both the suspect's and the public's expectations concerning the built-in adversariness of police interrogations do not encompass the notion that the police will knowingly fabricate tangible documentation or physical evidence against an individual. [The] manufacturing of false documents by police officials offends our traditional notions of due process. [Moreover,] manufactured documents have the potential of indefinite life and the facial appearance of authenticity." Thus, they "might be disclosed to the media as a result of the public records law" or find their way into the courtroom.

Many courts, however, balk at establishing a bright line between police deception generally and false documents or fake scientific evidence. "For these courts," observers Paul Marcus, *It's Not Just about Miranda*, p. 717 supra, at 615, "the question remains: With the falsified documents, is this considered action that would 'have induced a false confession.'?"

On the other hand, why should the *Cayward* approach be limited to forged documents or fake scientific evidence? Why shouldn't it go further? Consider Miriam S. Gohara, *A Lie for a Lie: False Confessions and the Case for Reconsidering the Legality of Deceptive Interrogation Techniques*, 33 Ford.Urb.L.J. 791, 833 (2006): "[There] is no principled distinction between a fake document and an officer's oral report to a suspect that he has failed a polygraph examination, which is a commonly used technique for eliciting confessions. * * * Forgery and oral representation differ from one another only in degree rather than in kind. [There] may be no documentation of the fact that the suspect did not in fact fail the polygraph, but there may very well remain documentation of the officer's report that he did fail."

8. *Offering to protect a prisoner from physical harm at the hands of other inmates.* Consider ARIZONA v. FULMINANTE, 499 U.S. 279 (1991) (other aspects of which are discussed at p. 1569). The case arose as follows: After defendant Fulminante's 11-year-old stepdaughter, Jeneane, was murdered, he was convicted of an unrelated federal crime and incarcerated in a federal prison. There he was befriended by another inmate, Sarivola, who was a paid informant for the FBI masquerading as an organized crime figure. Upon hearing a rumor that defendant had killed his stepdaughter, Sarivola brought up the subject several times, but defendant repeatedly denied any involvement in the murder. Then Sarivola told defendant that he knew he was "starting to get some tough treatment" from other inmates because of the rumor that he had killed his stepdaughter but that he, Sarivola, would protect defendant from his fellow inmates if he told him the truth about the murder. Defendant then confessed to Sarivola that he had sexually molested and killed Jeneane. The confession was admitted at defendant's trial and he was convicted of murder and sentenced to death. On appeal, the state supreme court held that the confession was coerced. Although it considered the question "a close one," a 5–4 majority of the Supreme Court, per White, J., agreed with the state supreme court:

"In applying the totality of the circumstances test to determine that the confession to Sarivola was coerced, the Arizona Supreme Court focused on a number of relevant facts. First, the court noted that 'because [Fulminante] was an alleged child murderer, he was in physical harm at the hands of other inmates.' In addition, Sarivola was aware that Fulminante was receiving 'rough treatment from the guys.' Using his knowledge of these threats, Sarivola offered to protect Fulminante in exchange for a confession to Jeneane's murder and 'in response to Sarivola's offer of protection [Fulminante] confessed.' Agreeing with Fulminante that 'Sarivola's promise was "extremely coercive," 'the Arizona Court declared: '[T]he confession was obtained as a direct result of extreme coercion and was tendered in the belief that the defendant's life was in jeopardy if he did not confess. * * * '

"We normally give great deference to the factual findings of the state court. Nevertheless, 'the ultimate issue of "voluntariness" is a legal question requiring independent federal determination.' Although the question is a close one, we agree [that] Fulminante's confession was coerced. The Arizona Supreme Court found a credible threat of physical violence unless Fulminante confessed. [A] finding of coercion need not depend upon actual violence by a government agent; a credible threat is sufficient. [As in *Payne v. Arkansas*, 356 U.S. 560 (1958)], where the Court found that a confession was coerced because the interrogating police officer had promised that if the accused confessed, the officer would protect the accused from an angry mob outside the jailhouse door, so too here, the Arizona Supreme Court found that it was fear of physical violence, absent protection from his friend (and Government agent) Sarivola, which motivated Fulminante to confess. Accepting the Arizona court's finding, permissible on this record, that there was a credible threat of physical violence, we agree that Fulminante's will was overborne in such a way as to render his confession the product of coercion."

Dissenting on this issue, Rehnquist, C.J., joined by O'Connor, Kennedy and Souter, JJ., was "at a loss to see how the Supreme Court of Arizona reached the conclusion that it did":

"Fulminante offered no evidence that he believed his life was in danger or that he in fact confessed to Sarivola in order to obtain the proffered protection. Indeed, he had stipulated that '[a]t no time did the defendant indicate he was in fear of other inmates nor did he ever seek Mr. Sarivola's "protection." 'Sarivola's testimony that he told Fulminante that 'if [he] would tell the truth, he could be protected,' adds little if anything to the substance of the parties' stipulation. The decision of the Supreme Court of Arizona rests on an assumption that is squarely contrary to this stipulation, and one that is not supported by any testimony of Fulminante.

"The facts of record in the present case are quite different from those present in cases where we have found confessions to be coerced and involuntary. Since Fulminante was unaware that Sarivola was an FBI informant, there existed none of 'the danger of coercion result[ing] from the interaction of custody and official interrogation.' *Illinois v. Perkins* [p. 615]. [The] conversations between Sarivola and Fulminante were not lengthy, and the defendant was free at all times to leave Sarivola's company. Sarivola at no time threatened him or demanded that he confess; he simply requested that he speak the truth about the matter. Fulminante was an experienced habitue of prisons, and presumably able to fend for himself. In concluding on these facts that Fulminante's confession was involuntary, the Court today embraces a more expansive definition of that term than is warranted by any of our decided cases."

B. COLORADO v. CONNELLY: DID THE COURT DECLINE TO EXPAND THE "VOLUNTARINESS" TEST OR DID IT REVISE THE TEST SIGNIFICANTLY?

In COLORADO v. CONNELLY, 479 U.S. 157 (1986) (also discussed at pp. 547–48, fns. b and c), the Court held, per REHNQUIST, C.J., that "coercive police activity is a necessary predicate to the finding that a confession is not 'voluntary' within the meaning of the Due Process Clause"; "[a]bsent police conduct causally related to the confession, there is simply no basis for concluding that any state action has deprived a criminal defendant of due process of law." The case arose as follows:

Respondent, a mentally ill person flew from Boston to Denver, approached a uniformed police officer on a downtown Denver street and, without any prompting, told the officer that "he had killed someone" and wanted to talk to the officer about it. Respondent was then handcuffed and informed of his Miranda rights. After stating that he understood his rights, respondent elaborated further on the initial statement. A homicide detective soon arrived on the scene. He readvised respondent of his rights, and asked him "what he had on his mind." Respondent then stated that he had come all the way from Boston because he wanted to confess to murdering a young girl, a crime he had committed in Denver nine months earlier. He then gave the detective the name of the victim. Next, respondent was taken to police headquarters, where records revealed that an unidentified female body had been discovered in the area respondent described. Connelly then made more incriminating statements and took the police to the place where he said the murder had occurred.

Respondent was initially found incompetent to stand trial. But he achieved competency after six months of hospitalization and treatment with antipsychotic and sedative medication. A psychiatrist, previously appointed to conduct a competency examination of respondent, testified for the defense that Connelly's statements to the police had resulted from "command auditory hallucinations," a symptom of his mental disorder. The "voice of God" had told Connelly to return to Denver to confess his crime. When he returned, the same voice became stronger and told him either to confess to the killing or to commit suicide. At that point, reluctantly following the voice's command, Connelly approached the first officer he could find and confessed. Because people suffering from command hallucinations feel they must do whatever the voice tells them, the psychiatrist was of the opinion that Connelly was unable to make a free and intelligent decision about whether to speak with, and to confess to, the police.

The trial court suppressed Connelly's statements because they were "involuntary"; respondent had not exercised "free will" in choosing to speak to the police, but had been "compelled" by his illness to confess. In upholding the trial court on this issue, the Colorado Supreme Court observed that "[o]ne's capacity for rational judgment and free choice may be overborne as much by certain forms of severe illness as by external pressure." The U.S. Supreme Court reversed:

"[The confession cases] considered by this Court over the 50 years since *Brown v. Mississippi* have focused upon the crucial element of police overreaching. [A]ll have contained a substantial element of coercive police conduct. Absent police conduct causally related to the confession, there is simply no basis for concluding that any state actor has deprived a criminal defendant of due process of law. * * *

"Respondent relies on *Blackburn v. Alabama*, 361 U.S. 199 (1960), and *Townsend v. Sain* [discussed briefly at p. 548, fn. c, a case some commentators had read as barring the use of confessions obtained from a person whose volitional power is seriously impaired, whatever the reason]. But respondent's reading of *Blackburn* and *Townsend* ignores the integral element of police overreaching present in both cases. In *Blackburn*, the Court found that [defendant] was probably insane at the time of his confession and the police learned during the interrogation that he had a history of mental problems.

"The police exploited this weakness with coercive tactics [and these] tactics supported a finding that the confession was involuntary. * * * *Townsend* presented a similar instance of police wrongdoing. In that case, a police physician had given Townsend a drug with truth-serum properties. The subsequent confession, obtained by officers who knew that Townsend had been given drugs, was held involuntary. These two cases demonstrate that while mental condition is surely relevant to an individual's susceptibility to police coercion, mere examination of the confessant's state of mind can never conclude the due process inquiry.

"[The] difficulty with the approach of the Supreme Court of Colorado is that it fails to recognize the essential link between coercive activity of the State, on the one hand, and a resulting confession by a defendant, on the other. The flaw in respondent's constitutional argument is that it would expand our previous line of 'voluntariness' cases into a far-ranging requirement that courts must divine a defendant's motivation for speaking or acting as he did even though there be no claim that governmental conduct coerced his decision.[a]

"The most outrageous behavior by a private party seeking to secure evidence against a defendant does not make that evidence inadmissible under the Due Process Clause. * * * [S]uppressing respondent's statements would serve absolutely no purpose in enforcing constitutional guarantees. The purpose of excluding confessions seized in violation of the Constitution is to substantially deter future violations of the Constitution. Only if we were to establish a brand new constitutional right—the right of a criminal defendant to confess to his crime only when totally rational and properly motivated—could respondent's present claim be sustained.

"We have previously cautioned against expanding 'currently applicable exclusionary rules by erecting additional barriers to placing truthful and probative evidence before state juries * * *.' *Lego v. Twomey* (1972) [p. 927]. We abide by that counsel now. [Respondent] would now have us require sweeping inquiries into the state of mind of a criminal defendant who has confessed, inquiries quite divorced from any coercion brought to bear on the defendant by the State. We think the Constitution rightly leaves this sort of inquiry to be resolved by state

---

a. Consider, e.g., United States v. Erving L., 147 F.3d 1240 (10th Cir.1998), which, relying on *Connelly*, upheld the admissibility of a confession coerced by the defendant's mother.

laws governing the admission of evidence and erects no standard of its own in this area. A statement rendered by one in the condition of respondent might be proved to be quite unreliable, but this is a matter to be governed by the evidentiary laws of the forum and not by the Due Process Clause * * *.''

Dissenting Justice BRENNAN, joined by Marshall, J., recalled that the *Blackburn* Court had observed: "Surely in the present stage of our civilization a most basic sense of justice is affronted by the spectacle of incarcerating a human being upon the basis of a statement he made while insane * * *." "[T]he use of a mentally ill person's involuntary confession," maintained Justice Brennan, "is antithetical to the notion of fundamental fairness embodied in the Due Process Clause." He argued that "[the] holding that involuntary confessions are only those procured through police misconduct [is] inconsistent with the Court's historical insistence that only confessions reflecting an exercise of free will be admitted into evidence" and that "[u]ntil today, we have never upheld the admission of a confession that does not reflect the exercise of free will."[b]

He continued:

"Since the Court redefines voluntary confessions to include confessions by mentally ill individuals, the reliability of these confessions becomes a central concern. A concern for reliability is inherent in our criminal justice system, which relies upon accusatorial rather than inquisitorial practices. * * *

"Because the admission of a confession so strongly tips the balance against the defendant in the adversarial process, we must be especially careful about a confession's reliability. We have to date not required a finding of reliability for involuntary confessions only because all such confessions have been excluded upon a finding of involuntariness, regardless of reliability. The Court's adoption today of a restrictive definition of an 'involuntary' confession will require heightened scrutiny of a confessions' reliability.

"The instant case starkly highlights the danger of admitting a confession by a person with a severe mental illness. The trial court made no findings concerning the reliability of Mr. Connelly's involuntary confession, since it believed that the confession was excludable on the basis of involuntariness. However, the overwhelming evidence in the record points to the unreliability of Mr. Connelly's delusional mind. * * *

"Moreover, the record is barren of any corroboration of the mentally ill defendant's confession. No physical evidence links the defendant to the alleged crime. Police did not identify the alleged victim's body as the woman named by the defendant. Mr. Connelly identified the alleged scene of the crime, but it has not been verified that the unidentified body was found there or that a crime actually occurred there. There is not a shred of competent evidence in this record linking the defendant to the charged homicide. There is only Mr. Connelly's confession.

---

b. The dissenters took sharp exception to the majority's reading of *Townsend*: "[Although the majority maintains that the confession in that case was obtained by officers who knew that a police doctor had given defendant a drug with truth-serum properties], in fact [as the *Townsend* Court pointed out], 'the police * * * did not know what [medications] the doctor had given [the defendant].' And the *Townsend* Court expressly states that police wrongdoing was not an essential factor:

" 'It is not significant that the drug may have been administered and the questions asked by persons unfamiliar with [the drug's] properties as a "truth serum," if these properties exist. Any questioning by police officers which *in fact* produces a confession which is not the product of a free intellect renders that confession inadmissible. The Court has usually so stated the test.' (Emphasis in original.)"

"Minimum standards of due process should require that the trial court find substantial indicia of reliability, on the basis of evidence extrinsic to the confession itself, before admitting the confession of a mentally ill person into evidence. I would require the trial court to make such a finding on remand. To hold otherwise allows the State to imprison and possibly to execute a mentally ill defendant based solely upon an inherently unreliable confession."

Notes and Questions

1. *What if the Ku Klux Klan had kidnapped and tortured a murder suspect?* The *Connelly* Court tells us that "the most outrageous behavior by a private party" would not make the resulting confession inadmissible under the Due Process Clause and that suppressing the confession under such circumstances "would serve absolutely no purpose in enforcing constitutional guarantees." Do you agree? Suppose the Ku Klux Klan kidnapped an African–American suspected of murder, hanged him by a rope to the limb of a tree, let him down, then hung him again, and when he was let down the second time, still protesting his innocence, tied him to a tree and severely whipped him until he confessed?[a] Suppose, further, that the state supreme court held the confession admissible, noting that it had been corroborated by extrinsic evidence. Would (should) the U.S. Supreme Court hold the confession admissible? Consider *Commonwealth v. Mahnke*, 335 N.E.2d 660 (Sup.Jud.Ct.Mass. 1975), which arose as follows: When a young woman disappeared, many suspected her boyfriend (the defendant) of foul play. After harassing the defendant for months, a group of friends and relatives of the missing woman assaulted and kidnaped defendant and drove him to an isolated, snowbound hunting cabin 128 miles away. There he was questioned by three and then five people for at least six hours. The questioning was interspersed with extremely rough language and threats that the defendant would never leave alive. Finally the defendant confessed. He was convicted of second-degree murder. The trial judge ruled that all statements the defendant made to his kidnappers prior to leaving the cabin were inadmissible, but ruled that, because of a "break in the stream of events," statements he made later were admissible. The Supreme Judicial Court of Massachusetts, per Tauro, C.J., agreed, but directed a verdict of a lesser degree of guilt. Massachusetts' highest court condemned the use of statements obtained at the cabin as follows:

"[The prohibition against the use of coerced confessions applies] even though the statements were extracted by private coercion unalloyed with any official government involvement. [A] statement obtained through coercion and introduced at trial is every bit as offensive to civilized standards of adjudication when the coercion flows from private hands as when official depredations elicit a confession. Statements extracted by a howling lynch mob or a lawless pack of vigilantes from a terrorized, pliable suspect are repugnant to due process mandates of fundamental fairness and protection against compulsory self-incrimination."

2. *Is "the (exclusionary) tail wagging the (due process) dog"?* Consider Laurence Benner, *Requiem for Miranda: The Rehnquist Court's Voluntariness Doctrine in Historical Perspective*, 67 Wash.U.L.Q. 59, 136–37 (1989):

"[The *Connelly* Court] concluded that in the absence of coercive police misconduct 'suppressing [Connelly's] statements would serve absolutely no pur-

---

   a. The coercion imposed on the defendant in the hypothetical case is essentially the coercion experienced by the defendant in the first fourteenth amendment due process confession case decided by the U.S. Supreme Court, *Brown v. Mississippi* (1936) (p. 548), except that law enforcement officials were involved in extracting the confession in the *Brown* case. See generally Morgan Cloud, *Torture and Truth*, 74 Texas L.Rev. 1211, 1213–15 (1996); Michael J. Klarman, *The Racial Origins of Modern Criminal Procedure* (quoted at p. 49).

pose in enforcing constitutional guarantees.' From this narrow premise, the Court then leaped to the broad conclusion that the use of Connelly's deranged statements as evidence against him did not violate the due process clause.

"But surely this is the (exclusionary) tail wagging the (due process) dog, for the upshot of the Court's position is that unless exclusion will deter someone in an official capacity, there can be no due process violation no matter how unjust the result. By allowing the deterrence rationale for the exclusionary rule to control the nature of the due process inquiry, the Court thus permits the logic of deterrence to shape the actual content of due process itself. Under this formula any concern for justice is excluded from the equation. Indeed, any attempt to develop a coherent theory of justice under the due process clause is precluded."

3. Confessions vs. guilty pleas. The *Connelly* Court balked at requiring "sweeping inquiries into the state of mind of a criminal defendant who has confessed, inquiries quite divorced from any [police] coercion brought to bear on the defendant." Would such inquiries be any more burdensome than constitutionally required inquiries into a defendant's competency to stand trial, to waive her right to counsel, or to be executed? See Benner, supra, at 137. Connelly, recalls Professor Benner, "was found incompetent to stand trial immediately following the making of his custodial confession. Does it not therefore appear incongruous that Connelly could not have pled guilty in open court, on the same day he sealed his fate with a confession obtained within the precincts of the Denver police headquarters?"

4. Should the admissibility of a confession turn on whether in fact it is the product of a "free will" or whether in fact it is voluntary? What is the *Connelly* dissenters' argument? That a confession by a mentally ill (or drugged) person is inherently unreliable or at least highly suspect? Or that the use of a mentally ill (or drugged) person's confession violates due process regardless of how impressively corroborated or otherwise reliable the confession turns out to be? Or both? If a confession is not the product of police overreaching and doubts about its reliability have been dispelled, why should it matter whether it was in fact involuntarily made?

(a) Changing the facts of the *Townsend* case: In *Townsend*, the defendant was suffering from severe heroin withdrawal symptoms. A police doctor was called in to treat this condition and injected the suspect with a drug that, unknown to the doctor or the police who subsequently questioned him (according to the record), had the properties of a "truth serum." About an hour later, defendant confessed.

Suppose that Townsend's sister had visited him in his cell and given him pills to relieve his suffering and that, unknown to her, these pills had the properties of a "truth serum." Suppose further that after taking these pills Townsend had told a guard that he wanted to confess and then had proceeded to do so. Would (should) such a confession be excluded? Why (not)?

Is the confession in the hypothetical *Townsend* case any more an exercise of "free will" or any less involuntary in fact than the confession in the actual *Townsend* case? If there is a distinction, is it that in the actual case the police doctor or the police who subsequently questioned Townsend were negligent? That even if the "truth serum" were not the result of police wrongdoing, it was still the result of their doing?

(b) Changing the facts of the *Connelly* case: Suppose that Connelly had never returned to Denver, but had phoned a Denver police officer from Boston and—with the "voice of God" ringing in his ears—had made a detailed confession over the phone. Or suppose Connelly had stayed in Boston and—with the "voice of God" doing the dictation—had written out a detailed confession and mailed it to the Denver police department. Would (should) such confessions be admissible? What would Justices Brennan and Marshall say? How, if at all, are the confessions in the hypotheticals different from the statements Connelly made in the actual case?

(c) A court should care whether a confession is the product of police wrongdoing or whether it is reliable, but why should it care whether it is voluntary or involuntary in fact? If a confession is neither the product of impermissible police methods nor untrustworthy (i.e. if doubts about its reliability have been removed), why should the confession's voluntariness be a relevant constitutional question?

5. *Does the Connelly case mark the decline and fall of the "reliability" element?* As we have seen (pp. 549–50), the reliability of a confession does not necessarily make it admissible. But should the unreliability of a confession (or the absence of substantial indicia of reliability) render a confession inadmissible as a matter of federal constitutional law? Compare George Dix, *Federal Constitutional Confession Law: The 1986 and 1987 Supreme Court Terms*, 67 Tex.L.Rev. 231, 272–76 (1988) with Albert Alschuler, *Constraint and Confession*, 74 Denv. U. L.Rev. 957, 959 (1997).

Professor Dix finds "the rejection of reliability as a relevant consideration in federal constitutional law" "the most surprising aspect" of *Connelly*. The opinion, comments Dix, "misleadingly represents that the Court's prior decisions definitively settled the matter, when in fact, until *Connelly*, reliability played an important role in traditional confession law analysis." Dix concludes that "at least in the absence of more thorough consideration than *Connelly* demonstrates, a total deconstitutionalization of traditionally important reliability issues is unjustified."

"Just as the Constitution does not mandate the exclusion of unreliable eyewitness testimony," maintains Professor Alschuler, "it does not mandate the exclusion of unreliable confessions. [The] Constitution requires the exclusion of unreliable eyewitness testimony only when improper governmental conduct—for example, an impermissibly suggestive police line-up—has produced it. The rule should be no different for unreliable confessions. Unless improper governmental conduct has generated a confession, the Constitution should give the defendant only a right to present evidence of the confession's unreliability to the jury."

THE IMPACT OF *MIRANDA* ON THE "VOLUNTARINESS" TEST

Consider Steven B. Duke, *Does Miranda Protect the Innocent or the Guilty?*, 10 Chapman L.Rev. 551, 562–64 (2007):

"[A] weighty counterbalance is the effect that *Miranda* warnings have on judges: psychologically, politically and doctrinally. If warnings were delivered by the police and a waiver was given or signed, it is almost impossible to persuade a judge that the resultant confession or admission is 'involuntary.' * * *

"Before *Miranda*, a major concern of the Supreme Court was the voluntariness of confessions. The Court was developing some rather stringent (if unclear) requirements on the admissibility of confessions. *Miranda*, however, has been a major contributor to the demise of that concern and to an inversion of the law governing involuntary confessions. Many confessions that would have been found involuntary in 1966 are considered voluntary today.

" * * * Even more important than its articulation of voluntariness criteria is the message the Supreme Court sends to the lower courts in its case selection and decision patterns. In the three decades prior to *Miranda*, the Supreme Court held that confessions were involuntary in at least twenty-three cases. In the four decades since *Miranda*, [the] Court has decided only three voluntariness cases and has only held two confessions involuntary: *Mincey v. Arizona* [Casebook, p. 552

n.c.] and *Arizona v. Fulminante* [Casebook, p. 727]. The Court has also moved from a voluntariness test related to the reliability of the confession to a doctrine that explicitly rejects such a concern. Police misconduct, not reliability, is now the sole determinant of involuntariness. [In] what has become essentially a faux remedy, the *Miranda* warning regime has virtually replaced a vibrant and developing voluntariness inquiry that took into account the vulnerabilities of the particular suspect as well as the inducements and conditions of the interrogation. As far as the Supreme Court is concerned, that protection of the innocent has vanished from the law of confessions."

THE CENTRAL PARK JOGGER CASE—AND FALSE CONFESSIONS GENERALLY

"Like many criminal justice officials, most people appear to believe in what [Richard Leo] has labeled 'the myth of psychological interrogation': that an innocent person will not falsely confess to a serious crime unless he is physically tortured or mentally ill. This myth is, of course, easily dispelled by the literature on miscarriages of justice, as well as the psychological and sociological literature on coercive persuasion and interrogation-induced false confession."

—Steven A. Drizin & Richard A. Leo, *The Problem of False Confessions in the Post–DNA World*, 82 N.C.L.Rev. 891, 910 (2004).

———

"As both experimental and field studies have demonstrated, criminal officials and jurors often place almost blind faith in the evidentiary value of confession evidence—even when, as in all the cases [of false confessions] in this study, the confession was not accompanied by any credible corroboration and there was compelling evidence of the defendant's factual innocence. Criminal justice officials and lay jurors who prosecute and convict false confessors in such high percentages appear to treat confession evidence as more probative than any other piece of case evidence and thus as essentially dispositive of the defendant's guilt—even when the confession lacks corroboration and is almost certainly the product of psychological coercion and/or police misconduct."

—Id. at 996.

———

"The problem with the empirical case for greater due process regulation [of confessions] is that we have no idea what rate of false confessions is produced by the [interrogation] tactics that the critics have targeted. * * * Maybe even more important, we do not even know if the tactics identified by the critics produce *disproportionate* numbers of false confessions. Perhaps they do not. * * *

"[It] would not surprise me if the vast majority of custodial interrogations involve the features condemned by critics. If so, the fact that a study of false confessions will frequently disclose the use of the interrogation tactics identified by [some professor] provides no basis to conclude that these features increase the likelihood that a confession is false."

—Lawrence Rosenthal, *Against Orthodoxy: Miranda Is Not Prophylactic and the Constitution Is Not Perfect*, 10 Chapman L.Rev. 579, 616–17 (2007).

———

The Central Park Jogger case is one of the most dramatic illustrations of how false confessions are obtained in high-profile cases. On the night of April 19, 1989, a woman jogger was brutally beaten, raped, and left for dead in New York City's Central Park. Nearly thirty Black and Latino male teenagers were questioned about their activities in Central Park that night. "Demonstrating remarkable efficiency, within forty-eight hours of the attack, the detectives assigned to the case had secured written, oral, and/or videotaped confessions from five teenage suspects."[a] SHARON L. DAVIES, *The Reality of False Confessions—Lessons of the Central Park Jogger Case*, 30 NYU Rev. of Law & Social Change 209, 215 (2006).

The five suspects ranged in age from fourteen to sixteen. Before making incriminating statements, each had been advised of their rights, but waived them and agreed to talk to the police without counsel present. "While each of the teens admitted *some* involvement in [the assault of the jogger], each minimized his own role and none admitted to having intercourse with her. But their statements plainly made them accomplices to rape under the state's 'acting in concert' law." Davies (at 216).

Without the confessions of the five defendants, there would have been no case. Because of her serious injuries, the victim was unable to identify her attackers and no other eyewitness placed any of the defendants on the scene. Moreover, pre-trial tests on the blood and semen found inside the jogger's body and nearby failed to link the defendants to the jogger's rape and assault. But DNA test in 1989 were still in their infancy and the prosecution could explain away the failure of science to support his case by maintaining that at least one other participant in the crime (and presumably the source of the semen found at the scene) had not been apprehended.

Before the trial began, the trial judge issued a comprehensive memorandum concluding that the interrogation methods used to obtain the statements from the five defendants satisfied all legal requirements. If so, comments Professor Davies (at 223): "[It] follows that it is possible for the police to obtain a confession that is false without constitutional error. This acknowledgment has potentially devastating implications for a system committed to taking all proper steps to bringing the guilty to justice while avoiding the conviction of the innocent. If the time-tested interrogation techniques used in the Central Park case could produce five false confessions within a forty-eight hour period, it is likely that the same techniques produced similar results in the past, and will produce them again."

At the conclusion of two severed trials, all five defendants were convicted of charges related to the jogger's rape and assault and sentenced to lengthy terms of imprisonment.

Thirteen years after the Central Park Jogger defendants had been convicted, and at a time when all but one of the five convicted teenagers had served their sentences and been released, Matias Reyes, a known serial rapist and convicted killer, confessed that he, and he alone, had raped and beaten the Central Park jogger. DNA analysis of the semen found at the scene of the crime confirmed that indeed he had done so.

In retrospect, it is easy to second-guess the conviction of the five teenagers. But consider Professor Davies (at 213): "[Even] had I not been appointed to serve as a federal prosecutor just after the trial of [the Central Park Jogger defendants], I am sure that I would have found (as so many others found) the teenagers' confessions to the crime sufficiently trustworthy and their pre-trial recantations of those confessions sufficiently implausible, to justify their convictions. It was

---

a. Although the police videotaped some of the confessions, they did not tape any of the interrogations which preceded the confessions.

simply impossible for many to believe that anyone could be compelled to falsely admit to having participated in such a vicious attack."[4]

STEVEN A. DRIZIN & RICHARD A. LEO, *The Problem of False Confessions in the Post–DNA World*, 82 N.C.L.Rev. 891, 905 (2004), report that of 140 convicted prisoners released and exonerated as a result of DNA testing at the time they wrote their article, approximately 25% of these wrongful convictions were caused by false confessions. Professors Drizin and Leo reported and analyzed 125 proven false confessions, all of which occurred in the post-*Miranda* era (55% between 1993–2003) and were struck by the fact (id. at 995–96) that—

"more than four-fifths (81%) of the innocent defendants who chose to take their case to trial were wrongfully convicted 'beyond a reasonable doubt' even though their confession was ultimately demonstrated to be false. [An] additional fourteen false confessions in this study * * * chose to accept a plea bargain rather than take their case to trial—despite their innocence—typically to avoid the death penalty. Remarkably, then, 86% (or almost nine of every ten) of the individuals in our sample whose false confessions were not discovered by police or dismissed by prosecutors before trial were eventually convicted. * * * This study adds to a growing body of research demonstrating the power of confession evidence to substantially prejudice a trier of fact's ability to even-handedly evaluate a criminal defendant's culpability."

Professor Leo considers it highly significant that more than 80% of the 125 false confessions analyzed in the 2004 study he did with Professor Drizin occurred in homicide cases and that 80 percent of the false confession studied by Professor Samuel Gross and his colleagues occurred in murder cases. See RICHARD A. LEO, *Police Interrogation and American Justice* 245 (2008). Professor Leo, id. at 246, suggests why this is so: "Police are under greater institutional pressure to solve serious and high-profile cases and therefore put more time, effort and pressure into interrogating suspects—conducting longer and more intense interrogations—and trying to elicit confessions. Investigators are thus more likely to use psychologically coercive techniques or simply wear down a suspect. In homicides, the fact that the victim is dead and police frequently lack any eyewitnesses makes getting a confession even more important."

As discussed earlier, see Notes 28 and 29 at pp. 671–72 supra, the mentally retarded and juveniles are more vulnerable to the pressures of interrogation and thus less likely to withstand accusatorial police interrogation. As a result, they are disproportionately represented in the reported false confession cases. Drizin and Leo (at 920) emphasize, however, that most reported false confessions "are from cognitively and intellectually normal individuals."

"The risk of harm caused by false confessions could be greatly reduced," maintain Professors Drizin and Leo (at 997), "if police were required to electronically record the entirety of all custodial interrogations of suspects." They give three reasons:

(1) taping "creates an objective comprehensive, and reviewable record of the interrogation";

---

4. Welsh White addresses the widespread skepticism that an innocent suspect can be compelled to confess falsely (absent physical abuse) in Welsh White, *Miranda's Waning Protections* 139 (2001) ("Even if the police employ interrogation techniques that exert considerable pressure, most people believe that a normal suspect would not confess to something he did not do.").

(2) taping "leads to a higher level of scrutiny (by police officials as well as others) [that will] improve the quality of interrogation practices and thus increase the ability of police to separate the innocent from the guilty"; and

(3) a taping requirement "creates the opportunity for various criminal justice officials to more closely monitor both the quality of police interrogation and the reliability of confession statements" and to enable all the participants in the criminal justice system "to more easily detect false confessions and thus more easily prevent their admission into evidence."

Drizin and Leo (at 948) deem it noteworthy that, of those cases in which the length of interrogation could be determined, most of the false confessors were subjected to questioning for an extraordinarily long time:

"More than 80% of the false confessors were interrogated for more than six hours, and 50% [were] interrogated for more than twelve hours. The average length of interrogation was 16.3 hours, and the median length of interrogation was twelve hours. These figures are especially striking when they are compared to studies of routine police interrogations in America, which suggest that more than 90% of normal interrogations last less than two hours. These figures support the observations of many researchers that interrogation-induced false observations tend to be correlated with lengthy interrogations in which the innocent suspect's resistance is worn down, coercive techniques are used, and the suspect is made to feel helpless, regardless of his innocence."[a]

In his recent book, recalling his 2004 study with Drizin, Leo favors setting time limits for police interrogations (at 311–12): "Lengthy incommunicado interrogation is not only inherently unfair, [but] far more common in false confession cases than other ones. * * * Specifying a time limit on interrogations of no more than four hours should diminish the risk of eliciting false confessions while maintaining the ability of police to elicit true confessions from the guilty. [For, as the authors of a widely-used police interrogation manual have] pointed out, 'rarely will a competent interrogator require more than approximately four hours to obtain a confession from an offender, even in cases of a very serious nature.'"

More generally, Professor Leo tells us (at 230), "once interrogation commences, the primary cause of police-induced false confessions is psychologically coercive methods." Leo continues:

"By psychological coercion, I mean either one of two things: police use of interrogation techniques that are regarded as inherently coercive in psychology and law; or police use of interrogation techniques that, cumulatively, cause a suspect to perceive that he has no choice but to comply with the interrogators' demands. Usually, these amount to the same thing."

More specifically, Professor Leo is quite troubled by police interrogators' promises of leniency and threats of punishment. Drawing upon an earlier study he did with Richard Ofshe, Leo maintains (at 309) that "in the modern era" "promises of leniency and threats of punishment, whether implicit or explicit, are the primary cause of police-induced false confessions." Leo continues (at 309–10):

"Appellate courts need to create an unambiguous, bright line rule prohibiting under all circumstances any implicit or explicit promise, offers, or suggestion of leniency in exchange for an admission. This would include any inducement that reasonably communicates a promise, suggestion, or offer of reduced charging, sentencing, or punishment; freedom; immunity; or police, prosecutorial, judicial, or juror leniency in exchange for an admission or confession. Appellate courts also

---

    a. According to Susan Saulny, *Why Confess to What You Didn't Do?*, N.Y.Times, Dec. 8, 2002, at 5, the five teenage suspects in the Central Park jogger case were questioned for fourteen to thirty hours.

need to create an unambiguous rule prohibiting, under all circumstances, any implicit or explicit threat or suggestion of harm in the absence of an admission. This would include any inducement that reasonably communicates higher charging, a longer prison sentence, or other harsher punishment in the absence of an admission or confession. * * * Appellate courts must exclude all promises of leniency (or their functional equivalents) because they create an unacceptable risk that police will elicit false, unreliable, or untrustworthy confessions."

As noted earlier (see p. 734), LAWRENCE ROSENTHAL, *Against Orthodoxy: Miranda is Not Prophylactic and the Constitution is Not Perfect*, 10 Chapman L.Rev. 579 (2007), has considerable difficulty understanding why the false confession studies should lead to greater due process regulation of confessions generally. He suggest that the police probably use the same interrogation techniques in the vast majority of custodial interrogations. Therefore the fact that these techniques appear in false confession cases "provides no basis to conclude that these [techniques] increase the likelihood that a confession is false." Id. at 617–18. Professor Rosenthal continues (at 618–20):

"At best, it is probably reasonable to presume that more aggressive interrogation techniques will produce a higher rate of confessions than more passive approaches, but it is entirely unclear that the rate of false confessions will also increase through more aggressive techniques.[167]

" * * * [Even] if courts could somehow divine error rates, how are they to decide what constitutes an unacceptable rate of error? Three percent? Ten percent? * * * And what about the large number of guilty offenders who will go unpunished if courts brand as impermissible investigative tactics that are far more likely to produce accurate than false convictions but that nevertheless produce error rates that are thought to be unacceptable?

" * * * The advocates of due process regulation of interrogation * * * seek additional protection, based on evidence that [certain interrogation] techniques produce some nontrivial (although as yet unascertained) error rate. As a doctrinal matter, the absence of any historical support for prophylactic due process regulation of interrogation techniques based on a presumed risk of error might itself doom the case for new regulation. Even putting that problem aside, however, no one could tenably read the Due Process Clause as a prohibition of error in the criminal justice system. Surely 'due process' accommodates that much reality."

SECTION 7. *MASSIAH* REVISITED; *MASSIAH* AND *MIRANDA* COMPARED AND CONTRASTED

A. THE REVIVIFICATION OF *MASSIAH*

"Until the Christian burial speech case [*Brewer v. Williams*, set forth below] * * * lasting fame had eluded *Massiah v. United States* [p. 557]. It was apparently lost in the shuffle of fast-moving events that reshaped constitutional-criminal procedure in the 1960s. [In] constitutional-criminal procedure circles, 1964 was the year of *Escobedo v. Illinois* [p. 559], and *Massiah* was understandably neglected in the hue and cry raised over the Illinois case. To the extent that *Massiah* was remembered at all, it was [only as a] stepping stone to *Escobedo* * * *.

"*Escobedo* may have seized the spotlight from *Massiah*, but *Escobedo* was soon shoved offstage by that blockbuster, *Miranda*, [a case that] '[did] not

---

167. To be sure, one can build an anecdotal case that investigators sometimes persuade a suspect that his position is so hopeless that he has no realistic chance but to confess, [citing several commentators], but this says nothing about the rate at which the same tactics induce a guilty suspect to provide an accurate confession.

[enlarge] *Escobedo* as much as [it] displaced it.' Assuming that *Escobedo* had not already done so, did *Miranda* also displace *Massiah*? After Miranda, was the institution of judicial proceedings, by way of indictment or otherwise, no more constitutionally relevant than whether the investigation had 'begun to focus on a particular suspect?' [If] one searches the *Miranda* opinion for answers to these questions, [one] discovers that *Massiah* is never mentioned—not once in Chief Justice Warren's sixty-page opinion for the Court, nor in any of the three dissenting opinions, which total another forty-six pages. Yet very little else even remotely bearing on the general subject is left out."

—Kamisar, *Police Interrogation and Confessions* 160–64 (1980).

BREWER v. WILLIAMS (WILLIAMS I)
430 U.S. 387, 97 S.Ct. 1232, 51 L.Ed.2d 424 (1977).

JUSTICE STEWART delivered the opinion of the Court. * * *

On the afternoon of December 24, 1968, a 10–year-old girl named Pamela Powers went with her family to the YMCA in Des Moines, Iowa. [When] she failed to return from a trip to the washroom, a search for her began. The search was unsuccessful.

Robert Williams, who had recently escaped from a mental hospital, was a resident of the YMCA. Soon after the girl's disappearance Williams was seen in the YMCA lobby carrying some clothing and a large bundle wrapped in a blanket. He obtained help from a 14–year-old boy in opening the street door of the YMCA and the door to his automobile parked outside. When Williams placed the bundle in the front seat of his car the boy "saw two legs in it and they were skinny and white." Before anyone could see what was in the bundle Williams drove away. His abandoned car was found the following day in Davenport, Iowa, roughly 160 miles east of Des Moines. A warrant was then issued in Des Moines for his arrest on a charge of abduction.

On the morning of December 26, a Des Moines lawyer named Henry McKnight went to the Des Moines police station and informed the officers present that he had just received a long distance call from Williams, and that he had advised Williams to turn himself in to the Davenport police. Williams did surrender that morning to the police in Davenport, and they booked him on the charge specified in the arrest warrant and gave him the [*Miranda* warnings]. The Davenport police then telephoned their counterparts in Des Moines to inform them that Williams had surrendered. McKnight, the lawyer, was still at the Des Moines police headquarters, and Williams conversed with McKnight on the telephone. In the presence of the Des Moines Chief of Police and a Police Detective named Leaming [a captain and 20–year veteran of the Des Moines police department], McKnight advised Williams that Des Moines police officers would be driving to Davenport to pick him up, that the officers would not interrogate him or mistreat him, and that Williams was not to talk to the officers about Pamela Powers until after consulting with McKnight upon his return to Des Moines. As a result of these conversations, it was agreed between McKnight and the Des Moines police officials that Detective Leaming and a fellow officer would drive to Davenport to pick up Williams, that they would bring him directly back to Des Moines, and that they would not question him during the trip.

In the meantime Williams was arraigned before a judge in Davenport on the outstanding arrest warrant.[a] The judge advised him of his *Miranda* rights and committed him to jail. Before leaving the courtroom, Williams conferred with a lawyer named Kelly, who advised him not to make any statements until consulting with McKnight back in Des Moines.

Detective Leaming and his fellow officer arrived in Davenport about noon to pick up Williams and return him to Des Moines. Soon after their arrival they met with Williams and Kelly, who, they understood, was acting as Williams' lawyer. Detective Leaming repeated the Miranda warnings, and told Williams:

> " * * * we both know that you're being represented here by Mr. Kelly and you're being represented by Mr. McKnight in Des Moines, [and] I want you to remember this because we'll be visiting between here and Des Moines."

Williams then conferred again with Kelly alone, and after this conference Kelly reiterated to Detective Leaming that Williams was not to be questioned about the disappearance of Pamela Powers until after he had consulted with McKnight back in Des Moines. When Leaming expressed some reservations, Kelly firmly stated that the agreement with McKnight was to be carried out—that there was to be no interrogation of Williams during the automobile journey to Des Moines. Kelly was denied permission to ride in the police car back to Des Moines with Williams and the two officers.

The two Detectives, with Williams in their charge, then set out on the 160–mile drive. At no time during the trip did Williams express a willingness to be interrogated in the absence of an attorney. Instead, he stated several times that "[w]hen I get to Des Moines and see Mr. McKnight, I am going to tell you the whole story." Detective Leaming knew that Williams was a former mental patient, and knew also that he was deeply religious.

The Detective and his prisoner soon embarked on a wide-ranging conversation covering a variety of topics, including the subject of religion. Then, not long after leaving Davenport and reaching the interstate highway, Detective Leaming delivered what has been referred to [as] the "Christian burial speech." Addressing Williams as "Reverend," the Detective said:

> "I want to give you something to think about while we're traveling down the road. * * * Number one, I want you to observe the weather conditions, it's raining, it's sleeting, it's freezing, driving is very treacherous, visibility is poor, it's going to be dark early this evening. They are predicting several inches of snow for tonight, and I feel that you yourself are the only person that knows where this little girl's body is, that you yourself have only been there once, and if you get a snow on top of it you yourself may be unable to find it. And, since we will be going right past the area on the way into Des Moines, I feel that we could stop and locate the body, that the parents of this little girl should be entitled to a Christian burial for the little girl who was snatched away from them on Christmas Eve and murdered. And I feel we should stop and locate it on the way in rather than waiting until morning and trying to come back out after a snow storm and possibly not being able to find it at all."[b]

---

a. At the time *Williams* was decided, it did not seem to matter that the defendant was arraigned on the charge of abduction, not the charge of murder that grew out of the abduction. Evidently the Court assumed that when the Sixth Amendment right to counsel attached to the abduction charge it attached to the factually related crime of murder as well. But see *Texas v. Cobb*, p. 754.

b. Although no member of the Supreme Court discussed, or even noted, this point, Captain Leaming offered two different versions of the "Christian burial speech." The captain's first version was given at a pretrial hearing to suppress evidence; his second version, the only one quoted and discussed by the Supreme Court and lower federal courts, was given four weeks later

Williams asked Detective Leaming why he thought their route to Des Moines would be taking them past the girl's body, and Leaming responded that he knew the body [was near] Mitchellville—a town they would be passing on the way to Des Moines.[1] Leaming then stated: "I do not want you to answer me. I don't want to discuss it further. Just think about it as we're riding down the road."

As the car approached Grinell, a town approximately 100 miles west of Davenport, Williams asked whether the police had found the victim's shoes. When Detective Leaming replied that he was unsure, Williams directed the officers to a service station where he said he had left the shoes; a search for them proved unsuccessful. As they continued towards Des Moines, Williams asked whether the police had found the blanket, and directed the officers to a rest area where he said he had disposed of the blanket. Nothing was found. The car continued towards Des Moines, and as it approached Mitchellville, Williams said that he would show the officers where the body was. He then directed the police to the body of Pamela Powers.

[The trial judge admitted all evidence relating to or resulting from statements Williams made in the car ride. He found that "an agreement" had been made between defense counsel and the police that Williams would not be questioned on the return trip to Des Moines, but ruled that Williams had waived his rights before giving such information. Williams was convicted of murder. The Iowa Supreme Court affirmed. On federal habeas, the District Court concluded that] the evidence in question had been wrongly admitted at Williams' trial. This conclusion was based on three alternative and independent grounds: (1) that Williams had been denied his constitutional right to the assistance of counsel; (2) that he had been denied [his *Miranda* rights]; and (3) that in any event, [his] statements [had] been involuntarily made. [The] Court of Appeals appears to have affirmed the judgment on [the first two] grounds. We have concluded that only one of them need be considered here.

Specifically, there is no need to review the [*Miranda* doctrine] [or the] ruling [that] Williams' self-incriminating statements [were] involuntarily made. For it is clear that the judgment before us must in any event be affirmed upon the ground that Williams was deprived of a different constitutional right—the right to the assistance of counsel. * * * Whatever else it may mean, the right to counsel * * * means at least that a person is entitled to the help of a lawyer at or after the time that judicial proceedings have been initiated against him—"whether by way of formal charge, preliminary hearing, indictment, information, or arraignment." *Kirby v. Illinois* [p. 769].

There can be no doubt in the present case that judicial proceedings had been initiated against Williams before the start of the automobile ride from Davenport to Des Moines. A warrant had been issued for his arrest, he had been arraigned on that warrant before a judge in a Davenport courtroom, and he had been committed by the court to confinement in jail. The State does not contend otherwise.

---

at the trial. See Kamisar, *Foreword: Brewer v. Williams—A Hard Look at a Discomfiting Record,* 66 Geo.L.J. 209, 215–18 (1977). For the view that these two versions are significantly different, see id. at 218–33.

Justice Stewart notes that the captain addressed Williams as "Reverend," and then gives the captain's *second* version of the speech and related testimony *in its entirety*. But Captain Leaming did not testify that he addressed Williams as "Reverend" in the second version, only in the first. Justice Stewart may have called attention to the "Reverend" address because the Attorney General of Iowa was sufficiently troubled by it to go outside the record to explain in his brief why Captain Leaming employed it. See Kamisar, supra, at 223. For a discussion of the significance of the " 'Reverend' ploy," see id. at 221–23.

1. The fact of the matter, of course, was that Detective Leaming possessed no such knowledge.

There can be no serious doubt, either, that Detective Leaming deliberately and designedly set out to elicit information from Williams just as surely as—and perhaps more effectively than—if he had formally interrogated him. Detective Leaming was fully aware before departing for Des Moines that Williams was being represented in Davenport by Kelly and in Des Moines by McKnight. Yet he purposely sought during Williams' isolation from his lawyers to obtain as much incriminating information as possible. Indeed, Detective Leaming conceded as much when he testified at Williams' trial:

"Q. In fact, Captain, whether he was a mental patient or not, you were trying to get all the information you could before he got to his lawyer, weren't you?

"A. I was sure hoping to find out where that little girl was, yes, sir.

"Q. Well, I'll put it this way: You [were] hoping to get all the information you could before Williams got back to McKnight, weren't you?

"A. Yes, sir."[6]

[The] circumstances of this case are thus constitutionally indistinguishable from those presented in *Massiah*. [That] the incriminating statements were elicited surreptitiously in [*Massiah*], and otherwise here, is constitutionally irrelevant. Rather, the clear rule of *Massiah* is that once adversary proceedings have commenced against an individual, he has a right to legal representation when the government interrogates him.[c]

[The] Iowa courts recognized that Williams had been denied the constitutional right to the assistance of counsel. They held, however, that he had waived that right during the course of the automobile trip from Davenport to Des Moines.

[It] was incumbent upon the State to prove "an intentional relinquishment or abandonment of a known right or privilege." *Johnson v. Zerbst*. [That] strict standard applies equally to an alleged waiver of the right to counsel whether at trial or at a critical stage of pretrial proceedings. [Judged by that standard,] the record in this case falls far short of sustaining the State's burden. It is true that Williams had been informed of and appeared to understand his right to counsel. But waiver requires not merely comprehension but relinquishment, and Williams' consistent reliance upon the advice of counsel in dealing with the authorities refutes any suggestion that he waived that right. [His] statements while in the car that he would tell the whole story after seeing McKnight in Des Moines were the clearest expressions [that] he desired the presence of an attorney before any interrogation took place. But even before making these statements, Williams had effectively asserted his right to counsel by having secured attorneys at both ends of the automobile trip, both of whom, acting as his agents, had made clear to the police that no interrogation was to occur during the journey. Williams knew of that agreement and, particularly in view of his consistent reliance on counsel, there is no basis for concluding that he disavowed it.

Despite Williams' express and implicit assertions of his right to counsel, Detective Leaming proceeded to elicit incriminating statements from Williams. Leaming did not preface this effort by telling Williams that he had a right to the presence of a lawyer, and made no effort at all to ascertain whether Williams

---

6. Counsel for the State, in the course of oral argument in this Court, acknowledged that the "Christian burial speech" was tantamount to interrogation * * *.

c. Isn't the clear rule of *Massiah* that once adversary proceedings have commenced against an individual, he has a right to counsel when the government *deliberately elicits* incriminating information from him (whether or not the government's efforts to obtain information constitute "interrogation" within the meaning of *Miranda*'s Fifth Amendment rights)? See Note 2 following this case.

wished to relinquish that right. The circumstances of record in this case thus provide no reasonable basis for finding that Williams waived his right to the assistance of counsel.

The Court of Appeals did not hold, nor do we, that under the circumstances of this case Williams *could not*, without notice to counsel, have waived his rights under the Sixth and Fourteenth Amendments. It only held, as do we, that he did not.

* * * Although we do not lightly affirm the issuance of a writ of habeas corpus in this case, so clear a violation of the Sixth and Fourteenth Amendments as here occurred cannot be condoned.

[The] judgment of the Court of Appeals is affirmed.[12]

[concurring opinions of Justices Marshall, Powell and Stevens are omitted.]

CHIEF JUSTICE BURGER, dissenting.

The result in this case ought to be intolerable in any society which purports to call itself an organized society. It continues the Court—by the narrowest margin—on the much-criticized course of punishing the public for the mistakes and misdeeds of law enforcement officers, instead of punishing the officer directly, if in fact he is guilty of wrongdoing. It mechanically and blindly keeps reliable evidence from juries whether the claimed constitutional violation involves gross police misconduct or honest human error.

Williams is guilty of the savage murder of a small child; no member of the Court contends he is not. While in custody, and after no fewer than five warnings of his rights to silence and to counsel, he led police to the concealed body of his victim. The Court concedes Williams was not threatened or coerced and that he spoke and acted voluntarily and with full awareness of his constitutional rights. In the face of all this, the Court now holds that because Williams was prompted by the detective's statement—not interrogation but a statement—the jury must not be told how the police found the body.

[In] a variety of contexts we inquire whether application of the rule will promote its objectives sufficiently to justify the enormous cost it imposes on society. [Against] this background, it is striking that the Court fails even to consider whether the benefits secured by application of the exclusionary rule in this case outweigh its obvious social costs. Perhaps the failure is due to the fact that this case arises not under the Fourth Amendment, but under *Miranda*, and the Sixth Amendment right to counsel. The Court apparently perceives the function of the exclusionary rule to be so different in these varying contexts that it must be mechanically and uncritically applied. * * *

JUSTICE WHITE, with whom JUSTICE BLACKMUN and JUSTICE REHNQUIST join, dissenting.

---

12. The District Court stated that its decision "does not touch upon the issue of what evidence, if any, beyond the incriminating statements themselves must be excluded as 'fruit of the poisonous tree.'" We too have no occasion to address this issue, and in the present posture of the case there is no basis for the view of our dissenting Brethren [that] any attempt to retry the respondent would probably be futile. While neither Williams' incriminating statements themselves nor any testimony describing his having led the police to the victim's body can constitutionally be admitted into evidence, evidence of where the body was found and of its condition might well be admissible on the theory that the body would have been discovered in any event, even had incriminating statements not been elicited from Williams. In the event that a retrial is instituted, it will be for the state courts in the first instance to determine whether particular items of evidence may be admitted.

[On retrial, the state court ruled that the body of Pamela Powers "would have been found in any event" and Williams was again convicted of murder. The U.S. Supreme Court upheld the state court's use of the "inevitable discovery" exception. See *Williams II*, p. 775.]

[I disagree with the majority's finding that no waiver was proved in this case.] That respondent knew of his right not to say anything to the officers without advice and presence of counsel is established on this record to a moral certainty. He was advised of the right by three officials of the State—telling at least one that he understood the right—and by two lawyers. [The] issue in this case, then, is whether respondent relinquished that right intentionally.

Respondent relinquished his right not to talk to the police about his crime when the car approached the place where he had hidden the victim's clothes. Men usually intend to do what they do and there is nothing in the record to support the proposition that respondent's decision to talk was anything but an exercise of his own free will. Apparently, without any prodding from the officers, respondent—who had earlier said that he would tell the whole story when he arrived in Des Moines—spontaneously changed his mind about the timing of his disclosures when the car approached the places where he had hidden the evidence. However, even if his statements were influenced by Detective Leaming's above-quoted statement, respondent's decision to talk in the absence of counsel can hardly be viewed as the product of an overborne will. The statement by Leaming was not coercive; it was accompanied by a request that respondent not respond to it; and it was delivered hours before respondent decided to make any statement. Respondent's waiver was thus knowing and intentional. * * *

JUSTICE BLACKMUN, with whom JUSTICE WHITE and JUSTICE REHNQUIST join, dissenting. * * *

The Court rules that the Sixth Amendment was violated because Detective Leaming "purposely sought during Williams' isolation from his lawyers to obtain as much incriminating information as possible." I cannot regard that as unconstitutional per se.

First, the police did not deliberately seek to isolate Williams from his lawyers so as to deprive him of the assistance of counsel. Cf. *Escobedo*. The isolation in this case was a necessary incident of transporting Williams to the county where the crime was committed.

Second, Leaming's purpose was not solely to obtain incriminating evidence. The victim had been missing for only two days, and the police could not be certain that she was dead. Leaming, of course, and in accord with his duty, was "hoping to find out where that little girl was," but such motivation does not equate with an intention to evade the Sixth Amendment.[d] * * *

Third, not every attempt to elicit information should be regarded as "tantamount to interrogation." I am not persuaded that Leaming's observations and comments, made as the police car traversed the snowy and slippery miles between Davenport and Des Moines that winter afternoon, were an interrogation, direct or subtle, of Williams. Williams, after all, was counseled by lawyers, and warned by the arraigning judge in Davenport and by the police, and yet it was he who started the travel conversations and brought up the subject of the criminal investigation.

[In] summary, it seems to me that the Court is holding that *Massiah* is violated whenever police engage in any conduct, in the absence of counsel, with the subjective desire to obtain information from a suspect after arraignment. Such

---

d. But see Kamisar, *Police Interrogation and Confessions* 146–47 (1980), maintaining that although at one point Leaming did testify that he was "hoping to find out where that little *girl* was," in light of the entire record he apparently meant the girl's *body*. Leaming testified that he heard Williams' lawyer say to him over the phone that he would have to tell the police "where *the body* is" when he got back. Leaming also testified that before he drove to Davenport to pick up Williams, Williams' lawyer told him that the girl "was dead when [Williams] left the YMCA with her."

a rule is far too broad. Persons in custody frequently volunteer statements in response to stimuli other than interrogation. * * *

NOTES AND QUESTIONS

1. *Was it constitutionally irrelevant whether the "Christian burial speech" constituted "interrogation"?* Did the Court deem it necessary (or at least important) to classify Leaming's speech as a "form of interrogation" or "tantamount to interrogation"? If so, why? Once the Court chose the "Sixth Amendment—*Massiah*" route over a "Fifth Amendment—*Miranda*" approach, did the question whether Leaming engaged in "interrogation" become, or should it have become, constitutionally irrelevant? Did the secret government agent engage in "interrogation" in *Massiah*?

2. *More on "interrogation" vs. "deliberate elicitation."* Although Justice Stewart misspoke in *Brewer v. Williams* when he talked about "interrogation" in the context of *Massiah* [see the text of his *Williams* opinion at fn. c], he, in effect, corrected himself when, three years later, he wrote footnote 4 to his opinion of the Court in *Rhode Island v. Innis* [p. 608]. In that footnote, Stewart pointed out that any suggestion in *Brewer v. Williams* that the terms "interrogation" and "deliberate elicitation" are interchangeable was erroneous. Justice Stewart then cited a law review article criticizing his use of the term "interrogation" in *Brewer v. Williams*.

Unfortunately, confusion over these terms has persisted in the lower courts. Hopefully, the Court put an end to this in *Fellers v. United States*, 540 U.S. 519 (2004). In the course of ruling that the Court of Appeals had committed reversible error in ruling that the absence of an "interrogation" foreclosed petitioner's *Massiah* claim, the Supreme Court, per O'Connor, J., underscored the distinction between "interrogation" within the meaning of *Miranda* and "deliberate elicitation" within the meaning of *Massiah*. The *Fellers* Court recalled that *Massiah* [p. 557] had held that "an accused is denied 'the basic protection' of the Sixth Amendment 'when there [is] used against him at his trial evidence of his own incriminating words, which [the police have] deliberately elicited from him after he has been indicted and in absence of his counsel.'"

The "interrogation"/"deliberate elicitation" distinction is especially important in the "jail plant" situation. *Miranda* is not implicated when the suspect is *unaware* that he is speaking to a law enforcement officer or his agent because a "police-dominated atmosphere" and "compulsion" are not present. Recall *Illinois v. Perkins*. However, *Massiah* can be implicated if a suspect has already been indicted even though he is speaking freely with someone he believes to be a fellow inmate. See *United States v. Henry*. A person cannot be "interrogated" within the meaning of *Miranda* unless he is aware of it, but he can be subjected to police efforts to "deliberately elicit" statements from him without being aware of it.

3. *Even if Brewer v. Williams were deemed a "Miranda case," would whether Leaming engaged in "interrogation" still be the wrong question?* Since Williams had asserted both his right to remain silent and his right to counsel several times before he was driven back to Des Moines, should the relevant question have been whether Leaming "fully respected" or "scrupulously honored" Williams' *Miranda* rights? Cf. *Michigan v. Mosley*, p. 635. How could it be said that Leaming did, when he "deliberately and designedly set out to elicit information" from Williams?

Brewer v. Williams was decided four years before *Edwards v. Arizona*, p. 636. Looking back at *Williams* in light of *Edwards*, if *Williams* were a *"Miranda* case," should the relevant question have been whether, after expressing his unwillingness to talk to the police without his lawyer, *Williams* changed his mind on his own initiative or whether Leaming "persuaded" or "prompted" him to change his mind?

4. Does the "fruits" doctrine apply to Massiah violations? As we have seen, the Court has balked at applying the "poisoned fruits" doctrine to violations of the *Miranda* rules, except for the most extraordinary circumstances. See *Elstad* (p. 697), *Patane* (p. 699) and *Seibert* (p. 702). What about *Massiah* violations? In *Nix v. Williams* (p. 903) (the *Williams* case on retrial), the Supreme Court *assumed* that the "poisoned fruit" doctrine did apply to *Massiah* violations. But in *Fellers*, Note 2, supra, the Court remanded the case to the Court of Appeals to address this issue in the first instance.

On remand, UNITED STATES v. FELLERS, 397 F.3d 1090 (8th Cir. 2005), the court held, per Wollman, J., that the "poisoned fruit" doctrine did not apply:

"We conclude that the exclusionary rule is inapplicable in Fellers' case because, as with the Fifth Amendment in *Elstad*, the use of the exclusionary rule in this case would serve neither deterrence nor any other goal of the Sixth Amendment. Both the deterrence of future Sixth Amendment violations and the vindication of the Amendment's right-to-counsel guarantee have been effectuated through the exclusion of Feller's initial statements. Although the officers acknowledged that they used Feller's initial jailhouse statements (obtained after securing a *Miranda* waiver) in order to extract further admissions from him, there is no indication that the interrogating officers made any reference to Feller's prior uncounseled statements in order to prompt him into making new incriminating statements. * * *

"[The] similarities between the Sixth Amendment context at issue in Feller's case and the Fifth Amendment context at issue in *Elstad* support our conclusion that the *Elstad* rule applies when a suspect makes incriminating statements after a knowing and voluntary waiver of his right to counsel, notwithstanding earlier police questioning in violation of the Sixth Amendment. * * * * "

5. What constitutes a valid waiver of the "Sixth Amendment—Massiah" right? PATTERSON v. ILLINOIS, 487 U.S. 285 (1988), per White, J., rejected "petitioner's argument, which has some acceptance from courts and commentators, that since 'the sixth amendment right [to counsel] is far superior to that of the fifth amendment right' and since '[t]he greater the right the greater the loss from a waiver of that right,' waiver of an accused's Sixth Amendment right to counsel should be 'more difficult' to effectuate than waiver of a suspect's Fifth Amendment rights." The Court ruled instead that "[a]s a general matter [an] accused who is [given the *Miranda* warnings] has been sufficiently apprised of the nature of the Sixth Amendment rights, and of the consequences of abandoning those rights, so that his waiver on this basis will be considered a knowing and intelligent one."

The case arose as follows: Patterson and other members of a street gang were arrested in the course of investigating the murder of Jackson. Patterson was advised of his *Miranda* rights and agreed to answer questions, but denied knowing anything about Jackson's death. He was held in custody while the investigation continued. Two days later, Patterson and two other gang members were indicted for the murder of Jackson. The same officer who had questioned him earlier told him that because he had been indicted he was being transferred from the lockup, where he was being held, to the county jail. Patterson asked the officer which of the gang members had been indicted for Jackson's murder, and upon learning that one particular gang member had not been indicted, responded: "[W]hy wasn't he indicted, he did everything."

Patterson then began to explain that a witness would support his account of the crime. At this point, the officer handed Patterson a *Miranda* waiver form and read the warnings aloud. Patterson initialed each of the warnings, signed the form and made a lengthy incriminating statement. He subsequently made additional statements. He was found guilty of murder, but maintained that the warnings he received, although they protected his *Miranda* rights, did not adequately inform him of his Sixth Amendment right to counsel during postindictment questioning. A 5–4 majority disagreed:

"[The] key inquiry in a case such as this one must be: Was the accused, who waived his Sixth Amendment rights during postindictment questioning, made sufficiently aware of his right to have counsel present during the questioning, and of the possible consequences of a decision to forgo the aid of counsel? In this case, we are convinced that by admonishing petitioner with the *Miranda* warnings, [the State] has met this burden and that petitioner's waiver of his right to counsel at questioning was valid. * * *

"Our conclusion is supported by petitioner's inability, in the proceedings before this Court, to articulate with precision what additional information should have been provided to him before he would have been competent to waive his right to counsel. * * *[8]"

As a general matter, then, an accused who is admonished with the [*Miranda* warnings] has been sufficiently apprised of the nature of his Sixth Amendment rights, and of the consequences of abandoning these rights, so that his waiver on this basis will be considered a knowing and intelligent one.[9]

"[While] our cases have recognized a 'difference' between the Fifth Amendment and Sixth Amendment rights to counsel, and the 'policies' behind these Constitutional guarantees, we have never suggested that one right is 'superior' or 'greater' than the other, nor is there any support in our cases for the notion that because a Sixth Amendment right may be involved, it is more difficult to waive than the Fifth Amendment counterpart.

"[W]e require a more searching or formal inquiry before permitting an accused to waive his right to counsel at trial [see *Faretta v. California*, p. 107] than we require for a Sixth Amendment waiver during postindictment questioning—not because postindictment questioning is 'less important' than a trial [but]

---

8. [Some courts have suggested] that, in addition to the *Miranda* warnings, an accused should be informed that he has been indicted before a postindictment waiver is sought. Because, in this case, petitioner concedes that he was so informed, we do not address [this issue].

Beyond this, only one Court of Appeals—the Second Circuit—has adopted substantive or procedural requirements (in addition to *Miranda*) that must be completed before a Sixth Amendment waiver can be effectuated for postindictment questioning. See *United States v. Mohabir,* 624 F.2d 1140 (1980). [Stressing that the "strict standard" governing waiver of counsel at trial should apply to an alleged waiver of the *Massiah* right to counsel as well, the *Mohabir* court exercised its supervisory power over federal criminal justice to hold that a valid waiver of the "Sixth Amendment—*Massiah*" right "must be preceded by a federal judicial officer's explanation of the content and significance of this right."] As have a majority of the Court of Appeals, we reject *Mohabir's* holding that some "additional" warnings or discussions with an accused are required in this situation or that any waiver in this context can only properly be made before a "neutral * * * judicial officer."

9. This does not mean, of course, that all Sixth Amendment challenges to the conduct of postindictment questioning will fail whenever the challenged practice would pass constitutional muster under *Miranda.* For example, we have permitted a *Miranda* waiver to stand where a suspect was not told that his lawyer was trying to reach him during questioning; in the Sixth Amendment context, this waiver would not be valid. See *Moran v. Burbine* * * *.

Thus, because the Sixth Amendment's protection of the attorney-client relationship—"the right to rely on counsel as a 'medium' between [the accused] and the State"—extends beyond *Miranda's* protection of the Fifth Amendment right to counsel, there will be cases where a waiver which would be valid under *Miranda* will not suffice for Sixth Amendment purposes.

because the full 'dangers and disadvantages of self-representation,' *Faretta*, during questioning are less substantial and more obvious to an accused than they are at trial. Because the role of counsel at questioning is relatively simple and limited, we see no problem in having a waiver procedure at that stage which is likewise simple and limited."

Justice Stevens, joined by Brennan and Marshall, JJ., dissented:

"Given the significance of the initiation of formal proceedings and the concomitant shift in the relationship between the state and the accused, I think it quite wrong to suggest that *Miranda* warnings—or for that matter, any warnings offered by an adverse party—provide a sufficient basis for permitting the undoubtedly prejudicial—and, in my view, unfair—practice of permitting trained law enforcement personnel and prosecuting attorneys to communicate with as-of-yet unrepresented criminal defendants.

"[The] majority premises its conclusions that *Miranda* warnings lay a sufficient basis for accepting a waiver of the right to counsel on the assumption that those warnings make clear to an accused 'what a lawyer could "do for him" during the postindictment questioning: namely, advise [him] to refrain from making any [incriminating] statements.' Yet, this is surely a gross understatement of the disadvantage of proceeding without a lawyer and an understatement of what a defendant must understand to make a knowing waiver. The *Miranda* warnings do not, for example, inform the accused that a lawyer might examine the indictment for legal sufficiency before submitting his or her client to interrogation or that a lawyer is likely to be considerably more skillful at negotiating a plea bargain and that such negotiations may be most fruitful if initiated prior to any interrogation. Rather, the warnings do not even go so far as to explain to the accused the nature of the charges pending against him—advice that a court would insist upon before allowing a defendant to enter a guilty plea with or without the presence of an attorney."[a]

NOTES AND QUESTIONS

(a) In addition to his principal contention, Patterson also argued (unsuccessfully) that someone in his situation should be equated with a preindictment suspect who asserts his right to counsel, thereby triggering *Edwards*. Even if this is so, didn't Patterson, when being transferred to the county jail, "initiate" further communication with the police within the meaning of *Edwards*?

(b) Reconsider fn. 9 to the majority opinion in *Patterson*. Is the Court saying that even if a postindictment interrogatee were unaware that a friend or relative had retained a lawyer on his behalf, a waiver of his Sixth Amendment right to counsel would not be valid unless the police informed him that he had a lawyer and that that lawyer was trying to reach him? If so, why? Does this view make the Sixth Amendment right to counsel "superior" to the Fifth when somebody happens to retain a lawyer for the defendant, but not when the defendant is too unlucky or friendless for this to occur? Should the test for waiver of the Sixth Amendment right to counsel vary at different times "depending on the fortuity of whether [the suspect's family] happens to have retained counsel [for him] prior to interrogation"? Cf. *Moran v. Burbine*.

6. *If the government obtains incriminating statements from a defendant after her right to counsel has attached, but the government does so for legitimate reasons unrelated to the gathering of evidence concerning*

---

a. Blackmun, J., wrote a separate dissent, "agree[ing] with most of what Justice Stevens said." He would equate someone in Patterson's situation with a suspect who asserted his Fifth Amendment right to counsel, thus invoking the protection of *Edwards*.

charges to which the right to counsel has attached (e.g. to investigate a report that defendant plans to harm a witness), are the statements admissible at the trial of the crimes for which formal charges had already been filed? No, answered the Court, per Brennan, J., in MAINE v. MOULTON, 474 U.S. 159 (1985):

"In *Massiah*, the Government also contended that incriminating statements obtained as a result of its deliberate efforts should not be excluded because law enforcement agents had 'the right, if not indeed the duty, to continue their investigation of [*Massiah*] and his alleged criminal associates.' [We] rejected this argument, and held:

" 'We do not question [that] it was entirely proper to continue an investigation of the suspected criminal activities of the defendant and his alleged confederates, even though the defendant had already been indicted. [But] the defendant's own incriminating statements, obtained by federal agents under the circumstances here disclosed, could not constitutionally be used by the prosecution as evidence against him at his trial.' (Emphasis omitted.)

"We reaffirm this holding, which states a sensible solution to a difficult problem. The police have an interest in the thorough investigation of crimes for which formal charges have already been filed. They also have an interest in investigating new or additional crimes. Investigations of either type of crime may require surveillance of individuals already under indictment. Moreover, law enforcement officials investigating an individual suspected of committing one crime and formally charged with having committed another crime obviously seek to discover evidence useful at a trial of either crime. In seeking evidence pertaining to pending charges, however, the Government's investigative powers are limited by the Sixth Amendment rights of the accused. To allow the admission of evidence obtained from the accused in violation of his Sixth Amendment rights whenever the police assert an alternative, legitimate reason for their surveillance [in this case, to insure the safety of their secret agent and to gather information concerning a report that defendant was planning to kill a witness] invites abuse by law enforcement personnel in the form of fabricated investigations and risks the evisceration of the Sixth Amendment right recognized in *Massiah*. On the other hand, to exclude evidence pertaining to charges as to which the Sixth Amendment right to counsel had not attached at the time the evidence was obtained, simply because other charges were pending at that time, would unnecessarily frustrate the public's interest in the investigation of criminal activities. Consequently, incriminating statements pertaining to pending charges are inadmissible at the trial of those charges, notwithstanding the fact that the police were also investigating other crimes, if, in obtaining this evidence, the State violated the Sixth Amendment by knowingly circumventing the accused's right to the assistance of counsel."

Chief Justice Burger, joined by White, Rehnquist and O'Connor, JJ., dissented, maintaining that "application of the exclusionary rule here makes little sense."

"We have explained, [that] 'the deterrent purpose of the exclusionary rule necessarily assumes that the police have engaged in willful, or at the very least negligent, conduct which has deprived the defendant of some right.' Here the trial court found that the State obtained statements from respondent 'for legitimate purposes not related to the gathering of evidence concerning the crime for which [respondent] had been indicted.' Since the State was not trying to build its theft case against respondent in obtaining the evidence, excluding the evidence from the theft trial will not affect police behavior at all. The exclusion of evidence 'cannot be expected, and should not be applied, to deter objectively reasonable law enforcement activity.' *Leon*. Indeed, [it] is impossible to identify any police 'misconduct' to deter in this case. In fact, if anything, actions by the police of the type at issue here should be encouraged. The diligent investigation of the police in this case may have saved the lives of several potential witnesses and certainly led to the prosecution and conviction of respondent for additional serious crimes."

B. "PASSIVE" vs. "ACTIVE" SECRET AGENTS

The *Massiah* doctrine probably reached its high point in UNITED STATES v. HENRY, 447 U.S. 264 (1980), which applied the doctrine to a situation where the FBI had instructed its paid government informant, ostensibly defendant's "cell-mate," not to question defendant about the crime, and there had been no showing that he had. Nevertheless, a 6–3 majority, per Burger, C.J., rejected the argument that the incriminating statements were not the result of any "affirmative conduct" on the part of the government agent to solicit evidence. The informant "was not a passive listener; rather he had 'some conversations with Mr. Henry' while he was in jail and Henry's incriminating statements were 'the product of this conversation.'" Moreover, and more generally—

"[Even if we accept the FBI agent's statement that] he did not intend that [the informant] would take affirmative steps to secure incriminating information, he must have known that such propinquity likely would lead to that result. [By] intentionally creating a situation likely to induce Henry to make incriminating statements without the assistance of counsel [after Henry had been indicted and counsel had been appointed for him], the government violated [his] Sixth Amendment right to counsel."

This broad language would seem to prohibit the government from "planting" even a completely "passive" secret agent in a person's cell once adversary proceedings have commenced against him. But the *Henry* Court cautioned that it was not "called upon to pass on the situation where an informant is placed in [close] proximity [to a prisoner] but makes no effort to stimulate conversations about the crime charged."

Moreover, concurring Justice Powell made it plain that he could not join the majority opinion if it held that "the mere presence or incidental conversation of an informant in a jail cell would violate *Massiah*." The *Massiah* doctrine, emphasized Powell, "does not prohibit the introduction of spontaneous statements that are not elicited by governmental action. Thus, the Sixth Amendment is not violated when a passive listening device collects, but does not induce, incriminating comments."[a]

As *Kuhlmann v. Wilson* (discussed below), well illustrates, the line between "active" and "passive" secret agents—between "stimulating" conversations with a defendant in order to "elicit" incriminating statements and taking no action "beyond merely listening"—is an exceedingly difficult one to draw.

---

a. Dissenting Justice Blackmun, joined by White, J., contended that "the Court not only missteps in forging a new *Massiah* test; it proceeds to misapply the very test it has created. The new test requires a showing that the agent created a situation 'likely to induce' the production of incriminating remarks, and that the informant in fact 'prompted' the defendant. Even accepting the most capacious reading of both this language and the facts, I believe that neither prong of the Court's test is satisfied."

In a separate dissent, Justice Rehnquist maintained "that *Massiah* constitutes such a substantial departure from the traditional concerns that underlie the Sixth Amendment guarantee that its language, if not its actual holding, should be re-examined."

KUHLMANN v. WILSON, 477 U.S. 436 (1986), arose as follows: Respondent Wilson and two confederates robbed a garage and fatally shot a dispatcher. He admitted that he had witnessed the robbery and murder, but denied any involvement in the crimes and denied knowing who the robbers were. After his arraignment for robbery and murder, Wilson was placed in a cell with a prisoner (Lee) who was a secret police informant. According to his arrangement with the police, Lee was not to ask any questions, but simply to "keep his ears open." Without any prompting, Wilson told Lee the same story he had told the police. Lee advised Wilson that his story "didn't sound too good" and that "things didn't look too good for him," but Wilson did not alter his story at that time. However, several days later, after a visit from his brother, who mentioned that members of the family were upset because they believed he had killed the dispatcher, Wilson changed his story. He admitted to Lee that he and two other men had planned and carried out the robbery and killed the dispatcher. Lee reported these incriminating statements to the police.

The trial court denied Wilson's motion to suppress his statements. Wilson was convicted of murder. The conviction was affirmed and he was denied federal habeas relief. However, following the decision in *Henry*, Wilson relitigated his claim. This time the Court of Appeals for the Second Circuit granted federal habeas relief, viewing the circumstances of his case indistinguishable from the facts of *Henry*. The Supreme Court, per Powell, J., reversed:

"[Since] the Sixth Amendment is not violated whenever—by luck or happenstance—the State obtains incriminating statements from the accused after the right to counsel has attached, *Moulton*, a defendant does not make out a violation of that right simply by showing that an informant, [reported] his incriminating statements to the police. Rather, the defendant must demonstrate that the police and their informant took some action, beyond merely listening, that was designed deliberately to elicit incriminating remarks. It is thus apparent that the Court of Appeals erred in concluding that respondent's right to counsel was violated under the circumstances of this case. [It failed] to accord to the state trial court's factual findings the presumption of correctness expressly required by 28 U.S.C. § 2254(d).

"The state court found that, [following police instructions, Lee] 'at no time asked any questions' of respondent concerning the pending charges * * *. The only remark made by Lee that has any support in this record was his comment that respondent's initial version of his participation in the crimes 'didn't sound too good.' [The] Court of Appeals focused on that one remark and gave a description of Lee's interaction with respondent that is completely at odds with the facts found by the trial court. [The Court of Appeals' conclusion] that the police 'deliberately elicited' respondent's [statements] conflicts with the decision of every other state and federal judge who reviewed this record, and is clear error in light of the provisions and intent of § 2254(d)."[b]

Dissenting Justice Brennan, joined by Marshall, J., maintained that "the state trial court simply found that Lee did not ask respondent any direct questions about the crime for which respondent was incarcerated. [The Court of Appeals] expressly accepted that finding, but concluded that, as a matter of law, the deliberate elicitation standard of *Henry* and *Massiah*, encompasses other, more subtle forms of stimulating incriminating admissions than overt questioning. [The court] observed that, while Lee asked respondent no questions, Lee nonetheless stimulated conversation concerning respondents' role in [the] robbery and murder by remarking that respondent's exculpatory story did not "sound too good" and

---

b. Chief Justice Burger, the author of *Henry*, joined the opinion of the Court, but also wrote a brief concurring opinion noting "a vast difference between placing an 'ear' in the suspect's cell and placing a voice in the cell to encourage conversation for the 'ear' to record."

that he had better come up with a better one. Thus,[it] concluded that the respondent's case [was] virtually indistinguishable from *Henry*.

"[Like the police informant in *Henry*,] Lee encouraged respondent to talk about his crime by conversing with him on the subject over the course of several days and by telling respondent that his exculpatory story would not convince anyone without more work. However, unlike the situation in *Henry*, a disturbing visit from respondent's brother, rather than a conversation with the informant, seems to have been the immediate catalyst for respondent's confession to Lee. While it might appear from this sequence of events that Lee's comment regarding respondent's story and his general willingness to converse with respondent about the crime were not the immediate causes of respondent's admission, I think that the deliberate elicitation standard requires consideration of the entire course of government behavior.

"The State intentionally created a situation in which it was foreseeable that respondent would make incriminating statements without the assistance of counsel. [While] the coup de grace was delivered by respondent's brother, the groundwork for respondent's confession was laid by the State. Clearly the State's actions had a sufficient nexus with respondent's admission of guilt to constitute deliberate elicitation within the meaning of *Henry*."[c]

Notes and Questions

1. *The distinction between placing an "ear" in the defendant's cell and placing a "voice" there to encourage conversations.* As a practical matter, is there any difference, let alone "a vast difference" (see fn. b, supra), between placing an "ear" in the cell and placing a "voice" there? Doesn't the "voice" go with the "ear"?

Is a defendant likely to make incriminating statements to a "cellmate" unless the latter has developed a relationship of trust and confidence with the defendant? Doesn't a police informant have to exchange remarks with the defendant if only to avoid "alerting" the defendant that something is amiss? If two people share the same cell for days or even weeks, don't they both talk—and talk back and forth? How likely is it that the flow of conversation and the progression of various conversations can be accurately reconstructed? How much incentive does the informant have to do so? Once formal proceedings have been initiated, is the only effective way to prevent police interference with the attorney-client relationship to prohibit any government agent from approaching a defendant in the absence of counsel? See the remarks of Professor Kamisar in Choper, Kamisar & Tribe, *The Supreme Court: Trends and Development*, 1979–80 (1981) at 107–08.

2. *Are the courts asking the wrong questions in cases like Henry and Wilson? Is the true issue in these cases "privacy"?* Yes, maintains H. Richard Uviller, *Evidence from the Mind of the Criminal Suspect*, 87 Colum.L.Rev. 1137, 1191, 1195 (1987):

"The fourth amendment is the guardian of privacy and the questions the courts should be asking are: Did the defendant enjoy a protected expectation of privacy in the circumstances, and if so did the state have a properly predicated warrant to encroach, or some good basis for the lack of it? * * *

"[W]hile a defendant may be required to bear the risk of ordinary disloyalty among trusted associates, it does not follow that he must also bear the risk that the government is engaging in surreptitious invasions. The fact that informers are

---

c. Stevens, J., filed a separate dissent, agreeing with Justice Brennan's analysis of the merits of respondent's habeas petition.

commonplace in the councils of criminals does not deprive the criminals of reasonable expectations of privacy for fourth amendment purposes any more than the frequency of wiretaps in Mafia investigations excuses the government from the duty to take its case to a judge for advance authorization of an electronic surveillance. [The *Hoffa* Court, see p. 470] should have regarded Partin as the human bug he was and treated his intrusion as a search and seizure (unless, of course, the government was right in the claim that they had not 'placed' him in Hoffa's company).

"Thus, Stewart[, who wrote the opinion of the Court in both *Hoffa* and *Massiah*,] unnaturally distorted the sixth amendment's promise of a skilled advocate in order to narrow the interval in which the suspect's mind could be probed and unwisely shortened the reach of the fourth amendment's guarantee of security by permitting the government deliberately to insert a human spy into the suspect's private space to report on declarations and behavior that might betray a guilty mind."

3. But consider James Tomkovicz, *An Adversary System Defense of the Right to Counsel Against Informants: Truth, Fair Play, and the Massiah Doctrine*, 22 U.C.Davis L.Rev. 1, 36–38 (1988):

"[If the fourth amendment] were the real basis for protection against government informants, the resulting doctrine would have to be considerably different than the current *Massiah* doctrine. For example, fourth amendment protection would not depend either on the initiation of adversarial proceedings or on active elicitation.

"More important, *Massiah*'s substantive sixth amendment protection is radically different than the substance of prospective fourth amendment shelter. The prohibition against 'unreasonable' searches would provide a limited safeguard against the informant surveillance itself. The *Massiah* right, on the other hand, raises an absolute barrier not to the surveillance, but to the use of its products at trial. Consequently, one cannot rationalize the current *Massiah* entitlement upon a fourth amendment foundation. Both the doctrine and the right belie any fourth amendment roots.[175]"

4. *Private citizens vs. state agents.* As pointed out in Tomkovicz, supra, at 72 n. 283, "lower courts have struggled to discern standards for determining when private citizens become state agents for *Massiah* purposes," relying upon several interrelated criteria: the existence of an explicit agreement or prearrangement between law enforcement and an informant; the source of an informant's motivation; the benefits accruing to the informant; and the governmental involvement in placing the informant near the defendant. Should the *Massiah* doctrine govern an informant's conduct "if a reasonable person would conclude that the informant has secured and reported inculpatory remarks at least in part because of affirmative governmental encouragement"? See id. at 74.

---

175. This statement is not meant to imply that the Court's unease with its repeated refusals to accord any fourth amendment protection against informant surveillance [has] not contributed to the birth and perpetuation of the *Massiah* doctrine. Although not a principled basis, the Court's discomfort cannot be discounted entirely as an actual influence upon the law in this area.

In addition, the textual discussion is not meant to imply that the fourth amendment should not have a role in informant contexts. [Rather,] the point [is] that the *Massiah* doctrine is not fourth amendment law in disguise.

ONCE THE SIXTH AMENDMENT RIGHT TO COUNSEL ARISES, DOES IT ATTACH TO ALL OTHER OFFENSES CLOSELY RELATED TO THE PARTICULAR OFFENSE CHARGED?

TEXAS v. COBB

532 U.S. 162, 121 S.Ct. 1335, 149 L.Ed.2d 321 (2001).

CHIEF JUSTICE REHNQUIST delivered the opinion of the Court.

[Respondent confessed to the burglary of a home, but denied knowing anything about the disappearance of a woman and child from the home. He was indicted for the burglary and counsel was appointed to represent him. While in police custody, he waived his *Miranda* rights and confessed to the murders of the woman and child who had disappeared from the home. (After the woman had confronted him during the burglary, he had killed her and buried her and her baby.) He was convicted of capital murder and sentenced to death. The Texas Court of Appeals reversed respondent's conviction, concluding that his Sixth Amendment right to counsel had attached on the capital murder charge even though he had not yet been charged with that offense: "Once the right to counsel attaches to the offense charged, it also attaches to any other offense that is very closely related factually to the offense charged." But the U.S. Supreme Court disagreed.]

In *McNeil v. Wisconsin* [p. 663], we explained [that when the Sixth Amendment right to counsel] arises "[it] is offense specific. It cannot be invoked once for all future prosecutions, for it does not attach until a prosecution is commenced * * *." Accordingly, we held that a defendant's statements regarding offenses for which he had not been charged were admissible notwithstanding the attachment of the Sixth Amendment right to counsel on other charged offenses.

Some [lower courts], however, have read into *McNeil*'s offense-specific definition an exception for crimes that are "factually related" to a charged offense. * * * We decline to do so.

[Respondent] predicts that the offense-specific rule will prove "disastrous" to suspects' constitutional rights and will "permit law enforcement officers almost complete and total license to conduct unwanted and uncounseled interrogations." Besides offering no evidence that such a parade of horribles has occurred in those jurisdictions that have not enlarged upon *McNeil*, he fails to appreciate the significance of two critical considerations. First, there can be no doubt that a suspect must be apprised of his rights against compulsory self-incrimination and to consult with an attorney before authorities may conduct custodial interrogation. In the present case, police scrupulously followed *Miranda*'s dictates when questioning respondent.[2] Second, it is critical to recognize that the Constitution does not negate society's interest in the ability of police to talk to witnesses and suspects, even those who have been charged with other offenses.

[Although] it is clear that the Sixth Amendment right to counsel attaches only to charged offenses, we have recognized in other contexts that the definition of an

---

2. Curiously, while predicting disastrous consequences for the core values underlying the Sixth Amendment, the dissenters give short shrift to the Fifth Amendment's role (as expressed in *Miranda* and *Dickerson*) in protecting a defendant's right to consult with counsel before talking to police. Even though the Sixth Amendment right to counsel has not attached to uncharged offenses, defendants retain the ability under *Miranda* to refuse any police questioning, and, indeed, charged defendants presumably have met with counsel and have had the opportunity to discuss whether it is advisable to invoke those Fifth Amendment rights. Thus, in all but the rarest of cases, the Court's decision today will have no impact whatsoever upon a defendant's ability to protect his Sixth Amendment right. * * *

"offense" is not necessarily limited to the four corners of a charging instrument. In *Blockburger v. United States*, [discussed in *United States v. Dixon*, p. 1140], we explained that "where the same act or transaction constitutes a violation of two distinct statutory provisions, the test to be applied to determine whether there are two offenses or only one, is whether each provision requires proof of a fact which the other does not." We have since applied the *Blockburger* test to delineate the scope of the Fifth Amendment's Double Jeopardy Clause, which prevents multiple or successive prosecutions for the "same offence." We see no constitutional difference between the meaning of the term "offense" in the contexts of double jeopardy and of the right to counsel. Accordingly, we hold that when the Sixth Amendment right to counsel attaches, it does encompass offenses that, even if not formally charged, would be considered the same offense under the *Blockburger* test.[3]

While simultaneously conceding that its own test "lacks the precision for which police officers may hope," the dissent suggests that adopting *Blockburger*'s definition of "offense" will prove difficult to administer. But it is the dissent's vague iterations of the " 'closely related to' " or " 'inextricably intertwined with' " test that would defy simple application. The dissent seems to presuppose that officers will possess complete knowledge of the circumstances surrounding an incident, such that the officers will be able to tailor their investigation to avoid addressing factually related offenses. Such an assumption, however, ignores the reality that police often are not yet aware of the exact sequence and scope of events they are investigating—indeed, that is why police must investigate in the first place. Deterred by the possibility of violating the Sixth Amendment, police likely would refrain from questioning certain defendants altogether.

It remains only to apply these principles to the facts at hand. [As] defined by Texas law, burglary and capital murder are not the same offense under *Blockburger*. [Accordingly,] the Sixth Amendment right to counsel did not bar police from interrogating respondent regarding the murders, and respondent's confession was therefore admissible. * * *

JUSTICE KENNEDY, with whom JUSTICE SCALIA and JUSTICE THOMAS join, concurring. * * *

As the facts of the instant case well illustrate, it is difficult to understand the utility of a Sixth Amendment rule that operates to invalidate a confession given by the free choice of suspects who have received proper advice of their *Miranda* rights but waived them nonetheless. The *Miranda* rule, and the related preventative rule of *Edwards v. Arizona*, serve to protect a suspect's voluntary choice not to speak outside his lawyer's presence. The parallel rule announced in *Michigan v. Jackson* [p. 659], however, supersedes the suspect's voluntary choice to speak with investigators. [While] the *Edwards* rule operates to preserve the free choice of a suspect to remain silent, if *Jackson* were to apply it would override that choice. [The] Sixth Amendment right to counsel attaches quite without reference to the suspect's choice to speak with investigators after a *Miranda* warning. It is the commencement of a formal prosecution, indicated by the initiation of adversary judicial proceedings, that marks the beginning of the Sixth Amendment right. These events may be quite independent of the suspect's election to remain silent, the interest which the *Edwards* rule serves to protect with respect to *Miranda* and the Fifth Amendment, and it thus makes little sense for a protective rule to attach absent such an election by the suspect. We ought to question the wisdom of

---

3. In this sense, we could just as easily describe the Sixth Amendment as "prosecution specific," insofar as it prevents discussion of charged offenses as well as offenses that, under *Blockburger*, could not be the subject of a later prosecution. And, indeed, the text of the Sixth Amendment confines its scope to "all criminal *prosecutions*."

a judge-made preventative rule to protect a suspect's desire not to speak when it cannot be shown that he had that intent.

Even if *Jackson* is to remain good law, its protections should apply only where a suspect has made a clear and unambiguous assertion of the right not to speak outside the presence of counsel, the same clear election required under *Edwards*. Cobb made no such assertion here, yet Justice Breyer's dissent rests upon the assumption that the *Jackson* rule should operate to exclude the confession no matter. * * *

Justice Breyer defends *Jackson* by arguing that, once a suspect has accepted counsel at the commencement of adversarial proceedings, he should not be forced to confront the police during interrogation without the assistance of counsel. But the acceptance of counsel at an arraignment or similar proceeding only begs the question: acceptance of counsel for what? It is quite unremarkable that a suspect might want the assistance of an expert in the law to guide him through hearings and trial, and the attendant complex legal matters that might arise, but nonetheless might choose to give on his own a forthright account of the events that occurred. A court-made rule that prevents a suspect from even making this choice serves little purpose, especially given the regime of *Miranda* and *Edwards*.

JUSTICE BREYER, with whom JUSTICE STEVENS, JUSTICE SOUTER, and JUSTICE GINSBURG join, dissenting. * * *

This case focuses [upon] the meaning of the words "offense specific." These words appear in this Court's Sixth Amendment case law, not in the Sixth Amendment's text. See U.S. Const., Amdt. 6 (guaranteeing right to counsel "[i]n all criminal prosecutions"). The definition of these words is not self-evident. [This] case requires us to determine whether an "offense"—for Sixth Amendment purposes—includes factually related aspects of a single course of conduct other than those few acts that make up the essential elements of the crime charged.

We should answer this question in light of the Sixth Amendment's basic objectives as set forth in this Court's case law. At the very least, we should answer it in a way that does not undermine those objectives. But the Court today decides that "offense" means the crime set forth within "the four corners of a charging instrument," along with other crimes that "would be considered the same offense" under the test established by *Blockburger*. In my view, this unnecessarily technical definition undermines Sixth Amendment protections while doing nothing to further effective law enforcement. * * *

Jackson focuses upon a suspect—perhaps a frightened or uneducated suspect—who, hesitant to rely upon his own unaided judgment in his dealings with the police, has invoked his constitutional right to legal assistance in such matters. * * * *Jackson* says that, once such a request has been made, the police may not simply throw that suspect—who does not trust his own unaided judgment—back upon his own devices by requiring him to rely for protection upon that same unaided judgment that he previously rejected as inadequate. In a word, the police may not force a suspect who has asked for legal counsel to make a critical legal choice without the legal assistance that he has requested and that the Constitution guarantees. [The] Constitution does not take away with one hand what it gives with the other. * * *

Justice Kennedy [criticizes] *Jackson* on the ground that it prevents a suspect "[from] making th[e] choice" to "give [a] forthright account of the events that occurred." But that is not so. A suspect may initiate communication with the police, thereby avoiding the risk that the police induced him to make, unaided, the kind of critical legal decision best made with the help of counsel, whom he has requested.

Unlike Justice Kennedy, the majority does not call *Jackson* itself into question. But the majority would undermine that case by significantly diminishing the Sixth Amendment protections that the case provides. That is because criminal codes are lengthy and highly detailed, often proliferating "overlapping and related statutory offenses" to the point where prosecutors can easily "spin out a startlingly numerous series of offenses from a single * * * criminal transaction." Thus, an armed robber who reaches across a store counter, grabs the cashier, and demands "your money or your life," may through that single instance of conduct have committed several "offenses," in the majority's sense of the term, including armed robbery, assault, battery, trespass, use of a firearm to commit a felony, and perhaps possession of a firearm by a felon, as well. A person who is using and selling drugs on a single occasion might be guilty of possessing various drugs, conspiring to sell drugs, being under the influence of illegal drugs, possessing drug paraphernalia, possessing a gun in relation to the drug sale, and, depending upon circumstances, violating various gun laws as well.

[The] majority's rule permits law enforcement officials to question those charged with a crime without first approaching counsel, through the simple device of asking questions about any other related crime not actually charged in the indictment. Thus, the police could ask the individual charged with robbery about, say, the assault of the cashier not yet charged, or about any other uncharged offense (unless under *Blockburger*'s definition it counts as the "same crime"), all *without notifying counsel*. Indeed, the majority's rule would permit law enforcement officials to question anyone charged with any crime in any one of the examples just given about his or her conduct on the single relevant occasion without notifying counsel unless the prosecutor has charged every possible crime arising out of that same brief course of conduct. What Sixth Amendment sense—what common sense—does such a rule make? The majority's approach [will] undermine the lawyer's role as " 'medium' " between the defendant and the government. And it will, on a random basis, remove a significant portion of the protection that this Court has found inherent in the Sixth Amendment.

[In] *Brewer v. Williams*, the effect of the majority's rule would have been even more dramatic. Because first-degree murder and child abduction each required proof of a fact not required by the other, and because at the time of the impermissible interrogation Williams had been charged only with abduction of a child, Williams' murder conviction should have remained undisturbed.[a] [This] is not to suggest that this Court has previously addressed and decided the question presented by this case. Rather, it is to point out that the Court's conception of the Sixth Amendment right at the time [that] *Brewer* [was] decided naturally presumed that it extended to factually related but uncharged offenses.

At the same time, the majority's rule threatens the legal clarity necessary for effective law enforcement. That is because the majority, aware that the word "offense" ought to encompass something beyond "the four corners of the charging instrument," imports into Sixth Amendment law the definition of "offense" set forth in *Blockburger*, a case interpreting the Double Jeopardy Clause of the Fifth Amendment, which Clause uses the word "offence" but otherwise has no rele-

---

a. But see Craig M. Bradley, *Seas, Bogs and Police Interrogation*, Trial, Oct. 2001, pp. 71, 73: "It is true that under *Cobb*, the fact that Williams had a right to counsel as to the kidnapping charge would not protect him from interrogation on the murder charge. But there are several reasons why *Williams* would still come out the same way even after *Cobb*. The first is that, unlike Cobb, Williams was not given his *Miranda* warnings before the interrogation in the police car. Second, Williams had been given *Miranda* warnings earlier and had indicated that he didn't want to speak to the police without counsel. Thus, although Williams might not have a *Sixth* Amendment right to counsel, his *Fifth* Amendment rights would still have been violated. Third, the police had promised counsel that they would not interrogate him during the car trip, so they may have violated William's due process rights when they broke that promise."

vance here. Whatever Fifth Amendment virtues *Blockburger* may have, to import it into this Sixth Amendment context will work havoc.

[The] simple-sounding *Blockburger* test has proved extraordinarily difficult to administer in practice. Judges, lawyers, and law professors often disagree about how to apply it. [The] test has emerged as a tool in an area of our jurisprudence that The Chief Justice has described as "a veritable Sargasso Sea which could not fail to challenge the most intrepid judicial navigator." Yet the Court now asks, not the lawyers and judges who ordinarily work with double jeopardy law, but police officers in the field, to navigate *Blockburger* when they question suspects. Some will apply the test successfully; some will not. Legal challenges are inevitable. The result, I believe, will resemble not so much the Sargasso Sea as the criminal law equivalent of Milton's "Serbonian Bog ... Where Armies whole have sunk."

There is, of course, an alternative. We can, and should, define "offense" in terms of the conduct that constitutes the crime that the offender committed on a particular occasion, including criminal acts that are "closely related to" or "inextricably intertwined with" the particular crime set forth in the charging instrument. This alternative is not perfect. [Yet] virtually every lower court in the United States to consider the issue has defined "offense" in the Sixth Amendment context to encompass such closely related acts. * * *

One cannot say in favor of this commonly followed approach that it is perfectly clear—only that, because it comports with common sense, it is far easier to apply than that of the majority. One might add that, unlike the majority's test, it is consistent with this Court's assumptions in previous cases [citing *Maine v. Moulton* and *Brewer v. Williams*]. And, most importantly, the "closely related" test furthers, rather than undermines, the Sixth Amendment's "right to counsel," a right so necessary to the realization in practice of that most "noble ideal," a fair trial.

The Texas Court of Criminal Appeals, following this commonly accepted approach, found that the charged burglary and the uncharged murders were "closely related." All occurred during a short period of time on the same day in the same basic location. The victims of the murders were also victims of the burglary. Cobb committed one of the murders in furtherance of the [burglary,] the other to cover up the crimes. The police, when questioning Cobb, knew that he already had a lawyer representing him on the burglary charges and had demonstrated their belief that this lawyer also represented Cobb in respect to the murders by asking his permission to question Cobb about the murders on previous occasions. The relatedness of the crimes is well illustrated by the impossibility of questioning Cobb about the murders without eliciting admissions about the burglary. * * *

SHOULD MASSIAH BE OVERRULED?

Should the Cobb Court have abolished Massiah altogether? Consider SHERRY F. COLB, *Why the Supreme Court Should Overrule the Massiah Doctrine and Permit Miranda Alone to Govern Interrogations*, <http://writ.news.findlaw.com/colb/20010509.html> (May 9, 2001):

"[When the Court handed down its decision in *Miranda*], [m]any of us expected *Massiah* eventually to disappear. After all, once *Miranda* was decided, it seemed no longer necessary and even counterproductive to apply different legal standards to interrogations, depending on whether a suspect had been indicted.

"[In] defense of *Massiah*'s 'indictment' distinction, the Court has claimed that indictment is 'a critical stage' in prosecuting a defendant, for then the defendant can harm himself irreparably by statements he makes before a lawyer arrives on the scene, before the trial even begins. Fair enough. But that argument simply suggests that *Massiah* rights should be triggered long before trial—without explaining why they should not be triggered long before indictment, too.

"There is nothing to stop a pre-indictment suspect from doing exactly the same self-inflicted harm as his post-indictment counterpart. Indeed, a suspect may do even greater harm prior to indictment, since an indictment can serve to put a suspect on notice that a prosecutor has made the decision to target him in particular and that he therefore ought to exercise discretion.

"*Massiah* rights will thus often come into being too late to be of any use to the defendant. The fortuity of when the prosecution decides to charge him with a particular crime, a matter over which the defendant has no control, can therefore be decisive.

"The *Cobb* Court could—and should—have gotten rid of *Massiah*'s distinction, and let *Miranda* alone protect suspects. But it did not.

"[The] *Cobb* dissenters argued [that] *Miranda* does not sufficiently protect suspects from interrogation they feel ill-equipped to handle on their own. The dissenters may be right. [But] whether one agrees with the majority or with the dissent, it should be *Miranda*—not *Massiah*—that is at issue.

"The dissent's arguments are really arguments for expanding *Miranda*. [They] are not, however, arguments for preserving *Massiah*'s groundless distinction between those who have, and those who have not, been indicted.

"The Court should abandon the separate *Massiah* doctrine, and conduct the important debate that is waiting in the wings, about the scope of *Miranda*. That debate will probably turn largely on the perceived desirability of obtaining voluntary (but ill-advised) confessions from criminal suspects. * * *"

CHAPTER 10

LINEUPS, SHOWUPS AND OTHER PRE-TRIAL IDENTIFICATION PROCEDURES

■ ■ ■

"Of all investigative procedures employed by police in criminal cases, probably none is less reliable than the eyewitness identification. Erroneous identifications create more injustice and cause more suffering to innocent persons than perhaps any other aspect of police work."

—International Association of Chiefs of Police, *Training Key #600: Eyewitness Identifications* (2006).

———

"[N]umerous analyses over several decades have consistently shown that mistaken eyewitness identification is the single largest source of wrongful convictions."

—Gary L. Wells & Eric P. Seelau, *Eyewitness Identification and Legal Policy on Lineups*, 1 Psychology, Pub. Pol'y. & L. 765 (1995).

———

"Since DNA testing became available in the late 1980s, more than 250 innocent people have been exonerated by postconviction DNA testing. [Did] the first 250 DNA exonerations result from unfortunate but nevertheless unusual circumstances? Or were these errors the result of entrenched practices that criminal courts rely upon every day?

[The] role of mistaken eyewitness identifications in these wrongful convictions is now well known. Eyewitnesses misidentified 76% of the exonerees (190 of 250 cases). [Two] related problems recurred: suggestive identification procedures and unreliable identifications."

—Brandon L. Garrett, *Convicting the Innocent: Where Criminal Prosecutions Go Wrong* 5–6, 48 (2011).

———

"We can't come close to estimating the number of false convictions that occur in the United States, but the accumulating mass of exonerations gives us a glimpse of what we're missing. We have located 328 exonerations since 1989, not counting at least 135 defendants in the Tulia and Rampart mass exonerations, or more than 70 convicted childcare sex abuse defendants. Almost all the individual

760

exonerations that we know about are clustered in two crimes, rape and murder. They are surrounded by widening circles of categories of cases with false convictions that have not been detected: rape convictions that have not been reexamined with DNA evidence; robberies, for which DNA identification is useless; murder cases that are ignored because the defendants were not sentenced to death; assault and drug convictions that are forgotten entirely. Any plausible guess at the total number of miscarriages of justice in America in the last fifteen years must be in the thousands, perhaps tens of thousands.

"We can see some clear patterns in those false convictions that have come to light: who was convicted, and why. For rape the dominant problem is eyewitness misidentification—and cross-racial misidentification in particular, which accounts for the extraordinary number of the false rape convictions with black defendants and white victims. * * * "

—Samuel R. Gross, Kristen Jacoby, Daniel J. Matheson, Nicholas Montgomery & Sujata Patil, *Exonerations in the United States 1989 Through 2003* (2004).

SECTION 1.   *WADE* AND *GILBERT*: CONSTITUTIONAL CONCERN ABOUT THE DANGERS INVOLVED IN EYEWITNESS IDENTIFICATIONS

The Supreme Court recognized the potential reliability problems with eyewitness identification procedures over forty years ago in UNITED STATES v. WADE, 388 U.S. 218 (1967).[a] As Justice BRENNAN, writing for a majority of the Court, explained:

"[T]he confrontation compelled by the State between the accused and the victim or witnesses to a crime to elicit identification evidence is peculiarly riddled with innumerable dangers and variable factors which might seriously, even crucially, derogate from a fair trial. The vagaries of eyewitness identification are well-known; the annals of criminal law are rife with instances of mistaken identification. [A] major factor contributing to the high incidence of miscarriage of justice from mistaken identification has been the degree of suggestion inherent in the manner in which the prosecution presents the suspect to witnesses for pretrial identification. A commentator has observed that '[t]he influence of improper suggestion upon identifying witnesses probably accounts for more miscarriages of justice than any other single factor—perhaps it is responsible for more such errors than all other factors combined.' Wall, *Eye-Witness Identification in Criminal Cases* 26 [1965]. Suggestion can be created intentionally or unintentionally in many subtle ways. And the dangers for the suspect are particularly grave when the witness' opportunity for observation was insubstantial, and thus his susceptibility to suggestion the greatest.

"Moreover, '[i]t is a matter of common experience that, once a witness has picked out the accused at the line-up, he is not likely to go back on his word later on, so that in practice the issue of identity may (in the absence of other relevant evidence) for all practical purposes be determined there and then, before the trial.'

"The pretrial confrontation for purpose of identification may take the form of a lineup, also known as an 'identification parade' or 'showup,' as in the present case, or presentation of the suspect alone to the witness, as in *Stovall v. Denno*. It

---

a. The Court decided two other pretrial identification cases the same day: *Gilbert v. California*, 388 U.S. 263 (1967), and *Stovall v. Denno*, 388 U.S. 293 (1967), both discussed infra.

is obvious that risks of suggestion attend either form of confrontation and increase the dangers inhering in eyewitness identification. But as is the case with secret interrogations, there is serious difficulty in depicting what transpires at lineups and other forms of identification confrontations. [The] defense can seldom reconstruct the manner and mode of lineup identification for judge or jury at trial. [The] impediments to an objective observation are increased when the victim is the witness. Lineups are prevalent in rape and robbery prosecutions and present a particular hazard that a victim's understandable outrage may excite vengeful or spiteful motives. In any event, neither witnesses nor lineup participants are apt to be alert for conditions prejudicial to the suspect. And if they were, it would likely be of scant benefit to the suspect since neither witnesses nor lineup participants are likely to be schooled in the detection of suggestive influences.[13] Improper influences may go undetected by a suspect, guilty or not, who experiences the emotional tension which we might expect in one being confronted with potential accusers. Even when he does observe abuse, if he has a criminal record he may be reluctant to take the stand and open up the admission of prior convictions. Moreover any protestations by the suspect of the fairness of the lineup made at trial are likely to be in vain; the jury's choice is between the accused's unsupported version and that of the police officers present. In short, the accused's inability effectively to reconstruct at trial any unfairness that occurred at the lineup may deprive him of his only opportunity meaningfully to attack the credibility of the witness' courtroom identification.

"[The] potential for improper influence is illustrated by the circumstances, insofar as they appear, surrounding the prior identifications in the three cases we decide today. In the present case, the testimony of the identifying witnesses elicited on cross-examination revealed that those witnesses were taken to the courthouse and seated in the courtroom to await assembly of the lineup. The courtroom faced on a hallway observable to the witnesses through an open door. [One witness] testified that she saw Wade 'standing in the hall' within sight of an FBI agent. Five or six other prisoners later appeared in the hall. [Another witness] testified that he saw a person in the hall in the custody of the agent who 'resembled the person that we identified as the one that had entered the bank.'

"The lineup in *Gilbert* was conducted in an auditorium in which some 100 witnesses to several alleged state and federal robberies charged to Gilbert made wholesale identifications of Gilbert as the robber in each other's presence, a procedure said to be fraught with dangers of suggestion. And the vice of suggestion created by the identification in *Stovall* was the presentation to the witness of the suspect alone handcuffed to police officers. It is hard to imagine a situation more clearly conveying the suggestion to the witness that the one presented is believed guilty by the police. * * *

"Insofar as the accused's conviction may rest on a courtroom identification in fact the fruit of a suspect pretrial identification which the accused is helpless to subject to effective scrutiny at trial, the accused is deprived of that right of cross-examination which is an essential safeguard to his right to confront the witnesses against him. And even though cross-examination is a precious safeguard to a fair trial, it cannot be viewed as an absolute assurance of accuracy and reliability. Thus in the present context, where so many variables and pitfalls exist, the first line of defense must be the prevention of unfairness and the lessening of the hazards of eyewitness identification at the lineup itself. The trial which might determine the accused's fate may well not be that in the courtroom but that at the

---

13. An additional impediment to the detection of such influences by participants, including the suspect, is the physical conditions often surrounding the conduct of the lineup. In many, lights shine on the stage in such a way that the suspect cannot see the witness. [In] some a one-way mirror is used and what is said on the witness' side cannot be heard. * * *

pretrial confrontation, with the State aligned against the accused, the witness the sole jury, and the accused unprotected against the overreaching, intentional or unintentional, and with little or no effective appeal from the judgment there rendered by the witness—'that's the man.' "

Because of the "grave potential for prejudice, intentional or not, in the pretrial lineup," the *Wade-Gilbert* Court held that a post-indictment lineup is a critical stage of the prosecution giving the accused person a right to have counsel present. See supra Ch. 4, Sec. 1.B. Absent notification and an "intelligent waiver" of that right, the Court adopted a *per se* rule excluding any reference to the out-of-court identification at trial:

"No substantial countervailing policy considerations have been advanced against the requirement of the presence of counsel. Concern is expressed that the requirement will forestall prompt identifications and result in obstruction of the confrontations. As for the first, we note that in the two cases in which the right to counsel is today held to apply, counsel had already been appointed and no argument is made in either case that notice to counsel would have prejudicially delayed the confrontations. Moreover, we leave open the question whether the presence of substitute counsel might not suffice where notification and presence of the suspect's own counsel would result in prejudicial delay. And to refuse to recognize the right to counsel for fear that counsel will obstruct the course of justice is contrary to the basic assumptions upon which this Court has operated in Sixth Amendment cases. We rejected similar logic in *Miranda,* concerning presence of counsel during custodial interrogation.

"[In] our view counsel can hardly impede legitimate law enforcement; on the contrary, for the reasons expressed, law enforcement may be assisted by preventing the infiltration of taint in the prosecution's identification evidence. That result cannot help the guilty avoid conviction but can only help assure that the right man has been brought to justice.

"Legislative or other regulations, such as those of local police departments, which eliminate the risks of abuse and unintentional suggestion at lineup proceedings and the impediments to meaningful confrontation at trial may also remove the basis for regarding the stage as 'critical.' But neither Congress nor the federal authorities have seen fit to provide a solution. What we hold today 'in no way creates a constitutional strait-jacket which will handicap sound efforts at reform, nor is it intended to have this effect.' *Miranda.*"

In *Wade* itself, the prosecution had not attempted to introduce evidence of the out-of-court identification at trial.[b] Rather, the trial court had permitted the eyewitnesses to identify the defendant in the courtroom over a defense objection that the in-court identification should be excluded because Wade had been denied counsel at the out-of-court-pre-trial line up. The Supreme Court refused to adopt a *per se* rule regarding the admission of later courtroom identifications:

"We come now to the question whether the denial of Wade's motion to strike the courtroom identification by the bank witnesses at trial because of the absence of his counsel at the lineup required, as the Court of Appeals held, the grant of a new trial at which such evidence is to be excluded. We do not think this disposition can be justified without first giving the Government the opportunity to establish by clear and convincing evidence that the in-court identifications were based upon observations of the suspect other than the lineup identification. * * * Where, as here, the admissibility of evidence of the lineup identification itself is not involved, a *per se* rule of exclusion of courtroom identification would be

---

b. In *Gilbert,* however, the Court applied its *per se* exclusionary rule to the testimony of various prosecution witnesses that they had also identified petitioner at a pretrial lineup. See fn. c infra.

unjustified. [A] rule limited solely to the exclusion of testimony concerning identification at the lineup itself, without regard to admissibility of the courtroom identification, would render the right to counsel an empty one. The lineup is most often used, as in the present case, to crystallize the witnesses' identification of the defendant for future reference. We have already noted that the lineup identification will have that effect. The State may then rest upon the witnesses' unequivocal courtroom identification, and not mention the pretrial identification as part of the State's case at trial. Counsel is then in the predicament in which Wade's counsel found himself—realizing that possible unfairness at the lineup may be the sole means of attack upon the unequivocal courtroom identification, and having to probe in the dark in an attempt to discover and reveal unfairness, while bolstering the government witness' courtroom identification by bringing out and dwelling upon his prior identification. Since counsel's presence at the lineup would equip him to attack not only the lineup identification but the courtroom identification as well, limiting the impact of violation of the right to counsel to exclusion of evidence only of identification at the lineup itself disregards a critical element of that right.

"We think it follows that the proper test to be applied in these situations is that quoted in *Wong Sun v. United States* [p. 894], ' "[W]hether, granting establishment of the primary illegality the evidence to which instant objection is made has been come at by exploitation of that illegality or instead by means sufficiently distinguishable to be purged of the primary taint." Maguire, *Evidence of Guilt* 221 (1959).' Application of this test in the present context requires consideration of various factors; for example, the prior opportunity to observe the alleged criminal act, the existence of any discrepancy between any pre-lineup description and the defendant's actual description, any identification prior to lineup of another person, the identification by picture of the defendant prior to the lineup, failure to identify the defendant on a prior occasion, and the lapse of time between the alleged act and the lineup identification. It is also relevant to consider those facts which, despite the absence of counsel, are disclosed concerning the conduct of the lineup.[33]"

The *Wade* majority then vacated the conviction pending a hearing to determine whether the in-court identifications had an independent source, or whether, in any event, the introduction of the evidence was harmless error under *Chapman v. California* [Ch. 27, § 5].[c]

NOTES ON THE MEANING OF THE *WADE-GILBERT* RULE

1. *How far does the Wade–Gilbert rule extend?* Justice White, joined by

Justices Harlan and Stewart, dissented from the majority's decision in *Wade* and described the Court's opinion as "far-reaching:"

---

33. Thus it is not the case that "[i]t matters not how well the witness knows the suspect, whether the witness is the suspect's mother, brother, or long-time associate, and no matter how long or well the witness observed the perpetrator at the scene of the crime" [quoting from Justice White's dissenting opinion in *Wade*]. Such factors will have an important bearing upon the true basis of the witness' in-court identification. * * *

c. Compare *Gilbert,* where various witnesses who identified petitioner in the courtroom also testified, on direct examination by the prosecution, that they had identified petitioner at a prior lineup. "That [pretrial lineup] testimony," ruled the Court, "is the direct result of the illegal lineup 'come at by exploitation of [the primary] illegality.' *Wong Sun.* The State is therefore not entitled to an opportunity to show that that testimony had an independent source. Only a *per se* exclusionary rule as to such testimony can be an effective sanction to assure that law enforcement authorities will respect the accused's constitutional right to the presence of his counsel at the critical lineup. [That] conclusion is buttressed by the consideration that the witness' testimony of his lineup identification will enhance the impact of his in-court identification on the jury and seriously aggravate whatever derogation exists of the accused's right to a fair trial. Therefore, unless the [state supreme court] is 'able to declare a belief that it was harmless beyond a reasonable doubt,' *Chapman,* Gilbert will be entitled on remand to a new trial * * *."

"It proceeds first by creating a new *per se* rule of constitutional law: a criminal suspect cannot be subjected to a pretrial identification process in the absence of his counsel without violating the Sixth Amendment. If he is, the State may not buttress a later courtroom identification of the witness by any reference to the previous identification. Furthermore, the courtroom identification is not admissible at all unless the State can establish by clear and convincing proof that the testimony is not the fruit of the earlier identification made in the absence of defendant's counsel—admittedly a heavy burden for the State and probably an impossible one. To all intents and purposes, courtroom identifications are barred if pretrial identifications have occurred without counsel being present.

"The rule applies to any lineup, to any other techniques employed to produce an identification and *a fortiori* to a face-to-face encounter between the witness and the suspect alone, regardless of when the identification occurs, in time or place, and whether before or after indictment or information. It matters not how well the witness knows the suspect, whether the witness is the suspect's mother, brother, or long-time associate, and no matter how long or well the witness observed the perpetrator at the scene of the crime. The kidnap victim who has lived for days with his abductor is in the same category as the witness who has had only a fleeting glimpse of the criminal. Neither may identify the suspect without defendant's counsel being present."

Is that an accurate description of the majority opinion?

2. Will counsel's presence at a pre-trial line up enhance the reliability of identification procedures? Justice White, in his *Wade* dissent did not think so: "I would not extend [the adversary] system, at least as it presently operates, to police investigations and would not require counsel's presence at pretrial identification procedures. Counsel's interest is in not having his client placed at the scene of the crime, regardless of his whereabouts. Some counsel may advise their clients to refuse to make any movements or to speak any words in a lineup or even to appear in one. [Others] will hover over witnesses and begin their cross-examination then, menacing truthful factfinding as thoroughly as the Court fears the police now do. Certainly there is an implicit invitation to counsel to suggest rules for the lineup and to manage and produce it as best he can. I therefore doubt that the Court's new rule, at least absent some clearly defined limits on counsel's role, will measurably contribute to more reliable pretrial identifications. My fears are that it will have precisely the opposite result. * * * "

Notice that the *Wade* majority disagreed with him about what role counsel would play at a pre-trial identification procedure. Who is correct? What should the role of defense counsel be at a pre-trial lineup? Consider the Commentary to the *Model Pre–Arraignment Code* at 429–33:

"The two extreme positions might be stated thus:

"(1) Counsel is to be present merely as an observer to assure against abuse and bad faith by law enforcement officers, and to provide the basis for any attack he might wish to make on the identification at trial.

"(2) The lineup procedure is to be a fully adversary proceeding in which the counsel for the suspect may make objections and proposals, which if they are proper or even reasonable must be respected.

"The cases and commentaries, as well as the practice since *Wade* would indicate that the first interpretation of the counsel's role comes closer to describing the general interpretation of the constitutional requirement and to describing the practice under it. The major difficulty with this interpretation is that by forcing counsel into the role of a merely passive observer it gives him a job which at best can be accomplished in a large variety of ways including video recording and at worst is uncomfortable or demeaning.

"[On] the other hand, any attempt to give counsel at identification a more active role is fraught with difficulties not only for the police but for counsel himself. For the police the difficulty is that a procedure which is often under the supervision not of lawyers but of police officers will be subject to manipulation and objection by a trained legal counsel for one side only.

"[The] assigning of a more active role to counsel has perils for counsel as well. If he is entitled to make objections at the lineup procedure, will he be held to have waived these objections if he does not make them at the procedure and he wishes later to question the fairness or accuracy of the identification at trial? If such a possibility of waiver exists will he not almost be under an obligation to raise every conceivable objection? Moreover, this hard choice would be imposed on a lawyer at a very early stage of his contact with the case. Indeed the lawyer who did this work is often likely to be a junior member of the public defender's staff assigned on rotation to do 'lineup work,' and thus would not likely be the lawyer to handle the case at trial."

3. Waiver. If *Wade* seeks to protect the reliability of the identification process and to make available testimony about the conditions under which such process is carried out, why should the right to counsel at the lineup be subject to waiver? Permitting waiver of *Miranda* rights may be defended on the ground that an important, legitimate object is served by permitting suspects to bear witness to the truth under conditions which safeguard the exercise of responsible choice, but what comparable value is served by allowing suspects to waive counsel at the identification process?

4. When will an in-court identification be considered a fruit of an illegal out-of-court identification? Justice Black concurred in the *Wade* Court's establishment of a *per se* exclusionary rule for out-of-court identifications obtained in the absence of counsel, but dissented from its application of the fruits doctrine to later courtroom identifications: "The 'tainted fruit' determination required by the Court involves more than considerable difficulty. I think it is practically impossible. How is a witness capable of probing the recesses of his mind to draw a sharp line between a courtroom identification due exclusively to an earlier lineup and a courtroom identification due to memory not based on the lineup? [In] my view, the Fifth and Sixth Amendments are satisfied if the prosecution is precluded from using lineup identification as either an alternative to or corroboration of courtroom identification. If the prosecution does neither and its witnesses under oath identify the defendant in the courtroom, then I can find no justification for stopping the trial in midstream to hold a lengthy 'tainted fruit' hearing. * * * "

Does it follow, as Justice Black maintained, that therefore *every* courtroom identification made subsequent to an illegal police lineup (so long as not supplemented or corroborated by the earlier lineup) should be admitted? Or do the very reasons advanced by Justice Black—the great difficulties, if not impossibility of ascertaining the "taint" or lack of it—suggest that *no* courtroom identification preceded by an illegal police lineup should be allowed?

Is the requirement that the prosecution establish by clear and convincing proof that the courtroom testimony is untainted by the earlier illegal identification a "heavy" and "probably an impossible" burden, as Justice White maintained in his *Wade* dissent? If pre-trial identifications are held in violation of the suspect's right to counsel, does the *Wade-Gilbert* rule, as Justice White claimed, bar all courtroom identifications "to all intents and purposes"? Consider the remarks of

A.J. Davis, *The Role of the Defense Lawyer at a Lineup in Light of the Wade, Gilbert and Stovall Decisions,* 4 Crim.L.Bull. 273, 294–95 (1968) (panel discussion), a year after the lineup cases were decided:

"How [is the defense lawyer] going to prove that the in-court identification that the victim is about to make is the fruit of [the invalid police lineup]? The Supreme Court may say the burden of proof is on the prosecution, but you know and I know that the attitude of the trial judge is going to be that the burden of proof is on [the defense lawyer] as a practical matter to convince that judge. He is not going to be terribly sympathetic to these cases.

"What is the prosecution going to do? The prosecution is going to put the victim on the stand and the victim is going to say, 'When this robber came to me and put that gun in my face, I looked at him and I formed a mental picture. [Then,] I had this lineup and I compared this portrait in my mind with the people in the lineup and I picked out that defendant. Now I am in court and what am I doing? I am not paying any attention to the lineup. I am again conjuring up that [mental picture] which I evolved in my mind at the time of the robbery, and I am taking that [picture] and putting it next to this defendant at the counsel table and I am saying that they are precisely the same,' and the judge is going to say, 'Whoopie, there's an independent origin,' and you can attempt to prove from today to tomorrow that the pre-trial identification was unfair, but the trial court has a finding of fact to make here, and nine times out of ten, unless you have a very exceptional trial court, he is going to find against you on this issue."

Mr. Davis has turned out to be a better prognosticator than Justice White. The cases support the conclusions of commentators that when confronted with invalid pre-trial identifications the lower courts have "easily found an 'independent source' for an in-court identification," Note, 55 Minn.L.Rev. 779, 818 (1971), and have "readily avoided reversing convictions by stretching, often beyond reason and logic, the doctrines of independent source and harmless error," Joseph D. Grano, *Kirby, Biggers, and Ash: Do Any Constitutional Safeguards Remain Against the Danger of Convicting the Innocent?,* 72 Mich. L. Rev. 717, 722 (1974) [hereinafter "Grano"]; see also CRIMPROC § 7.3(f) (collecting cases).

    5. *Lineups and the self-incrimination clause.* In *Wade* and *Gilbert*, a 5–4 majority of the Court relied on *Schmerber v. California* (discussed supra p. 30 and infra p. 855) to hold that requiring a person to appear in a lineup and speak for identification (*Wade*) or provide a handwriting exemplar (*Gilbert*) did not violate the privilege against self-incrimination. The privilege, observed the Court, "protects an accused only from being compelled to testify against himself, or otherwise provide the State with evidence of a testimonial or communicative nature." Because the lineup is not protected, the prosecution may comment on a suspect's refusal to cooperate. The refusal is considered circumstantial evidence of consciousness of guilt. On occasion, courts have utilized civil or criminal contempt to coerce or punish the suspect who refuses to comply with a court order to participate in some identification proceeding. Still another possibility is for the police to proceed to conduct the identification proceeding over the suspect's objection. See CRIMPROC § 7.2(c).

    6. *Identification procedures and the Fourth Amendment.* The Supreme Court has suggested in dicta that it might be permissible to detain individuals for fingerprinting on less than probable cause. See *Hayes v. Florida,* 470 U.S. 811, 816–17 (1985); *Davis v. Mississippi,* 394 U.S. 721, 727–28 (1969). Does this mean that police can seize individuals for the purpose of an identification procedure on the basis of reasonable suspicion? See Charles H. Whitebread & Christopher Slobogin, *Criminal Procedure* 524 (5th ed. 2008) (suggesting yes). Courts have generally found no Fourth Amendment violation when a person *lawfully in custody for one crime* is ordered into a lineup for other crimes for which there is no probable cause to arrest him. But some courts have indicated that even under these circumstances there must be a "reasonable suspicion" that the person committed the crimes. See generally Note, 45 Fordham L.Rev. 125–32 (1976). However, why should *the viewing* of suspects by witnesses—as opposed to *the basis for detaining* them in order to permit the viewing—raise any Fourth Amendment problems? Cf. *United States v. Dionisio*, 410 U.S. 1 (1973), infra Ch.11, p. 816.

7. *The Wade Court's legislative invitation.* Notice that the *Wade* majority suggested that legislatures or regulatory bodies could implement procedures that would "remove the basis for regarding the [pretrial identification] stage as 'critical.' " What alternative procedures would be sufficient? If a jurisdiction adopted pre-trial identification procedures to promote reliable identifications and later gave juries cautionary instructions about the dangers of misidentification, would that be sufficient? Consider cases discussed infra Section 4, Notes 3–6.

8. *Another "prophylactic" rule?* The *Wade* majority cited *Miranda* when it suggested that it was not intending to create "a constitutional strait-jacket which will handicap sound [legislative or regulatory] efforts at reform." This prompted Justice White, in his dissent, to characterize the *Wade* holding as "prophylactic":

"[The] Court apparently believes that improper police procedures are so widespread that a broad prophylactic rule must be laid down, requiring the presence of counsel at all pretrial identifications, in order to detect recurring instances of police misconduct. I do not share this pervasive distrust of all official investigations. None of the materials the Court relies upon supports it.

"[There] are several striking aspects to the Court's holding. First, the rule does not bar courtroom identifications where there have been no previous identifications in the presence of the police, although when identified in the courtroom, the defendant is known to be in custody and charged with the commission of a crime.[d] Second, the Court seems to say that if suitable legislative standards were adopted for the conduct of pretrial identifications, thereby lessening the hazards in such confrontations, it would not insist on the presence of counsel. But if this is true, why does not the Court simply fashion what it deems to be constitutionally acceptable procedures for the authorities to follow? Certainly the Court is correct in suggesting that the new rule will be wholly inapplicable where police departments themselves have established suitable safeguards. * * * "

Is Justice White correct that the *Wade-Gilbert* rule is prophylactic? If so, could Congress replace the rule? Consider the constitutionality of Title II of the Omnibus Crime Control and Safe Streets Act of 1968, 18 U.S.C. § 3502, designed to "repeal" the *Wade-Gilbert* rule in federal prosecutions: "The testimony of a witness that he saw the accused commit or participate in the commission of the crime for which the accused is being tried shall be admissible in evidence in a criminal prosecution in any trial court ordained and established under article III of the Constitution of the United States." As one commentator has emphasized, as a practical matter, § 3502 "has proved to be meaningless," because the lower courts have considered themselves bound by the *Wade-Gilbert* rule. See Judge Carl McGowan, *Constitutional Interpretation and Criminal Identification,* 12 Wm. & Mary L.Rev. 235, 249–50 (1970). What if that changed and lower courts began to

---

d. Consider Grano at 785: "[A]n identification more unreliable than the witness's familiar selection of the conspicuous defendant, frequently after scanning the courtroom for dramatic effect, is difficult to imagine. In effect, [these identifications are] one-man showups, albeit in the courtroom." How can defense counsel avoid or minimize the impact of a suggestive confrontation between a witness and defendant in the courtroom?

rely on § 3502? Would the *Wade-Gilbert* rule be upheld as *Miranda* was in *Dickerson* (discussed supra p. 677) or should it be treated differently?

9. *Application of fruits doctrine to other Sixth Amendment violations.* In both *Wade* and *Nix v. Williams*, 467 U.S. 431 (1984) (discussed at p. 761 and p. 903), the Supreme Court applied the "fruit of the poisonous tree" doctrine when considering the admissibility of evidence obtained as a result of a Sixth Amendment violation. The Eighth Circuit, however, has declined to apply fruits doctrine to the admissibility of second statements obtained in violation of *Massiah*. See *United States v. Fellers*, 397 F.3d 1090 (8th Cir. 2005) (discussed at p. 746) (applying the *Elstad-Seibert* rule). Is that holding in tension with *Wade* and *Nix* or not?

SECTION 2.   THE COURT RETREATS:
KIRBY AND *ASH*

1. *Pre–Indictment identification procedures.* Although *Wade* and *Gilbert* both involved post-indictment lineups, the language in *Wade* seemed broadly applicable to all pre-trial identification procedures. Five years after it announced the *Wade-Gilbert* rule, however, the Supreme Court decided KIRBY v. ILLINOIS, 406 U.S. 682 (1972), in which it refused to apply the rule to a pre-indictment show-up:[e]

"[In] a line of constitutional cases in this Court stemming back to the Court's landmark opinion in *Powell v. Alabama,* it has been firmly established that a person's Sixth and Fourteenth Amendment right to counsel attaches only at or after the time that adversary judicial proceedings have been initiated against him.

"This is not to say that a defendant in a criminal case has a constitutional right to counsel only at the trial itself. [But] the point is [that] *all* of [the right to counsel cases] have involved points of time at or after the initiation of adversary judicial criminal proceedings—whether by way of formal charge, preliminary hearing, indictment, information, or arraignment.[f]

"The only seeming deviation from this long line of constitutional decisions was *Escobedo* [which] is not apposite here for two distinct reasons. First, the Court in retrospect perceived that the 'prime purpose' of *Escobedo* was not to vindicate the constitutional right to counsel as such, but, like *Miranda,* 'to guarantee full effectuation of the privilege against self-incrimination. * * *' Secondly, and perhaps even more important for purely practical purposes, the Court has limited the holding of *Escobedo* to its own facts, and those facts are not remotely akin to the facts of the case before us.

"The initiation of judicial criminal proceedings is far from a mere formalism. It is the starting point of our whole system of adversary criminal justice. For it is only then that the Government has committed itself to prosecute, and only then that the adverse positions of Government and defendant have solidified. It is then that a defendant finds himself faced with the prosecutorial forces of organized society, and immersed in the intricacies of substantive and procedural criminal law. It is this point, therefore, that marks the commencement of the 'criminal prosecutions' to which alone the explicit guarantees of the Sixth Amendment are applicable.

---

e. Although Justice Stewart wrote for a plurality of the Court in *Kirby* (Justice Powell concurred only in the result), a majority of the Court has subsequently relied on and cited the ruling in *Kirby*. See, e.g., *Brewer v. Williams*, 430 U.S. 387, 398 (1977) (discussed at p. 739).

f. After *Rothgery v. Gillespie County*, 554 U.S. 191 (2008) (discussed at p. 85), readers should add "first formal hearing" to this list.

"[Abuses of other pretrial identification procedures] are not beyond the reach of the Constitution. [When] a person has not been formally charged with a criminal offense, [the Due Process Clause] strikes the appropriate constitutional balance between the right of a suspect to be protected from prejudicial procedures and the interest of society in the prompt and purposeful investigation of an unsolved crime."

Is the Court's reasoning in *Kirby* consistent with *Wade*?

2. *Wade and Powell.* Did the early right to counsel precedents, as Justice Stewart indicates, mandate the result in *Kirby*? Consider Grano at 727: "*Powell v. Alabama* [and its pre-*Gideon* progeny] relied on the fourteenth amendment due process clause rather than on the sixth amendment. Since the protections under the fourteenth amendment are not limited to any particular stage of a criminal proceeding, the fact that the defendants in these cases had already been charged is irrelevant."

3. *"Custody" vs. "the initiation of adversary judicial criminal proceedings."* Is it sound to view (as does Justice Stewart for the plurality in *Kirby*) the "initiation of judicial criminal proceedings [as] the starting point of our whole system of adversary criminal justice"? Is it realistic to say (as Justice Stewart does for the *Kirby* plurality) that "it is only then [that] the adverse positions of Government and defendant have solidified"? Is the postcustody police attitude supposed to be "neutral" or merely "investigative" rather than "accusatory"? Didn't the Court explicitly recognize in *Miranda* that the accusatory function begins very soon after the defendant is taken into custody? Again, see Grano at 726–27. Recall the statement in *Escobedo*—over Justice Stewart's strong dissent— that "it would exalt form over substance to make the right to counsel, under these circumstances, depend on whether at the time of the interrogation the authorities had secured a formal indictment. Petitioner had, for all practical purposes, already been charged * * *."

4. *Alley confrontations.* To what extent did *Kirby* reject the "custody" approach because such an approach would pose a serious threat to the common police practice of conducting "alley confrontations," i.e., prompt confrontations with the victim or an eyewitness at the scene of the crime? See Grano at 731. Prior to *Kirby*, most courts exempted these identifications from the right to counsel requirement. See, e.g., *Russell v. United States,* 408 F.2d 1280 (D.C.Cir. 1969) (Bazelon, C.J.). For the view that all the psychological assumptions on which *Russell* and similar cases are premised—(a) the victim or witness to a crime can be counted on to form an accurate mental image of the offender; (b) this image will be more accurate on the scene immediately after the crime than at the police station some hours later; and (c) the suggestion inherent in one-man confrontations is insignificant in light of the other factors—are speculative and questionable, see Grano at 734–38.

5. *Photographic versus corporeal identifications.* One year after the Court decided *Kirby*, it again limited the scope of the *Wade-Gilbert* rule when it declined to apply the rule to a post-indictment, photographic identification procedure in UNITED STATES v. ASH, 413 U.S. 300 (1973). Justice Blackmun wrote the majority decision:

"[Although the right to counsel guarantee has been expanded beyond the formal trial itself], the function of the lawyer has remained essentially the same as his function at trial. In all cases considered by the Court, counsel has continued to act as a spokesman for, or advisor to, the accused. The accused's right to the 'Assistance of Counsel' has meant just that, namely, the right of the accused to have counsel acting as his assistant.

"[The] function of counsel in rendering 'Assistance' continued at the lineup under consideration in *Wade* and its companion cases. Although the accused was not confronted there with legal questions, the lineup offered opportunities for prosecuting authorities to take advantage of the accused.

"[A] substantial departure from the historical test would be necessary if the Sixth Amendment were interpreted to give Ash a right to counsel at the photographic identification in this case. Since the accused himself is not present at the time of the photographic display, and asserts no right to be present, no possibility arises that the accused might be misled by his lack of familiarity with the law or overpowered by his professional adversary.

"[Even] if we were willing to view the counsel guarantee in broad terms as a generalized protection of the adversary process, we would be unwilling to go so far as to extend the right to a portion of the prosecutor's trial-preparation interviews with witnesses. Although photography is relatively new, the interviewing of witnesses before trial is a procedure that predates the Sixth Amendment. [The] traditional counterbalance in the American adversary system for these interviews arises from the equal ability of defense counsel to seek and interview witnesses himself.

"That adversary mechanism remains as effective for a photographic display as for other parts of pretrial interviews. No greater limitations are placed on defense counsel in constructing displays, seeking witnesses, and conducting photographic identifications than those applicable to the prosecution. Selection of the picture of a person other than the accused, or the inability of a witness to make any selection, will be useful to the defense in precisely the same manner that the selection of a picture of the defendant would be useful to the prosecution.

"[Pretrial] photographic identifications [are] hardly unique in offering possibilities for the actions of the prosecutor unfairly to prejudice the accused. Evidence favorable to the accused may be withheld; testimony of witnesses may be manipulated; the results of laboratory tests may be contrived. In many ways the prosecutor, by accident or by design, may improperly subvert the trial. The primary safeguard against abuses of this kind is the ethical responsibility of the prosecutor * * *. If that safeguard fails, review remains available under due process standards. These same safeguards apply to misuse of photographs. * * *"

Justice Stewart concurred in the judgment:

"[The *Wade* Court held] that counsel was required at a lineup, primarily as an observer, to ensure that defense counsel could effectively confront the prosecution's evidence at trial. Attuned to the possibilities of suggestive influences, a lawyer could see any unfairness at a lineup, question the witnesses about it at trial, and effectively reconstruct what had gone on for the benefit of the jury or trial judge.*

"A photographic identification is quite different from a lineup, for there are substantially fewer possibilities of impermissible suggestion when photographs are used, and those unfair influences can be readily reconstructed at trial. It is true that the defendant's photograph may be markedly different from the others displayed, but this unfairness can be demonstrated at trial from an actual comparison of the photographs used or from the witness' description of the display. Similarly, it is possible that the photographs could be arranged in a

---

* I do not read *Wade* as requiring counsel because a lineup is a "trial-type" situation, nor do I understand that the Court required the presence of an attorney because of the advice or assistance he could give to his client at the lineup itself. Rather, I had thought the reasoning of *Wade* was that the right to counsel is essentially a protection for the defendant at trial, and that counsel is necessary at a lineup in order to ensure a meaningful confrontation and the effective assistance of counsel at trial.

suggestive manner, or that by comment or gesture the prosecuting authorities might single out the defendant's picture. But these are the kinds of overt influence that a witness can easily recount and that would serve to impeach the identification testimony. In short, there are few possibilities for unfair suggestiveness—and those rather blatant and easily reconstructed. Accordingly, an accused would not be foreclosed from an effective cross-examination of an identification witness simply because his counsel was not present at the photographic display. For this reason, a photographic display cannot fairly be considered a 'critical stage' of the prosecution. * * * "

Justice Brennan, joined by Justices Douglas and Marshall, dissented:

"[To] the extent that misidentification may be attributable to a witness' faulty memory or perception, or inadequate opportunity for detailed observation during the crime, the risks are obviously as great at a photographic display as at a lineup. But '[b]ecause of the inherent limitations of photography, which presents its subject in two dimensions rather than the three dimensions of reality, [a] photographic identification, even when properly obtained, is clearly inferior to a properly obtained corporeal identification.' P. Wall, *Eye-Witness Identification in Criminal Cases* 70 (1965). * * *

"Moreover, as in the lineup situation, the possibilities for impermissible suggestion in the context of a photographic display are manifold.

"[A]s with lineups, the defense can 'seldom reconstruct' at trial the mode and manner of photographic identification. It is true, of course, that the photographs used at the pretrial display might be preserved for examination at trial. But 'it may also be said that a photograph can preserve the record of a lineup; yet this does not justify a lineup without counsel.' Indeed, in reality, preservation of the photographs affords little protection to the unrepresented accused. [For] retention of the photographs [cannot] in any sense reveal to defense counsel the more subtle, and therefore more dangerous, suggestiveness that might derive from the manner in which the photographs were displayed or any accompanying comments or gestures. * * *

"[C]ontrary to the suggestion of the Court, the conclusion in *Wade* that a pretrial lineup is a 'critical stage' of the prosecution did not in any sense turn on the fact that a lineup involves the physical 'presence of the accused' at a 'trial-like confrontation' with the Government. And that conclusion most certainly did not turn on the notion that presence of counsel was necessary so that counsel could offer legal advice or 'guidance' to the accused at the lineup. On the contrary, *Wade* envisioned counsel's function at the lineup to be primarily that of a trained observer, able to detect the existence of any suggestive influences and capable of understanding the legal implications of the events that transpire. Having witnessed the proceedings, counsel would then be in a position effectively to reconstruct at trial any unfairness that occurred at the lineup, thereby preserving the accused's fundamental right to a fair trial on the issue of identification.

"There is something ironic about the Court's conclusion today that a pretrial lineup identification is a 'critical stage' of the prosecution because counsel's presence can help to compensate for the accused's deficiencies as an observer, but that a pretrial photographic identification is not a 'critical stage' of the prosecution because the accused is not able to observe at all. * * * "

6. *The different readings of Wade.* The *Ash* majority looks back on *Wade* as concluding that "the lineup constituted a trial-like confrontation" requiring counsel in order "to render 'Assistance' [to a suspect] in counterbalancing any 'overreaching' by the prosecution," implying that counsel is to be an active adversary at this stage. Was the *Ash* majority compelled to so interpret *Wade* because its historical analysis led it to the conclusion that the lawyer's assistance is limited to the *immediate* aid he can give his client? See Note, 64 J. Crim. L. C. & P.S. 428 (1973). Notice that both Justice Stewart and Justice Brennan disclaim this reading and suggest that counsel is necessary at pretrial identification procedures in order to ensure a meaningful confrontation and the effective assistance of counsel at trial. Which interpretation is more consistent with the cases, commentaries, and practice since *Wade?*

   7.   *The significance of defendant's right to be personally present.* As noted by the Court, the defendant in *Ash* did not claim the right to be personally present at the photographic display. But does the right to counsel *only* exist when the defendant is entitled to be personally present? Voluntary absence or contumacious conduct (see *Illinois v. Allen,* Ch. 25, § 3) may cause a defendant to lose his right to be present at trial, but does it follow that he also loses his right to counsel? Defendants on appeal have the right to counsel, but do they have the right to be personally present? See generally Grano at 764–67.

   8.   *Justice Stewart's concurring opinion.* Is Justice Stewart correct that photographic displays are less vulnerable to improper suggestion, are easier to reconstruct at trial, and are less indelible in their effect upon a witness? Consider Grano at 767–70 (sharply challenging these conclusions); see also Section 4 infra.

   9.   *Photographic displays and other pretrial interviews of prospective witnesses.* Both the majority and concurring opinions in *Ash* indicated concern that granting a right to counsel at photographic displays might lead to the extension of the right to counsel to all pretrial interviews of prospective witnesses. But consider Note, 26 Stan. L. Rev. 399, 416–17 (1974): "[The] basis for extending the right to counsel to the identification context was that identifications by eyewitnesses—like confessions—are such damning evidence that they may completely decide the guilt or innocence of the accused. Photographic identifications can be just as critical to the future outcome of a trial as can corporeal identifications. Routine interviews between the prosecutor and his witnesses, on the other hand, do not have the potential for such damaging results, at least assuming good faith on the part of the prosecutor."

   10.   *The limits of Ash.* Is a post-indictment corporeal lineup recorded on video tape and played for the trial court at the suppression hearing a "critical stage" within the meaning of *Wade?* What if a witness identifies the defendant in a photograph of a lineup—does *Wade* or *Ash* govern? Compare Justice Brennan dissenting in *Ash* ("[A] photograph can preserve the record of a lineup; yet this does not justify a lineup without counsel.") with *United States v. Barker,* 988 F.2d 77 (9th Cir.1993) (*Ash* applies because the defendant's absence at the time the photo of the lineup is shown means that he cannot be "misled" or "overpowered").

SECTION 3.   DUE PROCESS LIMITATIONS

   The Supreme Court first discussed when an identification procedure would be "so unnecessarily suggestive and conducive to irreparable mistaken identification" as to violate a suspect's due process rights in STOVALL v. DENNO, 388 U.S. 293 (1967)—decided the same day as *Wade* and *Gilbert*.[g] In that case, the stabbing victim (Mrs. Behrendt), was hospitalized for major surgery. Without affording petitioner time to retain counsel (an arraignment had been promptly held but then postponed until petitioner could retain counsel), the police, with the coopera-

---

   g. In *Stovall,* the Court held that the *Wade-Gilbert* principles would not be applied retroactively, but would affect only those identification procedures conducted in the absence of counsel after the date the *Wade* and *Gilbert* decisions were handed down. See Ch. 29 for a discussion of retroactivity principles.

tion of the victim's surgeon, arranged a confrontation between petitioner and the victim in her hospital room. Petitioner was handcuffed to one of the seven law enforcement officials who brought him to the hospital room. He was the only black person in the room. After being asked by an officer whether petitioner "was the man" who had stabbed her, the victim identified him from her hospital bed. Both Mrs. Behrendt and the police then testified at the trial to her identification in the hospital. Despite the suggestiveness of the confrontation, the Court denied Stovall's due process claim. Justice Brennan, writing for the majority, observed:

"The practice of showing suspects singly to persons for the purpose of identification, and not as part of a lineup has been widely condemned. However, a claimed violation of due process of law in the conduct of a confrontation depends on the totality of the circumstances surrounding it, and the record in the present case reveals that the showing of Stovall to Mrs. Behrendt in an immediate hospital confrontation was imperative. [As the Court of Appeals stated]:

" 'Here was the only person in the world who could possibly exonerate Stovall. Her words, and only her words, "He is not the man" could have resulted in freedom for Stovall. The hospital was not far distant from the courthouse and jail. No one knew how long Mrs. Behrendt might live. Faced with the responsibility of identifying the attacker, with the need for immediate action and with the knowledge that Mrs. Behrendt could not visit the jail, the police followed the only feasible procedure and took Stovall to the hospital room. Under these circumstances, the usual police station line-up, which Stovall now argues he should have had, was out of the question.' "

As *Stovall* illustrates, and as the Court reiterated the following year in a case involving a pretrial photographic identification, the question under the Due Process Clause is whether the identification procedure "was so impermissibly suggestive as to give rise to a very substantial likelihood of irreparable misidentification." *Simmons v. United States*, 390 U.S. 377 (1968). It remained unclear after *Stovall* and *Simmons*, however, whether pretrial identifications that were impermissibly suggestive would be *per se* excluded at trial as unreliable or whether, despite their suggestiveness, out-of-court identifications that possessed certain features of reliability could be admitted into evidence at trial. The Supreme Court addressed that question in *Manson v. Brathwaite*, discussed below.

MANSON v. BRATHWAITE
432 U.S. 98, 97 S.Ct. 2243, 53 L.Ed.2d 140 (1977).

JUSTICE BLACKMUN delivered the opinion of the Court. * * *

[Several minutes before sunset, Glover, a black undercover police officer, purchased heroin from a seller through the open doorway of an apartment while standing for two or three minutes within two feet of the seller in a hallway illuminated by natural light. A few minutes later, Glover described the seller to a back-up officer, D'Onofrio, as being "a colored man, approximately five feet eleven inches tall, dark complexion, black hair, short Afro style, and having high cheekbones, and of heavy build. He was wearing at the time blue pants and a plaid shirt."

[On the basis of the description, D'Onofrio thought that respondent might be the heroin seller. He obtained a single photograph of respondent from police files and left it at Glover's office. Two days later, while alone, Glover viewed the photograph and identified it as that of the seller. At respondent's trial, Glover testified that there was "no doubt whatsoever" that the person shown in the photograph was respondent. Glover also made a positive in-court identification.

No explanation was offered by the prosecution for the failure to utilize a photographic array or to conduct a lineup.

[After the Connecticut Supreme Court affirmed respondent's conviction, he sought federal habeas corpus relief. The Second Circuit, per Friendly, J., held that because the showing of the single photograph was "suggestive" and concededly "unnecessarily so," evidence pertaining to it was subject to a *per se* rule of exclusion.]

Neil v. Biggers, 409 U.S. 188 (1972) concerned a respondent who had been convicted [of] rape, on evidence consisting in part of the victim's visual and voice identification of Biggers at a [one-person] station-house showup seven months after the crime. [The] Court expressed concern about the lapse of seven months between the crime and the confrontation, [but pointed out that the] "central question" [was] "whether under the 'totality of the circumstances' the identification was reliable even though the confrontation procedure was suggestive." Applying that test, the Court found "no substantial likelihood of misidentification. The evidence was properly allowed to go to the jury."[h]

Biggers well might be seen to provide an unambiguous answer to the question before us: The admission of testimony concerning a suggestive and unnecessary identification procedure does not violate due process so long as the identification possesses sufficient aspects of reliability. In one passage, however, the Court observed that the challenged procedure occurred pre-*Stovall* and that a strict rule would make little sense with regard to a confrontation that preceded the Court's first indication that a suggestive procedure might lead to the exclusion of evidence. One perhaps might argue that, by implication, the Court suggested that a different rule could apply post-*Stovall*. The question before us, then, is simply whether the *Biggers* analysis applies to post-*Stovall* confrontations as well to those pre-*Stovall*. * * *

Petitioner at the outset acknowledges that "the procedure in the instant case was suggestive [because only one photograph was used] and unnecessary" [because there was no emergency or exigent circumstance]. The respondent, in agreement with the Court of Appeals, proposes a *per se* rule of exclusion that he claims is dictated by the demands of the Fourteenth Amendment's guarantee of due process. He rightly observes that this is the first case in which this Court has had occasion to rule upon strictly post-*Stovall* out-of-court identification evidence of the challenged kind.

Since the decision in *Biggers,* the Courts of Appeals appear to have developed at least two approaches to such evidence. See Pulaski, *Neil v. Biggers: The Supreme Court Dismantles the Wade Trilogy's Due Process Protection,* 26 Stan. L.Rev. 1097, 1111–1114 (1974). The first, or *per se* approach, employed by the Second Circuit in the present case, focuses on the procedures employed and

---

h. The *Biggers* Court, per Powell, J., observed:

"The victim spent a considerable period of time with her assailant, up to half an hour. She was with him under adequate artificial light in her house and under a full moon outdoors, and at least twice, once in the house and later in the woods, faced him directly and intimately. [Her] description to the police, which included the assailant's approximate age, height, weight, complexion, skin texture, build, and voice [was] more than ordinarily thorough. She had 'no doubt' that respondent was the person who raped her. [The] victim here, a practical nurse by profession, had an unusual opportunity to observe and identify her assailant. She testified at the habeas corpus hearing that there was something about his face 'I don't think I could ever forget.'

"There was, to be sure, a lapse of seven months between the rape and the confrontation. This would be a seriously negative factor in most cases. Here, however, the testimony is undisputed that the victim made no previous identification at any of the showups, lineups, or photographic showings. Her record for reliability was thus a good one, as she had previously resisted whatever suggestiveness inheres in a showup. Weighing all the factors, we find no substantial likelihood of misidentification."

requires exclusion of the out-of-court identification evidence, without regard to reliability, whenever it has been obtained through unnecessarily suggested confrontation procedures.[10] The justifications advanced are the elimination of evidence of uncertain reliability, deterrence of the police and prosecutors, and the stated "fair assurance against the awful risks of misidentification."

The second, or more lenient, approach is one that continues to rely on the totality of the circumstances. It permits the admission of the confrontation evidence if, despite the suggestive aspect, the out-of-court identification possesses certain features of reliability. This second approach, in contrast to the other, is ad hoc and serves to limit the societal costs imposed by a sanction that excludes relevant evidence from consideration and evaluation by the trier of fact. * * *

Wade and its companion cases reflect the concern that the jury not hear eyewitness testimony unless that evidence has aspects of reliability. It must be observed that both approaches before us are responsive to this concern. The *per se* rule, however, goes too far since its application automatically and peremptorily, and without consideration of alleviating factors, keeps evidence from the jury that is reliable and relevant.

The second factor is deterrence. Although the *per se* approach has the more significant deterrent effect, the totality approach also has an influence on police behavior. The police will guard against unnecessarily suggestive procedures under the totality rule, as well as the *per se* one, for fear that their actions will lead to the exclusion of identifications as unreliable.

The third factor is the effect on the administration of justice. Here the *per se* approach suffers serious drawbacks. Since it denies the trier reliable evidence, it may result, on occasion, in the guilty going free. Also, because of its rigidity, the *per se* approach may make error by the trial judge more likely than the totality approach. * * * Certainly, inflexible rules of exclusion that may frustrate rather than promote justice have not been viewed recently by this Court with unlimited enthusiasm. * * *

We therefore conclude that reliability is the linchpin in determining the admissibility of identification testimony for both pre-and post-*Stovall* confrontations. The factors to be considered are set out in *Biggers*. These include the opportunity of the witness to view the criminal at the time of the crime, the witness' degree of attention, the accuracy of his prior description of the criminal, the level of certainty demonstrated at the confrontation, and the time between the crime and the confrontation. Against these factors is to be weighed the corrupting effect of the suggestive identification itself.

We turn, then, to the facts of this case and apply the analysis:

1. *The opportunity to view.* Glover testified that for two to three minutes he stood at the apartment door, within two feet of the respondent. The door opened twice, and each time the man stood at the door. * * * Natural light from outside entered the hallway through a window. There was natural light, as well, from inside the apartment.

2. *The degree of attention.* Glover was not a casual or passing observer, [but] a trained police officer on duty—and specialized and dangerous duty—when he [made the heroin purchase]. Glover himself was a Negro and unlikely to perceive only general features of [black males].

---

10. Although the *per se* approach demands the exclusion of testimony concerning unnecessarily suggestive identifications, it does permit the admission of testimony concerning a subsequent identification, including an in-court identification, if the subsequent identification is determined to be reliable. The totality approach, in contrast, is simpler: if the challenged identification is reliable, then testimony as to it and any identification in its wake is admissible.

3. *The accuracy of the description.* Glover's description was given to D'Onofrio within minutes after the transaction. It included the vendor's race, his height, his build, the color and style of his hair, and the high cheekbone facial feature. It also included clothing the vendor wore. No claim has been made that respondent did not possess the physical characteristics so described. * * *

4. *The witness' level of certainty.* There is no dispute that the photograph in question was that of respondent. Glover, in response to a question whether the photograph was that of the person from whom he made the purchase, testified: "There is no question whatsoever." This positive assurance was repeated.

5. *The time between the crime and the confrontation.* Glover's description of his vendor was given to D'Onofrio within minutes of the crime. The photographic identification took place only two days later. We do not have here the passage of weeks or months between the crime and the viewing of the photograph.

These indicators of Glover's ability to make an accurate identification are hardly outweighed by the corrupting effect of the challenged identification itself. Although identifications arising from single-photograph displays may be viewed in general with suspicion, we find in the instant case little pressure on the witness to acquiesce in the suggestion that such a display entails. D'Onofrio had left the photograph at Glover's office and was not present when Glover first viewed it two days after the event. There thus was little urgency and Glover could view the photograph at his leisure. And since Glover examined the photograph alone, there was no coercive pressure to make an identification arising from the presence of another. The identification was made in circumstances allowing care and reflection. * * *

Surely, we cannot say that under all the circumstances of this case there is "a very substantial likelihood of irreparable misidentification." Short of that point, such evidence is for the jury to weigh. [Juries] are not so susceptible that they cannot measure intelligently the weight of identification testimony that has some questionable feature. * * *[i]

JUSTICE MARSHALL, with whom JUSTICE BRENNAN joins, dissenting.

Today's decision can come as no surprise to those who have been watching the Court dismantle the protections against mistaken eyewitness testimony erected a decade ago in [*Wade, Gilbert* and *Stovall*]. But it is still distressing to see the Court virtually ignore the teaching of experience embodied in those decisions and blindly uphold the conviction of a defendant who may well be innocent.

[In] determining the admissibility of the *post-Stovall* identification in this case, the Court considers two alternatives, a *per se* exclusionary rule and a totality-of-the-circumstances approach. The Court weighs three factors in deciding that the totality approach, which is essentially the test used in *Biggers,* should be applied. In my view, the Court wrongly evaluates the impact of these factors.

First, the Court acknowledges that one of the factors, deterrence of police use of unnecessarily suggestive identification procedures, favors the *per se* rule. Indeed, it does so heavily, for such a rule would make it unquestionably clear to the police they must never use a suggestive procedure when a fairer alternative is available. I have no doubt that conduct would quickly conform to the rule.

---

i. Stevens, J., concurring, joined the Court's opinion, but emphasized that although "the arguments in favor of fashioning new rules to minimize the danger of convicting the innocent on the basis of unreliable eyewitness testimony carry substantial force, [this] rulemaking function can be performed 'more effectively by the legislative process than by somewhat clumsy judicial fiat,' and that the Federal Constitution does not foreclose experimentation by the States in the development of such rules."

Second, the Court gives passing consideration to the dangers of eyewitness identification recognized in the *Wade* trilogy. It concludes, however, that the grave risk of error does not justify adoption of the *per se* approach because that would too often result in exclusion of relevant evidence. In my view, this conclusion totally ignores the lessons of *Wade*. The dangers of mistaken identification are, as *Stovall* held, simply too great to permit unnecessarily suggestive identifications. * * *

Finally, the Court errs in its assessment of the relative impact of the two approaches on the administration of justice. The Court relies most heavily on this factor * * *.

First, the *per se* rule here is not "inflexible." Where evidence is suppressed, for example, as the fruit of an unlawful search, it may well be forever lost to the prosecution. Identification evidence, however, can by its very nature be readily and effectively reproduced. The in-court identification, permitted under *Wade* [if] it has a source independent of an uncounseled or suggestive procedure, is one example. Similarly, when a prosecuting attorney learns that there has been a suggestive confrontation, he can easily arrange another lineup conducted under scrupulously fair conditions. * * *

Second, other exclusionary rules have been criticized for preventing jury consideration of relevant and usually reliable evidence in order to serve interests unrelated to guilt or innocence, such as discouraging illegal searches or denial of counsel. Suggestively obtained eyewitness testimony is excluded, in contrast, precisely because of its unreliability and concomitant irrelevance.

[For] these reasons, I conclude that adoption of the *per se* rule would enhance, rather than detract from, the effective administration of justice. In my view, the Court's totality test will allow seriously unreliable and misleading evidence to be put before juries. * * *

Even more disturbing than the Court's reliance on the totality test, however, is the analysis it uses. [The] decision suggests that due process violations in identification procedures may not be measured by whether the government employed procedures violating standards of fundamental fairness. By relying on the probable accuracy of a challenged identification, instead of the necessity for its use, the Court seems to be ascertaining whether the defendant was probably guilty. * * *

[It] is my view that, assuming applicability of the totality test enunciated by the Court, the facts of the present case require [exclusion of the identification testimony].

I consider first the opportunity that Officer Glover had to view the suspect. Careful review of the record shows that he could see the heroin seller only for the time it took to speak three sentences of four or five short words, to hand over some money, and later after the door reopened, to receive the drugs in return. The entire face-to-face transaction could have taken as little as 15 or 20 seconds. But during this time, Glover's attention was not focused exclusively on the seller's face. He observed that the door was opened 12 to 18 inches, that there was a window in the room behind the door, and, most importantly, that there was a woman standing behind the man. Glover was, of course, also concentrating on the details of the transaction—he must have looked away from the seller's face to hand him the money and receive the drugs. The observation during the conversation thus may have been as brief as 5 or 10 seconds.

As the Court notes, Glover was a police officer trained in and attentive to the need for making accurate identifications. [But] the mere fact that he has been so trained is no guarantee that he is correct in a specific case. * * * Moreover, "identifications made by policemen in highly competitive activities, such as undercover narcotic [work], should be scrutinized with special care." P. Wall, *Eye-Witness Identification in Criminal Cases* 14 (1965). Yet it is just such a searching inquiry that the Court fails to make here.

Another factor on which the Court relies—the witness' degree of certainty in making the identification—is worthless as an indicator that he is correct. Even if Glover had been unsure initially about his identification of respondent's picture, by the time he was called at trial to present a key piece of evidence for the State that paid his salary, it is impossible to imagine his responding negatively to such questions as "is there any doubt in your mind whatsoever" that the identification was correct. * * *

Next, the Court finds that because the identification procedure took place two days after the crime, its reliability is enhanced. While such temporal proximity makes the identification more reliable than one occurring months later, the fact is that the greatest memory loss occurs within hours after an event. After that, the dropoff continues much more slowly. * * *

Finally, the Court makes much of the fact that Glover gave a description of the seller to D'Onofrio shortly after the incident. [But the description was only] a general summary of the seller's appearance. We may discount entirely the seller's clothing, for that was of no significance later in the proceeding. Indeed, to the extent that Glover noticed clothes, his attention was diverted from the seller's face. * * * Conspicuously absent is any indication that the seller was a native of the West Indies, certainly something which a member of the black community could immediately recognize from both appearance and accent.

From all of this, I must conclude that the evidence of Glover's ability to make an accurate identification is far weaker than the Court finds it. In contrast, the procedure used to identify respondent was both extraordinarily suggestive and strongly conducive to error. [By] displaying a single photograph of respondent to the witness Glover under the circumstances in this record almost everything that could have been done wrong was done wrong.

In this case, [the] pressure [to identify respondent] was not limited to that inherent in the display of a single photograph. Glover, the identifying witness, was a state police officer on special assignment. He knew that D'Onofrio, an [experienced] narcotics detective, presumably familiar with local drug operations, believed respondent to be the seller. There was at work, then, both loyalty to another police officer and deference to a better-informed colleague. * * *

NOTES ON THE *STOVALL-BRATHWAITE* DUE PROCESS TEST

1. ***The threshold inquiry.*** Before considering whether there is "a very substantial likelihood of irreparable misidentification," the Court asks whether the procedure used to obtain the out-of-court identification was unnecessarily or impermissibly suggestive. Why impose that threshold requirement? If, as the *Brathwaite* Court says, "reliability is the linchpin in determining the admissibility of identification testimony," shouldn't all identifications that involve a very substantial likelihood of irreparable misidentification be excluded regardless of how they were obtained? Would such a test overwhelm the criminal justice system? Cf. *State v. Henderson*, 27 A.3d 872, 923 (N.J. 2011) (allowing reliability hearings in all eyewitness cases would overwhelm the system).[j] At the very least,

---

j. The New Jersey Supreme Court held that reliability hearings should be conducted only after the defendant presents some evidence of suggestiveness. In explaining its holding, the court

if suggestive procedures increase the likelihood of a mistaken identification, shouldn't courts consider the reliability of any identification obtained by virtue of a suggestive procedure, whether it was necessary or not? Consider Gary L. Wells & Deah S. Quinlivan, *Suggestive Eyewitness Identification Procedures and the Supreme Court's Reliability Test in Light of Eyewitness Science: 30 Years Later*, 33 Law & Hum. Behav. 19 (2009) ("[F]rom a scientific perspective, whether the suggestive procedure was necessary or not necessary has no bearing at all on the power of the suggestive procedure to induce mistaken identifications.") [hereinafter "Wells & Quinlivan"].

2. When is an identification procedure unnecessarily suggestive? *Stovall*, *Biggers*, and *Brathwaite* make it clear that a one-person show up or single photographic identification procedure is suggestive, but when are such procedures necessary? The Supreme Court thought that Mrs. Behrendt's identification of Stovall was necessary. Do you agree? Consider Judge Friendly's opinion, dissenting from the lower court judgment in *Stovall*, 355 F.2d 731, 744–45 (2d Cir. 1966):

"[The argument that law enforcement officials were confronted with an emergency] ignores the huge amount of circumstantial identification the excellent police investigation had produced; moreover, if the state officials were motivated [by] solicitude [for Stovall], the natural course would have been to ask Stovall whether he wanted to go. The emergency argument fails both on the facts and on the law. [If] Mrs. Behrendt's condition had been as serious as my brothers suppose, nothing prevented the prosecutor from informing the state district judge at the preliminary hearing that Stovall had to be taken immediately before her, and suggesting that counsel be assigned forthwith for the limited purpose of advising him in that regard—rather than standing silent when Stovall told the judge of his desire to have counsel and then carting him off to a confrontation by the victim which counsel might have done something to mitigate."

Lower courts have not only followed *Stovall* in similar cases of serious injury to the victim or a witness but have applied it to situations where the *suspect* is seriously injured. See Commentary to § 160.5 of the *Model Pre–Arraignment Code* at 451–52. Is a "showup" in such cases necessary? Could a photographic array be utilized? If the suspect is hospitalized for an extended period, could the witness be taken to several hospital rooms? See *Model Code* at 452.

3. Does the unnecessarily suggestive identification procedure have to be arranged by the police or does any identification obtained under suggestive circumstances satisfy the threshold requirement? The Supreme Court answered this question in PERRY v. NEW HAMPSHIRE, 132 S.Ct. 716 (2012), which involved the following facts: Around 3:00 a.m., police responded to a call that an African–American male was trying to break into cars in an apartment parking lot. They found Perry in the parking lot holding two car-stereo amplifiers in his hands. The owner of the amplifiers then appeared in the parking lot indicating that his neighbor had just told him that she saw someone break into his car. One police officer stayed in the parking lot with Perry while another went to speak to the neighbor. When the officer asked the neighbor to describe the man she saw break into her neighbor's car, she pointed to her kitchen window and said that the person she saw was standing in the parking lot next to the police officer. Perry later moved to suppress this out-of-court identification on due process grounds, but the New Hampshire courts denied his motion, holding that the Due Process Clause only required a trial court to assess the reliability of an out-of-court identification when the police employed suggestive identification techniques.

---

noted that, "[i]n 2009, trial courts in New Jersey conducted roughly 200 *Wade* hearings .... [If any claim of possible unreliability] could trigger a hearing, that number might increase to nearly all cases in which eyewitness identification evidence plays a part." 27 A.3d at 923.

Here, the courts held, the identification was not police-orchestrated. The Supreme Court, per Justice GINSBURG, agreed:

"[Perry] contends [that] it was mere happenstance that each of the *Stovall* cases involved improper police action. The rationale underlying our decisions, Perry asserts, supports a rule requiring trial judges to prescreen eyewitness evidence for reliability any time an identification is made under suggestive circumstances. We disagree.

"Perry's argument depends, in large part, on the Court's statement in *Brathwaite* that 'reliability is the linchpin in determining the admissibility of identification testimony.'

"[Perry] has removed our statement in *Brathwaite* from its mooring, and thereby attributes to the statement a meaning a fair reading of our opinion does not bear. [The] *Brathwaite* Court's reference to reliability appears in a portion of the opinion concerning the appropriate remedy *when the police use an unnecessarily suggestive identification procedure*. The Court adopted a judicial screen for reliability as a course preferable to a *per se* rule requiring exclusion of identification evidence whenever law enforcement officers employ an improper procedure. The due process check for reliability, *Brathwaite* made plain, comes into play only after the defendant establishes improper police conduct. The very purpose of the check, the Court noted, was to avoid depriving the jury of identification evidence that is reliable, *notwithstanding* improper police conduct.

"[Perry] ignore[s] a key premise of the *Brathwaite* decision: A primary aim of excluding identification evidence obtained under unnecessarily suggestive circumstances, the Court said, is to deter law enforcement use of improper lineups, showups, and photo arrays in the first place. Alerted to the prospect that identification evidence improperly obtained may be excluded, the Court reasoned, police officers will 'guard against unnecessarily suggestive procedures.' This deterrence rationale is inapposite in cases, like Perry's, in which the police engaged in no improper conduct.

"[Perry] place[s] significant weight on *United States v. Wade*, describing it as a decision not anchored to improper police conduct. In fact, the risk of police rigging was the very danger to which the Court responded in *Wade* when it recognized a defendant's right to counsel at postindictment, police-organized identification procedures. '[T]he confrontation *compelled by the State* between the accused and the victim or witnesses,' the Court began, 'is peculiarly riddled with innumerable dangers and variable factors which might seriously, even crucially, derogate from a fair trial.' 'A major factor contributing to the high incidence of miscarriage of justice from mistaken identification,' the Court continued, 'has been the degree of suggestion inherent in the manner in which *the prosecution* presents the suspect to witnesses for pretrial identification.' To illustrate the improper suggestion it was concerned about, the Court pointed to police-designed lineups where 'all in the lineup but the suspect were known to the identifying witness, ...the other participants in [the] lineup were grossly dissimilar in appearance to the suspect, ... only the suspect was required to wear distinctive clothing which the culprit allegedly wore, ... the witness is told by the police that they have caught the culprit after which the defendant is brought before the witness alone or is viewed in jail, ... the suspect is pointed out before or during a lineup, ... the participants in the lineup are asked to try on an article of clothing which fits only the suspect.' Beyond genuine debate, then, prevention of unfair police practices prompted the Court to extend a defendant's right to counsel to cover postindictment lineups and showups.

"Perry's [argument] thus lacks support in the case law he cites. Moreover, his position would open the door to judicial preview, under the banner of due process, of most, if not all, eyewitness identifications. External suggestion is hardly the only factor that casts doubt on the trustworthiness of an eyewitness' testimony. [Many] other factors bear on 'the likelihood of misidentification'—for example, the passage of time between exposure to and identification of the defendant, whether the witness was under stress when he first encountered the suspect, how much time the witness had to observe the suspect, how far the witness was from the suspect, whether the suspect carried a weapon, and the race of the suspect and witness. There is no reason why an identification made by an eyewitness with poor vision, for example, or one who harbors a grudge against the defendant, should be regarded as inherently more reliable, less a 'threat to the fairness of trial,' than the identification [in] this case. To embrace Perry's view would thus entail a vast enlargement of the reach of due process as a constraint on the admission of evidence.

"Perry maintains that the Court can limit the due process check he proposes to identifications made under 'suggestive circumstances.' Even if we could rationally distinguish suggestiveness from other factors bearing on the reliability of eyewitness evidence, Perry's limitation would still involve trial courts, routinely, in preliminary examinations. Most eyewitness identifications involve some element of suggestion. Indeed, all in-court identifications do. Out-of-court identifications volunteered by witnesses are also likely to involve suggestive circumstances. For example, suppose a witness identifies the defendant to police officers after seeing a photograph of the defendant in the press captioned 'theft suspect,' or hearing a radio report implicating the defendant in the crime. Or suppose the witness knew that the defendant ran with the wrong crowd and saw him on the day and in the vicinity of the crime. Any of these circumstances might have 'suggested' to the witness that the defendant was the person the witness observed committing the crime.

"[In] urging a broadly applicable due process check on eyewitness identifications, Perry maintains that eyewitness identifications are a uniquely unreliable form of evidence. We do not doubt either the importance or the fallibility of eyewitness identifications. Indeed, in [*Wade*,] we observed that 'the annals of criminal law are rife with instances of mistaken identification.'

"[T]he potential unreliability of a type of evidence does not alone render its introduction at the defendant's trial fundamentally unfair. [The] fallibility of eyewitness evidence does not, without the taint of improper state conduct, warrant a due process rule requiring a trial court to screen such evidence for reliability before allowing the jury to assess its creditworthiness.

"Our unwillingness to enlarge the domain of due process [rests,] in large part, on our recognition that the jury, not the judge traditionally determines the reliability of evidence. We also take account of other safeguards built into our adversary system that caution juries against placing undue weight on eyewitness testimony of questionable reliability. These protections include the defendant's Sixth Amendment right to confront the eyewitness. Another is the defendant's right to the effective assistance of an attorney, who can expose the flaws in the eyewitness' testimony during cross-examination and focus the jury's attention on the fallibility of such testimony during opening and closing arguments. Eyewitness-specific jury instructions, which many federal and state courts have adopted, likewise warn the jury to take care in appraising identification evidence. The constitutional requirement that the government prove the defendant's guilt beyond a reasonable doubt also impedes convictions based on dubious identification evidence.

"State and federal rules of evidence, moreover, permit trial judges to exclude relevant evidence if its probative value is substantially outweighed by its prejudicial impact or potential for misleading the jury. In appropriate cases, some States also permit defendants to present expert testimony on the hazards of eyewitness identification evidence.

"[For] the foregoing reasons, [we] hold that the Due Process Clause does not require a preliminary judicial inquiry into the reliability of an eyewitness identification when the identification was not procured under unnecessarily suggestive circumstances arranged by law enforcement."

Justice SOTOMAYOR was the lone dissenter:[k]

"This Court has long recognized that eyewitness identifications' unique confluence of features—their unreliability, susceptibility to suggestion, powerful impact on the jury, and resistance to the ordinary tests of the adversarial process—can undermine the fairness of a trial. Our cases thus establish a clear rule: The admission at trial of out-of-court eyewitness identifications derived from impermissibly suggestive circumstances that pose a very substantial likelihood of misidentification violates due process. The Court today announces that that rule does not even 'com[e] into play' unless the suggestive circumstances are improperly 'police-arranged.'

"Our due process concern, however, arises not from the act of suggestion, but rather from the corrosive effects of suggestion on the reliability of the resulting identification. By rendering protection contingent on improper police arrangement of the suggestive circumstances, the Court effectively grafts a *mens rea* inquiry onto our rule. The Court's holding enshrines a murky distinction—between suggestive confrontations intentionally orchestrated by the police and—, as here, those inadvertently caused by police actions—that will sow confusion. It ignores our precedents' acute sensitivity to the hazards of intentional and unintentional suggestion alike and unmoors our rule from the very interest it protects, inviting arbitrary results. And it recasts the driving force of our decisions as an interest in police deterrence, rather than reliability. Because I see no warrant for declining to assess the circumstances of this case under our ordinary approach, I respectfully dissent.

"[The] majority maintains that the suggestive circumstances giving rise to the identification must be 'police-arranged,' 'police rigg[ed],' 'police-designed,' or 'police-organized.' Those terms connote a degree of intentional orchestration or manipulation. The majority categorically exempts all eyewitness identifications derived from suggestive circumstances that were not police-manipulated—however suggestive, and however unreliable—from our due process check. The majority thus appears to graft a *mens rea* requirement onto our existing rule.[4]

"As this case illustrates, police intent is now paramount. [Perry] was the only African–American at the scene of the crime standing next to a police officer. For the majority, the fact that the police did not intend that showup, even if they inadvertently caused it in the course of a police procedure, ends the inquiry. The police were questioning the eyewitness [about] the perpetrator's identity, and were intentionally detaining Perry in the parking lot—but had not intended for

---

k. Justice Thomas filed a concurring opinion in which he criticized the entire *Stovall* line of cases noting that the cases are all "premised on a 'substantive due process' right to 'fundamental fairness'" and arguing that "those cases are wrongly decided because the Fourteenth Amendment's Due Process Clause is not a 'secret repository of substantive guarantees against "unfairness."'" As a result, he indicated that he would "limit the Court's suggestive eyewitness identification cases to the precise circumstances that they involved."

4. The majority denies that it has imposed a *mens rea* requirement, but by confining our due process concerns to police-arranged identification procedures, that is just what it has done. The majority acknowledges that 'whether or not [the police] intended the arranged procedure to be suggestive' is irrelevant under our precedents, but still places dispositive weight on whether or not the police intended the procedure itself.

[the eyewitness] to identify the perpetrator from her window. Presumably, in the majority's view, had the police asked [the eyewitness] to move to the window to identify the perpetrator, that could have made all the difference.

"I note, however, that the majority leaves what is required by its arrangement-focused inquiry less than clear. In parts, the opinion suggests that the police must arrange an identification 'procedure,' regardless of whether they 'inten[d] the arranged procedure to be suggestive.' Elsewhere, it indicates that the police must arrange the 'suggestive circumstances' that lead the witness to identify the accused. Still elsewhere it refers to 'improper' police conduct, connoting bad faith. Does police 'arrangement' relate to the procedure, the suggestiveness, or both? If it relates to the procedure, do suggestive preprocedure encounters no longer raise the same concerns? If the police need not 'inten[d] the arranged procedure to be suggestive,' what makes the police action 'improper'? And does that mean that good-faith, unintentional police suggestiveness in a police-arranged lineup can be 'impermissibly suggestive'? If no, the majority runs headlong into *Wade*. If yes, on what basis—if not deterrence—does it distinguish unintentional police suggestiveness in an accidental confrontation?

"The arrangement-focused inquiry will sow needless confusion. If the police had called Perry and [the eyewitness] to the police station for interviews, and [the eyewitness] saw Perry being questioned, would that be sufficiently 'improper police arrangement'? If Perry had voluntarily come to the police station, would that change the result?

"[The] majority regards its limitation on our two-step rule as compelled by precedent. Its chief rationale is that none of our prior cases involved situations where the police 'did not arrange the suggestive circumstances.' That is not necessarily true.[1] But even if it were true, it is unsurprising. The vast majority of eyewitness identifications that the State uses in criminal prosecutions are obtained in lineup, showup, and photograph displays arranged by the police. Our precedents reflect that practical reality.

"[Indeed,] it is the majority's approach that lies in tension with our precedents. [We] once described the 'primary evil to be avoided' as the likelihood of misidentification. *Biggers*. Today's decision, however, means that even if that primary evil is at its apex, we need not avoid it at all so long as the suggestive circumstances do not stem from improper police arrangement.

"The majority gives several additional reasons for why applying our due process rule beyond improperly police-arranged circumstances is unwarranted. In my view, none withstands close scrutiny.

"[The majority's reading of our precedent as focusing on deterrence] mischaracterizes our cases. We discussed deterrence in *Brathwaite* because Brathwaite challenged our two-step inquiry as *lacking* deterrence value. [Our discussion of deterrence in that case was not a] list of 'primary aim[s].' Nor was it a ringing endorsement of the primacy of deterrence. [To] the contrary, we clarified that deterrence was a subsidiary concern to reliability, the 'driving force' of our doctrine.

---

1. Earlier in the dissent, Justice Sotomayor suggested that *Wade* might not have involved police-orchestrated suggestiveness: "In *Wade* itself, we noted that the 'potential for improper influence [in pretrial confrontations] is illustrated by the circumstances . . . [i]n the present case.' We then highlighted not the lineup procedure, but rather a preprocedure encounter: The two witnesses who later identified Wade in the lineup had seen Wade outside while 'await[ing] assembly of the lineup.' Wade had been standing in the hallway, which happened to be 'observable to the witnesses through an open door.' One witness saw Wade 'within sight of an FBI agent'; the other saw him 'in the custody of the agent.' In underscoring the hazards of these circumstances, we made no mention of whether the encounter had been arranged; indeed, the facts suggest that it was not."

"[The] majority emphasizes that we should rely on the jury to determine the reliability of evidence. But our cases are rooted in the assumption that eyewitness identifications upend the ordinary expectation that it is 'the province of the jury to weigh the credibility of competing witnesses.' [Jurors] find eyewitness evidence unusually powerful and their ability to assess credibility is hindered by a witness' false confidence in the accuracy of his or her identification.

"[The majority also] suggests that applying our rule beyond police-arranged suggestive circumstances would entail a heavy practical burden, requiring courts to engage in 'preliminary judicial inquiry' into 'most, if not all, eyewitness identifications.' But that is inaccurate. [As] is implicit in the majority's reassurance that Perry may resort to the rules of evidence in lieu of our due process precedents, trial courts will be entertaining defendants' objections, pretrial or at trial, to unreliable eyewitness evidence in any event. The relevant question, then, is what the standard of admissibility governing such objections should be.

"[Finally,] the majority questions how to 'rationally distinguish suggestiveness from other factors bearing on the reliability of eyewitness evidence,' [and] more broadly, how to distinguish eyewitness evidence from other kinds of arguably unreliable evidence. Our precedents, however, did just that. We emphasized the 'formidable number of instances in the records of English and American trials' of 'miscarriage[s] of justice from mistaken identification.' *Wade.* We then observed that 'the influence of improper suggestion upon identifying witnesses probably accounts for more miscarriages of justice than any other single factor.' *Id.* [The] majority points to no other type of evidence that shares the rare confluence of characteristics that makes eyewitness evidence a unique threat to the fairness of trial.

"[It] would be one thing if the passage of time had cast doubt on the empirical premises of our precedents. But just the opposite has happened. A vast body of scientific literature has reinforced every concern our precedents articulated nearly a half-century ago. [Over] the past three decades, more than two thousand studies related to eyewitness identification have been published.

"[The] empirical evidence demonstrates that eyewitness misidentification is 'the single greatest cause of wrongful convictions in this country.' Researchers have found that a staggering 76% of the first 250 convictions overturned due to DNA evidence since 1989 involved eyewitness misidentification. Study after study demonstrates that eyewitness recollections are highly susceptible to distortion by postevent information or social cues; that jurors routinely overestimate the accuracy of eyewitness identifications; that jurors place the greatest weight on eyewitness confidence in assessing identifications even though confidence is a poor gauge of accuracy; and that suggestiveness can stem from sources beyond police-orchestrated procedures. The majority today nevertheless adopts an artificially narrow conception of the dangers of suggestive identifications at a time when our concerns should have deepened."

4. *The relationship between the two prongs.* According to *Brathwaite*, if a court finds that the police used impermissibly suggestive identification procedures, then the trial judge should weigh the corrupting effect of the process against its five reliability factors. But, as one state supreme court has observed, "three of those factors—the opportunity to view the crime, the witness' degree of attention, and the level of certainty at the time of the identification—rely on self-reporting by the eyewitnesses; and research has shown that those reports can be skewed by the suggestive procedures themselves. [Thus, the test] may unintentionally reward suggestive police practice [rather than deterring it.]." *State v. Henderson*, 27 A.3d 872, 918 (N.J. 2011); see also Wells & Quinlivan at 9 ("[T]he use of suggestive procedures can lead the eyewitness to enhance (distort) his or her retrospective self-reports in ways that help ensure the witness' high standing on the *Manson* [*v. Brathwaite*] criteria.'').

5. *The practical result of the Brathwaite approach.* The practical result of the broad discretion conferred on the trial court by *Brathwaite*, observes Robert P. Mosteller, *The Duke Lacrosse Case, Innocence, and False Identifications: A Fundamental Failure to "Do Justice"*, 76 Fordham L.Rev. 1337, 1386 (2007), "is a paucity of decisions finding a due process suggestivity violation and excluding the identification evidence. If a violation is found under *Brathwaite*, the witness or, most poignantly, the victim is not allowed to identify the defendant in the courtroom." As Richard Rosen has written, *Reflections on Innocence*, 2006 Wis. L.Rev. 237, 251: "This places an almost intolerable burden on an (often elected) trial judge who must not only find that the identification was so flawed that the witness cannot be believed, but then has to tell the witness, often the victim of the crime, that she will not even be allowed to tell the jury what she honestly believed she saw. This would be a different thing to tell any witness, but imagine looking a rape victim in the eye, one who swears that she can identify the man who violated her, and telling that woman she will not even be allowed to tell her story to a jury. It is no wonder that few identifications have been suppressed for due process violations."

SECTION 4. SOCIAL SCIENCE RESEARCH ON IDENTIFICATION PROCEDURES AND THE NEED FOR REFORM[m]

As Justice Sotomayor emphasized in her dissenting opinion in *Perry v. New Hampshire* (discussed supra Note 3, p. 780), recent developments in the social science literature, coupled with revelations from DNA exoneration cases regarding the prevalence of misidentifications, demonstrate that the problem of mistaken eyewitness identifications may be worse than the Court originally thought. Human memory is far from perfect. Even when people are paying close attention, they have limited abilities to process multiple stimuli in their environment. Witnesses cannot simultaneously observe the height, weight, age, clothing, and physical features of a criminal suspect. As a result, witnesses often have memory gaps that they later unconsciously fill in based on stereotypes or expectations. People often see what they expect to see. This tendency to fill in memory gaps with inaccurate details is exacerbated by the fact that memory fades over time, and that new information that a person learns will affect and shape her memory of an event.

In addition to these general problems with memory, there are a host of situational circumstances that can affect a witness's ability to perceive events. Social science research has identified two categories of variables that contribute to the well-recognized problem of mistaken identifications—estimator variables and system variables.

1. *Estimator variables.* Estimator variables are factors over which the legal system has no control and include the characteristics of the witness, the characteristics of the perpetrator, and the circumstances of the witnessed event. Some people are better at being witnesses than others. Young children and the elderly are less able to make accurate identifications than young adults, and sober

m. The social science research analyzing the reliability of eyewitness identification testimony is vast. For an excellent summary of the research discussed in this section, see *State v. Henderson*, 27 A.3d 872 (N.J. 2011) (discussing the current state of the research after a hearing that "probed testimony by seven experts and produced more than 2,000 pages of transcripts along with hundreds of scientific studies").

individuals are better at making accurate identifications than those who are intoxicated. The characteristics of the suspect can also affect the reliability of an identification. Research reveals that the use of disguises—including hats, sunglasses, masks, wigs—severely inhibits witnesses' abilities to later identify someone. Moreover, there is robust research documenting problems with cross-racial identifications. People have a much harder time identifying the facial features and distinguishing among people of a different race. The circumstances of the event can also affect reliability. A brief or fleeting exposure to a suspect is less likely to produce an accurate identification than a prolonged one. An identification made at a great distance or in bad lighting conditions is more likely to be inaccurate than one made up close with good lighting. Research has shown that witnesses are particularly bad at identifying suspects who have used weapons to commit their crimes due to a phenomenon known as "weapon focus." Witnesses focus on the weapon itself rather than focusing on the person holding it. Moreover, studies reveal that high levels of stress can diminish an eyewitness's ability to recall details and make an accurate identification later.

Notice that, under the current due process test, these estimator variables are only relevant if there was an unnecessarily suggestive identification procedure. In light of this research, should the Court revisit that requirement?

2. *System variables.* System variables are factors—like identification procedures—that are within the legal system's control. Witnesses are very susceptible to suggestion. Even the most subtle comment or action by a police officer can affect a witness's selections, and police comments made after an identification praising or congratulating the witness can improperly reinforce a shaky identification and engender a false sense of confidence. The composition of the lineup or photo array can also be suggestive. Sometimes, if a witness does not select the suspect out of a photo array, the police will then conduct a live lineup in order to get the witness to make an identification. Research on the "mugshot exposure effect" reveals that presenting a suspect to the witness multiple times increases the likelihood that the witness's later identification of the suspect is based on her memory of having seen the earlier photograph rather than her memory of the crime itself. Witnesses are often anxious to make an identification and naturally believe that the culprit is in the lineup or photospread. As a result, they will frequently identify the person who most resembles the witnesses' memory *relative* to other people in the lineup or photospread. If the suspect is the only person in the lineup or photospread that fits the general description of the perpetrator, witnesses will pick the suspect because they want to be helpful and he looks *most* like their memory of the perpetrator. Moreover, once the witness makes a selection, she becomes committed to the identification and will psychologically reinforce her choice.

* * *

Given research demonstrating that jurors often overestimate the reliability of eyewitness identification testimony and place a high value on such testimony, police departments, courts, and legislatures around the country have begun to consider ways to enhance the reliability of identifications and protect against misidentifications.

3. *Changes in identification procedures.* Social scientists have long advocated the following requirements for lineups and photospreads:[n]

---

n. See Gary L. Wells, et al., *Eyewitness Identification Procedures: Recommendations for Lineups and Photospreads*, 22 Law & Hum. Behav. 603 (1998); Gary L. Wells & Eric P. Seelau, *Eyewitness Identification: Psychological Research and Legal Policy on Lineups*, 1 Psych., Pub. Pol'y. & Law 765 (1995), for a representative discussion of these recommendations.

- *The person conducting the lineup or photospread should not be aware of which member of the lineup or photospread is the suspect.* (Research shows that lineup administrators familiar with the suspect will consciously or unconsciously leak that information to the witness and affect the witness's behavior.)

- *Eyewitnesses should be told explicitly that the suspected offender might not be in the lineup or photospread, and therefore that they should not feel they have to make an identification.* (The danger of false identification arises from a tendency for eyewitnesses to identify the person who most closely resembles the offender relative to the others in the lineup.)[o]

- *The suspect should not stand out in the lineup or photospread as being different from the fillers on the basis of the witness's previous description of the offender or other factors that would draw special attention to the suspect.* (E.g., the suspect should not be the only one dressed in the type of clothes the victim said was worn by the offender or the suspect's photo should not be taken from a different angle than the other photos.)

- *Lineups or photospreads should include a minimum of five people other than the suspect and should not feature more than one suspect.* (Having at least five fillers and only one suspect decreases the possibility of "lucky guesses" and increases the reliability of the process.)

- *Pre- and post-identification feedback of any kind should be avoided.* (Information received by witnesses both before and after an identification can affect their memory.)

- *At the time the identification is made, a clear statement should be taken from the eyewitness regarding his degree of confidence that the person identified is the actual offender.* (Research shows that witnesses who were highly confident in the accuracy of their identifications at the time the identifications were made were more likely to have made accurate identifications. Confidence statements from eyewitnesses can be greatly affected by postidentification events that have nothing to do with the witness's memory. E.g., an eyewitness might learn, after his identification, that another witness has identified the same person or that the person he has identified has a prior record for offenses of the same type.)

- *Police should not permit witnesses to view a suspect (or a filler) more than once.*

- *The lineup or photospread should be presented to one witness at a time.*

- *People (or photos in a display) should be shown to witnesses one at a time— sequentially—rather than in a group at the same time.* (The sequential method reduces the chance that witnesses will simply pick the person who looks most like the perpetrator of the crime rather than compare the person in front of them against their memory of the crime.)

- *Videotape and audiotape the identification procedure whenever possible.*[p]

A number of police departments and state attorneys general have recommended adopting some or all of these requirements. See, e.g., Office of the Attorney Gen., Wis. Dep't of Justice, *Model Policy and Procedure for Eyewitness*

---

o. *Cf.* Randolph N. Jonakait, *Reliable Identification; Could the Supreme Court Tell in Manson v. Brathwaite?*, 52 U. Colo. L. Rev. 511, 525 (1981); Gerald Lefcourt, *The Blank Lineup: An Aid to the Defense*, 14 Crim. L. Bull. 428 (1978), advocating the use of "blank" lineups. This entails the viewing of two separate lineups. The witness should be told the suspect may or may not be in the first lineup. Thereafter, the suspect is presented in the second lineup.

p. New Jersey requires the police to make a written record detailing what occurred at any identification procedures. See *State v. Delgado*, 902 A.2d 888 (2006).

Identification 1 (2005) (recommending double-blind sequential photo arrays and lineups with non-suspect fillers chosen to minimize suggestiveness, non-biased instructions to eyewitnesses, and immediate confidence assessments); see also Dallas Police Dep't, *Dallas Police Department General Order* § 304.01 (2009); Denver Police Dep't, *Operations Manual* § 104.44 (2006); Police Chiefs' Ass'n of Santa Clara County, *Line-up Protocol for Law Enforcement* (2002); International Association of Chiefs of Police, *Training Key #600: Eyewitness Identifications* (2006); U.S. Dep't of Justice, *Eyewitness Evidence: A Guide For Law Enforcement* (1999). Some state legislatures have written many of these requirements into state law. See N.C. Gen. Stat. § 15A–284.50 to –.53 (mandating pre-lineup instructions and blind, sequential lineup administration); 725 Ill. Comp. Stat. 5/107A–5 (mandating that lineups be photographed or recorded and requiring pre-identification instructions); Md. Code. Ann. Pub. Safety § 3–506 (requiring police to revise identification procedures in light of social science); Ohio Rev. Code Ann. § 2933.83 (requiring blind identification procedures when possible and imposing a recording requirement); W. Va. Code Ann. § 62–1E–1 to –3 (requiring pre-identification instructions and recording of procedures and creating a task force to develop further procedures); Wis. Stat. § 175.50 (recommending double blind, sequential identification procedures). If a police officer violates these requirements, however, there is typically not a *per se* exclusionary remedy. It might, however, be a sufficient indicator of suggestiveness as to merit a hearing on the reliability of the identification.

    4. *Expert testimony.* Another possibility is to present social science experts to the jury to explain the frailty and fallibility of eyewitness testimony. But the admissibility of expert testimony is largely a matter of trial court discretion. And in the main the judicial response to such defense efforts has been very cool. For a discussion—and strong criticism—of the arguments against the use of expert testimony on eyewitness identification, see James Murphy, *An Evaluation of the Arguments Against the Use of Expert Testimony on Eyewitness Identification*, 8 U. Bridgeport L. Rev. 21 (1987). For more recent articles evaluating the arguments for and against the admissibility of expert testimony concerning eyewitness identification, see Thomas Dillickrath, *Expert Testimony on Eyewitness Identification: Admissibility and Alternatives*, 55 U. Miami L. Rev. 1059 (2001); Edward Stein, *The Admissibility of Expert Testimony About Cognitive Science Research on Eyewitness Identification*, 2 Law, Probability & Risk 295 (2003); see also Jennifer L. Devenport & Brian L. Cutler, *Impact of Defense–Only and Opposing Eyewitness Experts on Juror Judgments*, 28 Law & Hum. Behav. 569, 574 (2004) (concluding that expert testimony often fails to sensitize jurors).

    5. *Jury instructions.* Some courts have been receptive to defense requests for enhanced jury instructions to help jurors accurately assess the reliability of eyewitness identifications. New Jersey has been at the forefront of this development. See, e.g., *State v. Henderson*, 27 A.3d 872, 878 (N.J. 2011) (directing the drafters of the model jury instructions to revise the instructions to address both system and estimator variables); *State v. Romero*, 922 A.2d 693 (N.J. 2007) (requiring instruction that witness's confidence level may correlate with reliability); *State v. Cromedy*, 727 A.2d 457 (N.J. 1999) (requiring instruction on reliability of cross-racial identifications); see also *State v. Ledbetter*, 881 A.2d 290 (Conn. 2005) (requiring instruction that failure to give pre-identification instructions can affect reliability); *United States v. Telfaire*, 469 F.2d 552 (D.C. Cir. 1972). Some scholars question how effective jury instructions are at educating jurors. See e.g., David Starkman, *The Use of Eyewitness Identification Evidence in Criminal Trials*, 21 Crim. L.Q. 361, 376–77 (1979); Brian L. Cutler & Steven D. Penrod, *Mistaken Identification: The Eyewitness, Psychology, and the Law* 255–64 (1995).

6. More expansive due process tests under state law. Some states provide more protection against misidentification by expanding on the *Biggers/Brathwaite* factors that are used to assess the reliability of an identification. See, e.g., *State v. Henderson*, 27 A.3d 872, 919–20 (N.J. 2011) (allowing all relevant system and estimator variables to be explored and weighed at pretrial hearings once suggestiveness is shown); *State v. Hunt*, 69 P.3d 571, 576 (Kan. 2003) (expanding on the due process analysis's reliability factors and requiring cautionary instructions); *State v. Ramirez*, 817 P.2d 774, 780–81 (Utah 1991) (same). Other states have adopted requirements that more severely restrict the admissibility of show ups. See, e.g., *State v. Dubose*, 699 N.W.2d 582, 584–85 (Wis. 2005) (adopting a *per se* exclusionary rule for evidence about pre-trial show ups unless they are necessary); Commonwealth v. Johnson, 650 N.E.2d 1257, 1261 (Mass. 1995) (same); People v. Adams, 440 N.Y.S.2d 902, 423 N.E.2d 379, 384 (N.Y. Ct. App. 1981) (same).

Would you support a rule of *per se* exclusion whenever the police used a suggestive identification procedure? Consider Wells & Quinlivan at 9: "Imagine, for instance, that a victim-witness had been abducted and held for 3 months during which the culprit's face was never covered and there was full light (repeated opportunity to view), the victim studied the face repeatedly (repeated attention), the victim described the face in great detail, including unique features (excellent description), and the witness identified the suspect with total certainty within minutes after escaping. Surely, in this case we would not care if the identification procedure had multiple characteristics of a highly suggestive procedure."

7. Preventing resort to the ultimate punishment. Consider Margery Malkin Koosed, *The Proposed Innocence Protection Act Won't—Unless It Also Curbs Mistaken Eyewitness Identifications*, 63 Ohio St.L.J. 263, 265 (2002): "While cautionary instructions and expert testimony may be helpful, these have not proved strong enough in our battle to assure against mistaken identification. Altering the *Manson* standard for admission of the in-court identification and returning to the *Stovall* inquiry of whether the pretrial procedure was 'conducive to irreparable mistaken identification' (or an analogous 'any likelihood of misidentification will exclude the in-court testimony' standard) may further improve our arsenal. But the better approach would be for legislatures to simply bar the State from seeking death when suggestive procedures have been used."

CHAPTER 11

GRAND JURY INVESTIGATIONS

■ ■ ■

Not all criminal investigations are conducted by the police. Certain types of criminal activity are more commonly investigated by the prosecutor's office, largely by using the grand jury and its subpoena power. Section 1 provides a general introduction to grand jury investigations (and to alternative investigative authority that also relies upon the subpoena power). Sections 2–5 discuss the primary legal issues raised by grand jury investigations.

SECTION 1.   THE ROLE OF THE INVESTIGATIVE GRAND JURY[a]

A.   THE INVESTIGATIVE AUTHORITY OF THE GRAND JURY

1.   *Dual functions*. The grand jury is often described as providing both a "shield" and a "sword" to the criminal justice process. A "shield" against mistaken and vindictive prosecutions is provided by granting to the grand jury the decision as to whether or not to issue an indictment. In making that determination, the grand jury's role is to "screen" the prosecution's decision to charge, ensuring that no person is charged on evidence insufficient to justify a prosecution. On the other side, the grand jury is said to act as a "sword," combating crime, in the use of its investigative authority. Here, the grand jury's role is to uncover evidence not previously available to the government and thereby secure convictions that might otherwise not be obtained. The shielding function of the grand jury will be discussed in Chapter Sixteen.[b] In this Chapter we will concentrate upon the operation of the grand jury in its investigatory role. It should be kept in mind, however, that the two functions of the grand jury commonly are performed by the same grand jury. In particular, once a grand jury investigation is complete, the same group of grand jurors ordinarily will then be called upon to determine whether the evidence produced is sufficient to issue an indictment.[c]

---

a.   For citations to relevant source materials, as well as a much more detailed and comprehensive discussion of grand jury investigations, see Sara Sun Beale, William C. Bryson, James E. Felman, & Michael J. Elston, *Grand Jury Law and Practice* (2d Ed. 1997) (hereafter cited as Beale et al.); Susan W. Brenner & Lori E. Shaw, *Federal Grand Jury : A Guide to Law & Practice* (2d ed. 2006) (hereafter cited as Brenner & Shaw); CRIMPROC §§ 8.1–8.15.

b.   Various aspects of the grand jury's procedure and structure relate both to its screening and investigatory functions. Those aspects that have a major impact upon its investigatory performance are discussed in this Chapter. Others that have a less significant bearing on investigations are discussed in Chapter 16. The composition of the grand jury, because it arguably has a greater impact on the screening function, is discussed in Chapter 16.

c.   A small group of "information states," though continuing to use grand juries for occasional investigations, do not utilize prosecution by indictment (either because prosecution by informa-

2. *Historical development.* At the time of the adoption of the Constitution, the grand jury was an institution revered not only for its independence in screening, but also for its service as a "public watchdog," uncovering and proceeding against criminal activity that government officials chose to ignore. The colonial grand juries not only refused to issue indictments in infamous prosecutions sought by the Crown (e.g., in the Peter Zenger case), but also brought charges (to which the Crown was opposed) against various royal officials (including British soldiers). It was the screening function of the grand jury that was guaranteed as a constitutional safeguard for the accused in the grand jury clauses of various state constitutions and in the Fifth Amendment of the federal constitution. These provisions also recognized, however, in an indirect way, the investigative authority of the grand jury. The grand jury clauses required that prosecutions for felonies be brought by a grand jury's "indictment" or "presentment." The indictment was the charging instrument issued by a grand jury on finding that the evidence presented to it by a prosecuting official was sufficient to justify forcing the accused to trial. The presentment was the charging instrument issued by the grand jury on its own initiative (i.e., not at the request of prosecuting officials). Presentments often were based on information provided initially by citizen complainants (or by a grand juror), which then was supplemented through the use of the grand jury's investigative authority. Thus, in recognizing the presentment, the grand jury clauses arguably assumed the continued use of the grand jury's investigative authority.

Over the first half of the nineteenth century, grand juries, particularly in the western states, actively reviewed a wide range of grievances presented by citizens, and gained a reputation as the foremost "public watchdog" as a result of their investigations of governmental corruption and organized evasions of the law. Over that last half of that century, however, several developments combined to alter the character and significance of grand jury investigations.

As local police departments became a major element of law enforcement administration, and expanded their investigative capabilities, there was less need for grand juries to be involved in the investigation of many types of offenses that had previously attracted their attention. At the same time, local prosecutors came to exercise a virtual monopoly over the decision to prosecute, and private parties were no longer able to institute prosecutions after first having received the investigative and charging assistance of the grand jury. As a result, the grand jury came to be called upon to investigate only where the prosecutor requested its assistance, and then did so under the leadership of the prosecutor.

Moreover, in a growing number of states, the grand jury was no longer a continuously functioning body, and that development restricted its investigative role even in assisting the prosecutor. Many states, as part of a sweeping reform movement, eliminated the requirement that all felony charges be screened and approved by a grand jury. They granted prosecutors the option of proceeding either by grand jury indictment or by a prosecutor's information. With indictments no longer required, many counties in such states discontinued the practice of having standing grand juries. A prosecutor seeking the investigatory assistance of a grand jury would have to petition the court for impanelment of a special grand jury, and that imposed administrative and political costs that caused prosecutors to act only in exceptional cases.

---

tion is required by state law or because that law eliminates the procedural advantages of utilizing an indictment rather than an information). See Notes 5–6, pp. 1015–17. In these states, when a grand jury finishes an investigation, it may issue a report urging prosecution (sometimes described as a "presentment"), but the prosecutor makes the final decision as to charging, and the charging instrument is an information. Compare fn. d infra and fn. a, p. 1042, as to other types of grand jury "presentments".

Over the twentieth century, the investigative role of the grand jury varied considerably among the states (and sometimes among counties within a state). Where grand juries continued to be used for screening, the common pattern was to also continue to make use of their investigative authority, but only for a select group of crimes. Use of the grand jury for investigations tended to be less frequent in those states that commonly prosecuted by information and therefore did not have standing grand juries. In some, prosecutors regularly sought the assistance of specially impaneled grand juries, but did so for an even narrower band of offenses than prosecutors in indictment jurisdictions. The two groups of offenses most often calling for the grand jury's investigative assistance were offenses involving complex financial transactions and offenses involving the widespread distribution of illegal services. The latter investigations led to the popular description of the grand jury as the nation's "number one instrument of discovery against organized crime." In other information jurisdictions, prosecutors rarely, if ever, sought the impanelment of grand juries (in part, because these prosecutors simply did not deal with the offenses that most clearly required the investigative tools of the grand jury).

Perhaps the most prominent state grand jury investigations of the twentieth century were the criminal investigations of public corruption.[d] As in the nineteenth century, although with less frequency, those investigations were at times largely the product of the initiative of the grand jurors. While some states now restricted the grand jury to investigating matters put before it by the prosecutor, and others adopted procedural barriers to grand jury initiated investigations (e.g., prohibiting citizens from conveying their complaints directly to the grand jury), most states retained what was described at common law as the "independent inquisitorial authority" of the grand jury. Of course, that authority was subject to severe practical restraints if the grand jury could not commandeer the resources available to the prosecutor, but in some instances, reluctant prosecutors acceded to the grand jurors' wishes when the jurors threatened otherwise to become a "runaway grand jury," and in other instances, the grand jury successfully petitioned the court for assistance through the appointment of a special prosecutor.

The federal criminal justice system undoubtedly made the most extensive use of the grand jury's investigative authority throughout most of the twentieth century. The federal system dealt far more frequently than the states with offenses that could be uncovered only by unraveling a complex criminal structure or obtaining and analyzing extensive business records. Federal investigations of white collar crime, regulatory offenses, and the various transactions of criminal "gangs" and "families" naturally called for use of the investigative powers available to the grand jury. Federal success in the prosecution of these crimes added luster to prosecutorial use of the grand jury's investigative authority, but the potential for misuse of that authority was highlighted by other federal grand jury investigations (in particular, the investigations of alleged criminal activities of radical groups—characterized by some observers as directed more at harassment than developing supportable indictments). The latter investigations led to a series of proposed reforms aimed at restricting the investigative authority of grand juries

---

d. The grand jury's "public watchdog" image historically rested on two quite different aspects of its investigative authority: (1) the investigation of criminal activity, leading to indictments and presentments; and (2) the investigation of inefficiency, negligence, and malfeasance in public administration, leading to grand jury reports, issued to the community. While the grand jury's reporting authority has been restricted or eliminated in many jurisdictions, it has been retained in many others, with grand juries even assigned by statute the duty of periodically investigating and reporting on certain aspects of public administration (e.g., conditions in jails). The discussion in this chapter is limited to the grand jury's investigative authority as used in the criminal justice process. As for grand jury reports (called "presentments" in some states) and investigations conducted in connection with those reports, see CRIMPROC § 8.3(h).

and expanding the rights of grand jury witnesses. Those proposals met with some success at the state level, where, for example, over twenty states adopted legislation allowing grand jury witnesses to be accompanied by counsel (see Note 10, p. 847). Congress, however, consistently rejected the proposed reform legislation. It left the regulation of federal grand jury investigations to the federal judiciary (which largely continued with the standards of the common law) and to the Justice Department's internal regulations (which did adopt some of the procedural protections that had been part of the reform proposals). The call for reform of federal grand jury investigations has been renewed in the twenty-first century, but Congress remains unpersuaded.

3. *Current status.* Only eighteen states still require prosecution by indictment in all felony cases, and most of those states continue to utilize the investigative authority of the grand jury on a fairly regular basis. While the vast majority of the cases brought before the grand jury have been fully investigated by the police, in a small percentage, the grand jury's investigative authority will be used to "finish off" the investigation, and in a still smaller percentage, the primary investigation will be conducted by the prosecution through the grand jury. This latter group will involve crimes in which the grand jury's investigative authority offers one or more of the advantages over police investigative authority that are discussed in Pt. B infra. In states in which prosecutions are traditionally brought by information, grand juries tend to be used only in the investigation of the most pressing of such offenses. In some counties in such states, as a result of prosecutors not encountering such crimes or lacking adequate resources, grand jury investigations are not simply rare, but nonexistent.

In the federal system, on the other hand, use of the grand jury's investigative authority continues to be ubiquitous (although not a feature found in the majority of federal prosecutions). Indeed, in the more heavily populated federal districts, where several grand juries will be sitting at the same time, one or more of those grand juries will be assigned to investigations that are likely to run at least several months. Such grand juries are likely to be impaneled not under Federal Rule 6(a), but under the Organized Crime Control Act (18 U.S.C.A. §§ 3322–34), which provides for an 18-month grand jury term that can be extended to 36 months.

B. INVESTIGATIVE ADVANTAGES

Compared to police investigations, grand jury investigations are expensive, time consuming, and logistically cumbersome. Accordingly, the grand jury ordinarily is used to investigate only when it has a distinct investigative advantage over the police. The grand jury's advantages in investigating criminal activity stem primarily from the six elements of its investigatory processes discussed below—(1) the use of the subpoena ad testificandum, (2) the psychological pressure imposed by the grand jury setting, (3) the use of immunity grants, (4) the use of the subpoena duces tecum, (5) grand jury secrecy requirements, and (6) public confidence attributable to lay participation. These advantages become significant where criminal investigators must gain the assistance of victims or witnesses who are reluctant to cooperate, unravel a complex criminal structure, obtain information contained in extensive business records, or keep a continuing investigative effort from the public gaze. Criminal activities that often present one or more of these difficulties include public corruption (e.g., bribery), misuse of economic power (e.g., price-fixing), the widespread distribution of illegal services and goods (e.g., gambling and narcotics distribution), complex fraudulent schemes, and various regulatory violations. Most grand jury investigations are directed at such offenses, but a particular advantage of the grand jury's investigative authority may lead to using the grand jury in an occasional investigation of the type of crime that ordinarily would be successfully investigated by the police alone (e.g., where a key witness to an assault refuses to give testimony and must be compelled to do so through a grant of immunity).

1. *Subpoena ad testificandum.* The basic investigative advantage provided by the grand jury is its authority to compel the production of evidence through the subpoena authority of the court that impaneled it. The subpoena duces tecum (discussed in Note 4 infra) is available to compel the production of tangible evidence, while the subpoena ad testificandum is available to compel persons to appear before the grand jury and give testimony. Both subpoenas are supported by the court's authority to hold in contempt any person who willfully refuses, without legal justification, to comply with the subpoena's directive.[e]

The contempt sanction makes the subpoena ad testificandum particularly useful in obtaining statements from persons who will not voluntarily furnish information to the police. While those persons have the right to refuse to cooperate with the police, their refusal to comply with a grand jury subpoena invokes the threat of a possible jail sentence. Faced with that threat, a recalcitrant witness often will have a change of heart and will give to the grand jury information that he previously refused to give to the police. Of course, if the information sought could be incriminating, the witness (unless granted immunity) may still refuse to cooperate by relying on his privilege against self-incrimination. However, many persons unwilling to furnish information to the police, will willingly testify before the grand jury without regard to whether the self-incrimination privilege might offer an avenue for refusing to do so. Thus, the victim of a fraudulent gambling operation or a loansharking operation may be either too embarrassed or too fearful to voluntarily furnish information to the police, yet be willing to furnish that information to the grand jury when faced with the threat of contempt. Similarly, an employee may wish to avoid the appearance of voluntarily assisting officials investigating his employer, yet testify freely under the compulsion of a subpoena.

The grand jury subpoena ad testificandum also has the advantage of requiring witnesses to testify under oath. If a witness fails to tell the truth, he may be prosecuted for perjury. Generally, a person who gives false information to a police officer will not have committed a crime (though there is such a crime as to federal investigators). Accordingly, where a witness might be willing to talk to the police, but also is likely to "shade his story," requiring him to testify before a grand jury may produce more complete and truthful statements. Even where a witness is willing to give an entirely truthful statement to the police, there may be value in requiring him to testify before the grand jury. Arguably, a person who has testified under oath before the grand jury will be somewhat more hesitant to "change his story" when he testifies at trial. Also, if the witness does change his story and his prior statement is used to impeach him, the petit jurors may give greater weight to his prior grand jury testimony than they would to a prior statement he made to the police.

---

e. The contemnor may be held in either civil or criminal contempt. Civil contempt is used to coerce the contemnor into complying with the subpoena. The contemnor is sentenced to imprisonment or to a fine (which may increase daily), but he may purge himself of the sentence by complying with the subpoena. As courts have frequently noted, he "carries the keys to the prison in his pocket." The civil contemnor who refuses to purge himself will remain under sentence until the grand jury completes its term and is discharged. Moreover, if the information the contemnor possesses is still needed, he may be subpoenaed by a successor grand jury and held in contempt again if he continues to refuse to supply that information. Where the contemnor's testimony is no longer needed, or civil contempt will not convince the contemnor to testify, the contemnor may be prosecuted for criminal contempt, typically punished at the same level as an obstruction of justice offense.

2. *Psychological pressure.* Standing apart from the compulsion of the subpoena, the psychological pressure of grand jury interrogation is cited as an additional factor that frequently enables the grand jury to obtain statements from witnesses unwilling to cooperate with the police. Of course the pressure accompanying police custodial interrogation may be greater, but a prerequisite for such interrogation is the probable cause needed to take a person into custody. Persons can be called to testify before the grand jury without probable cause (or even reasonable suspicion).

Proponents of grand jury investigations claim that the psychological pressure of grand jury interrogation stems from the moral force exerted by the grand jury. Thus, two prosecuting attorneys noted:

> Most witnesses before grand juries feel a moral compulsion to be honest and forthright in discharging their duties as citizens, because their peers, the members of the grand jury, have also been taken away from their jobs, businesses, and private pursuits, and have accepted the inconvenience of becoming involved. The grand jurors manifest a serious purpose and are persons with whom witnesses can identify. Thus, even though their associates may be determined not to cooperate, certain witnesses may be ashamed to engage or persist in deceitful or obstreperous conduct to deny the grand jury the information it needs. John Keeney & Paul Walsh, *The American Bar Association's Grand Jury Principles: A Critique From A Federal Criminal Justice Perspective,* 14 Idaho L.Rev. 545, 579 (1978).

On the other side, critics of grand jury investigations claim that the psychological pressure stems primarily from what they describe as the "star chamber setting" of grand jury interrogation. "In all of the United States legal system," they note, "no person stands more alone than a witness before a grand jury; in a secret hearing he faces an often hostile prosecutor and 23 strangers with no judge present to guard his rights, no lawyer present to counsel him, and sometimes no indication of why he is being questioned." As to many jurisdictions, this description of the pressure presented by the witness' predicament is clearly overstated, as the witness may consult with counsel (located within the grand jury room in some jurisdictions, and in an outside anteroom in others) prior to answering a troubling question. See Notes 9-10, pp. 847–48. However, even here, the witness faces the pressures of being subjected to a far ranging inquiry, without knowing in advance what will be asked (or sometimes, even the subject matter under inquiry), while aware that answers deemed false could well lead to a perjury prosecution. At the same time, the witness may fear that repeated consultations with counsel will be viewed by the grand jury as an attempt at evasion.

3. *Immunity grants.* An immunity grant is a court order granting a witness sufficient immunity from future prosecution to supplant the witness' self-incrimination privilege. Once the recalcitrant witness has been granted immunity, he may no longer rely upon the privilege. Since immunity grants are tied to the exercise of the privilege by a person under a legal obligation to testify, they are not available for persons who simply refuse to give a statement to the police. At the investigatory stage, almost the only way the prosecution can make use of an immunity grant is in conjunction with a subpoena directing the uncooperative witness to testify before the grand jury. The immunity grant may be needed to gain information from various types of recalcitrant witnesses. For example, immunity quite frequently is given to a lower-level participant in organized crime in order to obtain testimony against higher-level participants. It also often is used to force testimony from witnesses who are not themselves involved in criminal activities, but desire not to give testimony that may hurt others. Although the privilege is not available simply to protect others (see Note 4, p. 841), witnesses who do not actually fear personal incrimination have been known to falsely claim that they do in order to avoid testifying against their friends. Since such claims are difficult to dispute, the prosecutor may simply prefer to grant the witness immunity.

4. *Subpoena duces tecum.* The grand jury subpoena duces tecum offers several advantages over the primary device available to the police for obtaining documents and other physical evidence—the search pursuant to a warrant. Unlike the search warrant, the subpoena duces tecum can issue without a showing of probable cause. Moreover, even where probable cause can be established, there are times when the subpoena duces tecum will offer administrative advantages. These advantages are less likely to prevail where documents are sought from the target of the investigation, as there is often a concern that the target will destroy, conceal, or alter the documents rather than properly comply with the subpoena. However, there are instances in which the target would find it too risky to take such actions (typically the case as to records that have been shared with employees or advisors), and here the subpoena might be used even though a search warrant alternative is available. For example, there may be a need to seize so many records from various locations that a search would be impractical. With a subpoena duces tecum, the recipient of the subpoena is required to undertake the extensive task of bringing together the records from several different locations and sorting through them to collect those covered by the subpoena. Also, the subpoena may broadly describe the documents sought, thereby ensuring that no relevant documents are missed (a risk not so readily avoided in meeting the "particularity of description" requirement of a search warrant). A subpoena also has the advantage of keeping the grounding of the investigation from the target, as it will include only a brief, very general description of the subject of the grand jury's inquiry. A search warrant, on the other hand, requires an affidavit setting forth the specifics of the probable cause supporting the search, and that affidavit is available to the target (absent a not-readily-obtainable sealing order).[f]

Although the Supreme Court has held that the Fourth Amendment does not preclude use of a search to obtain documents from a disinterested third party (e.g., a bank) (see Note 2, p. 288), the subpoena duces tecum remains the standard vehicle for obtaining documents from such third parties, both where the government has and does not have probable cause to seize the documents. The primary concerns here are to avoid the disruptive impact of a search upon the third party (typically a commercial entity) and to gain that party's cooperation and expertise in identifying and locating the records sought.

Finally, the subpoena avoids the risk of a complete loss of evidence. Where the search was made pursuant to a warrant so deficient as to preclude police reliance

---

f. These potential advantages of the grand jury subpoena may, in turn, be offset by certain administrative advantages presented by the search warrant process, even where there is no serious concern that the target would conceal, destroy, or alter the documents identified in the subpoena (a risk avoided by the search process, as it comes without advance notice). Those administrative advantages of the search warrant include: (1) the search gives the government immediate access to the documents (the subpoena must provide a reasonable time for delivery and delivery may be further delayed by a motion challenging the subpoena); (2) the search places an officer in a position to examine a larger body of documents in seeking to identify these specified in the warrant, and should the officer find in plain view any incriminating documents beyond those the government had anticipated, the officer can seize those documents; (3) the officer executing the warrant may gain valuable information from discussions with the target or the target's employees in the course of executing the search; (4) the disruptive impact of the search may convey to the target the message that the government is taking a tough, aggressive stance; (5) the use of a search may be publicized and convey a similar message to the public, whereas the issuance of a grand jury subpoena cannot be made public by the government, and (6) an individual (though not an entity) may raise a self-incrimination objection to the required production of documents under a subpoena, but that objection is not available where the documents are seized by the government (see Note 7, p. 856).

upon the "good faith" exception to the exclusionary rule (see Note 7, p. 240), or the execution exceeded the search warrant and was therefore unconstitutional (see Note 6, p. 327), the government loses the use of unconstitutionally seized documents and any additional evidence that falls within the "fruit of the poisonous tree doctrine". On the other hand, where a subpoena duces tecum is impermissible in scope or issuance, the challenge must be raised prior to the response and the consequence of a successful challenge is a quashing of the subpoena. This allows the government to refashion the subpoena to meet the sustained objections, so there is no loss of evidence that could have been obtained through a curable illegality.

   5. Secrecy. Grand jury secrecy requirements vary somewhat from one jurisdiction to another, but even the weakest of secrecy requirements is thought to add to the grand jury's effectiveness as an investigative agency. All jurisdictions prohibit the prosecutor, the prosecutor's staff (including investigative agents), the grand jurors, and the grand jury stenographer from disclosing grand jury testimony and other information relating directly to grand jury proceedings (e.g., what persons have been subpoenaed), unless such disclosure is authorized by the court upon a special showing of need. Although several jurisdictions extend this obligation of secrecy to grand jury witnesses (who thereby are prohibited from disclosing their participation and their testimony to persons other than counsel), the vast majority (including the federal system) do not attempt to hold a witness to a secrecy obligation. Here, witnesses are free to disclose publicly or privately both their own testimony and whatever information was revealed to them in the course of giving that testimony.

   In *United States v. Procter & Gamble Co.*, 356 U.S. 677 (1958), the Supreme Court noted five objectives of grand jury secrecy requirements imposed in the federal system:

   > (1) to prevent the escape of those whose indictment may be contemplated; (2) to insure the utmost freedom to the grand jury in its deliberations, and to prevent persons subject to indictment or their friends from importuning the grand jurors; (3) to prevent subornation of perjury or tampering with the witnesses who may testify before grand jury and later appear at the trial of those indicted by it; (4) to encourage free and untrammeled disclosures by persons who have information with respect to the commission of crimes; (5) to protect the innocent accused who is exonerated from disclosure of the fact that he has been under investigation, and from the expense of standing trial where there was no probability of guilt.

   While the second objective cited by the Court relates primarily to the screening function of the grand jury, the remaining four promote the grand jury's effectiveness as an investigative agency. The first objective—preventing the flight of the person being investigated—depends initially upon the grand jury having no need to subpoena the target as that would clearly put the target on notice (indeed, in the federal system and many states, a subpoenaed party will be informed if he, she, or it is a target of the investigation). Assuming information is sought only from witnesses, there remains the need to ensure that the witnesses do not inform the target of the inquiry. In the vast majority of jurisdictions, since the witnesses are not sworn to secrecy, this depends upon the inclination of the witnesses (although court orders prohibiting disclosure during an ongoing investigation may be possible in some jurisdictions).

   Grand jury secrecy arguably makes a more substantial contribution to the third objective noted in *Procter & Gamble*—precluding subornation of perjury and witness tampering. Even should some of the initial witnesses inform the target of the ongoing investigation, that information may not be sufficiently detailed to allow the target to anticipate who else will be called before the grand jury, and once the witnesses have testified under oath, a major shift in their later testimony is likely to raise suspicions of witness tampering. Where the target correctly identifies (and seeks to influence) potential witnesses, he still faces the obstacle of having no means to be certain that a witness testified as the target suggested. The witness has the protection of testifying in a closed proceeding (even counsel, who may have been provided by the target, is excluded in the federal system and many states). Thus, what the target learns of a witness' testimony is only what the witness chooses to tell the target (subject to the possibility of post-indictment discovery as discussed below).

The fourth objective noted in *Procter & Gamble* probably is the most significant for investigatory success. Witnesses often are much more willing to testify if they know that their identity will be kept from the target and the public (typically because they fear attempts at intimidation, fear economic or social repercussions, or simply seek to avoid notoriety). Though the jurisdiction does not swear witnesses to secrecy, witnesses know that, if they decide not to reveal their participation and testimony, the obligation of secrecy imposed on the grand jurors and prosecution personnel provides assurance that those persons will not reveal that information.

Of course, if an indictment is issued and the grand jury witness is called as a trial witness (indeed, in some jurisdictions, if the prosecution simply anticipates possibly calling him as a trial witness), his participation (and his grand jury testimony) will become known to the defendant (and probably the public).[g] However, an indictment also can issue without such disclosure; the grand jury witness may not be needed as a prospective trial witness (the witness' testimony may be unnecessary in light of leads he and others provide to more incriminating evidence) or a trial may not occur (e.g., the defendant may plead guilty). Moreover, if the grand jury witness can be assured that his identity will be revealed only in connection with the issuance of an indictment, he may have fewer qualms about testifying fully and truthfully. He may be less wary of being criticized as an "informer" if he knows that his role will be revealed only after a grand jury has supported his judgment and veracity by issuing an indictment.

The fifth objective noted in *Procter & Gamble* serves, in part, to justify the sweeping investigative power granted to the grand jury. Where an investigation can be based on "tips" and "rumors" (see *Dionisio* at p. 819), there is special need to protect the reputation of the target of the investigation (who may well be innocent). That protection is provided by secrecy requirements that prohibit those involved in the grand jury investigation from disclosing to the media and others the identity of those under investigation. This shield of secrecy is thought to be especially important in the investigation of public figures, and, indeed, needed to overcome a natural hesitancy to pursue investigations of such persons in the absence of strong evidence of criminality.

Critics contend, however, that grand jury secrecy requirements are practically worthless in the investigation of high profile targets. They note that, in the vast majority of jurisdictions, the secrecy requirements do not extend to grand jury witnesses, and a witness hostile to the target may be eager to inform a curious media of questioning relating to the target. In many jurisdictions, those secrecy requirements also do not bar a prosecutor from releasing to the media a carefully

---

g. Where a witness testifies at trial, all jurisdictions will make his prior grand jury testimony (where recorded) available to the defense for impeachment purposes. See CRIMPROC § 24.3(c). In many jurisdictions, the prosecution must disclose in pretrial discovery the names of its intended witnesses and their prior recorded statements (which includes grand jury testimony). In others, including the federal system, pretrial disclosure of the names of prospective witnesses is not required. See CRIMPROC §§ 8.5(f), 20.3(i).

worded description of the investigation and its targets that simply avoids reference to the activities of the grand jury itself. Where the target is aware of the investigation and is a corporate enterprise, it will have an obligation to investors to reveal that it is the target of a grand jury investigation. Above all critics argue, even where the target, the witnesses, and the prosecutor all desire to keep "under wraps" the investigation of a high profile target, there remains a distinct possibility of an "unauthorized leak" by investigators or other prosecution personnel. Here, it is claimed, the potential sanctions for violating grand jury secrecy through improper leaking of grand jury testimony lose their effectiveness as a deterrent as the person leaking that information generally can do so through a reporter who will not only publish the information but also protect the identity of her source (even if that means, where a reporter's privilege affords no protection, risking a contempt sanction for refusing to reveal that source in a subsequent judicial inquiry into the leak).[h]

6. *Maintaining public confidence.* Where the subject to be investigated is a matter of public knowledge (as in the case of investigations into matters already given considerable media coverage), grand jury participation often helps in maintaining community confidence in the integrity of the investigatory process. This is especially important where the person under investigation is a public official. The community tends to be suspicious of partisan influences in such investigations, especially where the investigation results in a decision not to prosecute. As one court noted: "Where corruption is charged, it is desirable to have someone outside the administration [i.e., the grand jury] act, so that the image, as well as the fact of impartiality in the investigation can be preserved and allegations of cover-up or white-wash can be avoided." *Losavio v. Kikel,* 529 P.2d 306 (Colo.1974). The prosecutor may also look to the grand jury to help allay other public concerns, as in cases in which investigated parties are almost certain to claim police and prosecutor harassment.

C. ALTERNATIVE ROUTES TO INVESTIGATION BY SUBPOENA

The primary investigative tool of the grand jury is the subpoena, and many jurisdictions grant the subpoena power to other agencies for either criminal investigations or civil investigations that may uncover evidence of criminal activities. As discussed below, to some extent, the law governing grand jury investigations also bears on those agencies as well.

1. *Alternative criminal investigative authority.* A small number of states have created investigate authorities which are roughly similar to the grand jury, except that they utilize judges or other officials rather than lay grand jurors. These investigative alternatives include the "one man grand jury" (a judge acting, in effect, as a grand jury, assisted by a specially appointed prosecutor), the "John Doe" proceeding (a prosecutorial inquiry into the commission of specified criminal activity, conducted before a judge), and the special crime commission (typically a state commission assigned to investigating and reporting on a particular type of crime). In some instances, these investigative authorities can actually bring criminal charges, while in others the prosecutor must decide whether to proceed on the results of their investigation.

---

h. Since press reports discussing the internal operations of grand jury investigations of high-profile targets almost invariably attribute the information reported to an anonymous source, whether such information commonly comes from government personnel is a matter of pure speculation. Courts conducting inquiries aimed at identifying such anonymous sources have rarely been successful, and when they have managed to identify the source, it typically has been someone other than government personnel (e.g., a witness, an agent of a high-profile target, or a person indicted in another aspect of the investigation).

Several states authorize the local prosecutor to use subpoenas in the investigation of some or all offenses. Some condition such authority on the prior approval of the court in the individual case (requiring a showing of need), while others allow the prosecution to issue subpoenas on its own initiative (although they are then subject to challenge in court). Still other states grant investigative subpoena authority to the state's Attorney General as to certain types of offenses.

In the federal system, Congress has granted to U.S. Attorneys and other Justice Department attorneys the authority to issue administrative subpoenas in the investigation of specific areas of potential criminal liability, including: health care offenses and offenses involving the sexual exploitation of children, 18 U.S.C.A. § 3486 (limited to the production of records or other tangible); offenses relating to controlled substances, 21 U.S.C.A. § 876 (subpoena may compel production of records and attendance and testimony of witnesses); racketeering offenses, 18 U.S.C.A. § 1968 (civil investigative demand, which operates as an administrative subpoena duces tecum); and fraud in government contracts, 31 U.S.C.A. § 3733 (also a civil investigative demand). These subpoenas, or subpoena-counterparts, operate in the same fashion as the administrative agency subpoenas discussed in Note 2 infra. See *In re Administrative Subpoena*, 253 F.3d 256 (6th Cir.2001). In providing for the investigation of terrorism, Congress had gone a step further and given the F.B.I. the authority to obtain court orders that are the equivalent of subpoenas, and the authority to obtain a limited class of records from certain service providers using directives to produce ("national security letters"), which may be enforced by a court order to comply. See pp. 540–41; Kriss & Wilson, fn. b., p. 539.

2. *Civil administrative subpoenas.* Most federal administrative agencies and many state administrative agencies are given administrative subpoena authority, to be used in the investigation of possible violations of regulatory provisions (which may often constitute criminal as well as civil violations, as on the case of S.E.C. violations). The administrative subpoenas (also called "summonses") may compel the production of documents or the appearance and giving of testimony. Administrative subpoenas, unlike grand jury subpoenas, do not utilize the process of the court (which use, in the grand jury context, places on the recipient the legal obligation of either complying or challenging the subpoena by a motion to quash). To enforce an administrative subpoena, the agency must bring an independent civil action. Should the administrative investigatory process produce evidence of a criminal violation, that evidence may be turned over to the prosecutor with a request for prosecution.

3. *Legal similarities and differences.* The alternative routes to investigation by subpoena tend to differ in several important respects from the grand jury subpoena. Apart from the grand jury counterparts (e.g., the one-man grand jury), they do not ask that testimony be given (or documents produced) in a closed proceeding. Where a witness is required to appear to give testimony, that witness may be accompanied by counsel. A rejected challenge by the witness readily can be appealed since the judicial enforcement of the subpoena presents a final judgment subject to the process generally applicable to a civil judgment (in contrast to the enforcement of a grand jury subpoena, where the party directed to comply ordinarily can gain review only by being held in contempt). Since the administrative subpoena is commonly tied to the investigation of a limited class of offenses and often subject to other statutory limits as well, the standard of judicial review may be somewhat more rigorous than the very limited Rule 17(c) standard applied to grand jury subpoenas (see e.g., *R. Enterprises, Inc.*, p. 823).

On the other hand, the Fourth Amendment standard applied to subpoenas duces tecum are similar for grand juries, grand jury counterparts, and administrative subpoenas. The application of the self-incrimination privilege is identical, and thus one of the leading cases on the application of the privilege to the production of documents (see *Fisher*, p. 856) involves an Internal Revenue Service summons rather than a grand jury subpoena. Similarly, where the applicable state or federal law allows the prosecutor or agency given subpoena authority to replace the self-incrimination privilege with an immunity order, the same constitutional standards apply to immunity granted in that setting as immunity granted in the grand jury setting (see Pt. B. pp. 848–52).

D. JUDICIAL REGULATION: SOME DIFFERING PERSPECTIVES

1. *CRIMPROC § 8.2(c).* "The grand jury investigation is frequently described as introducing an 'inquisitorial element' into a criminal justice system that is basically accusatorial. Critics argue that the grand jury's investigative authority should therefore be viewed as an anomaly and kept within narrow confines by close judicial supervision. They recognize that this position faces difficulties if history reveals that the grand jury inquest was accepted from the outset as an institution that coexisted with the accusatorial elements of the Anglo–American criminal justice process. The critics argue, however, that a careful reading of the history of the grand jury reveals no such accommodation. First, they note, the early grand juries did not frequently exercise the basic element of its modern investigative authority—its power to compel testimony—but instead relied primarily upon information known to the jurors or the voluntary testimony of aggrieved persons. Secondly, they argue, the investigative role of the grand jury was not critical to its initial acceptance in this country. It was the shielding role of the grand jury that earned it a place in the Bill of Rights and the early state constitutions. The grand jury's investigatory role was then viewed as entirely secondary and not necessarily distinct from its screening role. Today, it is argued, the significance of the two roles has been reversed.

"Supporters of the grand jury respond that the early history of the grand jury clearly establishes the legitimacy of its extensive investigative authority. The power of the grand jury to compel testimony was recognized well before the adoption of the Constitution and was used in some of the most notable grand jury inquests. At the time of the Constitution's adoption, the grand jury was a revered institution not simply because it served as a buffer between the state and the individual, but equally for its service as a watchdog against public corruption and its capacity to ferret out criminal activity that local officials either chose to ignore or were unable to investigate. The importance of this investigative authority was implicitly recognized, it is argued, in constitutional and statutory provisions authorizing the institution of prosecution by presentment as well as indictment.

"With few exceptions, American courts have accepted the position that the history of the grand jury provides a solid foundation for its broad investigative authority. The Supreme Court's discussion of that authority in *Blair v. United States* [see Note 2 infra] is typical.[i] The Court there noted that the grand jury's authority to resort to compulsory process had been recognized in England as early as 1612, and the inquisitorial function of the grand jury was well established at the time of the Constitution's adoption. Both the Fifth Amendment and the

---

i. Consider, however, Niki Kuckes, *The Useful Dangerous Fiction of Grand Jury Independence*, 41 Amer.Crim.L.Rev. 1 (2004), arguing that the Supreme Court opinions have just as frequently sustained the broad investigative authority of the grand jury not because of the grand jury's role as a law enforcement agency (highlighted in *Blair*), but because of its role as a "protective bulwark," reasoning that such investigative powers are needed to ensure that it properly exercises its screening function (i.e., "the Supreme Court has broadly claimed that the grand jury is given broad investigative powers for the putative defendant's benefit"). The author cites as illustrative the last paragraph of the *Dionisio* opinion, quoted at p. 819.

earliest federal statutes recognized an investigative authority of the grand jury that included the 'same powers that pertained to its British prototype.' The Supreme Court would not view that authority with suspicion and subject it to new limitations. * * *

"Critics of the grand jury also contend that even if a broad investigative authority is sanctioned by history, the same historical sources also indicate that authority was tied to an assumption of substantial grand jury independence. * * * Today, the critics argue, the sweeping powers of the grand jury are exercised in reality by the prosecutor alone. Working with the police, the prosecutor determines what witnesses will be called and when they will appear. He examines the witnesses and advises the grand jury on the validity of any legal objections the witnesses might present. If a witness refuses to comply with a subpoena, it is the prosecutor who seeks a contempt citation. If a witness refuses to testify on grounds of self-incrimination, it is the prosecutor who determines whether an immunity grant will be obtained. The grand jury must, almost of necessity, rely upon the prosecutor's leadership. Few investigations can succeed without the investigative work, skillful interrogation, legal advice, and even the secretarial assistance, provided by the prosecutor and his staff. So too, grand jurors are neophytes in the field of criminal investigation and are participating only on a part-time basis; it is only natural that they are disposed to rely upon the prosecutor—the 'professional' who commands the expertise necessary to their venture.

"Critics argue that this change in the nature of the investigative grand jury, which [they say] has converted it into the 'prosecutor's puppet,' requires a corresponding change in judicial attitudes. The courts should not, they argue, feel bound by precedent that was developed during an era when grand juries were independent bodies. Instead, they should 'pull back the veil of history and view the investigating grand jury as one would view any other investigatory instrument of government.' The power of the grand jury should be subject to the same kinds of limitations as are imposed upon other weapons in the prosecutor's investigative arsenal.

"Supporters of the grand jury readily acknowledge that the prosecutor plays a substantial role in directing today's grand jury investigations. They suggest that this is a beneficial development that makes the investigatory authority more effective and helps to ensure that it is not misused. Moreover, it is noted, this development dates back over one hundred years, preceding many of the decisions that speak most eloquently of the necessary breadth of the grand jury's investigative authority. The key to the historical grant of that authority, they argue, was a legal structure that rendered the government's use of the grand jury's investigative powers subject to the veto of the jurors, who sat as community representatives. That structure has not been substantially altered, and its very presence, the argument continues, serves to hold the prosecutor in check and to distinguish grand jury investigations from investigatory tools granted directly to the prosecutor or the police.[j] The fact that the grand jury only occasionally exercises its power

---

j. See e.g., Justice Black's oft-quoted dissent in *In re Groban,* 352 U.S. 330 (1957). Commenting on the distinction between a grand jury proceeding (where Justice Black agreed that "a witness cannot insist, as a matter of constitutional right, on being represented by counsel") and a fire marshall's closed inquiry (where Justice Black, disagreeing with the *Groban* majority, argued that the witness had a constitutional right to be accompanied by counsel), Justice Black emphasized the special role of the grand jurors: "They bring into the grand jury room the experience, knowledge and viewpoint of all sections of the community. They have no axes to grind and are not charged personally with the administration of the law. No one of them is a prosecuting attorney or law-enforcement officer ferreting out crime. It would be very difficult for officers of the state seriously to abuse or deceive a witness in the presence of the grand jury. Similarly the presence of the jurors offers a substantial safeguard against the officers' misrepre-

to override the prosecutor does not detract from the significance of that power. The prosecutor must respect the existence of that power and act in a way that he knows, from past experience, will be acceptable to the jurors."

2. BLAIR v. UNITED STATES, 250 U.S. 273 (1919). Responding to a grand jury witness' challenge to a subpoena on the ground that the federal government lacked constitutional authority to regulate, and the federal grand jury therefore lacked jurisdiction to investigate, the campaign practices of a candidate in a state primary election for U.S. Senator, PITNEY, J., speaking for a unanimous Court, noted:

"[T]he giving of testimony and the attendance upon court or grand jury in order to testify are public duties which every person within the jurisdiction of the Government is bound to perform upon being properly summoned, and for performance of which he is entitled to no further compensation than that which the statutes provide. The personal sacrifice involved is a part of the necessary contribution of the individual to the welfare of the public. The duty, so onerous at times, yet so necessary to the administration of justice according to the forms and modes established in our system of government is subject to mitigation in exceptional circumstances; there is a constitutional exemption from being compelled in any criminal case to be a witness against oneself, entitling the witness to be excused from answering anything that will tend to incriminate him; some confidential matters are shielded from considerations of policy, and perhaps in other cases for special reasons a witness may be excused from telling all that he knows.

"But, aside from exceptions and qualifications—and none such is asserted in the present case—the witness is bound not only to attend but to tell what he knows in answer to questions framed for the purpose of bringing out the truth of the matter under inquiry. He is not entitled to urge objections of incompetency or irrelevancy, such as a party might raise, for this is no concern of his. On familiar principles, he is not entitled to challenge the authority of the court or of the grand jury, provided they have a *de facto* existence and organization. He is not entitled to set limits to the investigation that the grand jury may conduct. * * * It is a grand inquest, a body with powers of investigation and inquisition, the scope of whose inquiries is not to be limited narrowly by questions of propriety or forecasts of the probable result of the investigation, or by doubts whether any particular individual will be found properly subject to an accusation of crime."

3. IN RE GRAND JURY PROCEEDINGS (SCHOFIELD I), 486 F.2d 85 (3d Cir.1973). Rejecting the government's claim that a grand jury witness should be held in contempt for failing to respond to a grand jury subpoena with no more showing as to the grounding of the subpoena than "what appears on the face of the subpoena", the Third Circuit (per Gibbons, J.) noted:

"[I]t is well to start with some fundamental propositions. First, although federal grand juries are called into existence by order of the district court, Fed.R.Crim.P. 6(a), they are 'basically . . . a law enforcement agency.' They are for all practical purposes an investigative and prosecutorial arm of the executive branch of government. Second, although like all federal court subpoenas, grand jury subpoenas are issued in the name of the district court over the signature of the clerk, they are issued pro forma and in blank to anyone requesting them. Fed.R.Crim.P. 17(a). The court exercises no prior control whatsoever upon their use. Third, although grand jury subpoenas are occasionally discussed as if they were the instrumentalities of the grand jury, they are in fact almost universally instrumentalities of the United States Attorney's office or of some other investiga-

---

sentation, unintentional or otherwise, of the witness statements and conduct before the grand jury."

tive or prosecutorial department of the executive branch. Grand jury subpoenas then, when they are brought before the federal courts for enforcement, for all practical purposes are exactly analogous to subpoenas issued by a federal administrative agency on the authority of a statute * * *. [A] court's determination under 28 U.S.C. § 1826(a) [the civil contempt enforcement provision] of the existence or nonexistence of just cause for refusing to obey a subpoena entails the same full judicial consideration as in the administrative subpoena cases."

4. **UNITED STATES v. WILLIAMS**, 504 U.S. 36 (1992). The *Williams* majority opinion held that a federal court could not on its own initiative impose a duty on the government to present to the grand jury material exculpatory evidence within its possession, and the court accordingly could not dismiss an indictment because the prosecutor failed to present such evidence. Explaining the limited authority of federal courts to mandate grand jury procedures beyond those "specifically required by the Constitution or Congress," Justice Scalia noted:

" '[R]ooted in long centuries of Anglo–American history,' the grand jury is mentioned in the Bill of Rights, but not in the body of the Constitution. It has not been textually assigned, therefore, to any of the branches described in the first three Articles. It 'is a constitutional fixture in its own right.' In fact the whole theory of its function is that it belongs to no branch of the institutional government, serving as a kind of buffer or referee between the Government and the people. * * * Although the grand jury normally operates, of course, in the courthouse and under judicial auspices, its institutional relationship with the judicial branch has traditionally been, so to speak, at arm's length. Judges' direct involvement in the functioning of the grand jury has generally been confined to the constitutive one of calling the grand jurors together and administering their oaths of office. * * * The grand jury requires no authorization from its constituting court to initiate an investigation, nor does the prosecutor require leave of court to seek a grand jury indictment. And in its day-to-day functioning, the grand jury generally operates without the interference of a presiding judge. It swears in its own witnesses, Fed.Rule 6(c), and deliberates in total secrecy.

"True, the grand jury cannot compel the appearance of witnesses and the production of evidence, and must appeal to the court when such compulsion is required. And the court will refuse to lend its assistance when the compulsion the grand jury seeks would override rights accorded by the Constitution * * *. Even in this setting, however, we have insisted that the grand jury remain 'free to pursue its investigations unhindered by external influence or supervision so long as it does not trench upon the legitimate rights of any witness called before it.' *United States v. Dionisio* [p. 819]. Recognizing this tradition of independence, we have said that the Fifth Amendment's 'constitutional guarantee *presupposes* an investigative body "acting independently of either prosecuting attorney *or judge*" . . . .' *Dionisio*.

"Given the grand jury's operational separateness from its constituting court, it should come as no surprise that we have been reluctant to invoke the judicial supervisory power as a basis for prescribing modes of grand jury procedure. Over the years, we have received many requests to exercise supervision over the grand jury's evidence-taking process, but we have refused them all, including some more appealing than the one presented today. [Citing *Calandra,* Note 4, p. 822]. * * * These authorities suggest that any power federal courts may have to fashion, on their own initiative, rules of grand jury procedure is a very limited one, not remotely comparable to the power they maintain over their own proceedings."

SECTION 2. FOURTH AMENDMENT CHALLENGES TO THE INVESTIGATION

A. THE INITIAL APPROACH

BOYD v. UNITED STATES
116 U.S. 616, 6 S.Ct. 524, 29 L.Ed. 746 (1886).

[Customs officials seized 35 cases of glass, imported by the partnership of Boyd and Sons, and instituted a forfeiture proceeding. That proceeding was brought under a statute providing that any importer who defrauded the government and thereby avoided payment of customs revenue was subject to fine, incarceration, and forfeiture of the imported merchandise. Utilizing an 1874 statute, the government's attorney obtained a court "notice" directing Boyd to produce an invoice covering 29 of the cases of glass. That statute authorized the trial judge, on motion of the prosecutor describing a particular document and indicating what it might prove, to issue a notice directing the importer to produce the document. The importer could refuse to produce without being held in contempt (which distinguished the "notice" from a subpoena), but the consequence of a failure to produce was that the allegation of the prosecutor as to what the document stated was "taken as confessed." The defendants produced the invoice in compliance with the notice, but objected to the validity of the court's order, and objected again when the invoice was offered as evidence. The jury subsequently found for the United States, and a judgment of forfeiture against the 35 cases was granted.]

BRADLEY, J.

The clauses of the Constitution, to which it is contended that these laws are repugnant, are the Fourth and Fifth Amendments. * * * [I]n regard to Fourth Amendment, it is contended that * * * [the Act of 1874], under which the order in the present case was made, is free from constitutional objection, because it does not authorize the search and seizure of books and papers, but only requires the defendant or claimant to produce them. That is so; but it declares that if he does not produce them, the allegations which it is affirmed they will prove shall be taken as confessed. This is tantamount to compelling their production; for the prosecuting attorney will always be sure to state the evidence expected to be derived from them as strongly as the case will admit of. It is true that certain aggravating incidents of actual search and seizure, such as forcible entry into a man's house and searching amongst his papers, are wanting, and to this extent the proceeding under the act of 1874 is a mitigation of that which was authorized by the former acts; but it accomplishes the substantial object of those acts in forcing from a party evidence against himself. It is our opinion, therefore, that a compulsory production of a man's private papers to establish a criminal charge against him, or to forfeit his property, is within the scope of the Fourth Amendment to the Constitution, in all cases in which a search and seizure would be; because it is a material ingredient, and effects the sole object and purpose of search and seizure.

The principal question, however, remains to be considered. Is a search and seizure, or, what is equivalent thereto, a compulsory production of a man's private papers, to be used in evidence against him in a proceeding to forfeit his property for alleged fraud against the revenue laws—is such a proceeding for such a purpose an "*unreasonable* search and seizure" within the meaning of the Fourth Amendment of the Constitution? or, is it a legitimate proceeding? * * *

As before stated, the [predecessor] act of 1863 was the first act in this country, and, we might say, either in this country or in England, so far as we have been able to ascertain, which authorized the search and seizure of a man's private papers, or the compulsory production of them, for the purpose of using them in evidence against him in a criminal case, or in a proceeding to enforce the forfeiture of his property. Even the act under which the obnoxious writs of assistance were issued did not go as far as this, but only authorized the examination of ships and vessels, and persons found therein, for the purpose of finding goods prohibited to be imported or exported, or on which the duties were not paid, and to enter into and search any suspected vaults, cellars, or warehouses for such goods. The search for and seizure of stolen or forfeited goods, or goods liable to duties and concealed to avoid the payment thereof, are totally different things from a search for and seizure of a man's private books and papers for the purpose of obtaining information therein contained, or of using them as evidence against him. The two things differ *toto coelo*. In the one case, the government is entitled to the possession of the property; in the other it is not. * * *

In order to ascertain the nature of the proceedings intended by the Fourth Amendment to the Constitution under the terms "unreasonable searches and seizures," it is only necessary to recall the contemporary or then recent history of the controversies on the subject, both in this country and in England. * * * Prominent and principal among these was the practice of issuing general warrants by the Secretary of State, for searching private houses for the discovery and seizure of books and papers that might be used to convict their owner of the charge of libel. * * * The case [which] will always be celebrated as being the occasion of Lord Camden's memorable discussion of the subject, was that of *Entick v. Carrington and Three Other King's Messengers,* reported at length in 19 Howell's State Trials, 1029. The action was trespass for entering the plaintiff's dwelling-house in November, 1762, and breaking open his desks, boxes, & c., and searching and examining his papers. The jury rendered a special verdict, and the case was twice solemnly argued at the bar. Lord Camden pronounced the judgment of the court in Michaelmas Term, 1765, and the law as expounded by him has been regarded as settled from that time to this, and his great judgment on that occasion is considered as one of the landmarks of English liberty. * * * As every American statesmen, during our revolutionary and formative period as a nation, was undoubtedly familiar with this monument of English freedom, and considered it as the true and ultimate expression of constitutional law, it may be confidently asserted that its propositions were in the minds of those who framed the Fourth Amendment to the Constitution, and were considered as sufficiently explanatory of what was meant by unreasonable searches and seizures. * * *

After describing the power claimed by the Secretary of State for issuing general search warrants, and the manner in which they were executed, Lord Camden says [in *Entick*]:

     * * * Papers are the owner's goods and chattels; they are his dearest property; and are so far from enduring a seizure, that they will hardly bear an inspection; and though the eye cannot by the laws of England be guilty of a trespass, yet where private papers are removed and carried away the secret nature of those goods will be an aggravation of the trespass, and demand more considerable damages in that respect. Where is the written law that gives any magistrate such a power? I can safely answer, there is none; and therefore, it is too much for us, without such authority, to pronounce a practice legal which would be subversive of all the comforts of society. * * *

     Lastly, it is urged as an argument of utility, that such a search is a means of detecting offenders by discovering evidence. I wish some cases had been shown, where the law forceth evidence out of the owner's custody by process.

There is no process against papers in civil causes. It has been often tried, but never prevailed. Nay, where the adversary has by force or fraud got possession of your own proper evidence, there is no way to get it back but by action. In the criminal law such a proceeding was never heard of; and yet there are some crimes, such, for instance, as murder, rape, robbery, and house-breaking, to say nothing of forgery and perjury, that are more atrocious than libeling. But our law has provided no paper-search in these cases to help forward the conviction. Whether this proceedeth from the gentleness of the law towards criminals, or from a consideration that such a power would be more pernicious to the innocent than useful to the public, I will not say. It is very certain that the law obligeth no man to accuse himself; because the necessary means of compelling self-accusation, falling upon the innocent as well as the guilty, would be both cruel and unjust; and it would seem, that search for evidence is disallowed upon the same principle. Then, too, the innocent would be confounded with the guilty.

* * * The principles laid down in this opinion affect the very essence of constitutional liberty and security. They reach farther than the concrete form of the case then before the court, with its adventitious circumstances; they apply to all invasions on the part of the government and its employees of the sanctity of a man's home and the privacies of life. It is not the breaking of his doors, and the rummaging of his drawers, that constitutes the essence of the offence; but it is the invasion of his indefeasible right of personal security, personal liberty and private property, where that right has never been forfeited by his conviction of some public offence,—it is the invasion of this sacred right which underlies and constitutes the essence of Lord Camden's judgment. Breaking into a house and opening boxes and drawers are circumstances of aggravation; but any forcible and compulsory extortion of a man's own testimony or of his private papers to be used as evidence to convict him of crime or to forfeit his goods, is within the condemnation of that judgment. In this regard the Fourth and Fifth Amendments run almost into each other. * * *

Reverting then to the peculiar phraseology of this act, and to the information in the present case, which is founded on it, we have to deal with an act which expressly excludes criminal proceedings from its operation (though embracing civil suits for penalties and forfeitures), and with an information not technically a criminal proceeding, and neither, therefore, within the literal terms of the Fifth Amendment to the Constitution any more than it is within the literal terms of the Fourth. Does this relieve the proceedings or the law from being obnoxious to the prohibitions of either? We think not; we think they are within the spirit of both.

We have already noticed the intimate relation between the two amendments. They throw great light on each other. For the "unreasonable searches and seizures" condemned in the Fourth Amendment are almost always made for the purpose of compelling a man to give evidence against himself, which in criminal cases is condemned in the Fifth Amendment; and compelling a man "in a criminal case to be a witness against himself," which is condemned in the Fifth Amendment, throws light on the question as to what is an "unreasonable search and seizure" within the meaning of the Fourth Amendment. And we have been unable to perceive that the seizure of a man's private books and papers to be used in evidence against him is substantially different from compelling him to be a witness against himself. * * * We are also clearly of opinion that proceedings instituted for the purpose of declaring the forfeiture of a man's property by reason of offences committed by him, though they may be civil in form, are in their nature criminal. In this very case, the ground of forfeiture * * * consists of certain acts of fraud committed against the public revenue in relation to imported merchandise, which are made criminal by the statute * * *. As, therefore, suits for penalties and forfeitures incurred by the commission of offences against the law, are of this quasi-criminal nature, we think that they are within the reason of criminal proceedings for all the purposes of the Fourth Amendment of the Constitution, and of that portion of the Fifth Amendment which declares that no person shall be compelled in any criminal case to be a witness against himself; and we are further of opinion that a compulsory production of the private books and papers of the owner of goods sought to be forfeited in such a suit is compelling him to be a witness against himself, within the meaning of the Fifth Amendment to the Constitution, and is the equivalent of a search and seizure—and an unreasonable search and seizure—within the meaning of the Fourth Amendment.

Though the proceeding in question is divested of many of the aggravating incidents of actual search and seizure, yet, as before said, it contains their substance and essence, and effects their substantial purpose. It may be that it is the obnoxious thing in its mildest and least repulsive form; but illegitimate and unconstitutional practices get their first footing in that way, namely, by silent approaches and slight deviations from legal modes of procedure. This can only be obviated by adhering to the rule that constitutional provisions for the security of person and property should be liberally construed. A close and literal construction deprives them of half their efficacy, and leads to gradual depreciation of the right, as if it consisted more in sound than in substance. It is the duty of courts to be watchful for the constitutional rights of the citizen, and against any stealthy encroachments thereon. Their motto should be *obsta principiis.* * * *

JUSTICE MILLER, with whom was The Chief Justice concurring:

I concur in the judgment of the court * * * and in so much of the opinion of this court as holds the 5th section of the act of 1874 void as applicable to the present case. * * * The order of the court under the statute is in effect a subpoena duces tecum, and, though the penalty for the witness's failure to appear in court with the criminating papers is not fine and imprisonment, it is one which may be made more severe, namely, to have charges against him of a criminal nature, taken for confessed, and made the foundation of the judgment of the court. That this is within the protection which the Constitution intended against compelling a person to be a witness against himself, is, I think, quite clear.

But this being so, there is no reason why this court should assume that the action of the court below, in requiring a party to produce certain papers as evidence on the trial, authorizes an unreasonable search or seizure of the house, papers, or effects of that party. There is in fact no search and no seizure authorized by the statute. No order can be made by the court under it which requires or permits anything more than service of notice on a party to the suit. * * *

Nothing in the nature of a search is here hinted at. Nor is there any seizure, because the party is not required at any time to part with the custody of the papers. They are to be produced in court, and, when produced, the United States attorney is permitted, under the direction of the court, to make examination in presence of the claimant, and may offer in evidence such entries in the books, invoices, or papers as relate to the issue. The act is careful to say that "the owner of said books and papers, his agent or attorney, shall have, subject to the order of the court, the custody of them, except pending their examination in court as aforesaid." . . .

The things . . . forbidden [by the Fourth Amendment] are two—search and seizure. * * * But what search does this statute authorize? If the mere service of a notice to produce a paper to be used as evidence, which the party can obey or not as he chooses is a search, then a change has taken place in the meaning of words, which has not come within my reading, and which I think was unknown at the time the Constitution was made. The searches meant by the Constitution were such as led to seizure when the search was successful. But the statute in this case uses language carefully framed to forbid any seizure under it, as I have already pointed out. * * *

NOTES AND QUESTIONS

1. *A civil liberties icon.* *Boyd* has been praised by commentators and courts as a landmark civil liberties case. Dissenting in *Olmstead v. United States*, 277 U.S. 438 (1928), Justice Brandeis noted: "*Boyd v. United States* [is] a case that will be remembered as long as civil liberty lives in the United States." See also William J. Stuntz, *Privacy's Problem and the Law of Criminal Procedure*, 93 Mich.L.Rev. 1016 (1995) ("*Boyd* is conventionally seen as the *Miranda* of its day, a criminal procedure case that courageously protected the rights (particularly the privacy rights) of individuals against the government. Its passing—essentially nothing in *Boyd's* holding is good law anymore—is mourned as a sign of citizens' diminished protection against an overly aggressive criminal justice system").

What made *Boyd* a civil liberties icon? Was it the statement in the last paragraph of the majority's opinion on the need for liberal construction of constitutional safeguards—a statement quoted with approval in numerous Supreme Court opinions? Was it the Court's attempt to bring together the Fourth and Fifth Amendment guarantees—its linking of the constitutional protection of "the privacies of life" not only to the restrictions on search and seizure but also to the privilege against self-incrimination? See Stuntz, supra. Was it the Court's focus on consequence rather than procedural form—its treatment of the court order to produce a document as the functional equivalent of a search and the production of an incriminating document through a search as the functional equivalent of being compelled to testify as to the incriminating contents of that document? See Note 1, p. 852.

2. Commentators also have suggested that many aspects of the reasoning of *Boyd* do not "ring true" for a civil liberties icon. Thus, *Boyd* has been described as a product of "nineteenth century legal formalism" that was founded "on the view that adjudication proceeds by deduction from virtually absolute principles rooted in natural law and enshrined in both the common law and the Constitution." Note, 90 Harv.L.Rev. 943 (1977). See also William J. Stuntz, *The Substantive Origins of Criminal Procedure*, 105 Yale L.J. 393 (1995) (comparing *Boyd* to the Supreme Court's pre-1930's substantive due process cases). Also, *Boyd* is characterized as a ruling grounded more on the protection of private property than the protection of privacy. See e.g., Stanton D. Krauss, *The Life and Times of Boyd v. United States (1886–1976)*, 76 Mich.L.Rev. 184 (1977) ("[C]onfidentiality was not the interest the Court sought to protect. Whether the Boyds had kept the invoice a secret to the world or whether they had made its contents a matter of public knowledge was irrelevant; either way the government's action was illegal"). The key to *Boyd*, under this view, was that the invoice was properly possessed private property—i.e., not contraband or the fruits of a crime.

Boyd, unlike most other civil liberties icons in the criminal procedure field, dealt with investigative techniques "far removed from ordinary criminal law." Stuntz, supra. As noted in Stuntz, Note 1 supra: "In the decades following the Court's decision, few ordinary criminal investigations led to *Boyd*-type claims, either in the form of challenges to subpoenas or as trespass actions against officers. On the other hand, regulatory cases were common. In a number of bankruptcy cases, the debtor sought to avoid certain kinds of compelled disclosure. Antitrust cases began to crop up following the Sherman Act in 1890, with defendants raising Fifth Amendment objections to subpoenas or questioning.

Railroad regulation disputes were especially numerous and especially high-profile, with corporate officials striving to avoid testifying or producing documents in ICC proceedings." Indeed, Professor Stuntz argues, it was concern for the barriers *Boyd* posed to economic regulation that led to the first step in the dismantling of *Boyd* in *Hale v. Henkel* (Note 1, infra). See also the Stuntz quotation at p. 814.

3. *The dismantling of Boyd. Boyd* and its reasoning survived intact for less than two decades. Yet its dismantling took almost a century, and some would argue that at least a small remnant of the *Boyd* analysis has current vitality. See Note 1, p. 863. But see *Krauss*, Note 2 supra (*"Boyd* is dead").

Initially, the Court in *Hale* (Note 1, infra) separated *Boyd's* Fifth Amendment and Fourth Amendment analyses, concluded that corporations had no self-incrimination privilege, and announced a separate (and more lenient) Fourth Amendment standard for the subpoena of documents. In later cases examining *Boyd's* commentary on the Fourth Amendment and searches, the Court first held that a search and seizure could extend to private property that constituted the instrumentality of the crime, *Marron v. United States*, 275 U.S. 192 (1927), then in 1967 rejected the reading of *Boyd* as prohibiting a search for private property that constituted no more than "mere evidence" of a crime, *Warden v. Hayden* (p. 286), and finally in 1976 held that Fourth Amendment did not prohibit a search for documents, *Andresen v. Maryland* (p. 286). The major developments in the Court's dismantling of *Boyd's* Fifth Amendment analysis and ruling are discussed in section 5 of this chapter.

B. THE OVERBREADTH DOCTRINE

1. *Hale v. Henkel (the introduction of the overbreadth doctrine).* In HALE v. HENKEL, 201 U.S. 43 (1906), the Court had before it a challenge to a subpoena directing the petitioner to produce before a grand jury (which was conducting an investigation into possible violations of the antitrust laws) various corporate documents. Petitioner's challenge was based on the combined impact of the Fourth and Fifth Amendments, but the Court initially separated those claims. Cases subsequent to *Boyd,* it noted, had "treated the Fourth and Fifth Amendments as quite distinct, having different histories, and performing separate functions." Turning first to the petitioner's self-incrimination claim, the Court found that claim clearly unsupportable since the statute authorizing the subpoena granted petitioner immunity from prosecution (see Note 1, p. 848) and the corporation itself had no self-incrimination privilege (see Note 2, p. 853). The petitioner's Fourth Amendment claim did have merit, but for reasons other than that which might have been assumed from *Boyd*. Speaking for the Court, Justice Brown, noted:

"Although * * * we are of the opinion that an officer of a corporation * * * cannot refuse to produce the books and papers of such corporation, we do not wish to be understood as holding that a corporation is not entitled to immunity, under the Fourth Amendment, against *unreasonable* searches and seizures. A corporation is, after all, but an association of individuals under an assumed name and with a distinct legal entity. In organizing itself as a collective body it waives no constitutional immunities appropriate to such body. * * * We are also of opinion that an order for the production of books and papers may constitute an unreasonable search and seizure within the Fourth Amendment. While a search ordinarily implies a quest by an officer of the law, and a seizure contemplates a forcible dispossession of the owner, still, as was held in the *Boyd* case, the substance of the offense is the compulsory production of private papers, whether under a search warrant or a subpoena duces tecum, against which the person, be he individual or corporation, is entitled to protection. Applying the test of reasonableness to the present case, we think the subpoena duces tecum is far too sweeping in its terms to be regarded as reasonable. It does not require the production of a single contract, or of contracts with a particular corporation, or a limited number of documents, but all understandings, contracts, or correspondence between the MacAndrews & Forbes Company, and no less than six different companies, as well as all reports made, and accounts rendered by such companies from the date of the organization of the MacAndrews & Forbes Company, as well as all letters received by that company since its organization from more than a dozen different companies, situated in seven different States in the Union.

"If the writ had required the production of all the books, papers and documents found in the office of the MacAndrews & Forbes Company, it would scarcely be more universal in its operation, or more completely put a stop to the business of that company. Indeed, it is difficult to say how its business could be carried on after it had been denuded of this mass of material, which is not shown to be necessary in the prosecution of this case, and is clearly in violation of the general principle of law with regard to the particularity required in the description of documents necessary to a search warrant or subpoena. Doubtless many, if not all, of these documents may ultimately be required, but some necessity should be shown, either from an examination of the witnesses orally, or from the known transactions of these companies with the other companies implicated, or some evidence of their materiality produced, to justify an order for the production of such a mass of papers. A general subpoena of this description is equally indefensible as a search warrant would be if couched in similar terms."

Justice McKenna, concurring separately in *Hale,* questioned the Court's Fourth Amendment analysis: "It is said 'a search implies a quest by an officer of the law; a seizure contemplates a forcible dispossession of the owner.' Nothing can be more direct and plain; nothing more expressive to distinguish a subpoena from a search warrant. Can a subpoena lose this essential distinction from a search warrant by the generality or speciality of its terms? I think not. The distinction is based upon what is authorized or directed to be done—not upon the form of words by which the authority or command is given. 'The quest of an officer' acts upon the things themselves—may be secret, intrusive, accompanied by force. The service of a subpoena is but the delivery of a paper to a party—is open and aboveboard. There is no element of trespass or force in it. It does not disturb the possession of property. It cannot be finally enforced except after challenge, and a judgment of the court upon the challenge. This is a safeguard against abuse the same as it is of other processes of the law, and it is all that can be allowed without serious embarrassment to the administration of justice."

2. *Explaining the overbreadth doctrine.* As Judge Friendly noted in *In re Horowitz,* 482 F.2d 72 (2d Cir.1973), "the Fourth Amendment portion of the *Boyd* decision was surely not based on the overbreadth of the Government's demand; the Government [there] sought only a single invoice of unquestionable relevance." Although relying on *Boyd, Hale v. Henkel*

> left the applicability of the Fourth Amendment to subpoena duces tecum in a most confusing state. None of the Justices seemed to think that such a subpoena could be issued only "upon probable cause, supported by oath or affirmation," as would be required for a search warrant. Nevertheless, except for Mr. Justice McKenna, all were of the view that an overbroad subpoena duces tecum against an individual would be an unreasonable search and seizure.

Judge Friendly suggested in *Horowitz* that the overbreadth doctrine of *Hale* might find firmer support in the due process clause than in the Fourth Amendment. Although a due process grounding for the doctrine is suggested in *Oklahoma Press*

Publishing Co. v. Walling, 327 U.S. 186 (1946) (a leading case on the application of the overbreadth doctrine to an administrative agency subpoena[a]), more recent cases have referred to the doctrine as based on the Fourth Amendment.

Accepting the Court's premise that the Fourth Amendment does apply to the subpoena duces tecum, why should the overbreadth doctrine be the sole Fourth Amendment limitation as to the subpoena duces tecum? One explanation is that the requirements of the Fourth Amendment's warrant clause are inapplicable in light of (1) the long history of subpoenas issued without regard to probable cause (particularly in the trial context, see Fed.R.Crim.P. 17), and (2) the lesser intrusion upon privacy resulting from a subpoena (as compared to the traditional search). This leaves applicable only the Fourth Amendment's general mandate of "reasonableness," which is reflected in the overbreadth doctrine. See Wayne R. LaFave, *Search and Seizure* § 4.13(e) (4th ed. 2004). This explanation makes *Hale* the forerunner of the Supreme Court's later line of cases which looked to similar factors in concluding that the Fourth Amendment permits administrative searches (e.g., health inspections) without a case-specific showing akin to probable cause or reasonable suspicion. See Ch. 6, § 9. But consider CRIMPROC § 8.7(a), responding that this explanation would seem to call for a standard of reasonableness that is more rigorous where there is a greater invasion of privacy due to the heightened confidentiality of the particular document (distinguishing for example between the subpoena of business documents and diaries), a position not suggested in *Hale*. "Also, such an analysis does not lead to protection conditioned on the subpoena compelling production of a substantial body of documents (as *Hale* seemed to suggest) and would not test overbreadth by reference to the economic burden imposed upon the individual or entity by being forced to relinquish those documents (as *Hale* clearly did)." Ibid.

A second explanation of *Hale* builds upon Justice McKenna's suggestion that the *Hale* majority found the Fourth Amendment applicable only when the subpoena was overly broad. The theory here is that the subpoena is not comparable to search, except where it potentially is too sweeping. Calling for a mass of documents without regard to what is relevant, necessarily requires a sifting through those documents to identify those that are relevant. Whether that sifting takes place on the premises of the owner or in the offices of the prosecutor assisting the grand jury, it would constitute a search, and therefore the Fourth prohibits a subpoena where it clearly is so sweeping as to include the relevant and the irrelevant. Commentators challenging this explanation note that it renders irrelevant a key component of *Hale*'s analysis—the heavy burden that compliance with the subpoena imposed upon McAndrews & Forbe. They also note that the explanation does not fully support the criteria courts subsequently have applied in

---

a. Speaking to petitioners' claim that enforcement of the subpoena duces tecum would violate rights secured by the Fourth Amendment, Justice Rutledge noted that the "short answer" to this contention was that "these cases present no question of actual search and seizure" as they involved no attempt by government officials "to enter petitioners' premises against their will, to search them, or to seize or examine their books." He later added: "The primary source of misconception concerning the Fourth Amendment's function lies perhaps in the identification of cases involving so-called 'figurative' or 'constructive' search with cases of actual search and seizure. Only in this analogical sense can any question related to search and seizure be thought to arise in situations which, like the present ones, involve only the validity of authorized judicial orders."

Oklahoma Press set forth three prerequisites for administrative agency subpoenas: (1) the investigation must be for a "lawfully authorized purpose within the power of Congress"; (2) the documents sought must be "relevant to the inquiry"; (3) the element of "particularity" must be satisfied by a "specification of the documents to be produced adequate, but not excessive for the purpose of reasonable inquiry." Lower courts have described this standard as lenient, but not as lenient as "the lowest standard [which] is reserved for federal grand jury subpoenas." *Oman v. State,* 737 N.E.2d 1131 (Ind. 2000).

assessing unreasonableness in *Hale* (see Note 3 infra), as the relevancy standard, in particular, can require quashing a subpoena that demands production of just a few documents, if clearly unrelated to the investigation.

A third explanation, stresses the different investigative focus of searches and grand jury subpoenas. The underlying premise of this explanation is that a Fourth Amendment that looks to the invasion of privacy would not on that ground draw a distinction between searches and subpoenas to produce documents.[b] Rather, the key to that distinction is "substantive necessity," as reflected in the character of the crime typically investigated by documentary subpoena as opposed to the crimes typically investigated through physical searches. See William J. Stuntz, *O.J. Simpson, Bill Clinton, and the Transsubstantive Fourth Amendment*, 114 Harv.L.Rev. 842 (2001): "[I]f the government is to regulate business and political affairs—the usual stuff of white-collar criminal law—it must have the power to subpoena witnesses and documents before it knows whether those witnesses and documents will yield incriminating evidence." Though *Hale* did not point to this reality in explaining its "lax" Fourth Amendment standard, the Court did so in another portion of the opinion (see Note 2, p. 853), where it rejected *Hale's* Fifth Amendment argument "in a pair of dismissive sentences," noting: "[T]he privilege claimed would practically nullify the whole [Sherman Act]. Of what use would it be for the legislature to declare these combinations unlawful if the judicial power may close the door of access to every available source of information upon the subject?" Commentators challenging this explanation note that the Court has never suggested applying a Fourth Amendment standard more rigorous than *Hale* for subpoenas issued in the investigation of a crime that would not be revealed primarily in the internal documents of a business enterprise. They also ask why such regulatory concerns have not been reflected in the Fourth Amendment standards governing searches for documents. See *Andresen v. Maryland*, p. 286, and Note 1, p. 863.

3. *Applying the overbreadth doctrine.* Lower courts applying the overbreadth doctrine in the grand jury setting frequently note that the doctrine requires a fact-specific judgment, with each ruling tied to the circumstances of the individual case. At the same time, they have sought to develop some general criteria to guide that judgment. Initially, the subpoena carries with it a presumption of regularity that will be called into question only if the subpoena has "sufficient breadth to suggest either that compliance will be burdensome or that the subpoena's scope may not have been shaped to the purposes of the inquiry." CRIMPROC § 8.7(c). If the subpoena has such breadth, the courts will then examine its scope in light of three criteria: (1) whether it "commands only the production of documents relevant to the investigation being pursued"; (2) whether

---

b. See William J. Stuntz, *Privacy's Problem and the Law of Criminal Procedure*, 93 Mich. L.Rev. 1016 (1995): "When the police search a car, they see anything that happens to be in the car, not just guns or drugs. A subpoena, on the other hand, asks only for the evidence being sought; nothing else need be disclosed. This difference could suggest that searches by their very nature invade privacy more than subpoenas do * * * [but] the line is incoherent in privacy terms. * * * The relevant privacy interest is the interest in keeping secret whatever the government is examining."

Consider also, Christopher Slobogin, *Subpoenas and Privacy*, 54 DePaul L.Rev. 805 (2005): "The fact that it is the target * * * rather than the police who locates the documents obviously does not change the nature of the revelations [the documents] contain, which can include information about medical treatment, finances, education, the identity of one's communicants, and even the contents of one's communications. The target's ability to challenge a subpoena, while it may inhibit some fishing expeditions, at most will only delay government access to the records, unless something beyond the current relevance standard is applicable [to subpoenas]. * * * And if the notion that searches only occur when government engages in physical invasion of private space were correct, then electronic surveillance and technologically-assisted physical surveillance of the home would not be a search, since neither usually requires a trespass or use of force."

the specification of the documents is made with "reasonable particularity" (measured by reference to both the subpoenaed party's ability to identify what "he is being asked to produce" and any "unreasonable business detriment" flowing from collecting and relinquishing the quantity and range of the documents requested); and (3) whether the documents to be produced cover "only a reasonable period of time." Ibid. Applying these criteria, courts have upheld subpoenas requiring production of as much as 50 tons of documents, see *Petition of Borden,* 75 F.Supp. 857 (N.D.Ill.1948); yet they also have rejected requests for records that presumably would have occupied no more than a single filing cabinet. See e.g., *In re Certain Chinese Family Benevolent Ass'n,* 19 F.R.D. 97 (N.D.Cal.1956) (rejecting subpoenas requiring various Chinese family associations to produce available membership lists, income records, and membership photographs, dating back to the association's origin, for use in an investigation of immigration fraud).

Although the overbreadth doctrine is a separate ground for challenging a subpoena duces tecum, as to federal courts, it may largely overlap with the Rule 17(c) objection discussed in *R. Enterprises* (p. 823), which imposes a similar limitation. See e.g., *In re Grand Jury Subpoena Duces Tecum Dated November 15, 1993,* 846 F.Supp. 11 (S.D.N.Y. 1994) (Rule 17(c) objection sustained, looking to reasoning of the Second Circuit in analyzing Fourth Amendment overbreadth of a subpoena requiring production of the full content of three filing cabinets in which an accountant had stored the records of a defunct business enterprise that may have been used as a vehicle for fraud; the Second Circuit noted that the cabinets had been used to store various documents of the target-owners, including those relating to matters that occurred long before the allegedly fraudulent scheme, and the government had made no effort to "define classes of potentially relevant documents or [impose] limitations as to subject matter or time period"; here a similar flaw was present in the challenged subpoena's demand for all computer hard drives and floppy diskettes, ignoring the possibility of identifying relevant materials by key words or particular categories of documents).

   4. *Third-party objections.* As discussed in Note 6 p. 517, *United States v. Miller* holds that a target of an investigation may not raise a Fourth Amendment objection to a subpoena directing a third party service provider (in *Miller,* a bank) to produce records of the transactions of its customer/target, even though some of the records (e.g., checks) were originally created by the target. Some states have refused to follow *Miller,* granting the customer/target standing under state law to raise a Fourth Amendment objection to such third party subpoenas, and some courts have distinguished *Miller* as to certain types of target records transmitted to third party service providers. See CRIMPROC §§ 8.5(d), 9.1(c), and *United States v. Warshak,* at p. 504. Criticism of *Miller* has focused on its application to various records that reveal personal information, such as loan applications, personal checks, travel records, and requests for medical reimbursement. Christopher Slobogin notes, however, that *Miller* is not the only culprit in failing to provide sufficient Fourth Amendment protection for such records; even if the target had standing to challenge the subpoena directed to the service provider, the *Hale* standard of reasonableness could be easily be met by the government. Professor Slobogin urges reconsideration of both *Miller* and *Hale* as applied to subpoenas for personal documents. He points, in particular, to the special context in which the governing doctrine was developed and the changed circumstances that have dramatically altered the impact of that doctrine:[c]

------

   c. Professor Slobogin also finds flawed the rationales that have been advanced in support of the current "regulatory regime," insofar as it permits subpoenas of personal records without probable cause and without giving the target any opportunity to object where those records are in the possession of a third party. He identifies (and rejects) six justifications for that regime ("the first and last of which apply to all subpoenas and the rest of which are relevant only to third

"[T]he Court's de-regulation of subpoenas came in cases [like *Hale*] involving government attempts to regulate *businesses*; not a single one of them involved searches of personal papers. Because, as far as the Court was concerned, personal records held by the person himself or herself—i.e., most personal records— remained protected by the Fifth Amendment's prohibition on compelling persons to give testimony, the virtual elimination of Fourth Amendment protection against subpoenas [in *Hale* and related cases] had no impact in that area. Two developments * * * have changed all that. First, within the past three decades, the Supreme Court has radically altered its approach to the Fifth Amendment privilege, so that now personal records held by the target are almost as unprotect- ed as corporate records as far as that constitutional provision is concerned. Far more importantly, the modernization of society has rendered the Fifth Amend- ment's application to personal records largely irrelevant in any event. That is because, in contrast to nineteenth century culture, so much more of our personal information is now recorded and held by third parties. When third parties are ordered to produce information via a subpoena, they cannot, under any plausible interpretation, be said to be incriminating themselves. * * * Since today most subpoenas for personal documents are aimed at third party recordholders, the upshot of these developments is that government is almost entirely unrestricted, by either the Fifth Amendment or the Fourth Amendment, in its efforts to obtain documentary evidence of non-business crime."

C. COMPELLING TESTIMONY (AND IDENTIFICATION EXEMPLARS)

UNITED STATES v. DIONISIO

410 U.S. 1, 93 S.Ct. 764, 35 L.Ed.2d 67 (1973).

JUSTICE STEWART delivered the opinion of the Court.

A special grand jury was convened in the Northern District of Illinois in February 1971, to investigate possible violations of federal criminal statutes relating to gambling. In the course of its investigation the grand jury received in evidence certain voice recordings that had been obtained pursuant to court orders. The grand jury subpoenaed approximately 20 persons, including the respondent Dionisio, seeking to obtain from them voice exemplars for comparison with the recorded conversations that had been received in evidence. Each witness was advised that he was a potential defendant in a criminal prosecution. Each was asked to examine a transcript of an intercepted conversation, and to go to a nearby office of the United States Attorney to read the transcript into a recording device. The witnesses were advised that they would be allowed to have their attorneys present when they read the transcripts. Dionisio and other witnesses refused to furnish the voice exemplars, asserting that these disclosures would violate their rights under the Fourth [Amendment]. * * * Following a hearing, the district judge rejected the witnesses' constitutional arguments and ordered

---

party subpoenas"): "The first justification, offered over a century ago, is that subpoenas are not 'searches' under the Fourth Amendment because they do not involve physical intrusion. The second, put forward by the modern Court, is that third party subpoenas are not searches because the information they seek is already exposed to others. The next three reasons are not as clearly stated in Supreme Court opinions but are implicit in the language of some of its cases or are found in lower court decisions: the records obtained through third-party subpoenas belong to the third party, not the target; third party record-holders are not different from third party witnesses who have information about a suspect; and third parties have an obligation to provide informa- tion to the government. The final reason given for leaving subpoenas essentially unregulated is the one most commonly seen in Supreme Court and lower court opinions: imposition of rigorous Fourth Amendment requirements on subpoenas would stultify important government investiga- tions." See also Christopher Slobogin, *Privacy at Risk* 154 –67 (2007).

them to comply with the grand jury's request. * * * When Dionisio persisted in his refusal to respond to the grand jury's directive, the District Court adjudged him in civil contempt and ordered him committed to custody. * * *

The Court of Appeals for the Seventh Circuit reversed. * * * The court found that the Fourth Amendment applied to the grand jury process * * *. Equating the procedures followed by the grand jury in the present case to the fingerprint detentions in *Davis v. Mississippi* [Note 1, p. 437], the Court of Appeals reasoned that "[t]he dragnet effect here, where approximately 30 persons were subpoenaed for purposes of identification, has the same invidious effect on fourth amendment rights as the practice condemned in *Davis*."[d] The Court of Appeals held that the Fourth Amendment required a preliminary showing of reasonableness before a grand jury witness could be compelled to furnish a voice exemplar, and that in this case the proposed "seizures" of the voice exemplars would be unreasonable because of the large number of witnesses summoned by the grand jury and directed to produce such exemplars. We disagree. * * *

As [this] Court made clear in *Schmerber v. California* [p. 30], the obtaining of physical evidence from a person involves a potential Fourth Amendment violation at two different levels—the "seizure" of the "person" necessary to bring him into contact with government agents, see *Davis v. Mississippi,* and the subsequent search for and seizure of the evidence. * * * The constitutionality of the compulsory production of exemplars from a grand jury witness necessarily turns on the same dual inquiry—whether either the initial compulsion of the person to appear before the grand jury, or the subsequent directive to make a voice recording is an unreasonable "seizure" within the meaning of the Fourth Amendment.

It is clear that a subpoena to appear before a grand jury is not a "seizure" in the Fourth Amendment sense, even though that summons may be inconvenient or burdensome. Last Term we again acknowledged what has long been recognized, that "[c]itizens generally are not constitutionally immune from grand jury subpoenas...." *Branzburg v. Hayes* [Note 3, p. 831]. * * * [*Branzburg* and other decisions] are recent reaffirmations of the historically grounded obligations of every person to appear and give his evidence before the grand jury. "The personal sacrifice involved is a part of the necessary contribution of the individual to the welfare of the public." *Blair v. United States* [Note 2, p. 804].

The compulsion exerted by a grand jury subpoena differs from the seizure effected by an arrest or even an investigative "stop" in more than civic obligation. For, as Judge Friendly wrote for the Court of Appeals for the Second Circuit:

"The latter is abrupt, is effected with force or the threat of it and often in demeaning circumstances, and, in the case of arrest, results in a record involving social stigma. A subpoena is served in the same manner as other legal process; it involves no stigma whatever; if the time for appearance is inconvenient, this can generally be altered; and it remains at all times under the control and supervision of a court."

Thus, the Court of Appeals for the Seventh Circuit correctly recognized in a case subsequent to the one now before us, that a "grand jury subpoena to testify is not

---

d. In *Davis*, petitioner and 24 other black youths were taken into custody, and questioned and fingerprinted, in connection with a rape for which the only leads were the victim's general description of the assailant and fingerprints around a window. The Supreme Court subsequently held that petitioner's prints should have been excluded from trial because they were obtained in violation of the Fourth Amendment. The Court left open the possibility that a court order directing that a person be detained briefly only for the purpose of obtaining his fingerprints could be sustained under the Fourth Amendment even though the individualized suspicion fell short of "probable cause in the traditional sense."

that kind of governmental intrusion on privacy against which the Fourth Amendment affords protection, once the Fifth Amendment is satisfied." * * *

This case is thus quite different from *Davis v. Mississippi,* on which the Court of Appeals primarily relied. For in *Davis* it was the initial seizure—the lawless dragnet detention—that violated the Fourth and Fourteenth Amendments—not the taking of the fingerprints. * * * *Davis* is plainly inapposite to a case where the initial restraint does not itself infringe the Fourth Amendment.

This is not to say that a grand jury subpoena is some talisman that dissolves all constitutional protections. The grand jury cannot require a witness to testify against himself. It cannot require the production by a person of private books and records that would incriminate him. See *Boyd v. United States.* The Fourth Amendment provides protection against a grand jury subpoena *duces tecum* too sweeping in its terms "to be regarded as reasonable." *Hale v. Henkel.* And last Term, in the context of a First Amendment claim, we indicated that the Constitution could not tolerate the transformation of the grand jury into an instrument of oppression: "Official harassment of the press undertaken not for purposes of law enforcement but to disrupt a reporter's relationship with his news sources would have no justification. Grand juries are subject to judicial control and subpoenas to motions to quash. We do not expect courts will forget that grand juries must operate within the limits of the First Amendment as well as the Fifth." *Branzburg v. Hayes.*

But we are here faced with no such constitutional infirmities in the subpoena to appear before the grand jury or in the order to make the voice recordings. There is * * * no valid Fifth Amendment claim. There was no order to produce private books and papers, and no sweeping subpoena *duces tecum.* And even if *Branzburg* be extended beyond its First Amendment moorings and tied to a more generalized due process concept, there is still no indication in this case of the kind of harassment that was of concern there.

The Court of Appeals found critical significance in the fact that the grand jury had summoned approximately 20 witnesses to furnish voice exemplars. We think that fact is basically irrelevant to the constitutional issues here. The grand jury may have been attempting to identify a number of voices on the tapes in evidence, or it might have summoned the 20 witnesses in an effort to identify one voice. But whatever the case, "[a] grand jury's investigation is not fully carried out until every available clue has been run down and all witnesses examined in every proper way to find if a crime has been committed." * * * The grand jury may well find it desirable to call numerous witnesses in the course of an investigation. It does not follow that each witness may resist a subpoena on the ground that too many witnesses have been called. Neither the order to Dionisio to appear, nor the order to make a voice recording was rendered unreasonable by the fact that many others were subjected to the same compulsion.

But the conclusion that Dionisio's compulsory appearance before the grand jury was not an unreasonable "seizure" is the answer to only the first part of the Fourth Amendment inquiry here. Dionisio argues that the grand jury's subsequent directive to make the voice recording was itself an infringement of his rights under the Fourth Amendment. We cannot accept that argument. In *Katz v. United States* [p. 264], we said that the Fourth Amendment provides no protection for what "a person knowingly exposes to the public, even in his home or office...." The physical characteristics of a person's voice, its tone and manner, as opposed to the content of a specific conversation, are constantly exposed to the public. Like a man's facial characteristics, or handwriting, his voice is repeatedly produced for others to hear. No person can have a reasonable expectation that others will not know the sound of his voice, any more than he can reasonably expect that his face will be a mystery to the world. * * *

Since neither the summons to appear before the grand jury, nor its directive to make a voice recording infringed upon any interest protected by the Fourth Amendment, there was no justification for requiring the grand jury to satisfy even the minimal requirement of "reasonableness" imposed by the Court of Appeals. A grand jury has broad investigative powers to determine whether a crime has been committed and who has committed it. The jurors may act on tips, rumors, evidence offered by the prosecutor, or their own personal knowledge. *Branzburg v. Hayes.* No grand jury witness is "entitled to set limits to the investigation that the grand jury may conduct." *Blair v. United States.* And a sufficient basis for an indictment may only emerge at the end of the investigation when all the evidence has been received. * * * Since Dionisio raised no valid Fourth Amendment claim, there is no more reason to require a preliminary showing of reasonableness here than there would be in the case of any witness who, despite the lack of any constitutional or statutory privilege, declined to answer a question or comply with a grand jury request. Neither the Constitution nor our prior cases justify any such interference with grand jury proceedings.[14]

The Fifth Amendment guarantees that no civilian may be brought to trial for an infamous crime "unless on a presentment or indictment of a Grand Jury." This constitutional guarantee presupposes an investigative body "acting independently of either prosecuting attorney or judge," whose mission is to clear the innocent, no less than to bring to trial those who may be guilty. Any holding that would saddle a grand jury with mini trials and preliminary showing would assuredly impede its investigation and frustrate the public's interest in the fair and expeditious administration of the criminal laws. The grand jury may not always serve its historic role as a protective bulwark standing solidly between the ordinary citizen and an overzealous prosecutor, but if it is even to approach the proper performance of its constitutional mission, it must be free to pursue its investigations unhindered by external influence or supervision so long as it does not trench upon the legitimate rights of any witness called before it. * * *

JUSTICE MARSHALL, dissenting.[e]

* * * There can be no question that investigatory seizures effected by the police are subject to the constraints of the Fourth and Fourteenth Amendments. *Davis v. Mississippi.* * * * Like *Davis,* the present cases involve official investigatory seizures which interfere with personal liberty. The Court considers dispositive, however, the fact that the seizures were effected by the grand jury, rather than the police. I cannot agree. * * * [I]n *Hale v. Henkel,* the Court held that a subpoena *duces tecum* ordering "the production of books and papers [before a

---

14. Mr. Justice Marshall in dissent suggests that a preliminary showing of "reasonableness" is required where the grand jury subpoenas a witness to appear and produce handwriting or voice exemplars, but not when it subpoenas him to appear and testify. Such a distinction finds no support in the Constitution. The dissent argues that there is a potential Fourth Amendment violation in the case of a subpoenaed grand jury witness because of the asserted intrusiveness of the initial subpoena to appear—the possible stigma from a grand jury appearance and the inconvenience of the official restraint. But the initial directive to appear is as intrusive if the witness is called simply to testify as it is if he is summoned to produce physical evidence.

e. In the companion case of *United States v. Mara,* 410 U.S. 19 (1973), the Court applied *Dionisio* to reject a lower court ruling that a preliminary showing of reasonableness was needed to justify a grand jury subpoena directing a witness to produce handwriting exemplars for the purpose of determining whether he was the author of certain writings. Justice Marshall's dissent was to both rulings. The separate dissents of Justices Douglas and Brennan are omitted. Justice Douglas' dissent proceeded from the premise, described as now being "common knowledge," that "the grand jury, having been conceived as a bulwark between the citizen and the Government, is now a tool of the Executive."

grand jury] may constitute an unreasonable search and seizure within the Fourth Amendment," and on the particular facts of the case, it concluded that the subpoena was "far too sweeping in its terms to be regarded as reasonable." Considered alone, *Hale* would certainly seem to carry a strong implication that a subpoena compelling an individual's personal appearance before a grand jury, like a subpoena ordering the production of private papers, is subject to the Fourth Amendment standard of reasonableness. The protection of the Fourth Amendment is not, after all, limited to personal "papers," but extends also to "persons," "houses," and "effects." It would seem a strange hierarchy of constitutional values that would afford papers more protection from arbitrary governmental intrusion than people.

The Court, however, offers two interrelated justifications for excepting grand jury subpoenas directed at "persons," rather than "papers," from the constraints of the Fourth Amendment. These are an "historically grounded obligation of every person to appear and give his evidence before the grand jury" [p. 817], and the relative unintrusiveness of the grand jury subpoena on an individual's liberty.

In my view, the Court makes more of history than is justified. The Court treats the "historically grounded obligation" * * * as extending to all "evidence," whatever its character. Yet, so far as I am aware, the obligation "to appear and give evidence" has heretofore been applied by this Court only in the context of testimonial evidence, either oral or documentary. * * * In the present case, * * * it was not testimony that the grand jury sought from respondents, but physical evidence. * * *

The Court seems to reason that the exception to the Fourth Amendment for grand jury subpoenas directed at persons is justified by the relative unintrusiveness of the grand jury process on an individual's liberty. * * * It may be that service of a grand jury subpoena does not involve the same potential for momentary embarrassment as does an arrest or investigatory "stop." But this difference seems inconsequential in comparison to the substantial stigma which—contrary to the Court's assertion—may result from a grand jury appearance as well as from an arrest or investigatory seizure. Public knowledge that a man has been summoned by a federal grand jury investigating, for instance, organized criminal activity can mean loss of friends, irreparable injury to business, and tremendous pressures on one's family life. Whatever nice legal distinctions may be drawn between police and prosecutor, on the one hand, and the grand jury, on the other, the public often treats an appearance before a grand jury as tantamount to a visit to the station house. Indeed, the former is frequently more damaging than the latter, for a grand jury appearance has an air of far greater gravity than a brief visit "downtown" for a "talk." The Fourth Amendment was placed in our Bill of Rights to protect the individual citizen from such potentially disruptive governmental intrusion into his private life unless conducted reasonably and with sufficient cause.

Nor do I believe that the constitutional problems inherent in such governmental interference with an individual's person are substantially alleviated because one may seek to appear at a "convenient time." In *Davis v. Mississippi,* it was recognized that an investigatory detention effected by the police "need not come unexpectedly or at an inconvenient time." But this fact did not suggest to the Court that the Fourth Amendment was inapplicable * * *. No matter how considerate a grand jury may be in arranging for an individual's appearance, the basic fact remains that his liberty has been officially restrained for some period of time. In terms of its effect on the individual, this restraint does not differ meaningfully from the restraint imposed on a suspect compelled to visit the police station house. Thus, the nature of the intrusion on personal liberty caused by a grand jury subpoena cannot, without more, be considered sufficient basis for denying respondents the protection of the Fourth Amendment. * * *

Whatever the present day validity of the historical assumption of neutrality which underlies the grand jury process, it must at least be recognized that if a grand jury is deprived of the independence essential to the assumption of neutrality—if it effectively surrenders that independence to a prosecutor—the dangers of excessive and unreasonable official interference with personal liberty are exactly those which the Fourth Amendment was intended to prevent. So long as the grand jury carries on its investigatory activities only through the mechanism of testimonial inquiries, the danger of such official usurpation of the grand jury process may not be unreasonably great. Individuals called to testify before the grand jury will have available their Fifth Amendment privilege against self-incrimination. Thus, at least insofar as incriminating information is sought directly from a particular criminal suspect, the grand jury process would not appear to offer law enforcement officials a substantial advantage over ordinary investigative techniques.

But when we move beyond the realm of grand jury investigations limited to testimonial inquiries, as the Court does today, the danger increases that law enforcement officials may seek to usurp the grand jury process for the purpose of securing incriminating evidence from a particular suspect through the simple expedient of a subpoena. * * * Thus, if the grand jury may summon criminal suspects [to obtain handwriting and voice exemplars] without complying with the Fourth Amendment, it will obviously present an attractive investigative tool to prosecutor and police. For what law enforcement officers could not accomplish directly themselves after our decision in *Davis v. Mississippi*, they may now accomplish indirectly through the grand jury process.

Thus, the Court's decisions today can serve only to encourage prosecutorial exploitation of the grand jury process, at the expense of both individual liberty and the traditional neutrality of the grand jury. * * * [B]y holding that the grand jury's power to subpoena these respondents for the purpose of obtaining exemplars is completely outside the purview of the Fourth Amendment, the Court fails to appreciate the essential difference between real and testimonial evidence in the context of these cases, and thereby hastens the reduction of the grand jury into simply another investigative device of law enforcement officials. By contrast, the Court of Appeals, in proper recognition of these dangers, imposed narrow limitations on the subpoena power of the grand jury which are necessary to guard against unreasonable official interference with individual liberty but which would not impair significantly the traditional investigatory powers of that body. * * *

NOTES AND QUESTIONS

1. *Subpoenas and "seizures."* Are there any circumstances under which a grand jury subpoena might be viewed as producing "a 'seizure' in the Fourth Amendment sense" (see *Dionisio* at p. 817)? What if the subpoena calls for "forthwith" compliance, i.e., the immediate production of evidence for presentation to the grand jury or the immediate appearance of the witness before the grand jury? See CRIMPROC § 8.7(e) ("federal courts have refused to hold forthwith subpoenas per se invalid, [reasoning] that the forthwith subpoena cannot be used like a search or arrest warrant" to allow agents to engage in an immediate search or seizure of the person over the opposition of a subpoenaed party who desires to contest the subpoena in court; they also have "rejected the contention that * * * [immediate] compliance [by the party subpoenaed] is so suspect as to assume an involuntary relinquishment of rights," determining

voluntariness instead by reference to "the [particular] circumstances of the case"). A Department of Justice internal policy restricts use of forthwith subpoenas to situations in which "swift action" is needed (e.g., a strong possibility that the subpoenaed material will otherwise be destroyed or secreted). Brenner & Shaw § 10:15. Where there is a strong possibility that a prospective grand jury witness would flee, the witness may be detained under the material witness provision of the bail reform act. See Note 3, p. 352; CRIMPROC § 12.4(g).

2. *Other identification procedures.* Does the reasoning of *Dionisio* extend to a grand jury subpoena directing the subpoenaed party to appear in a lineup? Several courts have held that it does, although some (to preclude the use of such orders simply to assist a police investigation, see Note 4, p. 834) have required that such a subpoena be approved by the grand jury itself. See *In re Melvin*, 546 F.2d 1 (1st Cir.1976). Consider also *In re Kelley*, 433 A.2d 704 (D.C.App.1981) (suggesting that a lineup is distinguishable from the identification procedures presented in *Dionisio* and *Mara* because "it entails the humiliation of standing on a stage, under floodlights, removed from counsel, subject to being compelled to speak certain words and perform actions directed by the police, all at considerably more risk of mistake and misidentification"; in any event, to prevent the prosecutor from utilizing a "grand jury pass through" to avoid the "reasonable suspicion" standard that must be met to obtain a court order directing a non-arrested suspect to appear in a lineup, court will exercise its supervisory power to mandate that "a grand jury subpoena to appear in a lineup [be supported] by an affidavit * * * mak[ing] a minimal factual showing sufficient to permit the judge to conclude that there is a reason for the lineup which is consistent with the legitimate function of the grand jury").

Courts have agreed that a special showing is needed as to the taking of blood, which has long been held to constitute a search when performed at the direction of the police (see Note 4, p. 360), but have divided as to whether the presence of a grand jury subpoena alters the character of the required showing. Compare In re Grand Jury Proceedings (T.S.), 816 F.Supp. 1196 (W.D.Ky.1993) (grand jury subpoena is not available; search warrant must be obtained); *Woolverton v. Multi-County Grand Jury, Oklahoma County*, 859 P.2d 1112 (Okla.Crim.App.1993) (subpoena may be used if supported by probable cause); *Henry v. Ryan*, 775 F.Supp. 247 (N.D.Ill.1991) ("individualized suspicion" sufficient, since grand jury subpoena affords an opportunity to challenge prior to taking blood, and as Supreme Court noted in *R. Enterprises* (p. 823), at the investigatory stage of a grand jury proceeding, "the government cannot be required to justify * * * a grand jury subpoena by * * * probable cause").

4. *Underlying Fourth Amendment violations.* In UNITED STATES v. CALANDRA, 414 U.S. 338 (1974), grand jury witness Calandra was asked questions about certain records (evidencing "loan-sharking" activities) that had been seized by federal agents in connection with a search of Calandra's office. Calandra initially invoked his privilege against self-incrimination, but subsequently was granted immunity. He then requested and received a postponement of the grand jury proceedings so that he could present a pre-charge motion for return and suppression of the seized evidence under Federal Rule 41(e). The district court granted the motion, holding that the search had been unconstitutional. The district court also held that "Calandra need not answer any of the grand jury's questions based on suppressed evidence," since such questions constituted the fruit of the poisonous tree. A divided Supreme Court (6–3), per Powell, J., reversed.

"In deciding whether to extend the exclusionary rule to grand jury proceedings, we must weigh the potential injury to the historic role and functions of the grand jury against the potential benefits of the rule as applied in this context. It is evident that this extension of the exclusionary rule would seriously impede the grand jury. Because the grand jury does not finally adjudicate guilt or innocence, it has traditionally been allowed to pursue its investigative and accusatorial functions unimpeded by the evidentiary and procedural restrictions applicable to a criminal trial. Permitting witnesses to invoke the exclusionary rule before a grand jury would precipitate adjudication of issues hitherto reserved for the trial on the merits and would delay and disrupt grand jury proceedings. Suppression hearings would halt the orderly progress of an investigation and might necessitate extended litigation of issues only tangentially related to the grand jury's primary objective. The probable result would be 'protracted interruptions of grand jury proceedings,' effectively transforming them into preliminary trials on the merits. In some cases the delay might be fatal to the enforcement of the criminal law. Just last Term we reaffirmed our disinclination to allow litigious interference with grand jury proceedings. *United States v. Dionisio.*

"Against this potential damage to the role and functions of the grand jury, we must weigh the benefits to be derived from this proposed extension of the exclusionary rule. * * * [The Court here considered the "incremental deterrent effect which might be achieved by extending the exclusionary rule to grand jury proceedings," and for reasons discussed in Note 1, p. 247, found "unrealistic" the assumption that such an extension would significantly further deterrence of illegal searches.] We decline to embrace a view that would achieve a speculative and undoubtedly minimal advance in the deterrence of police misconduct at the expense of substantially impeding the role of the grand jury."[f]

SECTION 3. OTHER OBJECTIONS TO THE INVESTIGATION

UNITED STATES v. R. ENTERPRISES, INC.
498 U.S. 292, 111 S.Ct. 722, 112 L.Ed.2d 795 (1991).

JUSTICE O'CONNOR delivered the opinion of the Court.

This case requires the Court to decide what standards apply when a party seeks to avoid compliance with a subpoena *duces tecum* issued in connection with a grand jury investigation.

Since 1986, a federal grand jury sitting in the Eastern District of Virginia has been investigating allegations of interstate transportation of obscene materials. In early 1988, the grand jury issued a series of subpoenas to three companies—Model Magazine Distributors, Inc. (Model), R. Enterprises, Inc., and MFR Court Street Books, Inc. (MFR). Model is a New York distributor of sexually oriented paperback books, magazines, and videotapes. R. Enterprises, which distributes adult materials, and MFR, which sells books, magazines, and videotapes, are also based in New York. All three companies are wholly owned by Martin Rothstein. The grand jury subpoenas sought a variety of corporate books and records and, in Model's case, copies of 193 videotapes that Model had shipped to retailers in the Eastern District of Virginia. All three companies moved to quash the subpoenas, arguing that the subpoenas called for production of materials irrelevant to the grand jury's investigation and that the enforcement of the subpoenas would likely infringe their First Amendment rights.

---

f. In *Gelbard v. United States,* 408 U.S. 41 (1972), the Court held that the statutory exclusionary remedy of the federal wiretap Act (see Note 9, p. 525) gave grand jury witnesses the right to object to the grand jury's use of information derived from illegal electronic interception of wire and oral communications.

The District Court, after extensive hearings, denied the motions to quash. As to Model, the court found that the subpoenas for business records were sufficiently specific and that production of the videotapes would not constitute a prior restraint. As to R. Enterprises, the court found a "sufficient connection with Virginia for further investigation by the grand jury." The court relied in large part on the statement attributed to Rothstein that the three companies were "all the same thing, I'm president of all three." Additionally, the court explained in denying MFR's motion to quash that it was "inclined to agree" with "the majority of the jurisdictions," which do not require the Government to make a "threshold showing" before a grand jury subpoena will be enforced. Even assuming that a preliminary showing of relevance was required, the court determined that the Government had made such a showing. It found sufficient evidence that the companies were "related entities," at least one of which "certainly did ship sexually explicit material into the Commonwealth of Virginia." * * * Notwithstanding these findings, the companies refused to comply with the subpoenas. The District Court found each in contempt and fined them $500 per day, but stayed imposition of the fine pending appeal.

The Court of Appeals for the Fourth Circuit upheld the business records subpoenas issued to Model, but remanded the motion to quash the subpoena for Model's videotapes. Of particular relevance here, the Court of Appeals quashed the business records subpoenas issued to R. Enterprises and MFR. In doing so, it applied the standards set out by this Court in *United States v. Nixon*, 418 U.S. 683 (1974). The court recognized that *Nixon* dealt with a trial subpoena, not a grand jury subpoena, but determined that the rule was "equally applicable" in the grand jury context. Accordingly, it required the Government to clear the three hurdles that *Nixon* established in the trial context—relevancy, admissibility, and specificity—in order to enforce the grand jury subpoenas. The court concluded that the challenged subpoenas did not satisfy the *Nixon* standards, finding no evidence in the record that either company had ever shipped materials into, or otherwise conducted business in, the Eastern District of Virginia. The Court of Appeals specifically criticized the District Court for drawing an inference that, because Rothstein owned all three businesses and one of them had undoubtedly shipped sexually explicit materials into the Eastern District of Virginia, there might be some link between the Eastern District of Virginia and R. Enterprises or MFR. It then noted that "any evidence concerning Mr. Rothstein's alleged business activities outside of Virginia, or his ownership of companies which distribute allegedly obscene materials outside of Virginia, would most likely be inadmissible on relevancy grounds at any trial that might occur," and that the subpoenas therefore failed "to meet the requirements [*sic*] that any documents subpoenaed under [Federal] Rule [of Criminal Procedure] 17(c) must be admissible as evidence at trial," citing *Nixon*. * * * We granted certiorari to determine whether the Court of Appeals applied the proper standard in evaluating the grand jury subpoenas issued to respondents. We now reverse.

The grand jury occupies a unique role in our criminal justice system. * * * [It] "can investigate merely on suspicion that the law is being violated, or even just because it wants assurance that it is not." *United States v. Morton Salt*, 338 U.S. 632 (1950). The function of the grand jury is to inquire into all information that might possibly bear on its investigation until it has identified the offense or has satisfied itself that none occurred. As a necessary consequence of its investigatory function, the grand jury paints with a broad brush. * * * A grand jury subpoena is thus much different from a subpoena issued in the context of a prospective criminal trial, where a specific offense has been identified and a particular defendant charged. * * *

This Court has emphasized on numerous occasions that many of the rules and restrictions that apply at a trial do not apply in grand jury proceedings. This is especially true of evidentiary restrictions. The same rules that, in an adversary hearing on the merits may increase the likelihood of accurate determinations of guilt or innocence do not necessarily advance the mission of a grand jury, whose task is to conduct an *ex parte* investigation to determine whether or not there is probable cause to prosecute a particular defendant. * * * The teaching of the Court's decisions is clear: A grand jury "may compel the production of evidence or the testimony of witnesses as it considers appropriate, and its operation generally is unrestrained by the technical procedural and evidentiary rules governing the conduct of criminal trials." *United States v. Calandra* [Note 4, p. 822].

This guiding principle renders suspect the Court of Appeals' holding that the standards announced in *Nixon* as to subpoenas issued in anticipation of trial apply equally in the grand jury context. The multifactor test announced in *Nixon* would invite procedural delays and detours while courts evaluate the relevancy and admissibility of documents sought by a particular subpoena. We have expressly stated that grand jury proceedings should be free of such delays. * * * *United States v. Dionisio.* Additionally, application of the *Nixon* test in this context ignores that grand jury proceedings are subject to strict secrecy requirements. See Fed. Rule Crim.Proc. 6(e). Requiring the Government to explain in too much detail the particular reasons underlying a subpoena threatens to compromise "the indispensable secrecy of grand jury proceedings." Broad disclosure also affords the targets of investigation far more information about the grand jury's internal workings than the Federal Rules of Criminal Procedure appear to contemplate.

The investigatory powers of the grand jury are nevertheless not unlimited. Grand juries are not licensed to engage in arbitrary fishing expeditions, nor may they select targets of investigation out of malice or an intent to harass. In this case, the focus of our inquiry is the limit imposed on a grand jury by Federal Rule of Criminal Procedure 17(c), which governs the issuance of subpoenas *duces tecum* in federal criminal proceedings. The Rule provides that "the court on motion made promptly may quash or modify the subpoena if compliance would be unreasonable or oppressive." * * * This standard is not self-explanatory. As we have observed, "what is reasonable depends on the context." In *Nixon,* this Court defined what is reasonable in the context of a jury trial. * * * But, for the reasons we have explained above, the *Nixon* standard does not apply in the context of grand jury proceedings. In the grand jury context, the decision as to what offense will be charged is routinely not made until after the grand jury has concluded its investigation. One simply cannot know in advance whether information sought during the investigation will be relevant and admissible in a prosecution for a particular offense.

To the extent that Rule 17(c) imposes some reasonableness limitation on grand jury subpoenas, however, our task is to define it. In doing so, we recognize that a party to whom a grand jury subpoena is issued faces a difficult situation. As a rule, grand juries do not announce publicly the subjects of their investigations. A party who desires to challenge a grand jury subpoena thus may have no conception of the Government's purpose in seeking production of the requested information. Indeed, the party will often not know whether he or she is a primary target of the investigation or merely a peripheral witness. Absent even minimal information, the subpoena recipient is likely to find it exceedingly difficult to persuade a court that "compliance would be unreasonable." As one pair of commentators has summarized it, the challenging party's "unenviable task is to seek to persuade the court that the subpoena that has been served on [him or her] could not possibly serve any investigative purpose that the grand jury could legitimately be pursuing." S. Beale & W. Bryson, *Grand Jury Law and Practice* § 6:28 (1986).

Our task is to fashion an appropriate standard of reasonableness, one that gives due weight to the difficult position of subpoena recipients but does not impair the strong governmental interests in affording grand juries wide latitude, avoiding minitrials on peripheral matters, and preserving a necessary level of secrecy. We begin by reiterating that the law presumes, absent a strong showing to the contrary, that a grand jury acts within the legitimate scope of its authority. * * * Consequently, a grand jury subpoena issued through normal channels is presumed to be reasonable, and the burden of showing unreasonableness must be on the recipient who seeks to avoid compliance. Indeed, this result is indicated by the language of Rule 17(c), which permits a subpoena to be quashed only "on motion" and "if *compliance* would be unreasonable" (emphasis added). To the extent that the Court of Appeals placed an initial burden on the Government, it committed error. Drawing on the principles articulated above, we conclude that where, as here, a subpoena is challenged on relevancy grounds, the motion to quash must be denied unless the district court determines that there is no reasonable possibility that the category of materials the Government seeks will produce information relevant to the general subject of the grand jury's investigation. Respondents did not challenge the subpoenas as being too indefinite nor did they claim that compliance would be overly burdensome. The Court of Appeals accordingly did not consider these aspects of the subpoenas, nor do we.

It seems unlikely, of course, that a challenging party who does not know the general subject matter of the grand jury's investigation, no matter how valid that party's claim, will be able to make the necessary showing that compliance would be unreasonable. After all, a subpoena recipient "cannot put his whole life before the court in order to show that there is no crime to be investigated." Consequently, a court may be justified in a case where unreasonableness is alleged in requiring the Government to reveal the general subject of the grand jury's investigation before requiring the challenging party to carry its burden of persuasion.[a] We need not resolve this question in the present case, however, as there is no doubt that respondents knew the subject of the grand jury investigation pursuant to which the business records subpoenas were issued. In cases where the recipient of the subpoena does not know the nature of the investigation, we are confident that district courts will be able to craft appropriate procedures that balance the interests of the subpoena recipient against the strong governmental interests in maintaining secrecy, preserving investigatory flexibility, and avoiding procedural delays. For example, to ensure that subpoenas are not routinely challenged as a form of discovery, a district court may require that the Government reveal the subject of the investigation to the trial court *in camera,* so that the court may determine whether the motion to quash has a reasonable prospect for success before it discloses the subject matter to the challenging party.[b]

Applying these principles in this case demonstrates that the District Court correctly denied respondents' motions to quash. It is undisputed that all three companies—Model, R. Enterprises, and MFR—are owned by the same person, that all do business in the same area, and that one of the three, Model, has shipped sexually explicit materials into the Eastern District of Virginia. The District Court could have concluded from these facts that there was a reasonable possibility that the business records of R. Enterprises and MFR would produce information relevant to the grand jury's investigation into the interstate transportation of

---

a. The United States Attorneys' Manual directs that subpoenas contain an "advice of rights" statement (see Note 6, p. 845), which includes the following: "The grand jury is conducting an investigation of possible violations of Federal criminal laws involving: (state here the general subject matter of inquiry, e.g., conducting an illegal gambling business in violation of 18 U.S.C. § 1955)." U.S.A.M. 9–11.151.

b. Justice Scalia did not join this paragraph of the Court's opinion.

obscene materials. Respondents' blanket denial of any connection to Virginia did not suffice to render the District Court's conclusion invalid. A grand jury need not accept on faith the self-serving assertions of those who may have committed criminal acts. Rather, it is entitled to determine for itself whether a crime has been committed.

Both in the District Court and in the Court of Appeals, respondents contended that these subpoenas sought records relating to First Amendment activities, and that this required the Government to demonstrate that the records were particularly relevant to its investigation. The Court of Appeals determined that the subpoenas did not satisfy Rule 17(c) and thus did not pass on the First Amendment issue. We express no view on this issue and leave it to be resolved by the Court of Appeals. * * *

JUSTICE STEVENS, with whom JUSTICES MARSHALL and BLACKMUN join, concurring in part and concurring in the judgment.

Federal Rule of Criminal Procedure 17(c) * * * requires the district court to balance the burden of compliance, on the one hand, against the governmental interest in obtaining the documents on the other. A more burdensome subpoena should be justified by a somewhat higher degree of probable relevance than a subpoena that imposes a minimal or nonexistent burden. Against the procedural history of this case, the Court has attempted to define the term "reasonable" in the abstract, looking only at the relevance side of the balance. Because I believe that this truncated approach to the Rule will neither provide adequate guidance to the district court nor place any meaningful constraint on the overzealous prosecutor, I add these comments. * * *

The moving party has the initial task of demonstrating to the Court that he has some valid objection to compliance. This showing might be made in various ways. Depending on the volume and location of the requested materials, the mere cost in terms of time, money, and effort of responding to a dragnet subpoena could satisfy the initial hurdle. Similarly, if a witness showed that compliance with the subpoena would intrude significantly on his privacy interests, or call for the disclosure of trade secrets or other confidential information, further inquiry would be required. Or, as in this case, the movant might demonstrate that compliance would have First Amendment implications.

The trial court need inquire into the relevance of subpoenaed materials only after the moving party has made this initial showing. And, as is true in the parallel context of pretrial civil discovery, a matter also committed to the sound discretion of the trial judge, the degree of need sufficient to justify denial of the motion to quash will vary to some extent with the burden of producing the requested information. For the reasons stated by the Court, in the grand jury context the law enforcement interest will almost always prevail, and the documents must be produced. I stress, however, that the Court's opinion should not be read to suggest that the deferential relevance standard the Court has formulated will govern decision in every case, no matter how intrusive or burdensome the request. * * *

NOTES AND QUESTIONS

1. *Assessing relevancy.* In IN RE GRAND JURY PROCEEDINGS, 616 F.3d 1186 (10th Cir. 2010), the grand jury subpoenas at issue related to investigation of possible fraud in the submission of government forms. In order to preserve grand jury secrecy, the 10th Circuit opinion (per Ebel, J.) did not set forth the specifics of the subpoenas, but it did describe the subpoenas as designating "broad overarching" categories of material, followed by "still broad sub-categories."

Illustratively, "the overarching category" in one subpoena was a request for "all documents and/or records regarding [Employee's] involvement in completing the federal forms for [Appellee]". The twelve sub-categories here included " 'any and all correspondence' with particular individuals and 'questionnaires/forms including drafts' completed for [redacted] process." The district judge, in response to a motion to quash, had required the production of certain documents for in camera review, and had subsequently ordered partial production, including redactions as to "personal information of the Appellee's [family members]." The 10th Circuit concluded that, in light of *R. Enterprises*, the district court committed three errors in this process: "[W]e believe the district court abused its discretion in three ways: (1) by redefining the categories of subpoenaed material for purposes of assessing relevancy; (2) by engaging in a document-by-document and line-by-line analysis of relevancy after finding categories of material relevant; and (3) by engaging in an *in camera* review of documents to assess relevancy when such a procedure was unnecessary to applying the *R. Enterprises* standard of relevancy." In explaining these rulings, the court offered the following analysis:

"At the outset, we find it helpful * * * to review the district court's basic approach to relevancy in this case. First, the district court identified specific categories. These categories, however, were not those delineated in the subpoena. The district court then concluded that some materials within these court-defined categories could potentially produce relevant information. Nonetheless, the district court, concerned that some potentially irrelevant information would also be produced if it ordered production of the entire court-defined categories of material, required that the documents be produced for *in camera* review so that irrelevant documents could be excluded from production. The district court then engaged in a document-by-document, and at times a line-by-line, review of the subpoenaed material for relevancy. The district court ordered the production of documents it deemed relevant, and either quashed the subpoena as to irrelevant documents or ordered redactions of irrelevant information in otherwise relevant documents.

"The district court committed a legal error by redefining the categories of material sought by the Government in order to assess relevancy and further engaging in a document-by-document and line-by-line assessment of relevancy. In *R. Enterprises*, the Supreme Court explained that the district court must deny a motion to quash a subpoena based on relevancy unless 'there is no reasonable possibility that the *category of materials the Government seeks* will produce information relevant to the general subject of the grand jury's subpoena.' (emphasis added). [p. 826] * * * First, the reference to a 'category of materials' contemplates that the district court will assess relevancy based on the broad types of material sought by the Government. This broad analysis forecloses the document-by-document or line-by-line approach to assessing relevancy that the district court took in this case. The district court's approach entails a much more exacting assessment of relevancy than the relaxed, categorical approach articulated by *R. Enterprises*. * * * Second, the standard articulated by *R. Enterprises* does not refer to just any category of material; rather, it specifically refers to the category 'the Government seeks.' Id. This language indicates that the district court is bound to assess relevancy based on the category of materials sought by the government, and it cannot create new categories for purposes of assessing relevancy.

"In accord with Rule 17(c)(2), we conclude that the district court may modify the subpoena by quashing entire categories or sub-categories of material as irrelevant, but, under *R. Enterprises*, the district court cannot go further and quash the subpoena as to specific documents within those sub-categories (or specific lines within relevant documents). Thus, the district court may consider the relevancy of each category or sub category contained in the subpoena. * * *

"A non-categorical approach to relevancy, as the district court employed in this case, * * * unduly disrupt[s] the grand jury's broad investigatory powers and its unique function 'to inquire into all information that might possibly bear on its investigations.' *R. Enterprises.* A non-categorical approach forces the Government to justify the relevancy of hundreds or thousands (or more) of individual documents, which it has not yet even seen, or even lines within those documents, as opposed to merely explaining how a broad category of materials could contain possibly relevant material-a much more manageable task at this stage of the proceedings. The Government often is not in a position to establish the relevancy with respect to specific documents, much less specific lines, because (a) it may not know the precise content of the requested documents or particular lines and (b) it may not know precisely what information is or is not relevant at the grand jury investigative stage. * * * In fact, it is for this reason that 'subpoenas duces tecum are often drawn broadly, sweeping up both documents that may prove decisive and documents that turn out not to be.' * * * Such a process necessarily involves a fishing expedition by the grand jury, but such fishing is permissible so long as it is not an arbitrary fishing expedition and satisfies the *R. Enterprises* relevancy standard. See R. *Enterprises* [p. 825] (noting that '[g]rand juries are not licensed to engage in arbitrary fishing expeditions').

"By way of example, we look to the district court's conclusion that only materials related to certain questions on [Form 2] were relevant. While the questions on [Form 2] that relate directly to the possible misrepresentations on [Form 1] for which Appellee is under investigation indisputably relate to the grand jury investigation, other questions also have a 'reasonable possibility' of producing relevant information. If Appellee misrepresented information on other questions, that information could lead to an expanded investigation into other charges of misrepresentation. It would also reflect on motive and intent. This type of fishing relates directly to the current investigation, and is not arbitrary. On the other hand, if Appellee answers other questions honestly, a grand jury could perceive that as exculpatory evidence with respect to the misrepresentations apparently currently under investigation. This type of fishing is also not arbitrary because part of a grand jury's broad investigatory responsibilities include satisfying itself that no crime has occurred.[19] * * *

"The district court's non-categorical approach also risks thwarting the grand jury's broad investigation because in assessing relevancy the court must rely on its necessarily incomplete understanding of the investigation. As the Government points out, 'given a district court's limited role in the proceedings, it is simply not possible for the court to accurately determine whether an individual document or portion thereof has possible relevance to the investigation.' * * * Although the Government could mitigate this problem by fully disclosing to the district court the breadth of the investigation in full detail, this solution undermines another important interest: grand jury secrecy. To justify a categorical relevancy conclusion, the Government would need to supply the district court (and, if necessary, the objector), with only a general picture of the investigation. This case illustrates, however, that a document-by-document approach to relevancy may require increased and undue disclosure about the investigation. Here, for example, the Government had to disclose additional information to the Court to demonstrate the relevance of additional questions on [Form 2], and this information was ultimately transmitted to Appellee. * * *

---

19. Another example of the district court's intrusion into the grand jury's broad investigatory powers involves its decision to authorize the redaction from documents of the social security numbers of Appellee's [family members]. Social security information is often an especially effective investigatory tool, and when considered in a categorical sense, has a "reasonable possibility" of leading to relevant information.

"Finally, a non-categorical approach to relevancy would invite delays in grand jury proceedings that could slow its investigation to a crawl and allow the target of an investigation to exploit the delay. * * * This case is a paradigm of such delay as the district court's diligent document-by-document and line-by-line in camera review delayed the grand jury's receipt of relevant documents and wholly prevented it from obtaining some information that fell within *R. Enterprises'* categorical standard of relevance. Had Appellee appealed the district court's orders to produce relevant documents, this delay would have been further exacerbated. The categorical approach we adopt in following *R. Enterprises* avoids this problem by allowing the district court to make a generalized finding that there is a 'reasonable possibility' that a broad category of subpoenaed material contains information relevant to the grand jury investigation.

"We can sympathize with the district court's desire to prevent the grand jury from subpoenaing wholly irrelevant information. Incidental production of irrelevant documents, however, is simply a necessary consequence of the grand jury's broad investigative powers and the categorical approach to relevancy adopted in *R. Enterprises*. Other limitations beyond the relevancy requirement exist and may, in appropriate circumstances, preclude production of otherwise relevant material, although they too must be tightly circumscribed to avoid unnecessary interference with the grand jury function.

"Because, * * * we conclude that the district court could have, and should have, made its relevancy determination by assessing the broad categories contained in the subpoena, we also conclude that the district court abused its discretion in engaging in an in camera review of subpoenaed material to assess relevancy.[20] We do not adopt in this case the Government's argument that a district court is per se barred from ever engaging in an in camera review to assess relevancy, although, even assuming, without yet deciding, that in camera review may be available in appropriate circumstances, only highly unusual circumstances would warrant such a procedure for assessing relevancy."

2. *Balancing.* Would the balancing approach discussed in Justice Stevens' concurring opinion in *R. Enterprises* permit consideration of such factors as: (1) the seriousness of the crime being investigated (as argued in Stuntz, Note 2, p. 814); (2) the likelihood that the evidence subpoenaed would only duplicate evidence previously received (e.g., where the grand jury has previously received from a bank an individual's checking account records and now subpoenas those records from the individual); (3) the breadth of the information likely to be disclosed by compliance (e.g., where the subpoena requires all financial records for a substantial period of time), and (4) the likelihood that the documents will disclose "personal" (as opposed to "organizational") information (as argued in Slobogin, Note 4, p. 815)? Lower courts generally have rejected applying a case-by-case balancing of such factors in Rule 17(c) rulings. Does *In re Grand Jury Proceedings,* supra, indicate that *R. Enterprises* deprives them of the authority to weigh such factors in assessing relevancy? On the other hand, as illustrated by Notes 3, 4, and 5 below, the lower courts are divided on imposing an additional review standard, more rigorous than the *R. Enterprises* relevancy standard, in several special settings.

3. *"Chilling effect": First Amendment objections.* Lower courts have divided as to the standard to be applied where the subpoenaed party claims that compliance would have a chilling impact upon the exercise of a First Amendment right. In *Branzburg v. Hayes,* 408 U.S. 665 (1972), the Supreme Court rejected the

---

20. [Transposed] Although the issue of relevancy must be resolved with the categorical approach set forth in *R. Enterprises,* there may be a limited need to examine some documents to determine other issues, such as privilege, whether a document falls within the relevant category, or ownership. These other issues are not presented to us on this appeal.

contention that the First Amendment prohibited a subpoena compelling reporters to testify before the grand jury as to information received in confidence (including the identity of their confidential sources) absent a government showing of "compelling need." The Court concluded that even if requiring reporters to appear and testify might have a negative impact upon news gathering by deterring future confidential sources, that impact did not outweigh the interest of the public in the grand jury's investigation of crime. The majority noted (and Justice Powell's concurring opinion stressed in particular) that judicial control of the grand jury process was always available to provide an appropriate remedy if the grand jury process was used to "harass the press."

Relying on *Branzburg*, the Fourth Circuit, on remand in *R. Enterprises*, rejected the First Amendment claim that had not been considered by the Supreme Court. See *In re Grand Jury 87–3 Subpoena Duces Tecum*, 955 F.2d 229 (4th Cir.1992). The Fourth Circuit found unpersuasive the reasoning of the Ninth Circuit in *Bursey v. United States*, 466 F.2d 1059 (9th Cir.1972). *Bursey* had distinguished *Branzburg* as a case involving only a peripheral First Amendment concern. It had insisted upon the government showing a "substantial connection" between the information sought by the grand jury and an overriding government interest in the subject matter under investigation where disclosure of that information would bear directly on the exercise of First Amendment rights (the case there, as the grand jury sought information relating to the activities of the Black Panthers and their publication of a newspaper, which had reported a threat against the president). The Fourth Circuit read *Branzburg* as having rejected requiring any such special showing of need. The Supreme Court there had concluded that relying upon the district court's capacity to prevent the "bad faith" use of the subpoena authority to "harass" was sufficient in "striking a proper balance" between the "obligation of all citizens to give relevant testimony with respect to criminal conduct" and the possible chilling impact on the exercise of First Amendment rights.

Compare the court's analysis in *In re Grand Jury Investigation of Possible Violation of 18 U.S.C. § 1461 et seq.*, 706 F.Supp.2d 11 (D.D.C. 2009). The court there quashed a grand jury subpoena insofar as it sought to compel Company X, a distributor of "expressive material" (thought by the government to be pornographic), to produce records of customer purchases that revealed the identity of the purchaser. Revealing purchasers' names, the court reasoned, clearly implicated a First Amendment right, as expressive material is entitled to presumptive First Amendment protection, and while the government "assumed that the films being investigated are obscene, as of yet there has been no judicial determination they are in fact obscene." *Branzburg* therefore was distinguishable, as the Supreme Court there had not "held [that] a First Amendment right was implicated by the subpoenas being reviewed." Looking to several federal lower court rulings, the court adopted "a two-part test to determine whether to enforce a subpoena that may infringe on First Amendment rights * * *; the government must show that they have a compelling interest in obtaining the sought after material and that there is sufficient nexus between the subject matter of the investigation and the information they seek." The government could not meet this burden in its argument that all purchasers names were needed (1) to assist in establishing the "engaged in business" element of the pornographic distribution statute (presumably, under a statutory presumption requiring sales of 2 or more copies of 5 or more titles), or (2) to protect grand jury secrecy as to the identity of those purchasers who were actually government agents (by not seeking the identity-records only as to their purchases). As to the first interest, there were alternative means of establishing the element without requiring disclosure of the names of all purchasers (e.g., relying on the purchases made by the government agents). As to the second, "revealing all the customer names * * * to protect the government's minimal interest in grand jury secrecy would prove too much as it might infringe on the legitimate First Amendment interests of Company X's customers."

4. *"Chilling effect": Attorney subpoenas.* Assume that a grand jury subpoenas the attorney representing one of several targets in an organized crime investigation and asks that attorney for information of possible relevancy to the investigation that is not protected by the attorney-client privilege (e.g., whether that target arranged for the legal representation of certain persons thought to be members of the same organized crime "family"). Should a special showing of need, similar to that imposed in *Bursey,* Note 3 supra, be required to overcome the "chilling impact" that such questioning may have upon the lawyer-client relationship?[b] The several circuit courts considering the issue have all refused to impose such a requirement as a general rule (although some dissenting judges would have done so). See CRIMPROC § 8.8. They have noted that: (1) the target has no constitutional right to counsel with respect to the grand jury proceeding (see Note 8, p. 846); (2) the attorney-client privilege provides adequate protection of the attorney-client relationship; (3) it is at most a "speculative" and "abstract possibility" that the attorney's testimony before the grand jury will lead to his or her disqualification as defense counsel should the target eventually be indicted; and (4) the target is asking, in effect, for the "same kind of preliminary showing which the Supreme Court had disapproved [in *Dionisio* and *Branzburg*] as causing indeterminate delays in grand jury investigations." At the same time, some of these rulings recognize a district court authority to quash such a subpoena under "compelling circumstances." See *In re Grand Jury Matters,* 751 F.2d 13 (1st Cir.1984) (attorneys were currently representing same client in a state criminal proceeding).

In 1990, the ABA amended Rule 3.8 of the Model Rules of Professional Conduct to deal specifically with attorney subpoenas. Model Rule 3.8(e) currently provides that a "prosecutor in a criminal case * * * shall not subpoena a lawyer in a grand jury or other criminal proceeding to present evidence about a past or current client unless the prosecutor reasonably believes: (1) the information sought is not protected from disclosure by any applicable privilege; (2) the evidence sought is essential to the successful completion of an ongoing investigation or prosecution; and (3) there is no other feasible alternative to obtain the information." The traditional view is that ethical standards govern only disciplinary proceedings and do not establish a ground for relief by a litigant. See CRIMPROC § 1.7(j).[c] Would it be an appropriate use of a court's supervisory

---

b. As a matter of internal policy, the Department of Justice does impose special prerequisites for subpoenaing an attorney to furnish information before a grand jury regarding a past or current client. U.S. Attorneys' Manual 9–13.410 authorizes use of attorney subpoenas (upon approval of an Assistant Attorney General) where (i) there exists "reasonable grounds to believe that a crime has been or is being committed and that the information sought is reasonably needed for the successful completion of the investigation," (ii) "all reasonable attempts to obtain the information from alternative sources shall have proved to be unsuccessful," (iii) the information is not "protected by a valid claim of privilege," and is not "peripheral or speculative," and (iv) "the need for the information * * * outweigh[s] the potential adverse effects upon the attorney-client relationship" (in particular, "the risk that the attorney will be disqualified from representation of the client as a result of having to testify against the client").

c. Under the McDade Amendment (also known as the Citizens Protection Act), 28, U.S.C.A. § 530B, federal attorneys are subject to "state laws and rules and local federal court rules governing attorneys * * * to the same extent and in the same manner as other attorneys in that State." Federal courts are in agreement that professional responsibility standards made applicable under the McDade Amendment do not create a right to relief within the criminal justice process. Thus, *United States v. Colorado Supreme Court,* 189 F.3d 1281 (10th Cir. 1999), although holding the state replication of Model Rule 3.8(e) applicable to federal prosecutors, also concluded that a Rule 3.8(e) violation does not constitute grounds for quashing a subpoena, as there was no power to adopt the standards of its state-counterpart of Model Rule 3.8(e) in reviewing a motion to quash a subpoena? Consider *State v. Gonzalez*, 234 P.3d 1 (Kan. 2010), adopting the standard of the state professional conduct rule replicating Model Rule 3.8(e) as the "analytical rubric for a district judge considering a prosecutor's motion for issuance of a subpoena to compel criminal defense counsel to testify about a current or former client's confidential information." Considering a challenge to a preliminary hearing subpoena, the *Gonzales* court pointed to the authority of the judiciary "independent of statutory privilege," to prevent the "misuse * * * of compulsory process," and to the frequent overlap of an "ethical duty and a legal duty [imposed] as a part of substantive law."

5. ***Oppressive burdens.*** Rule 17(c) and similar state provisions authorize quashing subpoenas where compliance would be "unreasonable or oppressive." Does oppressiveness constitute an alternative and distinct ground for quashing a grand jury subpoena? Consider in *In re Grand Jury Proceedings (Danbom)*, 827 F.2d 301 (8th Cir.1987). The Eighth Circuit acknowledged that a subpoena seeking records of all wire transfers of $1,000 or more over a 2 year period from Western Union's major Kansas City office met relevancy requirements for a grand jury investigating drug trafficking, but concluded that, under Rule 17(c), consideration could be given to Western Union's concern that the publicity resulting from its production of the records of many innocent persons would lead such persons to stop transmitting funds through Western Union.

NOTES ON MISUSE OBJECTIONS

1. Both federal and state courts traditionally have recognized witness objections to alleged prosecutorial misuse of the grand jury process (i.e., using the process for purposes other than furthering the grand jury's investigation). Such instances of misuse include: (1) employment of the grand jury process "primarily" to elicit evidence for use in a pending or future civil action; (2) employment of the grand jury process "for the sole or dominating purpose of preparing an already pending indictment for trial"; (3) employment of the grand jury process to further independent investigations by police or prosecutor rather than to produce evidence for grand jury use; and (4) calling a witness for the purpose of "harassment," with "harassment" described as encompassing various objectives other than producing relevant evidence, such as burdening the witness with repeated appearances or seeking to punish the witness by forcing him into a situation where he will refuse to answer (or lie) and be held for contempt (or perjury). See CRIMPROC § 8.8.

2. As noted in CRIMPROC § 8.8, a common thread running through the judicial treatment of misuse objections is that "a presumption of regularity" attaches to the grand jury proceeding and the objecting party bears a substantial burden in seeking to overcome that presumption. It clearly is not sufficient simply to show that the use of the process has (or will) benefit the government with

---

indication that Congress intended through McDade to alter Federal Rule 17(c) and the substantive standards for subpoena issuance developed under that rule. Other federal courts, in dealing with different state versions of Rule 3.8(e) have suggested that McDade may not incorporate professional responsibility standards replicating Rule 3.8(e). The McDade Amendment directed the Department of Justice to adopt implementing regulations, and the DOJ responded with a narrow reading of McDade's reference to "rules governing attorneys." Initially, the DOJ regulation states that McDade does not encompass standards "in state and local rules of professional responsibility * * * [that] alter federal substantive, procedural, or evidentiary law." Secondly, the regulations state that McDade makes applicable to federal prosecutors only rules that "prescribe ethical conduct" and therefore excludes "rules of procedure, evidence, or substantive law whether or not such rule is included in a code of professional responsibility." Both exclusions arguably apply to Rule 3.8(e). See CRIMPROC § 1.7 at notes 265.1–265.57.

respect to civil discovery, criminal discovery on a pending indictment, or some other alleged improper purpose. Courts have stressed that misuse exists only if the "sole or dominant" prosecutorial purpose is improper, and that the prosecutor will not be enjoined from carrying forward a legitimate grand jury investigation simply because one byproduct may be the production of evidence useful in other proceedings in which the government has some interest. To gain an evidentiary hearing on a claim of alleged misuse, the objecting party ordinarily must at least point to surrounding circumstances "highly suggestive" of improper purpose.

What should constitute such a showing? Where a grand jury investigation was instituted shortly after the target's legal challenges stymied the government's civil investigation, does that suggest misuse notwithstanding a substantial overlap in the applicable civil and criminal law governing the activities in question? Cf. *In re Grand Jury Subpoenas, April, 1978,* 581 F.2d 1103 (4th Cir.1978). Where a grand jury is investigating the same basic activities that led to indictment of the objecting party, and that party alleges that some of the witnesses to be called before that grand jury may be defense witnesses, does that establish a sufficient grounding for an evidentiary hearing notwithstanding a government response that the grand jury investigation is aimed at determining whether others had also been involved in the offense? Cf. *United States v. Doe (Ellsberg),* 455 F.2d 1270 (1st Cir.1972).

3. Even where the surrounding circumstances strongly suggest improper use to obtain civil discovery or discovery on a pending criminal indictment, courts have expressed a reluctance to judge the dominant purpose of the investigation while it is still ongoing. The objecting party, it is noted, should not be allowed to "break up the play before it was started and then claim the government was offsides." *United States v. Doe (Ellsberg),* supra. A preferable remedy, courts note, is to allow the investigation to continue to its completion and then judge its purpose if the government should attempt to utilize the fruits of its alleged misuse in another proceeding. Where the alleged improper purpose is the development of evidence for a civil proceeding, the Rule 6(e) motion needed for judicial authorization of disclosure to civil attorneys ordinarily will provide the objecting party with an opportunity to challenge the purpose of the investigation. See *In re Grand Jury Subpoenas, April, 1978,* Note 2 supra. Where the alleged improper purpose is gaining additional information for use in the trial on a pending indictment, the judge presiding at that trial can determine whether to require an inquiry into the dominant purpose of the post-indictment grand jury investigation when (and if) the government makes use in its prosecution of the fruits of that allegedly tainted investigation. See *United States v. Doe (Ellsberg).*

4. Claims that the grand jury process is being used to further independent police investigations commonly are presented where the individual subpoenaed to appear before the grand jury is offered the opportunity to avoid the grand jury appearance by giving a statement to the police or prosecutor. Although noting that it is improper to use the grand jury subpoena "as a ploy to secure the attendance of a witness at the prosecutor's office," courts have held that offering the witness the option of presenting information informally is not misuse where the prosecutor intends (after screening) to present that information to the grand jury. CRIMPROC § 8.8. So too, they note, where the witness was first approached by the police and refused to provide information, the prosecutor could properly take that factor into account in converting the investigation into a grand jury inquiry and seek the same information by subpoena. Ibid.

Since searches and subpoenas offer different investigative advantages, prosecutors may appropriately use search warrants and subpoenas to obtain related material in the same investigation, sometimes from the same party. Does misuse arise, however, where the subpoena is used to circumvent the consequences of substantial government misconduct in its prior execution of a search warrant? *United States v. Comprehensive Drug Testing, Inc.* 621 F.3d 1162 (9th Cir. 2010) (en banc), concluded that the district court had not abused its discretion in quashing a subpoena under Rule 17(c) where the circumstances suggested that was the strategy underlying the subpoena. [d]

NOTES ON THIRD PARTY SUBPOENAS

1. ***Third party subpoenas.*** Grand jury subpoenas duces tecum are commonly directed to individuals or entities other than the target of the investigation with the objective of obtaining records that reveal the activities of the target. These so-called "third party subpoenas" are commonly directed to service providers and seek records reflecting such activities as monetary transfers, credit card use, airline travel, telephone calls, e-mails, and documents sent to "the cloud." While the third-party can object to the subpoena, its interests and those of the target may be very different. Accordingly, a major issue presented by the third-party subpoena is whether the target has standing to challenge the subpoena and, if so, on what grounds. Where targets do have a right to challenge, a second issue is whether the target also must be given notice of the issuance of the subpoena so as to facilitate the exercise of that right. Providing the answers to these questions are a combination of court rulings and, as to some types of records, statutory requirements.

2. ***Target standing.*** As discussed in Note 6, p. 517, *United States v. Miller* concluded that a target of an investigation lacks standing to raise a Fourth Amendment challenge to a subpoena demanding from a third party its records relating to the target, even where those records were originally created by the target. Lower courts have held, however, that where a challenge to a third party subpoena is based on a grand jury misuse that impacts the rights of the target, then the target may challenge that subpoena. Thus, *In re Grand Jury Proceedings (Fernandez Diamante)*, 814 F.2d 61 (1st Cir.1987), held that an indicted defendant could move to quash a subpoena directing a travel agency to produce records relating to defendant's airline travel where the defendant alleged that the government was misusing the grand jury subpoena to obtain discovery in the criminal case pending against him. The First Circuit acknowledged that, unlike certain cases recognizing victim standing in other contexts, the defendant here did not have any property interest in the travel agency's records and could not allege that production of those records would violate some privilege of non-disclosure to which he was entitled. However, standing to challenge the subpoena could also be based on "the harm to [petitioner's] interest as a defendant in a criminal trial and as a victim of a systematic abuse of the powers of the grand jury." The court found support for such standing in Supreme Court precedent recognizing a civil

---

d. The district court's order was grounded on the following combination of activities by the government: (1) the government had originally sought by grand jury subpoena, issued in the Northern District of California, to obtain all drug testing records and specimens pertaining to major league baseball players in the possession of Comprehensive Drug Testing (CDT); (2) when CDT and the Players' Association filed a motion to quash, the government, to cut off that litigation, obtained warrants, in two other federal districts allowing searches for records of specific players; (3) in executing those warrants the government willfully disregarded various limitations, established in the warrant and Ninth Circuit caselaw, on warrant execution, resulting in motions under Rule 42(g) for the return of the seized material and records and prohibiting duplicating the records; (4) the government then returned to the Northern District and had the grand jury issue a subpoena for all the material it had seized, seeking to use that subpoena as an "insurance policy" in "an attempt to moot any future proceedings for a return of property"; and (5) the government failed in these multiple proceedings to "fully disclose to each judicial officer prior efforts in other judicial fora to obtain the same or related information and what those efforts had achieved."

defendant's right to challenge the government's improper disclosure of grand jury material for possible use against it in a civil suit. *See United States v. Sells Engineering, Inc.*, 463 U.S. 418 (1983). The court further noted that it was not carrying standing as far as suggested in a Third Circuit decision, *In re Grand Jury (Schmidt)*, 619 F.2d 1022 (3rd Cir.1980), which could be read as allowing a corporate employer to challenge subpoenas aimed at the harassment of its witness-employees.

Targets traditionally have had standing to challenge a third-party subpoena where presenting a claim under a privilege that bars disclosure. See e.g., *New York Times v. Gonzales*, 459 F.3d 160 (2d Cir.2006) (reporters challenge to prospective subpoena directing telephone provider to reveal reporters' telephone records, claiming that records are shielded from grand jury's subpoena by reporter's privilege protecting the identity of confidential sources). *In re Grand Jury*, 111 F.3d 1066 (3d Cir.1997), went a step beyond those rulings in recognizing the standing of the victims of a privately executed illegal wiretap to quash a grand jury subpoena directing the perpetrator of the wiretap to produce the recordings of the intercepted communications. The court majority noted that, in light of the statutory prohibition against use of illegally intercepted wire communication in grand jury proceedings (see fn. f, p. 823), the interests asserted by the wiretap victims (the target of the grand jury investigation and her husband) could "fairly be said to resemble a privilege," but in light of the reasoning of *Schmidt*, supra, it "need not characterize their interests as such in order to find standing." At stake here was a privacy interest, given "maximum protection" by a federal statute, which would be further violated by any unlawful disclosure to the grand jury. The petitioners here met the "jurisprudential concerns" of standing doctrine: they presented a claim based on their own statutory right, rather than that of the witness; that claim presented "a precise question arising from a specific grievance," rather than an "abstract question"; and since the subpoena recipient was the alleged perpetrator of the unlawful recordings, it was "the interveners and not the witness herself who are best suited to assert [the statutory] claim." While "recognition of standing in situations such as this one will undoubtedly result in delays in grand jury investigations," a motion to quash "had not traditionally been regarded an unreasonable burden on grand jury proceedings" where filed by the subpoena recipient, and should not be so viewed where filed by "a third party with an important interest as stake." The dissenting opinion disagreed, in particular, with this last prong of the majority's analysis. It concluded that "the majority's holding that a third party, such as a target * * *, may move to quash the subpoena issued to a witness during the grand jury investigation * * * runs counter to well-established precedent [e.g., *Dionisio*] disallowing procedures that would delay and disrupt grand jury proceedings."

3. *Target notification.* To make effective use of any standing to quash a subpoena issued to a third party, the target needs notification of the issuance of the subpoena in time to intervene before the third party complies. In *Securities and Exchange Commission v. Jerry T. O'Brien, Inc.*, 467 U.S. 735 (1984), in the context of an administrative agency subpoena (see Note 2, p. 801), the Supreme Court concluded that, assuming arguendo that the target of an investigation had standing to challenge a subpoena requiring a third party (here a brokerage firm) to produce records relating to the target's activities, the administrative agency had no obligation to notify the target of the issuance of the subpoena. Requiring such notice, the Court noted, would be highly burdensome for the agency and would "substantially increase the ability of persons who have something to hide to impede legitimate investigations" by informing them that they are being investigated. The Court would not impose such a notification requirement where Congress had failed to do so.

In the grand jury setting, the secrecy obligation imposed on the prosecution precludes it from informing a target that the grand jury has issued a subpoena to a third party. In the vast majority of jurisdictions, including the federal system, the witness is not subject to a secrecy obligation. Thus, the witness is free to inform the target, and is likely to do so where the target is a customer of the third party witness (as in *Fernandez Diamante*, Note 1 supra). Several federal courts have recognized an inherent judicial authority to issue an order prohibiting witnesses from making such disclosures during an ongoing investigation upon a prosecution showing of "compelling need" (e.g., that the informed target will seek to obstruct justice). Others suggest, however, that such authority is preempted by the Rule 6(e) directive that "no obligation of secrecy may be imposed except in accordance with Rule 6(e)(2)(B)" (which lists the persons subject to secrecy and does not include witnesses). See CRIMPROC § 8.5(d).

4. *Legislative grants of standing and notification.* In several instances, Congress has granted to potential targets standing to challenge third party subpoenas on specific grounds, and has implemented that right by generally requiring notification. The most prominent of such statutes are the Right to Financial Privacy Act (RFPA), 12 U.S.C.A. §§ 3401–3420, and Title II of the Electronic Communication Privacy Act (ECPA), 18 U.S.C. §§ 2701–2712 (also known as the "Stored Communications Act"). Although similar in some respects, these Acts take quite different approaches as to grand jury subpoenas.

(a) *The RFPA.* The RFPA, in general, places conditions on the use of federal process to obtain from financial institutions (which include not only the usual variety of banks, but also "consumer finance institutions" and issuers of "credit cards") the financial account records of a limited class of their customers (basically individuals and small partnerships). As to both "administrative" and "judicial" subpoenas, the RFPA provides for: (1) customer notification, (2) a waiting period prior to actual disclosure by the financial institution, and (3) a right of the customer to challenge the subpoena during the waiting period on the grounds that "the financial records are not relevant to the legitimate law enforcement inquiry stated by the Government authority in its notice [to the customer]" or that "there has not been substantial compliance with this chapter" (although the notice speaks generally of challenging relevancy or advancing "any other legal basis for objecting to the release of the records"). See 12 U.S.C.A. §§ 3405, 3407, 3410. The RFPA also provides, however, that the notification required under the administrative subpoena and judicial subpoena provisions may be delayed by court order upon a finding that: (1) the investigation being conducted is "within the lawful jurisdiction of the Government authority seeking the financial records," (2) there is reason to believe that the records are "relevant" to that investigation, and (3) notification will result in either (i) endangering the life or safety of any person, (ii) flight from prosecution, (iii) "destruction of or tampering with evidence," (iv) intimidation of a potential witness, or (iv) "otherwise seriously jeopardizing the investigation." 12 U.S.C.A. § 3409. The mandated delay ordinarily is limited to 90 days, with the customer thereafter receiving notice that the subpoena was issued and the identified documents were delivered to the government by the financial institution.

The basic RFPA provisions do not apply to grand jury subpoenas, as RFPA's exemption provision excludes disclosures to the grand jury (as well to the IRS and intelligence agencies). The grand jury exemption provision means that the RFPA does not create customer standing to challenge the subpoena and does not require customer notification as to a grand jury subpoena. In general, the RFPA leaves disclosure of a grand jury subpoena to the secrecy provisions of Federal Rule 6 (see Note 5, p. 798), which would permit the subpoenaed financial institution, at its option, to notify the customer. However, the RFPA does authorize the grand jury to obtain a judicial order that bars the financial institution from notifying the customer as to the "existence of the subpoena or the information furnished." That order is to be issued by the court for the period specified, and under the procedures established, in the § 3409 delayed-notice provision described above. In addition, § 3420 contains a seemingly permanent prohibition against disclosure to the target where the investigation relates to drug offenses and crimes against a financial institution.

(b) *Title II of the ECPA.* Title II governs the use of federal or state process to obtain a variety of stored account information from different types of interstate network service providers. Initially, as discussed in Pt. D, p. 534, Title II allows certain records containing "content information" to be obtained only through a search warrant, thereby narrowing the otherwise permissible use of grand jury subpoenas. Secondly, where Title II sets forth conditions under which information can be obtained by a subpoena, it refers to grand jury subpoenas as well as administrative subpoenas, treating both alike (in contrast to the RFPA, which exempts grand jury subpoenas). Thus, where Title II requires that a specific showing be made to obtain a particular type of record by subpoena, that showing applies to the use of grand jury subpoenas, even though it may require more than the *R. Enterprise* standard. Similarly, where Title II requires customer notification as a condition for obtaining certain types of information, that requirement applies as well when a grand jury subpoena is used to obtain that information. Notification may be delayed, however, if the government obtains a notification-delay order under a Title II provision that is similar in its general requirements to the notification-delay provision of the RFPA.

SECTION 4.   GRAND JURY TESTIMONY AND THE PRIVILEGE AGAINST SELF–INCRIMINATION[a]

A.   GRAND JURY TESTIMONY

1. *Application of the privilege.* *Counselman v. Hitchcock,* 142 U.S. 547 (1892), put to rest any doubts as to whether the privilege against self-incrimination was available to a grand jury witness. The grand jury witness testifies pursuant to a subpoena so the requisite element of "compulsion" clearly is present. However, the Amendment states only that a person shall not be compelled to be a witness against himself "in a criminal case." *Counselman* initially concluded that the grand jury proceeding was part of the "criminal case" (a broader term than the "criminal prosecution" used in the Sixth Amendment). The Court went on to note, however, that "criminal case" refers to the proceeding in which the compelled testimony is eventually used, not the proceeding in which the testimony is compelled. The Fifth Amendment, it concluded, applies to a witness "in any proceeding" who is being compelled to give testimony that might incriminate him in a criminal case (as illustrated by cases that had recognized the right of a witness in a civil proceeding to claim the privilege). Thus, as the Court later held, the privilege also could be relied upon by persons subpoenaed in those judicial and administrative investigative proceedings that serve as an alternative to grand jury investigations (see Notes 1–3, pp. 800–802).[b]

---

a. The grand jury witness may also utilize any other testimonial privileges recognized in the particular jurisdiction. Thus, the privileges applicable before federal grand juries are those generally recognized in federal courts. See Fed.R.Evid. 1101(d)(2), 501. We have focused here on the privilege against self-incrimination because it provides "what is undoubtedly [the witness'] most significant safeguard in responding to a subpoena ad testificandum." CRIMPROC § 8.10(a).

b. In *Chavez v. Martinez,* set forth at p. 690, the opinions of Justice Thomas and Justice Souter reexamined the grounding of the various rulings that allowed witnesses to claim the

2. ***The nature of "incriminating" testimony.*** As *Counselman* noted, the privilege only applies to testimony which is "incriminating"—i.e., to testimony which may "tend to show" that the witness himself "had committed a crime." What standard is applied in determining whether particular testimony has that tendency and who makes that determination? The leading case on both questions is HOFFMAN v. UNITED STATES, 341 U.S. 479 (1951). In that case, a witness subpoenaed before a federal grand jury relied on the privilege in refusing to answer questions as to his current occupation and his contacts with a fugitive witness. The district court found that there was "no real and substantial danger of incrimination" and the privilege therefore was inapplicable. When the witness persisted in his claim, he was held in contempt. In reversing that conviction, the Supreme Court (per Clark, J.) set forth the following guidelines for the district courts:

"The privilege afforded not only extends to answers that would in themselves support a conviction under a federal criminal statute but likewise embraces those which would furnish a link in the chain of evidence needed to prosecute the claimant for a federal crime. But this protection must be confined to instances where the witness has reasonable cause to apprehend danger from a direct answer. The witness is not exonerated from answering merely because he declares that in so doing he would incriminate himself—his say-so does not of itself establish the hazard of incrimination. It is for the court to say whether his silence is justified, and to require him to answer if 'it clearly appears to the court that he is mistaken.' However, if the witness, upon interposing his claim, were required to prove the hazard in the sense in which a claim is usually required to be established in court, he would be compelled to surrender the very protection which the privilege is designed to guarantee. To sustain the privilege, it need only be evident from the implications of the question, in the setting in which it is asked, that a responsive answer to the question or an explanation of why it cannot be answered might be dangerous because injurious disclosure could result."

It has been suggested that under the *Hoffman* guidelines, it will be a "rare case" in which a court can reject a grand jury witness' assertion of the privilege. See CRIMPROC § 8.10(a).[c] Consider in this connection the *Hoffman* case itself, where the Court had no difficulty in concluding that the district court erred in denying petitioner's claim of the privilege. The Court reasoned that, since the district court was aware that the grand jury was investigating racketeering, it should have recognized that questions concerning Hoffman's current occupation might require answers relating to violations of federal gambling laws. It also should have recognized that information concerning Hoffman's contacts with the

---

privilege in various non-criminal proceedings. Justice Thomas noted that the privilege would not be violated unless the compelled testimony was later used against the witness in a criminal case. However, the witness was allowed—and, indeed, required—to assert the privilege at the point of being questioned. That position had been adopted because otherwise, the witness would have to testify and then object to any subsequent use of his testimony in the criminal case, overcoming uncertainty as to whether his testimony had actually been compelled, or was in fact voluntary (for simply being required by subpoena to testify does not preclude voluntarily responding to a particular question, even though the answer might be incriminating). Justice Thomas described the "evidentiary privilege" allowing and requiring assertion of the privilege at the point of questioning as a "prophylactic rule," designed to ensure that a compelled statement was not subsequently allowed in evidence in a criminal case under the mistaken impression that it was voluntary. See pp. 692–93. Justice Souter described this branch of the self-incrimination caselaw as resting on "law outside the Fifth Amendment's core," which provided complimentary protection to the core's prohibition of "courtroom use of a criminal defendant's compelled self-incriminatory testimony".

c. *Hiibel v. District Court* [Note 10, p. 619] is cited as providing an illustration of one of those rare exceptions. Although *Hiibel* did not involve a testifying witness, the Court noted that witnesses, notwithstanding self-incrimination protection, were commonly required to do what defendant *Hiibel* refused to do—identify himself by name.

fugitive witness might tie him to efforts to hide that witness. See also *Ohio v. Reiner*, 532 U.S. 17 (2001) (state court erred in holding that privilege would not have been available to babysitter who later testified, under an immunity grant, that she had never shaken deceased infant or his twin brother and "she was unaware of and had nothing to do with the * * * injuries" to the two infants, as her testimony also acknowledged that she "spent extended periods of time alone with the children in the weeks immediately preceding discovery of their injuries" and "was with [the deceased infant] within the potential time frame of [his] fatal trauma"; the standard of "reasonable cause to apprehend danger" by providing a "link in the chain of evidence" recognizes that "truthful responses of an innocent witness, as well as those of a wrongdoer, may provide the government with incriminating evidence").

3. *Incrimination under the laws of another sovereign.* For many years, American courts took the position that the privilege protected only against incrimination under the laws of that sovereign which was attempting to compel the incriminating testimony. In applying this rule, said to be derived from the English common law, the Supreme Court treated as separate sovereigns not only separate nations but also each state and the federal government. Thus, if a witness appearing before a federal grand jury did not face potential incrimination in the federal system (e.g., he had been granted immunity from federal prosecution), he could not refuse to testify on the ground that he risked incrimination under state law. However, the Warren Court, in one of its seminal rulings, *Murphy v. Waterfront Comm.*, 378 U.S. 52 (1964), rejected this "separate sovereign" precedent as applied to state and federal inquiries. Noting that a "separate sovereign" limitation would permit a witness to be "whipsawed into incriminating himself under both state and federal law," the Court concluded that the "policies and purposes" of the Fifth Amendment required that the privilege protect "a state witness against incrimination under federal as well as state law and a federal witness against incrimination under state as well as federal law."[d] *Murphy* left open the question of whether the privilege would also be available where a witness in a state or federal proceeding feared incrimination only in a foreign country.

In *United States v. Balsys*, 524 U.S. 666 (1998), the Court majority (7–2) held that the separate sovereign doctrine continued to apply as to incrimination under the laws of a foreign country. Thus, respondent Balsys, a resident alien subpoe-

---

d. *Murphy's* analysis here included a passage explaining these "policies and purposes" that "continues to be cited by the Supreme Court and lower courts, and [has] * * * provided the starting point for analysis of the scope of the privilege in hundreds of state and federal cases." CRIMPROC § 2.10(d). The Court noted:

It [the self-incrimination privilege] reflects many of our fundamental values and most noble aspirations: our unwillingness to subject those suspected of crime to the cruel trilemma of self-accusation, perjury or contempt; our preference for an accusatorial rather than an inquisitorial system of criminal justice; our fear that self-incriminating statements will be elicited by inhumane treatment and abuses; our sense of fair play which dictates "a fair state-individual balance by requiring the government to leave the individual alone until good cause is shown for disturbing him and by requiring the government in its contest with the individual to shoulder the entire load," * * * our respect for the inviolability of the human personality and of the right of each individual "to a private enclave where he may lead a private life," * * * our distrust of self-deprecatory statements; and our realization that the privilege, while sometimes "a shelter to the guilty," is often "a protection to the innocent." * * * Most, if not all, of these policies and purposes are defeated when a witness "can be whipsawed into incriminating himself under both state and federal law even though" the constitutional privilege against self-incrimination is applicable to each.

Later cases, while referring to this passage and a similar explanation of the privilege's "complex of values" in *Miranda v. Arizona* (p. 575), have acknowledged that "the privilege has never been given the full scope which the values it helps to protect suggests." *Schmerber v. California*, Note 6, pp. 855–56. See also *United States v. Balsys*, infra; *Doe v. United States*, Note 6, pp. 855–56; *Fisher v. United States* (pp. 857–58).

naed to testify about his possible participation in Nazi persecution during World War II, could not utilize the privilege to refuse to provide testimony that could subject him to a "real and substantial danger of prosecution in Lithuania and Israel." (The only consequence of his testimony in this country was deportation, long established as having a "civil character"). The Court majority acknowledged that *Murphy* included reasoning that supported a complete rejection of the separate sovereign limitation. Thus, the two dissenting justices (Ginsberg, J. and Breyer, J.) relied in part on *Murphy's* reading of the history of the privilege (including its application under English common law), and on *Murphy's* analysis of the purposes of the privilege, both described in *Murphy* as inconsistent with a separate sovereign limitation. As to legal history, the *Balsys* majority rejected *Murphy's* conclusion that pre-*Murphy* Supreme Court precedent had misread the English common law (*Murphy* having concluded that the English common law actually had rejected, rather than accepted, the separate sovereign limitation). As to policy,[e] the Court noted that, while *Murphy* catalogued multiple "aspirations" of the self-incrimination clause (see fn. d, supra), some of which might support the privilege's extension to the fear of foreign prosecution, *Murphy* had failed "to weigh the host of competing policy concerns that would be raised in a legitimate reconsideration of the Clause's scope." Those costs included the loss of evidence in domestic law enforcement, due to the government's inability to grant immunity that would extend to foreign prosecution.

The *Balsys* majority concluded that *Murphy* was better read as resting on an "alternative rationale," which tied its rejection of the separate sovereign limitation to the applicability of the self-incrimination privilege to both the federal and state governments. The Court explained that *Murphy* was a product of the application of the self-incrimination clause to the states (via the Fourteenth Amendment) in *Malloy v. Hogan* (fn. a, p. 27), decided on the same day as *Murphy*. Once the states become bound by the Fifth Amendment guarantee, the self-incrimination clause "could no longer be seen as framed for one jurisdiction (i.e., state or federal government) alone, each jurisdiction having instead become subject to the same claim of privilege flowing from the one limitation." The concept of a single guarantee, moreover, was consistent with a "feature unique to the [self-incrimination] guarantee," an "option to exchange the privilege for an immunity to prosecutorial use of any compelled testimony." That option remained available by viewing the state and federal governments as extending their immunity to prosecutions by the other (a step taken in *Murphy*, see Note 2, p. 849). Neither state nor federal government, however, could grant immunity as to a prosecution by a foreign nation.

4. Waiver. Once a grand jury witness begins to provide incriminating information on a particular subject, does that action bar raising the privilege as to subsequent questions dealing with the same subject? If the answer might be incriminating as to a different offense, the privilege clearly is available, but that may not be the case where the only potential for incrimination is to the same offense suggested by the earlier testimony. Here the applicable standard is that set forth in *Rogers v. United States*, 340 U.S. 367 (1951). The Court there noted that "disclosure of [an incriminating] fact waives the privilege as to details," as the further disclosure does not then present "a reasonable danger of further incrimination in light of all the circumstances, including [the] previous disclosures." To allow a claim of the privilege as to details "would [only] open the way to distortion of facts by permitting a witness to select any stopping point in the testimony."

---

e. Justices Scalia and Thomas did not join Part IV of the opinion for the Court, which considered relevant both *Murphy's* discussion of self-incrimination policies and competing policy concerns not presented in *Murphy*.

Application of the *Rogers* standard is not always easy, as the division of the Court in *Rogers* itself suggests. In that case, a grand jury was seeking various records of the Communist Party branch in Denver. The witness Rogers admitted that she had been treasurer of the branch, but stated that she had turned the records over to another person. When asked to name that person, she initially refused to do so on the ground that she would not subject other persons to "the same thing that I'm going through." After consulting with counsel, she shifted to reliance on her privilege against self-incrimination. A divided Supreme Court (5–3) rejected that claim (described by the Court majority as a "pure afterthought"). The majority noted that the privilege was "purely personal" and could not be utilized to protect others. Rogers had already incriminated herself by admitting her party membership and her prior possession and transfer of the records; the "mere disclosure of the name of the recipient of the books" presented no more than an "imaginary possibility" of "increasing the danger of her prosecution" for a possible conspiracy to violate the Smith Act. While it was true that "at least two persons are required to constitute a conspiracy, * * * the identity of the other members [is] not needed inasmuch as one person can be convicted of conspiring with persons whose names are unknown." The dissenters saw the matter quite differently. There was a clear potential for additional incrimination, they noted, since petitioner's conviction could well "depend on testimony of the witnesses she was * * * asked to identify." The Court's analysis, they contended, made the "protection [of the privilege] dependent on timing that was so refined that lawyers, let alone laymen, will have difficulty in knowing when to claim it."

5. *Exercise of the privilege by the target.* The self-incrimination privilege has long been held to prohibit the prosecution from forcing a defendant to appear as a witness at his own trial. Should the prosecutor similarly be prohibited from forcing the target of an investigation who desires to exercise the privilege to appear before the grand jury, or is the Fifth Amendment satisfied by simply allowing the target-witness, like any other witness, to refuse to respond to individual questions where his answer might be incriminating? A few state courts have argued that the target of an investigation is, in effect, a "putative" or "de facto" defendant, and he therefore should be allowed to exercise his privilege in much the same manner as a "de jure defendant" at trial. They suggest that, unless the target expressly waives his self-incrimination privilege, the prosecution cannot use the grand jury's subpoena authority to force him to appear. See CRIMPROC § 8.10(c). Consider also Justice Brennan's opinion in *United States v. Mandujano*, discussed in Note 6 infra. On the other side, the federal courts and most state courts have taken the position that the Fifth Amendment, as to the target as well as any other grand jury witness, presents only an "option of refusal and not a prohibition of inquiry." *O'Connell v. United States*, 40 F.2d 201 (2d Cir.1930).[f] The "obligation to appear," the Supreme Court stated in a *Dionisio* (p. 816) footnote, is "no different for a person who may himself be the subject of the grand jury inquiry."

---

f. Internal Justice Department guidelines provide that, to avoid the possible "appearance of unfairness," where the testimony of a grand jury "target" (see fn. g infra) might be helpful, an effort should first be made to secure the voluntary appearance of the target. However, the grand jury and U.S. Attorney may jointly agree to subpoena the target in exceptional cases. In making that determination, the grand jury and U.S. Attorney are directed to give "careful attention" to the importance of the testimony sought from the target, whether the substance of that testimony could be provided by other witnesses, and whether the "questions the prosecutor and the grand jurors intend to ask * * * would be protected by a valid claim of the privilege." United States Attorneys' Manual 9–11.150. Should the subpoenaed "target * * * and his or her attorney state in writing, signed by both, that the 'target' will refuse to testify on Fifth Amendment grounds, the witness ordinarily should be excused," but the "grand jury and United States Attorney [may] agree to insist on appearance" based on the considerations "which justified the subpoena in the first place." U.S.A.M. 9–11.154.

What justifies the different treatment of the trial defendant and the grand jury target, even when that target is so close to indictment that a court will refer to him as a "putative" defendant? Consider the following arguments: (1) the defendant's right of silence grew out of the early common law rule on the incompetency of parties to testify, which had a bearing only on the trial; (2) the defendant's right not to take the stand at trial is aimed, in part, at protecting the defendant from being placed in a position where he may be forced to refuse to answer questions on self-incrimination grounds in the presence of the jury (who may conclude that he therefore has something to hide), but that protective feature has less significance in the grand jury setting since that body simply decides whether to charge and its proceedings therefore need not be conducted "with the assiduous regard for the preservation of procedural safeguards which normally attends the ultimate trial of the issues"; (3) the grand jury, having an obligation to "run down every clue," cannot ignore the possibility that the target's testimony may lead to the identification of others who also participated in the criminal enterprise; (4) the grand jury, having an obligation to "shield the innocent," must be able to seek the target's own testimony to determine whether it might not "explain away" the evidence against him; and (5) determining whether a witness is a "target" is not easy under any standard for establishing that status, so that a prohibition against compelling a target to appear invariably would lead to after-the-fact disputes as to whether a later-indicted witness actually had been a target.[g]

6. Self-incrimination warnings. To what extent, if any, does the Fifth Amendment require that grand jury witnesses be advised prior to testifying of their right to exercise the privilege against self-incrimination? In UNITED STATES v. MANDUJANO, 425 U.S. 564 (1976), there was considerable discussion bearing on that question, although the Court found it unnecessary to resolve the issue. The defendant Mandujano, known by the prosecutor to be a narcotics user, was called before the grand jury in the hope that he would furnish information about significant dealers. Instead, he steadfastly denied any involvement in the sale of narcotics and specifically disclaimed having sought within the year to make a purchase for a third-party for $650.00. The latter statement was a lie since (as the prosecutor already knew) Mandujano had recently tried to make such a purchase for a person who was actually an undercover agent. Subsequently prosecuted for perjury, Mandujano moved to suppress the grand jury testimony that was the basis of the charge. The trial court granted the motion on the ground that Mandujano had not been given full *Miranda* warnings prior to testifying. He had been informed of his privilege against self-incrimination, and he had been advised that he could retain a lawyer, to be located outside the grand jury room for the purpose of consultation. However, when Mandujano responded that he could not afford a lawyer, the prosecutor did not state that an indigent would receive appointed counsel (the last portion of the *Miranda* warnings).

---

g. The United States Attorneys' Manual, in its provisions on target subpoenas (see fn. f supra) and target notification (see Note 7 infra), uses the following definition of a target: "[A] person as to whom the prosecutor or the grand jury has substantial evidence linking him or her to the commission of a crime and who, in the judgment of the prosecutor, is a putative defendant." The target is distinguished from a "subject of an investigation," who is "a person whose conduct is within the scope of the grand jury's investigation." U.S.A.M. 9–11.151.

Concurring in *United States v. Mandujano*, discussed in Note 6 infra, Justice Brennan described the "target" as "one against whom [the government] has probable cause—as measured by an objective standard." Justice Brennan noted that "others have argued for a rule which would combine objective elements with the prosecutor's subjective intent subsequently to charge the individual by indictment * * * but this subjective intent requirement may pose grave administrative difficulties."

The Supreme Court unanimously concluded that even if the warnings were viewed as inadequate, that would not constitute a defense to a perjury charge. The Court had previously held that sanctions could be imposed for perjury "even in instances where the perjurer complained that the Government exceeded its constitutional powers in making the inquiry." Six of the justices also went on to speak to the adequacy of the warnings.

Speaking for four justices, Chief Justice Burger's plurality opinion concluded that the warnings given clearly were adequate, as *Miranda* certainly did not apply to the grand jury witness. The *Miranda* Court itself, in distinguishing custodial interrogation in a police station from interrogation "in courts or other official investigations where there are often impartial observers to guard against intimidation or trickery," had recognized that investigations "such as grand jury questioning take place in a setting wholly different from custodial interrogation." "Indeed," it was noted, "the Court's opinion in *Miranda* reveals a focus on what was seen by the Court as police coercion derived from 'factual studies' [relating to] police violence and the third degree * * *—beating, hanging, whipping—and to sustained and protracted questioning incommunicado in order to extort confessions. * * * To extend these concepts to questioning before a grand jury inquiring into criminal activity under the guidance of a judge is an extravagant expansion never remotely contemplated by this Court in *Miranda*; the dynamics of constitutional interpretation do not compel constant extension of every doctrine announced by the Court."

Chief Justice Burger added in a footnote that, since "warnings were provided in this case to advise respondent of his Fifth Amendment privilege," it was "unnecessary to consider whether any warning is required." However, in discussing the availability of the privilege, the Chief Justice suggested that grand jury witnesses, like witnesses in trial and administrative proceedings, were not constitutionally entitled to a warning even where the question posed had obvious potential for incrimination. The plurality opinion noted: "The very availability of the Fifth Amendment privilege to grand jury witnesses suggests that occasions will often arise when potentially incriminating questions will be asked in the ordinary course of the jury's investigation. * * * [T]he witness can, of course, stand on the privilege, assured that its protection 'is as broad as the mischief against which it seeks to guard.' *Counselman v. Hitchcock* [Note 1 supra]. The witness must invoke the privilege however, as the 'Constitution does not forbid the asking of criminative questions.' *United States v. Monia*, 317 U.S., at 433 [1943] (Frankfurter, J., dissenting):

> The [Fifth] Amendment speaks of compulsion. It does not preclude a witness from testifying voluntarily in matters which may incriminate him. If, therefore, he desires the protection of the privilege, he must claim it or he will not be considered to have been "compelled" within the meaning of the Amendment.

Absent a claim of the privilege, the duty to give testimony remains absolute."

Justice Brennan, joined by Marshall, J., responded to what he viewed as a "denigration of the privilege against self-incrimination" in the Chief Justice's opinion. Justice Brennan did not challenge the Chief Justice's efforts to distinguish *Miranda*, but criticized instead the Chief Justice's "mechanical" reliance upon *United States v. Monia*. Justice Brennan noted that *Monia* involved a deportation proceeding, and the Court had noted that the tribunal there had no notice of the likely incriminating quality of the witness' answer unless that potential was brought to its attention by the witness. But where the government is "acutely aware of the potentially incriminating nature of the disclosures sought," a knowing and completely voluntary waiver should be required. Just as a grand jury could not call an indicted defendant before it and interrogate him concerning the subject matter of the charged crime, absent an intelligent and voluntary waiver, the same should be true of a *de facto* defendant. Accordingly, Justice Brennan noted: "I would hold that, in the absence of an intentional and intelligent waiver by the individual of his known right to be free from compulsory self-incrimination, the Government may not call before a grand jury one whom it has probable cause—as measured by an objective standard—to suspect committed a crime and by use of judicial compulsion compel him to testify with regard to that crime. In the absence of such a waiver, the Fifth Amendment requires that any testimony obtained in this fashion be unavailable to the Government for use at trial. Such a waiver could readily be demonstrated by proof that the individual was warned prior to questioning that he is currently subject to possible criminal prosecution for the commission of a stated crime, that he has a constitutional right to refuse to answer any and all questions that may tend to incriminate him, and by record evidence that the individual understood the nature of his situation and privilege prior to giving testimony."

Relying on the *Mandujano* plurality opinion, the lower federal courts generally have assumed that self-incrimination "warnings" are not constitutionally mandated even as to targets. Several state courts, however, viewing the target grand jury witness as distinct from witnesses in other proceedings, have held that self-incrimination warnings for target witnesses are constitutionally required. See CRIMPROC § 8.10(d). In the federal system, internal prosecutorial guidelines require that both subpoenaed "targets" and "subjects" (see fn. g supra) be informed of the self-incrimination privilege, both by an "advice of rights" statement appended to the subpoena and by "warnings * * * [given] on the record before the grand jury" after the witness is sworn. The prescribed content includes informing the witness that "you may refuse to answer any question if a truthful answer to the question would tend to incriminate you" and that "anything that you do say may be used against you by the grand jury or in a subsequent legal proceeding." United States Attorneys' Manual 9–11.151. Warnings on the record also are common in state practice, at least as to targets, and are required by statute in roughly 10 states. See Beale et al., § 6.24.

7. Target warnings. In UNITED STATES v. WASHINGTON, 431 U.S. 181 (1977), the Court answered one of the issues left open in *Mandujano*: a witness need not be warned that he is a target of the grand jury investigation. Noted the Court (per Burger, C.J.):

"After being sworn, respondent was explicitly advised that he had a right to remain silent and that any statements he did make could be used to convict him of crime. It is inconceivable that such a warning would fail to alert him to his right to refuse to answer any questions which might incriminate him. * * * Even in the presumed psychologically coercive atmosphere of police custodial interrogation, *Miranda* does not require that any additional warnings be given simply because the suspect is a potential defendant; indeed, such suspects are potential defendants more often than not. Respondent points out that unlike one subject to custodial interrogation, whose arrest should inform him only too clearly that he is a potential criminal defendant, a grand jury witness may well be unaware that he is targeted for possible prosecution. While this may be so in some situations, it is an overdrawn generalization. In any case, events here [which included prior questioning by the prosecutor] clearly put respondent on notice that he was a suspect in the motorcycle theft. * * * However, all of this is largely irrelevant, since we do not understand what constitutional disadvantage a failure to give potential defendant warnings could possibly inflict on a grand jury witness, whether or not he has received other warnings. * * * Because target witness status neither enlarges nor diminishes the constitutional protection against compelled self-incrimination, potential defendant warnings add nothing of value to protection of Fifth Amendment rights."

Justice Brennan, joined by Justice Marshall, dissented, relying in substantial part on his discussion of the need for warnings in *Mandujano*. Several state courts, relying on a state statute or state constitutional provision, have held that target witnesses must be warned of their target status. United States Attorneys' Manual 9–11.151 states that the prosecutor should "advise witnesses who are known 'targets' that their conduct is being investigated for possible violation of federal criminal law." As to targets who are not witnesses, prosecutors are encouraged to provide notification of target status in "appropriate cases" (not the "routine clear case" or the case presenting a potential for flight or evidence tampering) in order to permit that person to request the opportunity to testify voluntarily. U.S.A.M. 9–11. 153.

8. *Constitutional right to counsel.* In UNITED STATES v. MANDUJA-NO (described in Note 6 supra), Chief Justice Burger's plurality opinion also spoke to the grand jury witness' right to counsel. Initially, in rejecting the lower court's extension of *Miranda*, the plurality opinion also rejected the contention that the "*Miranda* right to counsel, fashioned to secure the suspect's Fifth Amendment privilege," should apply to grand jury questioning. Turning to other possible sources of a constitutional right to counsel, the plurality added: "Respondent was also informed that if he desired he could have the assistance of counsel, but that counsel could not be inside the grand jury room. That statement was plainly a correct recital of the law. No criminal proceedings had been instituted against respondent, hence the Sixth Amendment right to counsel had not come into play. *Kirby v. Illinois* [p. 769]. A witness 'before a grand jury cannot insist, as a matter of constitutional right, on being represented by his counsel....' *In re Groban*, 352 U.S. 330 (1957). Under settled principles the witness may not insist upon the presence of his attorney in the grand jury room. Fed. Rule Crim. Proc. 6(d)."

Justice Brennan's separate opinion in *Mandujano* also challenged this portion of the plurality opinion. The statement from *Groban* quoted by the plurality was dictum that should be reexamined in light of *Miranda* and *Escobedo v. Illinois* [p. 559] and their "recognit[ion] of the 'substantive affinity' and therefore the 'coextensiveness' in certain circumstance of the right to counsel and the privilege against self-incrimination," and their rejection of the regime of "squalid discrimination" that distinguished between those "wealthy enough to hire a lawyer" and the indigent. Similarly, the plurality's reliance on *Kirby* was inappropriate because the line drawn there as to when "criminal proceedings had been instituted" (the "initiation of adversary judicial proceedings") assumed that the self-incrimination privilege was not "implicated." Also, once "the putative defendant is called and interrogated before the grand jury," he is "faced with the prosecutorial forces of organized society and immersed in the intricacies of substantive and procedural law," in much the same fashion as the person who is the subject of an adversary judicial proceeding.

Justice Brennan argued that, at a minimum, the putative defendant was entitled constitutionally to be told "that he has a right to consult with an attorney prior to questioning, that if he cannot afford an attorney one will be appointed for him, that during the questioning he may have that attorney wait outside the grand jury room, and that he may at any and all times during questioning consult with the attorney prior to answering any question posed." Justice Brennan also opened the door to a possibly broader constitutional protection: he noted that several commentators had argued that "the presence of counsel inside the grand jury room is required," and added that there "certainly * * * is no viable argument that allowing counsel to be present in the grand jury room for the purposes of consultation regarding testimonial privileges would subvert the nature or functioning of the grand jury proceeding."

The *Mandujano* plurality opinion generally is viewed as having put to rest any possible Sixth Amendment grounding for a constitutional right to counsel. See also Note 1, p. 90. Several lower courts, however, following an analysis similar to that advanced by Justice Brennan, have suggested a Fifth Amendment grounding for the right to counsel. Beale et al. § 6.26, suggests that this grounding has "broad implications that some courts may be hesitant to accept"—such as applicability to witnesses in other settings (e.g., administrative and civil proceedings relating to transactions that could conceivably involve criminality), recognizing a right to appointed counsel as well as a right to retained counsel, and creating a right to the effective assistance of counsel (at least as to advice relating to the exercise of the privilege).

A due process grounding for a right to counsel has also been suggested. Here, the right would flow from a general liberty interest of the individual to expend his resources to seek counsel's assistance whenever that assistance would not disrupt or alter the basic character of the proceeding involved. See CRIMPROC § 8.14(a) (finding support in the statement in *Powell v. Alabama,* p. 70, that an "arbitrary" denial of a right to be represented by retained counsel even in a civil case would be a due process violation). In treating the issues discussed in Notes 9 and 10 below, several courts appear to have assumed the existence of such a due process right to retain and consult with counsel.

9. *Federal practice.* Pursuant to internal guidelines, all federal grand jury witnesses are advised that they may retain counsel (who may be located in the anteroom) and that "the grand jury will permit you a reasonable opportunity to step outside the grand jury room to consult with counsel if you so desire." United States Attorneys' Manual, 9–11.151. Where the witness requests the assistance of counsel, but notes that he is indigent, that request is often conveyed to a federal district judge, who may then request that the federal defender or private counsel (in districts without defenders) assume representation. However, the Criminal Justice Act does not provide for appointment of counsel for grand jury witnesses. See 18 U.S.C. § 3006A(a)(1).

Lawyers representing federal grand jury witnesses commonly urge their clients to take full advantage of the opportunity to leave the grand jury room and consult with counsel. Indeed, some lawyers insist that their clients consult after each question, which allows the lawyer to construct a complete record of the questions asked. "Many federal courts permit such a practice, while others go almost that far, limiting witnesses to departures after every few questions." CRIMPROC § 8.14(c).

10. *State practices.* Most states follow a practice similar to the federal practice as to notification of the right to consult with retained counsel and providing through an informal arrangement public defender assistance for the indigent witness who requests counsel (indeed, several states have statutes providing for the appointment of counsel for indigent target witnesses). State courts may be somewhat less liberal, however, in allowing the witness to leave the grand jury for consultations. Those states that are less liberal commonly justify that position on two grounds—avoidance of "undue delay" and restricting counsel to his proper role. If witnesses are allowed to consult after each question, no matter what its nature, they may, it is argued, simply "wear down the grand jury." Moreover, if the attorney's advice properly is limited to counseling the witnesses on the exercise of testimonial privileges, there simply is no reason to allow consultation when the question clearly poses no such difficulty. See e.g., *People v. Ianniello,* 235 N.E.2d 439 (N.Y.1968) (where witness had been immunized and had previous opportunity to consult with counsel on the same line of questioning, grand jury appropriately refused to allow him to leave for the obvious purpose of obtaining "strategic advice" rather than counseling as to any legal right that would allow him to refuse to answer).

11. *The location of counsel.* Roughly twenty states now have statutes permitting at least certain witnesses to be assisted by counsel located within the grand jury room. See CRIMPROC § 8.14(b). Most of these provisions apply to all witnesses, but several are limited to targets or to witnesses who have not been immunized. The statutes commonly contain provisions limiting the role of counsel while before the grand jury. Several state that the lawyer may "advise the witness," but "may not otherwise take any part in the proceeding." One jurisdiction also allows counsel to "interpose objections on behalf of the witness." See Kan.Stat.Ann. § 22–3009(2).

Proponents of such statutes argue that they are needed to adequately protect the rights of the grand jury witness. They contend that even the most liberal right to leave the grand jury room to consult with counsel imposes substantial burdens upon the client's access to counsel and counsel's ability to advise the client. Those opposing the presence of counsel in the grand jury room acknowledge that the location of counsel outside the grand jury room poses certain difficulties for the witness and counsel, but claim that those difficulties are not so great as to undermine the witness' ability to exercise his rights, particularly as to the privilege against self-incrimination. They see any additional protection of witness rights as clearly outweighed by the detrimental effect that counsel's presence would have upon the grand jury's capacity to conduct effective investigations. They argue that, notwithstanding statutory prohibitions, counsel accompanying witnesses would find techniques, such as stage whispers and objections presented through the witness, for challenging the prosecutor's questions, and conveying counsel's arguments to the jurors. With no judge present to put an immediate stop to such tactics, the end result would be disruption and delay of the investigation. They further argue that with counsel at the witness' side, more witnesses will reply to questions by merely parroting responses formulated by counsel—responses that too often furnish as little information as possible or are purposely ambiguous so as to avoid potential perjury charges. The critics draw an analogy to the trial, where the defendant, once taking the stand, is not allowed to interrupt his testimony for further discussions with counsel. Finally, it is noted that, in some instances, the witness may be wary of counsel's loyalty and therefore prefer not to have counsel present. The witness may be forced to accept counsel provided by others (e.g., his employer) and fear retaliation if the full scope of his testimony is carried back to such persons. Once the law permits counsel to be present, the witness will be under pressure to allow counsel to accompany him, and will lose the capacity to be selective in the disclosure of his testimony to counsel.

B. IMMUNITY GRANTS

1. *Constitutionality.* The use of an immunity grant to preclude reliance upon the self-incrimination privilege dates back to the English practice known as providing "indemnity" against prosecution. See *Kastigar v. United States,* Note 2 infra (also noting the use of immunity grants in the American Colonies). Immunity grants were first upheld under the federal constitution in *Brown v. Walker,* 161 U.S. 591 (1896). A divided Court there concluded that the Fifth Amendment could not be "construed literally as authorizing the witness to refuse to disclose any fact which might tend to incriminate, disgrace, or expose him to unfavorable comments." The history of the Amendment, the majority noted, indicated that its object was only to "secure the witness against criminal prosecution." Thus, the

self-incrimination privilege had been held inapplicable where the witness' compelled testimony would relate only to an offense as to which he had been pardoned or as to which the statute of limitations had run. So too, the privilege did not apply where the witness' response might tend to "disgrace him or bring him into disrepute" but would furnish no information relating to a criminal offense. The majority reasoned that, once it is accepted that the object of the privilege is limited to protecting the witness against criminal prosecution, the constitutionality of the immunity grant necessarily follows. Since the grant removes the danger against which the privilege protects, the witness can no longer rely upon the privilege.

2. Scope of the immunity. *Counselman v. Hitchcock,* 142 U.S. 547 (1892), struck down a federal immunity statute that granted the witness protection only against the use of his immunized testimony as evidence in any subsequent prosecution. The Supreme Court concluded that such limited protection was not sufficient to replace the Fifth Amendment privilege. The Court stressed that there was no protection against derivative use of the witness' testimony. Thus, the statute "could not, and would not, prevent the use of his testimony to search out other testimony to be used in evidence against him." At the conclusion of its opinion, however, the Court spoke in terms of even broader protection. "To be valid," it noted, an immunity grant "must afford absolute immunity against future prosecution for the offense to which the question relates." This statement was read as indicating that the immunity grant must absolutely bar prosecution for any transaction noted in the witness' testimony. Accordingly, Congress adopted a new immunity statute providing for "transactional immunity." It provided that a witness directed to testify or produce documentary evidence pursuant to an immunity order could not be prosecuted "for or on account of any transaction, matter, or thing concerning which he may testify or produce evidence." The constitutionality of this provision was upheld in *Brown v. Walker,* supra, and subsequent state and federal immunity statutes were largely patterned upon the *Brown* statute.

Subsequent decisions—and the language of later statutes—established two limitations on the scope of transactional immunity. First, transactional immunity does not preclude a prosecution for perjury committed in the immunized testimony. Second, transactional immunity does not extend to an event described in an answer totally unresponsive to the question asked. Thus, the witness cannot gain immunity from prosecution for all previous criminal acts by simply including a reference to those acts in his testimony without regard to the subject on which he was asked to testify.

In *Murphy v. Waterfront Commission,* Note 3, p. 840, the Court first upheld immunity that was not as broad in scope as the traditional transactional immunity. After rejecting the separate sovereign doctrine as a limitation on the privilege's availability where incrimination remains possible under either federal or state law, *Murphy* turned to the scope of the immunity that must be granted to supplant the privilege as it related to prosecution in that other jurisdiction. It concluded that the immunity granted in one jurisdiction (federal or state) need not absolutely bar prosecution in the other; it was sufficient to bar both use and derivative use of the witness' testimony in the other jurisdiction. This ruling allowed the Court to fashion an immunity for state witnesses that would be sufficiently broad to replace the privilege. Congress' preemptive legislative authority permitted it to grant an immunity that extended to state proceedings, but the states lacked authority to legislate as to federal proceedings. However, to accommodate "the interests of State and Federal governments in investigating and prosecuting crime," the Court could (and would) exercise its supervisory power to prohibit the federal government from using in federal courts state immunized testimony or the fruits thereof.

Following *Murphy,* Congress adopted a general immunity provision that granted federal witnesses protection only against use and derivative use as to both federal and state prosecutions. The statute provided that "no testimony or other information compelled under the [immunity] order (or any information directly or indirectly derived from such testimony or other information) may be used against the witness in any criminal case, except a prosecution for perjury, giving a false statement, or otherwise failing to comply with the order." 18 U.S.C. § 6002. In KASTIGAR v. UNITED STATES, 406 U.S. 441 (1972), a divided Court (5–2) upheld the new federal provision.

Justice Powell's opinion for the *Kastigar* majority discounted the "broad language in *Counselman,*" which suggested the need for transactional immunity, as inconsistent with the "conceptual basis" of the *Counselman* ruling. The crucial question, as *Counselman* noted, was whether the immunity granted was "coextensive with the scope of the privilege against self-incrimination." Both *Murphy* and the cases applying the exclusionary rule to confessions obtained through Fifth Amendment violations indicated that the constitutional privilege required no more than a prohibition against use and derivative use. The new federal statute clearly met that standard: "The statute provides a sweeping proscription of any use, direct or indirect, of the compelled testimony and any information derived therefrom. This total prohibition on use provides a comprehensive safeguard, barring the use of compelled testimony as an 'investigatory lead,' and also barring the use of any evidence obtained by focusing investigation on a witness as a result of his compelled disclosures."

The *Kastigar* majority rejected the argument, relied on by the dissenters, that the bar against derivative use could not be enforced effectively. Appropriate procedures for "taint hearings" could ensure that derivative use was not made of immunized testimony. Those procedural safeguards were described as follows: "As stated in *Murphy:* 'Once a defendant demonstrates that he has testified, under a state grant of immunity to matters related to the federal prosecution, the federal authorities have the burden of showing that their evidence is not tainted by establishing that they had an independent, legitimate source for the disputed evidence.' This burden of proof, which we reaffirm as appropriate, is not limited to a negation of taint; rather, it imposes on the prosecution the affirmative duty to prove that the evidence it proposes to use is derived from a legitimate source wholly independent of the compelled testimony. This is very substantial protection, commensurate with that resulting from invoking the privilege itself. * * *'"

3. In a companion case to *Kastigar, Zicarelli v. New Jersey State Comm. of Investigation,* 406 U.S. 472 (1972), the Court upheld a state counterpart of 18 U.S.C. § 6002, providing for use/derivative-use immunity in state proceedings. Since *Zicarelli* was decided, a substantial number of states have moved from transactional to use/derivative-use immunity. The A.B.A. and N.C.C.U.S.L. have urged retention of transactional immunity, however, and roughly twenty states continue to provide the broader immunity, see Beale et al., § 7.8. Those opposing a shift to use/derivative use immunity have argued that the opportunity it offers to prosecute based on independently obtained evidence is too insignificant as a practical matter to offset the risk that derivative use will not be detected by a taint hearing. Those supporting use/derivative-use immunity contend that taint hearings are effective and that instances allowing permissible prosecutions of immunized witnesses, though small in number, should not be cut off where that is not constitutionally required. They also argue that use/derivative-use immunity affords substantial advantages apart from the possibility of a subsequent prosecution. They maintain that such immunity encourages the immunized witness to provide as much detail as possible so as to make it more difficult for the government to survive a taint hearing should it subsequently decide to prosecute. They also contend that the absence of an absolute protection against subsequent prosecution makes the immunized witness' testimony more credible to the jury.

4. *Subsequent prosecutions and the problem of taint.* While use/derivative-use immunity leaves open the possibility of prosecuting an immunized witness, the prosecution must meet the prerequisite of establishing that its evidence is independently derived, as described in *Kastigar.* Lower courts have read *Kastigar* to be satisfied by application of a preponderance of the evidence standard to this burden. See CRIMPROC § 8.11. Also, some courts have been willing to hold the *Kastigar* taint hearing after trial, thereby allowing the government to proceed to trial without providing the broad pretrial disclosure that is inherent in a pretrial taint hearing. Ibid. Nonetheless, prosecuting an immunized witness is not lightly undertaken, and commonly requires advance planning at the time the witness gives the immunized testimony.

The *Kastigar* burden is most readily met when the prosecution has completed or substantially completed its investigation before the witness is immunized. Thus, a prosecutor can readily meet the *Kastigar* burden where immunity was granted to force the testimony of a defendant who had already been convicted, but who had claimed the privilege because his appeal was still pending, and the prosecutor now seeks to reprosecute after an appellate reversal of that earlier conviction; the prosecution here can simply restrict itself to the evidence introduced at the earlier trial, which obviously was uncovered without the aid of the subsequent grant of immunity.

The *Kastigar* burden can also be met, although not as easily, in cases in which the prosecution had sufficient evidence to prosecute, and had intended to prosecute, but had a need to first gain the prospective defendant's testimony in a prosecution against another participant in the same general criminal enterprise. A similar possibility is presented where the prosecution was well on its way to obtaining an indictment when another governmental agency (a prosecutor in another jurisdiction or a legislative body) required the prospective defendant to testify under a grant of immunity. The preferred practice in such cases is for the prosecutor to make a record of all of the evidence collected prior to the grant of immunity, to file that record with the court, and then at the taint hearing, note its intent to utilize only that previously acquired evidence and further evidence directly acquired from that evidence. To ensure that no evidence was derived from the immunized testimony (as opposed to the previously acquired evidence), the prosecutor's office will establish a "Chinese Wall," keeping the staff in charge of the prosecution from being exposed to the immunized testimony.[h] This procedure is not foolproof, however. Where the immunized testimony was not presented in a closed proceeding, the government's witnesses may become aware of that testimony, and the government then has the burden of showing that their trial testimony was not influenced by the immunized testimony. See e.g., *United States v. North,*

---

h. Such a barrier may also be useful in establishing that the prosecutor did not make tactical use of the immunized testimony. Lower courts have divided over whether *Kastigar* bars "nonevidentiary uses of immunized testimony." CRIMPROC § 8.11 (c). Where a court views *Kastigar* as imposing such a bar, a taint issue may arise even though the prosecution relied entirely on evidence known to the government prior to the grant of immunity. Where the prosecutor was aware of the immunized testimony, there is the possibility that it was used tactically to shape the prosecution (e.g., to determine the appropriate level of the charge or to decide not to present a particular witness). Courts concluding that *Kastigar* "forbid[s] any prosecution use of the [immunized] testimony, not merely that which results in the presentation of evidence * * * [do] not go so far as to hold that prosecutor familiarity with the immunized testimony establishes a per se taint." CRIMPROC § 8.11(c). Still, that familiarity creates substantial difficulties under such precedent.

910 F.2d 843 (D.C. Cir. 1990) (witness exposure to immunized testimony in a Congressional hearing could require "line-by-line" examination of his trial testimony as that testimony was tainted even if the immunized testimony shaped it simply by refreshing the witness' memory); *United States v. Slough*, 641 F.3d 544 (D.C. Cir. 2011) (district court committed error in striking testimony of witnesses who had been exposed to immunized testimony without more careful examination as to whether parts of that stricken testimony did not overlap with the immunized testimony and whether an independent source existed where there was overlap).

5. *Prosecutorial discretion.* Although immunity statutes commonly require that the immunity order be issued by the court, the judge's role in ruling on a request for such an order often is limited to ensuring that the procedural requirements of the statute are met (e.g., under the federal statute, that the application was approved by one of the statutorily designated higher echelon Justice Department officials and that the order properly states the scope of the immunity). Under such provisions, the judge may not refuse to grant the order because it disagrees with the prosecutor's judgment that a grant of immunity is in the public interest. United States Attorneys' Manual 9–23.21 directs the appropriate Justice Department official, in making that judgment, to consider a wide range of factors, including the following: (1) the importance of the investigation; (2) the value of the person's testimony; (3) the likelihood of prompt and full compliance, and the effectiveness of available sanctions if there is no compliance; (4) the person's relative culpability; (5) the possibility of successfully prosecuting the person prior to compelling testimony through immunization; and (6) the likelihood of adverse collateral consequences to the person if compelled to testify.

SECTION 5. SELF–INCRIMINATION AND THE COMPELLED PRODUCTION OF DOCUMENTS

A. THE DISMANTLING OF *BOYD*

1. *Self–Incrimination and Boyd.* In sustaining the petitioner's challenge to the compelled production of a document, Boyd v. United States, set forth at p. 806, relied upon the Fifth Amendment's prohibition against "compelling a man 'in a criminal case to be a witness against himself,'" as well as the Fourth Amendment prohibition against unreasonable searches. Commentators and courts have offered various explanations of the self-incrimination grounding of *Boyd*. Consider, for example, the following:

(a) *Boyd* recognizes that the self-incrimination clause prohibits compelling a person to produce physical evidence that would be incriminating. Thus, *Boyd* was not limited to the production of documents, as recognized in *United States v. White*, 322 U.S. 694 (1944), where the Court spoke of the privilege as protecting the individual "from any disclosure, in the form of oral testimony, documents, or *chattels*, sought by legal process against him as a witness." (emphasis added). See Richard A. Nagareda, *Compulsion "To Be a Witness" and the Resurrection of Boyd*, 74 N.Y.U.L.Rev. 1575 (1999), arguing also that this interpretation of the self-incrimination clause finds support in the text of the Fifth Amendment, the content of related constitutional guarantees, and the history of the privilege against self incrimination.

(b) *Boyd* recognized that the self-incrimination privilege serves to protect "a private inner sanctum of individual feeling and thought," *Bellis v. United States*, 417 U.S. 85 (1974), and that this area of privacy is invaded not only in compelling a witness to testify but also in compelling him to disclose his writings. See

Brennan, J., in *Fisher v. United States* (p. 861) ("Many of the matters within an individual's knowledge may as easily be retained within his head as set down on a scrap of paper. I perceive of no principle which does not permit compelling the disclosure of the contents of one's mind but does permit compelling the disclosure of the contents of that scrap of paper by compelling its production.") *Boyd*, of course, did not involve a document authored by anyone associated with Boyd and Sons, but in looking to *Entick's* characterization of the individual's papers as his "dearest property," the *Boyd* opinion recognized that the compelled disclosure of certain documents written by others (e.g., letters) also could bear upon the individual's personal privacy of thought by revealing his knowledge of the often-personal contents of these documents. Cf. Marshall J., concurring in *Fisher* (p. 862).

(c) *Boyd*, in merging Fourth and Fifth Amendment, advanced a much larger privacy protection, which extended to all documents, as the compelled production of documents necessarily spells out the "private information" of the person who possesses those documents. See Stuntz, fn. b, p. 814.

(d) *Boyd* simply viewed the person compelled to produce a document as compelled, in effect, to recite the contents of the documents (and thereby to give testimony). See Note, 95 Harv. L.Rev. 945 (1977).

2. *The entity exception.* *Hale v. Henkel*, 201 U.S. 43 (1906), decided only two decades after *Boyd*, not only reconstructed *Boyd's* Fourth Amendment analysis (see Note 1, p. 811), but also added a major exception to its Fifth Amendment rationale. *Hale* held that the self-incrimination privilege was not available to a corporation and therefore *Boyd's* self-incrimination analysis did not bar a grand jury subpoena duces tecum requiring production of corporate documents. *Hale* reasoned that the privilege against self-incrimination was a personal right, and therefore was not available to the corporation. The corporation, unlike the individual was a "creature of the state," subject to the "reserved right" of the state to compel its assistance in assuring that it had not "exceeded its powers."[a] The Court also stressed the enforcement needs of the government in compelling, the production of corporate documents: if such production were precluded by a self-incrimination on behalf of the corporation, "it would result in a failure of a large number of cases where the illegal combination was determinable only upon such papers."[b]

---

a. This reserved right was not seen as depriving the corporation of the protection of the Fourth Amendment, and the *Hale* subpoena was quashed on that ground. See Note 1, p. 811. Consider also the availability (and unavailability) to the collective entity of other constitutional rights, such as: the Fifth Amendment protection against being placed twice in jeopardy (assumed to apply); the Fifth Amendment right to prosecution by grand jury indictment (not applicable, according to the Ninth Circuit, since the potential punishment, imposed on corporations does not include imprisonment, and therefore is not "infamous"); and the Sixth Amendment right to a jury trial (applicable). See Peter Henning, *The Conundrum of Corporate Criminal Liability: Seeking A Consistent Approach to the Constitutional Rights of Corporations in Criminal Prosecutions*, 63 Tenn.L.Rev. 783 (1996).

b. In *Hale*, the corporate official called upon to produce the documents had been immunized, so he could not claim that production of the records posed a self-incrimination risk as to himself. *Wilson v. United States*, 221 U.S. 361 (1911), subsequently rejected such a claim by a corporate official who had not been immunized. The State's "reserved power of visitation," the Court noted, "would seriously be embarrassed, if not wholly defeated in its effected exercise, if guilty officers could refuse inspection of the records and papers of the corporation." As the records were those of the corporation, not personal records, and were held "subject to the corporate duty," the official could "assert no personal right * * * against any demand of the government which the corporation was bound to recognize." The subpoena in *Wilson* was directed to the corporation, but *Dreier v. United States*, 221 U.S. 394 (1911), held that the result was the same where the subpoena was directed to a specific individual in his capacity as corporate custodian. See Note 6, p. 866 as to the reconsideration of this issue under the act-of-production doctrine.

3. In UNITED STATES v. WHITE, 322 U.S. 694 (1944), the Court (per Murphy, J.) extended the *Hale* exception to other entities. *White* held that the president of an unincorporated labor union could not invoke his personal privilege to a subpoena demanding union records. Characterizing the Court's previous reliance on the State's visitorial power as "merely a convenient vehicle for justification of governmental investigation of corporate books and records," the *White* Court concluded that the exception recognized in *Hale* was derived from the inappropriateness of affording the privilege to an impersonal collective entity, whether or not that entity took the corporate form. The privilege against self-incrimination, the Court noted, "was essentially a personal [privilege], applying only to natural individuals," as evidenced by its underlying functions. The privilege grew out of "the high sentiment and regard of our jurisprudence for conducting criminal trials, and investigatory proceedings upon a plane of dignity, humanity, and impartiality." It was "designed to prevent the use of legal process to force from the lips of the accused the evidence necessary to convict him or force him to produce and authenticate any personal documents that might incriminate him," and "thereby avoided * * * physical torture and other less violent but equally reprehensible modes of compelling the production of incriminating evidence." These concerns did not apply to the entity, which lacked the qualities of human personality and therefore could not suffer the "immediate and potential evils of compulsory self-disclosure".

The *White* majority also spoke to regulatory considerations "underlying the restriction of the constitutional privilege to natural individuals acting in their own private capacity." It noted: "The scope and nature of the economic activities of incorporated and unincorporated organizations and their representatives demand that the constitutional power of the federal and state governments to regulate those activities be correspondingly effective. The greater portion of evidence of wrongdoing by an organization or its representatives is usually to be found in the official records and documents of that organization. Were the cloak of the privilege to be thrown around these impersonal records and documents, effective enforcement of many federal and state laws would be impossible. The framers of the constitutional guarantee against compulsory self-disclosure, who were interested primarily in protecting individual civil liberties, cannot be said to have intended the privilege to be available to protect economic or other interests of such organizations so as to nullify appropriate governmental regulations."

4. The *White* opinion characterized the labor union as an organization with "a character so impersonal in the scope of its membership and activities that it cannot be said to embody or represent the purely private or personal interests of its constituents, but rather to embody their common or group interests only." In *Bellis v. United States*, 417 U.S. 85 (1974), however, the Court concluded that the entity exception remained applicable even though the entity embodied personal as well as group interests. The functional key was that the organization "be recognized as an independent entity apart from its individual members." Thus, a small law firm, organized as a partnership, was an entity for this purpose even though it "embodie[d] little more than the personal legal practice of the individual partners." The partnership was not an "informal association or a temporary arrangement for the undertaking of a few projects of short-lived duration," but a "formal institutional arrangement organized for the continuing conduct of the firm's legal practice." State law, through the Uniform Partnership Act, imposed a "certain organizational structure"; the firm maintained a bank account in the partnership name; it had employees who worked for the firm as such; and, the firm "held itself out to third parties as an entity with an independent institutional identity."[c]

---

c. *Bellis* left open the possibility that a "small family partnership" might be treated different-ly, as might a temporary arrangement for undertaking a short-lived project, or an association

5.   The "required records" exception. *Shapiro v. United States*, 335 U.S. 1 (1948), expanding upon some dictum in *Wilson* (fn. b, p. 861), held that the self-incrimination clause is not violated by requiring a person to keep records of certain business activities and to make those records available for government inspection. Accordingly, a grand jury subpoena requiring the production of required records could not be successfully challenged on self-incrimination grounds even though the records were those of a business conducted as an individual proprietorship rather than an entity. See *Grand Jury Subpoena Duces Tecum (Underhill)*, 781 F.2d 64 (1986). Business records will not be classified as required records under *Shapiro* unless three prerequisites are met: (1) the governmental requirement that records be kept must be "essentially regulatory" in nature; (3) the records must be "of a kind which the regulated party has customarily kept," and (3) the records "must have assumed some 'public aspects' which render them at least analogous to public documents." *Grosso v. United States*, 390 U.S. 62 (1968).

6.   The "testimonial" limitation. A series of Supreme Court cases dealing with production of identification evidence (see Note 5, p. 767) made clear that the *Boyd* analysis was limited to the production of documents. *Schmerber v. California*, 384 U.S. 757 (1966), was the most prominent of those rulings. *Schmerber* held that the privilege did not prohibit the compelled extraction of a blood sample from an accused and the subsequent admission of that sample as incriminatory evidence at his trial. The Court reasoned that the history of the privilege limited its application to compelled production of an accused's "communications" or "testimony." While this protection extended beyond words compelled from "a person's own lips" and extended to "communications * * * in whatever form they may take," it did not encompass "compulsion which makes a suspect or accused the source of 'real or physical' evidence." Citing *Boyd*, the *Schmerber* opinion distinguished the non-testimonial compulsion in identification procedures from the "compulsion of responses which are also communications, for example, compliance with a subpoena to produce one's papers."

Schmerber's analysis was carried over to the compelled writing of a document in *Doe v. United States*, 475 U.S. 201 (1988), (commonly cited as *Doe II*, to distinguish the earlier *United States v. Doe*, Note 1, p. 863). The Court there held that a judicial order requiring an individual to sign a form directing any foreign bank to release the records of any account he might have at that bank did not compel "testimony" for Fifth Amendment purposes. This was so since the government did not seek to use the signed form itself as a factual assertion of the individual. Indeed, the form was carefully drafted so that the signing party noted that he was acting under court order and did not acknowledge the existence of any account in any particular bank. The compelled writing did not indicate whether the requested documents existed, and offered no assistance to the government in later establishing the authenticity of any records produced by the bank. Thus, while the signed form did constitute a communication, it did not constitute "testimony." The individual, in signing a directive containing only government-prescribed content, was not revealing the "content of his mind" and the government was "not relying on the 'truthtelling' of Doe's directive to show the existence of, or his control over foreign bank account records."[d]

---

based on some "pre-existing relationship of confidentiality among the partners." Lower courts view any such exception as quite narrow. A corporation, even a one-person corporation or a closely held family corporation, will be viewed as an entity no matter how closely it would otherwise resemble the possible "small-family-partnership" exception noted in *Bellis*. See CRIM-PROC § 8.12(b).

   d.   In dissent, Justice Stevens argued that compelling the consent directive was compelling more than a physical act, as it "compelled [Doe] to use his mind to assist the prosecution." Justice Stevens noted in this regard: "He may in some cases be forced to surrender a key to a

The Court acknowledged that the directive could result in the production of incriminating evidence, but rejected Doe's contention that this result, in itself, made the privilege applicable. Doe contended that the "policies of the privilege," as set forth in *Murphy v. Waterfront Comm'n* (fn. d, p. 840), required the Government "to obtain evidence against an accused from sources other than his compelled statements, whether or not the statements make a factual assertion or convey information". The Court responded that this contention was foreclosed by *Schmerber*, where the Court had rejected such a "complex of values" contention (see fn. d, p. 840). *Schmerber* had recognized that, "despite the impact upon the inviolability of the human personality and upon our belief in an adversary system in which the Government must produce the evidence against an accused through its own independent labors, the prosecution is allowed to obtain and use * * * evidence which although compelled is generally speaking not 'testimonial.'" Since "the societal interests in privacy, fairness and restraint of governmental power are not constitutionally offended by compelling the accused to have his body serve as evidence that leads to highly incriminating testimony, as *Schmerber* and its progeny make clear," the same would follow when "compelling a suspect to make a nonfactual statement that facilitates the production of evidence by someone else."

7. *The "personal compulsion" limitation.* In *Andresen v. Maryland* [p. 286], in the course of sustaining a search for documents, the Court rejected the claim that the seizure was prohibited by the Fifth Amendment. The Court noted that the broad language of *Boyd* no longer governed, as later cases had emphasized that application of privilege required the "compulsion of the accused." Thus, *Couch v. United States*, 409 U.S. 322 (1973), held that a taxpayer could not assert the privilege as to a summons served on the taxpayer's accountant requiring the accountant to produce the taxpayer's personal business records. The records were not in the possession of the taxpayer and the taxpayer was "not asked to say or do anything."[e] The same was true where it was law enforcement officers who searched for and seized the target's documents.

8. *The act-of-production analysis.* The most far reaching development in the dismantling of the *Boyd* analysis was the adoption of act-of-production doctrine, discussed below. That is the doctrine to which the courts now look in determining whether the privilege applies to a subpoena requiring an individual to himself produce non-entity documents in his possession (assuming these documents are not required records).

B. THE ACT-OF-PRODUCTION DOCTRINE
FISHER v. UNITED STATES
425 U.S. 391, 96 S.Ct. 1569, 48 L.Ed.2d 39 (1976).

JUSTICE WHITE delivered the opinion of the Court.

In these two cases we are called upon to decide whether a summons directing an attorney to produce documents delivered to him by his client in connection

---

strongbox containing incriminating documents, but I do not believe he can be compelled to reveal the combination to his wall safe—by word or deed." The majority responded: "We * * * disagree with the dissent's conclusion that the execution of the consent directive at issue here forced petitioner to express the contents of his mind. In our view, such compulsion is more like 'be[ing] forced to surrender a key to a strongbox containing incriminating documents' than it is like 'be[ing] compelled to reveal the combination to [petitioner's] wall safe.'"

  e. *Couch* noted that "situations may well arise where constructive possession is so clear or the relinquishment of possession is so temporary and insignificant as to leave the personal compulsions upon the accused substantially intact," and therefore allow that person to assert the privilege. In large part, this exception has been limited to settings in which an office employee has been subpoenaed to produce documents of an employer who has equal access to the records. See e.g., *In re Grand Jury Subpoena (Kent)*, 646 F.2d 963 (5th Cir.1981) (where proprietor actively participated in management of a small office, and the subpoenaed employee was "never delegated the exclusive responsibility for the preparation and custody of the subpoenaed records," proprietor could assert the privilege).

with the attorney-client relationship is enforceable over claims that the documents were constitutionally immune from summons in the hands of the client and retained that immunity in the hands of the attorney. In each case, an Internal Revenue agent visited the taxpayer or taxpayers and interviewed them in connection with an investigation of possible civil or criminal liability under the federal income tax laws. Shortly after the interviews * * *, the taxpayers obtained from their respective accountants certain documents relating to the preparation by the accountant of their tax returns. Shortly after obtaining the documents * * *, the taxpayers transferred the documents to their lawyers—each of whom was retained to assist the taxpayer in connection with the investigation. Upon learning of the whereabouts of the documents, the Internal Revenue Service served summonses on the attorneys directing them to produce documents listed therein. [Those documents were accountants' work sheets, retained copies of income tax returns, and the accountants' copies of correspondence between the accounting firm and the taxpayer]. * * * In each case, the lawyer declined to comply with the summons directing production of the documents, and enforcement actions were commenced by the Government. * * *

All of the parties in these cases and the Court of Appeals have concurred in the proposition that if the Fifth Amendment would have excused a *taxpayer* from turning over the accountant's papers had he possessed them, the *attorney* to whom they are delivered for the purpose of obtaining legal advice should also be immune from subpoena. Although we agree with this proposition for the reasons set forth * * * infra, we are convinced that, under our decision in *Couch v. United States,* [Note 7, p. 856], it is not the taxpayer's Fifth Amendment privilege that would excuse the *attorney* from production.

The relevant part of that Amendment provides:

> "No person . . . shall be *compelled* in any criminal case to be a *witness against himself.*" (Emphasis added.)

The taxpayer's privilege under this Amendment is not violated by enforcement of the summonses involved in these cases because enforcement against a taxpayer's lawyer would not "compel" the taxpayer to do anything—and certainly would not compel him to be a "witness" against himself. The Court has held repeatedly that the Fifth Amendment is limited to prohibiting the use of "physical or moral compulsion" exerted on the person asserting the privilege. In *Couch v. United States,* supra, we recently ruled that the Fifth Amendment rights of a taxpayer were not violated by the enforcement of a documentary summons directed to her accountant and requiring production of the taxpayer's own records in the possession of the accountant. We did so on the ground that in such a case "the ingredient of personal compulsion against an accused is lacking." Here, the taxpayers are compelled to do no more than was the taxpayer in *Couch.* The taxpayers' Fifth Amendment privilege is therefore not violated by enforcement of the summonses directed toward their attorneys. This is true whether or not the Amendment would have barred a subpoena directing the taxpayer to produce the documents while they were in his hands. * * *

The Court of Appeals suggested that because legally and ethically the attorney was required to respect the confidences of his client, the latter had a reasonable expectation of privacy for the records in the hands of the attorney and therefore did not forfeit his Fifth Amendment privilege with respect to the records by transferring them in order to obtain legal advice. It is true that the Court has often stated that one of the several purposes served by the constitutional privilege against compelled testimonial self-incrimination is that of protecting personal privacy. See e.g., *Murphy v. Waterfront Comm'n* [fn. d, p. 840]. But the Court has never suggested that every invasion of privacy violates the privilege. Within the limits imposed by the language of the Fifth Amendment, which we necessarily observe, the privilege truly serves privacy interests; but the Court has never on any ground, personal privacy included, applied the Fifth Amendment to prevent the otherwise proper acquisition or use of evidence which, in the Court's view, did not involve compelled testimonial self-incrimination of some sort.

The proposition that the Fifth Amendment protects private information obtained without compelling self-incriminating testimony is contrary to the clear statements of this Court that under appropriate safeguards private incriminating statements of an accused may be overheard and used in evidence, if they are not compelled at the time they were uttered, *Katz v. United States* [p. 264], and that disclosure of private information may be compelled if immunity removes the risk of incrimination. *Kastigar v. United States* [Note 2, p. 850]. If the Fifth Amendment protected generally against the obtaining of private information from a man's mouth or pen or house, its protections would presumably not be lifted by probable cause and a warrant or by immunity. The privacy invasion is not mitigated by immunity; and the Fifth Amendment's strictures, unlike the Fourth's are not removed by showing reasonableness. The Framers addressed the subject of personal privacy directly in the Fourth Amendment. * * * They did not seek in still another Amendment—the Fifth—to achieve a general protection of privacy but to deal with the more specific issue of compelled self-incrimination.

We cannot cut the Fifth Amendment completely loose from the moorings of its language, and make it serve as a general protector of privacy—a word not mentioned in its text and a concept directly addressed in the Fourth Amendment. We adhere to the view that the Fifth Amendment protects against "compelled self-incrimination, not [the disclosure of] private information." * * * Insofar as private information not obtained through compelled self-incriminating testimony is legally protected, its protection stems from other sources—the Fourth Amendment's protection against seizures without warrant or probable cause and against subpoenas which suffer from "too much indefiniteness or breadth in the things required to be 'particularly described,' " the First Amendment, or evidentiary privileges such as the attorney-client privilege.[7]

* * * [While the] taxpayers have erroneously relied on the Fifth Amendment without urging the attorney-client privilege in so many words, they have nevertheless invoked the relevant body of law and policies that govern the attorney-client privilege. In this posture of the case, we feel obliged to inquire whether the attorney-client privilege applies to documents in the hands of an attorney which would have been privileged in the hands of the client by reason of the Fifth Amendment. * * * This Court and the lower courts have * * * uniformly held that pre-existing documents which could have been obtained by court process from the client when he was in possession may also be obtained from the attorney by similar process following transfer by the client in order to obtain more informed legal advice. * * * It is otherwise if the documents are not obtainable by subpoena duces tecum or summons while in the exclusive possession of the client, for the client will then be reluctant to transfer possession to the lawyer unless the

---

7. The taxpayers and their attorneys have not raised arguments of a Fourth Amendment nature before this Court and could not be successful if they had. The summonses are narrowly drawn and seek only documents of unquestionable relevance to the tax investigation. Special problems of privacy which might be presented by subpoena of a personal diary, *United States v. Bennett*, 409 F.2d 888, 897 (C.A.2 1969) (Friendly, J.), are not involved here. First Amendment values are also plainly not implicated in these cases.

documents are also privileged in the latter's hands. Where the transfer is made for the purpose of obtaining legal advice, the purposes of the attorney-client privilege would be defeated unless the privilege is applicable. * * *

Since each taxpayer [here] transferred possession of the documents in question from himself to his attorney in order to obtain legal assistance in the tax investigations in question, the papers, if unobtainable by summons from the client, are unobtainable by summons directed to the attorney by reason of the attorney-client privilege. We accordingly proceed to the question whether the documents could have been obtained by summons addressed to the taxpayer while the documents were in his possession. The only bar to enforcement of such summons asserted by the parties or the courts below is the Fifth Amendment's privilege against self-incrimination. * * *

The proposition that the Fifth Amendment prevents compelled production of documents over objection that such production might incriminate stems from *Boyd v. United States* * * *. Several of *Boyd's* express or implicit declarations have not stood the test of time. The application of the Fourth Amendment to subpoenas was limited by *Hale v. Henkel* [Note 1, p. 811] and more recent cases. Purely evidentiary (but "nontestimonial") materials, as well as contraband and fruits and instrumentalities of crime, may now be searched for and seized under proper circumstances, *Warden v. Hayden* [p. 286]. Also, any notion that "testimonial" evidence may never be seized and used in evidence is inconsistent with [various cases] approving the seizure under appropriate circumstances of conversations of a person suspected of crime. See *Katz v. United States* [p. 264]. It is also clear that the Fifth Amendment does not independently proscribe the compelled production of every sort of incriminating evidence but applies only when the accused is compelled to make a *testimonial* communication that is incriminating. See *Schmerber v. California* [Note 6, p. 855]. * * * Furthermore, despite *Boyd,* neither a partnership nor the individual partners are shielded from compelled production of partnership records on self-incrimination grounds. *Bellis v. United States* [Note 4, p. 854]. It would appear that under that case the precise claim sustained in *Boyd* would now be rejected for reasons not there considered.

The pronouncement in *Boyd* that a person may not be forced to produce his private papers has nonetheless often appeared as dictum in later opinions of this Court. * * * To the extent, however, that the rule against compelling production of private papers rested on the proposition that seizures of or subpoenas for "mere evidence," including documents, violated the Fourth Amendment and therefore also transgressed the Fifth, the foundations for the rule have been washed away. In consequence, the prohibition against forcing the production of private papers has long been a rule searching for a rationale consistent with the proscriptions of the Fifth Amendment against compelling a person to give "testimony" that incriminates him. Accordingly, we turn to the question of what, if any, incriminating testimony within the Fifth Amendment's protection, is compelled by a documentary summons.

A subpoena served on a taxpayer requiring him to produce an accountant's workpapers in his possession without doubt involves substantial compulsion. But it does not compel oral testimony; nor would it ordinarily compel the taxpayer to restate, repeat, or affirm the truth of the contents of the documents sought. Therefore, the Fifth Amendment would not be violated by the fact alone that the papers on their face might incriminate the taxpayer, for the privilege protects a person only against being incriminated by his own compelled testimonial communications. *Schmerber v. California,* supra. The accountant's workpapers are not the taxpayer's. They were not prepared by the taxpayer, and they contain no testimonial declarations by him. Furthermore, as far as this record demonstrates, the preparation of all of the papers sought in these cases was wholly voluntary, and they cannot be said to contain compelled testimonial evidence, either of the taxpayers or of anyone else. The taxpayer cannot avoid compliance with the subpoena merely by asserting that the item of evidence which he is required to produce contains incriminating writing, whether his own or that of someone else.[11]

The act of producing evidence in response to a subpoena nevertheless has communicative aspects of its own, wholly aside from the contents of the papers produced. Compliance with the subpoena tacitly concedes the existence of the papers demanded and their possession or control by the taxpayer. It also would indicate the taxpayer's belief that the papers are those described in the subpoena. The elements of compulsion are clearly present, but the more difficult issues are whether the tacit averments of the taxpayer are both "testimonial" and "incriminating" for purposes of applying the Fifth Amendment. These questions perhaps do not lend themselves to categorical answers; their resolution may instead depend on the facts and circumstances of particular cases or classes thereof. In light of the records now before us, we are confident that however incriminating the contents of the accountant's workpapers might be, the act of producing them—the only thing which the taxpayer is compelled to do—would not itself involve testimonial self-incrimination.

It is doubtful that implicitly admitting the existence and possession of the papers rises to the level of testimony within the protection of the Fifth Amendment. The papers belong to the accountant, were prepared by him, and are the kind usually prepared by an accountant working on the tax returns of his client. Surely the Government is in no way relying on the "truth telling" of the taxpayer to prove the existence of or his access to the documents. The existence and location of the papers are a foregone conclusion and the taxpayer adds little or nothing to the sum total of the Government's information by conceding that he in fact has the papers. Under these circumstances by enforcement of the summons "no constitutional rights are touched. The question is not of testimony but of surrender."

When an accused is required to submit a handwriting exemplar he admits his ability to write and impliedly asserts that the exemplar is his writing. But in common experience, the first would be a near truism and the latter self-evident. In any event, although the exemplar may be incriminating to the accused and although he is compelled to furnish it, his Fifth Amendment privilege is not violated because nothing he has said or done is deemed to be sufficiently testimonial for purposes of the privilege. This Court has also time and again allowed subpoenas against the custodian of corporate documents or those belonging to other collective entities such as unions and partnerships and those of bankrupt businesses over claims that the documents will incriminate the custodian despite the fact that producing the documents tacitly admits their existence and their location in the hands of their possessor. The existence and possession or control of the subpoenaed documents being no more in issue here than in the above cases, the summons is equally enforceable.

Moreover, assuming that these aspects of producing the accountant's papers have some minimal testimonial significance, surely it is not illegal to seek

---

11. The fact that the documents may have been written by the person asserting the privilege is insufficient to trigger the privilege. *Wilson v. United States* [fn. b, p. 853]. And, unless the government has compelled the subpoenaed person to write the document, the fact that it was written by him is not controlling with respect to the Fifth Amendment. Conversations may be seized and introduced in evidence under proper safeguards * * * if not compelled. In the case of a documentary subpoena the only thing compelled is the act of producing the document and the compelled act is the same as one performed when a chattel or document not authored by the producer is demanded.

accounting help in connection with one's tax returns or for the accountant to prepare workpapers and deliver them to the taxpayer. At this juncture, we are quite unprepared to hold that either the fact of existence of the papers or of their possession by the taxpayer poses any realistic threat of incrimination to the taxpayer.

As for the possibility that responding to the subpoena would authenticate the workpapers, production would express nothing more than the taxpayer's belief that the papers are those described in the subpoena. The taxpayer would be no more competent to authenticate the accountant's workpapers or reports by producing them than he would be to authenticate them if testifying orally. The taxpayer did not prepare the papers and could not vouch for their accuracy. The documents would not be admissible in evidence against the taxpayer without authenticating testimony. Without more, responding to the subpoena in the circumstances before us would not appear to represent a substantial threat of self-incrimination. * * *

Whether the Fifth Amendment would shield the taxpayer from producing his own tax records in his possession is a question not involved here; for the papers demanded here are not his "private papers," see *Boyd v. United States,* supra. We do hold that compliance with a summons directing the taxpayer to produce the accountant's documents involved in this case would involve no incriminating testimony within the protection of the Fifth Amendment.

JUSTICE STEVENS took no part in the consideration or disposition of these cases.

JUSTICE BRENNAN, concurring in the judgment.

Given the prior access by accountants retained by the taxpayers to the papers involved in these cases and the wholly business rather than personal nature of the papers, I agree that the privilege against compelled self-incrimination did not in either of these cases protect the papers from production in response to the summonses. See *Couch v. United States.* I do not join the Court's opinion, however, because of the portent of much of what is said of a serious crippling of the protection secured by the privilege against compelled production of one's private books and papers. * * * [I]t is but another step in the denigration of privacy principles settled nearly 100 years ago in *Boyd v. United States.* * * *

Expressions are legion in opinions of this Court that the protection of personal privacy is a central purpose of the privilege against compelled self-incrimination. * * * The Court pays lip-service to this bedrock premise of privacy in the statement that "[w]ithin the limits imposed by the language of the Fifth Amendment, which we necessarily observe, the privilege truly serves privacy interests." But this only makes explicit what elsewhere highlights the opinion, namely, the view that protection of personal privacy is merely a byproduct and not, as our precedents and history teach, a factor controlling in part the determination of the scope of the privilege. This cart-before-the-horse approach is fundamentally at odds with the settled principle that the scope of the privilege is not constrained by the limits of the wording of the Fifth Amendment but has the reach necessary to protect the cherished value of privacy which it safeguards. * * *

* * * [The Court's] analysis is patently incomplete: the threshold inquiry is whether the taxpayer is compelled to produce incriminating papers. That inquiry is not answered in favor of production merely because the subpoena requires neither oral testimony from nor affirmation of the papers' contents by the taxpayer.[f] To be sure, the Court correctly observes that "[t]he taxpayer cannot

---

f. Justice Brennan's opinion also questioned whether the Court's reasoning was consistent with its own analysis: "I also question the Court's treatment of the question whether the act of

avoid compliance with the subpoena *merely* by asserting that the item of evidence which he is required to produce contains incriminating writing, whether his own or that of someone else." For it is not enough that the production of a writing, or books and papers, is compelled. Unless those materials are such as to come within the zone of privacy recognized by the Amendment, the privilege against compulsory self-incrimination does not protect against their production.

We are not without guideposts for determining what books, papers, and writings come within the zone of privacy recognized by the Amendment. * * * *Couch v. United States* expressly held that the Fifth Amendment protected against the compelled production of testimonial evidence only if the individual resisting production had a reasonable expectation of privacy with respect to the evidence. * * * A precise cataloguing of private papers within the ambit of the privacy protected by the privilege is probably impossible. Some papers, however, do lend themselves to classification. Production of documentary materials created or authenticated by a State or the Federal Government, such as automobile registrations or property deeds, would seem ordinarily to fall outside the protection of the privilege. They hardly reflect an extension of the person. Economic and business records may present difficulty in particular cases. The records of business entities generally fall without the scope of the privilege. But, as noted, the Court has recognized that the privilege extends to the business records of the sole proprietor or practitioner. Such records are at least an extension of an aspect of a person's activities, though concededly not the more intimate aspects of one's life. Where the privilege would have protected one's mental notes of his business affairs in a less complicated day and age, it would seem that protection should not fall away because the complexities of another time compel one to keep business records.

Nonbusiness economic records in the possession of an individual, such as canceled checks or tax records, would also seem to be protected. They may provide clear insights into a person's total lifestyle. They are, however, like business records and the papers involved in these cases, frequently, though not always, disclosed to other parties; and disclosure, in proper cases, may foreclose reliance upon the privilege. Personal letters constitute an integral aspect of a person's private enclave. And while letters, being necessarily interpersonal, are not wholly private, their peculiarly private nature and the generally narrow extent of their disclosure would seem to render them within the scope of the privilege. Papers in the nature of a personal diary are *a fortiori* protected under the privilege. * * *

JUSTICE MARSHALL, concurring in the judgment.

* * * I would have preferred it had the Court found some room in its theory for recognition of the import of the contents of the documents themselves. * * * Nonetheless, I am hopeful that the Court's new theory, properly understood and applied, will provide substantially the same protection as our prior focus on the contents of the documents. * * * Indeed, there would appear to be a precise inverse relationship between the private nature of the document and the permissibility of assuming its existence. Therefore, under the Court's theory, the admission through production that one's diary, letters, prior tax returns, personally maintained financial records, or canceled checks exist would ordinarily provide

---

producing evidence is 'testimonial.' I agree that the act of production implicitly admits the existence of the evidence requested and possession or control of that evidence by the party producing it. It also implicitly authenticates the evidence as that identified in the order to compel. I disagree, however, that implicit admission of the existence and possession or control of the papers in this case is not 'testimonial' merely because the Government could readily have otherwise proved existence and possession or control in these cases. I know of no Fifth Amendment principle which makes the testimonial nature of evidence and, therefore, one's protection against incriminating himself, turn on the strength of the Government's case against him."

substantial testimony. The incriminating nature of such an admission is clear, for while it may not be criminal to keep a diary, or write letters or checks, the admission that one does and that those documents are still available may quickly—or simultaneously—lead to incriminating evidence. If there is a "real danger" of such a result, that is enough under our cases to make such testimony subject to the claim of privilege. Thus, in practice, the Court's approach should still focus upon the private nature of the papers subpoenaed and protect those about which *Boyd* and its progeny were most concerned. * * *

The Court's theory will also limit the prosecution's ability to use documents secured through a grant of immunity. If authentication that the document produced is the document demanded were the only testimony inherent in production, immunity would be a useful tool for obtaining written evidence. So long as a document obtained under an immunity grant could be authenticated through other sources, as would often be possible, reliance on the immunized testimony— the authentication—and its fruits would not be necessary, and the document could be introduced. The Court's recognition that the act of production also involves testimony about the existence and possession of the subpoenaed documents mandates a different result. Under the Court's theory, if the document is to be obtained, the immunity grant must extend to the testimony that the document is presently in existence. Such a grant will effectively shield the contents of the document, for the contents are a direct fruit of the immunized testimony—that the document exists—and cannot usually be obtained without reliance on that testimony. * * *

NOTES AND QUESTIONS

1. ***The demise of Boyd?*** In UNITED STATES v. DOE, 465 U.S. 605 (1984) (commonly described as *Doe I*, to distinguish it from *Doe II*, see Note 6, p. 855), the subpoena at issue directed a sole proprietor to produce for grand jury use a broad range of records, including billings, ledgers, canceled checks, telephone records, contracts and paid bills. The district court sustained the proprietor's claim of privilege, applying *Fisher's* act-of-production analysis. It concluded that compliance with the subpoena would require the proprietor to "admit that the records exist, that they are in his possession, and that they are authentic" and that each of these testimonial elements of production was potentially incriminatory. The Third Circuit agreed with this reasoning, but added that the privilege also applied because compelled disclosure of the contents of such documents in itself violated the Fifth Amendment. Relying upon a privacy analysis of *Boyd*, it reasoned that the contents of personal records were privileged under the Fifth Amendment and that "business records of a sole proprietorship are no different from the individual's personal records." Justice Powell's opinion for the *Doe I* Court affirmed the rulings below insofar as they relied on the act-of-production doctrine of *Fisher*, but rejected the Third's Circuit conclusion that the self-incrimination privilege also applied because it protected the contents of the papers.

Justice Powell initially acknowledged that the Court in *Fisher* had "declined to reach the question whether the Fifth Amendment privilege protects the contents of an individual's tax records in his possession" (see p. 861). The "rationale" underlying *Fisher's* holding, however, was equally persuasive as to such records and the records here. *Fisher* had emphasized that "the Fifth Amendment protects the person asserting the privilege only from compelled self-incrimination." That a record was prepared by a subpoenaed party and is in his possession is "irrelevant to the determination of whether its creation * * * was compelled." The business records here, like the accountant's workpapers in

Fisher, had been prepared voluntarily, and therefore only their production, and not their creation, was compelled. The contention that the Fifth Amendment created a "zone of privacy" that protected the content of such papers had been rejected in *Fisher*, and that rejection had been reinforced by the *Andresen v. Maryland* (Note 7, p. 286), which sustained a search for personal business records. The respondent could not avoid compliance with a subpoena "merely by asserting that the item of evidence which he is required to produce contains incriminating writing, whether his own or that of someone else."

Although *Doe I* dealt with business records, the opinion did not suggest any opening for separate treatment of diaries (see fn. 7 of *Fisher*) or other documents of a more intimate nature. Justice O'Connor, in a separate concurring opinion, sought to shut the door on any such exception. She noted: "I write separately * * * to make explicit what is implicit in the analysis of [Justice Powell's] opinion: that the Fifth Amendment provides absolutely no protection for the contents of private papers of any kind. The notion that the Fifth Amendment protects the privacy of papers originated in *Boyd v. United States*, but our decision in *Fisher v. United States*, sounded the death-knell for *Boyd*. 'Several of *Boyd's* express or implicit declarations [had] not stood the test of time * * * and its privacy of papers concept ha[d] long been a rule searching for a rationale.' *Fisher*. Today's decision puts a long overdue end to that fruitless search."

Justice O'Connor's opinion brought forth a response from Justice Marshall, joined by Justice Brennan. "This case," Justice Marshall noted, "presented nothing remotely close to the question that Justice O'Connor eagerly poses and answers." The documents in question here were business records, "which implicate a lesser degree of concern for privacy interests than, for example, personal diaries." It accordingly could not be said that the Court had "reconsidered the question of whether the Fifth Amendment provides protection for the content of 'private papers of any kind.'"

As to the post *Doe I* lower court treatment of this issue, see CRIMPROC § 8.12(f): "In the years since *Doe I*, lower courts usually have found it unnecessary to decide whether anything remains of *Boyd*. 'If the contents of papers are protected at all,' they note, 'it is only in rare situations, where compelled disclosure would break the heart of our sense of privacy.' That might be the case as to subpoena compelling production of 'intimate papers such as private diaries and drafts of letters or essays,' but it certainly would not cover the business and other financial records that typically are in issue. * * * A growing number of courts, however, have come to the conclusion that the rationale of *Doe* and *Fisher* precludes self-incrimination protection of the contents of a voluntarily prepared document, no matter how personal the document. Thus, courts have held that the act-of-production doctrine provides the only protection for such personal records as diaries and pocket calendars. In all of those cases, however, once the concept of a *Boyd*-based content protection was rejected, the government was able to overcome an act-of-production objection because the documents had been shared with others and their existence, possession, and authentication were established as foregone conclusions. Ordinarily such documents are kept more privately and the individual required to produce them would implicitly be giving testimony as to those elements and therefore be entitled to the protection of the privilege."

2. *Authentication and the foregone conclusion doctrine.* *Fisher's* reasoning as to why the implicit admission of the existence and possession of accountant's workpapers did not "rise to the level of testimony under the protection of the Fifth Amendment" (p. 860) came to be known as the "foregone conclusion" doctrine. In *Doe I*, the Court described that doctrine as extending also to implicit admissions of authentication. The lower courts there had sustained Doe's claim that the act of producing the subpoenaed documents would "tacitly admit their existence and his possession" and would "reliev[e] the government of the need for authentication" under Fed. R. Evid. 901.[g] The Supreme Court, in turn, also accepted that claim, based upon its traditional "reluctan[ce] to disturb findings of fact in which two courts below concurred." The Court noted that findings of the lower court as to the testimonial components of production were "sufficient to establish a valid claim of the privilege against self-incrimination," but it then added: "This is not to say that the government was foreclosed from rebutting respondents claim by producing evidence that possession existence, *and authentication* were a 'foregone conclusion.' *Fisher*. In this case, however, the Government failed to make such a showing." 465 U.S. at 614, fn. 13. (emphasis added)

3. *The rationale of the foregone conclusion doctrine.* As Justice Brennan noted in *Fisher* (see fn. f, p. 861), in determining whether a witness' testimony is protected by the privilege, courts look solely to whether the facts acknowledged in the testimony carry a potential for incrimination; they do not further inquire as to whether the prosecution might establish those same incriminatory facts without relying on the witness' testimony. Does the *Fisher* ruling that the privilege does not apply when "possession, existence, and authentication" are a "foregone conclusion" require precisely that inquiry in determining whether the act of production is testimonial (and therefore subject to protection by the privilege)? If so, why this different treatment of the act of production (as opposed to traditional testimony)? Consider in this connection, Robert Mosteller, *Simplifying Subpoena Law: Taking the Fifth Amendment Seriously,* 73 Va.L.Rev. 1, 32–33 (1987):

"More plausibly, the Court is suggesting [in its 'foregone conclusion' analysis] that when an implicit as opposed to an explicit communication is involved, it is necessary to consider whether the government is really asking a 'question' through the subpoena. Granted, the defendant's response to a documentary subpoena always reveals that the item does or does not exist; the government cannot eliminate the implicit question about the document's existence no matter how it phrases the subpoena's demand. But if the government already knows the answer to that question and is truly uninterested in the implicit answer provided by production, the witness' gratuitous communication of it should not violate the fifth amendment. In short, the *Fisher* decision suggests that constitutional rights are not violated by implicit communications that are inherent in a response to a documentary subpoena where those communications are unwanted because, though technically admissible, they are not substantially relevant to the prosecution's case given its other evidence."

4. *Potential incrimination.* Assuming that the government does not establish that possession, authentication, and existence are a foregone conclusion, under what circumstances will the privilege nonetheless not be applicable because the likelihood of incrimination is not "substantial and real" (see *Doe I*, discussed below)? Note in this regard *Fisher*'s comments on the incriminatory aspects of producing records that were authored by another and clearly could be lawfully possessed. What did the Court mean when it said that, "at this juncture," it was

---

g. Fed. R. Evid. 901 provides that authentication "is satisfied by evidence sufficient to support a finding that the matter in question is what its proponent claims." Subdivisions (1)–(10) of Fed. R. Evid. 901 offer illustrations of evidence that may support such a finding, including testimony of a witness with knowledge (subdivision 1), expert and nonexpert testimony as to the genuineness of handwriting (subdivisions 2 and 3), and distinctive characteristics of the document as contained in its "appearance, contents, substance, internal patterns, or other distinctive characteristics, taken in conjunction with circumstances" (subdivision 4). Doe's claim apparently was that his act of production would have provided authentication under subdivision (1). Some of the documents may have been capable of authentication under subdivision (4), without reliance on Doe having produced the documents, but there was no discussion of this possibility.

unwilling to hold that either the existence of the papers or their possession posed a realistic threat of incrimination (see p. 861)? Are the possible contents of the papers irrelevant to the determination of potential incrimination since the privilege does not protect the contents but only the act of production? Assuming that the contents of the tax work papers were incriminatory, wouldn't possession suggest knowledge of that content and thereby pose a realistic threat?

One answer is that the Court in *Fisher* may simply not have been willing to conclude, on the record before it, that a realistic threat existed that the contents were incriminatory. *Fisher* involved an IRS investigation, with no criminal overtones, and in that context, lower courts have commonly required more than a "blanket claim" (encompassing all records subpoenaed and offering no explanation) to establish a realistic threat of incrimination. See CRIMPROC § 8.13(b).

In *Doe I*, the Court returned to the issue of incrimination in its footnote 13. That footnote responded to the government's contention that, even if the act of production there did have "testimonial aspects," any incrimination would be "so trivial" that the Fifth Amendment would not be implicated. The risk of incrimination here, the Court noted, was "substantial and real," meeting the *Hoffman* standard (Note 2, p. 839), since the act of production established the existence and possession of the business records in question (points "not conceded" by Doe) and relieved the government of the need to otherwise establish "authenticity" under Fed. R. Evid. 901. No reference was made to the general character of the documents, although, as in *Fisher*, they certainly were documents that could be "lawfully possessed," and in some instances, may have been authored by others. *Doe I*, in contrast to *Fisher*, involved a grand jury investigation.

5. *Act of production immunity.* The government in *Doe I* maintained that, accepting arguendo the lower court's finding of testimonial self-incrimination, the district court should nevertheless have enforced the subpoena and granted to Doe immunity as to his act of production. The government argued that it had, in effect, offered such immunity by telling the district court that it would not use the act of production against Doe. The Court responded that the government, if it wanted to grant act-of-production immunity, must make a proper application pursuant to the immunity statute. (see Note 5, p. 852). It did, however, reject Doe's contention that the immunity granted under the statute must extend to the contents of the documents subpoenaed. The Court reasoned: "Respondent argues that any grant of use immunity must cover the contents of the documents as well as the act of production. We find this contention unfounded. To satisfy the requirements of the Fifth Amendment, a grant of immunity need be only as broad as the privilege against self-incrimination. *Murphy v. Waterfront Commission* [Note 2, p. 849]. * * * [T]he privilege in this case extends only to the act of production. Therefore, any grant of use immunity need only protect respondent from the self-incrimination that might accompany the act of producing his business records." 465 at 617, fn. 17.

6. *Production by an entity agent.* In BRASWELL v. UNITED STATES, 487 U.S. 99 (1988), the petitioner, a corporate president and sole shareholder, was subpoenaed to produce various corporate records. Raising the privilege against self-incrimination, petitioner sought to distinguish earlier precedent holding a corporate agent could not raise the privilege in such a situation (see fn. b, p. 853). He argued that: (1) the earlier rulings had assumed that the availability of the privilege flowed from the privacy rationale of *Boyd* and protected the contents of the records to be produced (which did not include entity records); (2) *Fisher*, however, had shifted the focus to the incrimination of the act of production, and (3) such testimonial incrimination also occurred where a corporate agent was required to produce corporate documents which that agent had created or used. A closely divided Supreme Court rejected that contention, although it did provide the custodian with a layer of protection that went beyond the earlier precedent. Speaking for the majority, Chief Justice Rehnquist reasoned:

"To be sure, the holding in *Fisher*—later reaffirmed in *Doe* [*I*]—embarked upon a new course of Fifth Amendment analysis. We cannot agree, however, that it rendered the collective entity rule obsolete. * * * From *Wilson* forward, the Court has consistently recognized that the custodian of corporate or entity records holds those documents in a representative rather than a personal capacity. Artificial entities such as corporations may act only through their agents, and, a custodian's assumption of his representative capacity leads to certain obligations, including the duty to produce corporate records on proper demand by the Government. Under those circumstances, the custodian's act of production is not deemed a personal act, but rather an act of the corporation. Any claim of Fifth Amendment privilege asserted by the agent would be tantamount to a claim of privilege by the corporation—which of course possesses no such privilege. * * *

"The *Fisher* court cited the collective entity decisions with approval and offered those decisions to support the conclusion that the production of the accountant's workpapers would 'not * * * involve testimonial self-incrimination.' * * * In a footnote, the Court explained: 'In these [collective entity] cases compliance with the subpoena is required even though the books have been kept by the person subpoenaed and his producing them would itself be sufficient authentication to permit their introduction against him.' n. 14. The Court thus reaffirmed the obligation of a corporate custodian to comply with a subpoena addressed to him.

"That point was reiterated by Justice Brennan in his concurrence in *Fisher*. Although Justice Brennan disagreed with the majority as to its use of the collective entity cases to support the proposition that the act of production is not testimonial, he nonetheless acknowledged that a custodian may not resist a subpoena on the ground that the act of production would be incriminating. * * * [For] 'one in control of the records of an artificial organization undertakes an obligation with respect to those records foreclosing any exercise of his privilege.' Thus, whether one concludes—as did the Court—that a custodian's production of corporate records is deemed not to constitute testimonial self-incrimination, or instead that a custodian waives the right to exercise the privilege, the lesson of *Fisher* is clear: A custodian may not resist a subpoena for corporate records on Fifth Amendment grounds. * * *

"We note further that recognizing a Fifth Amendment privilege on behalf of the records custodians of collective entities would have a detrimental impact on the Government's efforts to prosecute 'white-collar crime,' one of the most serious problems confronting law enforcement authorities. 'The greater portion of evidence of wrongdoing by an organization or its representatives is usually found in the official records and documents of that organization. Were the cloak of the privilege to be thrown around these impersonal records and documents, effective enforcement of many federal and state laws would be impossible.' *White* [Note 3, p. 854]. If custodians could assert a privilege, authorities would be stymied not only in their enforcement efforts against those individuals but also in their prosecutions or organizations. * * *[h]

---

h. Responding to this contention, the dissent (per Kennedy J.) noted: "The majority's abiding concern is that if a corporate officer who is the target of a subpoena is allowed to assert the privilege, it will impede the Government's power to investigate corporations, unions, and partnerships, to uncover and prosecute white collar crimes, and otherwise to enforce its visitatorial powers. There are at least two answers to this. The first, and most fundamental, is that the text of the Fifth Amendment does not authorize exceptions premised on such rationales. Second, even if it were proper to invent such exceptions, the dangers prophesied by the majority are overstated."

"Petitioner suggests, however, that these concerns can be minimized by the simple expedient of either granting the custodian statutory immunity as to the act of production, 18 U.S.C. §§ 6002–6003, or addressing the subpoena to the corporation and allowing it to choose an agent to produce the records who can do so without incriminating himself. We think neither proposal satisfactorily addresses these concerns. Taking the last first, it is no doubt true that if a subpoena is addressed to a corporation, the corporation 'must find some means by which to comply because no Fifth Amendment defense is available to it.' The means most commonly used to comply is the appointment of an alternate custodian. But petitioner insists he cannot be required to aid the appointed custodian in his search for the demanded records, for any statement to the surrogate would itself be testimonial and incriminating. If this is correct, then petitioner's 'solution' is a chimera. In situations such as this—where the corporate custodian is likely the only person with knowledge about the demanded documents—the appointment of a surrogate will simply not ensure that the documents sought will ever reach the grand jury room; the appointed custodian will essentially be sent on an unguided search.

"This problem is eliminated if the Government grants the subpoenaed custodian statutory immunity for the testimonial aspects of his act of production. But that 'solution' also entails a significant drawback. All of the evidence obtained under a grant of immunity to the custodian may of course be used freely against the corporation, but if the Government has any thought of prosecuting the custodian, a grant of act of production immunity can have serious consequences. Testimony obtained pursuant to a grant of statutory use immunity may be used neither directly nor derivatively. 18 U.S.C. § 6002. And '[o]ne raising a claim under [the federal immunity] statute need only show that he testified under a grant of immunity in order to shift to the government the heavy burden of proving that all of the evidence it proposes to use was derived from legitimate independent sources.' *Kastigar* [Note 2, p. 850]. Even in cases where the Government does not employ the immunized testimony for any purpose—direct or derivative—against the witness, the Government's inability to meet the 'heavy burden' it bears may result in the preclusion of crucial evidence that was obtained legitimately.

"Although a corporate custodian is not entitled to resist a subpoena on the ground that his act of production will be personally incriminating, we do think certain consequences flow from the fact that the custodian's act of production is one in his representative rather than personal capacity. Because the custodian acts as a representative, the act is deemed one of the corporation and not the individual. Therefore, the Government concedes, as it must, that it may make no evidentiary use of the 'individual act' against the individual. For example, in a criminal prosecution against the custodian, the Government may not introduce into evidence before the jury the fact that the subpoena was served upon and the corporation's documents were delivered by one particular individual, the custodian.[i] The Government has the right, however, to use the corporation's act of

---

i. The dissent characterized this ruling as revealing the inherent flaw in the majority's reasoning. It noted: "Beginning from ordinary principles of agency, the majority proceeds to the conclusion that when a corporate employee, or an employee of a labor union or partnership, complies with a subpoena for production of documents, his act is necessarily and solely the act of the entity. * * * [But] the heart of the matter, as everyone knows, is that the Government does not see Braswell as a mere agent at all * * *. The Government explained at oral argument that it often chooses to designate an individual recipient, rather than the corporation generally, when it serves a subpoena because '[we] want the right to make that individual comply with the subpoena.' This is not the language of agency. By issuing a subpoena which the Government insists is directed to petitioner personally, it has forfeited any claim that it is simply making a demand on a corporation that, in turn, will have to find a physical agent to perform its duty. What the Government seeks instead is the right to choose any corporate agent as a target of its

production against the custodian. The Government may offer testimony—for example, from the process server who delivered the subpoena and from the individual who received the records—establishing that the corporation produced the records subpoenaed. The jury may draw from the corporation's act of production the conclusion that the records in question are authentic corporate records, which the corporation possessed, and which it produced in response to the subpoena. And if the defendant held a prominent position within the corporation that produced the records, the jury may, just as it would had someone else produced the documents, reasonably infer that he had possession of the documents or knowledge of their contents. Because the jury is not told that the defendant produced the records, any nexus between the defendant and the documents results solely from the corporation's act of production and other evidence in the case.[11]"

7. What is the grounding of the evidentiary-use prohibition imposed by *Braswell*? See Peter Henning, *Finding What Was Lost: Sorting Out the Custodian's Privilege Against Self-Incrimination From the Compelled Production of Records*, 77 Neb.L.Rev. 34 (1998) (asking whether the Court here has established a "quasi-constitutional" prohibition or a standard based upon its "supervisory power.")

The prohibition of evidentiary use of the act of production does not bar use of the contents of the documents against the custodian. But would a bar against such use be required in the situation described in the second paragraph of footnote 11 of *Braswell*? The Second Circuit has suggested that, if the government does not identify the sole-shareholder as the source of the documents, any resulting inference would not justify such a ban. See *In re Grand Jury Subpoena Issued June 18, 2009*, 593 F.3d 155 (2d Cir. 2010): "Although the inference would be strong, it would not be automatic. The jury might believe the Government obtained the document entirely on its own, * * * and even if the jurors learned that the Government obtained the documents by subpoena, they might infer the corporation engaged a third party to search its records and make the production on its behalf. * * * The decision to incorporate is freely made and generates benefits, such as limited liability, and burdens, such as the need to respond to subpoenas, * * * and [one-person corporations should not be] effectively immune from regulation by virtue of being beyond the reach of the Government subpoena power."

8. *The non-documentary act-of-production.* The implications of the several doctrines discussed in this section were brought together in an unusual setting in *Baltimore City Department of Social Services v. Bouknight*, 493 U.S. 549 (1990). The Supreme Court there rejected a self-incrimination objection to a subpoena directing respondent Bouknight to produce her infant son, an abused

---

subpoena and compel that individual to disclose certain information by his own actions. * * * The majority gives the corporate agent fiction a weight it simply cannot bear. In a peculiar attempt to mitigate the force of its own holdings, it impinges upon its own analysis by concluding that, while the Government may compel a named individual to produce records, in any later proceeding against the person it cannot divulge that he performed the act. But if that is so, it is because the Fifth Amendment protects the person without regard to his status as a corporate employee; and once this be admitted, the necessary support for the majority's case has collapsed."

11. We reject the suggestion that the limitation on the evidentiary use of the custodian's act of production is the equivalent of constructive use immunity barred under our decision in *Doe* [see Note 5, p. 866]. Rather, the limitation is a necessary concomitant of the notion that a corporate custodian acts as an agent and not an individual when he produces corporate records in response to a subpoena addressed to him in his representative capacity.

We leave open the question whether the agency rationale supports compelling a custodian to produce corporate records when the custodian is able to establish, by showing for example that he is the sole employee and officer of the corporation, that the jury would inevitably conclude that he produced the records.

child who had previously been declared a ward of the court. The Court noted that the respondent could not claim the privilege based upon "anything an examination of the [child] might reveal," as that would be a claim based upon "the contents or nature of the thing demanded." However, the mother could conceivably claim the privilege because "the act of production would amount to testimony regarding her control over and possession of [the child]." While the state could "readily introduce [other] evidence of Bouknight's continuing control over the child" (including the court order giving her limited custody and her previous statements reflecting control), her "implicit communication of control over [the child] at the moment of production might aid the state in prosecuting Bouknight [for child abuse]." The Court had no need to decide, however, whether "this limited testimonial assertion is sufficiently incriminating and sufficiently testimonial for purposes of the privilege." In receiving conditional custody from the juvenile court, the mother had "assumed custodial duties related to production" (analogous to that of an entity agent) and had done so as part of noncriminal regulatory scheme which included a production component (analogous to regulations sustained under the required records doctrine). The Court added that it had no need in the case before it "to define the precise limitations that may exist upon the State's ability to use the testimonial aspects of Bouknight's act of production [against her] in subsequent criminal proceedings," but the "imposition of such limitations," as was done in *Braswell*, was not "foreclosed."

9. _Hubbell._ The Court's latest ruling applying the act-of-production doctrine, _United States v. Hubbell_, set forth below, addressed several of the issues that the lower courts had found most troubling in that doctrine's application.

UNITED STATES v. HUBBELL
530 U.S. 27, 120 S.C. 2037, 147 L.Ed.2d 24 (2000).

JUSTICE STEVENS delivered the opinion of the Court.

The two questions presented concern the scope of a witness' protection against compelled self-incrimination: (1) whether the Fifth Amendment privilege protects a witness from being compelled to disclose the existence of incriminating documents that the Government is unable to describe with reasonable particularity; and (2) if the witness produces such documents pursuant to a grant of immunity, whether 18 U.S.C. § 6002 prevents the Government from using them to prepare criminal charges against him.

This proceeding arises out of the second prosecution of respondent, Webster Hubbell, commenced by the Independent Counsel appointed in August 1994 to investigate possible violations of federal law relating to the Whitewater Development Corporation. The first prosecution was terminated pursuant to a plea bargain. In December 1994, respondent pleaded guilty to charges of mail fraud and tax evasion arising out of his billing practices as a member of an Arkansas law firm from 1989 to 1992, and was sentenced to 21 months in prison. In the plea agreement, respondent promised to provide the Independent Counsel with "full, complete, accurate, and truthful information" about matters relating to the Whitewater investigation.

The second prosecution resulted from the Independent Counsel's attempt to determine whether respondent had violated that promise. In October 1996, while respondent was incarcerated, the Independent Counsel served him with a subpoena duces tecum calling for the production of 11 categories of documents before a grand jury sitting in Little Rock, Arkansas. See Appendix, infra.[j] On November 19,

---

j. The Appendix to Justice Stevens' opinion set forth verbatim the "subpoena rider," which identified the 11 categories of documents in paragraphs (A)-(K). In essence, the 11 categories

he appeared before the grand jury and invoked his Fifth Amendment privilege against self-incrimination. In response to questioning by the prosecutor, respondent initially refused "to state whether there are documents within my possession, custody, or control responsive to the Subpoena." Thereafter, the prosecutor produced an order, which had previously been obtained from the District Court pursuant to 18 U.S.C. § 6003(a), directing him to respond to the subpoena and granting him immunity "to the extent allowed by law." Respondent then produced 13,120 pages of documents and records and responded to a series of questions that established that those were all of the documents in his custody or control that were responsive to the commands in the subpoena, with the exception of a few documents he claimed were shielded by the attorney-client and attorney work-product privileges.

The contents of the documents produced by respondent provided the Independent Counsel with the information that led to this second prosecution. On April 30, 1998, a grand jury in the District of Columbia returned a 10–count indictment charging respondent with various tax-related crimes and mail and wire fraud. The District Court dismissed the indictment relying, in part, on the ground that the Independent Counsel's use of the subpoenaed documents violated § 6002 because all of the evidence he would offer against respondent at trial derived either directly or indirectly from the testimonial aspects of respondent's immunized act of producing those documents. Noting that the Independent Counsel had admitted that he was not investigating tax-related issues when he issued the subpoena, and that he had "learned about the unreported income and other crimes from studying the records' contents," the District Court characterized the subpoena as "the quintessential fishing expedition." * * *

The Court of Appeals vacated the judgment and remanded for further proceedings. The majority concluded that the District Court had incorrectly relied on the fact that the Independent Counsel did not have prior knowledge of the contents of the subpoenaed documents. The question the District Court should

---

(each subject to a time frame limit of "January 1, 1993 to the present") were: (1) all documents "reflecting, referring, or relating to any direct or indirect sources of money or other things of value received by Webster Hubbell, his wife or children [collectively, the 'Hubbell family'] * * *, including but not limited to the identity of employers or clients of legal or any other type of work"; (3) all documents "reflecting, referring, or related to any direct or indirect sources of money or other things of value" received by the Hubbell family, including "billing memoranda, draft statements, bills, final statements and/or bills for work performed or time billed"; (3) copies of all bank records of the Hubbell family, including "statements, registers, ledgers, canceled checks, deposit items and wire transfers"; (4) all documents reflecting, referring, or related to "time worked or billed by Webster Hubbell," including "original time sheets, books, notes, papers, and/or computer records"; (5) all documents reflecting "expenses incurred by and/or disbursements of money by Webster Hubbell for work performed or to be performed"; (6) all documents "reflecting, referring, or relating to Webster Hubbell's schedule of activities," including "all calendars, daytimers, time books, appointment books, diaries, records of reverse telephone toll charges, credit card calls, telephone message slips, logs, other telephone records, minutes databases, electronic mail messages, travel records, itineraries, tickets for transportation of any kind, payments, bills, expense backup documentation, schedules, and/or any other document or database that would disclose Webster Hubbell's activities"; (7) all documents "reflecting, referring, or relating to any retainer agreements or contracts for employment" of the Hubbell family; (8) all "tax returns, tax return information, including but not limited to all W–2s, form 1099s, schedules, draft returns, work papers, and backup documents filed, created or held by or on behalf of [the Hubbell family], and/or any business in which [the Hubbell family] holds or has held an interest"; (9) all documents "reflecting, referring, or relating to work performed or to be performed for the City of Los Angeles, the Los Angeles Department of Airports or any other Los Angeles municipal or governmental entity, Mary Leslie, and/or Alan Arkatov"; (10) all documents "reflecting, referring, or related to work performed by [the Hubbell family] on the recommendation, counsel, or other influence of Mary Leslie and/or Alan Arkatov"; and (11) all documents related to work performed for or on behalf of specified entities (e.g., Lippo Ltd.) and specified individuals (e.g., James Riady) "or any affiliate, subsidiary, or corporation owned or controlled by or related to the aforementioned entities or individuals."

have addressed was the extent of the Government's independent knowledge of the documents' existence and authenticity, and of respondent's possession or control of them. It explained: "On remand, the district court should hold a hearing in which it seeks to establish the extent and detail of the [G]overnment's knowledge of Hubbell's financial affairs (or of the paperwork documenting it) on the day the subpoena issued. It is only then that the court will be in a position to assess the testimonial value of Hubbell's response to the subpoena. Should the Independent Counsel prove capable of demonstrating with reasonable particularity a prior awareness that the exhaustive litany of documents sought in the subpoena existed and were in Hubbell's possession, then the wide distance evidently traveled from the subpoena to the substantive allegations contained in the indictment would be based upon legitimate intermediate steps. To the extent that the information conveyed through Hubbell's compelled act of production provides the necessary linkage, however, the indictment deriving therefrom is tainted."

In the opinion of the dissenting judge, the majority failed to give full effect to the distinction between the contents of the documents and the limited testimonial significance of the act of producing them. In his view, as long as the prosecutor could make use of information contained in the documents or derived therefrom without any reference to the fact that respondent had produced them in response to a subpoena, there would be no improper use of the testimonial aspect of the immunized act of production. In other words, the constitutional privilege and the statute conferring use immunity would only shield the witness from the use of any information resulting from his subpoena response "beyond what the prosecutor would receive if the documents appeared in the grand jury room or in his office unsolicited and unmarked, like manna from heaven."

On remand, the Independent Counsel acknowledged that he could not satisfy the "reasonable particularity" standard prescribed by the Court of Appeals and entered into a conditional plea agreement with respondent. In essence, the agreement provides for the dismissal of the charges unless this Court's disposition of the case makes it reasonably likely that respondent's "act of production immunity" would not pose a significant bar to his prosecution. The case is not moot, however, because the agreement also provides for the entry of a guilty plea and a sentence that will not include incarceration if we should reverse and issue an opinion that is sufficiently favorable to the Government to satisfy that condition. Despite that agreement, we granted the Independent Counsel's petition for a writ of certiorari in order to determine the precise scope of a grant of immunity with respect to the production of documents in response to a subpoena. We now affirm. * * *

Acting pursuant to 18 U.S.C. § 6002, the District Court entered an order compelling respondent to produce "any and all documents" described in the grand jury subpoena and granting him "immunity to the extent allowed by law." In *Kastigar v. United States* [Note 2, p. 850], we upheld the constitutionality of § 6002 because the scope of the "use and derivative-use" immunity that it provides is coextensive with the scope of the constitutional privilege against self-incrimination. * * * We particularly emphasized the critical importance of protection against a future prosecution "based on knowledge and sources of information obtained from the compelled testimony." * * * [W]e held that the statute imposes an affirmative duty on the prosecution, not merely to show that its evidence is not tainted by the prior testimony, but "to prove that the evidence it proposes to use is derived from a legitimate source wholly independent of the compelled testimony." * * * The "compelled testimony" that is relevant in this case is not to be found in the contents of the documents produced in response to the subpoena. It is, rather, the testimony inherent in the act of producing those documents. The disagreement between the parties focuses entirely on the significance of that testimonial aspect.

The Government correctly emphasizes that the testimonial aspect of a response to a subpoena duces tecum does nothing more than establish the existence, authenticity, and custody of items that are produced. We assume that the Government is also entirely correct in its submission that it would not have to advert to respondent's act of production in order to prove the existence, authenticity, or custody of any documents that it might offer in evidence at a criminal trial; indeed, the Government disclaims any need to introduce any of the documents produced by respondent into evidence in order to prove the charges against him. It follows, according to the Government, that it has no intention of making improper "use" of respondent's compelled testimony. The question, however, is not whether the response to the subpoena may be introduced into evidence at his criminal trial. That would surely be a prohibited "use" of the immunized act of production. But the fact that the Government intends no such use of the act of production leaves open the separate question whether it has already made "derivative use" of the testimonial aspect of that act in obtaining the indictment against respondent and in preparing its case for trial. It clearly has.

It is apparent from the text of the subpoena itself that the prosecutor needed respondent's assistance both to identify potential sources of information and to produce those sources. See Appendix [fn. a supra]. Given the breadth of the description of the 11 categories of documents called for by the subpoena, the collection and production of the materials demanded was tantamount to answering a series of interrogatories asking a witness to disclose the existence and location of particular documents fitting certain broad descriptions. The assembly of literally hundreds of pages of material in response to a request for "any and all documents reflecting, referring, or relating to any direct or indirect sources of money or other things of value received by or provided to" an individual or members of his family during a 3–year period, is the functional equivalent of the preparation of an answer to either a detailed written interrogatory or a series of oral questions at a discovery deposition. Entirely apart from the contents of the 13,120 pages of materials that respondent produced in this case, it is undeniable that providing a catalog of existing documents fitting within any of the 11 broadly worded subpoena categories could provide a prosecutor with a "lead to incriminating evidence," or "a link in the chain of evidence needed to prosecute."

Indeed, the record makes it clear that is what happened in this case. The documents were produced before a grand jury sitting in the Eastern District of Arkansas in aid of the Independent Counsel's attempt to determine whether respondent had violated a commitment in his first plea agreement. The use of those sources of information eventually led to the return of an indictment by a grand jury sitting in the District of Columbia for offenses that apparently are unrelated to that plea agreement. What the District Court characterized as a "fishing expedition" did produce a fish, but not the one that the Independent Counsel expected to hook. It is abundantly clear that the testimonial aspect of respondent's act of producing subpoenaed documents was the first step in a chain of evidence that led to this prosecution. The documents did not magically appear in the prosecutor's office like "manna from heaven." They arrived there only after respondent asserted his constitutional privilege, received a grant of immunity, and—under the compulsion of the District Court's order—took the mental and physical steps necessary to provide the prosecutor with an accurate inventory of the many sources of potentially incriminating evidence sought by the subpoena. It was only through respondent's truthful reply to the subpoena that the Government received the incriminating documents of which it made "substantial use . . . in the investigation that led to the indictment." Brief for United States 3.

For these reasons, we cannot accept the Government's submission that respondent's immunity did not preclude its derivative use of the produced documents because its "possession of the documents [was] the fruit only of a simple physical act—the act of producing the documents." Brief, at 29. It was unquestionably necessary for respondent to make extensive use of "the contents of his own mind" in identifying the hundreds of documents responsive to the requests in the subpoena. The assembly of those documents was like telling an inquisitor the combination to a wall safe, not like being forced to surrender the key to a strongbox. *Doe II* [fn. d, p. 855]. The Government's anemic view of respondent's act of production as a mere physical act that is principally non-testimonial in character and can be entirely divorced from its "implicit" testimonial aspect so as to constitute a "legitimate, wholly independent source" (as required by *Kastigar*) for the documents produced simply fails to account for these realities.

In sum, we have no doubt that the constitutional privilege against self-incrimination protects the target of a grand jury investigation from being compelled to answer questions designed to elicit information about the existence of sources of potentially incriminating evidence. That constitutional privilege has the same application to the testimonial aspect of a response to a subpoena seeking discovery of those sources. Before the District Court, the Government arguably conceded that respondent's act of production in this case had a testimonial aspect that entitled him to respond to the subpoena by asserting his privilege against self-incrimination. * * * On appeal and again before this Court, however, the Government has argued that the communicative aspect of respondent's act of producing ordinary business records is insufficiently "testimonial" to support a claim of privilege because the existence and possession of such records by any businessman is a "foregone conclusion" under our decision in *Fisher v. United States*. This argument both misreads *Fisher* and ignores our subsequent decision in *Doe I* [Note 1, p. 863]. * * * Whatever the scope of this "foregone conclusion" rationale, the facts of this case plainly fall outside of it. While in *Fisher* the Government already knew that the documents were in the attorneys' possession and could independently confirm their existence and authenticity through the accountants who created them, here the Government has not shown that it had any prior knowledge of either the existence or the whereabouts of the 13,120 pages of documents ultimately produced by respondent. The Government cannot cure this deficiency through the overbroad argument that a businessman such as respondent will always possess general business and tax records that fall within the broad categories described in this subpoena. The *Doe I* subpoenas also sought several broad categories of general business records, yet we upheld the District Court's finding that the act of producing those records would involve testimonial self-incrimination.

Given our conclusion that respondent's act of production had a testimonial aspect, at least with respect to the existence and location of the documents sought by the Government's subpoena, respondent could not be compelled to produce those documents without first receiving a grant of immunity under § 6003. As we construed § 6002 in *Kastigar*, such immunity is co-extensive with the constitutional privilege. *Kastigar* requires that respondent's motion to dismiss the indictment on immunity grounds be granted unless the Government proves that the evidence it used in obtaining the indictment and proposed to use at trial was derived from legitimate sources "wholly independent" of the testimonial aspect of respondent's immunized conduct in assembling and producing the documents described in the subpoena. The Government, however, does not claim that it could make such a showing. Rather, it contends that its prosecution of respondent must be considered proper unless someone—presumably respondent—shows that "there is some substantial relation between the compelled testimonial communications implicit in the act of production (as opposed to the act of production standing alone) and some aspect of the information used in the investigation or the evidence presented at trial." Brief for United States 9. We could not accept this submission without repudiating the basis for our conclusion in *Kastigar* that the statutory guarantee of use and derivative-use immunity is as broad as the constitutional privilege itself. This we are not prepared to do. Accordingly, the indictment against respondent must be dismissed. The judgment of the Court of Appeals is affirmed. * * *

CHIEF JUSTICE REHNQUIST dissents and would reverse the judgment of the Court of Appeals in part, for the reasons given by Judge Williams in his dissenting opinion in that court, 167 F.3d 552, 597 (C.A.D.C.1999).[k]

JUSTICE THOMAS, with whom JUSTICE SCALIA joins, concurring.

Our decision today involves the application of the act-of-production doctrine, which provides that persons compelled to turn over incriminating papers or other physical evidence pursuant to a subpoena duces tecum or a summons may invoke the Fifth Amendment privilege against self-incrimination as a bar to production only where the act of producing the evidence would contain "testimonial" features. I join the opinion of the Court because it properly applies this doctrine, but I write separately to note that this doctrine may be inconsistent with the original meaning of the Fifth Amendment's Self–Incrimination Clause. A substantial body of evidence suggests that the Fifth Amendment privilege protects against the compelled production not just of incriminating testimony, but of any incriminating evidence. In a future case, I would be willing to reconsider the scope and meaning of the Self–Incrimination Clause.

The Fifth Amendment provides that "[n]o person ... shall be compelled in any criminal case to be a witness against himself." The key word at issue in this case is "witness." The Court's opinion, relying on prior cases, essentially defines "witness" as a person who provides testimony, and thus restricts the Fifth Amendment's ban to only those communications "that are 'testimonial' in character." None of this Court's cases, however, has undertaken an analysis of the meaning of the term at the time of the founding. A review of that period reveals substantial support for the view that the term "witness" meant a person who gives or furnishes evidence, a broader meaning than that which our case law currently ascribes to the term.[1] * * * If this is so, a person who responds to a

---

k. Judge Williams reasoned that, since the prosecution had "relied on the documents only for the information they contained," it had not made use of any testimonial elements of the act of production with respect to Hubbell's possession or authentication. As to "existence," the *Fisher* reasoning should appropriately limit the testimonial element of the act of production to the act's acknowledging "responsiveness of the documents to the subpoena." That would prohibit the government from "referring back to the subpoena to identify the documents and to clarify relationships that were not clear on their face." But it would not extend to "existence in a quite different sense—the fact that these particular pieces of paper are in being," for that "is quite easily confirmed by these papers own physical existence." Whether or not the government could previously establish that physical existence as a foregone conclusion, the act of production was not testimonial in establishing that existence, just as the act of providing a blood sample or a handwriting exemplar is not testimonial in establishing what third persons observe—that blood or handwriting come from the particular person. Thus, just as the prosecutor could make use of data drawn from the blood and handwriting (blood type, DNA, or handwriting idiosyncracies), the prosecutor could use the contents of the documents.

l. Justice Thomas cited the following sources from that period: (1) dictionary definitions of the term "witness"; (2) state constitutional provisions that granted a right against compulsion "to give evidence" or to "furnish evidence"; (3) the use of similar wording by the four states that proposed inclusion of a self-incrimination provision in the Bill of Rights, and the lack of any indication that Madison's "unique phrasing" in the proposal he offered to Congress was designed to narrow those state proposals; and (4) the Sixth Amendment's compulsory process clause, which the Court had long held to encompass the right to secure papers as well as testimony. For a more extensive review of this historical material, see Richard A. Nagareda, *Compulsion "To Be A*

subpoena duces tecum would be just as much a "witness" as a person who responds to a subpoena ad testificandum.[1] * * *

This Court has not always taken the approach to the Fifth Amendment that we follow today. The first case interpreting the Self–Incrimination Clause—*Boyd v. United States*—was decided, though not explicitly, in accordance with the understanding that "witness" means one who gives evidence. * * * But this Court's decision in *Fisher v. United States*, rejected this understanding, permitting the Government to force a person to furnish incriminating physical evidence and protecting only the "testimonial" aspects of that transfer. In so doing, *Fisher* not only failed to examine the historical backdrop to the Fifth Amendment, it also required—as illustrated by extended discussion in the opinions below in this case—a difficult parsing of the act of responding to a subpoena duces tecum. None of the parties in this case has asked us to depart from *Fisher*, but in light of the historical evidence that the Self–Incrimination Clause may have a broader reach than *Fisher* holds, I remain open to a reconsideration of that decision and its progeny in a proper case.

NOTES AND QUESTIONS

1. ***Establishing a foregone conclusion.*** Does *Hubbell* in its discussion of the lack of a sufficient "foregone-conclusion" showing in that case, and the presence of a sufficient showing in *Fisher*, adopt, in effect, the "reasonable particularity" standard advanced by the Court of Appeals (see p. 872)? See *In re Grand Jury Subpoena, Dated April 18, 2003*, 383 F.3d 905 (9th Cir.2004) (applying a "reasonable particularity" standard and citing *Hubbell* as supporting that standard); Robert Mosteller, *Cowboy Prosecutors and Subpoenas for Incriminating Evidence: The Consequences and Correction of Excess*, 58 Wash. & Lee L.Rev. 487 (2001) (questioning significance of Court's failure to adopt the lower court's standard).

2. To what extent must the preexisting knowledge establishing a forgone conclusion relate to a specific document? Consider CRIMPROC § 8.13(a) (2d ed. Supp., 2001), asking what the government would have needed to meet the foregone conclusion standard as to its demand for "tickets for transportation" (see fn. j, p. 871, category 6): "Must [the government] identify the specific [travel] document as one known to be in the party's possession (e.g., an airline ticket for a known trip on a particular day) or may it refer to a somewhat broader grouping of documents upon showing that the party had engaged in a particular type of travel activity which involved receipt of such documents (e.g., airline tickets from a specific airline which the subpoena party regularly used)?" Is it significant in this regard that *Hubbell* described the government's prior knowledge in *Fisher* "as relating to [the accountant's] workpapers as a group, not as relating to the specific documents within that grouping"? Ibid. Consider *United States v. Ponds*, Note 5 infra.

3. In *Grand Jury Subpoena, April 18*, Note 1 supra, the Ninth Circuit held that the government had failed to meet the foregone conclusion standard as to its subpoena to Doe (a former salesman for the target corporation) for the production of all documents "relating to the production or sale of * * * DRAM [a computer

---

Witness" and the Resurrection of Boyd, 74 N.Y.U.L.Rev. 1575 (1999), *also cited by Justice Thomas.*

1. Even if the term "witness" in the Fifth Amendment referred to someone who provides testimony, as this Court's recent cases suggest without historical analysis, it may well be that at the time of the founding a person who turned over documents would be described as providing testimony. See Amey v. Long, 9 East. 472, 484, 103 Eng. Rep. 653, 658 (K.B.1808) (referring to documents requested by subpoenas duces tecum as "written . . . testimony"). * * *

memory chip], including * * * handwritten notes, calendars, diaries, daybooks, appointment calendars, or notepads, or any similar documents." The government had established a prior knowledge of specific conversations between Doe and a competitor's employee regarding the pricing of DRAM (indeed, Doe acknowledged those meetings), and (2) the types of materials sought from Doe "were found in the employee records of other DRAM salesmen (including Doe's successor)." The Ninth Circuit reasoned that the government was not required "to have actual knowledge of each and every responsive document," but the "reasonable particularity" standard required more knowledge than it had here. The "government probably could identify * * * phone records corroborating that Doe spoke to his competitors, and records establishing the meetings with certain competitors because Doe made substantial admissions * * * [in his] interview regarding these documents" but the government had "failed to draft the subpoena narrowly" so as to limit it to such documents. Its "argument that a salesman such as Doe will always possess business records describing or memorializing meetings or prices" failed, in light of *Hubbell*, to "establish the reasonably particular knowledge required."

    4. *Hubbell* describes *Fisher* as a case in which the "Government already knew the documents were in the attorney's possession (p. 874)." Since the attorneys there raised the attorney-client privilege in response to the subpoena, they had to acknowledge that they currently possessed the documents. To establish existence and possession as foregone conclusions, must the government show that it not only has knowledge that the documents were created and placed in the possession of the subpoenaed party, but also knowledge that documents remain in the possession of the subpoenaed party on the day of the issuance of the subpoena? If so, can the government rely on the documents being records of a type ordinarily preserved for at least a few years, or must it show that this particular party has a practice of retaining such records? See Mosteller, supra Note 1 (a strict requirement of proof as to current possession would present a substantial "practical problem for prosecutors" as to "readily destructible items, such as specific documents").

    5. Assuming that the government has prior knowledge of the existence and possession of particular types of documents relating to specific events, does the foregone conclusion standard, in light of *Hubbell*, also require that the subpoena's description of the documents permit the subpoenaed party to identify the documents without using the "contents of his own mind" (p. 874)? Must the documents be identified "by reference to such features as letterhead, signature, or location," rather by a relationship that will require the subpoenaed party to utilize "his or her special knowledge of historical fact," CRIMPROC. § 8.13(a)? Consider Richard Uviller, *Fisher Goes On The Quintessential Fishing Expedition and Hubbell is Off the Hook*, 91 J.Crim.L. & Criminology 311 (2001) (such a restriction "goes too far" as "virtually every custodian * * * must use his or her own mind to sort out the files and to cull and organize documents * * * [and] the process of recognition and implicit voucher of authenticity * * * are, of course, the predicates of *Fisher*")

    In *United States v. Ponds*, 454 F.3d 313 (D.C.Cir. 2006), the court concluded that attorney Ponds' possession of documents relating to the payment of legal fees for client Harris was established as a foregone conclusion, and therefore Ponds' production of documents in response to a subpoena demanding all documents "that refer or relate to payments of legal fees by or on behalf of Jerome Harris" was not testimonial, even if Ponds did have to use the "contents of his mind" to identify the documents. The court noted: "The failure of the government to identify each produced document specifically is of no moment. To be consistent with *Fisher*, in which there is no indication that the government know of each document within the set of documents of which it was aware, the 'reasonable particularity' standard cannot demand that the subpoena name every scrap of paper that is produced."

6. *Act-of-production immunity*. Does *Hubbell* render act-of-production immunity as broad in its reach as suggested by Justice Marshall in *Fisher* (p. 863)? Does that immunity invariably prohibit any evidentiary use of the content of the documents produced as long as the immunity was needed because the government lacked previously knowledge of the existence and possession of the documents sufficient to satisfy the foregone conclusion doctrine? *United States v. Ponds*, supra note 5, rejected the contention that an immunized act of production "taints" the contents of produced documents only where that act makes "extensive testimonial representations" through "locating, cataloging, and assembly," as in *Hubbell*. Acknowledging that "the Supreme Court has not defined the precise amount of cognition on the part of an immunized party necessary to render a subpoena response 'testimonial'," the *Ponds* court reasoned that, nonetheless, immunized production here, pursuant to a somewhat more specific subpoena (e.g., for "records of employees of [Pond's] law office"), certainly required sufficient assistance from Ponds to be deemed testimonial. Since the act of production communicated the existence and location of documents previously unknown to the government, the contents of those documents were fruits of that immunized testimony.

7. *Compelled-to-give-evidence*. Does the position for which Justice Thomas urges reconsideration find support in any aspect of *Boyd* other than its precise holding? See Note 1, p. 852. Would the replacement of *Fisher* with a "compelled-to-give-evidence" standard also require reconsideration of the Court's modification of other aspect of *Boyd's* analysis (e.g., the recognition of a "collective entity exception")? Would adoption of that standard require that the Court also reject *Schmerber* (Note 6, p. 855)? Nagareda, fn. l., p. 875, notes that, while the concept of "giving evidence" is hardly limited to documentary evidence, in the identification-procedure cases, a distinction can be drawn where the government is not requiring an affirmative act of production, but simply is "taking the evidence" from the body of the person.

CHAPTER 12

THE SCOPE OF THE
EXCLUSIONARY RULES*

■ ■ ■

SECTION 1. "STANDING" TO OBJECT TO THE ADMISSION OF EVIDENCE (OR "THE EXTENT OF A PARTICULAR DEFENDANT'S RIGHTS UNDER THE FOURTH AMENDMENT")**

A. HISTORICAL BACKGROUND AND OVERVIEW

1. Must the person asserting a Fourth Amendment claim have been the victim of the challenged search or seizure? Long before the Supreme Court authoritatively resolved the issue, the lower courts had developed the doctrine that a defendant lacked "standing" to challenge evidence seized in violation of a third party's constitutional rights. The early basis for this doctrine seems to have been "the joint foundation of the Fourth Amendment and the self-incrimination clause of the Fifth," Comment, 58 Yale L.J. 144, 156 (1948). The rule was also "based on the theory that the evidence is excluded to provide a remedy for a wrong done to the defendant, and that accordingly, if the defendant has not been wronged he is entitled to no remedy." *People v. Martin,* 290 P.2d 855, 857 (Cal.1955) (Traynor, J.).

Six years before *Mapp,* the California Supreme Court's emphasis on the deterrence rationale for the exclusionary rule led it to abolish the "standing" requirement. *People v. Martin,* supra. "Such a limitation," observed the California court, "virtually invites law enforcement officers to violate the rights of third parties and to trade the escape of a criminal whose rights are violated for the conviction of others by the use of the evidence illegally obtained against them." Id.[a]

California's abolition of the "standing" requirement was "enthusiastically endorsed by most commentators," SEARCHSZR § 11.3 (j) (citing thirteen commentators), and when, in *Linkletter v. Walker* (1965), 381 U.S. 618 (1965), the Court seemed to explain and to justify the Fourth Amendment exclusionary rule as "the only effective deterrent to lawless police action," there was reason to think that the High Court, too, might scrap the "standing" requirement. Thus, two years after *Linkletter* and two years before *Alderman* infra, one commentator pointed out that "a system of classification based on 'victimness' provides no deterrence" against "searches that turn up evidence against persons other than

---

* Harmless error is treated elsewhere; see pp. 1558–69.

** *Rakas v. Illinois* (1978) (discussed at p. 884).

a. *In re Lance W.,* 694 P.2d 744 (Cal.1985), held that Proposition 8, an initiative approved by California voters in 1982, had abolished *Martin's* "vicarious exclusionary rule."

the victim" and concluded that "the standing requirement is inconsistent with the presently accepted general deterrence theory of the exclusionary rule." Note, 34 U.Chi.L.Rev. 342, 358 (1967).

However, in ALDERMAN v. UNITED STATES, 394 U.S. 165 (1969), the Court, per White, J., reaffirmed "the established principle [that] suppression of the product of a Fourth Amendment violation can be successfully urged only by those whose rights were violated by the search itself, not by those who are aggrieved solely by the introduction of damaging evidence. Coconspirators and codefendants have been accorded no special standing."[b] The Court was unmoved by the ascendancy of the deterrence rationale: "[We] are not convinced that the additional benefits of extending the exclusionary rule to other defendants would justify further encroachment upon the public interest in prosecuting those accused of crime and having them acquitted or convicted on the basis of all the evidence which exposes the truth."

Concurring in part and dissenting in part, Fortas, J., argued that there was much to be said for abolishing the "standing" requirement: "The Fourth Amendment, unlike the Fifth, is couched in terms of a guarantee that the Government will not engage in unreasonable searches and seizures. It is a general prohibition[,] * * * not merely a privilege accorded to him whose domain has been lawlessly invaded. [It] is an assurance to all that the Government will exercise its formidable powers to arrest and to investigate only subject to the rule of law."[c]

2. Does Alderman represent a genuine effort to strike a balance between the costs of exclusion and the need for deterrence? Daniel Meltzer, *Deterring Constitutional Violations by Law Enforcement Officials: Plaintiffs and Defendants as Private Attorneys General*, 88 Colum.L.Rev. 247, 275 (1988) finds it hard to so understand the Court's standing doctrine: "It is possible, of course, that an effort to strike a desirable balance would result in a standing doctrine limited to those whose rights were violated by the illegal search. But such a result would be extremely surprising, as there are factors more relevant to the need for and benefits of deterrent remedies. These include the seriousness of the harm caused by the search; the likelihood of detection; the perception of the sanction's severity; whether the violation was obvious or intentional; how susceptible to deterrence the search is; and how easily the resulting rules can be administered. A truly deterrence-focused standing doctrine would at least consider such factors, rather than simply assume that the optimal result is reached when only those who were victims of the search are empowered to suppress evidence."

3. The tension between the standing requirement and the exclusionary rule. Consider Joshua Dressler & Alan C. Michaels, *Understanding Criminal Procedure* 329–30 (5th ed. 2010): "Professor Anthony Amsterdam once noted that there are two competing perspectives on the Fourth Amendment. One view, the

---

b. A quarter-century later, in *United States v. Padilla*, 508 U.S. 77 (1993) (per curiam), a unanimous Court quoted this language from *Alderman* in rejecting a so-called "coconspirator exception" to the standing doctrine. Under this exception, developed by the U.S. Court of Appeals for the Ninth Circuit, a coconspirator obtained a legitimate expectation of privacy for Fourth Amendment purposes if she had either a supervisory role in the conspiracy or joint control over the place of property involved in the challenged search or seizure. Such an exception, observed the *Padilla* Court is "not only contrary to the holding of *Alderman*, but at odds with [the expectation of privacy approach taken in *Rakas*, p. 884, that now] govern[s] the analysis of Fourth Amendment search and seizure claims. Participants in a criminal conspiracy may have [exceptions of privacy and property interests], but the conspiracy itself neither adds to or detracts from them."

c. Justice Fortas' view is supported in Donald Doernberg, *"The Right of the People": Reconciling Collective and Individual Interests under the Fourth Amendment*, 58 N.Y.U.L.Rev. 259 (1983); Richard B. Kuhns, *The Concept of Personal Aggrievement in Fourth Amendment Standing Cases*, 65 Iowa L.Rev. 493 (1980).

'atomistic' perspective, is that the Fourth Amendment is 'a collection of protections of atomistic spheres of interest of individual citizens.' That is, the Fourth Amendment protects isolated individuals ('atoms'), in the sense that the amendment 'safeguard[s]' *my* person and *your* house and *her* papers and *his* effects against unreasonable searches and seizures.'[13] The second view, the 'regulatory' perspective, is that the Fourth Amendment functions 'as a regulation of governmental conduct.' In other words, the amendment is intended to safeguard the collective 'people'—as in 'we, the people'—from governmental overreaching.

"As Fourth Amendment jurisprudence has developed, standing—based as it is on the premise that a person may only raise a Fourth Amendment challenge only if she *personally* was a victim of unreasonable police activity—is based on the atomistic philosophy. In contrast, the exclusionary rule is regulatory in nature, in that its purpose [is] to deter police misconduct, in order to safeguard society as a whole. Understood this way, the standing requirement and the exclusionary rule act, at least in part, in opposition to each other. Evidence seized in violation of the Fourth Amendment is excluded at trial in order to deter police misconduct; but, the requirement of standing to raise a Fourth Amendment claim often undercuts this deterrence goal, as it limits the number of people ('atoms') who can bring the misconduct to the attention of the courts so that the exclusionary rule can be applied."

As an example, Professors Dressler and Michaels cite the *Payner* case, discussed in the next Note.

4. ***The use of the federal courts' "supervisory power" to overcome the standing requirement.*** If there has ever been a case that called for the exercise of the federal courts' supervisory power to break out of the standing restriction it was UNITED STATES v. PAYNER, 447 U.S. 727 (1980) (also discussed at p. 35). Nevertheless, a 6–3 majority, per Powell, J., was unmoved.

Payner arose as follows: An IRS investigation into the financial activities of American citizens in the Bahamas focused on a certain Bahamian bank. When an official of that bank visited the United States, IRS agents stole his briefcase for a time, removed hundreds of documents from the briefcase, and photographed them. As a result of this "briefcase caper," Payner—precisely the kind of offender the IRS agents were seeking when they violated the bank official's rights—was convicted of federal income tax violations. Hemmed in by the standing requirement, but outraged by the government's "purposefully" illegal tactics, the federal district court invoked its supervisory power to exclude the tainted evidence.

But the Supreme Court rejected the federal court's "substitution of individual judgment for the controlling decisions of this Court." "The values assigned to the competing interests do not change," pointed out Justice Powell, "because a court has elected to analyze the question under the supervisory power instead of the Fourth Amendment. In either case, the need to deter the underlying conduct and the detrimental impact of excluding the evidence remain precisely the same."[d]

The *Payner* Court cautioned that exclusion of evidence in every case of illegality must be "weighed against the considerable harm that would flow from

---

13. Anthony G. Amsterdam, *Perspectives on the Fourth Amendment*, 58 Minn.L.Rev. 349, 367 (1974).

d. "The Court's decision to engraft the standing limitations of the Fourth Amendment onto the exercise of supervisory powers," protested dissenting Justice Marshall, joined by Brennan and Blackmun, JJ., "appears to render the supervisory powers superfluous. In order to establish that suppression of evidence under the supervisory powers would be proper, the Court would also require Payner to establish a violation of his [constitutional rights]. This approach is totally unfaithful to our prior supervisory power cases [see generally pp. 34–38], which, contrary to the Court's suggestion, are not constitutional cases in disguise."

indiscriminate application of an exclusionary rule" (emphasis added), and that "*unbending application* of the exclusionary sanction * * * would impede unacceptably the truthfinding functions of judge and jury" (emphasis added). But consider Kamisar, *Does (Did) (Should) the Exclusionary Rule Rest on a "Principled Basis" Rather than an "Empirical Proposition"?*, 16 Creighton L.Rev. 565, 638 (1983):

"The relevant question in *Payner* [was] not whether the exclusionary rule should *always* be applied when police illegality is somewhere in the picture, but whether it should *ever* be applied—taking into account the seriousness or flagrancy of the illegality—when the defendant lacks 'standing.' The question was not whether the exclusionary rule should be given 'unbending application,' but whether *the 'standing' requirement* should be. By deciding that even in a case like *Payner* a federal court is *unable* to exercise its supervisory powers to bar the evidence—by holding that 'judicial impotency is *compelled* in the face of such scandalous conduct' [SEARCHSZR § 11.3(h)]—the Court gave us its answer."

5. *"Automatic" standing.* In *Jones v. United States*, 362 U.S. 257 (1960), the defendant was charged with various drug offenses, which permitted conviction largely on proof of unexplained possession of narcotics. The lower court denied standing because defendant had failed either to assert a sufficient interest in the apartment where the search occurred[e] or to allege ownership or possession of the narcotics, although doing so would have "forced" him to allege facts that would tend to convict him. The Supreme Court reversed: The "same element in this prosecution which has caused a dilemma, i.e., that possession both convicts and confers standing, eliminates any necessity for a preliminary showing of an interest in the premises searched or the property seized, which ordinarily is required when standing is challenged." To hold otherwise "would be to permit the Government to have the advantage of contradictory positions as a basis of conviction."

However, the Court subsequently held, in *Simmons v. United States*, 390 U.S. 377 (1968), that testimony given by a defendant in order to establish his "standing" "may not thereafter be used against him at trial on the issue of guilt." Were it otherwise, "a defendant who wishes to establish standing must do so at the risk that the words which he utters may later be used to incriminate him."

On the basis of *Simmons*, the Court subsequently abolished the *Jones* "automatic standing" rule and held that "defendants charged with crimes of possession may only claim the benefits of the exclusionary rule if their own Fourth Amendment rights have in fact been violated." UNITED STATES v. SALVUCCI, 448 U.S. 83 (1980). Observed the Court, per Rehnquist, J.: "The 'dilemma' identified in *Jones* [was] eliminated [by] *Simmons*, [which] not only extends protection against [the] risk of self-incrimination in all of the cases covered by *Jones*, but also grants a form of 'use' immunity to those defendants charged with nonpossessory crimes."

As for the vice of prosecutorial contradiction, the Court stated it need not decide whether that "could alone support a rule countenancing the exclusion of probative evidence on the grounds that someone other than the defendant was denied a Fourth Amendment right," for at least after *Rakas* [p. 884] it is clear that "a prosecutor may simultaneously maintain that a defendant criminally possessed the seized good, but was not subject to a Fourth Amendment deprivation, without legal contradiction." For a "person in legal possession of a good seized during an illegal search has not necessarily been subject to a Fourth Amendment deprivation. * * * We simply decline to use possession of a seized

---

   e. For this aspect of *Jones*, see Note 6 infra.

good as a substitute for a factual finding that the owner of the good has a legitimate expectation of privacy in the area searched."[f]

6. *Residential premises.* It has long been true, and is still so under the current expectation-of-privacy approach discussed in the next subsection, that one with a present possessory interest in the premises searched, e.g., a member of the family regularly residing in a home, may challenge that search even though not present when the search was conducted. As the *Alderman* Court explained: "If the police make an unwarranted search of a house and seize tangible property belonging to third parties [the] home owner may object to its use against him, not because he had any interest in the seized items [but] because they were the fruits of an unauthorized search of his house, which is itself expressly protected by the Fourth Amendment." The *Alderman* majority thus concluded that a person should have standing to challenge the legality of electronically overheard conversations in which he participated "or *conversations occurring on his premises,* whether or not he was present or participated in those conversations" (emphasis added).[g]

In *Jones v. United States,* Note 5, the Court held that "anyone legitimately on premises where a search occurs may challenge its legality." The defendant not only had permission to use the apartment of his friend, but had a key to the apartment with which he admitted himself on the day of the search. He also kept some possessions in the apartment. In the more recent *Rakas* case (below), the Court rejected the *Jones* "legitimately on premises" *formulation*—this phrase "creates too broad a gauge for measurement of Fourth Amendment rights"—but it did not question *the result* in that case. The *Jones* holding "can best be explained," observed the *Rakas* Court, "by the fact that Jones had a legitimate expectation of privacy in the premises he was using [even] though his 'interest' in those premises might not have been a recognized property interest at common law."

Thirty years after *Jones* was decided, the Court held in *Minnesota v. Olson,* 495 U.S. 91 (1990) that defendant's "status as an overnight guest" showed that he had "an expectation of privacy in the home that society is prepared to recognize as reasonable." Thus he had a sufficient interest in the home to challenge the legality of the warrantless entry there.

7. *Business premises.* In *Mancusi v. DeForte,* 392 U.S. 364 (1968), where state police seized records belonging to a union local from an office defendant shared with several other union officials, the Court viewed the "crucial issue" as "whether the area was one in which there was a reasonable expectation of freedom from governmental intrusion." The Court answered in the affirmative. Even though defendant shared an office with others, he "still could reasonably have expected that only those persons and [their guests] would ever enter the office, and that records would not be touched except with their permission or that of union higherups."

"Consistent with *Mancusi,* courts have held that a corporate or individual defendant in possession of the business premises searched has standing, and that an officer or employee of the business enterprise has standing if 'there was a demonstrated nexus between the area searched and the work space of the defendant.' Exclusive use would seem clearly to establish standing, but (as

---

f. See also *Rawlings v. Kentucky,* p. 885.

g. Justice Harlan, joined by Stewart, J., argued that this should not be so when the eavesdropped occurred without physical penetration, for then the absent householder's property interest has not been disturbed, and he can claim no privacy interest in conversations in which he did not participate.

Mancusi teaches) there can be a justified expectation of privacy even absent exclusivity." CRIMPROC § 9.1(c).

B. THE CURRENT APPROACH

Can a Passenger in a Car Other than His Own Challenge the Legality of a Search of that Car?

In RAKAS v. ILLINOIS, 439 U.S. 128 (1978), as Charles H. Whitebread & Christopher Slobogin, *Criminal Procedure* 141 (5th ed. 2008), observe, "the Court explicitly recognized the connection between search and standing analysis. That is, the Court held that standing should depend on whether the police action sought to be challenged is a search (i.e., a violation of legitimate expectations of privacy) *with respect to the person challenging the intrusion*."

In *Rakas*, in the course of affirming a ruling that when the police stopped and searched a car, which petitioners neither owned nor leased but were occupying as passengers, the police violated none of *their* rights,[a] Rehnquist, J., speaking for a 5–4 majority, asked "whether it serves any useful analytical purpose to consider [the principle that Fourth Amendment rights are personal rights] a matter of standing, distinct from the merits of a defendant's Fourth Amendment claim." He answered that inquiry in the negative: "[W]e think the better analysis forthrightly focuses on the extent of a particular defendant's rights under the Fourth Amendment, rather than on any theoretically separate, but invariably intertwined concept of standing. * * * Analyzed in these terms, the question is whether the challenged search or seizure violated the Fourth Amendment rights of a criminal defendant who seeks to exclude the evidence obtained during it. That inquiry in turn requires a determination of whether the disputed search and seizure has infringed an interest of the defendant which the Fourth Amendment was designed to protect."

---

a. Suspecting that the vehicle might have been the "getaway car" in a recent robbery, police stopped the car in which petitioners were riding. After the occupants of the car (petitioners and two female companions) were ordered out, the police searched the interior of the vehicle and discovered a sawed-off rifle under the front passenger seat and a box of rifle shells in the glove compartment (which had been locked). Because petitioners did not assert ownership of the rifle or the shells and because they conceded that they did not own the automobile, but were simply passengers (the owner of the vehicle had been driving it at the time of the search), the trial court ruled that they lacked "standing" to contest the search and seizure. Thus the judge denied their motions to suppress the evidence, without ever reaching the question whether the police conduct involved was lawful.

Applying its new approach to what had traditionally been called "standing" problems, the U.S. Supreme Court agreed that "petitioners' claims must fail": "They asserted neither a property nor a possessory interest in the automobile, nor an interest in the property seized. And [the] fact that they were "legitimately on [the] premises" in the sense that they were in the car with the permission of its owner is not determinative of whether they had a legitimate expectation of privacy in the particular areas of the automobile searched. It is unnecessary for us to decide here whether the same expectations of privacy are warranted in a car as would be justified in a dwelling place in analogous circumstances. [But] here petitioners' claim is one which would fail even in an analogous situation in a dwelling place, since they made no showing that they had any legitimate expectation of privacy in the glove compartment or area under the seat of the car in which they were merely passengers. Like the trunk of an automobile, these are areas in which a passenger *qua* passenger simply would not normally have a legitimate expectation of privacy."

"[*Jones v. United States* (1960)] involved significantly different factual circumstances. Jones not only had permission to use the apartment of his friend, but had a key to the apartment with which he admitted himself on the day of the search and kept possessions in the apartment. Except with respect to his friend, Jones had complete dominion and control over the apartment and could exclude others from it. [Jones] could legitimately expect privacy in the areas which were the subject of the search and seizure [he] sought to contest. No such showing was made by these petitioners with respect to those portions of the automobile which were searched and from which incriminating evidence was seized."

Is there still something to be said for treating "standing" and the issue whether a Fourth Amendment violation has occurred at all as distinct inquiries? Consider SEARCHSZR, § 11.3 at 121: "[It] is important to keep in mind that the question traditionally labeled as standing (did the police intrude upon *this defendant's* justified expectation of privacy?) is not identical to, for example, the question of whether any Fourth Amendment search has occurred (did the police intrude upon *anyone's* justified expectation of privacy?), and that therefore the [issues traditionally called "standing" issues] are still rather discrete and deserving of separate attention, no matter what label is put on them."[b]

In *Rakas*, it should be noted, Justice Rehnquist could "think of no decided cases of this Court that would have come out differently had we concluded, as we do now, that [the standing requirement] is more properly subsumed under substantive Fourth Amendment doctrine." He also told us that although he believed that the traditional standing requirement "belongs more properly under the heading of substantive Fourth Amendment doctrine," he was "under no illusion that by dispensing with the rubric of standing * * * we have rendered any simpler the determination of whether the proponent of a motion to suppress is entitled to contest the legality of a search and seizure."

In *Rakas*, as pointed out earlier, neither passenger asserted ownership in the items taken from the car. The Court seemed to imply that if the passengers had done so, they could have challenged the police conduct. But RAWLINGS v. KENTUCKY, 448 U.S. 98 (1980), rejected the argument that one could challenge a search of an area (in this instance another person's purse) simply because he claimed ownership of the property seized during the search. The case arose as follows:

On the day of the challenged police conduct, petitioner and Ms. Cox, who had been his companion for several days, were visitors at the house of one Marquess. Shortly before six police officers arrived, armed with a warrant for the arrest of Marquess, petitioner, who had been carrying a large quantity of illegal drugs, dumped them into the purse of Ms. Cox. Although there was a dispute about their discussion, petitioner testified that he had asked Ms. Cox "if she would carry this for me, and she said 'yes.' "(Although unclear, one plausible inference is that petitioner had put the contraband in the purse because he had seen police approaching the house.)

While unsuccessfully searching for Marquess in his house, the police came upon evidence of drug violations. Two of the officers then left to obtain a warrant to search the house, while the remaining officers detained the occupants, including petitioner and Cox, allowing them to leave only if they consented to a body search. Upon returning with the search warrant some 45 minutes later, the officers ordered Cox to empty her purse onto a table. As she poured out the contents of her purse, Cox told petitioner "to take what was his" and petitioner immediately claimed ownership of the drugs. Considering the "totality of the circumstances," including petitioner's admission at the suppression hearing that he did not believe that Cox's purse would be free from governmental intrusion, the state supreme court concluded that petitioner had no "standing" because he had failed to make "a sufficient showing that his legitimate or reasonable expectations of privacy were violated by the search of the purse." A 7–2 majority, again per Rehnquist, J., found no reason to overturn that conclusion:

"[1] At the time petitioner dumped thousands of dollars worth of illegal drugs into Cox's purse, he had known her only a few days. [2] According to Cox's uncontested testimony, petitioner had never sought or received access to her purse

---

b. See also Joshua Dressler & Alan C. Michaels, *Understanding Criminal Procedure* 328–29 (5th ed. 2010).

prior to that sudden bailment. [3] Nor did petitioner have any right to exclude other persons access to Cox's purse. [4] In fact, [a third person] a longtime acquaintance and frequent companion of Cox's had free access to her purse. [5] [Moreover,] even assuming that petitioner's version of the bailment is correct [,the] precipitous nature of the transaction hardly supports a reasonable inference that petitioner took normal precautions to maintain his privacy. [6] [Finally] the record also contains a frank admission by petitioner that he had no subjective expectation that Cox's purse would remain free from governmental intrusion * * * c

"Petitioner contends nevertheless that, because he claimed ownership of the drugs in Cox's purse, he should be entitled to challenge the search regardless of his expectation of privacy. We disagree. While petitioner's ownership of the drugs is undoubtedly one fact to be considered in this case, *Rakas* emphatically rejected the notion that 'arcane' concepts of property law ought to control the ability to claim the protections of the Fourth Amendment. Had petitioner placed his drugs in plain view, he would still have owned them, but he could not claim any

---

c. According to SEARCHSZR § 11.3(c) at 154, none of the points made by Justice Rehnquist "can withstand close scrutiny." He then responds to Justice Rehnquist's points as follows (id. At 154–58):

(1) The fact that Rawlings had only known Ms. Cox for a few days "hardly establishes the absence of a justified expectation of privacy."

(2) Rawlings' expectation of privacy was not diminished because this was the first time he had used Ms. Cox's purse. Otherwise, "we would be left with the curious notion that a first-time bailment [would] not carry with it a justified expectation that one's goods are secure in the hands of the bailee."

As for (3), "while a 'right to exclude' may be an easy way to establish the requisite legitimate expectation of privacy, it hardly follows that it is the *only* way * * *. Reliance on this 'right to exclude' factor is also inconsistent with the later [holding] of *Minnesota v. Olson* (1990) [p. ___], [that] an overnight guest had [a legitimate expectation of privacy in the premises] without regard to whether the guest 'had complete dominion and control over the apartment and could exclude others from it.' "

(4) The fact that a third party had access to Ms Cox's purse should not matter. The issue was not whether Rawlings "reasonably believed he was free from intrusion by *anyone*," but " 'whether the area [searched] was one in which there was a reasonable expectation of privacy from *governmental* intrusion.' "

As for (5), the argument that Rawlings did not take adequate precautions to maintain his privacy, "a container does not have to be locked to give rise to that especially strong expectation of privacy which makes the warrant clause of the Fourth Amendment applicable and thus it can hardly be said that an unlocked container carries with it no justified privacy expectation at all." Furthermore, if it can be said that Rawlings did not take adequate precautions in putting his effects into a closed container with the owner's consent, "then surely Ms. Cox likewise had no justified expectation of privacy in the same purse because she did not better safeguard her effects in that purse."

(6) The "frank admission" by Rawlings that "he had no subjective expectation that Cox's purse would remain free from governmental intrusion" turns out to be a "No, sir" answer when asked at the suppression hearing whether he thought the purse would be free from police intrusion. Rawlings was being asked "what he thought was going to happen *after* the police were on the scene and *after* they told him and others that a warrant was being sought and they could leave prior to the warrant execution only by submitting to a personal search. [But] if one can be deprived of Fourth Amendment standing by being informed in advance by the police of the intrusion they intend to make, [then] Rawlings likewise had no standing with respect to his own person, which he also expected would be intruded upon by the police."

According to Professor LaFave, id., "*Rawlings* is best viewed as an unusual case in which the result is more attributable to certain undercurrents in the case than to the reasoning offered by the Court." LaFave notes at this point that although none of the lower courts specifically found that Ms. Cox had not consented to the bailment, "the trial court was somewhat 'skeptical about [Rawlings'] version of events' and seemed to think that [he] probably saw the police approaching the premises and then thrust the controlled substances onto Cox over her objection. The thrust of the majority opinion in *Rawlings* strongly suggests the Court was influenced by an assumption that this latter version was correct."

legitimate expectation of privacy. Prior to *Rakas*, petitioner might have been given 'standing' in such a case to challenge a 'search' that netted those drugs but probably would have lost his claim on the merits. After *Rakas*, the two inquiries merge into one: whether governmental officials violated any legitimate expectation of privacy held by petitioner."

Blackmun, J., joined the Court's opinion, but also wrote separately. He agreed with the majority that determining (1) whether the defendant has a "legitimate expectation of privacy" that has been invaded by the police and (2) whether "applicable cause and warrant requirements have been properly observed" " 'merge into one' in the sense that both are to be addressed under the principles of Fourth Amendment analysis developed in *Katz* and its progeny." But he did not read *Rawlings*, or *Rakas*, "as holding that it is improper for lower courts to treat these inquiries as distinct components of a Fourth Amendment claim." "Indeed," he added, "I am convinced that it would invite confusion to hold otherwise. It remains possible for a defendant to prove that his legitimate interest of privacy was invaded, and yet fail to prove that the police acted illegally in doing so. And it is equally possible for a defendant to prove that the police acted illegally, and yet fail to prove that his own privacy interest was affected."

Can a Passenger in a Car Other than Her Own Challenge the Legality of a Police Stop of that Car?

In BRENDLIN v. CALIFORNIA, 127 S.Ct. 2400 (2007), a unanimous Court per Souter, J., held that when a police officer makes a traffic stop he "seizes" a passenger as well as the driver "within the meaning of the Fourth Amendment" and thus a passenger, as well as the driver, may challenge the constitutionality of the stop.

"After two deputy sheriffs stopped a car to check its registration without any grounds to believe the vehicle was being operated unlawfully, one deputy recognized defendant, a passenger in the car, and verified that he was a parole violator. Defendant was ordered out of the car, arrested and searched. The deputies found methamphetamine paraphernalia on his person. The deputies then searched the car and found more evidence of methamphetamine use. Charged with possession and manufacture of that substance, defendant sought to exclude the evidence, maintaining that the traffic stop was an unlawful seizure of his person and that the items found on him and in the car were the fruits of the unlawful seizure. Even though it recognized that the officers lacked any grounds for stopping the car, the Supreme Court of California held the evidence admissible, reasoning that defendant had not been "seized" by the traffic stop because the driver of the car was its exclusive target. The state court also maintained that once the police pull a car off the road, any passenger "would feel free to depart or otherwise to conduct his or her affairs as though the police were not present." The U.S. Supreme Court disagreed:

"[Defendant] did not assert that his Fourth Amendment rights were violated by the search of [the] vehicle, cf. *Rakas v. Illinois*, but claimed only that the traffic stop was an unlawful seizure of his person. [A] person is seized by the police and thus entitled to challenge the government's action [when] the officer, 'by means of physical force or show of authority,' terminates or restrains his freedom of movement. *Florida v. Bostick*, 501 U.S. 429 (1991), '*through means intentionally applied*,' *Brower v. County of Inyo*, 489 U.S. 593, 597 (1989) (emphasis in the original). Thus, an 'unintended person [may be] the object of the detention,' so long as the detention is 'willful' and not merely the consequence of 'an unknowing act.' Id. Cf. *Sacremento v. Lewis* [p. 31].

"When the actions of the police do not show an unambiguous intent to restrain or when an individual's submission to a show of governmental authority takes the form of passive acquiescence, there needs to be some test for telling when a seizure occurs in response to authority and when it does not. The test was devised by Justice Stewart in *United States v. Mendenhall* [446 U.S. 544 (1980)] ([a] seizure occurs if 'in view of all of the circumstances surrounding the incident, a reasonable person would have believed that he were not free to leave'). Later on, the Court adopted [this test], but added that when a person 'has no desire to leave' for reasons unrelated to the police presence, the 'coercive effect of the encounter' can be measured better by asking whether 'a reasonable person would feel free to decline the officers' requests or otherwise terminate the encounter,'" *Florida v. Bostick.* * * *

"We resolve the question [whether defendant was 'seized'] by asking whether a reasonable person in [his] position when the car stopped would have believed himself free to 'terminate the encounter' between the police and himself. We think [that] any reasonable passenger would have understood [that] no one in the car was free to depart without police permission. [An] officer who orders one particular car to pull over acts with an implicit claim of right based on fault of some sort, and a sensible person would not expect a police officer to allow people to come and go freely from the physical focal point of an investigation into faulty behavior or wrongdoing. [Our] conclusion comports with the views of all nine Federal Courts of Appeals, and nearly every state court, to have ruled on the question.

"[The] State Supreme Court reasoned that [the defendant] was not seized by the stop because [the deputy] only intended to investigate [the driver] and did not direct a show of authority toward [defendant]. [But applying] the objective *Mendenhall* test of what a reasonable passenger would understand [leads] to the intuitive conclusion that all the occupants were subject to like control by the successful display of authority. The State Supreme Court's approach, on the contrary, shifts the issue from the intent of the police as objectively manifested to the motive of the police for taking the intentional action to stop the car, and we have repeatedly rejected attempts to introduce this kind of subjectivity into Fourth Amendment analysis.

"[The] Supreme Court of California assumed that [the defendant] 'as the passenger, had no ability to submit to the deputy's show of authority' because only the driver was in control of the moving vehicle. But what may amount to submission depends on what a person was doing before the show of authority. [Here, the defendant] had no effective way to signal submission while the car was still moving on the roadway, but once it came to a stop he could, and apparently did, submit by staying inside. * * *

"Holding that the passenger in a private car is not (without more) seized in a traffic stop would invite police officers to stop cars with passengers regardless of probable cause or reasonable suspicion of anything illegal. The fact that evidence uncovered as a result of an arbitrary traffic stop would still be admissible against any passengers would be a powerful incentive to run the kind of 'roving patrols' that would still violate the driver's Fourth Amendment right. [The defendant] was seized from the moment [the] car came to a halt on the side of the road, and it was error to deny his suppression motion on the ground that seizure occurred only at the formal arrest."

Under What Circumstances Can a Guest or Visitor in Another Person's Home Challenge the Legality of a Search of that Home?

MINNESOTA v. CARTER

525 U.S. 83, 119 S.Ct. 469, 142 L.Ed.2d, 373 (1998).

CHIEF JUSTICE REHNQUIST delivered the opinion of the Court.

[A confidential informant told a Minnesota police officer (Thielen) that he had walked by the window of a ground-floor apartment and had seen people putting a white powder into bags. After looking in the same window through a gap in the closed blind and observing three men engaged in the bagging operation (respondents Carter and Johns and the apartment's lessee, Ms. Thompson), the officer notified headquarters, which began preparing affidavits for a search warrant. When respondents left the building in a previously identified vehicle, they were stopped and arrested. A later police search of the vehicle turned up cocaine. After seizing the vehicle, the police returned to the apartment and arrested the occupant, Ms. Thompson. A search of the apartment pursuant to a warrant revealed more evidence of cocaine.]

[The police later learned that Carter and Johns had never been in Thompson's apartment before and were only in it for 2 ½ hours, and that they had come to the apartment for the sole purpose of packaging the cocaine. In return for the use of the apartment, Carter and Johns had given Thompson one-eighth of an ounce of the cocaine.]

[Respondents were convicted of state drug offenses. The trial court held that (a) since they were only temporary out-of-state visitors, respondents could not challenge the legality of the government intrusion into Ms. Thompson's apartment; (b) Officer Thielen's observations through a gap in the closed blind was not a "search" within the meaning of the Fourth Amendment. The state supreme court reversed, holding that respondents did have "standing" because they had a " 'legitimate expectation of privacy in the invaded place' "(quoting *Rakas*). The court went on to hold that the officer's observation constituted an unreasonable "search" of the apartment. The U.S. Supreme Court reversed without reaching the question whether the officer's observation was a "search."]

The Minnesota courts analyzed whether respondents had a legitimate expectation of privacy under the rubric of "standing" doctrine, an analysis which this Court expressly rejected 20 years ago in *Rakas*. * * * Central to our analysis [then] was the idea that in determining whether a defendant is able to show the violation of his (and not someone else's) Fourth Amendment rights, the "definition of those rights is more properly placed within the purview of substantive Fourth Amendment law than within that of standing."

[The Fourth] Amendment protects persons against unreasonable searches of "their persons [and] houses" and thus indicates that the Fourth Amendment is a personal right that must be invoked by an individual. See *Katz.* ("[T]he Fourth Amendment protects people, not places"). But the extent to which the Fourth Amendment protects people may depend upon where those people are. We have held that "capacity to claim the protection of the Fourth Amendment depends [upon] whether the person who claims the protection of the Amendment has a legitimate expectation of privacy in the invaded place." *Rakas.*

The text of the Amendment suggests that its protections extend only to people in "their" houses. But we have held that in some circumstances a person may have a legitimate expectation of privacy in the house of someone else. In *Minnesota v. Olson* [p. 883], for example, we decided that an overnight guest in a house had the sort of expectation of privacy that the Fourth Amendment protects.

[Respondents] here were obviously not overnight guests, but were essentially present for a business transaction and were only in the home a matter of hours. There is no suggestion that they had a previous relationship with Thompson, or that there was any other purpose to their visit. Nor was there anything similar to the overnight guest relationship in *Olson* to suggest a degree of acceptance into the household.[1] * * *.

Property used for commercial purposes is treated differently for Fourth Amendment purposes than residential property. [And] while it was a "home" in which respondents were present, it was not their home. Similarly, the Court has held that in some circumstances a worker can claim Fourth Amendment protection over his own workplace. See, *e.g. O'Connor v. Ortega*, 480 U.S. 709 (1987). But there is no indication that respondents in this case had nearly as significant a connection to Thompson's apartment as the worker in *O'Connor* had to his own private office.

If we regard the overnight guest in *Minnesota v. Olson* as typifying those who may claim the protection of the Fourth Amendment in the home of another, and one merely "legitimately on the premises" as typifying those who may not do so, the present case is obviously somewhere in between. But the purely commercial nature of the transaction engaged in here, the relatively short period of time on the premises, and the lack of any previous connection between respondents and the householder, all lead us to conclude that respondents' situation is closer to that of one simply permitted on the premises. We therefore hold that any search which may have occurred did not violate their Fourth Amendment rights. [Thus] we need not decide whether the police officer's observation constituted a "search." * * *

JUSTICE SCALIA, with whom JUSTICE THOMAS joins, concurring.

I join the opinion of the Court because I believe it accurately applies our recent case law, including *Minnesota v. Olson*. I write separately to express my view that that case law—like the submissions of the parties in this case—gives short shrift to the text of the Fourth Amendment, and to the well and long understood meaning of that text. Specifically, it leaps to apply the fuzzy standard of "legitimate expectation of privacy"—a consideration that is often relevant to whether a search or seizure covered by the Fourth Amendment is "unreasonable"—to the threshold question whether a search or seizure covered by the Fourth Amendment *has occurred*. If that latter question is addressed first and analyzed under the text of the Constitution as traditionally understood, the present case is not remotely difficult.

[The] obvious meaning of the [Fourth Amendment] is that *each* person has the right to be secure against unreasonable searches and seizures in *his own* person, house, papers, and effects. The Founding-era materials that I have examined confirm that this was the understood meaning. [Justice Scalia then discusses various historical materials.]

[Thus,] in deciding the question presented today we write upon a slate that is far from clean. The text of the Fourth Amendment, the common-law background against which it was adopted, and the understandings consistently displayed after its adoption make the answer clear. * * * We went to the absolute limit of what

---

1. Justice Ginsburg's dissent would render the operative language in *Minnesota v. Olson*, 495 U.S. 91 (1990), almost entirely superfluous. There, we explained the justification for extending Fourth Amendment protection to the overnight visitor: "Staying overnight in another's home is a longstanding social custom that serves functions recognized as valuable by society ... We are at our most vulnerable when we are asleep because we cannot monitor our own safety or the security of our belongings." If any short-term business visit by a stranger entitles the visitor to share the Fourth Amendment protection of the lease holder's home, the Court's explanation of its holding in *Olson* was quite unnecessary.

text and tradition permit in *Minnesota v. Olson*, when we protected a mere overnight guest against an unreasonable search of his hosts' apartment. But whereas it is plausible to regard a person's overnight lodging as at least his "temporary" residence, it is entirely impossible to give that characterization to an apartment that he uses to package cocaine.

[The] dissent believes that "[o]ur obligation to produce coherent results" requires that we ignore this clear text and four-century-old tradition, and apply instead the notoriously unhelpful test adopted in a "benchmar[k]" decision that is 31 years old, citing *Katz*. In my view, the only thing the past three decades have established about the *Katz* test (which has come to mean the test enunciated by Justice Harlan's separate concurrence in *Katz*) is that, unsurprisingly, those "actual (subjective) expectation[s] of privacy" that society is prepared to recognize as "reasonable" "bear an uncanny resemblance to those expectations of privacy that this Court considers reasonable. When that self-indulgent test is employed (as the dissent would employ it here) to determine whether a "search or seizure" within the meaning of the Constitution has *occurred* (as opposed to whether that "search or seizure" is an "unreasonable" one), it has no plausible foundation in the text of the Fourth Amendment. That provision did not guarantee some generalized "right of privacy" and leave it to this Court to determine which particular manifestations of the value of privacy "society is prepared to recognize as 'reasonable.' "

[The] dissent may be correct that a person invited into someone else's house to engage in a common business (even common monkey-business, so to speak) *ought* to be protected against government searches of the room in which that business is conducted; and that persons invited in to deliver milk or pizza (whom the dissent dismisses as "classroom hypotheticals," as opposed, presumably, to flesh-and-blood hypotheticals) ought *not* to be protected against government searches of the rooms that they occupy. I am not sure of the answer to those policy questions. But I am sure that the answer is not remotely contained in the Constitution, which means that it is left—as *many*, indeed *most*, important questions are left—to the judgment of state and federal legislators. * * *

Justice Kennedy, concurring.

I join the Court's opinion, for its reasoning is consistent with my view that almost all social guests have a legitimate expectation of privacy, and hence protection against unreasonable searches, in their host's home.

[The] homeowner's right to privacy is not an issue in this case. The Court does not reach the question whether the officer's unaided observations of Thompson's apartment constituted a search. If there was in fact a search, however, then Thompson had the right to object to the unlawful police surveillance of her apartment and the right to suppress any evidence disclosed by the search. [Our] cases establish, however, that respondents have no independent privacy right, the violation of which results in exclusion of evidence against them, unless they can establish a meaningful connection to Thompson's apartment.

[In] this case respondents have established nothing more than a fleeting and insubstantial connection with Thompson's home. For all that appears in the record, respondents used Thompson's house simply as a convenient processing station, their purpose involving nothing more than the mechanical act of chopping and packing a substance for distribution. * * *

We cannot remain faithful to the underlying principle in *Rakas* without reversing in this case, and I am not persuaded that we need depart from it to protect the homeowner's own privacy interests. * * *

JUSTICE GINSBURG, with whom JUSTICE STEVENS and JUSTICE SOUTER join, dissenting.

The Court's decision undermines not only the security of short-term guests, but also the security of the home resident herself. In my view, when a homeowner or lessor personally invites a guest into her home to share in a common endeavor, whether it be for conversation, to engage in leisure activities, or for business purposes licit or illicit, that guest should share his host's shelter against unreasonable searches and seizures.

I do not here propose restoration of the "legitimately on the premises" criterion stated in *Jones*, for the Court rejected that formulation in *Rakas* * * *. First, the disposition I would reach in this case responds to the unique importance of the home—the most essential bastion of privacy recognized by the law. See *United States v. Karo*, [p. 280]. Second, even within the home itself, the position to which I would adhere would not permit "a casual visitor who has never seen, or been permitted to visit, the basement of another's house to object to a search of the basement if the visitor happened to be in the kitchen of the house at the time of the search." *Rakas*. Further, I would here decide only the case of the homeowner who chooses to share the privacy of her home and her company with a guest, and would not reach classroom hypotheticals like the milkman or pizza deliverer.

[A] home dweller places her own privacy at risk, the Court's approach indicates, when she opens her home to others, uncertain whether the duration of their stay, their purpose, and their "acceptance into the household" will earn protection. * * * Human frailty suggests that today's decision will tempt police to pry into private dwellings without warrant, to find evidence incriminating guests who do not rest there through the night. * * * *Rakas* tolerates that temptation with respect to automobile searches. See Gerald D. Ashdown, *The Fourth Amendment and the "Legitimate Expectation of Privacy,"* 34 Vand.L.Rev. 1289, 1321 (1981). * * * I see no impelling reason to extend this risk into the home.

Our leading decision in *Katz* is key to my view of this case. There, we ruled that the Government violated the petitioner's Fourth Amendment rights when it electronically recorded him transmitting wagering information while he was inside a public telephone booth. We were mindful that "the Fourth Amendment protects people, not places," and held that this electronic monitoring of a business call "violated the privacy upon which [the caller] justifiably relied while using the telephone booth." Our obligation to produce coherent results in this often visited area of the law requires us to inform our current expositions by benchmarks already established.

[The] Court's decision in this case veers sharply from the path marked in *Katz*.[2] I do not agree that we have a more reasonable expectation of privacy when we place a business call to a person's home from a public telephone booth on the side of the street, see *Katz*, than when we actually enter that person's premises to engage in a common endeavor. * * * *[a]

---

2. In his concurring opinion, Justice Kennedy maintains that respondents here lacked "an expectation of privacy that society recognizes as reasonable" because they "established nothing more than a fleeting and insubstantial connection" with the host's home. As the Minnesota Supreme Court reported, however, the stipulated facts showed that respondents were inside the apartment with the host's permission, remained inside for at least 2 1/2 hours, and, during that time, engaged in concert with the host in a collaborative venture. These stipulated facts [demonstrate] that the host intended to share her privacy with respondents, and that respondents, therefore, had entered into the homeland of Fourth Amendment protection. * * *

a. Although Justice Breyer concurred in the judgment because he did not believe that Officer Thielen's observation of the apartment, "made from a public area outside the curtilage,"

NOTE ON CARTER

Consider Craig Bradley, *The Fourth Amendment's Iron Triangle: Standing, Consent and Searchability*, Trial, Aug. 1999, p. 75: "Who may be searched? Who may consent to a search? Who has standing to protest a search? These three, seemingly unrelated, questions frequently arise in criminal cases. But though these issues have always appeared to the Supreme Court to be unconnected, consideration of two recent cases, *Wyoming v. Houghton* [p. 393] and *Minnesota v. Carter*, has led me to the conclusion that these three questions hinge on exactly the same issue: *What is the subject's interest in or connection to the place to be searched?* Further, they should all have the same answer. That is, if a person has authority to consent to a search, he also has standing to protest it, and is searchable if found at the scene of the search, and vice versa. Recognition that the answer to these questions is the same means that once the Court has put one side of this equilateral triangle into position, the position of the other two sides has been resolved as well. Moreover, it may cause decision makers to think more carefully about finding no standing for passengers in a car, for example, if they realize that will lead to a reduction in authority of such passengers to consent to a search and their 'searchability' by virtue of their presence in that car."

SECTION 2. THE "FRUIT OF THE POISONOUS TREE"

A. HISTORICAL BACKGROUND AND OVERVIEW

"In the simplest of exclusionary rule cases," observes CRIMPROC, § 9.3(a), "the challenged evidence is quite clearly 'direct' or 'primary' in its relationship to the prior arrest, search, interrogation [or lineup] [e.g., a confession made in response to impermissible interrogation or physical evidence obtained by an illegal search]." Not infrequently, however, points out CRIMPROC, "challenged evidence is 'secondary' or 'derivative' in character. This occurs when, for example, a confession is obtained after an illegal arrest[a] [or] physical evidence is located after an illegally obtained confession.[b] [In] these situations, it is necessary to determine whether the derivative evidence is 'tainted' by the prior constitutional or other violation. To use the phrase coined by Justice Frankfurter, it must be decided whether that evidence is 'the fruit of the poisonous tree.' "[c]

1. *Genesis of the rule; the doctrine of "attenuation."* (a) The genesis of the "taint" or "fruit of the poisonous tree" doctrine, as it came to be called, appears in *Silverthorne Lumber Co. v. United States*, 251 U.S. 385 (1920), where, in holding that the government could not use information obtained during an illegal search to subpoena the very documents illegally viewed, the Court, per Holmes, J., pointed out: "The essence of a provision forbidding the acquisition of evidence in a certain way is that not merely evidence so acquired shall not be used before the Court but that it shall not be used at all. Of course this does not mean that the facts thus obtained become sacred and inaccessible. If knowledge of them

---

constituted an "unreasonable search," he "agree[d] with Justice Ginsburg that respondents can claim the Fourth Amendment's protection."

a. See, e.g., *Brown v. Illinois*, p. 895.

b. See, e.g., *New York v. Quarles*, p. 621.

c. *Nardone v. United States*, Note 1(b).

is gained from an independent source they may be proved like any others, but the knowledge gained by the Government's own wrong cannot be used by it in the way proposed."

Did *Silverthorne* mean that illegally seized *evidence* may never be used by the government although the *facts* revealed by that evidence may be obtained from an independent source? See Robert M. Pitler, *"The Fruit of the Poisonous Tree" Revisited and Shepardized,* 56 Calif.L.Rev. 579, 589 (1968).

(b) In *Nardone v. United States,* 308 U.S. 338 (1939), which first used the phrase "fruit of the poisonous tree," the Court, per Frankfurter, J., refused to permit the prosecution to avoid an inquiry into its use of information gained by illegal wiretapping, observing that "to forbid the direct use of methods [but] to put no curb on their full indirect use would only invite the very methods deemed 'inconsistent with ethical standards and destructive of personal liberty.' "[a] The case also established the "attenuation" doctrine, being the first to authoritatively recognize that even where the challenged evidence did not have an "independent source" it might still be admissible: "Sophisticated argument may prove a causal connection between information obtained through illicit wire-tapping and the Government's proof. As a matter of good sense, however, such connection may have become so attenuated as to dissipate the taint."

2. *Verbal evidence as the "fruit" of illegal search and seizure.* In WONG SUN v. UNITED STATES, 371 U.S. 471 (1963) (other aspects of which are discussed at pp. 206, 655), six federal narcotics agents illegally broke into Toy's laundry, chased him into the living quarters at the back of his shop, where Toy's wife and child were sleeping, and handcuffed him. Toy then told the agents that Yee had been selling narcotics. The agents immediately went to Yee, who surrendered heroin to them and implicated Toy and a third party, Wong Sun. A 5–4 majority, per Brennan, J., held that both Toy's declarations, upon being handcuffed in his bedroom, *and* "the narcotics taken from Yee, to which [Toy's] declarations led the police" had to be excluded as the "fruits" of the agents' unlawful entry into Toy's bedroom and the "bedroom arrest."

The Court recognized that "traditionally" the exclusionary rule had barred only "physical, tangible materials," but concluded that "verbal evidence which derives so immediately from an unlawful entry and an unauthorized arrest [as here] is no less the 'fruit' of official illegality than the more common tangible fruits of the unwarranted intrusion."[b] Not "all evidence is 'fruit of the poisonous tree' simply because it would not have come to light but for the illegal actions of the police. Rather, the more apt question in such a case is 'whether, granting establishment of the primary illegality [the evidence] has been come at by exploitation of that illegality or instead by means sufficiently distinguishable to be purged of the primary taint.' J. Maguire, *Evidence of Guilt* 221 (1959). We think it clear that the narcotics [taken from Yee] were 'come at by the exploitation of that illegality [the lawless search and seizure of Toy]' and hence that they may not be used against Toy."

On the other hand, although Wong Sun had also been unlawfully arrested, his confession was not the "fruit" of his illegal arrest. Since he had been released on his own recognizance after a lawful arraignment and had returned voluntarily

---

a. But cf. *United States v. Calandra,* p. 247, holding that a witness may not refuse to answer grand jury questions on the ground that they are based on evidence obtained from him in an earlier unlawful search.

b. The dissenters, Clark, J., joined by Harlan, Stewart and White, JJ., did not challenge the manner in which the Court applied the "fruits" doctrine, but maintained that Toy's arrest was lawful and thus provided "no 'poisonous tree' whose fruits we must evaluate."

several days later to make the statement, "the connection between [Wong Sun's] arrest and [his] statement had 'become so attenuated as to dissipate the taint.' "

NOTES AND QUESTIONS

(a) *The relevant question.* Does the *Wong Sun* Court's talk of "purging the primary taint" obfuscate the relevant question—whether the admission of the secondary evidence will significantly encourage police misconduct in the future? See Pitler, supra, at 588–89; Note, 115 U.Pa.L.Rev. 1136, 1147 (1967).

(b) *"Purging the taint" of Fourth Amendment violations.* Are there events short of release from custody (which occurred in *Wong Sun*) which operate to "purge the taint" of an illegal arrest or search? Can the mere passage of time suffice? Or would such a rule only "postpone the testing" of the fruit but "not diminish its temptation"? See *Collins v. Beto,* 348 F.2d 823, 828 (5th Cir.1965). Would *Miranda* warnings purge the taint of an illegal arrest? See *Brown v. Illinois,* below.

3. *"Independent source"; "inevitable discovery."* The *Wong Sun* Court quoted from *Silverthorne,* supra, the proposition that the exclusionary rule has no application when "the Government learned of the evidence 'from an independent source.' " This means that if not even a "but for" test can be satisfied, the challenged evidence is not a fruit of the prior violation—a violation of a person's rights should not put him beyond the law's reach if his guilt can be established by evidence unconnected with or "untainted" by the violation.

A variation of the "independent source" exception is the "inevitable discovery" or "hypothetical independent source" rule, a doctrine long utilized by many lower courts and recently accepted by the U.S. Supreme Court.[a] This doctrine differs from the "independent source" exception in that the question is not whether the police *actually* acquired certain evidence by reliance upon an untainted source, but whether evidence in fact obtained illegally would inevitably or eventually or probably have been discovered lawfully.

The doctrine is most palatable, and has been most frequently applied, when the police misconduct occurred "while an investigation was already in progress and resulted in the discovery of evidence that would have eventually have been obtained through routine police investigatory procedure. The illegalities in such cases, therefore, had the effect of simply accelerating the discovery." Note, 74 Colum.L.Rev. 88, 90 (1974).

Because mechanical application of the "inevitable discovery" doctrine would seem to encourage unconstitutional shortcuts, and one purpose of the exclusionary rule is to discourage such shortcuts, it has been argued that the doctrine should be permitted only when the police have not acted in "bad faith" to accelerate the discovery of the challenged evidence. See, e.g., SEARCHSZR, § 11.4(a). But the Court rejected such a limitation in *Nix v. Williams,* p. 903.

4. *Confession as the "fruit" of an illegal arrest.* BROWN v. ILLINOIS, 422 U.S. 590 (1975), arose as follows: Following his illegal arrest, petitioner, a murder suspect, was taken to a police station where, after being given the *Miranda* warnings and waiving his rights, he made incriminating statements within two hours of the arrest. The state supreme court affirmed the murder conviction, taking the view that "the *Miranda* warnings in and of themselves" purged the taint of the prior illegal arrest. The Court, per Blackmun, J., reversed:

"The exclusionary rule, [when] utilized to effectuate the Fourth Amendment, serves interests and policies that are distinct from those it serves under the Fifth.

---

a. See *Nix v. Williams,* p. 903.

[E]xclusion of a confession made without *Miranda* warnings might be regarded as necessary to effectuate the Fifth Amendment, but it would not be sufficient fully to protect the Fourth. *Miranda* warnings, and the exclusion of a confession made without them, do not alone sufficiently deter a Fourth Amendment violation."

"[If] *Miranda* warnings, by themselves, were held to attenuate the taint of an unconstitutional arrest, regardless of how wanton and purposeful the Fourth Amendment violation, the effect of the exclusionary rule would be substantially diluted. [Illegal arrests] would be encouraged by the knowledge that evidence derived therefrom hopefully could be made admissible at trial by the simple expedient of giving *Miranda* warnings. Any incentive to avoid Fourth Amendment violations would be eviscerated by making the warnings, in effect, a 'cure-all' * * *."

Although the Court rejected the *per se* rule of the Illinois court whereunder the *Miranda* warnings were deemed to break the causal connection between the arrest and confession, it declined to adopt a *per se* or "but for" rule running in the other direction. It concluded instead that such taint issues "must be answered on the facts of each case. No single fact is dispositive. [The] *Miranda* warnings are an important factor, to be sure, in determining whether the confession is obtained by exploitation of an illegal arrest. But they are not the only factor to be considered. The temporal proximity of the arrest and the confession, the presence of intervening circumstances and, particularly, the purpose and flagrancy of the official misconduct, are all relevant. The voluntariness of the statement is a threshold requirement. And the burden of showing admissibility rests, of course, on the prosecution."

The Court then concluded that the prosecution had failed to sustain its burden: "[Petitioner's] first statement was separated from his illegal arrest by less than two hours, and there was no intervening event of significance whatsoever. * * * We could hold [petitioner's] first statement admissible only if we overrule *Wong Sun*. We decline to do so. [The] illegality here, moreover, had a quality of purposefulness. The impropriety of the arrest was obvious. [The] detectives embarked upon this expedition for evidence in the hope that something might turn up."

Justice White expressed agreement with the Court insofar as it "holds (1) that despite *Miranda* warnings the Fourth and Fourteenth Amendments require the exclusion from evidence of statements obtained as the fruit of an arrest which the arresting officers *knew or should have known* was without probable cause and unconstitutional, and (2) that the statements obtained in this case were in this category" (emphasis added), and therefore concurred in the judgment.

Justice Powell, joined by Rehnquist, J., joined the Court insofar as it rejected the Illinois courts' *per se* rule, but "would remand the case for reconsideration under the general standards articulated in the Court's opinion." In Justice Powell's view, "the flagrantly abusive violations of Fourth Amendment rights, on the one hand, and 'technical' Fourth Amendment violations, [on the other] call for significantly different judicial responses":

"I would require the clearest indication of attenuation in cases in which official conduct was flagrantly abusive of Fourth Amendment rights. [In such cases] I would consider the equalizing potential of *Miranda* warnings rarely sufficient to dissipate the taint. [At] the opposite end of the spectrum lie 'technical' violations of Fourth Amendment rights where, for example, officers in good faith arrest an individual in reliance on a warrant later invalidated or pursuant to a statute that subsequently is declared unconstitutional. [In such cases] I can see no legitimate justification for depriving the prosecution of reliable and probative evidence. Thus, with the exception of statements given in the immediate circumstances of the illegal arrest—a constraint I think is imposed by existing exclusionary rule law—I would not require more than proof that effective *Miranda* warnings were given and that the ensuing statement was voluntary in the Fifth Amendment sense."

In *Dunaway v. New York,* other aspects of which are discussed at p. 438, the Court, per Brennan, J., reaffirmed the view that *Miranda* warnings, by themselves, are not necessarily sufficient to attenuate the taint of an unconstitutional arrest: "The situation in this case is virtually a replica of the situation in *Brown.* Petitioner was also admittedly seized without probable cause in the hope that something might turn up, and confessed without any intervening event of significance. [To] admit petitioner's confession in such a case would allow 'law enforcement officers to violate the Fourth Amendment with impunity, safe in the knowledge that they could wash their hands in the "procedural safeguards" of the Fifth' [Comment, 25 Emory L.J. 227, 238 (1976)]."

Justice Stevens joined the Court's opinion but added a comment on "the significance of two factors that may be considered when determining whether a confession has been obtained by exploitation of an illegal arrest":

"The temporal relationship between the arrest and the confession may be an ambiguous factor. If there are no relevant intervening circumstances, a prolonged detention may well be a more serious exploitation of an illegal arrest than a short one. Conversely, even an immediate confession may have been motivated by a prearrest event such as a visit with a minister. The flagrancy of the official misconduct is relevant, in my judgment, only insofar as it has a tendency to motivate the defendant. A midnight arrest with drawn guns will be equally frightening whether the police acted recklessly or in good faith. Conversely, a courteous command has the same effect on the arrestee whether the officer thinks he has probable cause or knows that he does not. In either event, if the Fourth Amendment is violated, the admissibility question will turn on the causal relationship between that violation and the defendant's subsequent confession."[a]

The *Brown-Dunaway* rule was applied to a complicated set of facts in *Taylor v. Alabama,* 457 U.S. 687 (1982). A 5–4 majority, per Marshall, J., held that petitioner's confession was the impermissible fruit of his illegal arrest even though (a) six hours had elapsed between the illegal arrest and the time petitioner confessed; (b) petitioner was advised of his rights three times; and (c) he was allowed to visit briefly with his girlfriend and his neighbor shortly before he confessed.

Dissenting Justice O'Connor joined by the Chief Justice, and Powell and Rehnquist, JJ., maintained that *Brown* and *Dunaway* required a contrary result. As the dissent saw it, "[t]he petitioner's confession was not proximately caused by his illegal arrest, but was the product of a decision based both on knowledge of his constitutional rights and on the discussion with his friends."

Compare the *Brown–Dunaway—Taylor* line of cases with *Rawlings v. Kentucky* (1980), discussed at p. 885. Petitioner argued that his admission of the ownership of drugs which had been found in Ms. Cox's purse (after the contents of the purse had been emptied, pursuant to a police order) was the fruit of an illegal detention. The Court, per Rehnquist, J., disagreed. Assuming that Rawlings and

---

a. Rehnquist, J., joined by Burger, C.J., dissented, maintaining that the police had acted in "good faith and not in a flagrant manner" and that in such cases "no more [should be required] than that proper *Miranda* warnings [be] given and that the statement be voluntary within the meaning of the Fifth Amendment."

others were illegally detained in a house while the police obtained a search warrant for the premises, the Court noted, inter alia, that the detention was in a "congenial atmosphere"; that petitioner's admissions were "apparently spontaneous reactions to the discovery of his drugs in Cox's purse" and not the product of the initial illegality, and the police action "does not rise to the level of conscious or flagrant misconduct requiring prophylactic exclusion of petitioner's statements. Contrast *Brown*."[b]

    5. *Identification of a person as a "fruit" of an illegal arrest.* UNITED STATES v. CREWS, 445 U.S. 463 (1980), arose as follows: Immediately after being assaulted and robbed in a public restroom, the victim gave the police a full description of her assailant. Crews, who matched the suspect's description, was illegally taken into custody, photographed, and then released. Thereafter, when shown an array of eight photographs, the victim selected Crews' photograph as that of the man who had robbed her. At a court-ordered lineup, Crews was again positively identified. Finally, Crews was identified at the trial. Crews was convicted of robbery, but the District of Columbia Court of Appeals held the victim's in-court identification inadmissible, viewing it as obtained by official "exploitation" of the "primary illegality"—Crews' unlawful arrest.[a] The Court, per Brennan, J., disagreed:

    A victim's in-court identification has "three distinct elements": "[1], the victim is present at trial to testify as to what transpired between her and the offender, and to identify the defendant as the culprit. [2], the victim possesses knowledge of and the ability to reconstruct the prior [crime] and to identify the defendant from her observations of him at the time of the crime. And [3], the defendant is also physically present in the courtroom, so that the victim can observe him and compare his appearance to that of the offender. In the present case, none of these three elements 'has been come at by exploitation' of the defendant's Fourth Amendment rights."

    As for (1), the victim's presence and cooperation were "surely not the product of any police misconduct"; as for (3), because an "illegal arrest, without more, has never been viewed as a bar to subsequent prosecution," the defendant was "not himself a suppressible 'fruit,'" and the illegality of his detention cannot deprive the Government of the opportunity to prove his guilt through the introduction of evidence wholly untainted by the police misconduct."

    As for (2): "Nor did the illegal arrest infect the victim's ability to give accurate identification testimony. Based upon her observations at the time of the robbery, [she] constructed a mental image of her assailant. At trial, she retrieved this mnemonic representation, compared it [to] defendant, and positively identified him as the robber. No part of this process was affected by [the] illegal arrest."

    Because it was clear that prior to his illegal arrest, the police both knew defendant's identity and had some reason to believe he was involved in the robbery, Justice Brennan would have reserved judgment as to whether a defendant's face could ever be considered a suppressible "fruit" of an illegal arrest.[b] But a majority of the Court, in two separate concurring opinions, explicitly rejected this possibility.

---

    b. Dissenting Justice Marshall, joined by Brennan, J., maintained that "petitioner's admissions were obviously the fruit of the illegal detention."

    a. The trial court had excluded both the photographic and lineup identifications as the "fruits" of Crews' illegal arrest and on appeal the government conceded that both were inadmissible. Why? Wasn't *the lineup identification* admissible for the same reasons the Supreme Court held that the in-court identification was?

    b. As Justice Brennan noted, this part of his opinion was joined only by Stewart and Stevens, JJ.

6. **Confession as the "fruit" of a Payton violation.** *Payton v. New York* (p. 376) holds that the Fourth Amendment prohibits the police from effecting a warrantless entry into a suspect's home in order to make a routine felony arrest. In NEW YORK v. HARRIS, 495 U.S. 14 (1990), a 5–4 majority, per White, J., held that where the police have probable cause to arrest a suspect, the exclusionary rule does not bar the use of a statement made by the suspect *outside* his home even though the statement is obtained after an *in-house* arrest in violation of *Payton*.

The police had probable cause to believe Harris had killed a woman. They went to his apartment to take him into custody, but did not first obtain an arrest warrant. After being advised of his *Miranda* rights and waiving them, Harris reportedly admitted that he had committed the homicide. He was then taken to the station house, where, after again being advised of his rights and again waiving them, he signed a written inculpatory statement. Since the state did not challenge the trial court's suppression of Harris' statement to the police while still inside his home, the sole issue was the admissibility of the statement he made at the station house. The New York Court of Appeals ruled that it was the inadmissible fruit of the *Payton* violation, but the Supreme Court reversed:

"Nothing in the reasoning of [*Payton*] suggests that an arrest in a home without a warrant but with probable cause somehow renders unlawful continued custody of the suspect once he is removed from the house. [Because] the officers had probable cause to arrest Harris for a crime, Harris was not unlawfully in custody when he was removed to the station house. [For] Fourth Amendment purposes, the legal issue is the same as it would be had the police arrested Harris on his door step, illegally entered his home to search for evidence, and later interrogated Harris at the station house. Similarly, if the police had made a warrantless entry into Harris' home, not found him there, but arrested him on the street when he returned, a later statement made by him after proper warnings would no doubt be admissible. * * *"

"Harris's statement taken at the police station was not the product of being in unlawful custody. Neither was it the fruit of having been arrested in the home rather than someplace else. The case is analogous to *Crews*. In that case, we refused to suppress a victim's in-court identification despite the defendant's illegal arrest. The Court found that the evidence was not 'come at by exploitation [of] the defendant's Fourth Amendment rights,' and that it was not necessary to inquire whether the 'taint' of the Fourth Amendment violation was sufficiently attenuated to permit the introduction of the evidence. Here, likewise, the police had a justification to question Harris prior to his arrest; therefore, his subsequent statement was not an exploitation of the illegal entry into Harris's home. * * *"

"[S]uppressing the statement taken outside the house would not serve the purpose of the rule that made Harris's in-house arrest illegal. The warrant requirement for an arrest in the home is imposed to protect the home, and anything incriminating the police gathered from arresting Harris in his home, rather than elsewhere, has been excluded, as it should have been; the purpose of the rule has thereby been vindicated.[a] [The] principal incentive to obey *Payton* still obtains: the police know that a warrantless entry will lead to the suppression of any evidence found or statements taken inside the home. If we did suppress statements like Harris's, moreover, the incremental deterrent value would be minimal. Given that the police have probable cause to arrest a suspect in Harris's position, they need not violate *Payton* in order to interrogate the suspect."

---

a. In *Hudson v. Michigan*, the "knock and announce" case discussed at p. 907 infra, the opinion of the Court, per Scalia, J., rested in part on similar reasoning.

Dissenting Justice Marshall, joined by Brennan, Blackmun and Stevens, JJ., deemed *Brown v. Illinois* controlling:

"An application of the *Brown* factors to this case compels the conclusion that Harris' statement at the station house must be suppressed. About an hour elapsed between the illegal arrest and Harris' confession, without any intervening factor other than the warnings required by *Miranda*. This Court has held, however, that '*Miranda* warnings, *alone* and *per se*, . . . cannot assure in every case that the Fourth Amendment violation has not been unduly exploited.' *Brown*. Indeed, in *Brown*, we held that a statement made almost *two* hours after an illegal arrest, and after *Miranda* warnings had been given, was not sufficiently removed from the violation so as to dissipate the taint."

"[The] officers decided, apparently consistent with a 'departmental policy,' to violate Harris' Fourth Amendment rights so they could get evidence that they could not otherwise obtain. As the trial court held, 'No more clear violation of [*Payton*], in my view, could be established.' Where, as here, there is a particularly flagrant constitutional violation and little in the way of elapsed time or intervening circumstances, the statement in the police station must be suppressed. * * *

"Perhaps the most alarming aspect of the Court's ruling is its practical consequences for the deterrence of *Payton* violations. Imagine a police officer who has probable cause to arrest a suspect but lacks a warrant. [The] officer knows that if he breaks into the house without a warrant and drags the suspect outside, the suspect, shaken by the enormous invasion of privacy he has just undergone, may say something incriminating. Before today's decision, the government would only be able to use that evidence if the Court found that the taint of the arrest had been attenuated; after the decision, the evidence will be admissible regardless of whether it was the product of the unconstitutional arrest. Thus, the officer envisions the following best-case scenario if he chooses to violate the Constitution: he avoids a major expenditure of time and effort, ensures that the suspect will not escape, and procures the most damaging evidence of all, a confession. His worst-case scenario is that he will avoid a major expenditure of effort, ensure that the suspect will not escape, and will see evidence in the house (which would have remained unknown absent the constitutional violation) that cannot be used in the prosecution's case-in-chief. The Court thus creates powerful incentives for police officers to violate the Fourth Amendment. In the context of our constitutional rights and the sanctity of our homes, we cannot afford to presume that officers will be entirely impervious to those incentives."

7. ***A warrant search as the fruit of an illegal entry and occupation of the premises.*** SEGURA v. UNITED STATES, 468 U.S. 796 (1984), arose as follows: When Segura, a suspected narcotics violator, entered his apartment building one evening, he was immediately arrested and taken to his apartment. The agents entered the apartment without requesting or obtaining permission. Four other people were there. The agents told them that Segura was under arrest and that a search warrant for the premises was being obtained.

The agents then conducted a limited security check of the apartment, in the process observing drug paraphernalia. They then took Segura and the other occupants of the apartment to headquarters. Two agents remained in the apartment awaiting the warrant. Because of "administrative delay," the search warrant was not issued until some 19 hours after the initial entry. When the agents executed the warrant they discovered narcotics and records of narcotics transactions.

Since the government did not dispute the rulings below that the initial entry and security search were unlawful, "the only issue" before the Court was whether items "not observed during the illegal entry and first discovered by the agents the day after the entry, under an admittedly valid search warrant, should have been suppressed."[a] A 5–4 majority, per Burger, C.J., answered in the negative. The legality of the initial entry had no bearing on the admissibility of the challenged evidence "because there was an independent source for the warrant under which that evidence was seized": "No information obtained during the initial entry or occupation of the apartment was needed or used by the agents to secure the warrant. [The] valid warrant search was a 'means sufficiently distinguishable' to purge the evidence of any 'taint' arising from the entry."

Dissenting Justice Stevens, joined by Brennan, Marshall and Blackmun, JJ., maintained that "the controlling question" was "whether the deterrent purposes of the exclusionary rule would be served or undermined by the suppression of this evidence." He thought the deterrence rationale "plainly applicable": "The agents impounded the apartment precisely because they wished to avoid risking a loss of access to the evidence within it. Thus, the unlawful benefit they [obtained] was exactly the benefit [that] motivated [them] in the case to violate the Constitution."

In MURRAY v. UNITED STATES, 487 U.S. 533 (1988), the Court, by a 4–3 vote (Brennan and Kennedy, JJ., not participating), declined to read *Segura* narrowly and held that evidence observed by the police during an illegal entry of premises need not be excluded if such evidence is subsequently discovered during the execution of an otherwise valid search warrant sought and issued on the basis of information *wholly unconnected* to the prior entry. After receiving information that a warehouse was being used for illegal drug activities, federal agents forced their way into the warehouse and observed in plain view bales of marijuana. The agents then left without disturbing the bales and applied for a search warrant. In their application, they did not mention the prior entry or include any recitations of their observations during that entry. Upon issuance of the warrant, the agents reentered the warehouse and seized the bales and other evidence of crime. In upholding the admissibility of the evidence, the Court, per Scalia, J., observed:

"Knowledge that the marijuana was in the warehouse was assuredly acquired at the time of the unlawful entry. But it was also acquired at the time of entry pursuant to the warrant, and if that later acquisition was not the result of the earlier entry there is no reason why the independent source doctrine should not apply. Invoking the exclusionary rule would put the police (and society) not in the *same* position they would have occupied if no violation occurred, but in a *worse* one. See *Nix v. Williams* [p. 903]. We think this is also true with respect to the tangible evidence, the bales of marijuana. [S]o long as a later, lawful seizure is genuinely independent of an earlier, tainted one (which may well be difficult to establish where the seized goods are kept in the police's possession) there is no reason why the independent source doctrine should not apply."

"The ultimate question, therefore, is whether the search pursuant to warrant was in fact a genuinely independent source of the information and tangible evidence at issue here. This would not have been the case if the agents' decision to seek the warrant was prompted by what they had seen during the initial entry, or if information obtained during that entry was presented to the Magistrate and affected his decision to issue the warrant. [The] District Court found that the agents did not reveal their warrantless entry to the Magistrate and that they did not include in their application for a warrant any recitation of their observations in the warehouse. It did not, however, explicitly find that the agents would have

---

a. Such illegal entries, observed the Court, are sufficiently deterred by the officers' realization that "whatever evidence they discover as a direct result of the entry may be suppressed." The four dissenters found the suggested distinction a puzzling one: "If the execution of a valid warrant takes the poison out of the hidden fruit, I should think that it would also remove the taint from the fruit in plain view."

sought a warrant if they had not earlier entered the warehouse. [Thus], we vacate the judgments and remand these cases [for] determination whether the warrant-authorized search of the warehouse was an independent source of the challenged evidence in the sense we have described."

Dissenting Justice Marshall, joined by Stevens and O'Connor, JJ., maintained that "the Court's decision, by failing to provide sufficient guarantees that the subsequent search was, in fact, independent of the illegal search, emasculates the Warrant Clause and undermines the deterrence function of the exclusionary rule":

"[When], as here, the same team of investigators is involved in both the first and second search, there is a significant danger that the 'independence' of the source will in fact be illusory, and that the initial search will have affected the decision to obtain a warrant notwithstanding the officers' subsequent assertions to the contrary. It is therefore crucial that the factual premise of the exception— complete independence—be clearly established before the exception can [apply]. I believe the Court's reliance on the intent of the law enforcement officers who conducted the warrantless search provides insufficient guarantees that the subsequent legal search was unaffected by the prior illegal search. * * *

"*Segura* is readily distinguished from the present case. The admission of evidence first discovered during a legal search does not significantly lessen the deterrence facing the law enforcement officers contemplating an illegal entry *so long as* the evidence that is seen is excluded. This was clearly the view of [the *Segura* majority]. [E]xtending *Segura* to cover evidence discovered during an initial illegal search will eradicate this remaining deterrence to illegal entry. Moreover, there is less reason to believe that an initial illegal entry was prompted by a desire to determine whether to bother to get a warrant in the first place, and thus was not wholly independent of the second search, if officers understand that evidence they discover during the illegal search will be excluded even if they subsequently return with a warrant."[a]

———

Consider Craig M. Bradley, *Murray v. United States: The Bell Tolls for the Search Warrant Requirement*, 64 Ind.L.J. 907, 920 (1989):

"While I agree with the dissent in *Murray* that the decision 'emasculates the Warrant Clause,' I don't necessarily disagree with the result. This is [because] nothing in the amendment itself or, apparently, in the minds of its framers, requires a warrant as a prerequisite for a reasonable search; it only requires probable cause as a prerequisite for a warrant. [I]nstead of claiming that there is a warrant requirement and then, as recently illustrated in *Murray*, repeatedly finding ways to ignore it, the Court ought to adopt one of two models of the fourth amendment * * *.

[Professor Bradley then discusses the 'no lines' or 'general reasonableness' model, under which obtaining a warrant is only one of a number of relevant factors; and the 'bright line' approach, under which a warrant is *always* required for *every* search and seizure when it is practicable to obtain one.] With *Murray*, the Court clearly shows its preference for [a] reasonableness approach to fourth amendment law. *Murray* reeks of 'reasonableness' analysis and cannot be reconciled with the proposition that a search warrant is, in any meaningful sense, required."

———

a. While Stevens, J., joined Justice Marshall's dissent, he noted in a separate dissent that he "remain[ed] convinced that the *Segura* decision itself was unacceptable" because it provided government agents with an "affirmative incentive" to conduct illegal searches.

8. *The "tainted" witness.* UNITED STATES v. CECCOLINI, 435 U.S. 268 (1978), grew out of the following facts: An officer in a flower shop on a social visit illegally picked up an envelope and found it to contain money and policy slips. He then learned from his friend, Ms. Hennessey, an employee of the shop (who did not notice his discovery), that the envelope belonged to the defendant, the owner of the shop. The information reached the FBI four months later. An agent questioned Hennessey about defendant, without specifically mentioning the illegally discovered policy slips. She said she was willing to help, and she testified against defendant both before the grand jury and at his trial for perjury.

A 6–2 majority of the Court (Blackmun, J., not participating) held Hennessey's testimony admissible. Although it declined to adopt a *per se* rule that the testimony of a live witness should always be admissible,[a] the Court, per Rehnquist, J., pointed out that various factors indicate that "the exclusionary rule should be invoked with much greater reluctance where the claim is based on a causal relationship between a constitutional violation and the discovery of a live witness than when a similar claim is advanced to support suppression of an inanimate object":

"The greater the willingness of the witness to freely testify, the greater the likelihood that he or she will be discovered by legal means and, concomitantly, the smaller the incentive to conduct an illegal search to discover the witness. Witnesses are not like guns or documents which remain hidden from view until one turns over a sofa or opens a filing cabinet. Witnesses can, and often do, come forward and offer evidence entirely of their own volition. And evaluated properly, the degree of free will necessary to dissipate the taint will very likely be found more often in the case of live-witness testimony than other kinds of evidence."

"Moreover, exclusion of testimony" would perpetually disable a witness from testifying about relevant and material facts, regardless of how unrelated such testimony might be to the purpose of the originally illegal search or the evidence discovered thereby. [S]ince the cost of excluding live-witness testimony often will be greater, a closer, more direct link between the illegality and that kind of testimony is required."

Dissenting Justice Marshall, joined by Brennan, J., did not see how "the same tree, having its roots in an unconstitutional search or seizure, can bear two different kinds of fruit, with one kind less susceptible than the other to exclusion on Fourth Amendment grounds." The dissent charged the majority with "judicial 'double counting' ": "The majority allows a court to consider whether the witness came forward and then, if he did not, to consider that generally (but not in this case) witnesses come forward." As for the majority's argument that often the exclusion of live-witness testimony will be very costly to society, "at least as often the exclusion of physical evidence [will be equally] costly * * *."

B. THE "INEVITABLE DISCOVERY" DOCTRINE: THE SEQUEL TO *BREWER v. WILLIAMS*

Consider NIX v. WILLIAMS (WILLIAMS II), 467 U.S. 431 (1984), which arose as follows: After his conviction was overturned (see *Brewer v. Williams*, p. 739), Williams was retried and again found guilty of first-degree murder. At Williams's second trial, the prosecution did not offer Williams's statements into evidence. Nor did it seek to show that Williams had directed the police to the child's body. The only evidence admitted was the condition of the victim's body as it was found, articles of the victim's clothing, and the results of post mortem

---

a. Concurring Chief Justice Burger would adopt such a rule.

medical and chemical tests on her body. The trial court concluded that the State had proved by a preponderance of the evidence that, even if the search had not been suspended and Williams had not led the police to the victim, the searching party would still have discovered the body in essentially the same condition as it was actually found. The trial court also ruled that if the police had not located the body, "the search would clearly have been taken up again where it left off, given the extreme circumstances of this case, and the body would [have] been found *in short order*" (emphasis added).

The U.S. Court of Appeals for the Eighth Circuit reversed the district court's denial of habeas relief, maintaining that an "inevitable discovery" exception requires proof that the police did not act in "bad faith" and the record could not support such a finding. A 6–3 majority, per Burger, C.J., reversed:

"[The] core rationale consistently advanced by this Court for extending the Exclusionary Rule to evidence that is the fruit of unlawful police conduct has been that this admittedly drastic and socially costly course is needed to deter police from violations of constitutional and statutory protections. [On] this rationale, the prosecution is not to be put in a better position than it would have been in if no illegality had transpired.

"By contrast, the derivative evidence analysis ensures that the prosecution is not put in a *worse* position simply because of some earlier police error or misconduct. The independent source doctrine allows admission of evidence that has been discovered by means wholly independent of any constitutional violation. [The] independent source doctrine teaches us that the interest of society in deterring unlawful police conduct and the public interest in having juries receive all probative evidence of a crime are properly balanced by putting the police in the same, not a *worse*, position than they would have been in if no police error or misconduct had occurred. [There] is a functional similarity between [the independent source and inevitable discovery doctrines] in that exclusion of evidence that would inevitably have been discovered would also put the government in a worse position, because the police would have obtained that evidence if no misconduct had taken place. Thus, while the independent source exception would not justify admission of evidence in this case, its rationale is wholly consistent with and justifies our adoption of the ultimate or inevitable discovery exception to the Exclusionary Rule."

"[If] the prosecution can establish by a preponderance of the evidence that the information ultimately or inevitably would have been discovered by lawful means—here the volunteers' search—then the deterrence rationale has so little basis that the evidence should be received. Anything less would reject logic, experience, and common sense.

"The requirement that the prosecution must prove the absence of bad faith, [would] place courts in the position of withholding from juries relevant and undoubted truth that would have been available to police absent any unlawful police activity. Of course, that view would put the police in a *worse* position than they would have been in if no unlawful conduct had transpired. And, of equal importance, it wholly fails to take into account the enormous societal cost of excluding truth in the search for truth in the administration of justice. Nothing in this Court's prior holdings supports any such formalistic, pointless, and punitive approach.

"The Court of Appeals concluded [that] if an absence of bad faith requirement were not imposed, 'the temptation to risk deliberate violations of the Sixth Amendment would be too great, and the deterrent effect of the Exclusionary Rule reduced too far.' We reject that view. A police officer who is faced with the opportunity to obtain evidence illegally will rarely, if ever, be in a position to calculate whether the evidence sought would inevitably be discovered.

"[On] the other hand, when an officer is aware that the evidence will inevitably be discovered, he will try to avoid engaging in any questionable practice. In that situation, there will be little to gain from taking any dubious 'shortcuts' to obtain the evidence. Significant disincentives to obtaining evidence illegally—including the possibility of departmental discipline and civil liability—also lessen the likelihood that the ultimate or inevitable discovery exception will promote police misconduct. In these circumstances, the societal costs of the Exclusionary Rule far outweigh any possible benefits to deterrence that a good-faith requirement might produce.

"[On] this record it is clear that the search parties were approaching the actual location of the body and we are satisfied, along with three courts earlier, that the volunteer search teams would have resumed the search had Williams not earlier led the police to the body and the body inevitably would have been found."

Justice Stevens, concurring in the judgment, observed:

"The uncertainty as to whether the body would have been discovered can be resolved in [the prosecution's] favor here only because, as the Court explains, petitioner adduced evidence demonstrating that at the time of the constitutional violation an investigation was already under way which, in the natural and probable course of events, would have soon discovered the body. This is not a case in which the prosecution can escape responsibility for a constitutional violation through speculation; to the extent uncertainty was created by the constitutional violation the prosecution was required to resolve that uncertainty through proof."[8]

Dissenting Justice Brennan, joined by Marshall, J., underscored the distinction between the inevitable discovery and the independent source doctrines:

"The inevitable discovery exception necessarily implicates a hypothetical finding that differs in kind from the factual finding that precedes application of the independent source rule. To ensure that this hypothetical finding is narrowly confined to circumstances that are functionally equivalent to an independent source, and to protect fully the fundamental rights served by the exclusionary rule, I would require clear and convincing evidence before concluding that the government had met its burden of proof on this issue."[a]

NOTES AND QUESTIONS

1. *Must the independent line of investigation be underway?* In his dissent, Justice Brennan describes the *Williams II* majority as "conclud[ing] that unconstitutionally obtained evidence may be admitted at trial if it inevitably would have been discovered in the same condition by an independent line of investigation *that was already being pursued* when the constitutional violation

---

8. I agree with the majority's holding that the prosecution must prove that the evidence would have been inevitably discovered by a preponderance of the evidence rather than by clear and convincing evidence. An inevitable discovery finding is based on objective evidence concerning the scope of the ongoing investigation which can be objectively verified or impeached. Hence an extraordinary burden of proof is not needed in order to preserve the defendant's ability to subject the prosecution's case to the meaningful adversarial testing required by the Sixth Amendment.

a. For an in-depth analysis of the Supreme Court's opinion in *Williams II*, see Silas J. Wasserstrom & William J. Mertens, *The Exclusionary Rule on the Scaffold: But Was it a Fair Trial?* 22 Am.Crim.L.Rev. 85, 130–79 (1984). For an incisive treatment of the "fruit of the poisonous tree" problems raised by the second *Williams* case, or Williams II, prior to the Supreme Court's decision in that case, see Phillip E. Johnson, *The Return of the "Christian Burial Speech" Case,* 32 Emory L.J. 349 (1983).

occurred." (Emphasis added.) Consider also concurring Justice Stevens' observation to the same effect. Moreover, dissenting in *Hudson*, p. 252, Justice Breyer, joined by three other Justices, comes very close to saying the same thing. Is *Williams II* limited along the lines suggested by these Justices? Should it be?

When was the search in *Nix v. Williams* underway? When the appropriate official decided to conduct it? When the official told somebody else of her decision? When the group that was going to conduct the search assembled? When the group took the field?

Consider Albert W. Alschuler, *The Exclusionary Rule and Causation: Hudson v. Michigan and Its Ancestors*, 93 Iowa L.Rev. 1741, 1812–13 (2008): "Active pursuit is significant only as evidence, and it is not the only significant evidence. * * * The active-pursuit limitation guards against self-serving police testimony, but it restricts the inevitable discovery exception artificially."

2. ***Primary evidence vs. secondary evidence.*** *Nix* applied the inevitable discovery exception to secondary or derivative evidence, but most federal courts of appeals have also applied the exception to primary evidence (evidence acquired during the course of the search itself). See Robert M. Bloom, *Inevitable Discovery: An Exception beyond the Fruits*, 20 Am.J.Crim.L. 79, 87 (1992). Should a distinction between primary and secondary evidence be drawn on the ground that application of the inevitable discovery rule to secondary evidence does not excuse the unlawful police action by admitting what was obtained as a direct result of the initial misconduct, but that application of the rule to primary evidence constitutes an after the fact purging of initial wrongful conduct? See id. at 87–94.

3. ***The significance of Murray v. United States***. Recall that in *Murray*, an *independent source* case, bales of marijuana (primary evidence) were discovered as the result of an illegal entry. Nevertheless, the Court allowed for the introduction of the bales, provided that the subsequent lawful entry with a warrant was not based on information related to the initial illegal entry. Does *Murray* support the use of the *inevitable discovery exception* to avoid suppression of primary evidence? See Bloom, supra, at 92–94.

4. ***The relatively easy case.*** As pointed out in CRIMPROC § 9.3(e), "lower courts have had the least difficulty in applying the inevitable discovery doctrine where that discovery would have come about through a routine procedure invariably applied under the particular circumstances. That commonly is the case where the government argues that the evidence discovered through an illegal warrantless search would have been uncovered in an inventory search. The inventory search ordinarily will have been performed even after the discovery through the illegal search, thereby lending support to the contention that it was an inevitable procedure."

But consider Alschuler, supra, at 1813–14: "[I]n every inevitable discovery case, the government makes one of two arguments. It says either 'if we hadn't done it wrong, we would have done it right' or 'if we hadn't done it wrong, someone else would have done it right.' Neither of these claims is attractive, but the claim that 'someone else would have done it right' is less troubling. This claim is less likely to rest on the testimony of the offending officers themselves and is less likely to describe a discovery that they anticipate. Perhaps the inevitable discovery exception should be limited to cases in which a private party or a governmental agency other than the offending law enforcement agency would have discovered the unlawfully obtained evidence."

5. ***Inevitable discovery and the warrant requirement; "could have" or "might have" vs. "would have."*** If the police have probable cause to conduct a search, but do not bother to obtain a warrant, although they had plenty of time to do so, can (should) the inevitable discovery exception be used to avoid the need for a warrant?[a] Consider Bloom, supra, at 95:

"Because the *Nix* decision dealt with a Sixth Amendment violation, the Court probably was not focusing on the effect this exception would have on the Fourth Amendment warrant requirement. To the extent that the *Nix* Court concluded that there would be a limited deterrence effect by utilizing the inevitable discovery exception, its reasoning was flawed with regard to the warrant requirement.

"[The] existence of the inevitable discovery exception *will* provide the police with an incentive to avoid the warrant requirement. The police might seek the most expeditious method of obtaining the evidence without regard to its illegality, knowing that, as long as they could have obtained the evidence legally, their efforts will not result in its suppression. [For] example, if the police can demonstrate that they *could* have gotten a search warrant, what incentive will there be for them to go actively through the procedural hassle of actually obtaining one, since the effects of an illegal warrantless search could be nullified by the application of the inevitable discovery exception?"

See also Easterbrook, J., observing in *United States v. Brown*, 64 F.3d 1083, 1085 (7th Cir.1995), that in a situation where the police have probable cause, but do not, as they should, obtain a warrant, "what makes a discovery 'inevitable' is not probable cause alone [but] probable cause plus a chain of events that would have led to a warrant (or other justification) independent of the search." Otherwise, adds Judge Easterbrook, "the requirement of a warrant for a residential entry will never be enforced by the exclusionary rule."

The "inevitable discovery" exception permits the use of unlawfully obtained evidence if it "ultimately or inevitably *would* have been discovered by lawful means. *Nix v. Williams* (emphasis added). According to Wayne LaFave, the exception does not apply simply because the police *could* have or *might* have obtained the evidence lawfully—or simply because "the police had *the capacity* (which they did not exercise)" to proceed lawfully. CRIMPROC § 9.3 (emphasis added).

Cf. Scalia, J., speaking for the Court in *Kyllo v. United States* (p. 274): "The fact that equivalent information could sometimes by obtained by other means does not make lawful the use of means that violate the Fourth Amendment. The police, might, for example, learn how many people are in a particular house by setting up year-round surveillance; but that does not make breaking and entering to find out the same information lawful."

6. *More on the "inevitable discovery" exception and the "attenuation" doctrine.* In HUDSON v. MICHIGAN, 547 U.S. 586 (2006) (set forth at p. 252), in the course of holding that a violation of the "knock-and-announce" rule did not require exclusion of the evidence found in the search of the defendant's home, a 5–4 majority, per Scalia, J., observed:

"[E]xclusion may not be premised on the mere fact that a constitutional violation was a 'but-for' cause of obtaining evidence. Our cases show that but-for causality is only a necessary, not a sufficient, condition for suppression. In this case, [the] constitutional violation of an illegal *manner* of entry was *not* a but-for cause of obtaining the evidence. Whether that preliminary misstep had occurred *or not*, the police would have executed the warrant they had obtained, and would have discovered the gun and drugs inside the house. But even if the illegal entry here could be characterized as a but-for cause of discovering what was inside, we have 'never held that evidence is "fruit of the poisonous tree" simply because "it

---

   a. A similar question may be asked about illegal searches of vehicles which turn up items that would have been discovered through an inventory search.

would not have come to light but for the illegal actions of the police." ' *Segura v. United States.*"

After recalling that the *Nardone* Court had pointed out that even where the challenged evidence did not have an "independent source" it might still be admissible if the causal connection had "become so attenuated as to dissipate the taint," Justice Scalia continued:

"Attenuation can occur, of course, when the causal connection is remote. Attenuation also occurs when, even given a direct causal connection, the interest protected by the constitutional guarantee that has been violated would not be served by suppression of the evidence obtained. 'The penalties visited upon the Government [because] its officers have violated the law must bear some relation to the purposes which the law is to serve.' Thus, in *New York v. Harris*, where an illegal warrantless arrest was made in Harris' house, we held that 'suppressing [Harris'] statement taken outside the house would not serve the purpose of the rule that made Harris' in-house arrest illegal.'

"For this reason, cases excluding the fruits of unlawful warrantless searches say nothing about the appropriateness of exclusion to vindicate the interests protected by the knock-and-announce requirement. Until a valid warrant has issued, citizens are entitled to shield 'their persons, houses, papers and effects.' Exclusion of the evidence obtained by a warrantless search indicates that entitlement. The interests protected by the knock-and-announce requirement are quite different—and do not include the shielding of potential evidence from the government's eyes. [Since] the interests that *were* violated in this case have nothing to do with the seizure of the evidence, the exclusionary rule is inapplicable."

Dissenting Justice Breyer, joined by Stevens, Souter and Ginsburg, JJ., maintained that the majority had misunderstood the inevitable discovery doctrine:

"The majority first argues that the 'constitutional violation of an illegal *manner* of entry was *not* a but-for cause of obtaining the evidence.' But taking causation as it is commonly understood in the law, I do not see how that can be so. Although the police might have entered Hudson's home lawfully, they did not in fact do so. * * *

"Moreover, separating the 'manner of entry' from the related search slices the violation too finely. [We] have described a failure to comply with the knock-and-announce rule, not as an independently unlawful event, but as a factor that renders the *search* 'constitutionally defective.' *Wilson v. Arkansas*.

"[The] inevitable discovery doctrine rule [does] not refer to discovery that would have taken place if the police behavior in question had (contrary to fact) been lawful. The doctrine does not treat as critical what *hypothetically could* have happened had the police acted lawfully in the first place. Rather, 'independent' or 'inevitable' discovery refers to discovery that did occur or that would have occurred (1) *despite* (not simply *in the absence of*) the unlawful behavior and (2) *independently* of that unlawful behavior. The government cannot, for example, avoid suppression of evidence seized without a warrant (or pursuant to a defective warrant) simply by showing that it could have obtained a valid warrant had it sought one.[a] Instead, it must show that the same evidence 'inevitably *would* have been discovered by *lawful* means.' *Nix v. Williams.*

---

a. But see Akhil Reed Amar, Slate article: *The Battle of Hudson Heights*, June 19, 2006:

"With *Hudson* on the books, state and federal prosecutors should now try to find the Next Perfect Test Case, which would look something like this: The cops have very good reasons (what lawyers call 'probable cause') to conduct a given search and thus the police could easily get a warrant from a judge. But they decline to get the warrant because they reasonably—though it turns out erroneously—believe that the facts fall into one of the umpteen categories for which the court has said that warrants are not required. Armed with probable cause and good faith (but no

"[The] inevitable discovery exception rests upon the principle that the remedial purposes of the exclusionary rule are not served by suppressing evidence discovered through a 'later *lawful* seizure' that is '*genuinely independent of* an earlier, tainted one.' *Murray v. United States* (emphasis added).

"Case law well illustrates the meaning of this principle. In *Nix*, police officers violated a defendant's Sixth Amendment right by eliciting incriminating statements from him after he invoked his right to counsel. Those statements led to the discovery of the victim's body. The Court concluded that evidence obtained from the victim's body was admissible because it would ultimately or inevitably have been discovered by a volunteer search party effort that was ongoing—whether or not the Sixth Amendment violation had taken place. In other words, the evidence would have been found *despite*, and *independent of*, the Sixth Amendment violation. * * *

"Of course, had the police entered the house lawfully, they would have found the gun and drugs. But that fact is beside the point. The question is not what police might have done had they not behaved unlawfully. The question is what they did do. Was there set in motion an independent chain of events that would have inevitably led to the discovery and seizure of the evidence despite, and independent of, that behavior? The answer here is 'no.' "

A QUESTION ABOUT HUDSON

Does *Hudson* clarify the scope and logic of inevitable discovery, as Professor Amar indicates (see p. 908, fn. a) or does *Hudson* confuse the "independent source" rule with the "inevitable discovery" doctrine? See Joshua Dressler & Alan C. Michaels 1 *Understanding Criminal Procedure*, 386–92 (5th ed. 2010); Sharon L. Davies & Anna B. Scanlon, *Katz in the Age of Hudson v. Michigan: Some Thoughts on "Suppression as a Last Resort,"* 41 U.C. Davis L.Rev. 1035 (2008); James J. Tomkovicz, *Hudson v. Michigan and the Future of Fourth Amendment Exclusion*, 93 Iowa L.Rev. 1819 (2008).

C. IS A CONFESSION OBTAINED IN VIOLATION OF THE *MIRANDA* RULES A "POISONOUS TREE"?

[See UNITED STATES v. PATANE, p. 699; MISSOURI v. SEIBERT, p. 702; and the Notes and Questions following these cases.]

D. IS A "SECOND CONFESSION" FOLLOWING A FAILURE TO COMPLY WITH THE *MASSIAH* DOCTRINE ADMISSIBLE?

In *Nix v. Williams* all the Justices seemed to assume that the "fruit of the poisonous tree" doctrine applied to statements obtained in violation of *Massiah*.

---

warrant), the cops search and find a smoking gun or a bloody knife—proof positive of a violent crime.

"Similar cases have come before the court previously, and the justices have at times mindlessly suppressed the evidence. But none of the court's past cases has squarely addressed the strong argument of the inevitable discovery (combined with police good faith). With *Hudson* now on the books clarifying the scope and logic of inevitable discovery, the government can argue in our Perfect Test Case as follows: 'The cops *could have* easily gotten a warrant and surely *would have* done so, had they only better understood the often-complex court doctrine. Because the cops acted in good faith and because the evidence would have been found if the cops had strictly complied with the Fourth Amendment—a warrant would inevitably have been issued, had it been sought— the case should be treated just like *Hudson*.' "

Otherwise, why would there have been any need to establish that the case came within the "inevitable discovery" *exception* to the "poisonous tree" doctrine?) However, in *Fellers v. United States*, 540 U.S. 519 (2004) (discussed at p. 745), the Court reversed the conviction and remanded the case to the Eighth Circuit to determine whether the defendant's "second confession" should have been suppressed as the fruit of the initial Sixth Amendment violation and whether *Oregon v. Elstad* (p. 697) "applies when a suspect makes incriminating statements after a knowing and voluntary waiver of the right to counsel notwithstanding earlier police questioning in violation of Sixth Amendment standards." On remand, the Eighth Circuit concluded that *Elstad* did apply to violations of the Sixth Amendment and upheld the admissibility of the "second confession." *United States v. Fellers*, 397 F.3d 1090 (8th Cir. 2005).

Consider *Kansas v. Ventris*, p. 917 infra, holding that statements obtained in violation of the *Massiah* doctrine are admissible for impeachment purposes. Although it is not perfectly clear, a plausible reading of Justice Scalia's opinion is that *Massiah*, like *Miranda*, is a "prophylactic rule." At one point, Justice Scalia refers to "the Fifth and Sixth Amendment prophylactic rules" (which could well mean both *Miranda* and *Massiah*). At another point, Scalia describes the right to counsel at trial as "the core of the right to counsel" (apparently as opposed to the prophylactic rule protecting against jailhouse informants and other police manipulation). Cf. Sherry Colb, *Kansas v. Ventris: The Supreme Court Misconstrues the Right to Counsel*, <http://writ.news.findlaw.com/colb/20090610.html> (June 10, 2009). According to Professor Colb, although Justice Scalia's opinion for the Court in *Ventris* "did not explicitly say that *Massiah* is a prophylactic rule," the Court "seems in reality to be relying on the assumption that the *Massiah* right is 'prophylactic,' rather than being at the 'core' of the Sixth Amendment."

If this reading of *Ventris* is correct, does it signify that the 'fruit of the poisonous tree' doctrine does not (or soon will be held not to) apply to *Massiah* violations?

SECTION 3.   USE OF ILLEGALLY OBTAINED EVIDENCE FOR IMPEACHMENT PURPOSES

A.   THE EXPANSION OF A ONCE–NARROW EXCEPTION

1. In *Walder v. United States*, 347 U.S. 62 (1954), defendant, charged with various illegal narcotics transactions, asserted early on his direct examination that he had never possessed any narcotics or sold or given any narcotics to anyone in his life. The Court held, per Frankfurter, J., that this assertion "opened the door," for purposes of attacking the defendant's credibility, to evidence of heroin seized from the defendant's home, in his presence, in an earlier, unrelated case. "Of his own accord," observed the Court, "the defendant went beyond a mere denial of complicity in the crimes of which he was charged and made the sweeping claim that he had never dealt in or possessed any narcotics. [A defendant] must be free to deny all the elements of the case against him without thereby giving leave to the Government to introduce by way of rebuttal evidence illegally secured by it, and thereby not available for its case in chief. Beyond that, however, there is hardly justification for letting the defendant affirmatively resort to perjurious testimony in reliance on the Government's disability to challenge his credibility."

The instant situation, emphasized the *Walder* Court, is to be "sharply contrasted" with that presented by *Agnello v. United States*, 269 U.S. 20 (1925).

There, the government sought to "smuggle in" the tainted evidence on cross-examination by asking the defendant whether he had ever seen narcotics before, and eliciting the expected denial. In *Agnello,* the defendant "did nothing" to waive his constitutional protection or to justify cross-examination with respect to the illegally seized evidence.

2. HARRIS v. NEW YORK, 401 U.S. 222 (1971), often called the first blow the Burger Court struck *Miranda,* arose as follows: Petitioner, charged with selling heroin to an undercover officer, took the stand in his own defense. He admitted knowing the officer, but denied making a sale of heroin. Statements made by petitioner immediately following his arrest which partially contradicted his direct trial testimony were used to impeach his credibility. According to the Court, petitioner made no claim that the statements were coerced or involuntary,[b] but they were preceded by defective *Miranda* warnings, and thus inadmissible to establish the prosecution's case in chief. A 5–4 majority, per Burger, C.J., held that under the circumstances "petitioner's credibility was appropriately impeached by use of his earlier conflicting statements."

The Court noted that "[s]ome comments in the *Miranda* opinion can indeed be read as indicating a bar to use of [a statement obtained in violation of *Miranda*] for any purpose," but dismissed this discussion as "not at all necessary to the Court's holding" and not "controlling."[c] The Court noted, but also seemed untroubled by the fact, "that Walder was impeached as to collateral matters included in his direct examination, whereas petitioner here was impeached as to testimony bearing more directly on the crimes charged." The Court next observed:

"The impeachment process here undoubtedly provided valuable aid to the jury in assessing petitioner's credibility, and the benefits of this process should not be lost [because] of the speculative possibility that impermissible police conduct will be encouraged thereby. Assuming that the exclusionary rule has a deterrent effect * * * sufficient deterrence flows when the evidence in question is made unavailable to the prosecution in its case in chief.

"[The privilege to testify in one's defense] cannot be construed to include the right to commit perjury. [The] prosecution here did no more than utilize the traditional truth-testing devices of the adversary process. [The] shield provided by *Miranda* cannot be perverted into a license to use perjury by way of a defense, free from the risk of confrontation with prior inconsistent utterances."

Dissenting Justice Brennan, joined by Douglas and Marshall, JJ., criticized the majority for disregarding language in *Miranda* and for selectively quoting from *Walder.* The dissent emphasized that "*Walder* was not a case where tainted evidence was used to impeach an accused's direct testimony on matters directly related to the case against him," but only such testimony "on matters *collateral* to the crime charged." Continued the dissent:

"While *Walder* did not identify the constitutional specifics that guarantee 'a defendant the fullest opportunity to meet the accusation against him [and] permit him to be free to deny all the elements of the case against him,' in my view *Miranda* identified the Fifth Amendment's privilege against self-incrimination as

---

b. According to Alan Dershowitz & John Hart Ely, *Harris v. New York: Some Anxious Observations on the Candor and Logic of the Emerging Nixon Majority,* 80 Yale L.J. 1198, 1201 (1971), "the record is clear" that he did.

c. But consider Geoffrey Stone, *The Miranda Doctrine in the Burger Court,* 1977 Sup.Ct.Rev. 99, 107–08: "Rightly or wrongly, *Miranda* was deliberately structured to canvass a wide range of problems, many of which were not directly raised by the cases before the Court. This approach was thought necessary in order to 'give concrete constitutional guidelines for law enforcement agencies and courts to follow.' Thus, a technical reading of *Miranda,* such as that employed in *Harris,* would enable the Court to label many critical aspects of the decision mere dictum and therefore not 'controlling.'"

one of those specifics. [It] is fulfilled only when an accused is guaranteed the right 'to remain silent unless he chooses to speak in the *unfettered* exercise of his own will' (emphasis added). The choice of whether to testify in one's own defense must therefore be 'unfettered' * * *. [But] the accused is denied an 'unfettered' choice when the decision whether to take the stand is burdened by the risk that an illegally obtained prior statement may be introduced to impeach his direct testimony denying complicity in the crime charged against him."[d]

3. *The Fourth Amendment vs. the Fifth.* Should the Court have considered the significance of *Miranda's* Fifth Amendment underpinning before applying (or extending) the Fourth Amendment *Walder* case to *Harris?* Is impeachment by means of evidence obtained in violation of the Fourth Amendment more defensible than such use of evidence obtained in violation of the Self–Incrimination Clause of the Fifth because the Fourth's "exclusionary rule" is a court-created device designed to deter the police and as the link between police illegality and subsequent evidence becomes more attenuated it becomes less likely that exclusion would affect future police conduct? On the other hand, is the essence of the constitutional wrong under the Fifth the *use* against him of a defendant's compelled testimony, not the mere act of compelling him to speak (otherwise no immunity statute would be constitutional)? Doesn't the Self–Incrimination Clause by its own terms seem to prohibit the use of statements obtained in violation of its command? See Dershowitz & Ely, fn. b supra, at 1214–15; Stone, fn. c supra, at 110–111.

4. The Court went a step beyond *Harris* in *Oregon v. Hass,* 420 U.S. 714 (1975). In *Hass,* after being advised of his rights, the defendant *asserted* them—he asked for a lawyer. But the police refused to honor his request and continued to question him. A 6–2 majority, per Blackmun, J., ruled that here, too, the resulting statements could be used for impeachment purposes. "One might concede," wrote the Court, "that when proper *Miranda* warnings have been given, and the officer then continues his interrogation after the suspect asks for an attorney, the officer may be said to have little to lose and perhaps something to gain by way of possibly uncovering impeachment material. This speculative possibility, however, is even greater where the warnings are defective and the defect is not known to the officers. In any event, the balance was struck in *Harris,* and we are not disposed to change it now."

But wasn't a *different* balance struck in *Hass?* Dissenting Justice Brennan, joined by Marshall, J., thought so: "Even after *Harris,* police had some incentive for following *Miranda* by warning an accused of his [rights]. If the warnings were given, the accused might still make a statement which could be used in the prosecution's case-in-chief. Under today's holding, however, once the warnings are given, police have almost no incentive for following *Miranda's* requirement that '[i]f the individual states that he wants an attorney, the interrogation must cease until an attorney is present.' If the requirement is followed there will almost surely be no statement since the attorney will advise the accused to remain silent. If, however, the requirement is disobeyed, the police may obtain a statement which can be used for impeachment if the accused has the temerity to testify in his own defense."

5. In UNITED STATES v. HAVENS, 446 U.S. 620 (1980), what had "started out in *Walder* as a narrow and reasonable exception" to the exclusionary rule took on "awesome proportions," CRIMPROC § 9.6(a). On direct examination, defendant denied being involved with his codefendant in the transportation of cocaine and on cross-examination denied being involved in sewing a pocket (in which drugs were found) into his codefendant's clothing or having in his own

---

d. Black, J., also dissented, without opinion.

suitcase cloth from which the swatch was cut to make the pocket. Defendant's testimony was impeached by admitting the illegally seized cloth, but the Fifth Circuit reversed, maintaining that illegally seized evidence could be used for impeachment only if it contradicts a defendant's direct testimony. A 5–4 majority, per White, J., disagreed:

"[The] policies of the exclusionary rule no more bar impeachment here than they did in *Walder, Harris,* and *Hass.* [The] incremental furthering of [the ends of the exclusionary rules] by forbidding impeachment of the defendant who testifies was deemed insufficient to permit or require that false testimony go unchallenged, with the resulting impairment of the integrity of the fact-finding goals of the criminal trial. We reaffirm this assessment of the competing interests, and hold that a defendant's statements made in response to proper cross-examination reasonably suggested by the defendant's direct examination are subject to otherwise proper impeachment by the government, albeit by evidence that has been illegally obtained."

Dissenting Justice Brennan, joined by Stewart, Marshall and Stevens, JJ., on this point, protested: "The identical issue was confronted in *Agnello,* which determined—contrary to the instant decision—that it was constitutionally impermissible to admit evidence obtained in violation of the Fourth Amendment to rebut a defendant's response to a matter first raised during the Government's cross-examination. [The] exclusionary rule exception established by *Harris* and *Hass* may be fairly easily cabined by defense counsel's unwillingness to forego certain areas of questioning. But [today's holding] passes control of the exception to the Government, since the prosecutor can lay the predicate for admitting otherwise suppressible evidence with his own questioning."

Justice Brennan (joined only by Marshall, J., on this point) then voiced "a more fundamental difference with the Court's holding here, which culminates the approach taken in *Harris* and *Hass*":

"[T]he Court has undertaken to strike a 'balance' between the 'policies' it finds in the Bill of Rights and the 'competing interest' in accurate trial determinations. This balancing effort is completely freewheeling. Far from applying criteria intrinsic to the Fourth and Fifth Amendments, the Court resolves succeeding cases simply by declaring that so much exclusion is enough to deter police misconduct. That hardly conforms to the disciplined analytical method described as 'legal reasoning,' through which judges endeavor to formulate or derive principles of decision that can be applied consistently and predictably.[a] [More] disturbingly, by treating Fourth and Fifth Amendment privileges as mere incentive schemes, the Court denigrates their unique status as *constitutional* protections."

6. *The Court refuses to extend the impeachment exception to defense witnesses other than the defendant.* In JAMES v. ILLINOIS, 493 U.S. 307 (1990), the Court halted nearly forty years of the impeachment exception's expansion. A 5–4 majority, per Brennan, J., refused to expand the "impeachment exception" to the exclusionary rule to permit the prosecution to impeach the testimony of *all defense witnesses* with illegally obtained evidence. According to the majority, expanding the impeachment exception to such an extent "would not further the truthseeking value with equal force but would appreciably undermine the deterrent effect of the exclusionary rule."

The case arose as follows: A day after a murder occurred, the police took James, a suspect, into custody. He was found at his mother's beauty salon sitting

---

a. Support for this criticism may be found in James Kainen, *The Impeachment Exception to the Exclusionary Rules: Policies, Principles and Politics,* 44 Stan.L.Rev. 1301 (1992).

under a hair dryer; when he emerged, his hair was black and curly. When the police questioned James about his prior hair color, he told them it had been reddish-brown, long, and combed straight back. When questioned later at the police station, James stated that he had his hair dyed black and curled at the beauty parlor in order to change his appearance. Because the police lacked probable cause for James' arrest, both statements regarding his hair were suppressed.

At the trial, five eye witnesses testified that the person responsible for the murder had long, "reddish" hair, worn in a slicked-back style and that they had seen James several weeks earlier, at which time he had the aforementioned hair color and style. James did not testify in his own defense. He called as a witness Jewel Henderson, a family friend. She testified that on the day of the shooting James' hair had been black. The state then impeached Henderson's testimony by reporting James' prior admissions that he had reddish hair at the time of the shooting and had dyed and curled his hair the next day in order to change his appearance. James ultimately was convicted of murder. The Illinois Supreme Court concluded, that, in order to deter "perjury by proxy," the impeachment exception ought to allow the state to impeach the testimony of defense witnesses other than the defendant himself. The U.S. Supreme Court reversed:

"Expanding the class of impeachable witnesses from the defendant alone to all defense witnesses would create different incentives affecting the behavior of both defendants and law enforcement officers. As a result, this expansion would not promote the truthseeking function to the same extent as did creation of the original exception, and yet it would significantly undermine the deterrent effect of the general exclusionary rule. Hence, we believe that this proposed expansion would frustrate rather than further the purposes underlying the exclusionary rule.

"The previously recognized exception penalizes defendants for committing perjury by allowing the prosecution to expose their perjury through impeachment using illegally obtained evidence. [But] the exception leaves defendants free to testify truthfully on their own behalf; they can offer probative and exculpatory evidence to the jury without opening the door to impeachment by carefully avoiding any statements that directly contradict the suppressed evidence. The exception thus generally discourages perjured testimony without discouraging truthful testimony.

"In contrast, expanding the impeachment exception to encompass the testimony of all defense witnesses would not have the same beneficial effects. First, the mere threat of a subsequent criminal prosecution for perjury is far more likely to deter a witness from intentionally lying on a defendant's behalf than to deter a defendant, already facing conviction for the underlying offense, from lying on his own behalf.

"More significantly, expanding the impeachment exception to encompass the testimony of all defense witnesses likely would chill some defendants from presenting their best defense—and sometimes any defense at all—through the testimony of others. [Defendants] might reasonably fear that one or more of their witnesses, in a position to offer truthful and favorable testimony, would also make some statement in sufficient tension with the tainted evidence to allow the prosecutor to introduce that evidence for impeachment. [As] a result, an expanded impeachment exception likely would chill some defendants from calling witnesses who would otherwise offer probative evidence.[6]

---

6. * * * [The] dissent embraces the Illinois Supreme Court's suggestion that prosecutors could be allowed to impeach witnesses only when their testimony is in "direct conflict" with the illegally seized evidence. [But] the result of [an] inquiry distinguishing between "direct" and "indirect" evidentiary conflicts is far from predictable. [The] uncertainty whether a court might

"This realization alters the balance of values underlying the current impeachment exception governing defendants' testimony. [Given] the potential chill created by expanding the impeachment exception, the conceded gains to the truthseeking process from discouraging or disclosing perjured testimony would be offset to some extent by the concomitant loss of probative witness testimony. Thus, the truthseeking rationale supporting the impeachment of defendants in *Walder* and its progeny does not apply to other witnesses with equal force.

"Moreover, the proposed expansion of the current impeachment exception would significantly weaken the exclusionary rule's deterrent effect on police misconduct.

"[Expanding] the impeachment exception to *all* defense witnesses would significantly enhance the expected value to the prosecution of illegally obtained evidence. First, this expansion would vastly increase the number of occasions on which such evidence could be used. [Moreover,] due to the chilling effect identified above, illegally obtained evidence holds even greater value to the prosecution for each individual witness than for each defendant. The prosecutor's access to impeachment evidence would not just deter perjury; it would also deter defendants from calling witnesses in the first place, thereby keeping from the jury much probative exculpatory evidence. * * *"[a]

Dissenting Justice Kennedy, joined by Rehnquist, C.J., and O'Connor and Scalia, JJ., maintained that the majority had given the exclusionary rule excessive protection but had afforded the truth-seeking function of the criminal trial inadequate weight:

"[The] line drawn by today's opinion grants the defense side in a criminal case broad immunity to introduce whatever false testimony it can produce from the mouth of a friendly witness. [A] more cautious course is available, one that retains Fourth Amendment protections and yet safeguards the truth-seeking function of the criminal trial.

"[To] deprive the jurors of knowledge that statements of the defendant himself revealed the witness' testimony to be false would result in a decision by triers of fact who were not just kept in the dark as to excluded evidence, but positively misled. The potential for harm to the truth-seeking process resulting from the majority's new rule in fact will be greater than if the defendant himself had testified. It is natural for jurors to be skeptical of self-serving testimony by the defendant. Testimony by a witness said to be independent has the greater potential to deceive. And if a defense witness can present false testimony with impunity, the jurors may find the rest of the prosecution's case suspect, for ineffective and artificial cross-examination will be viewed as a real weakness in the State's case. Jurors will assume that if the prosecution had any proof the statement was false, it would make the proof known. The majority does more than deprive the prosecution of evidence. The State must also suffer the introduction of false testimony and appear to bolster the falsehood by its own silence."

NOTES AND QUESTIONS

(a) *The "Pinocchio defense witness" (a defense witness other than the defendant who lies at trial to benefit the defendant).* Consider Note, 1990 U.Ill.L.F. 375, 473: "Although Pinocchio is deterred from lying by the threat of perjury prosecution, cases abound where defense witnesses nevertheless commit perjury. [Mean-

---

find a witness' testimony to pose a "direct" conflict and therefore trigger the impeachment exception likely will chill defendant's presentation of potential witnesses in many cases.

a. Stevens, J., who joined the opinion of the Court, also wrote a separate opinion.

while, the defendant, Stromboli (in the Pinocchio story the puppeteer who caused Pinocchio to become a liar)], benefits from the lies by receiving an acquittal. To further the truthfinding function of the criminal justice system, the goal of judicial integrity, and the policy against perjury, Stromboli also must be deterred from resorting to Pinocchio's perjurious testimony. [If] perjurious testimony is an affront to the legal system, it does not matter whether the perjury comes from the defendant's own lips or the lips of the Pinocchio defense witness."

(b) *The dissent's selective assumptions.* The *James* dissent, notes James Spira, *James v. Illinois: A Halt to the Expansion of the Impeachment Exception,* 15 So.Ill.U.L.J. 27, 51 (1990), "is willing to assume that a defense witness, un-schooled and unfamiliar with the law, will be well versed in the quantum of proof necessary for a perjury conviction, but is unwilling to assume that police, who are in and out of court constantly, will not realize that the discovery of illegally obtained evidence will aid a conviction in light of an expanded impeachment exception."

(c) *Why should the impeachment of defense witnesses be restricted more severely than impeachment of defendants?* Consider James Kainen, *The Impeachment Exception to the Exclusionary Rules: Policies, Principles, and Politics,* 44 Stan.L.Rev. 1301, 1322–23 (1992):

"Although he argued that limitations on the impeachment of defense wit-nesses were necessary to confine the incentive to gather proof illegally to an acceptable level, Justice Kennedy was unable to explain why identical restrictions should not also be applied to the impeachment of defendants. Alternatively, if the impeachment of defendants should not be restricted, then such restrictions are similarly unnecessary to protect defense witnesses. As a result, Justice Kennedy could not demonstrate that extending the exception as he proposed would effect net gains, just as the majority could not demonstrate that its result would effect net losses when both truth-seeking and deterrence costs were tallied. * * *

"Justice Kennedy's truth-seeking analysis contended that contradiction of defense witness testimony is particularly important because juries are more likely to believe such testimony. [If so,] witness testimony should be more readily impeached than that of defendants."

(d) *Are the impeachment exception cases based on a faulty premise?* Do *James* and other cases dealing with the impeachment exception rest on the premise that it is possible to accommodate both rules of evidence and principles of constitution-al criminal procedure within a neutral framework? Is this premise sound? Are the contradictory values reflected in constitutional criminal procedure principles and evidentiary concepts susceptible to neutral accommodation? Should any analysis of the scope of the exclusionary rules be recast exclusively as an issue of constitu-tional procedure, rather than as a compromise between those rules and the rules of evidence? See Kainen, supra, at 1304–05, 1326–27, 1362–72.

B. WHAT KINDS OF CONSTITUTIONAL OR OTHER VIOLATIONS ARE ENCOMPASSED WITHIN THE IMPEACHMENT EXCEPTION?

1. *New Jersey v. Portash,* 440 U.S. 450 (1979) held, per Stewart, J. that testimony given by a person in response to a grant of legislative immunity could not be used to impeach him at his subsequent trial for extortion and misconduct in office. "Central to the decisions" in *Harris* and *Hass,* emphasized the Court, was the fact that the defendant made no claim that the statements were coerced. But testimony before a grand jury in response to a grant of use immunity "is the essence of coerced testimony." Balancing of interests was thought to be necessary in *Harris* and *Hass* "when the attempt to deter unlawful police conduct collided with the need to prevent perjury. Here, by contrast, we deal with the constitutional privilege against compulsory self-incrimination in its most pristine form. Balancing, therefore, is not simply unnecessary. It is impermissible."

2. In *Mincey v. Arizona* (1978), p. 911, the Court also distinguished *Harris* and *Hass* and made clear that the use of an "involuntary" or "coerced" statement even for impeachment purposes would constitute "a denial of due process of law." But the Court's discussion seemed to overlook the possibility that an "involuntary" statement may be trustworthy in a particular case.

3. In KANSAS v. VENTRIS, 556 U.S. 586 (2009), a 5–4 majority, per Scalia, J., held that a defendant's incriminating statement to a jailhouse informant, concededly obtained in violation of the *Massiah* doctrine, could be used to impeach the defendant's trial testimony:

"Whether otherwise excluded evidence can be admitted for purposes of impeachment depends upon the nature of the constitutional guarantee that is violated. [The privilege against compelled self-incrimination] is violated whenever a truly coerced confession is introduced at trial, whether by way of impeachment or otherwise. [In the case of the Fourth Amendment, however, which says nothing about excluding the evidence], exclusion comes by way of deterrent sanction rather than to avoid violation of the substantive guarantee. Inadmissibility has not been automatic, therefore, but we have instead applied an exclusionary rule balancing test. The same is true for violations of the Fifth and Sixth Amendment prophylactic rules forbidding certain pretrial police conduct. * * *

"It is illogical to say that the [*Massiah* right] is not violated until trial counsel's task of opposing conviction has been undermined by the statement's admission into evidence. A defendant is not denied counsel merely because the prosecution has been permitted to introduce evidence of guilt—even evidence so overwhelming that the attorney's job of gaining an acquittal is rendered impossible. In such circumstances the accused continues to enjoy the assistance of counsel; the assistance is simply not worth much. The assistance of counsel has been denied, however, at the prior critical stage which produced the inculpatory evidence. * * * We have never said officers may badger counseled defendants about charged crimes so long as they do not use information they gain. The constitutional violation occurs when the uncounseled interrogation is conducted."

Justice Scalia emphasized that the instant case did not involve "the prevention of a constitutional violation, but rather the scope of the remedy for a violation that has already occurred." In such circumstances, "the game of excluding tainted evidence for impeachment purposes is not worth the candle. The interests safeguarded by such exclusion are 'outweighed by the need to prevent perjury and to assure the integrity of the trial process.' "

Moreover, "even if 'the officer may be said to have little to lose and perhaps something to gain by way of possibly uncovering impeachment material,' " continued Justice Scalia, "we have multiple times rejected the argument that this 'speculative possibility' can trump the costs of allowing perjurious statements to go unchallenged. We have held in every other context that tainted evidence—evidence whose very introduction does not constitute the constitutional violation, but whose obtaining was constitutionally invalid—is admissible for impeachment."

Dissenting Justice Stevens joined by Ginsburg, J., protested:

"The pretrial right to counsel is not ancillary to, or of lesser importance than, the right to rely on counsel at trial. * * * We have never endorsed the notion that the pretrial right stands at the periphery of the Sixth Amendment. To the contrary, we have explained that the pretrial period is 'perhaps the most critical period of the proceedings' during which a defendant 'requires the guiding hand of counsel.' *Powell v. Alabama* [pp. 71, 73]. Placing the prophylactic label on a core Sixth Amendment right mischaracterizes the sweep of the constitutional guarantee."

"Treating the State's action in this case as a violation of a prophylactic right, the Court concludes that introducing the illegally obtained evidence does not itself violate the Constitution. I strongly disagree. [The] use of ill-gotten evidence during any phase of criminal prosecution does damage to the adversarial process—the fairness of which the Sixth Amendment was designed to protect.

"[When] counsel is excluded from a critical pretrial interaction between the defendant and the State, she may be unable to effectively counter the potentially devastating and potentially false,[1] evidence subsequently introduced at trial. Inexplicably, today's Court refuses to recognize that this is a constitutional harm."

Contrasting the Massiah *Right with Fourth Amendment Rights*

"What makes an illegal search objectionable," observes Sherry Colb, *Kansas v. Ventris: The Supreme Court Misconstrues the Right to Counsel*, <http:/writ.news.findlaw.com/colb/20090610.html> (June 10, 2009), "is the unjustified invasion of a person's privacy and security. [Although an illegal search or seizure may be *motivated* by a desire for a later prosecution (a motive which suggest that the misbehavior will be responsive to an exclusionary rule), the harm has already occurred by the time of trial and indeed requires no trial to be cognizable: If you are searched in violation of the Fourth Amendment, you may sue the police whether or not you are charged with a crime and, indeed, whether or not the police ever found evidence in the course of their search.]"

"What makes an uncounselled interrogation objectionable, by contrast, has everything to do with the later trial and evidence. [For] *Massiah* purposes, [the state's elicitation of statements from the defendant] does not inflict any harm unless a trial follows at which resulting statements are offered in evidence.

"[There] is nothing inherently objectionable [about] deliberately saying something to a suspect that motivates him to confess (assuming the police have not behaved in a coercive manner that would trigger Fifth Amendment concerns). It is thus very peculiar for Justice Scalia to suggest that even absent later admission into evidence, police conduct whose illegality turns entirely on whether a suspect has already been charged, would represent a Sixth Amendment violation. If no trial takes place, the suspect in [a case like *Brewer v. Williams*, the Christian Burial Speech Case,] (though asked, without counsel where the body was buried) suffers no Sixth Amendment harm. He would presumably not, therefore, be able to sue the police under § 1983 [for] a deprivation of his right to counsel."

C. USE OF DEFENDANT'S PRIOR SILENCE FOR IMPEACHMENT PURPOSES

1. *Doyle v. Ohio*: *impeachment by use of defendant's silence after being given the Miranda warnings.* After being arrested for selling marijuana to an informant, defendants were given the *Miranda* warnings and chose to remain silent. At trial, each defendant claimed that he had been "framed" by narcotics agents. In an effort to undercut their testimony, the prosecution was

---

1. The likelihood that evidence gathered by self-interested jailhouse informants may be false cannot be ignored. * * *

allowed to ask each defendant why he had not told this story to the arresting officer. In *Doyle v. Ohio,* 426 U.S. 610 (1976), a 6–3 majority, per Powell, J., held such use of a defendant's post-arrest silence, after receiving the *Miranda* warnings, impermissible. Not only is "every post-arrest silence * * * insolubly ambiguous because of what the State is required to advise the person arrested," but use of the silence to impeach would be "fundamentally unfair" given the fact that the *Miranda* warnings contain the "implicit" "assurance" that "silence will carry no penalty."[a]

2.   *The "English warnings": what, if after advising a suspect of her right to remain silent, the officer added: "However, it may harm your defense later if you do not mention, when questioned, something you rely on in court"?* This change would make the *Miranda* warnings essentially the "English warnings." In England, observes Craig M. Bradley, *Should American Courts Heed the 'English Warnings'?,* TRIAL, Dec. 2007, p. 62, "if you don't mention an alibi, cite self-defense, or say something else that you would naturally be expected to tell the police and then raise it as a defense in court, your earlier silence during the interrogation can be used against you." If such a warning were given to American suspects, could their silence be used to impeach them?

Yes, maintains Professor Bradley, supra: *Doyle* "rested entirely on a due process rationale and was not grounded on the Fifth Amendment right to silence." Moreover, notes Bradley, two post-*Doyle* cases, *Fletcher v. Weir* and *Jenkins v. Anderson* (both discussed below) indicate that a change from the *Miranda* warnings to the English warnings would be permissible.

"Most telling," adds Bradley, is *South Dakota v. Neville,* 459 U.S. 553 (1983) (also discussed at p. 610, n. a), which upheld the admissibility of a drunk-driving suspect's refusal to take a blood-alcohol test, "allow[ing] police officers to avoid the *Doyle* problem by the simple expedient of warning a suspect that noncooperation may be used against him or her in some way."[b]

Aren't most suspects likely to be confused by the "English warnings"? Aren't they likely to wonder how they can have *a right* to remain silent when asserting that right can harm their defense later on? If a suspect asks the average police officer to explain that, is he likely to do so in less than a few hundred words?

3.   *Use of defendant's prearrest silence for impeachment purposes.* In *Jenkins v. Anderson,* 447 U.S. 231 (1980), where at his murder trial petitioner claimed self-defense, the prosecutor was allowed to question him about the fact that he had not surrendered to the authorities until two weeks after the killing. In closing argument, the prosecutor again referred to petitioner's prearrest silence, noting that he had "waited" at least two weeks before "reporting" the stabbing to anyone, suggesting that he would have spoken out if he had truly killed in self-defense. The Court, per Powell, J., held (1), relying heavily on *Raffel v. United*

---

a.   However, after receiving the *Miranda* warnings, a defendant may be impeached for his inconsistent *statements.* See *Anderson v. Charles,* 447 U.S. 404 (1980) (per curiam). After giving a different version of the crime to the police than he subsequently did when he testified in his own defense, defendant was asked on cross-examination why he did so. The Court had little difficulty permitting such cross-examination: "[*Doyle*] does not apply to cross-examination that merely inquires into prior inconsistent statements. Such questioning makes no unfair use of silence, because a defendant who voluntarily speaks after receiving *Miranda* warnings has not been reduced to remain silent."

b.   However, Professor Bradley balks at using suspects' silence after they have asserted their right to counsel or after they have consulted with counsel. He regards "silence based on an expressed desire to speak with counsel [as] 'insolubly ambiguous' as the silence in *Doyle.* Moreover, assertion of the right to counsel "is a suspect's cry for help, whereas asserting the right to remain silent shows the suspect's awareness that he or she is in control of the situation" But doesn't a suspect's invocation of the right to counsel show that he is in control of the situation just as much, or maybe even more, than does the assertion of the right to remain silent?

States, 271 U.S. 494 (1926), that the Self–Incrimination Clause is not violated by the use of prearrest silence to impeach a defendant's credibility;[c] and (2) *Doyle* presents no obstacle for "no governmental action induced petitioner to remain silent before arrest. The failure to speak occurred before petitioner was taken into custody and given *Miranda* warnings."[d]

Dissenting Justice Marshall, joined by Brennan, J., contended that the Court's holding "has three patent—and in my view, fatal—defects": (1) Considering the various possible explanations for silence (e.g., Jenkins' story would have implicated him in the homicide), "the mere fact of prearrest silence is so unlikely to be probative of the falsity of the defendant's trial strategy that its use for impeachment is contrary to [due process]." (2) "[T]he drawing of an adverse inference from the failure to volunteer incriminating statements impermissibly infringes the privilege against self-incrimination." (3) "[T]he availability of the inference for impeachment purposes impermissibly burdens the decision to exercise the constitutional right to testify in one's own defense."

4. *Use of defendant's post-arrest silence for impeachment purposes.* When arrested, Weir, a murder suspect, said nothing, but the "significant difference" between this case and *Doyle* is that Weir did not receive any *Miranda* warnings during the period in which he remained silent immediately after his arrest. When Weir testified at his trial that he had acted in self-defense, the prosecutor cross-examined him as to why, when arrested, he had not offered this exculpatory explanation. *Fletcher v. Weir,* 455 U.S. 603 (1982) (per curiam), held that "in the absence of the sort of affirmative assurances embodied in the *Miranda* warnings" a state may permit cross-examination about post-arrest silence when a defendant chooses to take the stand. The Court rejected the argument that an arrest, by itself, is "governmental action which implicitly induces a defendant to remain silent," deeming such "broadening of *Doyle* * * * unsupported by the reasoning of that case and contrary to our post-*Doyle* decisions."

NOTES AND QUESTIONS

(a) Suppose, when arrested, Weir had said, "I believe I have a perfectly valid defense, but I don't think I should talk to you until I first have a chance to talk to my lawyer." Could that statement and/or the subsequent post-arrest silence be used for impeachment purposes?

(b) Suppose, when being driven to the station house, a suspect asks the arresting officer, "Do I have a right to remain silent?" Or, "Do I have a right to discuss my situation with a lawyer before saying anything about it to a police officer?" How should the officer respond?

(c) Suppose, when being driven to the station house, a suspect asks the arresting officer whether he has a right to remain silent or whether his silence can be used against him at the trial and the officer meets such questions with a stony silence? What result if the suspect then says nothing during the rest of the drive?

---

c. For strong criticism of this portion of the opinion, see Stephen A. Saltzburg, *Foreword: The Flow and Ebb of Constitutional Criminal Procedure in the Warren and Burger Courts,* 69 Geo. L.J. 151, 204–05 (1980).

d. But see Craig M. Bradley, *Havens, Jenkins, and Salvucci, and the Defendant's "Right" to Testify,* 18 Am.Crim.L.Rev. 419, 434–35 (1981), maintaining that the silence in *Jenkins* was just as equivocal as that in *Doyle* for "an individual's reluctance to hand himself over to the police and admit a stabbing, in self-defense or otherwise," is not probative of guilt. "Anyone who believes that volunteering information to police is 'natural' for a resident of Detroit's inner-city has an unusually optimistic view of human nature." See also Note, 94 Harv.L.Rev. 77, 84–85 (1980).

What result if the suspect then starts talking and makes incriminating statements?

D. USE OF POST-*MIRANDA* WARNINGS SILENCE OR ASSERTION OF RIGHTS TO REBUT DEFENSE OF INSANITY

May a defendant's post-Miranda warnings silence or request for counsel be offered not to impeach but as substantive evidence to rebut defendant's defense of insanity at the time of the offense? No, answers *Wainwright v. Greenfield,* 474 U.S. 284 (1986). On three occasions shortly after his arrest in Florida for sexual battery, Greenfield was given the Miranda warnings. Each time he exercised his right to remain silent and stated that he wished to speak with an attorney before answering any questions. Greenfield later pled guilty by reason of insanity. At his trial two police officers described the occasions on which Greenfield had exercised his right to remain silent and had expressed a desire to consult with counsel. In his closing argument, the prosecutor reviewed this police testimony and suggested that Greenfield's responses to the warnings demonstrated a degree of comprehension inconsistent with his claim of insanity. Greenfield was convicted and sentenced to life imprisonment. The Court, per Stevens, J., overturned his conviction, holding that *Doyle* applied to his case:

"The point of [*Doyle*] is that it is fundamentally unfair to promise an arrested person that his silence will not be used against him and thereafter to breach that promise by using the silence to impeach his trial testimony. It is equally unfair to breach that promise by using silence to overcome a defendant's plea of insanity. In both situations [the State] implicitly promises that any exercise of these rights will not be penalized."[a]

E. HOW MUCH LEEWAY DO THE "IMPEACHMENT" CASES AND "FRUIT OF THE POISONOUS TREE" CASES GIVE A "BAD MAN OF THE LAW"?

"Ten years ago, Albert Alschuler hypothesized about the advice that 'Justice Holmes' 'bad man of the law' " might offer in a [police] training manual.[134] Alschuler thought that a bad officer, one who cared only about the material consequences of and not the reason for his conduct, might author a manual advising police to continue to interrogate a suspect who asked for counsel or wished to remain silent. Alschuler's writing proved prescient. In deciding [such cases as *Harris, Hass, Tucker* and *Elstad*] the Court could not have intended to give police grounds to disobey this portion of *Miranda* deliberately, but this disregard is the natural consequence of these decisions. [These cases] provide an unfortunate opening for the quintessential 'bad man of the law.' "

---

a. Rehnquist, J., joined by the Chief Justice, concurred in the result because one of the prosecutor's remarks was "an improper comment on respondent's silence." But he maintained that "a request for a lawyer may be highly relevant where the plea is based on insanity"—"there is no 'insoluble ambiguity' in the request; it is a perfectly straightforward statement tending to show that an individual is able to understand his rights and is not incoherent or obviously confused or unbalanced"—and he did not read the warnings "as containing any promise, express or implied, that the words used in responding to notice of the right to a lawyer will not be used by the State to rebut a claim of insanity."

134. Albert W. Alschuler, *Failed Pragmatism: Reflections on the Burger Court,* 100 Harv. L.Rev. 1436, 1442 (1987) (quoting O. W. Holmes, *The Path of the Law,* 10 Harv.L.Rev. 457, 459 (1897)).

—Charles D. Weisselberg, *Saving Miranda* 84 Cornell L.Rev. 109, 132 (1998).

———

Pointing to police training materials uncovered in the course of litigation seeking to stop officers in two California police departments from questioning custodial suspects after they have asserted their *Miranda* rights, Professor Weisselberg, supra, reports that "[in] California and, to a certain extent in other states, police have developed the tactics of questioning 'outside *Miranda*,' meaning questioning over the direct and unambiguous assertion of Fifth Amendment rights." The police are instructed to go "outside *Miranda*" in order to obtain the "fruits" of any statement the suspect may make or to obtain statements that may be used later for impeachment purposes. The full transcript of the videotape of a deputy district attorney instructing the police to this effect is reprinted in the Appendix to Weisselberg's article.

SECTION 4. ALLOCATION OF THE BURDENS OF PROOF

PEOPLE v. BERRIOS
270 N.E.2d 709 (N.Y.1971).

SCILEPPI, JUDGE.

In each of [these] appeals, the defendants have been charged with possession of heroin and arresting officers have testified that glassine envelopes containing narcotics were dropped on the ground as the defendants were approached by the police.[a] We have been called upon to decide whether, in these "dropsy" cases, or for that matter whenever a warrantless search is presented, it is the People who must bear the burden of proving the legality of the search and seizure. [In each of the cases before the court, an officer testified that as he made a movement toward the defendant—leaving his car in one case, instructing the defendant to stop in another—the defendant dropped a glassine envelope containing narcotics. The officer was undercover in one case and in uniform in another.]

Simply stated, [defendants] have contended that the police testimony in these cases is inherently untrustworthy and the product of fabrication; hence, the argument is advanced that we should require that the People bear the burden of proving admissibility and depart from our present rule which places the burden of showing inadmissibility on the defendant. No argument is proffered that this departure is required by either the State or Federal Constitutions; rather, it is

---

a. In New York, as in most jurisdictions, challenges to the admissibility of evidence on the ground that it was illegally obtained must be presented by a pretrial motion to suppress. The motion must set forth the objection with sufficient particularity, which usually requires that the defense specify the nature of the alleged illegality in the acquisition of evidence (e.g., that a statement was obtained in violation of *Miranda*, or that the search in question was incident to an arrest not supported by probable cause). See CRIMPROC § 10.1(b). Assuming the form of the motion is correct, the trial judge will then hold a pretrial hearing at which both sides can offer its testimony regarding the acquisition of the evidence and cross-examine the other side's witnesses. Denial of the pretrial motion does not allow an immediate appeal by the defense, but the prosecution often can appeal the granting of the motion. See Ch. 28. § 3.

In those jurisdictions that do not require a pretrial motion, an objection may be made at trial, contemporaneously with the introduction of the evidence. An objection at this point ordinarily requires the trial court to recess the trial in order to conduct a hearing on the suppression objection. Whether a state requires a pretrial motion or a contemporaneous objection, failure to make a timely objection can result in the procedural forfeiture of the objection. See *Wainwright v. Sykes,* p. 1583; and CRIMPROC § 10.2(a).

asserted that the change in burden of proof is necessary to alleviate the possibility of perjured police testimony. It is noted by this court that the District Attorney of New York County has joined defense counsel in [one] case in suggesting the change in burden of proof. This concession does not, however, relieve us from the performance of our judicial function and does not require us to adopt the proposal urged upon us. [W]e are not persuaded that a change in burden of proof is indicated.

Thus far, we have made it clear that where a defendant challenges the admissibility of physical evidence or makes a motion to suppress, he bears the ultimate burden of proving that the evidence should not be used against him. [Since] such a person makes the claim because he contends that he is aggrieved and requests the court to give redress to an alleged wrong, it is most reasonable to require him to bear the burden of proof of that wrong. The People must, of course, always show that police conduct was reasonable. Thus, though a defendant who challenges the legality of a search and seizure has the burden of proving illegality, the People are nevertheless put to "the burden of *going forward* to show the legality of the police conduct in the first instance". These considerations require that the People show that the search was made pursuant to a valid warrant, consent, incident to a lawful arrest or, in cases such as those here, that no search at all occurred because the evidence was dropped by the defendant in the presence of the police officer.

* * * We have been told that with the advent of *Mapp v. Ohio*, there has been a great incidence of "dropsy" testimony by police officers. Hence, this court has been asked to infer that the police are systematically evading the mandate of *Mapp* by fabricating their testimony. [We] reject this frontal attack on the integrity of our entire law enforcement system. * * * Some police officers, as well as some in other callings may be tempted to tamper with the truth. But there is no valid proof that all members of law enforcement agencies or that all other citizens who testify are perjurers. Therefore, all policemen should not be singled out as suspect as a matter of law.

The fact that some witnesses may lie does not require a change in the burden of proof for it is our view that the proposal made in this appeal is no more effective in preventing perjury than the present burden of proof. Under both the suggested change and the present system, the defendant must still refute the testimony of the police officer. Thus, even where the officer testifies that glassine envelopes were dropped by the defendant or to facts which would sustain a warrantless search, the court would still be faced with the same credibility question. Since a change in the burden of proof would be ineffective to combat the alleged evil about which the defendants herein complain, principles of *stare decisis* do not allow a departure from our present rule of burden of proof.

[There] are more appropriate methods of dealing with the abuses about which the defendants complain. For example, [police departments] can effectively formulate internal procedures and policies within the department to eliminate any such abuses. [The] district attorneys of this State should evaluate the testimony of police officers, as they do the testimony of all witnesses, in determining what proof will be offered in the prosecution of a case. * * *

FULD, CHIEF JUDGE (dissenting).

[The] District Attorney of New York County informs us [that]: "For the last ten years participants in the system of justice—judges, prosecutors, defense attorneys and police officials—have privately and publicly expressed the belief that in some substantial but indeterminable percentage of dropsy cases, the testimony [that a defendant dropped narcotics or gambling slips to the ground as a police officer approached him] is tailored to meet the requirements of search-and-seizure rulings" and "it is very difficult in many [such] cases to distinguish between fact and fiction." When so able and dedicated a prosecutor as District Attorney Frank Hogan believes that there is basis for questioning the truthfulness of the testimony in a "substantial * * * percentage of dropsy cases," the conclusion seems to me inescapable [that] the integrity of the judicial process demands that there be a reallocation of the burden of proof. * * *

Underlying the Fourth and Fourteenth Amendments is the basic proposition that "no man is to be convicted on unconstitutional evidence." In light of the situation as it today exists, the present rule—which imposes upon the accused the burden of proving the illegality of a seizure on a motion to suppress—subverts this principle by making it possible for some defendants to be convicted on evidence obtained in violation of constitutional guarantees. This follows from the fact that a trial judge who is unsure whether the prosecution's account of the seizure is credible must, nevertheless, resolve his doubt in favor of the People and admit the evidence. To thus increase the likelihood of a conviction on proof of dubious constitutionality must be stamped as highly unreasonable and unfair. A change in the rule will help assure that a defendant's constitutional rights will not be violated since, by placing the burden on the People, the judge will be permitted to suppress evidence in cases where, for instance, he finds the testimony of each side evenly balanced on the scales of credibility and is unable to make up his mind as to who is telling the truth.

[Those] who recognize the problem and favor a change in the burden of proof rule do not, contrary to the majority's assertion, intend an "attack on the integrity of our entire law enforcement system." Rather, their concern is solely to promote adherence to the principles articulated in *Mapp v. Ohio*.

[Reason] and the imperative of judicial integrity, as well as substantial authority, dictate that the burden of proving the lawfulness of a search or seizure should be cast on the People in all narcotics and gambling cases when the search or seizure has been effected without a warrant. To do less, to shift the burden of proof to the People only in the classic dropsy situation, seems to me, as it does to the New York County District Attorney, "unrealistic." This is so, as he observes, not only because an "untruthful officer fearing rejection of tailored dropsy testimony could easily shift to the other scenarios which are familiar in narcotics and gambling cases in the lower courts" but also because "it is the experience of many prosecutors and judges that the problems of credibility and fact-finding raised [are] not limited to literal dropsy cases [but] appear in all types of possessory narcotics and gambling cases."

BURKE, JASEN and GIBSON, JJ., concur with SCILEPPI, J. FULD, C.J., dissents and votes to reverse in a separate opinion in which BERGAN and BREITEL, JJ., concur.

NOTES AND QUESTIONS

1. How common is police "falsification"? As pointed out in Gabriel J. Chin & Scott C. Wells, *"The Blue Wall of Silence" As Evidence of Bias and Motive to Lie: A New Approach to Police Perjury*, 59 U.Pitt.L.Rev. 233, 234 (1998), in 1994 the Mollen Commission, established to investigate police misconduct in New York, "reported that police 'falsification'—which includes 'testimonial perjury, * * * documentary perjury, [and] falsification of police records'—is one of the most common forms of police corruption facing the nation's criminal justice system. In fact, the Mollen Commission indicated that in New York, 'the practice of police falsification [is] so common in certain precincts that it has spawned its own word: "testilying." See also Morgan Cloud, *Judges, "Testilying," and the Constitution*, 69 S.Cal.L.Rev. 1341 (1996); Donald A. Dripps, *Police, Plus Perjury,*

Equals Polygraphy, 86 J.Crim.L. & C. 693 (1996); Christopher Slobogin, *Testilying: Police Perjury and What to Do About It*, 67 U.Colo.L.Rev. 1037 (1996).

2. Was there police perjury in the O.J. Simpson case? Detective Mark Fuhrman tried to defend the warrantless search of Simpson's residential property shortly after the murder of his former wife by testifying that at the time of the search the police did not know "if we have a murder-suicide, a kidnapping, another victim" and "we had to find out if there's anybody in the residence that's injured, to save their life, to save other people's lives." Despite the incredulous public response to the claim, two judges denied Simpson's suppression motions. For a discussion of why the police testimony about the purpose of the search of Simpson's residence "raised the specter of perjury designed to shield the fruits of an illegal search," see Morgan Cloud, supra, at 1357–61.

3. State variations. Aside from the justification of a search on the basis of consent—where the burden universally is placed on the prosecution—states vary considerably in the allocation of both the burden of going forward and the ultimate burden of proof (the burden of persuasion) on Fourth Amendment claims. Ignoring minor variations, the state's position on these burdens usually will fall within one of four general categories:

(a) Under the New York approach, as noted in *Berrios,* the prosecution has the burden of going forward—i.e., introducing evidence that, if accepted, would establish the legality of the search. Thus, in a case involving a search incident to arrest, the prosecution would initially introduce the testimony of an officer showing that probable cause for the arrest existed and that the search was within the scope permitted incident to an arrest. The burden of persuasion would then be on the defendant to rebut this evidence and prove that the search was invalid.

(b) Several states place *both* burdens of proof on the defendant. This position has been justified on several grounds: "(a) the burden should be upon the moving party, (b) there is a presumption of regularity attending the actions of law enforcement officials, (c) relevant evidence is generally admissible and thus exceptions must be justified by those claiming the exception, and (d) [this allocation] will deter spurious allegations wasteful of court time." SEARCHSZR § 11.2(b).

(c) A majority of the states follow the pattern of allocation adopted in the federal courts—if the search was pursuant to a warrant, the defendant has the burden of proof, but if the police acted without a warrant, the burden is on the prosecution. The burden of going forward follows the burden of proof. Where there was a search without a warrant, the defendant must make a prima facie showing of that fact before the prosecution is put to its burdens. Very often, however, the parties will agree as to how the evidence was obtained and an allegation of seizure without a warrant will be sufficient.

As noted in SEARCHSZR § 11.2(b), the federal pattern's "warrant-no-warrant dichotomy is typically explained on the ground that when the police have acted with a warrant 'an independent determination on the issue of probable cause has already been made by a magistrate, thereby giving rise to a presumption of legality,' while when they have acted without a warrant 'the evidence comprising probable cause is particularly within the knowledge and control of the arresting agencies.' Moreover, it is said that '[w]ithout such a rule there would be little reason for law enforcement agencies to bother with the formality of a warrant.'"

(d) In some jurisdictions, the prosecution has both burdens of proof on all Fourth Amendment objections. The reason commonly given as noted in SEARCHSZR § 11.2(b), is that "the state is the party which seeks to use the evidence and thus ought to bear the burden of establishing that it was lawfully come by."

4. Practical consequences of the allocation. Of what practical significance is the allocation of the ultimate burden of proof on Fourth Amendment claims? Compare the views of the majority and dissent in *Berrios* on the relation of the burden of proof to judicial treatment of police testimony in "dropsy" cases. Assuming one shared the objective of the dissent, would a better solution have been a direction to the lower courts to subject such testimony to "close scrutiny," in much the same way that a jury is directed that testimony of an accomplice or paid informer should be "scrutinized and received with care"? See Comment, 60 Geo.L.J. 507, 519–20 (1971).

Comments of defense counsel suggest that the allocation of the burden of going forward, and even the specificity required in the motion to suppress, may be more significant than the allocation of the ultimate burden of proof. Thus, Anthony Amsterdam, *Trial Manual for the Defense of Criminal Cases* § 252 (5th ed.1988), notes that a basic tactical objective of the defense is to avoid first disclosing its factual theories, lest the police "conform their testimony" to evade those theories. If defendant is required to go forward with the evidence, he often must, as a practical matter, first take the stand to tell "his side of the story." Although the officers, as prospective witnesses, usually may be excluded from the courtroom while this testimony is given, the defendant still is not in as good a position to rebut their testimony as he would be if he testified last. The defense bearing the burden of production may seek to satisfy it without using the defendant's testimony by calling the officers as its own witnesses. However, this tactic may backfire if the court is unwilling to treat the officers as "adverse" witnesses subject to impeachment. Id. at § 253.

5. Constitutional requirements. Why was it that the defendants in *Berrios* failed to argue that the federal constitution required the prosecution to bear the burden of proof? *Bumper v. North Carolina,* p. 459, held, as a matter of constitutional law, that when a prosecutor relies upon consent "he has the burden of proving that the consent was, in fact, freely and voluntarily given." If the Fourth Amendment requires that the prosecution bear the burden on this issue, why not on others? The Supreme Court has stated in various opinions that the Fourth Amendment generally requires a search warrant, and "the burden is on those seeking [an] exemption from [that] requirement to show the need for it." See, e.g., *Chimel v. California,* p. 363. Do such statements imply that, where a search is conducted without a warrant, the prosecution must bear the burden of proving facts that justify the search under one of the recognized exceptions to the warrant requirement, or do the statements refer only to the state's burden in appellate argument of justifying any request that the Supreme Court recognize a new or expanded exception to the warrant requirement? See SEARCHSZR § 11.2(b) (the former interpretation seems closer to the mark).

6. Confessions. Most jurisdictions place on the prosecution both the burdens of production and persuasion in responding to a claim that a confession was involuntary. A few states, however, place the burden of proving involuntariness on the defendant. *Lego v. Twomey,* discussed at Note 9, raises serious doubts as to the constitutionality of this practice. Though concerned primarily with the applicable standard of proof, *Lego* indicated that it was the constitutional obligation of the prosecution to meet that standard of proof.

7. Identification testimony. *United States v. Wade,* p. 761, indicates that, once the Sixth Amendment is shown to be applicable, the prosecution carries the burden of establishing that defendant intelligently waived his right to counsel at a lineup. But what is the proper allocation of the burden on an objection that a lineup or other identification procedure was so unfairly conducted as to violate due process? Several courts have assumed, without extensive discussion, that the defendant, as the moving party, bears the burden of establishing the due process violation. CRIMPROC § 10.4(d). But compare *People v. Young,* 176 N.W.2d 420 (Mich.App.1970), holding that the prosecution bears the burdens of production and persuasion whenever the identification procedure was conducted "out of the presence of defendant's attorney." Does *Young* constitute an open invitation to defense "fishing expeditions," that will be "automatically available in all lineup-cases"? See *State v. Bishop,* 183 N.W.2d 536 (Minn.1971).

8. *Exclusionary rule limitations.* Once a constitutional violation is established, does the burden of proof necessarily lie with the prosecution to establish that its evidence is not the fruit of the poisonous tree? See e.g., *Wade,* p. 761 (as to proof that the in-court identification was not tainted by the unconstitutional lineup); *Nardone,* p. 894 (once illegal wiretap established, government must convince the trial court that its proof had an independent origin). Consider also *Nix v. Williams,* p. 903, as to the government's burden in establishing that the same evidence would have inevitably been discovered by lawful means.

9. *Standards of proof.* Assuming that the prosecution bears the burden of persuasion on a particular exclusionary rule objection, what standard of proof should apply? In LEGO v. TWOMEY, 404 U.S. 477 (1972), the Court rejected the contention that the voluntariness of a confession must be established by proof beyond a reasonable doubt and accepted a preponderance of the evidence standard. Justice White's opinion for the Court reasoned that *In re Winship,* 397 U.S. 358 (1970), requiring proof beyond a reasonable doubt at trial, was not controlling: "Since the purpose that a voluntariness hearing is designed to serve has nothing whatever to do with improving the reliability of jury verdicts, we cannot accept the charge that judging the admissibility of a confession by a preponderance of the evidence undermines the mandate of *In re Winship.* * * * *Winship* [only] confirm[ed] the fundamental right that protects 'the accused against conviction except upon proof beyond a reasonable doubt of every fact necessary to constitute the crime with which he is charged.' A high standard of proof is necessary, we said, to ensure against unjust convictions by giving substance to the presumption of innocence. A guilty verdict is not rendered less reliable or less consonant with *Winship* simply because the admissibility of a confession is determined by a less stringent standard."

Lego also rejected the contention that application of a reasonable doubt standard was necessary "to give adequate protection to those values that the exclusionary rules are designed to serve": "Evidence obtained in violation of the Fourth Amendment has been excluded from federal criminal trials for many years. The same is true of coerced confessions offered in either federal or state trials. [But] no substantial evidence has accumulated that federal rights have suffered from determining admissibility by a preponderance of the evidence. Petitioner offers nothing to suggest [otherwise]. Without good cause, we are unwilling to expand currently applicable exclusionary rules by erecting additional barriers to placing truthful and probative evidence before state juries and by revising the standards applicable in collateral proceedings. [The] exclusionary rules are very much aimed at deterring lawless conduct by police and prosecution and it is very doubtful that escalating the prosecution's burden of proof in Fourth and Fifth Amendment suppression hearings would be sufficiently productive in this respect to outweigh the public interest in placing probative evidence before juries for the purpose of arriving at truthful decisions about guilt or innocence."[a]

---

a. Powell and Rehnquist, JJ., did not participate in the *Lego* decision. Dissenting Justice Brennan, joined by Justice Douglas and Marshall, argued that "the preponderance standard does not provide sufficient protection against the danger that involuntary confessions will be employed

10. Is *Lego* inconsistent with the philosophy underlying *Chapman v. California* (Ch. 28, § 5)? Cf. Note, 7 Harv.C.R.-C.L.L.Rev. 651 (1972), suggesting that the reasoning that led the *Lego* majority to conclude that implementation of a constitutional right did not require proof beyond a reasonable doubt could just as readily have led the Court in Chapman to conclude that there was no need to require the especially stringent harmless error standard imposed there. The dissent in *Lego* (see fn. a supra) also argued that the majority's position there was inconsistent with "the rule that automatically reverses a conviction when an involuntary confession was admitted at trial." Cf. Stephen A. Saltzburg, *Standards of Proof and Preliminary Questions of Fact*, 27 Stan.L.Rev. 271 (1975), arguing that a reasonable doubt standard should have been required in *Lego* because, inter alia, the test of involuntariness (as opposed to other exclusionary rule standards) is designed to exclude unreliable evidence and the admission of unreliable confessions is especially dangerous because juries give such evidence great weight.

11. The Supreme Court noted in *Lego* that, while due process was satisfied by application of the preponderance standard, the states were always "free, pursuant to their own law, to adopt a higher standard." Several states have done exactly that. See CRIMPROC § 10.4. On the other hand, the states uniformly have held that the standard of proof applicable to Fourth Amendment claims, except on the issue of consent, will be the preponderance standard. Id. In a jurisdiction that has adopted the reasonable doubt standard for the determination of the voluntariness of confession, why shouldn't the same standard apply to search and seizure claims? See Saltzburg, supra.

12. *Waiver of Miranda rights*. In COLORADO v. CONNELLY (p. 728) the Court held that the state need only prove a waiver of *Miranda* rights by the preponderance of the evidence. The majority, per Rehnquist, C.J., reasoned:

"[The state supreme court] held that the State must bear its burden of proving waiver [by] 'clear and convincing evidence.' Although we have stated in passing that the State bears a 'heavy' burden in proving waiver Miranda,[b] we have never held that the 'clear and convincing evidence' standard is the appropriate one. [In] *Lego v. Twomey,* [we] upheld a procedure in which the State established the voluntariness of a confession by no more than a preponderance of the evidence [for] two reasons. First, the voluntariness determination has nothing to do with the reliability of jury verdicts; rather, it is designed to determine the presence of police coercion. [Second,] we rejected Lego's assertion that a high burden of proof was required to serve the values protected by the exclusionary rule. [If,] as we held in *Lego* [a case the Court reaffirmed in *Connelly*], the voluntariness of a confession need be established only by a preponderance of the evidence, then a waiver of the auxiliary protections established in *Miranda* should require no higher burden of proof. * * * *"[c]

---

at trial." The preponderance standard, noted the dissent, was accepted in civil cases on the assumption that it was no more serious an error to have an erroneous decision in favor of one party or another, but the same could not be said for errors relating to the admission of confessions."

b. In dissent, Justice Brennan, joined by Marshall, J. argued that the Court's ruling ignored both "the explicit command of *Miranda*" in describing the state's burden as "heavy" and the implications of *Wade*, which specifically referred to the "clear and convincing" standard in describing the prosecution's burden of establishing that an in-court-identification was not tainted by an unconstitutional identification.

c. In dissent, Justice Brennan argued that *Lego* was distinguishable because it involved a situation in which the defendant was not in custody. The special setting of custodial interrogation, because it poses an increased danger of police overriding, justified "plac[ing] a higher burden of proof on the government in establishing a waiver of *Miranda* rights."

Does *Connelly* make *Miranda* "a much less prophylactic rule and a substantially more direct application of the fifth amendment compulsion standard"? Does *Connelly* "fuse" the fifth amendment compulsion standard with *Miranda*? See Mark Berger, *Compromise and Continuity: Miranda Waivers, Confession Admissibility, and the Retention of Interrogation Protections,* 49 U.Pitt.L.Rev. 1007, 1040–41 (1988). What follows from the fact that *Miranda* establishes special prophylactic rules governing custodial police interrogation? That special procedural requirements regulating the waiver process are also called for? Or that further protections governing the waiver process are unnecessary and undesirable, because likely to interfere unduly with appropriate police questioning? See id. at 1062.

13. ***The trier of fact.*** The factfinder on the constitutionality of a search has traditionally been the judge, but prior to *Jackson v. Denno,* 378 U.S. 368 (1964), many states followed one of two procedures that gave factfinding responsibility to the jury in judging the voluntariness of a confession. In states following the "Massachusetts rule," the trial court initially ruled on the admissibility of the confession. If the judge found the confession involuntary, that ruling was final. However, if the judge found the confession voluntary, it was then admitted subject to the jury's independent determination of voluntariness. In states following the "New York rule," the judge would make an initial determination as to whether reasonable persons could differ on the issue of voluntariness and if they could the issue went to the jury.

Jackson held the New York procedure unconstitutional. The crux of *Jackson's* reasoning was subsequently summarized in *Lego:* "We concluded that the New York procedure was constitutionally defective because at no point along the way did a criminal defendant receive a clear-cut determination that the confession used against him was in fact voluntary. The trial judge was not entitled to exclude a confession merely because he himself would have found it involuntary, and, while we recognized that the jury was empowered to perform that function, we doubted it could do so reliably. Precisely because confessions of guilt, whether coerced or freely given, may be truthful and potent evidence, we did not believe a jury [could] ignore the probative value of a truthful but coerced confession; it was also likely, we thought, that in judging voluntariness itself the jury would be influenced by the reliability of a confession it considered an accurate account of the facts. * * * "

14. As the Court noted in *Lego,* the *Jackson* case "cast no doubt upon" the Massachusetts procedure,[d] and many states continue to use that procedure (although most follow the "orthodox" procedure of having voluntariness determined initially and finally by the judge). Why should a defendant be given a "second crack" at the voluntariness issue, before the jury, where no such opportunity is given as to Fourth Amendment or other constitutional violations?

Of course, even under the orthodox procedure, the defendant may bring to the jury's attention the circumstances surrounding the confession for the purpose of challenging its credibility. Indeed, in *Crane v. Kentucky,* 476 U.S. 683 (1986), a

---

d. In distinguishing the Massachusetts procedure, the Court stressed that the judge there "himself resolves evidentiary conflicts and gives his own answer to the coercion issue" and the jury therefore only considers those confessions the judge believes to be voluntary. The dissenters responded that the acceptance of the Massachusetts rule revealed the "hollowness" of the Court's holding. They argued that the distinction between the New York and Massachusetts rule was more theoretical than real. They suggested, in particular, that in "cases of doubt," a judge operating under the Massachusetts rule was likely to "resolve the doubt in favor of admissibility, relying on the final determination by the jury."

unanimous Court held that a trial court's foreclosure of a defendant's attempt to introduce testimony about the "physical and psychological environment" in which the confession was obtained deprived defendant of his "fundamental constitutional right to a fair opportunity to present a defense." As the Court there noted, "The [*Jackson*] requirement that the [trial] court make a pretrial *voluntariness* determination does not undercut the defendant's traditional prerogative to challenge the confession's *reliability* during the course of the same trial."

15. Does it follow from *Lego* that it would be improper for a trial court to hear testimony on a constitutional challenge to the admissibility of evidence without first excluding the jury? Consider WATKINS v. SOWDERS, 449 U.S. 341 (1981). *Watkins* involved two state cases in which hearings on the admissibility of identification testimony were held in the presence of the jury. In each case, in challenging an in-court identification, the defense sought to establish that the identification was based on a pretrial identification procedure that was so suggestive as to violate due process. Over defense objection, the challenge was heard in the presence of the jury, and was rejected by the trial judge. The Supreme Court, per STEWART, J., found no constitutional error:

"The Court in *Jackson* did reject the usual presumption that a jury can be relied upon to determine issues according to the trial judge's instructions, [but only] because of the peculiar problems the issue of the voluntariness of a confession presents. [Where] identification evidence is at issue, however, no such special considerations [apply]. It is the reliability of identification evidence that primarily determines its admissibility. *Manson v. Brathwaite* [p. 774]. And the proper evaluation of evidence under the instructions of the trial judge is the very task our system must assume juries can perform. * * *"

"A judicial determination outside the presence of the jury of the admissibility of identification evidence may often be advisable. In some circumstances, not presented here, such a determination may be constitutionally necessary. But it does not follow that the Constitution requires a *per se* rule compelling such a procedure in every case."[e]

---

e. The dissenting justices (Brennan, J., joined by Marshall, J.) argued that "the powerful impact that such eyewitness identification evidence has on juries, regardless of its reliability, virtually mandates that, when such evidence is inadmissible, the jury should know nothing about the evidence."

INDEX

References are to Pages

A.B.A. STANDARDS and MODEL RULES
Attorney subpoena by prosecutor, 822–23
Conflict of interest, 187
Defense counsel's investigative obligation, 151, 168, 169
Frivolous claims, 218
Ineffective assistance, and, 136–37, 140, 150–52, 168, 169
Model for state law, 22
Reimbursement for appointed counsel, 79
Supporting services for counsel, 185

ACCESS TO SUSPECT
See Confessions.

ADVERSARY JUDICIAL PROCEEDINGS, INITIATION OF
See Counsel, Right To; Identification Procedures.

ADVERSARY SYSTEM
See Counsel, Right To; Counsel, Role Of.

"ALLEY CONFRONTATIONS"
See Identification Procedures.

AMERICAN BAR ASSOCIATION STANDARDS
See A.B.A. Standards.

ANONYMOUS INFORMERS
See Informants; Searches and Seizures.

APPEALS
See also Counsel, Right To; Counsel, Role Of; Equal Protection; Harmless Error; Indigent Defendants; Sentencing.
Appellate courts, 18
Constitutional right, not a, 102
Counsel on,
    Appointed counsel, right to, 100–07
    Control over issues raised, 210
    Effective assistance, 132–33, 210
    Frivolous appeals and counsel withdrawal, 218–20
    New counsel on, 129, 136
    Role of appointed counsel, 210, 218–20
Defendants most likely to appeal, 18
Defense appeals, right to, 99–107
Discretionary review, 102–07
Frivolous claims, 218–20
Ineffective assistance claims,
    Limited review, 135–36
    Record restriction, 135
    Requiring collateral review, 135
    Same counsel, 129, 134, 136
Reversal rate, 19
Sentencing, 17

APPEARANCE BEFORE MAGISTRATE
See Magistrates.

APPOINTED COUNSEL
See Counsel, Right To; Counsel, Role Of.

APPOINTMENT OF COUNSEL
See Counsel, Right To; Counsel, Role Of; Indigent Defendants.

ARRAIGNMENT
Description, 16
First appearance, distinguished, 13

ARREST
See also Police; Search and Seizure Remedies; Searches and Seizures; Seizure of the Person.
Arrest on probable cause for crime other than that charged, 336–37
Black males, see Racial Minorities.
Booking record and, 10, 336–37
Citation and summons alternative, 10, 348–52, 361–62
Common law acceptance, 337–38
Custody, relation to, 362, 425–32, 614–17
Deadly force in executing, 339–42
Disposition statistics, 12
Entry of premises after, 367
Entry of premises to, 376–83
Excessive force in executing, 339–42
Fabrication of probable cause, 308
Illegal arrest,
    Agency regulations and, 246
    Confessions following, 894–97
    Constitutional but unlawful, 246, 351–52, 362
    Identification following, 898
"In presence" test, 337–38
Material witness, 352–53
Misdemeanor, 337–38
Minor offenses, arrests for, 55, 337–38, 353–58
No-knock entries, 383
Non-arrest seizures, see Seizure of the Person.
On-scene arrests, 7
Police discretion, 10, 24
Post-arrest judicial review, 13, 340–43
Post-arrest presentment, see First Appearance.
Pretext, 348–58
Probable cause, 305
Search incident to,
    Person, 343–4, 359–61
    Premises, 363–67
    Vehicles, 398–407
State law and legality, 246, 351–52, 362
Stop distinguished, see Seizure of the Person.

ARREST—Cont'd
Traffic arrest, 343–58
Warrant, issuance of, 323
Warrant, need for,
    Arrest, 332–39
    Entry of premises, 376–83
    Exigent circumstances entry, 380–83
    Search warrant, 380–83
Warrant, use of, 10, 323–26
Warrantless, 10, 332–35, 376–83

ASSIGNED COUNSEL
See Counsel, Right To; Counsel, Role Of.

ASSISTANCE BEYOND COUNSEL
See Equal Protection; Indigent Defendants.

"ATTENUATED CONNECTION"
See "Fruit of the Poisonous Tree" Doctrine.

ATTORNEY–CLIENT PRIVILEGE
See Self–Incrimination.

ATTORNEY GENERAL
See Prosecutor.

AUTOMOBILES
See Searches and Seizures.

BILL OF RIGHTS
    See also Due Process; Fourteenth Amendment; Supreme Court.
Applicability to states, 25–26
Arms, Second Amendment, 25–27
Incorporated rights, 26–27, 564–5
"Incorporation," theories of, 26–27
Independent content, due process, 28–32
Interpretative approaches, see Supreme Court.
New federalism and, 38–39
Preference for specific guarantees, 27–32
Significance of differing formulations, 27–32
Specificity, lack of, 27–32
State court interpretation of parallel state rights, 38–39
Unincorporated rights, 26, 36

BLACK MALES
See Racial Minorities.

BLOOD TESTS
See Due Process; Identification Procedures; Searches and Seizures; Self–Incrimination.

BODILY EXTRACTIONS
See Due Process; Searches and Seizures; Self–Incrimination.

BOOKING
Description of, 10
Grounds for arrest and, 336–37

"BUGGING"
See Network Surveillance; Secret Agents.

BURDEN OF PROOF
Confessions, 926
Consent to search, 925
Counsel,
    Ineffective representation by, 140–41, 173–74

BURDEN OF PROOF—Cont'd
Counsel—Cont'd
    Waiver of trial assistance, 117
Degrees of proof,
        See also entries for specific claims, this heading.
    Clear and convincing evidence, 763
    For non-guilt issues, 927–28
    Preponderance of evidence, 851, 927
    Reasonable doubt, 927–28
Dropsy cases, 922–24
Elements of the offense, 927
Entrapment, 489
Exclusionary rule limitations, 927
Identification testimony, 763
Immunity taint, 851–52
Inevitable discovery, 903–09
Practical consequences of burden, 926
Search and seizure objections, 925–26
Waiver of Miranda rights, 595–96, 628–33, 648–59, 928–29

CAPITAL PUNISHMENT
Counsel conflict of interest, 191–200, 201–02
Counsel investigation of mitigating factors, 144–45, 147, 166–73
Effective assistance of counsel, capital cases, 166–67
Error rates, capital cases, 166–67
Right to counsel, 73
Right to counsel, collateral attack, 141
Suggestive eyewitness identification and, 790

CITATION
See Arrest.

COMMUNITY CONTROL
Responsiveness of officials, 24

COMPLAINT
See Arrest.

CONFESSIONS
    See also Postconviction Review, Federal; Counsel, Right To; "Fruit of the Poisonous Tree" Doctrine; Impeachment, Defendant and Defense Witnesses; McNabb–Mallory Rule; Motion to Suppress; Standing to Object to Illegally Obtained Evidence.
Central Park jogger case, 734–36
Coerced, see Voluntariness test, this heading.
Consular post notification, 674–75
Counsel, right to,
    Adversarial trial, analogy, 556–64
    Arrest and, 556–64
    Assertion of right, what constitutes, 634–35, 645–48
    Assertion of right, consequences of, 635–37
    "Break in custody," 637–42
    Charged defendant, 557–59, 738–59
    "Cellmate," obtaining statement from, 615–17, 750–53
    Custody, what constitutes, 601–08
    Exclusionary rule and, 752–53

CONFESSIONS—Cont'd

Counsel—Cont'd

Fifth amendment privilege, protection of, 576–83, 585–88

Informing suspect of counsel's presence, 665–70

Initiation of adversary judicial proceedings, 556–63, 741–43

Interrogation, violation without, 745

Jail plants, 615–17

Offense specific nature of Sixth Amendment right to counsel, 748–50, 754–59

Police deception of counsel, 665–70

Request for counsel at first appearance, 659–63

Secret agents, 750–55

Self-incrimination supplement, 577, 587–88

Sixth Amendment protection, 557–64, 738–59

Sixth Amendment starting point, 557–64, 738–46

Sixth Amendment warnings, 746–48

State agents, private persons as, 753

Waiver of, 628–34, 648–59, 746–48

Custody,

Definition of, 602–08

Focus compared, 601–02

"In the home" questioning, 602–03

Objective standard, 602–08

"On the street" questioning, 602–03

Probationer, 603

Roadside questioning, 602

Stationhouse questioning, 602–03

Traffic stops, 602

Voluntary stationhouse visit, 602

Deception or trickery, see Voluntariness test, this heading.

English Judges' Rules, 581, 585

"English warnings," 581, 919

False confessions, 631, 734–38

Focus, 557–63, 601–02

Habeas corpus,

Coerced confession claim, 672–74

Miranda claim, 672–74, 1579

Historical development of Supreme Court doctrine, 543–66

Interrogation by police,

Administrative questioning, 609–10, 617–19

Booking question exception, 617–19

Christian burial speech, 739–46

Conversation between officers, 608–13

Deception, post-Miranda, 718–26

Definition of, 608–13

Hostage negotiator, 602, 624

Incommunicado questioning, 669

Inquiries attendant to arrest, 609–10

Jail "plants," 615–17, 750–53

Juvenile suspects, 672

Magistrate questioning and, 689

Mentally retarded suspects, 671–72

Need for, 556, 566, 583–84, 587

Police interrogation manuals, 545, 560, 572, 586, 658

Psychological ploys, 572–73, 632, 718–26

CONFESSIONS—Cont'd

Interrogation by police—Cont'd

Secrecy of, 572, 628, 630–31

Surreptitious interrogation, 572, 628, 630–31

Massiah doctrine, 557–59, 739–58

McNabb–Mallory rule, 34, 554–55, 676–77

Miranda, oral arguments, 566–71

Miranda ruling,

Administrative questioning, 609–10, 617–19

Alternative procedures, 576, 676, 689–90

Brennan, memo to Warren on draft opinion, 576

Congressional "repeal" of, 676—85

Consular post notification and, 674–75

Forty-six years of interpretation, 589–95

Habeas review, 672–74, 1579

History and, 547–66, 575

Impeachment rule undermining, 590–91, 910–13

Waiver undermining, 631–34, 651–59

Miranda warnings,

Additional warnings, need for, 599–600

Adequacy of, 597–98

Consent to search, 461

Consequences of silence, 599, 918–21

Curing illegal detention, 592, 895

Custody and, 601–08

Grand jury witness, 843–45

Initiation of communication following assertion of counsel right, 642–45

Interrogation and, 608–17

Invocation of rights, 634–42, 663–65

Juvenile suspects, 672

Mentally retarded suspects, 671–72

Public safety exception, 621–25

Questioning "Outside Miranda," 922

Rescue doctrine, 624–25

Resumption of questioning following exercise of rights, 642–59

Silence following, see Impeachment, Defendant and Defense Witnesses.

Subject matter of investigation, 599–60

Omnibus Crime Control Act, 589, 676

Oral arguments in Miranda, 566–71

Oral arguments in Patane, 689–99

Oral arguments in Thompkins, 649–51

Police methods test, 549–51

Prompt presentment and, 554–55

Psychiatric examination, 670–71

"Public Safety" questioning, 621–25

Second confessions, see "Fruit of the Poisonous Tree" Doctrine.

Section 3501, 589, 676

Self-incrimination privilege and police interrogation,

Advice as to, 576–81, 597–601

Fifth Amendment applied to police station, 564–66, 574–77

Fifth Amendment applied to states, 26, 564–66, 575–76

Historical purpose, 574–76, 585–87

Legal compulsion limitation, 574–76, 585–87

Response to officer's question, 619–21

Voluntariness test and, 547, 564–66

Waiver of privilege, 628–34, 648–59

CONFESSIONS—Cont'd
Tape recording requirement, 628–31
"Third degree," 543–45
Torture to obtain information, 543–46, 625–28
Undercover agent, questioning by, 557–59, 615–17, 750–53
"Voluntariness" test,
    Ambiguity, 551–54
    Complex of values, 551–54
    Deception or trickery, 717–28
    Due process foundation, 547–51
    Habeas review, 653–54, 1582
    Harmless error and, 1562
    Historical background, 543–66
    Legal question, not factual, 551
    "Police methods" test, 548–50
    Police wrongdoing, illustrations of, 548–51
    Police wrongdoing rationale, 548–50
    Post–Miranda issue, 728–33
    Promise of leniency, 724–26
    Proof difficulties, 551–53, 579, 717–18, 724–26
    Psychological coercion, 552–53, 572–74, 717–26
    Shortcomings, 551–64
    State of mind of accused, 728–34
    Swearing contests, 552, 628–31
    Untrustworthiness rationale, 547–51, 733
"Volunteered" statements, 580, 587–88
Waiver of rights,
    Burden of proof, 579, 628–31, 928
    Deception following, 718–28
    Implied waiver, 631–32, 648–59
    "Intelligent and knowing" test, 579, 631–32, 633–34
    Qualified or constitutional waiver, 633–34
    Refusal to sign form, 631, 633, 649

"CONSECUTIVE CONFESSIONS"
See Confessions.

CONSENT
See Searches and Seizures; Waiver.

CONVICTING THE INNOCENT
See Innocent Convicted Defendants

COUNSEL, OBLIGATIONS OF
See Counsel, Right To; Counsel, Role Of.

COUNSEL, RIGHT TO
    See also Confessions; Counsel, Role Of;
        Grand Jury Witness; Guilty Pleas;
        Identification Procedures; Indigent
        Defendants; Self–Representation,
        Right to.
Adversary judicial proceedings, 86–87
Appointed counsel, characteristics of,
    Caseloads, 78, 176
    Client mistrust, 127, 217
    Comparative performance, 77–78, 148
    Compensation of, 77–78, 148, 176, 183
    Funding, adequacy of, 53–57, 77–78, 176
    Funding, litigation challenging, 176–77
    Funding, prison funding compared, 53
    Major types
        Contract counsel, 77–78
        Private attorney, 77–78

COUNSEL, RIGHT TO—Cont'd
Appointed counsel—Cont'd
    Major types—Cont'd
        Public defenders, 77
    Variations, 77–78
    Withdrawal obligation, 183
Appointed counsel, defendant's preference,
    Consideration under state law, 128
    Constitutional right, rejection of, 124–25, 128
    Continuance to facilitate, 128–29
    Meaningful relationship, 128–29
    Replacement of, 128–29, 217
Appointed counsel, delivery systems,
    Contract counsel, 77
    Federal courts, 77
    Individual appointments, 77–78
    Indigency, See Indigent Defendants,
    Public defenders, see public defenders, this heading.
Appointed counsel, right to,
    Appeal, on, 100–107
    Capital cases, 73
    Civil contempt, 97–98
    Collateral attack, 98, 133
    Common law, 70
    Courts-martial, 96
    "Criminal case" requirement, 82–85
    Custodial interrogation, see Confessions.
    Defense funding, 148, 176, 183
    Due process, 70–73, 93–98, 100–107
    Equal protection, 99–107
    Expert services, right to, and, 183–86
    Felony defendants, 71–79
    Grand jury witness, 846–47
    Interrogation, see Confessions.
    Juvenile delinquency, 95
    Lineups, see Identification Procedures.
    Misdemeanors,
        Conviction without incarceration, 81–85
        Enhancement of sentence, 83–84
        Probation and, 84–85
        Suspended sentence and, 84–85
    Parental status, termination proceedings, 96
    Pre-charge prison administrative detention, 87
    Prior uncounselled misdemeanor, 83–84
    Probation and parole revocation proceedings, 93–95
    Quality of indigent defense, 78, 176–86
    Recoupment of state payments, 79
    Sentencing, 93
    Special circumstances test, 71–73
    Systemic deficiencies, challenges to, 176–86
    Systems of appointment, 77–78
    Waiver of, see Waiver, this heading
Bail hearing, 91–92, 178–79, 181
Beginning of right, 85–93
Consent to search and, 461
"Critical stages" of prosecution, 85–93, 178–79, 181, 763, 771–72
Forfeiture of, 121
Harmless error, see Harmless Error
Hybrid representation, 112
Indigence of accused, see Indigent Defendants.

COUNSEL, RIGHT TO—Cont'd

"Prosecution," requirement of, 86–88
Psychiatric evaluations, 92
Public defenders,
  Assigned counsel, compared, 77–78, 148
  Counties using, 77–78
  Courthouse workgroup, 24
  Local agencies, 77–78
  Overburdening of, 77–78, 148, 176–83
  Retained counsel, compared, 78, 148
  Selection, 77–78, 128–29, 217
  Statewide programs, 77–78
Recidivist statutes and uncounseled convictions, 99–100
Retained counsel, defendant's choice,
  Appeals, 129
  Asset freeze and, 129–30
  Conflicting government interests, 125–30, 202–09
  Conflict of interest disqualification, see Counsel, Role of.
  Continuance to facilitate, 127–28
  Denial, per se error, 121–27
  Denial, showing of prejudice, 121–27
  Fee forfeiture and, 129–30
  Out-of-state attorney, 127
  Prosecutorial control over, 130, 208
  Six Amendment right, 121–27
Retained counsel, right to,
  Absolute right, 73
  Comparative performance, 78, 148
  Forfeitures and, 129–30
  Scope, compared to appointed counsel, 133, 850
Standby counsel, 111–14
Waiver,
  General understanding, 114–21
  Guilty plea and, 115–16
  Judicial advice and inquiry, 114–21
  Pretrial stages, 116–17
  Self representation and, see Self Representation, Right to.
  State requirements, 117
  Variation with stage, 116–17

COUNSEL, ROLE OF

See also Counsel, Right To; Professional Ethics.
Appeals, meritless, 218–220
Attorney/client disagreements, 217
Attorney/client relationship, 128, 217
Client perjury, 153–54
Communication breakdown, 217
Conflicts of interest,
  A.B.A. Rules of Professional Conduct, 187, 207
  Actual conflict, 187, 200, 201, 204
  Adverse effect, showing of, 193, 200–202
  Defender's offices and, 188
  Deference to trial court, 201, 203–07
  Disqualification of counsel, 203–09
  Employer retained attorney, 190–91
  Federal Rule 44 (c), 188
  Harmless error, 193
  Joint defenses, 188

COUNSEL, ROLE OF—Cont'd

Conflicts of interest—Cont'd
  Judicial interests supporting disqualification, 202–07
  Judicial responsibility for, 188–91, 197
  "Manufactured" conflicts, 204, 208
  Multiple representation, 187, 188–91, 201–09
  Postconviction review, 191–202
  Potential conflicts, 187, 202–07
  Prejudice presumed, 190
  Presumption of ethical response, 189–90
  Range of conflicts, 187, 208
  Same law office, 187
  Testimony by counsel, 201
  Trial court inquiry, 201
    Counsel informing court, 188–89, 192
    Constitutional obligation, 188–200
    Failure to inquire, consequences of, 191–200
    Non-constitutional requirements, 188
    "Reasonably should know" standard, 190–91
    Scope of inquiry, 191
  Waiver of conflict-free counsel, 203–04, 208–09
Constructive denial of counsel, 174–76
Defense strategy, control over,
  Consult, duty to, 210–13, 216
  Counsel binding client, 209–10, 214–17
  Defendant's pro se right and, 210
  Defendant's refusal to participate, 210–13
  Habeas corpus and, see Postconviction Review, Federal.
  Personal vs. strategic decisions,
    Appeal issues, 210
    Conceding guilty, 210, 212
    Decision to appeal, 216–17
    Distinction explained, 214–17
    Rights identified, 210–11
    Violation of discovery order, 211
  Prejudice and,
    Failure to consult, 216–17
    Per se ineffective assistance, 216–17
Effective assistance, see Incompetent performance, this heading.
Incompetent performance,
  ABA Standards, 150–52
  Adversarial process benchmark, 133–34, 149
  Appeals, failure to timely file, 216–17
  Argument to jury, 151, 166
  Attorney practice, 149–50
  Capital cases, 139, 145, 166–73
  Categorical vs. judgmental approach, 136–37
  Collateral proceedings, at, 133
  Competency standards, see Strickland standards, this heading
  Constitutional right prerequisite, 132
  Counsel's acted thought, 161, 165
  Counsel's testimony, 136
  Deferential review, 140–41, 155–63
  Exclusionary rule errors, 152
  Experts; use of, 155–63
  Excusing procedural defaults, 159

COUNSEL, ROLE OF—Cont'd
Incompetent performance—Cont'd
Federal habeas review, 154–63
Guidelines approach, 137, 141, 150–52
Guilty pleas, 147–48, 168
Inferential approach, 173–74
Institutional deficiencies and, 176–83
Isolated error, 165–66
Limited investigation, 141, 166–73
Mitigating factors, capital cases, 144–45, 147, 166–73
Non-guilt related errors, 152–53
Prejudice standard,
Applied, 146, 163, 169–71, 172
Constructive denial of counsel, 174–76
Factual innocence, 153
Grounding of, 149
Legal guilt, 153–54
Presumed prejudice, 173–74
Reasonable probability, 143
Sleeping counsel, 175
Raising the issue, 134–36
Retained vs. appointed counsel, 131–32
Right to counsel, relation to, 131
Strickland standards
Appellate counsel and, 147
Civil action challenges and, 177–83
Criticism of, 148–49
Exceptions to, 173
Guilty pleas, 147
Local practice, 149–50
Lower court rulings, 154
Order of analysis, 144
Performance prong, see Incompetent performance, this heading
Prejudice prong, see Prejudice standard, this heading
Interference with counsel, 176
Lineup, role at, 765–66
Plea bargaining, see Guilty Plea Negotiations.
Preliminary hearing strategy, see Preliminary Hearing.
Presentence investigation, capital cases, 144–45, 147, 166–73
Public statements, see Newspapers and Television, Trial by.
Sentencing, see Sentencing; Capital Punishment.
State interference,
Closing argument prohibited, 176
Defendant's testimony, order of, 176
Grand jury subpoena of attorney, 832–33
Interrogation of accused, see Confessions.
Late appointment, 173–75
Law office searches, 291
Presumed prejudice, 176
Prohibiting client consultation, 176
Strategic decisions, 155–63, 166
Systemic (structural) deficiencies, challenges to, 177–83
Withdrawal on appeal, 218–20

COURTS
See Appeals; Magistrates; Trial Court.

CRIME CONTROL ACT
See Omnibus Crime Control and Safe Streets Act.

CRIMINAL JUSTICE ACT
See Counsel, Right To; Indigent Defendants.

CRIMINAL JUSTICE PROCESS
See also Legal Regulation, Sources of.
Administration of, 23–24
Administrative interactions, 24
Caseload pressures, 24, 78, 148, 183
Community influences, 24
Crime rates and, 51–53
Described, 1
Discretion,
Discretionary decisions, 23–24
Legal authorization, 23
Significance of, 23–24
Diversity in, 3–4, 19, 23–24
Federal system, 3, 5, 19, 22
Funding, bearing of, 54, 55–57, 78, 148, 176, 183
Legal Regulation, 19–22
Legislatures and, 53, 54–57
Officials of, 4–6, 19–20
Substantive law, influence of,
State systems,
Described, 2, 4–5, 19–20
Diversity in laws, 19–22
Models followed, 22

CRIMINAL JUSTICE PROCESS: OVERVIEW OF STEPS
Appeals, 18–19
Arraignment, 16
Arrest, 9–10
Bail, 14
Booking, 10–11
Charge, decision to,
Grand jury screening, 15
Police screening, 11
Preliminary hearing screening, 14–15
Prosecutor post-filing screening, 12–13
Prosecutor pre-filing screening, 11–12
Chronology of steps, 5–6
Collateral remedies, 19
Complaint,
Filing of, 13
Magistrates probable cause determination, 13
Defense counsel, providing for, 14
Discovery, 16
Diversion, 12
Felony/misdemeanor distinction, 4, 22
First appearance, 13–14
"Gerstein" review, 13
Grand jury review,
Indictment decision, 15
Investigation, 9
Guilty plea, 15–17
Indictment, the, 15
Information, the, 16
Major/minor crime distinction, 22
Misdemeanor/felony distinction, 4, 22
Outcomes of arrest, 12
Outcome of charges, 12

CRIMINAL JUSTICE PROCESS: OVERVIEW OF STEPS—Cont'd
Post-arrest investigation, 11
Postconviction remedies, 19
Pre-arrest investigation,
    On-scene arrests, 7
    Proactive, 8–9
    Reactive, 6–8
Preliminary hearing, 14–15
Pretrial motions, 16
Prosecutorial investigations, 9
Reported crimes, 6
Sentencing, 17–18
Trial, 17

CRIMINAL JUSTICE STATISTICS
Appeals,
    Convictions, percentage appealed, 18
    Reversal rates, 19
Appointed counsel, 77–78
Arrest, timing of, 26, 323
Arrest warrants and caseloads, 323–26
Attrition of arrests, 12
Capital cases, error rates, 166–67
Crime clusters, 8
Exclusionary rule, impact of, 229–30, 236
False confessions, DNA exonerations, 629
Federal criminal filings, 19
Federal police agencies, 5
Forensic evidence, 7
Grand jury screening,
Guilty plea rate, 12
Indictment waivers, 1043
Ineffective-assistance claims, 148, 155
Miranda waivers, 632,
Misdemeanor/felony ratio, 6
National security letters, 541
Police agencies, 4
Prosecutor screening, 12
Pro se defendants, 110–11
Public defenders, 77–78
Race, auto stops, 356–57
Race, driver searches, 356–57
Section 215 orders, 541
State prosecutions, 4, 19
Trial,
    Acquittal rates, 17
    Disposal without trial, 12,
    Frequency of, 17
    Length, 17
    Time to trial, 17
Wiretap orders, 7, 524–25

CRITICAL STAGE IN CRIMINAL PROCESS
See Counsel, Right To.

"CUSTODIAL INTERROGATION"
See Confessions.

CUSTODY
See Arrest; Confessions; Postconviction Review, Federal; Seizure of the Person.

DEATH PENALTY
See Capital Punishment.

DEFENSE COUNSEL
See Counsel, Right To; Counsel, Role Of.

DELAY IN BRINGING BEFORE MAGISTRATE
See Confessions; McNabb–Mallory Rule.

DISCRETION
    See also Police.
Administrative culture and, 24
Community influence, 24
Defined, 23
Diversity and, 23–24
Factors influencing, 24
Significance of, 23

DIVERSE LEGAL REGULATIONS
See Criminal Justice Process; Legal Regulation, Sources Of.

"DOMESTIC SECURITY"
See National Security.

DOJ GUIDELINES
See Internal Guidelines.

"DROPSY" TESTIMONY
See Burden of Proof.

DUE PROCESS
    See also Bill of Rights; Fourteenth Amendment; Supreme Court.
Altering balance of adversary process, 120–130
Appeal, right of, 100–02
Asset forfeitures and defense capacity, 129–130
Bill of Rights, applicability to states, see Bill of Rights
Blood tests and, 29–30
Bodily extractions and, 27–31
Burden of Proof, see Burden of Proof.
Coerced confessions, see Confessions.
Confessions and, see Confessions.
Counsel, effective assistance, 123, 131, 149
Counsel, right to, and, 71–85, 93–98, 100–07
Deference to states, 61–62
Entrapment and, 480–85, 487–89
Evidentiary sufficiency, 927
Experts, services of, 185
Eyewitness identification, see Identification Procedures.
"Free–standing," 32–34
Fundamental fairness standard, 32–34, 71–73
Grand jury indictment, requirement of, 26
Historical acceptance of procedure, 32
Identification procedures and, see Identification Procedures.
Independent content, 33
Indigent's right to expert services, 183–86
Juvenile proceedings, 95
Postconviction DNA testing, 33–34
Preference for specific guarantees, 31, 32
Probation and parole revocation, 94
Psychiatrist, assistance of, 183–85
Reasonable doubt standard, 927
"Shocks the conscience" test, 27–31
Specific guarantee distinguished, 31, 32
"Stomach pumping" and, 28–29
Terrorism, war on, and, 40–48
Undercover agents, 472

EAVESDROPPING
See Network Surveillance; Searches and Seizures; Secret Agents.

EFFECTIVE ASSISTANCE OF COUNSEL
See Counsel, Role Of.

ELECTRONIC COMMUNICATION PRIVACY ACT
See Network Surveillance.

ELECTRONIC SURVEILLANCE
See Network Surveillance; Searches and Seizures; Secret Agents; Standing to Object to Illegally Obtained Evidence; Technological Surveillance.

"ENCOURAGEMENT"
See Entrapment.

ENTRAPMENT
Due process, 480–85, 487–89
Fourth Amendment and, 489
Inducement, 480–86
Internet and, 499–500
Objective test, 486
Predisposition, 489–97
Private entrapment, 498–99
Subjective approach, 486
Vicarious and derivative entrapment, 489–99

ENEMY COMBATANTS
See Due Process

EQUAL PROTECTION
See also Counsel, Right To; Fourteenth Amendment; Indigent Defendants; Prosecutor's Discretion.
Aid in addition to counsel, 183–86
Counsel, right to, on appeal, 100–07
Filing fees, 99–100
Investigative stops, 422
Racial discrimination, see Racial Minorities.
Traffic stops, 356–58
Transcript and other materials, right to, 185

ETHICS
See Professional Ethics.

EXCLUSIONARY RULES
See Bail; Confessions; "Fruit of the Poisonous Tree" Doctrine; Identification Procedures; Impeachment, Defendant and Defense Witnesses; McNabb–Mallory Rule; Motion to Suppress; Network Surveillance; Search and Seizure Remedies; Standing to Object to Illegally Obtained Evidence.

EXONERATIONS
See Innocent Convicted Defendants.

EXPERTS, RIGHT TO FREE
See Counsel, Right to; Equal Protection.

EXTRADITION
See Arrest; Jurisdiction.

EYE–WITNESS IDENTIFICATIONS
See Identification Procedures.

FEDERAL COMMUNICATIONS ACT OF,
See Network Surveillance.

FEDERAL HABEAS CORPUS
See Postconviction Review, Federal

FEDERAL SUPERVISORY AUTHORITY OVER ADMINISTRATION OF CRIMINAL JUSTICE
See McNabb–Mallory Rule; "Supervisory Authority" Over Federal Criminal Justice.

FEDERALISM
See Bill of Rights; Postconviction Review, Federal; Fourteenth Amendment; State Constitutions.

FELONIES
See also Counsel, Right To.
Distinguished from misdemeanors, 4, 22
Magistrates, and, 5
Procedural distinctions, 5
Prosecutions annually, 4

FINGERPRINTING
See Arrest; Identification Procedures.

FIRST AMENDMENT
See Grand Jury Witness; Searches and Seizures.

FIRST APPEARANCE
See also Counsel, Right To; Magistrates.
Description, 13–14
Timing, 13,

"FOCUS"
See Confessions.

FOREIGN INTELLIGENCE SURVEILLANCE ACT (FISA)
See National Security.

FORFEITURE OF RIGHTS
See Waiver.

FOURTEENTH AMENDMENT
See Bill of Rights; Due Process; Equal Protection; Supreme Court.

FREE COUNSEL
See Counsel, Right To.

FREE TRANSCRIPT
See Appeals; Counsel, Right To; Equal Protection.

FRISK
See Searches and Seizures.

"FRUIT OF THE POISONOUS TREE" DOCTRINE
Attenuation doctrine, 893–94
Confessions as a poisonous tree, 697–709
Confessions as the fruit, 894–97
Consent to search as the fruit, 460
Consequences of Miranda warnings, 677–709, 895–88
Gerstein violations as poisonous tree, 343
Historical background, 893–903
Identification as fruit, 898
Illegal entry as poisonous tree, 899
In court identification, lineup fruit, 763–64, 766–67
"Independent source," 895

"FRUIT OF THE POISONOUS TREE" DOC-TRINE—Cont'd

"Inevitable discovery," 903–07
Miranda violations as poisonous tree, 697–708
"Purging" the taint, 894–95
"Tainted" witnesses, 903
Testimony as fruit, 903
Trial identification and illegal lineups, 764, 766–67, 769
Verbal evidence as the fruit, 894
Warrant search as the fruit, 900–901

"GOOD FAITH" EXCEPTION
See Search and Seizure Remedies.

GRAND JURY
See also Grand Jury Witness.
Alternative investigative agencies, see Investigation by Subpoena
Description of, 15
Dual functions, 9, 15
Investigations, character of, 9, 794–95
Investigative advantages,
    Contempt sanction, 795
    Immunity grants, 796–97
    Psychological pressures, 796
    Public confidence, 800
    Search warrant comparison, 797–98
    Secrecy, 798
    Subpoena ad testificandum, 795
    Subpoena duces tecum, 797–98
    Testimony under oath, 795
Judicial perspectives on, 802–05
Judicial supervisory regulation, 804–05
Juror independence, 792–93, 802–05, 820
Presentments, 792
Privacy Protection Act, see Investigation by Subpoena
Reports, 791–92, 793
Screening function, 15, 791
Secrecy,
    Coverage of, 798–800
    Defense discovery, and, 799
    High profile targets and, 799
    Jencks Act disclosure, 798
    Objectives of, 798
    Public figure, and, 799
    Trial witness' grand jury testimony, 799
    Violations of, 800
    Witness exemption, 798
Self-initiated prosecutions, 792
Supervisory power, federal, 805
Use in states, 793

GRAND JURY SUBPOENA
See Grand Jury Witness.

GRAND JURY WITNESS
Boyd doctrine,
    Boyd ruling, 806–10
    Civil liberties icon, 810
    Dismantling of, 811–12, 852–56, 859, 863–64, 875–76, 878
    Fourth Amendment grounding, 811–12
    Privacy and, 810, 814, 815–16
    Self-incrimination grounding, 852–53, 859, 875–76, 878

GRAND JURY WITNESS—Cont'd
Challenge to,
    Attorney subpoena, 832–33
    Balancing analysis, 830
    Basis for subpoena, 804, 811–15, 816–21, 823–30
    Electronic surveillance, questioning based upon, 823, 836
    First Amendment infringement, 830–32
    Fourth Amendment violations, see Fourth Amendment, this heading.
    Identification evidence production, 816–21, 822
    Illegal search, questioning based upon, 822–23
    Misuse, see Misuse objections, this heading,
    Oppressive burdens, 833
    Overbroad subpoena duces tecum, 811–15
    Relevancy, 815, 823–30
    Rule 17, reasonableness under, 815, 823–30, 833
    Subject of investigation, 804
    Third party subpoenas, see Third party subpoenas, this heading
Citizen duty to testify, 804, 817, 820
Contempt sanction, 795, 801
Counsel, right to,
    Appointed counsel, 846–47
    Constitutional right, 846–47
    Federal practice, 847
    Location of, 848
    Notification of right, 846–47
    Reform movement, and, 794
    State practice, 847
Fourth Amendment,
    Business records influence, 810, 814
    Deregulation of subpoenas, 816
    Forthwith subpoena, 821–22
    Overbroad subpoena as search, 812–22
    Questions based on illegal search, 822–23
    Subpoena as search alternative, 797–98
    Subpoena as a seizure, 817, 821–22
    Subpoena duces tecum as search, 806–14
    Third party records, see Third party subpoenas, this heading
Identification evidence production, 816–21, 822
Lineup appearance, 822
Misuse objections, 833–35, 835–36
Recalcitrant witnesses, 795
Self-incrimination privilege,
    Applicability to grand jury testimony, 838
    Dual sovereignty, 840—41
    Entity claim, see Production of documents, this heading.
    Immunity grants,
        Act of production, 866, 870–75, 878
        Constitutionality, 848–49
        Foreign prosecution, 841
        Independent source, 851–52
        Procedures, 852
        Prosecutorial discretion, 852
        Scope, 849–852
        State/federal prosecution, 840–41
        State variation, 850–51
        Subsequent prosecution, 851–52
        "Taint" determination, 851–52

GRAND JURY WITNESS—Cont'd
Self-incrimination privilege—Cont'd
Immunity grants—Cont'd
Use, 796–97
"Incrimination" standard, 839–40, 865–66
Incrimination under laws of another sovereign, 840–41
Partial testimony, 841–42
Production of documents,
Act of production doctrine, 856–63, 866–69, 874–75
Applicability of privilege, 806–10, 852–63
Authentication, 800, 864–65
Attorney-client privilege and, 858–59, 877
Boyd analysis, 852–53
Corporate records, 853
Document category descriptions, 827–29
Entity agent's obligation, 853, 866–69
Entity agent, production use, 867–69
Entity records, 853–54
Establishing existence, 860, 873–74, 877–78
Establishing possession, 860, 873–74, 877–78
Executing prescribed document, 855–56
"Foregone conclusion" doctrine, 860, 865, 876–78
Partnership records, 844
Potential incrimination, 865–66
Privacy analysis, 852–53, 858, 861–62, 863–65
Private papers, 810, 852
Production immunity, 866, 870–75, 878
Reasonable particularity standard, 876
Relevancy standards, 825–26, 827–30
Required records, 855
Search for documents, 286, 797, 856
Single person corporation, 869
Testimonial limitation, 855–56
Third party production, See Third party subpoenas, this heading
Production of identification evidence, see Identification Procedures.
Production of non-documentary items, 869–70
Target exercise, 842–43
Waiver, 841–42
Warnings as to rights,
Constitutional requirements, 843–46
Federal practice, 847
Perjury and, 844
Prospective defendant standard, 843
State practice, 847
Target warnings, 845–46
Target of investigation,
Called as witness, 842–43
Duty to appear, 842–43
Notification of status, 842, 845–46
Target defined, 843
Voluntary appearance, 842
Warnings, 845–46
Third party subpoenas,
Electronic Communication Privacy Act, 836
Financial Privacy Act, 837–38

GRAND JURY WITNESS—Cont'd
Third party subpoenas—Cont'd
Fourth Amendment objections, 517–18, 814, 835
Misuse objection, 835–36
Privacy analysis, 517–18, 814
Privilege objection, 836
State law, 518
Stored Communications Act, 837–38
Target notification, 836–37
Target standing, 835–36
Wiretap objection, 836

HABEAS CORPUS
See Counsel, Right To; Postconviction Review, Federal.

HANDWRITING SAMPLES
See Grand Jury Witness; Identification Procedures; Searches and Seizures; Self–Incrimination.

HARMLESS ERROR
Counsel, right to,
Conflict of interest, 143, 153
Constructive denial, 174–76
Counsel of choice, 123–24
Failure to file appeal, 216–17
Interference with, 176
Trial access to defendant, 176
Disciplining prosecutors and, 34–38
Self-representation denied, 111
Supervisory power and, 34–38

IDENTIFICATION PROCEDURES
See also Motion to Suppress; Self–Incrimination.
Blood tests, 29–31, 767, 822
Counsel, right at lineup,
Adversary judicial proceedings test, 769–70
Alternative safeguards, 768–69
Critical stage, 763, 770–73
Custody test, 770
Exclusionary remedy, 763–64, 766–67, 769
Increasing identification accuracy, methods of, 787–790
Initiation of right, 769–70
Role of, 765–66
Substitute counsel, 763
Waiver of, 766
Counsel at other procedures,
Handwriting exemplars, 767
Photographic displays, 770–73
Courtroom identifications,
Independent source, 763–64, 766–67
Suggestiveness, 768
Unconstitutional lineup and, 762–64
Detention for, 437–38, 767–68
Due process limitations, 773–86
DNA Tests, 453–54
Eye-witness identification, fallibility of,
Capital cases, 790
Expert testimony, 789
Jury instructions, 789
Procedures responding to, 787–790
Psychological literature, 786–87
Totality of circumstances, 774–790
Unnecessary suggestiveness, 774–85

IDENTIFICATION PROCEDURES—Cont'd

Eye-witness identification—Cont'd
    Wrongful convictions, 760–61
Fourth Amendment and, see Searches and Seizures.
Grand jury subpoena for,
    Handwriting samples, 815–21
    Lineup participation, 822
    Other procedures, 822
    Voice exemplar, 816–21
Handwriting exemplars, 860
Lineups,
    Blank lineups, 778
    "Blind," administration of lineup, 788
    Counsel, see Counsel, right at, this heading.
    Courtroom identification compared, 768
    Due process, 773–786
    Expert psychological testimony, 789
    Grand jury subpoena, 822
    Sequential, 788
    Trial identification, relation to, 768
Omnibus Crime Control Act, eyewitness provisions, 769
Photographic displays,
    Counsel, right to, 770–73
    Due process, 773–86
Self-incrimination, 767, 855–56, 860, 878
Show-ups,
    Alley confrontations, 770
    Due process, 773–86
    State-action requirement, 770–73
Trial-like confrontation, requirement of, 770–73
Voice exemplars, 767, 816–21

ILLEGAL DETENTION

See Arrest; Confessions; Identification Procedures; McNabb–Mallory Rule; Seizure of the Person.

IMMUNITY

See Grand Jury Witness.

IMPEACHMENT, DEFENDANT AND DEFENSE WITNESSES

Defense witness impeachment,
    Defense strategy and, 913–16
    "Pinocchio" defense witness, 913–16
    Prohibited impeachment, 916–17
Exclusionary rule and, 910–13
Immunized testimony, 916–17
Prior silence, 918–21
Standing testimony, 882–83
Suppression hearing testimony, 882–83
Use of illegally seized evidence,
    Coerced confession, 917
    Illegal search, 910–12
    Massiah violations, 917–18
    Miranda violations, 911–12

INCOMPETENT COUNSEL

See Counsel, Role Of.

"INCORPORATION" OF BILL OF RIGHTS

See Due Process.

INCRIMINATING STATEMENTS

See Confessions; Impeachment, Defendant and Defense Witnesses; Self–Incrimination.

"INDEPENDENT ORIGIN"

See Identification Procedures.

"INDEPENDENT SOURCE"

See "Fruit of the Poisonous Tree" Doctrine.

INDIGENT DEFENDANTS

See also Counsel, Right To; Equal Protection.
Aid in addition to counsel,
    "Basic tools," 185–86
    Due process grounding, 185
    Ex parte hearings, 185
    Experts, 183–86
    Filing-fees, 99–100
    Particularized need, 185–86
    Reversible error, 186
    Statues providing, 186
    Support services, 185–86
    Transcripts, 99–100
Appeal by, 100–107
Choice of counsel, see Counsel, Right To.
Determination of indigency, 78–79
Funding of defense services, 53–57, 77–78, 176,183
Inquiry into indigency, 14
Obligation to repay, 79
Poverty, impact on adversary system, 59–65
Quality of defense services, 59–65, 78, 148, 176–83
Recoupment programs, 79
Standards to determine indigency, 78–79

"INEVITABLE DISCOVERY"

See "Fruit of the Poisonous Tree" Doctrine.

INFORMANTS

See also Entrapment; Searches and Seizures; Secret Agents.
Disclosure to magistrate, 310
Fictitious sources, 308
Informer's privilege, 308–10
Proactive investigations and, 8
Probable cause based on, 292–305

INFORMERS

See Informants; Searches and Seizures; Secret Agents.

INITIAL APPEARANCE BEFORE MAGISTRATE

See First Appearance.

INITIATION OF ADVERSARY JUDICIAL PROCEEDINGS

See Confessions; Counsel, Right To; Identification Procedures.

INNOCENT CONVICTED DEFENDANTS

Capital punishment, and, 57–63
DNA exonerations, 58–63
False confessions, and, 631, 734–38
Statistics, 57–61, 63
System flaws and, 58–63

References are to Pages

INTERNAL GUIDELINES
IRS regulations, 246
Judicial remedies for violations, 246
U.S. Department of Justice guidelines
    Attorney subpoena, 832
    Confidential informants, 478
    Grand jury practice, 832, 842–43, 845, 847
    Racial profiling, 67–68
    Searching & seizing computers, 537
    U.S. Attorneys' Manual, 832, 842, 843, 845, 847

INTERROGATION
See Confessions; Grand Jury Witness; Police.

INTRUSIONS INTO THE BODY
See Due Process; Searches and Seizures; Self–Incrimination.

INVESTIGATIONS BY SUBPOENA
Advantages and disadvantages, see Grand Jury
Civil administrative subpoenas, 891
Grand jury authority, see Grand Jury, Grand Jury Witness
John Doe proceeding, 800
Legal similarities and differences, grand jury and other subpoenas, 801–02
National security orders, 541
One-man grand jury, 800
Prosecutor authority, 801
Subpoena ad testificandum, see Grand Jury
Subpoena duces tecum, see Grand jury
Witness challenges, see Grand jury Witness

INVOLUNTARY CONFESSIONS
See Confessions.

JUDGES
See Magistrates; Supreme Court; Trial Court.

"JUDGES' RULES"
See Confessions.

JUVENILES
Confessions, 603–08, 672, 735–36
Counsel, delinquency proceedings, 95

LEGAL REGULATION, SOURCES OF
    See also Bill of Rights; Criminal Justice Process; Fourteenth Amendment; State Constitutions.
Common law heritage, 21
Federal constitution, 19–21
Federal courts' supervisory power, see "Supervisory Authority" Over Federal Criminal Justice.
Federal statutes, 21
Judicially created standards, 34–38
Models for,
    American Bar Association, 22
    Federal law, 22
Procedural subsets
    Capital offenses, 22
    Felony/misdemeanor, 22
State constitutions, 38–39
State law, 19, 21–22

LINEUPS
See Identification Procedures.

MAGISTRATES
Arrest review, 13, 340–43
Arrest warrants, 13, 323–26
Description of court, 5
Federal system, 5
First appearance, 13–14
Functions of, 5, 13–14
"Gerstein" review, 13, 340–43
Neutrality of, 316–17
Post-arrest review, 13
Probable cause determination by, 323, 340–43
Role in felony and misdemeanor cases, 5
Search warrants, 316–17, 319–20
State magistrate courts, diversity of, 5

MASSIAH DOCTRINE
See Confessions.

MATERIAL WITNESS
See Arrest.

McNABB–MALLORY RULE
Omnibus Crime Control Act, 589, 676
Rule explained, 34–35, 51–52, 554–55

MIRANDA REQUIREMENTS
See Confessions; Police.

MISDEMEANORS
    See also Counsel, Right To; Magistrates.
Appointed counsel, 80–85
Arrests for, see Arrests.
City ordinance violations, 4
Defined, 4
Distinguished from felonies, 4
Jurisdictional limit, 5, 22
Miranda warnings, 597–60
Petty offenses, 80
Procedures, compared to felonies, 22
Ratio to felonies, 4

MOTION TO SUPPRESS
    See also Burden of Proof; "Fruit of the Poisonous Tree" Doctrine; Impeachment, Defendant and Defense Witnesses; Search and Seizure Remedies; Standing to Object to Illegally Obtained Evidence.
Burdens of proceeding and persuasion, see Burden of Proof.
Contemporaneous objection, 922
Defense testimony, 882
Establishing standing, 882
False warrant affidavits, 307–08
Informer's privilege, 308–10
Pretrial objection, 922
Standard of proof, see Burden of Proof.
Trier of fact, 929
Warrant issuance, review of, 229–38, 307–08

MULTIPLE REPRESENTATION
See Counsel, Role Of.

NATIONAL SECURITY
Checkpoints, 442
Domestic surveillance, and, 539–40
Foreign Intelligence Surveillance Act (FISA), 540–41
Monitoring abroad, 539–40

NATIONAL SECURITY—Cont'd
National Security Letters, 541
Profiling, 66–68
Section 215 orders, 541
USA Patriot Act, 541–42

NETWORK SURVEILLANCE
See also National Security; Searches and
    Seizures; Technological Surveillance;
Carnivore, 531–32
Customer notification of subpoena, 837
Electronic Communications Privacy Act,
    519–20
Expectation of privacy.
    Cordless phones, 597–98
    E-mail privacy, 501–02
    Non-content information, 510–15
    Personal computer, 501–05, 508–09
    Postal mail, 505, 515
    Private searches, 509
    Telephone privacy, 505–08, 510–15
    World wide web, 509
Non-content network information
    Dialed telephone numbers, 510–15
    Mail covers, 515
    Internet addresses, 515–16
    Pen registers, 510–15
    Stored account records, 516–17
Packet sniffers, 531–32, 533–43
Pen Register statute,
    Basic structure, 532–33
    Caller–ID services, 533
    Cell site data, 533
    Definitions, 532
    Packet sniffers, 533–34
    Telephone bills, 533
State constitutional protections, 517
Statutory protections, 518–39
Stored Communications Act.
    Account records, 534–35
    Contents of communications, 534–35
    Entities regulated, 535–36
    Notice to subscribers, 539
    Opened e-mails, 536–37
    Subpoenas, application to, 837
    Voluntary disclosures, 538–39
Wiretapping,
    All-party consent statutes, 529–30
    Bugging, 523
    Consensual recording, 529–30
    Covert entry, 525
    Extension telephone, 529–530
    Foreign intelligence wiretapping, see Na-
        tional Security
    Grand Jury witness, 823
    Interception defined, 522
    Interstate communications, 531
    Provider exceptions, 526
    Remedies, 525–26
    Use and disclosure, 524–25
    Wiretap orders, statistics on, 7, 724–25

**OMNIBUS CRIME CONTROL AND SAFE
STREETS ACT**
See Confessions; Identification Procedures;
    McNabb–Mallory Rule; Network Surveil-
    lance.

"PETTY OFFENSES"
See Counsel, Right To.

PHOTOGRAPHIC DISPLAYS
See Identification Procedures.

"POISONOUS TREE" DOCTRINE
See "Fruit of the Poisonous Tree" Doctrine.

POLICE
See also Arrest; Confessions; Network Sur-
    veillance; Entrapment; Identification
    Procedures; Informants; Searches
    and Seizures; Secret Agents.
Alternative investigative agencies, 4
Black males, see Racial Minorities.
Charging discretion, 11
Community influence, 24
Court's influence on, see Judicial control, this
    heading.
Deadly force, 339–40
Discretion, 4, 11, 24
Encouragement and related practices, see En-
    trapment.
Excessive force, 339–40
Federal agencies, 5
Grand jury investigations compared, 9, 795,
    797
Investigations, 6–9, 11
Judicial control of, 49–53, 55, 224–27, 238–39,
    242–43, 353–58
Legislative non-control, 53
Localism and, 24
Perjury by, 238–39, 307–10
Prosecutor, relations with, 24
Race relations, see Racial Minorities.
Supreme Court and, 49–50, 55–57
"Sworn officers," 4
Variety of agencies, 4–5

POLICE INTERROGATION
See Confessions.

POLICE OFFICER TESTIMONY
See Motion to Suppress.

POSTCONVICTION REVIEW, FEDERAL
Assistance of counsel,
    Ineffective on collateral attack, 133
    No constitutional right, 133
"Collateral" nature, 19
Constitutional basis for, 40–48
Guantanamo detainees, 40–48

POSTCONVICTION REVIEW, STATE
General description, 19
Ineffective-assistance claims, 134–36

POVERTY
See Indigent Defendants.

PRO SE, RIGHT TO PROCEED
See Self–Representation, Right to.

PROBABLE CAUSE
See Arrest; Searches and Seizures.

**PROBATION AND PAROLE REVOCATION
PROCEEDINGS**
Counsel, right to, 93–94

PROBATION AND PAROLE REVOCATION PROCEEDINGS—Cont'd
Hearing, right to, 94
Illegally seized evidence, use of, 247–48

PROFESSIONAL ETHICS
ABA Rules of Professional Conduct
    Attorney subpoena, 832–33
    Conflicts of interest, 187
    Grand jury subpoena, 832–33
Citizen Protection (McDade) Act, 832–33
Frivolous appeals, 218
Judicial disqualification of counsel, 203–04, 207

PROFILING
See Racial Profiling.

PROOF, STANDARDS OF
See Burden of Proof.

PROOF BEYOND A REASONABLE DOUBT
See Burden of Proof; Due Process.

PROPHYLACTIC RULES
See Supreme Court.

PROSECUTOR
Courtroom workgroup, 24
Disciplining of,
    Judicial sanctions, 36–37
    Other sanctions, 832–33
Discretion, 23–24
Ethics Code,
    Citizen Protection (McDade) Act, 832–33
    Model Rules, see Professional Ethics
Federal, 5
Grand jury, relation to, 9, 793, 803–04, 820–21
Investigation, 9
Local prosecutors, 5
Number of offices, 5
Organizational ethos, 24, 61–62
State Attorneys General, 5
Subpoena power, 801

PUBLIC DEFENDER
See Counsel, Right To.

QUESTIONING
See Confessions.

RACIAL MINORITIES
    See also Equal Protection; Racial Profiling;
        Supreme Court.
Arab–Americans, 66–68
Black males,
    Police encounters, 64–65, 356–58, 418, 422
    Police harassment, 64–65, 356–58, 418, 422
    Sub citizen status, Fourth Amendment,
        64–65
Middle Easterners, 66–68
Race, legal relevancy of, 353–58, 418, 422
Racial origins, modern criminal procedure,
    49–50

RACIAL PROFILING
    See also Racial Minorities.
African–Americans, 64–65
Arab–Americans, 64–65
Department of Justice policy guideline, 67–68
Fourth Amendment limits, 64–65, 355–58, 418

RACIAL PROFILING—Cont'd
Investigative stops, 418
Middle–Easterners, 66–68
Police attitudes and, 64–68
Relevancy of race, 64–65, 353–58, 418, 422
Terrorists and, 66–68
Traffic stops, 64–65, 353–58

REASONABLE DOUBT
See Burden of Proof.

REVOCATION OF PAROLE
See Probation and Parole Revocation Proceedings.

REVOCATION OF PROBATION
See Probation and Parole Revocation Proceedings.

RIGHT TO COUNSEL
See Counsel, Right To.

ROADBLOCKS
See Searches and Seizures.

SEARCH AND SEIZURE REMEDIES
    See also "Fruit of the Poisonous Tree" Doctrine; Motion to Suppress; Searches
        and Seizures; Standing to Object to
        Illegally Obtained Evidence.
Constitutional tort, 242–43
Dismissal of criminal charges, 246–47
Exclusionary rule,
    Agency regulation violations, 246
    Application to the states, 222–29
    Contingent, 243
    Criticism of, 241–43
    Deterrence function, 223, 225, 229–43,
        252–64
    Effects of, 229–30, 238–39
    Electronic surveillance, 264–67, 526, 823
    Evidence from other agency, 248
    Foreign search, 251–52
    Good-faith exception, 229–41
    Justifications for, 224–39, 247–46
    Negligent act, 258–64
    No-knock violation, 252–57
    Nonpolice government violations, 250–51
    Private violations, 249–50
    Proceedings applicable,
        Collateral attack, 230
        Deportation, 249
        Forfeiture proceedings, 248
        Grand jury proceedings, 247
        Parole and probation revocation proceedings, 247–48
        "Quasi-criminal" proceedings, 248–49
        Sentencing, 247
    Reliance on unconstitutional case law,
        244–46
    Reliance on unconstitutional statute,
        243–44
    Remedies, alternative to the rule, 241–43
    Seriousness of offense, 241
Illegal arrest alone, 246
Warrant authorized searches and, 229–38

SEARCH WARRANTS
See Searches and Seizures.

SEARCHES AND SEIZURES
See also Arrest; "Fruit of the Poisonous Tree" Doctrine; Grand Jury Witness; Impeachment, Defendant and Defense Witnesses; Informants; Motion to Suppress; Network Surveillance; Search and Seizure Remedies; Secret Agents; Seizure of the Person; Standing to Object to Illegally Obtained Evidence: Technological Surveillance.
Administrative and regulatory inspections and seizures,
Alien traffic not at border, 441
Border searches, 440–41
Business premises, 440
DNA testing, 453–54
Driver's license and vehicle registration checks, 441–42
Driving-while-intoxicated checks, 441
Drug tests, 443–44
Fire investigations, 440
Parolees and probationers, supervision of, 444–53
Safety inspections of dwellings, 439–40
Special needs vs. balancing of interests, 439, 444–53
Students, 442–43
Terrorist checkpoints, 442
Airport investigations, 421, 425–26, 442
Arrest and,
See also Arrest.
Person, search incident to, 343–47, 359–61
Premises, search incident to, 363–68
Search preceding, 361–62
Search warrant, need for, 380–83
Vehicle, search incident to, 398–407
Automobile, of,
Border search, 40–41
Driver location, 398–405
Effects within, 388–405
Expectation of privacy, 383–87
Forfeiture, 383–88
Incident to arrest, 398–407
Inventory search, 407–08
Motor home, 383–88
Moving vehicle exception, 383–88
Packages within, 388–98
Passenger search, 393–96
Passenger seizure, 417–18
Probable cause for, 388
Scope of search, 388
Blood tests, 360
Bodily extractions, 360–61
Body searches, 360–61
Booking, search incident to, 359
Border searches, 440–41
Bright line standards, 332, 344–45, 348–49
Citation, search incident to, 361
Common law, relevance of, 338
Consent to,
Burden of proof, 454–59
By third parties, see Third-party consent, this heading.
Claim of authority, 459
Custody, importance of, 460
Deception to obtain, 461

SEARCHES AND SEIZURES—Cont'd
Consent to—Cont'd
Denial of guilt, 460
Emotional state, 460
Incarceration threat, 460
Nature of, 454–62
Place in law enforcement, 462
Prior police illegality, 460
Relevant factors, 459–62
Right to counsel and, 416
Scope, 461–62
Show of authority, 459
Theories of, 454–62
Voluntariness standard, 454–61
Waiver and, 456–58
Warnings and, 461
Containers, warrantless search of,
Cellphone, 347
Delivered and re-searched, 397–98
Incident to arrest, 343–48
Inventory search, 359, 407–08
Laptop, 393, 441
Within automobiles, 389–98
Detention of effects, 432–34
Diary, search for, 288
Disinterred third parties,
Search of, 288–91
Subpoena alternative, 288–91, 797–98
Documents, search for, 286–92
Dog sniffs, 277–78
Drug testing of employees, 443
Effects (personal), warrantless search of, 343–47, 359–62, 398–408
Exclusionary rule, see Search and Seizure Remedies.
Exigent circumstances, 360, 368–75, 380–82
First Amendment and, 288–92
Foreign officials, search by, 251–52
Grand jury subpoena, see Grand Jury Witness.
Habeas corpus review, see Postconviction Review, Federal.
"Immediate control" (area of) test, 363–68, 398–405
Impoundment, search incident to, 407–08
Informers,
Perjury as to, 309–10
Privilege as to, 308–10
Reliance upon, 292–305
Inventory searches,
Automobile, 407–08
Personal effects, 359, 407
"Mere evidence" rule, 286,
Newspaper offices, 288–91
Perjury concerning, 238–39, 308–10
Person, of,
Automobile passenger, 388, 417–18
Blood tests, 360
Bodily extractions, 350–61
Border search, 440–41
Fingernail scrapings, 362
Frisks, see Seizure of the Person.
Incident to arrest, 343–47, 359–61
Incident to booking, 359
Incident to citation, 361
Jail searches, 359–61
Presence at premises search, 324–25

SEARCHES AND SEIZURES—Cont'd
Person—Cont'd
   Probable cause and, 343–47, 359
   Scientific tests, 360–61
   "Stomach pumping," 28–29
   Strip Search,
     Arrestee, 361
     Border, 440
     Student, 442–44
   Surgery, 351
   Traffic arrestee, 343–47
   Without arrest, 324–25, 360–61
Plain view doctrine, 368, 397–98
Premises, of
   Accompanying arrestee, 367–68
   Entry to arrest,
     Arrest warrant required, 376–83
     Confessions following illegal entry, 899–900
     Exigent circumstances, 381–82
     Hot pursuit, 381–82
     Knock and announce, 383
     Search warrant required, 382–83
     Third party's residence, 382–83
     Traffic offense, 381–82
   Exigent circumstances, 368–76, 381–82
   Inspection following arrest, 365–67
   Plain view within, 365–67
   Protective sweeps, 366–67
   Search incident to arrest, 363–67
   Securing to obtain warrant, 372–74
   Warrant obtained after illegal entry, 900–01
   Warrants authorizing search, see Warrants this heading.
Pretext arrest to justify, 353–58
Private persons, search by, 249–50
Probable cause,
   Administrative inspections, 439–54
   Anticipatory warrant, 306–07
   Arrest or search distinction, 305–06
   Border searches, 440–41
   Collective police knowledge, 315
   Common enterprise, 310–12
   Definition of, 296–98
   Degree of probability, 310–13
   Entry of premises to arrest, 376–83
   Hearsay, use of to establish, 292–304
   Inference of possession, 310–13
   Informants, unnamed, 292–304, 308–10
   Multiple suspects, 310–13
   Night searches, 321
   Obscene publications, 290
   Police expertise, 314–15
   Police observations as basis, 314–15
   Police orders as basis, 315
   Police records as basis, 315
   Post-arrest review by magistrate, 13, 340–43
   Probationer search, 444–53
   Student search, 442–43
   Two-pronged test, 292–304
   Victim's information as basis, 314
   Warrant or not distinction, 305–06
Protected areas and interests,
     See also Network Surveillance, and Technological Surveillance.

SEARCHES AND SEIZURES—Cont'd
Protected areas and interests—Cont'd
   Aerial surveillance, 270–72
   Binoculars, 274
   Bookstores, 291–92
   Business premises, 272
   Business records, 286–88
   Canine detection, 277–78, 428–29
   Congressional offices, 292
   Containers, apparent contents, 396–98
   Containers previously searched, 397–98
   Containers, squeezing, 273–74
   Curtilage, 269–72
   Data aggregation and mining, 284–85
   Detention facilities, 272
   Electronic eavesdropping, 505–07
   E-mails, 501–05
   Eviction from premises, 267
   Expectation of privacy standard, 264–67
   Garbage, 267–69
   GPS tracking, 279–84
   Internet addresses, 515–17
   Library, 291–92
   License plate recognition, 284
   Luggage, 273–74
   "Open fields," 269–72
   Overflights, 270–72
   Pen registers, 510–15
   Photographic magnification, 278
   Physical penetration, necessity of, 467, 505–07
   Plain view, see Plain view doctrine, this heading.
   Private areas in public places, 272
   Sensory enhancing equipment, 274–85
   Telephone booths, 264–67
   Thermal imaging, 274–77
   Third party records, 504, 517–18
   Trash bins, 267–79
   Trespass doctrine, 264–65, 278–84, 467, 505–07
   Vehicles,
     Lesser privacy interest, 383–88
     Paint scrapings, 273
     VIN, 273
Roadblocks, 441–42
Scientific tests, 360–61
Self-incrimination and, 266, 286–88,
Subpoena duces tecum, see Grand Jury Witness.
Surgery, 360
Third-party consent,
   Antagonism, 467,
   Apparent authority, 462–65
   Bailor-bailee, 467
   Common authority, 462–67
   Co-tenant, 466
   Defendant refusal, 467–69
   Defendant's instructions, 467
   Employer-employee, 466–67
   Fourth Amendment reasonableness, 462–65
   Hotel clerk, 464–65
   Landlord, 466
   Parent-child, 466
   Spouse, 466
   Theory of, 462–65

SEARCHES AND SEIZURES—Cont'd
Warrantless,
  See this heading; Administrative and regulatory inspections and seizures; Automobile, of; Exigent circumstances; Person, of; Premises, of.
Warrants,
  Administrative inspections, 439–54
  Affidavits for, 297–99, 307–08, 319–20
  Anticipatory, 306–07
  Challenge to, see Motion to Suppress.
  Computer Searches, 329–31
  Electronic surveillance, 264–67, 507, 524–25
  Execution of,
    Delivery of warrant, 329
    Detention of persons on premises, 325–27
    Gaining entry, 312–24
    Intensity and duration, 312
    Magistrate involvement, 233
    Media attendance, 328
    Private person accompanying or aiding, 328–29
    Search of persons on premises, 324–25
    Sneak-and-peak, 322
    Time of, 321–22
    Unnamed items, seizure of, 327–28
  False information, 307–08
  First Amendment and, 288–291
  Good faith reliance upon, 229–41
  Information beyond affidavits, 307
  Neutrality of magistrate, 233, 316–17
  Network surveillance, see Network Surveillance.
  Notice of execution, delayed, 322,
  Preference for, 322
  Premises, description of, 317–18
  Reliance on affidavits, 319–20
  Seizable items, description of, 318–19
  Third party premises, 382–83

SECRECY
See Grand Jury.

SECRET AGENTS
  See also Confessions; Due Process; Entrapment; Informants; Network Surveillance; Searches and Seizures.
Attorney General guidelines, 478
Confidential informants, 470
First Amendment limits, and, 477–78
Foreign languages, 476
Identification of informer, 308–10,
Informer's privilege, 308–10
Jail plants, 615–17, 750–53
Passive vs. active, 750–53
Probable cause and, see Searches and Seizures.
Reasonable expectation of privacy, 474–77
Supervisory power, and, 477
Use of, recording devices, 475–76

SEIZURE OF THE PERSON
  See also Arrest; Confessions; Identification Procedures; Searches and Seizures.
Action short of,
  Airport encounters, 418, 421, 425–26
  Bus sweeps, 415–16, 418

SEIZURE OF THE PERSON—Cont'd
Action short of—Cont'd
  Flight by suspect, 416–17
  Unintentional collision, 416–17
Checkpoints and vehicle stops,
  Border patrol, 440–41
  Driver licenses, 441–42
  Drunk driving, 442
  Terrorist, 442
Custody, relation to, 408–18, 425–32
Detention at border, 440–41
Detention at station, 437–39
Detention for identification procedures,
  Court ordered, 437–38
  Fingerprinting, 437–38
  Handwriting exemplars, 438,
  Lineups, 438,
  Probability standard, 437–39
Detention of effects, 432–34
"Dragnet" procedures, 437–39,
Grand jury subpoena,
  Forwith subpoena, 821–22
  Subpoenas to provide identification evidence, 822
  Subpoena to testify, 817–18
Identification of suspect, 437–38
Least intrusive alternative, 426–27
Removal from car, 361
Show of authority, 415–18
Stationhouse, removal to, 437–39, 820
Stop and frisk,
  Anonymous tips, 422–24
  Drug courier profile, 421
  Duration of stop, 425–27
  Flight, 416–17, 421–22
  Force, show or threat, 425
  Fourth Amendment and, 408–15
  Grounds for, 419–25
  Identification, requiring, 427–28
  Informant's tip, 422–24
  Movement of suspect, 425–26
  Passenger in vehicle, 417–18
  Past criminal activity, 420
  Reasonable suspicion, 419–25
  Recording stop, 432
  Scope of detention, 425–32
  Scope of frisk, 413–14, 434–37
  Termination of stop, 431–32
  Time limits, 426–27
Subpoena for identification purposes, 822
Temporary detention for investigation, 437–39
Traffic stop, 343–58, 361–62, 428–29,
Vehicle checkpoints and spot checks, 441–42

SEIZURES
See Search and Seizure Remedies; Searches and Seizures; Seizure of the Person.

SELECTIVE INCORPORATION, THEORY OF
See Due Process.

SELF–INCRIMINATION
  See also Confessions; Grand Jury Witness; Identification Procedures.
Attorney-client privilege and, 858–59
Blood tests, 29–31

SELF–INCRIMINATION—Cont'd
Bodily extractions, 27–31
Burdens imposed upon exercise, 882
Coercive interrogation, standing alone, 690–96
Compelled-to-give-evidence interpretation,
    27–31, 852, 855–56, 875–76, 878
Compelled writings, See Grand Jury Witness,
    Compulsion,
        Choice between rights and, 882
        Informal, 551–54, 575, 582–85
Confessions, and, See Confessions
Consent to search and, 461
Core protection, 839–40
Custodial interrogation, and, see Confessions.
Documents, subpoena of, see Grand Jury Wit-
    ness.
Dual sovereignty, 840–41
Entity's position, see Grand Jury Witness.
Exclusionary rule and, 226, 287–88, 808–09
Executing prescribed document, 845–56
Federal/state prosecution, 840–41
Foreign prosecution, 841
Grand jury witness, see Grand Jury Witness.
History of, 574–75, 841, 848–49
Identification evidence, compelled production,
    29–30, 767, 855–56, 860, 878
Identity, disclosure of, 619–20, 839
Immunity grants, see Grand Jury Witness.
"Incrimination" defined, 839–40
Incrimination determination, 839–40, 865–66
Incrimination under laws of another sovereign,
    840–41
Invocation of Miranda rights, 634–35
Judicial proceedings, applicability in, 692–93,
    838–39
Lineup participation, see Identification Proce-
    dures.
"Link in the chain," 839–40
Police interrogation and, see Confessions.
Pre-charge stage, see Confessions; Grand Jury
    Witness.
Privacy and, 840, 852–53, 858, 861–62, 863–64
Production of documents, see Grand Jury Wit-
    ness.
Prophylactic rules and, 692–93, 838–39
Regulatory disclosures, 855
Required records, 855
Search and seizure and, 286–78, 797, 856
Standing for suppression motion, 882–83
Subpoena duces tecum and, see Grand Jury
    Witness.
"Testimonial" requirement,
    Acts and, 28–31, 617–19, 855–56, 860
    "Act of production" doctrine, see Grand
        Jury Witness.
    Basis for, 855–56
    Defined, 855
Values underlying, 840–41, 856
Voice samples, see Identification Procedures.
Waiver, see Waiver.
Witness claim, see Grand Jury Witness.

SELF–REPRESENTATION, RIGHT TO
Appeals and, 111
Competency to waive counsel, 117–20
Constitutional right, 107–11
Control over counsel, see Counsel, Role of.

SELF–REPRESENTATION, RIGHT TO—Cont'd
Forfeiture of, 121
Guilty plea and, 115–16
Harmless error, 111, 1563
Ineffective representation, 108, 114
Limits on right, 118–21
Mentally ill defendants, 118–21
Notification of right, 114
Outcomes, compared to represented defen-
    dants, 110–11
Standby counsel
    Function, 111–13
    No constitutional right, 113
    Ineffective assistance, 114
    Limits on participation, 111–13
    Lower court rulings, 113–14
    Selection of, 113
Timely assertion, 114
Warnings and inquiry, 114–18
Waiver of counsel and, 108–09, 114–18

SHOW–UPS
See Identification Procedures.

SILENT, RIGHT TO REMAIN
See Confessions; Self-incrimination.

**STANDING TO OBJECT TO ILLEGALLY OB-
TAINED EVIDENCE**
Automatic standing, 882–83
California approach, 879
Deterrence and, 879–81
Expectation of privacy test, 884–87
Federal supervisory authority and, 35–36,
    881–82
Illegal search of car, 887–80
Illegal stop and, 887–88
Possessory interest in premises, 883, 889–90
Shared privacy, 889–92
State constitutions and, 517
Standing of,
    Bailor, 885–86
    Co-conspirator, 880
    Employee sharing office, 883–84
    Family members, 883
    Guest in dwelling, 889–93
    Passenger in another's car, 884–85
Target standing, 87
Third party subpoenas, 504, 517–18, 835
Third party standing, 879–80
Victim limitation, 879–80

STATE CONSTITUTIONS
New federalism, 38–39
Supreme Court and, 38–39

STATE LAW, ROLE OF
See Criminal Justice Process; Legal Regula-
    tion, Sources of; State Constitutions.

STATISTICS
See Criminal Justice Statistics.

"STOMACH PUMPING"
See Due Process; Self–Incrimination.

"STOP AND FRISK"
See Searches and Seizures.

STORED COMMUNICATIONS ACT
See Network Surveillance.

SUBPOENA
See Grand Jury Witness; Investigation by Subpoena; National Security Searches and Seizures; Self–Incrimination.

SUMMONS
See Arrest; Bail; Searches and Seizures.

"SUPERVISORY AUTHORITY" OVER FEDERAL CRIMINAL JUSTICE
Agency regulation violations and, 246
Congressional overruling, 676–9
Counsel waiver, police interrogation, 37–38
Court rule, conflict with, 36–37
Constitutional ruling , conflict with, 35–36, 881–82
Disciplining prosecutors, 36–37
Exclusion of evidence, 35–37, 246, 544–55
Harmless error doctrine, 36–37
McNabb–Mallory rule, 34–35, 554–55
Source of authority, 34
Third-party standing, 35–36, 881–82

SUPPRESSION
See Motion to Suppress; Search and Seizure Remedies.

SUPREME COURT
See also Due Process; Equal Protection; Fourteenth Amendment; Police; "Supervisory Authority" Over Federal Criminal Justice.
Approaches to constitutional interpretation,
Common law history, emphasis upon, 338, 805, 807, 848–49
Particularistic decisions vs. bright-line rules, see Search and Seizure.
Prophylactic rules, 597, 637, 638, 682–83, 685–87,692–93, 696, 838–39
Certiorari authority, adequate state ground, 38–39
Congressional reaction to decisions, 589, 676
Enforcement needs and, 51–53
Effectiveness of rulings, 54–57
Legislative responses, 53, 54–57, 676
Police and, 49–53
Racial disparities, influence of, 49–50, 53, 64–68

SURVEILLANCE
See Network Surveillance; Searches and Seizures.

TECHNOLOGICAL SURVEILLANCE
See also Network Surveillance; Search and Seizure.
Caller ID services, 533
"Carnivore," 531–32
Cellular phone tracking, 533
Cordless phones, 507–08
Data aggregation and mining, 284–85
Electronic bugs, see Network Surveillance.
E-mail, 501–04
GPS tracking, 278–84

TECHNOLOGICAL SURVEILLANCE—Cont'd
License plate recognition, 284
Photographic magnification, 285–86
Thermal imager, 274–77
Wiretapping, see Network Surveillance.
World Wide Web, 509
USA Patriot Act, 519

TELEPHONE RIGHTS
See Confessions.

TERRORISM, WAR ON
See Due Process; Postconviction Review, Federal

TORTURE
See Confessions.

TRANSCRIPT AND OTHER MATERIALS, RIGHT OF INDIGENT TO
See Appeals; Counsel, Right To; Equal Protection; Indigent Defendants.

TRIAL
Acquittal/conviction rates, 17
Competency (mental), 117, 120
Defendant's testimony, access to counsel, 176
Described, 17
Frequency of trials, 17
Length of, 17
Outcome statistics, 17

TRIAL COURT
Caseloads, 24
Courthouse workgroup, 24
Trier of fact, suppression motions, 929–30

UNDERCOVER INVESTIGATIONS
See Entrapment; Secret Agents.

UNREASONABLE SEARCHES AND SEIZURES
See Arrest; Search and Seizure Remedies; Searches and Seizures; Seizure of the Person.

USA PATRIOT ACT
See National Security.

U.S. DEPARTMENT OF JUSTICE
See Prosecutors; Internal Guidelines.

VOICE PRINTS
See Grand Jury Witness; Identification Procedures.

VOICE SAMPLES
See Identification Procedures; Searches and Seizures; Self–Incrimination.

WAIVER
Burden of proof on, 926
Consent to search, 454–59
Counsel, appointed, see Counsel, Right To.
Counsel, conflict-free, 204–05, 208–09
Counsel, right to, See Counsel Right To.
Counsel and interrogation, see Confessions.
Counsel at lineup, 763–66
Forfeiture, as contrasted with, 121
Knowing and intelligent, 114, 115–116, 456–57

WAIVER—Cont'd
Personal participation of defendant, need for, 209–13
Procedural forfeitures, 121
Self-incrimination privilege,
    Grand jury witness, 841–42
    Partial testimony, 841–42
    Police interrogation, see Confessions.
    Witness awareness, 844
Self-representation and, see Self–Representation, Right To.
Silent record and, 114
Venue, 112–14
Voluntary relinquishment, 454–59

WARNINGS
See Confessions; Grand Jury Witness; Searches and Seizures.

WARRANTS
See Arrest; Magistrates; Searches and Seizures.

WARREN COURT
See Police; Supreme Court.

WIRETAPPING
See Network Surveillance.

WRIT OF HABEAS CORPUS
See Postconviction Review, Federal; Postconviction Review, State.

†